(2) 1122 BoB
0523

This book is dedicated to the memory of
Kathleen Marguerite Lea 1903–1995
and Tutor of Lady Margaret Hall, Oxford, 1936–1971,
and Vice Principal, 1947–1971.
One of those who cast light on our path.
only be furious / With things that are spurious" (K.M.L.)

The True Story of the Novel

ss Cataloging-in-Publication Data

Anne.
y of the novel / by Margaret Anne Doody.

iographical references and index.
-2168-8
Technique.   2. Fiction—History and criticism.

1996
                              94-39574
                                CIP

g-in-Publication information available

"The Great Artemis" of Ephesus: triple crowned, Cybele's lions on her shoulders, bulls' testes at her breast, and sacred animals (including bees) on her skirt. In antiquity her hands were probably made of gold.

Fellow

The
True S
of the N

>—•—‹••‹

MARGARET AN

RUTGERS UNIVERSITY PRESS
New Brunswick, New Jersey

"And let

Library of Cong

Doody, Margare
    The true sto
        p.   cm
    Includes bi
    ISBN 0-813
    1. Fiction–
    I. Title.
PN3355.D66
809.3—dc20

British Catalogi

CONTENTS

>-+-◦-+-◦-+-◦-+-◦-<

>-+-◦-+-◦-<

PART ONE   *The Ancient Novel*

>-+-◦-+-◦-<

PART TWO   *The Influence of the Ancient Novel*

PART THREE   *Tropes of the Novel*

ACKNOWLEDGMENTS

➤─┼─✦➤─○─◄✦┼─◄

I am grateful to the American Council of Learned Societies, which gave a grant that enabled me to travel to Greece and Italy in 1988. I wish to acknowledge the assistance given this project by two great universities, Princeton University and Vanderbilt University. Both helped me on my way and supported work on this book. I am particularly grateful to Vanderbilt University for its generous support, which has enabled me to travel not only in Europe but also in Asia Minor in 1990 and 1991.

In working on this book, I have had occasion to realize afresh how wonderful is the "community of scholars"—a phrase that has gained new meaning for me in the years this project has taken. I want to express my thanks to the many friends and associates who have helped with this work, especially those fellow scholars who have discussed the material with me, and who have been kind enough to read part or all of this work, or to help in its planning stages. These include Peter Brown, Maria DiBattista, George Forrest, William Franke, Jayne Lewis, John McCarthy, Elaine Phillips, Omar Pound, Enrique Pupo-Walker, David Quint, William Race, Peter Sabor, James Tatum, James Turner and Froma Zeitlin. Particular thanks go to Bob Brown, the copyeditor, for his care, patience, and interest. For expert knowledge brought to bear on problems of translation, I am ever indebted to Antonina Gove, Idit Dobbs-Weinstein, Margaret Miner, and William Race—and particularly grateful to Anthony Grafton and David Quint who, when called upon at the eleventh hour, came through with invaluable assistance on two particularly quirky and recalcitrant pieces of Renaissance prose. All errors in translations are my own property.

My thanks to Gregory Klyve for the Greek lessons, and my assurances that my defects are not his fault. I have particular reason to feel deeply obliged to Yu-Fang Han, who introduced me properly to the Chinese novel, and who has explained language and concepts. I am happy to express my obligation also to Elizabeth Wichmann for sharing with me information about Chinese literature, and for allowing me to read her translations of some Beijing operas. Useful information has been imparted by many people, but I particularly wish to thank Vilsoni Hereniko, Roger Long, Rachel Roth, and Angela Saylor. I am profoundly grateful to the numerous curators of museums and archaeological sites in Britain, Greece, Italy, and Turkey who have answered so many questions for me during my travels. My thanks to the Turkish Board of Tourism for letting me use photographs of objects and sites in that most beautiful country. Libraries and museum curators have helped me in all the institutions where I have had access to books or graphic works, particularly those where I have obtained photographs. I want to extend special thanks to Dr. Margherita Carboni Mariutti, librarian at the Marciana, and to Despina Vlassi, librarian at the Istituto Ellenico (both in Venice), and also to William Braesher at the Ägyptisches Museum in Berlin for his help and advice regarding papyri.

I am grateful to the many libraries that have supplied me with books and manuscripts and offered assistance. These libraries include The Bodleian Library, Oxford; The British Library, London; The William Andrews Clark Library, Los Angeles; The Huntington Library, Pasadena; The Istituto Ellenico, Venice; The Marcian Library, Venice; The National Library of Austria, Vienna; The Pierpont Morgan Library, New York; The Vatican Library, Vatican City, Rome.

I have reason to be heartily grateful to Leslie Mitchner, my editor, for her patience (which has been sometimes tried) and her literary judgment as well as her energy and enthusiasm. In preparing this manuscript, I have been very fortunate in having the assistance of Dianne Fasshauer, Carolyn Levinson, and Angela Saylor. To Angela in particular, who has had to live with this monster from day to day, my heartfelt thanks.

Wendy Barry should know how very grateful I am for sorely needed help in compiling the bibliography. I wish to extend my gratitude and heartfelt compliments to David Macey for skilled and valiantly persevering labor on the index.

I feel sad at remembering that long ago John J. Winkler promised to read what I wrote; everyone who knew the late and great Jack Winkler will share with me the sense of loss. I am very grateful to James Tatum for having included me in the International Conference on the Ancient Novel in 1989; attending that conference was an important and heartening experience.

My gratitude goes to Lindy Jordan and the late Jack Jordan for their hospitality in Andalusia during a memorable Holy Week in 1988. I welcome the opportunity to thank Marjorie Barton for driving me about Sicily in 1989 so I could see the mosaics at Piazza Armorina. Many thanks to Ihsan Aknur, my driver in Turkey in 1990 and 1991, who acted as constant interpreter, got us into apparently closed museums, and was willing to go to unknown sites over unusual roads.

My heartiest thanks to my sister Freda Bradley, who approaches the world from a different perspective. Talking with her has been an education and a stimulus, as well as providing valuable reality checks.

Everyone who teaches will recognize how much I must owe to my students over the years for challenge, discussion, and stimulation. I particularly wish to express my gratitude to students at Vanderbilt, especially those in the "Comic Novel" class in Comparative Literature.

This book is dedicated to the memory of Katherine Marguerite Lea, my tutor at Lady Margaret Hall in 1960–1962 and friend forever after. I had discussed the new project with her at its outset. As a Renaissance scholar, Kate was pleased to hear of my work on the ancient novels in the Renaissance, and expressed the opinion that Achilles Tatius had not been properly dealt with. Now, I am selfishly sad that I cannot give her a copy of this book, or ever again have the chance to talk anything over with "Miss Lea." She would have found much in the new book to disagree with—and much to like—and we would have had some good conversation. I am grateful to all of my teachers, students, and colleagues over the years for giving me the priceless gifts of questions and new approaches. Above all, I am fortunate in having led a life that abounded and abounds in friendship and good company.

A special debt of gratitude is owed, as always, to my dear friend Florian Stuber, always a stimulating questioner and fine reasoner, and to a recently departed friend, Irving Piper.

LIST OF ILLUSTRATIONS

ANCIENT NOVELS: CHRONOLOGICAL LISTING

▷─┤◆▷─○─◁◆├─◁

Ancient Novels	Contemporary Works	Events
	Euripides 485–406 B.C.: *Medea*, 431 B.C.	
	Herodotus: *Historiai*, pre 425 B.C.	
	Euripides: *Ēlektra*, 417 B.C.	
Xenophon c. 428 B.C.– c. 354 B.C.: *Cyropaedia*, pre 354 B.C.		
	Menander c. 342–292 B.C.	Alexander the Great 356– 323 B.C. founded Alexandria, 331 B.C.
Joseph and Aseneth, 100 B.C.– A.D. 100		Roman and Italian residents of Asia Minor killed under Mithridates, 88 B.C.
Ninus, 100 B.C.–A.D. 140		
Chariton: *Chaireas and Kallirrhoé*, 50 B.C.–A.D. 140		
	Cicero: *De officiis*, 44 B.C.	Murder of Julius Caesar 44 B.C.
		Battle of Philippi 42 B.C.
	Horace: *Satires* c. 30 B.C.; *Odes* c. 23 B.C.	Antony & Cleopatra's suicide, 31 B.C.; Octavian virtual dictator
		Octavian given title of "Augustus," 27 B.C.
	Virgil: *Aeneid*, 30–19 B.C.	
	Ovid: *Ars Amatoria*, 1 B.C.; *Metamorphoses*, A.D. 2–17	Death of Augustus, A.D. 14
	Epistulae, A.D. 9–17	
	Seneca (exile A.D. 41): plays c. A.D. 20–30; *Epistulae*, c. A.D. 40–65	
		Nero, Emperor A.D. 54–68
Petronius: *Satyricon*, by A.D. 66	Lucan: *Pharsalia*, A.D. 60–65	Seneca's suicide, A.D. 65
		Petronius' suicide, A.D. 65
		Nero's suicide, A.D. 68
		Pompeii destroyed by volcanic eruption, A.D. 79
	Quintilian: *Institutes*, c. A.D. 90	Domitian, Emperor A.D. 81–96
	Statius: *Thebaid*, by A.D. 96	
	Juvenal: *Satires*, c. A.D. 96– 130	

The Ass, c. A.D. 100

Chion of Heraklea, c. A.D. 100

Herpyllis, c. A.D. 125

Antonius Diogenes: *Wonders beyond Thule,* c. A.D. 150

Achilles Tatius: *Kleitophon and Leukippé,* c. A.D. 150

Kalligonē, c. A.D. 150

Lucian: *Vera Historia,* c. A.D. 170

Apuleius: *Golden Ass,* c. A.D. 160–180

"Xenophon of Ephesus": *Ephesiaka,* A.D. 100–200

Metiochos and Parthenopé, A.D. 100–200

Sesenchōsis, A.D. 100–200

Ps. Clemens: *Recognitiones,* A.D. 150–250

Lollianos: *Phoinikika,* A.D. 150–200

"Paul and Thekla," c. A.D. 160

Iamblichus: *Babyloniaka,* A.D. 165–180

Iolaos, pre A.D. 200

Longus: *Daphnis and Chloé,* c. A.D. 200

Alexander (Greek version), c. A.D. 250

Dictys Cretensis: *Ephemeris belli Troiani,* c. A.D. 250

Dares Phrygius: *De excidio Troiae historia* (?)

Chionē, A.D. 150–300

Heliodorus: *Aithiopika* c. A.D. 250–380

Historia Apollonii regis Tyri, Latin version A.D. 400–600

Plutarch: *Lives,* c. A.D. 100

Marcus Aurelius: *Meditations,* pre A.D. 180

Tertullian: *Apologeticus,* A.D. 197

Philostratus the Elder: *Imagines,* c. A.D. 200

Origen: *Contra Celsum,* pre A.D. 254

Plotinus (c. A.D. 205–270): *Enneads* pre 270

Porphyry (c. A.D. 233–c. 305): *On the Cave of the Nymphs,* pre A.D. 305

Augustine: *Confessions,* A.D. 397–401; *The City of God,* A.D. 913–926

Marcus Aurelius, Emperor A.D. 161–180

A.D. 256–260, persecution of Christians

A.D. 313, Edict of Milan under Constantine legalizes Christianity

A.D. 326, foundation of Constantinople

Julian, Emperor A.D. 360–363

A.D. 391, Temple of Artemis at Ephesus officially closed

A.D. 410, Visigoths sack Rome

PREFACE

After sailing for three days we arrived in Alexandria. My entrance was by the Sun Gate, as they call the portal, and immediately I was dazzled by the beauty of the city, and my eyes were filled with pleasure. . . . I set my eyes to looking into every street, but my vision was still unsated, and I could not succeed in seeing the whole beauty. While I was looking at some things, I was about to see some others; some things I wanted to see, others I wanted not to pass over. What I was seeing held my gaze, but so did what I was about to see. I wandered then through every street, and to my eyes still sick with desire I exclaimed, exhausted, "Eyes—we are conquered!"

—Achilles Tatius, *Kleitophon and Leukippé*

*T*he Zeitgeist whispers now of a revival of interest in the classical novel, but I came upon my subject in an unusual way. Writing a sequel to my novel *Aristotle Detective* (1978)—a sequel that remains unpublished (alas!) to this day—I decided to include in it some reference to or gesture towards every genre known in Aristotle's day. This brought me to the question of the Novel—where and when? It seemed to become visible around the time of Alexander the Great or just after—say, at the end of Aristotle's life or a little later. Reading Arthur Heiserman's *The Novel before the Novel* (1971), I became fully aware of the plots, the substance, and the importance of the ancient novels; I was more excited than Heiserman (who was wedded to the concept of Romance) about the connections of ancient fiction with our own. I had long felt dissatisfied with the version of the history of the novel on which I had been bred in the 1950s and 1960s, though even when I wrote my book on Richardson (published in 1974) I had accepted that history, if with some modifications (the inclusion of seventeenth-century fiction and works by women writers). To change the "background" to the eighteenth-century novel, it would be necessary, I realized, to go very far back indeed.

This book is an attempt to trace connections rather than to assert division. Of course it is true that many exciting divisions can be described and explored, but it seems to me that we cannot deal properly with subsets until we know more of the whole set. Once we know more of the range of fiction, new groupings and subgroupings will be available to us, and we can invent new terms. Sets and subsets are not stable entities but fluid variables dependent on the conceptual interests of those who deal with them. I believe the concept of "Romance" as distinct from "Novel" has outworn its usefulness, and that at its most useful it created limitations and encouraged blind spots. If I assert the interconnectedness of a history, and boldly venture to treat an admittedly protean form as if constantly visible from century to century, I do not mean that that is the only way to treat the subject. It merely seems necessary that now somebody should do so, in order to help us to see the range of surviving forest and not merely the individual trees or, at best, small groves. I personally am not inimical to the idea of historical change. My most recent book was a literary biography of one individual writer living in changing times. I traced the course of the life of Frances Burney (1752–1840), followed practically every line she wrote, pointed out the great differences between one of her novels and the next, indicated cultural shifts from one decade to the next. Having studied the matter of the novel at the micro level, crawling along a century with my magnifying glass in hand, I feel entitled to make use of the telescope and look over a period of two thousand years. If I emphasize continuities, it is because discontinuity, absolute division, has been harshly and hastily asserted before now. The fences have been too sturdy or too barbed—it is good sometimes to leap over fences, or even to break them down.

Undertaking the study of the Novel as I wanted to do it, however, was a tall order. I realized I would have to learn Greek. Endeavouring to learn Greek took a while; I cannot say I have mastered it, I do not "have" Greek, but I am no longer reliant on translators. That this is important was proved to me when I found that the translator of one work, when dealing with the dream-vision of a woman that crowns the story, had left out her divinity. In this book, translations from works in various languages including Latin and Greek are my own, unless otherwise indicated. For original texts of classical novels I have customarily relied upon the Loeb or Budé editions. I have, however, checked translations against new translations, including those in that valuable publication edited by B. P. Reardon, *Collected Ancient Greek Novels* (1989). That volume (hereinafter abbreviated to *CAGN*) was the upshot of the International Conference on the Ancient Novel (ICAN) held in 1979. The second ICAN at Dartmouth College in 1989 had, among other issue, the book *The Search for the Ancient Novel* (1994; here abbreviated as *TSAN*), edited by James Tatum. The conferences, and these and other recent books, are among the signs that the world is becoming more interested in the ancient novel. In 1979, as I began my study of Greek, I did not know about this heartening development. If I rarely quote the translations in Reardon's volume and others, it is not because I do not admire them. I prefer, throughout this book, to grapple on my own with passages quoted, because translators, if much more learned, often ignore the very nuances I wish to bring out. Such is the case in the epigraph from Achilles Tatius, with Kleitophon's *dyserōtiōn*, which Gaselee (in the Loeb) translates as "unsatisfied" and John J. Winkler, more happily (in *CAGN*), as "like a luckless lover." I wanted to sustain the sense of continuous desire, the eros concealed in the word. Kleitophon's love-longing for the city of Alexandria is not unrequited, he is not "luckless" (as in being rejected); rather, his erotic gaze is dysfunctional from a kind of lovesickness, he is in a state of intense yearning for the complex city, like the *desire* of the novel reader. I cannot rely on translators; we are hunting different snarks.

This fact makes me the more uneasy about including in Part III references to works in languages that I cannot read at all, with which no dictionary can help me. Yet it would not be right or reasonable to omit all reference to Russian novels, for instance. I have had expert assistance. When any text is quoted in a language not know to me, I have gone over the passage in the standard translation with someone who truly does know the language.

The barrier is obviously stronger elsewhere; a heavy wall rises between myself and works in Chinese or Japanese. China and Japan both have great novel traditions, but I can come upon their works only through translators, and without much real knowledge of the culture represented. Western translators unconsciously Westernize the works they translate, so I have no way of knowing whether the "tropes of fiction" I deal with are found in a particular novel or not. So I thought at first. When I began to write this book I intended to emphasize that this is a Story of Fiction *in the West,* and to assert the impermeable wall between myself, or my story, and the so-called Far East—even though my theory of the novel includes an emphasis upon what used to be called its "Oriental" elements and aspects. I found the belief that I should stick to "the West" hard to sustain in the face of the evidence. Classical Chinese novels, for instance, novels written before contact with our modern Western forms could have affected them, seem much more clearly related to the Western novels (including our antique novels) than I should have thought likely. Some references to Eastern novels have, irresistibly as it seemed, made their way into the discussion. It would, on reflection, be surprising if Chinese or Japanese novels had none of the Western tropes, but it would also be surprising if there were not important differences, including the presence of material (especially that related to a religious tradition) that is practically invisible to Western eyes. It is to be hoped that Chinese and Japanese writers will tell their own "Story of the Novel" and explain the traditions and tropes of their own fiction. After all, there have been contacts between East and West through the millennia; if there had not, the West would have no novel, or a different one. When we read in one of the very earliest Western novels, written in Greek, that the Great King of Persia possesses a sword made by the Chinese, we realize that the cultural boundaries have never been impermeable.

Part I of this book, the more orthodox section, contains a discussion of "classical novels"—a phrase that seems to some an oxymoron. These novels are not unknown, and a number of classicists have given some attention to them, but they are largely unknown to general readers and to students of English or other modern literatures. My view of them often differs from the classicists'. Classical scholars tend themselves to accept literary definitions learned in school and are rarely trained to connect literature in Greek or Latin with modern literature. If it is presumptuous of me to enter a field usually reserved for classicists, I do so in an Alexandrian spirit. Multiculuralism begins at home. My defense must be that I know some things classicists often do not know. My work on eighteenth-century fiction has given me some insight into fiction both later (including the 1990s) and earlier; eighteenth-centuryists have Janus vision. Classicists tend to think that the nature of the Novel is established, that it is a settled, stable, and above all realistic form with none of the strangeness that hangs about the ancient novel. But we have not really settled the modern novel's hash. The entire matter of the Novel in all eras is now open for discussion. The real relationships between old and new can be clearly seen when both classicists and modernists agree that there are many questions to be asked, and *many* novels to be read.

In order to prevent a clutter of notes, references are usually cited with (brief) title and page number in the text; a full reference awaits anyone who turns to the Bibliography. Standard sources customarily used for the Greek or Latin text of an ancient novel are given in the list I A of the Bibliography, and will not be fully cited where the work under discussion is clear; page references allude to the Greek or Latin passage, even when the work is quoted in English translation. Similarly, texts in modern languages (German, French, Italian) will be quoted as translated while the page reference will allude to the passage in original-language text. Any translator other than myself will always be acknowledged by name at the point where quotation occurs. When a passage in another language from a text not accessible to the reader is quoted, there part or all of the original-language text will be supplied either in the text or in the Notes. Such quotation is necessary in, for instance, reference to a Renaissance editor's Latin preface. Where the original-language version is readily available (e.g., *Inferno, Der Tod in Venedig*), passages will not be given in original language as well as translation.

In the case of traditional names in common use (Socrates, Plato, Thucydides), I have sustained common English spellings, rather than transliterating from the Greek according to the new system. In the case of moderately well-known ancient novelists (Heliodorus, Longus), I have likewise yielded to tradition. In the case of the names of the novels' characters I have endeavored to adhere to a modern style of transliteration reasonably faithful to Greek spelling, and I have preferred, for example, *Aithiopika* and *Ephesiaka* to the Romanized *Ethiopica* and *Ephesiaca*, partly in order to remind us that these novels do not emanate from a Latin world. There are a variety of usages among scholars; I cannot regret an apparent inconsistency since, in the English-language study of antiquity, perfect consistency is not possible. In English we all write "Psalms" and "Sappho" instead of "Salms" or "Psappho." I have also inherited the inconsistency whereby we refer to "Plato" and "Chariton" instead of "Platon" or "Charito."

In transliterated Greek I have written *upsilon* as *y* according to older rather than newer practice, in order to help the English-speaking reader to recognize significant words like *psychē* and *pyra*. In the case of *hubris*, however, I have left in the well-known *u*. Accent marks are used in transliteration only to distinguish by a macron two "e" and "o" forms from each other. Except for an acute mark helping with the pronunciation of female names, Greek proper names transliterated will not carry accent marks unless italicized, when *ēta* and *ōmega* will be distinguished by macron.

The "Chronological Listing" of Ancient Novels is offered for the guidance of the reader, but the dating of the novels is most uncertain. Scholarly guesses about the period of composition can range over centuries; some fresh discovery of a papyrus fragment may alter the dating of one work or another at any time.

The True Story of the Novel

INTRODUCTION

> ►–◄►–○–◄►–◄

In Search of the Ancient Novel

> ►–◄►–○–◄►–◄

Now let us, by a flight of imagination, suppose that Rome is not a human habitation but a psychical entity with a similarly long and copious past—an entity, that is to say, in which nothing that has once come into existence will have passed away and all the earlier phases of development continue to exist alongside the latest one. This would mean that in Rome the palaces of the Caesars and the Septizonium of Septimus Severus would still be rising to their old height on the Palatine . . . the same piece of ground would be supporting the church of Santa Maria sopra Minerva and the ancient temple over which it was built. And the observer would perhaps only have to change the direction of his glance or his position in order to call up the one view or the other.

There is clearly no point in spinning our phantasy any further, for it leads to things that are unimaginable and even absurd.
—Freud, *Civilization and Its Discontents*, trans. James Strachey

> ►–◄►–○–◄►–◄

*T*his book is the revelation of a very well-kept secret: that the Novel as a form of literature in the West has a continuous history of about two thousand years. This is no "secret" at all, of course. Any book offering a complete history of the novel has mentioned the novels of antiquity, but it has been customary to mention them dismissively, often merely in footnotes. We seem to have had a large investment in producing the Novel triumphantly as *the* form of modern times, and as an ultra-Western form too. Students in the English-speaking world have been bred to believe in the picture of "the Rise of the Novel" offered by Ian Watt in his important book of that name (1957). Watt's picture is amplified but not really changed by Michael McKeon in his more recent book, *The Origins of the English Novel, 1600–1740* (1987). British and American critics of Protestant descent or under the influence of Protestant history have often "explained" the development of the Novel in connection with the rise of Protestantism and of the new capitalist bourgeoisie. I do not wish in the least to deny the importance of Protestantism and capitalism as both social and philosophical developments, or their relation to all forms of literature in certain times and places. The English-speaking critics' penchant for looking at English Puritans and merchants for the *origins* of the Novel, however, indicates a very parochial view of the genre and history. This parochialism betrays itself in the incessant assertion that the Novel should always be separated from the Romance; there is a symptomatic determination to play down the inconvenient fact that other European literary languages make no such distinction.[1] A certain chauvinism leads English-speaking critics to treat the Novel as if it were somehow essentially English, and as if the English were pioneers of novel-writing—ignoring, for instance, the very visible Spanish novels of the sixteenth and early seventeenth centuries. A consideration of Spanish phenomena alone would lead to an admission that Catholicism and a premodern economic setting could also give rise to the Novel. English criticism of the Novel has by and large taken place within sound of the parish pump.

European criticism cannot be guilty of the same kind of chauvinism, which would deny Continental cultural production. Continental critics in general are more interested than the English in the prose fiction of the Renaissance. Mikhail Bakhtin, though a native of another country which came late to the Novel, was a student of Renaissance prose fiction as well as a literary theorist. In his (not unrepresentative) view, for modern purposes it was essentially the Renaissance that invented the Novel, whereas English critics (in defense of English belatedness) do not allow it to be "invented" until the eighteenth century, when the English came on strong. Bakhtin at least makes room for some discussion of Greek and Roman novels of antiquity, although he then rejects them as imperfect, indeed archaic, specimens. In placement and use of time (the "chronotope") these books are "static," "immobile," with "no potential for evolution, for growth, for change." I strongly disagree; a similar disagreement with Bakhtin's formulation here has been expressed by David Konstan (*Sexual Symmetry*, 11; 46–47). Bakhtin claims "the ancient world did not succeed in generating forms and unities that were adequate to the private individual and his life" (*The Dialogic Imagination*, trans. Emerson and Holquist, 110). Ancient novels have nothing important to say about the individual. In all that follows in Part I, I implicitly argue against this view. Bakhtin's language ("evolution," "growth") betrays the nineteenth-century origins of current views of literary kinds. The tendency to identify a past literature with the "static," the unchanging (in contrast to our own ebullient developmental change), is itself a form of pastoralism. Such idyllic notions have been useful to great industrial empires as they pursue their courses, murmuring "Better fifty years of Europe than a cycle of Cathay."

Twentieth-century historians and critics defending the Novel have emphasized the Novel's role as *superseding* something else. Sometimes it is treated as if its leading quality were its capacity to act as superseder, successor, or perhaps a sort of legitimate usurper, like a good republic replacing monarchy after a well-fought revolution. The Novel's nature is to be understood in terms of displacement. Traditionally, what the Novel was thought to displace—and *re*place—was the Epic. And for this view the antique novel itself bears some responsibility; Heliodorus figures the displacement of the *Odyssey* in the comic apparition of a grumbling Odysseus to one of the characters in his novel.

Some modern critics have even assumed an inevitably tidy relationship between epic/antiquity and novel/modernity, though few have been as absolute as Georg Lukács, who believed in a clear and ascertainable difference between historical phases; Lukács comments in puzzlement over *Don Quijote*, "We have here the curious case of a novel form existing in a period whose absolute belief in God really encouraged the epic" (*The Theory of the Novel* [1920], trans. Bostock, 101). Here is someone who lives in a neat universe. The Past = Belief in God = Epic; Modernity = Disbelief = Novel. Critics who are not, like Lukács, Marxists may still prefer such a paradigm. It rumples such tidiness to say that the age of early Christianity was really also an Age of the Novel—but so it was.

In twentieth-century criticism the Novel is seen also as not only displacing but *re*placing myth, or religious narrative, or rather religion—customarily, Christianity—itself. A book like Frank Kermode's *The Sense of an Ending* (1969) is based on that assumption. We accept such a view as literal history (instead of as an image) only at the cost of ignoring the facts. Actually, more people living on this globe in the 1990s have read some or all of the Christian Bible than have read any or all of *Don Quijote* or *Madame Bovary* or *War and Peace*—or even the books on the *New York Times* best-seller lists. So too for the Torah and the Koran, which, like the New Testament, are much more widely read than novels. The number of readers for any novel in any period is fairly limited. Eighteenth-century novels caused a stir, but they were not enormously widely read.[2] It has been estimated that the number of purchasers of the top best-seller would about fill Shea Stadium—compared to movie audiences, this seems indeed trifling. To admit these facts is not to degrade the novel, for books do have impact, if a slow-acting cumulative impact. Nevertheless, no novel is read as much as Scripture. To say this is not to state some kind of division between the ignorant and the sophisticated. Indeed, reading Scriptures (of some kind) can enable the reading of novels (and vice versa). Some twentieth-century readers and writers are atheists—and some are not. Many are agnostic. Some twentieth-century novels of repute have been written—and read—by theists and Scripture readers. We tend to deal with that fact, however, only when we deal with the individual author—André Gide, say, or Muriel Spark. Cultural simultaneity is something we find difficult to admit as a historical truth. Such zig-zagging on the part of the individual author, such untidiness on the part of the Zeitgeist, distresses the world-picture involved in some critical claims.

A world-picture is not a historical but a mythical view. Ours represents the absorption into literary theory of the idea of "progress" as the industrial world has conceived of progress, as well as Enlightenment ideas about emancipation from superstition. The Novel replaces the Romance as Reason replaces Superstition, and as the Model-T Ford replaces the horse and carriage. The charms of this simple progressivism may be diminishing, but it has certainly put its stamp upon our ideas about literature—even among those who urge us to read the valuable works of the past. During World War II, Erich Auerbach, a learned scholar in exile in Istanbul, wrote without access to libraries (so legend has it) his monumental study of narrative in the West. Auerbach's *Mimesis: The Representation of Reality in Western Literature* (1946) is a search for the origins and development of realism in literature from antiquity on. *Mimesis* relies on analysis of large chunks of various famous prose works. As a stylistic study it is still unequaled, but everything denotes a foregone conclusion. *Mimesis* assumes the displacement of (particularly Biblical) myth by realism. Auerbach spotlights in styles of narrative only those points congruent with the kinds of narrative realism he is looking for. We can see now that it might be possible to queer the pitch by inserting into his sequence some Post-Modernist works of literature more congruent with the "older" forms, thus disturbing the chronology, which is of course a chronology of progress—if not altogether of happy progress. Auerbach feared an imminent levelling of narrative into excessive simplicity! Biblical narrative is progressively displaced by history and then by the fully developed realistic novel. In selecting his passages, Auerbach can guarantee his results.

We should not think the criticism of fiction an arcane or ineffectual practice. Although the number of individual readers of criticism may be small, the effect can be very great. Literary criticism offers us the frameworks whereby we do our thinking. What critics say about the Novel is related to what those critics think about history, psychology, sociology, and their analyses in turn will affect history-writing and the making of history, as well as theories of sociology, psychology, and so on. At present the entire Western tradition is being overhauled and put to question—mainly, no doubt, because of Western contact with other nations and peoples, some of whom are not going to be subjugated to the West but already have some power over us. Within the academy, as within political circles, there is strong debate about the value of presenting "the Western tradition" in universities. The question is not really quite whether we should present the Western tradition (because we Westerners are bound to do so, whatever we discuss), but whether we present the Western tradition as one entire and perfect chrysolite, or as permeable, various, and subject to alteration. Are our "Great Books" material for discussion or a sort of sacred Scripture? The idea of a sacred canon (as distinct from a canon as a convenience) entails a high value to be set on exclusion, and many works—including many by "dead white males"—have been excluded. In order to make the picture conform to a desirable ideal there has been a good deal of suppression, including suppression of some works by "great" writers. The "canon," for instance, has deleted the Lucianic Henry Fielding almost entirely, so we can have the realist magistrate who writes the authoritative *Tom Jones*. Cervantes is "great" on the strength of *Don Quijote*, which we are so often told put an ending to that stupid form, the Romance, and announces the happy advent of modernity. It would embarrass our world-picture to mention the fact that Cervantes' last work, the work for which he wrote a moving preface on his deathbed, is a "romance" called *Persiles y Sigismunda* (1617). Revisions of canons are needed to do justice, even to some very established figures; the changes do not mean our attention will be drawn away from them, but that they will look different.

The vigorous and provocative criticism of the last forty years that rocked the halls of learning first in France and then in Britain and America is, probably, a herald of change rather than the major change itself. By defining interpretation, by questioning, by pointing out a wealth of signs and of cultural relations, critics have performed an invaluable service of clarification. We can no longer take cultural monuments for granted as idols (letting the lichens grow on them the while). Nor can we presume on our alleged disinterestedness. The prophetic gifts of our new criticism, visible in its power to disconcert, to give things a good shake and to call us to repentance (of a kind), seem inspired by millenarian feelings. It is part of our underconsciousness that we are entering not merely a new century but a new millennium. We may not want to carry in our baggage various styles of thinking, philosophies, mental and social habits that have served us for a long while. Political events (in the broadest sense of "political") indicate that nation is going to speak unto nation more often than hitherto, and in a different way. If writers and critics who, like myself, are undeniably Western want to explain to ourselves and others who we are and what we in the West have been doing and thinking during our history—say in the past couple of millenia or so—we need to be ready to correct and amplify the story that we tell ourselves. Otherwise we will mislead ourselves and others.

In Western Europe and America we have not been quite truthful during the last couple of hundred years in the story we have told about ourselves. A revised consideration of the Novel will mean a revised view of what constitutes the Western understanding of "personality." We will likewise have to augment and modify our view of family relations. For instance, Lawrence Stone has told us in *The Family, Sex and Marriage in England 1500–1800* (1977) that, in effect, familial love began about 1650, before which time (or thereabouts) men did not feel much affection for their wives, nor did husbands and wives feel more than slight emotional interest in their children. A number of literary scholars have relied upon this opinion. Even feminists. who do not share Stone's approval of "affectional individualism" and "companionate marriage" as ideals, seldom doubt his findings. Accepting a view like Stone's can also entail a dangerous tendency to suppose that other unenlightened people who have not "progressed" like ourselves (the poor, natives of Third World countries) do not have access to the feelings that grace our own refined relationships—a form of snobbery that can find even brutal and violent (as well as merely callous) expression.

Yet one has only to look at tombstones in ancient Athens to see very clearly that men and women have loved each other and their children for a long time. The monument to a dead little girl put up by her sorrowing family (a monument now in the National Museum in Athens) shows, as well as the wealth of the family, of course, the extent to which a mere girl child could be loved, cherished, and lamented; the sculptor has caught the affection in portraying the girl with her rabbit, a pet that may symbolize future life (Plate 1). Consider likewise Jairus' anxiety and grief for his dying daughter, and Jesus' concern for Jairus and the child (Luke 8:41–56). A great many important if subtle emotional changes may well have taken place in the period historians now call "Early Modern," but we do ourselves an injury if we accept coarse generalizations—not to mention the injury we can do our ancestors.

The idea of "personality" in any form must be bound up with ideas about the family, its structure, the individual's development and place in it. It is also inevitably bound up with the question of erotic love. At times one encounters a strange kind of anti-pastoral pastoralism that feels a nostalgia for an era when we were innocent of personality, and also innocent of erotic love—when we did not have to cope with the heavy intricacies of (modern) breathing human passion. Devout Jews, Christians, and Muslims may feel that heterosexual love is morally dubious and at best distracting from important spiritual concerns. Devout Marxists and feminists feel so too. To some feminists, such as Ruth Perry in *Women, Letters, and the Novel*, heterosexual love as an ideal is an aspect of a kind of conspiracy against women, and the novel that developed to promote it encouraged women in isolation and fantasy.[3] If love is a conspiracy, it is much older than the age of "bourgeois individualism" in which some historians tend to locate it;

nostalgia for an age that knew no Eros is hard put to find a home. There has admittedly been a tendency for classicists to present their age as secure from that awkward feminizing influence. Plato's Eros, is after all, homosexual, but Socrates does not indulge it, and Love between persons, being only a matter of beauty, should be but the first rung in the ladder that leads to higher things. Friedrich Wilhelm Nietzsche and C. S. Lewis have perhaps nothing else in common, but they both share the nineteenth century's desire to keep the grand classical age free of love stories. I was taught by C. S. Lewis, through reading his *The Allegory of Love* (1936), that what we know as "romantic love," heterosexual eroticism with an emphasis on personal emotions, began in the Middle Ages. C. S. Lewis gave heterosexual (or indeed homosexual) romantic love a rather low place in the scheme of things, as can be seen in his *The Four Loves* (1960). It is an irony that since the dramatization of his life in *Shadowlands* (1988), later a motion picture (1994), Lewis has become the "hero" of a love story and bids fair to be set, in company with his wife Joy Davidman, in the niche reserved for legendary great lovers, along with Abelard and Eloise. Truly, Eros, as the Greek novelists said, is a trickster, and he takes his revenge.

Eros is full of surprises. One of the surprises may be his literary presence. If one is taught that certain statements about Love are conceits and clichés of the Middle Ages, clichés later revived by Sidney and Spenser (not to mention John Lyly), then it is a surprise to read a passage such as this: "As soon as I saw her, I was lost. Beauty indeed wounds deeper than an arrow, and strikes through the eyes unto the soul, for the eye is the route of love-wounds" (Achilles Tatius, *Kleitophon and Leukippé*, 14). "Romantic love," with the poetic conceits that express it, is much, *much* older than the Middle Ages, and there is a great continuity in our dealings with it. Along with "romantic love" in the novels of antiquity can be found scenes, expressions, gestures, narrative tones entirely consonant with what we have come to know as "sentimentalism" and associate with the late seventeenth and the eighteenth centuries. A belief in Providence, joined with the secularization of that belief, has often been attributed to the readers and writers of the so-called "early novel" of the eighteenth century; recent critics in the British-American tradition (such as Watt and Damrosch) have made a good deal of the supposed connection of our fiction with Protestant Puritanism.[4] But a belief in Providence, or a reference to it, is neither Puritan nor Protestant. It is not even necessarily Christian or Jewish. We will find the pagan novel writers playing upon providence, the providence of god, *theou pronoia*.

The development of sentiment and erotic passion in prose narratives dealing with individual characters—this is a much older literary event than most of us are told about in college. If "Character" and "Sentiment" are to be found in works of late antiquity, we must change the story we have been telling about the modern age. Nietzsche in his first book, *The Birth of Tragedy from the Spirit of Music* (*Die Geburt der Tragödie aus dem Geiste der Musik*, 1872), rejects the novel on the same principles as those by which he rejects Judaism, Christianity, and democracy. Greek tragedy, he says, was an Apollonian embodiment of Dionysiac understanding of the truth of things, a truth that music, rather than any other art, conveyed. The noble tragedy of Aeschylus and Sophocles is not interested in the personal and does not represent "characters." Dionysian art dissolves boundaries and recognizes individuation as a curse. Greek culture underwent a kind of Fall, according to Nietzsche's system, when its glorious tragedy was brought to an end by the associated villains, Euripides and Socrates. Both of these deny *die Mysterien-lehre der Tragödie* (the mystery-teaching of Tragedy) which is "the underlying be-lief in the unity of all that is, the consideration of Individuation as the original basis of evil [*als des Urgrundes des Übels*], Art as the joyful hope that the curse of Individuation may be broken as the foreshadowing of a restored unity" (Sec. 10, 73–74).

According to Nietzsche, Euripides debased the drama by introducing or-dinary men as characters—which Nietzsche also presents figuratively as a kind of vulgar revolution brought about by Mr. Average Man himself: "The man of everyday life [Der Mensch des alltäglichen Lebens] pushed forward from the au-ditorium onto the stage" (Sec. 11, 77). Euripides inaugurated the era of indi-viduation and personal concern, including the care of personal survival and per-sonal immortality. Socrates likewise denied the Dionysiac in asserting belief in the power of reason; he diverted ancient culture from its nobler pessimism to the debased optimism that accompanies dialectic. This whole movement is craven and effeminate—and *feminine*, "this womanish flight [*diese weibische Flucht*] be-fore the serious and the terrible" (79).

Nietzsche projects the Enlightenment of the eighteenth century back-wards to the fifth century B.C. and accuses Euripides and Socrates of introducing the modern world, inaugurating a debased era of individualism, personal con-sciousness and trust in reason, all giving rise to the sway of Christianity, the de-velopment of democracy, and the bourgeois life and morality of the nineteenth century A.D. The Novel was an inevitable, if despicable, product of this first En-lightenment. Plato, a debased and querulous celebrant of Socrates' new shallow doctrine of the rule of reason, is responsible for the novel as well as for Platonism:

> The Platonic dialogue was, as it were, the lifeboat in which the ship-wrecked older Poesy rescued all her children; they crowded together in a narrow space and, timidly submissive to their only steersman, Socrates, sailed off to a new world, which could never be tired of looking at the fantastic images of this spectacle. Really, Plato had given to the whole of Posterity the model of a new art form, the model of the *Novel* [*das Vorbild des "Romans"*], which can be characterized as an endlessly amplified Aesopic fable in which Poesy holds a position in relation to dialectical Philosophy very like the position which for many hundreds of years Philosophy itself held in relation to Theology; namely as ancilla. (Sec. 14, 95)

That is, Nietzsche indicates, in the Novel, literature—poetic quality, poesy—is merely a handmaid to reason. Aesopic low smartness and Socratic reason, with its scientific spirit and endless *prosy* dialogue, produce a work which has long bid farewell not only to the true Dionysiac spirit but even to the true Apollonian. The new world belongs to the "Alexandrian man" who is not only writer and reader of this new nonliterature but also the essential librarian and the archetypal critic, without desire or art (*ohne Lust und Kraft, der alexandrinische Mensch*: Sec. 18, 122).

We need not (and I presume we do not) share Nietzsche's values in order to entertain something of his vision of profound change in European culture—without his hatred for the fruits of such change. Nor need we believe in such abrupt and heavily marked departures in antiquity in order to acknowledge the possibility that alterations parallel and similar to those we now attribute to the seventeenth or eighteenth centuries A.D. may have been occurring before and during the Age of Rome. Such a recognition will at least prevent our overstressing the world-historical alterations that took place in the West during the era often called the Enlightenment. Nietzsche is himself of course responding to both the Enlightenment and nineteenth-century Romanticism; *The Birth of Tragedy* is partly intended as a repudiation of the prevalent fantasy of a white marble Greekness, a calm Greekness that Nietzsche terms "Apollonian" and counters in the name of Dionysios. But his "Dionysian" is but a white Greekness with blood, fire, and will. The fantasy of white marble Greekness, of perfect Athenian beauty and calm civilization, had been fostered since the late eighteenth century, and it harmonized with one of our most repellent currents of thought, certainly to be found in Nietzsche—the exaltation of the Western European (pseudo-scientifically to be termed "Aryan") in terms of an idealized Greek, either the intellectual Athenian or hardy Spartan. Usually it is the Athenian citizen who is metamorphosed into the noble Greek, becoming the ideal cultural Father. In Him we are always culturally justified in whatever horrors of colonizing or ethnic cleansing we set out to pursue. Such a bolstering belief, which assisted the English, French, and Germans in the advancing stages of their colonial ventures, was bound to make all literary issues racial issues. Martin Bernal in his *Black Athena: The Afroasiatic Roots of Classical Civilization* (1987; 1991) has pointed out to what an extent the image of Greece and the Greeks has been whitened and history rewritten in order to preserve the notion of racially pure, handsome, rational Greeks.[5]

When Nietzsche writes "Alexandrian" he does so with an obvious sneer, for that which is "Alexandrian" stands for that which is racially mixed, impure, and cosmopolitan. Alexandria was always on a crossroads of commerce and exchange of ideas; open to all comers it was sophisticated, contaminated by the presence of Semitic and African people, and full of the babble of many voices. It was tolerant and thus degenerate—all matters, I think, in the mind of Laurence Durrell when he wrote *The Alexandrian Quartet* (1957–1960). Such exchange or such tolerance is not at all what Nietzsche means by the dissolution of boundaries, for Alexandrian tolerance must admit both difference *and* individuation; it does not dissolve and it does not reject. Spiritually speaking, the novel that we know (though not the Platonic dialogue) does come from Alexandria. "Alexandria" symbolizes the new world of Hellenistic culture, and of urban self-consciousness.

Alexandria was founded in 331 B.C. by Alexander the Great. It was one of the great cities of antiquity to be founded in historical time. A city such as Thebes or Athens or Rome had some story about its foundation, but the foundation itself took place in the dim mist of long ago. The cities had been there from time immemorial. Alexandria was visibly created in history, its nature recorded; it was even planned. It is thus not just a city but a city that knows that cities are man-made. It became very handsome (as Achilles Tatius' hero found—see the epigraph to my "preface"). It was the center of a new humanism, of cultural cooperation. It was also a city that liked reading; its scholars and librarians collected the manuscripts of a great library. Alexandria believed in *translation*—that strange activity acknowledging that there may be some good in somebody else's culture, or indeed that a number of cultures could combine on occasion without losing identity. Cultural identity is not locked away in a precious box, reserved for the few. There were Greek-speaking Jews in Alexandria, and this city produced the *Septuagint*—the Greek translation of the Hebrew Scripture. Alexandria thrived on exchange and on openness.

The Novel grew among a motley collection of various peoples living in the Mediterranean basin; many of the readers lived in upper Egypt and there were probably many novel-readers in Alexandria itself. Some of the earliest novels of this new "modern" period were probably Egyptian.[6] The ancient novel began to flourish—to the despair of later classicists. Nietzsche's contempt is only a very strongly expressed example of a general contempt for the Novel shared by classicists who do not share Nietzsche's dislike of Euripides, Socrates or Plato. Part of the trouble with trying to get hold of the ancient novel and to understand it is the tone of fastidious distaste prevalent (at least until very recently) among classicists who have traditionally treated the ancient novel as something not fit to be an object of a gentleman's attention. Such an attitude is, of course, also consonant with certain negative attitudes to the modern novel. In Part III of this book I hope to explain *why* this repudiation has been so widespread, even though the majority of all our Western novelists for 2000 years have been male. Yet, of course, the Novel has never been really repudiated, either; it is always being read. No genre can claim to have given more consolation or sheer pleasure, though many genres would claim they were more edifying or profitable. The pleasure a novel gives is often considered a superficial matter; I consider it a deep one, and hope to explain why. But these larger matters must wait for the last part of this book.

The first task of this book in Part I must be to recover the ancient novels for the reader, first through description of major examples of novels in Greek and Latin, and then through consideration of their topics, themes, and techniques. Part II explains first how the novels in Greek and Latin survived and influenced the literature of the Middle Ages and then how, in an onrush of renewed appearance, they became a decided influence on literary developments from the fifteenth to the eighteenth century.

Part III departs from the historical method and turns to themes. I here examine thematic metaphors or images, or, as I call them, "tropes of fiction." The approach will be topical and not chronological. Novels of different periods will rub shoulders; novels of A.D. 250, 1560, 1840, 1980, 1750—these may be placed together in surprising combination to point out resemblances and continuities. Throughout, additional information and issues of modern criticism not essential to the main design will be dealt with in the Notes. Authors quoted in the text will be cited in the text.

It is my purpose in *this* book to deal with continuities and to make a point of connectedness. Such an interest does not preclude a respect for difference. It is simply that difference is not my subject here; I write because I feel our comments on some kinds of differences have recently tended to obfuscate connections and to blot out continuities. There are continuities and connections in the Western world, after all. That this is so can be felt very acutely in a study of graphic design and ornamental patterns. Swags used to adorn a Macedonian underground tomb

of the sixth century B.C. may adorn a Roman dining-room of the first century
A.D., and then be seen functioning as Christmas decoration in a Canadian department store in the twentieth century A.D. If you stumble on an ancient mosaic in
Ostia you may be looking at your linoleum. We forget much less than we think—
even though we like to flatter ourselves that the modern world is all rush-rush,
with no memory.

The study of one particular novel, Samuel Richardson's *Clarissa, or The History of a Young Lady* (1747–1748), has been a recurrent pursuit or obsession
through most of my adult life. Trying to understand it fully is like trying to understand the entire history of the West. I now see that this novel has a larger
context and deeper roots than I could have guessed when I wrote my first book,
A Natural Passion (1974). The story of the righteous virgin is a story we have been
perpetually telling and trying to interpret. I no longer think we can talk about
temporal changes until we have a finer temporal register, and a wider view of the
Novel's own history. That does not mean I repudiate any critical approach—
Marxist, historical, psychological, feminist, structuralist, deconstructionist—all
are viable. Neither do I believe it is possible to eliminate works from consideration
on the basis of preconceived strict notions of the *genre*. My only criteria are related
to those qualities of which Nietzsche complains: I believe that a novel includes
the idea of length (preferably forty or more pages), and that, above all, it should
be in *prose*. The novel, like Molière's M. Jourdain, talks prose, descends to our
daily unpoetic level—however skilled the prose may be. Yet I do not promise
never to mention *Evgeny Onegin* or *The Golden Gate*, and some short fictions, folk
tales, or antique and modern novellas, come within my range of view. If anybody has called a work a novel at any time, that is sufficient—so Xenophon's
Cyropaedia, Bunyan's *Pilgrim's Progress*, Voltaire's *Candide*, J. M. Barrie's *Peter Pan*,
can all be admitted. When we are trying to discover what a genre might be (and
the idea of "genre" is itself at once loose and arbitrary) it is too soon to impose
strict definitions and qualifications. Nothing is precluded by my theory, which
comes not to destroy but to fulfill.

Freud—in the passage figuring as epigraph to this Introduction—imagines a Rome in which all its monuments and images of all eras are perpetually
present. He conjures up this image of our single and collective psyche and then
repudiates it, almost with horror. It is "absurd'; we need spatial order and temporal sequence in order to comprehend life. Yet—why not suppose the Novel as
a form to be that Rome with all its elements synchronously present? The Novel
may be the "place" where most readers, without discomfort, obtain that experience of simultaneous contact with the earliest and latest levels of our consciousness—a consciousness always both individual and collective. The novel—any
novel—can be such a "place." The Novel is neither a place nor a time, and yet we
call it "broad" and "long." It gives the impression of amplitude, of allowing room
for our desires to play in. The experience of reading a novel may be a bit like
Kleitophon's experience of his first visit to Alexandria. You cannot take it all in at
one go, it requires a deal of noticing, eyes always on the stretch. I think the novelist creates Kleitophon's experience of Alexandria as a figure for the reader's experience of Achilles Tatius' own ostentatiously witty, brilliant, and various work

of fiction. You cannot take in all the beauty of it at first reading, driven by the restless desire to see more.

If I think I have some clues as to the nature of the Novel, I must remember that clues lead to labyrinths. I shall try not to let my work become a dark and intricate labyrinth, for the object, as of the Eleusinian mysteries, for all the going down to the deeps, is that the reader should experience some degree of illumination.

PART ONE

>─┤◆├─○─┤◆├─<

The Ancient Novel

>─┤◆├─○─┤◆├─<

Woodcut illustration of *Kynge Appolyn*, 1510.

CHAPTER I

›—‹⁜›—‹

The Ancient Novel

›—‹⁜›—‹

Let us leave it to the Reviewers to abuse such effusions of fancy at their leisure, and over every new novel to talk in threadbare strains of the trash with which the press now groans. Let us not desert one another; we are an injured body. Although our productions have afforded more extensive and unaffected pleasure than those of any other literary corporation in the world, no species of composition has been so much decried.
                                                        —Jane Austen, *Northanger Abbey*

[I will stitch together for you various fables in this Milesian conversation, and will soothe your benevolent ears with a sweet murmuring—that is, if you do not disdain to look at an Egyptian papyrus written upon with a sharp Nile-reed pen—so that you may marvel at the figures and fortunes of men transformed into other shapes and then in a reciprocal intertwining changed back again.]
                          —Apuleius, *Asinus Aureus*

At ego tibi sermone isto Milesio varias fabulas conseram auresque tuas benivolas lepido susurro permulceam—modo si papyrum Aegyptiam argutia Nilotici calami inscriptam non spreveris inspicere— figuras fortunasque hominum in alias imagines conversas et in se rursum mutuo nexu refectas ut mireris.

›—‹⁜›—‹

*R*omance and the Novel are one. The separation between them is part of a problem, not part of a solution. The enquiry of this book includes (ultimately) an enquiry into the reasons why we have wanted since the eighteenth century to keep these two apart. The Anglo-Saxon tradition in particular since the mid-eighteenth century has exhibited a constant anxiety that fiction should adhere to the criteria posed by "realism," and the standard of "realism" has often prevented British and American critics from taking a good square look at the Novel. "Romance" is a dismissive term, especially in English usage; other European languages have admitted the unity of Romance and Novel: a novel is *le roman, der Roman, il romanzo*. Only the English speakers have maintained a perpetually stern attitude to despised Romance. "Romance" has been used to describe a mood or mode rather than a genre, strictly speaking; Northrop Frye has pursued this use *à l'outrance*. I am indebted to his work and admire that of Patricia Parker in *Inescapable Romance*, but I have very different interests. When the term is not being used to allude to a rather cloudy literary mode characterized by wishful thinking—and best left to Shakespeare in his late plays—"Romance" is despicable, a term reserved for a certain low section of the bookstore appealing to women only. "Romance" is most often used in literary studies to allude to forms conveying literary pleasure the critic thinks readers would be better off without.

It describes works that fail to meet the requirements of realism. But realism has faded away like the Cheshire cat, leaving its smile of reason behind; when novels by admired novelists deal with barons living in trees and with girls born with green hair it is time to drop the pretense that the primary demand of a long work of prose fiction is that it should be "realistic."

As the supposed distinction between Romance and Novel has in the past been employed somewhat disingenuously (and exploited not without purpose), and as the emphasis on that supposed distinction has often done more harm than good, I propose to do without it altogether. I shall call all the works I am dealing with "novels," as that is the term we feel most positively about, and the word "novel" is an encouraging word, describing something inviting to a reader. I am employing few and simple criteria of classification. A work is a novel if it is fictional, if it is in prose, and if it is of a certain length. Even these criteria are somewhat elastic (as explained in the Introduction), although the difference between poetic and prose narrative is of importance. Poetic narrative does not spring from quite the same sources or use the same techniques and tropes as prose narrative; in the end, they seem to serve different gods. A more troubling concept is the "fictional," for there is a very real sense in which all history and most written discourse is fictional (from *fingere*, to shape, mold or model); that is, it is something made or made up. It is disturbing to realize that we know about Julius Caesar in the same way that we know about Don Quixote. That is, both are mediated to us chiefly through texts—with a few graphic illustrations thrown in, which also (like dramatizations) become texts in turn. As we shall see, novels have always been playing around with history and history-writing, cultivating the "True Life Novel." [1] Characters in a work of fiction are often historical personages—or, to refine upon the point, bear historical names. At any moment a new novel can emanate from the idea of Napoleon, and historians proper (i.e., persons likely to be found in Departments of History) are powerless to prevent it.

The story of the Novel, its history and its nature, has often been told, but the story was told differently in the late Renaissance from the way in which it was told by the beginning of the nineteenth century. From the Renaissance to the early eighteenth century a less abridged and restricted history of the novel had considerable currency. In Part II, I shall deal with critical opinions about the novel in the Renaissance. Here I shall cite only one major critic, Pierre-Daniel Huet, Bishop of Avranches. Huet is an important critic of the Novel, at large and in detail. His treatise first appeared as a preface to *Zayde* (1670), a novel by Mme de Lafayette. Huet's discussion, amplified, was published as *Traité de l'origine des romans* (*Treatise on the Origin of Novels*), and went through edition after edition; the first English translation was published in 1672. Huet is one of the most vocal of modern enthusiasts for the novel. He says that he read Honoré d'Urfé's *L'Astrée* (1607–1628) in his youth and, having reread it, appreciates it even more. Huet's attitude is not at all rule-bound; his view of the value of probability does not entail adherence to a strict idea of realism. Huet believes that we are creatures naturally inclined to love fiction: "In my opinion, it comes from the fact that the faculties of our soul being of too great an extent and too vast a capacity to be filled with present objects, the soul seeks in the past and in the future, in truth and in lies, in imaginary spaces and even in the impossible, something to occupy and exercise them" (192–193).² The human soul will never be satisfied only with what is present, or even only with what is possible. The tendency of Huet's compatriots and contemporaries to devise rules for literature he treats with some skepticism. "These rules are known to so few people, that good judges are perhaps rarer than good Novelists [*Romanciers*] or good Poets. . . . The art of narration, which everybody practices and which so few people understand, is easier to understand than to practice well."³ Huet is more interested in the pleasures that novels, ancient as well as modern, can offer, and he concerns himself with tracing a continuous history of prose fiction. He acknowledges that it did not begin in France or Spain: "It is neither in Provence, nor in Spain, as many believe, that we must hope to find the first beginnings of this agreeable amusement of good idle folk [*des honnêtes paresseux*]. We must go to seek them in the most distant countries, and in the most remote antiquity" (2).⁴

But, Huet insists, even when we have got back to the most remote antiquity we have not found the origin of the novel if we expect it to be simply Greek or Roman. Where do novels come from?

> We must look for their first origin in the nature and spirit of man, man the inventive, lover of novelties and fictions, desirous to learn and to communicate what he has invented and what he has learned; and this inclination is common to all mankind in all eras, and in all places: but the Orientals have always appeared much more strongly possessed of it than others, and so their example has made such an impression on the most ingenious and polite of Occidental nations. When I say "Orientals," I mean the Egyptians, the Arabs, the Persians, the Indians, and the Syrians. You will admit it without doubt, once I have shown you that the majority of the great Novelists of antiquity [*grands Romanciers de l'antiquité*] came from these peoples. (12–13)⁵

It is the Eastern peoples—*les Orientaux*—who show to the fullest extent the human capacities for quickness of thought, speech, and imagination, and it is these qualities, put best to use first by "les Orientaux" that gave us our novel, of which the first practitioners were largely Syrians, Persians, Egyptians and so on.

Huet is not without some of those prejudices that Edward Said has bitterly summed up in *Orientalism*.⁶ Huet thought that "Oriental" fiction was uncultivated and luxuriant, and that the Greeks or the Greek language gave better form to Eastern expression, bringing the form under the rule of the epic and joining the diverse parts into one perfect body of harmonious construction. Yet he is consistently emphatic about the imaginative power, sense of beauty, and wit to be found in the "Eastern" peoples, who gave us literature of all kinds, including fables, not to speak of the stories of Job, Esther, Judith, and the Song of Songs. The Milesian fables, so often alluded to (and of which no examples survive) were produced, Huet thinks, by a people in Ionia who had first learned from the Persians the art of making novels, if rather risqué ones. Among the "Eastern" and "foreign" sources of course Africa is included. Huet is sometimes not very complimentary about "African" style. The Africans, "these rhyming peoples" (*ces peuples rimeurs*), introduced rhyme to European poetry, and are fond of jingles of sound. You find in African authors a certain stiffness and affectation, he says—

St. Augustine is an example among nonfiction writers, and Apuleius among the novelists. Yes, Huet has his prejudices at times, but they do not interfere with his knowledge or his enjoyment. The big thing about Huet's *Traité* is that he sets the novel in a large context; he insists upon its polyglot energies, its multiracial origins. It is wonderfully refreshing to read Huet after reading Ian Watt. Huet really *likes* almost all the antique novels, and he is one of the first (and few) critics to compare ancient novels with recent ones.

Classicists who study the ancient novel customarily cite Huet, though scholars of modern literatures tend to ignore him. Huet's essential point is not disputed by modern scholars, although knowledge has grown with fresh discoveries of papyri. The Novel was produced in antiquity by people from non-Greek and non-Roman areas, by writers who came from the Near East and from Africa. The Novel, that is, is a "foreign" import—or rather, it is the product of combination, of contact between Southern Europe, Western Asia, and Northern Africa. And behind these regions, the regions of Greece and Syria and Ethiopia and Egypt, there lie other areas, hinterlands not without influence. We can assume the possibility of story and style filtering in from the Balkans and the Celtic lands in the West, from Persia and India in the East, from the Sudan and Kush and Katanga in the South. The homeland of the Western Novel is the Mediterranean, and it is a multiracial, multilingual, mixed Mediterranean.

An influential American classicist, Ben Edwin Perry in his book *The Ancient Romances* (1967), memorably defended the essential Greekness of the literature, as well as the idea of individual authorship, as against the claims of Mediterranean mixtures and communal or general developments. He wrote what has become almost an epigram in certain circles: "The first romance was deliberately planned and written by an individual author, its inventor. He conceived it on a Tuesday afternoon in July, or some other day or month of the year" (175). Perry had come to detest the idea of literary development, of anonymous cooperation that submerges the Author—even though he himself has his theory of origins to promote: "Greek Romance is essentially Hellenistic drama in narrative form" (78). Perry sniffs with Nietzsche at the decline of a culture into cosmopolitan and democratic-tending messiness:

> Whatever in literary or dramatic art is meant to be accommodated to the understanding and taste of the cosmopolitan masses is thereby debased in proportion to the degree in which it is popularly exploited. Quality cannot be spread abroad in a *big* world. . . . Literature made popular in an open society, such as that of the Hellenized age or the present, is progressively externalized, mechanized, sensationalized, and impoverished. . . . That which reaches out for everything loses its own shape . . . the novel . . . is the open form *par excellence* for the open society. (47)

Perry was perhaps reacting against the ideas current among the young in the 1960s. One Romanticism opposes another. Perry's typical response is a far cry from Huet's, with its candid enthusiasm for the various humanity of the Mediterranean shores. Perry's form of romanticism leads him to espouse the cause of the lonely independent author. Yet, though Perry wants the "origin" to be the creative individual, the romantic unit, it seems scarcely worthwhile to be the unhappy genius who is the origin of so foul a form. Reading Perry's book, one sees how difficult it has been until recently in classical studies to get the ancient novel accepted: "externalized, mechanized, sensationalized, and impoverished"—Perry might be talking of daytime TV rather than of the ancestors of *Don Quijote* and *Wuthering Heights*.

We never, of course, encounter a founding author, the "He" who "conceived it" (but could he gestate it?) on the Tuesday in July or any other time. The Father of the Novel . . . we may seek "him" in vain. Some have claimed that role for various writers, chiefly Xenophon and Chariton. Xenophon's *Cyropaedia* (400 B.C.) seems something of a special case, although its influential presence in the novel tradition (up to *Tristram Shandy*) cannot be ignored. Huet said that the novel as we know it did not begin until after Alexander the Great, and most modern scholars agree with him. Chariton's *Chaireas and Kallirrhoé* appears at present to have the best claim to be the earliest surviving complete work—but dating may change at any time.

The "origins" of the novel, as Huet pointed out, lie in the various cultures of the Mediterranean basin. This very believable view has encouraged a number of scholars to investigate certain specific phenomena in relation to the Novel; the only problem with these searches is that individual scholars tend to wed themselves to specific "sources" as providing absolute answers. A number of seekers after *Quellen* have proposed origins: Platonic dialogue (Nietzsche); Euripides, New Comedy, and Hellenistic drama (Perry, after Nietzsche); school exercise, love-elegy, and travel story (Erwin Rohde); history and historical biography (Ludikovsky); fables, *fabliaux*, and oral stories (Sophie Trenkner); Sumerian myths of fertility and divine kingship (Graham Anderson).[7] There is no reason to deny any of these—and obviously these multitudinous "sources" do not contradict the insights of Huet. Some very interesting suggestions are offered by Karl Kerényi in *Die Griechisch-Orientalische Romanliteratur in religionsgeschichtlicher Beleuchtung*, which could be rendered as *Greco-Oriental Novels in the Light of Religious Writings* (1927); and by Reinhold Merkelbach in *Roman und Mysterium in der Antike* (1962). Both posit a religious origin for the novel. Kerényi suggested that the literary novel still carried traces of Isis-worship and unfolded from the story (or stories) of Isis and Osiris. Merkelbach elaborates upon Kerényi's theory by relating the novel to the several mystery religions, including the cults of Dionysius, Isis, and Mithras. Perry dismisses the work of both of these scholars with a loud sneer: "This is all nonsense to me" (336). It is not nonsense to me, however, and the theories of Kerényi and Merkelbach will be discussed later.

Who read the earliest novels? Who were the everyday men and women who pushed themselves into view in the works of fiction and saw their lives reflected and interpreted in these novels? And *when* did they start reading novels? The evidence is unsatisfactory and diffuse. The number of papyrus fragments of novels that have turned up in Egypt leads scholars to believe that novel-reading (and perhaps novel-writing) was popular among Egyptians in the second century A.D. and later. The tone of the *Satyricon* (by an author who died in A.D. 65), however, makes one wonder if there were not by the Age of Nero a great many novel-readers on the mainland of Italy. The *Satyricon*'s parodic comedy and stylistic playfulness would be lost on a readership with no idea of the patterns of Greek narrative prose fiction. The heyday of the Greek novel in antiquity has traditionally been related to the "Second Sophistic" (so called by Philostratus in his *Lives of the Sophists*, in the third century) since Erwin Rohde first discussed the movement and the novels in 1876. The "Second Sophistic," less a period than a state of rhetoric, was perhaps the first self-conscious literary movement in the West, something after the fashion of *préciosité* in France of the seventeenth century. In the second century A.D., in and after the time of the Emperor Hadrian (A.D. 117–138), both at court and among the upper classes generally, a strong philhellenism led to cultivation of the rhetorical arts and an elaboration of pure Greek style. The "sophists" or teachers of rhetoric were highly regarded as cultural experts; preservation of a self-conscious high culture may well have seemed all the more necessary in the face of an expanding and centrifugal empire. Small-town boys could make good by becoming exponents of this culture, highly paid rhetoricians who were good at making speeches; they could make their way as lawyers or as schoolmasters and tutors. The consciousness of literary style is evident in Lucian of Samosata in Syria, who sets himself the task of writing outrageously funny works, often very contemporary satires, in pure high Greek, the Greek of antiquity. Lucian, the most antitheistic and anticlerical of all Greek writers, recommended himself not only to the Byzantine courts but also to the monks; because of his purity of style (so useful for school teaching) the outrageous Lucian survives in profusion when more pious or sober writers have failed to be transmitted to us.

The conscious revival of "Greek" culture was paradoxically hospitable to ornate styles and rhetorical patterns of other Asian or African cultures, even while Greek grammar and vocabulary were being sustained. The Second Sophistic delighted in clever speech and writing. A number of the characters of the novels of the Second Sophistic themselves share the qualities of a skilled rhetorician. But we should beware. A century *before* the Second Sophistic, Petronius' antihero Encolpius possesses the characteristics of the wandering sophist, Latin model, and is, like his friend the rhetoric teacher Agamemnon, capable of flying off into elaborate rhetorical discourse at any moment. Well-educated or clever young men down on their luck have been favorite comic characters in works of novelists of all eras, from Petronius Arbiter and Achilles Tatius down through Alemán, Le Sage, and Dickens to Bellow and Richler.

The old idea that the Second Sophistic gave rise to the Greek novel has seemed increasingly less likely or even relevant with the new discoveries of papyrus fragments of Greek novels that clearly predate the era of the Second Sophistic. We can, however, certainly say that writers such as Achilles Tatius and Apuleius exhibit qualities much prized among the sophisticated *littérateurs* of their era, and it was the novels of the Second Sophistic that were to receive most attention in the West after the Renaissance, making not only their style but also their era represent a norm, or even a point of origin. It ought to be entertained as a possibility that the development of the novel in Greek (e.g. Chariton's *Chaireas and Kallirrhoé*) and in Latin (viz. Petronius' *Satyricon*) was itself a major influence *upon* the manner of the Second Sophistic, that the Novel (or individual novels) *contributed* to this "movement" and need not be considered merely a result of it.

When we discuss the Second Sophistic we are talking about the literary interests of the most highly educated men in the Roman Empire during a period of more than two hundred years. The picture of a sophist (or of his patron) is not exactly the image of the lowest common social denominator. Yet a number of modern classicists seem to be of divided mind; on the one hand they give some sort of recognition to the Second Sophistic as a feature in the cultivation of the Novel, while on the other hand they disdain that Novel as little better than literary garbage. Rather like Nietzsche, they are determined to see in the novel reader (the Common Reader) the doubtless unpleasant features of the Common Man— or worse still, the Common Woman. Ben Perry contemptuously calls this first reading audience for the Greek novels "the poor-in-spirit" (5, and elsewhere). They are the low—the uneducated, the powerless, the dim. Erich Segal, a classicist as well as the author of *Love Story*, suggested in an article in *The New York Times* that this first readership might have been—indeed probably was—largely women; B. P. Reardon tossed off a contemptuous reference to women's magazines. At least one physician in late antiquity (Priscianus) recommended reading such works to male patients of afflicted potency; some have assumed that numbers of these works operated as—and were written as—pornography.[8] The low, the uneducated—the impotent—*women*: these unenviable and even despised groups keep turning up as the putative readers of antique novels. The idea that writers of "classical times" might have written something that pleased *women* seems in itself enough to drive classicists into a frenzy of disapproval.

The Emperor Julian, famously the Apostate, one of history's salient victims of intense nostalgia, tried in the fourth century to restore not only pure Greek culture but also the purest religion. In a letter of advice to a priest of the old religion, Julian advises him to shun made-up stuff (*plasmata*) of seeming history such as love stories and all that kind of nonsense.[9] This sort of advice is often given in novel-reading ages. Jane Austen's truthful heroine Catherine Morland, opposing such advice, tries to explain why she likes fiction, and doesn't like "real solemn history': "with wars or pestilences, in every page; the men all so good for nothing, and hardly any women at all—it is very tiresome" (*Northanger Abbey*, 84). We are always being told that we ought to read the "real solemn history" and keep away from made-up stories, especially love stories, *erōtikai hypotheseis*. Yet serious history is customarily narrative, and the narrative has its fictional elements. A history is a *story*, and story is the same word as *historia*.

The word *history* originally meant *inquiry*. Herodotus (c. 484–424 B.C.), the first "Greek" historian whose work survives, did not come from mainland Greece but from Halicarnassus (modern Bodrum) in Asia Minor. He produced a work in nine books, his *Historiai* or *Inquiries*, designed to investigate the reasons for the conflict between Greece and Persia. His inquiries are open-minded, appreciative of the cultures of Asia and Africa, reflecting lively geographic and ethnographic researches, and offering sympathetic accounts of diverse societies. Thucydides of Athens (c. 464–401 B.C.) produced a very different history with no chatty investigation, deviations from central topic, or strange legends. His *History* is a narrative about the Peloponnesian war, one tense sequence of events as these affect one *polis* (Athens). Catherine Morland points out that most of the speeches in history books must be invention (hence fiction); Thucydides is the founder of the tradition of supplying invented rhetorical speeches for leaders. His narrative is dramatic, but it is also enclosed and nationalistic.

Naturally there are no emphatic references to women; Thucydides is the founder of the solemn history with "hardly any women at all." By contrast there are (it has been calculated) 375 references to women in Herodotus; British classicist John Gould thinks the variety of women and their roles constitute "evidence of Herodotus' distinctive awareness that the world of history is not a single-sex world" (*Herodotus*, 129–130). Most of the novelists came, like Herodotus, from Asia. Novel-writers of antiquity were attracted to Herodotus as a model; Herodotus' geographical spaciousness, his concern for various peoples, his interest in both women and men and their strange opinions and actions, and his stylistic inventiveness were obviously appealing, like his penchant for description of natural phenomena. When characters in the ancient novels discuss the nature of the phoenix, the lifestyles of marsh-dwellers, or the inundation of the Nile, they are overtly imitating Herodotus. Gould says Herodotus has tended to be rediscovered "at times when suddenly expanded horizons of knowledge made it necessary for contemporaries to try to understand the world in less insular and parochial terms" (127)—a time like the Hellenistic age, or the Roman Empire of Paul's time—a time very like the present, in short.

Plutarch, a mainland Greek of good family, around the end of the first century A.D. accuses Herodotus of maligning the Greeks in what Gould calls an "almost hysterical essay" (127), *Upon the Malice of Herodotus* (*Peri tēs Hērodotou Kakoētheias*). Plutarch thinks Herodotus is a barbarian-lover (*philobarbaros*, 28), unpatriotic enough to think the Greeks learned much from Egyptians and Persians. He spoils the good, like a rose-beetle (98). Plutarch had a strong interest in viewing superior Greekness as the admired civilizing aspect of the power of Rome. He fiercely resents, for instance, Herodotus' suggestion that the Ionians are not proud of that name (36). Plutarch is holding on to "Hellenic" civilization during an era when floods of foreigners from the Eastern Empire were coming into Greece and Rome. At the time that Plutarch (presaging the Romantics whom Bernal criticizes) found this xenophobic and patriotic outlet, novel writers and readers were drawing upon Herodotus and his methods of inquiry in contriving the entertainments of the expansive and multiracial novel.

Novelists accepted an expansion of horizons. Julian exemplifies a desire to limit horizons and to close the world; history becomes a great solemn stillness. Advice to shun fiction and to read history is always at bottom advice to read a certain kind of history, advice most easily given by those who believe that there is a settled authoritative history which will attune the reader to the proper social authority by contemplating a comprehensible and ultimately stable (or stabilized) past.

Julian's recommendation to avoid feigned histories and love stories by no means signifies that wise and learned men never read novels; indeed, it may be taken as signifying the contrary, for if the educated priests and Julian's serious friends would never dream of looking into a novel, the need for such advice would not have occurred to him. Perry's belief that no cultured *man* of the Roman Empire ever would, or ever did, write a novel is a bare assertion, indicating a traditional classicist's stubborn desire to free Greek and Roman antiquity as much as possible from the shame of having possessed novels.

The novels, however, are in evidence, as written works—and even as self-consciously writerly works. They are bookish and booklike—full of allusions to other works, aware of their own written form, and full of characters who read and write. They are not addressed to a folk-audience, but to a readership aware of the pleasures of reading. The percentage of peoples who can read and write in any of the older societies is small, and we find such people at or near the top of the social pyramid, though the literate class must also include educated slaves who acted as secretaries and business managers. Literate persons may well have read novels aloud to the illiterate, but there must have been a core-group of readers. Some of these were well-educated, able to appreciate the constant play of literary allusion within these works, the quotations from Homer and Herodotus, from Euripides and Demosthenes. Such allusiveness does not preclude lower classes of readers, of course, for any novel can be enjoyed by people who do not "get" all the literary play or by-play, but no such work exists without an author of some education postulating a readership of a similar education.

Ancient novels as physical objects also cost *money*. Just getting a novel or even part of one copied out was an expensive undertaking. There has been much discussion lately of "the commodification of literature," but the novel was a commodity when it was invented. We know that some people of wealth read and appreciated the novels. Elaborate mosaics have been recovered, with pictures apparently representing characters and scenes from a couple of novels known to us only from hearsay and fragments. Someone of wealth in Syrian Antioch wanted a representation of scenes from *Ninus* and from *Metiochos and Parthenopé*. He may have been "poor-in-spirit" but he certainly was not poor in pocket. Other mosaics or paintings—including Pompeiian wall paintings—seem to refer to novels that we simply do not know.[10] Mosaics relating to the love-story of Menander and Glykera (now at Princeton) suggest that these characters come from a novel (Plate 2). The dramatist and his courtesan-girlfriend are treated as fictional characters in a few letters in the *Letters of the Courtesans* by Alciphron (c. A.D. 200)— but is his the only fiction about these personages? May they not have figured in a novel, with a much bigger story (as indicated in the mosaics) than in Alciphron—which is, strictly speaking not a story at all? Perhaps his rendering is the parody of a well-known novel, the *Shamela* to some unknown artist's *Pamela*. Playful allusion and intertextuality are the order of the day in the novels themselves, and in other contemporary representations of characters and inner life. The Menander mosaics pose an interesting case of a historical person, himself a writer, becoming a narrative character. It seems right to posit an educated readership for the novelists, as for Alciphron, as long as we remember that *educated* is a broad term. The contention of a modern classicist that it took three years of *full-time* education to learn to read does not bear the inspection of experience. Tomas Hägg is willing to admit that the novels were read by the "educated classes of the Hellenistic cities of Asia Minor" (98), but we may believe that the novels were read also on the Greek mainland. We know they were read in North Egypt, source of a number of tantalizing fragments. These include the two contiguous pieces that form a major surviving portion of our *Metiochos and Parthenopé*, the hero's arrival at the house of Parthenopé's father and the beginning of the dinner-party (see Plate 3). The fragments are remnants of a papyrus originally written (c. A.D. 75–150) at Fayûm (H. Maehler, "Der Metiochos-Parthenope-Roman," 4). This particular example was part of a roll written on recycled paper—the back of the fragment is a tax account. The cursive nonscribal hadwriting of the narrative makes it easy to imagine that the Berlin text may have been a copy compiled by a reader rather than a commercial version of the novel.[11]

Scholarly findings on readership are wildly contradictory. Readers were many—they were few. They were all juveniles and women—they were all educated males. In thirty years the pendulum has swung from Perry's dismissive delineation of a humble, stupid, and female readership to a growing desire, as expressed by Ewan Bowie (among others), to demonstrate that the ancient novels could have been read as well as written only by educated males of a superior class.[12] As we shall see in Part II, when we come to look at the fortunes of the novel in Early Modern times, attribution of novel-reading to the juvenile and the female is always a politically charged gesture, both as an expression of anxiety and as a cover for it. The tendency to remasculinize the ancient novels in the 1990s suggests not so much any new discovery as a register of the fact that the Greek novel is going up in academic estimation, and is now to be reclaimed by mainstream classicists.

It is most likely that there was in late antiquity a fairly consistent novel readership of the comfortably off and moderately well educated, both men and women. Bowie argues that the women wouldn't have read the novels because the *paterfamilias* would not have approved: "The sexual forwardness of some experienced Greek women . . . is hardly what the heads of Greek *oikoi* would be happy to commend to their wives and daughters" ("The Readership of Greek Novels in the Ancient World," *TSAN*, 437). As an argument about reading this is peculiarly feeble; on such an assumption we could be sure that a Teresa of Avila would not and could not have read *Amadís* and the other stories we know she did read (see Teresa, *El Libro*, Part II, Chap. 10). The novels certainly imagine a context of literacy in both males and females; persons of both sexes write letters and read them. *Wonders beyond Thule*, in its convoluted mock-story of manuscript discovery at the end, contains a dedicatory epistle from the author Diogenes "to his sister Isadora'; within his account, the story was written down by Balagros for his wife Phila (Photius, *Bibliothēkē*, II : 147). The joke structure works only if literate women can be taken for granted. It is not unlikely that the novels, as well as appealing to a genteel audience, were appreciated by many of the poor and "low," including slaves, when they could get access to the books.

When manuscripts are to be copied, the work is laborious and circulation slow, but there will often be some copyists willing to work for nothing, and circulation may be continued, on cheaper paper and with increasing scribal error, so that a work or some part of it reaches a number of persons in a number of classes. Russian *samzidat* has operated on that principle in recent times. When there is a cultural appetite, works may be transmitted and devoured with surprising facility up and down the classes. Le Roy Ladurie has shown us that medieval illiterates in very small and remote towns relied on oral transmission of both written and recited material, and could be well versed in some of the most sophisticated poetry of the Provençal troubadours (*Montaillou*, 240).

The ancient novel comes into being and flourishes during a period—an extended period—of self-consciousness and of value for the individual. We can observe these developments in the graphic arts, in a new emphasis on portraiture that celebrates or records that "Individuation" so antipathetic to Nietzsche. On Egyptian coffins, for instance, the habit took hold of painting the likeness of the deceased; in the portraits from Fayûm, we do not see the dead one in that hieratic splendor of the traditional noble "mummy" but as *person* with specific characteristics, and haunting eyes. A similar interest in person—and in female person at that—can be felt in the painting known as "Sappho" from Pompeii (reproduced in Hägg) and in another picture nearby, the mosaic of the lady with the pearls and the large eyes (see Plate 4). Roman interest in commemoration of the individual can be seen in family tombstones of the period of the first Caesars. The dead declare their era by the fashion of their hair, and middle-class husbands and wives gaze out at us with a kind of nervous assurance, transmitting their household unity through that sign of marriage, the clasped hands. But in one tomb, shown in a British Museum exhibition in London called "The Age of Augustus" (1988), it is two women who clasp hands in the ancient ritual gesture, which always signified the relation of husband and wife (see Plate 5). Personal relations have altered the social signal, bent the customs of life and of memorial sculpture to reflect private arrangements.

The art of Pompeii, all of which was produced before 24 August A.D. 79, is elaborately decorative, as we should expect in such a grossly moneyed town, but it reflects this interest in the inward and the personal. The figures in paintings of mythological scenes look reflective, self-involved or self-questioning. In one great and shocking picture, Medea, at home in a private moment, communes with her shattered soul while her two boys, her destined victims, innocently play (Plate 6). Narcissus gazes at his own image (out of perspective). Pompeiian art also exhibits an interest in masks and theatricality, in actors and the moment when the mask is half-on, half-off (Plate 7). The slippage between private and public self likewise interests the first readerly audience for the novel. We can also sense the interest in the idea of a complex relation between the "natural" and the "artificial." The art itself is artifact-making—and one of the words for "fiction," *plasma* or (plural) *plasmata*, is a word for images or figures in clay or wax, hence anything that is involved in imitation, a forgery; it is related to the verb *plassō*, "I mold," also the source of our word "plastic." Fiction is a molding and shaping, an imitation that speaks its own imitatedness, like a figurine. Fiction may also be described as *drama*, and so may a painting; Achilles Tatius' Kleitophon, describing a picture of Perseus and Andromeda in vivid detail, finishes the description by saying "that was the *drama* of Andromeda" (*Kleitophon and Leukippé*, 150; italics mine). Drama is something that can be represented in verbal—and written—narrative, and in painting. It is something that can be appreciated for the aesthetic pleasure it brings, and analyzed.

The first readers of these early novels must have been people used to experiencing aesthetic pleasure, and to thinking about that experience. These were people accustomed to looking at paintings and statues—and to enjoying that contemplation as a private experience, not as an aspect of a civic or religious occasion. They analyze and reflect; when we look at the portraits we cannot help feeling that here are people capable of internal reflection, of introspection—like the characters in the novels, in fact.

The readers of the early novels, those who looked at statues and paintings of the era of Nero—or the eras of Hadrian or of Marcus Aurelius—were interested in representation, aware of the problems and fascinations of representation. The narrators of novels and the characters in novels talk about representative art; they also talk about their own arts of narrating. They feel the difference between presence and absence, and luxuriate in considerations of personal letters and portraits—those things which bridge the gap of absence with a substitute presence. You can see how "Ninus" in the mosaic illustration contemplates the *image* of his beloved Semiramis (see Plate 8). These matters will be seen more clearly as we pursue the stories of the novels themselves. It is time to give some account of the works of fiction extant.

Among the Greek novels we have four full and relatively long texts: Chariton's *Chaireas and Kallirrhoé* (50 B.C.–A.D. 140); Achilles Tatius' *Kleitophon and Leukippé* (c. A.D. 180–200); Longus' *Daphnis and Chloé* (c. A.D. 200); Heliodorus' *Aithiopika* (c. A.D. 250–380). Some works exist for us only in extensive plot summary. We are fortunate in Photius, ninth-century Patriarch of Constaninople, who kept track of his reading (or being read to) by recording plots as well as his opinions. Antonius Diogenes' *Apista hyper Thulēn* or *Wonders* (i.e., *Incredible Things) beyond Thule,* (c. A.D. 150–200) and Iamblichus' *Babyloniaka* (c. A.D. 165–180) are known to us only through Photius' *Bibliothēkē*. We can judge of Photius' accuracy and biases by his summaries of and comments on surviving novels. Another novel text, the *Ephesiaka* by "Xenophon of Ephesus" (which could be a pseudonym) may be a five-book abridgment of a novel originally in ten books; its most likely date is the second century A.D. There is one complete epistolary novella, known to us as *Chion of Heraklea* (*Chiōnos Epistolai*); it was probably written around the end of the first century A.D., or at the beginning of the second century. A very lively long novella or short novel is the *True History*, by Lucian of Samosata, a work often referred to by its traditional Latin title, *Vera Historia*. Lucian's (approximate) dates are A.D. 125–190, and he is thought to have written the *True History* during the time he lived in Athens, where he settled about A.D. 165. We have much more information about Lucian than about any other Greek writer of fiction. It has been suggested that the *True History*—or *True Story*—is among other things a parody of Diogenes' *Wonders beyond Thule*. Lucian was also traditionally credited with a work now not considered his, the Greek work simply referred to as *The Ass*, sometimes as *Lucius the Ass*.

As well as these works, which have substance and visible plot development, we have fragments whose stories can only be guessed at. Three substantial fragments of *Ninus* were discovered in the late nineteenth century. The heroine appears in these texts, but her name is not mentioned; we know it from other sources like the mosaics in the Syrian villa. The story was likely known to its original readers as *Semiramis and Ninus*; the name of the heroine customarily figured prominently in titles of novels of love, and novels were sometimes referred to by the name of the heroine alone. The *Phoinikika* (*Phoenician Story*) is a short collection of tantalizing fragments first published in 1972; the three fragments of *Metiochos and Parthenopé* were not connected and reconstructed until 1976, and the tantalizing small passage of the *Iolaōs* received definitive publication in 1974. There are some other very tiny fragments, now called *Sesonchosis, Herpyllis, Chionē,* and *Kalligonē* (see *CAGN*, 801–827). Tentative dates have been suggested, but these are often educated guesswork, mere approximations. The papyri, as physical fragments of evidence that can be dated by modern technology, furnish at least a latest date in every case. For the *Phoinikika* we have a named author, Lollianus.

The newly discovered fragments have altered classicists' opinions about the nature of the Greek novels. As Gerald N. Sandy says, "Until the publication of the *Phoenicica* [*sic*] and the slightly later publication of the Iolaus romance, extended fictional prose narrative of a salaciously realistic type was believed to be peculiar to Latin writers, in particular to Petronius" (Sandy in *CAGN*, 809). Sandy adds (regarding *Iolaus*), "the Greeks wrote fictional prose narratives about low life" (816). The identification of "low life" with "realism" is not altogether justified; one might just as well call these narratives "comically expressionistic."

As we shall see, there is comedy—and some "low life"—in the four major Greek novels, which could all be called "love-stories," or stories of love and adventure. Novelists writing in Greek are fond of highly stressed situations, which the narrators or characters may treat comically, pathetically, or dramatically at any point. The short fragment of *Herpyllis* deals with a storm at sea, which is probably going to end in the shipwreck so beloved of Greek novelists. The surviving comic and sensational material in *Phoenikika* or *Iolaos* is no guarantee that these novels did not contain highly dramatic moving scenes between lovers, or between tyrants and heroic personages. The very tiny fragment *Sesonchosis* deals with a famous Egyptian monarch as its hero, and the last part rather tantalizingly has a woman, Meameris, emotionally moved by seeing Sesonchosis (who is apparently in disguise); she returns to the banquet table, eating without appetite and remembering the handsome man—she reminds one of Potiphar's wife, and of Dido. This novel may have been contemporary with *Ninus*, or it may have been later—or earlier.

The Greek novelists were, as Arthur Heiserman has emphasized, interested in stories of *erōtika pathēmata*, erotic sufferings, (or *pathos erōtikon* as Chariton has it).[13] Words that indicate suffering are also words that indicate both emotion and experience. Novelists may have been writing prose stories about the engrossing experience of love even at the time of the great writers of Augustan literature, Ovid, Horace, and Virgil, all of whom contribute something to love poetry. Parthenius, who is supposed to have been Virgil's Greek teacher, sent his friend Cornelius Gallus a collection of stories of erotic suffering, suggesting that he draw on them for poetic treatment; Parthenius collects his love-stories from the poets and historians, but the interest in such stories of love-experience seems similar to the interest of authors and readers of the novels. Virgil's Dido is an example of a woman experiencing the torments of love, a victim of erotic suffering, and Virgil's treatment of her is novelistic. Virgil may have been the first major writer of epic who had actively to compete with the novel.

The "Greek" novelists were very fond of writing novels about famous people and places of the past that deal with characters from history. One can see that the "historical novel" was with us from the very beginning. In this the novelists in Greek are probably following an earlier Assyrian tradition; the only known early Aramaic literary text is part of an historical novel called *Ahiqar*: "The

Ahiqar novel . . .is set in Syria in the time of King Sennacherib, and makes use of names that may be historical. The piece itself was, in all probability, written after the catastrophe of Ninevah, but the Assyrian period is felt to loom large in the picture" (Walter Burkert, *The Orientalizing Revolution*, 32). Ninevah fell in 612 B.C.; one may guess that long after the fall of the Assyrian Empire the Assyrians consoled themselves, and retained the memory of what had been, through creating memorable fiction. So, too, after the conquests of Alexander and then the conquest of the East by Rome, writers of the East had reason to recall and reconstruct their past.

We tend, except in the case of Israel, to forget (the Romans certainly do not wish to remind us) that the Roman Empire was not felt everywhere as an unmixed benefit. Novelists in the Roman Imperial Age who set their works in another time emphasize that there was a cultural tradition aside from and before the Romans, and thus cultural alternatives, stretching back too before the post-Alexander hegemony of the Greek-speaking world. Most of our "Greek novelists" may write and even speak in Greek, but they are not of Athens, and they belong to mainland Greece far less even than Americans do to Britain. The use of the word *Ionia* became contaminated by a nineteenth-century desire to adopt anything valuable in Asia Minor as an extension of Aryan Greece. Hence, like people in Herodotus, I tend to shun the word *Ionia*, which means only one part of Western Asia Minor, colonized in prehistoric times by Greek peoples who intermixed with other peoples and were taken over first by Croesus of Lydia and then by Persia.

Psychologists tell us that a dream set in a dreamer's past is indicative, and can signify repressed material that needs to surface. In setting their novels in the past novelists can suggest anxiety about the historical dimension of present pain as well as the possibility that there are repressed or forgotten issues that need to be brought to light. The trope whereby a manuscript is *found*—used with notable emphasis in the preface to the narrative of "Dictys Cretensis"—can be read as an indicator of the need to recover something from the buried past. Critics of the ancient novels have often poured scorn on the lack of realism that results in a novel like *Ninus*, or the noncontemporary political world delineated by Heliodorus. But such use of the past is a strategy, rather than a pathology, whereby occupied or repressed peoples (including subgroups within a main group) bring important matter to the light under the pretense that it is merely harmless and antique.

There is a political dimension to imagining any kind of alternative to a present reality. The historical novel has many advantages. For one thing, it gives much less offense to governing powers than anything set in the present, and may escape censorship and censure. The only ancient novelist known to us who sets his work in the contemporary Roman Empire is the only one we know to have been sentenced to death by the emperor—Petronius was "allowed" by Nero to commit suicide. His example offered no encouragement to other novelists to get too contemporary. The historical novel allows writer and reader to speculate about and enjoy an alternative life, place, and power structure. Some of the best modern historical novelists (Scott is a salient example) have come from countries or cultures that have suffered serious overthrow; fiction allows the survival of what is officially vanquished.

When Greek novels are set in the past, although famous battles, etc., may be remembered, there is little or no attempt to recreate social conditions of a past era. There is, however, following Herodotus, an acknowledgment of different customs and manners pertaining among different peoples rather than between different times. The material may be very unhistorical history; as Sandy points out about *Ninus*, "a period of some fourteen hundred years has been telescoped to unite the most famous representatives of Assyria" (*CAGN*, 804). Perry is disgusted that such a powerful man as Ninus should be presented as a lover rather than as a patriotic hero of empire. He is even more put out that wicked Queen Semiramis, who according to legend was daughter of the goddess Derketo (in the novel transformed to the lady Derkeia), "a deity closely akin to Astarte and Ishtar," and "an amorous and voluptuous woman who kills her numerous lovers" (165), should be favorably represented as the shy teenager in love that she is in Fragment A of *Ninus*. Perry scolds *Ninus* and its unknown author as "trivial" and "non-patriotic" (sounding like Plutarch on Herodotus); he says testily, "Only an obscure Greek romancer addressing himself primarily to juveniles would write in *that* fashion about the national heroes of any country" (164). This is a good deal of animus to express toward a work so shotten by time that it takes up only four pages of printed text. The "romancer" may not have been "obscure" at the time, perhaps s/he was successful and popular, writing a kind of Assyrian *Gone with the Wind*. What Perry seems to react against is the respect accorded to a woman (apparently he feels Semiramis should never be mentioned without execration) as well as the psychologizing.

The most influential instance of a celebrated personage caught up in fiction is Alexander the Great. He seems to have appeared in different stories, but the most important is the work—or perhaps the tradition—incorporated in a work known as *The Alexander Romance*. According to Ken Dowden, who translates it for Reardon's collection, this work was compiled rather than created by a Greek writer of Alexandria between the mid-second and mid-fourth centuries A.D. This Alexandrian composed his work out of two other books, one "a varied collection of fiction concerning Alexander," and the other a rhetorical "history." With this he combines other material, including the Egyptian material concerning Nektanebos, Alexander's magician father. The finished "novel," *The Life and Acts of Alexander of Macedon*, was often ascribed to Callisthenes, the real court historian of Alexander (and relative of Aristotle). As Dowden comments, this was "antiquity's most successful novel'; there exist "eighty versions in twenty-four languages" (*CAGN*, 650). Alexander's impact upon the East was long remembered in the East. *The Life of Alexander* influenced Persian poets and traveled as far as India. The Latin translation by Julius Valerius Polemius was to influence European medieval writers; since Polemius' translation is, as Dowden says, "stylish . . . in the manner of Apuleius" (653), we can assume that the work was appreciated as a novel. The translation by Leo of Naples (c. 960), *Historia de Proeliis Alexandri*, was more widely known. The manuscript containing *Beowulf* (c. A.D. 1000) also contains a part of *Alexander*, and the Alexander story was to influence medieval heroic fiction, including the stories of King Arthur.

A salient fact about the novel's Alexander is the amount of narrated disapproval surrounding the hero and his actions. As he advances on other lands, he keeps encountering oracles, divine representatives or feminine powers who warn him that he should leave. He is always setting himself up against the feminine—most notably in the case of the Queen of the Amazons; the Amazons lose, but they are treated in a dignified manner by the narrative. Queen Candace of Meroe, the black queen, really gets the better of him. Alexander himself seems hung up on his mother, Olympias, and interestingly unresolved in his own sexuality or personality. Alexander's identity is always a problem to him; he claims both Philip and God (Ammon) as his father, but the narrative tells us he is the secret offspring of the Egyptian King-priest Nektanebos, who coupled with Olympias. In the end, Alexander dies, murdered, a victim of *Tychē*-Fortuna:

> I who crossed all the inhabited earth
> And the uninhabited places, and the places of darkness
> Was unable to evade fate.
>   (*The Greek Alexander Romance*, trans. Stoneman, 156)

Ancient readers were interested in stories of travel, and of marvelous, even fantastic travel. *The Wonders Beyond Thulē* and the section of the *Life of Alexander* known as the "Letter to Aristotle," where Alexander describes monsters at the edge of the world, both prefigure modern science fiction, as does Lucian's *Vera Historia*, which might be described as the first *satiric* work of science fiction. It parodies other histories and other fictions, offering us the inside story of the War between the Moon and Sun.

Ancient readers liked to read the story behind the story, "Secret History," to borrow a term from a kind of fiction popular in the seventeenth and early eighteenth centuries. Madame de Lafayette's *La Princesse de Clèves* (1678) is a fine example of the genre, which became popular with women writers in England, like Delarivier Manley, in the Age of Anne. "Secret History" is what Xenophon pretends to offer in *Cyropaedia*, and really manages to avoid. There is *no* secret life, Cyrus' public and private life are of a piece, according to the masculine ideal. Love, jealousy, anger, and uncertainty are deflected upon Cyrus' subordinates, in order that the author may carry out his novel-like project without falling into what he is evidently already aware of as novelistic traps. The novel as "Secret History" will not allow rulers and bigwigs to get away with the claim to be only public. The Novel's tendency, whether dealing with a Ninus or a Kleitophon, public man or private, is to exhibit that person outside the structure of power, in the midst of experience spiritually and emotionally realized. In the *Cyropaedia*, relations with others are instrumental only, as in a kind of business manual. In the later Greek novels, relationships are rarely instrumental merely, and no central character has the kind of obsessive control a Cyrus achieves. The novel is the true *Historia* in the sense of investigation, as it will not let us rest comfortable with the official biography, the approved version of our public life.

By the period of the Roman Empire, too, readers tended to want personality. This is the sort of "Secret History" that Plutarch objects to in Herodotus and other writers, such as comic poets, who can imagine that, for instance, Pericles was influenced by Aspasia and not motivated by his own *philotimia* (*Peri tēs Hērodotou Kakoētheias*, 24). Yet Plutarch himself says at the beginning of his own *Life of Alexander* that we can value jokes or slight incidents more in reading biography than the account of a battle. Ancient novel readers got accounts of battles along with the slight incidents and the jokes. Readers of *Alexander* were offered a picture of a driven man, plus various explanations of what caused him to be so driven. This novel, rather than functioning as "real, solemn history," offers a psychological reading of its subject and points out influences not under the king's control, even while giving the maximum possible space to the subject's own powers (including the power of self-consciousness). Love is a fascinating example of something both within and not within personal control, and most ancient novels are interested, intermittently or consistently, with love and its effects upon the individual. Even Xenophon's *Cyropaedia*, which functions mainly as a guide to political success and a management manual, includes a love episode at one remove, in the story of Panthea. Cyrus proves his managerial skills in keeping aloof from a passion whose power he respects.

So far we have dealt with the "Greek" novels only. These comprise a complicated body of material, and it is frustrating to realize how little is known, after all, about authors or even authorial nationalities, or dates. We know the titles of some works that have gone missing completely; Ptolemy Chennos in the second century wrote a novel called *The Sphinx*, for instance.[14] At any moment the desert sands, or a dry cave, or the bottom of an old trunk may offer to view the manuscript, early or late, of some completely "new" ancient novel—or perhaps more of one only partly known to us, like the *Babyloniaka*. We must always remember how much of ancient literature has simply been *lost*—including literature by authors held in the greatest reverence (unlike the novelists), as classics of our canon. Aeschylus wrote 90 plays; we have 7. Sophocles wrote 123 plays; we have 7. Euripides wrote about 65 plays, and we have 18. We have Aristotle to make generalizations about Greek drama for us, but of course we do not have all of Aristotle. His work on Comedy is notoriously missing—though it turns up as the subject of Umberto Eco's novel *Il Nome della rosa* (*The Name of the Rose*) (1980). We can draw no conclusions about the inferiority of works that did not "last."

We are on slightly firmer ground with the Roman novel than with the Greek. There are two major examples, both by named authors with an ascertainable biography. Petronius' *Satyricon* is a comic novel written in the reign of Nero, whose uneasy empire, with its social mobility, great wealth, and sudden violence, Petronius' novel so vividly records. The *Satyricon* parodies the formulae and plot situations best known to us in the Greek novels. We know these formulae from "Greek" novels of a later date than the work of Petronius, but the presence of the *Satyricon* reminds us that there must have been a wealth of this literature already sufficiently visible for a parodic use to be entertaining.

As noted above, modern finds among the papyri show that incidents of farce, violence, and comic sex are to be found in the "Greek" novels and not just the Roman ones; the earlier scholarly habit of keeping Greek and Roman fiction in separate watertight compartments will not work. The *Metamorphoses* of Apuleius—also known as *Asinus Aureus*, or *The Golden Ass* (c. A.D. 155)—has strong resemblances to *The Ass* in Greek; Photius suggested that Lucian had plagiarized a longer *Metamorphoses* in Greek for his shorter version. Both *The Ass* and the *Golden Ass* are stories of transformation; in both, the central character, a man with the vice of curiosity (as well as some lasciviousness and some cowardice) is transformed into a donkey, and undergoes various trials in that predicament—trials comic to the reader while comically pathetic to the ass. These stories lie behind other tales of transformation in modern literature—such as Swift's *Gulliver's Travels* (1726), Collodi's *Pinocchio* (1883) and Kafka's *The Metamorphosis* (1915). Apuleius' work is elaborate, elegantly told and ornamented, cunning in technique, and full of surprising effects. It is memorably our source for the "Cupid and Psyche" story, an episode of great length and intricacy. The novel has seemed to many readers to have a religious significance; the story does not end (as in the Greek *The Ass*) with the hero's enjoying his welcome return to human form, but with his spiritual search; he becomes a priest of Isis.

As well as these two well-known novels, there are others, more influential and better known in the Middle Ages than recently. *The Diary of the Trojan War* by "Dictys of Crete" (*Ephemeris Belli Troiani* by "Dictys Cretensis") is a short and packed Latin novel of the second or third century A.D. It is the story of the Trojan War narrated by a character who was there at the time as a soldier on the Greek side. Another short Latin work, *The History of the Trojan War* (*De Excidio Troiae Historia*) by "Dares of Phrygia," is also a story about the Trojan War. It may have been written originally in Greek; what we have is a Latin translation of the fifth or sixth century A.D. Also presenting a fictional eyewitness story, Dares' account takes the side of the Trojans.

Accepted history was likewise rewritten in a Jewish novel *Joseph and Aseneth* (originally perhaps first century B.C.) describing the Biblical Joseph's courtship and marriage; the version we have has been Christianized and Neoplatonized. The desire to revisit historical material and personages can be seen also in an early Christian novel, which likewise existed in a Greek version now lost. The *Recognitiones* is a work of the later second or early third century A.D., and, like Dictys' *Diary of the Trojan War*, it offers a first-person narrative by one who knew some celebrated people and was involved in an important movement. But here the celebrated person is the Christian Peter the Apostle, and the first-person narrator is "Clemens," purporting to be the Clement who became Peter's successor as Bishop of Rome. The narrator includes the story of a lost family whose scattered members become reunited, the substance of part of *Apollonius of Tyre*, in which the shipwrecked hero loses his wife and child and thinks them dead, but happily has them restored to him after many vicissitudes . . . material which Shakespeare is to work on in *Pericles*. In the *Recognitiones*, however, the hero is not the father but the son, who is reunited first with his brothers (though he does not know them when they first work together as fellow disciples of Peter), then with his mother, and last with his father. The parents are converted by the children. Another work often included in a discussion of Christian novels is the "Paul and Thekla" section of the apocryphal *Acts of Paul*, although this material was probably meant to be taken as truth and not as fiction, unlike *Recognitiones* with its title's witty reference to Aristotle on *anagnōrisis* (see Aristotle, *Poetics*, Sec. xi).

The preceding descriptions are merely preliminary sketches rather than analyses. As the major novels are not very familiar even to students of literature—and as the Greek novels are still much less known even than the Roman—it is necessary to offer an account of the major works.

CHAPTER II

⊨⊷⊶⊙⊷⊶⊨

Love and Suffering: The Stories of the Ancient Novels

⊨⊷⊶⊙⊷⊶⊨

I shall narrate a story of erotic suffering that happened in Syracuse.
—Chariton, *Chaireas and Kallirrhoé*

"I'll seize this dagger, and when I've filled my belly with food I'll kill myself before Daphnis' door. Then you'll have a job to summon your Gnatho-pet, as you always do in play."   —Longus, *Daphnis and Chloé*

"We were saved from the robbers—But we were reserved only for madness!"   —Achilles Tatius, *Kleitophon and Leukippé*

⊨⊷⊶⊙⊷⊶⊨

*I*n order to understand the ancient novels we need to know both what happens in them, and how those happenings can be expected to be interpreted by the reader. "The sufferings of love" is a generalizing phrase, but novels are never abstract, they deal always with particulars, and must aim to get the reader engrossed in specific characters, incidents, descriptions and observations. Yet it is not enough to follow the story; the reader must be interpretively engaged. A pursuit of three love novels in some detail will help us see the various ways in which "fate," "suffering" and "love" could be played out in ancient novelistic narratives, and how the reader might be expected to interpret them.

Like all novel characters, the hero and heroine of Greek novels undergo ordeals. Massimo Fusillo points out that the ancient novels adapt stories from tragedy, and borrow techniques from the tragic drama such as emotional monologue (Fusillo, *Il Romanzo greco* [1989], 36–40). The Novel is a strongly intertextual form, and the Greek novel is, as Fusillo says, "polyphonic," mixing a number of literary kinds to its own purposes. The inwardness achieved in certain forms of tragedy at certain moments is highly desired by these novels. The fundamental mode of the Novel, however, is comic, and the surviving long Greek novels are comic. In linking the comically plain and ordinary with the highly emotive, these novels seem to follow in the footsteps of Euripides. In that dramatist's *Ēlektra*, for instance, the peasant who has been forced on Elektra as her "husband" assures the visitor (Orestes) that the house can supply a meal: "A woman if she needs to / Can find many things to bring out for dinner. / There is sufficient in the house today / To fill up these hungry folk here for one day" (*Ēlektra*, lines 422–425). Here is one of the common men who pushed their way onto the stage, to Nietzsche's displeasure. There are statements against the hierarchies of power to be found in Euripides, statements in favor of the man of everyday life, like Orestes' speech in this very scene, in which he says that there is no good test for manliness

---

33

(*euandria*); the nobleman's son may prove a coward, a rich man mean-souled, while "a poor body may have a great spirit" (lines 369–372). Euripides' concerns (including his interest in women) vexed some contemporaries, as they later vexed Nietzsche; ancient novelists could find in the dramatist a helpful predecessor in linking story with daily life.

Ancient novels are on the whole more aggressively comic than Euripides' serious dramas. Satire had a part to play in their making. Ronald Paulson in *Satire and the Novel in Eighteenth-Century England* (1967) stressed the role of satire in creating the modern novel; as satire is the abode of the "low," the only "high" literary outlet for the base and mundane, it offered some modes of dealing with common experience. If this was true in the eighteenth century, it was true long before. Satirists of the Greek and Roman eras had found out ways of describing the relation of the individual to the material and social environment. Satirists also offered models for representing the daily conscious activity of the sensuous intellect making sense of the fragmentary world. We can see this activity, this inner commentary, at work in remnants of the first recorded Greek literary satirist, Archilochus (c. 680–640 B.C.) Horace (65–8 B.C.) made his own contribution to the resources of novelists (ancient and modern) in inventing his version of the satiric persona as commentator. His satirist, with his prosaic "pedestrian Muse" (Book II, Satire vi, line 17), creates the perceiving person jumbled about in the ordinary world, which is also an artificial world of institutions, customs, and made objects. Horace, the freedman's son, sometimes presents himself as the little man in the crowd—literally the man in the city street: "battling with the crowd and doing injury to the slow / 'What are you doing, you crazyman, and where do you think you're going?' some impudent person presses me / With irate curses" (lines 28–30). Horace as narrator is quite "novelistic," and novelists are sometimes quite "Horatian." (It is possible that Horace himself was nourished on antique novels now lost to us.) The satiric nature of the major Roman novelists, Petronius and Apuleius, needs little argument, but in almost any novel we come upon moments in which the techniques of satire are put to good use, even if satire is not the narrative's major concern. The comedy of the antique novels is, however, not simply reducible to satire. We should not expect the antique novels to be simple or naive, though they may (like Longus in his expert pastoral) play with simplicity and naiveté.

CHARITON: *CHAIREAS AND KALLIRRHOÉ*

Chariton tells us in his first sentence who he is: Chariton of Aphrodisias, secretary to the *rhetor* Athenagoras. He belonged to the educated professional class, like his employer the *rhetor*, a combination of politician, legislator, and lawyer. In mentioning the *rhetor* in his first sentence, Chariton already alerts us to the idea that as narrator he may be very much aware of *rhetoric*. We know he works in an office where the job is to manipulate words and fool with appearances. If a narrator tells me he works in a politician's or a lawyer's office, I am to be wary of assuming he is a simple soul or an artless speaker.

It was formerly suggested that Chariton (whose name indicates graciousness and gifts and comes from the same root-word as *charisma*) was a made-up name, and that his statement that he came from the city of Aphrodite was a mere allegory. But there was a real Aphrodisias, a thriving inland city among the hills of Caria; inhabited since the Bronze Age, it had been a sacred site of the Goddess when her name was Ishtar or Enana. The name "Aphrodisias" evidently came into use in about the second century B.C. This elegant marble city (now freshly excavated) was a cultural center of importance, and fostered learning in the arts and sciences. It was a city interested in its own local form of democracy, to judge from the gigantic statue of *Dēmos* in the theater, and it had a famous temple to Aphrodite, whose cult statue here somewhat resembles the image of Artemis in Ephesus. Aphrodisias could support rhetors and clerks. Most scholars now believe there really was a Chariton.[1] This author has an almost lawyerly interest in the law, and a big law case is an important feature of his novel. It is certainly not unsuitable that a man who lived in the city of Aphrodite should compose a story of love which honors that goddess.

As is customary in these novels, two lovers first meet at a religious celebration. In the *Ephesiaka* by the so-called "Xenophon" (probably a pseudonym) the young couple first see each other during the festival of Artemis. In that novel the hero, Habrokomes, contemns Eros, he has a bad case of narcissism, thinking none beautiful but himself. Eros pays him back by making him fall heavily in love with Anthia. Eros, we are told here, picks up the challenge: *philoneikos gar ho theos*: "for the god loves conflict" (4). Very similar words are used in *Chaireas and Kallirrhoé: philoneikos de estin ho Erōs* (50). There are a number of similarities between these two novels (the only ones extant to deal with married lovers); the *Ephesiaka* seems, however, not to be the complete text of a novel but a long epitome in which some parts are huddled up in rapid or confused summary, whereas Chariton's novel is complete. In Chariton's novel the first challenge to Eros does not come from the hero's hauteur but from the difference between the lovers' two families. During the official celebration honoring Aphrodite the two Syracusan lovers meet, at the corner of a street—by chance (or Fate) (*Tychē*). Both fall violently in love.

We have become so accustomed to the mutual-love-at-first-sight story that we forget its importance as a mental invention. In an important study, *Sexual Symmetry: Love in the Ancient Novel and Related Genres* (1994), David Konstan has pointed out how different these ancient Greek novels are from other classical material dealing with erotic love. Love is of course often portrayed as wrong, a debasement or distraction, but even when love is not dealt with in terms of Neoplatonic-Platonic aspirations or civic moralizing, the positions of lover and beloved are at odds in most classical literature. There must always be one who seeks and one who flees, unless the love is merely casual dalliance, often with hired persons or with slaves (as in Horace's *Odes*). The most emotive and spiritual literature about love is homoerotic, which is hopelessly tied to what Konstan calls "The Pederastic Paradigm" of inequality. A boy lover who grows of age and is an equal as a citizen should not remain a sexual beloved. Homosexual love is classically based on inequality, and such inequality proposes "a model of pursuit and seduction" (*Sexual Symmetry*, 66), which also characterizes many classical accounts of heterosexual love. Girls flee from lovers or from gods; sexual excitement lies in pursuit and control. Everywhere, Konstan claims, in classical literature the model of erotic love is a portrait of inequality. The Greek novels revolutionize love by proposing an equality between the lovers—in age, social status, and in emotional capacity. Hence the males in the Greek novels are as emotional as the females; they cry as easily. They are not valiant rescuers: "There are no scenes in which the valiant lover comes to the rescue of his lady. . . . Virtue is not conceived on the pattern of virile mastery" (*Sexual Symmetry*, 34). The women are as intellectual, resourceful, self-conscious, and intelligent as their sweethearts. The mutual and even simultaneous falling in love expresses an equality of the maximum importance.

If the lovers express a new possibility of equality, they have to make their way in a world structured on inequality. Chaireas' father is distressed to hear of his son's passion, because Kallirrhoé's father, Hermokrates, is of too high a rank. The heroine's father is supposed to be the Hermokrates who led the Syracusans in defeating the Athenians in their ill-fated Sicilian Expedition of 413 B.C.; that real-life Hermokrates is thought to have had a daughter who died, so the novel is improvising on the basis of some historical material.[2] The Sicilian expedition is a major subject of Thucydides, who tells the story from the Athenian point of view. Here we move to the world of the resistance. In drafting the anti-Athenian Sicilian hero as his heroine's progenitor, Chariton (not himself a Sicilian) seems to be making an anti-imperial point. "Sicily" comes to represent an escape from tyranny. At the end, some of the bravest among Persia's subjugated peoples (Greeks, Phoenicians, Egyptians, Cypriots) choose to join Chaireas in his return to a free land. A concept of political freedom, even political revolt, hovers behind *Chaireas and Kallirrhoé*.

There are many eligible suitors other than Chaireas for Kallirrhoé. The young people's patient suffering moves Hermokrates at last to consent to the marriage, and the hero and heroine are blissful for a short time. Jealous rivals, however, take a Sicilian revenge; Chaireas is made to believe (in a trick very like the one pulled in *Much Ado about Nothing*) that his wife has been unfaithful to him. Carried away by passion, and lacking sufficient voice to accuse his wife, he kicks her in the stomach. She falls down lifeless. Her family have a magnificent tomb quickly erected for her and Kallirrhoé is buried with great lamentation. Chaireas, who has learned of her innocence, begs the magistrates to pronounce sentence of execution upon him, but his father-in-law himself intercedes, saying his act was not intentional murder.

Kallirrhoé wakes up in her tomb, thinking she is awakening from sleep and expecting to feel her husband beside her; then she realizes where she is, but has not long to panic, for grave robbers break in to steal the fine things entombed with her. They take the living Kallirrhoé with them, at the command of the robber chief, Theron, and sail to Ionia, where Theron sells the girl to a middleman, who then sells her to the steward of rich Dionysios, the greatest landowner of those parts. Dionysios has just lost his wife and is grieving for her; he is disgusted with himself to find how strongly he is attracted to the slave-girl, who is so beautiful that the villagers think Aphrodite herself is visiting her shrine. Kallirrhoé is cool to Dionysios. But Fate makes her change her tune. The steward's wife, the slave Plangon, points out to the young woman that she is pregnant. Kallirrhoé does not see how she can endure to bear Chaireas' child and Hermokrates' grandchild in slavery. Plangon offers to help her with an abortion, but points out the advantages of marrying Dionysios instead. Since Dionysios realizes this girl must be high-born, he wants to marry her; with Plangon as go-between, all is arranged, and Kallirrhoé weds for the second time, though she cannot forget Chaireas, her first love.

This first husband visits her tomb, pretending he goes to make offerings but really intending to punish himself by committing suicide beside the corpse of his beloved. He finds the tomb empty. The Syracusans make up exploring parties to find the grave robbers. Theron eventually is forced to tell the truth; he is crucified in Syracuse, and Chaireas and his friends set out a second time to find Kallirrhoé on the coast of Ionia.

Chaireas' misfortunes and his expiation for his crime against Aphrodite (in committing the crime against his wife) are not over yet. He and his party get too close to Dionysios and his new bride. The steward, sensing the danger to Dionysios from these intruders, gets a party of bandits to murder Chaireas. Chaireas and his best friend Polycharmos are not murdered but sold into slavery; an even greater source of dole to Chaireas is that he now knows of his bride's remarriage. Kallirrhoé, meanwhile, has seen Chaireas in a dream, mournful and in chains. She cries out to him in her sleep—and that is the first time that Dionysios hears the name of her first husband. He is jealous when he finds out she was once married, but when Kallirrhoé gives birth to her child, Dionysios believes it to be his. Dionysios also believes that Chaireas was definitely murdered by the bandits. Kallirrhoé erects a beautiful tomb for Chaireas, the exact match of the one formerly made for her in Syracuse.

Love, Chariton tells us, delights in paradoxes: *ho Erōs . . . chairei tois paradoxois* (50). Eros the plot-maker loves paradoxes not only in the sense of marvels, surprises (which is what the Greek word meant) but also in the rhetorical sense implying parallels and symmetrical reversals. First, Chaireas believes Kallirrhoé unfaithful; then he realizes his error—and she *is* (in a sense) unfaithful. First Chaireas thinks Kallirrhoé dead; then she believes *him* to be dead. One ornate but meaningless tomb is balanced by another. There is a certain rhetorical playfulness about these symmetries. We are expected to be amused, but that does not mean we are not to be moved. The sequence after Kallirrhoé's discovery of her pregnancy is a strong instance of the *pathos* of the Greek novel, and its willingness to take female concerns seriously.

Kallirrhoé's first reaction on finding out that she is pregnant is misery. She blames Fortune—*Tychē*—for this culminating sorrow "that I should have a child who is a slave." When she is alone, she thinks of the necessity of killing the child to prevent further unhappiness, and addresses the child in her womb: "It will not be agreeable to you, Baby, to be born into a wretched life; even after being born you would flee it. Resist in freedom, untouched by suffering" (88). The rhetorical chime reinforces her words: *Apithi eleutheros, apathēs kakōn*. The words themselves are striking; in telling her foetus to resist (*apeitheō*) Kallirrhoé advises it to be disobedient, as a free person (*eleutheros*), to refuse to comply with the law that will impose evil upon it. Kallirrhoé's tone to the child in her womb is intimate and coaxing—her horror at herself for wanting to kill her own child (she thinks she is like Euripides' Medea) mingles with her strong desire that the child should not know the pains of slavery. This weight of decision—whether to let a child that will be born in slavery live or die?—is a female source of conflict, as well as an anguish that only a slave can know. In *Oroonoko* (1688), Aphra Behn presents the conflict as part of a male experience, in Oroonoko's decision to kill his wife Imoinda and their unborn child. The most powerful recent novelistic expression of this terrible dilemma is Toni Morrison's *Beloved* (1987); the story revolves around Sethe's central terrible deed, the killing of her infant daughter to save her from a life of slavery. As Sethe says defiantly later to her friend Paul D., another former slave, "It worked. . . . It's my job . . . to keep them away from what I know is terrible. I did that" (164–165). Morrison's entire novel deals with a kind of spiritual expiation for this necessary and terrible deed, and the reconciliation that must take place between the mother and the baby.

The mother's duty to keep the child from the ultimate horror and inhumanity of slavery even at the cost of its life is a duty nowhere recognized in law, or in the regulations of slave-owning and women-owning fathers. In Chariton's novel the decision about abortion has a peculiar intimacy, a special privacy; it is something to be discussed between women, between female slaves, secretly in back offices. Earlier Greek literature has presented noble slaves sympathetically—Cassandra is an instance—but they parade before us in haughty heroism or doom-laden sorrow; we do not see them living the life of slaves, nor are they presented in the private world of women. The sense that the mother has intimate possession of the womb-child, has the first relation to it, the right to decide its future—this is a highly unusual representation. Chariton narratively gives the decision about the child's life and destiny to the mother, as by right—this in a culture in which officially only a man has a right to a child. In ancient Greek and Roman society, a child was not decided to be member of the household, a person, until the father had picked it up and accepted it; without paternal acceptance it was a non-entity and could be exposed to the elements and left to die—or be picked up by the gladiator-trainer, professional beggar, or pimp.[3] Kallirrhoé overturns the accepted right of fatherhood, the basis of society, by taking the responsibility for her child's fate upon herself. Not the father but the *mother* is the decision-maker and life-giver, under Aphrodite—or colluding with wily Plangon behind the kitchen door.

Kallirrhoé does not, of course, think of herself as overturning the position of the father—she literally gives the baby's father a position in the discussion as she anxiously debates, in her second solitary crisis, whether she should marry Dionysios. Placing the portrait of Chaireas on her stomach (*tēn eikona Chaireou tēi gastri*), she says to it, "Well, here we are, the three together, husband and wife and child. Let us discuss our common concerns. I'll start first and state my opinion" (90). This piece of private playacting reconstitutes the family, but reconstitutes it as something in Kallirrhoé's mind. The portrait image (*eikōn*) of Chaireas is an important symbol of personal affection and loyalty, of personal relationship—yet at the same time Kallirrhoé can really choose who will be her baby's social "father." Plangon saw right away the advantage to herself and her husband if she could persuade Kallirrhoé to marry the prim master who desperately wants the lovely girl. Plangon asked all the practical questions; since Kallirrhoé is only two months' pregnant, the child to come will easily be passed off as Dionysios' issue if the girl marries her master right away. As Plangon points out, the child will be brought up rich and will have a wonderful inheritance. Plangon and Phokas also win their master's favor for persuading the wonderfully beautiful stranger to accept him.

Kallirrhoé does accept Dionysios—which is one of the novel's many deliberate ironies, for the reader wishes her to do so, even though Kallirrhoé is a champion of virtue—of *sōphrosynē*. A woman's *sōphrosynē* includes—or *is*—chastity, and Kallirrhoé is devoted to her husband in chaste but passionate love. But the narrative shows her virtue is given very limited choice in this peculiar situation: she can be cruel to her child (killing it or condemning it to slavery) or kind to it. And of course the marriage saves her from the threat of rape, a danger ever-present to a slave-girl. We are persuaded that Kallirrhoé loses no virtue in taking a second husband—her first husband even appears to her in a dream-vision, begging her not to kill their child. After the marriage to Dionysios, Kallirrhoé is forever burdened with a secret—a secret that is to become more complex when she finds her husband is alive. She does not doubt that she did right to have the baby and give it the best possible circumstances—maternal responsibility seems to take precedence over other duties. She presents the child to Aphrodite, looking, as Kallirrhoé always does, like Aphrodite herself. But this time she excels even Aphrodite, in a way. Chariton says: "First she took the child into her arms, and that was a most beautiful sight, finer than any paintings painted by painters or sculptures created by sculptors or stories made up by poets up to our own time; not a one of them has represented Artemis or Athena carrying a new-born babe in her arms" (110). In other words, Kallirrhoé is the "new" type, the Madonna.[4]

It is part of the comedy that Kallirrhoé gets all this glory by doing the very thing that has always given husbands and fathers the cold sweats—the very thing the masculine law has tried so hard to prevent. She lies, she marries under false pretenses, but above all she passes off another man's child as the father's own. She brings the cuckoo into the nest, in a sort of retrospective adultery. It was the mere *idea* of her adultery, her breaking the rule of belonging to him only, that drove Chaireas to such violence. He has to learn that Aphrodite, not himself, is in charge of the rules of sex and child-bearing. When he finds that Kallirrhoé is still alive but *married*, he is horror-stricken at this reversal, and complains that he is now forbidden to make love to the woman he loves, by the power of social law: "I would run the risk of being killed as an adulterer [*moichos*] with my own wife!" (107).

Chaireas' depression is reflected in the condition of slavery that he himself experiences almost immediately afterward. The conditions under which he labors are much more brutal than anything experienced by Kallirrhoé. The men are beaten severely for not accomplishing their field tasks, but Chaireas is not well enough or in spirits to do a full day's work. To spare him, his friend Polycharmos, who has stuck with him through thick and thin, asks the overseer to allot the two of them one piece of ground to work; Polycharmos then performs both his own work and most of his friend's. The magnanimity of Polycharmos as a slave, and the personal relationship between himself and his friend, like Kallirrhoé's personal decision-making under slavery, make evident the cruelty of slavery as a system. We also see in the characters the strength of a desire for freedom and the persistence of an ability still to act and think for oneself—to act as a person, and not as a possession.

Orlando Patterson, in the exciting first volume (1991) of his ambitious work *Freedom*, analyzes how freedom has been invented and developed so as to become "the supreme value of the Western world" (*Freedom in the Making of Western Culture*, ix). The idea of freedom, Patterson argues, is always based on the primary reality of slavery. "Who were the first persons to get the unusual idea that being free was not only a value to be cherished but the most important thing that someone could possess? The answer in a word: slaves" (ibid., 9). Prehistoric slaveholding communities created an identity for themselves by creating an internal dead enemy. If slaves are socially dead, they yet haunt the community, and its dreams are based on them.

Slavery defined the nature of power as power over others. One permanent aspect of our idea of freedom, called "sovereignal freedom" by Patterson, is constructed on the basis of control of others—this is the freedom of the King, or of the nation in relation to other groups. In aristocratic communities with a warrior class, as in Homer, male freedom is chiefly "sovereignal," based on victory in war. Personal freedom, according to Patterson, is not a male value; the males are threatened with death on the battlefield, not enslavement in defeat. It is their women who will be led away as slaves. We can feel the pang of the loss of liberty in Hector's speech to Andromache: "you, when some bronze-greaved Achaian / Will lead you away, weeping, robbed of freedom's day," *eleutheron ēmar apouras* (*Iliad*, VI, lines 454–455). Patterson cites this speech to illustrate the development of the idea of personal freedom, through its loss in slavery, and the fact that this jarring contrast was imaginable to heroic men only through the experience of their women. Still, warriors had to imagine not only the shadowy Hades that waited for themselves, but also the women's loss of liberty, of freedom's glad day.

When more complex social structures and economic arrangements made slavery a visibly permanent part of the social system, slaves were the purchased, not just the vanquished. They were associated with the idea of the foreign as well as of the despicable. The cooperation of the poorer classes of a city state's males could be bought by proclaiming their free citizenship, and allowing them some measure of participation in government. This idea of "civic freedom" is visibly opposed to the *non*-citizenship and *un*-freedom of male and female slaves. Ideologies and values of the ancient world, including democracy, were thus constructed, Patterson shows, on the free/slave opposition. Some of the thought of the Sophists and the Cynics exhibits a desire to get out of the free/slave binary system. But in the main, Patterson argues, a mental need for slavery persists in most antique philosophies; it is embedded in the thought of Plato, and in most forms of Stoicism, and it infected Christianity. Thus, the human body becomes the inferior, the *slavish*, aspect of the being—which must be harshly disciplined. The appetites, being rebellious *slaves*, should be chastised or obliterated. Reason is *free*, but habit *enslaves*—and so on.

The idea of "personal freedom" was itself frequently devalued, Patterson asserts, because the desire for personal freedom was felt most intensely by slaves—and by women. Aristocratic men had no such need. Yearning for a social condition (imagined as a spiritual condition) in which the male participates in imperial power and glory, having trampled on the ugly slaves, is too often encountered in antique thought, especially in high philosophic or religious thought. One should belong to the world of the Forms, or the Reason, or God the King—thus proving oneself removed from the lowly. Personal freedom is what is desired by the body, by unruly appetites, by slaves and women who want to be free of control.

Patterson believes that the development of an idea of personal freedom in the Greek-speaking world came largely from the women, the persons who, even among aristocratic castes in the heroic age, were most immediately threatened with slavery. For women and slaves, the other two forms of freedom, "sovereignal" and "civic," were practically impossible. Personal freedom could be imagined. As freedom from whipping, torture, rape, it could be imagined at a very simple and profound level. With the idea of such personal freedom comes the idea of individual rights over oneself. Women and slaves were thrown together in antique society; women spent the largest part of their days with children and with slaves, "the main adult company of nearly all [upper-class] women" (Patterson, *Freedom*, 108). Women's experience and their responses to their lives helped to shape the concepts of personal freedom expressed in Greek tragedies, Patterson believes. Men in the plays (especially Creon in Sophocles' *Antigone*, where this issue provides the central conflict) identify freedom with sovereignal power. Women in the plays (like Antigone, like Aeschylus' Elektra or Elektra's chorus of slaves) identify freedom as personal freedom—freedom of the self to act and be without the control of others. Freedom of the individual has mattered more to women than to men throughout Western history, Patterson argues, as men have often been addicted to other values and rewards, like honor and public praise. But the West has moved away from the aristocratic honor code in the direction of giving a progressively higher value to individual freedom, although (according to Patterson) Jesus' demands for love and his recognition of radical equality continue to mystify us.

If the dramatists seem incapable of approaching the issues of personal freedom save through women, this pattern is repeated in the so-called "Greek" novels—but with important variations. The male experience of slavery and the male desire for personal freedom has now to be included. Hence the importance of the fact that Chaireas, and not only Kallirrhoé, is enslaved. Both also are turned into slaves commercially, not as a result of war. The ancient novelists all show that contemporary slavery is a matter of trading in people as objects; the heroic justification of conquest is definitely absent. Patterson nowhere treats the ancient novels, save for a few references to the *Satyricon*, but the novels are consonant with his contention that the idea of personal freedom was stimulated by urban conditions (with their socioeconomic complexities), and constantly associated with women. The novels tend to put women at or near the center of experience—the novels written in Greek and coming from Asia Minor or North Africa are particularly likely to do so. Patterson has only very perfunctorily acknowledged the influence on the thought we tend to call "Greek" of other cultures, especially of Western Asia, and of a variety of religions, which should probably not be dismissed as "cults." The novels all reflect a religious sensibility, which is hard for us to define; these works commonly seem to come from a matrix less

well-known to us than the Greco-Roman pantheon or a philosophy such as Stoicism, for example.

What gives these novels such an ardent interest in personal freedom? The
freedom here reflected on is not one giving power over others. And where, we
may wonder, did these novels acquire their custom of displaying slavery—usually
for both heroes and heroines—as a melancholy evil that can be experienced by
good people? Aristotle had argued that slaves are slaves because they are naturally slavish; the noble-minded cannot "really" be slaves. He did not want to accept that slavery rests only on the imposition of power.[5] Authors like Chariton
know that it *is* the imposition of power that makes slavery, and that the power
now is not the grand force of war, but commercial interests. When we see Chaireas as a slave, we feel that the social identity (socially dead entity) and the reality
(living conscious human being) cannot be brought into any true focus or align-
ment. Yes, Chariton is light-years away from any idea of formal protest against
the system of things, but his story everywhere implicitly questions it.

The chain gang with whom Chaireas and Polycharmos are bound break
out in a desperate futile insurrection; all are sentenced to death, including our
hero and his friend. As they are being led to crucifixion, Polycharmos utters the
exclamation: "O Kallirrhoé, this is all your doing! You are the cause of all our
ills!" (119). The supervisor thinks that there is another person involved in the
plot, and he has the man taken before the owner, Mithridates, for questioning.
Polycharmos explains, narrating the entire story of Chaireas and Kallirrhoé—as
quickly as he can, for he is anxious to die with his friend. At the end he merely
requests Mithridates, "Order the executioner not to separate us on our crosses"
(121). His entire audience, much moved by his story and his demeanor, bursts
into tears and sobs (121). The gentlemen rush to the scene of execution, where
all have been killed save the hero, who is just ready to get up on the cross. "Chaireas," we are told, "aggrieved, got down from his cross. For it seemed a blessed
thing to be finished with a distressful life and an ill-fated love" (122).

Chaireas cheers up when Mithridates offers to help him get his wife back.
Dionysios, in a panic, appeals to the Great King of Persia. Dionysios realizes as
soon as he gets to Babylon that he was making a big mistake; all he has done for
himself is to advertise the beauty of his wife over the whole Persian Empire. He
was frightened of Mithridates, and now he has come to a city and court where
there are so many like Mithridates, so many rich noblemen who could get the
better of him. Menelaus could not keep Helen from Paris, even in virtuous
Sparta, he remembers, so what can he expect here: "so many Parises among the
Persians," he puns sadly (135).

Dionysios is throughout a well-drawn character.[6] He is comically unsuited
to his name. Instead of being all Dionysiac energy, he is all stiff self-consciousness.
I disagree with the view expressed by Consuelo Ruiz Montero, who argues that
Chariton's support of Dionysios' social class and function makes him exhibit in
this landowner an ideal *pepaideumenos*, an educated man of benevolent heart
and enlightened understanding (Liviabella Furiani, ed., *Piccolo mondo antico*, 136–
138). Dionysios would assent eagerly to such a description of himself, certainly.
It seems too bad that at present Chariton's novel, so long despised, cannot be
reclaimed for polite letters without being dragged into the role of supporter of

civic virtue as predefined by Roman culture. The values of society are indeed subjects of each of these novels. But every novel in its own way takes a very critical stance towards the normal or even the presumptively superior social values. Chariton's novel in particular is strangely, even perversely, democratic, and very resistant to Roman self-idealization. His central characters clearly do not wish to live under a foreign empire, and they are able to fight back against all sorts of tyranny, from the imperial to the domestic.

It is funny to hear Dionysios lauded with the epithets found on antique tombstones (Montero, in *Piccolo mondo*, 138) because in a way he is trying to be the man such a tombstone would describe. This anxious, even fussy, man takes very seriously his position as the biggest local landowner and tries always to act appropriately, like a sort of Ionian Mr. Allworthy, but a Mr. Allworthy troubled with sexual desire. This Dionysios is embarrassed by his own sexual desires and by his own need of comfort, for he wants to be strong. He is sincerely struck by sorrow at the death of his wife, and has also made his grief into a very powerful local *spectacle*; it is embarrassing to find that he falls in love with a slave. He takes himself severely to task for this falling in love:

> "Are you not ashamed, Dionysios, the first man among the Ionians in excellence of character [*aretēs*] and reputation, to whom satraps, kings, and cities do honor, to be afflicted by these adolescent troubles [*paidariou pragmata*]? One look made you fall in love, even while you were in mourning, before you had appeased the spirit of the dead. So this was why you journeyed into the country, in order to celebrate a wedding dressed in black, a wedding to a slave—and at that perhaps one who isn't your own property? For I never did see the contract of sale." (79)

Dionysios' self-scolding ruminations offer a vivid insight into an inner space of absurd theater, with almost endless possibilities for self-love and embarrassment. He finds relief from self-accusation about infidelity to his dead wife by drifting comically back into the realm of uneasy commercial practicalities (*was* there ever a proper contract for his ownership of Kallirrhoé?). Dionysios' lot is the harder because he cannot come to terms with the emotional and sexual life which he thinks he should disdain, identifying love as *paidariou pragmata*, the business of boys. That lofty attitude he identifies with his own virtue. But, we are told, "Eros aggressively put an end to all these fine reasonings, and to him that virtue [*sōphrosynē*] seemed but *hubris*" (79).

Dionysios gets his heart's desire in wedding Kallirrhoé—and getting that desire entails a constant state of anxiety. Dionysios is a man who is not loved. He thinks he ought to be, for he does everything correctly. He is a very good example of the Late Antique man described by Peter Brown; he is a victim of "the politics of *philotimia*" (*The Making of Late Antiquity*, 31). Although (presumably) pre-Antonine in conception, Dionysios (like Chaireas) is given to those sudden fits of anger and masochistic gestures that Brown notes as "besetting weaknesses" of the governing classes of the Antonine age (ibid., 40). Dionysios has also internalized a sense of sexual respectability of the kind that Brown so well describes in contemplating the pagan masculine ethos of Late Antiquity in *The Body and*

Society. His second marriage disrupts Dionysios' image of himself as wise and virtuous. Trying to defend that marriage in public leads him to Babylon, where he is himself seen as a mere slave of the Great King. Everyone is ultimately someone's slave—the word *doulos* echoes through the novel. Dionysios is not very good as a rhetorician nor very impressive as a man and a lover.

Babylon divides into parties. Among the men, the satraps and men in power take the part of the powerful Mithridates (and thus incidentally of Chaireas); the people, *to dēmotikon*, give their sympathy to Dionysios, whom they see as the victim of a more powerful man's attempt on his wife (137). Among the women, the parties line up differently. Rival beauties hostile to Kallirrhoé want to see her in effect raped by the claim of Mithridates. Others, the majority, want her to come happily out of the trial—which would mean the triumph of her legal husband Dionysios. The reader can see that the Persians' political readings of the legal case are invalid in relation to the complex state of affairs and to the leading characters' emotions. When Mithridates produces Chaireas as his surprise witness, Kallirrhoé is stunned. There is a sensation in the courtroom. The lovers hope to be reunited, but the Great King, who is falling in love with Kallirrhoé himself, cannot come to a decision. She remains locked up in the harem, protected by her kindest rival, the Queen Statira.

The men in Babylon again divide into two parties: one set for Chaireas, the other for Dionysios, who has done so much for the girl and given her a new life. The women also divide, some urging Kallirrhoé not to give up her true love, Chaireas, and her hope of seeing her home and father again. Others, less romantic, ask pointedly, "And suppose Chaireas gets mad again—then what? The tomb again?" (151). Kallirrhoé has to keep her own counsel; she could do too much damage to herself and to either or both men by voicing a preference, and she sees the lurking danger from the amorous Great King of Persia.

The Great King himself tries to fight against and conquer his rising passion. He is almost relieved when there is an Egyptian insurrection and he is called to war. He takes his women, including Queen Statira and Kallirrhoé, with him. Chaireas with Polycharmos joins the opposing Egyptians. Alert at last, the newly active Chaireas seizes the island where the Persian women have been in effect stored. Told of a recalcitrant but extremely beautiful woman who refuses to leave the temple sanctuary or to see her conqueror, Chaireas is curious; he comes to meet her and finds—at last—his Kallirrhoé. Even though the Great King once gave Dionysios his word he should have his wife again, the Persian powers are not capable of breaking up the restored union, since Chaireas has power over the queen. He and Kallirrhoé send Queen Statira and her ladies (and her jewels) back to the Great King, with many courteous messages. The Greek soldiers, with some of the many Egyptians and others who want to escape from Persian power, sail back with Chaireas in a great flotilla that finally lands in Syracuse.

There are many happy reunions, but not all are reunited. Kallirrhoé gives up something in leaving Dionysios—her child. Dionysios never knows during the entire course of the novel that this son is not his. Although we have a prophetic hint that Kallirrhoé's son will someday come to Syracuse and take up his grandfather's inheritance, such a resolution is far in the future. Dionysios got something out of the marriage. Kallirrhoé, heroine of virtue that she is, was polyandrous, and certainly does not hate her second husband. Chariton's story is a story of mixed emotions. The ironic situational paradoxes illustrate the mixed and mingled nature of life, and the difficulty of designing life—which is what Dionysios in particular tries to do. Eros, we are told, loves conflicts and changes.

LONGUS: *DAPHNIS AND CHLOÉ*

Eros also has explicit power in Longus' *Daphnis and Chloé* (c. A.D. 200). Eros is behind the major love plot and actually appears to one of the characters. Yet in this novel he shares power with the Nymphs and Pan, minor rustic deities whose major place in the action marks the novel as a pastoral narrative. In Lesbos, in the country outside of Mytilene, a goatherd finds one of his female goats suckling an infant boy. This beautiful baby, this "foundling" as George Thornley calls him in an English translation of 1657, is beautifully dressed in a purple cloak with a golden brooch, and there is a little dagger with a polished ivory handle by his side. Lamon and his wife Myrtale keep the baby (though Lamon was at first tempted just to take the valuables). They give the infant the name Daphnis, a pastoral name (Daphnis was a name of the supposed inventor of pastoral music). Two years later, a neighboring shepherd, Dryas, finds a beautiful baby girl suckled by a ewe in the Cave of the Nymphs. This infant is accompanied by fine tokens— a gold-embroidered girdle, solid gold ankle bands, gilt shoes. Dryas and his wife, Napé, adopt the child, and give it the name of Chloé—a *very* pastoral name meaning "green shoot," and associated with the offering of green shoots to Demeter.

The cave where Chloé is found is adorned with images of the Nymphs carved in stone, smiling, dancing barefoot, like the chorus of a theatrical dancing scene. This first reference to the Nymphs and to visual representation within the tale is not really the first reference either to Nymphs or to representation. In the frame story that begins the work, the nameless narrator tells us that in Lesbos he saw in the grove of the Nymphs a most beautiful painting of a story of love (*historia erōtos*). His own story (our novel) is, we are told, an attempt to vie with that picture by interpreting it in words. Longus' novel is thus offered as a re-representation, an artifice born of artifice. Longus is constantly interested in the connections between natural things and human arts, and his play with interfolding representations is also a play on the never-ending reciprocities of Art and Nature. The story is not just a present to the reader; it is a votive offering (*anathēma*) to Love, to Pan, and to the Nymphs, that is, to its subjects. It is, of course, an artificial offering, yet folded within the world of "Nature," of the Nymphs, as the original picture was displayed within the grove. These interreflections of redoubled mimeses at the outset warn the reader to be wary of complex artistries— Froma Zeitlin calls this "a hallucinating echo text" ("Poetics of *Erōs*," 438). We must not think this simple pastoral tale is really simple at all.

Longus turns the conventions of pastoral poetry as written by Theocritus and Bion (and by Virgil in Latin) into prose narrative—though we do not know whether he was the first to do that. The story incorporates well-known *topoi* of the poetic pastoral. The love between the two central characters is a love in the pastoral tradition, offering opportunity for reworking the addresses of a passionate shepherd to his nymph. The New Comedy style of *plot*, the story of the foundlings, is here welded to the *incidents* of pastoral. The language is poetic and inter-mixed with allusions to poetry. Sappho, perhaps because she is the poet of Lesbos, figures noticeably in the allusions, especially in the fruit-picking scene at the end of Book III, where only one great beautiful apple is left at the top of the tree and only Daphnis dares to climb so high and pick it—an allusion to Sappho's poem in which the unattainable perfect apple is the beloved herself (Sappho no. 105).[7]

As the reader must expect, Daphnis and Chloé, herding their flocks to-gether, fall in love—though they have never heard the word *love*. When she is thirteen and Daphnis fifteen, Chloé falls in love with her friend. After she has helped to rescue him from a pit set to trap wolves, she helps him to bathe off the dirt in the spring, and is suddenly stricken with the sight—and touch—of his lithe brown body. It arouses in her yearnings and disturbances, which she cannot understand. This scene is surely recollected in John Cleland's *Memoirs of a Woman of Pleasure* (1749), better known as *Fanny Hill*, when the beautiful Harriet de-scribes her first love, brought on, she tells us, when, all youth and still all inno-cence, she saw a beautiful naked youth swimming in a nearby stream, and was awakened to the perturbations of erotic longing: "new desires and strange wishes . . . not that I so much as knew precisely what was wanting to me . . ." (*Memoirs*, 102). (In that idyll of quite a different kind the young man rapes the ignorant girl.) When Chloé is judge in a contest between the shepherd Dorkon and Daphnis, she gives Daphnis the prize, a kiss. It is a kiss uneducated and un-skillful (*adidakton men kai atechnon*, 34) but it suffices to set Daphnis off into love. He is stunned and saddened, rather as if bitten than kissed. Now the young people must first make their love known to one another, and then decide what to do about it.

There are other incidents, distractions, and dangers posed to the pair, in-cluding the love of the shepherd Dorkon for Chloé, and the predatory habits of raiders, but these dangers are overcome, largely through the assistance of Pan. These incidents punctuate the developing and frustrating love of the two naïve young people. At the beginning of Book II, there is a scene in which an old man dressed in skins, Philetas, tells Daphnis and Chloé of his strange experience. He found a young boy romping about in his beautiful garden and feared that this hooligan child would injure his pomegranates and myrtles. This child bore myrtles and pomegranates in his hand and was lovely to see: "white as milk, shining haired like fire, glistening as if just washed. Naked he was, alone he was. He played about and picked the fruits as if the garden were his own" (70–72). Philetas ran after him, but the child easily eludes him, hiding under the roses or in the poppies like a partridge chick. As Thornley's translation has it, "this was a cunning piece and a thing that could not be caught." The old man, wearied, is won over by the child's laughter, and swears he will let him take whatever he likes if the child will but give him one kiss. With loud laughter the child tells him that would be too dangerous for him in his old age. The mischievous intruder reveals his identity: "No child am I though I seem a child, but older than Kronos and than all that is" (74). He was with Philetas in his courtship of Amaryllis; he comes to the garden and takes care of the groves, flowers, and fountains. He is taking care of Daphnis and Chloé. Philetas should rejoice that he has seen this boy in his old age. After this speech, the child springs into the myrtles like a young nightingale: "Then I saw his wings upon his shoulders and a bow and arrows between his wings . . . O children, you are consecrated to Love, and in the care of Eros" (70–77).

This poetically presented vision of Eros governs the whole book, which is itself an offering to Eros. As Froma Zeitlin points out, *Daphnis and Chloé* represents "a bold and provocative experiment (both psychological and artistic), that claims . . . to be an authoritative treatise on *erōs*." The novel combines various traditions in "an exercise (and lesson) in the poetics . . . of *erōs*" ("The Poetics of *Erōs*," 419–20). The entire novel is, as Zeitlin indicates, a complex study in desire, mimesis, and making, in which we are urged to experience the relations between nature and art, seeing even our own consciousness as the product of both art and time.

It is a bold experiment to bring Eros on stage, as it were. In Chariton's novel Eros is felt to be everywhere, and is rhetorically personified, but never directly represented. In Longus' story, Eros still does not quite appear directly—the embodiment of desire has appeared to one of the minor characters, who narrates the event to the hero, heroine, and reader. The Eros of Philetas' encounter is noteworthy, if only because he has such a decided resemblance to the Cupid we all know on Valentine's Day. In Hesiod, Eros is one of the primal gods; first comes Chaos, then Gaia, then Eros, "most beautiful of all the immortals," who overpowers the minds of both gods and men (*Theogony*, lines 120–172). This primary force is not necessarily a child, but he has become so by the Greek love poems of the *Anakreontika*, most of which date from the second century B.C. In Longus' story we have no doubt that we are meeting a god who is truly powerful and truly mischievous. Philetas' fear for his ruined garden is realized in Book IV when the jealous Lampis, in love with Chloé and wishing to make trouble for Daphnis and his father, rampages through Lamon's lovely garden and ruins the flowers. The power of love as a careless child fits in with the developing love of those carefree children, Daphnis and Chloé, to whom love is a progressive awakening to care.

After the Eros episode, the young people are more daring. They now know the *word* for love, and are assured that a god has authorized their feelings. They embrace and kiss often. Still frustrated, they start to study the sheep and goats around them, noticing what they do in the spring warmth. Daphnis tries leaping on Chloé from behind, but this is anticlimactic and depressing. Nature alone is not a sufficient teacher. A young married woman of the neighborhood, Lykainion—her name means "She-wolf"—has a hankering for Daphnis and decides to teach him what he wants to know. Daphnis, as we know, has a proclivity for falling into wolf traps. Our hero actually becomes an innocent adulterer (*moichos*), without knowledge of any law.

In a comic scene of seduction, Lykainion gets Daphnis to herself and then explains that she knows what his problem is, and that she can teach him. The whole scene is comically conducted in a language suited to the apprentice's shop or the schoolroom—a language of teaching and learning. Daphnis comically begs his mistress to teach him that lesson with the utmost speed: *taxista didaxai tēn technēn* (154). We can see the influence of this scene on Voltaire's *Candide* (1759), when Cunégonde watches doctor Pangloss "who was giving a lesson in experimental physics" (*une leçon de physique expérimentale*) to the maid, thus indirectly instructing the heroine, who "had a great disposition for the sciences" (180). Lykainion gives Daphnis instruction up to a certain point at which Nature (*Physis*) herself taught him the rest practical part (*autē gar hē physis loipon epaideuse to prakteon*)—Nature herself taking the lab course, as it were. When Lykainion has finished her "erotic pedagogy" (*erōtikēs paidagōgias*, 154), Daphnis wants to run off straight away and impart this instruction to Chloé. But Lykainion explains that he must expect Chloé to cry out and to bleed, since it will be her first time. This information shocks Daphnis very much. His ardor cools because he cannot bear the idea of hurting Chloé. He goes back thoughtfully and tells Chloé nothing of his lesson, but offers a convincing lie. He now has a secret, bigger than her secret about Dorkon's kiss.

The lesson in sex makes a man of Daphnis—not in giving him new power, and the new pleasure of potency, but in giving him responsibility. Both Daphnis and Chloé have been far from heroes of chastity so far. The comedy lies in their inability to finish with a chastity based on mere ignorance, a technical, unwanted chastity. Now Daphnis becomes a hero of chastity, not as an abstract *sōphrosynē* but because he does not want to hurt Chloé; his chastity is the fruit of a responsible friendship. His reluctance to engage in sex with Chloé arises from the fact that he sees it, for the first time, as a version of what Orlando Patterson means by "sovereignal freedom," of taking power over another. (In a way, that is what this woman-wolf did to him). His private and affectional chastity owes nothing to religious or human laws or prohibitions. Indeed, the young couple have behaved throughout as if they were ignorant of such laws or prohibitions. They have lived, Longus shows us, a life of "natural" innocent heterosexuality without social adult interference. But Lykainion is an adult and she has interfered. She herself, the victim of an unhappy marriage, heralds the advent of social cares and the practical and cultural problems surrounding marriage.

For it is *marriage* of which Daphnis now thinks—and so runs into the economical and social facts of a situation that had seemed free of such facts. A marriage seems unlikely because Chloé's (foster) parents are of a higher social status than Daphnis' (foster) parents. Indeed, Daphnis' foster parents are (it is now emphasized) *slaves*, serfs, and thus by implication Daphnis as their son is himself not a freeman. Chloé's fostering parents seem to be the humblest of freemen. Daphnis has no money to attract Chloé's family, who hope to make a very good match with such a beautiful girl. The Nymphs in a vision help him find a purse with three thousand drachmas—a fortune for such small people. Chloé's parents then agree, but Daphnis' adoptive father Lamon can do nothing until his master in town agrees.

Suddenly, the town intrudes harshly upon the country life. We realize that this rural area is an estate owned by a man who intends to profit by it. The name of the owner is Dionysophanes—"the showing forth of Dionysius"—and his name accords with the delicate but deliberate Dionysian themes of the novel, especially visible in the scenes of the fruit-picking and the vintage (III, paras. 33–34; IV, paras. 1–6). This Dionysius, as in a parable, sends his son Astylos before him to look over the land and the herds. Astylos forgives Lamon and Daphnis for the damage that the vengeful Lampis did, but this benefit is counterbalanced by a new terror. Astylos' parasite Gnathon ("Mouthful" or "Big-Mouth") is smitten by the beautiful Daphnis and tries to woo him. Daphnis repulses him, thinking homosexual love against nature; he points out (surely incorrectly?) that he-goats don't mount he-goats. Besides, Daphnis explains, he loves only Chloé. Gnathon, however, pleads with his friend Astylos to get this slave for him, and Astylos, although he laughs at Gnathon for falling in love with someone who is bound to smell of goats, agrees. Lamon, when he sees Astylos plans to take Daphnis to Mytilene as a toy-boy for Gnathon's use, is horrified and decides to reveal the tokens. They will prove that Daphnis is of too high a class to be made into a "woman" to do the woman's sexual job for Gnathon.

This scheme works even better than Lamon hoped. The tokens are recognized by Dionysophanes—*he* is Daphnis' father. Having too many children, he explains, he had the fourth child exposed. The tokens were not meant for future recognitions, but as funeral adornments. Two of his other children have died, so he is happy to have one back. He offers Daphnis the farm the boy has been living on.

Chloé, meanwhile, has lost her active part in the story. In the first part, she was an initiating force; she rescued Daphnis twice, she fell in love first. In the "natural" state woman seems to have an equal importance. But once Daphnis learned the secret of sex, the *technē* of love, the balance was altered. He did not consult Chloé about the decision not to consummate their affair; she was given no choice in the matter. It is he who begins to worry, about money, about the practicalities of marriage, about what will happen to his father and indeed himself as *slaves*. In this novel the man, not the woman, has to endure the burden of slavery, the fear of whipping—and even the fear of rape. The danger that Chloé was in from Dorkon in Book I is counterbalanced by the danger posed to Daphnis by Gnathon in Book IV.

Gnathon is of course a comic character; the parasite is a well-known satiric type. That he is both gourmet and gourmand (204; 213) links him with other greedy characters of satire, such as appear in Horace's description of a dinner party (Book II, Satire viii). If we knew more about the comedies of the period, the *mimes* (which did have speaking parts) we might know more of the sources of Gnathon's characterization.[8] (Terence, d. 159 B.C., was by now a very antique Old Master.) For men of superior rank—and Gnathon though a parasite, is free, and of rank enough to threaten to beat Lamon—the slave relation precludes respect. Gnathon's name ("Mouth," "Jaw") types him as a representative of oral fixation, including doubtless the interest in oral sex that the ancients identified as a characteristic of dwellers of Lesbos. Gnathon is pure slovenly greed, the most debased form of that desire which Eros makes life-quickening. The love-plaint of this perfect glutton when he threatens suicide is parodically comic: "I'll seize this dagger and when I've filled my belly with food I'll kill myself before Daphnis' door. Then you'll have a job to summon your Gnatho-pet, as you always do in play" (212). The word *paizōn*—"playfully," "in play" or "in sport"—indicates his attitude to sexuality—it is play. Astylos responds to Gnathon's plea on the understanding that this is all play, and when Astylos' other servants look forward to having the handsome Daphnis as one of their number in town, one sees that they too enjoy the prospect of new sport. This "play" is not what Daphnis has come to mean by love.

Daphnis' recognition by his father is an occasion for mixed emotions on his part. He has to bid farewell to the familiar things that he loves—and he causes laughter when after the recognition drama he starts talking about the needs of his goats. He must also explain that he wants to marry Chloé, but naturally his new papa thinks of grander things. Consent is given, however, and the large party departs for the city. Dionysophanes has a dream in which he sees the Nymphs petition Eros for permission to end matters with a wedding. Eros, unstringing his bow and laying aside his quiver, commands Dionysophanes to invite all of the nobility of Mytilene to a feast, and there to display Chloé's tokens. A great man, Megakles, the guest of honor, recognizes them, and exclaims that he left them with his daughter years ago. Megakles explains that he had overextended himself in spending money on warships and theater productions (two glory-making but expensive forms of civic service); after serving as *triērarchos* and *chorēgos* he had little money left and he did not know how he could afford to bring up his child, a daughter. The tokens were intentionally elegant and significant because he had hoped (unlike Daphnis' father) that someone would preserve the baby, and therefore he laid her in the cave of the Nymphs entrusted to the goddesses" (240). Since then he has grown richer every day, and has had no other children, not even a daughter. "But the gods, as if laughing at me for what I had done, sent me by night a dream explaining that a sheep would make me a father" (242).

This second recognition scene completes the round and knits up the families again. Yet, significantly, Daphnis and Chloé want to live in the country and escape from their families. They do *not* like the town, the abode of their new fathers, and they want to pick up their real life, the life *before* these mock-Aristotelian recognitions. Their wedding is held in the country, by the mouth of the cave of the Nymphs; there are rural songs, and the goats feed nearby, to the pleasure of Daphnis and Chloé—though not of the city folk! Hero and heroine are to have a son and a daughter, and will have the son suckled by a goat and their daughter by a sheep. They will adorn the cave of the Nymphs and will build an altar to Cupid the Shepherd and a temple to *Panos Stratiōtēs*, Pan the Soldier. But all this will happen later. On their wedding night they are led into the chamber to the sound of rural songs. Chloé at last finds out that "the things that they had done in the wood were only children's play."

The last words of the novel are "children's games" (or "toys"), "children's play" (*paidiōn paignia*). The novel plays on a variety of games and sports, including Daphnis' game of bird-catching when he is trying to get near Chloé's house. That winter scene of snow, with the myrtle bush, ivy, and birds is very attractive, and exhibits Longus' mastery of—and fondness for—detail. We see Daphnis, busy as the birdcatcher, and yet really watching Chloé's house all the time, hoping for some sort of excuse to get in to see her, since the winter has kept them apart: "But out of the cottage nobody came, not a man, not a woman, not so much as a dooryard fowl" (136). The little touch of the household fowl is characteristic of Longus. There are a number of birds involved in the story's various games, including the convincing gosling stolen by an eagle in Lykainion's made-up story that leads Daphnis on his goose-chase to her pudenda. And the birdlike Eros, like a nestling nightingale, plays his own game in Philetas' garden.

Spontaneous movement, active play are important in the figures of Longus' style, as well as in the themes of his novel. Yet as we see with the introduction of Gnathon, "play" can have its negative side, expressing a destructive attitude to the humanity of others. Where is the good "play" to be found? How to make games into seriousness, childhood into adulthood, without losing the joy?—these are central questions that Longus' novel poses. Of course, *Daphnis and Chloé* is itself a game; it playfully arouses a playful nostalgia in the reader, a nostalgia for the time when adult sexuality was intuited but not fully understood. Such nostalgia is burlesqued by Voltaire in the opening chapters of *Candide*, which parody Longus' novel, and is played upon in a different tone in Mark Twain's *Tom Sawyer* (1876). Not only childhood but adolescence is transformed by Longus into an idyll, represented with pastoral license as a free space without the encumbrances of social law. *Daphnis and Chloé* is thus a magical story about sex but not an immoral one (whatever impotences it may have been applied to curing). The novel presents the need for both friendship and passion in Eros. Like the other Greek novels, it shows us that the whole idea of "falling in love" depends on an idea of individuation. One person is *not* as good as the next, all cats are not grey in the dark. Dionysius, so often invoked in this novel, is yet here subordinate to Eros. Or rather, Eros becomes the true (if playful) Dionysius, as Eros does on some sarcophagi of the same period; the Eros of the Vintage is represented, as for instance, on a sarcophagus now in the Archaeological Museum in Istanbul, where the Cupidons who play in the garden of life and of material flesh (the vine and grapes) are also symbols and guarantors of individual life. In *Daphnis and Chloé*, Eros cares both for generation in general, and for the individual. Yet, to pursue such an ideal as *this* Eros represents places stress on the human players—stress that playful Eros himself, older than Saturn but forever a careless child, never has to share. We may see how true this is in this novel's Eros of the garden, as in its Pan—both the true original of James Barrie's hero in *Peter Pan*.[9]

Longus' novel is often spoken of as "charming," but many descriptions of it, while lingering over the scene with Lykainion, ignore the tensions of the second half, and the problems inherent in trying to imagine how to relate the charmed space of free growing affectional sexuality to the uncharmed space of marriage and property. Chloé is not a heroine of chastity, because she does not have to be. The first half of the story shows her physical development and her emotional involvement with Daphnis; the Nymphs and Pan approve of her, and her only worries are first whether Daphnis will love her and then whether they will get any satisfaction. Nobody seems to have spoken to her of chastity. In the second half her foster-mother suddenly remarks that they'd better marry her off, else she will give her virginity away to some shepherd; the maternal coarse practicality seems discordant, shocking.

Even more shocking is the condition of slavery that begins visibly to enclose Daphnis about the same time. Both hero and heroine become commodities. We find first their foster parents and then the city slickers all thinking how they may use or exchange the two young people. Longus shows us the problem, which he also indicates is a cultural, not a "natural," problem: the customs of society are such that fulfilling adult sexual destiny means entering a world of commodification and enclosure. Chloé's virginity is suddenly of concern to Daphnis' father. That father tried to destroy his son sixteen years ago; *now* he is all proper concern that this son should obtain a wife fit for him. Chloé must simply be privately grateful that she did not get her own earlier wish for the consummation of love, for the earlier fulfillment of her sexual desire would have been socially sadly disadvantageous. In pointing to the power of the god Dionysius in this novel, some commentators have stressed the significance of the name of Daphnis' real father "Dionysophanes." But our "epiphany of Dionysius" is a puzzle—a paradox, as Chariton might say. For *this* Dionysius is a grave and calculating man, not at all an exemplar of the Dionysiac spirit—even less so than Chariton's anti-hero. His good-natured elder son has an ambiguous name, which may mean something like "Citified" but also sounds very like "Unpropped," "Without a Pillar"; Astylos is a young man without any stay or center.

The novel's city folk seem luxurious, interfering, and somewhat enervated. Their presence forcefully recalls us to economic realities. These have not, however, been really absent in the first part of the novel: Winkler points to the details that describe a "scarcity economy," including the peasants' monotonous diet, and the high value of a piece of rope (*Constraints of Desire*, 107). Longus knows that the reader, like the rich characters but not the poor ones, desires to ignore harsh economic life in favor of pastoral pleasure. But shepherds—then as now—are engaged in an economic enterprise. In Turkey in November 1991 I encountered a magnificent shepherd striding over green fields through the mist with his flock. When I stopped to photograph him, I found (with the help of a translator) that this picturesque pastoral personage owns apartments and a taxi-business in Bursa; he follows his flocks himself because he enjoys the fresh air and thinks the life healthy. The flocks, however, are part of his wealth, like the taxi-business. I was reminded of Longus, who would have appreciated this twentieth-century shepherd. Longus, too, knows that the owner of flocks or vineyards has a financial stake in nature—but his urban landowners (unlike the Bursa shepherd) have detached themselves from their flocks and the fresh air, the daily labor that gets their riches. Longus knows we share a desire to elude such knowledge in favor of a "pure" (because imaginary) experience of escape into natural simplicity. But that desire is shown to involve a certain bad faith, as it aligns us with some very bossy and dull people in the novel, the city folk who use groves and fields as an investment but pretend they have a "natural" homecoming.

One of the major shocks of the last part of Longus' novel is the reader's forced recognition (*anagnōrisis*) that the beautiful pastoral places are someone's *property*. Their beauty is, partly, a got-up thing to please the property owner. Lamon's lovely garden lacks the attractions of Philetas' garden because so much emphasis is laid on it as a pleasure ground for the jaded city dweller. Rural laborers work hard to make the country look nice for the master from town. Lamon goes to work clearing out the fountains, and cleaning the yard so the lord and master will not be offended by the smell of dung. The peasants save some of the best grapes so that those from the city (*tois ek tēs poleōs*, 196) may have some of the fun of the vintage. The "natural" world of beauty and fertility is being trimmed up and played with to please a bunch of rich *tourists*. Dionysophanes and his entourage bring their urban world with them to the country; they even bring their own food. Daphnis and Chloé get some tidbits of the visitors' first big meal and are naïvely pleased at tasting the city dainties (212). Marriage and the construction of familial inheritance and importance seem to belong to the city world too.

No wonder Daphnis and Chloé are uncomfortable with that city world and make their own compromise. They will even try to reduplicate their experience with their own children, having them, too, nursed by the animals, who do not betray or abandon. Readers have often sought in *Daphnis and Chloé* a helping of nostalgic charm; George Moore introduces his translation by announcing, "I would escape from modern thought into Paganism" (*Pastoral Loves*, 5).[10] But the novel itself in its second half militates against the nostalgia that tempts us in its beginning. And "Paganism"—as we so quaintly like to call it—has its own problems, as the novel shows; religion is in transition, official custom and religion are defective, energies are misplaced—just as in "modern life" and "modern thought," in fact. Parents spend time and energy on city shows while throwing their children away. Dionysius, far from representing what Nietzsche nostalgically longed for, has obviously sold out to Big Business.

In *Daphnis and Chloé*, Dionysius is presented as confined and confining. Even the statue of the god Dionysius and the paintings of his deeds stand within that over-cared-for, over-civilized, anxious garden, the parodic (yet still attractive) *locus amoenus*. Dionysius has gone over to legalism and property. The real deities of the novel are the Nymphs, Pan, and Eros—a new trinity. These divinities are suitable to rural life, but Longus gives them a fresh significance in their combination. Pan rescues Chloé at one point, but the stories she keeps hearing of Pan—his treatment of Syrinx and of Echo—make her confidence fail. She says that Pan obviously will not punish Daphnis for infidelity, and makes Daphnis swear faith to her on a second vow, by the mother goat that nourished him. Pan stands for—or rather, Pan *is*—the justice of male sexuality, its righteousness, and Pan is here balanced against the Nymphs of the cave, who *are* the justice of femininity, and the female sexual energies that also go into childbearing and childrearing. The ewe suckles Chloé within the sacred female cave. Eros is in a good relation to both the Nymphs and Pan, and assists both sides in achieving harmony. A balance and harmony between male and female deities is the condition aspired to in the novel's images of art, and in the characters' dreams. Chloé's objection to Pan states a female cause, and permits us to notice the female cause as represented elsewhere in the story.

Longus can be accused of capitulating in the end, of accepting the conventions of marriage. We do not know, as Zeitlin points out, "what might have overtly motivated the apparent shift in Daphnis' perception" of "virgins and defloration" ("Poetics of *Erōs*," 458). Lykainion had told Daphnis forcefully that sex (heterosexuality) is a matter of dominion and pain. No Anthea Dworkin she, but she raises some of the same issues. Homosexual libertinism proves to have the same ingredients, though in libertinism (as not in marriage) pain can appropriately be played with—as in Gnathon's suicide threat. Daphnis' desire not to inflict pain on the one he sexually loves seems all the more unusual when we come to the last part of the book where an entire economy visibly depends on the authority to inflict pain. "Civilization" means slaveholding, whipping, the exposure of infants for financial reasons. We do begin to see that it might be possible to reach a higher plane—also a more pleasurable one. The harmony between Pan, the Nymphs, and Eros encourages the hope that male and female can reach some harmony.

As Longus knows, however, such a harmony demands an equality, a frankness, and even a hedonism not officially known to the world of ancient marriage, in which the wife should be the dutiful property of her civic-minded husband. The pastoral permits an escape from social law. As married lovers, Daphnis and Chloé consciously repastoralize their married life. But they are then out of the true pastoral world. They participate in a world of culture and artifice even as they design their country life.

ACHILLES TATIUS: *KLEITOPHON AND LEUKIPPÉ*

In Achilles Tatius' *Kleitophon and Leukippé* we have, not a pastoral tale, but a comically urbane—and urban—story of love-adventure: the hero and heroine dash from city to city. The threat of arranged marriage, which briefly hung over both Daphnis and Chloé, is the first problem of Kleitophon of Tyre; when he is nineteen his father plans his marriage (to his half-sister), but at that point "Fate began the drama" (*ērcheto tou dramatos hē tychē*, 12). His uncle sends his wife and daughter from Byzantium to take refuge from the wars. At the arrival of beautiful cousin Leukippé, Kleitophon falls in love with her immediately, and can hardly eat during the family banquet that follows. (The manners in this novel are not classical Greek manners: men and women eat together.) His cousin and best friend Kleinias sympathizes. Kleinias' young male lover is also threatened with an arranged marriage, but he does not live to marry, dying because of an accident caused by the horse Kleinias gave him. The heartbroken Kleinias is later willing to assist Kleitophon and to accompany the lovers on their journey: the hero's gay best friend is a feature of Greek novels.

Fortunately, lovely Kalligoné, the hero's half-sister and fiancée, is abducted by a Byzantine youth of quality, Kallisthenes, who turned pirate in order to abduct Leukippé but carries off Kalligoné instead. Kleitophon pursues the budding affair with Leukippé, persuading her to let him into her bedroom. The slave Satyros, after drugging Leukippé's mother's attendant, tells our hero, "Your Kyklops is sound asleep; make like the brave Odysseus" (104). Kleitophon makes his way into the girl's bedroom. Eroticism turns into comic farce, as Leukippé's mother, Pantheia, awakened by a nightmare (in which she sees a bandit cut open her daughter's belly with a sword) rushes in. Kleitophon jumps out of bed and runs away as fast as he can in the dark. He is trembling—Kleitophon is never very valiant, and never makes like a valiant Odysseus, except in persistent traveling. (Odysseus himself, however, is better known for getting out of tight situations than for sheer valor.) Leukippé gets out of her scrape by insisting that she doesn't know *who* was in her room—whether demon, demigod, or burglar. She has not lost her virginity, she insists, and of course she is technically correct, though it was not by her choice that she ended the evening in a virgin state.

Kleitophon decides they should both run away. They board a ship sailing to Alexandria, and it suffers the usual shipwreck. When Nietzsche described the shipwrecked older Poesy rescuing all her children on the lifeboat, he was sneeringly picking up a figure from the Greek novel, with its shipwrecks and family reunions. In this case, the crew rush into the lifeboat and leave the passengers to fend for themselves. Kleitophon and Leukippé, who cling to a piece of the prow when the ship breaks up, are carried through the corpse-laden sea to the shore at Pelousion. They then hire a little boat; but this boat is captured by bandits, who then take the virgin Leukippé to offer as a sacrifice. Kleitophon, who has escaped, is forced to watch from a distance as the bandits sacrifice Leukippé at their altar, ripping open her belly and disemboweling her (thus evidently fulfilling her mother's nightmare). The bandits make a sacramental meal of roasted entrails and then place the body in a coffin.

Kleitophon is about to kill himself by his beloved's coffin when the slave Satyros and a new friend from the journey, the gay Menelaos, arrive, having escaped from the gang. They tell him not to worry: "Your Leukippé will now come to life again" (170). They open her coffin and she does rise—a fearful sight, with entrails clinging about her. But all that has to be done is to remove a clever contraption of sheep-belly and animal guts contrived by Satyros and put under the girl's clothes. He and Menelaos had also tricked the bandit into using a stage dagger from the luggage of one of the bandit's victims, "one of those who recite Homer in the theatres" (174–76). This strolling actor's prop completed the effect of mock "death"—and the whole gruesome scene was a *coup de théâtre*.

Rejoiced at having his Leukippé resurrected and restored, Kleitophon is all for pressing ahead with consummation. But Leukippé has become more thoughtful about the matter. When she was lamenting the prospect of being sacrificed, the goddess Artemis appeared to her in a dream and promised to help her, telling her "Remain a virgin [*parthenos*], until I lead you as a bride; to no one but Kleitophon will you be given" (190). Comforted by Artemis' promise, Leukippé firmly insists on postponement of the consummation according to the goddess's decree. Leukippé has thus changed from the lustful teenager she was in the first two books, and has become a heroine of chastity. Heroism of chastity is thus also thrust upon Kleitophon.

The captain of the cavalry who freed the couple from bandits has no scruples about chastity, however, and wants Leukippé at once. Leukippé stalls for time; Menelaos tells the captain the girl has her menstrual period (one of the rare occasions when this is mentioned in any work of fiction before the twentieth century). The army officer insists that he will be content for a few days with close kissing—which plunges Kleitophon into agonies of jealousy. Any lovemaking on Leukippé's part is almost immediately precluded by her falling into a fit, and then going raving mad.

The men want to tie her up, but Kleitophon cannot bear to see his mad beloved in these restraining bonds. In *Jane Eyre*, Mr. Rochester will protest to Jane that if *she* were mad, he would still care for her: "if you raved, my arms should confine you, and not a strait waistcoat—your grasp, even in fury, would have a charm for me: if you flew at me . . . wildly . . . I should receive you in an embrace" (305). Kleitophon is truly put to the test. He begs the men to loose the bonds from those tender hands: "Leave me with her; I alone embracing her will be the bonds that bind her. Let her rage in her madness against me!" (208). For ten anxious days Kleitophon watches over his delirious sweetheart, as they travel through the muddy marshlands, the land-water area beside the Nile. Leukippé was, it turns out, poisoned by one Gorgias, an admirer who overdosed her on aphrodisiac. Leukippé recovers. She and Kleitophon, grateful to their new friend Chaireas, who has helped them in their medical crisis, enter Alexandria with renewed optimism. They should not be happy too soon. Leukippé is abducted by the treacherous Chaireas, and anguished Kleitophon from the deck of the pursuing boat sees her beheaded.

Kleitophon is in mourning for six months. His anguish is abating, when an astonishing piece of good fortune offers itself. A beautiful young woman of Ephesus, a widow whose husband was lost at sea, has fallen in love with Kleitophon and wants to marry him. His friends point out the advantages of acquiring a beautiful wife and a great estate together. Kleitophon meets Melitté—and the novel's second powerful woman enters the scene. She is very beautiful with milk-white skin, rosy cheeks, and long golden hair. She offers a delicious dinner, which she herself is unable to eat; she gazes upon our hero like Mrs. Waters upon Tom Jones at the Inn at Upton. Kleitophon finds her very lovely, and the kiss she gives him not disagreeable—but he is not as compliant as Tom Jones. He will not make love to Melitté in Alexandria because that is where he was last with Leukippé; he refuses to make love to Melitté on the boat going to Ephesus because they are sailing over the sea where he lost his Leukippé. But he agrees to consummate their love and become her husband once they get to Ephesus, and he intends to do so.

Melitté seems to have charge of everything. Although put out at times by the coyness of her new fiancé, she is evidently touched by the evidence of an amorous fidelity, which would be agreeable if directed towards herself. She has all the confidence of the mistress of a great estate; she is a fine hostess and a good talker. Once the couple arrive in Ephesus they visit Melitté's country estate; they are walking among the rows of trees in the orchard when suddenly a strange figure throws herself before them, a very dirty woman with shorn hair, carrying a hoe, wearing a short and wretched garment. This slave begs Melitté for pity and help as woman to woman—since she herself, she says, was born a freewoman. The slave identifies herself as Lakaina of Thessaly, sold into slavery by pirates and now abused by the steward Sosthenes, because she will not be a slave to his lusts. She shows her back scarred by the slave driver's whip. Melitté promises to help her and fires Sosthenes. She tells her own maids to look after this woman, to wash and dress her, and bring her to Ephesus. Having displayed her pity, quickness of mind, and executive powers, Melitté drives with her fiancé back to town, where they are to have an elaborate dinner at home before consummating their union.

In the middle of the dinner Kleitophon's own servant Satyros signals him to come out, and then secretly gives him a letter. He recognizes the writing straight away—it is Leukippé's! Of course the reader has already recognized that the dirty slave "Lakaina" *is* Leukippé . . . and that Kleitophon is a dolt. He *should* have recognized her—particularly since he should by now have got used to her habit of resurrection.

Leukippé's letter is a comic model of mixed emotions. She has heard that her former fiancé is about to marry the beautiful rich lady. She reminds him of all she has gone through on his account—she has been shipwrecked, sacrificed, sold, fettered, and made to till the ground and to undergo beatings. She has been faithful through these trials. Kleitophon, on the other hand, was never sold, never whipped—and now he is marrying! Leukippé's letter unites scorn and grievance, haughtiness and pleading. Kleitophon at least owes it to her to free her; if he will lend her the two thousand gold pieces Sosthenes paid for her, she will repay the money once she's back home in Byzantium. She concludes with sourly haughty good wishes: "Enjoy your new marriage. I who write this to you am a virgin [*parthenos*]." The last remark is a wonderful combined rebuke and appeal; Leukippé is still worth having because she is a virgin, and *she* has kept her chastity, though he has not.

Kleitophon, he tells us, was moved with many feelings. "I turned hot, I turned cold, I marvelled, I doubted, I rejoiced, I was distressed" (276). He writes back to her—a difficult exercise. "If you will wait to hear the truth," he tells her "you will learn that I have imitated your own virginity—if there is virginity in men [*ei tis esti kai en andrasi parthenia*]" (280–282). So Kleitophon answers the question rhetorically posed by Fielding's Lady Booby: "Did ever Mortal hear of a Man's Virtue! Did ever the greatest, or the gravest Men pretend to any of this Kind? . . . And can a Boy, a Stripling, have the Confidence to talk of his Virtue?" (*Joseph Andrews*, 32–33). Kleitophon tries to identify a new condition among men, male *parthenia*. He has an immediate problem with Melitté, who expects their wedding-night to proceed. He says he does not feel very well. Melitté goes to the newcomer, the Thessalian Lakaina, to ask her (since women of Thessaly are supposed to be witches) whether she cannot give her medicine to give Kleitophon to enable him to perform sexually—they have, she confides to the interested pseudo-Thessalian, been together for five nights and nothing has happened! Leukippé is thus reliably informed that Kleitophon has *not* been unfaithful to her with Melitté. But before any further clarifications can take place among this trio, a new disaster occurs.

Melitté's husband, Thersandros, another survivor of a shipwreck, returns. He bursts into their banquet and at once starts beating Kleitophon, who is astonished as to why this stranger is hitting him: "I, as if this were the celebration of some mystery rite [*hōsper en mystēriōi*], had no idea who this man was or why he was hitting me so ungraciously." Kleitophon takes this beating with his usual patience. "When he was tired of beating me and I of my philosophizing, I got up" (290). During this scuffle, his letter from Leukippé had fallen out of his clothes; Melitté, picking it up and quickly reading it, realizes the facts of the case. Thersandros has Kleitophon thrown into his own private prison, and bangs out of the house in a temper.

Melitté goes to the imprisoned Kleitophon and berates him—for tricking her, for laughing at her, and for lacking sympathy with a fellow-slave of Love. Now she can have no hope of marriage, but wants only one embrace, one lovemaking, as a little medicine against her long disease of love. She is not, she says proudly, afraid to allude to Eros' mysteries, for Kleitophon is an initiate. Remember the vow he swore on the altar of Isis, when he was willing to be her lover—he owes her that much. If he gives himself to her, she pleads, just this once, one short time, she will pray that he never loses Leukippé again. He owes her something, for it was through her that he came to Ephesus and recovered Leukippé. Eros speaks through her to Kleitophon, saying, "Grant this, Kleitophon, to me, your mystagogue. Do not go away and leave Melitté uninitiated, for her fire is mine" (298).

Kleitophon is moved by Melitté's terrific love-oration—as he says, Eros is a teacher of eloquent reasoning. And from many mixed motives, in which joy at the recovery for Leukippé and affection for Melitté mingle, he grants her wish. "I experienced a human feeling," he says (*epathon ti anthrōpinon*, 302). They make Love, just that once, in Kleitophon's prison room, but Eros cares nothing for aphrodisiac apparatus. The rite of Aphrodite is best not carefully planned; when it springs up naturally of its own accord, like a wild flower, it offers pleasure. Eros can make any place the site of his mystery.

This is one of the finest strokes of Achilles Tatius' novel. It is only when the weight of mourning has really been lifted from his spirit that Kleitophon is able to give Melitté the physical love she craves, when they both know that this has no future. Kleitophon sins against Leukippé (a fine paradox) just at the moment when he should renew his faith to her. He has now lost his *parthenia*, but not without good cause. One can see Achilles Tatius balancing the ideal (which he treats both comically and seriously) of heroic chastity with the claims of love and need, spontaneity and generosity. Melitté's desire is not reprobated by the author—she is an Ephesian "widow," but we are not required to laugh at *this* widow of Ephesus as some auditors do at the one in the tale in *Satyricon*.

Thersandros, whose own resurrection has pleased nobody, sulks, rages, and makes himself disagreeable. The slave Sosthenes (reinstated) offers him Leukippé as a fine new sex-partner; now that she is cleaned up, she is all too attractive. After preventing Kleitophon's escape (planned by Melitté) when the men catch that hero in the street in Melitté's clothes, Thersandros goes to Leukippé, whom he treats with a sentimental brutality. He enjoys her tears, cries with her, and then forces a kiss on her; when she resists, he hits her in the face. Leukippé disdains this fine masterly lovemaking; Sosthenes suggests whips and tortures will teach her. Thersandros' mode of lovemaking is a very marked contrast to Melitté's. Leukippé has no impulse to pity him, and ironically urges him and Sosthenes to do their worst:

> Bring your whips. Behold, my back—beat it! Bring in the fire. Behold, my body—burn it! . . . Be spectators at a new contest [*agōna*]! Against many torments one woman alone contends [*agōnizetai*] and is victorious over all. (344)

These are words and tones very similar to those employed by the Christian martyrs. Leukippé the agonist mocks male fondness for contests and shows of valor. Like a St. Catherine of Alexandria, Leukippé calls for the whips, the wheel, the fire, the sword. "I am naked, alone and a woman, but I have for armour my inner freedom [*en hoplon echō tēn eleutherian*] which cannot be beaten down with whips or cut off by the sword, or consumed by the fire . . . you will find no fire hot enough to burn it!" (346). Leukippé's words compare curiously with those attributed to Paul addressing the Ephesians (Ephesians 6:10–17). What is quite unlike the Pauline epistle is Leukippé's query as to how the villains dare outrage a virgin *in the city of the Virgin*, Artemis of Ephesus. Thersandros flings away, a victim of some very nasty mixed emotions, but his response to all this heroism is to resort to the law. He initiates a complex set of lawsuits, prosecuting Melitté for infidelity and Kleitophon for adultery. The penalty for a man who takes another man's wife is death, and that is what Thersandros tries for, figuring that once Kleitophon is dead Leukippé will be reasonable.

The seventh book is a comic law trial; both Thersandros and Melitté have a quantity of lawyers. Kleitophon muddies the whole matter. Led to believe, falsely, (yet again) that Leukippé is dead and murdered by Melitté's orders, Thersandros tries to turn the matter into a murder case. Matters get more complex as proceedings (and the torture of Kleitophon) are interrupted by a sacred embassy led by the priest of Artemis—and by none other than Leukippé's father, Sostratos. Kleitophon is unhappy at having to reveal his loss of Leukippé. But the maiden who is now seeking protection at the shrine of Artemis is none other than Leukippé herself. The priest of Artemis invites the family party to dinner. Dinner is somewhat embarrassing for the two young people—Kleitophon calls it "a symposium of shame" (*to symposion aidōs*, 396).

Once forgiven, the lovers narrate their adventures, and the priest of Artemis, sympathetic, makes mincemeat of Thersandros the next day in court. Thersandros, who wanted Kleitophon executed and Melitté punished for adultery, is thwarted on both counts. That Melitté is not a murderer of Leukippé is evident, and Melitté gets off the adultery charge by swearing (in words dictated by her husband) that she has not made love to Kleitophon during the time Thersandros was abroad. Thersandros, of course, has no idea that she and Kleitophon could have made love *after* his return, when Kleitophon was in jail. Meanwhile, Leukippé has displayed her right to claim the name of virgin by taking the test of entering Pan's cave, where if she is not a virgin she will disappear. The priest of Artemis is a bit doubtful about Leukippé's taking the test and advises prudence— it is possible, after all . . . but Leukippé proves herself triumphantly, pleasing her papa.

The young couple can marry, all the happier for the news that Kalligoné's piratical abductor has become a reformed character. Sostratos' praise of the reformed Kallisthenes is not the least comic section of this comic novel: "In other aspects of youthful behaviour, what a wonderful change! He would rise from his seat for his elders, and he would be the first to greet those whom he met with. And the reckless spending of his former dissolute life was changed into discretion" (448).

This is a wonderfully Gilbertian description of a reformed pirate. In offering near the very end such a reflection of the dullness of manners, the absurdity of a "sivilization" of the sort that offends Huck Finn, the author seems to be teasing us with the duality of ending. We want our characters to be safe and sound, united with their families and with each other—but that means being gathered in to the dull familiar round, and coming under the control of the fathers. What we really have enjoyed about the novel is not seeing young people act respectfully, but watching them have their own adventures and make their own mistakes. We have been made to sympathize with those who do not fit in with the patterns of paternalistic civil society. Melitté—who was after all an adulteress—

wins our sympathy, and Thersandros, who has all the rights of landowner, husband, and master, is a comic boor, a ruffian (his name means Beast-man) whom we want to see losing.

In Melitté's passionate speech to Kleitophon she begged him not to leave her "uninitiated.' She has been married and makes no claims to virginity—on the contrary, she seems very knowing. The initiation of which she speaks, initiation into "the mysteries of Eros," is different from initiation into the sexual act such as Daphnis and Chloé required. The *true* initiation, we gather, is to make love to someone who loves you. Loving and being loved take precedence over the sexual act itself. From that point of view, Kleitophon is, as Melitté says, an old hand at the mysteries of Love, not because he is sexually experienced (he is *not*) but because he has loved Leukippé so long and so hard.

LAW AND THE INDIVIDUAL

One might not have expected pagan ancients to take such delicate thought about what we now call the personal relationship. Against this new individuation of sacred love is set both the heavy world of slavery and the world of law. In many respects, the world of slavery and the world of law are one and the same. The painful truth of slavery is that men (and sometimes women) could purchase sexual toys and treat them as they pleased; the custom of slavery denies the individual. Melitté is accused by Thersander's lawyer in court of buying an effeminate male prostitute, importing him to Ephesus as pretty merchandise (*hōs phortion kalon*, 430). Sex is constantly being redefined in terms of commerce and ownership. The central characters in all these novels constantly resist this definition.

The world of Law—of property, of statutes, orders, and the fathers—looks serene and orderly. It asserts its ability to make the pain of sex and slavery disappear from view. The novel rescues such pain and will not allow it to be subsumed. The implicit claim of Law is brought to naught when the law in operation is represented in the ceremony of a trial within the narrative. Novelistic trials, more than dramatic ones, are exhibitions of the unsatisfactoriness of the law. Narratives seem suspicious of the definitive drama of the law court, which drama rather admires; narratives always point out how much is missing in that kind of theater. It is surprising how many novel characters (from ancient to modern times) are thrust into a law court at some point. The novels show that trying to make a person's real life coincide with what a court knows is comically—or sometimes perhaps tragically—doomed to fail. Chariton's Dionysios tries to keep his wife from her first husband in the law case that elicits so much difference of opinion in Persia. Thersandros resorts to the law to do his work for him and establish his rights over both his wife and his slave. The alternative source of power, to which characters are allowed to turn in the ancient novel, is the priesthood of Artemis/ Isis by which the Goddess can let her will prevail over the orders of the men. But to afford the "happy ending" of the narrative the heroine and hero must at last acquiesce in the civic order of things, just as in the end of *Daphnis and Chloé* the hero and heroine, with their spontaneous love, must be brought into line with the world of the city, the fathers, law, and property—considerations that nearly killed them in the first place. The civic dignity on which her father spent his wealth was literally almost the death of the infant Chloé.

The point of an ancient novel is not its ending. Closure is not really *telos*, though the ending of any novel interprets afresh for us what has gone before. The novel resides in the experience in which we are involved on the way. Each of these young people who function as characters in these novels is engaged in undergoing transformative experience. Such experience not only gives them some sort of claim upon the world to which they must attach themselves as adults, but also a claim to possess an identity which commands respect.

The processes of love and suffering *identify* them as persons. Reinhold Merkelbach claims in *Roman und Mysterium* that these novels reflect the rites of mystery cults, and that their plot points repeat episodes in the initiations of *mystai* as they progress towards a higher level of understanding. The relation of the Greek and Roman novel to the mystery religions is a very large matter and will be treated more fully later. Suffice it to say for the moment that I think Merkelbach's contention is basically true, perhaps truer than even he knows. Aristotle, as Walter Burkert paraphrases one of the fragments, had said "that those undergoing mysteries (*teloumenoi*) should not 'learn' (*mathein*) but should 'be affected,' 'suffer,' or 'experience' (*pathein*)" (Burkert, *Ancient Mystery Cults*, 69). So it is with the novels. We (and the characters) may learn (*mathein*) discursively about many things: the best mode of gardening, the arrangement of a picture, the reasons for the Nile floods, the habits of the crocodile or Phoenix. The higher learning, however, is in what we are able to experience (*pathein*) in these *erōtika pathēmata*. The novel conveys in its story what could not be conveyed aside from the story. Whether or not we think of the novelistic journey as a reference to the mystery religion's image of Isis setting out on her boat to search for the scattered body of Osiris, we must see that an experiential journey is inevitable. These novels insist that individual experience is a religious experience. That deepest individual experience of the voyage of life and its significance to the soul has to take place away from the civic realm where the laws and customs established by the fathers know the answers to all questions before they are asked.

CHAPTER III

>–+◆–O–◆+–◁

Goddesses and Virgins:
The Freedoms of Chastity

>–+◆–O–◆+–◁

"Be spectators at a new contest! Against all these torments one woman alone contends and is victorious over all."
  —Leukippé to Thersandros and Sosthenes, in *Kleitophon and Leukippé*

"If you wish to kill me, I am ready . . . But I do not choose to enter your bed, nor will I obey such an order."
  —Habrokomes to Manto, in Xenophon's *Ephesiaka*

"Because I would not marry Thamyris I was chased out of my city."
  —Thekla to Alexandros, "Paul and Thekla"

>–+◆–O–◆+–◁

ALTERNATIVE CULTURES AND CULTS

The novels certainly resemble the mystery religions in this, if nothing else: that they give great value to the experience, including the inner experience, of the individual. The period of the Roman Empire, the period of our first "Rise of the Novel," saw also the development and expansion of the mystery religions. The oldest of these, the cult of Demeter and Persephone at Eleusis, goes back to at least the sixth century B.C. and has a profound effect on the imagery and ideas of Socrates and Plato. The incorporation of many regions and peoples into the newly connected and communicating world of the Roman Empire assured the transmission of foreign and even new religions. The "cults," as we rather disdainfully call them, of Dionysius (Bacchus) and of the Magna Mater were fairly old. The cult of the Mother Goddess (whose lover Attis is castrated, dies, and is reborn) came into Rome during the war against Carthage in 204 B.C., long before the Imperial period. But that in itself is a fairly "modern" development compared to the long time in which the Mother Goddess had been worshipped in Asia Minor.

Even today the visitor who has come to Asia Minor (modern Turkey) to look at the antiquities of the Hellenistic and Roman eras may be immediately struck by the still-visible traces of a culture based on very different foundations from those of the Peloponnesus or Attica or Latium. The people of the kingdoms of Asia Minor adopted and adapted the styles of the Hellenes, but the fact that we see plenty of Corinthian columns and read Greek inscriptions everywhere should not blind us to the evident difference between this world and that of Athens or of Rome. The region had been populated before the coming of the Greeks—and the *Iliad* itself may be taken as an account of the impact of determinedly expansionist westerners (the Achaians) upon an "Oriental" people.

Homer himself (or themselves) may have belonged to Asia Minor. The language of the Homeric epics indicates an origin in Western Asia Minor, and among the seven regions that claimed him in antiquity, Smyrna (Izmir) and Chios have strongest claims (Rhodes is also a possibility). "Homer" provides an unforgettable poetic record of the confrontations of different peoples with each other; it is not surprising that tradition makes the poet a traveler and a wanderer. Homer may resonate differently for us if we consider the epic poet an observer of human variety from a viewpoint basically "Asian" and not Attic, even if Athens functioned in editing and transmitting these important texts, which were written in a non-Attic form of Greek. The story of the Trojan war as Homer tells it involves love, marriage, family, the attractions or weaknesses of the feminine. In one amazing section of the *Iliad* Diomedes manages actually to wound Aphrodite as she is carrying away her son Aineias: "He swung at the Cyprian the ruthless bronze / Recognizing her as a god lacking in war-strength [*analkis*]" (*Iliad* V, lines 330–331). The conquest and abjection of the female generative divinity seems an important objective of the Achaian cultural system in its conflict with the inhabitants of Asia Minor. The endearing side of what the Trojans stand for is seen in the well-known conversation of Hektor with Andromache and their baby son in Book VI of the *Iliad*. Respect both for sexuality and the familial affections do not, however, profit the Trojans very much. It seems not inappropriate to mention that the Turks of the present day see themselves as a highly romantic people, as well as family-oriented; certainly the air is full of love songs. But the modern Turks have not managed to transmit this image of themselves to the rest of the world.

That the "Trojan War" (whatever that may have been) was lost by the Asians allowed the Greek-speakers to push into Asia Minor and to settle, but they followed other populations, including Hittites and Assyrians. The rise of Persia under Cyrus meant a new influx of peoples from the Near East. In 546 B.C. Cyrus conquered Lydia, sacking the wealthy city of Sardis (ruled by Croesus the proverbially rich) and took other major western cities. Darius attacked mainland Greece itself. Heroic resistance by the Greeks during the Persian Wars (490–479 B.C.) at Marathon and Thermopylae brought about the decisive withdrawal of the Persians from attempts on the Greek mainland. Persia remained the major power in Asia Minor, however, including Greek-speaking Asia Minor, until the wars of Alexander the Great. (Chariton's *Chaireas and Kallirrhoé* looks back to that political state of affairs.) When Asia Minor fell to Rome, there was some discontent. The boasted "civilization" that it is the business of historians like Gibbon to exalt came to other peoples as oppression. Although the region of Ephesus had fallen peaceably into Roman hands, there was a revolt in 88 B.C., when one of the first things the people did was to overthrow all the Roman statues in Ephesus—then proceeding to massacre all the Italians in the area. Ephesus' attempt to revolt with the assistance of Mithridates, King of Pontus (from the Black Sea coast) was a failure; the city was deprived of its freedom until 47 B.C., suffering, with lesser cities, the exactions of Roman fines as well as the depredations of Roman bankers and tax-collectors.[1] We should not assume there was no sense of resentment or feeling of cultural difference. As Herodotus had noted long before the Roman era, the Greeks' "Asia" was inhabited by very mixed non-Attic populations, even in the areas with most Greek-descended colonists, the Ionian cities (*Histories*, I : 46). Asia Minor is not just a Graeco-Roman place.

Archaeological evidence strongly indicates that the regions of most of the great cities of late-antique Asia Minor had been largely settled for many centuries by peoples who worshipped the Great Mother, the *Megalē Mētēr* (Latin: *Magna Mater*), the goddess who ruled all fertility and procreation.[2] This female deity was also powerful in political and social affairs, and could be conceived of as the essential ruler of a city. The Anatolian deity Vanassa Preiia ruled over Perge; at length she became identified with Artemis, and a great temple was built to Artemis Pergaia. The great Goddess Kybele (Cybele) was worshipped in many regions of the west coast and mid-west; her image and her lions are frequently found— as in Sardis, the luxurious and beautiful city credited with inventing the city marketplace (*agora*). In the ruins of Sardis today, we can see her attractive if weather-worn lions not far from the remains of a fine synagogue with marble walls.

Kybele was worshipped in Ephesus from very ancient times. By the Hellenistic era, the most popular name for the Goddess seems to have become Artemis, although there is a strong following of Aphrodite. Images of Artemis and the remains of her temples abound. "Great is Diana of the Ephesians!" cry the excited crowds demonstrating against Paul in Acts 19 : 28 (*megalē hē Artemis Ephesiōn!*). Artemis of the bow, the queen and huntress chaste and pure, can be found in statuary and image, as for instance on the great frieze of the theater of Apollo at Hieropolis (modern Pamukkale). But the great and increasingly elaborated statues presented her in a majestic form, and covered with more emblematic images including bulls' heads and bees. (See Frontispiece.) We may tend to think of such images as "barbaric," but in fact they seem relatively "modern": earlier images of Artemis-Mother, such as the elegant gold statue found in Ephesus (now in the Ephesus Museum), are much simpler.[3] Art and literature of late antiquity tended towards elaboration, and delighted in emblematic multiplicity.

The many-breasted image of Artemis survives in some Christian images of the figure of *Caritas* (Charity). (See, e.g., Spenser, *The Faerie Queene*, I.x.30–31.) There is, in fact, some debate over whether what antique Artemis has on her front are breasts or bulls' testes. The image of the bull is very commonly associated with the image of the goddess, whether Cybele, Artemis, or Aphrodite, and in such representations the bull is, of course, subordinated to the goddess, his power under the sway of her power—a matter which might lead us to believe that Asia Minor produced the stories of Io and of Europa as different tales or images from those given us in most common tellings. The woman-with-bull may not be the victim of enchantment or rape, but a divine female in mastery of natural power, Artemis Tauropolis, as in the second-century limestone relief from Asia Minor, visible in the Royal-Athena gallery in New York in June 1993. In our westernized versions of such images not only are the women *not* divine, but they are also rendered helpless in the presence of a greater male force—we have the Rape of Europa, not the Ride of Europa. That was not always the case.

What we see in the images of Asia Minor, in its fragmentary mosaics and broken stones, are images of the female force. Political stimuli might urge service of Asia Minor's goddesses; Guy Rogers in *The Sacred Identity of Ephesos* (1991) has shown how worship of Artemis at Ephesus functioned to assure local citizens of their identity despite their precarious and subjugated position. The female force is good, just as snakes are good—in, for instance, the images of the Asklepion at Pergamon. It takes a little while to realize an obvious truth—that a very high proportion of the famous or creative women of antiquity came from Asia Minor: Artemisia, for instance, who not only built the Mausoleum at Halicarnassus in honor of her brother-husband, but also led the campaign against Rhodes; Queen Ada, who governed Halicarnassus after Alexander recovered it from the Persians; Aspasia, the mistress of Pericles, who came from Miletus; Sappho, the poet of Lesbos (the culture of the coastal islands such as Lesbos, Rhodos, and Kos should be considered as pertaining to the world of Asia Minor). To this list we could add the Empress Theodora, the sixth-century courtesan who married the Emperor Justinian, as well as the doughty Saint Thekla of Ikonion. It may seem more than happy chance that Ephesus has been considered the last home of Mary the Mother of Jesus Christ; a house thought to be hers just outside Ephesus is an object of pilgrimage and a site of veneration. It does not seem an accident that the most famous and most architecturally significant Christian church of Byzantium is Theodosius' fifth-century Church of the Holy Wisdom—*Hagia Sophia*—in which "Wisdom" is a feminine aspect of God. It is equally appropriate that the Third Ecumenical Council of the Christian Church met in Ephesus in 431, in the first church to be dedicated to the Virgin Mary, and established the description of Mary as the Mother of God. In both its pagan and Christian history the culture of Asia Minor has acknowledged the power and virtue of the feminine, and has at least included (and often given pride of place to) the female aspect of the eternal and divine.

The visitor to Asia Minor may begin to feel that all sorts of stories and figures are coming off differently from the "standard" version. There is, for instance, the powerful figure of Medusa—what are we to make of her? Certainly, her image persists throughout the Roman Empire, even to her late appearance in England, rendered at Cirencester by some puzzled colonist who makes her look like a little scared potato (see Plate 9). But the presence of this "Gorgon" in Asia Minor is beautiful and awe-inspiring. Contemplate, for example, Medusa at the center of the geometrical Roman-era mosaic at Pergamon (Bergama), or the gigantic statues in the cisterns of Justinian in Istanbul. See the enormous broken statue-head of Medusa (with its intellectual brow and snaky hair) at Didyma (modern Didim) in western Caria (Plate 10). We are used to thinking of the Gorgon as "bad." The ancient civilizations that we know best (in Jerusalem, Athens, and Rome) made clear separation between sky and earth, male and female, good and bad. In Hesiod we already find the earthy and the feminine regarded with suspicion. The ocean nymph Kallirrhoé, daughter of Ocean (source of the name of Chariton's heroine), for example, begets, according to Hesiod, a terrible female monster, Echidna. Echidna is half lovely nymph and half loathly flesh-eating snake who dwells underground (*Theogony*, II, lines 295–307). Woman's secret parts are horrific, man-eating, deathly, dirty, and hidden—*snaky*. (Compare Spenser's Duessa and Milton's Sin.) But the snake is a positive image in much Bronze Age religion; it is associated with regenerative powers of the earth—as it still is in its late Asculapian manifestations in pharmacy signs. Snakes are brandished aloft, not hidden from sight, by the priestesses or goddesses in Cretan representations. Freud thought the Medusa represented the female pubic hair and the female genitals—and *hence* was frightening to see. But the female genitals could be gazed on without horror. In Bronze Age amulets, as Lucy Goodison illustrates, the sun repeatedly appears just above the female pubic triangle; the sun *"is"* generative womb. The sun is not necessarily "male" in all cultures.[4] As Goodison argues in *Death, Women and the Sun* (1989), in the old world of the Eastern Mediterranean, woman could be both earth and sun: "in this culture it appears generally to have been the woman rather than the man who was most closely associated with the sun . . . the more powerful and generative (as opposed to reflective) of the heavenly bodies" (197). Goddess figures are associated with snakes and with the sun as a rayed star; the snake-radiating head of Medusa can be seen as combining both, even in her scared-potato avatar. In the story of Perseus as we have it (and it may be a form of rewriting old myth and bringing the goddess under control) to see the face of Medusa turns the gazer to stone, and Perseus himself cannot look directly upon her face. The sun is the heavenly body that one cannot look at directly, after all, and attempting to do so can bring on migraine, blindness, even epilepsy. Medusa makes a convincing figure of the sun goddess, with her rays of power, and her representative patronage—or matronage—of pubic hair and vulva is an aspect of her sun power. Medusa does not seem to have been displayed with fear and horror in Asia Minor, where she, like Eros, turns up constantly on sarcophagi, an image of the Life Force—which makes perfect sense, if she is the Sun. Medusa may indeed have the last laugh as we dicover more about her, and the best place to look is Asia Minor, now Turkey, where even harpies turn out to be good—as on the "Harpy Tomb" from Xanthus in Lykia, now reposing in the British Museum.[5] (See Plate 11.)

We may become capable of seeing female power, and of beholding female genitals, without horror. When naked Leukippé mockingly invites spectatorship, this immodest heroine becomes not the helpless victim but powerful Gorgon, allied with Artemis, whose arrows she invokes. The powerful new women of the novels are Medusas in that they are brazen and overt persons who must be witnessed, whether their spectators like it or not. The heroines of the Greek novels may largely be champions of virtue and chastity, *sōphrosynē*, but they are also reclamations of Medusa, unconquered.

If we entertain, even momentarily, the idea that Medusa could be an aspect of the Goddess as Sun, we begin to see the possibilities of reversal and recuperation involved in entertaining the imagery of the eastern Aegean and Asia Minor. The novels all entertain such imagery—usually along with that of Egypt as well. Kallirrhoé, that heroine of resistance, descended from a Sicilian general, who famously resisted Athenian rule, is a recuperation of Hesiod's sea-nymph. No monster-breeder, this very feminine Kallirrhoé, whose name means "lovely-flowing," flows in the direction of life, is potent for good, and is protected by the power of Aphrodite.

Medusa, when we look at her in the environment of Asia Minor, begins to seem a serious but not negative representation. On sarcophagi she reminds us of regeneration, as well as of the individual and collective human fate. She thus seems like another exemplar of a new deity, the new female god *Tychē* (Fate/

Luck/Chance) who became the deity of the Seleucid territories from about 300 B.C. onwards. Antioch in Syria had a famous fine statue of *Tychē*, a goddess incorporated into the Roman pantheon as *Fortuna*. *Tychē*, as well as Artemis, was a goddess of Ephesus; in that city her bust looks down from the center of the surviving arch of the temple of Hadrian (second century A.D.). A more optimistic aspect of *Tychē* is represented in the female deity Nike, or victory, also powerfully represented in Ephesus and Pergamon. The tendency towards elaboration resulted in overprogrammed images combining aspects of these female powers—as can be seen in the third-century bronze statuette of Isis, now in the Ephesus museum, which endows Isis with the crown of Kybele/Artemis, the quiver of Artemis, the shield of Athena, the wings of Nike and the cornucopia of *Tychē*/Fortuna.

The beliefs of the people living in the Greek cities of Asia Minor about the nature and power of the Great Goddess were bound to connect with the beliefs and practices associated with the Egyptian goddess Isis. The cult of Isis came into Rome before the Imperial period, even though it was repeatedly suppressed. The Roman Senate had a strong resistance to Isis and kept pulling down temples devoted to her. At last, in the age of Caligula, a great temple of Isis was put up on the Campus Martius (the Iseum in Pompeii was much older). An Egyptian priest had to be present to perform sacrifices and to teach initiates; devotees of Isis were distinguished by their shaven heads and linen clothes. Juvenal in his Sixth Satire (the satire against women) has some pungent things to say against Roman females who take up the cults of Phrygian Kybele or of Egyptian Isis. Women are particularly dangerous, according to Juvenal, when worshipping goddesses; they use the worship of the *bona Dea* to gratify their lusts, and, if men are lacking, they will put an ass to work (see Satire VI, lines 314–345). In taking up the foreign cults a Roman matron becomes particularly ridiculous:

> If white Io [Isis] should order it
> She will go off to the farthest end of Egypt;
> She'll bring back from hot Meroë the carefully-sought waters
> In order to sprinkle the temple of Isis
> Which rises next to the ancient sheepfold.
>
> (Ibid., lines 526–529)

Juvenal objects to the foreign as well as to the female. This monstrous new African temple, which turns women's minds to darkest, hottest Africa, has ruined the ancient simplicity of the old Roman sheepfold; metamorphosis of place stands for the ruination of the old virtuous (and male) pastoralism, a pastoralism also standing for tribal identity unadulterated. Isis is a sign of what we call "multiculturalism."

The religion of Isis was not only a cult religion (that is, prescribing prayers and sacrifices at certain locations before certain images) but also a mystery religion. There were ceremonies at which initiates underwent certain ritual ordeals and purifications. This was true also of the religion of Mithras, introduced to Rome, according to Plutarch, by Pompey's captives in 68 B.C. Mithras, Zoroastrian god of light, could be associated with the familiar Helios, or Phoebus Apollo the sun-god. The basic image of Mithraism is of a young man driving a sword into the neck of a prostrate bull. The Mithraism of the Roman world became extremely popular with the army, and shrines were put up wherever the Roman legions went. (A temple of Mithras was excavated in London in 1953.) This religion was organized with almost military efficiency: there were seven grades in its hierarchy of devotees. It is unusual among all the mystery religions for admitting no women. This is ironic, as the cult ceremony of initiation, the baptism of blood, the *taurobolium*, was apparently first practiced by devotees of the Great Mother.[6]

If you go now to Andalusia in spring, you may see a combination of celebrations at Eastertide involving not only the risen Christ but the much more dominant figure of Mary. Splendidly dressed cult statues of the Virgin Mother are taken in procession, and Easter Day is marked by a bullfight. In a region whose every cave is a site of the cult of the goddess and where bullfighting maintains its antique popularity in the face of modern objections, it is almost impossible to resist the conclusion that we have here one of the late survivals of the cult of Cybele-Attis (alias Venus-Adonis, Isis-Osiris) associated with the blood of the bull in an important archaic feature of goddess-worship.[7] Mithraism as the Roman Empire knew it may have been (one is tempted to speculate) a remasculinization of ritual, newly excluding both the goddess and female celebrants from what had once been rites of worship in honor of the goddess.

The other mystery religions (The Eleusinian Mysteries, the Dionysian, the Isiac) were receptive to women as candidates for purification and illumination. It is hard to imagine what must have been the effect upon the ordinary man or woman (*Der Mensch des alltäglichen Lebens* whom Nietzsche condemns) of undergoing rituals that promised the initiate not only freedom from pain but also the capacity to see life in a different way. An important aspect of these rituals, at least as they were known during the Roman Empire, seems to have been an assurance to the individual believer of immortal life. What would it be like, to have a glimpse of the divine plan, and then to come back to the very harsh world of Mediterranean reality?—to come back to the world of civic society, and of the law?

LAW, MARRIAGE, AND FAMILY

Roman law gave little emphasis to the individual, except when that individual was *paterfamilias*. W. K. Lacey, an expert on both Greek and Roman family life and law, sees the Roman concept as differing from the Greek. The Greeks emphasized the household, *oikos*, and the links of kinship both natural and artificial (as in *phratry* and *dēmē*). Roman law does not conceive society in this spreading network: "The law . . . shows a clear orientation towards *patria potestas* . . . and a structure of society in which wide discretionary powers are put in the hands of individuals [i.e., the fathers]." Lacey believes *patria potestas*, paternal power, "was the fundamental institution underlying Roman institutions," and that "in consequence, public life followed the assumptions of private life" (Lacey, "Patria Potestas," in Beryl Rawson, ed., *The Family in Ancient Rome*, 123).

Remarkably, a Roman son, as long as his father lived, could not acquire property save for his father, although he had a role in civic life *as if* he were an independent property owner. This unusual split between civic and financial power did not much affect women, as they were supposed to act under the guardianship of some male; a woman was automatically her brother's charge if her father were dead (at least until the time of Claudius, who allowed the father to choose another guardian). A woman was in tutelage, *in tutela*, though she might be "freed from *tutela* by virtue of having a certain number of children" (J. A. Crook, "Women in Roman Succession," in Rawson, ed., *The Family in Ancient Rome*, 67).

Roman women of the upper classes were much better off in many ways than Athenian women had ever been. They could separate from their husbands and even initiate divorce, and they could enter into certain businesses (some were moneylenders). Yet they had no claim upon their own children; a Roman woman could not, upon divorcing her husband, take her child and support it by her labors. Children were always the property of their father, and the ancient *patria potestas* had given the father unlimited right over them—including the theoretical right to kill them.[8] The accepted "scientific" biology (found in Aristotle and elsewhere) reinforced (or perhaps was invented with the unconscious purpose of reinforcing) the absolute right of the father. According to this biology, the child exists in complete if invisible miniature in the male sperm; the consort mother furnishes merely house-room and nourishment in her womb so that this complete infant can grow during the required time. Yet, though the importance of woman in the procreative process was thus kept to a minimum, women and marriage (distasteful as both might seem) were sadly needed in order to maintain a population. If the mystery religion looks to the individual's experience and future, marriage and marriage-law looks to the corporate and civic future.

The Roman world experienced spasms of severe anxiety about underpopulation. The most notable symptom of this acute worry (acute among the governing classes) is the well-known legislation brought in by Augustus Caesar. To increase marriage among the Roman higher classes, Augustus instituted a tax on single women over twenty and on bachelors over twenty-five.[9] By Augustus' law, widows under fifty were required by law to remarry within two years; despite common jokes about lascivious widows, some disobeyed, notably Mark Antony's daughter Antonia.

Augustus was concerned with ensuring the order and the fecundity of marriage and the perpetuating of Roman citizens. Notions of public order involved penalties for those who broke a marriage. So strong was the feeling against errant wives that when an early Christian writer suggested that a husband had a duty to receive back a penitent wife who had committed adultery, his statement aroused great dissension. Although the unnamed writer of *The Shepherd of Hermas* (c. A.D. 120) was really using this example of penitence and forgiveness in illustration, rather than as a main point, Tertullian (among others) berated writer and treatise, referring to "that apocryphal shepherd of adulterers [*pastor mœchorum*]."[10] It would be carrying Christianity much too far and upsetting all good civic order if forgiveness ran to the ridiculous extent of pardoning female adultery. An erring wife should be banished. As we have seen, Chariton's novel paradoxically exhibits Chaireas welcoming Kallirrhoé back to his life and his love after she has strayed into a liaison with Dionysius. Kallirrhoé committed her adultery deliberately; she did not have the excuse of the straying Melitté, that she thought her husband was dead. Religious speculation and novel-reading alike could lead to anticivic views of female adultery.

"Female adultery" is perhaps a slightly anachronistic phrase. The basic word for "adulterer" is really male. It is the male offender, the *seducer*, who is the conceptual legal entity (as in England in Mary Wollstonecraft's day).[11] "Adultery" paradigmatically meant a sexual affair involving a married woman and a male seducer, an "adulterer" (Greek *moichos*, Latin *moechus*). A man could divorce a wife even suspected of adultery. Divorce, including divorce by consent, was theoretically relatively easy to obtain in Rome. Divorce could also be obtained by a wife who could ask for her dowry back—but this could make real trouble for herself and her male relatives. Despite various claims about Roman freedom, there is little evidence that a woman could get a divorce without backing from strong male relatives and/or a politically powerful second husband in the offing.[12] A man's straying from his wife in affairs outside the home was not thought to concern her, but a wife's straying violates family life and the bloodline.

Augustus was not against divorce, but he made "adultery" into a criminal matter. Traditionally, the husband had had a right to kill both errant wife and her lover if he caught them in the act. Augustus restricted this right by legislation in 18 B.C., substituting legal action for revenge-killing. If a husband caught his wife in the act he was *required* by law to divorce her and to bring her to trial for adultery, though any such trial would center on the *moichos* as the active agent. Hence we have Thersandros' case against his wife and Kleitophon. In ancient Athens, the husband who caught his wife in the act of adultery was also required to divorce her; see Douglas M. MacDowell, *The Law in Classical Athens* (88). By traditional law an Athenian citizen had been entitled to kill a *moichos* caught in the act not only with his wife, but also with his mother, sister, or daughter (124).[13]

Seducing a woman—or raping her—was a crime only if the woman were a "free" woman, the daughter or wife of a free citizen. Male sexual crime began and ended with abusing the sexual property of another male (of rank). The display of women in brothels and arenas and the cruel abuse of some females was considered quite normal. Most lower working-class females, even if not officially slaves, were considered to be at everyone's disposal, in Christian as in pagan cities. As Peter Brown points out, "The bodies of such women counted for little." Brown quotes a legal statement of A.D. 326 pronouncing that chastity should be expected "from these women to whom the law applies" but that different standards were applied to low-life women (such as barmaids), "whose worthless life puts them beneath observance of the law." Brown adds pointedly, "It is the public voice of Constantine, the first Christian emperor" (*The Body and Society* [1988], 24). Women of the low classes could not claim a right to be chaste; their bodies should be available to service males of all classes. There is little if any legal or even moral thought about sexual misconduct on the part of males using such females—save that this is uncleanness, and the dirt of the women might sully the clear spirit of the citizen. Fornication between an unmarried woman and any man (married or single) is not adultery but merely *stuprum*—a word also applied to homosexuality between males. (The word seems to originate in ideas of pollution and of dullness or deficiency; "masturbation" comes from *manus-stuprare*, to commit hand-

stuprum.) A man who had an affair with a single woman of any class would not be prosecuted, and women (and boys) of the slave class could be purchased or borrowed with the owner's consent.

Augustus' interest in sexual morality concentrated on the need for settled marriages of citizens, which would produce numbers of legitimate children; he took cognizance of female adultery, because it affected legitimacy. As Beryl Rawson says, Augustus "aimed, first, to guard against married women bearing illegitimate children who would inherit an unsuspecting husband's name and property" ("The Roman Family," in *The Family in Ancient Rome*, 34). Rawson adds, "There seems to have been strong public opinion (at least in the upper classes) against all of Augustus's moral legislation, and a number of women made their own protest in Tiberius's time by registering themselves officially as prostitutes so that the law would not apply to them." Patrician women had noticed that the new criminal charge of adultery did not apply to slave women, actresses, or prostitutes, and were willing to change status. Rawson suggests that "The motive for this extraordinary action by women (apparently of rank) was surely women's liberation (to free women's private lives from intolerable interference by the state . . .)" (35). The government retaliated by making it a legal offense for a woman of rank to enter such a position. The Senate, with much tut-tutting over *libido feminarum*, forbade prostitution to women of the equestrian class. Women—ladies, rather—were not free to declare themselves prostitutes.

Women were not altogether without power of self-disposal. Widespread knowledge of certain methods of contraception gave them some degree of choice in childbearing. (The use of the sponge must have posed its own dangers in a hot climate where the inhabitants were ignorant of bacteria.) A Roman girl was supposed to consent to her own marriage, whereas in Athens of old a girl's consent was not necessary to her betrothal to a man she had never seen (MacDowell, *Law*, 86). Roman consent was, however, a technicality; a girl about to be married off by her family could not withhold her consent unless she could claim "that the proposed husband was of bad moral character" (Rawson, *Family*, 21). Recollections of all these practices haunt Western society and literature. In Richardson's *Clarissa* (1747–1748), the heroine tries to avoid an arranged marriage by making such a claim against the moral character of both Robert Lovelace and Roger Solmes, but her family regards her consent as a nugatory technicality and proceeds (as many a Greek and Roman family must have done before them) with wedding plans.

The world of Roman civic institutions, of Roman law, is a very tight world. The laws that affect the sexual and private life of every individual are designed to sustain the power of the *paterfamilias* and to prevent *turbatio sanguinis* (confusion of the bloodline). Into this world comes the extraordinary novel with its emphasis on sexuality—including female sexuality—as a matter of individual choice and personal control. And as soon as these ideas spring into view, we also see manifested the possibility—the revolutionary possibility—of chastity.

Chastity has not had a very good press lately, largely because we associate the concept, understandably, with the imposition of it on women in the male-ordered world, in which marriage involves the exchange of undamaged women between males. A wife should come virgin to her bridal and maintain chaste fidelity throughout marriage. Thus she shows her loyalty to the bloodline and does not disturb the transmission of property from male to male. Ancient Roman tombs praise the woman who is *univira*—a one-man woman—despite the Roman custom of remarriage after divorce or widowhood. The chastity that male-ordered marriage arrangements require of women should be given its own term—"imposed chastity" or "subordinate chastity." It is an act of obedience by the woman who behaves as her men tell her to do. That style of chastity also means marrying when the men who have guardianship tell the woman *in tutela* she must marry. A woman thus keeps her body, like a chest of polished plate in storage, so that it may be inherited and properly placed at the disposal of those for whom it is meant.

This is not the sort of chastity we are reading about in the novels. The novels, very like the stories of the early Christians, celebrate a voluntary and extravagant chastity—a chastity whose nature cuts against *utilitas*, and questions *gravitas*. Such an extravagant and willful chastity really offers to society a much greater *turbatio* than the occasional cuckoldry. Chastity becomes an oddly active virtue, and characters become heroines—and heroes—of chastity. It is true that in the novels the characters are only *temporarily* abstemious. They maintain *partheneia*, or remain *katharos*, until the union with the desired partner can take place—or can recommence, as in the case of the married lovers Habrokomes and Anthia in *Ephesiaka*. In Chariton's novel Kallirrhoé is unable for very particular reasons to preserve univiral chastity—she is a two-man woman—but it is part of Chaireas' purgation that he prove uniuxorious and take no woman other than his wife.

In the novels, both men and women are imagined as setting their own desire, and their own spiritual vision, against the forces of the state. Augustus Caesar was haunted by the idea of high-class citizens of the Empire (particularly Romans) wasting their valuable childbearing or child-begetting time. Young men and women are not supposed to rattle around the Mediterranean having adventures. They have a duty not to postpone their sober settling down into responsible married life.

Married life in the ancient world was heavily responsible. Gentlemen were supposed to maintain an even-tempered authority, gravity, and sobriety of character, which included a sanitary moderation in frequency of sexual intercourse, and a rational propriety during the act. Marital sexuality should be sober, the male subduing the excitability of the female, and both doing away with the violence of passion. As Peter Brown says in that most informative book *The Body and Society*, "The notion of eugenic sex" in the Late Antique world "committed both the man and the woman to codes of decorum in bed that were continuous with the public self" (21). That is, the Roman ideal is the ideal that Walter Shandy endeavors with such comic earnestness to put into practice. Walter, like the parish bull he so mistakenly esteems, "went through the business with a grave face" (*Tristram Shandy*, 496). Happily ignorant forever of the *turbatio sanguinis* his temperance and sobriety have led to within this own family, Walter holds stubbornly to the old Roman ideal of family life—which is, as Laurence Sterne knows, an antinovelistic ideal.

As Peter Brown explains, the new Christians of Christianity's first centuries hoped to challenge the "present age," the monotonous repetition of things and structures within the realm of Necessity:

> The "present age" might be a vast engine . . . its tyranny too intricate to trace in all its ramifications. But at least one part of that mighty current could be symbolically condensed in the sexual urge and in its manifest consequences, the endlessly repeated cycle of birth and death. In a world seemingly governed by iron constraints, the human body could stand out as a clearly marked locus of free choice. To re-nounce sexual intercourse was to throw a switch located in the human person; and, by throwing that precise switch, it was believed possible to cut the current that sustained the sinister *perpetuum mobile* of life in "the present age."   (*The Body and Society*, 84–85)

What might be called the "Sexual Revolution" at the beginning of the Christian era (in which others than Christians participated) was a revolution in favor of chastity, continence, and virginity. Not everyone had the eschatological interest in getting rid of the world and the flesh that the Christians had, but a deep dis-content with the ways of the world can be felt on many sides. We of the late twentieth century have been persuaded (and programmed by our advertisers) to imagine that we think of sex only in terms of pleasure and gratification. But people of other eras (and really of our own as well) have thought of it otherwise. "Because it was closely associated with the urge to overcome death through the begetting of children, sexual intercourse had always carried with it a tinge of sad-ness. For many ancient Greeks and Romans, their very need to sleep with women so as to obtain offspring was, in itself, a somber reminder of transience and the grave" (Brown, *Body*, 86). And of course for the "many ancient Greeks and Ro-mans" who were women this was no abstract matter; the marital embrace might indeed be a pathway to the grave.

FEMALE CHASTITY: PAUL AND THEKLA

As we have seen, the novelists suggest some of the difficulties involved in bringing their characters' loves to a "happy ending" in marriage. Marriage is the beginning of the serious troubles of Chaireas and Kallirrhoé, and Daphnis and Chloé have difficulty in coming to terms with a male-dominant and propertied idea of sex and marriage. The return to respectability is parodied in the figure of the re-formed pirate at the end of Achilles Tatius' novel. If we wish ancient prose nar-ratives would provide some other form of ending for characters such as we meet in the novels, we may turn to the "Paul and Thekla" section of the apocryphal *Acts of Paul*, (c. A.D. 180) a work composed, according to Tertullian, by a presbyter in Asia who lost his church office because of it (M. R. James, *Apocryphal New Testament* [1924], 270).

The story of "Paul and Thekla" is embedded within another narrative in-tended to be taken both as true and symbolically meaningful. "Paul and Thekla," which has often been considered along with ancient novels,[14] is a form of histori-cal novel, with touches of the "True Life Novel." It probably has some factual basis beyond the visit of Paul to Ikonion recorded in Acts 12–14. The description of Paul's appearance could have been transmitted by people who knew him. There were female disciples of Paul; some may have been travelers like Thekla. Yet the author uses some of the important techniques of the new fiction, and the names of some characters (Tryphaina, for instance) seem novelistic. What is most interesting for our present purposes is this story's consideration of the strong woman and her sexual and personal independence—and of such strength and independence as spiritual matters. Thekla, a virgin of Ikonion in Asia Minor, lives next door to the house in which Paul stays while visiting the town (see Acts 12: 51). Thekla watches his followers stream in to hear him, and she herself listens to his preaching for days from the window. Her anxious mother sends for her fiancé, Thamyris; he hopes to hear of a day set for marriage, but Thekla will have nothing to do with him, and declares her intention of living as a chaste virgin. Her mother declares angrily she does nothing but stick at that window "like a spider (*hēōsi arachnē*)" (164). Wounded and angry, Thamyris tries to bring Paul to justice for seducing his fiancée and the youth of Ikonion. Thekla, converted, leaves her home and city, and becomes Paul's disciple.

In Antioch, Thekla attracts the attention of a wealthy man, Alexandros, who thinks she is Paul's slave and offers money for her. Paul says he does not own her—Thekla physically beats off this civic dignitary, and is condemned to the wild beasts for "sacrilege." While she is being reserved for the games, she is looked after by a rich widow of the town, Tryphaina; in mourning for her own dead daughter, Tryphaina develops an affection for Thekla, which makes it harder for both when the execution festivities arrive.

The author is absolutely clear on the difference between the male and the female view of the condemnation of Thekla. At the sentencing, it is women who cry out "Vile sentence! unholy sentence!" ("*Kakē khrisis! anosia khrisis!*") (198). When Thekla is in the arena with the lions it is the women and children who cry out against the iniquities of the town. While the men are calling "Bring out the sacrilegious one!" the women are yelling: "Kill us all, Judge! bitter spectacle, evil sentence!" (208). They try to help Thekla by waving their perfumes and throwing them in the arena to stupefy the beasts—but the wild beasts have no disposition to harm Thekla. Thekla, naked and defenseless, behaves with great heroism. She astonishes the whole theater when, on seeing a tank full of sea-beasts, she plunges into it, for the baptism she has never had—there is a flash of flame, the beasts are dead, and a halo of fire plays about her, a *nephelē pyros* (212), symbol of her successful baptism. All efforts to kill her being unavailing, she is let go, having glorified God. Tryphaina, who swooned so her friends thought her dead during Thekla's ordeal, embraces her, happily now believing that her own darling daughter will live after death. Thekla, after catching up with Paul again, goes back to Ikonion to convert her mother, but then returns to life on the road as a missionary.

If any of these works were written by a woman, it is "Paul and Thekla." I am not saying it *is* the work of a woman (tradition firmly gives it to a male author). But it *could* be written by a woman. It focuses on the relations between women—not only individually, but also as a group. The women's yelling in the arena seems a fine and unexpected example of female solidarity. Thekla wins, and wins finally, a release from the dull confines of woman's place in the life of the small Mediterranean town. She ditches her dreary fiancé, she undertakes a life work, she travels. She is not baptized by Paul, but baptizes herself, dramatically. Early Christians had to wait a long while before being adjudged worthy of baptism. Thekla makes up her own mind, and her baptism is a matter between herself and God. The drama of the arena makes clear the false crudity of the civic disposition (which the female spectators reject).

When one reads true "classical" authors one realizes how trapped they were in the Roman world that could act as Alexandros and his other friends in high places act—the whole atrocity of the arena is something no one could combat. Seneca, for instance, in his fine *Letters* describes a most repellent scene, which he was obliged to witness. Naked swordsmen were set against each other; the winner who killed his opponent simply had to go on until he was killed at last. The only way out was death (*exitus pugnantium mors est*). The crowd meanwhile screamed at those who hesitated: *Occide, verbera, ure!* "Kill! whip! burn!" And wounded men are whipped, and whipped into wounding again. It is a hideous scene that Seneca describes. His moral is that one should not associate with crowds but should keep one's interior self, and retire into oneself as much as possible: *Recede in te ipse, quantum potes* (Epistle 7).

Seneca's Stoic answer is finely thought out, sensitive—and totally inadequate. Rather than having people receding gently and inwardly while sitting it out on their benches, we needed someone willing to get into that arena. Nietzsche's Man of Daily Life who pushed himself forward from the auditorium onto the scene was also the Christian Man—or Woman—who became the all-too-real actor on that patch of sand. In doing so, he—or she—made the inner self, the *te ipse*, something different, redefined both private and public self, and made object into subject.

The *woman* enduring torture *for a cause* is a figure of this new world. That the righteous virgin daring her tormentors is a crucial figure in literature does not mean that such individuals never existed. In modern times, Thekla is declared not to have existed, but she was a saint of the Church—particularly in Syria and Egypt—for centuries. In fact, she still is. Just outside Silifke (ancient Seleuceia ad Calycadnum) on Turkey's southern coast, there is the grotto where St. Thekla is supposed to have lived and died. The little grotto church has sadly few symptoms of its former glory, once lined with marble and mosaic. Yet Thekla's cult still survives, and her grotto is a place of worship at this day.[15] Thekla stands for an experience and a cause. It is noticeable that Achilles Tatius makes Leukippé stand for a cause—personal spiritual freedom—and not just for herself. *Echō tēn eleutherian*, she says, "I have my [inner] freedom."[16]

In "Paul and Thekla" as well as in the novels women are given a strong and central place. In the pagan novels, as well as in the writings of the new Christians, we can see a desire to overcome the world, or at least, in a kind of thought-experiment, to modify it. The social bases of the world of the *ius civile* and *ius gentium* are implicitly altered in the works that pay serious attention to women's passions—and to their choices. The novels permit the woman the unheard-of choice of disposing of her own body; a heroine decides when and with whom she shall engage in sexual intercourse. The position is most powerfully enunciated, however, in the story of Thekla, who deliberately decides to commit her own body to permanent celibacy, despite the outcry of the family, fiancé, city, and authority in general.

The fidelity of each heroine is an irritant to the system of things. During the time of the story she will not settle down. What is emphasized is her resistance. We are seeing the emergence of a new figure—the righteous and angry virgin. Wild beasts cannot conquer these women who stand for freedom. Anthia in *Ephesiaka* even kills a man who is trying to rape her—not an action the state readily encourages or even envisages. (Rome's Lucretia exhibited her chastity and propriety by killing *herself.*) Anthia's self-defensive violence is punished. She is locked up in a pit with savage dogs that are supposed to tear her to pieces—just as Thekla, after hitting Alexandros for his attentions to her person, is doomed to face the wild beasts for sacrilege.

Anthia, married to Habrokomes, is not, strictly speaking, a *parthenos*—a virgin or marriageable girl. But many of the heroines are *parthenoi*—like Leukippé, Thekla, and (very superbly) Heliodorus' Charikleia. A female virgin was *not* a person of consideration in antique society. A woman was thought of as a biologically inferior underdeveloped being, who wore her sexual organs inside whereas, had she been completely developed, they would have descended to visibility, like a man's. These interior organs cause a lot of trouble. A gynaecological text in the Hippocratic corpus, 'About Virgins" (or "About the Diseases of Young Girls") shows that girls who have not yet conceived are thought of as dangerous creatures. They were thought subject to delirium, to epilepsy, and to suicidal desires to strangle or hang themselves. They are hysterical (from *hyster*, womb), since the unfilled womb tends to run around inside the body. Such lists of symptoms may be not so much the result of observation as useful propaganda to scare girls into early marriage.[17] The undeflowered female is, according to Xenophon in his *Oikonomikos*, a wild thing—untamed, undomesticated (*admēs*). This savage must be married and brought into proper household order and domestic subordination before a man can even hold a conversation with her. Female virginity was not admired in the ancient world. The thing to be done with a virgin was to break her in and tame her for humble household use as soon as possible.

The ancient novels, by contrast, show us an admired virginity underwritten by the goddess. Resistance—framed as resistance to sexual violence—is recognized as heroic in the novels, if seldom elsewhere. Freud's well-known *Dora* seems an ingenious attempt to revisit, rewrite, and neutralize the Greek novel. The novel's typical story is reversed, so that the incestuous masculine desires are either passed over or vindicated, and female resistance is diagnosed as sickness.[18] Like Xenophon, Freud believes a virgin is a wild thing (*Sie war wirklich ein wildes Ding* [*Bruchstück*, 244]). The virgins in the stories are rather "wild"—they are uncontrollable. But their wild actions and their defiance are vindicated. Leukippé shouts at Thersandros and Sosthenes that they should not abuse a virgin in the city of the Virgin—Artemis. The goddesses in these novels support and assist female chastity—a chastity of choice, as it becomes, and not the subordinate chastity. Hapless Anthia, sold to a brothelkeeper (*pornoboskos*) is exposed to a multitude of men eager for the use of her charms:

> But she in this resourceless evil found a means (*technān*) of escape. For
> she fell on the ground and twisted her body and mimicked those suf-
> fering from the disease called "disease of the gods." Those who stood
> around left off the desire which had brought them together there, and
> felt pity together with fear (*eleos hama kai phobos*); they looked after
> Anthia.   (*Ephesiaka*, 65)

Medical doctrine would have pronounced that epilepsy, the "divine disease," was
in young women a symptom of lack of sex—Anthia's "condition" might be
"cured" by the very thing (or things) Anthia is trying so hard to escape. In her fit
the girl also reminds the men around her (in a kind of goddess-inspired irony) of
what was so feared by males in the sexual act—a loss of control. Sexual intercourse is a fit, a convulsion, uncannily like the falling sickness; as Peter Brown
tells us, "orgasm was a 'minor epilepsy'" (*Body*, 18). Anthia the recalcitrant *pornē*
ironically puts on a pornographic show of sorts—so terrific that it puts an end to
the customers' desire, as completely as if they had bought what they wanted. The
customers experience an abrupt *katharsis*, as Anthia offers a sort of short-order
tragedy, bringing her audience rapidly to the emotions of pity and fear so much
emphasized in Aristotle's *Poetics* and here ironically elicited. Anthia gets her way
by acting as a *parthenos*, as a wild untamed thing, out of anybody's control. So did
Thekla in her act of violence when she grabbed Alexandros, tore his military
cloak, and flipped the crown from his head, making him look ridiculous.

THE STANDARD OF MALE CHASTITY: *EPHESIAKA, JOSEPH AND ASENETH*

If the female virgin—the wild thing—is in these texts paradoxically admirable, it
is another paradox that the hero in these stories must hold himself to a standard
of chastity *in relation to the woman*—a standard little known to the ideals and practices of antique society. After Habrokomes and Anthia have been united in the
temple of Isis at the end of the *Ephesiaka*, Anthia has a question for her husband
during their first night together. First, she proclaims her own chastity: during all
her trials, by dint of many resources, she tells him, "I have remained entirely
chaste for you" (*menō soi pasan sōphrosynēs*, 76). But what about him? Has *he* forgotten his vows? Habrokomes then proclaims his own fidelity—no woman has
appeared beautiful to him once he parted from Anthia. He also swears to his own
chastity; he is just as she left him in the prison in Tyre. Chastity becomes an ideal
for the man, an injunction of the goddess mediated to the hero through the
woman he loves.

Men have often been warned to abstain from sex for reasons of health,
efficiency, or dedication to a cause. (Samson is always on view as an example of a
man who ruined his strength by "womanizing.") As we have seen, in the Late
Antique world men of position were supposed to be temperate in sex, not to
spend their strength or lose mental control. Male chastity has customarily been
goal-oriented (famously so in traditional athletic training). Such chastity, which
might be called "power chastity," is very frequently misogynistic. It is one of the
tragedies of the early Christian church that the old misogyny associated with
"power chastity" found its way into the revolutionary vision that offered a new

freedom and equality between male and female, bond and free. The novels present a male chastity that is—amazingly—not misogynistic. Even Kleitophon's departure from perfection with Melitté rather proves than breaks the rule, for he is not sneering, not triumphant, not misogynistic or even superior to Melitté's need. The idea of male chastity presented in the novels seems altogether a new venture—if a man can have *parthenia*, as Kleitophon wonders. This is a chastity sacred to a relationship—not a chastity to ensure getting ahead in matters in which women are at best hindrances; at worst, pollutants.

In reading the novels one is struck by the simple fact that what we call "romantic love" is not possible—either in idea or practice—without an idea of chastity of a fresh and personal—not institutional—nature. That chastity, too, must apply to both sexes. And it must be *chosen*, existentially, not dictated. Or rather, the goddess may dictate it, but not the fathers. One can see that if Love is truly to be freed, celibacy must be a possible option—including Thekla's choice, permanent celibacy. The sexual act is sanctified by a personal love, freely willed, which sees the other person as distinct and irreplaceable. The body becomes inwardly liberated—even while it is outwardly enchained. The body is no longer the property of *pater* or *oikos, polis* or *imperium*, agora or law-court. Only with a notion of willed chastity as an important possibility is it possible to think of the individual as both significant and free.

A notion of individuation—of the sacredness of individuality—is intimately bound with the possibility of chastity. The best-known traditional story involving *male* chastity is the Biblical story of Joseph, or rather the section of it dealing with the desire of Potiphar's wife for Joseph and his virtuous refusal (Genesis 39). Potiphar's wife certainly does not bother with the refinements of seduction, and Joseph is almost equally blunt:

> And it came to pass . . . that his master's wife cast her eyes upon Joseph; and she said, Lie with me.
>
> But he refused, and said unto his master's wife, Behold, my master wotteth not what *is* with me in the house, and he hath committed all that he hath to my hand;
>
> *There is* none greater in this house than I; neither hath he kept back any thing from me but thee, because thou *art* his wife: how then can I do this great wickedness, and sin against God?   (Verses 7–9 [KJV])

Gratitude, a sense of his place in the household, and a strong sense of the divine caveat against adultery are all maintained in Joseph. He sees the guilt of adultery as residing in the taking of another man's property; Potiphar's wife is his prize *thing*, and, after all, Potiphar has shared all the other things. Joseph's chastity is a male-bonded chastity. However powerful she may momentarily seem, Potiphar's wife is essentially not going to count against the more powerful order. Even though it gets him into prison for a while, Joseph's chastity is a species of power chastity, which puts the lustful woman in her place.

The story of Joseph, and analogues and variations of it, was one of the circulating stories of the ancient world, and it is very closely connected with the novel tradition. The material of the Joseph legend was rendered as a novel during the Late Antique period. *Joseph and Aseneth* is a Jewish novel of the first or second century (somewhat revised by Christians). This story may be taken as a *midrash* on the story of Joseph. Aseneth, daughter of an Egyptian priest (see the brief reference to her in Genesis 41:50) is here presented as a beautiful young woman who despises men and marriage. She chooses to live in a tower "exceedingly great and high" (*megas kai hypsēlos sphodra*), with seven virgins (*hepta parthenoi*) as handmaidens (132; 134). Aseneth's tower, with its three windows, connects her to the Moon and the Moon-Goddess. So, too, does the tower of the false goddess Luna, Simon Magus' girlfriend in *Recognitiones*; she makes the crowd marvel when she can be seen from all sides of her tower. Simon pretends that his Luna is *Sapientia* (Wisdom, Hagia Sophia) "brought down from the highest heavens" and mother of all things, *cunctorum genetrix* (45). Both the Christian novel and the Christianized Jewish novel have an uneasy relation with the goddess figure, who has to be introduced and yet removed. Aseneth is both a lively and somewhat haughty eighteen-year-old girl, and also the goddess to be deposed; her violet linen, gold bracelets and shoes, precious gems and tiara associate her strongly with Kybele or the Egyptian Neith, "goddess of the red crown."[19]

Aseneth is most irate when she hears of her parents' hopes that the highly important Joseph will make her his bride. She refuses to be excited by the prospect of an imminent visit from this potentate, protesting in aristocratic hauteur: "Wishest thou to give me over as a captive to an alien and a fugitive and one that hath been sold? . . . Is not this he who lay with his mistress, and his lord cast him into the prison of darkness, and Pharaoh brought him out from the prison inasmuch as he interpreted his dream, as the older women of the Egyptians also interpret?" (trans. E. W. Brooks, 27). Aseneth has heard the gossip (of course, we realize, rumor of that old affair of Potiphar's wife *would* get about). She has no esteem for alien fortune-tellers. Her disdain for this foreign slave who acts like an old woman is wiped out immediately as soon as she sees the beautiful Joseph. Ironically, Joseph has no desire to meet Aseneth; he has been wearied with offers of the wives and daughters of princes and satraps. When he hears that this young woman is "one who hateth every man" (Brooks, 31) he is relieved, and says her parents may bring her down. Aseneth's plunge into love is abrupt and humiliating, but Joseph's prayers for her conversion are fulfilled more thoroughly than he expected. An angel visits Aseneth in her tower, and she is converted by undergoing many magical ordeals, including having paradisal bees, white, purple, and gold, cover her "from foot to head" (*apo podōn heōs kephalēs*, 188), rather as if she were an image of Aphrodite. The Angel also talks to Joseph, who returns, proposes to the converted maiden, and asks her from Pharaoh. They marry, but their married life is at first shadowed by the jealousy of the sons of Leah, and by the envy and lust of Pharaoh's son, who wants Aseneth for himself. Escaping from the ambush set by Pharaoh's son, Aseneth, now wife and mother, proves herself again a heroine of chastity. The novel sustains Joseph's "power chastity," but modifies it in giving him a counterpart who is also dramatically interesting.

The potential of the story of Joseph as novelistic material is borne out by Thomas Mann, who found himself turning what he intended to be a *novella* into a four-volume novel written over a period of politically troubled years—*Joseph und seine Brüder* (1933–1943). Part of Mann's effect in the third part of the novel is to make of Potiphar's wife a sympathetic character, much more like Achilles

Tatius' Melitté than like the crudely peremptory lady of the Bible's account. Married off by her parents in youth to a socially eminent eunuch, Mut is sex-starved and lonely, but she struggles valiantly for a long while against her illicit passion. In such a use of the story Thomas Mann is emulating ancient novelists who took similar liberties with both legendary stories and established historical characters.

The Greek novels of late antiquity plunge their heroes into situations similar to Joseph's, but there is an important difference between the story in Genesis and the stories of males in the novels. These young men do not maintain a fidelity based on male-bonding, a reluctance to steal a woman as somebody else's property. Rather, they exhibit relational chastity, fidelity *to* a woman. In the *Ephesiaka*, Habrokomes, the hero, is sold into slavery and placed at the mercy of his mistress Manto, who is furiously in love with him. Even Anthia pleads with him that it is better to yield than to be killed—after hearing his proud answer to Manto's messenger: "I am a slave, but I know how to keep my vows. They have power over my body, but I have a free soul [*tēn psychēn de eleutheran echō*]. . . . I will never by my own will be unjust to Anthia!" (24). Unchastity in such a context is not pollution but injustice. Habrokomes will not wrong Anthia, deal with her unjustly (*adikeō*). Chastity becomes a form of justice in a relationship, not an abstraction, and not a frigid purity. When Manto (who is single) writes the hero a letter promising Habrokomes marriage if he is agreeable—or vengeance if he refuses to yield to her love—he writes a curt refusal: "Mistress . . . if you wish to kill me, I am ready; if you wish to torture me, torture as you will. But I do not choose to enter your bed, nor will I obey such an order" (25). In an interesting variation of the vengeance taken by the wives of Potiphar and Theseus, Manto runs to her father and complains to Daddy that the man made advances to his virgin daughter; she threatens suicide from shame if her father does not punish the offender. It is needless to add that the master is very angry and that brisk punishments are applied to Habrokomes. But they cannot make him repent his faith to Anthia. As we shall see, the hero of Heliodorus' *Aithiopika* is put in a similarly threatening situation, under the legal control of a powerful woman who is in love with him. Theagenes, like Joseph, maintains virtue—but he, too, maintains a chastity in relation to his beloved, and not out of respect for the lustful lady's absent husband.

The characters in these novels, in short, do not and will not act in accordance with the law. They ignore or override legal and social ordinances in fulfilling their own desires—which may be desires for chastity. Heroes and heroines alike often manifest their strength and independence (and the strength and independence of their own desires) by refusing to commit the sexual act with someone who orders them to—that someone customarily a person who has a legal and social right, according to the mores of the surrounding world, to make such a demand. We may be tempted to see the characters' sexual lives as simply political allegories, sex being the most convenient and visibly dramatic symbol for the crossing of public with private. But what is "allegorized" scarcely exists to be articulated outside the novels themselves, for the ancient world has little concept of the private self or of private rights over the body as person. The characters of the stories enact their own sense of their individuality in accordance with what much later generations would learn to think of as "rights."

The claims to sacred self-disposal of a highly valued and inalienable physical and sexual self, and to the possession of the "free soul" within the enslaved body, are in these early novels very largely underwritten by the Goddess (under whatever name she chooses to appear). A theological development of great moment would appear to have affected the pagan world, notably those areas of it (especially in Asia Minor) most strongly devoted to the practice of goddess-worship. The development within the goddess-religion of a sophisticated understanding of the claims of the individual human being fits in with the renewed and growing interest in the mystery cults, and their proffer of some sort of spiritual eternal life for ordinary people. Demeter democratizes. Early Jewish and Christian novels are under the somewhat awkward necessity of repudiating the Goddess while retaining her in some guise, so as to retain what she stands for. This feat is often performed by maintaining and incorporating some of the Goddess's emblems or personae, even while the female deity is, as it were, officially drummed out of one of the narrative's side doors. *Recognitiones* deals thus with untamed Luna, wicked in one aspect, but in another the representative of the mother who is partly the object of the hero's search. In *Joseph and Aseneth*, Aseneth–Moon Lady is chastened by a sublimer presence, but only by assuming *more* of the attributes of the goddess: covered with bees, Cybele's attribute, Aseneth in effect incorporates Cybele, though the bees are now reidentified as coming from God's paradise.

The Goddess blesses the selving of the flesh. Leukippé calls on her tormentors to see this: "Be spectators at a new contest! Against all these torments one woman alone contends and is victorious over all" (344). A concept of personal freedom and of rights prior to and anterior to the laws of family, property, and social organization is certainly at work in these powerful fables.

CHAPTER IV

> ⊱─◈─○─◈─⊰

Apollonius of Tyre and Heliodorus' Aithiopika: Fathers and Daughters, and Unriddling Mother's Plot

> ⊱─◈─○─◈─⊰

At first light he burst into his daughter's room, ordered the servant to go away, as if he was to have some private colloquy with his daughter, and then, urged by the force of his lust, despite his daughter's protracted resistance he tore apart the knot of her virginity. When the evil deed was done, he left the room. The girl, remaining amazed at the impious crime of her father, tried to conceal the flowing blood; but drops of blood fell upon the pavement.   —*Apollonius of Tyre*

"It snatched my daughter as I held her to my bosom—alas!—and carried her away to the ends of the earth, to a place full of dusky forms and shadowy figures . . ."   —Charikles to Kalasiris, *Aithiopika*

> ⊱─◈─○─◈─⊰

The novels discussed so far treat the question of sexual resistance somewhat playfully, on the whole. Even the works that are not exactly light-hearted, like "Paul and Thekla," make us believe in the straightforward possibilities of heroic freedom. We now turn to two books (in two different languages) which examine the cost of resistance, and indicate (in their different ways) the need for moral and political change. One of these novels, Heliodorus' *Aithiopika*, the longest of the surviving Greek novels, is a most sophisticated work. As we shall see later, it has had great influence on writers of modern centuries. The other, *Historia Apollonii Regis Tyri*, the *History of Apollonius King of Tyre*, is not nearly so highly regarded.[1] This Latin novel, generally thought a short version of some lost Greek original, is yet thoroughly embedded in Roman culture, as can be felt in the many echoes of Virgil, but its language is demotic and its style nonsophistic. David Konstan, who at least pays *Apollonius* the compliment of lengthy treatments, includes his discussion of this novel under the heading "Roman Novels: Unequal Love" (*Sexual Symmetry*, 100–113). Konstan wishes to make a clear distinction between the "Greek" novels, where one finds "sexual symmetry," and the "Roman" novels, which portray sexual inequality and asymmetry. *Apollonius*, instead of coming from some lost Greek original, is thus entirely *Roman*. Konstan supposes also that to portray such asymmetry is the same as to support it (see also his article on *Apollonius* in *TSAN*, 173–182). On the contrary, I think the "Roman" (i.e., those in Latin) novels are pursuing many of the same interests as the "Greek" ones, and diagnose similar problems, although their inquiry is pursued by different means.

Unlike the highly wrought *Aithiopika*, customarily treated with respect, *Apollonius* is frequently dismissed as simple or rambling; Hägg writes it off as "typical of trivial literature" (*Novel in Antiquity*, 153). Its subject seems anything but trivial. Its central subject is incest.

A discussion (even a fictional discussion) of father-daughter incest in the context of antiquity offers a considerable challenge to prevailing concepts of moral law. As L. William Countryman points out in *Dirt, Greed, and Sex* (1988), in the Torah (and mutatis mutandis in Gentile law as well) the rules against incest "were purity rules in that they forbade the combining of distinct social roles, but the social roles in question were themselves expressive of a sense of property and hierarchy" (163–164). Incest is important primarily when it is a violation of family hierarchy, as when a son takes one of his father's women, such as his own sister or—above all—the father's wife or concubine. Hence we find the great excitement aroused in the Greeks by the concept of Oedipus, and herein lies the interest of the "incestuous" love of Phaedra for her husband's son Hippolytus (who is not her own son). The feelings of women who are taken in incestuous rape (like Tamar, raped by her brother) are of little importance compared to the outrage suffered by the patriarch in such a case. But that the patriarch himself could suffer from lust for his own progeny is one of the unmentionable things that the ancient law does not want to look at. As woman has no rights in her own body but is the property of her father and often of her husband, it would be hard to discover in the context of ancient law the legal person to whom wrong is done in the case of father-child incest. The novels break the silence on the subject of females' rights to their own bodies, arguing for a personhood not only not unstricted as to gender but also unmodified by hierarchy.

Of all these novels, *Apollonius* takes the hardest look at the underside of both familial and cultural life. The *Aithiopika* takes an extensive view of the relation of the individual to different cultural groupings—including racial groupings—and imagines transformations of thought enabling new social concepts to emerge. Heliodorus' novel also acknowledges, though less harshly than *Apollonius*, the cost of arriving at even a perception or diagnosis of what is wrong in both public and private life. Both novels deal with the intersection of the "public" and the "private."

THE COST OF RESISTANCE: *APOLLONIUS OF TYRE*

That a woman is often not free to be a heroine of resistance is darkly set forth in *Historia Apollonii Regis Tyri*. At the very beginning of the story, King Antiochus, while thinking of marrying off his beautiful daughter, becomes enamored of her. Antiochus forcibly rapes his girl, despite her protracted resistance (*diu repugnanti*). The reader cannot readily forget the sight that the nurse sees when she comes in to the weeping girl after the event: "she saw the girl with tear-covered face, the floor sprinkled with blood, dyed rosy red" (*roseo rubore perfusam*). The unusually intense color words, the rose-red of pain and shame (*rubor*), color the rest of the story. Standing on the blood-spattered pavement, the princess laments to her nurse, "two noble names perished just now in this room." She intends to kill herself, but the nurse persuades her to live by cohabiting with her father. Antiochus says he will marry her off to any man who can solve his riddle. Into this situation walks the hero, Apollonius, as a suitor, and Antiochus puts his ironic question to him:

> Wickedly I ride, on Motherflesh I feed,
> I seek my brother, a husband of my mother.
> A son of my wife—I do not discover. [2]

No one is meant to understand Antiochus, but Apollonius gets the riddle much too quickly—and shows that he knows: "When you said 'wickedly I ride,' you were not lying; reflect upon yourself. And when you said 'on Motherflesh I feed,' neither were you lying then. Look at your daughter" (9–10). Antiochus then tries to kill this unriddler. Fleeing with a price on his head, utterly impoverished after a shipwreck, and entirely alone, Apollonius yet wins in Pentapolis the love of the King's daughter. After their marriage, they hear that wicked King Antiochus has been killed by a divine thunderbolt while lying with his daughter (presumably the daughter was killed too). Apollonius is to inherit Antiochus' kingdom and sets out on his journey with his young wife. She gives birth to a daughter during their voyage, but apparently dies after childbirth. Her weeping husband has her body coffined and thrown overboard. Apollonius sadly gives his daughter Tharsia to the care of his old friends in Tarsus, Stranguillo and his wife Dionysias, while he goes into Egypt. But the foster-mother Dionysias becomes jealous, for her own daughter's sake, of lovely Tharsia, and tries to have her killed. Tharsia (like Snow White) escapes, though Apollonius is later told she is dead and is shown her tomb.

Meanwhile, the princess is sold to a pimp in Lesbos and commanded to serve in a brothel—a service she successfully resists. When at last she meets her father, he is in a deep state of depression, coffining himself in the bowels of a ship and refusing to face the light of day. Tharsia goes down to him and attempts to rescue him from suicide by asking a series of riddles. The riddles serve to awaken his consciousness, but this therapy is only partially successful. Apollonius becomes angry with the girl and strikes her. The blow elicits her recital of her misfortunes and he realizes who this girl must be: "you are my daughter Tharsia, you are my only hope, you are the light of my eyes, whom, with your mother, I have been guiltily lamenting in tears (*conscius quam flens*) for fourteen years" (39).

Apollonius' speech, with its awkwardly placed *conscius* seems to indicate guilt or guilty knowledge. He was not *personally* guilty of his wife's death, nor was he responsible for the evil trick his former friends played in pretending his daughter was dead. Yet he is not utterly free of all agency in these matters. Apollonius' constant fate is guilt—a floating and imputed guilt. After he is burdened by the initial "guilty" knowledge of Antiochus' crime, his depression lifts only briefly during the courtship and marriage of his wife at the cheerful and musical court of Pentapolis. Archistrates' daughter was first attracted to him because he was so sad.

This novel investigates a condition of profound and perhaps insoluble unease. The story centers on the family, and yet the family is shocking. The possibility of family life—happy family life—seems precarious. There are four father-daughter pairs: the first three are (a) Antiochus and his daughter; (b) Archistrates and his daughter (who becomes Apollonius' wife); and (c) Apollonius and Tharsia. Archistrates' family is a sort of middle term; the father, bossy but kindhearted, orders his daughter to be polite to the stranger and to try to draw him out. This king seems exogamic and nonphobic; he and his child represent the norm insofar as there is one to be found. At an extreme end of the spectrum are Antiochus and his daughter, an obscene and violent spectacle. Apollonius should create some sort of opposite to that, a representation of the potential of good father-daughter relations. Instead, he gets rid of his daughter, effectually abandoning her.

The story of Antiochus as told here insists on the violence of the *father* in his libidinous possession of his daughter. In other ancient stories, we find the *woman* is customarily blamed in such a case—as with Lot's daughters (Genesis 19:31). Women have unnatural appetites, as in Ovid's story of Byblis, who loves her brother, and—even more relevant—the story of Myrrha, who loves her father Cinyras and contrives to sleep with him without his knowing their relationship. In Ovid's story of Myrrha, the daughter, as in *Apollonius*, threatens suicide in her trouble and confides in an old nurse, who likewise encourages her in a guilty continuance of life—but in this case the wicked desire is entirely the girl's. *Apollonius* might almost have been written to counteract the story of Myrrha as Ovid tells it. (See Ovid, *Metamorphoses*, Books IX and X.) [3] The unknown author of *Apollonius* makes evident that the terrible secret which lies behind family life is the secret of incest willed by the father. As the riddle-theme shows, such "secrets" are really not "secret" at all, but are known through being denied, or not discovered. There was no way out for Antiochus' daughter; she could either commit suicide at once or wait for the gods to strike her dead. Yet the sympathy of the narrative, in its opening paragraphs, demands that the girl not be canceled. Apollonius apparently escapes vengeance, but he cannot escape the horrific effect of his powerless knowledge. He becomes largely incapable of emotional function, especially after a bereavement for which he can feel partly responsible.

Tharsia alone apparently breaks free. Yet she can be freed, even partially, only by being exiled from her family, by undergoing the ordeal of slavery and resisting prostitution. When she is in the brothel in Mytilene in Lesbos, Tharsia's resistance and her appeals impress Prince Athenagoras, who comes as a customer. He is moved to spare her: "We know the chances of fortune; we are human. And I have a virgin daughter, for whom I might fear a similar fate" (30). Here then is the *fourth* father-daughter pair; within or without the brothel, the filial seems the inescapable relation. When he leaves the brothel, Athenagoras is asked, "how did the novice do by you?" He answers, "it could not be better, even to the point of tears [*usque ad lacrimas*]!" (31). Athenagoras' sentimental interlude with Tharsia, proving his own continence and magnanimity, thus seems itself poisoned by incest and ambiguity. Here is another riddle. Being moved substitutes for sexual motion; the daughterlike person to whom Athenagoras gave money gave him an orgasm—of a kind.

It becomes difficult while reading this novel to imagine sexual relations not poisoned by incest both cruel and sentimental, an incest that renders not only fatherhood but husbandhood itself perverse (Apollonius had said Antiochus' daughter should rather be called his *wife*). There are some hints of hope. Tharsia's mother did not die after childbirth; she was rescued by a doctor and his students, and she became a priestess of Diana at the temple of Ephesus—thus breaking out of the poisoned circle of family life. Her reunion with the family, rather than the reunion of father and daughter, is the climax of true reconciliation.

Tharsia herself has proved herself capable of acting unexpectedly and creatively. She thinks of a way to please the pimp and maintain herself in Lesbos by playing the lyre in public, attracting crowds of both men and women. (Tharsia is the only true working woman among the heroines of the ancient novel.) Later, the heroine shows she has learned from her trials. She exhibits unexpected charity to fellow-sufferers infinitely below her in rank. With her new status and wealth, she helps out the girls who were with her in the brothel: "Whatever you made by your bodies for that unlucky wretch [the pimp], that I render back to you for your own, and since you were once in slave-service with me, from now on enjoy liberty with me" (40). The narrative coincides with Tharsia's view in using the word "girls" (*puellae*) instead of any of the harsher words for whores. As we have seen, the daily abuse of such low wretches was taken for granted, even under Christian Constantine, but such abuse is not invisible to Tharsia, or to the author of *Apollonius*.

This novel has often been treated as if the most that could be claimed for it is that it "embodies an uncomplicated, satisfying morality" (Sandy, *CAGN*, 737). On the contrary, it seems quite a complex psychological narrative. *Apollonius*, I would suggest, is about rendering visible or knowable the psychosocial abuses that lie beneath the cultural surface. To render such open secrets knowable is to engage in the heavy psychic labor of unriddling. This labor oversets Apollonius. He wishes, in his most depressed phase, to sink back himself to the position of hiddenness, to become encrypted and cryptic, reaching that buried state which his truthful discernment had once disastrously disturbed. Hence he will not—or cannot—obey Athenagoras' command: "quit the shades and proceed towards the light" (34).

Tharsia's (relative) health seems to have resulted not in spite of her being separated from her family, but because of it. The capacity to exist outside the family and to make friends outside it is one of the great novelistic subjects. The "Family Romance," which is all we have been trained to see in such stories, is really a story of obsession, illness, and ill fate—unless and until the family becomes aerated and ameliorated by something other than family. The worst things done in *Apollonius* are done within the family or in the name of its values. Tharsia is nearly murdered by a woman who counts on advancing her own daughter through wanton destruction. Dionysias is really acting out of her own jealousy, not her daughter's will—she sees only herself and her desires reflected in her child. Tharsia counteracts such enclosed obsession by turning outward, befriending those who have helped her. Unlike Antiochus' imprisoned daughter in her terrible bedroom, Tharsia with her music calls crowds around her; she does not consent to enclosure.

The Christian novel *Recognitiones* (*Recognitions*), which may have been based (as Rohde thought) on some version of *Apollonius*, seeks to enfold that kind of story about a sundered family within a larger story in which family members acquire new interests, new friends. The really important friends here are St. Peter and his followers. Part of the "message" of the story is that you must love God more than family. Christ had directly—and shockingly—counteracted family piety: "For I am come to set a man at variance against his father, and the daughter against her mother. . . . He that loveth father and mother more than me is not worthy of me" (Matthew 10:35–37).

Indeed, the words of Jesus recorded in the Gospels are disconcertingly antagonistic to the whole system of morals and family life known to both Jews and Gentiles in the Mediterranean area in his time. Jesus does not recognize the family hierarchy that is the basis of all morality according to the best moral thought. "And call no man your father upon the earth: for one is your Father, which is in heaven" (Matthew 23:9). He repudiates the patriarchal pyramid. Jesus is in fact too revolutionary to sit well with contemporary respectability; as the Church gained in respectability it tended to compromise with the prevailing standards of family structure and social order. Hence we have Tertullian's horror at the *Shepherd of Hermas* suggesting forgiveness of an errant wife.

Yet, as the novels tell us, there were movements toward change within the "pagan" world and the pagan theologies. In *Recognitiones* itself we have the story of a "pagan" family, which is eventually Christianized, but not as a family—the children are converted first, and on their own. In the story of that family we see process of change; the family is split up and people make new connections.

When Clemens' mother, Matthidia, was shipwrecked and stranded on the island of Aradus (the same island where Kallirrhoé was reunited with Chaireas), a poor woman took her into her hut. Even after the restoration of her own children and her husband, Clemens' mother does not forget this woman, now palsied, and gets Peter to heal her. Matthidia originally embarked on the voyage that cost her so dear because she was threatened with incestuous love, a danger she did not know how to deal with at home:

> my husband's brother burned vehemently with illicit love for me, but as I valued modesty [*pudicitia*] above all things, and wished neither to acquiesce in such wickedness, nor to disclose to my husband the scandalousness of his brother, I thought about how I could escape unpolluted, without making my brother unfriendly and hostile or giving over all members of a noble family [*nobilis familiae*] to disgrace. I determined therefore to leave my native land and city with my twins until he should conquer his incestuous love [*incestus amor*], which was strongly agitated and inflamed by the very sight of me . . .
>
> ("Pseudo-Clemens," *Recognitiones*, 161)

Matthidia's story (similar to a story told in the *Life of Aesop*) exhibits the need for a woman at times to take the initiative. Social conditions have placed her in a bind so that she cannot just say "No." Modesty leads to a delicate dishonesty, the creation of distress-avoiding fiction: "In order that this could be done, I feigned that I had had a dream [*somnium finxi*], in which one who looked like some divinity came to me and instructed me that I should instantly leave the city with my twins" (161). The fiction of the dream works something like a riddle, indicating how Matthidia can arrange and represent her inner self, the being like a divinity who says "get out." Yet had she not had to lie for the sake of the pride of that "noble family," she and her twins would not have been endangered. One of the things that sometimes has to be done with the family is to get out of it. Recognition, reconciliation, and reunion can take place only when other things have happened. In the novels, things have happened through the courageous resistance of the women who have shown they have power to create change, even though no legal or social right of resistance resides in them.

The "new woman" in the Greek stories asserts the power to resist and the power to create change through the divinity she serves. Kallirrhoé serves Aphrodite; Leukippé, Artemis. Tharsia makes no direct appeal to the goddess in the brothel scene, yet we may presume that her mother's prayers to Artemis in Ephesus have been efficacious. When the mother appears at the end of the novel, she comes in queenly habit, adorned with gems and in a purple robe—it is as if the rare color words are trying to counteract the vivid red, the rubeous outrage, of the story's beginning. Tharsia's mother seems the image of the goddess. On seeing her, "Apollonius and his daughter and his son-in-law prostrated themselves at her feet. Such was the splendor of beauty that emanated from her, that they believed her to be the goddess Diana" (41–42). It is not only unusual but practically unheard-of for a man to kneel *to his wife*. Here is an inversion of all familial order, at present reconstituted by an extrafamilial order. Women serving the goddess choose chastity for themselves, and not out of dutiful service to men. To the overdutiful service by a woman of a particular man (in the sad case of Antiochus' daughter), Tharsia's mother, as representative of Diana, proposes a counterimage. But the example of Antiochus' daughter reminds us that not all are conquerors. The cost of resistance is sometimes very high, and the knowledge of what must be resisted can certainly be painful—even (as for the King of Tyre) incapacitating.

The therapy, as it were, that *Apollonius* proposes throughout is attention to riddles. Riddles are an invitation to approach a matter (especially the unsayable) from a different point of view. Frank Kermode, crisply paraphrasing Lévi-Strauss, says, "Puzzles and riddles, like incest, bring together elements that ought to be kept apart" (*The Art of Telling*, 79). Should we take Tharsia's riddles as an example of—and thus a collusion with—incest itself? On the contrary, Tharsia's riddles reenact some of the elements of incest, but as an antidote. As the novel has shown us, what is depressing is the normality of the breaking of the assumed taboo. In order to break out of the dull and painful normality created by the patterns or possessiveness we need to look at everything as if we had no ready-made understanding or definition of it—and that is what riddles do. Riddles figuratively enact the possibility of radical redefinition. Rhetorically they are *paradoxes*, in every sense—including the sense of surprise. Eros, who according to Chariton loves paradoxes, is something of a riddle himself in Longus ("I am not a boy, though I seem to be so, but am older than Kronos"). When Tharsia uses riddles, she engages in a serious erotic activity of self-preservation for her father and herself. She represents the desire of the mind to move outside the prison of custom. The way things are usually said to be need not remain the way they are to be. Attributed essences can change. Narrative itself always has something of this riddling quality, and never more than in the highly self-conscious narrative of the *Aithiopika*.

HELIODORUS' *AITHIOPIKA*: RACE, IDENTITY, AND PROPHETIC RIDDLES

One of the first riddles of the *Aithiopika* is its title.[4] How is this an *Ethiopian* story? *Ephesiaka*, the *Ephesian Story*, begins "There was a man in Ephesus . . ." The setting at once explains the title. When the *Ethiopian Story* begins, the characters are all far from home at the mouth of the Nile, the central pair seem to be Greeks, and no Ethiopians are visible. What have the white-skinned Greek-speaking characters we meet to do with Ethiopia? How will they come to terms with Ethiopia—a truly unknown place? A major motif of the novel is the racial motif, the relation between "black" and "white." A good many commentators, from the Renaissance to the twentieth century, do not care for this racial motif and try to suppress or ignore it. Reinhold Merkelbach, for instance, wants to get around the heroine's black heritage, flatly asserting, "Heliodorus' Ethiopia has nothing to do with the real Ethiopia," *Heliodors Äthiopien hat mit dem wirklichen Äthiopien nichts zu tun* (*Roman und Mysterium*, 293). For Merkelbach, the novel's Ethiopia must be a purely symbolic abode, a mere signifier for the place of the power of Helios—with no real black Africans involved.[5] It is evident, however, that Heliodorus, a Syrian identifying himself at the end as a Phoenician from Emesa who traces his lineage from the tribe of the Sun, takes a deep interest in issues of human difference, in what we would call matters of "race" or "regional culture." As John J. Winkler points out, Heliodorus is "unique in ancient literature for his continual attention to problems of language and communication. . . . To navigate one's way through this conspicuously polyglot world it is very helpful to know at least two languages, and several characters do" ("The Mendacity of Kalasiris," *Yale Classical Studies*, 27 [1982] 104). The novel's comments on language, on understanding or not being understood, constantly point to *difference*. Heliodorus, who came from Emesa, the present city of Oms in Syria, is even more aware than other "Greek" novelists of the ways in which people organize their identity, through language, region, nation, race, and religion. The novel poses a central question: how to harmonize the relation between black people and white people? Or between people of one culture and another?

Everything problematic in the novel focuses on the riddle of the heroine. At one time, the novel's title was simply her name, *Charikleia*. Charikleia, this radiantly beautiful girl who looks like an image of the goddess Isis, is a white woman of African parentage, who must claim her heritage and reinstate herself in her black family and kingdom. One of the unusual things about this novel is the fact that not only the central character but also the source of the plot is a woman. Were it not for the initial action taken by the heroine's mother, there would be no story. The women in the *Aithiopika* (both good and bad) do not wait to be kicked and enclosed in tombs, or shut up helplessly in coffins and tossed overboard. They display an unusual degree of initiative. Charikleia is one of the most striking exemplars of virtuous *parthenia*, but she is also distinguished for intellect. Her capacity for analysis is pressed into service by the narrative, and the narrative itself announces the need for analysis by pointing out, through successive narrative riddles, the difficulty of interpretation. Most unusually, the heroine is not named at the outset. The reader is required to plunge into commitment with no guarantee. The reader also rapidly begins to realize that what characters say to other characters need not necessarily be trusted.

The novel begins with a striking but mysterious scene. Disconcertingly, we share the view (and point of view) of a gang of bandits who come upon a strange scene at a beach on the western mouth of the Nile. Looking out to sea, they see a heavy-laden ship with no crew. Moving their gaze back towards the shore, they see a violent picture:

> The beach was covered with the corpses of men newly slain, of which some were entirely dead and others only half-killed, whose still-moving limbs signified that battle had just finished. And a strange battle—to judge from the apparent signs [*phainomena symbola*], for here were the wretched relics of an unfortunate feast. Some tables were still covered with food, while others, on the ground, were clutched by victims using them as shields in the fight that had occurred, as the battle was unexpected. Other tables served as shelter for men who tried to hide themselves under them. Wine-bowls were overturned; some had been dropped from the hands of drinkers in the act of drinking, while others had been used as missiles. . . . Here lay a man wounded by an axe, or struck down by a pebble supplied by the sea-beach itself, while others were broken up by a piece of wood . . . many were killed by many means. But the greatest number had fallen victim to arrows shot from a bow. (I : 2–3)

This violent scene—violent and yet peaceful in its way, a *nature* almost *morte*—is an obvious reminiscence of the banquet scene at the dénouement of the *Odyssey*, when the suitors are feasting and Odysseus, returned, levels his great bow against them. Eurymachos advises the other suitors, "hold the tables before you against the arrows," but he is immediately struck down, sprawling over the table, spilling the food and the two-handled beaker (*Odyssey* XXII, lines 74–86). Unlike the reader (or hearer) of the *Odyssey*, the reader here has no idea what on earth is happening. The well-known and completely comprehensible *climax* of one great (poetic) narrative is being turned around and used as the incomprehensible beginning of another (prose) narrative. It is a shock for the reader, almost like an impudence. The *mystery*—how did all this come to pass?—is still to be unraveled, and it will take many books of the work to complete the answer.

The bandits look about them, and see another strange sight. A beautiful young woman, crowned with laurel, sits pensively holding her bow. Chin in hand, she gazes sadly at a handsome young man apparently dying of his injuries. She then jumps up, her arrows rattling in her quiver and her gold-embroidered robe sparkling in the sun; her hair, worn loose under her crown like that of a Bacchante, floats freely down her back. The brigands wonder if she is Artemis or Isis. (Her bow would already have made the reader think of Artemis.) The strange woman then takes the bloodstained body of the young man in her arms and kisses him, raising wonder in the criminal observers; they ask, "Are these the works of a goddess? Would a divinity kiss a corpse so passionately?" (5–6). The reader, more acute, will already have sensed in the group formed by this heroine and her dying lover a reflection of the image of Venus mourning Adonis, or Isis mourning Osiris—this is the pagan Pietà. Throughout, the characters are presented in a complex background of mythical imagery, yet the characters are not to be treated themselves as divinities but as human beings in various kinds of predicament.

Who is this strange heroine? The first group of bandits do not find out; she utters a fine tragedy speech but they do not understand her language, and they are chased off by a second group of bandits, whose leader Thyamis almost at once begins to fall for the beautiful girl. The girl and her beloved are prisoners along with another Greek, the chatty and good-natured Knemon, who is skilled enough in medicine to heal the young man of his wounds, while telling them his own story, a variation of the story of Hippolytus and Phaedra. Loquacious Knemon may tell his own tale, but the fine couple are very discreet about theirs. The bandit chief Thyamis announces to a public meeting that he intends to marry Charikleia. She says modestly that it is unbecoming for a woman to speak in public—and then makes a long and convincing oration.

At his point we may think we are learning who the girl is. She *says* that the wounded man is her brother and that they are both from Ephesus, where she is a priestess of Artemis and her brother a priest of Apollo. They were going on a mission, traveling with a valuable cargo, and got caught in a storm; when they went on shore, the sailors attacked them in the middle of dinner. She asks only to be allowed to fulfill her original sacred mission and to make the offering to Apollo at Memphis before the wedding. Thyamis agrees, quite mollified. He is a priest himself, and this seems like a good ecclesiastical merger; he already told his troops that he wanted Charikleia as his booty, not for the pleasure of the works of Aphrodite (which priests despise), but so as to assure himself of posterity.

We may suppose we have heard the story, the background to the beach scene. Charikleia (whose name at least we now know) has remembered to touch on all the *phainomena*—but some things just do not ring true. In her ensuing dialogue with Theagenes, the young man approves of her saying they are brother and sister—for thus they will be allowed to remain together. But what does she mean by the rest of this fine rigamorole (*kalēs dēmēgorias*, lovely harangue)? And how can she break her faith to him—and marry this brigand! "I would pray to descend to my grave rather than my care and hopes of you should come to this end!" (I: 37).

Charikleia appeases him with embraces, but at the same time she is clearly offended. She is evidently proud of her own intelligence, her capacity to take care of herself—indeed, of both of them. She would have been in danger of rape had she not appeared to fall in with Thyamis' plan, she explains, but Theagenes should see that her story has won them some valuable time. Thyamis, feeling sure of her, will become calmer. There is a good deal of comedy in the *tone* of her discourse. We can feel her impatience. Has she not given Theagenes, she asks, enough proof of her fidelity in her past actions, has he not known enough of her behavior (*tōn ergōn*) so that he should not harbor jealous suspicions because of mere words (*ek logōn*) extorted from her by circumstances? (I : 36) Charikleia gets quite worked up during this conversation. She will guard her own virtue (*sōphronein*), she says; no one can force her to renounce it. But, she adds, with a good deal of asperity, "In one point I think I may have failed in discretion [*mē sōphronousa*]—when I first fell in love with you!" (36). The word *sōphrosynē* means virtue /discretion /self-control /wisdom—the French *sagesse* as well as English *virtue*. This lady evidently has a sharp tongue. She goes on to scold him: "How absurd [*atopos*] of you to think I would prefer a barbarian to a Greek, a bandit to the man I love!" (37)

Charikleia loves Theagenes indeed, but she scolds him in decided terms. She is quick to resent any reflection on herself and only too apt to be impatient when someone else does not keep up with her own nimble thought-processes. Throughout, Charikleia is customarily quicker-witted than Theagenes. Her eloquence (she speaks "like a siren," the narrative says), her intelligence, pride, and impatience are likely to seem familiar to anyone who knows another novel character—Samuel Richardson's Clarissa. Heliodorus' heroine, whose name (punned on in the novel) means something like "glorious grace," is a literary forerunner of Clarissa ("most famous, most shining"). Considering Charikleia's readiness with a convincing story, we can say of Heliodorus' heroine what Johnson said of Richardson's: "there is always something which she prefers to truth."[6] Like Matthidia, she knows the helpfulness of a good fiction. Charikleia here defends lying: "A lie [*to pseudos*] can be a very fine thing whenever it is useful to the speaker without injuring the hearer" (38). She has created a neat fiction about her own identity—and we still do not know who she is. Yet the eloquent Charikleia, we find out later, did not always know who she is either: her identity is truly unstable, subject to change and metamorphosis.

Thyamis is successfully cheated with a vision of happiness to come, but is soon overset by an attack (by bandit group the first). He hides his treasure, Charikleia, in the depth of a labyrinthine cave. The island within the marshes where the bandits hide out (as bandits also do in Achilles Tatius) is soon in a state of war. The reeds are set on fire, so the very ground seems to burn—a visually spectacular scene. Fearing he may lose the day, Thyamis vows not to lose Charikleia to another man even after his own death; he returns to the cave, finds the woman, and kills her.

Finding the dead body in the cave where he seeks his beloved, Theagenes laments in an agony and promises soon to join her. He is stopped from suicide by hearing the voice of Charikleia—the corpse is that of another woman, the treacherous Thisbe, who had caused Knemon trouble at home in Athens. Charikleia is alive. This resurrection scene of the restoration of Charikleia is (like much of the book) full of references to theatre, including Charikleia's knowledgeable question: "How probable was it, Knemon, that she [Thisbe] would get from the middle of Greece to the remotest parts of the land of Egypt as if she were sent by stage-machine [*ek mēchanēs*]?" (I : 55). Aristotle had said that it is inelegant to depend for dénouement on stage artifice (*Poetics*, 1454b); Charikleia seems jokingly to accuse the author of her own story of employing the creaking machinery in an improbable fashion. But Aristotle said one could explain matters outside the main dramatic plot by such a machine (*mēchanēi*), and so it is here—for Knemon's story, to which Thisbe belongs, is only a subplot (though Knemon never sees this).

Of all the ancient novelists, Heliodorus makes the strongest attempt to create the novel-plot as an equivalent of drama-plot, even while parodying that very connection. Sequential stories prove to be interrelated, in dramatic fashion. A novel like *Apollonius* relies on what might be called "thematic pressure" to create unity—the cumulative stories of fathers and daughters press us towards central recognitions. Thematic pressure is a major element in all novels, old and new; arguably, without such pressure no amount of plotting—or postmodernist refraining from plot—is going to work. A novel such as Dickens's serial-based *Old Curiosity Shop* (1840–1841), operates because we understand the thematic pressure while acknowledging the value of what seems random or episodic, as life in its progress may seem incoherent or episodic.

The *Aithiopika*, although fully conscious of the power of thematic pressure, brings plottedness to the fore, as an element to be discussed and examined. It constantly points out its own resemblances to—and differences from—dramatic works. One of its closest successors in this respect is Henry Fielding's *Tom Jones*, which impressed contemporaries in combining dramatic plot with narrative discursiveness. The reader gets the pleasures of apparently disconnected sequential lively incidents (with the attendant chance of meeting new characters) along with the opposing pleasures of tight dramatic plotted connection. In both *Tom Jones* and *Aithiopika*, the reader is understood to have absorbed the principles and techniques of criticism, even though the application of these may be imperfect—not to say self-satisfied, as in the remarks of complacent Knemon. Literary criticism itself is under question, as we pursue our hermeneutic way. To understand the theme of Heliodorus' story we have to be skilled at interpretation. As Heliodorus knows, neither episodes nor tight plots make real sense unless they are interpreted; defectiveness in a story may lie in the reader rather than in the author.

After Charikleia's wonderful return to life, the young people decide to escape in disguise, but Knemon is separated from the lovers, and lost. On the banks of the Nile he comes upon an old man with long white hair and a beard, apparently talking to the river. This old man, who says he would probably have told his story to the reeds (like Midas' barber) if Knemon had not happened by, takes the young Athenian home with him—not to his own home, for he too is a wanderer and a sojourner, but to the home of Nausikles, a hospitable merchant. Knemon is consumed with curiosity to know the old man's troubles, which include the loss of his children. His children, he says, are named Charikleia and Theagenes. Knemon is astonished. The old man explains that they are his children in a sense, "children born to me without a mother," "children born of my soul" (*apetekon hai psychēs*, I : 75). Knemon is dying to hear how his two young Greek friends and this venerable Egyptian are connected. Knemon has all the famed Athenian curiosity; he is chatty, quick, and shallow, and might be considered as a satire on Athenian life and culture, which in the work of this Syro-Phoenician novelist is certainly not represented as an ideal.[7]

The two, Kalasiris and Knemon, make an oddly satisfactory dinner, gratifying their own tastes at the table of Kalsiris' absent host. Kalasiris is a lifelong vegetarian who never touches animal food—how different from the King of Antioch who fed on *Motherflesh*, whose orientation was carnivorous and cannibalistic. They eat nuts and fruit, fresh figs and dates; Kalasiris drinks water while Knemon drinks wine. Two strangers in the house of a stranger, they make free with pleasure, and the hospitality they take for granted. Zeus—or rather the absent merchant—offers in their scrupulous and elegant supper. Julia Kristeva, in *Strangers to Ourselves* (*Etrangers à nous-mêmes*, 1991), speaks of the meeting and banqueting of strangers, as "a crossing of two othernesses." The "nutritive communion" of a meal offers a spiritual conjunction of the separated: "the banquet of hospitality is the foreigners' utopia—the cosmopolitanism of a moment, the brotherhood of guests who soothe and forget their differences, the banquet is outside of time" (trans. Roudiez, *Strangers*, 11). A description singularly appropriate this to the meal of Kalasiris and Knemon (save that, unlike Kristeva's banqueters, they do not start at the animal level of flesh-eating). This meal is the essence of the "cosmopolitanism" that Heliodorus is trying to convey. These characters are away from home and outside of the *family*—an abode of distress as we learn for Kalasiris, as for Knemon, and certainly for the absent Charikleia. Here, in a momentary but valuable conjunction not enslaved to time or social structure, they are exhibiting how the family may be reconstituted by not being family at all. The center here is the group of two strangers in the house of an absent third. At this point, in this place "outside of time" the storytelling begins and we go deeper into narrative, to explore the value of narrative itself.

Knemon (who has drunk the wine) urges the old man into narrative. "Dionysios, you know, Father, loves stories [*mythois*] and comedies" (I:76). "It is time to present your drama like a well-constructed piece on stage," he urges, equating the spoken narrative with dramatic performance and—how unlike Nietzsche!—feeling that prose narrative is Dionysiac. In an all-night sitting, the old sage Kalasiris tells his story, which is several stories interfolded.

Knemon listens as a connoisseur of narrative, a projection of the reader; he feels free to interrupt as he chooses (like Parson Adams in *Joseph Andrews*). At one point he says, "Enough of the wild herdsmen and of the satraps and of the kings . . . it's an episode, as the phrase is, which has nothing to do with Dionysius; return to your plot—you remind me of Proteus of Pharos who transforms himself into falsehood [*pseudomenēn*] and fluidity . . ." (78).[8] Knemon's reference to "episode" indicates that he, like Charikleia, knows his Aristotle. Kalasiris is indeed a Protean storyteller, animated and subtle, skilled in ventriloquizing the voices of others. Much of the center part of the novel consists of his narrative; instead of having the impersonal narrative Author, we have Kalasiris' voice, as the interruptions and questions of Knemon serve to remind us. And behind the character's implicit truthfulness we may suspect that Kalasiris, like Charikleia, and above all the Author, has a deep enjoyment of the *pseudomenēn*, that which is false, but seems true.

Kalasiris of Memphis is not only the narrator, but also a bridge between narratives; he knows more of the different stories than the other characters do, and he can connect them. He tells us how he came to leave Egypt, an overdetermined and uneasy migration, partly caused by a desire to preserve his widowed chastity,[9] partly caused by his anguish at the conflict between his sons, and his determination to escape the fate foretold, that he would see them fight each other. A priest of Isis, Kalasiris is interested in comparative theology; he came to Delphi in his travels, and became a friend of Apollo's priest Charikles, apparent (or pseudo) father of Charikleia.

Charikles tells him *his* story—how he was given a daughter in his old age, and how this daughter died on her wedding night, and his own wife soon after. Prevented by religious belief from committing suicide, the grieving Charikles had traveled. In Egypt, he was approached by a dignified young black man, who offered him a treasure; opening a purse, he took out many precious stones: pearls, emeralds, "hyacinths" (topazes or sapphires). The black man explains that the gems go with another gift of greater value, if he promises to use this gift well. The other "gift" of this riddling offer is a little girl, rescued by the black man from exposure "for I could not think it lawful in me to disregard and leave in danger a soul once it appeared in human form" (I : 88). Charikles takes the seven-year-old girl, radiantly beautiful, and the things exposed with her, not only the precious stones but also a silken band or girdle (*tainia*) with writing upon it—without doubt, the black man says, the mother of the child exposed with the infant these tokens of recognition (*gnōrismata*) (89). Charikles, having promised to treat the child well (and as a freeborn person, *eleutheran tautēn hexein*) is delighted to have a daughter again, and gives thanks to the gods.

In regaining a daughter, Charikles the depressed resembles Apollonius; he is also like the widow Tryphaina, who gains a substitute daughter in Thekla to replace her girl who died. But Charikles has behaved as if the point of the relationship were to cure his depression, and he innocently believes too simply in his own position as "father'—not realizing that everything is "as if." This daughter, of many *dōra* or gifts, to whom Charikles gave his own name, has been perfectly satisfactory, until her teens. Then she does not want to hear of marriage, having consecrated herself to Artemis. Charikles obviously cannot see his coaxing or coercing Charikleia into marriage as a breaking of his oath to treat her as *eleuthera*, "free," for he cannot see a woman's freedom in the terms of her own choice or her desire for personal freedom. The story makes him do penance for that, in the loss of his adoptive daughter, and in the long search for her that takes him to Africa. The unwittingly conventional Greek father asks Kalasiris to put Egyptian spells on the girl. Kalasiris should act as therapist to this father's *Dora*, making her acknowledge her nature as a woman (*hoti gynē*, 92). Otherwise, how is Charikles to have grandchildren?

This dangerous charge is accepted by Kalasiris in a partly ironic spirit, for he has knowledge of the girl's past that her adoptive "father" does not have. He is to become in fact the girl's new "father." Charikleia is thus the "child" of an Egyptian priest, an important position in ancient fiction; Aseneth was the daughter of an Egyptian priest, and, according to the *Alexander Romance*, Alexander the Great was the son of the Egyptian Nektanebos (who was a priestly magician as well as a king).[10] But it is important that Kalasiris is a priest of Isis, of the *goddess*. Unlike Freud, Kalasiris serves the mother who, like Demeter, has been deprived of a daughter. What Kalasiris does not tell Charikles is that he is already on a mission for Queen Persinna, to locate her lost child. Suppressing his active search and telling his story as if it were a drifting at random is, Winkler points out, "a deliberate narrative strategy on Kalasiris' part . . . an aspect of . . . his honorable mendacity." Kalasiris is, as Winkler emphasizes, fond of assuming roles. Like his author, he is a game-player aware of "the game-like structure of intelligibility involved in reading a romance" ("The mendacity of Kalasiris," 93; 101).

As Kalasiris knew, Charikleia was not going to be moved by her "father" Charikles' urging in favor of matrimony. But when Theagenes arrives with an embassy from Thessaly to take part in a grand Delphic procession, in which Charikleia also has a leading role, the two beautiful young people fall in love. Charikleia tries to keep her love secret—even from herself—but is understood by the wise Egyptian, who is also the confidant and counselor of Theagenes (like Friar Lawrence with the lovers in *Romeo and Juliet*). On a realistic level, Kalasiris is very engaging, partly because of his perpetual confidence that he can fix everything, as well as because of his ability to laugh at himself and others. Theagenes the stranger from Thessaly, however, is not the bridegroom Charikles has picked out for his "daughter."

Charikles commits the error of trying to make his love for his adoptive daughter shape her life entirely according to his views and plans. He literally cannot interpret that, for Charikles cannot read the silken band with the mysterious characters. He cannot hear—or read—the words of the Mother, the missing element, the coded riddle. Kalasiris, who borrows the band from Charikleia, sees that it is written in Ethiopic characters—in royal script (II:14). Unlike his *Greek* friends, African Kalasiris can read the story here inscribed—Mother's story.

Queen Persinna of Ethiopia addresses herself to her daughter, telling the sad story and explaining why she has had to expose the baby girl, whom she loves. In the royal bedchamber there hung pictures of Perseus and Andromeda, ancestors of the royal line. One hot afternoon as Persinna and her husband, the Ethiopian King Hydaspes, made love, she gazed at the image of white Andromeda. Persinna conceived, and the child was affected by the image (as according to contemporary science could be the case). Hence the child was unhappily born *white*—and as soon as she saw this, Persinna knew that she had to get rid of the girl, or her husband would accuse her of adultery.

The question of the plot is not, how can the girl physically return home by traveling to Ethiopia—but how can she be accepted when she gets there? What is required for the plot's resolution is a new level of interpretation of *phainomena symbola* on the part of the father, King Hydaspes. That such hermeneutic advance is difficult can be seen in the adopted "father," Charikles, who clings to an old and settled version of his own authority. Charikles, believing in his role as father, confides in his dangerous new friend, the wandering priest of Isis. The Delphic man, priest of Apollo, living at the center of Greek and Apollonian culture, cannot see that the gravely humorous and kindly Egyptian literally serves another god. The priest of the goddess may have different views of the freedom and destiny of the daughter. For Kalasiris, too, the mother is an important factor of the story, whereas to Charikles she is invisible.

Charikles is a sympathetic character even in his weakness and limitation, for he does love his girl. He is never more moving than when he recounts to Kalasiris a disturbing dream he has had. The adoptive father fears for his daughter, now in poor health (we know it is from pining with love for Theagenes). Charikles sees her death foretold in his dream: "My darling is about to depart from this life sooner than give herself in marriage as you fancy . . . for I dreamed that I saw an eagle fly from the hand of the Pythian [i.e., Apollo] and swooping to me as I held her to my bosom—alas!—it carried her away to the ends of the earth, to a place full of dusky forms and shadowy figures" (*zophōdesi tisin eidōlois kai skiōdesi plēthon*, II:23–24). Kalasiris bucks him up by offering a deliberately "false," or half-true and cheerful interpretation—the dream means that the girl will be married with the approval of Apollo. It is no wonder, however, that Charikles believes from this dream that his daughter is about to die, to go to the shades of Hades, the "place full of dusky forms and shadowy figures." For Charikles—as for some readers—Charikleia's true destiny, figured here, to return home to Ethiopia and her black people, is scarcely less dreadful. But that is the good destiny that Kalasiris sees and will try to bring about. One of Kalasiris' tasks (as he promised the Ethiopian Queen) is to try to restore Persinna's child. Now he is determined to do so, even if it means counteracting the dearest wishes of his friend Charikles.

The breaking up of the family is vividly conveyed in the elopement of Charikleia under the guidance of Kalasiris. Kalasiris, Theagenes, and Charikleia make up a new unit, composed of people who have broken out. They are a family-not-family, not connected by the bonds of blood or marriage—or even of sexual congress, for Charikleia makes Theagenes swear to observe chastity with her and not to perform the rites of Aphrodite until she has regained her own home and people. She asks him to swear by Apollo and Artemis and by Aphrodite herself and Eros. Theagenes swears, objecting, however, that requiring the oath does an injustice to his own capacity for moral virtue. Aphrodite herself, we see, is called in as a protector, a guarantor against the wrongful service of Aphrodite.

In their self-chosen company, bound by oaths of their own invention rather than by formal religious ceremony, far from any *polis* or nation they can call their own, the group journeys on. Kalasiris is the lovers' guide and companion through ensuing journeys and adventures, including the conflicts brought on by unwanted lovers of Charikleia. Kalasiris, winding up his narrative to Knemon, at last explains that amazing scene by the beach with which the story began—and which Charikleia had earlier covered by a mendacious explanation. We did not at that time have enough information to interpret the comically overdetermined *symbola*; Heliodorus' novel is an explosion—and exploitation—of semiotics.

As Kalasiris' story progresses, we are offered a new mode of interpretation, in the emphasis on prophecy and the prophetic. Though Kalasiris himself engages in relatively little hermeneutic explication while talking to obtuse Knemon, we begin to feel the prophetic pattern emerging through what he says. Part of the fascination of following the story is finding out how the puzzling prophetic clues (like Charikles' dream) will work out in the ensuing story. We begin to be persuaded that good narrative means prophetic narrative. The prophetic structure of the *Aithiopika* may powerfully remind us of the prophetic structure of sacred writings. The reading urged on us resembles the Christian mode of Scripture reading and interpretation, whereby prophecies in the Old Testament are fulfilled in the New, and prophecies in both are to be fulfilled at the end of the world. Of course, Hebrew Scripture has its own prophetic structure, or structures, and powerful Scriptural characters like Joseph, who can read signs, are good prophetic interpreters—the priestly role. What we call "paganism" has its equivalents. The highest "pagan" literature of the Roman Empire, the expression of the Roman right to empire, is Virgil's *Æneid*, which is structured according to a pattern of prophetic fulfillments.

The *Æneid* really works very much like the Scriptures as Christians have read them; a sequence of puzzling or disturbing prophecies works out in a logical yet surprising manner. It is of the nature of prophecy—literary prophecy—that it not be mere mechanical forecasting, while yet sustaining a certain literalism, if in a mode of paradox. The *Aithiopika* is extremely aware of prophetic patterns in literature; it is part of the reader's hermeneutic task to acquire such awareness. Any story about the Delphic oracle—and there were many stories—depends on the oddness of oracles and the puzzling nature of prophecy. The major prophecy of the novel emanates from Delphi.

The lovers seem to be supported by the gods, for the oracle at Delphi offers its own prophetic verse riddle:

> The one who begins in grace and ends in glory
> Regard, O Delphians, and him who is goddess-born [*theas genetēn*].
> Forsaking my temple and cleaving the billowing waves [*kuma*]
> They will come to the dark land burnt by the sun.
> There they will find the best reward for virtue,
> A white crown upon black brows   (I: 96)

Charikleia's name begins in grace (*charis*) and ends in glory (*kleia*); Theagenes' name means "goddess-born." The two together are destined to seek the "dark land." The journey to the "dark land" that is to be their home must inevitably be mysterious and troubled; the oracle indicates that their sacred destiny can be known to few. (It is part of the weakness of Knemon that having heard Kalasiris' story he wants to respond to it as *story*, and not to feel in it a call of destiny and virtue.) As in all good stories about prophecy, there is as much puzzle as promise in this oracular intervention. The last line is especially mysterious. Characters, like readers, never really know how prophecies are to be fulfilled until they find themselves in the midst of usually disconcerting fulfillment.

Kalasiris has great confidence in his ability to guide the lovers and control events. He does succeed in guiding them through many dangerous ways; he rescues Charikleia from slavery and promises to conduct both lovers to the Ethiopian home. So engrossed does he become in his prophetic role that he forgets the prophecies regarding himself and runs into the scene he had fled Egypt to avoid. As he and Charikleia come to Memphis, seeking Theagenes, Kalasiris suddenly sees his two sons, Thyamis and Petosiris, fighting each other outside the city wall, a scene resembling the fight between Akhilleus and Hektor (*Iliad*, XXII). Here, as not in the epic, there is a sudden and effective intervention. Kalasiris rushes towards them; when they do not recognize the old man dressed as a beggar, tears come into his eyes and he exclaims, "O children, it is I, Kalasiris!—I, the father of you both."

The recognition scene that follows is satisfyingly full of plays on Aristotelian *anagnōrisis*, augmented by the reunion of Theagenes and Charikleia. The spectators behold *skēnographikēs thaumatourgias*, scenographic wonders (II: 124). We are openly invited to notice the clever alteration into comedy from tragedy.

We may also note that epic values have been denied, or challenged; the epic demands slaughter, not reconciliation, and puts everything at the service of the state, including prophecy. Here reconciliation is possible and personal values prevail. This happy climax apparently leaves nothing wanting. Kalasiris, after giving thanks to Isis, goes to bed happy—and never wakens. His story is over.

The death of Kalasiris is nearly as great a shock to readers as to the hero and heroine. We have *all* come to rely upon Kalasiris. He is our guide, philosopher, and friend, our narrator and interpreter. But, for all his priestly confidence and his interest in prophecy, he overlooked his own death as a potential interruption to all their plans. His own intention was to bring matters to triumphant fulfillment, by conducting the chaste young couple home to the heroine's kingdom, and explaining everything personally to her parents. Kalasiris has great confidence in his own rhetorical powers: he could reassure Persinna and explain to Hydaspes. He *thought* he was in charge of the whole plot—but he wasn't. We were not in charge of events either, for we never factored in the possibility of losing Kalasiris. Charikleia had dreamed of losing her right eye and was told this augured the loss of her father. With the heartlessness of youth, she said she would sooner lose her father Charikles than her love Theagenes. (Of course she had already "lost" her biological father.) She never thought of the other "father" she could lose.[11]

There is a certain degree of comedy in the fact that Kalasiris, so busy, so happily officious in helping others, never saw his own death on the horizon. Kalasiris, that amiable character, has been too much occupied in being slightly untrustworthy (to Charikles and to the shallow Knemon) to think how he might be caught in the treachery of events. Kalasiris liked to keep all the reins in his own hand. Now he is gone—the narrative experiences stoppage, a gap. E. M. Forster's famously abrupt killing of a character ("Gerald died that afternoon")[12] pales beside the effect Heliodorus achieves in killing off Kalasiris. If we want meaning and progression, we can no longer count on the Egyptian priest to supply them—we are left on our own in the hermeneutic labyrinth. Kalasiris' own innocent *hubris* should warn us against too much pride in our capacities as readers.

Although Theagenes and Charikleia still have each other, at this low point in their fortunes they each have reason to feel alone and threatened. They are imprisoned in the realm of the Bad Mother. Queen Arsaké, a married older woman, falls in love with Theagenes, like Phaedra with Hippolytus (and like stepmother Demaineté with Knemon). With honeyed guile, Arsaké assures the couple of her care and keeps them prisoner. Motherly old Kybelé, Arsaké's former nurse and confidante, eggs Arsaké on (in scenes Racine drew upon for his *Phèdre*). Theagenes is threatened with whipping for his contumacy. Arsaké exclaims, with erotic sentiment, "how could I bear, ye gods! to see with my own eyes that body lacerated—that wonderful body!—or even just struck?" (III : 11) Kybelé assures her that just a *little* torture would make the boy see reason, and besides, Arsaké would not have to *watch*. Kybelé herself evidently would not mind watching.

The entire section of the novel set in the Persian palace is full of watching, looking, references to eyes. Everything is under the control of the gaze; it is a locus of paranoia, of the exhaustion of being seen. It is no wonder Kybelé's son is weak-eyed; with the reigning thirst for visual information, he is forced to satisfy himself mainly at keyholes. This weak-eyed boy wants Charikleia for his own sexual toy, but Arsaké, wanting Theagenes for herself, would like Charikleia out of the way. An attempt to poison Charikleia misfires; Kybelé dies instead. Charikleia is then accused of murder. After a quick and formal trial (how often novel characters appear in courts of law!) she is sentenced to be burnt alive for her "crime."

In this threatened execution Charikleia becomes a chief spectacle, a glorious object of interest as she is about to be set aglow. The flames, however, refuse to burn her, and she stands in the midst of them, encircled but not touched by fire, like a virgin bride (*nymph*) on a marriage bed of flame (*en pyrinōi thalamōi nympheuomenēn*, III:20).

At this moment she is both spectacle and omen, like Virgil's Lavinia when the divine fire from the altar plays about her head and crown and mantles her in yellow light (*Aeneid*, VII:71–80). But poor Lavinia is a passive instrument; Charikleia, an active agent. She rather resembles the martyr Thekla when she was baptized in a flash of flame and appeared in the center of the arena in "a cloud of fire" (*nephelē pyros*, 212). Seing the flames spare her, the Memphians shout, "The woman is innocent!" (as the female spectators of Antioch shouted for Thekla), and Charikleia, active as usual, jumps down from her pyre. Exasperated Arsaké grabs her, however, and scolds the people for their folly in letting this murderess go. Can they not see she is a sorceress? This is but fresh proof of her criminality. And Charikleia is thrown into a prison. As we constantly observe, everything depends on interpretation. Words are always subject to distortion, but there are no signs or wonders that are perfectly clear. Nothing speaks for itself in Heliodorus' story.

In the *Aithiopika*, the place where innocence meets power is in a place definitely and wrongfully female-controlled. We should not be too surprised that a Late Antique or early Byzantine critic gave a completely Neoplatonic or Gnostic allegorical reading of the novel in which Charikleia represents the soul and the other characters various sins, virtues, or temptations—nor even that this critic "Philip the Philosopher" can assert that the novel "presents more women and less men as famed for evil since there is more evil dispersed among the race of women" (trans. Lamberton, *Homer the Theologian*, 308).[13]

In this commentator likewise, Western arrogance has resumed its sway; he is assured that Ethiopia represents the invisible state of nonbeing, the darkness of precognition, while Delphi is associated with enlightenment and moral virtue. Yet Charikleia, the female Ethiopian, represents perfection of body and mind and spirit—she is a perfect 777. She is thus the highest possible representative of human life, an Everyperson. This willingness to allegorize total human experience as female experience can be seen also in the story of "Cupid and Psyche" in Apuleius.

"Philip the Philosopher" overcomes his general suspicions of fiction-reading to defend this book. The novel is "like Circe's brew" (307); take it in a profane manner only, and you are transformed into a pig. The unease about fiction-reading felt in Emperor Julian's remarks begins to gain shape and definition. "Philip" has to make the story accord with preconceived concepts of good and bad. He tends to forget the novel's bad *men*—and he is not interested in the fact that most characters are mixed, including even Arsaké. Allegory rescues the Neoplatonist reader from dangerous and profane ambiguities. The novel itself seems quite aware of—and even to play with—the kind of allegorical reading accorded it by "Philip the Philosopher" while repelling the reductionist conclusions of such readings. There is no need to attribute "Philip's" sort of misogyny to the novel, but undoubtedly Arsaké's poisonous palace is a Motherworld gone wrong.

On the way to that palace, Kalasiris and Charikleia encountered a witch trying to reanimate a corpse on a battlefield, and the Arsaké-sequence is full of references to witchcraft, poisonous or magical medicines, and sorcery. In Achilles Tatius' novel, when the heroine is enslaved and threatened with torture and the hero is imprisoned, they are simply in the control of the master of an estate in Ephesus. Melitté may have some Circean qualities, but she is not really to blame for what is happening—in fact, we feel sorry for her. Arsaké, though she resembles Melitté in inconveniently loving the hero who is pledged to another, has none of her charm. Arsaké is full of rage and power, and these emotions are further contaminated by self-regard and sentimentality. As a (substitute) ruler and queen she is a mother-figure, but she also likes playing the child and being "mothered" unwholesomely by scheming Kybelé, whose name is that of the Great Goddess, the *megalē Mēter*. When Kybelé calls her mistress "child" it casts a strange backward light on Kalasiris' address to his grown sons (*Ō tekna!*—"Oh, children!"). The Memphis atmosphere infantilizes.

The palace at Memphis is Persian-controlled, not Egyptian, an outpost of an infantilizing empire. Arsaké's palace is the most negatively drawn female *locus* in the extant Greek novel. Heliodorus seems to feel the need to balance a story of Aphrodite and Isis with a caution about what happens when the feminine goes wrong. Some sort of balance is needed. The Mother is still at the center of the story, and Charikleia, like a new Persephone, is seeking her mother and still under the protection of her true Mother. Her mother's gift, the magic *pantarbe* ("all-fear") stone that she wears, saves her from burning. (Charikleia had heard a prophecy about that gem which she had forgotten—so useful are oracular warnings.) Yet when the Father is most entirely absent the heroine is most subject to attack. Of course, the experience of enslavement, imprisonment, and threat seems a necessary experience for novel characters.

Hero and heroine are imprisoned. Chained, but sharing the same cell, they can at least talk. Theagenes tells his beloved of a dream he just had: Kalasiris came to him and uttered a short verse prophecy:

> "To the land of Ethiopia you will go, in company with a Maiden;
> From the prison of Arsaké tomorrow you will escape."

Gloomily, Theagenes interprets his dream, which seems clear to him: "For Ethiopia signifies the nether world and the company of a maiden signifies Persephone [*the* great *korē*], who will receive me after I have been freed of the prison of the body" (III: 24–25); "Sweetheart," says Charikleia, with the exaggerated sweet patience customarily produced by her impatience, "you are so accustomed to misfortunes that you always believe the worst. . . . The visionary dream seems to me to offer happier promises than you think. The girl is perhaps myself . . . you will go to my own country, my Ethiopia" (25).

They do indeed get to Ethiopia, if not at first under the happiest auspices. Taken prisoner by the Ethiopians, they are conducted to Meroë not only as prisoners but also as destined sacrifices—to be offered to the gods in thanksgiving for victory over the Persians. Even when he has recognized his daughter, Hydaspes, Brutus-like, still thinks it his duty to sacrifice her, as if she were Iphigenia, or the daughter of Jephthah (Judges 11:34–40). There are as many images of torment in Meroe as in Arsaké's Memphis. Hydaspes has to learn *how to value a daughter*.

The ending of the story records the Ethiopians' change of religious belief, under the guidance of the wise black gymnosophists, who apparently have learned the lore of India. Among these wise men is the man who gave Charikleia with her treasure and her mother's tokens to Charikles. The Ethiopians learn to forsake human sacrifice. But at first things look bad for the young lovers. Theagenes wants Charikleia to produce her tokens right away and save them, but the maiden is wiser:

> "When a demon has entangled the very beginnings of a complicated plot, it's impossible for that to come to an end save through a long-drawn-out process of multiple conclusions. Besides, something which has become increasingly more complicated over a long period of time cannot suddenly be unveiled and unknotted, especially when the chief worker of the whole piece, the weaver of the web, the one on whom my recognition depends—I mean Persinna, my mother—is not there." (III:69)

Charikleia explains that recognition tokens are only objects, cannot be real tokens (*gnōrismata*) except to the one who already can know (*gnōrizein*) what they are. Recognition needs cognition. The gems could merely announce to an onlooker that the young people were guilty of theft or brigandage. Or the things might remain objects not endowed with any meaning at all. Throughout, we have seen how vision can play one false, even among such eye-strainers as the Memphians. Even people are not recognizable: Thisbe was taken for Charikleia, Charikleia for Thisbe. At one point Theagenes did not recognize Charikleia in humble and dirty disguise. Appearances are riddles, as well as words.

The grand and sobering suggestion of Heliodorus' novel is that it may take a great cultural change to bring about an appropriate art of interpretation—a change as great as the imaginary change of religion brought about in Meroë by the black holy men who teach Hydaspes that sacrifice can be free from stain of blood. Sisimithres, the chief gymnosophist, the black man who rescued Charikleia and gave her to Charikles, speaks against blood sacrifice and the sacrifice of the daughter. A change of religion will make other things possible, including alliances and friendship among various nations, suggested in the descriptions of the embassies arriving at Meroë from Arabia and China. A different cultural framework could change the frame of understanding, and alter the realm of possibility. The packed and puzzling ending of Heliodorus' novel points far beyond the mere solution of the affairs of the hero and heroine, though, of course, it works itself out through their story.

Charikleia puts her faith in her mother. The final unworker of the plot, the clarifier, must be the weaver of the story. The mother noticeably wants to save the girl—be she black or white, virgin or deflowered, captive or ruler—unlike the father, who is obsessed with the idea of *sacrificing* the daughter. Persinna provides not only recognition, but also proof of undemanding love, saying, defiantly, that she does not care if her daughter prove virgin or not (thus suggesting another possible, if improbable, cultural change). Charikleia is, of course, magnificently chaste, though her love for Theagenes has been true erotic love as well as friendship. Her chastity has not been directed by compliance with parental values, but freely chosen and voluntarily defended.

Theagenes' own chastity is the equal of hers, and evidenced not only in his respect for Charikleia but also in his wily handling of his dangerous mistress Arsaké when he was serving as her cup-bearer. He then showed an address very like that of Mann's Joseph in his service in Mut's Egyptian palace. Both hero and heroine have suffered when others have tried to exert control over them—control always imagined as ownership. Even Charikles has not been guiltless on that score; he turns up at the end to ask for his daughter back. Though kindly treated in the end by the narrative, Charikles is also transcended. He is here repeatedly referred to as an old man (*presbytēs*); he is roughly dressed, and he is very sad. When he cannot at first find his daughter among the girls, he is "again dejected" (*authis katēphēsas*, III: 119). He is reunited with his foster "daughter" only to lose her to a larger destiny.

Both in *Historia Apollonii* and in *Aithiopika* the fathers are associated with dejection. *Apollonius* gives an almost clinical representation of depression. The *Aithiopika* exhibits Charikles' home as an abode of bad dreams and gloom, combined with well-meaning authoritarianism. What both novels show us is that Father's House is the abode of Depression, and Mother's House the breeding ground of Mania. It is the insane mothering of possessive Dionysias that stimulates her to kill Tharsia; the insane indulgent mothering of Arsaké by Kybelé brings on the attempted murder of Charikleia, and the frustrated manic passion of Queen Arsaké is reflected in the fire into which she would plunge her rival. To escape both mania and depression, it is necessary to flee.

In these novels, the original parents are found only to be superseded. The child finds parent at the time when the child has united with another and no longer needs the parent in the old way. An important aspect of the so-called Family Romance is the discovery of the inferiority or at least mistakes of parents, who belong to a past set of muddles requiring not only personal but cultural change. The "Family Romance" in prose fiction is always an ironic affair. In Jane Austen's *Emma*, silly old Mr. Woodhouse (a comically depressive father) laments "that young people would be in such a hurry to marry—and to marry strangers too" (158). But fiction is heartily in favor of union with the stranger. Theagenes of Thessaly is a stranger to Charikleia of (apparently) Delphi. If Kleitophon is a cousin to Leukippé of Byzantium, the two have not met until that significant first visit of Leukippé. Kleitophon rejects the incestuous union with his sister arranged by his father. Even in novels such as *Daphnis and Chloé*—or for that matter *Emma*—where the characters marry a neighbor, something has first to happen to make that neighbor seem *like* a stranger.

It is not only in cases of love and marriage that narrative favors the stranger. Characters in novels meet persons who are no kin to them, and establish friendships, aside from the interest of familial, sexual or commercial bonds. To become oneself a stranger in relation to another is a step on the road to knowledge. In the world of these Mediterranean novels, it is good to be mobile and polyglot. Getting to know the strangers forms an important part of every novel's story, most markedly in the exogamic *Aithiopika* and *Apollonius*. Antiochus carried Mr. Woodhouse's possessive greed too far in his perverse cutting out of the stranger who might take his daughter from him. (Mr. Woodhouse, too, is enveloped in riddles, but he is too foolish to pose any.) Exogamy itself represents a larger turning outward. Strangerhood is seen favorably in these novels, which encourage the possibility of new encounters, new bonds that go outside of the familial or linguistic or ethnic or religious groupings. And the reader shares in this cosmopolitanism, and this enthusiasm for the stranger. For, as we read, what are we doing but making friends with strangers (even foreigners!), developing an interest in persons whose lives and fortunes are unknown to us and alien when we first pick up the novel.

At the end of *Aithiopika*, hero and heroine have escaped from the realm of the legalistic Father (represented by Charikles) and from the dangerous realm of the possessive Mother (witch, Kybelé, Arsaké). They have even gone beyond the realm of the spiritual Father as counsellor and rule-giver (Kalasiris). They celebrate a wedding, a *hieros gamos*, that unites the male and female forces. The Ethiopians worship the Sun and Moon. Theagenes will be priest of the Sun and Charikleia a priestess of the Moon. Their worship will thus combine the worship of Apollo and Isis, as Sun and Moon. A harmony arising in the service of the gods will reflect a harmony between the sexes. Not only so, but even more remarkable, there will be a harmony between the races. The heroine's own body proves to bear the now-interpretable—and thus now visible—signs of that strange meaning, Charikleia *is* partly black; there is a circle of ebony flesh coloring the ivory of her arm. The last lines of the novel remind us of the vision set forth in the oracle of Delphi, which has now been fulfilled:

> They will come to the dark land burnt by the sun,
> There they will find the best reward for virtue [*per aristobiōn*],
> A white crown upon black brows

(III : 126)

"Virtue" is here best life, noblest living and the "prize" is *meg' aethlion*, "big prize" or major prize in an athletic contest. Hero and heroine are like someone who receives first prize in a race—but because of *aristobios*, good life, rather than classical *aristeia*, heroic feats. The whole passage seems similar to the end of the ninth chapter of I Corinthians: "Know ye not that they which run in a race run all, but one receiveth the prize [*to brabeion*]? So run that ye may obtain. . . . Now they do it to obtain a corruptible crown [*stephanon*]; but we an incorruptible" (vv. 24–25). The crown of reward for Theagenes and Charikleia, the white garland, would seem to bear more resemblance to Paul's incorruptible crown than to the mere fading wreath of the athlete.

The goodness—*aristobios*—of the righteous virgin proves powerful at last. It is powerful enough not only to bring about restoration and justice, but also to heal divisions between races, to erase signs of difference that have hitherto stood as socially all-powerful.

I can see that an African or an African American might have a different view of the novel and its band of black flesh in Charikleia—might see the book as still too white-oriented, as neocolonialist. On the other hand, one might wonder whether Heliodorus "of the race of the Sun" might not have had a partly African origin himself. The point is that *Aithiopika* should be discussed by experts in African and African-American literature and by many others—it is one of the "Great Books" of our tradition, one of the works that have influenced our vision as it transmitted itself through the tradition of the Novel. It should be noted that the narrative clearly shows Delphi as superseded. We move away from the heartland of Greece here, never to return. The narrative takes its way from Delphi via "Persia" (Asia Minor) and Egypt to Ethiopia, as if tracing the development of the novel itself back to some kind of heartland or origin. If Delphi represents the West—why, that West is not good enough. The novel cries out for more interpretation than it has ever had. This is a novel that absorbs interpretation, an hermeneutic sponge.

The traditional sign of the skin—black-white—is subsumed in the riddle at the end of the story, a riddle that still retains its power to perplex: "white garlands upon black brows." *Whose* are the "black brows"? Some translators have been uneasy about that riddle. Nahum Tate and the "Person of Quality" in their translation of 1686 go out of their way at times to make "black" synonymous with "ugly" ("seeing them so black and ugly," *Aethiopian History*, 5). As we will see, however, this attitude is out of keeping with the views of most Renaissance translators and commentators, who see in the Ethiopian king, black Hydaspes, a model monarch; Tate is unusually "modern" in his antipathy to the idea of black Africans. Tate plays some unauthorized tricks with the prophetic verse. At the novel's end he renders the last line as "And Snowy Wreaths from Sun-burnt Temples bear" (159); at the prophecy's first recitation the Oracle says, "And as their Virtues Coronation, there, / Loos'd from black Temples, shall white Garlands wear" (99). Tate is anxious to create a separation: snowy wreaths (or white garlands) are taken off the black "Temples" (brows or buildings?) and put on the white people. Most translators have more respect for the original version of the prophecy, which does not deal in separations or create a process of transmission from a plain black to a clear white. Instead, the verse collapses differences in an atemporal image: "white garlands upon black brows." Evidently in the end, under a new blessedness, a new dispensation, Charikleia and Theagenes partake of an honorary blackness. Black/White are no longer distinguishable in the traditional manner. Opposites unite, unlikes dissolve, as in Roland Barthes' noted figure S/Z. In the syntactic movement here, *leukon* becomes *melainomenōn*, white is black, or whiteness has achieved blackness. The real prize for *aristobios* is that one does not see life in the old ways.

CHAPTER V

Parody, Masculinity, and Metamorphosis: The Roman Novels of Petronius and Apuleius

I began to consider how lost to all modesty it was in me to confer verbally with that part of my body which the more serious sort of men are not accustomed to admit even to their thoughts.

—Encolpius in *Satyricon*

"Imagine," he said, "that I'm dead."   —Trimalchio in *Satyricon*

Therefore I have remembered and am thankfully grateful to my ass, because, concealed under his covering, I was exercised in various fortunes, and so the ass repaid me—though I was not so prudent—with a good deal of knowledge.   —Lucius in *The Golden Ass*

THE CASE OF THE TIRED PENIS: *SATYRICON*

The earliest major Roman novel is a parody of the genre exemplified by Heliodorus' later work. Petronius' *Satyricon* is, as its title indicates, an aphrodisiac story of libidinous life. It is not a novel with any affection for virginity. It is about characters who, as it were, have taken an aphrodisiac, or suffer insatiably from satyriasis; it is also a *satura*, a Roman satire (this time in prose) dealing in mixed modes with a mixture of topics, a variety of observations. This comic work seems even more experimental than it is, as we have lost so much of it.[1] It is both episodic and plotted; there are clear indications that incidents in the extant sections are connected with incidents in much earlier books, and that characters recur.

In this story we meet the sort of characters who serve in subordinate capacities in other novels—people like Kleitophon's homosexual friend Kleinias, or like the lewd and greedy Gnathon in *Daphnis and Chloé*. (These examples are of course later than *Satyricon*.) The love-story motifs are ironically shifted, so that comic homosexual males occupy center stage. Until recently it was customary to contrast the "realism" of Roman fiction as exemplified by Petronius with the "romantic" patterns of the Greek novel, but the discovery of more fragments of Greek novels has rendered that distinction dubious. Lollianus' *Phoinikika* (or *Phoenician Story*) (first edited 1972) clearly exhibits even in its tantalizing short fragments the existence of Greek works in the tradition most fully exemplified by Petronius.[2] Petronius' novel is visibly a member of the class it parodies. Like the Greek novels, it presents us with frustrated love, travel, the making of new acquaintances (including elders or father-figures, here comically unwise). There is at least one oracle, there are dreams and interpretations, symbolic paintings and other objects, and treasures, as well as comic recognitions (especially, in the surviving work, Tryphaena's and Lichas' *anagnōrisis* of Encolpius on board ship). There is a sea journey and a shipwreck.

The "hero," Encolpius, an impious Aeneas whose name means "In Crotch," is wandering with his homosexual beloved, Giton, whose name, "neighbor," has a sexual sense (very like the word "friend"). Encolpius and his Giton, when we first meet them, are in some unidentified town in the Naples area. The pair by this time has become a trio; the smooth Ascyltos ("Unwearied") has joined up with them and constantly tries to win Giton for himself. The trio get into trouble in watching Quartilla celebrating secret Priapic rites, and Ascyltos also literally loses his shirt, in which his fortune was sewn.

In search of a free dinner, Encolpius and Ascyltos, accompanied by Giton, attend a banquet at the house of preposterously wealthy Trimalchio. There is a superabundance of rich and complicated food, resembling (if surpassing) the display of food in the "Buffet Mosaic" in Antioch, an image of conspicuous consumption. The long sequence of the *Cena Trimalchionis*, Trimalchio's dinner, has been popular with schoolmasters and anthologists, not least because it seems easy to extract from it a clear and simple moral, a sermon against excess, in a work where the "moral" is unusually difficult to locate or define. Trimalchio, the newly rich freedman, represents obvious consumer excess and intellectual deficiency. The Roman Empire had just discovered "culture" in our modern sense; the use (or abuse) of knowledge of art and literature, as well as artistic objects, represents social status and power. The cultural blunders of Trimalchio and some of his friends are funny, because this rich man knows that a gentleman ought to know Greek literature, or at least the stories. The prized "culture," however, is indeed a commodity, and Encolpius, like Agamemnon and other teachers and rhetoricians, is one of those who scrape a living by selling that commodity. However "good" Encolpius' taste, however much he may despise cakes that spurt saffron, and silver piss-pots, he too is trying, as we say, to grab a piece of the action. Eumolpus, his associate, displays his cultural goods in bombastic poetry that sounds like Lucan on a very bad day. All of the characters share with Trimalchio the qualities of excess and show.

Trimalchio seems a figure with multiple meanings. On one level, he is simply a joke, an outrageous fat rich man trying to show off. He utters absurdities in a bad accent, treating us to enjoyment of our superiority as we watch him make cultural blunders: "I am quite devoted to silver. I have a hundred—more or less—urn-shaped drinking cups, in a design so that you can see Cassandra killed her sons and the dead boys lying there just as if they were alive. I have a thousand jugs, which my patron bequeathed, where Daedalus shut Niobe up in the Trojan horse" (104–106).

That is the Trimalchio of easy comedy, probably related to the comic mimes of the period. But there are more disturbing aspects of this ignoramus. The theme of death runs under the narrative; the Roman *memento mori* appears in unexpected guises, and not only in the silver skeleton shown at the start of the banquet. Towards the end of the banquet Trimalchio gets carried away with the wonders of the preposterous tombstone he is planning, and he then begins to plan his funeral, going so far as to act it out: "'Imagine,' he said, 'that I'm dead. Say something beautiful.'" (*'Fingite me,' iniquit, 'mortuum esse. Dicite aliquid belli'* [180]). The whole banquet is a kind of symposium in Hell, a comic feast of the underworld, as Graham Anderson points out, suggesting that the dinner with Trimalchio ("Thrice king") is the mock-epic visit to the underworld, with Trimalchio, whom Anderson calls "our King of the Campanian Waste Land" (*Ancient Fiction*, 187), figuring as a kind of comic Pluto. Trimalchio says (in a kind of wonderful Latin "Irish bull") that you can see "Cassandra's" (it should be "Medea's") dead boys as if they were alive. At his banquet, the dead pretend to be alive, and the technically alive Trimalchio pretends to be dead. The metamorphoses so strongly emphasized in this sequence involve life/death, death/life—and the metamorphosis of nature into art, about which Trimalchio is blunderingly serious, and about which the author (even more than Encolpius the narrator) has doubts.

Dinner with Trimalchio takes on the characteristics of burial alive; all the characters begin to undergo a *Scheintod*, to seem as if they are dead. Trimalchio's feast, apparently so jolly, so full of riddles and sensuousness, spirals down into melancholia and inertia. Here is Father's House as Depression, once again, after the manic sensuality of Mother's House, Quartilla's brothel. Trimalchio's realm casts a blight on Roman rule, on masculine authority in social and economic life, and on the display of all forms of phallic power, including cultural display.

Not unlike Trimalchio, other male characters claim a higher ground than can be substantiated by visible claims. They lack what Trimalchio has—money—but they know all about pretense and show, including the sophistic show of rhetoric. Giton the meretricious has almost frankly to engage in hypocritical show; his kisses, embraces, and intimate gestures are pieces of acting. Considerations of money play as large a part as the considerations of sex in Petronius' world. Characters know alike the price of their bodies and their minds, their sexual gestures and their words. The central characters are deracinated professionals, living on their wits in an urbanized world. Sexuality is never free of urban economic trammels—it is indicated to Encolpius that his rightful home is the brothel. Sex is always associated with physical and mental unease—or, most commonly, pain. Living on one's wits means one has time to notice the pain, as well as opportunity (even if unwelcome) to change one's appearance and status in perpetual labile play.

After the episode of the banquet of Trimalchio, Encolopus and his friends, now unwillingly united with the would-be poet Eumolpus, escape on board ship—of course fated to shipwreck. Encolpius and Ascyltos have had to pose as slaves—like Leukippé and even Charikleia at one point, they are in humble and dirty disguise. In Crotona they pretend to be slaves of a wealthy man (the disguised Eumolpus). Eumolpus' scheme for raising money, his pretending to be a dying millionaire who will make rich heirs of his friends, is the plot of Jonson's *Volpone*, in which Encolpius (with Ascyltos) is pressed to act the part of a Mosca. Obviously, this gang is going to get into trouble and will have to leave town in a hurry—like the Duke and the Dauphin in *Huckleberry Finn*. Eumolpus is like the Duke and the Dauphin combined; the slave Giton, stolen by the imposter, resembles Jim; Encolpius is an older and less virtuous Huck Finn with erotic problems. (The resemblances are not surprising; Mark Twain presumably read this novel.)

A beautiful married lady with the strongly indicative name of Circe falls in love with Encolpius, in his guise as a slave. The pair lie on the grass amidst flowers, in a *locus amoenus* suitable to love-poetry—and love-poetry is forthcoming, but naught else. Alas! for all the perfection of partner and setting, poor Encolpius can do nothing. The last part of the extant novel deals extensively with the hero's problem of impotence. Encolpius' offense against Priapus—perhaps some other deity too—is working out its penalty. Rejected and punished by women, comically self-accusatory, Encolpius goes to the old priestess of Priapus, Oenothea (or "wine-goddess") but offends again by killing the goose sacred to Priapus; the bad spell seems still to be taking effect when our version of the novel comes to an abrupt end.

Encolpius the narrator, the hero or anti-hero, is a complex comic creation, a man whose sophistication, including facility with words and literary works, is undercut by persistent naïveté. Encolpius is ever-ready to believe in Giton's carefully worded expressions of love, not allowing himself to see that Giton's interests are those of the prostitute. Encolpius, a sentimentalist even while he thinks he is hardboiled, naïvely in earnest just when he should not be, resembles Thackeray's Pendennis, or Stendhal's Julien Sorel, as well as Huck Finn. As naïve and sentimental lover, Encolpius fails—naïvely and sentimentally. His impotence is comically displayed for our consideration, not hidden as such a shameful matter should be. He is not "all man": Circe says to him on his second visit, "how is it, paralytic? have you come here today a whole man?" (*Quid est . . . paralytice? ecquid hodie totus venisti?*, 344). After his second failure, Encolpius threatens his own penis, addresses it, scolds it. Then he realizes what he is doing: "Not less when this disgraceful objurgation was finished did I repent of what was spoken, and, suffused with a secret blush, I began to consider how lost to all modesty it was in me to confer verbally with that part of my body, which the more serious sort of men are not accustomed to admit even to their thoughts" (*quam ne ad cognitionem quidem admittere severioris notae homines solerent*, 348). Encolpius knows perfectly well that Roman moralists would deeply disapprove of his conduct. The Roman ideal of grave serious self-control, of the masculinity of austere power, is not invisible to Encolpius—just impossible. He argues against it. In doing so, he in a manner demystifies the male body, which becomes, not the sign and instrument of power, but (like his words) *novae simplicitatis opus*, a work of new simplicity, subject to illness, failure, and pleasure. Encolpius' whole narrative might be taken as a monologue on the possibilities of *letting go*—including letting go of power. After all, Encolpius has already lost masculinity in allowing himself to be buggered (and thus "feminized") by the *cinaedus* or sodomite during the night of penitence in Quartilla's brothel. Encolpius' significant name tells us that in a sense this book is the male crotch speaking, but, even if gifted with authorship, this male crotch does not speak at all in an authoritarian manner—unlike the masculine members in Denis Diderot's *Les bijoux indiscrets* (1748).

What this novel appears not to have is women. The female characters who are so important in the Greek novels are absent—at least, at first glance. There are certainly no chaste virgins here. As we look more closely, the women come into focus, and we begin to see how much power the female presence has over the males, especially Encolpius. Quartilla looms over him asking for erotic revenge, Tryphaena threatens him and snatches back her love-pet Giton, causing a mock-heroic battle on board ship until she declares a truce. If Encolpius has trespassed by gazing on the secret rites of Priapus, he has offended (so one would think) against some *masculine* principle of power—yet throughout the story it is *women* who are the priestesses and custodians of that power, and women who have the power to terrify, punish and reward. Female power is very close to divine: Oenothea, the priestess of Priapus, bears the goddess in her name, and in her fragmented poetic speech promising to cure Encolpius she makes claims that equal those of Isis in Apuleius: "Whatever you see in the world belongs to me. The flowery earth, as I will, becomes dry and faint, its juices dried up, and as I will, pours forth its riches . . . to me the sea submits its calmed waves . . ." (354). She is only a poor old woman, yet her speech indicates the power of the Goddess lying below all things—including the presently powerless "thing" of Encolpius.

Circe, as lovely as the Melitté who seduces Kleitophon and even more insistent, knows she is not the mythical semidivinity, and yet she lays some claim to a reflected mythical status: "Didn't my maid tell you that I am called Circe? Indeed, I am not the offspring of the Sun, nor did my mother, while she pleased, stop the moving world in its course. I will, however, be in Heaven's debt, if the fates will unite us. Indeed, the god in his silent considerations is working out I don't know what. But not without cause does Circe love Polyaenus: always between these names a great flame blazes" (332). As Encolpius has taken on the pseudonym of Polyaenus, "much-praised"—an epithet for Odysseus—Circe weaves him into her version of the story of the *Odyssey*, imputing to both of them a powerful and fated legendary status which Encolpius is comically unable to act out. To pose the question whether Encolpius "should" or "should not" make love to this Circe seems an absurdity. Circe's self-consciously parodic part in the story is to raise the power of Woman as something that Encolpius cannot ignore and do without, even as the narrative simultaneously mocks the illusion that great literature like the *Odyssey* will or can do our living for us. We may not even know what great literature means. Prophecy fails and tumbles into slangy bathos: "the god is working out I don't know what" (*nescio quid*). To try to live in art invites the stasis that mirrors death: *Fingite me mortuum esse*. Ironically, the characters at the end of our fragment are living in Crotona, a ghost town.

The female "character" in the *Satyricon* that most readers best remember, the widow of Ephesus, is not really a character in the main narrative. Eumolpus, entertaining the company on board ship after the mock-heroic battle, tells the story of the widow, partly as a gibe against Tryphaena; he gives expression to some of the antifeminine sentiment felt at that moment by Encolpius himself. For once, Eumolpus is an effective narrator, telling his story in good prose instead of his awful poetry. He tells the story as something that he remembers, but the "Tale of the Ephesian Widow" is really a circulating folktale or fable, one of the satiric "Milesian Tales."[3] "Milesian Tales" were supposedly invented in Miletus in the second century B.C.; the generic name pertains to a short funny story, usually bawdy, sometimes dealing with the supernatural (or mock supernatural) and usually ending with some narrative twist. In the Middle Ages this kind of story is called the *fabliau*. Petronius amplifies the fable and makes it more dramatic. His is the best-known version of a story that can be briefly epitomized:

> A woman of Ephesus, very famous for her virtue, insisted on following her husband to the tomb, watching over his corpse and weeping night and day, neither eating or drinking. As she sat starving in the mausoleum, the governor had some robbers crucified nearby. The soldier who was set to watch over the robbers' corpses saw the light in the tomb and heard the groans; curiosity drove him to the vault. After he had persuaded the lady to live, he conducted a successful campaign against her chastity. Delighted with their lovemaking, they passed all their time enjoying themselves in the vault, so that the family of one of the crucified robbers took their man down and buried him. Seeing the empty cross, the soldier was sure he would be tried and sentenced to death, and was ready to commit suicide, when the lady saved him by having her husband's body put on the cross in place of the missing corpse.

Petronius has amplified and dramatized the fable. He creates the important subordinate character of the maid: it is the maid who is first overcome by the smell of food and gives in to human hunger at the humane invitation of the soldier. The soldier is no swaggering seducer here; he is motivated first by curiosity, then by humane pity, and only at last by lust. The lady's virtue, as Anderson points out (*Ancient Fiction*, 162) is "performance." She drew women from neighboring regions to look upon her (*ad spectaculum sui*, 268). She makes a *spectacle* of herself. In the tomb she becomes a story (*fabula*) and a pattern; she shone and glittered (*affulsisse*) as the true example of chastity and love. The light in her tomb, however, which attracts the soldier, becomes the light of love and not of spectacle; keeping their reality hidden, the unorthodox lovers are nearly undone by having to provide another exemplary spectacle that is occupied solely with death.

This story is one of the central riddles of the *Satyricon*. Like the main story, it offers the possibility of different "morals" to be derived from it. An early twentieth-century critic has said that its message is that "no man's honesty and no woman's virtue are unassailable" (F. A. Abbot, quoted in Walsh, *Roman Novel*, 11). Eumolpus tells his tale as an antifemale story, attacking women's evident fickleness, their lightness (*in muliebrem levitatem*). Eumolpus, however, is hardly a trustworthy guide either to morals or to literary meanings. Tryphaena blushes at the story, using her blush as an excuse to lay her face on Giton's neck. Others, like the sailors, find the story simply funny and laugh. Lichas, however, refuses to laugh but gets angry: his mind runs to law and penalties; he wants the woman to be punished: "If the governor were just . . . he should have put the body of the *pater familias* back in the monument, and affixed the woman to the cross" (276).

Lichas' reaction is instructive, as it is such a wrong reaction. He wants Augustan law reinforced. Lichas wishes to follow the path of death, which the widow of Ephesus tried to avoid. *Her* argument is that there has been too much death already. She does not argue that she has no love left for her husband, but that multiplying deaths cannot be the right answer: "May the gods forbid that at one and the same time I should look upon [*spectem*] the dead bodies of the two men dearest to me. I would rather hang a dead man than kill a living one" (276). Her previous notion of virtue, both as a show-off spectacular virtue and as a male-dictated ideal of self-destructive chastity, has been altered so that she repudiates the increase of deathly spectacles, instead of participating in them. Lichas sees that the widow has freed herself from the rule of male law, both as represented by the crucifying governor and by the customs that dictate female behavior. In freeing herself, she liberates her new "husband," the soldier, who has also turned away from the imposed task of looking at the spectacle of deaths wrought by the state. Lichas wants state and household rule to be reinstated and the woman's law done away with. Things should go in their right places. The body of the widow's husband should go where it belongs—into its tomb (which he calls *monument*). Lichas does not call this male the woman's *husband*, but the head of the household, the father, *pater familias*. The woman has offended against legitimate rule, and should be made an exemplary spectacle, fixed on the cross. Lichas has obviously missed the whole point.

The story itself, whatever Eumolpus' point of view, is not in favor of legal authorities, civic fathers, or exemplary spectacles. Exemplary spectacles, it indicates, are deathly. The story carries warnings, too, about the desire to achieve the status of a work of art, which in a way is Trimalchio's mad desire; Trimalchio not only possesses precious objects containing pictures of death (Medea's sons) but also makes himself into a spectacle of death ("Imagine that I'm dead"). The widow of Ephesus has learned at last to question artistic deathliness and spectacular fixity; she and the soldier do the work of life, not death.

The widow of Ephesus, doubly fictional within the novel, could be taken as the figure for the presiding genius of it. Ephesus is known as a place where female power is in the ascendant. The energy we have seen associated with Asia Minor's ladies seems especially concentrated in Ephesus. Charikleia soothes Thyamis by saying she is from Ephesus (a lie) instead of from Delphi (the truth); the bandit has hopes of her compliance, as evidently women of Ephesus are thought more sexually obliging than most. Ephesian women do not define themselves as sexual victims; they do not see themselves as seduced and abandoned, but as searching for satisfactory solutions. Ephesian women (such as Melitté or Anthia) respect their own sexuality and their right to sexual and other pleasures, including self-determination. Powerfully associated with the Goddess, Ephesus also represents new horizons, possibilities of female power and thus of female judgment. The decision of "the widow of Ephesus" represents a female ordering of things. That reordering involves, significantly, the exposure of the male body.

Throughout Petronius' novel, the male body is "exposed" not only in lust but also in weakness. If the penis is the hero of the story, it is a penis oft in danger, oft in woe. This penis is not "phallic," it is not the penis as tacit figure for the familial, social, and legal potency that rises to *imperium*. The importance of the *Satyricon* does not reside in its representation of homosexuality, still less in any invitation to us to "take sides" as to the value of homosexuality (to do so seems to be missing much of the main point, like Lichas).[4] *Satyricon*'s importance as a literary sexual document resides in its acknowledgment of the weakness of the flesh. It calls the bluff of the masculine ideal, the notion that male sexuality is easy, unspoken, authoritative, and authoritarian. Lichas, evidently cuckolded of yore, wants to restore that ethos. Frightened by the storm at sea, Lichas is anxious that Encolpius and his friends replace the robe and sistrum of Isis that they have stolen; some commentators point out that he is not rewarded for his pious concern about Isis, as he is the only character who dies in the shipwreck (see Walsh, *Roman Novel*, 101). We cannot really say that this indicates the goddess is not important in the novel; we know tantalizingly little about the theft from Isis. Encolpius may be working out his own penance for offending the goddess. But if Encolpius is wrong, that does not mean Lichas is right. Beyond Lichas' superstitious care there is his real offense against the goddess Artemis (and thus Isis) in condemning the justice wrought by the widow of Ephesus; when he says the woman should be stuck up on the cross, he may be sealing his own fate.

The *Satyricon* demystifies potency of all kinds. Rather than placing the narrative within a feminine history (as Chariton's or Heliodorus' novels do), the novel "feminizes" a male narrative, dealing comically and critically with the masculine ethos and the masculine experience. Its greatest successors in this vein include Rabelais' *Pantagruel*, especially in the *Tiers Libre* (1546) and *Quart Libre* (1548), and Laurence Sterne's *Tristram Shandy* (1760–1767). Characters in the *Satyricon* have immediate *rhetorical* access to the masculine ideal. Agamemnon, in the first scene that we possess, bursts into a (parodic) poem: "If a man solicits success in the severe art / And applies his mind to great things, let him first / Refine his character by an exact rule of frugality" (8). The characters all know this sort of stuff. The Augustan masculine ideal is to the *Satyricon*'s characters what her suicidal fidelity was to the Ephesian widow—an artistic but morbid idea ultimately not worth sustaining. Male characters are unable or unwilling to identify themselves with the traditional authoritative masculine image, the one kept up by men of the more serious sort (*severioris notae homines*).

There is a price to be paid for the freedom from the severer imperatives. Male characters in this novel, most particularly Encolpius, experience intermittent breakdowns of role behavior and of body parts. The dominant feeling-tone is not comic libidinousness so much as comic panic. They have claimed a freedom for themselves, which includes a primary freedom from the role of *pater familias* (the role that Trimalchio nervously overacts). But theirs is a freedom to wander and to suffer, oddly akin to the freedom found by the wandering virgins of other fictions.

GOLDEN ASININITY

The most celebrated Roman novelist to be considered here lived in reality the wandering life which Encolpius represents. Apuleius, born c. A.D. 120 in Madaura, an African town in present-day Algeria, made his way by the use of his wits, as did his equally successful contemporary Lucian, born on the banks of the Euphrates. Apuleius, like Lucian, journeyed about and gave what might be called performance lectures. His wanderings also gave him the opportunity to marry a wealthy widow; accused by her relatives of witchcraft he defended himself brilliantly in court, at least if we can trust his version of his speech, the *Apologia*. The works of both Lucian and Apuleius are built upon the customs of verbal performance, and they have a performative quality, though the elaborate stylistic techniques draw upon deliberate archaism and ostentatious ornament. Charles Burney in the eighteenth century snubbingly told his daughter Frances that no one had ever put up a statue to a novelist—but several statues were put up to Apuleius, apparently not to honor him as the author of *The Golden Ass* but to pay tribute to the wonder-working orator.

The opening of this novel is performative and successfully re-creates a turn from spoken to written language: "So—I will stitch together for you various fables in this Milesian conversation, and will soothe your benevolent ears with a sweet whispering—that is, if you do not disdain to look at an Egyptian papyrus written upon with a sharp Nile-reed pen—so that you may marvel at the figures and fortunes of men transformed into other shapes and then in a reciprocal intertwining changed back again. I shall begin. 'Who is he?' You'll have it in a few words" (Apuleius, *The Golden Ass* [*Metamorphoses*], I : 2). The reader who breaks in has a voice which can be "heard" by this narrator, even though the story has shifted in a clause from being told personally to being written by a pen on paper; personal telling, the sweet delightful murmur, is sublimated in the *sharp* art of writing, which has the power to make the reader *see* (rather than hear) wonderful figures and shapes.

The speaker, this writer with the "Nile reed," claims his cradle was the Attica of Hymettos, where he learned the Attic tongue in infancy; then he was trained in spoken Latin of Rome, but without a master, so you will have to pardon him if he makes a slip . . . he is really telling a *Greek* story: *Fabulam Græcanicam incipimus* (4). This "Greek" narrator is *not* the African Apuleius. The jokes about language point to the importance of language as something to be inspected throughout the novel.

The basic story told by this "Greek" narrator (whose name turns out to be Lucius) already existed in at least two other versions.[5] It is often assumed that Apuleius based his book, also entitled *Metamorphoses*, on a longer lost work, the old *Metamorphoses*, by "Lucius of Patras," and not on the extant *Ass* once falsely attributed to Lucian. Apuleius' book makes plain the cross-fertilization of Greek and Latin works. His novel was known in antiquity by its primary title, *Metamorphoses*, but it was also known as the *Asinus Aureus* (or *Golden Ass*); it is thus referred to by St. Augustine (in *De Civitate Dei*, XVIII : 18), who says that Apuleius gave it that title.[6] The primary tale (*Metamorphoses*), the statements regarding the "Greek" narrator, and the Greekness of the tale can be taken as a comic tribute to a Greek *Metamorphoses* now lost to us. Apuleius may even have expected his readers to know the earlier novel and thus to be able to appreciate his different rendition of the same material.

The basic "Ass-story" story concerns, in brief, a hero (named "Lucius" in all the versions) who is devoured by curiosity about witchcraft. Coming to Hypata in Thessaly, a city where witchcraft is practiced, Lucius makes love to his host's servant-girl, not just for pleasure but primarily in order to get her to help him observe her mistress's acts of witchcraft. The servant is very unwilling, and tries to dissuade him, but with her assistance the hero does eventually watch the witch-woman change herself into a bird. Consumed with desire to do likewise, he makes the girl give him the magic unguent—but alas! he applies the wrong vanishing cream, and finds himself transformed into an ass. He can be cured, the maid tells him, by eating roses, but his own impatience and the vicissitudes of fortune prevent his obtaining this cure. As an ass, but retaining the mind, sensibilities, and even the tastes of man, the poor Lucius is made to endure the service of various hard masters, with much buffeting and blows. His asinine experiences improve a little when some of his human characteristics are manifest, especially his ability to eat human food and to make love to a human woman. In *The Ass* the last master has the ass and the woman sent to the arena merely to show off; luckily, rose petals are strewn about this couch, and Lucius can eat them and return to his proper shape.

In Apuleius' tale the ending is very different; the ass is to be the executioner of a woman in the arena, torturing her by rogering her before she (and probably he too) must be torn by wild beasts. Deeply unwilling, the ass escapes this cruel and degrading show, and is rescued by Isis, who transforms him back into his own shape. In gratitude, this Lucius becomes a devotee of the goddess, and then a priest of Osiris.

The Ass is insouciant; Apuleius' *Metamorphoses* is not. What is a somewhat superficial—if highly entertaining—story in the work once attributed to Lucian is here a philosophical tale—or at least teases us with that possibility. We have not only Lucius the ass as narrator but a multitude of narrators. The most notable (and longwinded) of these other narrators is the old woman in the bandit's cave. Lucius, now the ass of the bandits who stole him, overhears the bandits' housekeeper comforting the distraught abducted bride, Charité. The housekeeper's story, the noble tale of Psyche and Cupid, runs from Books IV to VI of the novel. By placing this tale so centrally and making it so extensive. Apuleius poses an important riddle to the reader, indicating unmistakably that narrative demands interpretation. The story that the old woman tells, although at its first level simply a tale with a happy ending to cheer Charité up after her trials, is a story posing the problems of the soul's desire and its destiny. That this tale also concerns curiosity (in Psyche's desire to look upon her husband against his command) is sufficient in itself to alert us to possible connections between this fable and the main story of Lucius. Like Psyche, Lucius suffers after trying to gaze upon what he should not. He too is lonely and much-tried. A female deity—Fortuna—seems to be against him, as Venus is against Psyche. Like Psyche, he cannot fulfill the task that would set him free (eating roses) and must, in the end, be rescued by a female deity.

To the Platonist, the site of the storytelling is itself significant; the old woman tells this *fabula* in the cave—the abode of unknowing in Plato's *Republic*. In this darkness Charité (whose name means grace) and the metamorphosed ass are given glimpses of a higher light—a light superior to the light offered by the sexy maid Photis (whose name means light), or that of the torch that the disobedient Psyche brought to her marriage bed.

The old woman's story should perhaps cheer us up. It has a happy ending—the wedding in heaven, the feast celebrating the eternal union of Psyche and Cupid. Almost immediately the story seems to be fulfilled, as Charité's bridegroom, disguising himself as a bandit, rescues her (and thus the ass) in a stirring sequence of clever ruses and high-spirited action. Our belief in poetic justice is

soon overthrown, however, for the happy ending of Charité and her husband is
not the ending of their story. A jealous rival compasses the death of the young
husband and then woos Charité. In revenge upon her husband's murderer, Charité pierces both of his eyes with her sharp hairpin and then kills herself with her
husband's sword so she falls upon his grave. Charité turns out to be an extraordinary—and violent—heroine of chastity; bloody and resolute, she breathes
forth her "manly soul" (*perefflavit animam virilem*; II : 84).[7] Whether this (certainly
not happy) ending of Charité's story is a satisfactory response to the violence
around her we may wonder.

The stories after the Cupid-and-Psyche narrative become darker and more
grotesque. Murders and suicides abound; brutal or stupid husbands and faithless
or even murderous wives turn up in an alarming string of interwoven narratives,
including another version of the story of the lustful stepmother, a variant, like
Knemon's tale, of the story of Phaedra and Hippolytus. Such narratives contradict
the happy vision of the divine wedding, the *hieros gamos* of Book VI. Apuleius
promised us in his first sentence a "Milesian conversation," an interweaving texture of Milesian tales. Apuleius deploys the Milesian tales with great skill in the
Book IX, and they are narrated with energy—such as, for instance, the story of
the adulterous wife and the tub. Caught entertaining her lover by her husband,
the woman pretends she has found a purchaser for the great tub, and that her
lover (whom she hid under the tub) was merely inspecting it. The lover, forced
by the wife to part with a large sum of money for the tub, complains in *double
entendre* that the vessel is old and cracked and dirty. The husband goes under the
tub to clean it, while the good wife and her companion take their pleasure on the
bottom of the tub, over the ignorant husband's head (II : 132–136).

The ass not only overhears these stories but also participates in one; he is
himself the instrument of justice to reveal his mistress's crimes. When the baker's
wife is hiding her adulterer, Lucius as ass steps on the man's fingers, so the baker
discovers both hiding place and man. The husband then punishes this adulterer,
first by sodomizing him all night and then at dawn by beating him on the buttocks
like a young child (II : 174–178) The baker finishes by announcing to his wife
that he is divorcing her, and telling her to get out of the house instantly. The
cumulative effect of these numerous interwoven tales (both those reported in the
ass's hearing and those viewed by him) is to make the world of human business
and human sexuality seem more and more troubled.

Lucius the ass knows all these disturbing events because his curiosity continues unabated. He very comically consoles himself by comparing himself with
Odysseus: "Not unworthily has the divine author of the first poetry among the
Greeks, desirous to demonstrate the highest manly prudence, sung the man who
attained the highest virtues through visiting many cities and knowing various
peoples. Therefore I have remembered and am thankfully grateful to my ass, because, concealed under his covering, I was exercised in various fortunes, and so
the ass repaid me—though I was not so prudent—with a good deal of knowledge" (II : 148–150).

Lucius is a ridiculous Odysseus, and this is a ludicrous *solacium*. He is certainly less prudent than Odysseus. As he admits, he has no *prudentia* either at the
beginning or in his asinine form, despite his making-the-best-of-things gratitude

to "my ass" (*asino meo*). This consolation exhibits Lucius' desire to separate him-self from "my ass" as from an entirely other entity, but the more he tries this, the less likely the reader is to credit such separation, and the more likely to identify him with his assy shape.

The assy shape has its comic and sympathetic side. Nothing is more com-mon than the ass in the daily economy of much of the world, even now. Small trotting asses laden with enormous bundles are still a feature of Greek and Turk-ish life; "Ah, my friend," said my Turkish driver nodding jovially when we passed a donkey on the road, showing the persistence of a comic sense of affinity with this lowly, stubborn, and overloaded beast. A mosaic in the Mosaic Museum of Istanbul shows a defiant ass shaking off its bundles of faggots and kicking its mas-ter energetically. This beast is very like Lucius-as-ass losing his temper (as he does several times), and could serve as an illustration to the story. Stubbornness, re-sentment, and anger—as well as lust—these assy qualities are shared by many of the human beings Lucius-as-ass encounters.

In his asinine identity he exemplifies, if more innocently than the forni-cators or swindlers he comes upon, the weakness of human nature. He might be taken as illustrating everything that Saint Paul means by "the flesh" (*sarx*), e.g., "I know that nothing good [*agathon*] dwells in me, that is, in my flesh [*en tēi sarki*]" (Romans 7:18). The ass seems a symbol of the base nature of *sarx*, a rep-resentative of carnal will. This may be (neo)Platonically signified by Lucius' loss of his white horse, Candidus, who is restored to him after purification. The white horse recalls Plato's fable in the *Phaedrus* describing the soul as a charioteer with two horses: one is white in color, good (*agathos*) and noble; the other is thick, black and ugly, stubborn and hubristic. Reason the charioteer can control the noble will, but the flesh always resists (*Phaedrus*, 74). Plato's base horse has comi-cally slipped in Apuleius' fable, demoted from horse to ass. Yet Apuleius' story is by no means a dry fable of the loss of reason and the descent into a baser self. Like the other novels, *Metamorphoses* seems to search out and question both social structures and psychological formulas. The pain it conveys with all its comedy is very real.

One of the chief sources of pain in *The Golden Ass* seems to be masculinity itself, as a social-sexual construct or idea. As John J. Winkler notes, the ass is "a preeminently phallic animal." Lucius ironically represents and *is* the penis—ironically because in his ass form he is usually averse to the aggressive penile pleasures that others assume he both has and wants more of (see Winkler, *Auctor & Actor*, 174). It was an ancient joke that women would want a man with a virile member as large as an ass's—or failing that, the ass itself; Juvenal lays this charge against Roman matrons who worship foreign deities (like Isis) in all-female get-togethers (*Satire* VI, lines 314–334). The lady of Corinth in Apuleius' story acts out this fantasy, casting him on her bed of down and murmuring sweet words ("'I love' and 'I desire' and 'I want only thee'")—disturbing words because their use supposes a human "thou" as partner. The modest if not unwilling ass is afraid (like Daphnis) that he will hurt her, but she is fearless and insatiable, and (pre-posterously) they pass a night of joy. The archetypal story of the beautiful lady falling in love (or in lust) with an ass is also behind the story of Titania's sudden love for that other good-tempered ass Bully Bottom, in *A Midsummer Night's*

Dream. Such an ass-story is a humiliation not only for women but also for men; it expresses a male fear of being debased into the penis, measured only by the penis. Only as ass, embodied penis, might a male be sure of not being found wanting.

Lucius is reduced to being a penis, visibly representing what society hides. Lucius-as-ass makes explicit the painfully humble fleshly reality of the real male member, as distinct from its archetypal potent Form as phallus. Lucius is never aggressive—even when he is making love to Photis, she is the dominant partner and commands him until he is exhausted. The robbers of the cave threaten a hideous punishment to the ass and to Charité for escaping—Charité will be sewn up in the eviscerated ass's belly, and they will be left to die together in the tormenting heat. Lucius, designated an instrument of death, has pity for Charité as well as himself. But he is also designated an instrument of death when he is supposed to fuck the multiple murderess in the Corinthian arena—though on that occasion he does not want to pollute his body and his modesty with such a woman.

Society accounts the penis lethal and aggressive, base and destructive. It is made an instrument of the law—literally so, in the story's Corinth. Lucius' problems resemble the problem of Daphnis, when he was told by that she-wolf who seduced him that his entry into Chloé would hurt the girl. *Daphnis and Chloé* does not directly solve the problem raised, the problem of finding the unphallic, noninjurious use of the penis, escaping the imputation of its greed and cruelty. In Apuleius' novel the loss of the penis itself is directly threatened at one point, where a shepherd argues that the best way to deal with this troublesome beast is to castrate him: "I know not only many tame asses, but really even the fiercest stallions laboring under too much lust [*nimio libidinis*], but if they are treated with a bit of castration, once cut and gelded, they have been rendered gentle and mild, not unmanageable, bearing burdens and patiently submitting to other service" (II : 44–46).

This strongly resembles Gulliver's advice to the Houyhnhnms about the treatment of the Yahoos. The shepherd, in pseudokindness, speaks as if the *libido* itself were a burden under which the animal labors, an oppressive source of suffering that can kindly be removed. This solution impotent Encolpius momentarily proposed to apply to himself. The shepherd's answer to the problem of libido is (like Gulliver's) technologically correct (we *do* use such force on hapless animals), but it is not (Origen to the contrary) the answer for the human male. The castrated crew who serve the Syrian Goddess exhibit to the disgusted Lucius the failings of such an answer; renouncing physical masculinity is not a road to spiritual enlightenment, nor does it even truly modify unruly libido.

The world that this mock-Odysseus sees is a world comically caught up in repetitive libidinousness. Lucius transferred his libidinous desire to the wish to become a bird—to fly—to rise above the human condition, whereas he is destined to sink below it. The poor mistaken pilgrim is stuck at the outset with a lack of self-knowledge and an inability to find or face up to his identity. This inability is fully illustrated in the pretransformation part of the story, including the inset narratives. One of the important inset tales is that told in Book II at the banquet of that powerful rich lady Byrrhena, in whose atrium stands the warning statue of Diana and Actaeon, which Lucius admires without heeding.

Byrrhena begs her guest Thelyphron, "tell your story with your usual obligingness" (I:98); the story (*tuam fabulam*) is evidently already known. Thelyphron then relates how as a young man he came to Larissa in Thessaly (famous for its witches). He takes on the job of watching a corpse overnight; the grieving widow and her friends hire him to ensure that witches do not harm the body. Waking at cock crow, after a deep sleep, he is relieved to find the corpse unmolested. But when the funeral comes along the street, an old man complains that the corpse was a victim of murder and summons an Egyptian priest to rouse the dead man. The corpse not only confirms the charge (his adulterous wife poisoned him) but adds proof. The witches, the corpse says, cast the corpse-watcher into a sound sleep. Then they began to call the dead man by name, but it was Thelyphron who answered, because he had the same name. The watcher answered their call, and the witches cut off his nose and ears—a disfigurement intended for the corpse. They made him ears and nose of wax and fitted them on him. Astonished, Thelyphron feels his face and ears—and his nose and ears fall off! So from that time he has always had to cover up his ears with his long hair and his face with a cloth (I:98–120).

The story becomes more eerie when Thelyphron's position as narrator passes (within his story) to the dead husband, the corpse who is his mirror. Which of them is a dead man? What sort of identity does Thelyphron have if he can answer to a corpse's name and permit the plastic (or wax) surgery upon his members without noticing? Certainly, masculinity is under threat in this tale, comically castrated. Without self-knowledge enough even to know he was wounded, Thelyphron belongs to the novel's tribe of simpletons, among whom Lucius and even Psyche must be numbered.

What are we to make of Thelyphron's story? If we take it at its simplest level, it reflects a fear of marriage; do not marry or your wife will not only kill you but try to disfigure you, emasculate even your memory—women are powerful witches. But if Thelyphron's tale is to be taken as sheer fiction (and the tip-off is the gale of hearty laughter at Byrrhena's table) the victim is really gullible Lucius. His gullibility indicates that *we* should look at Thelyphron's tale as a clever story (*fabula*), and look for the significance of it in relation to the Lucius-themes.

Thelyphron's supposed experience is a "metamorphosis" parallel to the one about to afflict the imprudent hero. The images in Thelyphron's tale point to a divided and maimed masculine self—echoing the first tale told in the book, the witch story told by Aristomenes of the death of his un-Socratic friend Socrates, who literally did not know he was already dead after the witches cut his throat. Thelyphron's story confronts us with a divided masculine self, one half dead (or capable only of life-in-death), the other half unconsciously dismembered and disintegrated. The men in his *fabula*, faced with the challenge of keeping self together, sustaining an identity, do not fare very well. Lucius' own implication in the failure of Thelyphron is indicated in the fact that he immediately makes himself stunningly ludicrous.

Coming back to his host Milo's house after the party, Lucius sees three great strong men battering away at the door. Bravely, Lucius takes out his gallant sword and kills them all. The next day the citizens hale him out of bed and put him on trial for these homicides. Lucius is made to unveil the corpses of his "victims." He draws back the cloth—and "What a wonder! What a sudden change of my fortunes!" (*Quod monstrum! Quae fortunarum mearum repentina mutatio!*, I : 142). The three "men" are three great skins (i.e., bottles) inflated, but injured in various places where he wounded the "thieves." The whole assembly bursts out laughing—and Lucius is informed that he has just acted a special part in their Festival of Laughter. The transformation of the wineskins into the appearance of men was caused by the witch, Milo's wife, making a little mistake in her magic. But the city took advantage of this metamorphosis to make Lucius into a public *spectacle*. He has made himself into a spectacular simpleton. The mock-Dionysiac encounter is far from proving his manhood. This famous episode in Apuleius' novel lies behind Don Quixote's Battle with the Wine Skins, as Bakhtin and others have recognized (see *Don Quijote*, Part I, Chap. 35).[8]

The endeavors to represent masculinity bring on failure. Masculinity is a myth, a fable, a subject of laughter. One begins to notice what might be called the "hermaphroditic strain" in Apuleius' novel; if actual hermaphrodites, like the Syrian priests, are condemned, gender characteristics are constantly transposed. Charité in her heroic suicide dies babbling incomprehensible statements (which makes her like a child—or woman), but she breathed forth her "manly soul". . . Thelyphron's name is Greek for "female understanding" or "womanly spirit"— the *thēlē* part meaning very specifically "the nipple of the breast." Winkler, who points out that Thelyphron's name can be taken as meaning "female *animus*," suggests—but refuses to go into—the question "whether 'female *animus*' suggests *psyche* or Psyche, who also takes on a 'masculine *animus*'" (*Auctor & Actor*, 115). Thelyphron—female mind or spirit—or rather the two Thelyphrons (the mutilated and the dead) indicate something about assuming the feminine role. In Book IV the narrative itself assumes the female role—the female mind and soul— in the story told by one woman to another woman about a third woman. At that point the novel goes into its "feminine" mode, from which it never quite departs afterwards.

Psyche's story, a story inherited by Apuleius, though in his telling of it he has made it his own, is peculiarly elaborated and intense; yet it has the wide sky of the mythological realm, not the narrow focus of crowded small rooms that the novel associates with panic and witchcraft. Interpreters of the novel have often wanted to see in this telling of the story of Psyche a tale about the soul and its desire for union with the eternal Good. Other things can be said of it. Winkler points out that it works a bit like a detective story. We live the first part of the story through Psyche's ignorance: "the tale is told (mainly) from her point of view" (*Auctor*, 90). We are enchanted first by the mystery, then by the need to arrive at some means of reuniting the parted lovers, Cupid and Psyche. Psyche, a heroine of chastity, cannot pass all the tests set by Venus; what must happen is a change in the attitude of Venus herself, and a new relation between the two women. (Cupid may be the lover, but this is a mother-in-law story.)

The Cupid and Psyche story indeed teases us with the possibilities of allegory, and it has received allegorical interpretations. Fulgentius the mythographer offers a partial but detailed reading in his *Mythologies*. To this North African Christian of the evening of antiquity, Psyche is visibly the soul. Her two sisters are the flesh and the will. Venus (lust) envies the spirit and sends greed (*cupiditatem*) to it, but greed (or desire) can be to good as well as bad, and it unites itself with Psyche. Flesh and will compel her to learn the pleasure of greed, and the lamp is her hot desire, which spills out as hot sin (*Fulgentius the Mythographer*, trans. Whitbread, 88–90). It can readily be seen that Fulgentius' interpretation requires the complete sacrifice of Venus and all the goddesses. Not only so, but it requires the abjection of lovely Cupid into desire/greed/sin. There is no room here for any balance of male and female principles. All the powers that surround the soul are bad.

Among the many commentaries is a modern one, Erich Neumann's *Amor and Psyche: The Psychic Development of the Feminine* (originally published as *Amor und Psyche, mit einem Kommentar von Erich Neumann: Ein Betrag zur seelischen Entwicklung des Weiblichen* [1952]). Neumann, who takes the story seriously as a myth having psychological applicability within a Jungian framework, wavers between admiration for the humane implications of the myth and misogyny of the old-fashioned (or 1950s) kind. Narcissism is a phase "which in the masculine development is superseded" but is "permanently maintained in the woman" (trans. Manheim, 123). What Neumann apparently resists, in his insistence that the Psyche story offers a paradigm only of the development of the lowly *female* identity, is the truly startling implication of Apuleius' narrative: that the story of Psyche is universal, and thus that *general human experience can be universalized as female*. Instead of taking male experience as the norm, the benevolent or scrupulous reader, soothed by the sweet whisper that melts into the writing of the Niltoic reed, is invited to identify himself—or herself—with the female experience. The soul (*anima* or *psyche*) is known—known to itself—as "female." For Fulgentius, that was still possible. For Neumann, one feels, it would be a horror for the man to be identified with the female personification—a false impersonation.

In Book XI of Apuleius' novel, Lucius the ass, the poor wandering penis imprisoned in an awkward and risible flesh, is freed at last by the female power. Escaped from the noise and show of the arena at Corinth to a quiet beach, the ass falls asleep. He wakens to see the moon shining bright, as if she had emerged from the sea-waves. Then he remembers that this is the time when the goddess has most power and majesty, "all human things being entirely governed by her providence" (*resque prorsus humanas ipsius regi providentia*, II: 290). He plunges into the sea to purify himself, and then prays to the "Queen of Heaven" (*Regina caeli*) by whatever name she may be called—Ceres, Venus, Artemis, Prosperpina. His prayers are answered. From the midst of the sea arises the divine face, "venerated by the gods" (*venerandos diis*, 294). Then is seen the entire grand figure of the goddess, with her flowing hair, a light like the moon in the center of her forehead. Her vestments are multicolored, but her cloak is black; through it the stars can be seen. In her right hand she holds the sistrum and in her left a chalice of gold, with an asp upon the handle. The divinity speaks to Lucius, addressing him by name, and proclaiming her own identity:

> "I am [she proclaims] the parent of all things in nature, the mistress of elements, the first offspring of time, chief of divine powers [*summa numinum*], the queen of all the shades, the first of the heavenly powers, the one form and face of all gods and goddesses [*deorum dearumque*

facies uniformis]; I dispose with my command the luminaries of the highest heavens, the healthful blasts of the sea, the lamentable silences of the infernal regions; whose one divinity in multiform shapes, by various rites and by many names is adored throughout the whole world [*cuius numen unicum multiformi specie, ritu vario, nomine multiiugo totus veneratur orbis*]." (II : 296–298)

Lucius was right, evidently, to pray to her by the different names. What might be called "the new goddess theology" promotes the essential unity of all representations of female divinity. The Goddess explains that she is known to the Phrygians as Mother of the Gods; to the Athenians, Cecropian Minerva (i.e., Athena); to the Cyprians, Paphian Venus; . . . to the Eleusinians, she is Ceres; to some she is Juno, to others Bellona, Hecate, Rhamnusia (i.e., Nemesis). But the Ethiopians and Egyptians "call me by my true name, Queen Isis" (*appellant vero nomine reginam Isidem*, 300). The address to Isis and Isis' own speech reflect liturgies of Isis. The most complete religious aretology or statement of Isis' powers begins, "I am Isis, the ruler of all lands." [9]

That poor Lucius' absurd Odyssey has come to an end is signified by his coming to the Goddess and undertaking a spiritual pilgrimage to give meaning to the shifting world of mere experience, the bundle of knowings that the beaten-up ass acquired. As *ass*, James Tatum points out, Lucius is particularly antipathetic to Isis. Isis does not allude to Lucius specifically as "ass" but only generally as "monster" (*belua*). The ass-shape, or ass with a man's head, is firmly associated in Egyptian mythology and graphic arts with the figure of Seth, the enemy of Isis and slayer of Osiris, "the master of evil changes" (Tatum, *Apuleius*, 45). From falling into the power of the diabolical divinity who makes him see in *Tyche*-Fortuna only blind chance, Lucius is rescued, so that, as the priest tells him, he must now see himself in the guardianship of *Fortuna videns*, "sighted Fortune," the opposite of blind Fortune (*In tutelam iam receptus es Fortunae, sed videntis*, II : 320).

The goddess does not change Lucius' form right away, but commands him to join the great procession in her worship. The festival being celebrated in Corinth is the *Navigium Isidis*, the Journey of Isis. Reinhold Merkelbach has summarized the evidence relating to this festival's observances, and the symbols within it, relating it to the procession in Apuleius' novel. The Voyage of Isis entails the journey of the worshippers and celebrants, some in costume, some bearing holy objects, to the seashore, where a carefully decorated boat, the Ship of Isis, will weigh anchor and set sail. [10] In participating in the *Navigium* celebration, Lucius, the most landbound of all the ancient novel's characters, symbolically participates in the sea-journey that is the literal lot of so many heroes and heroines. (And he has already washed himself in the deep salt sea.) This festival comes from Egypt, where the water of the Navigium is the Nile. In the depths of Greece, in Corinth, the character is transported through symbolism to Egypt, becomes a wanderer through an Egyptian holy landscape. The wanderings of Kleitophon and Leukippé, and the journey of Charikleia and Theagenes, take them literally to Egypt, and their novels also deal with the celebrations of the Nile and of Isis. That fertilizing ground, that Nile mud of reeds, is theirs. Lucius, who seems so often to life in a world of reflected representations, gains relief in participating in the holy

"Matter of Egypt" without literally leaving the Greece where he dwells. Yet he is transformed.

The goddess told him that he must join the procession in which the priest will carry a garland of roses; and he must eat them. She further adds that he must give the rest of his life in her service; after death he will see her light shining in Hades. If he merits her divine help by tenacious chastity (*tenacibus castimoniis*, 304) she may prolong his life beyond the Fates' appointed time. Lucius of course does exactly as the goddess tells him. He narrates with great excitement the wonderful procession, and his happy retransformation.

Lucius has the support and counsel of two priests of Isis during his development of a new life. These priests (the one in the procession and the later spiritual advisor, oddly named Mithras) may remind us of that other priest of Isis, wise Kalasiris in the *Aithiopika*, as well as of the Egyptian priest who appeared in Thelyphron's tale, to rouse the dead man and make him speak. Lucius becomes a priest himself, tonsured and wearing a linen robe. Achieving the higher initiation, he becomes a priest of Osiris, and Osiris too appears to him in a dream, telling him that he will now become a very successful pleader in his court. And so the novel ends, with Lucius, who once valued hair, and then had been given too much of it (growing monstrous hairy about the face) going about openly with shaven head; "I was going about rejoicing"—*gaudens obibam*—the last words of the novel. John Winkler has commented upon the peculiarity of ending a large work with a word in an imperfect tense, "I was going about," and suggests it indicates "the incompleteness of the end '" (*Auctor*, 224). Lucius' story may not be really over.

The ending of the novel is as puzzling as the rest of the story. We may object to seeing our anti-hero turned into this modest monklike person, a sort of antique equivalent of a modern Western follower of Hare Krishna. This is the *truly* unexpected example of the figures and fortunes of men changed into other images. We should notice that Lucius makes a decided choice in opting out of the society he knew both before and during his asshood. Like Thekla, he lights out for spiritual territory, and he is still journeying (the last word indicates that he is in *motion*.) The chastity that Lucius chooses is not just a chastity of rejection—it is a relational chastity of a kind, for it arises from his relation to Isis. In the sections immediately before the crisis that brings on the vision of the Goddess, the ass-Lucius has been reveling in sensual pleasure. The ascetic response seems a counterbalance. Lucius has been tried through luxury—as were Charikleia and Theagenes in Arsaké's palace—as well as being tried through deprivation, enslavement, and blows. Lucius, unlike Heliodorus' characters, succumbs to practically every temptation. He comforts us in assuring us that, however foolish and stupid we may be, we may still hope to experience a transformation into a higher shape. Transformation is part of the experience of living. Charikleia (like Anthia and Leukippé) was metamorphosed into a slave, unrecognizable to her lover, as well as being transfigured by the divine light that hovers about her on the pyre.

The irony of the indeterminate and incomplete ending that Winkler notes points out to the reader that the story has developments but no final *telos*. Lucius is still in process of becoming. But why should a goddess-theology lead to Aristotelian climaxes? The aesthetic of Isis demands a kind of overriding of ending.

Metamorphosis is the business of living—so all these novels in their various ways tell us. *Satyricon* too might have been called *Metamorphoses*, for the characters change social "figure" and even physical appearance—as for instance when they try on golden wigs. It is not only characters who metamorphose, but also the divine. The vision of divinity alters. This is clearest in *The Golden Ass*, where Lucius complains of Fortuna and is led to understand *providentia*; but it is quite clear in the (presumably earlier) novel by Chariton, in which *Tychē* becomes identified with Aphrodite. At the end of *Aithiopika* the black gymnosophists endeavor to instruct Hydaspes and his court in a higher vision of the divine—in the only novel where that metamorphosis is made an overtly political matter. At the very end of Apuleius' novel we may be puzzled by the sudden if unemphatic swerve of Lucius towards Osiris, since the vision of Isis has had so great an impact not only on Lucius but also on the reader. Here, as at the ending of Heliodorus' novel, we seem to have an attempt to balance the worship of male and female divinities, as at the end of Heliodorus' novel the central characters are to serve Helios and Selene, Sun and Moon—male and female. Both novels seem to be working out the achievement of a higher harmony between complementary principles, a harmony also suggested in the story of Cupid and Psyche.

The problem in both *Metamorphoses* and *Aithiopika* (granted their many differences) seems to be how to reintegrate the masculine with the feminine after the *feminine* power has been made manifest. Once freedom has been defined—in contradistinction to phallic law and order—in terms of feminine heroism (Charikleia) and feminine *numen* (Isis), how do we reintegrate the masculine? One way of achieving integration is in storytelling itself. Knemon eggs Kalasiris on to tell his tale with the remark that "Dionysius likes stories." Presumably Isis also likes stories; her unwitting handmaid, the bandits' housekeeper, tells the prophetic story of Psyche that foreshadows what Isis has to say. Kalasiris and the bandits' servant, however, both die within the novels in which they appear; the role of story-maker or narrator is evidently fraught with peril.

▶┼◀▶┄○┄◀▶┼◀

The Novelistic Nature of Ancient Prose Fiction: Character, Dialogue, Setting, Images

▶┼◀▶┄○┄◀▶┼◀

What were we to do, wretched men shut up in a new kind of labyrinth?
—Petronius, *Satyricon*

"We should never have left Miletus!"
—Dionysios, *Chaireas and Kallirrhoé*

"I am an example . . . for I have suffered outrageously in the experience of love."
—Kleitophon, *Leukippé and Kleitophon*

She had a small forehead and her hair curled away from it, her brows ran to the edge of her cheekbones and almost met together over her eyes.
—Encolpius on Circe in *Satyricon*

▶┼◀▶┄○┄◀▶┼◀

*B*y this point we have become familiar with the stories of the major works of prose fiction that appeared during the time of the Roman Empire. Are these works "novelistic"—are they "really novels"? Such a question conceals a belief that the questioner already knows what constitutes a "novel," that the qualifications that admit a work to the genre are universally clear and well-defined. Such clarity does not really exist. The "general reader" relies on definitions of the novel carved out during the nineteenth century. Practitioners of the novel at the end of the twentieth century are much less likely to hold themselves bound to the practices and criteria that clearly marked a novel as a novel in the late nineteenth century—the works of Isabel Allende or Gabriel García Márquez or Douglas Adams can convince us of that fact. Yet, in order to persuade readers to accept the novels of antiquity, not as exotic curios but as part of our literary heritage, belonging on our shelves as much as, say, *Middlemarch* or *Der Zauberberg*, it would be only polite and politic to show as many genuine connections as possible with "the Novel" that we all thought we knew until the day before yesterday.

CHARACTER AND CHARACTERIZATION IN THE ANCIENT NOVEL

When I tell any general reader that I am working on the ancient novels and that there are such things as novels in antiquity, I find that one of the very first responses is, "Real novels? With *characters*?" We have been particularly trained by the nineteenth-century novel to define and respond to a concept of *character*. Novels are named after characters: Emma, Eugénie Grandet, Madame Bovary.

George Eliot may be taken as supplying a sort of ideal representation of "character" in the nineteenth-century sense with personages such as Tertius Lydgate and Dorothea Brooke. "Character" should be, as E. M. Forster was to put it so succinctly, "round," that is, given psychological depth and inwardness as well as being endowed with a capacity to participate in external and social action within a recognizable society. According to this criterion, authors like Dickens or the Thackeray of *Vanity Fair* do not come off very well. Dickens, Forster rather contemptuously thought, produced only "flat" characters.[1]

A complicating factor in any concept of the "roundness" of characters must lie in the fact that notions of "inner life" and self vary enormously from one era to another. Ruth Padel in *In and Out of the Mind* (1992) points out that antique Greek ideas of thought and feeling are expressed in highly visceral terms. Comprehension and emotion are the work of the heart, liver, or guts—or of *phrēn*, meaning midriff, lungs, and what we call "mind." A person who is wise and prudent, *sōphrōn*, has "a safe-*phrēn*" (Padel, *In and Out*, 23). Anxiety and indecision, as well as jealousy or rage, happen inside a highly active and vulnerable body with its heaving invisible organs; Padel suggests that Greek tragedy images these wild and dark parts, these receptive and reactive "innards," as feminine, leading to "a female model of mind" (112). Not only philosophers like the Stoics but civic leaders also represented to males the advisability of acquiring impassive control, avoiding subjection to such feminine parts or selves. Even so, to have access to inner thought, to cogitate and ruminate, is to have contact with the passionate viscera. Such a psychic model had many justifications, and offered many excitements; it also tended towards a perception of consciousness as fragmented, a perception that now may be more acceptable than it used to be. "It may be that consciousness is simply the kind of thing that is fragmented, and that the twentieth century is peculiarly able to perceive this as a truth" (*In and Out*, 46).

We may expect characters in Late Antique novels, even while possessing a strong idea of the value of the individual, to possess—and to represent also—an insight into fragmentation. The state of fragmentation is most vividly rendered in the condition of Lucius, both a "self" and alienated from his "self" as assy form. But there is also Kallirrhoé ventriloquizing her husband's portrait *on* her stomach and the baby *in* it. Cyrus in Xenophon's *Cyropaedia* represents avoidance of fragmentation above all other characters in ancient novels—unlike the tormented Alexander of the *Historia Alexandri*. But if Cyrus avoids passion and love, and hence fragmentation, his henchman Araspes is not so lucky. Araspes, who acts in the narrative as Cyrus' inferior and self-deluding *alter ego*, is trapped by "the wicked sophist Love" (Stoneman trans., *The Education of Cyrus*, 175). Araspes self-hatingly believes he must have two souls: one beautiful and one bad. The emotional side of himself, the part susceptible to the charms of a woman, is the "bad" soul; Araspes can excuse himself only on the supposition of tense and permanent self-division. Cyrus, in contrast, has transcended any such shameful need to suppose division within. Cyrus stands as a model of (impossible) integration, rather like the future Stoic Man, *in se ipso totus, teres atque rotundus*, as Horace satirically puts it (*Satires* II, vii, line 86): "entire within himself, polished smooth and round as a ball"—independent, unified, and self-absorbed. There is no place in the *Cyropaedia* for the recognition that suffuses the *Alexander Romance*—that the conqueror's desire of conquest is a form of erotic enslavement and an expression of the irrational.

We are at present arriving at a concept of "self" much less unified than that designed by the nineteenth century, with its models of organic maturation into wholeness; psychological work on multiple personality disorder begins to pose new possibilities for imaging the self. In developing new psychological images, ancient novels may prove helpful assistants. Characters in novels of the twenty-first century will not be just like characters in nineteenth-century novels, and we may find ancient "characters" much more congenial when we leave off setting them against one template. The belief in—or desire for—various kinds of novelistic "characters" depends on different religious and philosophical sets of beliefs about the nature of human subjectivity. Such beliefs are always undergoing shifts. Somewhat less addicted than hitherto to the conscientiously reflective and inwardly social personage as offering the only model, we still think (rightly) the "characters" of George Eliot and Henry James very fine. But we now accept with equanimity on certain occasions (i.e., in a particular reading experience) a heroine with green hair, or webbed feet, or a murder victim who keeps trying to talk on the telephone after he has been killed. We are less in the thrall of physical or psychological "realism."

At the same time, it is a mistake to think the nineteenth-century writers themselves always worked according to one template. Flaubert and Dickens offer very different kinds of "characters"—not only different from each other's, but differing within their own works, from novel to novel. In the nineteenth century a novelist was required to keep up a show of belief in individual psychological identity both free and shaped by pressure of social circumstances. That was a tall order, and novelists often escaped from it, creating characters who are slyly transcendent, or who form themselves into emblems (Milly Theale) or assume a mythic power even while reflecting in themselves apparently only a set of social productions (like Ebenezer Scrooge). "Characters," even in the Victorian novel, are often emblems, icons, or personifications.

Forster's "round" characters really stand for a late nineteenth-century idea of personality as having an essence once the idea of the "soul" was discounted. It is easier to discount the soul in theory than in practice. (George Eliot's works, for instance, "save the appearances" of the soul.) The first meaning of the very word "character" is sign, mark, or stamp; it comes from the Greek word for an instrument that cuts letters or signs, that engraves. The "character" is just a sign. The import of this sign in a novel is the response(s) it can arouse in the reader. In order for the writer to obtain response, some matters must be conventional, readily understood.

Like modern writers, ancient novelists had a store of stock "types" to draw on. Certain professions or activities were thought to coincide with certain qualities—cf. the modern "absent-minded professor." This particular type had its equivalent in the *scholasticus*, the learned fool, subject of many jokes, as Winkler reminds us, suggesting that Lucius has affinities with this type from the jokebooks and low mimes (*Auctor*, 160–163). Certain cities reflected certain qualities on their citizens, for instance Sybaris (vanished by 510 B.C.), which became the notorious—if imaginary—home of outrageous luxury; Sophie Trenkner lists the comic anecdotes of *Sybaritika* (*The Greek Novella*, 175–177). A Sybarite joke appears in *Chaireas and Kallirrhoé*; Theron pretends he bought Kallirrhoé from a Sybarite woman—hence she's a luxury item (68). Popular anecdotes and types, though they may indeed inculcate prejudice, at the same time educate tellers and hearers in the comic possibilities of human behavior, making it possible for them to comprehend more sophisticated material. There is no period of novel-writing in which stock types (of nationality, profession, physique) are not employed by novelists. We have in fact always accepted what Forster calls "flat" characters in literature, especially in the case of so-called minor characters, and in certain modes such as satire. We do not need "round" characters in *The Bonfire of the Vanities* (1987), nor in Boccaccio's story of Fra Cipolla in the *Decameron*. We are often happy to trade complex psychology for vividness of impression. A new character type in a novel does not have to be "round" in order to seem refreshingly "new." The pompous civic official delights us when incarnate as Lucius' acquaintance Pythias in *The Golden Ass* (I : 50–54), and the idea of a greedy but somewhat amiable businessman is nicely renewed in Edith Wharton's Elmer Moffat in *The Custom of the Country* (1913) and in Heliodorus' Nausikles in *Aithiopika*.

When we meet personages in novels, they are mere bundles of signs that ideally should bring to the reader's mind certain associations and sets of reactions that may vary widely (from, for instance, erotic response to historical analysis). Central characters (heroes or heroic villains) may function, as Peter Brooks suggests, "as 'desiring machines' whose presence in the text creates and sustains narrative movement through the forward march of desire" (*Reading for the Plot*, 39). Such characters, Brooks says, are "motors" that drive the plot and organize our experience. Brooks comes close to saying that the ambitious young man of so many French and English novels of the nineteenth century, including Eugène de Rastignac, Julien Sorel, and Philip Pirrip, constitutes a stock type with variations. However elaborated by psychology and social observation, each of these functions according to conventions that operate on us so we can read their story. The dynamic metaphor could be changed to a spatial one; characters who are strong 'desiring machines' are customarily represented in terms of space. We know where they're coming from . . . as we know straight away where Kleitophon or Lucius comes from, geographically and socially.

The original Greek term that performs characterological function is *ēthos*, a word that actually meant first "accustomed place," and then something like "habit" or "disposition"; we respond to someone's habitual behavior, conceived spatially as the place the individual is usually in—we know where that person is coming from. One of the primary modes of creating what we (not the Greeks) call "character" in prose discourse is through physical description—the body being a primary location or "place." The ancient novelists, as we might expect, engage in this, though in various degrees. Often it is enough to say of a character that he or she was excessively good-looking. All we are told of Habrokomes in the *Ephesiaka* is that he increased in beauty as he grew older, and with the beauty of his body there increased also the goodness of his soul. That is one way of saying he has an inner self and an outer self.

Habrokomes' inner self becomes the more convincing because he has a dream while in prison. That a person dreams is a sign of an inner self made mani-

fest. A dream (which in art *or* "real life" can be known only through being narrated) is a kind of high compliment to narration; it raises the possibility that our
very subconscious, the inner self, thinks narratively and that any glimmerings of
personality or person-hood cannot but be organized around narrative. So Freud
was to believe, but Freud bases his theory on Western narrative and dramatic
texts and their interpretations. He is the most novelistic of philosophers—which
does not mean he always attends to what the Novel has to say. That a literary
character is capable of having and describing a dream is a sign of perturbation and
persuades us of inner depths beneath the surface ripples. Men and women of
antiquity recorded their dreams, worried about them and took advice about
them. One second-century soothsayer, Artemidorus, wrote a book *On the Interpretation of Dreams* (*Oneirokritika*) based on his own experience as a counselor, and
taking into account "the individual dreamer's own cultural experience" (Winkler, *Constraints of Desire*, 28).

Novel-characters seem especially given to dreaming—although it should
be admitted that fictions of all kinds (epic, tragedy) and likewise religious and
historical writings are rich in dreams. But novels regularly reserve for dreams a
place of honor. "A dream can be the highest point of a life" says Ben Okri's hero
in the last sentence of the Nigerian novelist's *The Famished Road* (1991). Novel-
characters in their constant anxiety seem to be looking for counseling and interpretation not readily forthcoming; the other characters and even the narrator
either do not possess or withhold interpretation. The character, foregrounded in
wrestling with the dream, becomes the more engaging and convincing, mirroring
our own struggle with inwardness and identity. Charikles dreams that his daughter is taken from him by an eagle of Apollo, borne away to a shadowy land; nobody can give him a good interpretation of this dream, and it takes us the rest of
the novel before we "get" it, but Charikles' own anxiety and his capacity to produce such an interesting dream means he becomes for us a character with an
"inner self," and not merely the dry representative of patriarchy or social constraints. He is an individual.

The age of the Ancient Novel was an age of *individual* portraiture: attention was paid to that particular envelope of flesh in which an individual was
wrapped. But the flesh can never be just "envelope" to the novelist. Indeed, a
novel-character can never truly transcend the flesh; in order to be "character" or
sign, the personage must be represented as embodied, as physical. This does not
mean that a wealth of detail is always felt to be necessary. In the ancient novel,
heroines are not always described in detail: Charikleia is, but Kallirrhoé is not.
The very intriguing woman who is a little bit "bad" is apt to be quite fully described: we have a full description of Melitté as Kleitophon sees her, and a very
full description of the seductive Circe as Encolpius sees her: "Her hair poured
down in natural waves over her shoulders, she had a small forehead and her hair
curled away from it, her brows ran to the edge of her cheekbones and almost met
together over her eyes . . . . (*Satyricon*, 328). This is not just a general description
of a Lovely Lady; it has the effect of a detailed portrait of an individual. But so
does another description—of a male—from a very different narrative: "a man
small in size, with a bald head, his legs a little bowed, vigorous, his eyebrows
joined together [*synophryn*], nose somewhat hooked, a man full of grace" (*Actes
de Paul*, 150–152). This is the description of Saint Paul in *Paul and Thekla*, a

description that has been taken as representing the way the real Paul looked. But physical "characteristics" have almost always been thought of (especially by novelists) as bearing a meaning, being "characters" or signs of the person within. Did brows meeting together indicate (in both Melitté and Paul) firmness of nature, determination?

A novelistic description may have an ironic meaning, like Byrrhena's description of Lucius; exclaiming that he resembles his *mother*, she praises his looks: "a moderate height, well fleshed for all his graceful slimness, temperate in color, with blond and unfussy hair, eyes bluish but with a lively sparkling look, just like an eagle's, and with a face in the flower of health all over, handsome and unaffected in his gait" (I:62). It has sometimes been thought that this succulent description is of Apuleius himself. If so, it is a comic one—the portrait of the artist as a young sap. But there is no reason to believe that African Apuleius was himself a blond; it is more likely that there was a traditional physical type (slightly epicoene) associated with the man-who-turns-into-ass. Byrrhena uses a strange mixture of metaphors in her enthusiastic speech, mingling flowers and eagles, and her vocabulary is strangely chosen: *suculenta* (or "succulent"); *speciosus* (both "handsome" and "plausible"). Byrrhena describes a body extraordinarily congruous with that of the *mother*. She says Lucius inherited not only his *probitas* (or virtuous behavior) but also his physique from his mother Salvia (or "Healthy"). His body type is mathematically congruent with hers. Lucius then combines Male and Female in himself, being thus a kind of Everyperson or Everybody, a counterpart to Psyche, who is Everysoul. Perhaps Byrrhena herself worries about the epicoene mix, for she goes on to express relief that his gait is manly and not affected (like that of a homosexual?).

Lucius' looks are not fully expressive of character, as his "character" is not fully developed. The more detail we are given about him from Byrrhena's viewpoint, the less the readers can be sure about who Lucius at this point "really" is. He needs something to happen to him to get him out of being a mere repetition, a product of the parental mold—though the transformation that does happen is of course disproportionate to his initial deficiency in identity and significance. The description of Lucius' bodily form certainly makes us feel all the more forcibly the contrast when Lucius senses this good-looking and healthy body turning into that of the ass.

Byrrhena herself is an interesting and disturbing character. Like Aseneth, she is arrayed in gold and gems, suggesting goddess properties. Lucius sees the great lady in the marketplace and is surprised when this unknown woman in the gold ornaments greets him. She announces herself as his kinswoman and his mother's foster sister; furthermore, she is one of those who reared Lucius in infancy. The old-nurse character Byrrhena so nearly resembles is usually (like Heliodorus' Kybelé) somewhat sinister. Byrrhena has some of the qualities of a Mother Midnight—but of a very glamorous Mother Midnight.[2] She has married well and lives in great luxury. She shines as a hostess and enjoys her own dinner party; she seems to be the joker who sets Lucius up to hear tall tales. Byrrhena is a strong female character. There is enough description for us to recognize her and her quality of speech—though all Apuleius' characters speak "Apuleian." Later, on seeing Isis, we may recognize in Byrrhena Isis' earthly avatar. As a Profane

Isis, Byrrhena presides over an important sequence of the narrative, and her home bears emblems of the Goddess, in the figures of winged Victory and in the statue of Diana. Like the hero, however, we do not take in these mythological elements at first, but greet Byrrhena as a character, a talkative and hospitable matron, who yet eludes us; she does not fulfill the roles demanded of older women in Milesian tales.

Like most novelists of any era, novelists of antiquity prefer that any closely treated and highly focused characters (whether "flat" or "round") be neither completely villainous nor utterly angelic. The figural or symbolic dimensions of these characters (as with those of Dickens and Dostoevsky) should not detract from their particularity. Despite "Philip the Philosopher" and his style of allegorical reading, characters in ancient novels are usually mixed. The "mixed" character is certainly preferred for any sustained appearance. Even Charikleia, wonderful as she is, has a sharp tongue and indulges in a fit of depressed self-pity. On the other hand, the complacent and wealthy Nausikles is pleasantly affable, despite lecherousness and some greed. Ancient novelists, like modern ones, are skilled in exhibiting the psychological background and nature of a particular character emerging in a particular instance. In Chariton's *Chaireas and Kallirrhoé* we become used to Dionysios' anxious (and egotistical) self-communings. Because we know him so well, we can participate fully in the effects late in the novel, when Dionysios (in Persia) has lost all his local importance as well as the company of his wife. As the "biter bit," the man who tries to keep his wife by starting a lawsuit that almost guarantees he will lose her, Dionysios of Miletus is a figure from a "Milesian tale." But he does not see it that way. He is earnest and panicky as he tries to gain admission to Kallirrhoé, now locked away in the protection of the Great King's harem. Dionysios' self-pity finds outlet in addressing his baby son in a litany of tearful complaints: "O my poor baby, before I counted myself lucky in thy birth, but now how miserable. I have in thee the inheritance of thy mother and the memorial of my unfortunate love. . . . We should never have left Miletus! Babylon has undone us." He involves the baby both in his complaint and in the action, ordering the child to go in and plead to his mother for his father. Dionysios' speech is succinctly managed by the author so that we see the action going on at the same time: "Crying, kissing her, say to her 'Mother, my father loves you!' Do not reproach her. What's that you say, attendant? They won't let us into the King's apartments? O cruel tyranny! They lock out the son whom the father sends as ambassador to his mother!" (149).

Dionysios, filling his child with his own anxiety and self-pity, knocking on the heartless palace gates, is perfectly "in character." He now knows, as we know, that he has wrought a situation he cannot control. His characteristic tendency to demand approbation and sympathy is consistent with the large emotional demands he makes upon "his" tiny son.

DIALOGUE AND SETTING

Novelists have learned from Homer and from the dramatists how to set down speech that is socially engaged in the immediate situation and yet marked with "characteristic" qualities—habits or assumptions related to gender, class, condition and expectations as well as personal qualities. Some characters play double games in their speech to another, as Plangon does with Kallirrhoé. The most vivid socially marked speech is found in the mouths of the more comic characters. Gnathon in *Daphnis and Chloé* is a prominent example. But Daphnis and Chloé too have the social assumptions of their adoptive status and of their youth—in their delight at the city-style delicacies at dinner as a treat, for instance. Petronius offers us the most flourishing examples of low speech individualized in the speeches of Trimalchio and his friends at the banquet—speeches marked by ungrammatical or slangy Latin. Eric Auerbach points to the description of Trimalchio's wife given by a guest, in which not only Fortunata but the manners and values of the temporary narrator are represented as leading to "a more meaningful and more concrete illusion of life . . . the viewpoint is transferred to a point within the picture" (*Mimesis*, trans. Trask, 27). Auerbach thinks this effect probably unique in ancient literature, but something very close to it is found in Chariton's Dionysios' reaction to Persia. James Tatum claims that "The qualities of Petronius's characters are reflected in their speech," whereas "Such verisimilitude never appears in Apuleius. No matter how depraved a character may be, no matter how uncouth, his language is never anything less than elegant and grammatical" (Tatum, *Apuleius*, 149). But Apuleius does create characteristic talk. Not everything is in the same style. We get, for instance, the Corinthian lady's love-language in her monstrous wooing of her ass: "I hold thee," she said, "I hold thee, my little pigeon, my sparrow" (*"Teneo te" inquit "Teneo meum palumbulum, meum passerem,"* II: 256). The metaphors of endearment, the erotic sparrow (shades of Catullus!) are convincing, and risible, in this context, just when a real animal in the bed with the lady would seem to preclude such customary comparisons—an *ass* is so evidently not a sparrow. The lady's habit, her *ēthos*, has notably dictated her words.

The amount of theatrical reference in the ancient novels makes it very evident that the novelists know what they are borrowing from drama, though novelists tend to ignore the limits established by stage-genres. There is no reason why the novelist cannot run together effects found in low mimes, or in comic drama by Menander or Plautus, with effects similar to those found in high "literary" dramatists such as Sophocles and Euripides. Euripides, with his awareness of an aberrant irrational inner self, provided a constant model for the novelists (as Nietzsche noticed, in his uncomplimentary way). But novelists have the inestimable epic benefit of authorial description. A novel has a narrator, it is "diegetic" rather than "mimetic" like stage-plays; Chariton (or the-authorial-voice-calling-itself-Chariton) says, "I am going to tell [*diēgēsomai*] a story of love-suffering [*pathos erōtikon*] that happened in Syracuse" (50). The novel, like the epic, is *apangelia*; it is a relation, a telling out (see Aristotle, *Poetics*, 1448a, 1449b). A good novelist can assume characteristic points of view in the telling, just as Homer did, as Aristotle noted. Dialogue is embedded and does not have to act on its own; the novelist (except in epistolary works) can act as theater director, exhibiting speech in the light of other characters' responses, and the reader's response.

In Heliodorus' *Aithiopika*, after the troubled night in which Charikleia dreams she has lost an eye, hero and heroine then decide to disguise themselves as poor folk begging their bread. "'By Zeus,' said Knemon, 'and you do look exceedingly misshapen, especially Charikleia since she lost an eye just now. But in my opinion you seem fitter to beg "swords and urns" than scraps of food.' At this they smiled a little, but a constrained smile that went only as far as the lips . . ." (I: 68–69).

There is some wit in Knemon's reversal of an appropriate line in the *Odyssey* (XVII, line 222). He has a right to tease his friends, since they have just been teasing him, but he really wants to cheer them up. Knemon's intended raillery is labored, however, reflecting the strain they are all under; the author's commentary tells us that it was not an effective speech. The author can direct us to comprehend what the dialogue is doing; the unspoken responses of Theagenes and Charikleia here are as "characteristic" of them as Knemon's speech is of himself.

The nature of speaking itself is often a cause for concern or puzzlement, particularly for characters who know themselves to be somewhat ineffective speakers, like Dionysios or even the fluent Knemon. St. Peter in the *Recognitiones* is a sort of traveling sophist, and no bad speaker, but it is interesting to notice the rising tension when he has to debate the arch heretic Simon Magus. The Christian group gathers its forces, puts arguments together, and goes into practice sessions—rather like a modern political candidate and his handlers faced with an important debate. The low point of inability to speak is reached by the Ass Lucius when he tries to begin a speech but can render only his hee-hawing form of "O" (II: 116). Trying to speak, trying to speak appropriately, convincingly, to the right person—this takes up a lot of the attention of novel characters of all periods. All novel characters are afraid that they may not be able to use with success the words they desperately rely upon to create the bridge between outer world and inner self. The novelist (ultimately subject to the same fear) pursues and contains this anxiety.

Novelistic characters speak and think in particular circumstances, including a place—what we used to call "setting." The setting of ancient novels, like that of modern works, can be more or less specific. In general, the novelists favor adding substantial details. In their description of cities, for instance, we have a sense of a large and full economic and social world. These descriptions are not, however, reliable as data. Recent studies have pointed out anomalies and anachronisms. The cities we encounter in the novels may have characteristics and buildings borrowed from different time-periods; Heliodorus archizes his Delphi, while his Athens is "a montage." Chariton's description of Aradus include references to porticoed buildings of an Imperial style out of place in a town of the fourth century B.C., the ostensible time of the novel's action; the details are "obviously anachronistic" (Suzanne Saïd, "The City in the Greek Novel," *TSAN*, 216–236). This is not mere carelessness; the authors are concerned to create certain ideas—e.g., for Heliodorus, the idea of Delphi in its heyday of influence. Some details are much more important as figures than as facts—e.g., the *didymos limēn*, the double harbor, of the opening of *Kleitophon and Leukippé*, which functions, as Saïd says, as *mise-en-abîme* ("The City," 232). That does not mean we are not to take in readerly earnest the sights, sounds, smells, activities of the particular city we are in any particular novel. Certain details—a narrow lane, a painter's shop—we are to attuned to with sensitive and sensuous belief.

Longus makes the pastoral setting a very important aspect of *Daphnis and Chloé*, part of the novel's appeal. We remember the descriptions, the beauty of landscapes and orchards—even of the winter scene, and Chloé's shut house, with nothing coming out, not so much as a chicken. The effect of particularity is often closely associated with the idea of "realism," but, as C. S. Lewis pointed out in *An Experiment in Criticism* (1961), there are "realisms"; one can have "realism of content" (which involves the whole work in the demands of truth to life) or "realism of presentation"—when the circumstances are magical or improbable but the detail is diurnal and familiar (57–67).

For Eric Auerbach, the episode of "Trimalchio's Feast" in Petronius is useful in proving that antiquity could represent everyday life "only in the low style . . . and ahistorically," and that "these things mark the limits not only of the realism of antiquity but of its historical consciousness as well" (*Mimesis*, 33). Furthermore, Petronius (in Auerbach's reading) is made to stand in representative contrast to the later development (under Christianity) of figurative reading. Petronius writes only as a "man of culture," "from above," and has no interest in the sort of "figural meaning" that obsessed Christians (47–49). For Auerbach's system, it is necessary to ignore all forms of "figural meaning" within pagan prose writings in the earlier periods of the Roman Empire. It seems pertinent to insist that, on the contrary, Petronius is playing with—or playing off—various patterns of prophetic and figural meaning in epic and in prose fiction. That is, *Satyricon* may make more "sense" if it is seen as if it were a "post-modern" work, rather than being identified as an example of a semideveloped realism.

The "Trimalchio's Feast" episode in *Satyricon* is so sharply exaggerated in its semiotic and claustrophobic effects that it seems, rather than an effort of ancient realism, an expressionistic *tour de force* drawing upon and deliberately overgoing certain naturalistic effects. (It tempted Fellini into making a film in which the phantasmagoric surpasses the effect of the satiric.)

Novelistic detail can amplify our responses to both character and situation, without being unduly emphasized. In Chariton's novel, when Kallirrhoé comes to within the tomb, she cries out in the darkness, then touches the gold and silver ornaments buried with her—she makes them *sound*, and there is a *smell* of aromatic spices (62). Chariton skillfully conveys the experience, calling on senses other than sight. We imagine the silvery noise, and retain in unison the impression of the ringing sound and the sweet spice in the heavy air. These images are slightly comic in their delicate precision, and witty in the contrast between the pleasures of silver and spices and the threat of death. But the reader, also momentarily deprived of sight, has an unconscious impression of anxious darkness. The images make up the experience shared with the heroine, making us feel more empathy for her—and thus at the same time, she becomes more convincingly "real."

In the epistolary *Chion of Heraklea* the main story concerns the development of a young philosopher to the point where he becomes a man of action; at the end of the story, we know he is going off to kill the tyrant—and will himself be killed. The severer philosophical theme is embedded in the construction of convincing parent-child relations; when Chion goes to study in Athens, his father sends him presents, for which the son writes his thanks: "Phaidomos came and brought me the pickled fish, the five amphorae of honey and twenty jars of wine flavored with myrtle as well as three talents of silver" (*Chion*, 54–56). Even a budding gentleman philosopher, even a budding tyrannicide, has to live at college; Chion gains in credibility in acknowledging the sustenance of pickled fish and *retsina* as well as Platonic lectures.

One of the things we appreciate about novels is their quality of super-abundance—they offer that touch more, that graceful superfluity of detail. The attack on pompous Pumblechook in *Great Expectations* is so satisfyingly "Dickensian" not because the robbers stole from the seedsman, or beat and gagged him, but because they took this jowly, mouthy character and "stuffed his mouth full of flowering annuals" (442). Such an enjoyable superfluity can be found, for instance, in the *Aithiopika*, when Kalasiris, Knemon, and Nausikles are anxiously going in pursuit of Theagenes and meet a friend of Nausikles running along with a flamingo (*phoinikopteros*). Another example of the generous extra, more strictly tied in with the story line, can be found when Chaireas asks Kleitophon and Leukippé to dinner at his house on the island of Pharos, "pretending that it was his birthday" (*skēpsamenos genethliōn agein hēmeran*) (240).

If this was a culture that celebrated birthdays, it was a culture with a consciousness of both personal and historical time. Hence the importance of the characters' ages—they are youths growing older. We have recently tended to accept the contentions of historians such as Philippe Ariès, who asserts that taking account of age by year is a modern, or at least "Early Modern," phenomenon.[3] Ancient novelists *do* give the ages of characters. Kleitophon is nineteen; Charikleia, seventeen. Chloé and Daphnis are thirteen and fifteen, respectively, when they start herding their flocks together. Such particularity must give us pause. Age and time indeed matter in the ancient novels. Bakhtin's contention that "This Greek romance-time does not have even an elementary biological or maturational duration" is quite untenable; Bakhtin patently felt a particular interest in denying fictional mastery of time and time-consciousness until the Renaissance (see "Forms of Time and Chronotope in the Novel," in *Dialogic Imagination*, trans. Emerson and Holquist, 84–258, esp. 89–91). David Konstan also defies Bakhtin on this issue, asserting that "time is of the very essence in Greek novels" because "it is precisely the element of duration that engenders the love specific to the hero and heroine" (*Sexual Symmetry*, 46–47).

Yet to say this much is merely to situate the ancient novel within a predetermined framework of realistic time, which we have labeled "historical time." Novelists may not always be primarily interested in dealing with that sort of time, or with that alone. Sheila McKoy in a lecture has taught me to see within African-American and Caribbean literature the possibility of times alternative to what she calls "Western time" or "objective time." McKoy holds that peoples of the African Diaspora preserve cultural identity and understanding through such use of time.[4] In a situation with some parallels, subjugated peoples in the Roman Empire may have had reason to find consolation in a free play upon time and in fictional attention (if hidden attention) to alternative ritual time. We can easily see within modern fiction that, for instance, Sterne's *Tristram Shandy* and Emily Brontë's *Wuthering Heights* seem (in different ways) deliberately to overthrow or subvert "objective time." A novel that looks to alternative relations with time may also, as these two both do, insist *overtly* on temporal measurements and chronologies—those insistences, however, being partly ironic.

The novelists of the Mediterranean during the Roman Imperial period had, as we have seen, sufficient reason to treat "real time" or "objective time" with the greatest possible care. Real historical time is precisely the time that interests the despot, who becomes irritable if he thinks faults are being found with historical activities in contemporary time. Anachronism is a valuable camouflage. It always practiced by writers living under despotisms. The use of a partly mythical past, a historical but also anachronistic time (like the time of the Sicilian Expedition, or the Persian Empire), gave the novelists access to deep time, to ritual time as well as to "history." But the ancient novelists, like others, were not at all uninterested in duration, or biological development, or emotional change through time. The novels remind us of history and biology, of change and time. Longus employs a frame of time based on seasonal change rather than historical happenings. Seasonal change is biological change—which is the movement towards death, real change.

As any novel, no matter how "contemporary" or even "futuristic," is always already dealing with "the past" by the time it is under our eyes, the reading time is—or becomes—a mythical time in which one repeats the events of this now legendary time. I enter such a mythical time when I read Tolstoy or Jay MacInerney, Heliodorus or Hemingway. My rereading will not make the narrative any more—or any less—"anachronistic." Getting into a novel is getting into some form of deep time that is not really anybody's time. We speak of "cyberspace," but novels offer also a "cybertime."

To dwell in historical time is to experience constriction. Time-as-history is a weight. Within every one of these novels, no matter how "magical" its realism, the character must be content to be part of the stream of time, part of a *larger* history, like a larger city, or community or empire, in which the individual is in a sense buried. No matter what the relief of ritual time the Novel has to offer, no form is more likely than the Novel (of any period) to give the reader the sensation of enclosure, of imprisonment within all-powerful time—Time that (according to Trimalchio's puzzling anecdote) shrank the Cumaean Sibyl so that when Trimalchio was a little boy he saw the Sibyl hanging in a bottle (*Satyricon*, 100).

MYTHOLOGY AND THE IMAGES OF ART: EKPHRASIS

A novel, even a "realistic" novel, tends to develop mythological overtones, or at very least mythological reminiscences. At present I wish only to point to the overt expression of mythologizing in the ancient novels, partly as an aspect of setting, but also of characterization. Nowhere is this more evident than in the practice of introducing works of art, most particularly paintings, but also statues and other forms of plastic art. These works must be admired, described, and (customarily) interpreted by a character or the narrator (or both). Such an artistic description is termed *ekphrasis*; the word means merely "telling at length, description," but it acquired its specialized sense among the rhetoricians of the Second Sophistic, when exercises in describing and interpreting works of art begin to find a place in rhetorical handbooks (see Bartsch, *Decoding the Ancient Novel*, 8–10). Two

Greek works of the Second Sophistic exhibit the process of exploring and explaining (supposed) graphic works. The first of these, the *Kebētos Pinax*, commonly known as the *Table of Cebes*, a work traditionally attributed to Cebes, a pupil of Socrates, is apparently a late Stoic piece, generally now assigned to the first or second century. This narrative essay, partly in dialogue, describes a large complex picture, which an old man explains to the young viewer. The narrative work is a moral allegory like its imagined picture, a series of concentric circles and uphill climbs illustrating the temptations waylaying men on their way to True Knowledge. Each figure has a meaning, though that meaning is first hidden from the viewer, who sees only strange drawings. Each pictured personage is a temptation, a virtue, a victim, or a pilgrim. The mode of seeing and reading the *graphē* becomes itself a moral action. The *Table* makes clear that, without the key, the figures would be meaningless; the viewer acquires confidence in the rush of instruction that makes him a meaningful viewer.

A far less moral work is the *Eikones* or *Imagines* of Philostratus (c. A.D. 220). The *Imagines* is a series of descriptions of various pictures, described as if in an address to a young boy in the presence of an audience of older students; this frame-narrative offers a vision of (idealized) teaching by a successful sophistic rhetorician. Philostratus succeeds in the real *tour de force*, which surpasses the fictional brilliant lecture in the gallery; he makes his reader (who replaces the supposed audience) imagine with him these *eikones*, these images. He outdoes the graphic artists whom he fictitiously celebrates, though he says he himself studied painting in Asia Minor, and there is no doubt of his appreciation of artistic skill. The subjects of the artworks are, as the admiring Goethe noted, varied, including heroic tragic subjects, stories of love (Medea and Ariadne), as well as the works of Herakles, athletic contests, hunting scenes, and landscapes. The qualities Philostratus values in technique are the ones the Renaissance was to value—including perspective.

Philostratus knows that it is important for a gentleman to be able to confront and interpret a *graphē*—but Trimalchio knew that too; he just could not do it, lacking the education the rhetorician advertises. In order to be truly worthy, an artwork must have significance, which means a meaning has to be uncovered. Mimesis itself, Philostratus insists, is not enough. If we praise a painter for the way he rendered the skipping of his goats or the puckered lips of the pipe players, then "we should be praising a petty matter in the painting, something related only to imitation [*mimēsis*], and would not be praising its wisdom or sense of the fitting, though I believe these are the most excellent qualities of the art" (40). Realism is insufficient. A good painter includes allegorical and encoded meanings; the art of knowing a painting is hermeneutic. It is not that Philostratus does not appreciate the senses; his writing is very sensuous, and deals remarkably in synaesthesia, one sense running into another in imaginative play of sensibility. When we "look" at the picture of the Cupids gathering apples, he asks, "Do you get the sensation of this garden or are you dulled to it?" "But attend," he adds confidently, "for with my discourse the apples will approach you" (20). No writer was ever more confident of the ability of words to strike the senses than this sophisticated sophist—and we believe it all while we read, including the luxurious villa outside Napoli with a view of the Tyrrhenian Sea.[5]

We can see in Philostratus how *ekphrasis* unlocks the culture and the mind together. The mind's relation to itself is enhanced in contemplating a work of art; the longer you look at a picture the more you make of it, the more mastery you acquire over a range of myths, figures, objects. But this rush of mastery, this exercise of finding meanings in the world, can of course be rendered—and is so rendered by Philostratus—as totally the achievement of *words*. In admiring a described painting we show how the *logos* controls mere visible phenomena. The imagination can be provoked into supplying all that is needed. The novelists of the Second Sophistic were also discovering how true that is for the Novel—the Novel, which can take the reader anywhere, make the reader sense things, actions, characters, and muse upon their meaning. The Novel can create the imaginative substitute for actual sensation, the "virtual reality" whereby the apples come to us.

Novels of antiquity are ornamented with many *ekphraseis* that sharpen our skill as interpreters while reminding us that what we are reading is a verbal artwork. The appearance of *ekphrasis* in a fictional text not only recalls to us myth, legend, history, but also, and cardinally, reminds us that we have a moral, aesthetic, and intellectual duty not only to perceive—and to perceive in an orderly if stimulated way—but also to interpret the *entire* work at hand. *Daphnis and Chloé* represents itself indeed as entirely an extended *ekphrasis*. (That it is absurdly extended is part of the comedy.) The story begins with the Narrator's description of a painted picture (*eikona graptēn*) portraying a story of love (*historian erōtos*, 6). The Narrator wanted to write something that would "answer" this picture, and thus explain it, but also (it is implied) something that would "answer it back" (*antigrapsai tēi graphēi*). *Daphnis and Chloé* teases us by proposing itself as a commentary on a painting we, the readers, have never seen; the "original story," that is, the painter's story, may or may *not* be what this narrator, as ingenious hermeneut, has in mind.

A less formidable *ekphrasis* is found at the beginning of *Kleitophon and Leukippé* in the open-ended frame story. The first Narrator describes his view of a great painting in Sidon, a painting whose subject is Europa. Europa in art of late antiquity is treated as suggesting power and new life, as well as pleasure—as for instance in the dynamic mosaic in Kos, where the sexy lady, sensuous as a Boucher nude, seems to dominate her bull like a goddess, while the leaping dolphin echoes her pose as they both move through the waters, guided by Eros (see Plate 12). In Achilles Tatius' novel, the first Narrator's word-painting of this well-known subject provides an evocative image of possibilities, of fulfillment through venturing into the unknown. (So effective is this ekphrastic opening that it is imitated at the outset of Roberto Calasso's polemical mythology, *Le Nozze di Cadmo e Armonia*, 1988.) Achilles Tatius' detailed *ekphrasis* includes a connoisseur's interpretation, a commentary on artistic technique: the artist "had painted the shadows cast by the leaves . . . he had placed the girls, Europa's fellows, at one end of the meadow where the land met the sea . . . the sea was painted in two colors" (4). Such a description, with its praise of the exactness of the painter's observation, is also an ironic commentary on the realism of the novelist's own presentation, and an invitation to admire novelistic techniques. After we have seen the great painting, Kleitophon is introduced, as another spectator at the same scene.

The narrator's exclamation about the power of Eros rouses Kleitophon to eager agreement, as one who has also suffered outrages from Eros. So Kleitophon begins his long narrative; the reader must figure out the connections.

Kleitophon, like his author, is accomplished in *ekphrasis*. He describes the works of art seen at Pelousion including the pictures (signed by the artist) of Andromeda and Prometheus, both in chains (146–153). Both paintings are (re-)animated by the vivid verbal description designed to capture the paintings' supposed effects. Andromeda, a beauty in terror, has a beauty in the process of being quenched, like languishing violets. She is bound to her hollow rock, like a new tomb; her bound hands droop, her fingers white, like those of one dead; she is arrayed like one who is given to Hades in bridal. The painting may resemble the impressionistic painting from the villa at Boscotrecase near Pompeii (now in New York's Metropolitan Museum), with its delicate elongated Andromeda (Plate 13). Kleitophon describes a normal painterly subject; an Andromeda painting figures importantly in Heliodorus' narrative likewise.

The reader must admire Kleitophon's own artistry in description at the same time as admiring the animated images, symbols mysteriously pointing to meanings that we must draw for ourselves. What do the sufferings of Andromeda and Prometheus have to do with the sufferings of Kleitophon and Leukippé? Shadi Bartsch, in her excellent study *Decoding the Ancient Novel*, has shown how the described paintings operate in relation to the story. In their context, the Andromeda painting and the Prometheus painting refer forward to Leukippé's supposed disembowelment and her *Scheintod*. But at another level, Andromeda and Prometheus refer to hero and heroine who both await deliverance, moral and spiritual. At another level still, all four share the quality of being artworks, looking *as if* they were alive—the painter's world is an *as if*. In yet another interpretation, Andromeda is the soul of the reader, endangered, awaiting unknown salvation—or just the end of the story.

The animated and colorful use of such complex and kinetic images within the texture of the main story can frequently surprise us into thinking of the movies. Nothing is more "cinematic" than the Novel from the beginning, save only cinema itself. (Sometimes it seems surprising that we had to wait so long for an art that we seem to have had in mind for a long while.) Drama may *sometimes* be cinematic, but the Novel is always reaching for "cinematic" effects, arresting and complex visual images, striking montages, interesting relations between objects, the characters, and major situation. Characters' dream-images begin to team up with the images of their art galleries, seeking a connection between the personages' inner world and the dream-life of a public culture with its symbols. A novel like *Kleitophon and Leukippé* itself exists on this frontier between the concepts of the private and the public. The entire novel is a meta-reconciliation of private and public, conducted through the individual character(s).

In the second book of *The Golden Ass*, Lucius describes to us, with the minute aesthetic attention that we found in Kleitophon's scrutiny of the paintings, the statue of Diana that he saw in Byrrhena's house in the town of Hypata in mid-Thessaly. "Life-size" marble statues of the goddess-huntress with her dogs are not uncommon (there is a good example on the island of Kos), but Byrrhena's statue is more elaborate than any surviving piece of statuary. The image of the majestic goddess seems to confront those who enter the house. The dogs on each side of her threaten with flaring nostrils and grinning teeth. Behind the goddess is a carved cavern, with apples and grapes so lifelike that you would think it was autumn. If you bent down to look at the water which flowed around the feet of the goddess, you would see the grapes, and also the reflection of Actaeon already turning into a stag. As Winkler points out, this "frozen tale" is a paradigm of the novel's motifs; part of the irony may consist here in the investigative Lucius bending forward and looking into the fountain: "If you *did* lean forward and look into the water you would see not only a second Actaeon but yourself" (*Auctor*, 168–170). Lucius, naïve "Second Actaeon" is delighted, and of course does not hear the doubleness of Byrrhena's hospitable saying, "Everything you see is yours." The experience of *metamorphosis* that is Actaeon's in the elaborate statue will certainly be his. (And Artemis-Diana will be "his" too in a different sense, when he acknowledges the power of Isis.)

Ekphrasis connects setting with character, and character with reader. It appeals to artistic, cultural, and mythological tradition functioning both within and outside of the novel. *Ekphrasis* works in novels by modern novelists in the same way. Henry James, who is particularly fond of this device, employs it to effect in, for instance, *The Wings of the Dove* (1902), when Lord Mark shows Milly Theale "the Bronzino":

> the face of a young woman, all magnificently drawn, down to the hands, and magnificently dressed; a face almost livid in hue, yet handsome in sadness and crowned with a mass of hair rolled back and high, that must, before fading with time, have had a family resemblance to her own. The lady in question, at all events, with her slightly Michaelangelesque squareness, her eyes of other days, her full lips, her long neck, her recorded jewels, her brocaded and wasted reds, was a very great personage—only unaccompanied by a joy. And she was dead, dead, dead. Milly recognized her exactly in words that had nothing to do with her. "I shall never be better than this." (144)

Lord Mark can see only that the portrait is like Milly, but that Milly is "better," because "one doubts if she was good." Lord Mark is an example of the ignorant interpreter who makes the *ekphrasis* completed by the reader all the more impressive—and imperative. This fading lady is an Andromeda without hope of rescue. Milly is caught up with the painting as a harbinger of death. The novel reader must praise James for his creation or re-creation of a "Bronzino" while thinking about how the image stands as a figure for the novel itself—for his "Portrait of a Lady," to use an ekphrastic title from an earlier novel by James. And, of course, in admiring the *ekphrasis* we are laying some claim to a cultural understanding of all the implications of a Bronzino (and of a Lord Mark whose country-house gallery can contain one). Works of art function in novels as succinct reminders of wastes of historical time, including hosts of other viewers of this same work.

A graphic work (of any kind) treated to an *ekphrasis* in a novel is always an object located in a social space; no novel, ancient or modern, allows us to ignore how the character got to see it and what kind of social space the gazing viewer is occupying. A novel may contain many icons, but it refuses to believe in a purely iconic vision. Questions of social relations, religious pursuits, public and private spaces and meanings are all going to be raised. And so is the question of money. Lord Mark's "Bronzino" we know would cost a pretty penny. When the hero and heroine of *Kleitophon and Leukippé* see an ominous painting at an artist's *shop*, they are clearly aware of the commodification of art. Although only a Trimalchio would be unsubtle enough to talk about how much his objects of art and craft actually cost, the novelist is always aware of a relationship of artistry to the marketplace, as well as to other ideas and scales of value. Graphic arts are the stuff of our social world, the rendition of public values (which are also values of exchange) even while they may penetrate our inmost souls—or so characters may feel. The novelist shows us, always, how the character got to the gallery, as well as what sort of person is looking.

It is an aspect of the novelist's art to work everything together—characterization, dialogue, setting, *ekphrasis*—so that we as readers get a larger meaning than any character can arrive at, no matter how educated, intelligent, or all-round excellent that character may be. Even a bright character must often be perplexed by other persons, actions, and places, and by the connection of images to life—and the bright characters are severely hampered by not knowing they are in a story. One reason we like novel characters—"flat" or "round"—may be that they are always (even the best) our inferiors. The Author, however, as the Author is projected, is not. The Author (engaged in a sort of perpetual showing-off) must puzzle us and instruct us and raise our consciousness by making a new combination of elements.

CHAPTER VII

>-+→-○-←+-<

Literary Self-Consciousness and Ancient Prose Fiction: Allusion, Narrative, Texts, and Readers

>-+→-○-←+-<

A great historian, as he insisted on calling himself, glories in his copious remarks and digressions . . . But Fielding lived when the days were longer. . . . I at least have so much to do in unravelling certain human lots, and seeing how they were woven and interwoven, that all the light I can command must be concentrated on this particular web, and not dispersed over that tempting range of relevancies called the universe.   —George Eliot, *Middlemarch*

"I will be a great history, an incredible tale in books."
    —Lucius in Apuleius' *The Golden Ass*

Recognizing Kallirrhoé's handwriting he first kissed the letter, then opening it hugged it to his bosom as if she herself were present. . . .
    —Chariton, of Dionysios in *Chaireas and Kallirrhoé*

>-+→-○-←+-<

A novelist "ties everything together," weaving and unraveling the tissue of text. A novel must supply means by which the reader can create coherence. Without structures that induce coherence, even a story with very dashing characters or pretty settings or stunning *ekphraseis* will founder. We tend to think that what ensures sustained interest is "a good story"—what has been called "a good read." E. M. Forster with aesthetic *hauteur* famously despised "story" as an inevitable but low element in a novel, a sadly regrettable necessity ("Oh dear, yes—the novel tells a story").[1] For Forster, story is disgustingly oral, emanating from cavemen telling stories amid "offal and bones"; the "and then" of story is tied to the tyranny of time. One sees that to Forster *story* represents not only matter ("offal and bones") but also time and hence *death*. But matter, time, and death are no small things, and if story gives us those it gives us much.

Forster distinguishes between story and plot (plot introduces causality) but distances himself from Aristotelian pleasure in vulgar event. Story has had defenders in the twentieth century, including the Russian formalists like Vladimir Propp, who sought typological patterns in narratives; structuralists and post-structuralists acknowledge the central import of "what happens" and do not treat that as a mere tedious platform for interesting characters or sentiments. Temporality—which made Forster shudder—has interested some very sophisticated commentators, including Gérard Genette and Paul Ricoeur; there is something fascinating about the paradoxical novel, which represents itself as spatial form while also incessantly impressing us as sequential temporality. The time it takes to read a novel is part of its impact—as true for *Aithiopika* as for *Madame Bovary*. Length seems an important criterion for a novel—a short story has lyric intensity without implicit duration. Dealing with time, we are inevitably reminded of our mortality; the ideal reader of any novel is aware of personal death. Yet we can set mortality aside, too, paradoxically, in associating with our papery immortals, the imaginary people who were never born of flesh. We feel both the pressure of time (it takes a chunk of one's life to finish a substantial novel) and the mastery over time; we can cover huge tracts of the characters' lives, even from birth to death.

We also find in reading a novel an experience of a sort of new time; we acquire, through the novelist's use of varying repetitions, a new or artificial memory, always somewhat analogous to the ways in which we remember our own lives, but much better organized. Our discovery of this "artificial memory" is closely related to the novel's codes, and rises to our own consciousness whenever in the story signs are overtly treated as codes. For instance, in *Aithiopika*, Theagenes and Charikleia agree on two code words by which they will always recognize each other: "lamp" or "torch" (*lampas*) and "palm" (*phoinix*) (II : 44). The alert reader recalls that these objects were formerly held by Charikleia at Delphi at the moment when she and Theagenes first met. Like Theagenes, we have to recall both association and code later, when Charikleia is unrecognized by her lover in her beggarly attire and has to say "don't you remember the *lamp*?" (II : 124). By such devices we are sharply reminded of our own memory, and of the chance that (like Theagenes) we may fail at detection of significance, may not remember a code in time.[2] We must keep alert. It is the reader's duty to tie signs together, creating the "story" of the novel, which is a reflection of its temporality; as Peter Brooks says, "narratives are temporal syllogisms" (*Reading for the Plot*, 21). Forster, who could not acknowledge in oral literature any employment of the literary devices that support what he calls "the life of value," refused to see that the lowly "story" is itself an important image (or rather, set of images). Like other images, it cannot operate without interpretation.

We do care—despite Edmund Wilson—who killed Roger Ackroyd, but only because we are being taught as we read how to respond to and interpret a particular narrative. What makes the "story" coherent and significant, along with everything else (along with, for instance, Andromedas, gardens, lords, and Bronzinos) seems, among other things and paradoxically enough, to be the restrained capacity of the book to discuss its own writtenness, to assure us that there is a mind, large and in charge, which creates with artistic intention. *Somebody* has put meaning into the book, which makes it worth our while to try to dig meaning out of it. Books that we do not wish to go on reading either repel us by the quality of the mind we seem to encounter, or bore us with an inability to project any significant mind capable of ordering elements into meaning. The low phrase "a good *read*" turns out to have the right stress, for what we must do is acknowledge that we are reading. A good novel knows it gives us something both to peruse and to interpret.

We lose illusion to regain it; we cannot "escape" into a novel before we yield our allegiance to the shadowy but strong personality, the "implied author" in Wayne C. Booth's phrase,[3] who may constantly remind us that we are only reading, and even more constantly may exercise control over us. Part of the fun may, however, be our permission to dispute with the author, or exercise skepticism about what is said at any given moment. (These matters are taken up and made overt by the Author of Fielding's *Tom Jones*.) Part of the author's "right" to take on this jocular power rests in the assumption that the author has a good understanding of the cultural issues at stake, and can help us to interpret the world in which we live. There is and has always been a strong element of "wisdom literature" in the Novel. One of the handiest means of both displaying knowledge of cultural issues and inviting us to consider the nature of reading itself is the employment of literary allusion, a common device in most novels, and a symptom of a claim to mind and meaning.

LITERARY ALLUSION

As we have seen, *ekphraseis* offer points of "intertextuality" in a novel; we see at a particular juncture how our novel relates itself to mythology and to art of a "high" tradition. Ancient novels are also, however, richly related to literal or literary texts. Wolfgang Iser has contended that the "repertoire" of any given literary text consists of two elements: cultural norms and literary allusions. Literary allusions function "as a means of generalizing the repertoire," that is, of giving us ways of seeing and organizing the social and cultural norms of "the historical situation to which it [the work] is reacting" (Iser, *The Reality of Fiction*, 80). Borrowing Merleau-Ponty's phrase "coherent deformation," Iser contends that both cultural and literary elements are "deformed" in systematic ways by reacting against each other in one text. Within any novel, then, we might expect an abundance of literary allusions, because a novel, as it processes such an abundance of cultural givens, and questions—to some extent—a number of norms, must be greatly in need of the kind of assistance in organizing cultural understanding that literary allusion can give. Iser considers that literary quotations encompass "earlier answers to the problems—answers which no longer constitute a valid meaning for the present work" (79). That is, Iser would see the quotation or allusion as essentially *rejected* by its very inclusion. Such a conception of literary design seems too narrow. But an element of the parodic in the mocking sense is certainly often—if not always—present in literary allusion. The difficulty of knowing how to place the tone and register of a particular allusion constitutes an arousal of the reader's attentiveness and judgment, while the allusion is working to recall the culturally familiar and render it defamiliarized.

No form is more "intertextual" than the Novel, more given to quotation from other written works. Ancient novels, like modern, function on running sets of allusions and quotations—or misquotations. Like the works of Proust and Joyce, they court the danger of being described as *pastiche*, in a brash novelistic certainty that they are above such elementary abuse. Historians like Herodotus, all the dramatists from Aeschylus to Menander, the philosophers (particularly Plato)—all are quoted. The poets abound, including the lyric and erotic poets. Sappho's unreachable apple reappears in the fruit-picking scene in *Daphnis and Chloé* (where it gets picked); in *Chaireas and Kallirrhoé* the sad heroine when kissed by her fiancé resembles Sappho's extinguished lamp into which fresh oil is poured, burning with new brilliance (*Chaireas and Kallirrhoé*, 52). There seems to be an extra impudence in a novel's prosaic recall of a poetic work, a sort of insult in the novel's greedy swallowing of the picked apple of poetry. The poetic loses its incantatory magic in being taken over and surrounded by that which is doggedly nonpoetic.

Reading the work of ancient novelists calls, like the interpretation of a *graphē* such as a painting of Andromeda, for the kind and range of cultural knowledge that a Kleitophon can begin to claim and a Trimalchio signally fails to acquire. Undoubtedly, there are in ancient novels numerous embedded quotations and parodies referring to authors we do not know, so even we can never claim full mastery. In general, Greek novelists do not cite Latin authors, while Roman novelists quote Latin authors in addition to the Greek ones. Apollonius, for instance, is Virgilian (and speaking in almost-hexameter) when he first requires his unknown daughter to leave him in his depression: "Go, and I ask that you do not address me again; for you have only renewed my recent sorrow in me." (36). The last clause (*recentem enim mihi renovasti dolorem*) is a vivid echo of Aeneas' complaint to Dido when she asks him to tell his story: *Infandum, regina, iubes renovare dolorem*: "O queen, you command me to renew unutterable sorrow" (*Aeneid*, II, line 3). At such a moment of echoic allusion we as readers stumble out of the work in question, momentarily, in being reminded of our other reading, of other circumstances and characters. Then we bring these back into the work at hand. The moment of stumbling out, fetching and running back in may be very short—and of course this jolting exercise is not required at all of the ignorant reader who is given no such pause (one reason for the happy state of reading in childhood).

The experience of importing an allusion may seem almost instantaneous, but it breaks up the simplicity of illusion. The author has—we are aware—by this means deliberately achieved a new richness and perplexity, adding to the riddles of the text and enforcing the idea that more than one meaning is always at hand. Literary allusions are less stable than graphic ones. In the passage of *Apollonius* we can do the work of connection quickly, if we first recall Aeneas and then think of sorrow, wandering, and loss (including loss of a wife) shared by Aeneas and Apollonius. Both works, the great Roman epic and the humbler story, deal with the importance and power of memory. For their own health, both heroes must tell the story they do not wish to tell, a story they think untellable. But the text leaves it up to the reader to decide or hit upon all these relevant points, and more disturbingly in relation to a dialogue between father and daughter, whether to import that element of sexual attraction which must present itself whenever we think of Dido and Aeneas.

All the novelists, Greek and Latin alike, quote Homer, that great reservoir of allusion and meanings. One entire work, *The Diary of the Trojan War* (*Ephemeris Belli Troiani*), supposedly by a narrator called "Dictys Cretensis," is a fresh telling of the Trojan war story, with material culled from Homer and the dramatists but liberally altered. It registers itself everywhere as in strong dissent from Homer, but part of the point must be that the reader recollects the *Iliad*. The *Iliad* is found in just about every novel. It is quoted, for instance, in *Chaireas and Kallirrhoé*, just before the Sappho allusion mentioned above—and the two very different allusions disturb or "deform" each other. One can see why the notion that the Novel as a genre came to *supersede* something took root—for every novel makes itself out to be the supersessor to other works, setting aside and replacing other texts by playing with them.

Though the *Iliad* may be popular with novelists, the references to the *Odyssey* are particularly striking both in frequency and emphasis. In *Chaireas and Kallirrhoé*, again, when the steward Leonas brings Dionysios Kallirrhoé as a slave and refers to her brutally as such (77), Dionysios rebukes him with apposite lines of the *Odyssey*: "For the gods, like strangers from faraway countries, / Observe both the *hubris* and righteousness of human beings" (see. *Odyssey*, XVII, lines 485–487). Chariton not only proves his own wit with this apt allusion, but also makes us see that Dionysios is well-bred, pedantic, and moral. And we can see that this particular allusion serves to emphasize the motifs of strangeness and estrangement as they are working in the novel.

We need not go far into other novels to find allusions to the *Odyssey*. Kleitophon prowling to his girlfriend's bedroom is told to act like Odysseus in the Kyklops' cave, Encolpius is overtaken by a Circe, Lucius the Ass consoles himself that he has been learning from experience—just like Odysseus. The witch Meroe, punishing her absconding lover Socrates in Aristomenes' tale (at the very beginning of *The Golden Ass*), says sarcastically to her sister, "And I to be sure, deserted like Calypso by the cunning Ulysses, shall weep in eternal solitude" (I:26).

The *Aithiopika* not only begins with a scene reminiscent of the *Odyssey*, but also contains a vision of Odysseus. An old man appears to Kalasiris in a dream, a man with a cunning expression, wearing a leather helmet and with a wound in one leg. The description (Kalasiris' *ekphrasis*) of the vision is full of Homeric echoes, so the wise reader may solve the riddle before Kalasiris names the visionary man. This personage is angry at Kalasiris and his charges for not having paid tribute to him by visiting his home; since Kalasiris is neglectful of his fame, he and his friends may expect to undergo ordeals like his own, on land and sea. But the old man's wife sends greetings to the young girl and wishes her well on account of her chastity (*sōphrosynē*) (II:66–67).

This whole episode is an audacious game between author, character, and reader, eliciting our joint awareness of the many ways in which the *Odyssey* might be replayed. By the time Heliodorus was writing, the *Odyssey* itself had been used to supply moral allegorical meanings and terms. The epic had issued in large patterns of interpretation, invoked playfully here, in intimation that the author is aware of the kinds of reading his own text will evoke. Kalasiris' dream tells us that we already know how much can be said about *sōphrosynē*, and how *useful* the *Odyssey* has been. Odysseus as he appears here, only a dream figure, seems played out. He is a comic ghost (as he is in Horace's Fifth Satire of the Second Book). This antiheroic Odysseus speaks to Kalasiris with a sneering smile. His petulant anger we may take as standing for the hostility of the epic to its heir and successor, the Novel.

This "dream" does not affect us like characterological narrative dreams; we recognize it as an outrageous literary allusion that is also a clever use of *ekphrasis*, pointing to the relation of (and distance between) epic and novel. Odysseus may sneer at Kalasiris and his friends, but this novel, as it were, cocks a snook at the epic. However much epic quotation may be taken aboard, the Novel never succumbs to the epic. The Novel—any novel—always knows itself to be more than a match for what it quotes; it is a magpie that will pick up anything, an ostrich that can digest anything.

NARRATIVE MODES AND POINTS OF VIEW

The success of a novel in keeping us under its spell depends on its effective deployment of narrative modes and manners. Some sort of voice must be found to tell the story in—even while tale told becomes story read, the sweet soothing whisper metamorphosed into the scratchings of the Nilotic reed. Novelistic narrative, like the epic, allows—or even demands—the presence of the Author Who Knows All, the Authority. In novel criticism we have learned to call this Homeric personage the "omniscient author." Yet this may be a slightly mistaken term. I take seriously Meir Sternberg's contention that the Jewish Bible presents us with the only full and uncompromising "omniscient author" in our literature. The narrator of any book of the Bible (until we get to the Minor Prophets) is impersonal and utterly authoritative, speaking uniformly in full knowledge, though sometimes with ironic withholdings of information. This narrator, who "has free access to the minds ('hearts') of his dramatis personae, not excluding God himself" always "speaks with the authority of omniscience." The Bible thus "concretizes the opposition to the human norm" in its characters and readers alike; the author's "firm hold on the truth" contrasts with their "blindness, stumbling, wonder" (*The Poetics of Biblical Narrative*, 84–85). Unlike other authors, Western or Eastern, the authors of the biblical writings nowhere make any attempt to identify an individual narrating self; all writers have incorporated their telling into the magnificent voice of utter authority. Compared with this model, in which Omniscience is a central subject, even Homeric narration pales, exhibiting as it does fluctuating and illogical degrees of knowledge (88).

The voice we hear in the telling of a novel in third person, the "author" is a slightly more personalized entity in novels than in epic narration, and much less truly authoritative than the narrator in Exodus or Kings. A novel-relater, even in third person, has identity, human personality. This is true, for instance, of the Author who stands in for Henry Fielding and tells the story of *Tom Jones*; he gives his opinions, utters maxims, makes points based on his own observations of men and manners, and even comically introduces points of autobiography. Chariton and Heliodorus, among ancient novelists the notable practitioners of "omniscient" telling, tell us who they are. We should call this personalized but knowledgeable entity "the almost-omniscient author." Such an "author" can decide what is to be known and what is to remain unknown. Most Western narrators through the ages, even in third person, like to leave some moments of opacity, some reality that they cannot quite break through—as in Chaucer's "But God woot what that May thoughte in hir herte" ("Merchant's Tale," line 1851). This is true of Fielding's Author, who is sometimes sure of the motives of his characters, and sometimes professes only to suggest them: "Whether the insatiable Curiosity of this good Woman had carried her on to that Business, or whether she did it to confirm herself in the good Graces of Mrs. *Blifil* . . . I will not determine" (*Tom Jones*, 61).

George Eliot creates her own version of such a powerful Author in the *persona* that tells us the story of *Middlemarch*. She (or rather the authorial persona) sets up a comparison with Fielding:

> A great historian, as he insisted on calling himself . . . glories in his copious remarks and digressions as the least imitable part of his work, and especially in those initial chapters . . . where he seems to bring his arm-chair to the proscenium and chat with us in all the lusty ease of his fine English. But Fielding lived when the days were longer (for time, like money, is measured by our needs), when summer after-noons were spacious, and the clock ticked slowly in the winter even-ings. We belated historians must not linger after his example; and if we did so, it is probable that our chat would be thin and eager, as if delivered from a camp-stool in a parrot-house. I at least have so much to do in unravelling certain human lots, and seeing how they were woven and interwoven, that all the light I can command must be con-centrated on this particular web, and not dispersed over that tempting range of relevancies called the universe.   (*Middlemarch*, 96)

This is of course one of the many "copious remarks and digressions" of-fered by the Author who disclaims digression, this nineteenth-century narrator who is to be known as "George Eliot" (not Marian Evans). Part of the appeal of Fielding is his authorial ability to offer digressive remarks, including descriptions of generalities and general observations on human affairs, such as, "But it is with Jealousy, as with the Gout. When such Distempers are in the Blood, there is never any Security against their breaking out; and often on the slightest Occasions . . ." (*Tom Jones*, 63). "George Eliot" also interweaves a number of maxims and obser-vations into the texture of narrative: "Our vanities differ as our noses do" (*Middle-march*, 102); "Our passions do not live apart in locked chambers, but, dressed in their small wardrobe of notions, bring their provisions to a common table . . ." (ibid., 114–115). The omniscient historian may nudge us into accepting a par-ticular plot development by dint of judicious generalization: "It sometimes hap-pens that we find ourselves interested from the first glance in complete strangers, even before we have spoken to them" (Dostoevsky, *Crime and Punishment*, 9).

This assumed capacity or duty to act as the "historian" of human nature is one of the implicit duties—or prerogatives—of the novelist from the beginning of novel-writing in the West. What is possibly the earliest extant example of prose fiction narrative by the Omniscient Author—Chariton's *Chaireas and Kallirrhoé*—offers significant illustration of that capacity, as well as a number of other tech-niques associated with the All-Knowing Author. Chariton identifies himself in his first sentence, offering rather bluntly some autobiographical details, attesting to himself as historical being in time and space. But this "Chariton of Aphrodisias" soon becomes the large figure, the generalizing wise historian, who more than fulfills his promise, also found in the first sentence; "I am going to narrate [*diēgē-somai*] the suffering of love that befell in Syracuse." Once he has embarked on this narrative, Chariton is wise, witty, paradoxical, dry or dramatic, as suits the moment. He keeps us in his confidence: "Fate [*Tychē*] . . . now performed an extraordinary [*paradoxon*] deed, or, more correctly, even unbelievable [*apiston*]: it is worth *hearing* [emphasis mine] the way it happened [*ton tropon*]" (86). He encourages us, that is, to keep *listening*. Seriously present as relater, the one who knows what happens and what is going to happen, Chariton is also the serious (or mock-serious) historian of human nature. When Theron, the grave robber and bandit, newly come to Ionia, sees the crowd around the black-clad Dionysios, he bestirs himself to find out who the gloomy but important personage is; Chariton inserts the observation, "Man is by nature curious" (67–68). When that same Theron, in the little boat surrounded by the cadavers of his companions, decides to admit to the investigating Chaireas and his party that he is alive, Chariton offers a digressive observation: "By nature man is a lover of being alive [*philozōon*], and even in the worst combination of woes hopes that things will take a turn for the better. The Demiurge has sown this illusion [*sophisma*] in all men everywhere, so that they should not fly from a life of hardship" (100). A number of Chariton's maxims are generalizations applied to the deities or powers: "Eros loves conflict and enjoys unexpected turns [*paradoxois*]" (50). Chariton also slyly investigates characters' motives: for instance, when the Great King (*Basileus*) of Persia commands Dionysios to come for trial, his thoughts are political and prudent, but his decision is based on the hidden reasoning of private desire: "But another feeling urged him to summon the beautiful lady; in his solitude his only counselors were night and darkness, which recalled to him that part of the letter . . . that spoke of Kallirrhoé as the most beautiful woman in Ionia" (128–129). Chariton's manner is generally witty; he is playful about the strokes of Fate (*Tychē*) that he relates, and he wants to make sure that we are enjoying the effects. In comic conduct of the story he bears a resemblance to Fay Weldon.[4]

If in Chariton we see the flowering of the authorial narrative third-person manner, in Heliodorus we see third-person narration elaborated. There are interjections by the Authorial "I." For instance, the Authorial "I" intervenes as an audible commentator on the death of Arsaké: "But I think [*oimai*] that the soul of this wicked woman was more bitter than the poison" (*Aithiopika*, III: 15). Heliodorus, however, complicates his narrative by having many narrators, including Knemon and Charikleia. These inset narrators are all subordinated to the implied author; they are in ironic positions even when they can take pride in their own ability to deceive or conceal. A very large part of the novel is made over to Kalasiris, and Kalasiris' narrative extends the suspense. The temporal dislocation of the story line subordinates straight plot to narrative *telling*, I-narration focusing our attention on the teller (or tellers). We are made to realize how much we rely on a "voice"—an imaginary voice—to help us along; we see that narrative itself is what makes for coherence, and that coherence in a diegetic work is always imagined in terms related to personality. We are asked to *hear* these tellers, and in the hearing to gain a new memory, and a fresh sense of interconnection. The vital tellers themselves, whether third-person Author or first-person character-narrators (and whether continuous or intermittent), may not always know everything or put things together properly. Kalasiris, the amazing copious narrator of the middle of *Aithiopika*, is himself not always good at taking in what he is told—it seems no accident that he is, as he admits, just a little deaf (II: 37). But all these "voices" push us along, giving us a sense of unity arising from a conscious subject, a human center—and human centredness or consciousness, or even "subjectivity," is itself a subject of the Novel.

Ancient novelists rarely use the device known as free indirect discourse (or *style indirect libre*) whereby the authorial voice assumes the view and attitudes of a character. Sternberg believes there are some examples in the Bible, where it is "a biblical resource for capturing the inner life" (*Poetics of Biblical Narrative*, 52), although judging from his examples such moments are transient. The device seems not entirely absent from ancient novels, though not exploited as it will be in modern works. For instance, when Kybelé is praising Arsaké for the benefit of Theagenes, the third-person authorial voice seems to drop into the idiom and even sentence-form of its subject: "She greatly praised her mistress's loving disposition and made occasion for him to see her beauty, not just her appearance but under her clothes, and praised her sweetness of disposition and her condescension and her affection for all young men who were gentle and lively . . ." (II: 146). The tone and terms of Kybelé seem to persist here in the authorial relation—the phrase "under her clothes" is Kybelé's own manner, as well as the gushing sentence.

As we have seen, antiquity produced entire novels in first-person narrative; the stories told by Kleitophon, Encolpius, and Lucius are our prime examples. In this category should be included the first-person *Diary of the Trojan War* (*Ephemeris Belli Troiani*) by "Dictys of Crete"—a Latin novel for which we know there was a Greek original. Dictys of Crete claims first-person knowledge: "I served in the contingent which was formerly brought before Troy." This honest Cretan—a contradiction in terms, for proverbially "all Cretans are liars"—claims to describe events personally known to him. "Whatever happened afterwards, since I took part in it, I will explain as truthfully as I can" (11). Dictys ascribes motives to others when he thinks he knows them, and admits ignorance or doubt about others' state of mind when he feels he does not know—for instance, he does not know if Agamemnon ever knew the real fate of Iphigenia (20). Stefan Merkle has decided that the intention of the unknown author (or authors)—as distinct from the narrating "Dictys"—was to write a propaganda story against war. In a novel which offers an oblique rejection of Rome, the narrator describes and exhibits the moral decline of a war's victors, in a manner indicating that the author "had an ethical purpose: to reveal the disastrous effects of war on human character" ("Telling the True Story of the Trojan War," *TSAN*, 194). We see beyond Dictys to what he has to show.[5] Nor need we think the author of the *Ephemeris Belli Troiani* incapable of such irony.

In its use of what we may call the "found manuscript game," the Latin *Ephemeris* resembles Antonius Diogenes' *Apista hyper Thulēn*. Dictys' work (according to the preface) was buried in his grave in Crete and came to light in an earthquake. Nero then ordered it to be translated from ancient Phoenician into Greek, the translation to be stored in a library. In Antonius Diogenes' novel, we can see (even in Photius' summary) an extensive elaboration of the discovery and transmission of a manuscript. In this case, cypress tablets survived Alexander's siege of Tyre by being buried in a grave-vault. Both texts are thus, as it were, once declared officially dead, but proved living. They are resurrected, like heroines.

Both belong to an older or "other" culture not homogenous with the Greco-Roman. The story of the text *trouvé* seems in both cases to have political overtones. The moral *Ephemeris*, we might gather, is needed in Nero's reign. *Apista hyper Thulēn* barely escaped the dangers of imperialistic war and ruination. Important messages are attacked or hidden, texts are dead until we hear them. They come to light, but they need not only to be transcribed and translated, but also to be read properly. Textual transmission is dangerous and delicate. The found manuscripts need readers who can read with the right kind of attention. The framework of both these narratives indicates a keen and ironic awareness of the problems of textuality, sources, origins, and truth.

The immediate "truth" of a story depends on the trustworthiness of its narrator. First-person narrators in ancient fiction are frequently and even overtly untrustworthy. The obvious exception is the "Clemens" of *Recognitiones*, whose naïve candor is part of his charm. Other first-person narrators are more ambiguous.[6] The first-person narrator can, very obviously, be something of a rascal, as Encolpius is, for instance. It has often been recognized that there is a resemblance between early "picaresque fiction" of the modern West and the novels of Petronius and Apuleius.[7] Social criticism, sharp social comedy, become available through the mocking (if, at times naïve) eyes of the antique *picaro*, the down-on-his-luck semidelinquent trying to make his way through a greedy and divided society.

The persona of the sharp-eyed observer evidently bears some relation to the persona of the traditional Cynic observer. The Cynics were affected by the "naked philosophers" (gymnosophists) of an India newly opened by the travels and conquests of Alexander. In the *Alexander Romance*, the gymnosophists tell Alexander that they have nothing to give him and want nothing from him. They also mercilessly define him to his face: "You are a wild beast, and see how many other wild beasts you have with you, to help you tear away the lives of other beasts" (*Alexander*, trans. Stoneman, 132). Similar "gymnosophists" illuminate and correct the religious, familial and political life of Ethiopia at the end of the *Aithiopika*. The Cynic as observer is a negative gymnosophist who sees through the shams of culture and is alienated from society. The Cynics' negative dogmas precluded a search for fame through writing, but the effects of their satiric mode are to be found in Roman satires such as Juvenal's. The Cynic "school" (which could not be one) gave birth to the satires of the Syrian Cynic Menippus, who wrote in the mid-third century B.C. Menippus' satires, written in a mixture of prose and verse, are now lost to us, but they were known in the ancient world, and the mixture of prose and verse in *Satyricon* connects it with the works of Menippus.

Are the heroes of *Satyricon* and *Metamorphoses* speaking to us in the first person merely because they are rascals who can yet function as Cynic observers? Or can we see other elements in their self-presentation? First-person narration is usually brought up in relation only to the Roman comic novels, but the topic becomes more complex and interesting if we include the Greek first-person novels. In Achilles Tatius' novel, Kleitophon cannot be neatly pigeonholed as *picaro* or as Cynic observer. He is the hero of a love-story who is himself a distinctly comic character, but the comedy individualizes him rather than making him seem a general type. There are winning elements in his naïveté, his anxiety. His unheroic passivity has its own comic appeal—as when he describes being suddenly assaulted by the irate husband of Melitté: "I, as if I were the participant in some mystery rite, had no idea who the man was, or why he was hitting me. . . . When he grew tired of hitting me, and I of my philosophy, I got up, saying, 'Who are you, man? and why have you assaulted me?' But he got more angry . . ." (290).

Kleitophon is much more reasonable or "philosophic" than valiant. His self-portrayal suggests a change in the presentation of masculinity, a desire to explore various options, including being a love-object and/or striving for *parthenia en andrasi*. Sharply focused as it is, a first-person narrative like Kleitophon's consistently reminds us of the sheer difficulty of being human; the anxieties of existence come through apparently unmediated.

The ancient novel shows a very high respect for individual experience as reflected in narration. Even the ambitious *Aithiopika* is partly carried through first-person intercalated narration, the longest section being Kalasiris' tale, within which we also have the important story told by Charikles about his adoption of the little girl, as well as the written first-person narration of Persinna (decoded by Kalasiris). When any one of these narrating characters errs, or seems brusque or cruel or interfering—or, as in the case of Knemon, too timid—we are already supplied with information proved on our pulses, sufficient to carry our sympathies with our judgment. One important thing the multiple tellings do is to give us the decided impression that there is not one story, but *many* stories, each worthy of respect, even while the interests of some of these narrators may collide in the course of the plot.

In novels of all periods, part of the narration is usually carried out by some of the characters. Contributing to narration is a job characteristic of "characters." It makes this attribute no less "novelistic" to note that it is also an attribute of characters in the *Odyssey*, in which many narrators such as Nestor and Menelaus are in a kind of competition with the superb narrator Odysseus who spins his yarn to the Phaiakians.

EPISTLES IN ANCIENT NOVEL NARRATION

One non-epic manner of novelistic participation on the part of the characters of novels is the contribution of epistles. Characters in the ancient novels seem perpetually to be reading—or writing—letters. Kleitophon at the wedding banquet with Melitté is amazed to receive the letter from Leukippé. He exclaims upon it, aside to Satyros, and then carefully reads and rereads it: "I read the letter again, as if I could see herself in it, and acknowledged the reproach it contained. 'Justly you blame me, my darling! . . .'" (278).

Novel characters are not only letter-readers, but also careful *re*readers, as we know, for example, through Elizabeth Bennet's rereading of Darcy's letter in *Pride and Prejudice* (1813). Kleitophon, unlike Elizabeth Bennet, has the immediate problem of writing a reply to the letter he has perused so carefully, and not without blushes. He even asks Satyros to help him compose an answer to this epistle of resurrection: "But what I am to write?—for I am so violently astounded by what has come to pass that I am completely at a loss [*aporōs*]" (280). The reader's enjoyment of the epistle Kleitophon pens on this occasion is heightened by the knowledge of the circumstances of the letter, including the frustration and anxiety of its author. It is in writing this hasty but important epistle that Kleitophon strikes out one of his most interesting thoughts—his wondering if there can be *parthenia* in the male sex.

Kleitophon recognized Leukippé's *handwriting.* Similarly, in Chariton's *Chaireas and Kallirrhoé,* Dionysios recognizes the handwriting of Kallirrhoé (*ta Kallirrhoēs grammata*) when he receives the letter she secretly sent him (by Queen Statira) while on her way home with her first husband, Chaireas. "This alone she did apart from Chaireas." Kallirrhoé's secret epistle is very clever: it gives Dionysios thanks for liberating her from brigands and slavery, and emphasizes the bond between them in his son. She begs him to look after the boy—and not to give him a step-mother. She mentions Chaireas not at all; her last words are not only gracious but affectionate: "Goodbye, good Dionysios, and remember thy Kallirrhoé" (190–191). She knows how greatly Dionysios always desired to be—and to be thought—good (*agathos*). The reader's admiration is certain to be caught by this tactful epistle, but the pay-off comes when we see Dionysios in the process of receiving, reading, and interpreting it: "recognizing Kallirrhoé's handwriting he first kissed the letter, then opening it hugged it to his bosom as if she herself were present, and for a long while he held it so, not capable of reading it through his tears" (195).

When Dionysios is able to read, he reads carefully, trying to weigh each phrase. He is distressed, for a start, by her salutation: "Kallirrhoé to her benefactor Dionysios"; the word *benefactor* is displeasing: "'Alas!' he said, 'why not husband?'" He finds more to cheer him as he goes on, and reads the letter (or that part of it he regards as her *apologia,* or defense) many times, making himself believe that "it secretly indicated that she abandoned him unwillingly." "So nimble is Eros," the Author adds, "and so easy it is to seduce oneself into the belief that one is loved in return" (195). The reader participates in trying to interpret the epistle. The sending of Kallirrhoé's letter is a complex and ironic matter. Dionysios' deluded reading seems not *utterly* deluded. Kallirrhoé's primary objective is to care for her child, but she always wants to behave nicely, and it is not her way to forget anybody—she remembers in this important letter to send a warm greeting to Plangon, once her fellow-servant. Kallirrhoé is the sort of person who sustains relationships, keeps them going over distances and time. When she bids farewell to the Queen of Persia, who is going back to her Basileus, Kallirrhoé is very affectionate: "'Farewell, O Statira,' she said, 'and remember me and write to me often [*graphe moi pollakis*] in Syracuse'" (191).

"Write to me often in Syracuse"—ah, there we have the true novelistic note. Epic characters tend to be present to each other or absent, divided by absolute distances, living cleanly in a now. Novelistic characters are in a web of entanglements and connections, a web only partly signified by the entanglements and "threads" and "plot lines" of any plot. The possibility of *letters* means that nothing is quite ended, that private self and public self will continue to shift and slide into one another, that each soul knows relationships which are many, not one, and complex, not simple. Kallirrhoé wants to get letters from her female friend Statira—even back home in Syracuse, with her parents and devoted husband, she can imagine wanting some other communication, a network of personal affections stretching beyond the household, and even beyond romantic love. The very idea of epistles of that sort extends the possibilities of human connections. In Kallirrhoé we have the woman who writes. Surely she signifies a cultural shift. We have argued as much for the case of the women in France and England in the seventeenth century. Perhaps because of that interest we have been attracted to the Pompeiian picture, the "portrait of a lady" commonly referred to as "Sappho"—but she may be merely an image of a woman writing a letter, one of those devastating private letters that change the course of our individual histories.

My contemporaries and I, at one time, believed that the idea of letter-writing was intertwined with a respect for the importance of the individual related to Protestant religious faith and practice, and related also to the development of the new capitalist economy with its circulation of commodities, including printed books and posted letters. I, too, believed that the participation of the female character as heroine—as of the female writer as author—was closely bound up with the emergence of the epistolary narration, and that the appearance in 1669 of the epistolary novella *Lettres Portugaises* marked the beginning of a new era in fiction. We have not been allowing for older events and older traditions. The change from an oral to a writing culture was taking place with great rapidity in the time of the Roman Empire. The Alexandrian Man—and Woman—becomes more and more often a person who can read and write.

Embracing Kallirrhoé's letter, Dionysios acts as if it were her presence—*parousia*—though what he has is not her presence, not her absence either, but her letter. Of the many resurrections that characters in the novel go through this is not the least notable. It is Kallirrhoé's second coming, a life beyond life—the *Parousia* in Christian theology signifies the Second Coming of Christ, as in I Corinthians 15:23, a text itself emerging in a new era of private letter-writing. Saint Paul writes epistles, like the fictional Kallirrhoé, emphasizing that he has set down the letters with his own hand: "You see with what large letters I have written to you with my own hand" (*Idete pēlikois hymin grammasin egrapsa tēi emēi cheiri*: Galatians 6:11). So Kallirrhoé emphasizes to Plangon the personal touch: "This to thee I have written with my own hand" (*tauta soi gegrapha tēi emēi cheiri*, 191). The *writing hand* lies mysteriously, half elusively, behind the written words—somewhere there is a reality that the written words both are and are not. From this focus of interest upon writing, and upon the mysteriously personal nature of writing and the mysteriously important nature of the individual *person* ("He recognized her handwriting"), comes the epistolary narration within novels, and the novel in letters.

The epistolary novella *Chion of Heraklea* is short and philosophical. But it exhibits an appreciation of the ironic variability of letters, even those emanating from a single source; for instance, the hero tells Metris that the untrustworthy and disagreeable Archepolis has asked for a letter of introduction; this frank epistle (no. 7) is followed by the actual letter of introduction itself that Archepolis carries, which is a bland if guarded letter of recommendation. The ironies are apparent only if one has read the first letter (57–59). It is likely that there were many more antique prose stories in letters which are lost to us. But a novel does not have to be told in letters in order for letters to be prominent and functional features of narration. Letter-writing is one of the things novel characters do best, and do frequently—it comes naturally to them, like dreaming.

THE SELF-CONSCIOUS NOVEL OF ANTIQUITY

Ancient novels exhibit a profound consciousness of writing. They reflect upon their own writtenness. This is particularly true of *Asinus Aureus*. The first sentences of Apuleius' novel move us from voice to pen: we must inspect the written page, that mysterious *Egyptian* written page. Lucius-as-ass in the cave, listening to the old woman tell her tale of Psyche to Charité, wishes, absurdly enough, for writing implements: "But standing not very far away I lamented, by golly, that I did not have tablets and stylus to note down such a lovely story" (*tam bellam fabellam*, I: 354). Much good a stylus and tablets would do an ass! If Lucius in his asinine form is still writerly, the Lucius who is narrator is even more aware of writing and the written. He thinks of his *reader*. Perhaps, he says at one point in Book IX, the reader will wonder how the ass could have known all that was going on? "But perhaps you, scrupulous reader [*lector scrupulosus*], censuring my narrative, will make objection thus: 'How come, astute ass, you were able to know . . . what the women were up to?'" (II: 180).

In introducing this argumentative conference with the reader, Apuleius is, as Winkler points out, the forerunner of Laurence Sterne. There is always to be a precise, skeptical reader at the other end, a *scrupulosus lector*, weighing and thinking about what is going on. "Scrupulous reading . . . is a fictional attitude subsumed within the more complex performance of actually reading" (Winkler, *Auctor*, 62). The fun of authoring a narrative is in part the fun of imagining such a *lector*.

Lucius himself is prone to love the *lector*, and he almost idolizes books. More like Tristram Shandy than Laurence Sterne, Lucius seems to feel that existence is completed only by being *in* a book. He tells the dinner-party group that a Chaldean astrologer, back in Corinth, told his fortune, when Lucius asked about his present voyage: "he said really wonderful and quite various things: now that I will sufficiently prosper and boast of renown [*gloriam satis floridam*], now that I will be a great history, an incredible tale in books" (I: 82–84).

Such a passage reminds us, very forcefully, that Lucius who is "talking" to us, or writing everything down himself, is really a product of a book, shut up in a book. That, rather than his priesthood, is his ultimate *metamorphosis*—to be a character in a book. He is the hero of writtenness; that is his "glory," to feature in an incredible tale in a work of several volumes. But beyond that, he is "really" just a set of marks on a page.

It is clearly unkind to remind novel characters that that is all they are. Alice got into trouble in Wonderland for telling the Queen of Hearts and the whole court "You're nothing but a pack of cards!" (Chap. 12). Tristram Shandy, who has something at stake, ventures a digressive reproach to scholars dealing with the case of the Biblical Job:

> (in case there ever was such a man—if not, there's an end of the matter.—
>
> Though, by the bye, because your learned men find some difficulty in fixing the precise aera in which so great a man lived;—whether, for instance, before or after the patriarchs, &c.—to vote, therefore, that he never lived *at all*, is a little cruel,—'tis not doing as they would be done by—happen that as it may). . . (279)

The benevolent reader (with benevolent ears, *auresque tuas benivolas*) has a pudency about reminding novel "characters" of their status as mere paper; we know it is not doing as we would be done by, indeed. Like Lucius and Tristram Shandy—not to mention Don Quixote—we may in some sense envy the novel characters their papery position because of their fresh and flowering fame.

The novelists of antiquity seem fully aware of the division within the reader who is being constructed (as Wolfgang Iser has it) as "implied reader." As "implied readers" we, too, have been metamorphosed into paper. The desire to take the story very literally and to live within it is counteracted by an aesthetic desire to distance oneself and watch the narrative in operation. We know what we have is a virtual reality, an "as if" that we share in creating.[8] Most antique novelists seem to be as well aware of this division (and as eager to exploit it) as later novelists such as Cervantes and Fielding. The novels carry with the fable their own "meta-fable," consisting not only of explicit appeals to the reader but also of the manipulation of aesthetic and philosophical terms evoking the reader's knowledge of literary custom. The reader—even the reader genuinely caught up in the excitement, the adventure, the love-story—is seduced into amusement at seeing how literary customs are being set a-working here and now.

If ever any novelist knew all the contemporary terms and fashions and philosophies of literature, it is Heliodorus, who makes his own heroine, Charikleia, a paragon not only of heroic virtue but also of literary knowledge. In her first speech she casts herself as a personage in a drama; the bandits' murder of herself and her lover would be like the last scene in a tragedy. She is the channel for the reader's suspicion of the authorial machinery when she asks how Thisbe got into that cave so handily, as if she were brought to Egypt by the theater *machine*. But it is not only dramatic practice that Charikleia knows. She understands the principles of plot, and narrative plot, including such a plot as the one she figures in. She explains the plot's structure and principles to Theagenes, who desires a quick ending:

> "O sweetheart," she said, "the bigger the business, the greater the preparations. For when a demon has entangled the very beginning of a complicated plot, it's impossible for that to come to an end save through a long-drawn-out process of multiple conclusions. Besides, something which has become increasingly more complicated over a long period of time cannot suddenly be unveiled and unknotted, es-

pecially when the chief worker of the whole piece, the weaver of the web, the one on whom recognition depends—I mean Persinna, my mother—is not there." (III : 69)

Charikleia understands all about plot and the tangled web and the various plot threads—almost as well as George Eliot, whose riposte to Fielding ends with the same metaphorical language for the conduct of novelistic plot: "I at least have so much to do in *unravelling* certain human lots, and seeing how they were *woven* and *interwoven*, that all the light I can command must be concentrated on this particular *web*" (*Middlemarch*, 96). The "George Eliot" who is the invented Author of this novel (and thus also a sort of character in it) pretends that the threads of the human lots were woven together without her assistance, and that she merely illuminates the "web"—a pretense very close to Charikleia's.

It seems we require textured texts, that we like the imagery of weaving and web, the sense of the story as *plasmata*, madeness, textuality itself—textuality. Textuality becomes one with material texture in the knotted *quipus* of Graffigny's *Letters d'une Péruvienne* (1747) or in the soft band of silk, the *tainia* (or Greek *brassière*), Charikleia's sash, upon which is embroidered Persinna's story (*Aithiopika*, I : 89).

Who weaves the web? We remember in *Paul and Thekla* that Thekla's mother complained to the girl's fiancé, Thyamis, that Thekla, listening to Paul, stuck in the window "like a spider" (*hōs arachnē*, 164). This seems a homely simile enough, but is Thekla not an Arachne, a plot-weaver, in deciding to change her lot? Charikleia has a comical readiness to attribute everything that happens to the demon (*daimon*) who is in charge of her fate. When Theagenes has been captured while Knemon is happily celebrating his wedding, Charikleia goes into a passion of sorrowful rage, and speaks to her guardian divinity with the utmost sarcasm of which she is capable—which in Charikleia's case is quite lot: " 'Let us celebrate,' she said, 'let us praise in the dance this demon who has fallen to our lot, upon this fresh development! Let us offer him songs of mourning, and cheer him with the enactment of our miseries!' " (II : 97).

She is rather nicer about her demon after she has been saved from execution by burning: "This wonder . . . of my being saved undoubtedly seems like the divine work of some demonic power." But she is rapidly more doubtful. The misfortune which falls upon them so unremittingly, she says, indicates that the gods must be against them. Unless—she adds—"Unless this is a miracle wrought by some demon who enjoys casting us into the uttermost depths in order to save us from truly desperate situations" (*tōn aporōn*, III : 23).

It is the role of novel characters to find themselves in extremity or at a loss, confronted by aporias, no-exit signs; frustration is a normal condition. Charikleia's *daimon* or demonic power, who seems to take pleasure in creating complications and in plunging herself and her lover into impossible dangers, is reflected in a later major novel by a writer strongly influenced by Heliodorus. In *Don Quijote* the Don's "sage enchanter" fulfills the role of the *daimon* of Charikleia. Don Quijote at his first errant outsetting is pleased to imagine the power who is to record his exploits: "O thou, sage enchanter [*sabio encantador*], whosoever thou mayst be, to whom it is given to be the chronicler of this traveling history! Forget not, I pray, my good Rosinante . . ." (42). But once his niece blames the destruction of his library on some "enchanter," the historian-enchanter becomes malign; "He is a sage enchanter [*sabio encantador*], a great enemy of mine, who holds a grudge against me, because he knows by his arts and letters what is going to happen, and knows there will come a time when I will encounter in single combat a knight whom he favors, and that I will win . . . " (78). If at this point Don Quixote still thinks he has some freedom in opposition to the enchanter, as troubles accumulate he believes more and more heartily in the power of this mysterious and invisible opponent.

It is an open secret, as it were, of the novel *Don Quijote* that the "sage enchanter" who is both benevolent Historian and malign Fate must be none other than the Author himself, invisible but all-pervasive, even if hidden behind the narrating *personae* of both the Spanish Narrator and Cide Hamete Benengeli. It is equally an open secret of the novel *Aithiopika* that Charikleia's *daimon* is her *sabio encantador*, the Author of her novel. It is the Author who enjoys thwarting the heroine's plans and wishes for the sake of the plot, and shares with the reader a certain pleasure in plunging her into desperate situations and then snatching her out of them at the last minute.

Once we recognize the *Aithiopika*'s novelistic jokes about its own writtenness, become sensitive to its "self-consciousness" (in modern parlance), then we may employ this self-consciousness as a key to interpreting various circumstances in the novel. One of the passages that brings the matter of interpretation to the fore is Charikles' dream. Charikles interpreted his unhappy dream of the loss of his daughter as a prophecy of her imminent death (wrong). Kalasiris, to soothe him, tells him it prophesies the daughter's marriage (she *does* eventually get married, but not as Charikles at the moment would wish). The *reader*, now knowing the heroine's Ethiopian background, takes the dream-parable as a hidden prophecy of the heroine's journey home to Ethiopia—"the land of dark and shadowy forms." Her quest is to get home, and we believe this is what Kalasiris sees in Charikles' dream and keeps hidden from the dreamer.

The passages dealing with Charikles' dream are thus already sufficiently complex. But—is there not yet another possible interpretation of this puzzling dream-vision? The place full of dark and shadowy shapes—*eidōla*—may that not be the realm of the novel itself? What will happen to Charikleia ultimately is what happens to Lucius of the *Golden Ass*: she will have glory enough, featuring in a great history, an incredible tale in books. She belongs to the land of shadows; that is, she is a novel character, and her image or *eidōlon* is transmitted only through the dark shapes of the letters on the page. She belongs to the shadowiness and unreality of novel characters, placed there by the power of the Apollo who governs art. She is turned into a work of art; she is, after all, only the creation of *fiction*.

The ancient novel proves itself highly sophisticated—even in our own terms. But it is time to ask ourselves whether these are altogether the right or the only terms. Plot, characters, realism, setting, dialogue—these are the concerns of the nineteenth century. When we talk about narrative techniques, point-of-view, self-consciousness, we are turning to twentieth-century terms. But is the Novel—any novel—required to live according to our terms, talk our language, in order to prove itself?

Are there not a number of elements in the novels that have not been referred to, or remain developed—even after these last two all-embracing chapters in the present work? Suppose there were in these antique fictions and in other novels some other effects and meanings?—not destructive of the plot, dialogue, characters, narrative voice, and so on, but running beneath and within these things. Suppose—to put it strangely—there were an undersong to these novels, which we should hear? Perhaps the Novel of Antiquity is on a different errand from the sort of errand we have been accustomed to ascribe to novelistic fiction. And if so, then whatever that other errand is may be the task also of the Novel of Now.

CHAPTER VIII

>⊷<⊶<

The Ancient Novel, Religion, and Allegory

>⊷<⊶<

I, as if in a mystery-ritual, had no idea either who the man was or why
he was mercilessly beating me
          —Kleitophon in Achilles Tatius' *Leukippé and Kleitophon*

                a lovely and murky cave
sacred to the nymphs called Naiads
Within are kraters and amphoras
of stone, where bees lay up stores of honey.
Inside, too, are massive stone looms and there the nymphs
weave sea-purple cloth, a wonder to see. —Homer, *Odyssey*

>⊷<⊶<

*R*ather than requiring the Ancient Novel to take out its credentials and
prove itself by assured modern criteria (as if these existed), we may eventually
have to acknowledge that what we know of the Novel of Antiquity affects and
redefines novels of a much later date. Let us make no mistake about it; it is dangerous to look into such possibilities, for we may disturb our vision of the Western
Novel altogether.

    I mentioned earlier two important works: *Die Griechisch-Orientalische Romanliteratur in religionsgeschichtlicher Beleuchtung* ("Graeco-Oriental Novel-Writing
in the Light of Religious Writings") by Karl Kerényi, and *Roman und Mysterium in
der Antike* ("Novel and Mystery in Antiquity") by Reinhold Merkelbach. Both of
these works are well known in classical circles, at least among those classicists
who have much to do with the ancient novels, or with the religion (or religions)
of the Late Antique period.

    Karl Kerényi, a Hungarian of German culture, had a lifelong interest in
mythology. (He was later to work with Jung.) His interest in mythology led Kerényi to connect extant ancient novels according to their mythological content. Kerényi picks up Erwin Rohde's interesting question in relation to the ancient novel: "From what secret source did there arise in Greece something so
un-Greek?" Part of the problem, Kerényi sees, is whether one considers Greekland (*Griechenland*) as Greece (Hellas) or as the Greek-speaking world. In the
latter case, we are taken beyond the boundaries, ultimately not only of the
Greek mainland but also of what is usually considered Hellenism (see Kerényi, *Griechisch-Orientalische Romanliteratur*, 44–45). Kerényi emphasizes the
non-Greek origins of the authors of the novels—the first positive critic to do so
since Huet. He follows Huet in recognizing the "Oriental" (we ought to add
firmly, *African*) elements in Greek novels. The more we look at Egyptian and Oriental religion and religious literature, the clearer the novel becomes: "The 'entirely un-Greek' character of the Greek novels begins to lose its colorlessness for
us" (95). The novel is not Christian in origin; rather, the single definitely Chris-

tian novel, the Clementine *Recognitiones,* shares general themes and characteristics with non-Christian ones. On the other hand, there is a relationship between novelistic and Christian perceptions, a relationship that Kerényi feels is explicable in terms of motifs of older religions, especially the religion of Isis, now moving into centrality and eclipsing what was left of the vanishing Greek religion. The so-called "Greek novels" are each to be considered as "narrations of the *sufferings of divine Personages*" (or "stories of the trials of godly people"—*Erzählungen von Leiden göttlicher Personen,* 95). Novel-characters, as Kerényi works out his theory, are to be seen as reflections of a divine personage, imitating on a human level the trials of that holy being.

All the novels, that is, are to be illuminated by being considered as religious writings, tracing the progress of the soul in the service of a god or goddess. Isis plays a very important role, and the various goddesses are connected, as Isis says in *The Golden Ass.* According to such a scheme of interpretation, it becomes impossible to separate Greek from Roman novels, or fantastic from "realistic." The cave in which the old woman tells Charité the tale of Psyche is in some sense the same as the cave in which Charikleia and Theagenes are reunited. In fact, Kerényi believes Heliodorus must have read either Apuleius' novel or its lost progenitor, the vanished *Metamorphoses.*

The essential "story" is the salvation of the soul through the experience of death and resurrection to new life. Part of this death-experience entails being thrown into a tomb or a covered place, such as a pit or cave (*Höhle*). The tomb may be elaborated on—as is the case with Kallirrhoé's tomb in the beginning of Chariton's novel, and of Chaireas' tomb halfway through the book. "He [Dionysios] forgets that it was only a seeming funeral, and that they put up for Chaireas in place of a tomb (*taphos*) only a cenotaph (*kenotaphion*). But this sort of rhetorical *aposiōpēsis* [broken rhetorical figure] is characteristic of the "Greek novel" (Kerényi, *Griechisch-Orientalische Romanliteratur,* 35).

The reading of these novels was thus (if we believe Kerényi's propositions) something in the nature of a religious experience for their first readers; the fictions developed themes with which we are familiar in a context of Christian theology, but here, by and large, they occur in a context of a new pagan theology working out the soul's relation to the divine.

Reinhold Merkelbach a generation later develops the insights of Kerényi and makes matters more specific. In a brisk and efficient German much easier to follow than Kerényi's more elaborate prose, Merkelbach in *Roman und Mysterium* develops a thesis that the ancient novel is very closely related to the mystery religions of antiquity. The Novel turns out to be essentially a mystery-story indeed! Merkelbach takes Apuleius' *Golden Ass* as his primary text. He discusses the Eros and Psyche story first, as the model for the other narratives, and the story that, as it were, "gives away" the spiritual and even liturgical significance not only of its surrounding narrative (whose hero becomes a priest of Osiris) but also of the other ancient novels. Merkelbach believes that the ancient novels very openly and ostensibly present to us and to their first readers the images and practices and rituals of the mystery cults.

The cult of Isis was associated (as we know from external sources) with the journey. Isis set out in her boat to look for the scattered remains of Osiris (the *Navigium Isidis*). Isis was the patron of all navigation; port cities such as Alexandria celebrated her reign and the opening of the sailing season with enthusiasm. This great feast of Isis is described in the Book XI of the *Golden Ass*, but is also referred to in Heliodorus in Book IX, where commentary on the Nile is lengthy and important. The journey of Kleitophon and Leukippé to Egypt is a ritual journey: "The wandering journey is a penalty set by the Goddess Isis-Tyché" (Merkelbach, *Roman und Mysterium*, 139). When Leukippé drinks the Nile water, it is a purification "just as the Isis *mystēs* would be healed through the sacrament of Nile water" (136).

In Isis' Egypt Kleitophon meets the rich young widow Melitté: "Melitté is an Ephesian woman and as beautiful as a portrait of a goddess. Her husband is drowned at sea.—This woman is in a very remarkable way an 'image' of Isis: she is an Ephesian woman like Artemis-Isis, and her husband is drowned like Osiris. The loving advances of this woman are in reality a test, to see if Kleitophon is true to his bride" (Merkelbach, *Roman und Mysterium*, 139).

Kerényi had already offered an explanation for Kleitophon's passivity when he is set upon by Thersandros, pointing out Kleitophon's phrase, that he was as ignorant "as if in a mystery" (*hōsper en mystēriōi*). The expression of the whole passage where this occurs lets us believe "that the *whole* situation, and within it the complete passivity of the hero under the blows, is properly an initiation" (Kerényi, *Graeco-Orientalische Romanliteratur*, 127). Merkelbach quotes this, and adds, "The scene corresponds to the scourging and fettering of Leukippé" (*Roman und Mysterium*, 143).

If the characters in the novel, enacting the stages of the initiand in a mystery-religion, must be beaten, imprisoned, even left for dead, they are not without comforters or advice. Merkelbach believes that certain stock character types represent personages represented during actual mystery-ceremonies. The bandit-herdsmen (*boukoloi*) would have served as abductors and captors, moving the initiands about. The fisherman, in contrast, is always a good figure: "the Fisher, who seeks the fish in the sea, is a spiritual image [*ein Sinnbild*] for the spiritual father, who draws the mystic candidate [*den Mysten*] from the cleansing baptismal bath" (212). The birdcatcher is another symbolic figure, which is why Daphnis is presented as going to catch birds in the winter. We may be reminded of Mozart's Papageno (*Der Vogelfänger bin ich, ja*), and one way of clarifying what Merkelbach is talking about would be to listen to *The Magic Flute*, Mozart's opera imaging Masonic initiation; the Freemasons of the eighteenth century were as interested as Merkelbach in trying to reconstruct mystery lore and mystery initiations, though for different purposes.

Merkelbach dwells upon words or phrases frequently found in these novels, believing that they are "mystery words" (*Mysterienworte*). Especially important is the encouraging word *tharsei*. This word or its cognates also occurs very often in the Gospels; the King James version of the Bible customarily translates *tharsei* as "be of good cheer": as in Matthew 9:2: *tharsei, teknon, aphientai sou hai hamartiai* ("Take heart, child, thy sins are forgiven"). In the early novels, as Merkelbach points out, the word is frequently used. Chloé says it to Daphnis, Kalasiris says it to Theagenes (*Roman und Mysterium*, 242), and Knemon to both hero and heroine (255). The old woman in the cave in *The Golden Ass* says the Latin equivalent to Charité: *bono animo esto* (I:234). Other words are also "mystery words" such as "good hope," "seeking," and "finding" (*Roman und Mysterium*, 267). If there are recurrent words there are also recurrent symbols, such as the Phoenix.[1]

If even slight references to the Phoenix are significant, much more significant must be the moments of set *ekphrasis*, when an author deliberately invites us to contemplate important images. The beginning of *Kleitophon and Leukippé* has the important painting of Europa, which the nameless Narrator and Kleitophon (the main narrator) unite in contemplating. Merkelbach points out that the description of the picture is carefully worded: "Europa 'travels' on her bull, 'as if on a ship.' . . . Her robe blows out behind her 'like a sail.' This reminds us of the representation of Isis Euploia, who in her ship with blowing sail herself controlled the rudder. Europa is thus somehow identical with the Seafaring Isis, and her Zeus-bull with the divine bull Osiris-Apis (Serapis); referring to the Abduction of Europa, 'Zeus took on the semblance of an Egyptian bull,' says Achilles Tatius . . ." (*Roman und Mysterium*, 115).

The novel thus begins not with a lewd representation of a rape but with an image of Isis' loving search for Osiris, which itself can be imaged in the viewer's loving desire for completion. The picture "prefigures the whole story: a loving couple fly over the sea . . . and land eventually at the rescuing shore. One can also interpret it thus: Whosoever entrusts himself to God shall fare securely over the sea of life" (115). The image of Andromeda, so important in Heliodorus and Achilles Tatius, can be similarly interpreted. With Kleitophon we are shown the Andromeda picture in order to profit not only from its beauty but also from its meaning: "One should not overlook the extraordinary resemblance of Andromeda to the Psyche stuck upon her rock; Andromeda also is a symbol for the Death-journey [*Todesgefahr*] and unexpected deliverance of the mystery-candidate [*des Mysten*]" (125). The soul must be the bride of death before it can be saved and awakened into new life. Andromeda's story (*Mythos*) "became interpreted both as an emblem [*Sinnbild*] of the unhoped-for deliverance of Mankind from the greatest peril, and as a promise of the salvation of the soul through God" (11–12).

It does not seem reasonable (it is obviously *possible*) to dismiss the concepts and interpretations of Kerényi and Merkelbach. Once they have begun to show us the patterns, these strange "figures in the carpet" of the novel, the carpet looks different, but we can hardly deny that the figures are there. I can understand why Merkelbach has failed to convince. His approach is very abrupt. Using at times a religious vocabulary that would do credit to the most earnest preacher, he nevertheless holds himself above all religion and seems impatient in advance of his readers' potential emotional reactions.

One of the difficulties of figuring out exactly what went on in the secret religious rituals of the Roman Empire is that the ancient practitioners left no complete prayer books or books of rituals. Some prayers have survived (including some prayers to Isis), and some relevant works of graphic art, usually very puzzling, like the famous frescoes in the Villa dei Misterii in Pompeii. A complicating factor is the position of Merkelbach's key text, Apuleius' *Metamorphoses*, as itself our major single piece of *evidence* about Isiac ritual; any discussions of the novel in the light of Isiac practice are in immediate danger of circularity, if not of short-circuit.

All this having been granted, Merkelbach's *Roman und Mysterium* is very impressive, even though Merkelbach obliterates the novels as what we call "literature" in favor of what sometimes seems like a set of performative religious tracts. "The design of the characters," he says disdainfully "doesn't lie very deep in the Mystery-novel. Its personages are basically only figures in a holy drama" (337). (He does except minor or 'side' characters in Heliodorus, such as Knemon or Kalasiris, who are more fully drawn.) Merkelbach evidently feels that once these works' "real" meanings are discovered, the books are, as it were, "found out" and cease to be otherwise entertaining. This is utterly untrue. Our suspicion of a religious "meaning" or philosophical implication in a novel may increase our appreciation of its possible depths, but does not erase the surface or unweave the texture.

I feel equally disposed to quarrel with Merkelbach's determination to structure his own narrative so that he starts with Isis (in Apuleius) but proceeds to stories featuring (as he believes) worship of a male divinity, ending with Heliodorus as the winning contender, the author who finishes his story with the worship of a male god—Helios-Apollo. This bias (more or less unconscious?) may have something to do with Merkelbach's rather surprising refusal to discuss Chariton's novel in any detail; he really does not want to include it, and there he parts company with Kerényi. Chariton's story is very strongly a story of Aphrodite. It seems to me not an entirely unrelated matter that Merkelbach should remain so hostile to—or uninterested in—references to *black* Africa. He wants us to believe that the Ethiopians who feature so largely in Heliodorus' novel (particularly at the end) have nothing to do with *real* Ethiopians (293). The piety that he sees in the ancient novel is individual and has no political or social implications—a piety very suited to some kinds of Protestant German Christian piety, perhaps, but not intrinsic to a salvational theology, either of Christians or of the religious pagans whom Merkelbach would show us.

It is an inevitable deficiency of studies such as those of Kerényi and Merkelbach that they cannot deal with history but must deal with a timeless continuum. This is obviously a "fault" (if a deliberate "fault") of my own method as well, particularly in Part III; nevertheless, it seems right to pause in order to emphasize that there is no smooth and uniform era called Late Antiquity, particularly not for those who lived then. The people who became mystery-initiates or read the novels were living lives in historical time, with many pressures upon them. The emphasis upon pain, imprisonment, and torture in the mystery-rites and in the stories may have increased when arbitrary imperial power was becoming increasingly effective, and given to terrorism. The power of Stoicism lies partly in its affording support to the sufferer, who must likewise endure illness and bereavement and may be called upon also to bear imprisonment, torture, and execution. Wealth, status, or intellectual achievement could not save one, but on the contrary made one more visible and vulnerable, as Cicero, Petronius, and Seneca discovered.

The elements that move upon our minds never move abstractly. People living under the Roman Empire had already felt that times were changing. As Martin Bernal points out, there was a sense of a new age coming not restricted to Jewish Messianism. The change from the age of Aries to that of Pisces was an astrological event variously dated (from 50 B.C. to A.D. 150) but much discussed; Bernal thinks Virgil's Fourth Eclogue refers to "a cosmic or astral change of age" (*Black Athena*, I:126). Intermittent "New Age" feelings, as we may call them, persisted, exacerbated with the advent of each new emperor. Rome tried to harness such feelings by pointedly celebrating the thousandth year of the foundation of Rome, in the mid-third century, stimulating spurts of both patriotism and resentment. The world had changed since Augustus came to power; for a while, with Syrian women associated with the house of the Emperor, and even the advent of an Oriental emperor, "Philip the Arabian" (244–249), things must have looked brighter for those who did not belong to the central power-group, but hopes were dashed in new régimes and systematic persecutions.

The more the Emperor, Caesar, the Imperator, was declared "a god" the more people looked for the godlike in themselves. In such a turbulent time, during which change was repeatedly announced, people were drawn to trying to make sense of their own lives. The celebration of personal birthdays (noted before) is one symptom of the search for personal significance—though some, such as Origen, spoke against the new custom: Origen thought only carnal men would celebrate birthdays, which link them further to corruption and the temporal (Henri Crouzel, *Origen*, 236–237). More serious perhaps is the sophisticated discussion of the nature of the soul, engaged in by Jewish and Christian theologians and by "pagan" philosophers—almost all of these ransacking all available texts, including the scriptures of the Jews, the Christians and Zoroastrians, as well as the works of Plato. The human being becomes a multipartite and dynamic entity, with an exciting soul, bearing within it an image of God, however much covered over and defaced.

The discussion of human personality from this angle could yield surprising results. Origen (b. A.D. 185), a product of Christian Alexandria who lived part of his life in Palestine, describes the soul as the re-presentation of Mary, the *Theotokos* or God-bearer: "every soul, virgin and uncorrupted, which conceives by the Holy Spirit, so as to give birth to the Will of the Father, is the Mother of Jesus" (Origen, quoted in Crouzel, *Origen*, 124). As Crouzel says, according to Origen "every human soul is feminine, Wife and Mother" (125). (We see at once how far this is from the fear of gender-crossing that prohibits Erich Neumann from seeing in Apuleius' Psyche anything other than the representation of the lowly female, "narcissism" and all.) Nor need we think of Origen's "femininity" of the soul as purely passivity. To survive as a self is an activity of love; Origen recollected that Ignatius of Antioch had called Christ Eros. Personal significance and personal salvation may involve a time in the future, a place without or beyond torture (Origen was captured and tortured) in the timeless world. But, more interesting to the people who attended Christian churches and/or mystery-rites, the eternal is reflected in the soul here and now, and we are moved right now by our desire to be, and to be more fully.

As we can see, such self-contemplation cannot be conducted other than by the mode of *allegory*. This is true in the twentieth century when Freud and Jung gave us their allegories to play with, but these too are descendants of the bright and scattered multiplicity of images for the self that were developed during the first centuries of the Roman Empire. Allegory is not an academic trope, not dead matter, but a powerfully appealing mode of expression allowing one to think or sense what cannot otherwise be fully articulated. Only a very dull allegory says $x = y$ when both x and y are fully known and definable: "let the large lady with the striped shield = Britannia" is not the same sort of utterance as saying "the soul is the Virgin Mary." In the latter case, we could not begin to understand the new meaning of x until we have said y, and the implications go always towards activity.

The above serves in a manner as a defense of Kerényi and Merkelbach. We might have asked whether pagans of the first centuries of our new "Common Era" were capable of such allegorizing subtleties as Merkelbach wants to deal in. The short answer is "yes, they were"—though the long answer to Merkelbach involves a very definite assertion that the novels are not mere tracts whose allegorical meaning can be peeled off, the residue to be thrown away. The novels are not superficial statements of obvious pieties, but explorations. Nevertheless, the novelists that we know lived in an intellectual environment in which allegory and allegorical reading are quite common. We have already noted that a late Neoplatonic Christian critic could provide a quite extensive and well-thought-out allegorical reading of Heliodorus' novel. But there are other texts, written earlier and thus the more convincing in proving a readerly and writerly milieu familiar with subtle allegorizing.

This concept may take some getting used to. Many of us, particularly in English studies, have been bred to associate spiritual *allegoria* with the Middle Ages. Within the Christian Church, "fundamentalism" within the Protestant movement has tried to evade much allegory in Scripture, insisting on "literal" meaning, and insisting (as a corollary) that the Early Church was not guilty of allegorical thought and reading, which came in with Catholicism and medievalism. Outside the Church, certain forms of Enlightenment humanist thought have likewise regarded allegory as characteristic of bad medieval ways of thinking, and have tried to rescue all "classics" from it. We can illustrate the prevalence of sophisticated modes of allegorical reading within the Late Classical and Early Christian era by looking at Porphyry's essay "On the Cave of the Nymphs." Porphyry (born c. A.D. 233), a Phoenician from Tyre originally named Malkos (he gave himself his own name, like Voltaire later), was a student of Plotinus (d. 270), usually considered the founder of Neoplatonism. Porphyry, another example of the Alexandrian Man, the academic, was a valiant and prolific exponent of Neoplatonism, and a staunch enemy of the Christians.

In "On the Cave of the Nymphs" Porphyry considers in detail the levels of meaning to be found in a passage of Homer, a passage of the *Odyssey* (Book XIII) describing the cave in Ithaca where Odysseus at last landed:

> and at the head of the harbor is a slender-leaved olive
> and near by it a lovely and murky cave
> sacred to the nymphs called Naiads.
> Within are kraters and amphoras
> of stone, where bees lay up stores of honey.
> Inside, too, are massive stone looms and there the nymphs
> weave sea-purple cloth, a wonder to see.
> The water flows unceasingly. The cave has two gates,

the one from the north, a path for men to descend,
while the other, towards the south is divine. Men do not
enter by this one, but it is rather a path for immortals.

> (*Odyssey* XIII, lines 102–112, trans. Lamberton,
> *Porphyry on the Cave of the Nymphs*, 21)

Porphyry wonders about the different levels of meaning in this passage—levels which must exist, whether the author (Homer) were conscious of them or not. We should first consider, Porphyry tells us, how caves have been used in myth and literature. Well, "the ancients . . . made caves and caverns sacred to the cosmos" (Porphyry, "On the Cave of the Nymphs," trans. Lamberton, 24). Porphyry then undertakes a study of comparative religion and anthropology, pointing out that "the Persian mystagogues" explain to candidates the downward journey of souls and their return by reference to a "cave." Offerings are made in caves, "Demeter likewise raises Kore in a cave among nymphs" (25). Plato drew upon the image of the cave in the *Republic*. Theologians and writers of myth have made caves "symbols of the sensible cosmos" (26). The Naiad Nymphs indicate the presence of water, a substance associated with life and generation—*genesis*. Why does Homer call the cave, puzzlingly, "lovely and murky"—how can a place be both beautiful *and* shadowy and shapeless? The murkiness, like the dampness, represents the properties of *matter*. It is because of order, the Forms, that the cosmos is beautiful: "a cave might appropriately be called 'lovely' seen from the point of view of one who . . . perceives in it the participation of the forms—and, on the contrary, it might be called 'murky' seen from the point of view of one who sees more deeply into it . . ." (24–25). The souls coming into *genesis* are "nymphs," brides baptized in water and initiated into the material world. "For souls coming down into *genesis*, and the making of bodies . . . what could be a better symbol than the stone looms? . . . Flesh comes into being by means of bones . . . and stone represents these bones . . . . The sea-purple cloth would clearly be the flesh, woven of blood" (29). The presence of honey is also comprehensible and symbolic: "In view of its relation to purification, to the prevention of decay and to the pleasure of descent into the flesh, honey is an appropriate symbol" (31).

What saves this place for Porphyry is the presence of the olive tree; Homer had a religious purpose in placing it where he did:

> The olive tree belongs to Athena . . . In view of the fact that the goddess was born from the head [of Zeus], the theologian found an appropriate place when he enshrined the tree at the "head" of the harbor and he indicated through this tree the fact that the universe did not come to be spontaneously nor was it the work of irrational chance, but rather that it is the result of noetic [i.e., intellectual] nature and of wisdom. At the same time, the tree is something separate from the cave . . .   (Porphyry, *Cave*, Lamberton trans., 38)

It is quite evident that for Porphyry the Nymphs' cave is a peculiarly horrible place. It represents the degradation of material existence, the contamination of the pure soul by the damp and dirty flesh, and the constraints and miseries of mortal life. The olive tree represents the hope of the intellect. It teaches that all is not lost even in mortality. The tree of thoughtfulness, the sign of divine wisdom, is, however, clearly separate from the fleshly world. Porphyry evidently interpreted the whole of the *Odyssey*, treating the epic not only spiritually (Neoplatonically) but, as we would say "psychologically." In this surviving essay on the Cave, Porphyry says that the sequence of the blinding of the Kyklops really represents Odysseus succumbing to the temptation of suicide, the desire "to cast off this life of the senses simply by blinding it" (40). He has to conquer the passions, including the desire to get rid by violence of this material body; only after patient endurance will he be rewarded; "Odysseus . . . was the symbol of man passing through the successive stages of *genesis* and so being restored to his place among those beyond all wavecrash and 'ignorant of the sea'" (39). Robert Lamberton comments on this "fascinating internalization of the Polyphemus episode, transforming the crude and sensual cyclops into a symbol of Odysseus' own physical existence," pointing out that it reflects Porphyry's "personal concern" (42n). In his *Life of Plotinus*, Porphyry tells us that his master Plotinus knew he was intending to commit suicide, and advised Porphyry to leave Rome; Porphyry cured his depression by going on a trip to Sicily.

Porphyry is experienced, sensitive and sophisticated in his allegorizing. To be an allegorist of any effective kind is to be a mythographer (as Spenser and Dante and Freud are mythographers). Interpretations of life are available to those who know (and compare) *myths*—meaning not untruths, but powerful imagistic stories. Porphyry believes Homer too must be not only a mythographer but also an allegorist (like himself). In Porphyry's era writers were expected to be mythographer-allegorists.

Porphyry's reading is syncretistic and inclusive; not only written texts but the intellectual world of myth, story, and religion constitutes a sacred wood, made up of *forêts de symboles*. As Lamberton says, "Porphyry is one of the founders of that vast tradition of scholarship that has pursued the elusive goal of a universal encyclopedia of symbols, a tradition that has scored its most enduring successes, from Artemidorus of Daldis to Freud, in the study of dreams" ("Introduction," *Porphyry on the Cave*, 12). Porphyry is also one of the progenitors of George Eliot's Mr. Casaubon, who wanted to write a "Key to All Mythologies," as well as of Sir James Frazer of *The Golden Bough*.

The existence of Porphyry's essay tends to support the position of both Kerényi and Merkelbach. Modes of thinking of the Late Antique period, including the vision of the possibilities and manners of literature, were evidently extremely hospitable to the presence of allegory and symbol in narrative. Porphyry gives us an idea of what intelligent readers might have seen in a novel, or what an intelligent and intellectual author might have wanted to create, contemplate—or play with. Porphyry's essay is so supportive of the interpretive method of both Kerényi and Merkelbach that we may be surprised that they do not draw upon it. (Kerényi does not refer to either Plotinus or Porphyry; Merkelbach has some footnotes referring to Plotinus.) But on second thought there may be good reason for them not to draw upon it, for any prolonged contemplation of the essay "On the Cave of the Nymphs" throws up other very obvious possibilities of meaning in the Novel, major allegories that will not fit comfortably quite into the mold either of these scholars designed.

If we come to Porphyry's essay after a reading of the novels, the images

Porphyry deals with will immediately resonate for us. The cave—yes the cave. The cave in which the Ass hears the story of Psyche, the cave in which Charikleia is imprisoned—but most immediately the cave at the beginning of Longus' pastoral, the cave where Chloé is found: "It was the Nymphs' cave, a huge rock" (*Daphnis and Chloé*, 14). From the mouth of the cave there gushes the spring that runs off in a brook and waters the fresh meadow before it. As Porphyry points out, Demeter kept the Maiden (*Korē*) in a cave—and Chloé's name indicates her connection with both Demeter and Demeter's daughter. This is the cave of *genesis*, of the material, the water of matter and of generation. It does not disturb either Porphyry's or Longus' statements to add that the cave at another "level" indicates the womb, and that the nymphs, as well as standing for the soul taking material form, or the powers that preside over this activity, also symbolize the female genitals. Freud in *Dora* makes a lot of the fact that his anti-heroine saw in an exhibition a picture of a "thick wood," and "in the background of the picture there were *nymphs*." Freud labors away at proving that the nymphs indicate the *labia minora*, which lie in the background of the thick wood of the pubic hair. "That was a symbolic geography of sex!" (*Das war symbolische Sexualgeographie!* 261–262). But for Freud this *Sexualgeographie* is a more hostile terrain than the "sexual geography" we cover in the ancient novel.

The cave, as we have seen, disturbs Porphyry, even perhaps in something of the same way as Dora's vision of the nymphs disturbs Freud (Freud is not a Neoplatonist, to be sure, but he has a Neoplatonical streak in him.) Porphyry gives us, if not a Key to All Mythologies, a very good key to the mythologies of the Novel—but it will work only if we reverse Porphyry's reading. The cave, the honey, the water, are terrifying images to Porphyry, signifying the dirty imbecility of living. For the Novel, and thus for every novelist (even if the writer may be a Neoplatonist in daily life) *the world is good*. The Nymphs weave textures of deep purple or sea-purple (*haliporphyra*) or deep red, putting Porphyry in mind of the color of blood (represented incidentally in his own chosen name). So too, interestingly, works that other weaver, the Virgin Mary, according to the "Life of Mary," a pseudo-Christian account in the apocryphal *Gospel of Saint James* (probably written by a devotee of Isis). The priests of the Temple in Jerusalem called together the virgins of Israel to weave a curtain for the Temple; offered a choice of stuffs, Mary chose "the true *porphyry* and the scarlet (cochineal)," *hē alēthinē porphyra kai to kokkinon* (*Protevangelion*, Chap. 10 in *Le Protévangile de Jacques*, ed. Amann, 220).[2] In the former Church of Saint Saviour in Chora in Byzantium (now Kariye Camii in Istanbul), we can see the brilliant early fourteenth-century mosaics depicting the life of the Virgin Mother, the *Theotokos* or God-bearer. One large picture shows her receiving the undeniably red wool from the priest. This Byzantine image is in keeping with the symbols investigated by Porphyry; the Virgin Mother will incarnate the living lord, in her body weaving the texture of flesh and red blood. The Byzantine artists, unlike Porphyry, see this as matter for celebration; the youthful Mary is, as it were, a sacred nymph, her labor imaging the high value of divine Incarnation—and with divine Incarnation the human incarnation of each of us.

One of the most striking things about the ancient novels is that, unlike almost all other ancient literature, they are ruled by the "Feminine." It is this recognition that Kerényi and Merkelbach seem to try to resist. They notice that the Goddess recurs, that Isis / Fortuna / *Tychē* / Artemis / Aphrodite are one—yet at the same time, they do not really *want* to notice this. The novel, it is true, encodes a religious experience of birth, trial, acceptance of death, acceptance of sexuality, ignominious experience of physicality—and with all these things the possibility of renewal, of resurrection, even repeated resurrection. It is possible for the individual to achieve a life on a higher plane of being in this life, not (usually) by avoiding sexuality but by reinterpreting it. (Though the reinterpretation of life on the part of Thekla, Clemens, and Lucius involves abstention.) The Ancient Novel is—as the Novel has forever been—interested in moral life, in relations between one person and another, in trying to evolve some new responses or definitions— as when Kleitophon wonders if males can have *parthenia*.

Of all products of the Late Antique period aside from Christianity, the Novel seems the most heartily to endorse the possibilities of change. Here novels decidedly part company with Neoplatonism, for Neoplatonism deals with the eternal and unchanging and is hostile to all forms of earthly revolution. Change is in itself a symptom of corruption. Novel-characters accept birth, which is change, and biological time. They travel—it is one of the duties of characters in all novels to travel, even if, like Elizabeth Bennet, they get only as far as Derbyshire. Note that travel too, however greatly analogous to travail, is also a stimulant to continued existence; there is an Eros of travel, as Plotinus knew when he persuaded suicidal Porphyry to leave Rome and take a trip to Sicily. In traveling, novel-characters encounter strangers, foreigners, the "other." Not only do they encounter them (for encountering can be done aggressively, as in war-epics); they also make friends with these barbarians, outlanders, people speaking foreign tongues. "Write to me often in Syracuse." The endorsement of this life as valuable—as of spiritual value and promise—includes a suggestion of the possibility of new forms of political and social life. "Epic, Lyric poetry and Drama have their origin in religion. The learned—with the exception of Karl Kerényi—have believed they could otherwise explain the origin of the Novel. But now it is probable, on generally available evidence, that it is no different with the Novel than with the other remaining literary genres of antiquity. That the Novel in reality arose from religious roots, we shall prove in this book." So Merkelbach says in his Forward to *Roman und Mysterium*. Yes—we have traditionally acknowledged the other genres' religious origins and nature, and have denied such roots to the Novel. Merkelbach is right—the Novel is no different from other ancient genres in having a religious well-spring.

⊢•⊕•⊕•⊣

But it would be a very bad thing, and disastrous for the appreciation of the Novel as a form, if this understanding of its religious origins and nature left us staring blankly at a set of tracts. It would then have been a thousand times better not to have even hinted at the secret of religious origins, not to have coasted along the dangerous shore of allegory. We should never have alluded, however discreetly, to the element of *midrash* in a novel like *Joseph and Aseneth*, a revisiting of the Biblical Joseph combined with a story based on an earlier re-vision of the story of Dinah, and the fate of the imagined child of her rape. There is an element of what might be called *midrash* in non-Jewish and non-Christian novels as well, a "pagan *midrash*"—if this oxymoron can be permitted—in which we receive an extended commentary upon and suggestive amplification of religious stories and images. If Kerényi is remotely right, almost every one of the ancient novels constitutes a sort of *midrash* on the story of Isis. To some readers, a suggested relationship between the Novel and Religion must seem to draw the novel and the reader depressingly into the prison house of fetters and exhortation. But that state of fettering and exhortation is just what novel-characters experience and escape from. The novels are dynamic stories of release; at almost every point, they question authority. The "religion" of the novels is related not to a set of rules but to the understanding of a life lived hermeneutically, that is as something with meaning for individuals.

It would also be mistaken to set up a contrast: EITHER we have in novels characters who have significance(s) translatable into other terms, and in that sense allegorical, OR we have "real characters." That is a false dichotomy. "Characters" in a novel have to represent more than "themselves" in order to be "selves" at all—they need to escape being just marks on paper. Any commentary on a novel such as *Great Expectations* will show how inevitably we do read characters and their actions allegorically in order to read them at all. Here, for instance, is Peter Brooks reading *Great Expectations*: "The dream of Satis House is properly a daydream, in which 'His Majesty, the Ego' pleasures himself with the phantasy of social ascension and gentility. Miss Havisham is made to play the role of Fairy Godmother, her crutch become a magic wand . . ." (*Reading for the Plot*, 119).

Even less promising, distinctly minor, novelistic personages can provide, for a critic like Brooks, minable lodes of significance: "Mr. Wopsle's career . . . may exemplify a general movement in the novel toward recognition of the lack of authorship and authority in texts . . ." (*Reading for the Plot*, 134). With the aid of a dark prophet like Derrida as well as a first-rate mythographer (and allegorist) like Freud, Brooks is able to engage in an enjoyable performance of allegorization. Critics have a dual consciousness about this sort of thing, on the one hand crediting themselves with original cleverness, on the other, feeling that this play of meanings is "in" the text whether or not they were always in the front of the mind of the author. An author who can create a name like "Satis House" is evidently alert to allegory. Most criticism, including spoken appreciation, of novels would fail if everything that resembled allegory were to be barred. Reading, official or unofficial, is a process whereby we divine meanings.

We see novel-characters as creatures endowed with meaning; they are *worthy* of our contemplation, of our teasing out their meanings. The characters themselves—Habrokomes, Charikleia, Pip—are engaged in teasing out their own meaning, in becoming meaningful to themselves through processes (like dreams and interpretations) that we might term "self-allegorizing." Novels, these *plasmata*, succeed (a success often disapproved of) because their hermeneutic design, with its invitation to scrutinize for interpretive meanings, persuades us that *life has meaning*. We are also persuaded that *there is a self to be discovered*. On these two hypotheses hangs the success of the *erotikai hypotheseis* from age to age. Reading a novel does not seem like a waste of time because it indicates the possibilities of knowing and offers each reader ways of thinking about the self. Allegory is, then, deeply congenial, as we think of ourselves "allegorically"—if we think of ourselves at all. To contemplate "oneself" is to be already divided, to set up a *psychomachia* (or war between parts) or at least a psychodynamic of diversities. Self-consciousness is an exercise deeply, not superficially, related to what we call "the allegorical." Novels, supporting our private allegories with their own, persuade us that self-consciousness is valuable and the "self" worthwhile. They do thus support the *individuation* complained of by Nietzsche, for whom the spiritual activity of any individual—save the Superman, the *Übermensch*—is a matter for revulsion. To love oneself is, like loving God or one's neighbor, a religious activity—so the Novel says, in its prosy, comic and *un*priestly voice.

If we accept that the Novel has a religious well-spring, this does not mean that the Novel has to be—or ever had to be—written by pious people. In fact, it may be especially receptive to "infidel" or subversive authors. It values experience and exploration and play. But it has a religious grounding in the sense of the holy in human existence. And it has a high sense of the holy in all that may be called "feminine"—including the weak fleshly penis as distinct from the *phallos*, the penis that Encolpius addresses when he knows the severer sort of men, proper Romans, would not do so. The Novel above all genres celebrates the value of *incarnation*.

The reader who has come thus far with me may be willing to grant the general truth of what I have said regarding the *ancient* novels described. But—the reader may be saying—*has* all this anything to do with later novels in the West? Part II of this book takes up that question, conducting a chronological study, examining the history of the relation of novels of antiquity to later prose fiction. As we shall see, the ancient novels just examined—the ones we used not to allow in our canon—do touch and shape the novels of later centuries, certainly including the novels of the eighteenth century, a period which we in Western literary studies have always agreed produced "real novels." The interrelatedness becomes so undeniable that at last evidence will not allow us to make an absolute differentiation between Novels of Antiquity and Novels of Modernity. After this argument is made in Part II, we can reap the reward in Part III. The reader anxious to pursue the "elements of novelism" may wish to skip directly to Part III, but should do so only if truly convinced that ancient novels have played an important part in Western fiction from the Middle Ages through the Age of Reason.

My book is structured around a gap, like a Gothic castle or Roman house. We cannot get from one part to another all at once. A strategic delay is part of the plan. Matters such as those discussed in these last three chapters will not come to the fore again until Part III. In Part III, the reader and I will be released from all the bondage to history as chronology, and will be free to play with the tropes of fiction. Diverse works of diverse eras will be examined together, considered according to what connects them and not according to separation. But first, it is important to establish the humble but basic connection, to make clear that these ancient *plasmata* have been mingled with our plasma, have been part of the bloodline of Western fiction. We need to find out if we can accept them not as a disjointed curiosity but as an integral part of our tradition and thus inextricably present in modern novels.

PART TWO

>─┤─◆─○─◆─┤─<

The Influence of the Ancient Novel

>─┤─◆─○─◆─┤─<

The Amazons debate about Alexander's ultimatum. Illustration in a Byzantine manuscript of the *Alexander Romance*.

CHAPTER IX

> ⊱─┅•❀•┅─⊰

Ancient Novels and the Fiction of the Middle Ages

> ⊱─┅•❀•┅─⊰

And as for me, though that my wit be lite,
On bokes for to rede I me delyte.
       —Geoffrey Chaucer, Prologue to
          The Legend of Good Women

"A Gallehaut was that book, and he who wrote it."
   —Francesca da Rimini, in Dante's *Inferno*, Canto V

Incline your ears with no fickle understanding to new lines, which do not offer you the cruel conflagrations of ancient Troy, nor the sanguinary battles of Pharsalia. . . .
       —Giovanni Boccaccio, beginning of *Filocolo*

To have composed stories is clearly much more useful than injurious.
       —Boccaccio in *De Genealogia Deorum Gentilium*

"What makes you think Greek ladies are less clever than French ones? . . . We shall understand your Latin, no matter how obscurely you speak it."
       —Princess Carmesina of Constantinople
         in Joanot Martorell's *Tirant lo Blanc*

> ⊱─┅•❀•┅─⊰

CHANGE: THE MOVEMENT OF PEOPLES

It is difficult to trace the fate of fiction during the "Dark Ages" and the early part of what we have very loosely called "the Middle Ages." The whole of Europe was shaken by the incursion of new tribes, and the political and social structures of antiquity disappeared or were transformed. It is impossible to exaggerate the turmoil of the fifth and sixth centuries, not only in Europe but throughout most of Asia. An enormous number of human beings were on the move, including various tribes of Germanic peoples, Slavs, Asian Avars, and the Huns. Turkish people settling Manchuria drove the Mongolians through Persia; Arabs as well as Turks were to expand their holdings. The Roman world was sharply disturbed when the Visigoths first attempted to take Greece and then went on to sack Rome in A.D. 410. After other movements, including Visigothic settlement in what is now France, the progress of Vandals and then Visigoths into Spain and the check given to the Huns at the battle of Troyes (A.D. 453), the Ostrogoths moved into Greece and into Italy. As has often been noted, the Germanic tribes did not see themselves as destroyers of the Roman civilization they admired. Theodoric the

Ostrogoth wanted to reconcile the Roman and Gothic societies and cultures. But no one of the new tribes was strong enough to maintain the kind of absolute control the Romans had exercised for so long; the Ostrogothic empire was defeated by the Lombard invasion of Italy, and the weakness of the Goths allowed for the expansion of the Franks in Gaul. In the Eastern Empire, the Emperor Justinian (527–565) successfully warred against the Goths and Bulgars. Constantinople was able to hold on to its reduced territories, its language, and its independence while the Western Empire split up into various ethnic and linguistic and political divisions. A new outlook and world vision was to inspire the peoples, old and new, of the Middle East with the advent of Islam, which spread quickly after the death of Mohammed in A.D. 632.

The momentous sociopolitical earthquake that went on in tremor after tremor for about five centuries is enough to daunt any social or political historian. The historian of fiction is less troubled, for there is less information. What is clearly evident is that with the incursion of all these new tribes all sorts of new tribal stories, legends, and myths were to be added to an already very mixed stew, the traditions of fiction existing in the old Roman Empire. Less material was now written down, so the developments of fiction are less traceable in the West.

In the eastern part of that "West," where written tradition prevailed, what happened is more traceable. First, Greek culture survived very largely because it was studied by the non-Greeks at the borders of the old Roman Empire. Arabs and Persians were among the inheritors of "classical" Greek culture. Much of our biographical information about Aristotle, for instance, comes from two surviving Syriac and four surviving Arabic *Lives*. Much Greek writing was rescued from utter destruction by being cradled in the Eastern culture, like Moses among the bulrushes. The developing civilization is truly impressive. Baghdad, home of the new Abbasid Caliphate, the empire of Islam, was founded in the eighth century; a wealthy and highly populous urban center, in the next century it was probably the world's largest city. This is the city of Haroun al-Raschid, the magnet city of the civilization we best know through our versions of *The Thousand and One Nights*. The world of Arabic scholarship, this new culture of writing, preserved and developed enormous quantities of Greek material, as well as seeing the flowering of its own new literature. The ages that to us are "dark" were light in the East. There were important works of fiction, largely in poetry (unlike the "vulgar" *Thousand and One Nights*, or *Arabian Nights' Entertainments*). The poetic work best known to the West, the *Rubáiyát* of Omar Khayyám, was written by a poet who died in 1123.

BYZANTINE FICTION

The old Greek empire also preserved and developed Greek culture. But the literature of the Greek empire was also influenced both by the literature of the (now turbulent) West, and by the work of the freshly exciting East. As George Kehayióglou says, "During the second half of the eleventh century and in the years of the first Comnenian emperors, Byzantine interest in Eastern narrative fiction appears to have increased, and attempts at translating such works became more systematic" (Kehayióglou, "Translations of Eastern 'Novels' and Their Influence on Late Byzantine and Modern Greek Fiction," in Beaton, ed., *The Greek Novel*, 157). He points to "three 'novels' that became known to Byzantine Hellenism between the seventh and the eleventh centuries" (156); their English titles are *Barlaam and Joseph*, the *Fables of Bidpai* (also known as *Kalila and Dimna*), and the *Book of Sindbad the Philosopher*. These works "display an elaborate pattern of a frame-story with inserted stories." Rather less happily, with a typical modern European antipathy to the East, Kehayióglou thinks these stories introduce "frames of mind little known . . . to Christian Byzantium," including "Eastern fatalism and pessimism, exoticism and motifs of migration / journeys, scabrous narratives, complicated magic tales" (158). But of course all of these elements can be found in the earlier novel (see especially *The Golden Ass* by the man from Madaura).

Byzantine interest in creating new *prose* fiction seems to have waned, although the earlier prose fictions were certainly read and "republished" in full manuscript versions. Political events, in Byzantium as elsewhere, could provide a severe check to literature. As Roderick Beaton notes, "After the sack of Constantinople by the Latins in 1204 no more literary fiction seems to have been written in Greek for a hundred years" ("The Greek Novel in the Middle Ages," in Beaton, ed., *The Greek Novel*, 140). The later Middle Ages saw the advent of new very elaborate Greek narratives in verse, dealing with material similar to that in the prose works, such as *Rodanthé and Dosikles* by the poet Theodoreos Pródromos. Roderick Beaton notes, this poetic narrative is deeply indebted to the work of Achilles Tatius and Heliodorus, and is set in "the same Hellenistic world." "The element of nostalgia for the past glories of classical Greece that is present in the most of the ancient romances—which for instance never allude to the Roman Empire under whose rule all of them were written—is vastly developed and extended by Pródromos" (*The Greek Novel*, 137). There are other twelfth-century verse fictions (*Drosilla and Charikles*, *Hysmene and Hysmenias*), and later medieval works in similar (if more colloquial) style. Their techniques are often elaboration of the techniques of the earlier Greek novel: Corinne Jouanno points out the devotion of these authors to *ekphrasis*, and remarks that Byzantine authors are fascinated by optical illusions and reflections, by mirrors.[1]

There are new elements in plot and situation. The Byzantine *Kallimachos and Chrysorrhoé*, written in the early fourteenth century, exhibits an erotic sadism with no precedent in the ancient novel. In the story, the hero Kallimachos, son of a foreign emperor, enters an unguarded castle; he comes through a garden into a vaulted room. From the ceiling of this room a naked young woman is hanging by her hair; she tells him (from her uncomfortable position) that the castle belongs to a giant. Our hero hides—just in time, for the giant comes in and whips the naked lady. After the giant has eaten and gone to sleep, Kallimachos kills the giant, and after some pleasantries he and the lady Chrysorrhoé go into a healing bath, in which she not only gets over the pain of her beating but allows the consummation of their new love.

The narrative seems to emphasize spectatorship—Kallimachos spectates in a manner unknown to any earlier novel character, except perhaps Lucius the Ass. The reader's pleasure would seem to arise from participating in seeing the lady whipped, as well as in rescuing her. The other spectators in the room include the painted Aphrodite, who is portrayed in the fresco of the ceiling from which the young lady hangs. Only Aphrodite herself, the poet interjects, would be able to tell of the pleasures and graces found in that bath. The pleasures include the juxtaposition of pain with pleasure: the hero rubbed the maiden's wounds and unspeakable tender pleasure from her bruises . . . presumably he kisses to make it better, but the language of the poem lingers on the touch of female pain. In reading this anonymous poem, or these parts of it —for which I am indebted to Panagiotis A. Agapitos [2]—one is also struck by the recognition that the Byzantines possessed Christianity and the classical inheritance but were not participants in the ideology of chivalry. We have a narrative of magic, quest, adventure, and a giant—and the hero does what he ought to do—rescues the lady by killing the wicked giant. But he does not do it *chivalrously*. No fictional knight of chivalry would be able to watch a lady being brutally attacked by a wicked giant without intervening on the spot. Kallimachos is certainly the descendant of prudent and wily Odysseus, and not very closely related to Launcelot or Perceval. More to the point, he comes out of the Greek novel tradition in which, David Konstan argues with some exaggeration, "There are no scenes in which the valiant lover comes to the rescue of his lady" (*Sexual Symmetry*, 34).

MANUSCRIPTS OF NOVELS

The surviving manuscripts of the ancient novels, as of the medieval stories, come to us from the Middle Ages. That is to say, we would not have the ancient novels at all had people of the Middle Ages not read them. A few examples of these manuscripts are richly adorned and beautiful—none more so than the early fourteenth-century version of the *Alexander Romance* now in the Istituto Ellenico in Venice. From this richly illustrated manuscript comes my frontispiece to Part II (see Fig. 14), showing the red-dressed Amazons with their Queen discussing a communication from Alexander. This special edition of the *Alexander Romance*, probably expressly commissioned by an emperor of Trebizond, has numerous colorful illustrations, fully captioned. This copy later belonged to a Turkish reader, who has apparently translated the captions and some of the commentary, presumably adding comments of his own. Also in Venice, in the Marcian Library, is a beautifully made copy of Apuleius' *Golden Ass*, dated 1388; there is a delightful opening illustration of the Ass (see Plate 14).

Most manuscripts, however, are businesslike affairs, obviously written commercially, with different copyists' hands at work in the same book. These productions, with only the simplest of ornaments, if any, are meant for reading rather than display. In general, our novel manuscripts were produced from the eleventh to the fifteenth centuries. There are also manuscript editions and versions *after* the arrival of print; manuscript culture does not die out straight away. Although we have been taught to think that Greek manuscripts came to the West only after 1453, modern studies reveal that the boundaries between East and West were more porous, and Western collectors took what manuscripts they could from the East long before the fall of Constantinople; see D. C. Greetham, *Textual Scholarship: An Introduction* (1992). It is thus harder than we used to think to decide what works an author of Western Europe could or could not have come into contact with. It is hard to track the medieval transfer of manuscripts, or to decide what quantity of copies of any one work might reasonably be estimated as extant at any given time. That novels were popular is clear in the better-monitored early Renaissance, when scholars collected Byzantine manuscripts of novels as well as works of "higher" literature.

In the later fifteenth century, the learned Cardinal Bessarion, a native of Asia Minor, anguished over the downfall of the Greek Empire and systematically collected manuscripts, thus endeavoring to salvage the whole of Byzantine civilization so that it could be reconstructed. (He trustingly left his huge collection to Venice, believing that a library would be built straight away so that the understanding of the world of vanquished Constantinople would not be lost; but the Venetians left the material in its hundred or so crates for forty years while they argued over what kind of super library they would build.) This valiant collector of manuscripts did not at all despise novels. I would hazard the guess that he was particularly fond of the *Aithiopika*, since he acquired a number of versions of it. Some of the earliest copies we have were once in his possession. The Marcian Library owns parchment copies of the *Aithiopika*, one dating from the eleventh century (or very early twelfth), and one from the thirteenth century, as well as a fifteenth-century copy—all formerly Bessarion's.

In these medieval Greek copies, plain copies for serious readers, there is often (as with other manuscript texts) some editing in the production. Editorial remarks can be found at the beginning of a section, or in a (usually brief) introduction, commonly coming just after the title. Editorial comment may also figure in the margin. But the greatest contributors of commentary are readers. The fact that books were expensive did not deter readers from marking them up. Real readers in all centuries have tended to mark and annotate books—even if this is a habit that librarians identify with Goths and Vandals, it is probably a classic custom. I do not know of any study of the readerly marginalia in Byzantine manuscripts of the novels, but it is a subject worthy of exploration. My own necessarily cursory and inadequate studies indicate that readers most often wrote simply "GNŌ!," the Greek equivalent of "N.B." But they also inserted more detailed comments, particularly as a guideline to the subject matter at hand. A reader might insert a marginal note pointing out a fine phrase or beautiful description, writing *phrasis* or *ekphrasis*. Sometimes the admired detail is elaborated, as in *"Ekphrasis* of the Beauty of Theagenes" (Marcian, GR 409 Coll. 838; see Plate 15). Sometimes a plot-point is indicated in the margin such as that Charikleia is accused of murdering Kybelé. Such information or emphasis pointed the way to the late Renaissance's ambitious editorial supplying of indexes in printed versions of novels (see below, Chapter X).

Usually, only Greek comments appear in the margins of Greek texts, and Latin or Western vernacular comments in the margins of Latin novels. Occasionally there is a crossover. With the advent of the Renaissance, readers of the Roman West began to comment on the Greek works; Latin comment in a Greek manuscript is likely to be very late. For instance, in a copy of Chariton's novel called *Chariton of Aphrodisias' Loves of Chaireas and Kallirrhoé* there are readers' notes in Latin in the margins. But this is a copy of the novel written out by the humanist Antonio Marco Salvini (Salvinius) with his own hand, and is thus a very late production. It is annotated by at least two other people. One commentator marks a particular phrase in the first encounter of Theron and Dionysios: "Anastas oun ho Thērōn *periergon gar anthrōpou physis* [Theron then got up (*man is curious by nature*)]." The reader then adds in the margin: *"mitio generi humani Petronious in matrona Ephesi"* ("weakness of human nature—Petronius on matron of Ephesus"). This particular note is far too late to qualify as "medieval," but it indicates a habit of reading and making comparisons from one novel to another. This habit, although it may have become more deliberate during the Renaissance, cannot have been entirely absent during any century. The custom of marginal annotation shows that reading in both manuscript and print ages is felt to be participatory. Novels, as the notes show, are resorted to for excitement, pleasure, and knowledge; there is always an element of wisdom literature about novels, they are felt to supply truths about experience. "GNŌ!" —"Know this!" The pattern of personal annotation also shows that the individual reader expected to reread the novel—we mark books up partly because we expect to come back to them again.

That former things had not all passed away, that Greek popular literature of the earlier part of the first Christian millennium was still in the hands of readers at the end of that millennium, is indicated by various clues and infrequent documents. For instance, a landowner in eastern Asia Minor wrote a will in A.D. 1059 bequeathing his collection of books to a monastery. Fifty-seven of his volumes are Bibles, liturgies, or patristic writings. Five are saints' lives. Among the remaining seventeen secular books, one is a book on the interpretation of dreams, one an Aesop, one is a volume of the *Alexander Romance*, and one is a volume of Achilles Tatius' *Kleitophon and Leukippé* (Charlotte Roueché, "Byzantine Writers and Readers," in Beaton, ed., *The Greek Novel*, 126). This prosperous landowner's library shows that there was a literary culture outside Constantinople, and that novel-reading was thought not incompatible with the study of serious and even religious works (so Archbishop Photius also thought).

The narrative patterns of the Greek saints' lives have often evoked comment on similarities to the patterns of the Greek novel (*vide* Thekla). Such connections have aroused the distaste of some commentators, such as Ernest A. Baker, who, in *The History of the English Novel* (1924), blames what he calls "voluptuous Ionia" for both sensual "erotic romances" and "the innumerable legends of martyrs of virginity," finding these equally distasteful and unmanly. What Baker calls "the cult of chastity" is to him "a sign of sickness and degeneracy" and, like the erotic stories, equally the product of unwholesome Asia Minor, of what he calls "Ionian romanticism," "Ionian worldliness and sophistication" (47). Chastity and sensuality ignore British good sense: "A reasonable and balanced ideal, such as could be realized by those having refined tastes and powers of self-control, would not have struck home" (47–48). Baker wants to see the chastity stories as a hysterical undergrowth creeping into the Christian scene fairly late; discounting the goddess-oriented stories of chastity in the earlier novels, he also totally overlooks the value of an idea of chastity in permitting any real exercise of choice in sexuality, particularly for women.

Manuscripts of ancient novels, and new readers for them, are visible in the early Middle Ages in the Byzantine world. What of the West? What, indeed, was "Western" in the West of the end of one millennium and the beginning of another? Arab peoples had moved into Egypt in the seventh century, taking over Alexandria in 632; they then swept along the Mediterranean rim of North Africa and entered Spain. An eastern people (called the "Moors" by Europeans) thus occupied the furthest western point of the mainland of the continent of Europe. The "Moors" kept going, up into what is now France, trying to take the Rhône valley; they were defeated at Poitiers in A.D. 732 and retreated into Spain. Charles Martel's victory at Poitiers was a major historic event in Europe, signaling the resistance of the European people to Islam and the Arabs, and spelling the possibility of a new set of regional boundaries and political forces. Charles Martel's grandson Charles, who became called "the Great," *Carolus Magnus*, Charlemagne, was crowned Emperor in Rome on Christmas Day, A.D. 800. The Roman Empire never quite emitted its death-rattle; as an idea, it has been surprisingly durable if infinitely variable.

The new French (or Germanic) culture could flourish only if the Arabs were kept well back behind the Pyrenees. According to the chronicles, Roland, one of the "paladins" or peers of Charlemagne, was returning from an expedition against the Moors across the Pyrenees in 788 when he and his party were attacked by Basque raiders. In legend, the attack on Roland becomes the work of a party of "Saracens" or "Moors" who benefit from the doubleness of the traitor Ganelon. This story is the foundation of *Le Chanson de Roland* (early twelfth century). The *Chanson de Roland* (*Song of Roland*) is the most widely known of the *chansons de geste*, literally "songs about deeds," epic poems about heroic exploits. "Roland" or "Orlando" became the center of an expanding group of stories. The work of defending Christian Europe against the people who now occupied Spain seemed of the first importance to those engaged in it. A major historic labor produced a crop of new situations and characters for fiction: Roland, his companion Oliver, and also the heroine Angelica and the Moorish characters Ruggiero and the lady Marfisa. All of these existed as personages in stories long before Ariosto drew on this material for *Orlando Furioso* (1532).

SUBJECT MATTER AND FICTION: CAMELOT, ROME, AND TROY

Religion and History are the central, perhaps most truly the only, sources of new story-material. The great change in religion in the West, as Christianity took hold and commanded the philosophical and ethical center of the lives of millions of men and women, certainly had a great and even permanent effect upon literature, including narrative fiction. The impact of history as it is told depends upon the writers' (and readers') sense that history is important, that it has impact. Major historical events may set off a kind of fictional fission, giving rise to versions, elaborations, alterations of the stories that appear again and again for centuries.

According to the medieval poet Jean Bodel, "Ne sont que iii matières à nul homme atandant / De France, et de Bretaigne et de Rome la grant." "There are only three 'matters' [sets of subjects, packets of story-stuffs] that any man can draw on—the matter of France, of Britain, and of Rome."[3] This medieval division of the three great sources of fictional material has been picked up by modern scholars of medieval literature, who often refer to the "Matter of France" and "Matter of Britain" (or of *Bretagne*, "Brittany"). The "Matter of France" is material centrally related to the Charlemagne personages. The "Matter of Britain" is the story of Arthur with all its ramifications. The "Matter of Rome" covers all the material dealing with a historical or legendary-historical antiquity, including the Fall of Troy and the stories of Alexander. The Middle Ages, particularly from the twelfth to the fourteenth century, were earnestly concerned with history—understandably, for Europeans were just trying to grapple with the very turbulent and confusing events that had befallen them.

It is easy to understand why all the stories of Charlemagne, and his paladins, their friends and enemies, loomed so large in the European mind. It is not quite so easy to understand why a remote band of Celts living in Brittany, Wales, Ireland, and south-west England should attract so much attention, or why the rest of Europe thought King Arthur so significant, and knew all about Guenevere, Launcelot, Gawain, and so on—and also of course Tristan and Iseult. The "Matter of Britain," has proved amazingly durable, and haunts even modern history—we recall the Kennedy "Camelot" of the 1960s. The third package, the "Matter of Rome" covers stories that Europe was determined not to lose even though the knowledge of Greek had gone. Nobody in Western Europe was reading Homer, though a fair number of people read the *Æneid*.

The novels of antiquity that survived the Dark Ages and received medieval attention in the West tended to be those most overtly historical—the *Alexander Romance* and the *Diary of the Trojan War*. Benoit de Sainte-Maure wrote (c. 1160) *Le Roman de Troie*, a version of the Troy story based on Dictys Cretensis. This is one of the sources for Boccaccio's poetic *Filostrato*, and both Benoit de Sainte-Maure and Boccaccio are sources for Chaucer's *Troilus and Criseyde* (c. 1385), although Chaucer may have read Dictys Cretensis and Dares Phrygius for himself. Pieces of Alexander's story get reworked, including the fantastic voyage section, which helped to furnish medieval writers with a model for a kind of science fiction, the story of preposterously marvelous travel. On the north facade of the basilica of San Marco in Venice there is a bas-relief showing Alexander ascending into the sky between two griffins (see Plate 16). Not all of the prose fiction that caught readers' attention was as importantly "historical." *Apollonius of Tyre*, in which the interest is much more in sexual event and in familial and psychological trouble, seems to have been something of a Dark Ages best-seller. The eleventh-century manuscript providing us with *Beowulf* contains a segment of an Anglo-Saxon translation of *Apollonius*; it appears also in Old French and Middle High German as well as Byzantine Greek. Hägg reproduces photographs of a Latin manuscript c. A.D. 1000 (now in Bucharest) of this novel, with cartoon-strip-like illustrations (*Novel in Antiquity*, 150–151).

Chaucer seems to have read the original novel, and not just the version of the story in John Gower's *Confessio Amantis* (1390) when he describes the story

> of Tyro Apollonius,
> How that the cursed king Antiochus
> Birafte his doghter of hir maydenhede,
> That is so horrible a tale for to rede,

Whan he hir threw upon the pavement.
("Introduction to the Man of Law's
Tale," *Canterbury Tales*, B, lines 81–85)

Chaucer describes himself as an ardent reader: "On bokes for to rede I me delyte" ("Prologue" to *The Legend of Good Women*, line 30), and no one made fuller use of the manuscript culture for pleasure reading. But there are some tales Chaucer does not like—and he congratulates himself that *he* doesn't write "swiche cursed stories" (B, line 80). But of course he just has told the story (or part of it) in these very verses.

It cannot escape our notice that writers of the Middle Ages, from the tenth century to the fourteenth, tend to produce fiction primarily in verse. Poetry is— as it is for Chaucer—the preferred medium of storytelling. We may wish to ask ourselves *why* this should be so. An obvious answer is that wandering tribes tend to produce heroic lays, or lyric ballads; warlike activity, especially when combined with territorial dislocations, creates better conditions for verse, which is memorizable and thus portable, than for long prose pieces, which are not readily committed to memory and demand labor and materials for expensive written works that must then be carried about. Prose *was* written in the Dark Ages and early Middle Ages. Sermon literature that comes down to us exhibits considerable stylistic skill, including the graceful harmonies of Aelfric (d. 1020) and the stirring exhortations of Wulfstan (d. 1023). There seems, however, to have been little desire to compose new stories in prose, though in the "Dark Ages" there are signs of continuous reproduction of novels or parts of them, like *Apollonius* and the "Letter to Aristotle" of the *Alexander Romance*.

We may surmise that prose narrative largely disappeared because city life is essential to the production of novels as commodities. But cities like Baghdad and Constantinople had the necessary economic and population base for novel-production, and they did produce books. A third answer may be that in the hurly-burly of conquest and territorial movement the social center had shifted back into small court life. In Turkey and the Arabian lands, as well as in France and Germany, local chiefs, whether entitled kings or barons or emirs, were more important than subaltern and removable "kings" could have been under organized Rome. A revival of small court life would entail a high value given to the minstrel, the verse reciter-singer, the entertainer in the hall. There would follow a movement to improve and polish verse productions, which might become so valued that they got written down.

Something like this could explain why we have this quasi worldwide efflorescence of narrative poetry-writing just when we have had a semiglobal shifting of many tribes and the breakdown or radical dislocation of old empires and forms of social organization. A period of tenuous stability followed the most disrupted time, though not without outbreaks of aggression and renewed invasions. The Crusades were a movement (or attempted movement) from West to East. The incursions of Timur-Leng or "Tamerlane" (d. 1405) upset Turkey, Persia, and India. But local governments became stabilized. Meteorologists tell us there was a warming period beginning about A.D. 1000. Those brilliant spring mornings so common in medieval poetry may be reflections of fact. The friendlier climate was favorable to crop-growing and to settlement, to the building of manor houses and the construction of towns. New universities were founded (e.g., Oxford in 1167). New technologies were developed (the windmill, the water mill). Wealth accumulated and city life reemerged. Literature became produced again in elaborate manuscripts once the economy could afford this. The twelfth century is a time of notable cultural blossoming, and new literary production.

The aristocratic cast of society, prevailing at first even in the new world of the towns, meant that chiefs of tribes and men of important military descent were the patrons of literature. Such a structure naturally entails a shift towards aristocratic characters in literature. The shift is never entire; saints' lives, for example, provide a counterbalance in offering ideal portraits of persons of lower origins. The excellence of saints too (whatever the birth origin) is often somewhat antipathetic to aristocratic values.

An objection lodged against medieval literature is that it notoriously concerns itself with "unreal" things—with castles, knights, dragons, witches, magic objects, and the Quest. These things are the very essence of the "romantic." But castles and knights are really symptoms of a certain realism in medieval fiction; castles and mounted warriors were part of the scene, in both East and West. Fiction follows engineering. Witches and magic objects we have encountered in Heliodorus (and elsewhere). Dragons seem an interesting addition from Northern lore, though they could have come from China; the dragon (Greek *drakōn*) is known to Greeks and Romans as a guardian of treasure, but it appears in neither epics nor novels of classical antiquity—unless Scylla could stand in for one. Monsters appear only sparingly in the ancient novel (as distinct from the *Odyssey*); they are usually (as now) human monsters, such as the ever-popular werewolf.

The Quest has been seen as a truly new motif, especially as the Quest becomes focused upon the Grail. Jessie Weston, discussing the relation of the Grail-quest to folklore motifs, suggests that the grail as a holy receptacle or container is an emblem of the female genital organs, and "reproductive energy" (*From Ritual to Romance*, 75).[4] Jason as presented in Apollonius Rhodius' epic *Argonautika* (c. 230 B.C.) is on a quest to find the Golden Fleece, but ancient prose writings have no tales about gangs of young men going on a quest, exactly— though we do have men teaming up to attempt to rescue the girlfriend of the hero. The strongest "quest story" in the ancient novels is the story of Charikleia's quest for her home and parents, treated in the *Aithiopika* less as a *nostos*, a return home to the familiar, than as an exploration of the unknown that forms part of the charm of any "quest," as indeed of all journeys.

Once "Quest" is expanded into "Journey," then we see that all novels are really "about" journeys, and medieval fiction is relieved of what was supposed to be a primary distinguishing characteristic. For Northrop Frye (see *The Secular Scripture*, 1976), journeys, divided into forms of ascent and descent, but ultimately more or less circular, are a major structural feature of "romance," a feature often borrowed by modern fiction. Percy G. Adams in *Travel Literature and the Evolution of the Novel* (1983) summarizes the views of the symbolic critics of "romance" while insisting on a realistic substratum to voyage literature; there were "real journeys, short or long, that preceded the first imaginary journeys" (151). We know that some writers of imaginary journeys (notably Lucian) did take very considerable real-life journeys. The mock-hero narrator of Lucian's *True Story* (*Vera Historia*) says that he wants to explore the boundaries of the ocean and what lies beyond—a heroic quest for adventure here treated comically. Lucian may be parodying the *Apista hyper Thoulēn* (*Wonders beyond Thule*) of Antonius Diogenes, a novel offering a complex account of impossible voyages narrated in twenty-four books, which we possess only in Photius' summary. Photius thought the characters of Antonius Diogenes furnished the *paradeigma* or models for the heroes and heroines of Heliodorus, Achilles Tatius, and others in their "erotic wanderings" (*Bibliothēkē* II : 148). Whether on the ramble or seeking a fleece, a home, a clue, a lover; whether on a holiday tour or a business trip; willingly or unwillingly, characters in narrative fiction old and new, in verse and prose, are constantly given to traveling.

Medieval literature notoriously deals extensively in allegory. This is sometimes held to be another charge against it. We are now in a position to see that the use of allegory is not a medieval peculiarity, or invention. Allegory is offered as an interesting mode of reading, writing, and interpretation by critics like Porphyry in the later Roman imperial era—not to mention as far back as Plato. Dante has puzzled and intrigued us by setting up, in his famous letter to Can Grande, the scheme of four levels of interpretation.[5] He offers a suggestive way of treating his *Divina Commedia*, but much of what Dante has to say is a shorthand version of traditional schema. Christian scriptures suggest the potential of allegory, in Jesus' parables and in figures like "the whole armor of God" of Galatians 6. Dante's allegorical view is adumbrated by the early Christian Origen, the scholar from Alexandria, who stimulated the specifically Christian allegorical tradition eagerly picked up by St. Augustine. Thus, some of Dante's thought has its genuinely Alexandrian origins—he too is an *Alexandrinische Mensch*.

A movement towards allegory was common in intellectual communities outside the Christian one in Late Antiquity. Neoplatonism of course takes the lead. Judaism has sometimes liked to boast its relative freedom from Greek entanglements, its divine clarity of history, but (*pace* Meir Sternberg) even Judaism has its allegorical aspects. In Late Antiquity the Jewish relation to Scripture was becoming increasingly allegorical. Partly (as Jacob Neusner suggests) this was because the extreme stress experienced under the powerful assaults of Rome and the destruction of the Temple necessitated a reading of the Bible that reflected both the stressful present and a hopeful future, not just a vanished past. Bible history becomes an image, a set of symbols of the eternally present God. New attributions can be made—e.g., "Esau" becomes "Rome." Rabbinical Midrash is particularly rich in allegorical application. Every detail becomes usable symbolically. For instance, an Essene Midrash on Numbers 21 : 18, which describes princes of Israel digging a well, comments "*The Well* is the Law, and those who dug it were the converts of Israel . . . God called them all *princes* because they sought Him . . ." (Dead Sea scroll, quoted in Neusner, *What Is Midrash?*, 35).

Allegory is a mode of interpretation (both for artist and audience) perhaps most likely to become dominant in times of danger and disruption rather than of stability. The more we need a supply of meaning to find our way through very difficult times, the more overtly allegories will be announced. In times of tranquillity, allegory may be veiled. "Allegory" cannot exist on its own for it is related to the power of other literary or graphic or cinematic elements; any work with allegorical presence is also a complex and multilayered one. The presence of allegory helps us to grasp the possibility of many-layeredness. We feel an access of power and hope when we realize our own powers of seeing deeply, of inheriting multiplicity. Any culture that needs to deal with cultural pain, multiplicity, and confusion may have to employ allegory of some kind, if only to make its needs and pain known to itself . . . as the Japanese used "Godzilla" to express the horror of the bombing of Hiroshima. The 1740s in England had less need of allegory than the 1960s in the United States, when *Lord of the Rings* and the *Narnia* chronicles took hold.

The Middle Ages came out with some very sophisticated thought—as we can see in the work of St. Thomas Aquinas. Medieval thought, far from being "Gothic" and "primitive," is highly rational, systematic, thought-provoking, and detailed. Readers liked good stories with those characteristics, including the many layers that offer the reader a mode or various modes of interpretation. A narrative like the prose *Queste del Saint Graal* (c. 1220) offers very careful explainers of matters such as dream visions, just like *The Shepherd of Hermas*, in order to make sure that interpretation goes right—though at first narration of a scene or episode the reader is invited to see what can be made of this before the solution is given. In later medieval works less effort is needed to explain things to the (doubtless) trained reader. One may doubt, too, whether any medieval reader ever read in the strict, machinelike and negative manner proposed by D. W. Robertson, who would have us suppose that contemporary English readers of the fourteenth century saw in Chaucer's tales only workings out of understood moral and spiritual truths, virtuously reprehending all "bad" characters—seeing in the Wife of Bath, for example, only the Scarlet Whore of Babylon.[6] Such a mechanical application of the spirit seems to have little to do with the way Christian believers of any era actually deal with their art. It is admittedly unlikely that medieval readers did not want an allegorical reading for their text, whether or not that was spelled out by the author. New influences affected allegorical understandings. In Islam, mysticism and allegories were developed that affected European reading and seeing. The images of the East were often like those of the West—both had been affected by Neoplatonism. In both Christendom and Islam, a rose could be the rose of Paradise and light, the light of the Divine—and the rose could also be a lady, and the sunshine the light of her smile. On all sides, poetic narrative was supposed to provide (as always) pleasure and instruction—the pleasure, like the instruction, related to teasing out significances.

In the *Lais* of Marie de France (late twelfth century) we can recognize a secular narrative literature in which Northern Celtic and Mediterranean elements are woven together. A Norman dwelling in England, and delving into Breton folklore for elegant and pointed verse narrative, Marie frequently refers to the wider world. She endows her characters with coverlets of Alexandrian silk (*Guigemar*) and brocade from Constantinople (*Le Fresne*). *Le Fresne* offers the narrative motif (so familiar to us from *Aithiopika*) of the girl-child lawfully conceived but abandoned by the mother, with tokens. Her tokens are very similar to Charikleia's: a piece of striped silk from Constantinople, a ring or bracelet (*un gros anel*) of fine gold with *une jagunce* (a ruby), so that wherever she was found people might know "Que ele est nee de bone gent"—that she was born to good people, is of gentle birth (lines 123–134). The fiercely comic adultery story in *Equitan*, with its climax in the mixup of the murderous boiling bath, is reminiscent of the adultery stories in Apuleius. The great European stockpot of stories is now fully available.

Sustaining—indeed elaborating—the qualities and techniques of lyric while dealing with complex narrative material and psychologies is a grand achievement of the literature of the twelfth and thirteenth centuries. This achievement was to continue, as in the works of Chaucer and the anonymous English *Sir Gawain and the Green Knight* (fourteenth century). Poetic narrative of novelistic material has never gone away—viz. Elizabeth Barret Browning's *Aurora Leigh* (1856), or Vikram Seth's *The Golden Gate* (1983). Poetry is never a mistake. But perhaps the achievement could not long be sustained, the renewed weight placed on unheroic inner struggle, and on nice moral and social difficulties, ultimately bending the form back to prose.

One of the notable things about Marie's *lais* is that they are in the vernacular. Here we are close to the essence of what the Middle Ages called *roman*. A "Roman" or "Romaunt" is a lengthy narrative fiction, either in poetry or prose, written in a modern "Roman" language not Latin—such as French or Spanish. The great step made in setting up the vernacular as the literary language in various European countries in the twelfth and thirteenth centuries was a stimulus to vivid and differentiated literary production. The *vernacular* is the language of the household, the kitchen (from *verna*, meaning female household slave). Frequently looked down upon as the mere "mother-tongue," parochial kitchen-language, the vernacular is *the* medium for storytelling. The essence of "romance" lies not in castles or journeys, but in the use of a common language, a language of daily life. The fresh impulse given to the vernacular, it may be supposed, would inevitably lead at some point to the rediscovery of the powers of prose telling. Prose itself is the ultimate literary vernacular, the expression of the demotic, the democratic. In written prose fiction we find the reflection of what we all, like M. Jourdain, speak from day to day without knowing it.

The most ambitious achievement in the twelfth century's experiments with verse narrative is surely that of Chrétien de Troyes, who worked in the court of Marie de Champagne in the latter decades of the 1100s. Chrétien writes with the lightest of touches, in four-beat lines, pleasant, rapid, varied, and apparently unquenchable. In the work of Chrétien we have definitely come upon the verse-novel as *roman*. The exploits of *chansons de geste*, heroic stories about historical heroes told in verse, are borrowed only to be subdued. Heroes may perform astounding feats of valor, but that is incidental to the social and moral ordering of their lives. The *chansons de geste* belong to the epic world. Epic is always concerned with the fate of the tribal group and the foundation of political power. The world of the epic is a world in which private relationships must be subordinated or even vanquished—as Aeneas must vanquish Dido and his love for her. The novel demands that a value be set on the personal affection, and on individual desire. However brave some of Chrétien's heroes are, they are fated to live in a novelistic world—if not the world of the prose novel. Their personal lives are complex with the added complexities of the code of *amor courtois*, which to some degree licensed (or playfully pretended to license) adultery. Medieval love stories are not, however, inevitably adulterous—adultery is but one of the many complications of love. The Novel is always to some degree sympathetic to adultery (or to the impulses behind it), the more so when marriage is seen as an institution belonging to the state, to a realm of power that disregards individual choice.[7]

The interest of each of Chrétien's narratives lies in the characters' emotional reactions, especially to love-situations that place them under complicated stress. Chrétien, one of the most sophisticated narrators who ever set pen to paper, is a kind of poetic medieval Henry James with a more pronounced comic sense. All his elegant castles are so many Poyntons, sites of psychological turmoil and the anxieties of love and greed.

The reader is obviously invited to discuss a character's problems and solutions, as in one of the "debates of love" (débats d'amour) concerning the casuistry of Amor. Chrétien's stories often resemble meditations on earlier stories, as replayings, with complications. Fenice, the second-generation heroine of *Cligès* (c. 1172), says she does not want to live like Yseult, between two owners of her body. Yet Fenice, married off against her will to an unloved husband, is put to it to find a different solution from Yseult. She makes great efforts to preserve her virginity within that marriage, reserving herself for Cligès, her true love. Eventually she decides to stage her own *Scheintod*, appearing dead so that she may be entombed and then, her reputation saved, go off with her lover. Fenice succeeds in her plot, though not without unforeseen difficulty, as a physician who tries to revive her nearly burns her alive. The narrative has brilliantly comic unglamorous touches, like the daily inspection of the invalid Fenice's urine, and the feather mattress that Cligès puts into her sepulchre, so she won't have to lie on cold stone. Fenice's *Scheintod* seems like a brilliantly perverse reading (or strong misreading) of Chariton. Well is this heroine named "Fenice" meaning "Phoenix," not only because, as the narrator comments, she is a nonpareil for beauty, but because also she rises again from fire and death—like the Phoenix, or like those other Phoenix-heroines of the ancient novel, including Charikleia. In achieving her desires, Fenice is assisted by a Mediterranean "Mother Midnight," the old nurse called "Thessala" because she comes from the land of witches, spells, and diablerie (the land of Lucius' misadventures with Photis and a witch): "Por ce fu Thessala clamee / Qu'ele fu de Tessalle nee, / Ou sont feites les deablies" (lines 2965–2967).

Critics are nowadays less likely than of yore to discount the possibility of medieval writers' acquaintance with the classical novels; David Rollo traces connections between *The Golden Ass* and Chrétien (From Apuleius' Psyche to Chrétien's Erec and Enide," *TSAN*, 347–369). But commentators have long noticed the Byzantine elements in *Cligès*, a narrative braiding together of Celtic and Byzantine personages and stories. The action ranges from Constantinople to Oxford and back. It is eminently likely that Chrétien was influenced (and not just in this work) by Byzantine writers. He may have got wind of some of the new Greek narratives which were also drawing on the ancient Greek novels. A modern editor suggests that *Cligès* is largely a Byzantine story loosely attached by Chrétien to the more familiar Arthurian matter.[8] Perhaps the French poet did a disservice to

Byzantium by making Constantinople *too* luxurious, ornate, and attractive; the Fourth Crusade took place only a generation after the appearance of *Cligès*.

We have been taught in school that Greek culture was absolutely separated from the culture of the West until 1453, when the Ottoman Turks at last took Constantinople, and her scholars fled Westward, taking their ideas, language, and manuscripts with them. We tend to ignore earlier points of contact, and have been particularly efficient in forgetting one of the most distressing episodes of East-West relations. In 1204 the men who undertook the Fourth Crusade decided, rather than trying to free Jerusalem from the Saracens, that it would be more profitable to sack rich Byzantine cities. This largely Venetian-led expedition was ruthlessly successful; the "crusaders" sacked and burned Constantinople, with the intention of setting up their own empire. This outrage is triumphantly commemorated in huge paintings in the Doge's palace in Venice. Constantinople was stripped of wealth and art treasures. Count Baldwin of Flanders had himself crowned emperor in Hagia Sophia, which was turned into a Roman Catholic cathedral. The Empire of Nicaea was the largest remaining segment of the old Greek Byzantine Empire, and Nicaea's ruler managed to regain Constantinople in 1261. The sixty-odd years of "Latin rule" gave Byzantines a horror of the Roman West, which is one reason why they were unwilling to call for foreign assistance in the fifteenth century; the Turks were a kinder enemy. Yet the Fourth Crusade, this ugly episode, presents us with a high degree of contact between the Greek and Latin cultures. The Greek provinces, including Attica and Boeotia, fell to the lot of the Burgundians, and "Frankish" Greece endured until the Catalans dispossessed the French and took control in 1311.

Kos and Rhodes fell to Genoa and then to the Knights of St. John. In the meantime Sicily, one of the colonies of Magna Graecia and then a Roman possession, had fallen to the Normans, and the Normans were in turn chased out by the descendants of Frederick Barbarossa, the Holy Roman Emperor. In the late twelfth century, on the death of the Hohenstaufens, the pope made Charles of Anjou king of Naples and Sicily. Though the violent revolt known as the "Sicilian Vespers" put an end to the Angevin line and to French sway in 1282, Naples and Sicily remained joined under the rule of Pietro of Aragon and his descendants. Western Europeans were trying vigorously to expand throughout the Mediterranean Basin. The biggest check to their ambitions in the Eastern Mediterranean were the Osmanli or Ottoman Turks, who arrived in western Asia Minor in the early fourteenth century, taking place of the Selçuk Turks, who had been there since the thirteenth century. The Ottoman Turks built a great empire, and tried to expand throughout the Mediterranean world just as the West Europeans were attempting to do.

There was certainly plenty of contact—if often of a rather dismal sort—between various West Europeans and the Greek-speaking world. It is not very wonderful if through some direct or indirect routes Chrétien had made contact with some of the Greek literature. As we have seen, romantic narratives, novels in verse developed out of the earlier Greek prose fictions, were a feature of Byzantine literature in the century in which Chrétien was writing his major works. Most interesting is the technique of *entrelacement* developed by Chrétien (and others), a technique of interlacing narratives following the action of different characters, which seems ultimately to owe its successful practice to the example of Heliodorus. Chrétien presumably did not read Heliodorus—at least not unmediated; he seems to have been influenced, however, by works with Heliodorus in their background.

What is remarkably evident about the narrative fictions of the High Middle Ages, whether in poetry or (more rarely) in prose, is the high degree of intertextuality proclaimed. Stories are once more meant for readers rather than for hearer. And they belong to a larger tissue of literature, of story-writing. As Renate Blumenfeld-Kosinski says, "Unlike the epic and the Saint's Life, which derived their authority and significance from the national / historical and the religious / devotional sphere respectively, the romance is presented as a link in a chain of texts" (*The French Novel*, 2). The writing of novels or *romans* depended on familiarity with written literature—the novel proves itself always "bookish." Chrétien at the beginning of *Cligès* refers to the importance of books and tradition: "Par les livres que nos avons / Les fez des anciens savons / Et del siegle qui fu jadis" (*Cligès*, lines 25–27). ["By the books that we have / We know the deeds of the ancients / And of the era which was of old."] The "romance"/*roman* has its textuality always about it. As fictional narration shades back into prose once again, the textuality will become hidden, will most often come out not as source, but as quotation, especially as the stories become more free-standing, detached from the matter of Troy or Bretagne. Yet by the twelfth century we know once more that we have an audience of *readers*, that we are once more in the world of writing. The writer is a body in the library, at a remove from the tribal lay in the hall.

There *is* a medieval concept of authorship. Both "Marie" (of France) and Chrétien insert their names into beginning or end of the narrative, like Heliodorus or Chariton. Subject matter is not seen as exclusive—medieval authors have no objection to picking up other writers' story-material, usually with a basis in history or legend, and playing with it. A retelling of an old story will offer surprising turns, new language. We should be sympathetic, as the twentieth century has shown similar tendencies, both in the retelling of history as fiction, and in the retelling of legends as novel, as in Christa Wolf's *Kassandra* (1983). Even Biblical narratives can be turned into fiction, as in Joseph Heller's *God Knows* (1984) or Jeanette Winterson's use of the Noah story in *Boating for Beginners* (1985). Characters invented by earlier writers of fiction may be redeployed by later writers, who dare to employ Dickens's Estella or Conan Doyle's Irene Adler for their own purposes.

Medieval writers are quite sanguine about writing such continuations. The most remarkable case of discontinuous continuation is the case of the *Le Roman de la Rose*, begun in the first part of the thirteenth century by Guillaume de Lorris and continued (c. 1275–1280) by Jean de Meung. Guillaume de Lorris' story is an allegorical narrative, in which the narrator, the Lover or Dreamer, dreams that he is in a beautiful garden ruled by the God of Love; Cupid lays commands and restrictions upon the Dreamer as he desires to reach the most beautiful rose of all. The figures that invite him or fend him off obviously represent aspects of the lady's state of mind, such as *Bel-Accueil* or *Danger*, but she is also threatened by external forces such as Slander (*Male Bouche*); when Venus allows the Lover one kiss, Slander raises an outcry and a higher wall is built about the rose. In this story of courtship and desire, rendered in emblems of the lovers' states, we can see the old novelistic influences at work, even catch a glimpse of the fictional garden of antiquity as we saw it in *Daphnis and Chloé* or (further emblematized) in *Kleitophon and Leukippé*. In the use of its major conceit this *roman* leans ultimately on Sappho.

Guillaume de Lorris' poem breaks off (or ends) with the frustrated lover finding his beloved is further from him than ever. But the work is taken up by Jean de Meung, whose literary objectives are altogether different. One of his purposes is really to rebut or parody the basic suppositions of de Lorris' story of love-longing, eliminating, in so doing, the allegorical possibilities whereby the garden can represent the fertility of Earth itself, or even Paradise. In Jean de Meung's poem, hypocrisy is a major enemy, and the trappings of emblems and civilization are deceitful coverings or restrictions upon plan and simple Nature. Women are special objects of a wide-ranging attack that also turns against the more powerful orders of society. It is a little like finding Chaucer taken over by Swift. Both writers know that the *roman* can be very various. Both authors exhibit a knowledge of the resources of fiction, if not of prose fiction.

It takes prose fiction a while to catch up. When it appears, it has dynamic impact on other prose discourses. The relationship of novelistic narrative to other kinds of narrative has never been fully explored—and "exploration" is itself a narrative and partly novelistic idea. The presence of the Novel should not be registered as a cultural distraction; it makes other kinds of works possible. Marco Polo would not have written of his travels had he not met in a prison in Genoa a fellow prisoner, Rustichello of Pisa, a writer of French novels or "romance." Rustichello was co-author if not ghost writer, narrating the story of Polo in the style of the Arthurian fictions he had written before. Marco Polo's book ought to have an "as told to" statement beneath its title. Rustichello must not be thought of as in some way damaging the purity of Polo's "real" account; without the novelist there would have been no account.

One of the important prose works of the Middle Ages is the prose *Lancelot*, a work of the mid-thirteenth century, like the prose *Tristan*. Both deal with the "Matter of Britain" (or *Bretagne*); *Lancelot* closely follows the complicated relationships between Arthur, Lancelot, and Guenevere. In the first part, the proud and somewhat bitter Gallehaut plays an important role as a devoted friend of Lancelot and thus as a furtherer of the liaison between Launcelot and Guenevere. Gallehaut recognizes Launcelot's suffering from hopeless devoted love for Queen Guenevere, and wishes to relieve it. When the queen meets Launcelot and thanks him graciously for his deeds of prowess, Gallehaut is urgently explicit with her: "'Lady,' said Gallehaut '. . . have pity on him, who loves you better than himself . . . I plead to you for him . . . for you could never conquer a richer treasure . . . I pray you that you give him your love and take him for your own knight for ever. . . . Then kiss him in my presence [*Donc lo baissiez devant moi*] for the beginning of true love" (347–348).

This is the book to which Dante's Francesca di Rimini refers in Canto V of the *Inferno* when she says she and Paolo were reading the story of Lancelot's love when their eyes met and . . . "That day we read no more." Francesca blames the novel as a pandar: "Galeotto fu il libro e chi lo scrisse" ("A Gallehaut was that book, and he who wrote it") V, line 137). Does Francesca offer the first modern instance of *Bovarysme*? It may be indicated that part of her trouble (or sinful condition) was a desire to be *like* the characters in the books, that her lust was complicated by Lucius' sort of wish to figure in books, or at least to imitate those who do. (If she wanted to figure *in a book*, of course Dante's Francesca has certainly had her way.) Adultery here rests not on simple lust but on what has recently been called, through the influence of René Girard, "mediated desire," which is very often bookishness, of Don Quixote's or Emma Bovary's kind. (See Girard, *Mensonge romantique et vérité romanesque* [1961].) For the first time in the modern vernacular—and of course never for the last—we hear that warning note about the danger of reading fiction, a danger particularly acute where ladies are concerned, who are always likely to be carried away by love-stories, as poor Francesca is endlessly carried away in the everlasting mournful gust of her passion. But Dante never denies that he himself loved the literature of French chivalry. He too is a proponent (and protagonist) of the "love-story," even inventing a new form of fictionalized autobiography for his own love-story in the *Vita Nuova* (c. 1295) as he tries to work out how *amor* can be rendered spiritually good.

BOCCACCIO: *FILOCOLO*

The most important figure in the creation of the novel during the entire Middle Ages is one of Dante's warmest admirers, another Italian writer who differs very much from the poet of the *Divina Commedia*. My story of the novel should of course be a story without a hero. (And nowadays we are scarcely allowed to have "authors" at all, let alone to make them into heroes.) Yet my story cannot quite do without a hero, and, if I am allowed to have one, it is Giovanni Boccaccio. Boccaccio (1313–1375), the son of a Florentine merchant, had the good luck to be sent on a mission to the court of Naples from c. 1325 to 1340. He returned to Florence in time to witness the ravages of the Black Death in that city, an event commemorated in his most famous work, the *Decameron*. Employed on various diplomatic missions, he knew almost everyone of importance in North Italy of his time. Boccaccio was a close friend of Petrarch (a poet very different from himself). As well as being a diplomat and a writer, Boccaccio was a founder of the modern academy. He began modern criticism of modern writers in writing his own "Life of Dante" and in giving a course of public lectures on the *Divina Commedia*. He also, singlehandedly, established Greek studies in the Florentine academy; he invited a Greek scholar to come to Florence, and supported him. He introduced Homer to the modern Europeans by inducing his Greek scholar to write a Latin prose version of both the *Iliad* and the *Odyssey*. Boccaccio had a fondness himself for encyclopedic works and produced many (in Latin): *The Falls of Illustrious Men; Famous Women*, etc.

Such prodigious academic work was sufficient for one man, and enough to change the view of things. But Boccaccio was a steady and unstoppable "creative" writer, versatile in prose and poetry in his own Italian. He is best known for the *Decameron*, a collection of short stories with a frame story or *cornice* in the manner of the Eastern collections that had already been absorbed by the Byzantine Greeks. The *Decameron* was very popular in Boccaccio's own time, but so were his poetic narratives, such as the *Filostrato* (the source text for Chaucer's *Troilus and Criseyde*) and the *Teseida* or story of Theseus, source-text for Chaucer's "Knight's Tale" in *Canterbury Tales*. I choose here, however, to focus not upon Boccaccio's narrative poems, nor even solely upon the well-known *Decameron*, but rather upon two important novels that change the face of fiction. During his sojourn in Naples between the years 1336 and 1338 Boccaccio wrote his first prose narrative, the *Filocolo*. Boccaccio himself claims that the book was written to please his lady Maria, natural daughter of King Robert of Naples and Sicily, and under her inspiration. Legend and biography, taking their cues from Boccaccio himself, have emphasized the young Tuscan's love for this high-born (if not legitimately conceived) lady, and have seen her as the multi-faceted "Fiammetta" (Little Flame, Flamelette) who appears as the heroine in so many of Boccaccio's works. (Tradition has even made the Maria-Fiammetta whom Boccaccio loved a redhead, explaining the soubriquet.) Boccaccio's "Fiammetta" in her various guises in various books is more properly to be taken as Boccaccio's idea of the most interesting kind of woman, in all sorts of different aspects, rather than as a literal portrait. Boccaccio himself, however, emphasizes a personal level in his writing, and is eager for the reader to think of the author as a man in love.

The novel begins with a reference to the *Aeneid*, and to the descent of the Roman people from Aeneas; the *Aeneid* is the epic most played upon in the course of the novel. After praise of King Robert and his daughter, the narrator confides his own falling in love, and the vision of Amore; the author confesses to Amore, "I can fly you no longer, nor do I desire to flee, but submit myself, humbly and devotedly, to your pleasure." Then, he says, he was in a temple dedicated to the king of celestial birds (i.e., the Church of St. Gabriel), in which a priestess of Diana in white veil and dressed in black habit (i.e., a nun) guarded the sacred flame. There it came into his head to rehearse the story of valorous Florio, "reciting what happened to him in amorous words" (*con amorose parole*). The *gentilissima donna* encourages this project, and the present book is the result. Boccaccio then addresses his reader in playfully gilded language:

> Now then, O youths, who have hoisted the sail of our wandering bark
> to the winds blowing from the golden fanning wings of the young son
> of Cytherea, who dwelling on the amorous shores are desirous of arriving at the safe harbor with eager pace, I by his inestimable power
> pray that you should devoutly lend your intellect to this present work,
> because in it you may find how fickle fortune has dealt out various
> permutations and tempests to lovers of antiquity . . . whence you can
> see that you are not singular and not the first to endure adversity, and
> may firmly believe that you shall not be the last. From which you can
> take consolation, if it is indeed true that the miserable find solace in
> having company in their pain. And likewise, you can have secure hope
> of guerdon, which does not come without alleviation of your pain.
> And you, young amorous ladies [*giovanette amorose*] who in your delicate breasts carry the most secret burning flame of love, incline your

ears, with no fickle understanding, to new lines [*nuovi versi*], which do not offer you the cruel conflagrations of ancient Troy, nor the sanguinary battles of Pharsalia, which produce a certain hardness in the spirit. But you will hear the piteous adventures of the enamored Florio and of his Biancifiore, which will give you great pleasure. And hearing them, you can know how much it pleases *Amore* to make a young man sole lord of her mind, without giving vain attention to many arguments, because many times one thing is lost for another, as we say he who chases two hares sometimes catches one but often catches none. Therefore learn to love one alone, one who loves you perfectly, as did the good young woman [*la savia giovane*] who, through long sufferings, was brought by *Amore* to the desired end. And if the present matter, O young men and maidens, should generate in your spirits any fruit and pleasure, do not be ungrateful but offer devout thanks to Jove and to the new author [*al nuovo autore*].   (Branca, ed., *Filocolo*, 66–67)

This jocular outsetting creates the mood, in its elaborated, even "Alexandrian" language, and in its confidence in the presence of both author and reader, and in their roles. Boccaccio is using—as he and his readers both know—traditional material. The story of the lovers Florio (or Florizel) and Biancifiore (or Blanziflor) was a widely known medieval tale, and had been the subject of a French narrative poem. These are not "new" characters. But the manner of dealing with them is new, and Boccaccio is right to herald himself as a "new author." Boccaccio here equates poetic narrative and prose narrative, terming the lines he offers *versi* or verses, while at the same time jocularly defying the epic. Young people, after all, want to read love stories, not the incendiary tale of Troy or the bloody battles of Lucan's epic *Pharsalia*. The epic is a hard-hearted thing, Boccaccio jokes, it requires *nell'animo alcuna durezza*, a certain hardness of spirit or hardening of soul in its reader. This, the novel, is something with its own virtues, the chief among them being its power to give pleasure.

Actually there are in the novel scenes designed for the epic reader, scenes of bloodthirsty fights, and an incendiary threat hangs over the characters. It seems part of Boccaccio's joke that this exordium disclaiming bloodshed is immediately followed by a very violent episode: the heroine's father is killed in battle. His poor pregnant wife takes refuge with the King and Queen of Spain, and she and the Queen of Spain endure childbirth pangs at the same time. The Queen of Spain bears a son, and the poor refugee a daughter, on the same day. The girl's mother soon dies, however, and leaves the baby to be brought up by King Felice and his wife. The royal couple treat the baby girl well, but as the little girl Biancifiore (or "White-blossoms") grows up, she and little Florio, the King's son and heir, are inseparable playmates and friends. The innocence of childhood gives way after adolescence to a new feeling, as in *Daphnis and Chloé*. At first the young people, hardly even able to describe what is happening to them, keep their feelings for each other a secret. Eventually, however, love cannot be hidden, and all is consternation at the most agreeable of all possible castles.

Florio is sent away to be the squire of a distant noble, in order to get over his love, and Biancifiore is treated with displeasure. The royal couple discuss marrying her off to another, but she resists this idea. Florio also staunchly resists other enticements. Then the hero's parents have the bright idea of bringing about the judicial murder of the inconvenient girlfriend. Biancifiore is accused of attempting to serve poisoned peacock to the King at his birthday feast—and, sure enough, the peacock was poisoned; the dog who ate a piece died. Biancifiore is condemned to be burned at the stake. Florio comes to the rescue, urged on by the gods.

The king and queen pretend to be friendly and to accept the explanation of the mistake. But once Florio is out of the way again, his parents sell the girl to two merchants heading for Alexandria. After traveling to other ports, including Sicily and Rhodes, the merchants arrive at Alexandria, where Biancifiore attracts the attention of the *amiraglio*, "Admiral" (Emir) or chief officer of the King of Babylon. The potentate of Babylon is a very "oriental" personage, always seeking fresh subjects for his harem. The amiraglio buys Biancifiore as the prize of his collection and shuts her in a tower. We keep coming upon the lady confined or dwelling in a tower in fictional narratives. In *Aucassin et Nicolette*, a thirteenth-century French *chante-fable* or prose narrative with intermittent verses, the heroine likewise is imprisoned in a tower, from which she escapes by moonlight. Nicolette is a rather exotic heroine; she is a captive bought from Saracens, and her indeterminate background and ambiguous situation between Saracen and Christian cultures explain why Aucassin's family are so set against his relationship with the girl. The discovery of Nicolette's true identity reveals her to be the lost daughter of the king of Carthage (and thus a woman from Africa, like Charikleia). This story (which could have been in contact with Heliodorus at some point) might be an influence (direct or indirect) on *Filocolo*. Biancifiore is another exotic tower-dweller with Eastern and African associations. Miss White-flowers is a Moon-Lady, like Luna and Aseneth, or even Rapunzel.[9] But Moon-Ladies in towers are condemned to wax and wane in sterility; like Persephone-Rapunzel, they need to invite a man in, and eventually to get out.

Florio is told his beloved is dead; his parents, like the villains in *Apollonius of Tyre*, hold a funeral and (using a substitute corpse) create a monument, a tomb complete with epitaph. Florio ultimately sees through the substitution and goes on a quest to find his beloved. Shipwrecked, he is tossed up on the coast of Italy near Naples. While waiting for his ship to be repaired, he has a pleasant day in a beautiful garden with Fiammetta and her young friends, and hears a court-of-love dispute; Fiammetta, as crowned queen of the circle, must answer *questione d'amore* with her wisdom. Florio then retraces Biancifiore's route, hearing particular news of her in Sicily, and in Alexandria he finds out about her present situation. He gains the confidence of the warden of the tower, the eunuch Sadoc, by playing chess with him.

At last he is able to introduce himself into the tower, hidden in a basket of roses used for a special festival. Florio arrives in the erotic *roses* that counteract lunar sterility, becoming a sort of rose himself, in a neat reversal of gender imagery. Biancifiore's faithful servant Glorizia recognizes Florio and hides him in a closet. He emerges when the house is at last asleep, and climbs into bed beside the sleeping beloved, who had cried herself to sleep after praying that she could be reunited with Florio. After Florio's many tender and intimate caresses of the sleeping girl's body, she (not incredibly) awakens. Once she recognizes the answer to her prayer, she begins to return the kisses and embraces with equal enthusiasm. The couple then conduct their own marriage ceremony before the gigantic image of Cupid that dominates the room. Their wedding ring is the magic ring that Florio's relenting mother gave him when he set out on the quest. They then consummate their love, and enjoy the same pleasure the next night.

In the dawning, however, they are caught by the amiraglio, who orders them to be arrested and brought out naked, save for their bonds, to the meadow beneath the tower. Much of the population of Alexandria arrives to see the spectacle as the amiraglio has ordered that the couple be burned at the stake. Florio's seven friends put on a great show of fight and, assisted by Mars, engage in an energetic and bloody battle (not unlike something in Lucan's *Pharsalia*). The pyre is involved in smoke, and the friends believe the young couple must be dead. The two, however, clinging together, are saved both by the magic ring and by the intervention of the gods. The amiraglio, whose disposition to fight has been assuaged by this combat, becomes reconciled to Florio and his doughty companions. The young couple (now well dressed) are brought into Alexandria. The "amiraglio" turns out to be Florio's uncle on his mother's side. The last book is of course the book of the return, the book of explanations and reconciliation.

Boccaccio's narrative offers various pleasures. The young couple, especially in the early books, are sympathetically drawn but always remind us that they are teenagers in love. There is a constantly youthful quality to their complaints, and to Florio's inadequate if earnest confrontations with his father. The murder plot in Book II ("The Case of the Poisoned Peacock") is very nicely handled, with a lot of believable political plotting and mutual gangsterish reassurance among the king and his courtiers, a back-room atmosphere that contrasts with the elaborate public spectacle of the king's birthday feast, and the elegant public room that is its ultra-rich setting:

> The royal salon was ornamented with marble columns of diverse colors . . . and the windows were divided with columns of crystal, the capitals of which were of gold and silver . . . in that room there could be seen ancient stories sculpted in bas-relief in lucent marbles by the best master. . . . Here you could see the piteous ruins of Thebes, and the flaming pyre of the two sons of Jocasta, and the other cruel battles created by their division, together with the first and second destruction of proud Troy. Nor were there lacking any of the great victories of great Alexander. (203–204)

The wicked queen persuades Biancifiore to dress herself up to do honor to the occasion and the place, making her put on a new dress of vermilion samite. The wicked seneschal persuades the girl that the offering of the peacock ought to be made by her: "It is not suitable that the bird should be carried to the royal table except by the most gentle and beautiful virgin. . . . And therefore I earnestly beseech you that it will please you to consent to do this service . . ." (206). Of course Biancifiore consents, and, dressed in her *red* dress, she will appear a fittingly wicked woman when the accusation falls upon her.

A different kind of plot against the young lovers is devised by Florio's host, the duke, and his elderly friend Ascalion in the third book. Ascalion shrewdly argues that Florio could best be diverted from his love by "carnal conjunctions"; after all, "Florio has never had carnal delight with Biancifiore; and if we were able to bring it about that he had it with some other beautiful girl, it would be easy for him to forget what he has never had in favor of what he possessed; and even if he did not forget all about her afterwards, at least he would not think of her so much" (249). Two beautiful young ladies, who expect that one of them will gain Florio in marriage for her prize, are set to entrap him. They sit in the shade in a most beautiful garden, "dressed in the thinnest garments over their delicate flesh" (253), a raiment that shows the form of their breasts. These young ladies are extremely charming to Florio, but he remains loyal to his love—to their great distress, as they not only see the matrimonial prize slipping away, but fear the duke's anger. Florio is not unaroused by the girls' charms, but scolds himself into a better frame of mind:

> "Ah! crude man, not born of royal progenitors, but of the lowest stock, what betrayal is this that you have thought of just now? . . . Now how could you deign to love these, whose beauty is the smallest portion of that of Biancifiore? And if it were even much greater, so how would you ever be able to find one who should love you as perfectly as she loves you? Oh! if this should be known, would she not reasonably have occasion to wish never to see you again?—Yes, indeed." (255)

Florio is a true hero of chastity, of *parthenia en andrasi*. He proves his loyalty to the one love and his determination not to act like common young men. He is also heroic in his role as Biancifiore's rescuer when, alerted and spurred on by Venus, he sets out to rescue her from the stake to which she has been condemned for her alleged attempt on the king's life. But that rescue is very comic. We have been tensely following Biancifiore's fate in her windowless prison, under sentence, and see her near-hopeless condition as she is led out to be burned. Florio is on the way, true. But—he gets tired, and, as he and his posse have apparently plenty of time, he lies down for a short nap. The authorial narrator exclaims in horror, "O Florio, now what are you doing? You are acting contrary to the laws of love. No sleep suits the solicitous lover" (212). But Florio can be awakened only by the vision of Mars. Guilty, he proceeds on his way, and rescues his love in the nick of time. The momentary lapse of this inopportune slumber is reflected in the later lapse in Alexandria, when Florio, hearing of Biancifiore's long imprisonment, suffers from temporary wanhope. While he was on the quest, he had the quest to keep him going; on finding that he has arrived at his objective but the difficulties are as great as ever, he succumbs to a melancholy disbelief in his own abilities and in Biancifiore's fidelity.

The story rewards both the hero of chastity and the heroine, though there is much less emphasis on Biancifiore as a decision-maker in the narrative. She is a girl possessing *sōphrosynē*, she is, as Boccaccio says in his prologue, *la savia giovane*. But there are no prolonged or elaborated attempts on her chastity; the merchants who buy the girl are easily won over by her tears to do her no personal harm, and seem more interested in making a handsome profit (rather like the grave robbers in Chariton). Like all the girls caught for the ruler of Babylon, she must undergo a virginity test in a special section of the tower of ladies, a test very reminiscent of that near the end of *Kleitophon and Leukippé*.

The well-preserved chastity of both hero and heroine is rewarded with the most intense amorous delight. The delight is rendered in the text, in the narrative of their union, from Florio's scopophilic position in the closet to his approach to Bianciofiore's bed to his various activities within the bed. This is luscious and amorous prose, in a scene which presumably excited Boccaccio as well as his readers. That the *Filocolo*'s scene was thought of as erotic (if also lightly comic) by some early readers can be seen in the illustrations of the 1478 edition. The sequence of consummation, with the marriage before the image of Cupid, emphasizes the spontaneous, self-initiated, and free aspects of the couple's union. It is almost a disappointment later that the amiraglio, when he finds he is Florio's uncle, insists on the couple's undertaking a public wedding ceremony—as far as the pair privately are concerned, they *are* married—as married as Rapunzel and the Prince, who also unite by private agreement. Joyful consummation is interrupted by the ignominy of discovery—a sequence of Boccaccio's novel that was certainly recollected by Sir Philip Sidney in the *Old Arcadia* (c. 1580), in which Pyrocles enters Philoclea's bedroom and makes love to her, a pleasant time that leads to their disastrous discovery by angry Philanax (*Old Arcadia*, 202–211; 251–265). The prayers of Sidney's hero and heroine, each trying to spare the other, also echo the valiant attempts of Florio and Bianciofiore to prevail upon men and gods to spare the innocent partner.

The ordeal of threatened burning in Book IV of Boccaccio's novel seems both to echo and play with elements of Heliodorus' *Aithiopika*. In Heliodorus' novel the heroine, accused of being a poisoner, is sentenced to die by fire—just what happens to Bianciofiore in Book II of *Filocolo*. Charikleia is saved not by her lover (as Bianciofiore is at that juncture) but by the divine powers, and the power of her *pantarbe* stone. Charikleia on her pyre is surrounded by a ring of flames that do not touch her but only illuminate her beauty: she looks "like a bride in a fiery bridal-chamber" (*en pyrinōi thalamōi nympheuomenēn*, III: 20). In Boccaccio's novel, the hero and heroine really are bride and bridegroom, and the two are together not only in prison (as Charikleia and Theagenes are in Book VIII) but even unto death, when they are brought naked to the stake. Their tormentors intend to execute them separately, but Florio pleads successfully that they be burned together: "one will, one love has always bound and joined us . . . likewise let the same flame consume us" (520). Their generosity in passing the maternal magic ring back and forth and their close intertwining even at the apparent moment of death saves them both amid the flames (see 1478 illustration, Plate 17); Venus, concealed in a white cloud, encourages the pair and suppresses the flames nearest them.

The pyre in Alexandria is Bianciofiore's *second* experience of attempted execution by fire. Charikleia similarly undergoes a second fiery trial; on her return home in Africa she is about to be sacrificed by burning in a ritual fire, although in order to be a suitable thank offering she must prove a virgin. Similar repetition is involved in the fates of Boccaccio's young couple, and their experience is also an experience in Africa, where they prove (or rather, Florio does) to have blood-relatives; the chief man of Alexandria is Florio's maternal uncle.

In his first prose work Boccaccio seems to be holding together with a firm grasp the complicated threads of Western novelistic narrative, acknowledging and drawing upon both the recent medieval fictions and the novele of antiquity. His novel proclaims itself as novelistic, distinguishes itself from epic. Young people like to read love-stories rather than the bloody battles of the *Pharsalia*. Like the ancient novels that precede it, *Filocolo* playfully refers to and repudiates predecessor epics. The governing immediate epic in *Filocolo* is the *Aeneid*, invoked—to be dismissed—in the very first paragraphs, and constantly reappearing, as it were, in the negative mode. When he is shipwrecked on the Italian coast, near "Parthenope" as Boccaccio always terms Naples (Napoli) in this story set in a vague antiquity, Florio reproaches various powers: "And you, O highest Aeolus . . . temper your wrath, unjustly raised against me. Open your eyes, and know that I am not Aeneas, the great enemy of holy Juno: I am a young man who loves, just as you once loved" (373).

"I am not Prince Aeneas, nor was meant to be." The hero's protest resembles that of Dante's hero on a more serious occasion: "Io non Enea, io non Paulo sono" (*Inferno*, Canto II, line 32). Florio repudiates the epic role, and is aggrieved when it seems to be coming too near. Yet, as he and Boccaccio know, in "Parthenope" Florio is certainly treading epic ground. He sets out towards Virgil's tomb—but is diverted by the sound of young voices and musical instruments in a garden. A young person would quite rightly rather join a good party than seek out the ashes of a dead author. Yet Florio later goes in for intensive sightseeing, including not only the antiquities of Baiae, but also Monte Misenus, where Aeneas, led by the Sibyl, descended into the infernal regions; Florio also looks at the oratory of the Sibyl and makes an expedition around Lake Avernus. Later, when he and Biancifiore are returning homeward, they make a long stop in Parthenope and indulge in a similar round of sightseeing in a kind of honeymoon tour. We can imagine that the young Giovanni Boccaccio of Certaldo similarly engaged in touring the regions around Naples, seeing (as one can today) the landscape that Virgil knew and incorporated so memorably in the *Aeneid*.

But beyond the classicism of the *Aeneid*—recognizable and familiar—there is the other world of "antiquity" that was just coming into Boccaccio's vision, the Greek world of "Greek" fiction. "Greek" culture is undoubtedly connected by Boccaccio with the idea of fiction in general and of the novel in particular. This connection is indicated by the riddle that is the novel's title. The reader has no idea for a long while *why* the work is called *Filocolo*. Would the right title not be *Florio e Biancifiore*? The answer to the puzzle is not given until near the end of the third book. When he is setting out on his quest, Florio says that anybody holding his beloved captive would recognize his own name. To prevent his opponents from discovering his identity and making renewed attempts to conceal Biancifiore, he will take a pseudonym: "and the name which I have chosen is this: Filocolo. And truly such a name agrees with me much better than any other, and the reason why, I will tell you. Filocolo is composed of two Greek words, from 'philos' and from 'colon'; and 'philos' in Greek is as much as to say in our language 'amore' and 'colon' in Greek similarly corresponds in our language to 'fatica': whence joined together, one can say (transposing the parts) *fatica d'amore*" (357). Filocolo's new name means—or Boccaccio wants it to mean—"worn down by love." The story's hero is just like Kleitophon, who at the beginning of his story proclaims himself one who has suffered from Eros, undergone "many outrages from the experience of love" (*tosautas hubreis ex erōtos pathōn*, 8). Florio is one who has experienced the pain, the wearying travail of love, and has shown its effects. Boccaccio always uses the *philos* word for "lover" and "loving" rather than *eramai* and its derivatives for his Greek-derived "love," presumably because he wants to emphasize that affection (rather than lust only) is involved. As we have seen, and as David Konstan demonstrates, the Greek novels' *erōs* included affection, constancy, friendship as well as passion, but this was their innovation; Boccaccio has to reemphasize this content of the erotic.

Boccaccio's Greek is certainly not the best—it is the "Greek" of one who knows that the language exists, rather than of one who truly knows the language (rather like mine, in short). But he is fascinated by the idea of Greek words, Greek origins, Greek labels for fictions. Hence he entitled his best-known work the *Decameron* from *deka hēmera*, ten days, rather than *Historia dei dieci giorni* or some such title. In his play with the Greek words that provide a new kind of title for *Filocolo* Boccaccio shows himself very much aware of a leading theme in Greek erotic fiction—the pains or sufferings or trials of love, *erōtika pathēmata*. Boccaccio as "new author" is writing a modern story—that is, a *new* story written in and for the early fourteenth century. It is a lengthy and elaborate written work, making a number of allusions to modern as well as ancient literature, allusions that include quotations from the modern writer Dante—often in a delightfully ludicrous or unexpected context. But this new and highly ornamental story picks up and uses and points to the topics, patterns, and narrative preoccupations of the antique novel.

There is, of course, a mystery attached to *Filocolo*, beyond the inset riddle of the title (which some would-be helpful Renaissance editors explain to the reader straight away). How could Boccaccio have known anything about the Greek novel? The answer, I think, is given in the novel itself, in the very careful account of Florio's journey. Florio first arrives by happy accident at Parthenope, that rich abode of myth and culture—just as Giovanni Boccaccio first arrived at Naples/Parthenope, the Virgin's City where the inspired Virgil had lived. Florio and Boccaccio coincide there. We cannot know for certain that the rest of Florio's journey does not correspond to an actual physical journey undertaken by Boccaccio: Florio goes to Sicily, Rhodes, and Alexandria, and then retraces this journey on his return to Spain. But certainly in imagination Boccaccio had taken the great leap, looking eastward towards what he calls the "oriental lands," *gli orientali paesi* (553), and southward to Africa. The nodal point for this mental journeying is Sicily, the important island, once the habitat of the Kyklops, where Florio hears substantial news of his kidnapped beloved's whereabouts. On his return to Sicily, Florio makes a full narration of his love and adventures to the old woman, Sisife. The King of Naples was also the King of Sicily, and in the court at Naples Boccaccio would have met a number of Sicilians, and others who had traveled to those farther corners of the Mediterranean where Greek was still a living language and where the Greek culture was known. Sicily itself is a sort of "memory spot" in the Mediterranean; it has held to cultural material with remarkable tenacity and is unwilling to forget anything (for which service it has received no thanks). Even today on Sicily you can see the puppet shows involving the *personaggi* Rinaldo, Angelica, Ruggiero; Sicily has retained the stories rising from the "Matter of Charlemagne" for many hundreds of years.

Boccaccio was separated from the time of the last ancient novels by about seven centuries—that is, by the same length of time that lies between Boccaccio and ourselves. Almost twice as much time severs us from Charlemagne, yet Sicilians still recall the Charlemagne stories. In his journey to Naples, the most important single event in Boccaccio's life, the young Italian from a Tuscan village came into intoxicating contact with Mediterranean culture, represented most fully by Sicilians present at the court of Roberto. It is almost harder to believe that Boccaccio did not know Heliodorus (in some form) than that he did. He was hungry for literature of all kinds; contact with Naples revealed to him the vast possibilities the Mediterranean world offered to the writer. Boccaccio's energetic efforts to introduce the study of Greek to the Florentine academy proves his discovery of and commitment to the Greek world, which he would have known as mediated through men acquainted with the Byzantine tradition and culture. Boccaccio would not have been able to read Greek well enough to read complicated works (ancient or Byzantine) for himself, even if he had some instruction in the rudiments. It is most likely that some acquaintance or employee read aloud to him (or, more likely still, read aloud to a courtly group of ladies and gentlemen) from various written works, translating as he went. It is impossible not to believe that among the works Boccaccio came into contact with in some such manner were some of the Greek prose fictions—though we shall never know which ones, or which of the Byzantine romantic poems, Boccaccio heard, or heard of. (It is also quite probable that he knew—or knew of—some works that we no longer have.) Boccaccio, whose lifelong passion for fiction and for narrative in general is so very striking, was in Naples enriched by a cultural store that he could never have received in Florence. In Boccaccio we see the line of suture, the traceable point where Western fiction in prose in the new vernacular languages consciously aligns itself with the full European tradition, acknowledging that the story of fiction, the journey of fiction itself, links Spain with Alexandria as well as Naples with Sicily.

In the *Filocolo* Boccaccio created his own witty tribute to the graces and pleasures of love-fiction, wrapping up everything that had happened from Longus and Heliodorus through de Lorris, Chrétien de Troyes, and Dante. *Filocolo* is festive, fantastic, outrageously artificial, hyperbolically ekphrastic and super-sentimental in its topoi. It is a brightly colored, amusing, and highly self-conscious fiction.

The *Filocolo* was very well-known before the age of print; Chaucer draws upon this novel as well as upon Boccaccio's poetic narrative *Filostrato* in the creation of his novelistic poem *Troilus and Criseyde*. Chaucer himself calls attention to the intertextual referential nature of his own compositions; writers of the Middle Ages and early Renaissance tend to overstate indebtedness, in a teasing game that requires the reader to comprehend the function of the new poem and its originality in relation to the other works, which the ideal reader will also have read.

There is, however, no lack of the sense of the new—as Chaucer does not fail to remind us Petrarch is long *dead*, and in his coffin to boot. Imitation is not mere repetition, nor is allusion; writers write for the present, for readers alive *now*.

BOCCACCIO: *FIAMMETTA*

In Boccaccio's next novel, the *Elegia di Madonna Fiammetta* (composed between 1343 and 1344), he took a different approach, creating a simple nonfantastic narrative in which the emphasis is primarily psychological, and most of the interesting action is internal. It is a story of love and adultery; the married Fiammetta engages in an intense affair with young Panfilo (another of Boccaccio's recurring "Greek" names, meaning "love-all," i.e., the man loves all or many women and cannot be faithful). Panfilo leaves town, promising to return, but does not, and at length Fiammetta hears that he is married. Her shock and grief are the harder to bear as she cannot confide in anyone. Fiammetta's anxious husband—who is no brute and behaves impeccably throughout—notices her pallor, want of appetite, and melancholy, and he tries to entertain and distract her. The torment of attending festivities under such inner stress is brilliantly described—everything is vividly described, in fact, for we are told of experience firsthand. Fiammetta narrates her own story, and we are very strongly aware of the power (and limitations) of her point of view. In this novel, sensual happiness is not a long-sought objective reached at last (as in *Filocolo*) but a brief interlude at the beginning. Almost as soon as we come upon the scene of happiness, it starts to dissolve:

> We—he and I—as it befell, the weather being tiresomely rainy and cold, were in my chamber passing the silent night, one of the longest nights for love of the year, reposing on a rich bed together; and already Venus, much fatigued by us, vanquished had yielded, and a great light in one part of the room flushed his eyes with my beauty and made them happy, and did the same with his in mine. Afterwards, while I talked of various things, drinking deep draughts of happiness, as if inebriated by their light, I do not know for how little a space of time my eyes were overcome by cheating sleep, that took from me my words, and they fell shut. This sleep removing itself from me as sweetly as it had come, my ears heard regretful murmurs from my dear lover; and, suddenly worried about his health, I wished to say "What ails you?" But overtaken with a new prudence I kept silent, and with the sharpest eye and with sensitive ears turned to him from the other part of our bed, cautiously wondering, and listened to him for a short space. But no word of his reached my ears, although I realized he was troubled by lamentable sobbings, and his face and breast likewise were bathed in tears.   (*Fiametta*, ed. Marti, 457–458)

In *Fiammetta* Boccaccio does not eliminate the figures of the Greek novel, which he flourished so outrageously in *Filocolo*. Venus, the nymphs, Eros—these are all to be found, as is imprisonment and a death-in-life state. But essentially they are found as experiences *within* the perceiver. The entire story after this point of awakening is one long anxiety; the activity is Fiammetta's solitary self-enclosed awareness. Panfilo, the love-object, apparently does not intend faithlessness at the time; he seems genuinely reluctant to go, partly because he fears his own inevitable faithlessness. Fiammetta without him enters a void; there is nothing to take the place of that affair in her life. Boccaccio is always good on *ennui*, and certainly he never underestimates the part played by boredom in human existence. (It is because of his wearisome days that the eunuch Sadoc in *Filocolo* is so happy to play chess with Florio.)

Fiammetta writes her story for the benefit of other women, "gentle ladies," to make them wiser than she was herself; if her adultery does not pay, it does create a story of which she is the center. Unlike many later novelists, Boccaccio does not kill off his adulterous heroine, who lives to tell her tale. In the preface to her book, Fiammetta addresses her women readers and anticipates their compassion, as well as seeing herself as the benefactor warning them not to do as she has done:

> You alone who, as I know through myself, are yielding and piteous to the unfortunate, I pray you to read: in reading this you will not find Greek fables ornamented with many falsehoods, nor Trojan battles soaked in a quantity of blood, but amorous conflicts, stimulated by many desires, in which will appear before your eyes the wretched tears, the impetuous sighs, the lamenting voices and the tempestuous thoughts, which, molesting me with continuous goading, together took food, sleep, happy times and my loved beauty entirely away from me. (421)

This "prologo" to *Fiammetta* is, as the Latin chapter title to the Paduan edition of 1472 would have it, a *Prologus Artificiosus*, an artful (and artificial) prologue. Here again, as in the prefatory matter before *Filocolo*, we can see Boccaccio's insistence that what real young people (and especially ladies) really want to read and *should* read is not the epic material, the Trojan battles *sozzè per molto sangue*, but lively stories of the experience of love. Here, however, there are no ornamental falsehoods of "Greek fables" (as in *Filocolo*?), but plain experiential truth.

BOCCACCIO: *DECAMERON*

Boccaccio's great prose work, the *Decameron*, of course includes many lively stories of the experience of love—not least in the frame-story, or *cornice*, the story of the group of young people who leave Florence during the Black Death and escape briefly into the country, where they indulge in a complex game of storytelling. The frame-story reintroduces a number of Boccaccio's favorite characters, including "Panfilo" and "Fiammetta." Some of the characters in the frame-story are in love with each other (and some are heart-whole), but they are evidently able to behave with delicate civilized *sōphrosynē* during the house party. The storytellers act according to honor and chastity, though they are (briefly) outside the community, subject only to themselves. The license they take is a license to narrate— to recount all sorts of various possible reactions to the complexities of life, including those aspects of life involving sex and marriage.

The *Decameron* is multi-faceted, introducing a number of possible answers to vexing questions, while defying any sense that answers ought to be simple, or that there is only one answer. The storytelling sequence starts out by dealing with differences in culture and religion; many of the initial stories are about relations between Christians, Jews, and Muslims. The Islamic world (like the Oriental world altogether) is in general respectfully treated by Boccaccio. In these initial stories about religion, an impressive exemplar is provided by the story of the three rings: a father bequeaths a ring to each of his three sons, of which only one is genuine. Since it is impossible to tell which are the spurious rings, all three must be equally honored until the end—thus, too, nobody will know whether Christianity, Judaism, or Islam is the final "answer," the "real truth," until Judgment Day, so all must be honored in this life. Such tolerance has not exactly been typical of the West, and we are more likely to find it in fiction than in fact—but, as Boccaccio indicates, fiction can provoke thought and provide models for thinking. Within the meta-narrative of the *cornice*, the Florentine young people provide various reactions to and discussions of each story. A story with a strong and overt moralistic content (like the story of Patient Griselda) may meet with a strongly antipathetic response (as the tale of Griselda does) or with new interpretations.

In creating a collection of stories, Boccaccio is drawing upon the Eastern literature and collections such as the *Fables of Bidpai* or *Sindbad the Philosopher*; these, as we have seen, had already entered the bloodstream of Byzantine literature. But one of the chief models for the *Decameron* is Apuleius's *Asinus Aureus*, which also provides a sequence of stories combined with the observation of human life from an odd angle. Boccaccio is on record as a strong enthusiast for Apuleius. We know that he obtained an important manuscript of Apuleius' works, the Monte Cassinus Codex, a manuscript copied in the eleventh century by monks of Monte Cassino; Boccaccio took it to Florence. Petrarch, Boccaccio's friend, knew the *Metamorphoses* or *Asinus Aureus*, and quotes from it. In the fourteenth century it was suggested that a manuscript of Apuleius, likewise found in Florence, could have been transcribed by Boccaccio himself (Concetto Marchesi, c. 1338, quoted by Laura Sanguineti White, *Apuleio e Boccaccio*, 10–11). Boccaccio refers to Apuleius several times. In *De Genealogia Deorum Gentilium* he rehearses the story of *Cupid and Psyche* (Book V, Cap. 22). In the latter part of that encyclopaedic book (a little like poor Edward Casaubon's putative "Key to All Mythologies") Boccaccio points to the telling of the Cupid and Psyche story in Apuleius' work as an example of fiction's ability to cheer up spirits laboring under adversity: "Quam penes Charites, generosa virgo infortunio suo apud predones captiva, captivitatem suam deplorans, ab anicula fabule Psycis lepiditate paululum refocillata est" (Book XIV, Cap. 9). ("As in the case of Charité, the noble virgin in her misfortune, when captive among bandits, and lamenting her captivity, she was revived by taking a little pleasure in the old woman's story of Psyche.") Boccaccio defends fiction—stories are healthy: "Composuisse fabulas apparet utile potius quam damnosum"—"To have composed fables [stories] is clearly much more useful than injurious."

In the festival of *fabulae* that is the *Decameron*, Boccaccio pays the highest tribute to Apuleius in adopting two of his stories. The story of the husband, his wife, and the sneezing adulterer in the ninth book of Apuleius' *Golden Ass* or *Metamorphoses* turns up as the tenth story of the Fifth Day of the *Decameron*. The story of the clever use of the tub by the wife and her lover, also in the ninth book of Apuleius, turns up as the second story of the Seventh Day. The relations between these tales have been closely studied, and the verbal echoes pointed out: for instance, the wife in Apuleius' tub-story complains to her husband about her constant hard work to keep the family going: "At ego misera pernox et per diem lanificio nervos meos contorqueo, ut intra cellulam nostram saltem lucerna luceat" ("But I, wretched I, by night and by day twist my sinews in wool-spinning, just so that in our wretched hut we can at least have enough lamp-oil to light us," II : 134). Compare Boccaccio: "Credi tu . . . che non fo il dì e la notte altro che filare, tanto che la carne mi s'è spiccata dall'unghia, per potere almeno aver tanto olio, che n'arda la nostra lucerna?" *Decameron*, Day Seven, 595. ("Don't you believe . . . that there never passes a day or a night when I am not spinning, so that my flesh is worn off my fingers, just to be able to have at least as much oil as will light our lamp?" See Laura Sanguineti White, *Apuleio e Boccaccio*, 63.) Boccaccio certainly varies his stories; he adds detail, elaborating the characters, or taking them in new directions. As White points out, the wife in Boccaccio's version is less interested in presenting herself in an economic light than in an affective one (*Apuleio e Boccaccio*, 178). But part of the pleasure Boccaccio might have expected his best readers to share with him lies in their recognizing the reference to Apuleius and enjoying the stories thus revisited, replayed with new settings and new meanings.

Apuleius' earliest modern editor, Philippus Beroaldus (or Filippo Beroaldo), noted the connection in his extensive *Commentary* on Apuleius (first published 1500). In discussing the story of the Poor Man made Cuckold in Book IX of *The Golden Ass*, Beroaldus notes that it is a Milesian Tale:

> For there are two sorts of jesting stories: one diffuse, the other sharp and brief. In that kind of extended pleasantry our Lucius excels . . . so that he pleases with his facetious stories, and elegant short narratives, no less than do serious writers with their serious and grave doctrine. This is that very "Milesian writing" [*sermo milesius*] that I discussed in the beginning of this work—what Lucian calls *logon milesian*—by which a narrative of fiction is tastefully expanded.
>
> (*Apuleius cum commento Beroaldi* [Venice, 1516], 116ʳ) [10]

Boccaccio is brought in as a modern example of success in this mode.

> Giovanni Boccacio, a most expressive writer in vernacular eloquence, wrote a hundred stories of the most agreeable and humorous subject and style . . . among which he inserted this story of Apuleius. He transferred it most fittingly, and not as a translator, but as an author [*non ut interpres: sed ut conditor*]: this story our women listen to with no deaf ears, nor read unwillingly. (Ibid.) [11]

Beroaldus also notes the role of the reader in entering a story and considering its terms and meanings, although the ideal reader is not like the lustful greedy-eared women:

> for us also [Beroaldus continues] it is a pivotal story: here is our Lucius the artist of fable with a breadth of characterization, and graphic and most agreeable unfolding of the story so that we, stealthily hearing

> secrets, read and ponder carefully with ears, eyes, souls, all delighting:
> with such pleasures in digressions that readers are not only readers but
> truly are made into commentators [*non solum lectores: uerum etiam com-*
> *mentatores reficiantur*]. . . (Ibid.) [12]

Beroaldus is thinking of moral commentary (the understanding of the difference
between kinds of "poverty" for instance), but his discussion indicates the high
place given in Renaissance critical theory to readerly participation; the readers
may become (as Richardson was to say over two centuries later) "if not Authors,
Carvers." [13] Apuleius and Boccaccio share the capacity to conduct a story so that
the reader will be drawn in to read with "ears, eyes, souls." Boccaccio, according
to Beroaldus, is not merely quoting, he is re-authoring the stories of Apuleius, he
is *conditor*, not mere *interpres*. His own authorship, authority—or *auctoritee*, to borrow Chaucer's word—does not, however, detract from the authorial presence of
Apuleius.

In Boccaccio's works we can see a thorough and intelligent—even intellectual—absorption of the novelistic tradition, and very firm and conscious links
with the prose fiction of the past as an aspect of hopes and plans for prose fiction
of the present and future.

THE NOVEL IN SPAIN

The emphasis I have placed on Boccaccio in Italy may unjustly deflect attention
from developments in other parts of Western Europe, most particularly Spain.
Spanish literature developed enormously in the later Middle Ages, and Spain was
to take a primary part—arguably the leading role—in the production of prose
fiction in the vernacular. Ramón Lull of Mallorca produced a prose narrative,
Blanquerna (around 1285). Lull, who, like so many other Spanish writers, may
have been partly Moorish, took as his (doomed) mission the Christianizing of
Islamic North Africa. *Blanquerna* can be seen as a sort of extended sermon, which
makes prose a suitable medium for it, but it *is* a story; part of its appeal lies in its
use of mystic images and languages, elements in which it resembles the older
Grail stories.

Spain was an area divided among and controlled by different groups, with
different languages and three major religions: Judaism, Christianity, and Islam.
This situation was to be radically altered. Unfortunately, the dominant group was
not to share Lull's more peaceable notions about Christianizing. The union of
Aragon and Castile was effected in 1469 by the marriage of Ferdinand and Isabella. These, "the Catholic Kings," *los reyes católicos*, made a determined push to
drive the Moors out of Spain. They succeeded politically and militarily when they
took the last Moorish stronghold, the beautiful Alhambra at Granada. The year
1492 is most familiar to North American ears because that is the year in which
Columbus "discovered" America—on a mission also financed by Ferdinand and
Isabella. But to Europeans at the time, 1492 was important for the Conquest of
Granada. The expulsion of the occupants of Granada did not mean an instant end
to the Moorish presence in the whole of Spain; unfortunately, the Catholic Kings
and their successors instituted systematic persecutions of Muslims, people of
Moorish "blood," and in this hostile hunt for "infidels" the Jews were also in-

cluded. The Spanish believed that their nationhood and sovereignty depended on the thorough defeat of the Moors, and were always afraid that an Islamic force, funded by North Africa or Arabia, would make a determined comeback with the aid of local friends. Such political factors explain, if they do not justify, the paranoia about "infidels" in Spain, and clarify the reasons why the "Spanish Inquisition" was to become a byword not only for cruelty but also for thoroughness. The Spanish also participated in the Battle of Lepanto in 1571, an important naval conflict that ended Islamic hopes of gaining (or regaining) tracts of Western Europe; it was a sort of sixteenth-century equivalent of the Battle of Troyes. It was at Lepanto that Miguel de Cervantes lost (or lost the use of) his left hand, a war injury that did not prevent his participating in other campaigns against the Moors, especially against Tunis. But when he was trying to return home, the vessel in which he was sailing was seized by Turkish pirates, and he was a slave for five years (1575–1580) on an estate in North Africa until he was ransomed. Kidnapping has long been a way of life in the Mediterranean—as it is now, and as it was in the time of Chariton.

If the new and nationalistic rulers of Spain put an end to the Moorish state in 1492, before that time, during the gradual "Reconquest" (as the Spanish somewhat disingenuously term it), Spain was always a land with a frontier. Or rather, frontiers—and these could change in any local area depending on what leader's war-band was taking control. The actual conditions of the country meant that Christians and Moors were living in fairly close proximity. Spanish literature is continually sharpened by the awareness of an Other, of Otherness, and haunted by the fascination with what is at once familiar and exotic. In Spanish fiction, as not (unhappily) in Spanish political history, the possibility of positive relations between diverse groups is constantly canvassed. Nowhere is that more clear than in the short novel (or novella) *El Abencerraje* (or *Novela del Abencerraje y Jarifa*), first published in 1561, but emerging from earlier and now lost states in manuscript with a basis in oral tradition.

By the fifteenth century, prose fiction resumes her sway; we now see poetic *romanceros* being turned into prose narrative. *El Abencerraje* is a novelization. In this story, both Christians and Moors show themselves capable of acting according to the highest standards of honor and courtesy. Rodrigo de Narvaez and his men ambush a party of Moors and take the leader prisoner. Rodrigo is surprised at the signs of unvalorous depression in his chief prisoner; the Moor "gave a great and profound sigh." Rodrigo rebukes him for lamenting the fortunes of war, but promises that if the Moor has any secret reason of sorrow he will help him if he can. The Moor, whose name is Abindarraez, does have a reason for dole. He is, he says, one of the Abencerrajes of Granada, an important familial or tribal group that had suffered heavily in the Moorish civil wars of the fifteenth century. Abindarraez was sent in childhood to the alcaide of Cártama; this grandee had one child, a daughter whose mother had died in giving birth to her. "In our childhood we were often taken for brother and sister, because we wished so to call ourselves. Nothing happened to me which did not happen to both of us together. Together we cried, together we walked, together we ate and drank. There was born in this resemblance a natural love, which was always growing with our ages" (116). The modern Spanish editor draws a parallel to Longus and to "the medieval books of *Flores y Blancaflor*" (112). Fortuna/*Tychē* is the lovers' foe, *la fortuna, envidiosa de nuestra dulce vida* ("fortune, envious of our sweet life," 119). The King of Granada sends the alcaide to Coín, and the out-of-favor Abencerraje and his lovely Jarifa are separated, to his great sorrow. At last he has had a chance to see Jarifa; when her father left for Granada, he set out for Coín:

> "I was going from Cártama to Coín, a brief day's journey, although desire lengthened it greatly, the proudest Abencerraje who ever existed: I was going to call upon my lady, to see my lady, to enjoy my lady and to *marry* my lady. Look at me now!—wounded, captive and vanquished. And what I feel most of all is that the object and opportunity of all that is good for me must end this night. Permit me, then, Christian, to find consolation in my sighs, and do not judge them as weakness, since it is a very great thing to keep up one's spirits in suffering such a hardship." (122)

Rodrigo not only sympathizes, but also offers a solution: the captive may go on to Coín and consummate his plan, if he will return and yield himself prisoner in three days. Joyfully, Abindarraez agrees. He has an exciting time in Coín, arranging the elopement with the happy Jarifa, but their honeymoon is much shorter than she anticipated. He tells her he must return to be Rodrigo's prisoner; Jarifa says he cannot think that in yielding himself to be a prisoner she is still free, because she is not. "I want to accompany you in this journey, for neither the love which we share nor the fear which I have drawn upon myself of having offended my father will allow me to do anything else" (128). Abindarraez and his bride both show their *gentilesse* in yielding themselves prisoner, even at the height of a happiness that seems all too brief. Of course, Rodrigo is magnanimous likewise, and finds a way not only to free his noble hostage but also to reconcile Jarifa's father with his new son-in-law. The story begins with a simple conflict, and a simple idea of knighthood as consisting in acts of prowess against infidels, and then progresses to more complicated values. Everyone behaves well, everyone is happy, and everyone is in the end well treated; the person most badly treated would seem to be Jarifa's father, whose daughter did after all make a runaway match; but novels from antiquity to the modern age have had little use for paternal plans in the face of the individualized and individualizing love of the young. Once again in the "Western tradition" (which incessantly proves to be an Eastern tradition too) a mutual and adventurous erotic love crosses a number of borders, and brings into contact cultures that national or civic virtue would keep apart.

El Abencerraje was immensely popular, and the story is repeated in different versions in a number of other Spanish texts. There is a complete retelling of the novella in Montemayor's *Diana*, (1560) and a lengthy allusion to it in Alemán's *Guzmán de Alfarache* (1599; 1604); it is referred to in Cervantes' "El celoso extremeno" in *Novelas ejemplares* (1613). *El Abencerraje* is the most accessible example of a much larger tradition, that of "morisco" literature of Spain. Literature about or by Moors was closely related to the development of prose fiction in Spain, a prose fiction that was a very animated matter long before the sixteenth century. Spanish prose fiction was a presence in the fourteenth century, when the first versions of *Amadís de Gaula* were apparently composed.

The story material of *Amadís* is a deliberately artificial derivation from the "Matter of Bretagne"; no longer dealing with the original Arthurian characters, the authors of the *Amadís* created new parallels. *Amadís de Gaula* is consciously represented as a new kind of post-Arthurian novel. Amadís himself, as a recent translator remarks, is "a composite of Lancelot and Tristan" (Edwin B. Place, *Amadis of Gaul*, 13). Many episodes are modeled on stories in the Round Table cycles. Amadís is in many respects a model of virtue. Unlike Launcelot, he does not engage in adulterous love. He is a hero of male chastity in loving only one woman, the beautiful Oriana, to whom he is long secretly engaged. But our view of Amadís has been warped by the views of such defective readers as Don Quixote, for Quixote cannot deal with Amadís' sex-life and apparently suppresses it in his own mind. Cervantes certainly could expect his contemporary readers to notice this. When we come to *Amadís de Gaula* itself, we may be amazed at how lusty it is. Oriana and Amadís continually make love outside of wedlock. Part of the suspense lies in the reader's implicit question "What will they do about it—since they cannot tell Oriana's father?" At the end of the second long book, Oriana is pregnant. What will the pair do now?

The first version of Amadís' narrative seems to have been created in the fourteenth century by a Spanish author, possibly a cleric. In this version, Amadís' son Esplendián kills his father. In the fifteenth century, Garci Rodríguez de Montalvo radically rewrote this story, starting with the last book, the stories of Esplandián (who is no longer to kill his father). Some complete or nearly complete version of this material, the *Sergas de Esplandián* or *Feats of Esplandián*, was in circulation in manuscript by the 1470s. The *Sergas* was very popular; the name "California," incidentally, occurs first in the *Sergas*, where California is the land of cruel amazon women. Having written (or rewritten) the sequel first, Montalvo went back and dealt with all the Amadís material, which he linked by anticipation to the completed later parts. He finished the work and wrote his *prologo* or preface between 1492 and the time of his death (circa 1504).

At the beginning of *Amadís*, Elisena, daughter of the King Garinter of Little Britain, refuses all offers for her hand and is famously chaste and devout. When, however, Perion, king of Gaul, makes an unexpected visit to Garinter's castle he falls in love with her, and Elisena returns his passion. As she conceives an illegitimate child during this intense affair, Elisena must guard her reputation (like Charikleia's mother) by sending her child away. The baby is put in a little ark, a coffinlike boat of tarred boards, and set upon the sea; he is found by a British knight and brought up with his own child, given the name or nickname of "Child of the Sea." Amadís becomes a knight of peerless chivalry, his qualities of courage and magnanimity already visible in his childhood. In his adulthood he achieves great exploits, among them the rescue of Oriana, his beloved, from the Emperor of Rome, to whom her father, the King of Great Britain, has granted her in marriage.

The popularity of *Amadís* can hardly be exaggerated. Another great work of prose fiction produced on the Iberian Peninsula in the fifteenth century is the Catalan novel *Tirant lo Blanc*. This novel also had two authors, but in this case the second writer, Martí Joan de Galba, followed the intentions of the book's first author, Joanot Martorell of Valencia. Galba even incorporated some chapters of the latter part that the previous author had written before death interrupted him.

Tirant lo Blanc is, as its latest translator into English tells us, a book incorporating a good deal of fifteenth-century history. The first section is based on

English and French stories of Guy of Warwick, but this section also incorporates material from Martorell's own visit to England; the novel contains the earliest account of the foundation of the Order of the Garter. Sections of the novel dealing with the voyages to Sicily and Rhodes are related to the siege of Rhodes in 1444, when the Genoese on the island turned against the Catalans and allied themselves with the besieging Egyptians. After the expedition to Rhodes and Sicily, Tirant is sent by the King of Sicily to aid Constantinople against the Turks. The novel can thus be seen as a historical fantasy: Martorell was writing it about 1460 and the city of Constantinople had fallen in 1453, so the author is imagining that a current historical event had turned out differently. Yet he may also have had in mind a stroke of propaganda, for there was still the possibility that Western Europe might unite in a great expedition against the Turks for the recovery of Byzantium, and not all of Byzantium had as yet fallen (Rhodes held out until 1522).

In Martorell's novel the relief of the Byzantine Empire is brought about partly through an alliance between black Africa and white Europe. This was not merely the fantastic notion of a novelist, or even of white Europeans of the time; some non-Islamic Africans had had the same idea. In 1427 Ethiopia had sent ambassadors to Valencia, the Catalan capital, and in 1450 Prester John sent an Ethiopian envoy to Naples. In 1453 King Alfonso sent his ambassadors to Ethiopia. As David Rosenthal reminds us, these are the events behind the "African" section of the novel, and the good black King Escarino, who becomes a powerful ally of Tirant, "combines imaginary traits with those attributed to Prester John" (xvi). In *Tirant lo Blanc* we see again the tendency of the novel to represent international mixes and the bringing together of people of different races and cultures.

The centrally "different" culture in this novel, however, is the Byzantine world. As Rosenthal points out, "More than half of *Tirant lo Blanc* takes place in the Byzantine Empire" (xiii). Tirant falls in love with the Princess Carmesina, daughter of the Emperor of Byzantium. There is a lot of love-play among the young people, and a good deal of comedy—as when Tirant is hidden in the princess's room under a pile of clothes while she is combing her hair and talking to her mother; she begins slyly to comb his hair too, under the clothes, without letting her mother notice. The princess's lively young companion Stephanie makes love to her lover, and the princess, on seeing them, is consumed with envy. Sex is taken naturally and boisterously—constancy matters (as in *Amadís*) but not abstemious purity. Spanish medieval fiction, most of all where it touches Catalan culture, makes much less than the usual ado about female chastity, and places a strong emphasis on high spirits, sexual pleasure, and fidelity in both partners.

In much of medieval literature, from Marie de France to Martorell and Montalvo, women who have illicit sex do *not* have to come to a bad end. In *Tirant*, Stephanie and her lover marry and live happily. The tragedy is that Carmesina and Tirant put off their marriage, and the hero dies (a shock for the reader!) before the wedding. *Carpe diem*—it is a relief to remember that Carmesina had at last allowed illicit congress before the marriage. The novel's atmosphere is redolent of Byzantine erotic play and elegant décor—combined with the very stern business of fortifying a city and seeing to the rationing. We are reminded of the very close contact between the Byzantine and Greek-speaking areas and the Catalans, in a time when the Catalans were masters of much of the mainland of Greece itself. How to combine West with East is a question posed to the characters: "'What makes you think Greek ladies are less clever than French ones?' asked the princess. 'We shall understand your Latin, no matter how obscurely you speak it'" (*Tirant lo Blanc*, trans. Rosenthal, 194). Western stories are now transported Eastward. Just after Venus wounds Tirant as he gazes through the princess's transparent blouse, he is taken to a room ornamented "with splendid tapestries depicting the noble loves of Florice and Blanchfleur, Pyramus and Thisbe, Aeneas and Dido, Tristan and Isolde, Queen Guinevere and Launcelot and many others" (189). Female lovers, heroines of Western stories including Guinevere, Yseult and Dido, as well as the Greek ladies—Briseis, Penelope, Medea, and Phaedra—turn up as servants to the goddesses on the pageant platform created for the great joust in Constantinople: "There sat wise Sibyl, gazing now here and now there, while other masked goddesses sat at her feet, since in the past the pagans had thought them heavenly bodies" (*Tirant*, ibid., 327). If the "goddesses" are officially dismissed as pagan decoration, they still take an active part in the action, as does Eros, who is impersonated in an English pageant show.

The novel is somewhat hostile to Islamic culture and characters. The princess does not want to marry the Grand Sultan of Babylon, despite his generous proposal that "their sons be raised as Muslims and their daughters as Christians" (316). Yet it should be emphasized that Abdulla Solomon, the Sultan's envoy, is a truly wise and pious man. *Tirant lo Blanc* as a narrative has been in touch with the East; one of the stories is related to a tale in the *Arabian Nights*, mediated through an early thirteenth-century *Book of Fables* and the thirteenth-century collection *Cento novelle antiche* or *One Hundred Old Stories*.

In *Don Quxjote*, the priest and the barber, in their famous inquisition into Don Quixote's library, spare certain books from the fire—including the very first one they pick up, *Amadís de Gaula*. The priest does not want to spare *Amadís*, as it was the first of the novels of chivalry, the first begetter of a genre, and thus ought to be condemned to the flames "as expounder [*dogmatizador*] of such a bad sect," i.e., as an initiatory heretic. But the barber argues for preserving it, because it is the oldest, and "the best of all the books ever composed in this genre" (*el mejor de todos los libros que de este género se han compuesto*, 67). The discussion of *Amadís* is, however, tame, compared to that of *Tirant lo Blanc*. The priest loses his cold objectivity: "'God defend me!' said the priest, giving a great shout. 'So here is *Tirante el Blanco*! Give it here, friend; I account that book as possessing a treasure of pleasure and a mine of pastimes . . . . Take it home with you and read it, and you will see that what I'm telling you about it is true'" (72). The priest's detailed knowledge of the work shows that he has read it before, and thus (like a Don Quixote himself) he is both stimulated by the prospect of the pleasure of rereading, and wishes to share the pleasure of novel-reading with a friend.

Part of the joke of Cervantes' novel is that everyone—not just the book-crazed Don—reads novels, or has heard them read. When, near the end of Part I, the curé censoriously explains that the books of chivalry have turned Quixote's brain, the innkeeper is indignant and puzzled:

"I don't know how that can be; for in truth, to my understanding, there is no better reading in the world, and I have two or three of them, with other works on paper [*con otros papeles*], which truly have given me life—and not only to me, but to others. Because when it is harvest-time, during the holidays, many of the reapers come here, and always there are some among them who know how to read, and one of them will take one of these books in his hands, and we will gather around—more than thirty of us—and we are entertained with so much pleasure that it saves us a thousand grey hairs . . ." (321)

The innkeeper provides a defense of the novel from an unexpected quarter. He makes us wonder if perhaps those who wish to censor or erase the fictions are oppressing the poor in the name of saving Quixotes from themselves. The region of fiction-reading is certainly much larger than the gentleman's library. The arrival of printed books has obviously made this entertainment more accessible, even to the nonliterate. Yet the innkeeper's use of the intriguingly vague word *papeles* (papers, documents) poses the possibility that such entertainment was available *prior to* the invention of the printing press. Indeed in *Don Quijote* the immediately ensuing production of the *manuscript* of a story, "El Curioso Impertinente" ("The Inappropriately Curious Man") provides a case in point. One of the ways in which novels have been read is aloud. We notice in novel criticism, from antiquity to the Renaissance, metaphorical references to hearing the story with unwearied ears, taking in our benevolent ears the voice imparted by the pen. Novels have been read aloud, not just in deep antiquity, but in sixteenth-century pubs, in eighteenth-century parlors and Victorian drawing-rooms—and now drivers on long highways may be listening to recordings of *Madame Bovary* or *Crampton Hodnet* as they wend their late-twentieth-century way.

In emphasizing the power of the printing press, our histories have conventionally slighted the importance of the circulation of writing in the manuscript culture. Chaucer (or his narrative persona) is always determinedly "bookish" and frequently mentions his pleasure in reading—including that habit which modern parents and doctors have so much deplored, reading in the middle of the night, a pleasure that long pre-dates the invention of electric light.

> So when I saw I might not slepe
> Till now late, this other night,
> Upon my bedde I sat upright
> And bad oon reche me a book,
> A romaunce, and he it me tok
> To rede, and dryve the night away;
> (Chaucer, *The Book of the Duchess*
> [c. 1370], lines 44–49)

The "Middle Ages" are a number of centuries in which European authors undertook a great deal of strong writing—recycling, inventing, reinventing, and celebrating the nature of fiction. But writers can do that when and because there are readers—who will read aloud during the work-recess, or alone in the middle of the night.

CHAPTER X

The Ancient Novel in the Age of Print: Versions and Commentaries of the Renaissance

Nous ny pouons retourner si ce nest par le moyen de la lune.

[We cannot return if it is not by means of the moon.]
—Guillaume Michel, commentary on his trans., *Lucius Apulei de Lasne dore autrement dit de la Couronne Ceres,* 1522

Si per uos quodammodo renatus, & tanquam ab inferis reductus . . .

[If by you he is in a manner born again, just as if he were rescued from the lower depths . . .]
—Vincentus Obsopaeus, editor of first printed *Aithiopika,* 1534

Totam verò Historiam, veluti Tragicocomoediam dicentes, haud errauerimus: sicut ex Theagenes verbis lib. 5 patet.

[If we treated the whole History as if it were a Tragicomedy we should hardly err: as is evident in words of Theagenes in Book V.]
—Martinus Crusius, *Epitome* of Heliodorus' *Aithiopika,* 1584

*I*n her spiritual autobiography *El Libro de la Vida* (The Book of the [my] Life, or—punningly—The Book of Life) Teresa of Avila tells us that in early childhood she and her little brother ran away from home: "We planned to go to the country of the Moors, seeking it for the love of God, so that there they would behead us" (4).

We can see all the history of the Spanish attitudes to the Moors in this account. At least Teresa and her brother were not planning to fight but only to die, not recognizing that the martyrdom in Spain had been endured by the Moors themselves. Yet as well as the conscious desire for martyrdom Teresa's account offers some sense of the attraction of the mysterious *tierra de moros;* the exotic other place exercises its own fascination.

As well as saints' lives, a major source for the young Teresa's knowledge of the Moors would have been the novels of chivalry. We know she read these—and thus, almost all the novels extant in Spanish. Her mother, she tells us with some disapproval, was *aficionada a libros de caballerías* and from this *aficionada* Teresa herself caught the love of books of chivalry. Teresa read as much and as many as possible: "and it seemed to me no evil to waste many hours of the day and of the night in such a vain exercise, even though hidden from my father. I was so extremely absorbed in this, that if I didn't have a new book, I could not be happy" (6). Here indeed is the sin of *Bovarysme*, of female reading, which should be supervised by the father, subject to the proper authority—but is not: mother and daughter share the love of fiction, a hidden love.

The desire to have some *new* book at hand all the time is probably not a new desire at all. But the young Teresa of Avila (born 1515) belonged to the first generation for whom that desire was gratifiable. The appetite for reading seen in Saint Teresa no less than in Don Quixote is an appetite that could be at once stimulated and gratified by the new invention: the printing press. The printing press delivers the new faster. When Teresa read *Amadís* (printed first in 1508) it was not an old medieval classic, but a smart *new* book. At this point we have very definitely moved into the world of what has been called "print culture." This print culture was to change communication while accelerating the spread of new ideas. The enemy that the grown-up Teresa was to fight was to be not the Moors of her childish imagination, but the new Protestantism, its growth assisted by the very printing press that allowed the girl to read numerous *libros de caballerías*. In becoming a published writer herself, Teresa of Avila was to be a formidable force; her works spread her influence far beyond the confines of her convent, her country, and her century.

Our own attentiveness to the impact of the printing press, an attention now sharpened by our intuition that the computer is changing our lives in a parallel way, has sometimes blinded us to the existence and importance of written material and of reading in the pre-print era. The manuscript industry produced important editions, often illustrated, many with commentary set about the page in attractive and authoritative style. Authors wrote, and wrote for entertainment of a public (see Boccaccio's prefaces.) The historian, however, has a much better time of it once it is possible to turn to the records left by print. Here indeed are footprints and clues. The advent of print enables us to monitor not only the writing of the past but the manners and assumptions that accompanied the writing and reading. In the world of manuscripts we know ourselves in a fog; so much has been lost, so many things may have happened of which we have no record.

With the advent of print we arrive at an era that offers the historian of fiction huge amounts of data. We must, however, be careful to consider the limitations of the material. For instance, early editors themselves had no idea of how many manuscripts of some particular work (say of the *Aithiopika*) were still extant, and tended to claim that they had the only copy. The efforts made by Renaissance editors are so admirable as to be awe-inspiring—they founded the processes on which we rely. But they could not know everything to start with. For instance, they could not always know if a work had been translated before. The development of Greek studies in Europe after 1453 meant that those who dealt in texts and translations often had a strong academic bias. The university plays a larger part in the early print culture than in the manuscript culture, replacing the monastery, which ceases to be a center of literature.

Elizabeth Eisenstein in *The Printing Press as an Agent of Change* (1979) has pointed out that the work of the presses both created and facilitated conceptual change. Some elements of the change seem so "natural" to us that they are easily overlooked: the discovery or revival of the (Alexandrian) idea of alphabetical order, the use of arabic numerals, pagination, regularized punctuation, the index. Order, regularity and convenience of access to information become guiding principles related to the larger principle of exchange of ideas. The presence of multiple copies of the same edition fostered a new idea of objectivity. At the same time, the flow of new editions freshly corrected and improved detracted from any idea of perfect final statement. Scribal culture posits a steady deterioration of textual copying; one must get back to the earliest manuscript. In print culture, the latest copy is the best: "a sequence of corrupted copies was replaced by a sequence of improved editions" (109). Eisenstein points to the production of encyclopedias and their active growth: "Sixteenth-century editors and publishers, who served the Commonwealth of Learning, did not merely store data passively in compendia. They created vast networks of correspondents, solicited criticism of each edition, sometimes publicly promising to mention the names of readers who sent in new information or who spotted the errors which would be weeded out" (109). Knowledge became open-ended. "The closed sphere or single corpus, passed down from generation to generation, was replaced by an open-ended investigatory process pressing against ever advancing frontiers" (687). Eisenstein also suggests that the presence of the printers themselves was a factor in the new life of town, and in the development of a new intelligentsia.[1]

The printing press required educated workers as well as skilled labor; a printer would give entertainment and employment to scholars, translators, people of various expertise who would meet at his house or print-shop for the exchange of ideas. The idea of free exchange of information becomes a dominant notion, as it is to be in the Enlightenment. Sixteenth-century printers and authors of all sorts shared a belief in the community of the lettered (often including educated women) extending across national and other boundaries. At the same time, as national identities became more pronounced, printers and booksellers had to be aware of the local public, the purchasing public requiring books in a particular vernacular. Early printers had a sense of vocation, and a certain idealism emerges from the sources cited by Eisenstein and others. Yet, at the same time, the press was certainly a business, dealing in commodities—a fact sharply noted by Cervantes when he has Don Quixote visit a printer's shop. Don Quixote, that child of the print world, that reader begotten for other readers, is shocked to find out the basis of the production of texts (including the one he is in). The hack says he gives not a farthing for the fame of a book, and does not print for fame— he only wants to know if a book will succeed (*Don Quijote*, Part II, 999).

The new printing presses turned out fiction from the very outset. William Caxton edited and printed Thomas Malory's *Le Morte Darthur* at his press in London (established in 1476). Malory had completed his work, a powerfully emotive synthesis of various Arthurian material, about 1470, and it is through Malory's book, or some book derived from it, that English-speaking people through the modern centuries have sustained contact with the "Matter of Bretagne." Caxton himself tells us in his Preface to Malory's book that he published it by request. He started out by printing histories, including "hystoryal and worldly actes of grete conquerours and prynces," and also religious and moral works, "certeyn bookes of ensaumples and doctryne." But his public were not satisfied: "many noble and dyvers gentylmen of thys royaume of Englond camen and demaunded me many and oftymes wherfore that I have not do made and enprynte the noble hystorye of the Saynt Greal and of the moost renomed Crysten kyng, fyrst and chyef of the thre best Crysten, and worthy, Kyng Arthur . . ." (xiii). Here we find *male* readers demanding fiction. Caxton, however, addresses both male and female readers:

> humbly bysechyng al noble lordes and ladyes wyth al other estates, of what estate or degree they been of, that shal see and rede in this sayd book and werke, that they take the good and honest actes in their remembraunce, and to folowe the same; wherein they shalle fynde many joyous and playsaunt hystoryes and noble and renomed actes of humanyté, gentylnesse, and chyvalryes. For herein may be seen noble chyvalrye, curtosye, humanyté, frendlynesse, hardynesse, love, frendshyp, cowardyse, murdre, hate, vertue, and synne. Doo after the good and leve the evyl, and it shal brynge you to good fame and renommee.
>
> And for to passe the tyme thys book shal be pleasaunte to rede in, but for to gyve fayth and byleve that al is trewe that is conteyned herin, ye be at your lyberté. (xv)

Caxton's address imagines as wide an audience as possible—male and female readers, not only of the nobility but of "*all* other estates," in any degree. The work is morally instructive as it gives examples of good actions (a favorite claim about fiction). But the work offers the great benefit of *variety*, a variety imitated in Caxton's deliberately scrambled list. The reader will be pleasantly overwhelmed by diversity: love, friendship, cowardice, murder, hate, virtue, and sin. All human life is here. And the book is "pleasant" to read—it gives pleasure. Caxton impishly adds that we can believe it or not, as we like. We know, in effect, that what we are reading is not true, but is its own kind of truth—and here, as not in matters of religion, we are at our liberty to "believe" or not. Over a hundred years later, and in another country, Don Quixote is going to take advantage of that liberty of belief, and stubbornly to insist (with at least one part of his mind) on the creation of literal credence.

Caxton paid great attention to his edition of Malory, published in July 1485; it was an immediate success. Fiction had already made a big impact on the printing presses of continental Europe. The very first book ever printed in Padua seems to have been an edition of Boccaccio's *Elegia di Madonna Fiammetta* in 1472. *Filocolo* was published in Venice in the same year. European works of fiction appeared and reappeared. Translations multiplied and increased the audience of any one nation's works. For instance, a Spanish translation of *Fiammetta* was published in *la muy noble & leal ciudad de Salamanca* in 1497. And among the books to roll off the presses in the fifteenth and sixteenth centuries were the novels of antiquity.

Among these newly printed treasures of fiction, Apuleius' *Metamorphoses* or *The Golden Ass* takes pride of place. I propose to spend some time on the Renaissance reception and treatment of Apuleius' work, the most well-known of our complete novels, finding in the treatment of his work some important indicators for the Renaissance attitude to ancient prose fiction. I shall treat the versions of Heliodorus at some length also, commenting more briefly on the editing, criticism and translation of some other antique novels. When we are speaking of editorial practices we should not forget that some of the *manuscripts* are also editions, already containing major editorial material (such as chapter divisions and titles) and even prefatory commentary. Renaissance editors inherited practices of text management from their predecessors.

THE GOLDEN ASS IN PRINT

Apuleius had left a considerable body of writing, which strengthened his position in scholarly eyes. Scholars of the late fifteenth and the sixteenth centuries were very eager to see what it would have felt like to be a genuine early (neo) Platonist, and felt that the *Asinus Aureus* offered important clues. But of course the *Asinus Aureus* was already a well-known entertaining book, as we can see from Boccaccio's references to it. That the book was in Latin made it readable by all who were well educated. The aura of magic that hung about the author's life—he had been accused of being a magician—as well as about his novel offered an extra frisson.

The first printed edition of Apuleius' works, his *Opera*, was published in 1469; it is an elaborate large book looking as much like a manuscript as possible. It is dedicated to Cardinal Bessarion, and the editor enthusiastically emphasizes the author's Platonism. Early editors also attribute to Apuleius the authorship of two of the Hermetic dialogues of "Asclepius" and "Mercury Trismegistus" (or Hermes Trismegistus), a fact of which Laurence Sterne was presumably well aware when he had Walter Shandy insist (vainly) upon christening his child "Trismegistus." Marianus Tuccius, in Marsilio Ficino's 1512 edition of Apuleius, says in the prefatory Dedication to Cardinal Medici that fortunately some masters both of the Greek and Latin language escaped the barbarians after the fall of Rome: "Anyway it happened that in that conflict some among the Greek and Latin authors secretly escaped the conflagration, but (as is likely to happen in battle) these were either mutilated in some part or survived with almost innumerable wounds. Among which number is our Apuleius . . ." (Florence, 1512, aii[r])[2]

The editor congratulates both himself and Cardinal Medici (presumably punning on the medical meaning of "Medici") upon their modern ability to heal textual wounds, which makes them fitting rivals of Asclepius himself. (When you reach the sixteenth century you have to get used to the loud sounds of Renaissance editors congratulating themselves.) We note that a writer of prose fiction can be taken without apology as a major author whose rescue is a matter for rejoicing.

Once wounded texts were healed (more or less) and established, editors constantly felt the urge to annotate. Petrus Colvus, editor of Apuleius' *Works* (*Opera Omnia*) published by the Plantin house in Leiden in 1588, explains that he has consulted other editions (all of which are faulty) and has added notes, to explain variant readings or the more obscure passages, "which in this author are many" (*qui in hoc auctore multi*, *4[v]). He also includes a Life of the author, as was becoming standard practice. Colvus' edition is garnished by conventional blurbs in the form of (execrable) poems.

The most ambitious annotated version of Apuleius had already been produced, as Colvus notes, by Philippus Beroaldus in 1500; in 1516 illustrations were added. In Beroaldus' giant version, set up like the best and most ornate manuscript editions, the text is a neat island in mid-page, often accompanying its woodcut illustration, and around the text swirls the unstoppable fullness of the commentary. In his Preface, Beroaldus compares Apuleius' ass story with that of "Lucian" (i.e., *Onos*). After briefly rehearsing the plot of the Greek novel, Beroaldus engages in typical Renaissance comparison and contrast. "Our Apuleius" plays most elegantly with the Greek style of novel in imitating the Greek work, which he has really surpassed:

> and he himself among Roman authors wrote the eleven volumes of
> the *Golden Ass*, or *Metamorphoses* with a similar plot and in brilliant
> style, in which he shows himself elegant, erudite, and shrewd. And
> there is hardly any doubt that his vintage was drawn from the vine-
> stock of Lucian, and that he used Lucian's work almost as his own par-
> ticular private archetype. But there is a great difference between the
> Greek and the Latin ass. The Greek one is brief. This is copious. The
> Greek work is simple and briefly describes the transformation and
> reformation from man into ass and from ass into man. Our work truly
> is multiplex, and wipes out all weariness from the inward ear with
> seasonably interjected stories. (Venice, 1516, aiii^r) [3]

The editor picks up and plays with Apuleius' own figures of speech in his exordium, recalling the "benevolent ears" to be soothed by a delightful whisper.

Beroaldus urges us, "Let this writer become familiar to you as if his work were your handbook, and your Enchiridion" (*hortor: ut familiaris tibi fiat hic scriptor: sitque tuum quasi manuale: & Enchiridion*, aiii^r). This is a style of Renaissance hyperbolical exhortation still surviving in, for instance, Samuel Johnson's advice that the student should "give his days and nights to the volumes of Addison"—in both cases part of the effect is the slight blasphemy involved in treating amusing secular works as if they were doctrine. The editor highly approves of Apuleius' style; Beroaldus *likes* what is copious, and "multiplex" and highly wrought:

> And indeed he is very frequently a most elegant inventor of words, and
> with such propriety and grace that nothing could be more graceful or at-
> tractive. In short, just as this our Ass is called "golden" so the book itself
> appears of gold, with such a charming and cultivated style, such an
> elegant and harmonious combination of words not common in them-
> selves, that one could most justly say of it "The Muses would have
> spoken Apuleian, if the Muses wished to speak Latin." (1516, aiii^r) [4]

Beroaldus' Commentary itself speaks Latin loquaciously. As it surrounds the text the commentary endeavors to explain everything one might ever want to know about anything in it: what the powers of the moon are (among other things, it nourishes shellfish); who Ceres was and what she stood for, and so on. The woodcut illustrations to the big annotated edition are superb—and themselves also provide another aspect of the reading, another indicator of the way the book can be read. Words ekphrastic in themselves foster new icons. The tearful ass gazing at the moon is peculiarly poignant (See Plate 18).

We do not expect learned works to have illustrations—unless they are pictures of something of respectable antiquity. During the Renaissance—and later—illustrations were produced for both scholarly and popular editions. There is a good manuscript tradition behind this; we may recall the expensive illustrations to the prose *Lancelot* and *Tristan*, for instance. Individual printings could be treated like manuscripts, with special illustrations for a particular purchaser; see, for instance, the copy of Lucian's *Opera* in Latin, published in Venice in 1494, with illustrations by Benedetto Bordon for the Mocenigo family (now in the Austrian National Library, Vienna). The frontispiece is a detailed illlustration in delicate color of the hero of *Vera Historia* and his companions meeting the farmer and his son on their farm within the belly of the whale. Noble books deserved noble illustrations in the graphic Middle Ages—and in the early Renaissance. We might expect the translations of a work into a popular vernacular language to maintain a "popular" approach, but the Renaissance is often less likely than later eras to erect rational partitions between the "learned" and the "popular." The Paduan edition of Boccaccio's *Fiammetta* printed in 1472 emphasizes the book's appeal to the ladies, as of course the author's own Preface does, even though the headnotes and chapter titles are all in Latin, a language read by fewer ladies than gentlemen, and hardly read at all by the merchants and artisans or their wives.

Ancient novels were as subject to immediate translation as more recent works of fiction. Once an established text had been published, booksellers could easily commission translations, while translators knew they could find a public for their endeavors. Translations of the ancient novels poured from the presses of Europe during the sixteenth century. These translations indicate an engagement with the works and a certain equalizing familiarity with them. For example, as the initial statements of the *Golden Ass* were frequently printed as if forming a verse headnote to the main matter, translators could take advantage of this "poetical" opening to offer their own amplified (doggerel) verse.[5] So William Adlington's English translation (published in 1566), begins thus:

> The Preface of the author to his sonne Faustinus, and
> vnto the reader of this booke.

> That I to thee some ioyous iests
>   may shew in gentle glose:
> And franklie feede thy bended eares,
>   with passing pleasant prose.
>   . . .
> I wil declare how one by hap,
>   his humane figure lost.
> And how in brutish formed shape,
>   his loathed life he tosst. . .

> (London, 1586 ed., A4ᵛ)

Such a treatment allows plenty of opportunity for the editor-translator to insert himself into Apuleius' work. The introductory sentences were also seen to offer an opportunity of modernizing the novel—all the more if they could be treated in vernacular rhymed verse.

No one modernizes the novel as audaciously as Messer Agnolo Firenzuola of Florence, a literary experimenter who cites novel characters (Photis, Fiammetta) in his dialogues "On the Beauty of Women," with diagrams of female vase-shapes that may have stimulated Rabelais' diagram of *Le Dive bouteille* (*Beauty of Women*, 61–63). He turns Lucius' story in *The Golden Ass* into an autobiography: "Firenzuola, situated at the foot of the Mountains which stand between Florence and Bologna, is a small Citadel, but, as its name and its insignia demonstrate, it is noble. . . . And Sebastian my father was rich enough, and enjoyed an abundance of the gifts of Fortune" (1549, fol. 4 $^{r-v}$).[6] After this completely extraneous new material, the translator blends Lucius' story with his own. He studied in Siena, and then in Rome (as Lucius did), but he left off his professional life and set himself to cultivating the delectable gardens of the literary Muses. Apuleius' Lucius says, "let us begin a *Greek* fable"; Firenzuola offers to begin "a *Tuscan* fable" (*una Thosca fauola*, fol. 5 ^{r}). Firenzuola naturalizes the whole story to its new setting. Lucius had to travel to Thessaly; this narrator "had to go on some of my affairs to the region of Napoli." The novel is changed to an Italian story throughout. In Book II of Apuleius' story, Lucius woke up excited to realize where he was: "considering that I was now located in the middle of Thessaly, universally agreed to be the native home of the arts of magic and incantation celebrated throughout the whole world" (I:58). But in the Italian version, the character thinks "that I was in the middle of Bologna, where, according to unanimous opinion, as if in their own field there flourish the enchantments of the Magical arts . . ." (fol. 16 ^{r}).[7] The lady who gives a dinner-party and owns a statue of Diana is now named Laura.

Such a daring (not to say egotistical) liberty taken with Apuleius' "classic" sufficiently demonstrates that Renaissance readers were not filled with awe in the face of the re-edited antique novels. Nor—and this is even more important—did writers and readers feel themselves faced with cold marble works of a beautiful but dead past. The Renaissance attitude was adaptive and engrafting. Liberties were very freely taken. Niccolò Machiavelli, for instance, in 1517 began writing a poetic epic version of Apuleius' novel, *Asino d'oro* (left unfinished at his death in 1527). Machiavelli departs widely from his source, not only in introducing Circe as the agent of many men's transformations, but also in fashioning his story as a political meditation.

As we trace response to the ancient fictions through editors, commentators, translators, and preface writers, we can see a very hospitable readership (a readership partly composed of other writers). There is no great psychological or aesthetic distance between the "learned" texts undertaken by the zealous editors and the versions for the general reader produced in vernacular languages. A new edition of Firenzuola's book printed in Venice in 1566 acquires some of the apparatus of a learned edition (here it is the *Tuscan* that is corrected by an editor); at the same time it offers a number of pictorial illustrations—as Latin editions had already done. The common impulse appears to have been to modernize the old works, to assimilate them rather than to cordon them off in a special enclosure. The "discovery" of the ancient novels in the Renaissance seemed to authenticate the experience of fiction of the past few centuries, and to offer new models for new writers.

The ideology of any given novel could also be discussed and assimilated. We can see this very clearly in a French translation of *Asinus Aureus* in 1522. The translator, named on the last page as Guillaume Michel, "dict de Tours," begins with a Preface praising Apuleius' novel simply for the pleasures it can bring, and promising us a *melliflueux stille de diuerses sentences, varietez a nouuelles matieres* ("mellifluous style of diverse sentences varied to new subjects") (Ai^v). Drawing heavily on Beroaldus (as he acknowledges) the authorial translator offers us the moral: *Nous sommes faictez asnes perdant la forme dhomme quant par voluptez brutalles, pechez, et folies a la simillitude dung asne nous brutons.* ("We are made asses losing the form of man, when by so many brutal pleasures, sins and follies we brutalize ourselves to the similitude of an ass," Aii^{v-r}). Guillaume Michel then glides into the translation with a section entitled *La proposition de la(u)cteur a son filz Faustinus & aux lecteurs de ce present liure.* It takes a while for the reader to recognize that this translator is greatly rewriting Apuleius' own exordium: "Faustinus, my dear child, and you, all my benevolent readers, the labor of my little study is an effort to offer to set out for you and to describe some facetious, joyful and delectable fables, if I can delight your tender ears, and edify them, and with a whispering sound, joyous and *lepide*, dispose your sad heart to its full faculty of joyfulness" (*Faustinus mon chier enfant et vous tous lecteurs beniuoles, le labeur de mon petit estude cest efforce vous inserer planter et descripre quelques facessieuses, ioyeuses et delectantes fables si que ie puisse uos tendres oreilles demulser, lectifier, et par ung son susurrant, ioyeulx et lepide, vostre triste cueur en plein pouoir de ioyeusete mettre*) (Aii^v). We can see here an example of sixteenth-century inkhornism as the translator adapts words from his original that do not really exist in French (*lepide*) or have a somewhat precarious claim (*demulser* for *permulceam*). At the same time as he is capable of following his original's words so closely, the translator loves infinite expansion: there are a lot of elements here that do not belong in Apuleius. The reader's "sad heart" may look in vain for its equivalent in the Latin text. The first few sentences of Apuleius are spun out for nearly two pages, in a full example of Renaissance *amplificatio*. The translator, as we can see, is elevating himself to the position of his author and grants himself some authorial control—if not quite as much power of usurpation as Firenzuola. Sixteenth-century translators are very conscious of modernity as a potential aspect of their text. All novels are felt to be in some way contemporary.

This translation significantly bears an amplified title: *Lucius Apuleus de Lasne dore autrement dit de la Couronne Ceres, contenant maintes belles hystoires, delectantes fables, et subtilles inuentions de divers propos Speciallement de philosophie.* That the French translator offers an alternative title, *The Crown of Ceres* (or *Ceres Crowned*) shows that he is very interested in the novel's presentation of the figure of the Goddess. Michel regards his own interest as philosophical, related to the philosophical material in Apuleius. The book ends with a lengthy application, as if Apuleius' novel were some giant Aesopic fable for which the translator must supply a meaning and a moral. Some headings of his conclusion will suffice to indicate their tendency: "New Interpretation [*Sens nouuel*] of the Books of Lucius Apuleius' *The Golden Ass*" (OOii^v); "Of those who wish to fly and remain as beasts"; "Of the reversion of sin in the state of grace" (OOiv^r); The last part is, however, the crown, and that is entitled *De l'invocation de la Vierge Marie*:

We cannot return if it is not by means of the moon. [*Nous ny pouons retourner si ce nest par le moyen de la lune.*] That is to say, of the glorious Virgin Mary: who finally helps us for she never forsakes those who invoke her. Therefore it is necessary to call upon her from the sea of bitterness, sorrow, and unhappiness with one's sins, in washing one's conscience in that sea of contrition: as Apuleius did when he plunged therein as he invoked his goddess. Then by her means we are sent towards the great priest, Vicar of God Almighty, who will give us the garland of flowers and the crown of roses which hang from the Sistrum of the image of the goddess Ceres, that is as much as to say the cross of Jesus Christ which is of such good savor. There is the crown of roses which we must have if we wish to regain our lovely form of innocence. Then when we have reassumed it we shall dwell in continual praise of the glorious goddess Ceres, the Moon which in the heavenly sky and in the church militant shines forth in splendor.

We can note how ingeniously and painlessly this commentator has Christianized the novel's religious imagery without any sense of being in tension with the novel. As an allegorist he leaps over the character of Lucius to fasten his experience upon his author—*Apuleius* plunged into the sea of contrition. The novel allegorically relates spiritual experiences available to every reader. The emphasis on spiritual self-consciousness, on experiential inwardness, here appears perfectly compatible with Catholicism. Apuleius' Isis supports the dignity of the true Moon-goddess, the Virgin Mary, and the rest of this translator's crowning exordium is devoted to her:

> Let us then make ourselves holy in her immortal praise. Let us bless and celebrate the honor of god her spouse and of herself; as Lucius Apuleius did honor to Osiris and to his spouse, otherwise named the great goddess Ceres. This goddess under one only deity possessed and contained several names; thus too does the glorious Virgin, holy mother of God. She is Ceres the goddess of the grain fields [*Cest Ceres la deesse des bleds*]—she is Juno who aids each one. She is also Trivia by the three ways which she has in her care, for she is queen of the heaven, of hell, and of the world. It is that moon who so strongly relumes the night who is placed amidst the dark shadows of sin, enlightening her servants. She is on earth Diana of the chase, who once transformed Actaeon into a hart and gave chase to him; that is to say, set the devil of hell in confusion and chased him from the forest, that is the conscience of sinners. And she is in hell Proserpine by her power, for all the devils obey her and put away the aforesaid temptation from her servants. For she wishes so much to pray for us that we may have absolution from our sins. In the name of the father and of the son and of the blessed holy spirit. Amen. (Paris, 1522, 00v^v–00vi^r) [8]

In 1527 a new editor of *Le Roman de la Rose* (probably Clément Marot) appears to have been so impressed by this commentary on Apuleius that he borrows it in order to give a higher allegorical cast to *Le Roman de la Rose*: the rose, he says is a spiritual rose, like those in "the great Apuleius," who describes the chaplet of roses hanging from the sistrum of *Céres déesse des bledz* (I:91). Marot's assimilation of Michel's style of commentary betrays, like his entire *Exposition Moralle*, a Renaissance anxiety lest a medieval work be neither allegorical nor moral enough.

It is not surprising that Book XI of Apuleius' novel should be as extensively allegorized as it is in the 1522 version, for the original seems to demand some sort of allegorical treatment. Michel's application shows how much Christians had inherited of Porphyry's method, and how well suited the Renaissance is, because of training in allegorical thinking, to putting together cultural elements from diverse sources. What stands out in this instance is the strong support the writer feels able to give to the various pagan concepts and images of the Goddess. Multinamed with many strengths, she is the Virgin Mary—but that is to say she can also be called Ceres, or even Diana. The early Christian author ("Pseudo-Clemens") of *Recognitiones*, nervous of the figure of the goddess, incorporates her in his book as Luna, demon girlfriend of the wicked Magus Simon. But here we find Luna calmly acceptable to a French Christian of the sixteenth century. "We cannot return if it is not by means of the moon"—a sentiment worthy of Yeats, one feels, and yet unlike Yeats, for not only is the writer convinced he is a Christian, he is not agitated by contemplation of the "feminine" aspect of divine power in incarnate creation. Here at least the contemplation of the Goddess inspires no repugnance. It is felt to be not only possible but even a sovereign relief from pain and sorrow.

Of course, there are other ways of looking at Apuleius' novel, and Renaissance readers looked at it in a number of ways. It is only fair to mention, after Michel's enthusiastic reception of the Déesse, the complete aversion to the Goddess-book expressed by another French translator, "George [*sic*] de la Bouthiere Autunois," in the same century. In his *Epistre aux Lectevrs* he confides in us that when he came to reading the eleventh book he could hardly bear it. This book treated nothing but ceremonies, pomps and processions and sacrifices by priests of the Goddess Isis: "The whole so prolix and boring [*tant prolixe et ennuieux*] that I was greatly disgusted at ranking it with the others [*le mettre au rang des autres*]." But, he adds, in order not to leave poor Lucius in his asinine condition, he went back to the ending of Lucian's *Ass* (Latin version) and has restored that as the ending of *The Golden Ass*. He defends himself by treating the *Onos* as the original version and source—and anyway, he points out, another most learned Tuscan translator (Firenzuola) has set the example of taking liberties with this text (*Lucio Apuleyo* [Lyon, 1553], 13–14).

De la Bouthière sees in the last book of *The Golden Ass* a mistaken break with the work's own comic nature, which is much better served by *la plaisante & recreative conclusion de Lucian* (14)—this is to assume that the novel itself must be consistently pleasant, jocularly diverting. The comic nature of the novel can be variously defined. It can be turned into a satiric work, the *fabliau*-element emphasized. We can see such an interpretation simply by looking at the frontispiece-cum-title page of a Spanish translation of 1543 (see Plate 19). The illustration shows Lucius turning into an ass, in two stages. At least, that is one way of seeing it. But the woodcut can also be "read" as emphasizing female adultery, with reference to the story of the baker's wife in Book IX, and to the bestiality that figures in Book X. What the reader sees is the lady leading the ass himself, at the left, and on the right a lewd large figure, a human male with a shaggy breast and an ass's head, like Bully Bottom in his transformation. This figure, however, looks sardonic and knowing; it presides over the picture, gesturing mockingly at both the ass and the lady while turning to the immodestly naked presiding goddess. The story appears to be under the control of a demonic satiric power, which *knows* women. The title page advertises the merriment to be found within: "in which there are treated many histories and merry stories [*fabulas alegres*] . . . and you will see and hear the wickedness and treasons which bad wives inflict on their husbands." The advertisement of the book picks up themes that are sure to please a popular audience, connecting this book with other stories of the evils of women and the woes of marriage found in the *fabliaux*. This aspect of the book gets, as it were, "equal time" with the summary of the magical transformation. Altogether, the title page assures the reader, this book will make you laugh.

The Age of Print seems to bring in a new consciousness of females as readers. Not that women did not make part of the implied audience of fiction in the Middle Ages. Beroaldus, as we have seen, commented on the way greedy-eared women would read the stories of adultery in Boccaccio, and Boccaccio in all his works has an idea of a female readership, as we can see in his prologue to *Filocolo* and in Fiammetta's address to the gentle ladies who are to be her readers. Chrétien alludes to the ladies who will read his works. Dante certainly has something to say about (or against) female readership in Francesca's case, but it should be noted that she and Paulo were engaged in reading aloud as a *shared* activity; like the other writers, Dante envisages a mixed audience, male and female, for his works. With the proliferation of print, however, we begin to hear much more muttering about the dangers to which books—especially novels—expose the young and the female. This concern, which by no means inhibits the production of novels, is tied to other concerns over moral control.

Such moral and social concerns are not particularly English or particularly Philistine, or even particularly middle-class. They certainly cannot be tidily sorted by the application of the terms "Catholic" and "Protestant." One of the effects of the Renaissance, when people saw how diverse and complicated was the world of cultural thought, seems to have been a withdrawal, slight but definite, from the puzzling—or rather from the insoluble. The ardent quest for answers led to a certain coldness towards works that tease the reader with unanswered questions, or problems without solutions. A novel like *Apollonius*, with its harsh puzzles and unresolved tensions, is not so likely to succeed as the Renaissance mood gathers force. *Apollonius* was apparently much more highly esteemed in the fifteenth and early sixteenth centuries than later. There are good sixteenth-century printings. An English translation of 1510 is ornamented with beautiful pictures. In the Preface of this *Kynge Appolyn of Thyre* the translator Robert Copelande says he has taken it "out of the Frensche [*sic*] language," getting the copy from Wynken de Worde. In producing the novel, he thinks of himself as following "the trace of my mayster Caxton" (1510, A1 ᵛ). Yet even so, this translator feels the need to justify both translation and reading. In an English translation near the end of the century, Laurence Twine feels called upon to editorialize the title, making sure that the novel now spells out its moral themes: *The Patterne of painefull Aduentures: Containing the most excellent, pleasant and variable Historie of the strange accidents that befell vnto Prince Apollonius, the Lady Lucina his wife, and Tharsia his daughter. Wherein the uncertaintie of this world, and the fickle state of mans life are liuely described.* The sexual problematics of the novel are largely ignored or subordinated to the fashionable and most acceptable late Elizabethan theme of mutability. As Twine says in his "Epistle Dedicatorie," "the delectable varietie, and the often changes and chances contained in this present historie . . . cannot but much stirre vp the mind and sences vnto sundry affections" (London [1594?], A3ʳ). (The new Prayer Book seems to have influenced Twine's style here.)

To a Continental editor of the same period, however, the work is both questionable and somewhat distasteful; Chaucer's expressed distaste for "swiche cursed stories" emerges in double measure. This editor does not really expect the reader to enjoy this book: "If anyone is prepared to read so as to find gold and gems in a dunghill, he will be a suitable reader for this book . . . . Much in this same story is absurdly contrived, and much in its prose is barbarously put, although now and then there are spots of writing of better quality, and it is interspersed with some traces of antique manners and customs. . . ." ("Editorial Opinion," in *Narratio Eorum quae Contingervnt Apollonio Tyrio* [Augsburg, 1595], A2ʳ).[9] Is it mere crude Latin that gives offense—or does the incest theme evoke this proverbial allusion to the excremental? To find value in *Apollonius* is to dig for gold in a heap of shit.

We might propose that the antipathetic categories we should consider are not the Learned and the Vulgar, or the Old and the New, but the Clean and the Dirty. Print introduces a new self-consciousness about "dirt" on the page. This does not mean there is no place for bawdy or pornographic works—there may be more place for them than ever—but they ought to declare themselves according to theme and function. Problems arise when the dirty is what we might call "unresolved-dirty." *Apollonius* is a case *par excellence* of the unresolved-dirty, the incest problem at its basis never being capable of being explained away, tidied into a joke, or otherwise settled. The *Ass* of "Lucian" could be seen as pretty largely a set of jokes, to be perused *laxandi animi*, as Poggio of Florence advises Cosimo de Medici, sending Cosimo his Latin translation of *Onos*, his new *Asinus Luciani*. Stating that he knows jokes can soothe even the pains of gout, and that nature has made Cosimo facetious and ready-witted in jokes (*facetium . . . & iocos promptum*), Poggio has sent "this fable full of asinine pleasantries and wantonnesses" (*hanc fabellam asininae iocunditatis & lasciuiae plenam*) ("Praefatio," *Asinus Lvciani*, in *Poggio Fiorentini Oratoris Clarissimi* [Strasburg, 1513], 52ᵛ). Even *The Golden Ass* could be represented as a similar string of comic tales, emphatically bawdy in the style of traditional *fabliaux*. On the other hand, Apuleius' novel might be tidied by an allegorial reading resolving such jocund parts into sobering exhibitions of the pains of the lower self caught in brutish carnal experience.

Whichever solution is chosen, there is a constant drive towards clear resolution of some kind. Rabelais, born in the last decade of the fifteenth century, splendidly broke all the sixteenth-century taboos in connecting the drives of the physical body with the Renaissance's unquenchable thirst for learning. In Rabelais we cannot separate "clean" from "dirty." But Rabelais knew the fight that he was waging—he comes on so strong because he knows currently and prophetically the powers of the opposing side.

In literature of the Middle Ages (from the twelfth to the fifteenth centuries) one can see a love of the "multiplex." Dante proclaims to Can Grande that his *Divina Commedia* is polysemous, even if the *Commedia* is one of the most highly controlled works in the entire medieval Western corpus. In general, we can say that medieval writers like to put different kinds of experience side by side, circling round the same question or similar themes (as in Chaucer's *Canterbury Tales*) or connecting through one central movement, itself experiential, a multitude of thoughts and experiences—the pattern of the *Roman de la Rose* as well as the *Divina Commedia*. Writers have a strong confidence in their powers to organize intricate and vastly diverse material—a confidence better borne out in Dante's case than in that of Chaucer, who never finished his *Tales*. Medieval narrative is quite fond of uncompleted or unenclosed stories—this is true even in Dante, for the story of Dante the Pilgrim cannot truly be completely told while he remains in this life. Medieval literature offers experiments with unresolved multiplicities, setting up alternatives—as in Marie de France's *Lais*, read together, or the *Canterbury Tales*, or above all the *Decameron*. In reading—or writing—prose novels, medieval people seem to have expected similar pleasures in interfolding contrasted stories.

The Renaissance seems more anxious about ambiguity and the unenclosed. Our old schoolroom commonplace, whereby the Middle Ages is religious and moral, and the Renaissance secular, skeptical, and robustly pleasure-loving, does not get us very far. It would be hard to find literature more "secular" than the *Lais* or *Tirant lo Blanc*. A major difference lies in the fact that once the Age of Print got underway, literature was seen to have a *public* duty to perform. Our emphasis on the rise of the bourgeoisie as an economic development often inclines us to miss the political point. (There were "middle classes" in antiquity and in the "medieval" era; Blanquerna's father is the son and heir of a wealthy burgess.) The growth of the town is of great importance. So too is the new nationalism—a way of organizing one's individual identity as well as of centralizing the state and its powers. The full return to Europe of the republican ideas of the state and the civic idea of public life is of the utmost importance.

THE SENSE OF THE CIVIC

From the period we call "the late Middle Ages" through the sixteenth and seventeenth centuries political life changed markedly. Feudal and clan organization, and social organization around a small chieftain (baron or prince) and his small court dissolved into the city and the state. Small courts joined with cities to produce and share cultural and economic activities. The sense of the civic, of the value of *civitas*, points towards the desirability of participation in political life. Power spreads—which is what we mean by "the rise of the bourgeoisie." (The word "bourgeois," however, not only has been too abusively employed to be a truly helpful term, but also has most recently been used in misleading ways, as if the bourgeoisie were no more than "the middle classes" and these middle classes no more than flaccid "consumers.") Rich merchants indeed had reason to want more active participation in the institutions of church and state that supported them, but these institutions also gave shape to the merchant's desires and his notion of himself.

The desire for the civic can be felt in Dante, who deals with political life in his *Convivio*. As he defines it, "The radical basis of imperial majesty, according to the truth, is the necessity of human civility [*civilitade*], which is ordained to one end, that is to happy life; to which no one in himself is sufficient to arrive without some assistance, because man has need of many things, which one person on his own cannot satisfy. And therefore says the Philosopher [Aristotle] that man is naturally a companionable animal [*naturalmente è compagnevole animale*]" (*Convivio* [1966], Sec. 1V, 416). Government is necessary, and so is civic organization, for the pursuit of happiness. Dante reserves some of his most grotesque punishments and grimmest jokes in the *Inferno* for those who have cheated in city government office—the "barrators" or city swindlers of Lucca whom we see boiling in the cauldrons of pitch in the fifth pocket of the Malebolge (Cantos XXI–XXII). To lend oneself to civic corruption is to foil some of the best hopes of mankind and to do deep injustice to the common desire for the happy life, the *vita felice*.

The solution Europe found to answer its need for political form was not to be the grand common *imperium* envisaged by Dante, but the expanding nation-state ruled by a powerful monarch. Such a nation-state and its amoral ruler are clearly delineated by Machiavelli in *The Prince* (written in 1513), although the author sustained an ardent republicanism and the hope for a revival of civic virtue. The strong nation-states, however, were going to be in the condition of competition and hostility with each other that Dante imagined European empire would obviate. Some of these powerful states (first France, later Austria) invaded Italy, creating long-lived occupations that were to put a serious dent in the Italian sense of the civic. (Civic feeling is short-circuited by hostility to an occupying power; cheating the powers that be becomes a duty as well as a pleasure.) The new nation-states emphasized centrality and control; the model of kingship seems to thrust power further and further away from the people. Yet people were becoming more involved in civic life, if largely at a local level, while activation of the parliamentary system (in England and for a while in France) created the idea of national participation.

Protestantism is a powerful new force in creating a political sense. True, the intellectual Reformers or reforming theorists (Luther, Calvin, Tyndale) pronounced on the need of respect for the prince or "magistrate." Officially they disclaimed political interests. They were in conflict with the more radical reformers, such as the Anabaptists, who saw in governments only systematic evil. Yet both sides of that debate within Protestantism affected the sense of the political and the civic very profoundly. Anabaptists and others inculcated a sense of responsibility and self-respect in the poor, offering ideologies that allowed questioning and protest in the face of constituted authority. Lutheranism and Calvinism, which explicitly disclaimed revolution, were revolutionary. Both movements contributed to the increasing respect in which the secular is to be held. Calvin, for instance, insists that the magistracy is founded by God and that political life should reflect the divine plan. He carefully does not encourage his followers to interfere with a ruler already in authority. In setting up the theocracy of Geneva after 1541, Calvin himself became a ruler in the service of exhibiting complete unity of church and state. It was now his duty to root out heretics, and he had Servetus burned at the stake; both Catholicism and Protestantism went in for punishing thought-crime.

In outlining the advantages and benefits of the material and political life, Calvin planted in his followers a strong sense of the value and hopefulness of life in the man-made world. Luther's and Calvin's attacks on monasticism—not merely convents but even monastic values in themselves—reinforced the superior value of life lived in the world and in the community. The community included men and women, was family-centered, was engaged in getting and spending, and in moral self-improvement. Church government and the organization of church communities—in both Lutheran and Calvinistic models—divorced churchgoers from a pyramid of distant power and created a sense of immediate participation and responsibility, to be increased among various congregational sects. The church congregation becomes a true model of the civic. In the West, congregations have been nurturers of political action and organization—for Black American Protestants in the twentieth century as for English Protestants in the seventeenth.

This might seem an unmitigated success story, but there are some grave drawbacks to the new rise of the civic. Both the rise and the drawbacks are apparent by the sixteenth century. A strengthened political force can always lead to more efficient cruelty, and more brutal policing. Centralized state governments spied on their subjects and could do so more efficiently than in the past. Influxes of money created new senses of privilege. Almost all major Protestant thinkers urged church members to think of themselves as *stewards* of their wealth, but the emphasis came to be placed (as Calvin, perhaps inadvertently, places it) on not *wasting* money, on fine food and expensive clothing for instance, rather than on giving to the poor. There is little impetus to try to create situations in which there are no poor—we have been in the habit of throwing people out of work in employment cycles, then calling them "idle," and then creating workhouses or "programs" where they either do meaningless jobs or operate as slave-labor. Calvin argues very hotly against the Anabaptists and Libertines on the matter of individual property. Calvin cannot really *believe* that at any time in the Early Church's history Christian people had goods in common—despite Biblical evidence. When the author of Acts 4 says "no one called what he possessed his own," Calvin audaciously explains away the text. The New Testament account may seem quite clear:

> And the multitude of them that believed were of one heart and of one soul: neither said any *of them* that ought of the things which he possessed was his own; but they had all things common [*panta koina*]. . . .
>   for as many as were possessors of lands or houses sold them, and brought the prices of the things that were sold,
>   And laid *them* down at the apostles' feet: and distribution was made unto every man according as he had need.
>
> (Acts 4:32–35, K.J.V.)

The text does not seem to pose linguistic or exegetical problems. Yet Calvin decides to take it all as a figure of speech. We say of a generous man that he has "nothing of his own" since he is so openhanded—that is all that is meant here. These early Christians cannot *really* have combined their wealth in a heap—putting things "in such a pile of confusion." No, no. "Each retained his household goods and governed them by himself. But they had such fellowship that none suffered indigence" (*Against the Libertines*, trans. Farley, 287).

Calvin is really a civic writer. You cannot be a member of the *civitas* unless you have a household, and power to govern your property. This respect for property, which allowed Calvin to contradict an author he believes to be Saint Luke, can easily slide beyond respect for individual (meaning male) choice and ownership to an estimation of human value based on goods alone. The poor, if they work hard, may be worthy members of the community, contributors to common weal and commonwealth. But the poor person is not as valuable as the man of property. "Citizenship" becomes based on control and substance. Individualism can be thought of (as by Calvin's cleverest child, Rousseau) only in male and propertied terms. Rousseau's Emile is a good citizen when he marries and becomes fully propertied. Calvin's intellectual descendants were to object to being called "subjects" and to demand (forcefully in 1790) to be called *citizens*. The French Revolution's experiment in democratizing "citizenship" was very brief. "Citizenship" cannot be, like the state of being a king's subject, an inevitable condition. Citizenship is a right reserved to the worthy. Only the most democratic movements (stemming partly from the more "disreputable" sides of Protestantism) have begun to erode this view. The trouble with the republican ideal is that not everybody is thought good enough or worthy enough to handle *res publica*. The invention of the vote (or its spread) made clearer than before the difference between citizens (male, over 21, white, possessing property) and others—all women, idiots, minors, slaves, and "natives."

The Novel, though it flourishes during the rise of the civic ideal, and has been thought of as an epiphenomenon of the rise of the mercantilist middle class, has always been in partial conflict or tension with the civic ideal, just as it was in tension with the Roman ideal when novels gave voice to women, the young, foreigners, and slaves. Novels and novelists are (rather like those other sectarians) regarded as wild fringe groups and treated to abuse, termed deluded, insane, scatterbrained, and foolish.

William Tyndale, translator of the Bible into English, in *Obedience of a Christian Man* (1528) dismisses a range of fiction and fictional heroes, including stories of Hercules, Hector and Troilus, and Robin Hood as "fables of loue and wantonnes and of ribauldry, as filthy as hart can thinke." C. S. Lewis defends this as "the ordinary attitude of the humanist to medieval story" (*English Literature in the Sixteenth Century*, 185), but it is *not* the inevitable attitude of the humanist *per se*. Other humanists were spreading stories of Hercules and Hector in their classical forms, but Tyndale's style of comment would apply to fictions of any period. Yet the objective Tyndale has in view—that every Christian should be able to read the Scripture in his own language—proposes a radical social change enabling all members of society, including the poor and the female, to have access to the written word. Tyndale's English Bible project helped to create an enormous class or persons who would avail themselves of new printed texts of every description. From the secular point of view, one of the lasting changes effected by Protestantism was the advent of an ideal of universal literacy, with all that flows from that. The Novel, however ill-treated, could survive and flourish because the same printers' shop that could set out the Bible or religious pamphlets could also print off copies of fictions. Tyndale announced his desire that "a boy that driveth the plough" should be able to read Scriptures. He did not perhaps envisage that boy reading a lot of other things—nor did he consider the class-complexity created by the literate plowboy, perhaps because he himself believed so ardently in "degree," including the total possession of children by parents, and deep subordination of wife to husband. (See Lewis, *English literature in the Sixteenth Century*, 182–184.)

It can be seen as one of the tragedies of Christian history that hierarchies contaminate the idea of equal membership in Christ, and that the pagan idea of the civic all too readily contaminates the fellowship of Christians. When human beings in the Renaissance (and earlier) studied the civic in order to consider how to achieve the political state that makes for happiness, they had pagan models to turn to—chiefly Aristotle and Cicero. Aristotle's image of the authoritarian household, wherein the man governs his wife, children, and slaves was all too attractive, as was the idea of a *civitas* run by men of substance and property who were good at keeping wives, children, and slaves in subjection. Cicero goes even further, for he is the spokesman for the most attractive and elegant forms of oligarchy—and oligarchy was something about which Aristotle had his suspicions. For Cicero, it is obvious that the world should be run by the well-born and the well-educated, that is to say by the rich and influential. Cicero was a fantasist, for he dreamed of republicanism in a state that was actually a despotism. The short interval after the murder of Julius Caesar allowed him to try to put his political views into action; for this, Octavian and Mark Antony rewarded him with summary death. Ciceronian republicanism has always flourished as an idea rather than a reality; in the Renaissance and the Enlightenment it was an ideal. The *res publica*, the public thing, public matters, should be deserving of the respect and attention of the leading elite males. Participation is an ideal—but it is participation of the few. The idea of respect for *res publica*, for public matters, is certainly important. The new civic ideals are worthy of our respect—and for men of the time, the difference between cowering in one's hut while brigands of barbarian hordes tried to overrun it, or sitting in one's city of stone and brick, working on public committees making ordinances for safeguarding the property of ones townsmen—this difference was obvious.

But women and the poor, according to the best civic philosophies, are to have nothing to do with the running of *res publica*. Civic virtue is to be measured in part by the ability to keep women and the young in control—as in the days of Greece and Rome. As the new modes of getting and using property become more expansive, female possession of property comes to seem more and more anomalous, and regulations increasingly force women out of economic control or choice. Protestantism did not even allow women the choice of a celibate and scholarly or artistic life in a convent—a woman's destiny was to reproduce. Marriage is a means of control of production, a control both financial and emotional. True, some Protestant sects tried to rebel against the system of property and control that had become confused with Christianity on its secular side—but these groups were defeated. While Protestantism said the individual had no need of a priestly or papal mediator between himself and God, that did not mean forswearing strong efforts to govern the inner processes of piety itself. The Roman Church had been greatly vexed by this problem, which became acute in the early sixteenth century when the Church was much exercised, especially in Spain, by the issue of "mental prayer." Encouraged by some divines, like Dominican preachers, "mental prayer," inner devotion, was thought by others undesirable, especially by the Inquisition; some Inquisitors tried to stamp it out. Mental prayer gave low persons and women too high an opinion of themselves. (The first recorded instance is that of the Biblical Hannah, and Eli the High Priest thinks she is drunk.) In private direct address to God the individual constructs an idea of the self outside the authorities' control, and thus essentially antagonistic to civic and religious order. This antagonism to inner spiritual activity was one of the difficulties Saint Teresa had to contend with (see Rowan Williams, *Teresa of Avila*, 26–34).

It was widely felt that the mass of people had to be taught what to feel and think. Protestant clergy had the extra task of educating people in private devotions as well as in public rites, and the flood of devotional manuals and spiritual autobiographies supplied a giant "How to Do It" regulatory system. Ironically, these incursions into the representation of inner life were picked up by novels, which had never stopped dealing with the inner life. Her own early reading of novels was probably a deep help to Saint Teresa of Avila in writing works like *Interior Castle*. For Protestant religious as well as civic authorities (and the two were frequently combined), it was often more comfortable to turn outward, encouraging people to think about their jobs, public life, and productivity. Less time should be spent on thinking about one's soul in unproductive ways, and more energy expended in developing manifestations of the social virtues that monasteries and celibate clergy were thought so saliently to lack.

The civic ideal crystallized around the important individual man, of middle or upper class, with his property, his wife, his child and servants ranged round him. This ideal was liberating in some ways but highly restrictive in others. Aberration or eccentricity is looked at more askance, can be punished more severely. Exemplary punishment within the family and community—not to mention the school—seems to take an increasingly central role. The birching of boys in schools becomes in itself a kind of sadistic theater of Renaissance and Enlightenment life. Novel-reading was under renewed pressure from the civic ideal: for novels should breed or exemplify not only pious people, but also people of social value. Either that, or they should show people without social values coming to a sticky end. With both "secular" and "spiritual" (or ecclesiastical) territories grimly occupied by Protestant troops, there was very little space in which to turn. Fiction comes under a renewed suspicion; even if Christian or ostensibly so, fiction may be teaching people to waste time, to entertain not only idle thoughts but really subversive thoughts not conducive to good social order.

Theater comes under increasing censorship, suspected both for providing a playground and escape for the lower classes and for encouraging vulgar elements within the higher classes. Drama should be purified. And if drama—why not narrative? Distrust of censorship as practiced by the Roman Catholic Church was mitigated by some defensiveness about censorship when it concerns good civic order, as Milton found to his dismay when the Puritans took over London in 1644. Anything that encourages women, the young, and the poor to dream, to imagine things otherwise, may well be destructive of the civic order and of civic virtue as imagined by the dominant political theory. The Christian idea—or ideal—is that "we are all members one of another," an ideal that Calvin himself supports in explicitly refuting our right to distinguish between deserving and un-deserving poor when giving alms (*Institutes*, III : vii). From this idea we move to pagan images of gross inequality, of the belly and the members, the fable taught in Shakespeare's *Coriolanus*, whereby the "mob" must learn that they have no place of control in the civic arrangement, but must dumbly put up with their lot (*Coriolanus*, I, i., lines 52–167). The rise of civic virtue leads to a lot of nasty talk about the "mob."

The Novel joined in the political activity—the Novel in its various forms, including philosophical fantasy (More's *Utopia* might be classed with science-fiction), picaresque tale, coded political allegory, and satire, as in war-recording *Simplicissimus*. The Novel maintained its interest in people's lives in relation to power and in society. But the Novel itself was going to be looked at more closely, its faults detected. Its ultimate alienation from the civic ideal of Aristotle and Cicero is always suspected, even when the individual novel tries to pretend oth-erwise. A novel is better off if it can pretend that it is supporting the social virtues, without stimulating too much overt political thought on the part of characters and readers. But novel characters, though they are always "companionable ani-mals" as Dante puts Aristotle's phrase, do not trust magistrates, and novelists tend to see what is wrong with the civic enterprise—even to the point of giving voice to women, the young, or the poor.

EDUCATION AND MORAL WRITING

The Renaissance, like the Enlightenment later, is involved in a giant education project. The civic urge to educate may itself have been chiefly responsible for the thoroughgoing adoption of the printing press, and it substantiates Protestantism itself. Princes are now to be considered as *educable* beings. The presses bend with the weight of Mirrors for Magistrates and handbooks for Princes. But everybody is to be educated, (everybody above the laboring poor, and sometimes even those). Reading, however, must also be justified against its own pleasurable-ness. Discussions of the sin of sloth had traditionally included discussion of what we call "waste of time"—but there is a new acute sense of the injury of self-dissipation. As early as 1510 (before the Protestant movement had really got go-ing) the translator of *Kynge Appolyn* must defend reading (good books) as a way of avoiding the sins of laziness: "in the auoydynge of osiuyte and ydlenes por-tresse of synne" (1510, Aiᵛ). Reading is a matter to be actively scrutinized; does reading *this* book amount to an avoidance of *oisiveté*,—inaction, indolence?

Morality often had to be propitiated in feeble excuse for producing a work of fiction; for example, the author-compiler of *Amorous Tales and Sentences of the Philosophers* (1567) (a book containing a renarration of part of the *Aithiopika*) of-fers as his reason for supplying "amorous tales" that they tell us what to avoid: "The fruites which spring of hote Love and fleshly lust are declared in those Tales following" (A iiiᵛ). This common escape-hatch might be termed the Case of the

Exemplary Alibi—a moral meaning is to be discovered external to the story by treating the story as a *bad example*. The corollary of such a concern is that those books most worth reading display a clear moral. Fifteenth-century printings of Boccaccio, for instance, were already beginning to fret about how moral his works were. The postscript by "Hieronymo Squarzasigo Alexandrino" of a printing of *Fiammetta* in 1491 is addressed to Fiammetta's suspect audience of women in love, *donne innamorate*, and argues that fiction about love can be good in that it makes us see how *bad* it is. *Fiammetta* is useful as an example of what to avoid (Venice, 1491, 65ᵛ–66ᵛ). There should be something exemplary about a good fiction. A book should teach what to do and what to avoid—and teach clearly.

Protestantism set the cat among the pigeons in the matter of reading. Catholics insisted (correctly) that without guidance unlearned readers of Scripture would put their own personal constructions on practically everything. Protestants retorted that this would not be so, for the new readers of Scripture would have Protestant clergy to guide them—not the old Catholic priests who had wrong ideas, but new clergy, well educated in Greek and Hebrew, who knew the meanings of the Bible texts inside out. Groups of Protestants kept fissioning off, however, disagreeing on matters usually connected with reading and interpretation. The style of educated cleric the Anglicans and Presbyterians and early Lutherans had in mind was going to be subject to question by other Protestants—how vain is the work of mistaken human learning compared with the power of the Spirit! In the sixteenth century, however, the idea of the learned Protestant cleric had some success, and splinter movements were put down—only to rise again in the seventeenth century.

Arguably, in Protestant countries the larger investment lay in the education of the people, involving careful authoritative instruction. In Spain there was less of this schoolmasterly approach and thus, paradoxically, less drive towards uniformity, even though a powerful political force was bent on supporting orthodoxy; in Spain, then, the novel flourished more than it was to do at first in the newly Protestant countries. The Spanish produced more novels than anybody else, from *Amadís* to *Lazarillo*, from *Celestina* to *Diana*. In what might be called the "Big Bang" period of schism and sundering—from the ban on Luther in 1521 through the excommunication of Henry VIII in 1533 to the Council of Trent in 1545–1563—Western European energies were bent on matters ecclesiastical and doctrinal. The new movement excited in *both* Catholic and Protestant a renewed sense of inner and individual life, one of the effects of which was to make the prose novel all the more appealing. But a certain anxiety about interpretation remained, in a century battered by conflicts over hermeneutics. The craving for complexity in multiplex texts was balanced by a certain doubt as to whether a clear interpretation must not always be offered, to save the reader from going astray.

HELIODORUS IN PRINT

Heliodorus' *Aithiopika* on its first appearance in print was associated with the new Protestant movement. The first edition of the *Aithiopika* was published in 1534, in Basel, edited by Vincentus Obsopaeus, a humanist who translated some of

Luther's works from German into Latin. Obsopaeus' association with the new Lutheran movement may have made the novel the more appealing to new Protestants in northern countries. This 1534 printing should not be confused with the first appearance of the Heliodorus' novel in Europe. Many surviving manuscripts are of a fairly late date, suggesting that Heliodorus had a strong and constant readership throughout the Eastern Empire. Obsopaeus' manuscript comes from Hungary; Heliodorus was presumably read in Hungary, Bulgaria, and the regions formerly called Yugoslavia, as well as in Greece and Asia Minor.

Obsopaeus dedicates his edition (in a Preface dated 26 June 1531) to the senators of the Republic of Nuremberg, indicating that such a fine and moral work befits a virtuous Republic which is, and which wishes to be, founded on the best laws derived from the traditions of Germania of old. Heliodorus is "born again in this sunlight of the Germans" (*isto sole ac luce Germanorum Heliodorus renascatur*, Basel, 1534, a3ᵛ). It is interesting to see how the new republican ideal, as well as German national sensibility, gets intertwined with the idea of this novel. Obsopaeus thinks he has the sole manuscript, referring to it as if snatched from the barbarians of Asia; in fact it was taken from the sacking of the King of Hungary's library. If the editor of Apuleius speaks of the text as a wounded soldier, the editor of Heliodorus speaks of his text as a captive in a dungeon. Heliodorus owes the Republic no little gratitude if by their means he is recalled to life: "Nor indeed will he owe your Republic an ordinary gratitude if by you he is in a manner born again, just as if he were brought back from the underworld, that is from beetles and larvae, from prison and darkness, from mold and neglectful filth, and from annihilation which threatened to be next—that he should rise again, liberated into the light . . ." (Basel, 1534, a2ʳ–a2ᵛ).[10] The condition of being in manuscript form is now itself a condition of prison and bondage for a book. A book in manuscript form is always threatened by the depredations of moths and mold, menaced by physical annihilation.

The editor offers this book to "your greatnesses" because it is moral as well as excellent:

> as well as drawing in this history all human affections most perfectly in a real likeness (and to know these exactly is not the least part of wisdom), he has also drawn the most beautiful example of conjugal love and faith in Theagenes and Charikleia. I pass over the ornamented words and composition, and the highly-wrought speeches and other excellences of his writing, in which he does not come second to any other Greek author. (a2ʳ)[11]

The editor likes the fact that this is a big and complex book; it is an additional recommendation that it is geographically and ethnographically educational:

> Concerning the plot which is both various and multiplex, I shall offer no comment, except that this is a festive and agreeable and pure and chaste history related in a continuous narration. The author also most learnedly depicts many places with cosmographical science; he digs out and reveals the hidden causes of not a few things, and there are not a few peoples whose customs and manners he describes with

erudition. He explains the nature of a number of rivers, mountains, stones, plants and regions of Egypt and neighboring Ethiopia (unknown to the vulgar). All these he so mixes and tempers with the most beautiful digressions and most delightful supplementary artifices and adornments. . . . (a3ʳ) [12]

Obsopaeus echoes Virgil (*felix qui potuit rerum cognoscere causas*, in *Georgics*, II, line 490) and Lucretius (see *De Rerum Natura*, I, lines 144–145), in making Heliodorus out to be a type of Lucretian scientist, an explorer of the world of nature and of human activity. We can see here the Renaissance thirst for knowledge, as well as the accepted pleasure (which novel-readers in most ages have shared) of being led into new lands and introduced to strangers and foreigners. If the novel is encyclopedic and highly ornamented, it is also, the editor stresses, morally—and stylistically—trustworthy: "what is more, he left nothing rude or unpolished in the whole of his work, nothing that could give nausea to even the most delicate reader" (*adeo in toto opere nihil rude & impolitum reliquit, quod etiam delicatissimo lectori nauseam adferre queat* [a3ʳ]). Both in morality and taste, this book is irreproachable. We seem to hear at the beginning of the Renaissance the first whisper of the requirement that a novel should not bring a blush to the cheek of the young person. But the *delicatissimus lector* imagined by the editor is a reader who is in search of truly *polite* literature, polished, artificial, and developed in style and manner. When Rabelais, in a very backhanded compliment to the *Aithiopika*, introduces the novel in the *Quart Livre* of *Pantagruel*, he may have been thinking of Obsopaeus' "Epistola Dedicatoria." During a calm at sea, *Pantagruel tenent un Heliodore Grec en main sus un transpontin au bout des escoutilles sommeilloit* ("Pantagruel, stretched out on a cross-sail at the end of the hatchway, slumbered, holding a Greek Heliodorus in his hand" [II: 231]). The book that will not induce nausea might have been useful during the storm, but is obviously too tranquil for a dead calm.

We can also see in the Renaissance commentators' praise of digressions in narrative an assumed principle of worth touching not only complexity of plot but also the presence of additional material. Works are valued for variety and fullness, the sense of an extra. When Sterne's Tristram Shandy claims "Digressions, incontestably, are the sunshine;—they are the life, the soul of reading. . ." (55), he may be in amusing contravention of certain Enlightenment or neoclassical principles, but he is certainly in line with the ancient and the Renaissance tradition of the Novel.

We can sense elements of paradox in Renaissance criticism of the novel. On the one hand, commentators value formal multiplicity and skillful introduction of complex variety. Layers of material are more valuable than a slight straight story. A good storyteller like Heliodorus will know how to communicate even encyclopaedic information without breaking the threads of a complete narrative. But at the same time there should be unity of effect, and this unity of effect should be subordinate to strong moral outline. A book is to *announce* itself as valuable and educational—and there lies the rub, rather than in the idea that a novel should be valuable or even educational. We think it is because we ourselves are "modern" that we value ambiguity and do not make such demands—yet, as soon as we get back into medieval literature, or indeed antique novels, we find that they are congenial to ambiguity. They, too, may ask us to wait on meaning rather than having meaning thrust upon us. If the question "what did you learn from this book?" can be answered fully straight away, either book or reader is likely to be shallow. It might be years after first reading that I could feel I knew what *Aithiopika* or *Arcadia* or *Crime and Punishment* really "meant," or how they had "educated" me. Like some modern reviewers, however, Renaissance commentators feel that the answer as to intellectual worth and moral values should be available at once.

The requirements placed on the novel were not, of course, singular. Renaissance readers and critics demanded similar clarities of other kinds of reading matter. What is most endearing about the Renaissance readers and editors is their positive enthusiasm for reading matter—of all kinds—and the giant energy with which they dragged all sorts of texts back up into the light. Well might they present themselves as on an heroic mission—not unlike the characters in some novels. They fight battles, rescue captives, heal the sick. The Novel itself becomes like a heroine in a dungeon, buried alive but ever to be resurrected.

Renaissance editors and commentators stress the importance of *pleasure* in reading literature—and they are emphatic in their own professions of pleasure. The enthusiasm of Renaissance commentators can indeed be somewhat overwhelming at times. Coming to it from either direction, from the fourteenth century, say, or the eighteenth, one is struck by how *loud* the sixteenth century seems. The indefatigability, the sheer uproarious energy, was favorable to reading long books—a fact in itself favorable to the Novel. Renaissance critics are *not* likely to say something should be shorter. And, of course, long books could now be reproduced more easily, quickly and (ultimately) cheaply. There is even a detectable vogue for turning short fiction into novels, a habit visible from the earliest days of printing. In 1473 Franciscus Florius published his *De amore Camilli et Emilie*, a little Latin novel based on a brief story by Boccaccio. There is a general desire to lengthen, rather than to shorten, a desire favorable to the production of works—including novels—in a number of "books" or short volumes. The sixteenth century was very alert to the possibility of "book" as a division, inherited from antiquity but now used more and more as a rhetorical division of a long work with little reference to the mere exigencies of writing space.

Here I think we come to the advantage that Renaissance writers had—and took—which was also their means of getting around the ostensible unpopularity of ambiguity. Renaissance novelists tend to write books that have continuations, revisitings, and rethinkings. Such a "continuation" is not a part of the original concept, unlike Dante's *Purgatorio*, for instance, the ultraplanned sequel to *Inferno*. Instead, a genuine "new part" is both continuous and disjunctive; the effect on the reader is as of accompanying a thinking mind over a period of years, while that mind changes. In the interstices and disjunction, ambiguities and the lack of closure could be successfully implied. *Don Quijote* comes to mind as a stellar example of that kind of book. Part II both parodies and comments upon Part I, while engaging itself with material in the same way and differently. But Cervantes caught the form from the Renaissance, when the continuation might be called an *in*formal or hidden aspect of novelistic form. Sir Philip Sidney wrote his early

Arcadia (nowadays called *The Old Arcadia*) about 1580 and then revised it to make an almost completely new, more moral and stately, and much longer work. This unfinished work, published posthumously as the *New Arcadia* (1590), was then clapped together with the end of the old one and some editorial revisions as *The Countess of Pembroke's Arcadia* (1593), and that is what three centuries' readers mean by Sidney's *Arcadia*. *The Old Arcadia* had already had an audience, as it had circulated briskly in manuscript. This first version of the novel might be called *The Sexy Arcadia* and the printed one *The Exemplary Arcadia*.[13] *Guzman de Alfarache* moves on from Part I (1599) to Part II (1604), changing as it goes. A triumphant example of publication by lengthening into parts is Rabelais' sequence that we loosely call *Pantagruel*. The parts came out in a random series: 1532, 1534, 1546. Part IV emerges (partially) in 1548 and the rest not until 1552, while for the (posthumous) *Quint Livre* the reader had to wait until 1562. Rabelais' work seems to have caught on—with himself not least; when he began *Pantagruel*, he could not have known that it was to be the first installment of a multivolume book as gigantic as its hero. By turning that first book into the *second* of his series, Rabelais revised the notion of sequentiality, and, with every volume that emerged, it became the clearer that the *Pantagruel* series was much more than the jolly jest book the original volume could be assumed to be.

When Rabelais exhibits Pantagruel reading (or sleeping over) a Greek Heliodorus, we may be sure that giant-hero was, like Rabelais himself, learned in Greek and a staunch supporter of the education in the Three Languages, against the obscurantist wing of the Sorbonne, which was trying to put a stop to the teaching of Greek, fearing the development of heresy. But as long as *Aithiopika* remained in a printed Greek text, it was available to very few. As its Latin translator says, "in Greek it was retired as if in exile." The publication of the novel in Latin was of major importance in disseminating it and accelerating the progress of its influence. The big Latin translation (1552) was done by a Polish knight, Stanislaus Warschewiczki, who dedicates his work to the King of Poland, extoling the arts of peace in contrast to those of war. This novel, he indicates, like other examples of humane learning, can contribute to a civilization dedicated to the arts of peace. Warschewiczki emphasizes the *pleasure* the book affords, and its moral value. The *Aithiopika* offers not only changes (like Apuleius) but also images of virtue:

> For it is to the pleasure of the reader (*ad uoluptatem lectoris*) as well as to his profit that this narrative is wonderfully accommodated, with the exceptional elegance and charm of its prose, and its wonderful variety of counsels, events, and emotions. Not only many changes of fortune but also many images of virtue are here displayed. Among these is the description of Hydaspes, the king of Ethiopia, who is to be praised not only for his fortitude but also for his justice, clemency, and kindness towards those whom he has subdued (1552, a3ᵛ).[14]

Renaissance men believed in the moral good of contemplating examples of virtue. Such examples have power. We may be surprised to see neither the hero nor the *heroine* brought in as the image of human virtue, and pride of place given to Hydaspes. But the book is dedicated to the *King* of Poland, and the Renaissance was interested in pictures for princes, mirrors for magistrates, good examples with which to train rulers. It is interesting that such an example can be the black king of foreign Ethiopia.

Warschewiczki's book is a large, expensively produced and ambitious edition. He got a blurb for it from Philip Melancthon, Professor of Greek at Wittenberg, best known for his advocacy of the Reformation. Here again is the Protestant connection. This celebrated humanist, in an epistle dated 20 April 1551, recommends Heliodorus' book: "The prose is brilliant, and not bombastic. There is a wonderful variety of counsels, incidents, events and emotions; and it contains many images of life. Therefore it is useful to many to read it, and its variety can attract readers" (a4ʳ).[15] Melancthon has obviously read the dedicatory epistle prefixed to the 1534 Greek edition, which he echoes, while Warschewiczki in his own preface employs Melancthon's own phrases, even though he—or his publisher—is going to quote Melancthon's epistle itself. It may be salutary to realize that blurb-writing is practically as old as printing.

The Polish count's real innovation is not his Introduction, nor his blurb. It is his Index. The title page advertizes this valuable feature: *Item locuples rerum ac uerborum memorabilium Index* ("Likewise a richly stored Index of memorable things and words"). Warschewiczki's long Index, alphabetized in the approved up-to-date style, helps us to find not only useful facts, historical and geographical references, etc., but also various "counsels," useful or pithy statements, and interesting "sentiments"—as a later generation was to call them. We are also given numerous plot-points so that we can find things happening to or being done by the characters. (See Plate 20.) Thus we have, for instance, under "A": *Aegyptij cur deos pedibus coniunctis fingant* ("Egyptians, why they fashion their gods with joined feet"); and also *amoris nulla satietas uera* ("of love, no real satiety"); and also *Arsace Charicliam ueneficii crimine accusat* ("Arsaké accuses Charikleia of the crime of poisoning") (B2ᵛ). Everything in the novel is to be included; the Index displays itself as a mine of information, an encyclopedic guide offering in itself pithy essences of the novel, such as the *sentence* or sentiment "of love there is no real satiety."

The custom of treating novels as mines of information in themselves, and extracting that information or counsel from them, had already been established. It is not surprising that the education-mad Renaissance should so treat serious books, but most interesting to find the novel so firmly defined as instructive and instructional. Seldom has the novel's aspect as wisdom literature been so fully acknowledged. Sentiments, advice, and examples from *Amadís de Gaula* were turned into a highly popular book, a collection of excerpts from the novel called the *Trésor des livres d'Amadis*, first published in 1559, and (at least in France) from then on outselling Castiglione's *Il Cortegiano* (*The Courtier*) of 1525. The *Trésor* was translated into German and English. The English translator's prefatory "To the gentle Reader" we may proleptically term euphuistic in its praise:

> For truly it aboundeth with such eloquent orations and wyse counsels:
> with such sweete and delicate Epistles and letters especially of loue, so
> courteously and amiably handled: with suche exhortations and ad-
> monitions so prudently penned: . . . with suche lamentations & com-
> plaints so sorowfully [sic] and mournfully expressed . . . with re-

proches and tauntes so bitingly and bitterly spoken: . . . with excuses
so craftily and subtilly painted and coloured: with defyances so stoutly
and courageously sente to the aduersarie and receiued, that if a man
were astonied & much amazed, it would quicken him, and sodeynly
reuiue his spirites againe.

(*The most excelent and pleasaunt Booke . . . The treasurie of*
Amadis of Fraunce, [1567?], iii^v)

This list gives some idea of the virtues that Renaissance readers expected to find
in texts of fiction. These books might function sometimes as manuals for letter-
writers, sometimes as guides to the perplexed or self-help treatises, while offering
erotic pleasure: "What stonie and hard hearte hath he, that with the glittering
and twinkeling of the eye, the abundant teares . . . of his paramour (wherewith
this fine flattering booke is infarced) will not be mollifyed and melted?" (iii^v).
The pleasures of erotic cruelty and sensibility mingled were well understood long
before the age of sentimentalism.

Other novels had already been presented with a table of contents; in a
Venetian edition of Boccaccio's *Philocolo* (*sic*) in 1488 there is a *Tavola* offering
highlights, chapter by chapter. Beroaldus had offered a *Vocabvlorum Index* to Apuleius. Warschewiczki's innovation is to magnify vastly the concept of the contents.
He treats the *Aithiopika* as if it were a learned work of nonfiction in giving it its
encyclopaedic Index, but at the same time he follows out all the plot points, characteristic actions, and emotions. The Index is an index to that novel, and not just
to some information contained within it. Warschewiczki's example seems to have
influenced the presentation of other novels at the time. Guides to contents become more detailed, as in a Venetian *Filocolo* of 1575, or a *Fiammetta* "with the
Table at the end of the most notable things" (Florence, 1594).[16] Such "tables"
were consonant with an age in which, like Hamlet, a thoughtful person prepared
his own notebooks (tablets or "tables") of notable thoughts: "My tables—meet it
is I set it down" (*Hamlet* I.v.97–109). The popular Index to Heliodorus was repeatedly copied by translators of the *Aithiopika*. We can see that this example lies
behind Dr. Johnson's suggestion that there should be an *"Index Rerum"* to
Richardson's *Clarissa*. Richardson's collection of *Sentiments* culled from his three
novels likewise looks back to the florilegium culled from *Amadís* as well as to the
Latin edition of Heliodorus.[17]

The Latin translator came a little late into the field. The most important
translation of all had been made in 1547. Jacques Amyot, the arch-translator,
turned the *Aithiopika* into a French work, *L'Histoire Æthiopique*. Amyot, humanist
teacher, had been appointed as tutor of the two sons of Henri II. He had thus
profited by court patronage, but he made his mark as a first-rate popularizer,
bringing a number of classical works (including Plutarch) within reach of the
common reader. Amyot, witty and lucid, is an astounding and rare example of
the translator who can make a work seem natural in its new guise. A sensitivity
to language and to cultural nuances perhaps prompted him to see what few had
really seen: Amyot seems to be the first post-print commentator to treat the
Aithiopika not as a product of sheer classical culture, as "Greek," but as the admirable production of the East. Amyot, who wants to believe his author is the

Heliodorus mentioned by Flavius Philostratus in the second book of *Lives of the Sophists*, identifies his Phoenician author as an Arab, noting that "Philostratus surnames him 'the Arab,' and that Heliodorus himself at the end of his book says that he is a Phoenician, native of the city of Emesa, which is situated at the borders of Phoenicia and Arabia" (Paris, 1547, aiii^v).[18] There is certainly no desire here to disguise the Easternness, the Otherness, within the novel tradition. In Amyot's modern language the book was enabled to make its way rapidly into the libraries and minds of all sorts of readers.

Amyot, among all these editor-critics, tackles in his "Proesme" what might be called the "Pedagogical Problem" head on. Himself a teacher, he obviously feels some skepticism about both the demand that fiction should teach and the anxiety about its corrupting influence. He acknowledges that there are enemies to novel-reading, and knows what their arguments are. He begins by remarking that a philosopher has advised that nurses not tell stories to children for fear their heads will be filled with folly; perhaps grown-ups should not read fabulous books for fear their understandings will become accustomed to lies. But, after all, Amyot argues (following Aquinas) the weakness of our nature is such that our understandings cannot be always on the stretch to read grave and serious matter, any more than our bodies can endure hard labor without intermission. When our spirits are troubled or fatigued, we need some diversion, or rather some refreshment. The natural delectation for a good understanding is to see, hear, and understand something new, and for that there is nothing like history. But it has always seemed to some men of good judgment that the truth of history makes it a little too austere to be sufficiently entertaining, because history has to recite matters barely and simply, as they happened, and not so that they are pleasant to read.

Amyot seems as well aware as Jane Austen of the arguments that place "real solemn history" above lying airy fiction. But he can retort with the Aristotle-based argument that history is limited to describing merely what happened. Historical accounts are thus not capable of sustaining our hearts (*noz courages*) which want to experience passion in reading the deeds and fortunes of another. We read fiction to supplement the imperfection of "real history" (*au default de la vraye histoire*, Aii^v). Among fictions, those that please us best are those least distanced from *la nature*, and in which there is more of *verisimilitude*.

These terms will become increasingly familiar over the next two centuries; the standards will become those of the French Academy. The idea of "verisimilitude," however, undergoes much alteration. According to the sixteenth-century and even the seventeenth-century notions of "probability" and "verisimilitude," both the *Aithiopika* and *Daphnis and Chloé* are perfectly acceptable. Artistic shaping of plot and narration does not count against the verisimilar. We must even have a certain degree of the marvelous. Amyot, in an argument derived from Strabo, maintains that the art of poetic invention (in the novel as elsewhere) requires in the first place truthfulness; secondly, an ordering that can attract the reader; and thirdly, fictitiousness itself: "Thirdly [the art consists] in fiction, of which the object is the astonishment and delight which proceed from the novelty of things strange, and full of marvels" (1547, Aii^v).[19] Such marvels are denied to true history, and, in any case, Amyot says airily, most French histories fail on all counts, being ignorant, unpleasing, and as remote from the probable as the feverish dreams of an invalid. History is often defective—Fiction produces some of the best exercise for the mind.

It would be nice if the Emperor Julian could have read Amyot's defense of *plasmata*. Amyot belongs to an age in which it is becoming *necessary* to defend the fictional; a certain guilt attaches to reading stories—guilt for Catholics and Protestants alike. Amyot has to fall back on the by now conventional arguments for the merits of "this fabulous history of the loves of Chariclea and Theagenes." Besides the "ingenious fiction" there are "beautiful discourses drawn from Philosophy Natural and Moral" as well as pertinent *sentences* (or sentiments) and beautiful speeches exhibiting the art of eloquence. That is, the novel is educational in the most overtly instructive way. It is also exemplary: "everywhere the human passions are painted in so lifelike a manner, with such great honesty [or probity], that no one would know how to draw from them an occasion or example of ill doing. For of all illicit and bad affections he has made an unhappy ending: and, in contrast, he has wrought for the good and honest a desirable and happy end" (1547, Aiiiʳ).[20]

Fiction can be justified by declaring it more moral than other kinds of writing—but only if writers fulfill their obligations. As Miss Prism was to put it in Oscar Wilde's *The Importance of Being Earnest*, "The good ended happily, and the bad unhappily. That is what Fiction means." We can see how Aristotelian "poetic justice" is working out in a strict form in the Renaissance. It becomes the duty of the writer to create clear moral examples, with rewards and punishments clearly defined within the work. The reader—the young or impressionable reader—must understand the true moral values and not be swayed from civic virtue by ambiguities. This is obviously felt to be especially necessary in the new print age, now that vernacular reading matter extends to all classes and nearly all age groups. Fiction has the freedom and thus the duty to reward virtue and punish vice—as history often fails to do. Such ideas about poetic justice or the exemplary were the new humanist ideas, in the vanguard of thought, not the rearward. It was important that fiction be earnest. Yet there is a certain strain in holding to the didactic formulations too strictly. Amyot seems happier when he deals with the formal pleasures of the novel, and with reader response:

> But above all the arrangement of it is singular, for he [Heliodorus] begins in the middle of his story, as the Heroic Poets do. This causes a great astonishment to readers at first glance, and engenders in them a passionate desire to understand the beginning: and all the time he draws them on so well by the ingenious connections of his story, that you cannot determine what you find at the very beginning of the first book until you have read to the end of the fifth. And when you have arrived at that point, you have a still greater longing to see the ending than you did before to see the beginning. In this way the understanding always remains suspended, up until you come to the conclusion, which leaves the reader satisfied, after the manner of those who succeed at last in enjoying a good ardently desired, and long awaited. (1547, Aiiiʳ)[21]

There has seldom been a better expression of the erotics of reading—and how well Amyot understands the erotics of reading *Aithiopika*, with its singular and ingenious construction. Amyot justifies Heliodorus by an appeal to the epic example, but the epic example reminds Amyot of defects in the novel. It lacks grandeur (*la grandeur*), especially because Theagenes the hero performs no memorable military exploits (*nulz memorables exploitz d'armes*, Aiiiʳ). Thomas Underdowne in the later version of his English translation in 1577 is going to contradict Amyot on this point. Underdowne here compares Heliodorus favorably with the stories of Arthur and Amadís which "accompt violente murder . . . manhode" (*An Æthiopian Historie* [London, 1577], iiiʳ). This statement seems an echo of Roger Ascham, who, in *The Schoolmaster* (1570), decries *Morte Darthur*: "the whole pleasure of which book standeth . . . in open manslaughter and bold bawdry" (68–69). Ascham also hated modern Italian books newly translated: "Suffer these books to be read, and they shall soon displace all books of godly learning" (69). The prefatory material to Underdowne's *first* edition of *An Æthiopian Historie* in 1569 makes no such insulting comments on other fictions. We may surmise that Underdowne sensed during the 1570s a rising prejudice against fiction, particularly but not only medieval narratives. Underdowne's negative remarks against Arthur and Amadís, expendable old-fashioned medieval heroes as they now might seem, are defenses intended to shield the "new" Heliodorus from Puritan hostility. What Amyot, I think, misses in Heliodorus' narrative is not the Homeric epic so much as the good old medieval story, the matter of Bretagne and of Charlemagne, in which there was plenty of fighting and the heroes were all valorous. Without an emphasis on the warlike, a story lacks grandeur—cannot have Aristotelian magnitude as the Renaissance tended to interpret it. It is noticeable that Renaissance editors and critics (as distinct from other *novelists*) shrink from giving Charikleia central place; they are always trying to find the *hero*.

Having fulfilled his obligation to defend fiction, and to recite the virtues of Heliodorus' novel as a didactic and exemplary work (falling as it were into that customary trap), Amyot apparently then became slightly impatient with that style of defense. At the end of his "Proesme," he encounters the sixteenth-century civic moralists head on, with great *brio*. There are, he says, only two kinds of people who will not like this book:

> But with respect to those who are so perfectly disposed to virtue that they neither acknowledge nor receive any pleasure other than their duty, or to those who through an incurable fever of austerity have such a depraved taste that they find nothing good, and are displeased with themselves, if by chance they reprehend this affair of mine, I shall content myself with saying to them in response, That this book was never written, nor translated for them. For those first mentioned, because they have no use for it, for the others because they are not worthy of it. (1547, Aiiiᵛ) ²²

If you are too good, don't bother. If you are just a sour hater of pleasure, the book is too good for you, and you are incapable of understanding it. With a certain degree of flippancy, Amyot closes the argument. After all, novels are for real people, for readers who are neither saints nor hypocrites. If you are a Malvolio or a Tartuffe, let novels alone—they weren't written for you.

Amyot's translation bounded through Europe, and translations into other languages were based on it. It was Amyot's version, rather than the Greek or even Latin editions, that opened the novel to the general reader—and to numerous other novelists. By the end of the sixteenth century *Aithiopika* had appeared in English, German, and Italian. Scholarly interest kept pace. A second Greek edition (by Commelinus) was printed in Augsburg in 1596. The big dual-language (Greek-Latin) edition of Johannes Bourdelotius (Jean Bourdelot) in 1619 included one hundred and twenty-three pages of annotation, to be well mined by later editors. In his address to the well-disposed reader (*Lectori Fauenti*) who is judge (*Lector Arbiter*, in *Heliodori Æthiopicorum* [1619], avi[r]), Bourdelotius complains that other commentators still have not succeeded in straightening out the plot of Heliodorus' novel, which is really quite difficult to follow, "so involved in various winding stories [*ambagibus*] that you can scarcely follow it even on a third reading except in a fog" (1619, avi[v]).[23] Bourdelotius offers his own detailed plot summary. The editor echoes Amyot's commentary in saying it is unnecessary to refute "frivolous objections," such as that the author "very often erred in his narrative as when he represents Theagenes as not disposed to fight [*imbellem Theagenem exhibet*]" (aviii[r]).[24]

Bourdelotius finds truly objectionable the kind of criticism that rescues an author like Heliodorus by claiming "that under the names of human beings Chymistrie is being described." How can we give any faith to such a lying argument? Men of distinction (*uiri clarissimi*) have undertaken the treatment of the matter of Love (*materiem Amatoriam tractandum*), he argues, linking past with present by adding, in an aside, "as I now hear of the most accomplished Barclay." Could such distinguished writers have written only in order to deal with "Chymick trumpery [*nugas Chymicas*]?" In his allusion to John Barclay, he indicates that he must already have got wind of *Argenis*, not to be published until 1621; the complimentary reference to Barclay here may veil some implicit disapproval of *Euphormio*'s allegorical schematism and scientific bent. Jean Bourdelot's abrupt and vigorous rejection of certain kinds of allegorical reading—and thus also of allegorical writing—offers an unusual example of defense of the novel and its true subject (*materies Amatoria*). The Novel is abused, he indicates, if pressed into the service of another system of meaning, especially one not related to the feelings of individual persons. The Novel should not be treated as mere gilding to a pill of knowledge. Bourdelot seems to me to be the first critic to suggest that a novel betrays itself in espousing some intellectual system the story is simply designed to illustrate. He is also the first clear spokesman against reductionist criticism of a novel.[25] Bourdelot is certainly prophetic in his concern, for the novels of the seventeenth century were to be, as Clifton Cherpack points out in *Logos in Mythos*, largely devoted to allegorizing in the service of "ideas," not to say propaganda. *Argenis* was to be a political *roman à clef* rather than *materies Amatoria*.

Heliodorus, once in circulation in print, had many European imitators, both Catholic and Protestant. Almost every major fiction-writer of the sixteenth or early seventeenth century registers the impact of the *Aithiopika*. Heliodorus' influence can be felt throughout Jorge de Montemayor's *Diana* (1560), that best-seller of the later sixteenth century. His influence is equally apparent in Honoré D'Urfé's *L'Astrée* (1607–1628). Sidney's well-known *Arcadia* is a work openly undertaken in the light of Heliodorus, and Sidney's ideal reader is a reader already acquainted with that other novel cited by him in his *Apologie for Poetrie*. Detailed studies have been done pointing out Sidney's debts and allusions to *Aithiopika*, so there is no need to rehearse them again.[26] It has been generally less well recognized that Cervantes is also powerfully affected by Heliodorus' book, both in itself and as mediated and interpreted by other novelists such as Montemayor; the *Aithiopika*'s influence, and allusions to it, can be felt in all Cervantes' important writings, including not only *La Galatea* but also *Don Quijote*. It is, however, in his last novel, *Persiles y Sigismunda*, that the Spanish novelist very deliberately takes up the challenge of the *Aithiopika* and writes "a book that ventures to compete with Heliodorus," as Cervantes himself claims.[27] The Preface to the 1741 English translation of *Persiles* quotes from Pierre Bayle's *General Historical Dictionary* (1697–1706): "The Incidents are *numerous*, and vastly various. In some we see an Imitation of *Heliodorus*, and in others *Heliodorus* greatly improved; and in the rest a perfect Newness of Fancy shines forth in the most conspicuous Manner . . . . Briefly, this Performance is of a better Invention, more artificial Contrivance and of a more sublime Stile than that of *Don Quixote de la Mancha*" (*Persiles and Sigismunda* [1741], I: A4ʳ). Posterity has not agreed with this opinion, but Bayle's view could still be taken as standard in the first half of the eighteenth century, at the end of a novel-reading and novel-writing era in which imitating or overgoing Heliodorus figure as matters of current critical understanding.

Literary critics were affected by other literary critics pronouncing upon novels both old and new. Translators and writers of introductions were major mediators of critical and theoretical ideas. In their ponderings a modern critical theory of the novel began to be born. There were no individual books of criticism on the novel, although discussion of individual novels could become very animated. There was some thought of making Heliodorus' Greek novel a text for schools (as Lucian had been). A professor at Frankfurt in the 1580s produced a summary version or "epitome" of Heliodorus' novel, an easy-to-read potted version with a plot summary (in Latin) of each book (now made into a mere chapter) followed by "Observations" and Greek quotations, and annotations upon these. Young people could perfect their Greek without having actually to read the novel itself. (It is depressing to think that almost as soon as we get printed novels we get potted versions for schools.) The epitomizer, Martinus Crusius, begins his Preface, however, rather engagingly: "Last summer vacation I went back to Heliodorus' *Aithiopika*: partly so that I could refresh my spirit with amusing reading after my labors; partly in order to nourish anew my very moderate capacity in the Greek language by means of this most eloquent Writer" (*Martinus Crvsii Æthiopicae* [Frankfurt, 1584], 3).[28] Crusius, influenced by Amyot and Cinthio, says that Heliodorus is worthy the name of a poet: "*He carries his point entirely* (said Horace) *who mixes the useful and the agreeable*. Although this is said of Poets, it can be not ill-advisedly transferred to this Writer also: for his book is not dissimilar to a poem, granting that it is a continuous prose narrative. For it is not on account of its meter, but on account of its fiction that a work is fittingly adjudged a Poem" (ibid., 5).[29]

"It is not rhyming and versing that maketh a poet," exclaims Sidney in his *Apologie for Poetrie* (written c. 1580). Sidney follows Giambattista Giraldi Cinthio, whose critical work, the *Discorsi* (1554) discussing "Romanzi," Tragedy, and Comedy, was to influence many theorists who elaborate upon or contradict him. Cinthio, who tends naturally to emphasize the Italian contribution to literature, promulgates the Aristotelian idea that prose works can be numbered among works of poetic art (although he thinks prose an unsuitable medium for stage plays). Sidney, himself a novelist, is much more specific and enthusiastic in endorsing the poetic qualities of prose fiction. The examples he calls in aid are Xenophon's *Cyropaedia*, and Heliodorus' "sugred [*sic*] invention of that picture of loue in Theagines and Cariclea" (*An Apologie* [1595], C4ʳ). A good novel must be a good "poem." The defense of the novel as a species of poetry (not necessarily just of Epic) is long-lasting. In 1761 Denis Diderot is to claim for Richardson's novels the status of three great *poèmes*, on similar grounds.

The academic Martinus Crusius praises in Heliodorus what other commentators have praised, the plot displaying Providence and divine goodness (*prouidentia & bonitas diuina*, in *Martinus Crvsii*, 6), the various travels and adventures, the satisfactory bad endings of bad characters like Knemon's step-mother and Arsaké, and the good picture of a king in Hydaspes: *prudentis, fortis, clementis, munifici, felicis, sapientibus Consiliariis firmati* (ibid., 6–7). As for this king's daughter, Although Crusius admits that the infant girl grew up in beauty of form, vivacity of wit, and greatness of soul, he still has some strong doubts about Charikleia:

> Then, it was her own fault that was the cause of evils and calamities: so that after Theagenes of Thessaly abducted this virgin from Delphi, he, with her, had to contend against many hard mishaps. The girl's deed was certainly not laudable: she set aside the man who stood to her in the place of a parent, and, under promise of matrimony, gave over the young man to the uncertain chances ensuing (as she herself at length acknowledged). However, because of the signal chastity in all this, the fidelity, the constancy in their love for each other, they were in the end able to enjoy the tranquility they wished for, and a happy union. (Ibid., 6)[30]

Such moralizings about Charikleia strike a new note. This may be accounted the beginning of a new consciousness of literary "character," which gains new life at the cost of an imposed sententiousness. Characters are to be measured according to moral (and modern) concerns—measured minutely. Here is a *scrupulosus lector* indeed! We may note that to Crusius mixed genres are acceptable, but not mixed characters. A heroine should be *exemplary*—and Charikleia is not. There is also, as we have seen in other academic writings about this novel in the sixteenth century, a marked reluctance to accord too high a status to Charikleia. It is hard to imagine that readers in Heliodorus' time had anything like Crusius' reaction to the heroine—certainly Photius did not. As we have seen, "Philip the Philosopher" thought Charikleia the perfect 777, a representative of the human being at its most advanced, and an image of the human soul in its struggles and endeavors. Such a view, despite the Neoplatonism with which the sixteenth century seems at times almost awash, does not accord with the new civic consciousness and emphasis on duty.

Charikleia offends against civic propriety, against the laws and valuable mores of the family. Protestant theologians from Luther and Calvin on had emphasized the role of the nuclear family with the father at its head, giving a high place to duty within the family, especially for women. To female historians these Protestant developments have not been a cause of unmixed rejoicing. Protestant girls, for instance, had no mode of flight from the family; if, as Protestant clerics emphasized, they could not be walled up uselessly in nasty convents, they also could not run away from sexual and family duty in the name of a higher spiritual calling. Charikleia in the name of her own calling offends against the familial and civic proprieties; lurking behind Crusius' critique is a sense that Charikleia is *selfish*. We can see how strongly Charikleia's case, once it is viewed through this Renaissance lens, anticipates the case of Richardson's heroine: Clarissa also, as some eighteenth-century critics complained, did not behave laudably, in allowing herself to be run away with and in slighting her natural guardians.

Crusius gives Heliodorus credit for mixing effects and genres, and praises him for creating a kind of Tragicomedy, which true-seeming histories are likely to be: "In fact, if we treat the whole History as if it were a Tragicomedy, we shall hardly err; as is evident from the words of Theagenes in Book V" (ibid., 8).[31] Crusius points to Theagenes' despairing deliberations upon their dramatic fate in *Aithiopika*, Book V (II:45). "Therefore to our poets," Crusius believes, "from now on, if they like, this story will be occasion and matter for composing either Tragedies or Comedies" (*Ergo & nostris Poëtis, si velint, hinc occasio & materia componendi Comoedias & Tragoedias erit*, ibid., 8).

ACHILLES TATIUS IN PRINT

Kleitophon and Leukippé, an obviously less "moral" book than *Aithiopika*, nervously rode the coattails of Heliodorus. A Latin translation was issued before the Greek text: Annibale della Croce of Milan published a Latin translation of the last four books of the novel by an author he calls "Achilles Statius" in 1544, and the whole in Basel in 1554. He complains in this edition of the novel, now called *Of the Loves of Kleitophon and Leukippé* (*de Clitophontis et Leucippes amoribus*), that what once gave him pleasure (*uoluptatem*) had become wearisome labor. His edition, however, exhibits a deal of lively playfulness, not least in its employment of various emphatic typefaces, the sort of play with print in a work of fiction that long predates Richardson and Sterne. (See Plate 21.)

Translations of Achilles Tatius into modern languages quickly ensued: an Italian translation in Venice in 1546, and again in 1550; a French version by Belleforest in 1568 and another in 1573; the first English translation in 1579. By the mid-century, given a growing appetite for fiction, the production of an original-language text, edited in approved humanistic manner, is not necessary for the appearance or success of an ancient novel. The first Greek text of Achilles Tatius was not printed until 1601.

Apologists for Achilles Tatius tended to assimilate him to Heliodorus and to praise his *style*. Francisco Angelo Coccio, Achilles Tatius' first translator into a modern language, takes this line in the Dedication of his Italian translation, which appeared originally in 1550. He quotes or rather paraphrases Photius: "Achilles Tatius seems in style and structure to be artful because the style is both clear and expressive, and when he uses abrupt transitions he uses them very appropriately; the turns of his sentences are for the most part concise, open, and sweet, and with their sound offer delight to the ears; in the construction and form of the narrations he preserves a strong resemblance to those of Heliodorus" (Venice [1560], A5ʳ).³² Coccio omits Photius' strictures against *Kleitophon and Leukippé*'s "exceeding indecency and the uncleanness of its sentiments" (*to lian hyperaischron kai akatharton tōn ennoiōn*; see *Bibliothēkē*, II:11). The author could always be praised *dalla piaceuolezza della materia, & dalla dolce maniera del dire* ("for the pleasing nature of his material and of his sweet manner of putting it," A5ʳ). Coccio, however, goes further in defending Achilles Tatius. He knows that the reader may feel embarrassed or ashamed (*uergognarsi*) in turning to a work that is a love-story, *l'opera . . . di soggetto amoroso*, A6ʳ). Neoplatonic purists argue that we should contemplate divine things with the intellect and be ashamed of stooping to talk of love. Coccio paraphrases these purists' argument only to turn it against them with his own ingenious Neoplatonist excuse for the novel of love—and thus for his author's material. In almost all times, he argues, Love has given the most copious subject matter for writing. And with reason—for Love is the true and most learned master (*Amore è il uero & dotto maestro*, A6ᵛ), who teaches everything perfectly, and from him as from a most abundant fountain, springs the principle of all our activities.³³ Without *Amore* no one can possess within the self either virtue or good. Coccio thus argues that shame at reading love-stories is a false shame, and scorn of them a false scorn, a sign of pride rather than of spiritual achievement.

Renaissance novelists began to draw on Achilles Tatius as well as on Heliodorus and other novelists, old and new. Sir Philip Sidney, whose relation to Heliodorus is so marked in the *Arcadia*, was influenced also by the *Golden Ass*, *Amadís de Gaula*, Montemayor's *Diana*, and other works, including *Kleitophon and Leukippé*. The influence of Achilles Tatius' style, though this was largely communicated through translations (especially the French), is visible—audible, rather—in Lyly's *Euphues* novels (1578; 1580). Some of the qualities of "euphuism" can be traced to what some commentators were to call an "Alexandrian" or even "African" style in both Apuleius and Achilles Tatius of Alexandria. Looked at in this light, Lyly's famous style can seem a kind of "white rap."

The influence of Achilles Tatius seems to have entered sixteenth-century fiction shortly after the first Latin translation. In the amplified version of his *Quart Livre*, Rabelais includes in the new second chapter a mock-ekphrastic scene that appears to be a direct parody of the description of the painting of Philomela's story, including the tapestry, in Book V of *Leukippé* (see 240–242). Rabelais reports on the paintings Pantagruel and his men saw in Medamouthi (i.e., Nowhere), a great mart of the merchants of Africa and Asia. Panurge bought the painting of Philomela's tapestry. "Don't think, I beg you," implores the narrator, "that this was the portrait of a man coupling with a girl. That is too stupid and gross. The painting was quite different and more intellectual [*intelligible*]" (II : 37). This statement indeed applies to the elaborate work described by Kleitophon, which also avoids direct representation of the rape in favor of reflection upon it, rendering matters *intelligible*—appealing to the intelligence. The narrator adds airily, "You can see it in Thelema, on the left as you enter the upper gallery." Here we have ekphrasis, and a picture-market (as in Achilles Tatius), and furthermore the picture is now purchased, possessed and absorbed into the fantastic world of the new novel. In his last three books Rabelais becomes most conscious of the range and drive of large-scale narrative fiction, ancient and modern. If the *Tiers Livre* is in some sense the epic book, the *Aeneid*-book, the *Quart Livre*, though full of epic reference, is most conscious of the resources and implications of current prose fiction, including the newly restored ancient novels. Allusions to and plays on novels cluster here, the same volume in which we meet the reference to Heliodorus.

To any writer or reader with a sense of the comic, Achilles Tatius would possess attractions. In the seventeenth century, editions of Achilles Tatius multiplied, including the first translation into German (1670), and a new version in English in 1638. This new translation by Anthony Hodges, *The Loves of Clitophon and Leucippe. A Most Elegant History*, is well-presented, with a charming frontispiece, a poetical explanation of the frontispiece as it implicitly reflects Achilles Tatius' *ekphrasis* at the beginning of the novel, and a Preface in which the translator worries about the difficulty of maintaining "the elegancy of a Greeke author" (A3ʳ). His other anxiety arises from the immodesty of the text, a problem now solved by excision:

> The second thing which may excuse me, is, that by the exection of the two testicles of an unchaste dispute, and one immodest expression, I have so refined the author, that the modestest matron may looke in his face and not blush. . . . That little which I have spared to English [i.e., forborne to translate], prostituted my author not onely to the censure of the Patriarch of *Constantinople*, but also of some of these times, and would have appeared as a mole in his face . . . (Oxford [1638], A3ᵛ)

The "unchaste dispute" is the argument in Book II as to whether love of girls or love of boys is best. (In 1917 the Loeb editor slides into Latin in translating this section: see 128–133.)

The advertised castration of Achilles Tatius may seem a triumph of prudery. Yet the translator is undoubtedly right in thinking that, in his newly chaste, refined, and self-conscious age, the book thus revised could enjoy a wide circulation, just like contemporary fiction. The poet Richard Lovelace writes a blurb poem "To the Ladies" advising them to read the book:

> Faire ones, breathe: a while lay by
> Blessed *Sidney's Arcady*:
> Here's a Story that will make
> You not repent *Him* to forsake;
> And with your dissolving looke

Vntie the Contents of this Booke;
To which nought (except your sight)
Can give a worthie Epithite.
Tis an abstract of all Volumes,
A Pillaster of all Columnes
Fancie e're rear'd to wit, to be
Little *Love*'s Epitome,
And compactedly expresse
All Lovers Happy Wretchednesse.
      Brave *Pamela*'s majestie,
And her sweet Sisters modestie
Are fixt in each of you, you are
Alone, what these together were:
Divinest, that are really
What *Cariclea*'s feign'd to be;
That are every One, the Nine;
And on Earth *Astraea*'s shine;
Be our *Leucippe*, and remaine
In *Her*, all these o're againe.

. . .

      (Oxford [1638], A5ᵛ–A6ʳ)

We may wish to pause, to consider whether such a verse indicates a growing "feminization" of the reader in this period, as Danahy and others have argued.[34] There is no suggestion with *Amadís* or *Arcadia* or *Diana* or sixteenth-
century translations of Heliodorus and others that the larger readership for these
works is not masculine. Gentleman readers are always assumed. But the new
civic moralizing, the concerns over wasting time, may be pushing the novel officially more and more towards the young and the female. Lovelace's verse perhaps
makes Sidney's Pamela and Achilles Tatius' Leukippé less universally representative, more locally and specifically feminine. They are attractive models for young
ladies, exemplary in a more specialized way. Another prefatory verse, however,
by a less gifted author, suggests that Kleitophon offers a model for young *male*
readers, especially in teaching them what to avoid—such as modern Melittés.

We should also recognize in Lovelace's verse a certain joyful universality
that is not yet confined and limited. Lovelace is able still to share the sixteenth
century's happy contemporaneity. All literature is contemporary, all is present.
No gaps of time separate readers from books, or from characters. Modern and
ancient fiction are thoroughly intermixed in Lovelace's list; Sidney's Pamela and
Philoclea are equated with Charikleia and with D'Urfé's Astrée, and all with Leukippé. That is, *Arcadia* (1590), *Aithiopika* (c. 250–300), *L'Astrée* (1607–1627), and
Kleitophon and Leukippé (c. 250) can be contemporary. Each is present to all the
others.

Such an expansiveness of temporal view is one of the great advantages
enjoyed by the Renaissance. Constant *new* translations had dimmed any sense
that these works were particularly old—and to the Renaissance, in any case, the
antique "old" was not dusty or *passé*, but full of potential for the future. Lovelace's

verse well illustrates the naturalizing process of the sixteenth and the seventeenth centuries, as older and newer fictions alike were continuously presented and re-presented to an enthusiastic readership. The enthusiasm is even more undoubted than the moralizing—in fact, the moralizing would not have been so prevalent had the enthusiasm not been so uncomfortably real. But the process of naturalization was coming to an end by the time Richard Lovelace wrote his jocular lines. Readers of the sixteenth and early seventeenth century had cultivated the undisturbed enjoyment of a perpetual present. But commentators were soon to be more sharply aware of the historical nature of fiction itself.

CHAPTER XI

><+•>─0─<•+><

Novels in the Seventeenth Century: Histories of Fiction and Cultural Conflicts

><+•>─0─<•+><

The Persians first affected this kind of amorous literature . . . Certainly they gave to the Arabs the fashion of this same kind of writing and the genius for it. The Arabs then transmitted it to the Spanish. From the Spanish we Gauls in turn took it, and from them indeed it also went elsewhere.   —Salmasius, Preface to *Kleitophon and Leukippé*, 1640

. . . a Prayer stol'n word for word from the mouth of a Heathen fiction . . . , & that in no serious Book, but the vain amatorious poem of Sir Philip Sidneys *Arcadia* . . .   —John Milton, *Eikonoklastes*, 1649

POETRY, by which terme I meane, FICTION, in the largest extent. Under *this*, are comprehended the highest & noblest productions of man's wit, ROMANCES.
     —John Davies of Kidwelly, Introduction to *Astrea*, 1657

><+•>─0─<•+><

PRODUCING AND IMITATING THE ANCIENT NOVELS

The Renaissance festival of fiction-reading and fiction-creating, a festival which entailed the unselfconscious assimilation of the antique novel, continued unabated and reached some kind of peak in the early to mid-seventeenth century. Booksellers and printers could count on a widespread readership. Confidence in the market encouraged the production of elegant books, often very beautifully illustrated. There is, for example, *Les Amovrs de Clytophon, et de Levcippe* (Paris, 1635) with many pictures, including a frontispiece stressing the *ekphrasis* of Europa. (See Plate 22.) Illustrations were not restricted to old novels; new books were illustrated, too, customarily with frontispieces to each individual book of a novel, as with the novels of Madeleine de Scudéry. Nor were illustrations meant only for the unlearned; pictures accompanied texts in Greek and Latin.

The darling of the illustrators was—and always has been—Longus' *Daphnis and Chloé*. The Greek text was not printed until 1598 (in Florence). But Amyot, who had been so successful with Heliodorus, published his French translation of *Daphnis and Chloé* in 1559, and subsequent versions relied heavily on it. Longus' story becomes almost synonymous with "pastorals" (*pastoralia*), and its influence can be felt in Montemayor's *Diana*, in Sidney's *Arcadia*, Cervantes' *Galatea*, and other works; far-off echoes of it can be heard in the youthful loves of Tom and Becky in Twain's *Tom Sawyer*.

George Thornley wrote two prefaces for his translation of 1657. The second preface, "To the Criticall Reader," repeats testimonials by earlier Renaissance critics and editors to the excellence of Longus' work, and picks up "a Snapdragon Objection," that translation into English would spoil the poetry of the language. The first preface, "To young Beauties," is gallant, sexually flirtatious, and even broad: "This little, pleasaunt Laundschip of Love, by its own destiny, and mine, belongs most properly to your fair eyes, and hands, and happier laps. And then, who would not lay his legge over a book; although that, sometimes has been the complaint of a Schollar's solicitude?" (London [1657], A3ʳ). There is nothing to alarm you, says Thornley, in this account of ancient rural customs interspersed with "old and sweet Tales"; he teasingly protests, in a Sternean manner, that the sexuality is the reader's: "And in short, nothing to vex you, unlesse perchance, in your own conscience" (A3ᵛ). Thornley admits a masturbatory element in the reading of an erotic story—a male masturbation is indicated ("his legge") but perhaps female also ("happier laps"). Reading this story about desire could be sexually arousing. Thornley evidently imagines that both young men and young women will read the book, even though his full title is *Daphnis and Chloe. A Most Sweet, and Pleasant Pastorall Romance for Young Ladies*. The frontispiece to Thornley's book is a kind of awkward Valentine, advertising both the process of falling in love and the erotic power of the press that produces the book and the pictures (Plate 23).

The eighteenth century produced appealing rococo illustrations; see the picture of the old man and Eros in a 1718 French edition of *Daphnis and Chloé* (see Plate 24). The most notorious illustration of that novel is a mid-eighteenth-century picture that came to be known as "Les Petits Pieds"—"The Little Feet." This is a comic illustration, by one who signs himself only "a pupil of Picart," of the initiation of Daphnis by Lykainion. The viewer, like the puzzled dog (presumably belonging to Daphnis) cannot see the real scene itself, but only anatomical parts suggesting the whole. This picture appears facing a Greek text (see Plate 25), showing that seriousness was not implicitly associated with reading the learned language; the picture, however, was not restricted to the view of those who knew the learned language.

As Thornley's title shows, translators and editors felt at liberty to change the title of an ancient work to meet contemporary taste. Nowhere is the festive naturalization process better illustrated than in the repeated variation of title. Changes in literary fashion (and perhaps in readership) can sometimes be traced in the differing titles given to any one of the older novels from the sixteenth through the eighteenth centuries. We may be given a new emphasis on the love-story ("The Loves of Cleitophon and Leucippe"), or the stress may be placed on adventure ("The Adventures of Theagenes and Charikleia"). A version of 1720 gives us *The Amours of Clitophon and Leucippe. Illustrated, In Six Novels*—the six "Novels" being six important episodes, here given titles such as "The Disappointed Bride," a practice reminding us of the popularity of the short fictional form, the "novel" (or *novella*), in the late seventeenth and early eighteenth century. The presentation of any one of the ancient novels is likely to make it as up-to-date as possible. On the other hand, a truly new fiction could be introduced (and thus advertised) by relating it to a well-known novel, whether of ancient days or more recent times.

"NEW" ANCIENT NOVELS: PETRONIUS, CHARITON, XENOPHON

The later seventeenth century witnessed what was in effect the emergence of one truly "new" ancient novel, Petronius' *Satyricon*. The publication of the re-assembled *Satyricon* was a cause for celebration, even though the first text of the "restored" version (Amsterdam, 1669) was defective, and the next big edition (Rotterdam, 1694) contained forged material. A good deal had already been known about *Satyricon*, even in its previous severely defective state. There are some surprisingly pretty manuscripts, such as the one in Vienna with its first page set off in an elaborate border in pink, blue, green, and gold (MS Cod. Ser. n. 4755, see Plate 26). Such an illuminated manuscript indicates wealthy and sophisticated readers. As soon as Petronius' book came into print, it began to attract profuse commentary, though sixteenth-century editors and commentators had a severely truncated and mutilated text to work with. The editor of a 1587 Paris edition compares the work with the comic plays of Menander, and with Apuleius, suggesting a visible genre of comic novels to which this work belongs: *Hoc totum fabularum genus* ("all this genre of stories," iiiᵛ). Yet it must be admitted that the sense of any *narrative* genre is most indistinct. The prefatory section dealing with "this kind of writing" (*hoc scribendi genus*) deals with satire, basing the argument on Roman poetic satirists, and placing Petronius on a line running from Lucilius through Horace, as well as relating him to Menippus (ivʳ).

Petronius' *Satyricon* was a literary influence long before it was reassembled in its modern form. John Barclay in his youth published a *Satyricon* (1603–1607). This work (also known as *Euphormio*) is a novel exhibiting the influence of Petronius and Apuleius, as well as of all the Roman satirists alluded to by the 1587 editor of Petronius. *Euphormio*, an attack on the Jesuits (among other things) is a creative and contemporary employment of the Roman style of novel.[1] It is easy to suppose Barclay had read Firenzuola's free (not to say brassy) adaptive version of Apuleius. Had Barclay written his story in the vernacular, either English or French, his *Satyricon* might have passed permanently into the ranks of well-known Renaissance works, like its coeval, Thomas Nashe's *Unfortunate Traveller* (1594), a novel that may also bear the imprint of the *Satyricon* as well as the more open influence of the Spanish picaresque fictions. Barclay became better known for the moral *Argenis* (1621), and his earlier and more light-hearted work did not survive its century.

Petronius figures in another work of 1621, Robert Burton's *Anatomy of Melancholy*; Burton alludes not only to the well-known story of the widow of Ephesus (as proof that no widower should grieve over the loss of a wife) but also to Encolpius' first encounter with Eumolpus, and to the would-be poet's explanation of why poets are badly dressed (*Anatomy of Melancholy*, Pt. II: 183; Pt. I: 309). Burton has a good knowledge of the antique novels, a knowledge he expects readers to share; he cites both Charikleia and Kleitophon (with quotations) as exemplifying the symptoms of love (Pt. III: 134, 139).

Bourdelotius had produced a learned edition of Petronius in 1618, a year before his annotated Heliodorus. There is already too much material on this author, Bourdelotius complains; he comically laments the huge pile of scholarship confronting him: "Of the Critics who have written prefaces to Petronius Arbiter, there is not one who is not conscious of his wit even to a hair. So declares that huge heap of Emendations, Conjectures, Notes, Animadversions, Miscellanies, Excerpts, Clusterings, Sheaves, Symbols—and as many other new names as they can dress them up in—which seek out the reader already disgusted with stronger fare" ("Sweetly I admonish my reader" [Paris (1618), aiv^v).[2]

The list suggests that Bourdelotius had spent some time, not unprofitably, with Rabelais. He boasts that he can write what takes others three pages in as many lines—a valuable talent, even then, when summarizing studies of Petronius. The heap of material was to increase enormously with the advent of the fuller version of the novel. This new *Satyricon* was produced with handsome illustrations, even in relatively "learned" editions with extensive notes. The Latin-French edition published in Utrecht in 1709 has a very fine title page and frontispiece; the same edition has a good comic illustration of the old woman's wrath at Encolpius over the dead goose (Plate 27). The illustrations' deliberate mixture of a parodic stiff classicism with "low" material is obviously part of the fun, and offers some clues as to contemporary readings of Petronius.

The new *Satyricon* was eagerly absorbed into the gigantic body of new fiction. It became well-known (Addison refers to it in the *Spectator*), and its presence is fully felt in the novels of the eighteenth century. There is more than a little of the *Satyricon* behind Alain-René Le Sage's *Le Diable boiteux* (1707), while the breaks and peculiar montages of Petronius (the more apparent because of our actual loss of narrative) became an inspiration for Sterne's *Tristram Shandy*.

The ancient novel that is really excluded from the festival of novel-reading and novel publication from the early Renaissance to the Enlightenment is Chariton's *Chaireas and Kallirrhoé*. It seems to me that there are clear reasons why it was not printed in the sixteenth century, even though scholars were browsing through manuscript libraries, looking for works to translate or edit. The famous Byzantine manuscript in Florence, *codex Laurentianus*, containing Longus, Achilles Tatius, and Xenophon of Ephesus as well as Chariton, had long been available and visible. But the near-crucifixion of Chaireas could pose problems for the writer seeking a Christian public and not wishing to be accused of heresy. Mere sexual impropriety could be laughed at or slightly suppressed—but after all, Kallirrhoé is an adulterous wife who successfully commits polyandry. Chariton's novel was not available in the sixteenth and seventeenth centuries. In 1700 Salvinius (Antonio Salvini) wrote out a copy of the whole manuscript, intending to edit both Chariton and Xenophon of Ephesus; he was prevented by death. *Chaereas and Kallirrhoé* did not make its appearance until 1750, when M. Jacques-Phillipe D'Orville published the Greek text with notes and a Latin translation by Reiskius (J. J. Reiske). D'Orville prefigures Erwin Rohde in placing Chariton at the end of the novel tradition, noting with displeasure his inferior and idiomatic Greek. D'Orville is also the first critic to suggest that "Chariton of Aphrodisias" is a made-up *persona*, suited to the telling of an erotic novel. "Chariton" is to be praised if reservedly, for straightforward narration of the probable, without anything of the miraculous, "in which kind *Heliodorus* and *Achilles Tatius* indulge themselves from time to time" (*Charitōnos Aphrodisieōs* [Amsterdam, 1750], xix). And the novelist is moral: "he is certainly to be praised in this, that neither word nor sentiment is ever to be found in him at which even the severest reader could wrinkle his brow [*severissimus lector frontem corruget*]." In this respect Chariton far exceeds Xenophon and Achilles Tatius, but their offense is to be imputed to their supposedly earlier and more licentious period or age (*saeculum*). The eighteenth century has a newly developed (if often erroneous) sense of *period*.

These notions are repeated by Chariton's translators. Some translators share D'Orville's unease with the possibly low station of Chariton as secretary or amanuensis, a matter rehashed by Larcher in his French translation of 1763, which echoes D'Orville's repudiation of "Chariton of Aphrodisias" as a real identity. Both of the immediate Italian translations (1752; 1755) pick up the praise of the Greek author's scrupulous delicacy: "It contains nothing which could give the least offense to minds most tenderly observant of the proprieties, and of the most delicate modesty" (*Di Caritone Afrodisieo* [Venice, 1755], iv). It is scarcely surprising to find the first English editor, publishing *The Loves of Chaireas and Callirrhoe* in 1764, insisting that Chariton "cannot be too much applauded for the chastity of his pen; it not presenting a single image that may raise a blush in the most modest cheek" (*The Loves of Chaereas and Callirrhoe*, 2 vols. [London, 1764], a2ᵛ). Instead of merely censuring such pudency, we may admire it as a stratagem by which a rather difficult novel could be presented in a reassuring way.

The English editor seems, however, to have taken Chariton's modesty very literally. To prove that his author is utterly chaste, this editor explains that he set his female children to translating it—and that is how this version came about:

> With regard to this English version, it was at first no more than an extensive Exercise, I had set two of my Daughters; the enlightening of whose minds I have ever thought a more worthy object, than the advancing of my own fortune. . . . Their version, which I revised with as much attention as many other indispensable duties would permit, was first drawn from an elegant Italian translation of Chariton, printed in quarto at Rome, anno 1752. . . . It was afterwards compared with Mr. Reiskius's Latin translation of our author, and occasionally with the original, and Mr. D'Orville's notes. (London, 1764, a3ʳ–a3ᵛ)

This is hardly a prepossessing advertisement for the work, either for its scholarship or its entertainment value. Who wants to read a Greek novel taken out of the Italian by young girls doing their homework?

Chariton's book had the misfortune to arrive on the scene in the 1750s when the tide was turning against ancient novels and many other kinds of fiction hitherto popular. Xenophon of Ephesus had a slightly happier fate; Cocchius (Antonio Cocchi) printed the Greek first edition of *Ephesiaka* in 1726, and an Italian translation based on Salvini's version had already appeared (announcing itself as printed in London but more probably in Florence) in 1723. The translator admires *Degli Amori Di Abrocome e d'Anthia* for its fast action—"Happenings upon wonderful Happenings, wonderfully and clearly described" (*Accidenti sopra Accidenti maravigliosi e maravigliosamente e nettamente descritti*, "London," 1723, A8ᵛ). In the English version, *Xenophon's Ephesian History: or the Love-Adventures of Abrocomas and Anthia*, the translator explains that he has "given a different Turn to one Passage" as representing matter "entirely repugnant to the Genius and Customs of our Country" (3d ed., London, 1727, A4ʳ). The English translator has changed the love-story of Hippothous in Book III, turning it from a homosexual to a heterosexual account by the simple device of changing Hyperanth*es* into Hyperanth*e*, and having Hippothous see *her* "in a Dance" instead of *him* at the gymnastic exercises (ibid., 58). In spite of such free surgery, like the seventeenth-century translator's excision of "testicles" from Achilles Tatius, or more truly *because* of such moralizing liberty, editors could still be fairly sure of reaching a popular readership. Even as late as the 1720s, foreign, antique, or experimental works could still be absorbed into the literary bloodstream fairly quickly. It does not seem that *Ephesiaka* was wholly without influence. One may at least choose to detect it within Prévost's *Histoire d'une Grecque moderne* (1741), an ambiguous tale about a French ambassador's love for a Greek slave whom he liberates but wishes to possess. Françoise Létoublon has pointed out that in the very title the "modern Greek" heroine encourages the reader to think of the parallels, the stories of "ancient Greek" heroines. In her article "La 'Modernité' de la Grecque de Prévost et la Tradition Grecque du Genre Romanesque" (1989), Létoublon suggests Chariton as an analogue, but thinks it unlikely that Prévost could have come upon his novel. Xenophon's *Ephesiaka* is a more certain influence, but Prévost's Théophé, the beautiful Greek, is chiefly "a modern avatar of Charikleia" who becomes "a sort of Arsaké" (97). Although the heroine certainly bears a resemblance to Charikleia, she seems psychologically closer to the slyer, more elusive, Anthia—but an Anthia seen from without by a puzzled and imperfect observer. In Prévost's story, the heroine's duplicity is emphasized, as are the cultural pressures at work on her; we notice in the Greek novels themselves the duplicity of the heroines, and their ambiguous position, but in Prévost we see through a befuddled male narrator who resembles the unwanted and self-deluding suitors of the heroine in Greek novels—as if Kallirrhoé's Dionysios or Anthia's Perilaos had become central narrator. Prévost's novel is also a revisiting of Mme. de Lafayette's *Zayde*'s male protagonist Consalve.

A more ambitious European novel of the late eighteenth century overtly incorporates elements of many ancient novels. Christoph Martin Wieland's *Geschichte von Agathon* (1773–1794), a symbolic and argumentative novel set in antiquity, uses as its narrative base a variety of incidents and personages adapted from ancient fiction. It is related to the *Kebētos Pinax* as well as to Longus, Apuleius, Petronius, and Heliodorus—all cited in the text. The hero, having served in the temple at Delphi, is captured by pirates and sold into slavery. He falls in love with a *hetaira*, Danae, who later proves herself a purified beautiful soul (*schöne Seele*). After telling her story, the former prostitute begs Agathon, "Let thy Friend go under the name *Chariklea*" as this is the name she has taken in her new life (734). Agathon's other beloved is the fair and elusive Psyche, at last revealed to be his sister.

Wieland's knowledge of late antique fictions, like his interest in them, was very far-reaching. He was later to write *Menander und Glycerion* (1803), a novella fulfilling the suggestions found in Alciphron's *Epistolai*. It would not be surprising if the newly discovered Chariton should arouse Wieland's interest, and I believe that the experiences of Agathon bear some strong resemblances to the experiences and emotions of Chaireas. (The abduction by pirates, however, seems strongly to resemble an event in the Byzantine *Rodanthé and Dosikles*.) Chariton's hero, like Wieland's, has to learn what virtue is through a variety of harsh or puzzling, sometimes comic, experiences, frequently in separation from the female of choice. Wieland's hero is named after an important character in Plato's *Symposium*, and the novelist's chief concern is to find how to reconcile earthly desire and existence with spiritual being and yearning—a major problem of the Novel altogether. In playfully adapting the stories and styles of a number of fictions, old and new, Wieland obviously wishes to show himself as the successor of other synthesizing heroes of fiction such as Boccaccio. He is an important influence on Goethe, and beyond Wieland also we can see the coming shade of Thomas Mann.

If *Chaireas and Kallirrhoé* is one of the elements at work in Wieland's *Agathon*, that would represent the major claim of Chariton's novel to an influence on modern fiction. But, although the English editor could trumpet the golden recovery of *Chaereas* as "no inconsiderable acquisition to the republic of letters" (A7ʳ), Chariton's book came too late upon the scene (and with too little *empressement*) to participate in that vigorous process of naturalization begun in the fifteenth century. Its subsequent reputation has suffered from its belatedness.[3] The time of novelistic burgeoning that encouraged engrafting and intermixture of old and new was nearly at a close in 1750. Chariton was doomed to be swallowed up by the German scholars without having had much modern life.

That was not the case for the other ancient novels printed during the Renaissance. They kept on being visible until and even through the Enlightenment. The line between old and new had remained remarkably (and helpfully) blurred; ancient novels, Boccaccio's prose narratives, the works of Rabelais and of the new Cervantes had all blended into a world of acceptable fiction. Writers wrote for readers aware of both old and new novels. A modern writer of fiction such as Madeleine de Scudéry (writing under the name of her brother Georges) could imitate the style and manner of Heliodorus, at the same time offering a good deal of novelty, and challenging both classical and medieval ideas of the heroic. The beginning of Scudéry's *Clélie* (1654–1660) imitates the structure of the *Aithiopika*: an exciting and puzzling event takes place (a bride is abducted right after an earthquake) and the rest of the volume is, in essence, flashback explanation of all the background to this extraordinary incident, as narrated by the hero's friend Celère to the concerned Princesse de Leontins. The name of this princess brings to mind *Wonders beyond Thule*, in which the heroine Derkyllis is taken as a captive to the chief of the Leontins in Sicily, where she is unexpectedly reunited with her brother (Photius, *Bibliothēkē*, II: 143). Scudéry's works exhibit traces of the *Cyropaedia* and the *Alexander Romance*, as well as of the rarer *Wonders beyond Thule*, now available (since 1606) in a Latin printed version. But the *Aithiopika* is a major influence.

Heliodorus continued to be imitated in modern fiction. Richardson at the beginning of *Clarissa* seems to be imitating the Heliodoran opening gambit, if rather more quickly; we are offered an exciting and disturbing event, a sudden fight or "rencounter," bloodshed—and have to unriddle it by finding out the events that led up to this beginning. Frances Burney in *The Wanderer* (1814) also

imitates the initial confusion on a beach; the riddling opening demands explanation that comes by slow installments and is not complete until the middle of the
book.[4] Scudéry, a transmitter of the influences of the classical novel, remains on
the scene for a long while; the reading of the French *romans à longue haleine* proceeded with undiminished vigor up to the 1730s. If she imitates Heliodorus, Scudéry also looks forward to Proust; her characters (and her writing) are, like his,
discursive, anxious, and spatially conscious, if not as imagistic. Reading the two
writers during the same week may result in genuine confusions. Proust himself
pays tribute to Scudéry by referring to her celebrated "Carte de Tendre" in *Du côté
de chez Swann* (349), the first part of his own immense *roman à longue haleine*.
Long-breathed Kalasiris leads the way for these other long-breathed narrators of
lengthy and intricate fictions.

   In the late sixteenth century and in the seventeenth century new satiric
fictions, such as *Lazarillo de Tormes* (1553) or *Guzman de Alfarache* (1599–1604) or
Le Roman comique (1651), were assimilated all the more readily because their
readers had shared the reading of novels of the past, including the works of Apuleius, Boccaccio, and Achilles Tatius. Mateo Alemán's *Guzman d'Alfarache*, published in England, translated (by James Mabbe) as *The Rogue* in 1622, exhibits the
influence of Achilles Tatius as well as of Apuleius. There even appear to be direct
verbal echoes: "Now they being weary with punching vs, and wee with suffering
it" (London, 1622, 62): so Mabbe translates *Ya cansados de aporrcarnos, y nosotros
de suffrillo* (Madrid, 1599, 49). Alemán's wording seems to be an adaptation of
Kleitophon's *epei de ekamen, ho men tuptōn, egō de philosophōn* (290).

   The kind of receptivity we have observed entails an impatience with historical categorizing of the works themselves. In the fifteenth and sixteenth centuries, editors and commentators discuss *particular* novels; each book is a sort of
discrete sensation. Allusions to works other than those by the author under discussion are rare, and comparisons between modern works and the ancient novels
are at first almost nonexistent—which makes Underdowne's references to Arthur
and Amadís the more welcome. Critics refer to *hoc genus*, "that kind of writing"
without clarifying what they think that *genus* is. Nobody in the sixteenth century
took up the peculiar challenge that Cinthio threw out; there was much discourse
about literature in general, but very little about the novel as a genre. The sixteenth century had been most sensitive to the immediacy of all this "new" fiction,
whether it were really "new" like the works of Rabelais or Montemayor, or
freshly released from the prison of manuscript, whether it had been composed in
the thirteenth century or in the third. It was left to the seventeenth century to
organize the material according to a temporal scheme, in an era which was beginning to be freshly sensitive to the idea of eras and to temporal schemes. Analytical
history is itself a work of the Enlightenment.

CONSTRUCTING A HISTORY OF PROSE FICTION

The first important prose treatise to offer a history of fiction in this period is not
very long. It is in fact constituted by the dedicatory "Praefatio" and the address
"To the Reader" (*Ad Lectorem*) prefixed by Salmasius to his Greek-Latin edition of
Kleitophon and Leukippé, entitled *Erōtikōn Achilleōs Tatiou, Sive de Clitophontis & Lev-*

cippes Amoribus (*The Erotic Story of Achilles Tatius, Or, Of the Loves of Kleitophon and Leukippé*). This scholarly version of 1640 appears in a kind of pocket edition, suited to the traveler; perhaps Napoleon's copy (now in the Bodleian Library) was the resort of leisure moments during campaigns. Salmasius' edition, however scholarly, is obviously a book for pleasure-reading; it has a charming title-page vignette showing Eros guiding the lovers. (See Plate 28.) Salmasius (the French scholar Claude de Saumaise) was an internationally respected Protestant human-ist; he is best known to the English for having written the treatise against the killing of Charles I to which Milton wrote a rejoinder. Salmasius jokes that Achil-les Tatius' text as published before was in nearly as bad shape as its heroine: "his Leucippé was in no more filthy case, when whipped, with shaven head, in the role of a slave, she was not recognized by her own Clitophon even when she was standing in plain sight" ("Praefatio," Leiden, 1640, *3ᵛ).⁵ Achilles Tatius is said to have been a bishop, but Salmasius comments: "it is certain that he was not a Christian when he composed this book. What he writes of the love of boys, and what Clitophon admits about his own adultery, sufficiently argue a man alien to Christian discipline. That he might have been able to take the oath of allegiance to Christ afterwards, I am not willing to meddle with, as I am unable to refute whoever should say otherwise" (*Ad Lectorem*, *8ᵛ).⁶ Yet, the pious and learned Salmasius admires his author. Achilles Tatius and Heliodorus are the best and most outstanding authors of love stories (*optimi ac præstantissimi erōtikōn auctores*) of the works that have survived to this day and have reached the hands of men of leisure, desirous of an elegant inactivity, i.e., of tasteful relaxation (*manibus hominum otiosorum & elegantis inertiæ studiosorum*). Salmasius engages in a system-atic comparison of the two novelists:

> Heliodorus is more expressive in this kind [i.e., than Achilles Tatius, and Eustathius and Prodromos], and superior in the more highly wrought style, even advertising the eloquence that he promises and excels in. Certainly he is the more abundant, and with the clear and pleasant expansion of his diffuse discourse he allures his reader and holds him. But our author [i.e., Achilles Tatius] is the disciple of a simpler and more unaffected elegance, so that you can plainly see in him the acute expressiveness peculiar to home-born Alexandrians and the charm of their native speech, written with wonderful wit and pleasantry. Everywhere he is more succinct, and abruptly interjects his shimmering aphorisms. The variety of plot situations and turns of events are more wonderful in Heliodorus, although Achilles is not de-fective in that respect. Our author intermixes some *episodes* which are a bit more lascivious, whereas Heliodorus is always chaste. This kind of writing was altogether ancient; and further, it has been popular with many of the politer peoples formerly, and is so today. (1640, *8ᵛ–9ʳ)⁷

Salmasius thinks of Achilles Tatius as a specifically *Alexandrian* writer. A modern classicist will hasten to add that this just means a Greek-speaker from one par-ticular ancient city, for modern classicism has largely sought to erase African content or influence from classical sites. Yet Salmasius is certainly aware of the cosmopolitan nature of Alexandria. Arguably he intends, in stressing Achilles Tatius' existence as an *Alexandrinische Mensch*, some emphasis on this author as an African—though Salmasius is more explicitly interested in contact with India, pointing out that the author knows at least one Indian word and is aware of trade with India.

Salmasius does not get very far with a generic definition of the novel ("this kind of writing") but the matter of its *popularity* leads him to search for a history. He continues:

> The Persians first affected up this kind of amorous literature, whether in prose or in verse, or rhythmic speech, in which they excelled. And they can be seen in every period to delight in fables written in this mode. You will not find it hard to believe that of old they introduced the beginning [*originem*] of Milesian fables in Asia [i.e., Asia Minor] which they ruled. Certainly they gave to the Arabs the fashion of this same kind of writing and the genius for it. The Arabs then transmitted it to the Spanish. From the Spanish we Gauls in turn took it, and from them indeed it also went elsewhere. (1640, *9ʳ)[8]

Salmasius thus traces a clear line of *transmission* for the European novel. It stemmed ultimately from the Persians, came to Asia Minor (and thence to the classical world), then traveled with the Arabs (or Moors) to Spain, and thence spread through the whole of Europe. It is thus a truly Eastern form of literature, to which all Europeans are to some extent latecomers, but it is a form of literature enjoyed by the "politer" nations (*populis politioribus*), by all civilized people with a culture.

Salmasius is, I think, the first to propose such a very clear track for the novel, a map of its historical and geographical progress. But it is hard not to believe that he got his idea to some extent from Cervantes. Everyone who has read *Don Quijote* remembers that the putative Narrator of chapter nine comes upon a boy selling old paper and parchment in the streets of Toledo. The Narrator purchases a parchment book written in Arabic but is unable to read it. He needs an interpreter, a Castilian-speaking "morisco" who could read it to him, "and it wasn't very difficult to discover such a translator [*intérprete*], any more than it would have been hard, had I sought one, to find a translator for another greater and more ancient language" (*Don Quijote*, Part I, 93). The even older and better language is Hebrew; both Jews and "Moors" can still be found, despite the ban against them, and only through them do we have keys to the meanings of the most important writings, sacred and profane. They can *read*. The translating Moor reads, translates, and sometimes indeed interprets what is supposedly the book itself, the narrative about "Don Quijote," which is written in Arabic by the Moor Cide Hamete Benengeli (a last name that means "son of eggplant"). Cervantes has in jest and earnest drawn a line of transmission here, suggesting that Western fiction has a Moorish and Arab origin, and, like sacred Scripture itself, comes to us from the East.

Bishop Pierre-Daniel Huet makes the connection between Cervantes and Salmasius in his *Traité de l'origine des romans* (first version published in 1670).[9] Huet is somewhat indignant about Salmasius' giving the Novel to the Spanish, and one of his impulses is to claim a higher place for the French: "From the great number of novel writers that one sees in France from the beginning of the third dynasty of our Kings, we got many, many old Novels, of which one part is in print, another rots in the Libraries, and the rest has been consumed by length of years. And it is from us that Italy, and Spain which has been so fertile in Novels, took the art of composing them" (*Traité de l'origine des romans*, 8th ed. [Paris, 1711], 166).[10] Even "Geraldus" (Cinthio) admitted how much Italy owed to the troubadours (166–167). Provence is a cradle of the novel. "The late monsieur de Saumaise, whose memory I hold in singular veneration, both for his great learning and for the friendship which there was between us, believed that Spain, after having been taught by the Arabs the art of novelizing (*l'art de romaniser*), taught it by example to all the rest of Europe" (168–169).[11] But, Huet contends, such an opinion would require the dismissal of all Dark Age works composed before the time of Mohammed, and does not allow for the time required for Arab novels to circulate in Spain, and for Arab-influenced Spanish novels to circulate through the rest of Europe. It is wrong to believe that we owe the entire European novel to the Muslim Arabic-speakers of Spain, even though this popular belief comes to us from Cervantes:

> Miguel de Cervantes, one of the greatest geniuses Spain has ever produced, made a fine and judicious Critique of the matter in his Don Quixote, which he feigns to have translated from the Arabic of Cide Hamete Benengeli, thus making evident his error concerning the origin of Spanish Novel-writing (*Romancerie Espagnole*). The Curé of his hero's village and Master Nicholas the Barber hardly find among the great number [i.e., of Spanish novels] six which are worthy to be preserved. . . . But all of those are recent in comparison to our old Novels, which probably were the models of these. (174–176)[12]

Yet, though Huet gets so worked up in his patriotism, he himself poses a line of influence running from East to West, and from Africa to Europe. He is really more resentful of the claim of *Spain* than of the Arabs. As he says at the beginning of his *Traité*, "It is neither in Provence nor in Spain, as many believe, that we must hope to find the first beginnings of this agreeable amusement of good idle folk (*cét agréable amusement des honnestes paresseux*): we must go to seek them in the most distant countries, and in the most remote antiquity" (2).[13] One can see that Huet, who is tracking Salmasius, picks up and parodies Salmasius' defensive "men of leisure, desirous of elegant inactivity," turning these otiose personages into the less genteel "honest lazy folk" (*honnestes paresseux*).

Scholars of the seventeenth century do not shine as well when they are trying to draw a definite line of transmission as when they are discussing the complex and polyglot nature of the novel itself. As we can see, all agree on the novel's Eastern and African aspects. Growing nationalism has not yet enclosed the novel within narrow national boundaries. Neither has the temporal boundary found its later strength. In the seventeenth century, as in the sixteenth, there is a mingling of old and new, the remote with the neighboring.

The Renaissance festival of novel-reading lasted until the early or mid-eighteenth century. We can trace what is going on by looking at the occurrence of new editions and translation of the old novels. Heliodorus, for instance, is translated into English by Nahum Tate and a "person of quality" in the 1680s, translated again in 1717—and then not again until 1789, when, perhaps stimulated by Clara Reeve's hesitant and surprised remarks about Heliodorus in *The Progress of Romance* (1785), a new translator issues a modern version, comparing Heliodorus in his Preface to Richardson and Frances Burney.

But by the late eighteenth century another history of the Novel was being proposed, along with a definition of fiction (or fictions) that could have been consciously designed to obscure from view the glorious international history of the Western novel. Perhaps the writing of what Jane Austen's Catherine Morland would call "real solemn history" of the Novel itself was part of the problem. Novels were now palpably not peripheral phenomena, but part of the cultural mainstream. They found their way into Pierre Bayle's gigantic folio *Dictionnaire Historique et Critique* (1697), ancestor of the Enlightenment *Encyclopédie*. Bayle spends a good deal of space on Heliodorus, for instance, in various references as well as in the central entry. In this article, however, despite Bayle's respect for the author, he takes note of and quotes a recent work entitled *Parnasse Reformé*, in which Theagenes complains of the load of chastity his novelist (*mon Romaniste*) has laid upon him—and is joined in this complaint by Charikleia! (*Dictionaire* [1697], Vol. II, Part II, 38–39). As this adumbration of Enlightenment libertinism indicates, novels (with their attendant criticism) had become an important site of debate upon ideas and behavior. The presence of the new History of the Novel created by Salmasius and Huet had raised the form into public awareness as a strong literary and thus social force. Such a sharp consciousness of the form was probably bound to cause unease in members of a newly emerging structure of power that was developing a social and intellectual culture sympathetic to the aims not only of a new capitalism but also of a new domination of the world through science and conquest. The first formulation of the History of the Novel not only made its *foreign* stock apparent, but also celebrated the African and Oriental dimensions of this now unignorable literary form, which could appear treacherous to the new objectives.

Repudiation of the Novel, or its whole history did not, of course, happen abruptly. Neither can it be seen as a simple effect of "Puritanism," for Puritanism's true literary productions include the *Arcadia* and *The Pilgrim's Progress* (1678). For a hundred years after Salmasius' important essay, the Novel developed without too much hindrance, if with some embarrassment. For a while, both writers and readers seemed happy to accommodate the form while accepting its rich and variegated history. The late seventeenth century and early eighteenth century are times of very lively experiment in novel-writing, especially in France and in England. Women writers were increasingly entering the field, like Mme. de Lafayette, whose novel *Zayde* (about a foreign woman) occasioned the first version of Huet's treatise. Her novel *La Princesse de Clèves* (1678) builds on its predecessors, especially the work of Madeleine de Scudéry, and thus indirectly (as probably directly also) on the work of the ancient novelists, her novel being an ironic compression of many motifs of older fiction.

The seventeenth-century novel is by and large a political novel in a political age. Ideas of civic virtue in small monarchies had developed into more complicated European ideas of political life, ideas that were going to create structural change. The political, as it is understood in the disruptive but sophisticated Europe of the Fronde, the English Revolutions, and the Thirty Years War, is a focus of the deeply personal as well as of large-scale public affairs—and public tumult.

An endeavor to take over the Novel for political purposes characterizes much seventeenth-century literature and is, I think, the root of what Bourdelot complains of as early as 1619—writers produce systems, alchemical or otherwise, in their fictions in order to bend the reading public to specific views. This quarrel over the Novel as contested ground leads to the presence of the "ideas" which Clifton Cherpack traces in the French novel of the seventeenth century. If some writers attempt "to Christianize ancient religions in French romances," as Cherpack notes (*Logos in Mythos*, 64), that is part of a larger effort to sanitize the Novel and force it into the service of the civic. The fact that the Abbé d'Aubignac (François Hédelin) published in 1664 an incomplete novel *Macarise ou la Reine des Isles Fortunées*, subtitled *Histoire allégorique contenant la philosophie morale des Stoïques . . .* (*Macarise or the Queen of the Fortunate Isles: Allegorical History containing the moral philosophy of the Stoics . . .*) is significant. D'Aubignac, best known for his formulation of the rules of neoclassicism to be applied by the Académie Francaise in his *Pratique du Théatre* (1657), tried to shanghai the Novel into its proper place in the paternal and regulated order—with the aid, as Cherpack notes, of a great deal of "preparatory coaching" to enlighten the reader (64). The Novel was to be tamed into clearly referential allegory, and subordinated to the service of moral philosophy, directly inculcated. Novelists like Scudéry have their own "ideas," and these are displeasing to those who try earnestly in schoolmasterly fashion to counter them, often with indigestible and oddly parodic reworkings of the form. The only big success in that line is Fénelon's *Télémaque* (1699).

Novels of the period deal with what the eighteenth century was going to define as "happiness" at the nexus of the public and the private. Life is understood to be a political affair. Novels as diverse as Scudéry's *Artamène, ou le Grand Cyrus* (1649–1653), Hans J. C. von Grimmelshausen's *Simplicissimus* (1669), or Aphra Behn's *Oroonoko* (1688) are all politically conscious and analytical. D'Urfé's very popular multivolume novel *L'Astrée* is set in a deep past when the Gauls of France are resisting imperial Rome. This situation, which will remind the modern reader of *Astérix le Gaulois*, has, like *Astérix* itself, strong contemporary political implications, including a resistance to the absolute rule that was to emanate from Paris and (later) Versailles.

The long-breathed French novel of the earlier seventeenth century was readily understood by contemporaries to be allegorical. An English translator of *Le Grand Cyrus* comments, "the Intrigues and Miscarriages of War and Peace are better, many times, laid open and Satyriz'd in a *Romance*, than in a downright History, which being oblig'd to name the Persons, is often force'd . . . to be too partial and sparing" (*Artamenes* [1691], A4^v–A5^r). Novels can tell the true history, while historians are under pressures that make them false. As well as offering political allegories of the present, novels at a deeper level express the knowledge that individual human beings are subject to—and part of—human structures and arrangements over which they have little and sometimes no control—including war and slavery. In such a situation, even a heroic capacity for great deeds (as in the case of Scudéry's Cyrus, modeled on Xenophon's hero) will not be all sufficient—there will be not only "Intrigues" but "Miscarriages" in "War and Peace." Everyone wants power and feels the lack of it; even the great folks really have very little.

REJECTING THE NOVEL: NASTY FEUDAL MONARCHICAL ROMANCE

Catholics, Anglicans, Protestants—even Puritans—had a liking for these novels or "Romances" as long fictions were then called. But these offered a considerable challenge to the working-out of affairs of state (and church). That unfortunate monarch Charles I—certainly an example of a great personage who ultimately had very little power—displayed the political content of the Novel, not much helping his own cause or the Novel's. Charles quoted the *Arcadia's* imprisoned Pamela's prayer in his own propaganda, the *Eikōn Basilikē*, published shortly after his execution. It seems likely that this reference was genuinely hit upon by King Charles himself. Helpless, facing execution, he had reason to recall the stirring words of Sidney's heroine, who in a like situation had (like Charikleia and Leukippé) expressed her dauntless inner freedom. Charles saw himself as an innocent captive, a hero of *sōphrosynē* in a dungeon. His enemies did not see it at all like that. They poured contempt on the king for thinking of such irreligious trifles as a romance at such a moment, instead of his sinful soul. Milton leads the pack in his *Eikonoklastes* (1649), with his gibes at King Charles for lifting a prayer from Sidney's "vain amatorious poem."[14] Milton extends his attack on Sidney, so popular with royalists, into an attack on the tradition of the European novel. All such fiction gets associated with Bad King Charles: "For he certainly whose mind could serve him to seek a Christian prayer out of a Pagan Legend, and assume it for his own, might gather up the rest God knows from whence; one perhaps out of the French *Astraea*, another out of the Spanish *Diana*; *Amadis* and *Palmerin* could hardly escape him . . ." (367). The form of fiction represented by *Arcadia* came under heavy suspicion. While Sidney's 1590 *Arcadia* is certainly monarchist, it is also Protestant and could even be called "Puritan"—but such nice considerations did not count for much in England in the mid- and late seventeenth century. In England the Novel or "Romance" could be identified with all that was old-fashioned, feudal indeed.

There were some grounds for connecting the Novel with the aristocracy, all the more when the English aristocracy, especially during the Commonwealth period, took to writing historical fictions (carefully veiled) to convey their point of view. Barclay's *Argenis* had supplied an important model, and that novel was translated into English at the request of the king and dedicated to Charles I in 1629. (See Annabel Patterson, "The Royal Romance," in *Censorship and Interpretation*, 159–202.) Meanwhile in France the Novel also became connected with new ideas of courtly aristocracy and refinement. Social as well as dynastic changes taking place entailed both a strong movement towards a centralized and unifying government, led by Cardinal Richelieu. There were new modes both of organizing and questioning power structures. Richelieu, in a stroke of characteristic genius, set up the Académie Francaise (1634) to rule on the correctness of literature and of language. His form of "political correctness" was what we often and loosely term "conservative"; that is, he was determined that literature should favor strong central rule, and the control of a newly powerful absolute authority. But when he set up an Academy to discuss the French language, he seemed to many of the upper-class women of Paris to be inviting their participation, for women of course spoke their mother tongue. Aristocratic women had a claim, which they stressed, to understanding the niceties and proprieties of elegant French. Although not allowed to be members of the Académie, women of the leisured classes had become increasingly interested in reading and discussion. They held that it was possible for women to meet and know men as friends and to engage in interesting conversation without being bound by the intimacies of either sexual congress or familial bonds. They expressed their belief in inventing the *salon*. This French women's movement was to be far-reaching; ultimately our coeducational university arises from it.

The salon soon became a subject of the new novel, as in Scudéry's *Artamène* (1649–1653). The women of the salons, the discussions, and the fictions were all termed *Précieuses*. "Precious" was an abusive term dating back to the Middle Ages—a woman who thought too highly of her personal integrity or untouchability, who was too chary of sexual favors or unwilling to marry, was termed "precious." The *Précieuses* had a strong view of the importance of women and were visibly bringing about a social revolution. They disturbed the dynastic proprieties in their announced insistence on the right of a woman not to marry if she chose not to, and on her right to judge her suitor by her own standards of what is pleasing or intelligent.

Some backlash was inevitable, and it was likely to come when it did, when Louis XIV got his hands on the reins. There was no love lost between monarch and *Précieuses*, or monarch and novelists. The disturbances of the two revolts known as "La Fronde" in the 1640s had indicated an unnerving potential for revolution against the strongly centralized government and the new absolute ideal of monarchy. The loose coalition of nobles and bourgeois *parlements*, which tried unsuccessfully to tackle Mazarin, had been ideologically supplied by some of the new intellectuals. The men and women who frequented the salons were heavily implicated in the Fronde, including novelists like Scudéry. Novels such as Scudéry's are in themselves, it should be added, in their structure apart from content, somewhat unnerving to absolutism. They do not obey the unities, but travel over time and space. Far from having a single unified action lending itself to the controlling gaze of the ideal viewer (the eye of the Roi Soleil), they are deliberately diffuse and discursive, offering a variety of characters, events, and emotional responses. Early seventeenth-century French novels like *L'Astrée* and *Clélie* have multiple centers of interest (an inheritance from Heliodorus and Montemayor, among others). The novels' multicenteredness and variety of viewpoints pose an implicit structural critique of absolute rule.

Louis XIV needed to signal to France that the lax era of regencies and revolutions was over, and that there would be no time for the follies of the past. In 1659 Molière wisely staged his new comedy *Les Précieuses ridicules* before the young king. Molière displays the absurdity of two young provincial middle-class girls who have been seduced into a second-hand and ignorant version of *préciosité*.

Their absurdity is shown up by the fact that they are easily taken in by two valets masquerading as *précieux* aristocratic males.

REJECTING THE NOVEL: NASTY BOURGEOIS STUFF

Molière's bourgeois girls Magdelon and Cathos (nicknames alluding to the high-born Catherine, marquise de Rambouillet, and Madeleine de Scudéry) have learned to desire to be refined, and to be courted in a refined and respectful manner. They also want a life before a marriage concocted by the father. The meddling go-between that has contaminated their minds is the Novel. Although Molière's comedy rests ultimately (or pretends to) on the certainties of class, it betrays some anxiety about the standards of the *noblesse* moving ineluctably down the scale, which would make women of all classes, including those of the *petits-bourgeois*, much less tractable. These low-bred maidens have, for instance, read the aristocratic *Le Grand Cyrus*. Magdelon complains of their own vulgar names, "just one of these names would be enough to discredit the most beautiful novel in the world" (Scene 4). The Novel is already what it is feared to be in the eighteenth century, a poisonous conduit of discontent, giving girls (and vulgar boys, too, sometimes) ideas above their station.

The very success of novels like Madeleine de Scudéry's had become a cause of social concern by the 1650s. These novels connect what should be separate: history and lies; intellect and the boudoir; aristocracy and bourgeoisie; authority and women. Boileau fiercely attacks the novelists—with overt emphasis on Scudéry—in his *Dialogue des héros de roman* (written in the late 1660s). He claimed when he finally published it in 1710 that he had waited until Scudéry's death, out of delicacy—but he had circulated the *Dialogue*, even given performances of it, and supposedly illicit printings had appeared. In Boileau's *Dialogue*, Scudéry's characters are damned in Hades for usurping the names and titles of real heroes. As Joan DeJean points out, Boileau particularly resents Scudéry's offense against the civic, especially in creating "a model for heroes that threatened to weaken the male fiber on which the State relied" (*Tender Geographies*, 169). Characters become, as Boileau indicates, "effeminate." Perhaps novel-characters always are somewhat "feminine." Caught and scrutinized, they lack full grandeur, even when most grand. They give way to inner emotion, if only privately and internally—but the private and internal is the Novel's hunting ground. The Novel is thus always in danger of seeming to question both glory and civic virtue.

Boileau's attack is launched in the name of the rule of Louis XIV. Here the civic ideal serves a strong and militaristic nationalism. Monarchy is the acceptable figure for that nationalism, which focuses the civic ideal. It is easy in an English context to suppose that "Romance" must always be seen as monarchical, and as an enemy of the middle classes (as represented by the Roundheads). But the Novel (or Romance) can be attacked on the other side equally well. Boileau, taking the hint from Molière, is the first to think of the brilliant charge that the "Romance" or "Novel"—*le roman*—is *bourgeois*. At the end of the *Dialogue*, Scarron recognizes all of the novelistic heroes and heroines as "bourgeois de mon quartier" (*Oeuvres*, 309). Vulgarians all, despite the grand classical names they have adopted, the personages of these novels are suited only to middle-brow, middle-class readers. Boileau deserves credit for being the originator of the long-lived attack on the novel as a middle-class artifact and pastime—an attack, incidentally, most frequently launched by those who are (like Boileau) middle-class themselves.

In labeling the novels *bourgeois*, Boileau indicates that they are incapable of assisting in the development towards a higher, more lofty and more powerful *civitas*. They lack the lofty and powerful vision, and thus can only do harm. If in England the Novel was associated with the king's party, in France it was associated with the ragged alliance of nobles, gentry, and parliaments against the centralized state and its monarch. So the Novel got caught in its political affiliations and became both old-fashioned feudal monarchical antique *and* dangerously vulgar middle-class nuisance. Since that time, both sets of sticks have been used to beat it. The Novel is an enemy of the civic, in short—whether the civic represents itself as monarchical or republican.

Huet's *Traité* was written explicitly to counter Boileau, as well as to answer Salmasius. In order to counter the vision of the Novel as a middle-class upstart, and hence a wispy lightweight, Huet tried to give it a pedigree. He illustrated its depth, diversity and appeal in considering its age and ancestry. But his answer only intensified the fears of the Novel's enemies. This foreign and polyglot thing looks like an invader. It is in the civic world what Protestantism, or perhaps even secularism, is to the Pope's Christendom. The novel devalues civilization, disorders centralities, sets strange ideas afloat. In the French "culture wars" over *préciosité* and *le roman* we see the first example of an ideological dispute over aesthetics and popular culture. For the first time, we have an ideological social conflict not directly over religious doctrine. But the debate over the Novel did have implications for religion. Some Protestants were to find it advisable, even necessary, to attack the Novel. At best it is a distraction from true doctrine (just as secularized quarrels like the conflict between Boileau and Huet are distractions from religion.) At worst, the Novel is a sort of diabolical rival to the Reformation.

THE PURITAN ATTACK

In 1658, Jean Racine's Greek teacher, the sacristan of the Abbey of Port-Royal, twice tore up and burned the copies of the *Aithiopika* that the nine- or ten-year-old Racine was reading. The schoolmaster acts on the views of the Jansenist establishment, and acts out the Puritan desire to eliminate imperfection and false dreams. The boy Racine obtained a third copy of Heliodorus; this time he memorized the novel, and then gave the sacristan the paper copy to burn. Racine's memory may seem phenomenal, but the story illustrates the real difficulty of eradicating novels, which steal into the very places schoolmasters are trying hardest to guard, the hearts and minds of the young. The Novel is not only a temporary distraction from responsibility, while the reader wastes time reading it. It is a moral danger, because it warps future attention to responsibility, to duty, and to authority. This is the essence of the charge eloquently leveled against the genre in 1660 by a leading English Puritan, Nathaniel Ingelo. (Here again we find literary theory being established and contested in a preface; this Puritan antagonist to novels expressed his views in a preface to his own counter-novel, or Puritan allegory, *Bentivolio and Urania*.) Ingelo had reason to feel sour in 1660, when the Puritan cause was lost, republicanism had somehow evaporated, and Charles II was restored to the throne. It would have been dangerous to write too directly political a treatise, but Ingelo's attack on the Novel in his lengthy Preface is political in the larger sense.

Ingelo will not accept the plea of pleasure as a justification for the Novel; the pleasure received in such reading is largely folly. Novelists have no right to play with reality—including history—even if they have a moral design somewhere, for *"Romancers"* have "made the fabulous rind so thick, that few can see through it into the usefull sense" (*Bentivolio and Urania*, B2ʳ⁻ᵛ). Scudéry (and others) had dignified the Novel by including in its purview the ancient epics; Homer is one of the *"Romancers."* Ingelo retorts upon them by including Homer (and most other poets) in the attack on romances. He agrees with Justin Martyr: "*The whole Rhapsody of Homers* [sic] *Iliads and Odysseis . . . is but a Woman*" (B1ᵛ). As soon as we have fiction of almost any kind, there is too much of the *feminine* in play.

The reading of novels insidiously occupies the soul and disables its functions. Fictional narratives make "a deep impression" upon "the affectionate part':

> For men having indulg'd Imagination, and play'd carelessly with its Fantasms, unawares take vehement pleasure in things which they do not believe . . . and read Fables with such affections, as if their own or their friends [sic] best interest were wrapp'd up in them. . . . How unsatisfied are they till the End of a paper-Combate? . . . How are they taken with pleasure and sorrow for the good and bad success of the Romantick Lovers? They are apt also to draw to themselves or their friends such things as they read in far-fetch'd references: if the resemblances suite in some little points, they seem to do and suffer such things. . . . (C2ʳ⁻ᵛ)

We are Quixotes in reading novels—inevitably. All novels are therefore bad. Ingelo feels no need for historical or other division—he lumps together "that sort of books written in the *Greek, Latin, Italian* and *French* Languages" (D2ʳ). The writers' talents are perverted: "Excellent Wits thrown away in *writing* great stories of Nothing" (C1ᵛ). Such stories color our identification of the living world and haunt the inner mind: "they leave the Memory so full of fantasticall Images of things which are not, that they cannot easily dismisse them: the Fancy being held in the amusement of those foolish Dreames" (C1ᵛ–C2ʳ). Protestant divines, fascinated by the inner world of self, the new and hopeful region of cultivation, found to their disgust that the novelists had got there before them. The inner world could be otherwise colonized.

Fancy is at fault—Ingelo likes to imagine corporal punishment inflicted on errant Fancy, "a Naturall Faculty" of the soul, but under governance of Reason, who should whip it severely for straying: "out-staying its time in allowed diversions, or transgressing the limits of such Subjects as sound Judgement permits, it returns abus'd with hurtfull delight, and instead of being us'd decently, is unworthily prostituted" (D1ʳ). Fancy is here oddly gendered. Like a school*boy* straying out of school into unlawful play, sneaking off to prostitutes at midnight,

Fancy is yet also a *whore*, feminine and effeminate, "prostituted." The violence, the sexual horror, and the struggle for control in these images betray the amount of authority that is felt to be contested. No ground can be yielded to the claims of Fancy or Imagination.

In his preface, Ingelo specifically engages the arguments of John Davies of Kidwelly, translator of D'Urfé and of Scudéry. In introducing *Astrea. A Romance*, Davies had made enormous claims for the civilizing value of "POETRY": "by which terme I meane, FICTION, in the largest extent. Under *this*, are comprehended the highest & noblest productions of man's wit, ROMANCES . . ." (London, 1657, A2ʳ). Davies takes an anthropological and large-scale historical approach, unlike Huet's detailed historical inspection. Davies is also progressivist. "Romance" was the mode of pagan religious worship and contributed to civilization. Modern fiction is even better, the product of the rational mind, "calculated to the *meridian* of the most *criticall* and most *ingenious*" (A2ʳ). The *"extravagance"* that came from pagan religion "is now reconcil'd to *probability*, and restrain'd by *judgement*." D'Urfé's *Astrea* offers "a cleare *representation* of the Noblest and most generous *images of life*, and such an accompt of the *passions* and *actions* of *Men*, as few bookes of this nature afford so plentifull." Davies agrees with the dictum of the late Cardinal Richelieu, *"That he was not to be admitted into the Academy of* Wit, *who had not been before well read in ASTREA"* (A2ᵛ). Richelieu, who died in 1642, had been able to admire D'Urfé's novel when it first came out (its last volume appearing in 1628) because the Novel was not yet in his time fully associated with dangerous political and social trends. Because of revolutionary events in France and England, after the 1640s the Novel (or Romance) is going to be much more frequently under attack. Its defenders are conscious that it requires defending.

Novels were apparently growing in popularity at this time. Scudéry was widely read and eagerly translated. Novels rapidly crossed national and other boundaries. In the 1650s Dorothy Osborne, a Royalist in the countryside, was reading La Calprenède's *Cléopâtre* and Scudéry's *Artamène*, and passing the volumes on to her suitor William Temple, a Commonwealthsman in London. (She read the original French, having, as she said, "no patience . . . for these translators of romances"; *Letters*, 158). *L'Astrée* likewise continued to be read and translated; it certainly profoundly affected one English novelist, Aphra Behn, who took from it her pseudonym *Astrea*, evidently first used in love-correspondence with her "Celadon" and then as her self-chosen code-name as a spy for Charles II.

Heliodorus' *Aithiopika*, Scudéry's other "model" beside *Astrea*, was likewise faring well in editions and translations. The Renaissance festival of novel-reading was still going on. It helped the pro-novelists that people like Ingelo were consistent enough to damn Homer along with Heliodorus. Material prefixed to *The Adventures of Theagenes and Chariclia, A Romance* (1717) offers one of the strongest defenses of that novel, and of novels. This is not a merely academic matter. The title page of this version, not only emphasizing love and adventure, but also defining the novel's structure as a set of curious "Histories," advertises the novel's contents in terms congenial to contemporary tastes in fiction (see Plate 30). This edition is clearly aimed at a popular audience. The editor, C. G. (Charles Gildon?), in his "Dedication," is the first editor of the age of print clearly to give the position of central character to Charikleia: "CHARICLIA is evidently the chief Character of the ensuing *Poem* (for with ARISTOTLE, and other exalted Critic's, I must call it so, tho' in Prose . . .) 'tis on her the Author bestows his utmost Mastery, and in her has drawn a perfect Character of those *Social Vertues*. THEAGENES has but the second Place, and is every where subservient to the setting her Excellence in a more conspicuous Light" ("Dedication," London, 1717, iv).

The anonymous translator, a clergyman, praises Heliodorus highly as an originator, a founder: "one of the Noblest Genius's [*sic*] that any Age has produced; being the first Enterprizer of a way of Writing"—a position Henry Fielding will wish to reclaim. Heliodorus is "the first, who made Love the grand Subject of his Narrations, and in managing that Subject converted Poetry into Prose," though his story is "drawn up in the Epick way":

> this Book may be styl'd the *Mother Romance* of the World . . . yet I well
> know what a bad Name *Romances* go under . . . and . . . the Book might
> have gone down much better with some Readers, had that invidious
> Title been left out. But why Romances should all lie under this hard
> censure, I am yet to learn. It's true, Books of that Name, the Product of
> Barbarous Ages, that are stuff'd with nothing but Legendary Stories of
> Knights, Giants, Monsters and Dragons, are very idle in themselves,
> and fit only for Children and weak People to read. . . . But what is this
> to others of a finer Texture, that are filled with useful Precepts and
> wise Reflections, that imitate true History, and have this advantage
> over it in point of Instructiveness, that every Act has its due Conse-
> quence, and they shew not so much what Men are, as what they ought
> to be? ("Preface," xxiv–xxvii)

The translator goes on to praise novels for providing suitable diversion for the mind, good reading matter, especially for "young Ladies," whereas books of devotion and of history are not diverting to the fancy, while "News-Papers are too short" (xxviii). Heliodorus provides examples especially of chastity, but also of the other virtues as seen in Hydaspes (echoes of Renaissance commentators). The novelist has excellent characterization, good conversation ("His Table talk is wonderful agreeable"), and moving scenes. The whole is "all of a Piece, not a Character in it but what is interwoven with the grand Subject" (xxxiii). Heliodorus "rarely exceeds the just bounds of Probability"—for instance, "He does not strain your Belief, by empowering Youths of Seventeen, to chase whole Squadrons with their single Arm" (xxxiii–xxxiv). The argument here not only poises Heliodorus against Madeleine de Scudéry, but also picks up that old charge that Theagenes is *imbellus*.

THE IDEA OF CHARACTER

The translator of the 1717 *Adventures of Theagenes and Chariclia* is a sufficiently good Aristotelian to praise Heliodorus for interweaving all the characters into the "grand Subject," and thus implicitly subordinating characters to plot. Yet the emphasis on *exemplary* character, which this commentator insists on, is likely to make character seem much more important than plot. The "grand Subject," speaking morally, cannot be obtained without the character. We might wish to argue that novels have always been about individual persons closely observed, and that thus "character" has always been a leading feature, but "character" gains in theoretical importance in the seventeenth century. The more exemplary a character is or can be, the more that character asks us (as both Sidney's and Richardson's Pamelas do) to identify ourselves with that personage in an oddly intimate manner.

Charles Stuart, we may note, identifies himself with Sidney's princess Pamela. Charles is not committing a class trespass like Molière's *bourgeoises* imagining themselves to be Clélie or Mandane, but he does step across gender lines here—another cause for his opponents' scorn. Charles has proven himself a Quixote. He reads quixotically, projecting himself into the experience of a mere novelistic character, as if their experiences were in some sense on a similar plane of reality. Charles also appears to imagine that the female experience could be adopted as a universal one. Such a reading supplies material for Ingelo's heavy wit against the novel, and gives rise to his disgust at male readers who are apt, on the mere basis of fancied resemblances on some little points, to read themselves into the characters. Thomas Hobbes in his *Leviathan* (1651) had already treated such identification as commonplace. Hobbes may not approve such reading, but he assumes everyone will understand it as an easy illustration of what he calls "compound Imagination': "as when a man imagins himselfe [*sic*] a *Hercules*, or an *Alexander* (which happeneth often to them that are much taken with reading of Romants)" (*Leviathan*, Part I, "Of Imagination," 16). Such male mis-reading, possible with epic but (Hobbes assumes) prevalent among novel-readers, happens "when a man compoundeth the image of his own person, with the image of the actions of another man" (ibid.). Such a "compound" is not at all stable. Distinctions between self and other are confused. A new and somewhat monstrous being emerges in a metamorphosis creating an artificial hybrid. The novel or "Romant" attracts in offering the errant fancy a way to create an alternative "self." Not merely bodily self-image but the reader's own soul or sense of being goes out to inhabit the character—an action utterly revolting to moralists such as Ingelo. Part of the attraction of the Novel to the errant fancy lies in its power to offer an alternative self, another soul. Drama at least requisitions an actor (soul and body together) to inhabit the role. A novel character is disconcertingly free to let others inhabit it—or meet it—at will. Quixotic reading is not possible without a strong emotional relationship to "character."

In the seventeenth century, "character" begins to take a leading role in the idea of the Novel. A novel metaphorically becomes its (central) character. In prefaces of the time, we frequently encounter the game of treating the book as a person—its own person. Honoré D'Urfé introduces his novel *L'Astrée* as if it were the character, and that combined personification, that fusion of book /personage, as his daughter.

The author admonishing his shepherdess sounds like Frances Burney's Mr. Villars warning Evelina of the dangers of her "Entrance into the World" in his parental fear of the public world Astrée will encounter:

> If you knew what are the pains and difficulties to be met with along
> the path you undertake . . . perhaps you would wisely stop where you
> have been so long and tenderly loved. But your imprudent youth,

which has no experience of what I am telling you about, may perhaps make you imagine glories and vanities to befall you. . . . Nevertheless, since your resolution is as it is, and, if I oppose it, you threaten me with a prompt disobedience, remember at least that it is not by will but by suffrance that I permit it. And in order to leave you at your departure some earnest of the paternal affection I bear you, deposit carefully in your memory what I am about to say to you . . .

(*L'Astrée* [Rouen, 1616], aiii^{v})[15]

The book, in insisting upon being published, is a slightly naughty daughter—at least, she will not behave "sagement," she threatens "prompt disobedience." In this conceit, D'Urfé not only excuses publication of his novel, but also makes the novel itself feminine. He can oddly suggest that any imprudences within the novel may be manifestations of disobedience to himself, the higher author who is somehow powerless to prevent the book being what it is. Such an address to the personified novel is significant also in that it precludes propaganda from the outset, signing to us that we can happily dismiss the possibility that this novel is a mere set vehicle for predetermined ideas.

The English translator of the First Part picks up the personification. This book is now a traveling lady: "*Astrea* finding so good entertainment in her owne Countrey . . . is now encouraged to crosse the seas, and to try what welcome she shall meete with here in ENGLAND. And though it cannot be, but her riding-suite will take much away from her originall beauty . . . yet she is so confident of her owne worth, that she expects acceptance onely for herselfe, and not for her ornaments" (London, 1620, A3^{r}–A4^{v}).

The editor who introduces the posthumous Sixth Part of *L'Astrée* plays the same game; now the character is in mourning: "it is true that she is hidden in the crêpes and veils of her grief" (Paris, 1626, avi^{v}–avii^{r}).[16] Astrée in losing her author is a daughter who has lost a father. Don Quixote in similar conceit is conflated with his book, in John Stevens's translation of 1700, "*Don Quixote*'s third Sally amongst us, since he . . . now comes abroad again to seek Adventures. It is his fate to be Presecuted [*sic*] by Enchanters . . . and to be Ston'd by Gally-slaves, but still he finds Generous usage among Persons of Worth and Honour . . ." ("Preface," London [1700], A3$^{\mathrm{r-v}}$). This conceit survives to the mid-eighteenth century, when we find Prévost presenting *Clarissa* to Mme. de Graffigny as a young lady who will live with her daughters (her characters): *L'aimable Famille!* (1751, I:*2^{v}). Henry Fielding lamenting the critical mistreatment of his novel *Amelia* strikes the same note in resenting unmanly attacks upon *Amelia*, "my favorite Child."[17]

There is more than a mere conceit or little jest here. We see the advance of the importance of character. Nina Auerbach has complained of the treatment of novel characters as real people, attributing such a practice (which she thinks erroneous and sentimental) to the nineteenth century, but it was well established before then.[18] We can argue, of course, that it was established by the time Heliodorus' novel got called *Charikleia*, but in the late Renaissance and early Enlightenment the hermeneutics of novel-reading were bound to arrive at this near-obsession with the notion of "character."

Allegorical interpretation means that the reader should universalize the experience described. The first major step in thus universalizing is application to oneself. In *Le Roman de la Rose*, for instance, the reader must get into the position of the rose-seeker, creating a playful transference. In novels, the allegory is more and more inner-directed, even when there are layers of external allegory (e.g., political references) to pick up. In order to find meaning, the reader must make an application of the subject matter—and the easiest way to do that is to project the self upon the character. From highly intellectualized allegorical readings we have moved into an identification of feeling that gives the vehicle for feeling— the "character"—more and more power and a stronger position.

Thus, King Charles I can feel that Sidney's invention Pamela (rather than some historical or religious personage) is a companion in adversity. He does not only assimilate himself to her *while* he reads, but identifies her with himself as he is imprisoned. The patterns of identification necessary while reading a novel lead to ever-renewing emphasis on character. Such a state of affairs makes life more difficult for authorities and various cultural monitors, for they must find out not only what abstract ideas any given fictional work seems to inculcate, but also what its "characters" are like, and what emotional responses they may elicit. (It may be easy to scoff at such authorities and monitors, but it is difficult not to feel some sympathy with them in, for instance, the case of *Werther*, when young people were committing suicide in imitation of the novel's hero.)

We have little record of anxieties about Quixotic reading in antiquity, but that does not mean that self-identification with character did not occur. The stellar case of Quixotic reading—Alexander's self-identification with Homer's Achilles—is always touted as Homer's success story, instead of being looked at askance as aberrant. Augustine in the *Confessions* notoriously rejects his own earlier emotional identification with Dido: "weeping the death of Dido, which she brought about by loving Aeneas, and not weeping his own death, brought about by not loving thee, Lord" (I.xiii.38). Augustine is a strong voice against self-identification with a literary character—the stronger because he has experienced it. Such a sympathy turns us away from our real spiritual state. But for Augustine, as for the harsher Puritans who followed him, there is no real point in saying what some humanist antinovelists very much wished to say, that the (good) Epic is superior partly because it has built-in safeguards against such sloppy emotional identification with a character. If even the higher form, the Epic, cannot rely on the cultural safeguards of its classical height, its literary and political authority, to keep it safe from identification and undesirable projection, then the low form, the Novel, can claim no safeguards at all.

In the seventeenth century people worry about the Novel in new ways. Both political and literary theory led to an impasse. The apparently new solution to the dangers posed by the Novel—realism—did little to dissolve the problems of Quixotic reading of which people now were fully conscious. The last of these historical chapters will briefly trace some of the solutions and prohibitions introduced by the eighteenth century, as well as some important developments up to the twentieth century.

CHAPTER XII

►-+-◆►-0-◄◆-+-◄

The Eighteenth Century—and Beyond: The Rise of Realism, and Escape from It

►-+-◆►-0-◄◆-+-◄

Mr. Podsnap's world was not a very large world, morally; nor even geographically: seeing that although his business was sustained upon commerce with other countries, he considered other countries, with that important reservation, a mistake, and of their manners and customs would conclusively observe, 'Not English!' when, PRESTO! with a flourish of the arm, and a flush of the face, they were swept away.
—Charles Dickens, *Our Mutual Friend*

"Once I'm an owl, what is the spell or antidote for turning me back into myself?" Mr. Mohammed Sufyan, prop. Shandar Café and landlord to the rooming-house above, mentor to the variegated, transient and particoloured inhabitants . . . responded . . . with the above impromptu quip, stolen, with commendable mental alacrity for one aroused from his slumbers, from Lucius Apuleius of Madaura, Moroccan priest, A.D. 120–180 approx., colonial of an earlier Empire . . .
—Salman Rushdie, *The Satanic Verses*

►-+-◆►-0-◄◆-+-◄

GENDERING THE READER

One way of looking at prose fiction before the eighteenth century is to assume that it is an old-fashioned, feudal, and feminine thing, which it is necessary to turn into an appropriately modern and manly thing. Such an assumption is apparently behind Henry Fielding's *Joseph Andrews* (1742). In the fable of the babies swapped in their cradle, Joseph, "a poor sickly Boy," substituted for the former occupant, a girl, "a fat thriving Child," seems a figure for Fielding's new novel, which is to replace the old one (264). But another way of looking at the same process of history is to assume that prose fiction before the eighteenth century was manly and heroic, while in the new era it is domestic and feminine. The latter view has been popular of late—not that many critics are much interested in earlier prose fiction, but there has been some agreement on what has been called (to borrow the words of one title) "The Feminization of the Novel." The need to attach a gender to the form (a gender always in dispute) seems to arise out of a desire to attach a gender to the novel's *reader*—a matter likewise in dispute. Exemplary characterization and the questions of reader identification stimulate inquiry into the gender of the reader.

As we have seen, sixteenth-century editors spent some time on the case of the reader, anxious to reassure us that this particular story will be good for us. Amyot has the most impish defense—if you are too good, or too sour, then do not bother to read this book. Such excuses, or defenses, would seem to apply to readers of both sexes. So, too, one might imagine, would the common Renaissance defenses of reading based on the importance of pleasure. James Mabbe, translating Cervantes' *Exemplarie Novells*, claims only that these stories are "matter of harmlesse *Merriment*"; "I will not promise any great profit you shall reape by reading them: but I promise they will be pleasing and delightfull" (1640, a3ᵛ). But Mabbe is old enough to remember and sustain the Renaissance view of reading. By the middle of the seventeenth century, fiction-reading had become, as we have seen, a more complex and political affair. "Merriment" is not harmless if the novel is a political allegory. Pleasure itself may be suspect, especially if you ask the questions, "*who* is pleasured?" and "*how*"?

Prefatory material in novels of the seventeenth century seems more sharply aware of the particularity of readerships than prefaces of the sixteenth century. There are numerous dedications to women and addresses to readers of the "fair sex." Thornley, for instance, seems to pretend his *Daphnis and Chloe* is chiefly for female readers—the subtitle indicates as much. Lovelace's poetic address in front of Achilles Tatius' novel assumes female readers—though there is other prefatory material addressed to the male.[1] In the seventeenth century, at least during the first half of it, such instances can be seen as acknowledgments that women are a presence not only as patrons but also as *buyers* of fiction.

The second half of the seventeenth century brings with it, in France and England, new alarms. Part of the excitement arises from the now-unavoidable perception that women are new members of the writing fraternity. Recognition of this as a fact of modern life (rather than a mere freak) seems to have been delayed until the 1650s and 1660s. As we have seen, attacks against the *Précieuses* are related to the incursion of the female into the intellectual world, and into authority over readers. Defenders of the "Ancients" could look back to an all-male literary world. Defenders of the "Moderns" had to cope with the unnerving fact of the female presence—as support or contamination of the literary enterprise. According to Boileau, women writers produced heroes too soft, guilty of *mollesse*—male readers are thus now endangered by the works of female writers.

The work of gendering the reader takes place in a context of female writing of fiction—and that is ostensibly a new context. We do not *know* that it is entirely new. Waiving the female authors of poetic fiction in the Middle Ages, we can wonder if the novelists of antiquity may not have had women in their number. They could have published anonymously, or under a male name—just as Madeleine de Scudéry wrote under the name of her brother Georges, a disguise that at first served its turn, but became at last as transparent as "George Sand" and "George Eliot." There may well have been female novelists in antiquity, but we shall (presumably) never know. In the seventeenth century the presence of female novelists became a public fact. There is a certain promiscuity in the fact that neither men nor women write for an audience of one sex only.

At times, writers and critics of this period, especially those upholding the cause of the Ancients, speak as if the literary world can still be imagined as all male. Yet even such an all-male world still produces anxiety. As we see in Ingelo's argument, the male reader of fiction is constantly in danger from his own Fancy. A male harbors this partly-female entity, this Delilah-seductress Fancy within, who will team up with the wanton enticements in books. The Romantics are going to cope with this problem of the Fancy—which remains a problem for the entire eighteenth century—by celebrating Imagination as a very powerful and strictly masculine affair. This rejoinder had not yet been invented in 1660, or even in 1760, and indeed it was to do the Novel little good, for the Romantic *poets*, like Wordsworth writing on the German Gothic novels, were only too willing to throw the Novel over.

The threat posed by fiction (as by other kinds of writing) was often met by censorship. The Roman Catholic Church tried to regulate reading and printing by means of its *Librorum Prohibitorum Index* (List of Prohibited Books, which sometimes worked as an advertisement for the works, especially in Protestant eyes); a number of novels were included in the *Index* from its inception in the late sixteenth century until its abrogation in 1966. The habit of printing new or dangerous works in those European cities less prone to censorship persists through the seventeenth and eighteenth centuries; in Protestant countries censorship was local and less centralized. We note that the first "complete" edition of the dangerous new *Satyricon* was printed in Amsterdam in 1669. Amsterdam, London, and Geneva served not only as printing centers of dangerous works, but also as accommodation addresses. Books are sometimes given false places of publication in order to shield printer as well as author. Xenophon's *Ephesiaka* in Italian was cautiously published in 1723 with a fake place of publication on its title page—why would an Italian version be printed in "London"? The real place of printing was pretty certainly Florence. In January 1759, Voltaire had his *Candide ou l'Optimisme* published in Geneva, Paris, and Amsterdam, in order that the source should be uncertain and circulation unimpeded. In February there were official raids on the publishing houses, and copies of the book were seized, but *Candide* proved unstoppable. Voltaire had taken the precaution of keeping his name out of his philosophic novel, which was presented as "Translated from the German by Doctor Ralph," playfully supplying a (false) language and culture of origin. Translated books of course came under any local or ecclesiastical bans, but the idea of *translation* provided a sort of alibi. Translation and transmission are important Enlightenment ideas, supporting the ideal of the free flow of information and opinion, an ideal gestated in the matrix of the printing press.

Governments, however, including local governments, are rarely truly happy with an unregulated flow of words. The itch to control dubious communication is often scratched by the irritated rejection of fiction, the easiest form of written communication to attack (as "trivial"), as well as the one most deeply opposed by nature to the civic. In the mid-eighteenth century, an ingenious mental invention came to the rescue to accommodate both writers and civic authorities. This was Book Reviewing—in its modern form, in semipopular rather than in learned journals. Its rise can be traced simply by a glance at the fortunes of the *Gentleman's Magazine* in England; founded in 1731, it acquired its new format, including original material and reviews, in 1739, and the space devoted to reviews steadily increased thereafter.

Book reviewing emerged as a point of negotiation between the civic Establishment and the writers themselves. Magazines promised (implicitly) to sieve out books, scrutinizing novels and encouraging writers to write acceptable fiction correctly. Novel reviewing serves as a kind of gatekeeper for the *civitas*. It is official and responsible. Its rise in importance noticeably if subtly diminished the importance of novels' prefatory material. From the fifteenth century to the age of Prévost, Fielding, and Richardson, the preface(s) of a novel had constituted the *locus* where critical dialogue had been carried on and critical argument made. The sudden (and lasting) decline in the import of such material after the age of reviewing goes some way to explain why modern editors are so cavalier about excising authorial preliminary material in new printings of old books. Critical arguments are to be made in published Reviews—from the *Monthly Review* through the *Revue des Deux Mondes* to the *New York Review of Books*. In novel reviewing, which soon became a brisk trade, novelists themselves, co-opted as reviewers, can often be persuaded into ingenious forms of mutual policing. The arrival of novel reviewing is at least an admission that the Novel was not going to go away.

The standard reader of a novel in the early eighteenth century is still imagined as a male, who is under continual threat from his own treacherous mind and emotions. Male novelists have a greater duty than ever to see that their novel is sufficiently masculine, and not to play wantonly with male fancy. As we move into the eighteenth century, however, we notice that the reader is increasingly imagined as female. Heliodorus' 1717 translator emphasizes that novels make valuable diversion for the "Ladies." Yet he finds it necessary to add that Heliodorus can be valuable reading for serious males: "And yet I dare be bold to add, that there are many things in it, which even Men of grey Hairs, and advanced Judgments, need not be ashamed to employ a leisure hour upon. To understand Human Nature is a Study worthy of a Philosopher . . ." (xxx). That last sentence may well have influenced Fielding. It is easy to imagine that both Richardson and Fielding had come upon that Preface; the fiction to come is adumbrated in what is there said about the fiction of the past. A sixteenth-century editor was likely to say that this particular novel was worth the attention of a busy man in idle hours, and leave it at that. By the eighteenth century, a more specific appeal had to be made. The eighteenth century was to get into the irritating habit of stating that the reading of novels was the (dangerous) occupation of the groups succinctly described by Johnson: "these books are written chiefly to the young, the ignorant, and the idle, to whom they serve as lectures of conduct, and introductions into life" (*Rambler* no. 4 [March 1750], in *Works*, IV: 21). We can see thus the high compliment implied in Johnson's letter to Richardson about *Clarissa* when he said that novel will be "occasionally consulted by the busy, the aged, and the studious" (*Letters*, I: 48).

Johnson's tripartite list puts the age division ("the young") first, rather than gender. The other two groups seem to relate first to class (the "ignorant" being the poor and the "idle" the indolent rich) and second to undesirable moral states. All of these qualities (youth, ignorance, idleness) are negative; it is reasonable to look down on each group (to whom the "studious," "aged," and "busy" form an exact contrast). We note a similar condescension at work in Ingelo's earlier plea for a very clearly moral fiction, with nothing lying "in such deep conceits as but few can dive into the bottom of them" (*Bentivolio and Urania*, *1ʳ). An author should be a preacher, plainly aiming at the lowest common denominator.

Few writers can be cheered by the idea that their work is going to be read by teenagers, the stupid, and the workless. Yet at the same time, the idea of a youthful and idle nobility or gentry being led along by novels is not socially reassuring. The assumed "feminization" of the novel has much to do with the power of the marketplace to produce novels. Not only is the Novel not going to go away. With the help of big-city printing presses, it is going to proliferate.[2] Ways must be found of containing it, to limit any damage it may do. To pretend that the novel is primarily directed towards females (including those of both middle and upper classes) is reassuring, for women (unlike youthful male aristocrats) are theoretically disabled from bringing concepts into social currency.

Some historians have noted that during this period (the late seventeenth and eighteenth century) the development of mercantilism and a business world of large fortunes had moved women out of the businesses and the manorial production that had engaged them in earlier ages.[3] Women were edged out of the "public sphere." Feudalism had permitted some public functioning for women; occasionally, blue blood could override gender in the hierarchy, as it could not under the commercial system. The eighteenth century has been credited with (or blamed for) inventing the "private" sphere, the realm of the "domestic." "Public" and the "Private" are new ways of conceptualizing the civic. The private is what cannot be the civic, but ought to support it, as home is the nucleus of the system. The Novel is now urged to become at least officially both "private" and "domestic." I should say at once that, unlike many contemporary critics, I do not believe for a moment that this is a description of what *really* happened to the Novel, or to novels, though it is a true enough description of something wished for by cultural regulators.[4] The "domestic novel" in the eighteenth and even the nineteenth centuries is a vortex of energies, strong lines of force radiating outward from the home center and drawing foreign elements towards it. The walls of "home" are very porous; only sillies like Mr. Woodhouse think that one can shut off the world and keep an unbroken and static family circle. The private always is the public in the Novel—if only by virtue of the fact that we the readers constitute a public audience to what transpires. But, that aside, novel characters refuse to keep enclosed in a narrow private world, but are very dashing in all directions. Even in the work of that conservative Anglican spinster Charlotte Yonge, the supposedly home-centered Victorian family in *The Daisy Chain* (1856) has its girls rushing out to set up and teach schools and found churches. The novelistic "home" is best suited to metaphors from modern rather than antique atomic theory, as a system of particles in ceaseless (even somewhat chaotic) activity. Before the end of any novel, the home and its women (the angel in the house included) will have touched multiple aspects of the community, the culture, and history . . . as Charikleia did.

In 1717 "C.G." could state that Charikleia exemplifies the *"Social Virtues."* That is, Charikleia is still thought of as functioning in the "public" sphere, even though she does not exemplify *heroic* virtues. But the *"Social Virtues"* become more and more the masculine prerogative. By 1747 Richardson has to advertise his *Clarissa* as dealing with "The most Important Concerns of Private Life." The Novel should deal with the private sphere; should go where the women and the young are, and teach them how to be civic, or how to support the civic. Women become the officially designated readers of novels. The young, the ignorant, and the idle all belong (at least temporarily) to the private sphere. But women sum up all these qualities. Forever a minor before the law, a woman will almost certainly be "ignorant" in regard to Greek and Latin, and "idle" in that she engages in no public work. At least this characterization of the reader gives the novelist a somewhat educated and partly adult target audience.

The "feminization" of the Novel in France and England may be seen as a way of both succumbing to and resisting social pressure. By making the Novel so officially unimportant, so harmless, the definition permitted the Novel to continue, and novels to be bought. Such a definition even encouraged (if slowly) further writing by women, and the production of novels in which female characters play central roles, although, as we have seen, female characters playing central roles are *not* news in the history of the Novel. The "domestic novel" was not the invention of women, nor wrought by them, though it was to become a critical truism (as for Henry James) that women are good at that sort of thing because of their eye for the trivial details of daily life. Actually, women writers have never shrunk from scenes of battle and violence, of murder, of intrigue, of travel and adventure, and they are neither more nor less attracted to the fantastic than male writers. Following the career of a writer like Eliza Haywood, one can see the difficulty she had in adjusting her subjects and interests to the new requirements of the 1740s and 1750s. In 1736 she had produced the satiric and intelligent fantasy *Eovaii*, a novel set in "pre-Adamitic" times, and supposedly translated from the Pre-Adamitic language into the Chinese—thus ridding both characters and language of the prescriptions of Genesis. The age of such experimentation was over by 1750.

With the average reader imagined (no great compliment) as female, male novelists had a new inducement to write about female characters. That male authors wrote about women has come under some criticism recently. Nancy K. Miller in *The Heroine's Text* (1980) has criticized novelists of the eighteenth and nineteenth century for obsessively reinscribing "male scenarios of women's fragile fate" (154). According to Miller and others, female characters drawn by men are merely "female impersonators." This seems harsh—must every novelist be prohibited from dealing with characters of the so-called "opposite" sex? Scudéry spent a lot of time on her male characters and their inwardness (to Boileau's disgust). We ought to consider the other side of the case: that in colonialist, militaristic, and expansionist societies such as France and England of the time, male experience was in some respects becoming officially much smaller. Men are supposed to be rational and successful. Failure is for failures. Inner perturbation, dreams, nightmares and anxieties are to be permitted only to weak or villainous—and preferably lower-class—males. In the eighteenth century, it is the male sex that is perilously in danger of becoming the sex without a psyche. The failure, by and large, of tragedy, after the era of Racine and Otway, indicates a cultural inability to envisage men except in terms of rational success (a spell that Arthur Miller is still trying to break in *Death of a Salesman* [1949]). But women can be intelligent, sensitive, and benevolent beings who encounter undeserved hardship—without looking merely stupid. Women are not supposed to be in charge of fate.

Women, that is, become ever more interesting to male and female authors

alike because they represent the cultural locus of *Tychē* and the cultural repository of imagination, or of feeling—even of social criticism. Many novels of both
the eighteenth and the nineteenth centuries are named after female protagonists:
*Roxana, La Vie de Marianne, Clarissa, Lettres d'une Péruvienne, Amelia, Julie ou la Nou-
velle Héloïse, Sophie von Sternheim, Evelina*. We remember that the *Aithiopika* was
once *Charikleia* and that *Leukippé and Kleitophon* was once *Leukippé* (as Salmasius
says). The male half of the male-female pair in a title is now treated as fully
disposable.

It is assumed that the female protagonist need not be stupid to be ignorant
of the world she is entering, and she need not be satiric to be capable of telling
reflections. Marivaux in his "Avertissement" to the first part of his *Le Vie de Marianne* (1731) comments that although the taste nowadays is for nothing but adventures, his heroine has excluded none of her reflections upon what happened;
she writes to a female friend who loved to think (*aimait à penser*, 5), and
retirement from the world made her serious and philosophical. This preface assures us that *knowledge* is to be gained from a female who is a thinking being.
Such reassurance is necessary for the male reader, and the female protagonist
customarily addresses herself to males outside the novel). The presence of such a
thinking being on the scene is a sign of the world of feminine readers who could
easily become female writers. Mary Granville Delany is emboldened to write her
autobiography in the form of a novel, for the eyes of her best friend the Duchess
of Portland. In this form, as nowhere else, she could voice her anger over the
arranged marriage that imprisoned her youth.[5] Reading Mary Delany's private
account, one feels that autobiography might not have been possible for her at all
without the novels, with their veil of figurative language and, most important,
their modes of mythologizing the personal life. "Romance" allegorized a woman's
life for her.

It was always to be feared that the novel allowed both young men and
young women too much scope for protest and discontent. That is, it is inconvenient to society for young persons (or the poor) to feel their individual life as myth.
Such discontent was hastily labeled idle self-indulgence. *Bovarysme* is the result of
much novel-reading, as Molière had foreseen. The proliferation of conduct books
in the eighteenth century bears witness to social fears that females, influenced by
the pernicious novel, might get above themselves, take themselves too seriously.

As soon as the female reader was fully imagined as a cultural defense, she
became a cardinal source of anxiety. In his "Seconde Préface" to *Julie ou la Nouvelle Héloïse*, Rousseau, carrying matters to the extreme as he likes to do, says that
no chaste girl (*honnête fille*) ever reads novels (love-stories, *livres d'amour*, 23). Any
girl who would read this one was already lost. The virtuous female novel-reader
thus becomes practically a contradiction in terms. Novels inflame—no matter
how exemplary they may claim to be. Richardson and other such moral novelists,
Rousseau says, are merely setting the house on fire in order to try to put it out.
Yet if the reading of novels is sin, then everyone has fallen—everyone is contaminated. To permit the fancy to move at all, within either man or woman, is to
have lost that first virtue of sheerest ignorance and a lack of self-awareness, the
innocent bloom that novels, even the most virtuous, must always rub away. The
"exemplary novel" is paradoxical—indeed, impossible. The more successful a

novel is in relating us to the example, through force of emotion and image, the more wickedly seductive it is in arousing our fancy and exercising the psyche on that which is not.

Moralists were in danger of allowing their own psyches to become unduly exercised on that imaginary being, the gendered reader. For, whether imagined as male or female, the reader is always troubling as a social entity. Only in the contemporary academy is the novel-reader safely and respectably imagined. In the company of Iser and Brooks and Booth, we need worry no longer. Outside the academy, the reader is still a bit of a problem—the female more than the male. We produce anxious books on *women*'s reading of cheap paperback formulaic love-stories.[6] Nobody studies male reading in that way, although there is a tendency to agonize over what males are not reading: the Great Books. It is comforting to suppose that young men are kept from their rightful *Iliad* by the vicious interposition of feminists or multiculturalists, rather than to inspect young men's ingestion of Tom Clancy.

THE PROBABLE AND THE VERISIMILAR

The author of the anonymous preface to the 1717 *Adventures of Theagenes and Charikleia* notes ruefully that "romance" has become a dirty word, romances "being reckoned at least but vain sallies of Wit in them that write, and unthrifty spenders of time to those that read them." The Novel or Romance needs much more defense than it used to require. To counter the sweeping attack, a pro-novel critic of the late seventeenth or early eighteenth century must go back to the Renaissance's best Aristotelianism, sacrificing some fiction on the way. It has become a cliché by 1717 to decry the old barbarous fiction of knights, dragons, castles. That is, medieval fiction could be offered as a propitiatory sacrifice to the new doctrine of the "verisimilar."

In France, a critical movement centered on, though not limited to, the Académie Francaise had worked to bring drama into line with the highest humanist theory—and, not incidentally, into line with the unifying theory of the state. There is to be one action—no subplots—consistency of scenes, and unity of time and place. The new drama separated the nobles and the intellectuals from the lower-class folk who like tumbling and spectacle. Pure reason is not for them. In drama proper, all is to be subject to the Aristotelian probability, which in France is described chiefly as *vraisemblance*. This *vraisemblance* is subject to many restrictions. Nothing should be out of keeping with the eternal verities. Thus, Corneille was wrong to show a girl who loved her father's murderer, even if it actually happened in real life, because there is a higher Platonic (or perhaps really sociopolitical) *vrai*. Nothing is to be "low." Everything is to be truthful— *verisimilar*—but like life at its highest and most dignified capacities. This Aristotle-based but not truly Aristotelian theory was refitted to suit the Novel. What is troubling about the French "rules" in drama is not that people thought Aristotle's ideas worth pursuing, but that the matter became so prescriptive and formulaic. The Novel was threatened with a similar theoretical programming—although the Novel could be more evasive than the easily censored drama. The Novel, which has always had a friendship for popular forms of storytelling despite its own moneyed clientele, is not very happy with the sort of restraints the new French theory poses. In the seventeenth century, the "verisimilar" seems a largely abstract idea, productive of an art in which pure essence confronts pure essence in the formidable force of intellect—as with Racine's plays. But what is "truth"? What is the verity that the verisimilar story should respect? Nobody wanted to write much about knights or dragons anymore (castles were to be another matter) so that part was easy. But where does the real subject lie? French neoclassicism did not assume that the *vrai* and the *véritable* lay in the world of vulgar phenomena.

According to one tradition, the "Fancy" is really creative, or at least visionary, working more or less directly from the divine eternal template rather than copying the world of things. This defense is offered by Sidney for the golden world of his *Arcadia*. Margaret Cavendish, Duchess of Newcastle, in the introduction to her *Blazing World* (1666), glances at that theory but wishes to proclaim, in almost a Romantic way, the *creative* power of "Fancy": "Fancy creates of its own accord whatsoever it pleases, and delights in its own work." She labels herself "a Happy Creatoress" and boasts that though she cannot conquer worlds like Alexander "yet rather then [*sic*] not to be Mistress of one . . . I have made a World of my own: for which no body, I hope, will blame me, since it is in every ones [*sic*] power to do the like" (2d ed., 1668, "To the Reader," a3ᵛ–a4ʳ). "Margaret the First" was, however, an eccentric, an anomaly. In the seventeenth century it was possible to think that the artist's fidelity to the truth the soul knows could result in a work that is truth-ful, however wonderful or unlikely the events. This theory lies behind *Persiles y Sigismunda*, though Cervantes himself is unhappy about the amount of lie (*mentira*) in fiction, and his book might have been written to express some of the concerns of Ingelo. The truth, the verity, does not have always to be day-to-day reality—though it can include that, the *cosas humildes*, humble things, just as, Cervantes says, great paintings have grass and bushes in the corners (*Persiles y Sigismunda*, 371).

Such Neoplatonic verity was not to satisfy all the demands of new generations, although some concept like it has never been totally absent from novelwriting. The novelist is not writing a scientific document—though scientific documents of all kinds are sustained by myth and colored by metaphor. A novelist's primary calling is to give *a representation of what it feels like to be alive*. This can be done in many ways. But the sense of being alive, as an individual in time, is a mythic affair—no matter what the religious belief or absence of belief of novelists or readers. The concept of the creative power of "Fancy" allows the novelist to claim access to important truths other than those the scientific realist would emphasize. Living is not teapots and trains but a personalized legend of relationship to teapots and trains—or to other concepts of our minds, such as the Mediterranean sea, or a just society, or what it would feel like to fly. Yet with a Neoplatonic justification the novelist can never rest too satisfied, for Platonism of all kinds must at last slight the world of things and experiences in which the Novel is perpetually interested.

As the seventeenth century advanced, it became more and more incumbent upon fiction to pay overt homage to the laws of "nature," and to deal only with the *literally* possible as the *vrai*. This might be considered a kind of scientific method of fiction-writing. But of course the "possible" is itself very largely a mental construct. Where would we be if we could never imagine the thing that is not—or is not yet? The seventeenth century sees the burgeoning of a scientific thought counter to the scientific method in the emergence of the new fantastic form we have come to call *science fiction*. Such fiction, rooted in the comic fantasy of Lucian, especially in *Vera Historia*, as well as in its later serious offshoots such as *Utopia*, can be considered in part a parodic riposte to the new theories of naturalistic probability. It is highly visible from the time of Francis Godwin's novel of space travel, *The Man in the Moone* (1638), with its fresh application of Copernican science. This mischievous and valuable form has never left our side since, and before very long was taking on the exploration of ideas of the future, as Paul Alkon has demonstrated in *Origins of Futuristic Fiction* (1987).

Although science fiction has an ancient background in Aristophanes and Lucian, it is new in its deliberate play with scientific findings and cosmological relativism. When we imagine travel to planets, we are imagining not only technological but also social developments and alternatives. Science-fiction writers were among the first to realize that technological change is conceptual change— and *vice-versa*. Science fiction necessarily exhibits political consciousness. It progressed rapidly in the seventeenth century, but often as an outlaw form—as in the case of Cyrano de Bergerac's *Histoire comique des états et empires de la lune* (1656) and *Histoire comique des états et empires du Soleil* (1661), which suffered from censorship. These are not stories about what is, or what is likely—but they are stories that can change possibilities. It took 300 years of imagined space travel before we did get to the moon, but the writers helped to change the framework of possibility, and of probability. Of course, reading itself has technological implications. It can even be called a technological act. Arguably, the culture that produced *Aithiopika* and got us to follow the complicated interweaving of stories would eventually produce the Jacquard loom and all that ensues.

Reading fiction can hardly be an "idle" and unproductive act if it changes our mind-set, transforming the outlook and standards of society itself. But that argument makes fiction too tremendous. Few fiction writers wanted to defend themselves by pointing out their social and political consequence. The idea of the *exemplary* meant that the individual reader should be morally ironed out to conformity with the civic norm—rather than that society itself should be transformed. One theorist of the early eighteenth century did set out an argument of social transformation: Abbé Nicolas Lenglet-Dufresnoy in his *De l'usage des Romans* of 1734. The Abbé, who took a great interest in fiction (he was an editor of *Le Roman de la Rose*), advertises his book's relation to Huet's *Traité*, emphasizing the role of women that the novels bring to light. Once that role is recognized, he suggests there is no reason not to allow inheritance of nobility to pass through the womb alone. Although he is talking about aristocratic titles only, the Abbé's proto-feminist statement has obvious implications for the inheritance and use of all wealth and even for diffusion of political power. In contemporary eyes, his was a nightmare vision of Amazonian rule, of the destruction of proper civic society through the undermining influence of the Novel.

Such theoretical musings made Huet's ideas seem more noxious and alien than ever and provoked attack. One of the liveliest of these attacks was the anonymous *Voyage Merveilleux du Prince Fan-Férédin dans la Romancie* (1735) (which might be translated as *The Amazing Voyage of Prince Fan-Férédin in Novel-Land.*) The Prince, after passing through an underground cavern, emerges in a meadow with groves dispersed at proper distances from each other. He drinks of the fountains of love and hate and remedies the effects at the Lake of Indifference (a comic reminiscence of Scudéry's cartography of the Land of Tenderness in *Clélie*). In this place even the rocks are sensitive, the very echoes are docile, the trees are always green and even have a taste for music. Here he meets the shepherds and shepherdesses from the banks of Lignon (i.e., from *L'Astrée*), who never have to worry about the matrimonial knot but only about the tender signs of *amitié* (57).

The Prince notices some odd things about the inhabitants of Romancie. There are no children or old people, and no one is deformed or in bad health. We think the French pass for a good-looking nation, but with us you find people with long noses, wide mouths, comical chins—not so with the folk of Romancie. There a person with a slightly long nose, or rather small eyes, would be regarded as a monster. It is explained to the Prince that in order to understand the place you must realize that Romancie is divided into High and Low (*haute & basse*):

> The first is the domain of Princes and celebrated Heroes; the second has been abandoned to all the Subjects of the second Order, travellers, adventurers, men & women of mediocre virtue. It must even be admitted, to the shame of human nature, High Romancie has been for a long while nearly deserted . . . whereas low Romancie [*la basse Romancie*] becomes ever more and more populous. Also, the Fairies and the Genies seeing themselves neglected, and almost without a practice, have for the most part chosen to go away, some to imaginary spaces, others to the land of Dreams. That is why you no longer see Romancie adorned as it was of yore. (107) [7]

Le Voyage Merveilleux du Prince Fan-Férédin dans La Romancie is engagingly witty, and some points are well taken, like the one about fictional characters' looks—although the author seems to have forgotten the large number of novel characters, from Leukippé to Amadís and beyond, who get ill, disheveled, and dirty. If we expect the distinction between "high" and "low" Romancie to work in favor of realism, in the English manner, we will be disappointed. It is evidently the author's purpose to ridicule all fiction together for its unnaturalness, its conceit—and its very fictiveness. His satire ranges not only through the works of Scudéry and D'Urfé, but also through modern novels including *Gulliver's Travels* and Prévost's *Le Philosophe Anglais ou les Mémoires de Cleveland*, the first part of which had just appeared in 1732 (not be completed until 1739). The satirist is up-to-date, and impartial, for the absurdities of the *Odyssey* come in for their share of mockery, as well as *The Thousand and One Nights*—this latter being parodied in a truly novel title, *The Thousand and One Quarters of an Hour*.

The importance of fiction by women, as pointed out by Lenglet-Dufresnoy, here supplies the guiding light to the absurdity of the Novel altogether. Female writing only makes clear the vulgar fantasy of all narrative fiction. Significantly, only the schoolmasterly and civic-minded *Télémaque* is excepted and praised (200–202).

A much harsher attack on Huet, Lenglet-Dufresnoy, and the Novel is to be found in the Abbé Armand-Pierre Jacquin's *Entretiens sur les Romans* (1755). The origins of the Novel, according to Jacquin in this *Ouvrage Moral et Critique* as the subtitle calls it, are not as Huet said, for the Arabs were not good at prose fiction; rather, the stories enshrine the absurdities and superstition of former ages in Europe. The modern novel is a feminine invention. Jacquin is most concerned about the effect of this bad reading on males; even the brightest man may have his intellect contaminated if he takes to reading novels. Novels are pernicious to civic order: "this baleful reading-matter accustoms us to confound ideas of good with those of evil, ideas of vice with those of virtue. . . . Open these works, and you will see in almost all of them, the laws of divine and human justice violated; the authority of parents over their children set at naught; the sacred ties of marriage and of friendship broken" (225).[8] *Le Roman* accustoms people to blasphemous and presumptuous thoughts: "each Reader believes himself justified in arrogating to himself the same right [as the hero] . . . leaving to his caprice and his passions the care of dictating the maxims of his beliefs: so true it is that there is but one route which leads to the sanctuary of truth, and that those that lead to error are numberless!" (212–213).[9]

The novel is a quintessential Protestantism of its own kind, turning against monarchy, monoglot discourse, and unity of opinions. The Abbé remarks approvingly that in the reign of Louis XIV not many novels were written, and good sense was the rule. The return of novels in France is felt as a sort of political disease, a cultural plague: "Of all poisons, that which is presented in a gilded cup and with a charming outside is often the most dangerous" (289).[10] Novels threaten the social order.

Yet Jacquin, rather inconsistently, assures himself and us that novels are too feeble to be lasting or memorable. He asserts (against the evidence) that major new works of the kind have passed or are passing out of mind: "Was I wrong to prophesy to you [the Contesse] that the Novel *Pamela* would soon be forgotten? You were once its idolator; however, without your little bitch that you called by that name, would one idea of it remain with you? It was the same three years ago with *Tom Jones* and *Clarissa*" (101).[11] We notice that there is no attempt, such as the English love, to separate out the superior English works in the new mode and to classify them as essentially different from and superior to mere romances. All are pretty well trash alike. *Le Roman* is *le roman*—and a silly thing it is.

It was obviously much safer for the novelist to emphasize the private and exemplary nature of the novel, and never to make any open claim to large-scale social influence; still less should a novelist point to social change as a foreseeable or reasonable result of his or her work. In the critical discourse created in the seventeenth and eighteenth centuries, one encounters an implicit resistance to the idea that literature has an impact on the creation of "reality"—that it is not just a model of digesting already available reality. Novel-reading is most defensible if regarded as an individual moral therapy—like the conduct books.

The individual can be reformed by reading an exemplary tale. Yet novels themselves, ancient or modern, seem not to fit the model at all, and Jacquin is certainly right in pointing this out. In novels good girls run away from home, well-meaning boys get thrown in jail. Because they offer an image of the social norm itself altering, novels are dangerous and volatile. We may sense in the increasing pressure to produce novels that are lifelike, probable, verisimilar, an effort to tie the Novel down, to clip its wings so that it will not be guilty of the extravagances of moral imagining. The seventeenth century still has an abstract and loose idea of the "reality" to which fidelity must be maintained. But in England especially, under the control of Whig mercantilism and expansion, by mid-century there will be a demand for fidelity to a very close physical and social reality. We may suspect in that prescription a desire on the part of the authorities to sustain the *status quo.* Yet, there are still difficulties in defining "reality." As Samuel Johnson remarks, it is as morally dangerous to mirror what exists outside you as anything else—and if that is all the Novel does, you might as well live your own life unmediated: "If the world be promiscuously described, I cannot see of what use it can be to read the account; or why is may not be as safe to turn the eye immediately upon mankind . . ." (*Rambler* No. 4 [March 1750], *Works,* IV : 23). A novel cannot *really* be a mirror, reflecting without plan or pattern. On the other hand, therefore, any novel has improbability in the very nature of its being plotted—not to mention "absurdities," which novels are likely to fall into, *Manon Lescaut* and *Clarissa* included.

"Probability" and "verisimilitude" had been introduced to save the day, to discipline the form and make it acceptable. Let it but respect the verisimilar, the *vraisemblable,* and the proprieties (the *bienséances*), and the Novel might be admitted to the humblest plateau of Parnassus. At the price of getting rid of its medieval phase, the Novel (or "Romance") could enter the Kingdom of Literature—or the Republic of Letters. *Chaireas and Kallirrhoé,* for instance, could be accepted because it dealt with the probable, was not fantastic. (And at least Chariton's novel was translated in the 1750s; one doubts whether, if the whole of *Phoinikika* had been discovered and edited in 1972, that novel would have been issued in vernacular editions straight away.) In the eighteenth century the door was still open—open to the foreign and the past—but it was closing. Theorists forgot, however, to take into account the changeable nature of the "probable" and the "verisimilar." They thought they had hit on solid value, primary qualities in the Lockean sense. The "verisimilar," however, is fluid and iridescent.

"Verisimilar" fiction is as open to moral objections as fiction about knights and castles (themselves once verisimilar in their time). To the true anti-novelist, no book can be good that *does* give "an account of the *passions* and *actions* of Men"—at least in any way at all calculated to be moving. This is to display vice at large. It is also to involve the reader in fantasy, drawing him in to share and create an artificial memory, his mind being reinscribed with thoughts and feelings that were not there before, and which Church and State neither convey nor monitor. The more passionate or puzzlingly intricate the characters, the worse a book may be adjudged, for the reader's soul is jolted out of its desirable calm. John Davies of Kidwelly tries to placate that judgment in claiming that the Novel nowadays works only *gently* rather than in a harsh Aristotelian catharsis. The Novel "does now but gently enflame the minde" into emulation of virtue and "a *sympathy* for the weaknesse and sufferings it finds represented" (*Astrea,* 1657, A2ᵛ). The argument from *sympathy* is relatively new, though it rests on an Aristotelian basis. Aristotle imagines we want to be rid of a load of passion; Davies, that we desire to have emotions gently encouraged in us. The argument for virtuous sympathy is one way for the eighteenth-century novel-defender to stave off the severer critiques. But the "Puritan" side can always retort that our real power of sympathy is falsely leached off into artificiality. We imagine we have helped our neighbor because we have wept (like St. Augustine) over the trials of an imaginary personage.

THE RISE OF REALISM

"Realism" has been a feature of literature ever since literature became visible. Representation of common objects, of forms of speech, of personalities and emotions has been part of the work of prose fiction throughout its history. When we use a phrase like "The Rise of Realism" we are alluding to a particular formulation of that "realism" and its extension as a law of fiction. The novel that Ian Watt defines and sees as rising—at last!—in England in the eighteenth century is a form of the Novel that lies under Prescriptive Realism. From the mid-seventeenth to the early mid-eighteenth century, experimentation in fiction was tolerated, along with the kind of internal consistency that Corneille has said applied to Medea; if she is a witch throughout the play, she can have her magical car at the end. The *vraisemblable* could be (possibly) redefined and need not limit itself to what always happens at home. Those who are relatively powerless in "real life" can be granted extraordinary powers in fiction. But Prescriptive Realism tightened the grip of a *vraisemblable* redefined. This Realism's design makes it less possible to move out of one's own sphere.

The Rise of Realism can be seen as a political event, and a direct—if delayed—effect of Huet's establishment of the international history of the Novel. Huet's formulation, which was also a formulation that favored the power of women writers, had displayed the alarming and pernicious tendencies of the Novel to the opened eyes of pastors and masters. Undoubtedly there was a general repugnance, a "natural" aversion especially among the insular and provincial—if colonizing—English, to that which is "Oriental." The new Novel would define itself as home-grown, Aryan. The Novel is an inheritor of the epic of Homer—that much is admissible, for "Homer" is naturalized, and already stands among our cultural claims to superiority.

The great bard "Homer," sage and master of civilization, died in the eighteenth century. He passed away under the scrutiny of F. A. Wolf in his *Prolegomena ad Homerum* (1795). Wolf's Homer is what he saw the Hebrew Scriptures had already been shown to be, the ultimate result of many reworkings of early and even primitive elements transmitted from the period before writing was known or at least common. Folk-materials were perpetually reinterpreted, reshaped, and rerendered. "The Homer that we hold in our hands now" is but a constructed entity, "variously altered, interpolated, corrected, and emended from the times of Solon down to those of the Alexandrians" (*Prolegomena to Homer*, ed. and trans. Grafton, et al., 209).[12] Wolf's folkish Homer fits in with certain late eighteenth-century poetic and political interests in folk-culture, but he does not meet the needs of high culture as a support to imperial greatness. Wolf's Homer is fractured, rough, and foreign—and not an individual artist. By the time "Homer" had thus broken down, the English, after them all of Europe, had a new icon firmly in place, "Shakespeare," the modern unitary and consciously creative (if inspired) single genius. Shakespeare is what the novelists must try (usually, they are told, in vain) to emulate.

The culture of the Novel, the true "Great Tradition" stretching back not only to Boccaccio but to Apuleius and Heliodorus, was still the literary heritage of European and English readers and writers born at the turn of the eighteenth century. This inheritance included Spanish novels of the sixteenth century and French novels of the seventeenth century. The rise of Prescriptive Realism put an end to this culture of the Novel and made the Great Tradition largely invisible. The fog of invisibility fell over England first but was to be exported to the Continent. In France, a revulsion such as Jacquin's at the status of the Novel and the dangers it posed permitted a sympathetic Continental reception of English ideas as to how to restrict the Novel's activities. It might be argued not that a devotion to the realistic led incidentally to the loss of much fiction—but that a devotion to realism was invented by the English as an efficient excuse for shedding the tradition.

Realism does have its potentially idealistic aspect. There is much to be said for honoring the humble facts of life, for celebrating the diurnal. Realism has its potentially politically democratic aspects, such as are celebrated by some novelistic practitioners of the nineteenth century, like the early George Eliot. But the "realistic" is not *necessarily* more democratic than other modes. When one of the poorest of men wished earnestly to write a fictional narrative, he borrowed form and pattern from versions of medieval "romance." The indebtedness of John Bunyan's *Pilgrim's Progress* (1678; 1684) to *Guy of Warwick* and other stories has been well documented; Bunyan's story also bears a relationship to *Amadís* and *Persiles*. In writing his narrative Bunyan does not have to be true to the "realistic" as defined in public terms, according to which he is just a tinker and should write about what he knows (pots and pans) or preferably not write at all, not stepping out of his civic sphere. There is no reason in nature why the poor or oppressed should choose realistic material when they turn to writing fiction. The evidence offered by actual writers who are poor or female suggests otherwise. Had strict realism applied in France in the early 1750s, Mme. de Graffigny could never have written *Lettres d'une Péruvienne*. She had never even been to South America and was certainly not an Inca in a city sacked by the conquistadors.

Realism emerges not as a suggestion but as a kind of ideology. Unstandardized realism might have been left as one of the original modes, a possibility in the palette of the artist. Writers of 1700–1730 obviously enjoyed experimenting with the realistic as well as combining it with other modes. The advent of newspapers and magazines is sometimes invoked to explain the new dominance of realism—but one might as justly record the impact of fictional narration on newspapers themselves. There are many ways to tell "a story." Prescriptive Realism demanded that all novels admitted as Literature should be written only in certain ways, and should deal with certain subjects.

We can posit an almost exact date signaling the new Realism's usurpation of the major realms of prose fiction. Charlotte Lennox's *The Female Quixote* (1752) records this moment in describing the disillusionment of Arabella, quixotic reader of French novels by Scudéry and company. Her cousin and imposed fiancé

Mr. Glanville significantly refuses to read the works his beloved urges him to try. Glanville, obviously a disciple of Boileau, knows *without reading them* that they are trash. Arabella has to realize that the novels, her inheritance (as in the case alleged of Rousseau) from her *mother*, constitute a mere female tradition, which is useless and wrong and should never have got into the library. Arabella must relinquish her books and with them the idea that she can be of importance, meekly taking up the tameness of the imprisoning "real life" she is offered. As the Countess tells her, gentlewomen have no history and no "Adventures"—the very word "carries in it so free and licentious a sound" (327).

Lennox's own first novel, *The Life of Harriot Stuart* (1750), contained numerous elements of the older fiction, including voyage and shipwreck. Harriot, like Anthia in *Ephesiaka*, tries to kill a would-be rapist. In *The Female Quixote* Arabella has to believe not only that she should have no history, but—preposterously—that rape never happens outside of bad books written by women. Lennox is visibly chagrined at discovering the literary tradition she had inherited had just been declared defunct. Her next work, *Shakespeare Illustrated* (1753–1754), is a defense of the older fiction, as well as an attempted deconstruction of Shakespeare. Her critical discussion of Shakespeare's borrowing (a matter hitherto little understood) turns approvingly to his sources; writers such as Boccaccio, she contends, are fairer to women in their stories than Shakespeare (or his Augustan admirers).[13] But Lennox was practically alone in defending the old medieval and early Renaissance fiction against the new idol, who not only represented British superiority but was also to represent modern Europe's claims to civilization after the decline and fall of "Homer."

Not everyone ceased reading the older fiction in 1752. Anyone old enough to write in the 1750s could still remember the older literature. Sarah Scott in *A Journey through Every Stage of Life* (1754) alludes to Scudéry's *Clélie* as if assured that readers will easily recollect the incident: "I suppose you would sooner have attributed the breaking off of the intended Marriage to an Earthquake, like the Author of Clelia" (I: 173). But by the mid-1750s even Samuel Richardson, Lennox's supporter, had joined the cry against the tradition, in his *Sir Charles Grandison* (1753–1754). This is disingenuous, as *Grandison* itself betrays the influence of *Clélie* (among others). In *Grandison*, the heroine's grandmother confesses her own earlier reading of "Romances," which created a false desire for love, so that she did not want to marry the man her family proposed to her. (That is, she was becoming a *Précieuse*.) But she was persuaded: "Esteem, heightened by Gratitude, will soon ripen into Love: the only sort of Love that suits this imperfect state . . ." (III: 398). Besides, her family, with its many daughters, needed this match "of real benefit to your whole family." "Romances," once again, have militated against the civic ideal, according to which women should subordinate their desires to the larger unit's needs. Richardson's own *Clarissa* argues against such a position, and in *Grandison* itself he has distinguished the power of love. But he can rid himself of blame at the end of his novel by having Mrs. Shirley declaim, in a short of spoken essay, against all the older female-based literature, "that unnatural kind of writing," including *La Princesse de Clèves* in her structures (III: 398–400).

The older literature is now historicized, placed inexorably in the *past*. An old-fashioned corrupted taste has been corrected: "The present age is greatly obliged to the authors of the Spectators" (*Grandison*, III : 398). The *Spectators*, as advice to women, are now clearly ranged against the "Romances," and thus against all fiction, most especially that by or about women. Jane Austen shows she knows this, in her calculated outburst wittily accusing the *Spectator* papers of all the faults customarily ascribed to "romances," including being long-winded, improbable, unnatural, outmoded, and crude (*Northanger Abbey*, 21–22). The *Spectators* are now in turn historicized, at a moment when to be historicized is largely to be dismissed.

In both France and England, reading of the older fiction along with the new had continued unbroken until the 1730s, when Horace Walpole was reading Scudéry in his school days at Eton.[14] In France, the many editions of Scudéry's novels had sold well until the issue of *Clélie* in 1731. In both nations, copies of Scudéry's novels in private libraries sufficed to ensure that they were not entirely forgotten, even up to the French Revolution, and the same applies to a host of other novels, including the ancient novels. But they were losing circulation as live ideas. Constant reissue of the older novels ceases to be the norm. The 1730s sees the winding down of the festival of universal reading begun in the Renaissance. But violent and overt attack on all the older fiction emerges as a feature of the 1750s. Jacquin's polemic against the novel *holus bolus* appeared in the middle of that decade. Charlotte Lennox seems to have been acute in her diagnosis in 1752: there was an onslaught against most forms of the Novel, and any passable novel must display among its credentials a claim to Realism.

The judgmental remarks made by characters in *The Female Quixote* on the heroines cited by Arabella, including warriors and queens like Thalestris and Cleopatra, adumbrate one of the interests of the new Realism—that bad women be punished. New Realism, describing and controlling the highly domesticated novel, takes a renewed interest in monitoring female chastity. Heroines in fiction of the past included stellar proponents of *sōphrosynē*, like Charikleia, and not-so-stellar, like Leukippé. But there are also women who "fall," like Melitté and indeed in a sense Kallirrhoé, who succeed in avoiding censure and even in finding some happiness. In the medieval and Renaissance fiction, women who undertake sexual adventures might have a hard time emotionally—like Boccaccio's Fiammetta and Montemayor's Selvagia. But they remain on this side of the grave—or, if in a grave, like Fenice, they get out. In the eighteenth- and nineteenth-century realistic novels there is an enormous rise in female mortality. If Lennox's Arabella nearly dies as a result of imprudent contact with the Thames, Rousseau's Julie is killed as an effect of the contact with water. Water, once wont to disgorge heroines harmless, now becomes a means of killing those who stray—even in thought, like Maggie Tulliver. Drowning or elegant fever are among the better ways to depart. Mme. de Merteuil in *Les Liaisons dangereuses* (1782) catches small pox, and it would have been better for her to have died—she is horribly disfigured, *affreusement défigurée* (385). If Mme. de Merteuil is disfigured by smallpox, to which she has lost one eye, the heroine of Zola's *Nana* (1880) is both killed *and* disfigured—she too has lost one eye. Zola labors at the end to make sure we realize that Nana, the poor but eminently beautiful girl who became showgirl (playing the part of Venus) and prostitute to men of good standing, is neither admirable nor pitiable, but contemptibly rotten, a plague-carrier who is herself a sort of moral virus: "It seemed that the virus picked up by her in the gutters, on the heaps of tolerated carrion, this fermentation with which she had poisoned a people, had just returned into her own face and rotted it [*l'avait pourri*]" (439). Poxy Nana becomes a horrific corpse, pitilessly translated into an ekphrastic exemplar of the disgusting:

> a heap of humours and blood, a shovelful of corrupted flesh, thrown there, on a cushion. The pustules had invaded her entire face, one pimple touching the other; and, withered, collapsed, greyish like mud, they already seemed mold of the earth on that formless pap where one could no longer find any features. One eye, the left, had completely sunk into the boiling pus; the other, half open, was subsiding, like a black and decayed hole . . . Venus was decomposing. (438–439)

Nana's decayed eye stands in for the other hole, the wicked hole of her lawless sex, which has corrupted Paris. How one wishes to cry out to Zola, *Frères humains, qui après nous vivez / N'ayez les coeurs contre nous endurcis!*[15]

Zola has managed to surpass Flaubert, who had lingered on female decay in describing Emma Bovary, self-poisoned, dying slowly and grotesquely, her face "bluish, as if frozen in the exhalation of a metallic vapor," her eyes protruding, her body trembling and convulsed (*Madame Bovary*, 323). Not to be outdone in ruining human flesh, Tolstoy has his equally self-destructive and adulterous Anna Karenina throw herself under a train—though he relents and spares her head and "lovely face" from damage. The era of Realism's dominance is rich in dying women, from Manon through Camille and cousin Bette, from Clarissa to Milly Theale. These latter two both die lovely deaths, it is true, for they are innocent—yet they also err and are mysteriously afflicted by unnamed malady.

REALISM AND THE FOREIGN

It is hardly new to discuss questions of *gender* in relation to the development of the novel in the eighteenth and nineteenth centuries. After all, "masculinism" preceded modern feminism. A critic like Georg Lukács, as Michael Danahy notes, imposes the epic as the norm for narrative and encourages the novel to achieve manliness by trying to meet epic standards (see Danahy's *The Feminization of the Novel*, 57). Lukács is only replaying Fielding, who in *Tom Jones* offers specific commentary as to what may masculinize the Novel.

Whenever the Novel is freshly masculinized, women are warned to keep off. Women writers of the eighteenth and nineteenth century were, as we have seen, supposed to keep to the "private sphere," and the approved way to do that in novel-writing, if one must write, was to write only "domestic novels." Some modern feminist critics have welcomed the advent of the more feminine domestic novel and its host of women writers; others have seen such novels as condescending and delusive. A great deal of excellent work has been done in studying all such fiction, as by Vineta Colby, Elaine Showalter, Sandra Gilbert and Susan Gubar, and Nancy Armstrong—to name only a few.[16] There is no need for me to develop the matter further here, as Anglo-American criticism since the 1970s has examined so many aspects of the Novel of the eighteenth and nineteenth centuries, particularly investigating what women were able to achieve with the "domestic novel."

But there are two meanings of "domestic." On the one hand, we have the novel of the home, of the drawing-room, the woman's domestic sphere. But the realistic novel is "domestic" in the other sense, too. Thoroughly localized, whether in the capital or the provinces, it is nationally in-turned. It does not take kindly to foreignness, either for excursion or for importation. In 1715, a translator of Huet could admit that the Novel is more or less a foreign import; Stephen Lewis hopes that England will not have to rely solely upon the (largely French) supply, "but that some *English Genius* will *dare* to Naturalize *Romance* into our Soil" (*The History of Romances*, ix). Lewis takes Huet's *Traité* as a kind of "Teach Yourself Novel-Writing."[17] The English had sooon dared "to Naturalize *Romance*" to such a degree that they could deny the importation of the root stock. Once they had done their naturalizing, they dared to claim the entire form as their own—as Ian Watt and his successors are still doing.

One of the most striking aspects of the new domestic realistic novel, particularly as the English developed it, is its ability to *exclude*. It puts a stop to immigration and emigration. It does not on the whole care for ethnic mixing. The *domestication* of the supposedly realistic novel is not a matter only of gender, nor of gender and class, but of gender, class, and race. Aspiring young European writers, male and female alike, are to be told to write about what they know—what they experientially know—as if that were the sum of what is. They are encouraged to stay in the parish, and not imagine Ethiopia. It hardly seems coincidental that the cult of the "real" and the "normal" in fiction should have taken fiercest hold in England and that its rise coincides with the hardening of true Whig hegemony and the rise of British imperialism. In writing *Our Mutual Friend* (1864–1865) Charles Dickens brilliantly invented Mr. Podsnap, who incorporates the standards (and the source of the standards) of Prescriptive Realism of social control. Podsnap, who is the quintessence of respectability, wishes all the arts to be "sedately expressive of getting up at eight, shaving close at a quarter-past, breakfasting at nine . . ." He is perpetually anxious about "the young person," an "inconvenient and exacting institution, as requiring everything in the universe to be filed down and fitted to it. The question about everything was, would it bring a blush into the cheek of the young person?" (129). We recognize at once in Podsnap the embodiment of those severe or scrupulous readers who might wrinkle the brow. A host of schoolmasterly editors have also aggressively imagined the childlike reader, the "young person" who must be protected for he-or-she is somehow all cheek. Creeping progressively into the introductions to novels over the previous centuries, "Podsnappery" has long been making itself felt. But "Podsnappery" in Dickens's succinct term, includes the repudiation of everything that is Other. "Mr. Podsnap's world was not a very large world . . . seeing that although his business was sustained upon commerce with other countries, he considered other countries . . . a mistake" (128). Mr. Podsnap is the hideous embodiment of the civic ideal.

The *probable* and *vraisemblable* of the seventeenth century doffed their flowing robes and put on pantaloons, narrow jacket, tight cravat, and marched into the City of London. There they found a trade in many interesting things, including not only sugar and cotton, gold and pineapples, but also human beings, known as *slaves*. But it would not be polite to talk about these, and most novelists, at least after Behn and before Harriet Beecher Stowe, did not. What the eye did not see the novelist should not write about, for it is not "real" but would be "imaginary."

We can see that in asserting a manifest destiny to govern and exploit other peoples in many lands, the English and the French (and, later, other imperial powers) with their growing empires would find it more convenient to eliminate the idea of a fiction that has that awkward flavor of the Orient and of Africa. Even by the 1740s we are far removed from the temper and the vision of a Huet, who could even delight in the fact that we must search for the origin of our ancient fiction in the most remote countries and distant ages. The English performed a wonderful trick in persuading themselves that "The Rise of the Novel" took place in England in the eighteenth century. They eliminated the predecessors once so fully acknowledged, along with the transmissions outlined by Salmasius and Huet. Such historians had made the foreignness of fiction *too* visible. That foreignness at the root must be cut off. Only realistic novels could be viewed as literature—but even then, always as literature of an inferior kind. "Gentlemen read better books"—the cliché that Austen's Catherine Morland learns to parrot. According to this Catch-22, a novel must always be a somewhat inferior production because it is homely, limited, domestic, and gently emotional. Yet it cannot be allowed to exist if it is not those things, for then it supposedly becomes wild fantasy—now identified as "Romance."

The Novel becomes fully "domestic"—shutting out aliens. It is almost a definition of the kind of "Novel" meant in *The Rise of the Novel* that we must meet no Muslim characters. If there are Muslim characters, this is not a novel. Western fiction from Boccaccio to Scudéry had had Muslim characters; if not always well treated, at least they were there. Oddly enough, the presence of Jews is also a strain on Realism; when she writes about Jews in *Daniel Deronda* (1876), George Eliot is impatient enough with Realism partly to forego it. Montesquieu in a brave experiment created Muslim narrators in *Lettres Persanes* (1721), though of course his "Persians" really stand for various attitudes present in the West. Just before the gates, as it were, closed, the French had rushed off and brought in the *Mille et une Nuits*, a much-needed import, during the early years of the eighteenth century, injecting into the fictional system of Europe a strong infusion of new Oriental story. Voltaire took the lead in inventing the "Oriental tale." In short story or short novel of this type could be included all that was to be banned by realistic theory—not just magic but Muslims or, indeed, Zoroastrians as in *Zadig* (1747).

ESCAPE FROM PRESCRIPTIVE REALISM: THE INVENTION OF NEW FORMS

One of the cleverest things about the introduction of realism as a necessity for prose fiction is the apparent harmlessness of the concept; it is hard to argue against representation of "real life" (though what a wide, shimmering field that is!). We all value the details that pay homage to the pleasures and exigencies of physical life in the physical world, and of social life in the social world. What we often call "realism" is a particularly *fresh* observation of the physical and the social. Literary artists all employ special touches of "realism" when they find it appropriate. Chariton does so when he has Kallirrhoe upon awakening in her tomb sense the smell of spices and hear the tinkling litter of ornaments. But Apuleius does so too in his more fantastic story, as when the Ass makes use of the pantry. We can find useful C. S. Lewis's distinction between "realism of presentation" (found in touches in practically every literary narrative) and "realism of content" (*An Experiment in Criticism*, 59–73). I use "realism" for all sorts of literary drawing upon social and physical experience. This realism is part of the palette of every novelist. Even in the most fantastic narrative a certain realism of coherence is called for; thus, if you imagine a planet that has a green sun, you must imagine a green sunrise.

I use the capital letter on "Realism" to distinguish what I call Prescriptive Realism, the Realism new in the mid-eighteenth century and dominant in the nineteenth, that became considered as a *sine qua non* of fiction. This all-or-nothing Realism cuts out fantasy and experiment, and severely limits certain forms of psychic and social questioning. This demanding and hectoring Realism can be a dangerous thing for fiction.

As soon as the Novel appears to be tied up in Prescriptive Realism, authors have to rescue it; they do so by inventing other forms of the Novel that will do what the newly "risen" approved middle-class realistic novel says it will *not* do. Science fiction had already arrived and was to be a genre helpful to authors of the next three centuries. The manner and method of the Oriental tale eventually was to be more or less swallowed up in forms of science fiction, with which it has some affinity. (Voltaire's *Micromégas* is a comic science-fiction story.) Both forms allow the protest and thought-experiment disallowed by the regularized novel. Both kinds also not only permit but encourage large-scale traveling. If in the domestic novel (as Goldsmith notes satirically) "all our migrations [were] from the blue bed to the brown" (*The Vicar of Wakefield*, 9), in science fiction our migrations can be from planet to planet. In an Oriental tale you can get from continent to continent. This is a relief for novel characters, who are in the habit of a good deal of traveling.

It is noticeable that the eighteenth century, the first in which the Novel is apparently cramped into domesticity, is very alert at creating forms that are not to be dignified as Novel, or rather by the favored term, fictional "History." That century produces the Oriental tale, the fantastic apologue (*Candide, Rasselas*), the pornographic memoir (*Fanny Hill*). It also invents the "Gothic" novel, a momentous invention first wrought by women and homosexuals who could not be happy with the conceptual "reality" on which domesticated Realism was founded. Horace Walpole, partly in jest, led the way with *The Castle of Otranto* (1764). Ann Radcliffe, in calling her second book *A Sicilian Romance* (1790), announced her participation in an officially despised mode. Nobody was *supposed* to write *romance* anymore—but here it is.

The "Gothic" was always going to be unofficial; it takes up its residence on the dark marches outside the pale. Horror stories had and were to have some very powerful practitioners, including Schiller in the unfinished *Der Geisterseher*, but the story of horror, the "Gothic" novel in all its forms, remains an outsider, critically speaking, from the eighteenth century to the present. It moves back towards the domestic novel slantwise and sardonically, like the detective story, in which there is always a body in the library, and the domestic and civil worlds are rife with hatred and sudden death.

At the price of being disreputable, of not writing "good" fiction, artists of the wider or stranger fiction—and often very popular fiction, too—could create the liberty to say what they wished to say. Such novelists were—and are—almost always called "minor," whether they write thrillers, horror tales, or detective stories. Continental judgment has been more generous than the Anglo-British in allowing literary merit to an author like Poe, but such generosity is of a piece with Continental historical unease about the absolute claims of Realism as the British defined it. Goethe tried to prove in *Die Leiden des Jungen Werthers* (1774) that the domestic *is* the horrifying, but that too-popular book, which has its own way of redefining the realistic, was decried as morbid and sensational. The official charge against Goethe is that he is too "Romantic" in writing about suicide, but the sui-cide of a respectable middle-class male person itself takes place along with "low" subjects that polite writers agree not to mention. Thus it becomes an offense against the *vrai* and is aesthetically incredible—although actual suicides were re-corded in eighteenth-century newspapers and were not incredible.

"Romance"—i.e., the excludable—came back like the return of the re-pressed in the Gothic novel. "Romance" seemed to make a better comeback in another and more exalted form—the only one of the newly invented forms not to be shifted (at least at first) into the enduring "minor" category. The modern historical novel was invented. That is, the historical novel (with us since antiq-uity) was *re*invented. It provided a means of return to space, grandeur, action, adventure, and foreignness. Walter Scott is considered to have perfected the mode, but not before female predecessors had worked on it, as he himself ac-knowledges in his own notes to *Waverley* (1814). Jane Porter, for instance, in *Thaddeus of Warsaw* (1803), a novel admired by Napoleon which deals with the fall of Poland in the 1790s, had treated battle, invasion, and exile. In the historical novel, epic strengths were freshly reunited with the respectable realistic novel, mediating public and private life, and drawing the history of the common people.

A number of important nineteenth-century novels are historical novels, like Alessandro Manzoni's *I Promessi Sposi* (1825, 1842) and Leo Tolstoy's *War and Peace* (1865–1872). It took a while to bring this genre down, but we had done it by the early twentieth century, largely by decrying it for falseness to history and for "sensationalism" (but battle, executions, sieges, etc., may very well evoke sen-sations). The moving pictures' fondness for the historical novels' scenes and ef-fects only proved that this kind of novel was "low"—lowbrow and disreputable. The only kind of historical novel acceptable now is one set in a past within living memory. Everything else of the kind is considered "trash." Yet any historical novel, even a "trashy" one, offers a mode of interpreting history as well as mak-ing available the primary and even shocking truth that real people lived in the otherness of another time. We seem to have some sort of desire to familiarize to ourselves the foreignness of the "then"—but "then" is too foreign a country not to be suspect.

Science fiction, Gothic fiction, and detective stories, historical novels—a rich set of alternatives to the domestic novel, which is proper Literature. So they remain, in the categories of our bookshelves. Booksellers mysteriously know that Science Fiction is not Literature, Mystery Stories are not Literature. Another new kind of fiction invented in the eighteenth and nineteenth centuries offered ways of escaping the restrictions of realism. That is "Children's Fiction"—although this too has many subdivisions. Books written specifically for children and marketed for them first clearly emerge in the late eighteenth century. Despite Johnson's claim that babies like to read about giants, some writers for children, like the Edgeworths, were remorselessly realistic. But the fantasies (often religious and satiric) that had pleased grown-ups in the past and were now less in favor (as the work of mere "Fancy") migrated to children's shelves. *Pilgrim's Progress, Robinson Crusoe*, the *Morte Darthur* and *Gulliver's Travels* (expurgated) stayed there for a long while. Some very fine writers of the nineteenth and twentieth centuries were to write fantasy of different kinds, incorporating elements once allowed to general fiction on the plea that this was "just for the children." For talking animals we go to "children's literature," and for epic quests, also for travel, metamorphosis, and spiritual endeavor. We may be told that a work like *Winnie-the-Pooh* is a culture-specific fantasy, a merely local whimsy, but its positive reception by, for instance, a young Aboriginal girl in Australia as recorded in Sally Morgan in her autobiography *My Place* (1987), must give us pause.[18] The appeal of childrens' literature and its influence may be very great indeed.

THE SURVIVAL OF THE NOVEL

The cult of Realism affected critical practice and literary history far more than it did the creative practice of novel-writing. Undeniably there are many wonderful realistic novels—among them such "masterpieces" as *Père Goriot, Madame Bovary, War and Peace*, and *Middlemarch*. But the *novelists* of the nineteenth century (as distinct from the critics) were in touch with the entire tradition of fiction, and their deeper roots tapped into the great stream, even if that was running underground. There is hardly any great "master" of fiction in the nineteenth century who does not register some impatience with the demands of absolute Realism—not at realism itself, but at the idea that it must be all-in-all. Most nineteenth-century authors give themselves a holiday from Prescriptive Realism from time to time. It would scarcely be fair to cite Dickens, whose attachment to Realism is so notoriously loose. *A Christmas Carol* (1843), which is certainly not realistic, though it borrows what it wants from realism, has never been among the least popular of his works. But for very different "holidays from Realism" one might consider Balzac's *La Peau de chagrin* (1831), or Flaubert's *Salammbô* (1862). Dostoevsky's attachment to Realism is also disconcertingly loose; he can write stories in which corpses underground talk—a matter and a tone taken up in William Kennedy's *Ironweed* (1983).

In the English-speaking world, critical acceptance of nonrealistic practices in fiction—as of nonrealistic modes of fiction—has lagged far behind what real writers have been writing and real readers reading. Italo Calvino, with his own allegiances to myth and journey, offers not only in his own fiction but in essays such as "Levels of Reality in Literature" (1978) a view congruent with theories in and of the older fiction, that realism of detail need not preclude artifice of design, or symbolic or highly unreal events. All levels of reality in a literary text exist only as "part of the *written* word," and we find in any work only "the credibility peculiar to the literary text." What Coleridge called "suspension of disbelief" is "the condition on which the success of every literary invention depends" (Calvino, *The Uses of Literature*, trans. Creagh, 104–105). The base-text to which Calvino repeatedly returns is the *Odyssey*, that permanent favorite of all novelists from antiquity on, a superb narrative not subject to the laws of Realism. Like Scudéry and others, Calvino sees that the author of the *Odyssey* can be included among the *Romanciers* and the modern *Romanciers* can be assimilated to the author of the *Odyssey*. James Joyce in *Ulysses* had already played in a serious and parodic way with all the demands of Realism—including details (such as cooking and shitting) that neoclassical realistic theory—but not the classic novel—tends to leave out. Joyce ironically fulfills the prescription of masculinizing the novel by assimilating it to the epic, showing in the process the instability of authoritative concepts of both "epic" and "masculinity." The *Odyssey* remains the ever-novelizable resource, always superseded, yet perennially available. The novelist Samuel Butler had already impishly suggested in *The Authoress of the Odyssey* (1897) that the most realistic and most fantastic of epics was written (like a novel) by a woman. (A Mlle. Scudéry not only assimilates herself to Homer, but "Homer" could have been a Mademoiselle also!)

If the Homeric epics were visible in the nineteenth century, the ancient novels largely were not. They made some strange appearances from time to time. Edward Bulwer-Lytton's *The Last Days of Pompeii* (1834) refers overtly in its voluminous notes to Apuleius, but there are undeniable symptoms of Heliodorus, and probably some use of Achilles Tatius and even *Ephesiaka* as well. Bulwer-Lytton's book itself participates in the creation of the myth of the pure Aryan Greeks, with its impossibly purebred Greek hero and heroine Glaucus and Ione, far superior to the vulgar materialistic Romans. The novel, though purporting to be a novel *about*—if not *of*—antiquity, reflects and recapitulates literary history's recent repudiation of the African and Oriental. The Egyptian priest of Isis, whom we know as amiable friend in Kalasiris, is turned into this novel's villain, Arbaces the Egyptian, who must be clobbered on the head if the pure white Greeks are to survive. Flaubert's *Salammbô*, another gorgeous farrago but in better critical repute, was affected by Bulwer-Lytton's production and was also researched in a manner indicating direct contact with the ancient novels. Its heroine is a priestess of the goddess Tanit. Flaubert was fascinated by Apuleius, by the very stench of *l'encens et l'urine* in *The Golden Ass*, but his novel bears signs of contact with the other ancient novels, as well as with the East itself in his travels to the Levant.

It seems a poor thing to be looking for the once proud ancient novel only in the back alleys of a few odd historical novels. And indeed, that is not where they really are. As Calvino reminds us, "what books communicate often remains unknown even to the author himself . . . in any book there is a part that is the author's and a part that is a collective and anonymous work" ("Right and Wrong Political Uses of Literature" [1976], *Uses of Literature*, 99). Any book—certainly a novel—is written out of a cultural background and in a culturally shaped form.

It is in its own form and nature that the modern novel—historical novel or Gothic mystery, or sober account of daily life—retains and incorporates the novel of antiquity.

The waning of the Age of Realism allows us to see this now, although some elements in the literary establishment (newspaper reviews for instance) doggedly adhere to the old doctrines of Prescriptive Realism. The "Post-Modern" novel is what it is partly because of the dazzling impression made by South American novelists, who have deployed the traditional resources of the Spanish novel as well as of American Indian stories and traditions to great advantage. Once again, the Novel arises refreshed from mixing of peoples, the contacts of different tribes and their stories and images. Throwing off Realism as a set of stern laws, as a chain, does not mean that realistic novels cannot be written; the novelist is free to choose (even within different sections of the same work) from a number of modes. In a way, novels and novelists have just recovered the position they held in the later seventeenth century. Yet the possibilities and freedoms now so visible were in some sense *always* available, despite the dogged precepts of reviewers.

The Novel itself has always known better things. To put it simply, nineteenth-century novels were written by writers who had strong contact with writers of the eighteenth century. Those eighteenth-century writers, like Prévost, Marivaux, Richardson, and Fielding, had strong contact with seventeenth-century novels influenced by and adapted from everything from *Satyricon* to *Amadís* and *Célie*. And eighteenth-century novelists, at least until 1760 or 1770, came of age in a period when translations of the novels of antiquity were commonly accessible, and treated as current literature. The chain of connection at that time is short and direct, as well as indirect. In every novel there are threads pulling this way, pulling that way, connecting, tying in, and running back. It is not necessary to have read an antique novel in order to be touched by a mediated contact. Whoever has read *Pamela* or *Tom Jones* is in contact with Heliodorus, Longus, Amadis, Petronius. And you are in contact with them again if you read authors of the nineteenth or twentieth century who have read other authors who read those works.

To put it more grandly, the form itself has constantly contained within itself all its potential—like the eggs in an infant's ovaries. The Novel's genetic inheritance has always been present, even if certain characteristics have been suppressed, or seen as sources of embarrassment. Sometimes the embarrassment was so great that a novel (to borrow a plot motif from the ancient novel) had to be exposed, unowned by the official House of Fiction. A number of such illegitimate novels have been fortunate foundlings adopted by readers. The endeavor to throw out aspects of the form has met with but limited success—the bonfire of Don Quixote's books could not be rendered total. In the first full-length critical history of the Novel written after the ascendancy of the Age of Realism, *The Progress of Romance* (1785), Clara Reeve, herself a novelist, allows her discourse (cast as dialogue) to turn and wind in search of inclusiveness, introducing the Greek novel, for instance. At the very end of her *Progress*, she includes *Charoba*, an *Egyptian* story about a woman, thus rewinding the history. Robert Mack argues that Clara Reeve, herself the author of a "Gothic" story, desires "to view the history of prose fiction in all its grand, polyglot inclusivity" and that Reeve does not intend to turn the distinction between romance and novel into a hierarchy. Her inclusion of *Charoba* at the end illustrates "not only . . . Reeve's defense of Eastern tales, but . . . her larger argument for the romance as being 'of human growth'" (Introduction to *Oriental Tales*, xxxvi–xxxvii). Reeve is obviously aware of Huet. Yet her book was largely assimilated by her public as a support for the superiority of realistic novel over discarded older fiction—we are urged to see "progress" as movement from the worse to the better. But in bringing the story of the Egyptian Queen Charoba to the light, and thus even endeavoring to install it in the canon, Reeve unbalances the teleology of a simple concept of literary progress.

To start writing a novel—any novel, no matter how frivolous—is to start writing the Novel—and the author is in charge of something truly bigger than s/he is. The Novel of Antiquity, in quiet ways and passing along hidden streams, has always been the source and nurturer of our Western prose fiction. Through our own tradition Western writers and readers are—and have been—in touch with much larger dimensions of myth than we consciously require. We are also in touch with a variety of cultures, and enjoy a reenergizing contact with the East and South.

In the late eighteenth century the great and long-lived Novel of the West that Huet knew passed theoretically out of sight. The Ancient Novel became officially lost to view—it retired to the German universities. But fiction itself suffered no such occlusions, separations, or quarantines. It was never really severed from the vital East and South. *The Thousand and One Nights* (or *Arabian Night's Entertainment*) and Voltaire's *contes*, including *Zadig* and *Candide*, show that the Enlightenment could not require Realism to be the sole mirror of its reflections; like other thought-experiments, the Enlightenment necessitated full fictional possibility. The *Arabian Nights* become a legitimate source of Oriental allusion, its stories alluded to repeatedly by nineteenth-century novelists writing in the hot high noon of high Realism.

As the twentieth century draws to a close, we observe a return to fantasy, foreignness, and the larger novel. We have Muslims in the novel now—nay, there are novels in English (as well as translated into English, and other European languages) by Muslims. We no longer have just *A Passage to India*, but Indian passages to the West. The process of exchange and transformation is certainly not unproblematic. Salman Rushdie's notorious *Satanic Verses* (1988) elicited a fiercely antagonistic reaction, even to death threats—the extreme of censorship. Like Rabelais' work, which in some respects it resembles, Rushdie's fantastic novel plays with all the rules and forms, including religious language and forms, and narrative customs. It is not exemplary. Severest readers wrinkled their brows. In trying to negotiate a site between beliefs and cultures, Rushdie's novel signals its strong relation to the ancient novel. *The Golden Ass* is not only a source of inspiration, but also a direct ancestor openly alluded to within the novel: "Sufyan, meanwhile, offered further Apuleian sympathy. 'In the case of the ass, reverse metamorphosis required personal intervention of goddess Isis,' he beamed. 'But old times are for old fogies. In your instance, young master, first step would possibly be a bowl of good hot soup'" (*Satanic Verses*, 244). Sufyan addresses Chamcha, who has partly turned into a goat. Chamcha's "comic deformity" mirrors the comic deforming of the realistic novel in Rushdie's book. To deal with Indian characters in London is itself a "deforming" of Mr. Podsnap's notion of literature.

Any novel has a greater range of literary relationships than those indicated by its overt quotations or allusions. What any novel always has to draw on is the Novel itself, that great bizarre medley of the African, the Asian, and the European. The Western novel was strong enough to accommodate itself in appearance to the demands of Realism without losing its inner qualities—and if it had lost those it would have become fundamentally uninteresting, even to Leavisites. The Novel went on being itself basically, despite superficial differences. There must always, of course, be a multitude of differences between age and age, between author and author. The novels that we have enjoyed in the eighteenth, nineteenth, and twentieth centuries, some of which have been hailed as triumphs of Realism that beat the dreadful old "Romance" all to flinders, are siblings under the skin of the other novels we have been discussing—the works of antiquity, of the Renaissance. They share their true characteristics and their inner structure. Every novelist (good or bad, major or minor, fantastic or realistic) repeats the tropes of the Novel itself. The third and last part of this book will show how that is so.

Plate 1. Ancient Greek funerary monument to a dead little girl.

Plate 2. Menander and Glykera: mosaic picture (c. A.D. 200) of a love story.

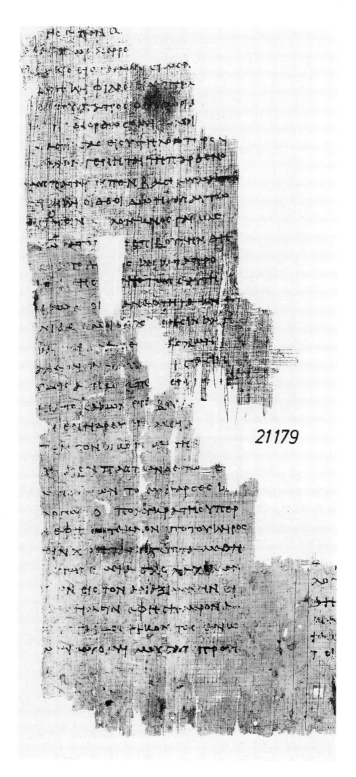

Plate 3. Hero and heroine meet: *Metiochos and Parthenopé* in Egyptian papyrus fragment, c. A.D. 100.

Plate 4. Portrait of a lady with pearls. Pompeiian mosaic, first century A.D.

Plate 5. Individual relationships triumph over convention: two Roman women in marital gesture on tomb, era of Augustus.

Plate 6. A quiet moment as Medea broods; Roman painting, Pompeii, first century A.D..

Plate 7. Roman actors: the masked unmasked. Pompeiian mosaic.

Plate 8. Looking at the beloved's picture: scene from *Ninus and Semiramis*, mosaic (c. A.D. 200) of Antioch area.

Plate 9. Frightened vege-
table, or Lady of the Sun?
Medusa in Romano-Briton
mosaic, Cirencester.

Plate 10. Giant head of Medusa, second century A.D., from Didyma, west coast of
Asia Minor.

Plate 11. A gentle harpy takes care of the soul: sculptures of fifth century B.C. on "Harpy Tomb," from Lykia, southwest Asia Minor.

Plate 12. Europa voyages, led by Eros, accompanied by dolphin: mosaic (c. A.D. 200) on island of Kos, near Asia Minor.

Plate 13. Beauty in terror, "like languishing violets": Andromeda painting from Julia's villa in Boscotrecase, c. 10 B.C..

Plate 14. Picture of ass and ornamental border around a clear text: first page of an illuminated *Golden Ass*, ms. A.D. 1388.

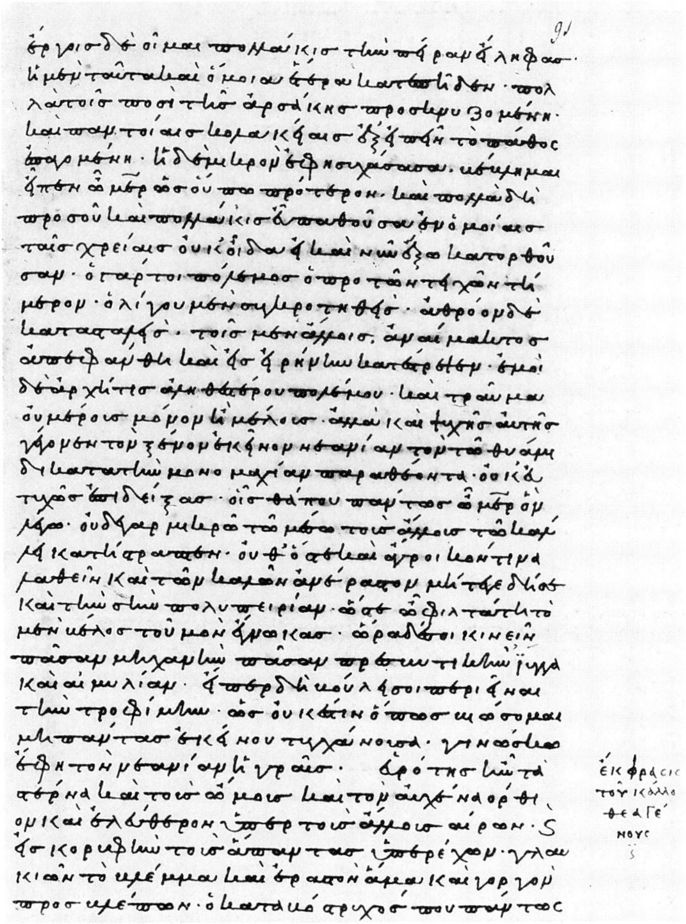

Plate 15. "Ekphrasis of the beauty of Theagenes": marginal comment in Byzantine manuscript of *Aithiopika*, drawing attention to Kybelé's rush of detailed praise of the hero (Book VII, c. x).

Plate 16. Alexander undertakes a space journey in a basket drawn by griffins, on the north side of the cathedral of San Marco, Venice.

Plate 17. Florio and Biancifiore at the stake: woodcut illustration of *Filocolo* (Napoli, 1478).

Plate 18. Ass and moon: the appeal to the goddess. Woodcut illustration to Apuleius' *The Golden Ass*, Book XI, in Beroaldus' annotated edition (1516).

Plate 19. The ass as satyr and *The Golden Ass* as satire: illustrative vignette, Spanish version, 1543.

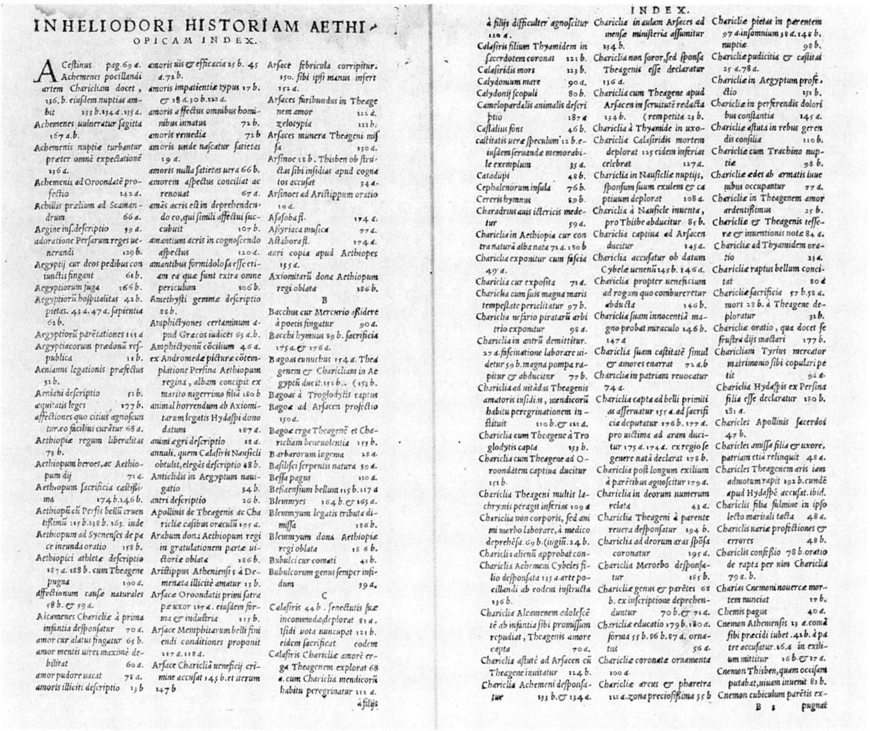
IN HELIODORI HISTORIAM AETHIOPICAM INDEX.

INDEX.

Plate 20. Turning a novel into a mine of information and advice; Warschewiczki's "Index" to Heliodorus, 1552.

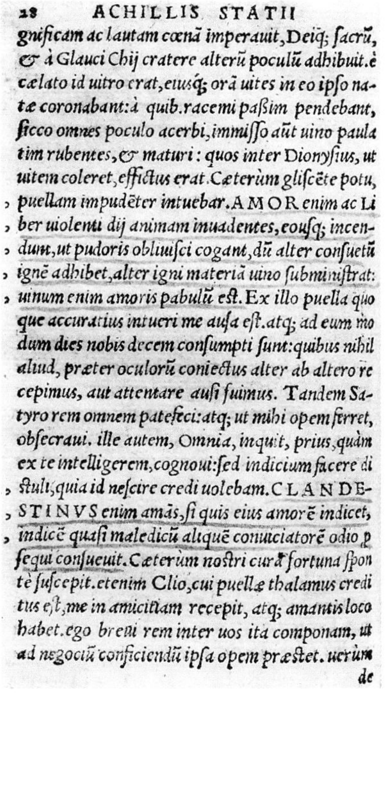
28 ACHILLIS STATII
gnificam ac lautam cœnã imperauit,Deiq; sacrũ,
& à Glauci Chij cratere alterũ poculũ adhibuit.è
cælato id uitro erat,eiusq; orã uites in eo ipso na-
tæ coronabant:à quib.racemi passim pendebant,
sicco omnes poculo acerbi,immisso aũt uino paula
tim rubentes,& maturi: quos inter Dionysius, ut
uitem coleret,effictus erat.Cæterùm gliscẽte potu,
, puellam impudẽter intuebar.AMOR enim ac Li
, ber uiolenti dij animam inuadentes,eousq; incen-
, dunt,ut pudoris obliuisci cogant,dũ alter consuetũ
, ignẽ adhibet,alter igni materiã uino subministrat:
, uinum enim amoris pabulũ est.Ex illo puella quo
que accuratius intueri me ausa est.atq; ad eum mo
dum dies nobis decem consumpti sunt:quibus nihil
aliud, præter oculorũ coniectus alter ab altero re
cepimus, aut attentare ausi fuimus. Tandem Sa-
tyro rem omnem patefeci:atq; ut mihi opem ferret,
obsecraui. ille autem, Omnia, inquit, prius,quàm
ex te intelligerem,cognoui:sed indicium facere di
, stuli,quia id nescire credi uolebam.CLANDE-
, STINVS enim amãs,si quis eius amorẽ indicet,
, indicẽ quasi maledicũ aliquẽ conuiciatorẽ odio p
sequi consueuit.Cæterùm nostri curã fortuna spon
tẽ suscepit.etenim Clio,cui puellæ thalamus credi
tus est,me in amicitiam recepit, atq; amantis loco
habet.ego breui rem inter uos ita componam, ut
ad negociũ conficiendũ ipsa opem præstet. uerùm
de

Plate 21. Emphatic typeface and expressionistic page in Renaissance translation (into Latin) of Achilles Tatius.

Plate 22. The Europa motif recollected: frontispiece of French version of *Kleitophon and Leukippé*, 1635.

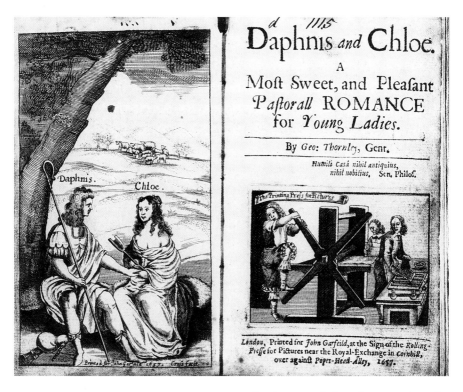

Plate 23. The erotics of print: frontispiece and title page of Thornley's version of Longus, 1657.

Philipus inv. et pinxit. 1714.   B.^tus *Audran Sculp.*

L'Amour apparoiſt a Philetas dans ſon Jardin.

Plate 24. Eros disturbs the old man's garden: French rococo illustration of Longus.

Plate 25. "Les Petits Pieds" or the erotics of concealment: eighteenth-century French illustration of the seduction of Daphnis by Lykainion.

Plate 26. First page of Petronius' *Satyricon* in late medieval illuminated manuscript.

rabioſo ſtridore circumſiſtunt trepidantem;
atque alius tunicam meam lacerat , alius
vincula calceamentorum *reſolvit* , ac
trahit : unus etiam dux ac magiſter ſævi-
tiæ non dubitavit crus meum : ſerrato
vexare morſu. Oblitus itaque nugarum,
pedem menſulæ extorſi , capiſque pugna-
ciſſimum animal armata elidere manu :
nec ſatiatus defunctorio ictu , morte me
anſeris vindicavi.

Tales Herculea Stymphalidas arte
coactas
Ad Cœlum fugiſſe reor , ſanieque
fluentes
Harpias , cùm Phineo maduere ve-
neno
Fallaces epulæ tremuit perterritus æ-
ther
Planctibus inſolitis , confuſaque Re-
gia Cœli
Viſa ſuas moto transcurrere cardine
metas.

Jam

Anſeris ob mortem ſævas Anus ardet in iras.

Plate 27. Scholarly editions also merit pictures: 1709 *Satyricon* text annotated, with illustration of the old woman's wrath over the death of her goose.

Plate 28. Eros leads the way: title page vignette in Salmasius' edition of Achilles Tatius' novel, 1640.

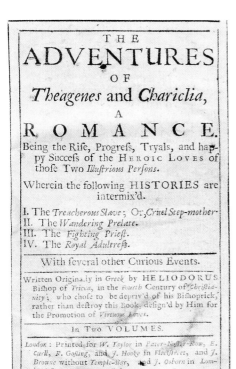

THE
ADVENTURES
OF
Theagenes and *Chariclia,*
A
ROMANCE.
Being the Rise, Progress, Tryals, and happy Success of the HEROIC LOVES of those Two *Illustrious Persons.*

Wherein the following HISTORIES are intermix'd.

I. The *Treacherous Slave;* Or, *Cruel Step-mother.*
II. The *Wandering Prelate.*
III. The *Fighting Priest.*
IV. The *Royal Adultress.*

With several other Curious Events.

Written Originally in *Greek* by HELIODORUS Bishop of *Tricca,* in the fourth Century of *Christianity;* who chose to be depriv'd of his Bishoprick, rather than destroy this Book, design'd by Him for the Promotion of *Virtuous Loves.*

In Two VOLUMES.

London : Printed for *W. Taylor* in *Pater-Noster-Row,* E. *Curll, F. Gosling,* and *J. Hooke* in *Fleetstreet,* and *J. Browne* without *Temple-Bar,* and *J. Osborn* in *Lombard-street.* 1717. Price 5 s.

Plate 29. Adventure and romance emphasized in 1717: Title page of new English translation of *Aithiopika.*

Plate 30. Charikleia in the marsh: seventeenth-century illustration.

Plate 31. Kleitophon and Leukippé marginalized by shipwreck on the beach: seventeenth-century version.

Plate 32. Clarissa in the prison room—a version of pit, hole and cave: illustration in late eighteenth-century edition of Samuel Richardson's *Clarissa*.

S. Wale del.   *C. Grianion Sculp.*

Plate 33. Eros whips two Psyches towards the muddy shore of generation: mosaic (c. A.D. 200) of Antioch area.

Plate 34. Eros and Psyche, as children: Roman statuary group, Ostia.

Plate 35. Damaged Eros: the devil Asmodeus, illustration to an English translation of *Le Diable boiteux*

Plate 36. Venus and Cupid with Florio and Biancifiore: illustration of *Philocolo*, 1478.

Plate 37. Venus on the half-shell, mistress of the sea of generation: Pompeiian painting.

Plate 38. An Ethiopian in a seventeenth-century illustration of *Aithiopika:* Charikleia's rescuer, Sisimithres, gives the seven-year-old girl to adoptive father, Charikles.

PART THREE

Tropes of the Novel

The Virgin Mary as life-spinner: Byzantine statue, Venice.

CHAPTER XIII

>–+-•>–0–‹•+–‹

Breaking and Entering

>–+-•>–0–‹•+–‹

The beach was covered with the corpses of men newly slain, of which some were entirely dead and others only half-killed. . . . Here lay a man wounded by an axe, or struck down by a pebble supplied by the sea-beach itself, while others were broken up by a piece of wood . . .
—Heliodorus, *Aithiopika*

"Oh, Kitty, how nice it would be if we could only get through into Looking-glass House! I'm sure it's got, oh! such beautiful things in it!"
—Lewis Carroll, *Through the Looking-Glass*

When the woman, her name is Violet, went to the funeral to see the girl and to cut her dead face they threw her to the floor and out of the church. She ran, then, through all that snow, and when she got back to her apartment she took the birds from their cages and set them out the windows to freeze or fly, including the parrot that said, "I love you."
—Toni Morrison, *Jazz*

>–+-•>–0–‹•+–‹

TROPES

The connection between the antique novel and the modern novel is ultimately inescapable, even if it takes a reorientation to entertain this possibility. The access of understanding and pleasure offered by a much wider tradition may at first be felt as a loss. Only by breaking with recent critical habits can we mend the ragged gap in our knowledge. In Part II the gap got mended, as we have looked at the Novel in terms of a history—from antiquity to the Middle Ages, from the Middle Ages through the Renaissance to the eighteenth century—and beyond. The Novel in the modern centuries (eighteenth through twentieth) is fully akin to the Novel of earlier periods—of the sixteenth century, or the fourteenth or the first. Various transmissions and readaptions effectively inscribed the Novel on Western consciousness. Any given novel not only is "a history" (like *The History of Tom Jones*) but also recaptures and reinterprets the history of the genre as a whole.

My story of the Novel has hitherto been largely a history—a word not without its dangers. To modern ears "history" urges concepts of change, supersession, *progress*. For Hippolyte Taine, for instance, in his influential *Histoire de la littérature anglaise* (1863), literature is a fossil shell, dead matter left by a past mode of existence. Shell and document alike are dead rubbish, *débris morts* (viii), until we read through them the conditions of life that called them into being. The history of literature offers us the dead productions of the past, which we can interpret as living phenomena, connecting race, religion, philosophy, and historical moment. Taine does not notice that he already "knows" what the answers to these things really are. He already "knows" about racial characteristics: for instance, that not much can be expected of Semitic art. He "knows" that the state depends on the family: "And what makes the family if not the sentiment of obedience whereby a wife and children act under the direction of a father and husband?" (xxxvi–xxxvii). He can "know" that Sidney's *Arcadia* reflects the violence of life in Protestant England, whereas Scudéry's novels exhibit aristocratic French (and implicitly Catholic) calm—thus Taine supresses the reflections of the Fronde in the French novels.[1] My readers will already have allowed for my own biases, and I should take warning by the seductive prejudices concealed in the authority assumed by Taine (who seduced Zola, among others). Taine made an important contribution (still far from exhausted) in connecting individual psychology with general cultural conditions. His method, however, is distinctly disingenuous. In the factory age, Taine thought of everything not in terms of the *marketplace* so popular in capitalist thought of the end of the twentieth century, but in terms of *product*: "Vice and virtue are products like vitriol and sugar" (xv). Literature is no less a *product*—an implicit definition that renders it inert. The observer is as safe from being caught by it as by the Darwinian tenantless curious shell. The use of literature by historians has often seemed to render it remote, even sterile—and quite safe. History puts things in the past and declares the past safely over. For literature, nothing is ever over. Literature never has a *Nachleben*—a posthumous existence—but only a *leben*, a life continuous.

If we want to look at the Novel's whole story, that entails at last looking into certain elements which might be called "formal" rather than "historical." But the word "form" can get us into as much trouble as the word "history." We soon pick up, like lint on a sleeve, the late nineteenth-century aesthetics, the cooing over perfection of form that tried to make the Novel a safe artifact without contact with "savages," or the poor of the industrial age, or the intrusive women. More disturbingly, we can be spun back to the Greek distinction between Good (Male) Form and Bad (Female) Matter—or between inferior Particulars and unified Whole. The Novel is famously resistant to form, constantly playing with it only to reject it, after some fashion. The Novel has little if any desire to be *in se ipso totus teres, atque rotundus*. It is, to adopt Henry James's famous phrase, "a loose baggy monster."[2] And it is so chiefly because it does not acknowledge the distinction between General and Particular, between Form and Matter. The distinction that separates pure *Form* from vulgar *Stoff*, from *hylē*, is the very distinction that the Novel itself seems to put into question. We might be better off not speaking of "formal" elements at all. If we do so, we must do so under the proviso that in using the metaphor of spatial shape we know that it is here a rather unimportant metaphor and must yield to others.

From now on, the discussion will concentrate not on history but on what I prefer to think of as the "deep rhetoric" of the Novel rather than its "form." I concentrate on what I call "Tropes of Fiction" in the Novel—as Tropes of the Novel itself. These tropes, I maintain, rather than anything describable in terms of spatial shape, characterize and thus define the Novel (insofar as it may be definable). These tropes are figures not of phrasing but of narrative. They are not techniques (like manipulating point of view). Nor are they modes of narrative (such as epistolary narration). The "Tropes of Fiction" are to be understood as something more like narrative symbols that move us through a novel's story. They supply its "meanings"—or rather, the sense that it is meaningful. They are in some sense metaphors, tropes as figures of rhetoric. But they also actively *trope* (from Greek *trepein*, to turn); in their moving, these "turns" of speech or thought turn our attention towards something, though it may be only our deep inward attention that is affected. The tropes of the Novel are far less like "figures" (visual shape again) than they are representations of experience; they operate on the experiential level, and not on the level of the picturesque. These tropes operate— to use an odd but germane analogy—like symbolic moments in a liturgy. The liturgical reference reminds us that we will eventually have to pick up that troublesome if interesting question raised in Chapter VIII of Part I. Is the Novel religious—somewhere in its murky "origins" and its slippery nature? And, if so, how does that "religious" element manifest itself in modern works?

Meanwhile, however, let us say that the tropes of a novel act like moments in a liturgy, or more precisely like ritual acts or observances. Symbolic moments that are focal and observant in the liturgical sense include, for instance, the fracture of the Host in the Eucharist, and also home liturgical observances, such as the lighting of Shabbat candles or a candle on a menorah. Such ritual acts and observances focus meaning, allow meaning to flow through. If we say that the tropes are "moments" (considering them temporally) they can also be imaged spatially, as "points," like the places on the Stations of the Cross, or special places sought out in the journey of a pilgrim, like the major sites of Mecca. When we come to a "tropic moment" in the reading of a novel, we have also come to a "tropic topos," a place of intensified significance, where important action can occur, as baptism can occur at the place of the font. But if the tropes of a novel act like "moments" or "points" in a liturgy, they do so with this grand difference: that whereas religious ritual must demand active participants aware of the symbolic value of what they are doing, the novel's ritual acts can be efficaciously undergone in a state of unawareness—or under-awareness. We may expect the *character* to be blithely unconscious of deep significance much of the time, but, in the case of the tropes, the unconsciousness extends to the reader—and even to the author.

It is usually not to the purpose of a novel's effect that the reader should be struck all of a heap by one of the novel's tropes. They often act subliminally. Authors pick up the tropes from other novelists and may use them quite ably without knowing that they do so. In my own case, for instance, in my detective novel *Aristotle Detective* (1978), I employed the labyrinth trope to be discussed below in Chapter XV. In my novel, the hero Stephanos is led by an old woman through the back alleys of Peiraeus: "I followed, like Theseus threading the labyrinth" (90). This notion is elaborated, with some knowledge of mythology, in the rest of the paragraph; as author, I was perfectly aware of my uses of Theseus and Orpehus and was even very deliberately drawing on Petronius for the back alleys of antique slumland and the sense of confusion (see *Satyricon*, paragraphs 6–7). I was, then, perfectly awake as I made my story, but I still did not know that the figures I was playing with constituted an important trope of the Novel in general. Rather than being (as I flattered myself) bookishly witty, I was really compelled in some sense by the Novel to stick my hero in a labyrinth.

I do not in the least accept the "Death of the Author" on this (or any other) account. But I am certainly personally convinced that Authors (though the report of their death has been greatly exaggerated) do more than they know. Not only the era and the language but also the genre speaks through the Novelist. Most novelists apparently use the tropes unconsciously, picking them up from the Novel itself. There are some possible exceptions, such as Thomas Mann, a mythographer who systematically examined metaphorical and mythic structures in his novels.

Mythography has been much in vogue at certain times in both the nineteenth and in the twentieth centuries. Its high development can be seen in both Mann and Karl Kerényi, and in the correspondence (the *Briefwechsel*) between them. Kerényi, who was to work with Jung during the latter part of Jung's career, offers us a clear connection between literary mythological theory and the development of working psychological hypotheses. Colonialism placed heavy demands on the mythological sense, as Western intellectuals were called upon to deal with beliefs and stories other than those of their own tribes and simultaneously to acknowledge and repudiate the beliefs and stories of others. The endeavors of ethnographers to find systems for developing the myths of various peoples, endeavors visible in *The Golden Bough* (1890–1915), came into high relief in the work of Claude Lévi-Strauss towards the end of the era of overt colonialism.[3] We must confess that the work of categorizing and interpreting the myths of other peoples suits the designs of our postindustrial era, and of countries and conglomerates interested in selling goods and services to Third World countries as well as in obtaining their raw materials and labor as cheaply as possible.

Anthropology and ethnography in effect created the primary structuralism of our era. Tools honed by ethnographers (often borrowed from earlier classicists) were utilized by Russian formalists such as Vladimir Propp, who traced the motifs of folktales, bringing multiplicity into a semblance of unifying order. Jessie L. Weston's *From Ritual to Romance* (1920) similarly offered patterns of order and connection, creating a bridge between what was perceived as archaic and more modern (or at least more familiar) cultural expressions.[4]

Classical and anthropological studies mingle, as they do in the work of the psychological mythographers, Freud being the greatest. The psychologists shared the nineteenth century's general belief in the historical and diagnostic value of myth, but came with a different declared purpose—the healing of sick individuals. Jung, who split off from Freud in his picture of the psyche and in his development of the archetypes, drew, like Freud, on a hermeneutic tradition already partly apparent within the Bible and the Platonists. The newly designed methods of analysis could, however, now be used *on* the Bible, and on Plato and the Platonists, just as Porphyry had deployed his own new thought-instruments on Homer, from whom he also derived them. Jung excited people by declaring, in effect, that myth was more than a historical curiosity. Jung made myth contemporary, but at the cost of appearing to suppose the archetypes to have objective "real" existence—a notion easily mocked by materialists.

With some reason, I shall be accused of belonging to all these groups. I am prepared to be called a formalist, an anthropological structuralist, a psychological mythographer, and a Jungian archetype-hunter. Certainly, I would not be carrying out such as study as Part III of this present volume without my twentieth-century background. I am probably closest of all to Northrop Frye, who made evident his own relation to Jung, and to the Jessie L. Weston who was an influence on Frye. Yet what Weston meant by "Romance" is not what I mean by Novel, and Frye's formulations are much too gravely hierarchical and too fond of limitations to sit comfortably with what the Novel itself is doing. I also stand at a different point in the river of time from Propp, Jung, Lévi-Strauss, or Frye.

Deconstruction has had a certain influence on me as on others. Jacques Derrida represents language, representation itself, as a sort of Fall, with written language as a second fall. Following Nietzsche, he unhitches history from objective truth. Derrida offers us an intellectual world without any objective external valid standnpoint. If we get rid of Aristotelian universality and generality we must admit there are no "truths universally acknowledged." It is Derrida who has taught us that "Origin" is a patriarchal concept, and that we should abandon the search for "origins." To undertake such a search is to comply with a plot of power; all origins are fictitious. We should forsake History in favor of Play. Only thus could we escape the sway of the masculine authoritative *logos* and defy "phallogocentrism," the rule of masculine authority mediated through the Word. The attractiveness of deconstruction at its own historical moment (1960s–1990s) is fully understandable. Some of its important concepts have passed into the currency of general thought, where they meet fairly agreeably with the mathematical physics of Chaos Theory. But I cannot be a true deconstructionist. If Derrida offers some help in getting rid of oppressive authority, he is oppressive in his turn—an owl of Minerva, a prophet of night. In him is reflected the West's constant tendency to see any swerve from traditional authorities as the End of Civilization, the descent into the Abyss. Derrida, however, likes the view from the Abyss and prefers dark holes to entities.

Our twentieth-century mythographers have not been totally helpful either within or outside literary critical theory. Freud as well as the Freudians used mythology to subjugate as well as to liberate. In psychoanalysis and psychotherapy there has been a chronic deafness to the voice of the female or the poor within both literature and myth. Some feminist critics have met this deafness with (metaphorical) voicelessness; following Derrida they have made not language but ululating noise, wordless moan, the voice of Woman. To fall into the trap of denigrating the Word (a trap baited by Derrida) is to give up the game, and to represent language as only and solely "male" is a pernicious and damaging fiction. Some structuralists became very conventional, reinforcing our notions of the civic in gloomy fashion, while the more serious deconstructionists left us little more than the Void to deal with, along with a general alibi for all moral action. They came on like Ezekiel, they exit looking like Harold Skimpole.

The Novel itself—if we let it *all* in—offers a road towards a new aesthetics. In the Novel, History and Play combine. It suggests a new "humanism," one that does not exclude the bulk of humanity, nor the earth, nor the religious consciousness. Yet the Novel is not a preacher. It is not a propper-up of the restrictive civic sense that already "knows" the only foundation of the State to be "the sentiment of obedience" in women and children. The general disposition to see in the Novel only an inferior and certainly *bourgeois* kind of writing has kept it from certain styles of examination. Generally, it is neither "folkish" enough for the Left, nor "righteous" enough for the Right—which in this century has perhaps been just as well for it. Looking at the chief mythographers of the twentieth century, one sees that (with the exception of practicing authors) they have dealt with the Novel only in a very random and occasional manner. If the Novel was Andromeda, none of the theorists made much effort to free her from the rock of Realism to which she had been bound.

We have a means of picking up the mythology the Novel so playfully (and so historically) offers us in examining its tropes. At the very least, picking up the tropes, the customs of fiction, offers us a means of escaping strict one-way historical lines. We can place novels of the third century, of the sixteenth century, of the twentieth century beside each other and keep nothing in separation. The reader of any particular novel may not notice the tropes. Focusing on other elements in the narrative ("character," say, or the portrayal of a certain society), the reader takes the deep structure of the work for granted. Yet it is possible for each of us to pick up a new novel and read it because the tropes are there. If we were to read a work that was really "new" in every respect, we could not understand it. Childhood reading prepares us for adult works in part by furnishing us with the tropes. I do not mean here the reading of fairy tales (though I think highly of those) but of novel-length works such as *Treasure Island*, or *The Wind in the Willows*. A good book is a good book. Working through its ancient powerful figures, any particular novel offers us the knowledge and the reassurance we require in order to engage with the new material every *novel* in its *novelty* must offer us.

The argument of Part III of this book is disrespectful of hierarchies and categories. Illustrations will draw on detective stories and children's books, as well as on contemporary popular works and undeniable "classics." It is also necessary, of course, not to keep to works in one language or one period. The breaking down of categories must form part of the argument. At this point, too, it is time to open the door to the literature of "the East," to novels from China and Japan. In the construction of an historical account of fiction in "the West," they were not included, but now that we are to look at the tropes of the Novel itself, they should be mentioned.

Nothing in my argument can rest upon Chinese and Japanese novels, written in languages that I can never hope to understand, and within cultures not familiar to me.[5] Yet, on turning to the novels of China at the end of the reading period for this book—even after chapters had been drafted—I was struck and surprised by the fidelity with which my supposed "Western" tropes are reflected. No Chinese or Japanese (or Korean or Burmese) reader should suppose that I imagine myself fully competent to discuss their literature. But to assert an eternal and hopeless divide by ignoring the novels of "the East" came to seem shortsighted, and less scrupulous than self-limiting as well as ungenerous. What we do not know is where and how "Western" and "Eastern" fiction met and mingled in much earlier times—before or during the time of Alexander, say. The Chinese are not utterly absent from our classical novels—where they are called "the Seres." The Persian king of Chariton's novel has a sword from the Seres. In *Aithiopika* the ambassadors of the Seres (*hoi Sērōn presbeytai*, III : 106) bring to Hydaspes fabric of threads "made by their spiders" (i.e., silk), a red robe and a white. Given the place of fabric and weaving within this novel as metaphors for its construction, this allusion to the Seres' woven stuffs is a strong reminder that the Chinese are also fabricators. As the Chinese are present to Charikleia of Ethiopia towards the end of her book, so let them be present to us in the last part of this one.

Individual novelists, although always educated in the terms of their time, have not as practitioners been limited by the views of their day. They have faithfully served the Novel in all its depths and capacities, and they have developed its tropes in a multitude of interesting ways, always giving the world something deeper than it thought it had. The concept of a "trope" calls for illustration. The rest of this chapter will be devoted to one example. Successive chapters will develop other tropes exemplified in novels seen outside of their merely historical framework.

THE CUT, THE BREAK

In the first paragraph of this chapter I have used the words "breaking" and "mend" in deliberate imitation of a novelistic figure associated with beginnings. The reader is thus alerted novelistically to a kind of new start in my own argumentative narrative. Novels often begin with a "break" or a "cut." These, or analogous words—"pierce," "sunder," "shatter," etc.—are likely to be found in the first paragraphs. This Breaking Trope may be used at large and emphatically, as in the great set scene opening Heliodorus' *Aithiopika*: "The beach was covered with the corpses of men newly slain, of which some were entirely dead and others only half-killed. . . . Wine-bowls were overturned; some had been dropped from the hands of drinkers in the act of drinking, while others had been used as missiles. . . . Here lay a man wounded by an axe, or struck down by a pebble supplied by the sea-beach itself, while others were broken up by a piece of wood" (I:1–2). Heliodorus focuses our attention on a great deal of disorder involving cutting, mangling, shattering, and severing. The effect is of course heightened here by the association of food and festivity with disorder and breakage. The description of breakage continues in the description of wounded Theagenes, and only the description of the unwounded and glorious Charikleia puts a stop to the chain of destruction at the beginning of the novel. Heliodorus' effect, attained so emphatically, was the object of conscious imitation by later novelists. Madeleine de Scudéry tries to outgo Heliodorus at the beginning of *Artamène*, in producing a destructive scene of unprecedented grandeur, like a cinematic scene directed by Eisenstein:

> The Conflagration of *Sinope* was so great, that the very Sky, the Sea, the Valleys and Tops of Mountains, tho far remote, were all illuminated by its Flames: so that notwithstanding the black mask of Night, all things might mournfully be discerned: never was object more terrible to Spectators than this; Twenty Ships might be seen burning all at once in the Port; which tho floating in the midst of water, did belch up Flames as high as Clouds. These affrighting Flames being blown by the Bellows of an impetuous wind, did oft times bend towards the Town; and as if but one huge faggot were set on fire, seem'd to

consume it all. They flasht from place to place in an instant; and there
was scarce one Quarter in all the Town, which by a dire communication did not feel its fury. All the Tackling, Cordage and Sails being set
on fire, flew horribly into the air, and fell down again in sparks upon
the houses, which being thus consumed, are forc'd to yield unto this
merciless Element, and tumble down in those Streets, unto which they
were before an Ornament. The hideous multitude of flames which
stream'd through several streets, and which had more or less fury, according to the subject upon which they seiz'd, did seem to Combat one
with another, by reason of the whirling Wind which countermoved
them; sometimes mingling together, sometimes parting, as if they did
dispute about the Glory of destroying this stately Town.

(*Artamène*, as *Artamenes*, English trans. [1691], para. 3)

The description itself glories in destructiveness and provides a spectacle of perverse activity on the part of inanimate objects and insensate elements. As in Heliodorus, we see a grand scene but do not know the cause of what we are viewing;
we share the point of view with a belated newcomer—in this case, the hero
Artamène. He has come to rescue his beloved, Mandane, and at first thinks with
horror that she must have perished terribly in this conflagration. Meanwhile, we
have been watching the flames creep towards a great castle, and have been able
to speculate how long the edifice could resist the flames. Buildings testify to "the
Magnificence of their Structure" and create "Compassion for their inevitable
ruin." We expect to see the great castle involved in such "inevitable ruin"—and
then we find out that Mandane the captive princess is in this castle. . . . We with-
draw some of our illicit pleasure in the uproar in order to invest in the plotful
pleasures of suspense—but not before we have enjoyed the effect. Burning Sinope is a place of continuous breakage, of the perishing of structures; fragmented
"Tackling, Cordage and Sails" metamorphose into detached pieces of burning ash
flying about and causing solid things to "tumble down." The stronger the structure, the more effective its destruction.

The Breaking Trope does not have to be employed with such cinematic
empressement, even if it is associated with large-scale events. Arthur Conan Doyle's
A Study in Scarlet (1887), the book that introduced Sherlock Holmes and Dr. Watson to the world, begins, like the two novels just mentioned, with warlike activity
and damage, but the tone is personal; an imperial battle is presented in terms of
personal fracture:

The campaign brought honours and promotion to many, but for me it
had nothing but misfortune and disaster. I was removed from my bri-
gade and attached to the Berkshires, with whom I served at the fatal
battle of Maiwand. There I was struck on the shoulder by a Jezail
bullet, which shattered the bone and grazed the subclavian artery. I
should have fallen into the hands of the murderous Ghazis had it not
been for the devotion and courage shown by Murray, my orderly, who
threw me across a packhorse, and succeeded in bringing me safely to
the British lines.   (Doyle, *A Study in Scarlet*, para. 2)

In Heliodorus' novel we see dying men, and a shattered survivor, Theagenes. In Doyle's novel, we see the shattered narrator—or rather, we do *not* see him, for Watson is not a spectacle, but an immediate subject, who experiences the wounds inflicted on him—unlike the corpses Holmes strikes with a stick, which we are shortly to hear about. Watson complains of "misfortune"; Tyché seems to be against him. He does not realize that *Tychē*-Fortuna is working for him, in sending him safely away from battle and towards his true love and *alter ego*, Sherlock Holmes, the real "home" to which he tends. Watson's real story begins—is allowed to begin—with the shattering wound.

The Breaking Trope is presumably so common because we—not the characters but the readers—really need some signal that we are to cut ourselves off from our own life. The opening of any long work of prose fiction has the tough job of getting the whole thing going, including moving the reader into the story. The reader may, for instance, be sitting in an easy chair worrying about money. It is necessary that this reader should launch into the unknown, should cast off or break the attachments that moor one in what we call "real life." As readers we likewise desire this, or we would not have picked up a novel. The beginning of a novel reflects both that necessity and that desire, in giving expression to cutting and departure, to division, separation, and mangling.

The beginning also imitates a kind of birth—the plunge into another existence, the cutting of the umbilical cord. This is rarely made as clear as it is, for instance, in Lewis Carroll's *Through the Looking-Glass* (1872).

> "Oh, Kitty, how nice it would be if we could only get through into Looking-glass House! I'm sure it's got, oh! such beautiful things in it! Let's pretend there's a way of getting through into it, somehow, Kitty. Let's pretend the glass has got all soft like gauze, so that we can get through. Why, it's turning into a sort of mist now, I declare! It'll be easy enough to get through——" She was up on the chimney-piece while she said this, though she hardly knew how she had got there. And certainly the glass *was* beginning to melt away, just like a bright silvery mist.   (*Alice's Adventures*, Chap. 1, para. 12)

The solid wall of glass turns into a membrane and then vanishes, a space for exit and emergence. The effect is different from that at the opening of *Alice's Adventures in Wonderland*, where the very first adventures repeatedly connect birth with the danger of cutting. Birth is emphasized in the long fall through the birth canal of the burrow (which also serves as entry to hole, pit, or cave). Alice's prolonged fall is to be echoed in the opening of James Joyce's *Finnegans Wake* (1939), a waking to both birth and death. During her descent, Alice forestalls breakage by not dropping the jar of "Orange Marmalade," but she is aware that she seems to be falling "right *through* the earth!" (11). In being born, Alice becomes the phallic child, herself the instrument that pierces and cuts. In this she represents a Joycean character in another novel, Stephen Dedalus, named as "Kinch, the knife-blade" by Buck Mulligan, who brings a *razor* to the first sentence of *Ulysses* (3–4).

The phallic role is subordinate in both cases to the antiphallic or "female" or "patient" role, of being born, being cut, being separated, being plunged into dangerous *hylē*. At the end of her fall Alice is soon significantly reminded of the monitory lessons about children "who had got burnt, and eaten up by wild beasts, and other unpleasant things, all because they *would* not remember the simple rules their friends had taught them: such as, that a red-hot poker will burn you if you hold it too long; and that, if you cut your finger *very* deeply with a knife, it usually bleeds. . . ." (21–22) The Looking-Glass World (but *not* Wonderland) reverses these rules: bleeding happens before cutting or piercing, and birth occurs without breakage. Alice's entry into Looking-Glass World contains no reference to breaking the glass; the idea of such breakage is supplied by the reader. In ordinary physics we know no way of making a hole through glass other than by breaking it. It is fitting that in Looking-Glass World the very trope is itself reversed.

The Breaking Trope perhaps requires a name; as Greek derivations have been fashionable lately, I suggest *Hrexis*—or *Rhexis*, as the more natural English spelling. There is a certain degree of violence in the Rhexis, the breakthrough which is also a birth, though it may be a concealed violence. Consider, for instance, the opening of Zola's *Thérèse Raquin* (1867):

> At the end of the rue Guénégaud, as you come from the quays, you find the alleyway of Pont-Neuf, a sort of narrow dark corridor which runs from rue Mazarine to the rue de Seine. This passage is thirty paces long and two paces in width, at most; it is paved with yellowish paving-stones, worn down, loose, always sweating an acrid humidity; the glass which covers the passage, cut at a right angle, is black with grime. . . .
>
> To the right, all the length of the passage, there extends a wall against which the small shopkeepers opposite have stuck their narrow cupboards; objects without a name, merchandise forgotten there for twenty years, are ranged along the narrow shelves painted a horrible color of brown. A merchant of fake jewelry is established in one of these cupboards; here she sells fifteen-sou rings, delicately arranged on a bed of blue velvet, at the bottom of a mahogany box. Above the glass rises the wall, black, crudely roughcast, as if covered with a leprosy and all seamed with scars. . . .
>
> At night, three gaslamps, closed in heavy foursquare lanterns, light the passage. . . . The passage takes on the sinister aspect of a veritable cut-throat's lair; great shadows stretch along the paving-stones, damp breaths come from the street, you would say it was a subterranean gallery vaguely lit by three funerary lamps. (Chap. 1, paras. 1–7)

According to some traditional categories, Heliodorus and Emile Zola should not be named in the same sentence, so far are they asunder. One is the author of a mere "romance" (and an old one), the other is a nineteenth-century modern, the great exponent of "naturalism." But there are resemblances between the opening of *Aithiopika* and the opening of *Thérèse Raquin*: in both we see a mysterious place, objects out of place, a mixture of the gross and the delicate, the banal and the sinister, connected by an omnipresent if unfixed violence. We can borrow a phrase from Scudéry, Zola's countrywoman and predecessor, and refer to *ce grand désordre* (*Au milieu de ce grand désordre*, in *Artamène*, I:4).

This unpleasant *corridor étroit et sombre* is the birth-canal of *Thérèse Raquin*. Zola offers us a birth-passage that is a hiding place of false treasure and an abode of the dead. In his adjectival way, he repeats effects, by small but incessantly repeated strokes creating a symbolism and a drama. The Rhexis emerges in a kind of pun, two different uses of the same word. We are told that the glass which covers the ugly passage is "cut at a right angle"—*coupé à angle droit*. The cutting in this sense is beneficent, ostensibly, the work of an artisan creating something, but the effect is harsh, the design of this straight roof of dirty glass shuts one in: paradoxically, a cut leads to enclosure. At night, the dirty passage *prend l'aspect sinistre d'un véritable coupe-gorge*. The passage may seem the abode of cutthroats, a likely place for them to lurk, but the language itself makes the walkway itself a *coupe-gorge*. We experience two cuts as we are jerked violently into the novel.

The Rhexis, which is most likely to occur within the first paragraphs of a novel, and is almost inevitably found within the first two chapters, need not be as emphatic as the examples above. It may appear in muted form, as merely an ordinary piece of working-day metaphor. Near the beginning of Jane Austen's *Emma* (1816), for instance, Mr. Woodhouse gives voice to it: "pray do not make any more matches, they are silly things, and *break up* one's family circle grievously" (11, italics mine). In Samuel Richardson's *Pamela* (1740) the Rhexis concerns the language of the novel itself, the language of dialogue and narration. The death of Pamela's former mistress and friend begins the novel, and the breaking off of words supplies the first Rhexis: "I was sobbing and crying at her Pillow, she could only say, My dear Son!—and so broke off a little, and then recovering— Remember my poor *Pamela!*—And these were some of her last Words! . . . Don't wonder to see the Paper so blotted!" (*Pamela*, para. 1). At the outset of Richardson's first novel, the Breaking Trope is neatly interfolded with the incompleteness of utterance, and the incompleteness of individual personal narration—the paper itself blotted, the words broken.

Mr. B's mother has died at the outset of *Pamela*. James Harlowe is merely threatened with death, in the mysterious and violent opening of Richardson's *Clarissa*, where he is cut into and bloodied. It does not matter whether the death at the outset of a novel is literal on the plot level, or threatened at the plot level, or merely reflected in the metaphors. The Rhexis may be a sign of birth, a cutting of the umbilical cord, a bringing us to birth within the realm of the novel. But at the same time it is closely associated with the threat of death.

THE FIRST SENTENCE OF DEATH

The opening of any long prose fiction contains, secretly or openly, a salute to death. The death so encountered must be worked away from, thrown off, conquered or recovered from during the beginning of the novel. This is so even in novels that are to finish with the death of the major protagonist, like *Clarissa* or *Madame Bovary*. The beginning of a novel is an encounter with death at the same time as it is a birth; or, perhaps one ought to say, the encounter with death provides the means for a birth.

The plunging child who breaks membranes is less phallic than fetal. To be born may be to be ruinous, to cause irreversible breakage. Alice manages not to smash the jar of Orange Marmalade, but many children are not so careful. The birth of the child may be the death of the mother—and the Mother is frequently the figure who dies at the beginning of a novel. Emma Woodhouse's mother (we are told in the second paragraph) died "long ago"; part of the comedy of the opening chapter is that Emma's father treats the departure of her governess and substitute mother *as if* it were a death ("Poor Miss Taylor!") although Miss Taylor (now Mrs. Weston) has left to be married and is going on to conceive, gestate, and produce a child (a new Emma) during the course of the novel. Pantagruel is too large to be born without killing his mother Badebec. We would expect (but for certain clues) that David Copperfield's mother will die in giving birth to him, but the death of his father is sufficient sacrifice for a while. (His mother dies of her next child.) Even when happily past childbirth dangers, the mother may be required at the hands of the novelist before the first paragraph is over; *Pamela* opens with the death of the adult hero's mother. Genji's mother, the Japanese Emperor's beautiful concubine, dies when her child (the hero) is three years old.

Genji's dying mother quotes a poem to the emperor:

> She looked sadly up at him. "If I had suspected that it would be so—"
> She was gasping for breath.
>
> > "I leave you to go the road we all must go.
> > The road I would choose, if only I could, is the other."
>
> It was evident that she would have liked to say more, but she was so weak that it had been a struggle to say even this much.
>
> *(The Tale of Genji,* trans. Seidensticker, 6)

There is almost always somebody at the beginning of the novel who is dead or dying, who will not accompany us down the road of life. The road of life becomes the novel itself. The dead character becomes part of the past within the novel, a function of the artificial memory we create in order to participate in the novel's world. A novel may even be built around that already-dead character, who becomes the focus of our artificial memory, as the dead girl Dorcas becomes in Toni Morrison's *Jazz* (1992). *Jazz* offers a startling example of the Breaking Trope, in the fourth sentence of the first paragraph: "When the woman, her name is Violet, went to the funeral to see the girl and to cut her dead face they threw her to the floor and out of the church" (3). Seldom have the cut and the death of a novel's beginning been as brilliantly or as shockingly combined, and this Rhexis thereafter governs the novel's language.

If the Angel of Death flies over the beginning of a novel, it sometimes flies very high, supplying only the shadow of a feather-tip across the page; on other occasions it may be very visible. In the long opening of Charles Dickens's *Little Dorrit* (1852–1853), for instance, the death motif is long-drawn-out and varied, with references to plague as well as to murder. The Rhexis is fulfilled with the references to the guillotine, the "national razor," which apparently awaits the man accused of murdering a woman, and in the description of the man's suspect hands, "with ugly scratches newly healed" (*Little Dorrit,* 41; Chap. 1, para. 9).

The Breaking Trope may be applied only to an object, as in the second paragraph of Chinua Achebe's *Arrow of God* (1967): "The eaves on this additional entrance were cut back so that sitting on the floor Ezeulu could watch that part of the sky where the moon had its door" (1). The Breaking Trope is here connected with expectancy, appearance, and fear, and with the power to see the new. Facade meets facade, opening matches opening. The idea of a building cut or cut into arouses some unease, even—or perhaps especially—in the expected presence of a moon both feared and desired. The many cuts and pressures on buildings in the opening of Balzac's *Eugénie Grandet* (1834) arouse very decided readerly unease. Balzac directs our attention to decaying houses in a country town. Like Scudéry, Balzac approaches Rhexis through images of the destruction of buildings, but instead of the excitement of burning Sinope we have a slow wearing-down through time. The human urge to construct and decorate is pathetically unable to withstand deconstruction.

> Here, pieces of transverse wood covered with slates draw blue lines along the frail walls of a dwelling terminated by an ornate carpentered roof, which the years have caused to buckle, whose rotten boards have been warped by the alternate action of rain and sun. . . . Beside the trembling house of board and plaster where the artisan has glorified his plane rises the *hôtel* of a gentleman where, in the very center of the lintel stone, there are visible some vestiges of his coat of arms, broken by the diverse revolutions that have agitated the country since 1789.
>
> (*Eugénie Grandet*, Chap. 1, para. 1)

Elegiac feeling seems at first provoked only by the sight of fragile man-made dwellings in a natural decay; the activity of decay is first attributed to nonhuman agency, to rain and sun. But by the end of the paragraph human agency is engaged in destruction. The emblematic arms in the stone have been broken (*brisées*) in the revolutions. It is the word *brisées* that supplies the Rhexis itself. Death and decay seem omnipresent, if impersonally located in nature and history. The thought of such death and decay inspires a melancholy, our key to the emotional entry into this novel.

Feelings of melancholy and thoughts about death may be focused on a character. One of the best examples in this manner is the opening of Boccaccio's *Fiammetta*:

> Accursed bee that day, and hated of me more than any other, in which I first enjoyed this common light. Howe happy had I beene (alas) if I had neuer beene borne, or if I had at the time of my unfortunate byrth, beene carryed to my grave, or had not breathed anie longer time, then the teeth sowne of Cadmus: or els, if Lachesis at one and selfe same howre, had begunne and cut in two her vitall thredde: because then, in that small time of life, those infinite Woes, which are nowe a sorrowfull occasion to putte my penne to Paper, should wyth the same haue been concluded.
>
> (Trans. Bartholemew Yong, 1587, Book I, A1ʳ)

Fiammetta wishes that her threads had been cut, broken, ruptured (*rotte*). Boccaccio wittily combines death, birth, and the Rhexis here: the Rhexis is what did *not* happen—the cutting of Fiammetta's vital thread. Fiammetta laments with such vitality that we cannot in the least share her melancholy; with every phrase she utters we rejoice the more that such splendid liveliness was not cut off on the day of her birth. And if that wish had been fulfilled, there would of course have been no story. We defy death for story—which is the secret of the openings of all novels.

MENDING

A novel may be considered as a sort of long convalescence from the threat and pain of its beginning. If the opening of a novel is characterized by breaking, it is equally characterized by its counterpart and opposite—what might be called *Henōsis*, in modern form "Enosis" or the Mending Trope. The beginnings of novels conventionally also contain references to making and mending. Wounds, holes, breakages—seen in the opening movement of the story—are to be repaired in some way. In the *Aithiopika*, we first see Theagenes grievously wounded, but soon the cheerful Greek Knemon offers to heal him: "I will procure an herb which will close your wounds [*henōsei tas plēgas*] in three days" (I, 12). His promise of healing is a promise of reintegration. Wounds are to be healed, rents or tears to be rewoven or at least patched together. Even the wounds on the hands of the murderer Rigaud in *Little Dorrit* are in the process of healing—simultaneously evident as cuts and at the same time as mended, "scratches newly healed."

A complex and highly comic expression of both tropes—breaking and mending—combined can be found in the case of Don Quixote's helmet. He soon realizes that he cannot be a knight without a proper helmet, but his ancestors have not left him this essential piece of equipment—so he has to create one. He contrives one out of his own industry and cardboard. Unfortunately, he tests this construction.

> It is true that in order to test if it was strong and could stand up to the hazards of a fight, he struck it with his sword dealing it two blows, and in the first stroke and in a moment cut to pieces [*deshizo*] what it had taken him a week to make. . . . he turned to making it anew, strengthening the back with a metal strip, in such a manner that he was satisfied of its strength, and, without trying to make any new test of it, he adopted it and took it for a fine and finished vizor.
>
> (*Don Quijote*, Part I; Chap. 1, para. 5)

Don Quixote's improvisation with the cardboard, his *bricolage*, is also a work of fiction. The making of fiction itself—or *the* fiction in which we are engaged, the present novel (whatever that may be)—is often figured in the references to mending, repair, and humble improvisatory making that accompany beginnings.

Such references may use the image of threads and sewing, reminding us of the thread of life (an image overtly used in the outset of Boccaccio's *Fiammetta*). At the beginning of *Through the Looking-Glass*, the black kitten and Alice are engaged in a game of unmaking-making: "the kitten had been having a grand game of romps with the ball of worsted Alice had been trying to wind up, and had been rolling it up and down till it had all come undone again; and there it was, spread over the hearth-rug, all knots and tangles" (*Alice*, Chap.1, para. 3). The tangled thread is a literal appearance of a very old metaphor, *plokē*, a metaphor for plot and story itself—a story being a weaving at apparent cross-purposes, an entanglement. This metaphor, we remember, is effectively employed by Charikleia, when she tells Theagenes they cannot expect a quick winding-up simply by producing their tokens: "When the demon [*ho daimōn*] has entangled the very beginnings of a complicated plot [*polyplokous*], it's impossible for that to come to an end save through a long-drawn-out process of multiple conclusions" (III:69). Alice's kitten playfully acts the role of the *daimōn* who causes plot by causing tangles. The story that we are reading when we read a novel is a magical entanglement that is simultaneously a mess and a weaving. The characters in their various chores of *bricolage* support the pattern of the weaving.

Women are often associated on the literal level with the Enosis or Putting-Together Trope, and their activity may be emphasized at various turns in the novel, not only at the first beginning. Women sewing, like Pamela flowering Mr. B.'s waistcoat, embody that which is healing and creative. In L. M. Montgomery's *Anne of Green Gables* (1908), the presence of Rachel Lynde, busybody though she is, at the outset of the story is benevolent; as Mrs. Lynde sits "knitting 'cotton warp' quilts" and keeping an eye on her neighbors, she embodies in homely guise the very spirit of story that Anne herself loves so much (Chap. 1, para. 2). The Mending Trope often does appear in very homely guise: "I'll just fetch a little sewing, and then I'll sit as long as you please," says Nelly Dean to Lockwood in Chapter 4 of *Wuthering Heights* (33). She sews as she begins her story, which is the narrative proper, and her sewing, her story (shocking as it is), and Lockwood's healing from his illness are connected.

The Mending Trope can, however, come in many forms; we need not peer anxiously about for women with needles or skeins in their hands. In Milan Kundera's *The Book of Laughter and Forgetting* (1978), the opening has two different Breaking Tropes in two successive short chapters; the airbrushing out of Clementis from the photograph of party leaders (Chapter 1), and Mirek's breaking of his arm (Chapter 2). Mirek's arm then undergoes the process of slow healing, while his diary and his efforts to preserve correspondence, to keep records in a political realm that keeps trying to destroy records, also express his effort to heal and create. Mirek tries to make a whole history, a full texture, a *fabric*, where authority wills only oblivion and gaps. In trying to assemble his documents he resembles all writers, and indeed reflects the author of this novel. The idea—and the value—of putting together is in Kundera's novel fully imaged in the reference to the car-repair shop, which here represents the particular embodiment of the Putting-Together Trope. The trope of Enosis or making-into-one-whole is a reassertion of unity that includes complexity. Mending or healing asserts itself against the break, the cutting, that initiates us into the story. The Mending Trope soothes, with its promise that damage is not utterly irrevocable, and that we may cheat death and disorder through humble human effort—under *Tychē*. Yet the work of any character whenever engaged in this work of recovery, this suture and *bricolage*, is likely to be somewhat absurd at any given moment, and certainly incomplete. Not every character is as visibly and defiantly absurd as Don Quixote, but the patchiness of the product or artifact that the character has worked on is usually evident. It is just as evident, in effect, in relation to Charles Bovary as to Don Quixote. At the very beginning of the novel in which Charles Bovary figures (not even the hero in his own novel), he is an awkward boy, a *nouveau* entering the schoolroom in awkward garments, "his hair *cut* straight along his forehead" (*les cheveux* coupés *droit sur le front*; in *Madame Bovary*, Chap. 1, para. 4, my emphasis). The air is riven with howls of mirth and derision from the other boys. Poor Charles, that dutiful drudge, labors away at his assignment: "looking up all the words in the dictionary, and taking a lot of trouble." Charles works as a writer of the humblest sort, a schoolboy translator, but this labor is pathetic, for although he knows the grammatical rules, he lacks elegance of expression. Charles Bovary's work as a physician, a healer, is likewise doomed; he cannot mend, improvise, unify—unlike his creator Flaubert, whose labor at bringing things and words together is much more fortunate.

Flaubert himself takes a risk in reminding us of the incompleteness of writing, the fallibility of most attempts at putting life together in words, or making sense through patterns. The suspense of any narrative itself must depend on its *not* achieving perfection and completeness in the opening paragraphs. Breakdown and effort struggle together, as they do in the Balzac opening quoted above, where the efforts of the workman's plane which the artisan glorifies (strictly, *deifies*) are struggling against the elements. The artisan's provincial carpentry has a certain ridiculousness of result. The opening of a novel (and any new departure in a narrative may also freshly employ the tropes of opening) offers us fear and hope, but what we may expect above all is a certain repetition of these effects. Characters heal—but they get ill again. Things are mended—but they tear.

CHAPTER XIV

꙳꙳꙳꙳

Marshes, Shores, and Muddy Margins

꙳꙳꙳꙳

The artist had placed the maidens at one end of the meadow where the land thrust out into the sea.
> —Kleitophon describing Europa picture,
> Achilles Tatius' *Kleitophon and Leukippé*

The Branch . . . that hung over a Canal, broke, and the poor Lad plumped over Head and Ears into the Water.
> —Henry Fielding, *Tom Jones*

Outside was a ditch, dry except immediately under the fire, where there was a large pool, bearded all round by heather and rushes.
> —Thomas Hardy, *The Return of the Native*

In these times of ours, though concerning the exact year there is no need to be precise, a boat of dirty and disreputable appearance, with two figures in it, floated on the Thames, between Southwark Bridge which is of iron, and London Bridge which is of stone, as an autumn evening was closing in.
> —Charles Dickens, first sentence of *Our Mutual Friend*

꙳꙳꙳꙳

LIMEN AND *LIMNĒ*

Achilles Tatius' *Kleitophon and Leukippé* begins with the description of a great painting in Sidon, a painting of the abduction of Europa by the bull. The narrator gives us a detailed description of the effects achieved by the artist, and the disposition of the figures: "The artist had placed the maidens at one end of the meadow where the land thrust out into the sea" (4). The central action of the story depicts what has happened at the edge of the water, and is now continuing in the sea, where Europa—triumphantly rather than passively—rides her bull. The novelist begins by focusing on a margin, on an important shore—and on a deep. The novel in its own story alludes to a number of shores and to deeps. The very first lines of the novel describe the seaside town Sidon, with its double harbor (*didymos limēn*), suggesting twinnedness, reduplication, choices among margins, reappearances of shores. The ekphrasis then emphasizes shore or strand, the area where earth and water meet.

The cut of the Rhexis Trope comes, most commonly, as a short delicate stroke, which readers are not obliged to notice consciously. The Trope of the Shore or Margin is presented at greater length, often calling a good deal of attention to itself. The first cut may be worked into the larger description of a margin, when beach or marginal land begin the novel. In *Kleitophon and Leukippé*, the description of the double harbor of Sidon includes the information that the second inlet or mouth (*stoma deuteron*) has been dug or cut through (*orōruktai*) to make the artificial protected inner harbor (just as the novel is hidden as the second story beyond this opening).

Seashores and riversides are not peculiar to the Novel. Epic literature in particular is very rich in them. Who can forget Chryses the priest of Apollo striding angrily along the beach of the many-sounding sea and praying to Apollo to avenge him (*Iliad* I, lines 33–42)? Odysseus' and Aeneas's wanderings mean they have very good acquaintance with beaches and harbors; Odysseus' arrival on the Phaiakian shore, including his appearance to Nausikaa on a beach, is one of the masterpieces of both social and natural description in ancient literature. I am content that we should include sea-journeys, storms, and shipwrecks among the properties the Novel borrowed or adapted from the Epic—although the roots of both forms in various kinds of story may indicate less borrowing than sharing. The Novel, however, makes much more of its beachfront property. It is more openly and insistently fascinated by the implications of the point at which water and land mingle. That ambiguous area—it cannot be called a territory—becomes a special kind of space or setting for the Novel.

Achilles Tatius at the outset gives unusual emphasis to the shore, but he is certainly not alone. Heliodorus begins his *Aithiopika* with a view of one of the mouths of the Nile, a harbor and a beach (para. 1). On the beach are arranged the bizarre signs, the *phainomena symbola*, which the narrative must help us to interpret. The effect is redoubled when the second set of bandits removes the central characters (and ourselves as viewers) to another place where land and sea meet. Theagenes and Charikleia are taken to a stronghold in the *marshes*. The authorial voice tells us about the lives of the marsh-dwellers, describing the scenes among the reeds. Evidently we are to focus, enjoyably, on this indeterminate setting, this place of watery land and earthy water. Artists dealing with a novel often play with such a setting, as in the early seventeenth-century picture of Charikleia being convoyed through the marsh. (See Plate 30.) Illustrators are also very fond of the watery margin of the beach, the place of shipwreck, as in the picture at the beginning of Book IV of *Kleitophon and Leukippé* in an edition of 1635. (See Plate 31.) The place where land and water meet is a place of genesis for a novel. The whole first action of the *Aithiopika* is played out on a stage which is nothing but limen—in a double or rather a punning sense, *hē limnē* (marsh), *ho limēn* (harbor). The action is liminal (from Latin *limen*, threshold), performed on a margin or threshold which is a home of the indeterminate.[1] This is a place where the characters are nameless, or improperly identified (as Charikleia misidentifies herself and Theagenes) or acting outside their proper function and role (e.g., Thyamis, priest turned bandit).

Elements become confused, paradoxes interact. Especially is this true in the war sequence at the end of Book I and beginning of Book II, where the marshland is set afire, and characters seek each other through the burning reeds. That sequence made a big impression on subsequent novelists—one can see how Cervantes in *Persiles* and Scudéry in *Artamène* try to imitate and even to outdo it. But the same liminal paradox of burning reeds, marshlands on fire, is employed with spectacular success in the Chinese novel with the evocative name of *The*

Water Margin, also known as *Outlaws of the Marsh*, or *Marsh Chronicles* (*Shui Hu Zhuan*). In this fourteenth-century novel, a group of heroic bandits rebels against an unjust government. (It is easy to see why this classic novel got banned in Mao's China.) The bandits create a stronghold in Liangshan Marsh and successfully resist an attempt to take them, sending fireships among the government boats: "The soldiers and their officers leaped for the bank, only to discover that they were surrounded by reeds and marsh, without a strip of solid ground. Then the reeds along the shore also burst into a flame, cutting them off completely. The wind was strong, the blaze was fierce" (Shi Nai'an, *Outlaws of the Marsh*, trans. Shapiro, I : 289). The scenes in the nineteenth chapter of this Chinese novel closely resemble those at the end of Book I and beginning of Book II of the Greek novel: "Once ignited, the flames flung themselves upon the nearby marsh [*helos*], devouring the many reeds that grew there so thickly, an indescribably strange sight, the brightness unbearable to the eye as the noise of the crackling fire was overwhelming to the ears" (*Aithiopika* I : 42).

Beaches and marshy margins are omnipresent in fiction, although they may not often be as emphatically presented as they are in *Aithiopika*. The shore (including approach to the shore) is a trope of the Novel.

The place between water and land functions most obviously and overtly as a threshold. Its presence signifies the necessity of passing from one state to another. It is liminality made visible and palpable. Whereas the Rhexis Trope is needed early, it is not necessary for a novel to begin with a river, lake, or sea, or with characters on a shore, strand, bank, or marsh—yet it is surprising how many novels do so. Consider the following works:

> *Lazarillo de Tormes* (1553)
> James Fenimore Cooper, *The Last of the Mohicans* (1826)
> George Eliot, *The Mill on the Floss* (1860)
> Charles Dickens, *Great Expectations* (1860–1861)
> Gustave Flaubert, *L'Education sentimentale* (1869)
> Kate Chopin, *The Awakening* (1899)
> Joseph Conrad, *The Heart of Darkness* (1899)
> Virginia Woolf, *To the Lighthouse* (1927); *The Waves* (1931)
> James Joyce, *Finnegans Wake* (1939)
> Ben Okri, *The Famished Road* (1991)

Examples could easily be multiplied. Contemplating this list of "important" works, it would be hard to deny the efficacy of beginning a novel with a watery limen. But in novels that do not employ this trope at the outset (and that may employ it at later junctures) there are effective substitutes emphasizing a margin or a place of change.

One of the most common manifestations of the Threshold Trope is a description of a building, wall, door, or room—a literal boundary and threshold. *Eugénie Grandet* begins with many descriptions of walls and doors. The novel first denies the marshland trope by insisting on the dryness of the things being described—the word *aridité* and the word *sec* both occur in the first paragraph—but that effect is counteracted almost immediately by the effect of our first entry into one of the dark cavernlike shops, *cette espèce d'antre humide*, a kind of damp cave.

We keep inspecting thresholds and even passing through them in a series of tentative initiations. Balzac's novel initially evokes a marginal world, a No Man's Land conjured up in the images of cloisters, ruins, and dull moorlands.

FRONTIER AND WILD SPACE

In novels that do not employ the beach or marsh, the effect is created of passing through a Debatable Land, an uncomfortably unoccupied and somewhat indefinable territory. In Anne Brontë's *The Tenant of Wildfell Hall*, for instance, the space between the home of the narrator, Gilbert Markham, and the heroine's Wildfell Hall, encountered in the second chapter, is such a territory:

> I . . . proceeded to mount the steep acclivity of Wildfell, the wildest and the loftiest eminence in our neighbourhood, where, as you ascend, the hedges, as well as the trees, become scanty and stunted. . . . The fields, being rough and stony and wholly unfit for the plough, were mostly devoted to the pasturing of sheep and cattle; the soil was thin and poor: bits of grey rock here and there peeped out from the grassy hillocks; bilberry plants and heather—relics of more savage wildness,—grew under the walls; and in many of the enclosures, ragweeds and rushes usurped supremacy over the scanty herbage;—but these were not *my* property.   (*The Tenant of Wildfell Hall*, 19)

In its immediate context, the rough stony soil represents, we might say, Helen's difficult life. The "relics of more savage wildness" suggest (like the name of her house) the "wild thing" that she is, as a single woman separated from her husband in a self-imposed recovered *parthenia*. The narrative also supports our need to recognize and respect such an unclaimed unpropertied area, even as we make the effort to pass through it. In order to get to his beautiful Helen, Gilbert must deliberately pass through the uncomfortable and chaotic frontier, a land of betweenness that has not been colonized and overcome by daily life, a borderland between two worlds.

The frontier in which elements are mixed is associated with journey, motion, and change. The opening of Thomas Mann's *Der Zauberberg* (1924) not only tells us that simple Hans Castorp is traveling in midsummer from Hamburg to Davos-Platz, for a three weeks' holiday, but also emphasizes that which lies between: the middle ground of frontiers and mixed elements: "From Hamburg to that point, that is indeed a long journey, too long for such a short sojourn. It goes through all sorts of people's countries, up hill and down dale, from the south German plateau to the shore of the Swabian Lake, and by ship over its dashing waters, onward over gorges that formerly were thought to be bottomless" (*Der Zauberberg*, Chap. 1, para. 2). Frontiers, margins, and dangers are suggested. Hans Castorp's journey takes him across foreign areas, through border after border, to a shore—and beyond. The journey, the *Reise* itself, impersonally appears able to conquer these dangers or distractions and not to be waylaid by them; it is the *journey* that takes ship, and then easily passes over the bottomless. Hans Castorp slights the deeps; there is some suggestion that his passage is too easy. Later, he is to be truly detained by a bank or shore. In the chapter called *Hippe*, Hans Castorp takes a walk in the mountains near the tuberculosis sanatorium; he comes upon a picturesque scene, a landscape of wildflowers by a waterfall and mountain stream, a *Wildbach* (126). By the wild rushing stream Hans Castorp descries *eine Ruhebank*—literally "a sleeping bank," a comfortable place by the pretty brook. Resting on his Ruhebank, listening to the music of the water—Castorp has a violent nosebleed, the beginning of the symptoms, hypochondriac or tubercular, that will long detain him in the Magic Mountain. His real story begins here.

Hans Castorp ironically passes over and beyond the shore of Lake Constance at the very outset of his story, but sometimes the shore or bank is too insistently present to be so easily transcended. The shore as riverbank or beach may accompany the representation of other frontier areas or boundaries, most especially the often-found facade of a building or buildings. The beginning of Mark Twain's *Pudd'nhead Wilson* (1894) illustrates such a combination in the description of Dawson's Landing: "on the Missouri side of the Mississippi":

> In 1830 it was a snug little collection of modest one- and two-story frame dwellings, whose whitewashed exteriors were almost concealed from sight by climbing tangles of rose vines, honeysuckles, and morning glories. Each of these pretty homes had a garden in front fenced with white palings and opulently stocked with hollyhocks, marigolds, touch-me-nots, prince's-feathers and other old-fashioned flowers; while on the windowsills of the houses stood wooden boxes containing moss-rose plants and terra-cotta pots in which grew a breed of geranium whose spread of intensely red blossoms accented the prevailing pink tint of the rose-clad housefront like an explosion of flame. When there was room on the ledge outside of the pots and boxes for a cat, the cat was there—in sunny weather—stretched at full length, asleep and blissful, with her furry belly to the sun and a paw curved over her nose. . . .
>
> The hamlet's front was washed by the clear waters of the great river; its body stretched itself rearward up a gentle incline; its most rearward border fringed itself out and scattered its houses about the base-line of the hills; the hills rose high, enclosing the town in a half-moon curve, clothed with forests from foot to summit.
>
> Steamboats passed up and down every hour or so.
>
> *(Pudd'nhead Wilson*, Chap. 1, paras. 2–5)

The description repeatedly insists on images of protection and enclosure, combined with prettiness and privilege, as in a reference to "the palace-bordered canals of Venice." Even the trees "at the outer edge of . . . sidewalks" are "protected by wooden boxing" (22). Yet each enclosure or protection only re-creates a frontier and emphasizes living on the edge.

The town is a succession of fronts and elaborate concealments, indicated in the exteriors almost concealed by the luxuriant colorful growths. Twain builds up the sensuousness of the flowers in order to explode with the violent color of the geraniums that turns into flame. The effect of this "explosion of flame" is in miniature similar to the effect of the conflagration of edifices that begins *Artamène*. In Twain's case one can see the social and moral reasons that might lead author and reader to desire some sort of metaphorically consuming attack on this smugness and enclosure. But the fronts and facades, unconsumed, continue to assert themselves. The cat sleeps contentedly on the ledge, a creature of the frontier.

Twain's hamlet itself is entirely on an edge. For all its willed coziness, Dawson's Landing is altogether a *shore* thing. As its name indicates, it has its identity as a beaching ground, as a place on the bank touching the water. "The hamlet's front was washed by the clear waters of the great river," like a face—the rest of the hamlet being "its body" (22). The face seems to require this cleansing. The steamboats remind us of the life of change and adventure that Dawson's Landing cannot escape; Twain heightens the effect at the end of paragraph 5 by stressing the regions visited by steamboats and river: "down through nine climates to torrid New Orleans." The river moves through many frontiers, many areas (like Hans Castorp's journey). Dawson's Landing (like Achilles Tatius' Sidon) is ineluctably on the water. It belongs essentially to that category of important fictional places where the land thrusts into the water, where elements meet.

We can see in Twain's opening paragraphs a most determined and elegantly repeated emphasis on the Threshold Trope. We are perpetually brought up against margin, perimeter, and facade, as we recognize in the vocabulary of the scene: "exteriors," "in front," "palings," "housefront," "ledge," "outer edge," "hamlet's front," "rearward border." Threshold and shore are buckled together in the phrase "palace-bordered canals of Venice," the allusion to Venice ostensibly being conjured up by nothing more than the striped barber-pole. In that quick phrase, Twain brings house-front and water-front closely together; he also conducts a reversal, the edifices now becoming a mere edging or "border" to the water.

RIVER AND POND AND REEDY MARSH

A much quieter use of the sign of the river bank to signify the threshold of entry into a novel is to be found in a very different work, by Twain's contemporary Henry James. The description of the edifice and garden with which James's *The Portrait of a Lady* (1881) opens presents us at both the beginning and the end of the second paragraph with a river: "It [the house] stood upon a low hill, above the river—the river being the Thames at some forty miles from London. . . . The river was at some distance; where the ground began to slope the lawn, properly speaking, ceased. But it was none the less a charming walk down to the water" (*Portrait of a Lady*, Chap. 1, para. 2). The Thames, seen at the bottom of the garden and thus marking both a pleasurable objective and a boundary, plays no overt part in the plot. It is employed here mainly for figurative value. In Kenneth Grahame's *The Wind in the Willows* (1908), on the other hand, the discovery by Mole of the River itself is a major event, and the description of the River is the climax of the first chapter. Animal characters (like Twain's cat in Dawson's Landing) dwell, it may be remarked, more safely on riverbanks and seashores than human characters in fiction usually do.

The shore is a site of restlessness, just as it is a place of promise for the future, including hope of love. The third movement of Proust's *A la recherche du temps perdu* is played out by the seaside; the two objects of Marcel's love, Saint-

Loup and Albertine, are associated with the seashore at the resort "Balbec." Marcel sees Saint-Loup coming in from the beach, "the sea that filled the hall windows to mid-height making a background for him" (*A l'ombre des jeunes filles en fleurs*, Part II, 105). Albertine and the "little band" of girlfriends attract his attention as they walk along the promenade. The narrator asks aesthetically, "Were there not noble and calm models of human beauty that I saw there, beside the sea, like statues exposed to the sun on a Grecian shore?" (174). But neither Albertine nor the love-affair that ensues reflects calm nobility. In a later reference to Balbec, the less happy narrator refers sourly to "the social disarray, the unquiet vanity, the wandering desires of the life of sea-bathing resorts" (*La Prisonnière*, 78). Riversides and seashores, even without the social glitter or resort hotels, awaken disquietude and *désirs errants*, errant and unfixed desires. Human characters are full of unease and longing as they pace upon a shore.

In *Eugénie Grandet*, the heroine takes a walk by the Loire with her father, the notary, and her young cousin Charles, and it is here, in *le sublime paysage de la Loire*, that her desires begin to crystallize, a love for Charles made evident to herself by her shock at her father's snubbing remark to the notary that he would rather throw his daughter into the Loire than marry her to her cousin. "The distant hopes which had begun to sprout in her heart suddenly flowered . . . and formed a bouquet which she saw cut and felled to the ground" (83). Old Grandet talks of planting poplars on the river bank, but it is his daughter's growing love that has rooted itself there.

A dominant meaning of the figure of the shore is sexual. Venus the sea-born seems closer there than elsewhere, and it is her warm image we may encounter by some *rivage de la Grèce*. Erotic awakening requires neither sea nor river to supply its shore, the interface of water and land. The exotic shore may also be presented as marshland, *limnē*—as it is too in the *Aithiopika*. In the ninth chapter of Part II of *Madame Bovary*, Emma and Rodolphe leave their horses and walk through the countryside: "He led her further on, to the side of a little pond, where duckweed made a greenness upon the waters. Faded water-lilies lay unmoving among the reeds. At the sound of their footsteps on the grass, frogs jumped to hide themselves" (165). The little pond is a marshland, an area where the elements are mixed. The duckweed makes not only green color but *une verdure*, like a garden, a display of vegetation on land. Reeds and waterlilies mingle. The little frogs, the amphibians *par excellence*, resemble the Lykian frogs surrounding the goddess Leto as she gave birth to Artemis and Apollo at the spring of Xanthos— or the mean-minded Lykians whom she turned into frogs.

The marshland is a threshold of sexuality, as of birth—sexuality itself, sexual engagement, is a kind of birth. It is at this point in *Madame Bovary* that Emma engages in adulterous sex with Rodolphe—the marsh, we might say, as much as anything else, has undone her in those final moments. Here *elle s'abandonna*—she abandoned herself. She crosses a threshold here in mid-novel, which is not the same as the threshold that figures at the novel's opening. There, we saw poor young Charles Bovary entering the schoolroom, trying to cross over into the public world. That dry (and comic) passing over a *limen*, trying to enter a new stage, has its counterpart this private ritual, a watery initiation into the pleasure of realized amorousness.

The marsh may appear less emphatically. In the description of the uncultivated wasteland around Wildfell Hall, the word "rushes" strikes a curious note; rushes belong in the wet, in marshy territory. There is a hint of the sexual marshland in this beautiful Helen's frontier. In Hardy's *The Return of the Native* (1878) Egdon Heath is dwelt upon at length as an untamed place. This large margin area at the very beginning of the novel not only appears perfectly wild ("the untameable, Ishmaelitish thing") but also very dry. Eustacia, an untameable *parthenos,* is associated with the wild thing. Yet, as we pursue Eustacia, and her story, the dryness becomes mitigated, and the initial fire becomes associated with a watery verge. As in *Aithiopika,* we get the paradoxical fire-in-a-marsh. In her love-longing Eustacia maintains a signal fire in a half-hidden place: "Outside was a ditch, dry except immediately under the fire, where there was a large pool, bearded all round by heather and rushes. In the smooth water of the pool the fire appeared upside down" (54). A little boy is supposed to tell Eustacia when he hears a frog jumping, though the "frog" will in fact be a stone cast into the pool by her lover Wildeve. The language describing this area of ditch and pool is restrainedly but palpably sexual. This is a feminine ditch, the small landscape of pool and plants mirroring the feminine genitals and pubic hair. Where there are rushes and reeds, there is sex also.

The editor of *Joseph et Aséneth* points to the recurrence in that novel of the phrase *hē hylē tou kalamou,* meaning "thick growths of rushes." The goddess Neith is the goddess of the rushes, and many attributes of this puzzling Jewish story's heroine are taken from Neith, whose name is echoed in her own. The *hylē* can refer not only to the density of the plants, but also to the mud in which they grow. *Hylē* ultimately means "primordial matter," "the matter of Neith" (Philonenko, *Joseph et Aséneth,* 78–79). In any novel when we come upon the mud and rushes, we are coming upon, or stumbling into, primordial matter. We pay tribute, nervously, to the first matter of the physical world of being, supplier of the very "nilotic reed," the *Niloticus calamus* with which *The Golden Ass* apparently gets written. Erotic love (the sexual marshland) and love of being and love of writing unite in this rush of power.

The shore (beach, bank, water edge) is the point of departure, of immersion into turbulence. In its role as harbor (*limēn* indeed) it is also potentially the shore of salvation where those who were immersed are recalled to life. D'Urfé opens his *L'Astrée* with an effective use of that special novelistic site, the place where the land thrusts out into the water. His characters, disconsolate Corydon and disdainful (because jealous) Astrée, are seated beside the river Lignon.

> The place where they were set, was a piece of earth somewhat
> mounted, against which the fury of the water beat in vaine, sustained
> in the bottome with a naked rock, but on the top covered with a little
> mosse. From this place the shepheard struck the river with his hooke,
> wherewith he raised not more drops of water, than he found divers
> sorts of thoughts that assayled him, which dashing on him like water,
> were no sooner come, then they were driven away by others more
> violent.   (*The History of Astrea,* trans. John Pyper [1620], Book I, 3–4)

In an interesting use of the Breaking Trope, the novelist makes his character break the glassy surface of the water by striking against it, turning undifferentiated river into violent drops of water, which represent his angry thoughts and mingle with them. Not satisfied with making such a break in the water and contributing to its "fury," Corydon deliberately jumps into the river:

> In this place was *Lignon* very deepe, and the streame strong: for there was a world of waters, and the casting back of the rocke made a kinde of counter-mount, so that the shepheard was long before hee could sinke to the bottome, and yet longer before hee could rise up; and when hee appeared, the first was a knee, and after an arme, and then ouer-whelmed suddainely with the working of the waves, hee was carried farre off under the water. (5)

Everything becomes chaotic. Corydon, taken over by the power of current and undertow, loses shape and form, appearing as a knee first and then an arm. Astrée thinks that he is dead, faints, and flops into the water herself. Actually the hero is carried downstream, comes up against a bank on the opposite shore, and is rescued by three aristocratic nymphs, who apply first aid. There is a good deal of somewhat bizarre comedy in the attempted suicide—including the comedy of an unconscious hero who has to have water and sand pumped out of him. There are two shores in this initial movement of the story—the shore by the rock from which Corydon jumps, and the other shore where he lands: the shore of immersion and the shore of salvation. The shore of salvation is more commonly dwelt upon in fiction—consider *Robinson Crusoe* (1719). But there are many instances of the shore of immersion: for instance, the Thames riverside, near Kew Gardens, site of Mirah's attempted suicide in George Eliot's *Daniel Deronda*, or the canal into which young Tom plops when trying to rescue Sophia's bird in *Tom Jones*. It is as if Corydon had heard the cryptic advice that echoes through Conrad's *Lord Jim* (1900): "In the destructive element immerse . . . " But Conrad is more likely to have caught this advice from Dostoevsky's Porfiry to Raskolnikov: "plunge straight into life [or "yield yourself to life"], without deliberation; don't be uneasy—it will carry you direct to the shore and set you on your feet. What shore? How should I know?" (*Crime and Punishment*, trans. Coulson, 441). Characters do not know, and we usually cannot know for them, what shore they are to come to through the bracing and destructive element. The differences between murderous Raskolnikov and comic Corydon do not cancel out their similarities.

THE SEA, THE SEA

The *navigium* of novel characters most commonly turns into a *naufragium*, journey into wreck. The destructive element, the sea of life, does at first seem only to destroy, though characters are commonly saved from the watery grave—Robinson Crusoe is normal, not exceptional. Nietzsche, as we have seen, was sarcastically parodic about the prevalence of shipwreck in the Novel, but he was not the only critic to notice this. Scudéry (Georges or Madeleine, or both together) commented on the prevalence of fictional shipwreck in the illuminating Preface to *L'Illustre Bassa* (1652):

> As for me, I hold, that the more naturall adventures are, the more satisfaction they give; and the ordinary course of the Sun seemes more

mervailous to me, than the strange and deadly rayes of Comets; for
which reason it is also that I have not caused so many Shipwracks, as
there are in some antient *Romanzes*. . . . So as one might think that
AEolus hath given them the Winds inclosed in a bagg, as he gave them
to *Ulysses*, so patly doe they unchain them; they make tempests and
shipwrack when they please, they raise them in the Pacifique Sea,
they find rocks and shelves where the most expert Pilots have never
observed any. . . . Howbeit I pretend not hereby to banish Shipwracks
from *Romanzes*, I approve of them in the workes of others, and make
use of them in mine; I know likewise, that the Sea is the Scene most
proper to make great changes in, and that some have named it the
Theater of inconstancie; but as all excess is vicious, I have made use of
it but moderately. . . .

> (*Ibrahim, or The Illustrious Bassa*, trans. Henry Cogan [1678], A4ʳ)

The over-use of shipwreck is to be faulted, but that does not mean that novelists
cannot or should not employ what Scudéry obviously sees as a motif or figure
rather than as just an event. We are reminded how sophisticated the seventeenth
century was about symbols, and how self-conscious: "the Sea is the Scene most
proper to make great changes in." The Sea with its *naufragium* appears in fiction
as the sign of great and necessary, if painful, change. The novelist when writing
should be aware of this, Scudéry implies, and conscious of the reasons for causing
a shipwrick. Shipwreck leads us (if we are blessed by *Tychē*-Providentia) to the
shore of salvation. The arrival at the saving shore can be narrated in a number of
ways, including the impressively sensational (as in *Robinson Crusoe*) and the pathetic (*Zayde*). It can certainly be comic, too, as in *Satyricon*, where Encolpius on
the beach mourns the unloved Lichas, the only one of their ship of fools to perish
in the wreck.[2] Encolpius comes up with an appropriate moral commonplace: "If
you calculate correctly, shipwreck is everywhere" (286).

Boccaccio's Filocolo complains about the elements' lack of decorum. The
winds and seas are treating him like an epic hero, he thinks, in subjecting him to
shipwreck near the city of Parthenope: "And you, O highest Aeolus . . . temper
your wrath . . . Open your eyes, and know that I am not Aeneas . . ." (373). But
in being tossed upon the sea's margin at the city of the Virgin, Filocolo has been
given the gift of civilization itself. This shore of salvation means for him (as for the
young Giovanni Boccaccio) the encounter with Napoli, civilization—and Fiammetta. What seems an interruption or frustration is really a gift.

The effect of traditional *naufragium* can be achieved without wrecking a
literal boat. Fay Weldon in *The Hearts and Lives of Men* (1987) supplies a wittily
comic example of the deliberate transformation of the shipwreck into modern
terms; a plane wreck in the Channel becomes a form of shipwreck, with the kid-
napper and the heroic child (a hidden princess with her emerald treasure),
brought up in the tail of the fuselage against the shore of France. Variations of the
motif lie readily to hand—like the parodic *naufragium* of *Anne of Green Gables*,
when Anne drifts in an untrustworthy dory as the unfortunate lily Maid of As-
tolat. Numerous small pleasure craft go down in thrillers and mysteries, as in
Daphne Du Maurier's *Rebecca* (1938). The means of wreckage of small craft are
just as available now as they were for George Eliot.

Eliot not only kills her heroine Maggie in a final glorious wreck in *The Mill on the Floss* (tossing her heroine and brother Tom together on the salvational shore of their *Liebestod*), but also contrives a death by drowning for *Daniel Deronda*'s villain Grandcourt, who falls off his boat. Poor Gwendolyn is supposedly guilty of thought-murder in not trying to save her detestable husband when he falls overboard, but an another level of the story we know that Aphrodite has rejected Grandcourt, and Tyché has judged him justly. At the end of *Catch-22* (when the hero is trying to escape the war in a small craft), we believe that Aphrodite and Tyché are on his side and that he will reach the shore of salvation, the place of desire and peace which is also the realm of profound change. In *Catch-22* that salvational shore is unromantically named Sweden, and Yossarian's friend Orr (for "or" or alternative?) has already arrived there. Heller's ending can be considered as a variation on the ending of Part I of *The Pilgrim's Progress*, for instance, in which the reader knows of the happy ending of Christian and Faithful as they cross the river, which is both death and life, but cannot yet know of the fate of the others (including the reader's own self).

VENICE

These journeys to the shore are always frightening. *The Pilgrim's Progress* makes very clear in its own determined allegory why the passage across water is emblematically scary. To cross the river is to die. Any passage across water may be a figurative death.

According to Hindu religious thought, the sea is an image of the illusion of life, the boat on the sea a figure for the soul trusting in *Maya*, the illusion of all existence. Ironically, *Maja* (or *Maya*) is the title of the pedantic hero's important novel, a weaving together of many characters' fates into one *Romanteppich*, or novel-tapestry in Mann's *Der Tod in Venedig* (192). Aschenbach is not to find it so easy to be lofty about *Maya*; he is *not* in control of illusion. In Western thought and literature the sea is also like Maia, mother of Hermes and in the Roman religion a goddess of all living things. The character's journey itself is (as suggested by both Heliodorus and Achilles Tatius) a reflection of the *navigium Isidis*, the questing journey of Isis, a pilgrimage in which all share, whether they know it or not. The boat on the sea is the illusion of the individual, and his or her craft, plans and projects. Shipwrecked, the individual is violently knocked into the deeps of life and made to change direction. As Achilles Tatius' Melitté remarks, when trying to encourage Kleitophon to have sex with her at sea, the ocean is Aphrodite's own element. "Where could Eros and the mysteries of Aphrodite be more at home than on the sea?" (268). "Love still has something of the Sea / From whence his Mother rose," as the seventeenth-century poet was to put it. The novelistic sea as an avatar of *Tyché* appears to choose whom to save, whom to cast on the shore of salvation after the *Naufragium*, which signifies the shattering of a previous life and the need for a new beginning. It is of the essence of novels that shipwreck can—and even must—happen to quite ordinary people and quite suddenly.

In this discussion of bank and shore, of coast and watery passage, as threshold, as amorous topos and as saving *telos*, a special place ought to be reserved for the role of Venice in Western fiction. In literature in general, Venice has been an abode of combined beauty and ugliness, from which greed and treachery emanate. In drama, Venetian characters are not only given to avarice and betrayal, but are also capable of abruptly surprising behaviors: see for instance *The Merchant of Venice, Volpone, Venice Preserv'd*. In prose fiction, Venice has been treated a little differently, although there are connections with the drama (indeed there is a modern novel, *The Fox*, based on *Volpone*). Novelists focus on the perpetual crossing of water, and on the watery interfaces of palazzo walls and marble steps, slime-encrusted, the water lapping against them.

Tony Tanner, in *Venice Desired*, associates Venice's rise as a novelistic "spectacle," "the city *as* art," with the fact that "Venice was fading out of history" and "disappeared from history altogether in 1797" (4). I connect Venice's manifestation as a novelistic topic, rather, with the rise of Realism. Venice itself provides a "real-life" antidote to Realism. It is a city often associated with dream and the dreamlike; it is a place of imagination, and to be imagined, as Proust's Marcel, long before he visits the city, fantastically inhales "the Venetian air, that marine atmosphere, inexpressible and particular like that of dreams, that my imagination had enclosed in the name of Venice" (*Du côté de chez Swann*, 464); his thoughts create a Grand Canal whose waves "of somber azure and of such noble emerald" break "at the feet of Titian paintings" (463). Venice is (as always) aesthetically conjured, but the Venetian idea includes the indescribably oceanic, and its melting dreamlike colors can readily become nightmare.

Venice first makes its presence felt, novelistically, in new alternative fictions, narratives of horror and mystery. Schiller uses Venice as the scene for his (unfinished) *Der Geisterseher* (*The Ghost-seer*) in the 1780s, complete with what must be the Caffè Florian. Venice is the setting for an early section of Ann Radcliffe's *The Mysteries of Udolpho* (1794). Radcliffe's heroine's little boat on the lagoon waters seems deliberately described as a drifting of the soul on the waters of *Maya*; the spires and domes of Venice appear in their illusory and shifting character. The heroine of *Udolpho* experiences what is customary for fictional visitors to (or denizens of) Venice—pleasure and betrayal.

Other fictional visitors to Venice are no happier, even though they too, like Radcliffe's Emily, take part in the festivity and sensuous pleasure also associated with Venice. Dickens's Little Dorrit is unhappy there; so, if differently, is Henry James's Milly Theale, who comes to Venice to die in *The Wings of the Dove* (1902). I think Mann got it right—: *Der Tod in Venedig, Death in Venice*. Venice has been an abode of fictional death—death covered by, yet recognizable in, the great beauty that constantly metamorphoses form. Venice teaches us that color can be more important than form, that forms change (mirrored in reflections on the water, shifting in haze and cloud). The very cityscape has an allegiance to changeability that is disturbing. The disturbance is connected with possibilities of great excitement, and excitation is felt by all central characters who proceed in their fictions to Venice—Mann's Aschenbach is an outstanding, but not singular, example.

The Maori novelist Witi Ihimaera in *The Matriarch* (1986) has his Maori narrator comment on the disorientation familiar to travelers to Venice: "I had left the real world and crossed some threshold between reality and fantasy . . . in which the senses were heightened by the conjunction of both. Venice . . . was the product of two worlds in collision, the supernatural with the real, the fantastic with the natural, the bestial with the sublime . . ." (431).

Part of Venice's disturbing charm is that it has always been an important interface between Byzantium and Rome, between East and West. For Ihimaera, it develops possibilities as a surprising interface between Maori and Western culture. Venice shares with Maori culture an ability and desire to bring myth to the surface; "here were the manaia, the marakihau and taniwha of a culture far to the south" (433). Venice is the bubble where myth surfaces. It has thus been valuable as a *limen* "between fantasy and reality," where worlds collide. It was soon moved from the Gothic to the "realistic" fictions to provide the shimmering mythical possibilities and disturbing symbolisms officially banned by the school of the Monday-morning novel. Prescriptive Realism had wished to assert that identity is certain. Venice says otherwise. Venice's disrespect for form and for realism has made it particularly congenial to "Post-Modernist" writers.

The excitement commonly connected with Venice in prose fictions is associated with fear of the loss of the self. Venetians, with their expertise in masking and Carnival, play with that exciting and fearful possibility. Whether one is deceiver or deceived, monster or prey (and Mann's Aschenbach is all these things), Venice threatens one with instability, fluidity. In Jeanette Winterson's *The Passion* (1987) the characters who cope best with Venice are physically amphibious, women with webbed feet. The dry heroine of Anita Brookner's *A Friend from England* (1987) is nearly submerged in antagonistic images of water and baffled by Venice's multiplicity of shores. For that is what Venice has above all: a multiplicity of shores. As novelists know, the psychic work of perpetually crossing water is both fulfilling and enervating. Every *rio*, every canal, is full of the possibilities of passage and transformation, of passion and baptism. Venice itself is also one great amorous marshland, as well as an emblem of shifting life perched precariously above the unknowable deep.

Venice is perhaps the most novelistic city the West possesses. Unlike Paris or London (used more regularly as settings) Venice cannot stand for the idea of Urbs or Megalopolis. It is not a type of just any city, but is our amorousness and death. It speaks of novelistic meaning—of too many meanings. In it we confront our own unknowability, the treachery of ourselves to ourselves. We associate Venice with brilliance, with illumination even, but never with cleanness. Its beauty is closely associated with dirt, its loveliness resting on mud. The "slime-encrusted marble of her palazzos" has become a cliché of description, but every visitor is truly struck by "the decay and rot of the ages" such as Ihimaera's narrator sees (or dreams he sees) on "the bellies of the bridges" (450). Venice teaches us to admit that we are dirty. If Venice is the flickering complex of shores, the amorous marsh, it is also the great slough.

DIRT

Bunyan's *The Pilgrim's Progress* ends with a beautiful river and shore, but it begins with a dirty great slough. Christian the pilgrim (along with the feeble Pliable), in his first attempts to undertake the way to salvation, falls into the Slough of Despond. If we think of that in terms of actual "sloughs" or miry holes in seventeenth-century roads, we realize that a variety of dirt, including sewage running through a watercourse, can be included the idea of a slough. Christian flounders helplessly, covered with mud and dirt: "they drew near to a very *Miry*

Slow that was in the midst of the Plain, and they being heedless, did both fall suddenly into the bogg. The name of the Slow was *Dispond*. Here therefore they wallowed for a time, being grievously bedaubed with the dirt; And *Christian*, because of the burden that was on his back, began to sink in the Mire" (12).

This miry Slough is a vivid expression of a novelistic topos. It is a direct ancestor of the variations of this topos—mire as quicksand—that provide so notable a feature of Victorian novels, like the Shivering Sand of Wilkie Collins's *The Moonstone* (1868), or the Great Grimpen Mire of Conan Doyle's *The Hound of the Baskervilles* (1902). These miry deeps that suck down human beings—these may not be true features of the geological world, but they function as appropriate images of both threshold and sexuality, and, in their nineteenth-century appearances, for the capacity for self-absorption. Despond is also a self-absorption. Yet it is impossible for novelistic characters not to be self-involved to some degree.

Christian in the Slough of Despond fulfills another "invisible duty" of novel characters—the duty to get dirty. The act of becoming dirty, involved in the mud, customarily occurs near the beginning of a novel, but may be associated with the first crossings of life-thresholds. Novel-characters are heroes of dirt and disorder; they are attracted to *hylē*. We especially admire, and like, a Sherlock Holmes who plunges fearlessly into *hylē* for our good, tracing muddy footprints and fingering cigar ash; we like feeling that the material world is never merely waste material. An occasion of "becoming dirty" or going "through dirt" offers a kind of baptism into the world of the novel.

Mud is often referred to in novels—even in elegant novels by "ladies" like Jane Austen. "As they splashed along the dirty Lane Miss Watson thus instructed and cautioned her inexperienced sister" (first paragraph of *The Watsons*, 275). Austen treats her heroine Elizabeth Bennet to noticeably muddy petticoats, drawing down the scandalized comment of Bingley's sisters: "I hope you saw her petticoat, six inches deep in mud, I am absolutely certain; and the gown which had been let down to hide it, not doing its office" (*Pride and Prejudice*, 30). Elizabeth, who has crossed a frontier, in her "scampering about the country" in order to join her sick sister (and Mr. Darcy) at Netherfield, has passed through the slough. Wading, as her detractors point out, "above her ankles [*sic*] in dirt," she has been baptized into the world of matter and of love; in crossing wet fields and puddles she has shown herself amphibious, a denizen of the sexual marshland, a sexual being. In the first chapter of *Emma*, Mr. Knightley proves to Mr. Woodhouse that he has brought in no mud on his shoes—a comic negative use of the trope, pointing to the sterility of Mr. Woodhouse's drawing room, and indicating the necessity of the hero and the heroine getting "muddier" before they can come together. The proposal scene at last takes place outdoors, in the garden after a heavy rain, and after Mr. Knightley has had "a wet ride" (*Emma*, 384).

D'Urfé's Corydon is comically immersed in the humid element mixed with earth and sand at the beginning of his novel. Movement in or around the fertile liminal area is often combined with ideas or images of dirtiness and disorder. The train travelers in the first chapter of Dostoevsky's *The Idiot* are all shabby and grimy, bound, as the second sentence tells us, on a journey in "damp and foggy" weather; their faces are all yellow, "the color of the fog" (27). They arrive in a damp and dirty city, which is too wet for comfortable walking. Hans Castorp in his railway journey, a *Reise* of apparent dry safety and efficiency, has his worthy book, *Ocean Steamships* (a dry book on a wet subject), sprinkled with dry dirt, *Kohlenpartikeln*, specks of soot (*Der Zauberberg*, 7). Richardson's Pamela as she sits on the bank of the "dashing Waters" of the fishpond and despondently meditates on suicide (151–153), is in a wounded and dirty and bloody condition, befitting her forthcoming rebirth here after a brief *Scheintod*.

The essence of dirtiness is birth, and birth involves dirt—valuable dirt as is expressed in the deceptively simple outsetting of Dickens's *David Copperfield* (1849–1850). The title of the first chapter is "I am Born" (an unusual use of the present of this verb), and the fourth paragraph begins, "I was born with a caul, which was advertised for sale, in the newspapers, at the low price of fifteen guineas" (49). The newborn's caul is thought a valuable preservative against *drowning*—and indeed it is not David who drowns, but Steerforth. The "caul" is eventually bought for under five shillings by an old lady who lives to the age of ninety-two and strictly avoids drowning: "her proudest boast, that she had never been on the water in her life." She strictly avoids immersion of the self in the deep element. The "caul" is the membrane enclosing the fetus in the womb, a portion of which sometimes still encloses the infant at birth. David is born still surrounded by the mother, attached to the feminine (some would read this psychologically as an essential sign of David's major problem). The "caul" is both himself and not himself—he is embarrassed, at age ten, to see it put up for sale: "I remember to have felt quite uncomfortable and confused, at a part of myself being disposed of in that way" (50). David's superstitiously valued "caul" is a dirty treasure, treasured dirt, organic sign of the passage into full life, a dirt paradoxically not hidden or disposed of but kept and displayed. It bears a symmetrical relation to the churchyard mound that signifies the father: "the mound above the ashes and the dust that once was he, without whom I had never been" (60). Viscous, bloody, transparent yet solid, the "caul" stands for all the coming-to-be of the flesh, which is both "dust and ashes" and living creature. The old lady, the caul-buyer who preserves a withered age by never going near the water, is a comic reminder that we are not meant to keep from the wet, that we must venture, even at risk of shipwreck, upon the deep.

Water is a sacred element, and it is treated as such in the Novel. Novels have a special affection for humid dirt. Grime and dampness combine in the first chapter of *The Idiot*, as they do in the opening description of *Thérèse Raquin*, where that sinister passageway is paved with yellowish paving-stones, "always sweating an acrid humidity" (*suant toujours une humidité âcre*). The Threshold Trope is carried on in that description of the narrow passage (like a birth-canal), and includes a reference to the river. The passageway assures us that there is a fructifying humidity present in the mean dirtiness. In Zola's *L'Assommoir* (1876) humidity and dirt combine in the wonderfully monstrous scene of the cheap washhouse to which Gervaise goes in the middle of the first chapter, an establishment located in the beautifully named rue Neuve-de-la-Goutte-d'or (New Street of the Drop of Gold). In a perpetually steamy fog, rows of women do their wash:

> They beat furiously, laughed, turned themselves about in order to
> shout a word in the uproar, bent over their tubs, filthy lewd women

[*ordurières*], brutal, ungainly, soaked as if caught in a downpour, their flesh red and steaming. Around them, under them, ran a great streaming, buckets of hot water carried about and emptied at one go, cold-water faucets open and pissing down, splashings of the laundry-bats, droppings from the rinsed wash, puddles where they paddled running in little brooks along the sloping flagstones. (32)

Zola does not explain (with a word like "from") the relation between the concourse of streams under and around the women and the buckets, etc.; he jams his list altogether to create a total impression. It is an impression of gigantic femininity, expressed in the gigantic humidity that seems to emanate (like piss) from the bodies of these ugly energetic female workers. The confused uproar (*vacarme*) is an aspect of the creative disorder of this festival, which is at once a festival of cleanliness and dirt, of sacred and horrifying dirt of flesh combined with water-made-dirty.

The horror (authorial) at such dirt is stressed in the sequence where Gervaise sets up shop as a laundress, taking in stinking dirty objects, closely associated with the fleshly body, its excretions and productions—underclothing, handkerchiefs, used towels, "socks eaten up and rotten with sweat." "She felt no disgust, being accustomed to filth [*ordure*]" (173). The job of a laundress as here described is an interface job, combining purification and carnality. Water must be perpetually made dirty, in order to cleanse objects that must return dirty again, signed by contact with the human body and its needs.

Water-made-dirty is a recurrent motif of *L'Assommoir*. In the second chapter, we are shown Gervaise visiting a six-story tenement building, which emits a trickle of rose-colored water: "a dyer's laboratory in its great boilings let out this stream of a tender rose color [*ce ruisseau d'un rose tendre*] running under the porch" (66). In the activities of the laundresses in their wet and streaming cavern, and in the trickle of rose-colored water, we may recognize a new manifestation of the Homeric nymphs who so impressed (and depressed) Porphyry: "And in the cave are long looms of stone, where the nymphs weave webs of purple dye [*haliporphyra*] wondrous to behold, and there are ever-flowing water-springs" (*Odyssey*, XIII, lines 107–109). This is the home of creation of the flesh, the site of Incarnation and its activities.

As well as the cut marking new beginning, as well as Threshold and Sexual Marsh and Salvational Shore, we may expect to find in a novel a tribute to the dirt of incarnation, an acknowledgement of that fertilizing world of embedded matter, which is the body itself.[3] So it is with Stephen Dedalus on the dirty Dublin beach, a themepark of *hylē*: "Signatures of all things I am here to read, seaspawn and seawrack, the nearing tide, that rusty boot. Snotgreen, blue-silver, rust: coloured signs. Limits of the diaphane. . . . Stephen closed his eyes to hear his boots crush crackling wrack and shells" (*Ulysses*, 31). Boot; snot; the feel of crackling shells—these remind one of the needful, productive, and powerful body that is neither transparent nor abstract. Not everything can be imaged and disposed of by Aristotelian visibility or reason. Soon, incarnate Stephen catches sight of a midwife coming down "the shelving shore": "What has she in the bag?

A misbirth with a trailing navelcord, hushed in ruddy wool. The cords of all link back, strandentwining cable of all flesh" (32).

Joyce picks up the "ruddy wool," the *haliporphyra*, of baby-making. Stephen is on a margin of incarnation, but it is a place of danger, of death as well as life: "Unwholesome sandflats waited to suck his treading soles, breathing upward sewage breath, a pocket of seaweed smouldered in seafire under a midden of man's ashes" (34). Dirt layered upon dirt offers dangers and pleasures at the edge of the gathering of waters, "loom of the moon" (41).

Heliodorus offers us an explanation of the peculiar holiness of shore and dirty margin in a context stressing the dangers of this conjunction. The analysis of what might be called "holy mud" comes just after the description of Hydaspes' successful siege of the city of Syene, which he vanquished by flooding. The flood left in its wake a thick mud, and a muddy pool (*telma*), which could swallow up horses and men—a precedent for the Great Grimpen Mire itself (III:50). The narrator of *Aithiopika* (in personal voice) gives a rational (or rationalizing) account of the meaning of the Egyptian religion: "to the initiated [*pros tous mystas*] it is proclaimed that Isis is the earth and Osiris is the Nile, real things partaking of these names" (III:51). The common people think that being and life are given to mankind by the conjunction of the primordial elements of moist and dry. Initiates likewise believe this, but also understand the names of the gods to be representations of one universal principle. The holy conjunction of humid with dry (*tēn hygras te kai xēras*), the holy syzygy, brings about the life-giving mud. The common people worship that which allows the crops to grow—in their eyes the river is a strong brown god. It is necessary for Heliodorus' interpretation of wet and dry to identify Isis with the earth, and water with masculinity. That is not always the case. As we have seen, the ocean is Aphrodite's own element, and sometimes the water-earth attributes may be reversed. In China's most famous novel, the eighteenth-century *Dream of the Red Chamber* by Cao Xueqin, the hero Bao-yu has a "feminine" nature and values the feminine. As a child he says, "Girls are made of water and boys are made of mud. When I am with girls I feel fresh and clean, but when I am with boys I feel stupid and nasty" (I:76). Bao-yu's infusion of the feminine principle gives him great sensitivity and insight, not always appreciated by his father. In Bao-yu's case, the margin is within him, he is a frontier at which Yin and Yang visibly meet. He thus offers possibilities for greater enlightenment, and even for cultural transformation.

The muddy margin is a place to start from—perpetually a point of departure and rebirth. The fertilizing ooze is both unpleasant and pleasurable, the ooze of reality, the undertone of the flesh and the flesh's remaking of itself. Its viscosity sticks to us, in the ineluctability of matter, as we watch the novelistic characters ritually engaged with their necessary dirt. The mud and dirt of borderland can be emphasized even in the description of a salvational shore—as well as most certainly in the representation of the sexual marshland. The references to coast, bank, shore, and to pool, muddy bank, humid verge, all remind us of the common pleasures and responsibilities of being alive. The seashore is a place of beginning, which both cleanses us and covers us with salt. Pond and marsh and riverbank offer the muddy site of our desire, where we begin again to confront the marshy stuff of sex, birth, love, change. The Novel tells us all these things, reminding us quietly of what we need, and of the place of our necessity—as for instance does D. H. Lawrence's *The Rainbow* (1915) in its first sentence: "The Brangwens had lived for generations on the Marsh Farm, in the meadows where the Erewash twisted sluggishly through alder trees, separating Derbyshire from Nottinghamshire" (7). We must farm that marsh, live on that borderland, washed by the "Erewash" that washed us of yore, always before (or ere) the paradoxical dirty cleansing of the particular novel we hold in our hands. We have lived on the marshes—or, as Philip Pirrip's relatives call them, "th' meshes" (*Great Expectations*, 21). We are enmeshed in that web of being, formed and woven by the twisting springs and the nymphs' yarns.

CHAPTER XV

>-+-◆>--0--◆-+--<

Tomb, Cave, and Labyrinth

>-+-◆>--0--◆-+--<

"Alas! . . . I am buried alive!"
>   —Kallirrhoe in Chariton's *Chaireas and Kallirrhoé*

"Gracious Creator of Day! to be buried alive for eighteen years!"
>   —Mr. Lorry in Charles Dickens's *A Tale of Two Cities*

"Watch what you're doing, my master; don't try to bury yourself alive, nor send yourself down there like a bottle put to cool in some pit."
>   —Sancho Panza in Cervantes' *Don Quijote*

An awful silence reigned throughout those subterranean regions, except now and then some blasts of wind that shook the doors she had passed, and which grating on the rusty hinges were re-echoed through that long labyrinth of darkness.   —Horace Walpole, *The Castle of Otranto*

>-+-◆>--0--◆-+--<

LIVING DEATH

In Chariton's *Chaireas and Kallirrhoé*, as we have seen, the heroine is buried alive, her husband believing he has killed her. The heroine's relatives console themselves with an impressive burial. In Hermokrates' magnificent (*megaloprepēs*) tomb by the sea Kallirrhoe is laid—and comes back to life to a strong aroma of spices amid a clutter of gold and silver objects. She cries aloud for help, and then bewails her fate: *Oimoi . . . zōsa katōrygmai!* ("Alas! . . . I am buried alive!" 62). Rescued inadvertently by Theron and his bandits, and newly "married" to Dionysios, Kallirrhoé can return the compliment of her spouse. Thinking Chaireas dead, she insists on creating a great cenotaph for him: "entirely the same as her own in Syracuse, in design, in size, in expensiveness" (116). As the narrator comments, this new grand tomb, this duplicate is also "the same" in a way Kallirrhoé does not suspect—it is also for one who still lives. Chaireas never gets into this tomb, but he does experience burial alive, elsewhere, in Caria, where he and his enslaved companions are thrown into the dark hut from which the sixteen desperadoes break out.

The characters in Xenophon's *Ephesiaka* experience similar restrictions and imprisonments. In order to keep her vow to Habrokomes—not only a formal marriage vow but a private mutual pledge—Anthia determines to resist the forced marriage to Perilaos. She buys what she thinks is a lethal poison from an Ephesian doctor and drinks it on the eve of the unwanted wedding. Like Shakespeare's Juliet, Anthia is to all appearances lifeless. The grieving Perilaos bewails his fiancée, the maiden bride-to-be, the "nymph." He takes her corpse to the city's cemetery (*tēs poleōs taphous*) and deposits her in a monumental funeral chamber (*en tini oikēmati*), with rich offerings (43). Anthia, like Kallirrhoé, awakes in the tomb; realizing the doctor tricked her, she awaits death—more calmly than Chariton's panicked heroine. Anthia too, however, is rescued by grave robbers.

On a later and more painful occasion, after Anthia has killed a bandit who would rape her, she is sentenced by the chief of the gang. Dragged from the cave in which she has been held, and where Anchialos attempted the rape, Anthia is thrown into a deep pit with two hungry Egyptian dogs. She is led "to the pit and the dogs" (*epi tēn taphron kai hoi kynes*, 54). The pit is covered over with great planks and earth. That this deliberately constructed living grave is dug near the Nile (*ēn de tou Neilou oligon apechousa*, 54) must instantly reassure us that life-giving aid will not be slow in coming. Deep in the Nile mud, Anthia must rise again. The brigand guard takes pity on her, gives her bread and water, and feeds the dogs. Later this guard quietly deserts the brigand band, digs up Anthia, and takes her to his new hideout, a cave. They live chastely together and happily—not excluding the dogs, who have become affectionate companions (*hoi kynes all' estergon synētheis genomenoi*, 60).

Taphos or *taphros*—tomb or trench, sepulchre or grave. The place of sepulture can be envisaged as miniature house of the dead (*oikēma*) or as the pit, the ditch. The place of sepulture gapes for novel characters, and they not uncommonly find themselves in the hole. The matter may be treated any number of ways by the novelist; it may indeed form the stuff of comedy. So it does, for instance, in Fielding's *Joseph Andrews*, in which the hero is attacked by footpads, robbed, stripped, and thrown into a ditch. The postilion of a passing coach tells the coachman "he was certain there was a *dead* Man lying in the Ditch, for he heard him groan" (41). This paradoxical statement (what the eighteenth-century English were wont to call an "Irish bull") captures both Joseph's deadness and his aliveness, his passing through the realm of death in his *taphros*. Fielding is, of course, deliberately drawing on the story of the Biblical Joseph, who pays a notable visit to the *taphros*:

> And Reuben said unto them, Shed no blood, *but* cast him into this pit that *is* in the wilderness, and lay no hand upon him: that he might rid him out of their hands, to deliver him to his father again.
>
> And it came to pass, when Joseph was come unto his brethren, that they stript Joseph out of his coat, *his* coat of *many* colours that *was* on him;
>
> And they took him, and cast him into a pit. . . .
>
> (Genesis 37:22–24)

Thomas Mann, novelizing the Biblical Joseph's story in *Joseph und seine Brüder* (1933–1943) offers some commentary on the idea of the pit, as Joseph meditates *In der Höle* ("In the Pit"):

> He had wept and wailed when big Reuben had given his voice that they should throw him into the pit; yet at the same time his reason had laughed as at a joke, the word used was so laden with allusions: "*Bor*" the brothers had said. And the monosyllable was capable of various

interpretations. It meant not only well, but prison; not only prison, but the underworld, the kingdom of the dead; so that prison and the underworld were one and the same thought, one being only a word for the other. Again, the well, in its property as entrance to the underworld, likewise the round stone which covered it, signified death; for the stone covered the round opening as the shadow covers the dark moon. . . . When the horror happened and the brothers hoisted him onto the edge of the well and on the margin of the pit, so that he must descend below the daylight with all the caution he could muster— then his quick mind had clearly understood the allegory of the star which one evening is a woman and in the morning a man and which sinks into the well of the abyss as evening star.

(Joseph and His Brothers, trans. H. T. Lowe-Porter, 390)

Mann's passage, like the novel as a whole, is concerned to present mythological symbols and to interpret them; it plays upon all the analogous *German* words while talking about the non-German *Bor*. Joseph's recognition of the word "one syllabled–many meaninged" (*einsilbig-vielsinnig*) is an act of thought; "his understanding laughed as at a piece of wit: *hatte sein Verstand gelacht wie über einen Witz* (II: 198–199). The word Lowe-Porter translates first as "joke" and second as "mind" refers to play on words or ideas, and to the intelligence itself; it is the word used by Freud in a work sometimes translated as *Wit and the Unconscious*. Mann demonstrates a cultural unconscious (not Joseph's individual psychology) that links all these meanings in the language itself.

Mann also points out, more overtly and consciously than any other Western novelist, the deep mythology within the Novel as well as within his own novels,—he does so not just in *Joseph* but in all of his mature works. In this instance, part of the mythic fun lies in the multiplicity of German words playing around the idea of "pit." In contrast to the compact *Bor* (which Joseph must unpack), the language is profuse in offering a number of synonyms for the *Bor* which is all of its own synonyms: we encounter *Höhle, Grube* (twice), *Brunnen*—as well as the unpacked meanings *Gefängnis, Totenreich, Unterwelt* (prison, kingdom of the dead, Underworld). A sense of potential puns hovers above the passage: *die Grube = das Grab*: pit = grave; *die Höhle = die Hölle*: empty cavern = Hell. Both Joseph and the author of this passage are evidently possessed of the wakeful wit that plays such games. The word Lowe-Porter translates as "allegory" is *Anspielung*, a word centrally conveying "play" or "game," *spiel* indicating a playfulness relying on allusion or connection. Only connect.

Mann wishes us to connect very large mythological ideas with the enforced descent of Joseph to the pit. "It was the abyss [*Abgrund*] into which the true son descends, he who is one with the mother and wears the robe by turns with her. It was the nether-earthly sheepfold, Etura, the kingdom of the dead, where the son becomes the lord, the shepherd, the sacrifice, the mangled god" (trans. Lowe-Porter, 390). Joseph, type of Jesus and Osiris, is one with the Mother, or Mother-Goddess. Torn like Adonis, he descends into the earth to rise again.

Well, of course the Joseph story *is* a religious story, and Christian interpretations have brought its connections with the myth of the mangled god to our attention. Mann's extremely emphatic interpretations here point out that the descent into the pit and burial alive are fates not reserved for characters who are already great religious and mythical heroes, but lying in wait for ordinary characters, in commonly known and quite easily read novels to which no archetypal religious significance has been attached.

What about the favorite set text for high-school reading, Dickens's *A Tale of Two Cities*? We first encounter Mr. Lorry of Tellson's bank, on his way to Paris on a peculiar errand: "He was on his way to dig some one out of a grave. . . . the passenger in his fancy would dig, and dig, dig—now, with a spade, now with a great key, now with his hands—to dig this wretched creature out. Got out at last, with earth hanging about his face and hair, he would suddenly fall away to dust" (46–47). We find out the meaning of these images on the literal level of the story: Doctor Manette has been rescued from the Bastille after lengthy incarceration: "Gracious Creator of day! To be buried alive for eighteen years!" (48). Dickens, as witty as Mann's Joseph, conflates the images of prison, grave, and underworld through Mr. Lorry's combining "fancy" which arms him with "spade" as well as "key," and emphasizes disinterment from the pit. The banker is well-named "Lorry," as the business of a British "lorry" is to move things from place to place, like a "metaphor" (and the word *metaphor* turns up nowadays on Greek moving-vans). Mr. Lorry carries meanings and connects them as well as connecting cities. He connects life and death. Readers remember Mr. Lorry's metaphorically cryptic message sent by Jerry Cruncher: "RECALLED TO LIFE" (41).

Jerry, the body-snatcher or resurrection-man, functions in the novel to focus our attention (while the rest of the "plot" is unwinding in the middle of the story) upon the various possibilities of "resurrection"—and upon the grave or pit. Jerry, a creature of the criminal underworld and of the grave as Underworld, is a custodian of the pit who supports the party of Death. Not of putting-to-death, of killing (like Madame Defarge), but of Death itself, of the final dusty pit. Jerry masks his deathly and dusty trade under the pretense that he is a fisherman, a pretense put to ironic use in the description of his midnight activity: "They fished with a spade, at first" (191).

Fishermen, connected with life-giving water, are in the antique novel, as Merkelbach points out, helpful folk, like the fisherman who assists Habrokomes in the fifth book of *Ephesiaka*. Merkelbach argues that "fisherman" has a mystical sense; the fisherman assists at rebirth or spiritual awakening, which is why the Isis-parade in Apuleius has a man dressed as a fisherman (*Roman und Mysterium*, 138–139).[1] Jerry proves at last true to his assumed character, even against his own wishes, when he is able to defend the good party by testifying to the absence of a corpse in the coffin he disinterred. The grave that he robs, under the eyes of his own son and of the reader, is indeed a cenotaph, like Kallirrhoé's tomb for the absent Chaireas, an empty grave, a marker from which death is absent. Yet this novel itself dwells, rather like Jerry, upon the edge of the pit, its major actions performed on the margins of the grave.

Dr. Manette's *Scheintod*, his seeming death, lasted for eighteen years before the opening of the novel. A character's *Scheintod*—a period of hiddenness, of being in the hole or the hold—is usually much briefer. In Richardson's *Pamela*, as we have seen, the heroine contemplates suicide on the banks of the fishpond; the watery bank is the site of decision and renewal. Pamela has earlier played at fishing there (113), and as "Fisher" Pamela proves herself capable of sustaining a life on the deep. She can come to her own aid, deciding against committing suicide. She is still in pain, having been beaten by inanimate objects in her vain effort to escape: "and bending my limping Steps towards the House, [I] refug'd myself in the Corner of an Out-house, where Wood and Coals are laid up for Family Use, till I should be found by my cruel Keepers . . . and there behind a Pile of Firewood I crept . . . with a Mind just broken, and a Heart sensible to nothing but the extremest Woe and Dejection" (154).

Pamela's period of "Woe and Dejection" in the wood-house is the interval of her seeming death in the eyes of her jailers. Discovered and aroused to life after beating and burial, Pamela nearly undergoes another beating by yokels armed with sticks, but she is then fully restored and recalled to life. Her occlusion in the place of wood and coal, of dry earth and dust, is happily very short.

Even shorter is the time in the pit spent by George Eliot's Eppie in *Silas Marner* (1861). Silas the weaver wonders how to discipline the foundling child, and his friend Dolly advises: "you might shut her up once i'the coal'hole" (185). Silas acts, on this recommendation reluctantly and briefly: "Silas let her out again, saying, 'Now Eppie 'ull never be naughty again, else she must go into the coal-hole—a black naughty place.'"

Silas's rueful belief that he has punished and frightened the child by placing her, like a very infantine Joseph, in the pit, receives a shock within the next hour: "He turned round again, and was going to place her in her little chair near the loom, when she peeped out at him with black face and hands again, and said, 'Eppie in de toal-hole!'" (188). Eppie has already undergone the *Scheintod* in participating in the death of the Mother whose memorial she is; instead of dying she was restored to life. Now Hepzibah-Eppie, whose nature is resurrection and whose constant task is to exhibit the powers of life and the future, refuses to respect the "black naughty place," the pit or Underworld into which she is thrust. For her, even more than for Mann's Joseph, it is all play, a jest, "ein Witz." Unlike Pamela in *her* coal-hole, Eppie feels no woundedness or self-pity, but resurrects at once. She is willing to descend and ascend, time and time again. The real victim of a "pit" is her greedy and cruel uncle Dunstan, who robbed Silas of his gold and then fell into "the Stone-pit," a sort of female orifice (despite its name) of "moist . . . clay," and "red, muddy water" (83). This Venus-place rejects him, finds him unworthy of life.

Eppie's black "toal-hole" is a grave, which is also a form of prison. In novels, the prison *cell* frequently operates as the symbolic grave. As we see—as in the case of Anthia thrown into the pit, or of Chaireas chained in the dark hut—prison and grave are often interchangeable. Richardson's Clarissa has a much harsher series of experiences than his Pamela. Her life is a sequence of habitation of prisons. The nadir of despair and sorrow is reached after the rape, when the prostitutes have her arrested for debt. Lovelace's friend Jack Belford, coming to bail her out, is appalled by the prison room he describes:

A horrid *hole* of a house, in an Alley they call a Court; stairs wretchedly narrow, even to the first-floor rooms; And into a *den* they led me, with broken walls, which had been papered, as I saw by a multitude of tacks, and some torn bits held on by the rusty heads. . . .

The windows dark and double-barred, the tops boarded up to save mending; and only a little four-paned eyelet-hole of a casement to let in air; more, however, coming in at broken panes, than could come in at That. . . . On the mantle-piece was an iron shove-up candlestick, with a lighted candle in it, twinkle, twinkle, twinkle, four of them, I suppose, for a peny [*sic*].

Near that, on the same shelf, was an old looking-glass, cracked thro' the middle, breaking out into a thousand points; the crack given it, perhaps, in a rage, by some poor creature, to whom it gave the representation of his heart's woes in his face. . . .

An old-half-barred stove-grate was in the chimney; and in that a large stone-bottle without a neck, filled with baleful Yew, as an Evergreen, withered Southernwood, dead Sweet-briar, and sprigs of Rue in flower. (VI: 272–273; italics mine)

There is nothing here that is not decaying—save only the remorseful rue. Identity crumbles. Clarissa, in disappearing for one whole day from the narrative, has experienced the inexpressible vigil *in der Hohle*. The novel's illustrators appreciate Richardson's expressive images of wasting and decay, though their pictures do not quite capture the closeness and darkness of the place (see Plate 32). The "baleful yew," tree of English churchyards, turns this *hole* or *den* into a grave. To enter it is like walking under the graveyard, into the invisible pit made visible.

Emblems of the pit can be nearly as self-consciously deployed by secret societies as by novelists, as Tolstoy ironically demonstrates. The Freemasons' objective in devising their rituals was, at least in part, to capture for modern enlightened use the rituals (insofar as these could be recovered) of the ancient mystery religions. (Among their primary sources were the ancient novels themselves.) In the early eighteenth-century (just the age of our conventional "Rise of the Novel") the elaborate apparatus of rites, symbols, and passwords was devised. In *War and Peace*, Pierre as initiate is first blindfolded and then taken to a dark room, where he is left to discover a Bible open at the Gospel of John, a lighted human skull, "a coffin full of bones" (trans. Edmonds, 416). Like Clarissa, Pierre is in a small, dimly lit room full of reminders of death and decay. Pierre, of course, knows that the whole show has been arranged, and dutifully tries to have the appropriate responses: "Trying to stir up a devotional feeling in himself, he peered around" (416–417). He tells the "tyler" or mystagogue "I . . . I . . . seek regeneration" (417). So does everyone in Tolstoy's novel—so does Russia itself. Tolstoy's comic if sympathetic treatment of this episode shows up the artifice and shallowness of the Masonic characters (including here Pierre), who are, as it were, trying to write their own novel around themselves. They want—and plan—to arrive at satisfactory results (enlightenment and resurrection) quickly, on the cheap, as it were.

Later in the novel Pierre undergoes the true descent into the pit. Pierre's real *Scheintod* (when he appears dead to his friends) includes captivity and the threat of burial. After he has been captured by the French and has been living an enslaved life as a prisoner in the dark shed with other men (an ordeal not unlike that of Chaireas), Pierre is nearly executed when supposed "incendiaries" are shot by their own grave: "a big pit had been freshly dug in the ground" (1142). In the course of his resurrection or birth to new life, Pierre is guided by his true mystagogue, the serf Platon Karatayev, the simple man whose name is significantly the name of the great Greek philosopher, author of the *Republic* with its Parable of the Cave. Pierre descends into the cave with a new Plato and finds the pit of darkness not a place of ignorance but of spiritual growth.

The Cave often figures in novels, where it plays a more ambiguous role than that allotted it in Plato's parable. Longus' Chloé is found in a cave, and Daphnis in a hollow dell, where he is suckled by a Dionysiac goat. Defoe's Robinson Crusoe finds the beautiful cave, the sparkling "Grotto," but the entrance is guarded by a frightening old goat, just dying—a Dionysiac emblem and sacrifice, that makes the place uncanny (177–179). A cave is a mysterious place, frightening even when it is the desired place of refuge. It may bear the meaning of "tomb" and even be interchangeable with *taphos/taphros*. Cervantes in the very first sentence of *Persiles y Sigismunda* connects tomb and prison with cave, recollecting the tomb of Lazarus, Hell, and Christ's sepulchre, and implicitly recalling also the Platonic parable: "The cruel Corsicurbo gave voice at the narrow mouth of a deep dungeon [*profunda mazmorra*], formerly a sepulchre which imprisoned many living bodies that had been buried in it. And, notwithstanding his terrible and frightening loud sound heard near and far, no one understood clearly the words he pronounced, except the miserable Cloelia, whose misfortunes kept her shut up in that deep confinement" (19).

The "mouth" (*boca*) of the cave or pit of hell expresses that which would extinguish life by swallowing it, in a common locution like the "gorges" (*Schlunde*) over which Hans Castorp passes so serenely in the initial journey of *Der Zauberberg*. In his Enlightenment journey, sustained by technology and science, he dismisses the ancient gorges that *formerly* seemed bottomless. His ironic mimicked complacence might warn us the hero has yet to encounter hell-mouth, the pit. Castorp's escape from the throat that would devour him is of a somber sort, for he is ultimately to perish in the hell of war. Cervantes' hero fares rather better, drawn out of his cavernous prison like a rising god, like Mann's Joseph, pulled towards the heavens. Buried alive, he is restored to light.

Yet a cave or cavernous place, even when it is a prison, seems to serve as a fostering place of transition. We note that in *Ephesiaka* Anthia is in the bandit's cave before she is thrown into the pit. Amphinomos rescues himself and Anthia by hiding in another cave (*en antrōi*, 59). The Cave is a house that Nature offers. It has many attractions, including the idea of it as original human dwelling and natural womblike place, like "the home under the ground" so constantly referred to in Barrie's *Peter Pan*. It is also uncanny (*unheimlich*) and may announce itself as uncomfortably free of the customary attributes of the domestic.

In Kafka's *Metamorphosis* (1915), Gregor Samsa, transformed into a monstrous bug, feels a sense of panic when the women of his family start to take the furniture out of his room, so he can have simple space in which to crawl about:

"he could not explain to himself . . . how in all seriousness he could have been anxious to have his room cleared out. Had he really wanted to have his warm room, comfortably fitted with furniture that had always been in the family, changed into a cave, in which, of course, he would be able to crawl around un-hampered in all directions but at the cost of simultaneously, rapidly, and totally forgetting his human past?" (*Metamorphosis*, trans. Corngold, 33). The room, de-natured by being dis-furnished, becomes a wild place and confirms Gregor's iden-tity as a monster, an outcast creature, *ungeheuer*, with no part in the family or in the domestic and civic world. Corngold's translation is perhaps a trifle optimistic here; in the original, Gregor wonders why he wanted *das warme, mit ererbten Möbeln gemütlich ausgestattete Zimmer in eine Höhle verwandeln zu lassen* ("to let the warm room so comfortably equipped with inherited furniture, turn into a pit" (*Die Verwandlung*, 80). Gregor fears seeing his room become a scooped-out hollow in which he is lost, thrown like a wild beast into a den or like Joseph into his *Höhle*. The room is becoming both cave (the more neutral concealment) and *pit*, the hole of lostness.

The Cave may be considered as the human aspect of the earthy dwelling which, considered in its animal aspect (and as animal-dominated), becomes a *den*. Robinson Crusoe, taking possession of the goat's den, his "Grotto," thinks of him-self as monstrous, *ungeheuer*, "like one of the ancient Giants, that are said to live in Caves, and Holes in the Rocks" (*Crusoe*, 179). When in *Ephesiaka* Anthia is thrown into the pit with violent animals, the *pit* then assumes its forbidding iden-tity as *den*. Anthia, however, partakes of the goddess-role of "Mistress of Ani-mals." With the practical help of Amphinomos, she turns those fierce dogs into social companions, and the story moves upward towards the more cheerful and social cave. In *Wuthering Heights*, the kitchen at the Heights may be read as Heath-cliff's cave, which is a pit or prison to young Catherine; yet she is mistress of the animals that frighten Lockwood: "Half-a-dozen four-footed fiends, of vari-ous sizes and ages, issued from hidden dens to the common centre" (*Wuthering Heights*, 15). The kitchen of Wuthering Heights is a den, at the center of other dens. Humans forced into *dens* are pushed towards the animal side of their iden-tity. Thekla, forced into a den (the arena with its wild beasts), also chooses one; she jumps into a wet den when she dives into the pit (*orygma*) of water-beasts (*phōkai*, 210–212). There are some values in coming into contact with dens—not the least being an acquisition of strength.

If characters like Thekla or Anthia (or even, comically, Brontë's Lock-wood) are thrown into wild-beast dens, Gregor Samsa has the psychologically harsher fate of seeing the space around himself becoming identified as a beastly pit. Lucius as Ass is in a den of himself—so is Gregor as Bug. The deepest and harshest imprisonment is that which Lucius as Ass and Gregor as unnameable Bug endure—claustration within a beast. The fleshly integument in no way an-swers the desires of the soul. Their plight may be considered as a special case of imprisonment, of being thrown into the pit. In the *Odyssey*, we know Circe's vic-tims only from the outside; we may choose what we will imagine of their expe-rience of being animalized. Lucious and Gregor take us unavoidably into that experience of deep and dumb incarceration.

In *The Golden Ass*, the ass and the human girl share an imprisonment within the bandits' cave in the mountains—a cave, not a den, a *spelunca* located amid beautiful scenery. Charité weeps at finding herself "in this stony prison locked up like a slave" (*inque isto saxeo carcere serviliter clausa*, I: 228). It is within this cave that the old woman, in order to console the girl, tells her long story of Cupid and Psyche. The cave is the place of storytelling, of the poetic art. But it is no wonder that novelists, dedicated to the arts of fiction—illusive as Plato thought them—should give a strong place to the cave.

That the cave is a good place for storytelling is known to Cervantes—and probably to Don Quixote. Don Quixote insists on spending an interval in the Cave of Montesinos: see Part II, Chapter 23, entitled "Of the wonderful things which the incomparable Don Quixote says that he saw in the deep Cave [*la profunda cueva*] of Montesinos, the impossibility and grandeur of which have caused this adventure to be held apocryphal" (702). Don Quixote is curious to see this cave associated with legendary heroes and insists on being lowered down into it at the end of six hundred feet of rope, though Sancho begs his master not to make the descent: "Watch what you're doing, my master; don't try to bury yourself alive, nor send yourself down there like a bottle put to cool in some pit [*en algún pozo*]" (699). Don Quixote, however, does deliberately put himself to cool in this under-world place which to him is not a pit but a miraculous cave. Returning, he claims to have had the most extraordinary encounters and conversations with the legendary dead—an adventure that the narrator (as Cide Hamete Benengeli) rejects. The reader is left to wonder whether Don Quixote fell into a visionary trance and dreamed up all this (highly disconcerting) material, or whether the Don himself is engaging in storytelling. The cave is here firmly attached to the idea of fiction, of fiction-making. This cave is a *mise en abîme* indeed! What Sancho interprets one way—perfectly appropriately—as "burial alive in a pit or sepulchre" is interpreted otherwise by both the Don and the narrator, as the encounter not with Death but with Fiction.

The Cave may be invited into the domestic scene, created in a *bricolage* that deliberately evokes the idea of the fictitious: "'A gloomy wood,' according to the one play-bill, was represented by a few shrubs in pots, a green baize on the floor, and a cave in the distance. This cave was made with a clothes-horse for a roof, bureaus for walls; and in it was a small furnace in full blast, with a black pot on it, and an old witch bending over it" (*Little Women*, 17). Here in Louisa May Alcott's *Little Women* (1868) the improvised "cave" announces Jo's connection with fiction, and her love of the fictional (the play being acted is her own).[2] This mock-up cavern, which puts to new use such mundane articles as a clotheshorse, also signifies a welcome escape from the domestic. Female characters in books by women may particularly welcome cave-dwelling and cave life, at least in their reveries, as an escape to a space of nurture without domestic rules. In Radcliffe's *The Mysteries of Udolpho*, Emily, the heroine, while in Venice expresses in her poem "the Sea-Nymph" (179–181) a wish to descend to the "secret caves" and "coral bow'rs" of the ocean deeps.

The happiest Cave in all literature is the dwelling of Mr. Badger in *The Wind in the Willows*, which is a glorious Den—a Den recuperated for domesticity.

Rat and Mole, lost in the Wild Wood in a snowstorm, are invited in by kindly Mr. Badger:

> He shuffled on in front of them, carrying the light . . . down a long, gloomy, and, to tell the truth, decidedly shabby passage, into a sort of central hall, out of which they could dimly see other long tunnel-like passages branching, passages mysterious and without apparent end. But there were doors in the hall as well—stout oaken comfortable-looking doors. One of these the Badger flung open, and at once they found themselves in all the glow and warmth of a large fire-lit kitchen. (51)

The description of the kitchen with its wide hearth, log fire, and high-backed settles is an idyllic celebration of the beauties of the traditional English farmer-yeoman's style of living. The place is not only domestic, we are assured, but also epic; not only personal but also clubbable:

Here Rat and Mole are restored by being fed and having wounds bandaged. Rebirth and escape from death are achieved not by arising out of the underworld (like Cervantes' Periandro) but by diving *into* it. Badger's Good Den seems in some respects a deliberate rewriting of that more ambiguous Den, the kitchen of *Wuthering Heights*, in which another snow-bewildered traveler, the urban Lockwood, found a difficult refuge. Badger's House is a salient example of the Den or Pit re-envisioned as happy Cave.

THE LABYRINTH

Badger's House is also an example of another and related trope—the trope of the Labyrinth. When Rat and Mole, cold and confused, first enter, they see the hall and "other long tunnel-like passages branching, passages mysterious and without apparent end." After they have eaten and slept, the more cheerful visitors are taken on a tour of Badger's residence:

> Crossing the hall, they passed down one of the principal tunnels, and the wavering light of the lantern gave glimpses on either side of rooms both large and small. . . . A narrow passage at right angles led them into another corridor, and here the same thing was repeated. The Mole was staggered at the size, the extent, the ramifications of it all; at the length of the dim passages, the solid vaultings of the crammed store-chambers, the masonry everywhere, the pillars, the arches, the pavements. (61)

Badger explains that his home is built on the site of an ancient human city, ruined and then reclaimed by natural forces, and at last taken over by animals like himself. His house is a labyrinth, partly man-made, now rehabilitated or decontaminated by innocent animal presence. We might say that Badger's House is a "Green" labyrinth. That Badger possesses such a vast labyrinth strengthens his position as a custodian of the good Earth, and a benevolent guardian of the Underworld.

The Labyrinth appears everywhere in novelistic fiction, for it is deeply novelistic, though its particular applications may widely differ. In *Middlemarch*, Will Ladislaw, disgusted at Dorothea's marriage to the elderly pedant Casaubon, exclaims, "You have been brought up in some of those horrible notions that choose the sweetest women to devour—like Minotaurs. And now you will go and be shut up in that stone prison at Lowick: you will be buried alive. It makes me savage to think of it!" (153). Ladislaw's mythological allusion is fairly complex. The Minotaur of Crete demanded an annual tribute of seven youths and seven maidens, until it was slain by Theseus with the help of Ariadne, who gave him the clue to guide him through the labyrinth where the Minotaur was kept. For the creature that dwelled in a stony prison, "buried alive," was the Minotaur itself, the monstrous (*ungeheuer*) offspring of King Minos' wife, Pasiphaë, who mated with a bull. Daedalus (*Daidalos*) of Athens, the cunning craftsman, made the labyrinth in which the monstrous offspring of Queen Pasiphaë's lust was to be hidden. The name of James Joyce's youthful hero thus refers to Stephen Dedalus not only as the cunning artificer but also as one who knows a secret (or who must learn a secret) related to the results of female sexual passion . . . and this Dedalus is both maker of labyrinths and a wanderer in a labyrinth (or several labyrinths).

Ladislaw's remark at its most obvious level simply refers to the social ideas taught to women as the "Minotaur." Dorothea, dutiful to her dull husband, will be the sacrifice to monstrous ideals of female submissiveness and self-suppression. As an elaboration of this meaning, poor Casaubon becomes the Minotaur, the monster who demands sacrifice. But there is another level at which Dorothea is herself both Queen and Minotaur, the hidden female sexual passion shut up in a secret stone tomb. Neither of these interpretations need suppress the other, but we must realize that the monster Casaubon is not for himself the beast at the heart of the maze, but the wanderer within the labyrinth: "Poor Mr. Casaubon himself was lost among small closets and winding stairs. . . . With his taper stuck before him he forgot the absence of windows, and in bitter manuscript remarks on other men's notions about the solar deities, he had become indifferent to the sunlight" (137). Casaubon is entombed in Plato's Bad Cave, the one inhabited by men indifferent to the Sun. It is now the Cave as Labyrinth, the Tomb in which one wanders.

The legend of the Minotaur need not be taken as the only focus of mythological meaning offered by the concept "Labyrinth." Archaeology and new influences in classical studies are in the course of changing our vision of what the Cretan Labyrinth actually was or signified—or might signify. Rodney Castleden in *The Knossos Labyrinth* (1990) boldly proposes that what Arthur Evans reconstructed as "the Palace of Minos" in Crete was not a palace but a temple, or temple complex, "dedicated to bronze age deities and their cults" (173).[3] Ariadne, the "feminine heart of Minoan civilization," is "princess, priestess, goddess" (175). The essential Minoan religion is goddess-worshipping, as we see in the images of the goddess or priestess with snakes in her hands. Castleden argues that the Labyrinth itself, the actual building at Knossos may well be the work of "a Minoan architect . . . trying to create a pictorial or narrative experience . . . that was unsettling, full of incident, drama, and surprise":

It seems as if it was intended to be experienced as a wonder-creating journey of the soul. Or rather, in its many entrances, interlocked sanctuaries and access passages, it set up for the worshipping pilgrim a series of journeys that we can no longer re-create. (179)

Religion, then, provided the original theme-park, guiding the visitor through a set of structures and paths that created experiences. As we shall see, this was what happened at Eleusis, in the Mysteries. Castleden's description of Knossos could almost be a description of the Novel or Romance as a form. Novelists in their own fashion do re-create the wondrous journey through the labyrinth. Or rather, they re-create multiple journeys. George Eliot, for example, treats Casaubon's wanderings with not-unsympathetic irony; this dry clergyman is a poor excuse for a Theseus and does not seize the clue that his Ariadne holds out to him. How can he get to the heart of his mystery when in his mythologizing he denies and overlooks the feminine?

The Labyrinth is a frightening place. It sustains something of its ability to frighten even in the most comic treatment, as when Harris and the others get lost in Hampton Court Maze in Jerome K. Jerome's *Three Men in a Boat* (1889). It can inspire adventurous horror, as it does for a child reading about Tom Sawyer's excursion with Becky Thatcher into the cave: "They wound this way and that, far down into the secret depths of the cave . . . and branched off in search of novelties to tell the upper world about" (*The Adventures of Tom Sawyer*, 192).

Heliodorus offers a most intricate and exhaustive representation of the Labyrinth in which he interconnects Labyrinth, Cave, and Tomb—and elaborates upon the interconnection. Thyamis the bandit, to keep Charikleia safe for himself, has her stored in a cave; when the battle goes against him he kills her (as he thinks). Theagenes, entering the cave in search of his beloved, weeps over what he thinks is her corpse —until the real living Charikleia appears. Heliodorus describes the cave with great care, laying particular emphasis on its tortuous intricacies. The narrow mouth (*stomion*, I : 40) is hidden under a secret chamber; the doorsill stone when moved allows descent into the depths. These caverns are man-made (like Daedalus' Labyrinth). This is a work of artifice (*technē*); the brigands in order to store their booty dug this cave (*orygma*). But it is no simple hollow or pit: "In the inmost recesses the openings and tunnels now appeared alone, making a straying detour, now tumbled upon one another, intertwined like tree-roots, all flowing together to one spacious hearthless room in the furthest depths, into which room through a slit came a dim light reflected from the face of the marsh" (I:40).

Heliodorus emphasizes the effect achieved by the Egyptian bandits' art, the effect of a *natural* randomness—the tunnels sometimes are intertwined like tree roots (*hrizēdon plekomenoi*). If the tree roots reflect the natural, the *plekomenoi* suggests artifice again, for it can mean "braided together," as twined by art, and bears a close relation to the web or weaving of the plot, its *plokē* as Charikleia defines it in Book IX, this demon's devising of interbraided (or entangled) threads (*polyplokous*). We note also that Charikleia is hidden in the very depths of the cave; the priestess (in this story) takes the place at the center, not the Minotaur. Having penetrated to the heart of the labyrinth, Charikleia is saved; another victim is sacrificed in her place, and she rises from this complex living tomb more bright than ever. Her *orygma* has a haunting suggestiveness and a set of meanings that the *orygma* of Xenophon's Anthia does not, for Anthia's pit is not a labyrinth. A Labyrinth may take the place of pit or rocky tomb, and perhaps it always has some of the characteristics of those two other important *topoi*. But a labyrinth is always something more. In its intricacy is power, and to move rightly through that intricacy and out again is to assume that power.

Norman Mailer in *Ancient Evenings* (1983) offers us the labyrinth-experience of an Egyptian soul reborn inside a tomb. This entity crawls out of the tomb, wanders through the Necropolis to the tomb of Menenhetet Two, whose reincarnation he in some sense is, and encounters the High Priest and King, Menenhetet One, his ancestor, who acts as his guide through the rest of the process of reincarnation. The Egyptian Priest leads the narrator-hero on a labyrinthine journey:

> Down we went along a promenade in the dark, down some low tunnel that made us stoop, and before us was the scuttling of rats, and a scattering of insects, while bats flew so near I all but heard the menace of their brain. . . . As I went on in this darkness, bathed in light behind my eyes, I seemed to pass through vales of heat and cold, the air collecting in chill pods like the void of a tomb; yet another five steps, and I was back in the balmy Egyptian night breathing the warm perfume I had first taken in on my great-grandfather's breath, a scent that did not seem to come from him so much as from the stone itself, until I began to feel as if we were not on our way up a steep narrow ramp so much as winding our passage from tent to tent of a mysterious bazaar. . . .
> (108–109)

Mailer is one of the most surprising modern exponents of the Egyptian element in the Novel, reintroducing us to such hallowed characters as the Egyptian Priest—"O! Shade of Kalasiris!" we might feel like remarking to this shady Menenhetet, although this cunning Priest-King-Spirit has a stronger resemblance to the wily Nektanebos of *The Alexander Romance*. Mailer's hero has a most literal experience of burial alive and of being recalled to life —"literal" and yet of course an experience far outside the boundaries of realism. The narrator's story is about rebirth, reincarnating; his *Scheintod*—his *Tod*, moreover—took place just prior to the story's beginning.

Mailer's intermingling of labyrinth-tomb with "bazaar" may alert us to the lurking labyrinth in other suggestively mysterious, enclosing, and erratic places, where goods are laid out in disorder. A fine example is the *magasin d'antiquités* in Balzac's *La Peau de chagrin*. This *magasin* is itself a series of *magasins*, of boutique after boutique in which objects, the wreck and leavings of all our civilizations, are jumbled together. The hero, a gambler on the point of suicide, wanders through it all in a sort of exhausted ecstasy, then in stupefaction.

> In climbing the interior stair that led to the rooms on the first floor, he saw votive tablets, suits of armor, sculpted tabernacles, figures in wood hung on the walls, set beside every step. . . He was pursued by the strangest forms, by marvelous creations poised on the frontiers between death and life. He walked in the enchantments of a dream, and,

> doubting his own existence, he was, like these curious objects, neither
> entirely dead, nor entirely living. (39; the apparent omission points
> are Balzac's punctuation)

Amid all this glorious and repellent débris of dead thought, the wanderer seems
increasingly moribund:

> A gleam about to depart from the sky having lit up a last red reflection
> in battling against the night, he raised his head, and saw a barely
> lighted skeleton which, pointing its finger, nodded its skull dubiously
> from right to left, as if to say to him
>   "The dead don't want you yet!" . . .
>   Passing his hand over his brow to chase away his sleepiness, the
> young man distinctly felt a cool breeze produced by some unidentifi-
> able hairy thing that brushed against his cheek . . . He shuddered.
> But, as there was a dull thud against the window-panes, he thought
> that this caress, cold and worthy of the mysteries of the tomb [*des mys-
> tères de la tombe*], had been given him by some bat. (44; Balzac's
> punctuation) [4]

This crowded place, quintessentially marginal, on the frontiers of life and death,
is a labyrinth partaking of "the mysteries of the tomb." Yet, like all labyrinths, it
demands constant efforts in forward motion and perception.

Balzac's weird shop serves as the model for other labyrinthine bazaars
such as Dickens's Old Curiosity Shop (in the novel of that name, 1841) and Mr.
Venus's shop in *Our Mutual Friend* (1865). The Sheep Shop in *Through the Looking-
Glass* also partakes of some of the qualities of the crowded labyrinth, a riddle
"solved" by dissolving into water, into a river, not unlike the way the enclosed
tomb dissolves in the mind of Mailer's narrator into the pleasant liquid Nile:

> I could still reach out an arm on either side, and the walls of the gallery
> were there to touch, yet I felt closer to the Nile on that one golden day
> I could remember of my boyhood, or, rather, as if much confused, like
> the Hebrew who could not separate what was to come from all that he
> might dream, I felt as if the river was washing along the floor, and the
> walls were riverbanks, and I was on the Nile once more. . . .
>
>   (*Ancient Evenings*, 109)

Or as Alice remarks in the Sheep Shop, "Things flow about so here!"
(*Through the Looking-Glass*, 176), a remark that connects the movement of objects,
and the movement of the mind through space, with movement of water—as does
Heliodorus' verbal adjective *syrreontes*, "flowing together," describing the tunnels
or passages of the underground caverns, which flow together towards the empty
space at the lowest depth (I : 40). Such touches remind us that the earthy or stony
labyrinth and the plashy bank and flowing water have their alliances. The hard
labyrinth may be closer to the life-giving river than we think—as it is for Tom
Sawyer when he "pushed his head and shoulders through a small hole and saw
the broad Mississippi rolling by!" (201).

Looking back at the above examples, we can see that the Labyrinth can reveal itself in two aspects—as empty space, or as a space tormentingly crowded with objects. The Labyrinth has—or is—a Via Negativa and/or Via Positiva. It stands for that where nothing is, where the self is constrained and pressed in gigantic emptiness. Or it is the place where too much is, a pressure of confusion of objects demanding the strained attention of the self. Even Heliodorus' man-made cavern system might abound in objects, for we are told initially that the bandits "had carefully scooped out this cavern for a place of security for their spoils" (*orygma pros skylōn phylakēn periergōs koilainomenon*, I : 40). We experience the cave-system during the narrative as a confusion of emptiness, darkness, absence, yet it could have been represented as a store of objects. In some sense it is such a store, for it contains a multiplicity of Charikleias. The Labyrinth is both one and the many.

The Egyptian bandits in Heliodorus made their cavern, which was not a work of nature but a work of art in imitation of nature (*alla technēs lēistrikēs tēn physin mimēsamenēs*, I : 40). Heliodorus himself created this cave-system (and his labyrinthine novel) in "imitation of nature"—in the Aristotelian sense. In certain types of novels labyrinths have a very visible formal work to perform; such labyrinths we are scarcely invited to appreciate on a "naturalistic" level. Medieval buildings offered the labyrinth of choice for Gothic novelists. Horace Walpole in *The Castle of Otranto* (1765) began the castle game, offering a very explicit connection of imaginative ideas. The heroine Isabella, fleeing from the villain Manfred, tries to escape by means of the secret "subterraneous passage" leading from the castle to the church of Saint Nicholas: "The lower part of the castle was hollowed into several intricate cloisters; and it was not easy for one under so much anxiety to find the door that opened into the cavern. An awful silence reigned throughout those subterraneous regions, except now and then some blasts of wind that shook the doors she had passed, and which grating on the rusty hinges were re-echoed through that long labyrinth of darkness" (25). The underground place is both tomb and prison, and yet associated too with the saving cave of retreat. We feel the sustained heaviness of the man-made building pressing us down—Ann Radcliffe's constant word for this kind of oppressive building is "edifice." Above all we notice the *intricacy*. The Labyrinth is associated with anxiety, with puzzlement, with strained attention. It presents an epistemological challenge. How is one to disentangle what is confused, how to locate a meaning and hence an objective? In heightened uses of the Labyrinth Trope, epistemological and moral problems of great force are represented in emblems of spatial disorientation, of the self in unknown space.

The experience of the Labyrinth is not essentially, as with cave or tomb, enclosure, but wandering through an obscure suite of enclosures that are also openings, opportunities. The mind must always be busy calculating these intricacies. Unlike the prisoner, or the patient buried alive, the lost one in the labyrinth is a traveler and must keep on the move to survive. The attention is dizzied by the constant fissioning, one thing leading to another in an associative scramble very like the mind itself. Heliodorus describes the labyrinthine tunnels branching off, *ataktōs schizomenon*, splitting off in an irregular apparently random manner. In the labyrinthine state one is close to the schizophrenic, having a divided mind, a mind splitting off in random thoughts or even alternative selves.

Movement through the labyrinth may be compelled. In Schiller's *Der Geisterseher* (*The Ghost-seer*, 1787), both the narrator and the hero are seized by officers
of the Venetian state and taken on an undesired mystery tour. They are first taken
to a canal and put in a gondola; then their eyes are bound. After going through
the labyrinthine canals, they are taken through an unknown building: "They led
us up a great stone staircase and then through a long winding passage over vaults,
as I deduced from the multitudinous echoes that responded under our feet. Finally we arrived at another stairway, which led us down twenty-six steps into the
depths. Here there opened a room, where they took the bandages off our eyes"
(53). This is a labyrinth, not really the pleasanter for their being conducted forcibly. Yet one might think they were merely being initiated into the Masons, like
Pierre.

Schiller refrains from using the word "labyrinth" here, reserving that
word for its apparently merely *rhetorical* function in a later passage. The Prince
begins to find his religious beliefs unsettled; the narrator comments on this with
concern:

> Religious controversies in general, so it seems to me more often then
> not, are to him who enters into them as if he had entered an en-
> chanted castle [*bezaubertes Schloss*], in which one cannot set his foot
> without horror, and a man would do a great deal better, would get
> through life with more honorable resignation, without courting this
> risk of setting himself to wander lost in its labyrinth [*sich in seinen La-
> byrinthen zu verirren*]. (105)

Schiller's narrator, a rather Doctor-Watson type, the good normal fellow,
supplies the word withheld before ("Labyrinth") and offers a whole set of meanings attached to the word. The word supplies precisely the connection between
abstract "realistic" historical concept (religious controversies) and imaginative
narrative image (enchanted castle). Schiller's interest evidently lies in presenting
the difficulties of both belief and enlightened nonbelief, and the social, intellectual, and psychic strain involved—not only for the individual but for the culture
at large—in examining the grounds of its belief, of descending into the dark labyrinth which is the *Urgrund* of the visible culture. When the word "labyrinth"
appears apparently as a flourish of rhetoric, a "mere metaphor," in a novel it is
always doing its deep work under the reassuring mask.

Gothic novels (among which *Der Geisterseher* can be numbered) became
very expert at creating their labyrinths. Their chief *loci*—castles, abbeys, convents, and so on—never require more than the slightest veiling of historical naturalism, and always proclaim themselves as not the works of Nature but works of
Art. We might call such labyrinths "Purpose-Built Labyrinths" for their evident
function is to *be* labyrinthine. They focus our attention upon the look, feel, and
nature of the enclosing maze. Characters in the novels are customarily free to
wander through the maze, but the *anxious* wandering is that stressed in Schiller's
verirrten, to wander astray. It is not the wandering of *spaziergang*, a cheerful chosen walk through open space. S/he who wanders in the labyrinth "errs"—by
definition. The Labyrinth is a place where it is impossible not to err.

In novels, Reason is of *some* avail when the character is lost in the labyrinth. Yet Reason alone is never enough. For one thing, Reason has never been able to keep us from the Labyrinth in the first place. As Schiller's narrator indicates, Reason is itself source of the sinister enchanted castle and of losing labyrinths. Perhaps Schiller was recalling Milton's devils, who engage in theological debates in Hell: "And found no end, in wandring [*sic*] mazes lost" (*PL* II, line 561). We would like to say —the Enlightenment would like to say —that Superstition is the Castle's dark cellarage and that Reason is the bright lamp. But for Enlightenment writers (of any era) matters become more complicated than that.

In Umberto Eco's *Il Nome della rosa* (*The Name of the Rose*, 1980), a mock-Gothic mock-detective story also functioning as a historical novel, the monastery library furnishes the labyrinth. It is entered at dead of night by the Sherlockian detective, the Franciscan Guglielmo da Baskerville, and his Watson, Adso da Melk. The Library has a special name in the story—it is referred to constantly as "the Edifice," *il Edificio* (a shrewd reuse of the Radcliffe tradition). Reason itself— knowledge, learning, wisdom—furnishes the labyrinth. The chapter title (under Second Day: Night) makes evident what is going on: "In which they at last penetrate the labyrinth, have strange visions, and, as happens in labyrinths, get lost" (*Dove si penetra finalmente nel labirinto, si hanno strane visioni e, come accade nei labirinti, ci si perde*, 173). The library's system of arrangement is obscure, full of maddening riddles; it seems impossible to remain oriented within this weird library. (Part of the comedy of the scenes in *Il Nome della rosa* lies in the fact that all libraries and all library cataloguing systems share some of the characteristics of *il Edificio*.) When Guglielmo and Adso first enter the *Edificio* through the secret passageway, Adso is horrified to find himself in the monastery's catacombs, among the bones of an ossuary: "In one niche I saw only hands, so many hands, by this time irremediably intertwined [*intrecciate*] one with another, in an entanglement [*in un intrico*] of dead fingers" (166). Here is *plokē*, the braidedness, combined with "mysteries of the tomb" indeed. Eco's words stress intricacy (also a Radcliffean word); we here first catch sight of the labyrinth image in the entanglement and intertwining of the dead hands—an image that literalizes in a macabre and jocular fashion the metaphor used by, for instance, George Eliot as a title of a section of *Middlemarch*: "The Dead Hand." Eco expresses what all "Gothic" writers have known and have also represented in their several ways: that the past (*dead hands*) is the source of structures, mental conflicts, and plots (*intricacies*). The Library is also the product of dead hands—very literally, in a manuscript culture. Gothic novelists, when they want to query the powers of historical structures, very often use the images and paraphernalia of the medieval Church, but that alone is never their true object. Eco shows us that the stuff which Reason uses to think with—literature, philosophy—has its dead and imprisoning aspects; all intellectual endeavor is an entry into a labyrinth. That labyrinth, like the overstuffed shop of *La Peau de chagrin*, is the culture itself, with its confusing inheritance. To try to think one's way through our superstructures and infrastructures is a strenuous task, which we carry out partly in the dark.

Eco's work is, of course, a comedy, a parody of the detective story (as well as a true detective story). In detective fiction we *expect* labyrinths. We make allowances for their appearance, as long as the author dresses them up in sufficiently realistic detail. Hospitals, office blocks, and large mansions have often been pressed into service. In "Gothic" fiction the Labyrinth shrugs off its realistic cerements and reveals itself for what it is. We have tended to apply special names or categories to novels in which certain tropes are emphasized, pushed to the limit. If the calm village houses and tame gardens of normal realism are expected to make room in their midst for some unignorable and gigantic form of trope—a lethal marsh, a lowering castle—we label this novel "Gothic" or "fantastic," or sometimes "experimental" (as with Kafka). But when the calm village disappears practically altogether (as in Mailer's *Ancient Evenings*, for instance) we have no name for the new kind of fiction. Mailer is considered an important male writer, so we do not feel socially free to insult him by calling what he writes "Romance"—though it is probably not the author we are worried about insulting so much as the reader. Mailer's novels seem to have something in common with the work of seventeenth-century writers like Madeleine de Scudéry, who attempted a similar disruption of norms in their novels set in a vivid imagined antiquity, works in which they are (relatively) free to push images and tropes towards extremity. Eco, like Mailer, works with a nonrealistic past in a take-off from the historical novel, in which he is to be free to play with images and tropes, but, more cautious than Mailer, Eco signals that his work is in that despised and low (but accessible) genre, the "mystery story," and that he knows how to mock the form while using it.

Eco's *Il Nome della rosa* is a comedy . . . in a way. It is also a book about comedy, about the missing text, Aristotle's treatise on Comedy. By focusing on Tragedy as the highest literary form, perhaps Western civilization has made itself grandiose and cruel. . . perhaps it has ignored other possibilities. Petronius' *Satyricon* is the most comic of our ancient prose fictions. Does it have any relationship to the matter and images of our most "Gothic" productions? Well, yes, for it, too, has the Labyrinth. As we have already seen, the dinner with Trimalchio is a descent into the Underworld. At one point, in the middle, Ascyltos and Encolpius, accompanied by Giton, try to leave. Trying to get out, and to escape the housedog, Ascyltus and Encolpius fall into the fishpond; Giton (as if appeasing Cerberus at the mouth of Hades) pacifies the dog with the bits of dinner he saved while the porter rescues the other pair. But the porter has bad news: "'You are wrong' he said, 'if you think you can go out here the way you came in. No one of the guests is ever let out by the same door. They come in one way and go out another.' What were we to do, wretched men enclosed in a new sort of labyrinth?" (*et novi generis labyrintho inclusi?*, in *Satyricon*, 166).

Trimalchio's house is a labyrinth, a crowded labyrinth that is also a tomb (*"Fingite me" inquit "mortuum esse,"* 180). Images of death and tombs abound in it. It is a comic place of erring in all sorts of ways. Like a Gothic hero and heroine, Petronius' protagonists here do get out, when the firemen come into the house, but it is apparently (texts are not clear here) just after this that they get lost in the dark town on their way to their lodgings—it is Giton who finds a way out of this new labyrinth because of his earlier prudence, like a little Hansel, in marking the way.

Whether a novel is "serious" or "funny" it takes us into the Labyrinth. For the Labyrinth is the Novel itself, as Jorge Luis Borges explained in his short story "El jardin de senderos que se bifurcan" published in *Ficciones* (1956).

> In this perplexity, there was sent to me from Oxford the manuscript which you have examined. I was caught, as is natural, by the phrase *I leave to various futures (not to all) My garden of paths that bifurcate*. Almost in the act I understood: *the garden of paths that bifurcate* was the chaotic novel; the phrase *various futures (not to all)* suggested to me the image of bifurcation in time, not in space. A general rereading of the work confirmed this theory. In all fictions there occurs a time when a man is confronted with diverse alternatives, opts for one and eliminates the others; in the case of the practically inextricable Ts'ui Pên, he opts—simultaneously—for all. He *creates* thus, diverse futures, diverse times, which likewise proliferate and bifurcate. Hence the contradictions of his novel. Fang, let us say, has a secret; an unknown person calls at his door; Fang resolves to kill him. Naturally, there are several possible *dénouements* [*desenlaces*]: Fang can kill the intruder, the intruder can kill Fang, both can be saved, they both can die, etcetera. In the work of Ts'ui Pên, all the *dénouements* occur; where one happens is the point of departure for other bifurcations. At some time, the paths of this labyrinth converge; for example, you arrive at this house, but in one of the pasts you are my enemy, in another my friend.
>
> (*Ficciones*, 111–112; cf. *Labyrinths*, 26)

The English collection in which this story occurs, translated by Donald A. Yates as "The Garden of Forking Paths," bears the title *Labyrinths*, and certainly Borges of this period is fascinated by the idea. He imagines a Chinese novelist—thus, one supposedly well insulated from the conventions of the modern west—who has created the perfect novel, the "ivory labyrinth," which fulfills all the labyrinthine nature of the Novel itself, and indeed set itself to do nothing else. Borges' Chinese novelist thus anticipates perfectly the scenarios of computer games, where the player can choose at critical moments which bifurcation to take; to the player the story may still be linear, but to the inventor it is a mathematical labyrinth. Stephen Albert, the Englishman speaking the passage quoted above, is allowed to articulate the critical insight that Borges wishes us to grasp—that prose fiction, the chaotic Novel (*la novela caótica*) is always a labyrinth. The customary translation of this story "Garden of Forking Paths" does not do justice quite to the strangeness of the verb *se bifurcan*; "bifurcate" is no more common in Spanish than in English, and to say "forking" misses the reflexively active activity of metamorphosing into two. The phrase *varios desenlaces*, here translated as "various dénouements," stresses what the English translator's "outcome" misses, the imagery of plaiting, knotting, braiding, the intricate *plokē*—and the need for unknotting, unplaiting. *Entrelacement* must eventually lead to *desenlace*, entangling to disentangling—in a language still very close to that of Heliodorus. The description of the labyrinth that is the Novel may remind us also of the labyrinth so magnificently set out by Heliodorus: "In the inmost recesses the openings and tunnels now appeared alone . . . now tumbled upon one another."

Borges brilliantly articulates something of which the Novel itself as a form seems (to use a popular kind of personification) deeply aware. The Labyrinth is one of the Novel's open secrets. The secret is shared by Italo Calvino, who in his own novels also indicates an intellectual interest in the tropes at the heart of the Novel. Calvino, like Borges, is at top form in the Labyrinth. In his novel *Se una notte d'inverno un viaggiatore* (1979), translated as *If on a winter's night a traveler*, the motif of labyrinthine *entrelacement* is first indicated by the criss-crossed railway tracks, and then becomes a novel within the novel: "the new and much awaited novel *In a Network of Lines that Enlace* [or, *In a Net of Entangled Lines*] by the famous Irish writer Silas Flannery" (*nuevo e tanto atteso romanzo* In una rete di linee che s'allocciano *del famoso scrittore irlandese Silas Flannery*, 117).

Both Borges and Calvino make us aware of the element of *repetition* in the Novel as a form (an element that interests Calvino slightly more than Borges). In being long, the Novel has to repeat itself. Its plot lines are going to carry a (sometimes reassuring) element of monotony as well as fear, horror, surprise, pleasure, etc. When we undertake to read a novel, we enter a labyrinth, as Borges so brilliantly remarks, of time rather than space.

At one level, the Labyrinth is certainly the plot itself, and the entanglements and confusions not only in the incidents, but also in the feelings aroused in characters—and in readers. This seems to have been quite well understood by earlier critics. In 1719, James Sterling praised Eliza Haywood in dedicatory verse for her talent as a novelist in portraying and raising passion:

> See! Love and Friendship the fair Theme inspires
> We glow with Zeal, we melt in soft Desires!
> Thro' the dire Labyrinth of Ills we share
> The kindred Sorrows of the gen'rous Pair. . .
> (*Love in Excess; or the Fatal Enquiry* a1ᵛ–a2ʳ)

The reading experience is to share the "dire Labyrinth" with the character. The novel is not only a formal labyrinth (as in Borges and Calvino) but also an emotional one—or rather, the emotion and the "form" are the same, and the labyrinth itself is formless form, emotional shape. But why do we desire to subject ourselves to the Labyrinth experience?

The experience of the Tomb as the Novel sets it forth seems to offer an expression of our own Knowledge of Death—a different matter from Death, *per se*. At the same time, the Tomb experience (with its reflections in various novelistic caves and prisons, well as tombs) offers a deep image of the negative aspects not of Death merely, but of Life. The individual finds him/herself entombed in a particular and separated body. Not only so, but each human being feels what is thought of as the Self to be buried alive in the cultural envelope—particularities of time, place, social class, civic role, relationships, and so on. These cannot but oppress even the healthiest and wealthiest from time to time. The novelistic experience of "burial alive" offers a channel for that feeling of oppression, with some hope of emerging from the living burial.

The Labyrinth Trope—which is more than just a network of crossed lines—offers us a way out. In a maze we must *not* be patient. We must keep going, we must think and move. The entity in the Tomb may be in suspended animation (like buried Kallirrhoé or Anthia). In the Labyrinth one is alive, active, searching, straining the faculties, trying to go forward. The *Aufsteigen* is no longer effortless— it cannot be wrought for us by grave robbers. Being there implies thought, choice, and feeling—as well as inevitable mistake, error, perplexity.

Some novels emphasize what might be called the *pleasures* of the labyrinth (as Borges himself does, with his "ivory labyrinth," his "garden"). In D'Urfé's *L'Astrée*, Galatée, one of the lovely nymphs just falling in love with Celadon, betakes herself to a pleasant garden with a little boskage of different kinds of trees, "which all together made such a gracious Labyrinth [*vn si gracieux Dedale*] where the paths in their diverse windings lost themselves confusedly one into another [*se perdissent confusément l'vn dans l'autre*] that they could not but be most agreeable in their ambiguities" (20). This pleasance, quite in the Borges style, is both locus and rhetoric (*gracious* and *ambiguous*); in the story, it obviously reflects and responds to Galatée's emotional perturbations. But Galatée here repeats a similar action undertaken earlier by the disconsolate heroine Astrée, who undergoes a more purely mental experience: "In this laborinth [*sic*] of divers thoughts, she went a long time wandring thorow the woods, without election of way" (*History of Astrea*, trans. Pyper [1620], 12). The Labyrinth is always a "laborinth of divers thoughts." The Novel—any novel—organizes for us our diverse thoughts, our perplexities and stresses; it allows us in entering this particular labyrinth to experience an irritated satisfaction giving us a kind of resignation to the constraints, indignities, and enclosures of our lives. Gabriel Garcia Márquez entitled one novel *El General en su laberinto* (1990). The title is justified by words reputedly spoken by Bolivár on his deathbed—which are in Marquez's novel the last words that his General Bolivár speaks: "Damn it," he sighed, "how will I ever get out of this labyrinth!" (*The General in His Labyrinth*, trans. Grossman, 267). He wishes to escape from death, but the only escape from his labyrinth of life is his dying.

In a very different novel, Dickens's *Great Expectations*, the word "labyrinth" is also given an unexpected possessive. In reading the novel, we have undergone the experience of entering the Tomb and wandering through the Labyrinth during Pip's first visit to Miss Havisham's house. It is strange, then, in a later chapter to find the older Pip giving a summary description of Miss Havisham's house as it looks when he sees it again, but withholding the word "labyrinth" from that edifice only to place it elsewhere:

> I had stopped to look at the house as I passed; and its seared red brick walls, blocked windows, and strong green ivy clasping even the stacks of chimneys with its twigs and tendons, as if with sinewy old arms, had made up a rich attractive mystery, of which I was the hero. Estella was the inspiration of it, and the heart of it, of course. But . . . I did not, even that romantic morning, invest her with any attributes save those she possessed. I mention this in this place, of a fixed purpose, because it is the clue by which I am to be followed into my poor labyrinth. (253)

Miss Havisham's house here is closed off, encrusted, externalized, even though it is the place of "attractive mystery." The real mystery lies elsewhere—

the "mystery" of Pip himself. His labyrinth ("*my* labyrinth") is not Miss Havisham's. It is the story he is telling, especially to himself. Pip's "poor labyrinth" is his poor self—not his body in itself, but his "life."

Pip in his poor labyrinth, and the General in his. You in your labyrinth, and I in mine. In novel-reading we are rescued from the solitude of our own poor labyrinth—by dint of entering another's and making it our own. When we read a novel, we know that the Labyrinth is neither merely the labyrinth of adventure, or of thought (considered abstractly), nor just the entrapments of culture and choices, but the labyrinth of individual life, in all its constraints, excitements, terrors, and hopes.

CHAPTER XVI

>─┤◆>─○─<◆┤─<

Eros

>─┤◆>─○─<◆┤─<

"I am not a child though I seem to be so, but am older than Kronos and all this universe."   —Eros to Philetas, Longus' *Daphnis and Chloé*

Sic ignara Psyche sponte in Amoris incidit amorem. Tunc magis magisque cupidine flagrans Cupidinis.   —Apuleius, *The Golden Ass*

A couple of human hearts skewered together with an arrow, cooking before a cheerful fire, while a male and female cannibal in modern attire . . . were approaching the meal with hungry eyes. . . . A decidedly indelicate young gentleman, in a pair of wings and nothing else, was . . . superintending the cooking.   —Dickens, *The Pickwick Papers*

"Provoking!" exclaimed Miss Ingram: "you tiresome monkey!" (apostrophizing Adèle) "who perched you up in the window to give false intelligence?"   —Charlotte Brontë, *Jane Eyre*

The Princess resembled Hanuman when she wielded a tree branch like a sword . . .   —Yukio Mishima, *The Temple of Dawn*

>─┤◆>─○─<◆┤─<

*E*ros, as Chariton tells us, is a lover of combat and delights in paradoxes (*Philoneikos de estin ho Erōs kai chairei tois paradoxois*, 50). The word *paradox* here means primarily "unexpected outcome," as in a twist of events, but it also contains a sense of something aside from, if parallel to, received opinion and normative expectation. The Labyrinth has its own paradoxes, its surprises and doubleness. The wanderer in a labyrinth is faced with perpetual contraries. One gallery opens here, and another one opposite or beside it—this is a realm of challenging and disturbing alternatives. In the Labyrinth choice is felt as hard necessity; the wanderer registers confusion and inadequacy. So too does the reader. So compelling is the trope that we are customarily not obliged to remain too long in the stony entrails of the figured maze.

    The Labyrinth can feel very gloomy. Eros—or Cupid/Amor/personified Love—can seem very cheering. Eros is warmth and light, activity and movement. He is usually winged—that is, he has freedom. Our contact with Eros is a kind of reward for undergoing the terrors of the labyrinth, and the burial in the tomb. Yet he is a reward which cannot be possessed.

    Eros (or Cupid) as a trope of fiction is a multiple and subtle signifier, even when introduced in apparently incidental embellishment. He stands, usually, outside the story proper, yet to come upon him is to encounter him, an experience always important for the reader, whether the character is conscious of Eros or not. The encounter itself fulfills the trope. If we have been winding along in time and process (grey time and dull unremitting process), when we run up against Eros-Cupid we run up against something sharp, bright, and timeless. If the labyrinth expresses (among other things) our subjection to time and to movement through time, Eros expresses (for both story and reader) something not subject to time. That which is outside time's law is less soothing than disconcerting—Eros is *lawless*.

EROS OF THE GARDEN

The most thorough explication of the nature of the novelistic Eros is given in Longus' *Daphnis and Chloé*, when old Philetas tells the young lovers how a child broke into his beautiful garden, a child *leukos hōsper gala kai xanthos hōsper pyr*, white as milk and shining as fire (70–72). For all Philetas' running, he cannot get the boy into his clutches; this was "a thing that could not be catched" (trans. Thornley). When he hears the boy's laugh, Philetas' anger is changed into yearning. He wants the child to give him just one kiss. But the laughing boy explains this would be dangerous to Philetas—and that he is not merely what he seems: "I am not a child though I seem to be so, but am older than Kronos and all this universe" Philetas is an old man (*presbytēs*) but this child is older (*presbyteros*)— older than everything that is, older than Time. Eros is necessary in order to make sense of Time—the time spent in the labyrinth of this life. Eros also "makes sense of" objects and nature surrounding us, the garden of which we are part. Eros links us to the world through the primal Love. Love visibly flourishes in the young (the young Philetas and Amaryllis, the young Daphnis and Chloé). Without sexual love, the world would not continue. But, as we can see in Longus' story, other loves are included—the love of Philetas for his beautiful and constantly tended garden is a manifestation of *erōs*.

Philetas thinks Eros is going to ruin his careful garden, break things and disarrange things. The first glimpse of Eros stirs a certain fear. Carefully ordered lives may be seriously disarranged by this mischievous delinquent. He comes to rob the orchard—the orchard of the Self. We do not like to admit that we would not "have" this orchard or any of the things in the ordered lives that we so value without Eros. Without Eros, one's life becomes not only a tomb-labyrinth, but a tomb-labyrinth totally sterile and immobilizing. Eros offers us freedom from the mazes that we would construct. The illustration to an eighteenth-century French translation of Longus' popular story represents this fact in a lively rococo manner—Eros flutters like a provocative Valentine image over the mazelike formal garden (see Plate 24).[1]

Without Eros there is nothing to love—as Eros tells Philetas, he is the cause why "your flowers and your plants are so beautiful" (74). It was perhaps because of this strong representation of the power of love in life that Goethe so highly valued Longus' *Daphnis and Chloé*, praising it as a work in which intelligence, craft, and taste were at their peak, a work that gave Virgil a run for his money.[2]

Philetas' description of Eros supplies us with an archetypal scene of the Novel—it illustrates in itself, that is, types and figures which lie behind the Novel as a form, manifesting themselves in different novels. Eros is removed from us in

Longus by being represented in an internal telling, appearing in the story Philetas tells the hero and heroine. Eros is thus partly active being, partly rhetorical turn or description. We sustain, however, a very sharp impression of his youthful, mischievous activity. Eros is an imp, a thief—a young hooligan of the neighborhood, in short, who ought to be under better control.

CUPID AND PSYCHE

Apuleius has left us the most lengthy and significant exploration of the appearance and meaning of Eros in the story of Cupid and Psyche told at length in *Asinus Aureus*, Books IV–VI. The story is told in the robbers' *cave* (both pit and labyrinth) by the old woman who is the robbers' servant. The garrulous old woman tells this tale in order to cheer up the captive Charité by such "old wives' tales" (*anilibus fabulis*). The dreamlike story is a means to rid the girl of the impressions of her bad dreams. The story is, as promised, *lepidus*—charming, agreeable—but it is also puzzling and even disturbing. It is told in an ironic context. *Should* one cheer up when one's marriage has just been violently ruptured and one is expecting to die? True, the story encouragingly tells the tale of another female (Psyche) whose marriage is violently interrupted, who becomes a tormented captive, but who ends in total happiness. The old woman has claimed, however, that dreams go by contraries. If that is so, the pleasures of the story's happy ending also become ambiguous, for the utterly gratifying outcome of this dream-like story may ironically augur Charite's sad fate here on earth. Lucius as ass absurdly regrets that he has no tablets and stylus with which to take down *tam bellam fabellam*. At the same time Lucius calls the source of the story *delira et temulenta illa . . . anicula*, "that demented and drunken old woman" (I: 354). The teller is out of her mind and in her cups. But perhaps she is intoxicated with divine inspiration? As with Lucius himself, perhaps a higher soul is hidden within a base manifestation. The drunken old woman's story, which invites allegorical interpretation, seems to be about how to get in touch with that higher soul or self.

In the story, which bears an obvious and often commented-upon relation to certain well-known European folk-tales like *Beauty and the Beast*, beautiful Psyche stirs up the jealousy of Venus, who asks her son to avenge her. Because of an oracle, delivered through Venus' prompting, Psyche is sacrificed to a cruel invisible monster who will come to the high rock and take her. Instead of suffering death, she is, like another Andromeda, delivered, though by invisible aid. She is transported to a palace and given all delights, including a tender spouse whom she can never see. Her jealous and hypocritical sisters persuade her that she is lying with a monster and must kill it. She lights the lamp at night, and discovers that she is lying with winged Love himself. The burning oil from her lamp wounds him and he awakens. Her action causes him to vanish.

Psyche must go through the world to seek her husband Cupid, enduring the punishment inflicted by Venus and performing strange and impossible tasks. Psyche undergoes shape-change in this metamorphosing story; Venus taunts her that she now seems such an ugly slave-girl (*tam deformis ancilla*) that she can hope to get lovers by nothing other than diligent service (*sedulo ministerio*) (I: 328). Like Leukippé, Psyche endures the trial not only of slavery, but also of temporary loss of her recognizable identity. Cupid himself seems to change in the story, from the wanton boy, Venus' mischievous baby, to a mature and tender husband, who can plead to Jupiter to reunite the separated pair. Cupid has already explained to Psyche that he had actually disobeyed Venus' orders. Venus had commanded him to make Psyche fall in love with someone base and ridiculous (that is, her plot was like that of Oberon against Titania in *A Midsummer Night's Dream*). Instead, Cupid flew to Psyche as her lover. Although he did that at first frivolously (*leviter*), he shot himself with his own arrow—Love had developed the power to love (I: 294).

Cupid is a mystery. *Quis ille?* ask the jealous sisters (I:280), unwittingly echoing the initial words of the novel's narrator, about himself: *"Exordior." "Quis ille?" "Paucis accipe."* ("'I shall begin!' 'Who is he?' 'In a few words you will hear.'") Cupid is originally accused—even by the narrator—of being an anticivic delinquent: "And without delay she called for her son, that boy who is winged and certainly bold enough, who with his bad manners and contempt for all public discipline, armed with his flames and arrows, runs about at night through other people's houses, breaking up everybody's marriages, who commits so many shameful acts with impunity and does absolutely no good at all" (I: 240). Can we simply dismiss this condemnation of Eros? It is not easy to dismiss it absolutely, for we all have some reservations about Eros, though these reservations may vary. The elders and officials of the Roman Empire were always worried about the power of the erotic to break up civic order and property-transmitting matrimony.

Such moralists (even among Christians) do not, on the other hand, seem worried about the use of sexuality to abuse the helpless. Looking at the images of Eros as winged boy, of *erōtes* doing cute things, that decorate so many houses in Pompeii, one must be struck by the unpleasant fact that these pretty pictures illuminated places (not only brothels but private homes) in which systematic abuse and degradation of the helpless was practiced in the name of Eros. (My own pleasure in the *Satyricon* receives a sharp check at the point where we see the seven-year-old girl in the brothel.) Sexuality in a wealthy slave-owning society is an area of massive consumption, control, and cruelty. Calling in Eros as an accomplice heightens the mess and confusion. But, of course, such abuses are no offense against what is meant by *disciplina publica*. Hardly any amount of brothel-frequenting, child abuse, and copulation with slaves (including rape of slaves) affected Roman "public discipline." The heart of public discipline is the tranquil marriage in which women behave themselves and acknowledge no desire. Cupid is a threat to that tranquillity, for Cupid, unlike the law, applies to men and women alike.

The problems of Cupid are the overt subject of many ancient novels, including Apuleius' *Golden Ass*. To know more about Eros (even considering Eros as only the power of sexual love) is to know more about ourselves. And to respect ourselves and Eros is to begin to wish to refrain from the enslavement and abuse of others, as all of the surviving ancient novels tend to show. These novels are all, after a fashion, captivity narratives. Repeatedly we see the good hero or heroine enslaved to some greedy person who wishes to make sexual use of him or her. In the power of the Novel, the hero or heroine can stand up against this cruelty—but that does not mean that hero or heroine is antierotic. On the contrary, in the novels the central characters increase in power and self-respect *because* they know Eros.

Yet, as we see in the Cupid and Psyche story, knowing Eros is difficult and dangerous. When Psyche (for the wrong reasons) dares to look upon the divine invisible spouse, she sees him complete in his beauty, the light shining from his curls. Beside him are his bow and arrows, and Psyche pricks herself on the point of one of the arrows in examining it: *sic ignara Psyche sponte in Amoris incidit amorem. Tunc magis magisque cupidine flagrans Cupidinis* . . . ("Thus ignorant Psyche of her own accord fell in love with Love [*Amor*]. Then burning with a greater and greater desire of Desire . . ." (I: 292). We may be reminded of Augustine's account of himself in Carthage: "I did not yet love, but I was in love with loving [*nondum amabam, et amare amabam*]," *Confessions*, I: 98).

Apuleius' story is the most complete version of the love of loving, the need of needing, the desire of Desire. The desire to know Cupid is destructive—or rather, it seems destructive, even painful. It leads to disruption, as the state of wedded bliss is destroyed for Psyche by her bringing her husband to the light. To know Desire is to increase desire.

The knowledge of desire destroys the first state of bliss of unconscious desiring—the unexamined life. The advent of a consciousness must always feel like a transgression. Just so, the simple pleasure in Story as Story is abolished, lost, or at very least superseded, when one acknowledges the nature and problematics of narration itself—as Apuleius repeatedly does. To know Story *as* Story, to examine its nature, to search for significances, interpretations—this is a loss, as well as a gain. Cupid must fly away, must be rediscovered, and not without pain and difficulty. Psyche goes through many trials before arriving at the happy marriage and the banquet of the gods and the immortality that Cupid helps bestow. Ancients (and many Moderns) have taken this story as an image of the progress of the individual soul—the *psyche*—from lower states through phases of painful experience to a higher state. This is certainly a story of resurrection and completion.

The story of Psyche universalizes our relation to Desire. We are all *in cupidine Cupidinis*. The desire that the young woman in the cave, the old woman's sole auditor (as she thinks), sustains so hopelessly is the basic desire for life itself—as well as the desire for the young bridegroom parted from her. The listening Ass has a desire for deliverance, like Charité, and also a desire like Psyche's—to be himself at a higher level. But Lucius got himself into this metamorphosed fix because of his *desire*. In Apuleius' novel (as in life), we are with Cupid before we know him or his name. Lucius in the early books is always the victim of his own desire—principally of his own desire to see "real" magic. His sexual desire for the maid Photis is a second best; he uses her to gain his objective. As he tells Photis, he is most ardently desirous to see magicians with his own eyes—*ardentissimus cupitor*. Photis says she would willingly give him what he wants, *quod cupis*, if it were not so difficult (I: 160–162). Very dangerously, Lucius says that he wishes, in making himself a winged being, to turn into Cupid "that I may stand beside you, a winged Cupid by my Venus" (I: 166). Foolish self-love and grandiosity could not be more clearly demonstrated. Lucius is not to be restrained by the admonitions of Photis (or Light). He has to take his own rough road to enlightenment.

Cupid and Psyche often figure in antique art. A puzzling mosaic of the third century A.D. from Daphne (Harbiye) near Antioch shows Eros driving a team of two Psyches, apparently through water to a sandy shore. So Eros harries and drives the powers of the soul. This picture (Plate 33) might be taken as a "rereading" of Plato's *Phaedrus* in the light of the Cupid and Psyche story. In the *Phaedrus*, Socrates suggests that the immortal soul might be represented in a dynamic composite figure: "a yoked pair of winged horses and a charioteer" (Rowe ed., *Phaedrus*, 60). In the gods' souls, winged horses and charioteer are alike noble, but in the case of humans the horses are at variance: "one of them is beautiful and good and of noble origin, while the other is the opposite, and of antithetical origin. So for our charioteer the driving is of necessity difficult and vexatious" (60). Human souls have sunk down from the heavenly realm because of the weakness of the bad horse: "For the weight of the bad horse preponderates and burdens them and pulls them towards the earth if the charioteer has not bred it well. Here the hardest labor, the harshest conflict, awaits the soul [*psychēi*]" (62). If it falls to earth, the soul is forced into it retribution for ill management of its base aspect—the punishment is incarnation as a human being.

In the *Phaedrus*, after having uttered conventional warnings against mischievous Eros, Socrates makes his recantation, his palinode to Eros. But the Eros that Socrates so memorably defends is the Eros that raises us upward, ultimately to love our heavenly realm, to love the good. The *good* Eros cannot truly be working in and for this world. Incarnation is the Fall. In rehabilitating Eros, we must lose the earth.

The Harbiye mosaic seems to represent the troubled moment of the incarnation of the soul, when the soul with its two "steeds" touches watery land under the urging of Eros as the angry charioteer.The two impatient if anguished beings he drives are not winged horses, but winged Psyches. They go through water, an element associated with desire, as also in the *Phaedrus*: "the runnings of that spring which Zeus in love with Ganymede named 'desire' [*himeron*]" (78). In the Harbiye mosaic, the Eros guiding us into life seems an angry power, and Love and the Soul(s) are in discord, Cupid lashing Psyche. A sort of Platonic anger at Love coming down to earth seems expressed, even with the acknowledgment of the power of Eros, who brings us into life and sustains life. The reeds at the water's edge closely resemble those in Botticelli's painting of Venus arising from the sea, but the mosaic picture is not as happy as Botticelli's about those reeds of fecundity and life, or about narrative itself, the Nilotic *calamus* that begins and "tells" Apuleius' story. There is shame and anger here in—and at—the Eros that drives us into living.

This strange and cruel representation of the relation between Eros and Psyche is a far cry from the customary classical use of those two figures. We see them everywhere as lovers, divine or childlike, usually embracing or gazing at each other. There is the famous statue at Ostia, of the two as embracing children—an image that captures the childlike unconscious state of both pre-pubertal innocence and sexual and existential unself-consciousness. (See Plate 34.) The most common appearance of Cupid and Psyche, however, is on tombs. The ancients frequently placed these two figures on sarcophagi—Psyche with her butterfly wings, like a windup toy, is familiar and easily recognizable.

Outside the museum in Ostia that carefully houses the cute statue there are several such sarcophagi—presently used as flower-planters. Psyche with her Cupid assures the mourner or spectator at the site of death that the soul lives—and lives on. Divine Love gives perpetual life to the soul. That is, *we have being*. Unlike the Harbiye mosaic, the common artistic representations of Eros with Psyche manifest not the state just before and during the process of incarnation, but the existence after the process of death. Yet Eros figures appropriately in all such contexts—coming-to-be, being, going on to be.

Cupid and Psyche together are often invoked in novels, although Eros is the more general and ubiquitous figure. In D'Urfé's *L'Astrée* we encounter an image of Cupid "with the hurt on his shoulder from the lampe of the curious *Psiche*" (Pyper trans., 30). The story of Cupid and Psyche is skillfully invoked in *Middlemarch*, when Mr. Casaubon asks poor Dorothea if she would like to go sightseeing:

> "Should you like to go to the Farnesina, Dorothea? It contains celebrated frescoes designed or painted by Raphael, which most persons think it worth while to visit."
>
> "But do you care about them?" was always Dorothea's question.
>
> "They are, I believe, highly esteemed. Some of them represent the fable of Cupid and Psyche, which is probably the romantic invention of a literary period, and cannot, I think be reckoned as a genuine mythical product. But if you like these wall-paintings we can easily drive thither; and you will then, I think, have seen the chief works of Raphael, any of which it were a pity to omit in a visit to Rome." (137)

Casaubon accuses this "fable" of being the invention of romantic literature—a novelistic invention, in short—and we can see how he despises the novelistic, not realizing, poor creature, that he is *in* a novel. The "fable" of Cupid and Psyche is not a "real" myth—so Casaubon can be justified in ignoring it. He would really do well to study both Raphael's and Apuleius' Cupid and Psyche. By his incapacity he imprisons himself; two paragraphs later, we find him lost in his windowless mental labyrinth.

EROS AND AUTOBIOGRAPHY

Eros may be represented with Psyche, or in relation to her, but he is even more frequently invoked on his own. In Achilles Tatius' *Kleitophon and Leukippé* as we have seen, the opening of the narrative displays to characters and readers the great Europa painting which inducts us into the story. "Around the bull dolphins sported, Cupidons played [*epaizon Erōtes*]. They were painted as if they moved [like moving pictures, cinematic things, *ta kinēmata*]. Eros led the bull. *Erōs*, a little boy [*mikron paidion*], his wings outstretched, wearing his quiver, carrying his lighted torch . . ." (8). Eros impresses the nameless narrator: " 'Look,' I said, 'that baby [*brephos*] rules heaven and earth and sea!' " Kleitophon picks up this exclamation and chimes in, claiming he knows how true that is: " 'I may take myself as an example,' he said, 'I have suffered so many outrages from Eros.' " The introduction of Eros seems to unleash confidences, stories of the personal life. That can be true even in fictional works that are not novels. In the most "novelistic" section of Virgil's *Aeneid*, Dido is deceived when Venus deliberately changes Ascanius into Cupid. Cupid successfully tempts Dido's disused heart into "lively love," *vivo amore* (I, line 721). It is while she is fondling this deceitful child that Dido asks Aeneas for his story, asks in such a way that he is bound to respond. The presence of Cupid seems to justify, or even in some sense to explain, the hero's talking at length about himself.

Cupid may preside over self-revelation in works that are neither epic nor novel, even works pretending not to be fictional. In Plato's *Symposium*, that powerful piece of prose fiction, Agathon praises Eros. Agathon denies the tradition that Eros is older than Kronos, for had he existed of old, the gods would not have done such terrible deeds. "For since this god grew into being, from love of the beautiful all good things have come to both gods and men" (158). Agathon claims it is the Divine Eros who allows such a banquet as their present symposium to be. Socrates answers and rebuts him, in—as he claims—the words of Diotima, denying Eros' power in favor of the power of the eternal unchanging Good. So far we have thesis and antithesis, the *agōn* of a two-sided debate. The arrival of Alcibiades adds a third element. Alcibiades arrives as an irruption—he comes in drunk, Dionysiac, crowned with ivy and violets. If Alcibiades resembles Dionysius, he is also an honorary Eros, the *enfant terrible* whose presence disturbs calm and order. Alcibiades as an honorary Eros also presides over personal history. He tells of his own unsuccessful attempt to have an affair with Socrates. Alcibiades represents himself as Eros-like, in his beauty and his weaponry of arrows: "Having shot off, as it were, my arrows, I thought he was wounded" (*kai apheis hōsper belē, tetrōsthai auton ōimēn*, 230). But, Alcibiades tells us, his loveliness and love-provoking words were ineffectual. In this fiction we have an Eros comically disarmed. Alcibiades wins our affection through an autobiographical narration presenting himself in a comic light. The coming of Alcibiades, with his Eros-presence and his erotic tale, makes the orderly dialogue turn novelistic. This attractive anti-hero moves us from objective debate towards acknowledgment of the power of represented personal experience.

Eros presides over egotism, narration, and embarrassing revelations. Another such mischievous character much given to personal revelation can be found in Augustine of Hippo. Augustine, looking back on his youth, presents himself as a young hooligan of the neighborhood, when he led his gang to rob the orchard:

> For I stole that, of which I had enough of my own, and much better. Nor did I wish to enjoy the thing which I had grasped by theft, but enjoyed the theft and sin itself. There was a pear tree in the orchard next to our vineyard, laden with fruit, not irresistible in either form or flavor. To shaking and robbing this a company of us bad young fellows [*nequissimi adulescentuli*] went late one night. . . . It was a foul deed, and I loved it [*foeda erat, et amavi eam*].   (*Confessions*, I : 76–78)

Augustine puzzles over *why* he stole those pears—as he did not want to eat them. The reader may come up with some suggestions that Augustine never thought of—such as that the pears are a sexual image of both scrotum and womb, and the desire to possess but not use them represents an adolescent sexual state. To Augustine, his own story is an example of a primary drive, the desire or *cupidity* that makes human life go awry. Yet young Augustine is not unattractive as a gang member. There may be a hint of pride in the superlative—*nequissimi*. They were most bad, "the baddest." The self-generated parable directs us to another overt aspect of Augustine's narration—that is, to Augustine's real and permanent love of himself. That love enables him to attend to the particulars of his own life and inner being throughout his *Confessions*. In this passage, Eros is reflected as Augustine's young self, the orchard-robber. Is that Eros really denied? Does Augustine fuel his narrative by presenting himself as Eros? Can he tell his story only with some assistance from Eros?

Autobiography novelizes, it appears. After all, Augustine grew up in a novelistic age—we know he knew of *The Golden Ass*.[3] But autobiography poses extra dangers, such as those suggested in some novelistic renderings of Eros-Cupid. It is dangerous to fall in love with Eros himself—as Eros points out to Philetas. Do not ask Cupid for a kiss. You could not stand the results. The only thing more dangerous than falling in love with Eros personified in another is to fall in love with oneself as Eros. Alcibiades charms us by courting that danger and then gracefully evading it, though the suggestive presence of his Eros elicits autobiography and biography. That arch-autobiographer Augustine does not seem to escape the danger figured forth in his own parable of the pears—of falling in love with his own desire for its own sake (the fault the parable officially reprehends). Augustine as narrator seems to fall in love with his desirability as an Eros-like mischievous generator of desire. In a fiction, a narrator like Kleitophon is able to deflect that danger; Kleitophon sees himself as one who is the victim of the *hubris* of Eros, a figure external to himself. The autobiographical Huck Finn is an Eros-figure who remains wonderfully and permanently innocent of his function, even as he works as both orchard-robber and light-bringer. Novelists can use the relation of Eros to the narrating character in diverse ways. But the serious autobiographer is always likely to run the risk of falling in love with Self as Eros.

Dante, who works best in an autobiographical mode, seems to have perceived this danger. In *Vita Nuova* (A.D. 1290–1294) he invents a new form of fictionalized (even novelized) autobiography, which permits the externalized representation of Eros-Amor. Eros is not here the mischievous little child, the *mikros pais*, but a great lord, a god of life, as in the latter part of Apuleius' story. And (like Kleitophon) the hero-narrator experiences *hubris* and tribulation from this deity and is not himself the source of *hubris*. "I was surprised by a sweet sleep in which appeared to me a marvelous vision. There seemed to come into my room a cloud the color of smoke, within which I discerned the figure of a man of fearsome aspect [*di pauroso aspetto*]" (*Opere Minori*, 156). The terrifying figure pronounces the sentence *Ego dominus tuus*, "I am thy lord." The fearsome lord carries Beatrice sleeping in his arms and in one hand a flaming heart. The apparition (who speaks Latin, like a priest) seems to say to the dreamer the words *Vide cor tuum*, "Behold thy heart" (11). This lord then awakens Beatrice and gives her the dreamer's heart to eat. Inexorable Love (*Amore*) apparently delights in cannibalism. Dante as dreamer and narrator is not an exciting source of mischievous desire—he is passive, under subjection. Something of Dante's frightening figure of Love, as both priest and god, lingers about representations of Eros in the High Middle Ages and the Renaissance. Even when representations are playful, there is a sense that this is a power dangerous to trifle with. A god so *pauroso* is not a figure to be identified with the Self. Yet it is the Overlord of that Self. "Ego dominus tuus," it says, "I am thy lord." In all eras, autobiography seems to command the presence of Eros, whether as solemn Overlord or mischievous imp. Any kind of autobiography demands some strong self-love and love of life, for which Eros is a necessity. For the Novel, even more than other literary kinds (plays, lyrics), acknowledgment of Eros is almost compulsory. The Novel is obliged to figure forth the self-love and the love of life that Eros manifests, and novelists of all ages have developed interesting ways of representing Eros.

REPRESENTATIONS OF EROS

The Child

Longus' *Daphnis and Chloé* can luxuriate in its bright and mischievous portrait of Eros, for that Eros appears safely outside of the story proper. A character other than hero or heroine has gone through the dangerous work of encountering him. But the Eros of the Novel will occasionally be visible as a child, sometimes infantile but more usually entering adolescence. Pip's Estella in *Great Expectations* is such an Eros-child, but, as Pip makes the cardinal error of falling in love with her, she belongs in the discussion of the distortions of Eros that follows. There are characters who can act as Cupid with impunity, because these personages are not recognized as Cupid by those about them. Rather than being beautiful works of art, child-characters who momentarily assume the role of Eros are lively and mischievous. They appear a distraction from the central story in which they manifest themselves. A good example of a child character who functions as Cupid without becoming the dangerous *eidolon* of Cupid is Mr. Rochester's illegitimate "brat" Adèle, in *Jane Eyre*. Adèle, the lighthearted strawberry-gatherer, offers searching criticism of Rochester's possessive vision of his life alone with Jane; eventually (and reluctantly) Jane is to take Adèle's implicit advice to heart.

Adèle reminds Jane of the erotic necessity of self-love for self-preservation. As unwanted child, Adèle is reflected in Jane's dream-sense that she is "burdened with the charge of a little child . . . which shivered in my cold arms, and wailed piteously in my ear" (284). This "unknown little child" reminds us that Desire is always Need. Eros as child expresses the nature of incessant demand, that greed for life which refuses to be dropped or stifled. Mr. Rochester is in danger of identifying his beloved Jane with Eros' self, as can be seen in his song "For glorious rose upon my sight / That child of Shower and Gleam" (274). As long as Rochester tries to make Jane into the shining elfin Child who will liberate him, their marriage is doomed. The presence of Adèle is necessary in this central part of the narration to deflect the child role and the Eros-work from Jane herself.

To be closely identified with Eros is a miserable fate for a character, including a child character, and a conscientious novelist like Charlotte Brontë must labor to decontaminate that child character, freeing it from this disturbing power, as Brontë (at the cost of some moralizing) frees the teenage schoolgirl Adèle. Most novelists only gesture towards the misery of such identification. Nabokov, however, presents it with the succinct and elegant brutality of which he is capable, near the beginning of *Ada or Ardor: A Family Chronicle* (1969), when he describes Van's view of the "hysterical lad from Upsala . . . with . . . the round creamy charms of Bronzino's Cupid," who is "much prized and tortured by a group of foreign boys" (32). Outrage is done upon Cupid; the perpetrator of *hubris* is the victim of *hubris*. Most novels turn away from the ill fate of the one forced to play the role of Cupid. Novelists tend to be more interested in the fate of the person who makes an identification of Eros with a human object of desire.

Dramatic and Rhetorical Artifice

Eros is at his happiest when we do not see him directly, or fully embodied, but can console ourselves with the idea of him, at the same time beholding him as artifice only. Dramatic representation offers one such mode of bringing Eros to light, in mock-embodiment. In *Tirant lo Blanc*, Amor is certainly physically visible, but in apparently harmless artifice. He is seen in a masque during a royal wedding's festivities. Knights assail a mock castle, which remains closed until the queen approaches and asks who the master is. "They told her it was the God of Love, and he stuck his head out the window" (trans. Rosenthal, 64). The joyous god leads his worshippers into a sumptuously furnished (if insubstantial) castle, where the guests can party to their hearts' content. Both characters and readers can knowingly enjoy the artifice, neither denying nor affirming what the masque represents.

Cervantes offers a variant of the God of Love's masque in Part II of *Don Quijote*. Rich Comacho the farmer has been give the beautiful Quiteria to marry, and he is making a royal splash of the wedding feast. His rival Basilio is in despair. Prenuptial festivities include a play or "speaking masque" in which a castle is attached by rival teams, "one led by the god Cupid and the other by Interest." Worldly Interest seems to win by throwing a great purse of money at the castle, whereupon it collapses, leaving the maiden within defenseless. This show of *el dios Cupido* satirically points out the economic constraints upon a god who seems so powerful. In Longus' pastoral as in Cervantes', money (along with class) separates the two lovers. In the upshot of Cervantes' story of Basilio, rich Comacho is proved wrong in thinking he with his wealth could be lord of Cupid.

Eros-Cupid does win—in stories. In the novels we notice how regularly Eros-Cupid insists on the value of individual desire. The forces arrayed against Eros include all those things that deny value to the individual and to the individual's desires. For Quiteria's family, evidently, her desires did not count; they were looking only for that general type, "a rich husband." Even the ardent Mr. Rochester is in conflict with Eros when, once he thinks he has won Jane, he tends to conflate her with his other women, meriting Adèle's sharp comments. Eros—the novelist's Eros—respects the personal, while at the same time reminding us of the strong impersonal force charging along through the generations.

Rhetorical Figure and Pictorial Image

The force of Cupid and his power to upset all our arrangements is an inducement to novelists not to let his presence get out of control. Often Eros is present as a mere passing figure, his garden a mere flower of rhetoric. Thackeray in *Vanity Fair* modulates between characterization and rhetoric when he makes shrewd Becky Sharp call conceited George Osborne by Cupid's name (291). She suspects that he, like Alcibiades (though without the self-reflexive irony), is in love with himself, sees himself as all-lovable. We have seen the effect he has upon Amelia: "He beamed on her from the drawing-room door—magnificent, with ambrosial whiskers, like a god." Thackeray hastens to assure us that this god is "an ass" arrayed "in the splendour . . . of her imagination" like Bottom the Weaver; he is really a Lucius (159). Becky is not enamored of this drawing-room Alcibiades. "Captain Cupid" is shrewdly identified with the erotics of his self-love. Yet Becky's joke does save the narrative from exhibiting George fatuously identifying *himself* with Eros; what might be personification is turned into figure of speech.

Cupid often appears in novels as a figure of speech, sometimes apparently inert, as in Mary Wollstonecraft's description, in *The Wrongs of Woman* (1798), of the heroine's strange love affair within a madhouse where both she and the new man in her life are imprisoned. The pair have "an animated conversation, in which love, sly urchin, was ever at bo-peep . . . Love the grand enchanter, 'lapt them in Elysium'" (101). Although the references seem decorative, and serves to increase our sense of skepticism about this relationship, the "sly urchin" is not without the power of his traditional representations—aspects of both Longus' Eros and Dante's are here recalled.

At times reduced to mere rhetorical reference, a glancing verbal allusion, Eros-Cupid may at any moment, in novels old or new, blossom forth again in full *ekphrasis* as a visual image. We may remember, for instance, the giant image in Boccaccio's *Filocolo*, the statue in Biancifiore's tower bedroom, the *Cupido* with golden wings and great eyes of luminous carbuncle (471–472). This imaged idol-deity hugely presides over the lovers' sexual union.

But Eros may enter the scene in the lightest of visual emblems, as in Trollope's *Barchester Towers* (1857), where he appears in the adornment of that comic siren, the self-styled Signora Vesey Neroni: "Across her brow she wore a band of red velvet, on the centre of which shone a magnificent Cupid in mosaic, the tints of whose wings were of the most lovely azure, and the colour of his chubby cheeks the clearest pink" (95). Since for Madeline love or love-making is all in the mind, it is fitting that she puts the emblem on her forehead and not her heart. But her Italian ornament, the Cupid in mosaic, presides over this entire comic novel, and not merely over the Signora's playful schemes.

In the modern novel, Cupid may well be hidden in the *décor*, eluding us by looking like a trifle, disappearing before we catch his eye. In Barbara Pym's *The Sweet Dove Died* (1978), James, the young man beloved of so many, owns a fruitwood mirror set round with cupids. Both of his women, young Phoebe and the older Leonora Eyre, want this mirror. Leonora the ruthless takes it, not only because it reminds her of James but because it makes her look, she thinks, "fascinating and ageless" (87)—like Cupid the ever young. She endeavors to appropriate the power of the *Erōtes*. This *fruit*wood mirror is a puzzle. Wood of what fruit tree, we may ask—Edenic apple or Augustinian pear? The cupid-beset looking glass is a dangerous narcissistic object, and young Phoebe, whose name indicates an affiliation with the chaste moon-goddess, is better off without it.

In Salman Rushdie's *The Satanic Verses*, Eros likewise appears amid the *décor*. The room of the actor Saladin Chamcha is overfull of objects: "And everywhere, on the walls, in the movie posters, in the glow of the lamp borne by bronze Eros, in the mirror shaped like a heart, oozing up through the blood-red carpet, dripping from the ceiling, Saladin's need for love" (174). This description recalls the scene of the crime of passion in Hardy's *Tess of the D'Urbervilles*: "The oblong white ceiling, with this scarlet blot in the midst, had the appearance of a gigantic ace of hearts" (369). Amidst the tormented redness of Saladin's angry need, Eros glows, *xanthos hōsper pyr*, the bearer of illumination. Eros is next to the mirror, but, fortunately for Saladin, Eros is here not mirror but lamp. Eros as mirror: Eros as lamp. Here are the two representations that M. H. Abrams has taught us to see as the emblems of romantic imagination, or of Mind itself. Eros with the mirror, however, is usually a symptom of a difficult self-love in the gazer. That Saladin's Eros holds up a *lamp* is indicative of some hope for his desiring, some possibility that Love can bring light, even in the face of gaping need and potential violence. We should not be fooled by an Eros disguised as *décor*. Eros may look passive and decorative, but he is always on duty, and always dangerous.

He customarily turns up in artifice, our Cupid of Prose. He may be overpoweringly present, but he has an alibi: it was not he but his *representation* we gazed upon. The need for Cupid in novels to be artificial is explained by a remark of Italo Calvino:

> The thick symbolic armor beneath which Eros hides is no other than a system of conscious or unconscious shields that separate desire from the representation of it. From this point of view all literature is erotic, just as all dreams are erotic. In the explicitly erotic writer we may therefore recognize one who uses the symbols of sex to give voice to something else, and this something else . . . may in the last instance be redefined as another and ultimate Eros, fundamental, mythical, and unattainable.   ("Considerations on Sex and Laughter,"
> trans. Creagh, *The Uses of Literature*, 66)

At the time he was writing this essay of 1969, Calvino was reading and responding to Northrop Frye's *Anatomy of Criticism* (1957). Calvino was impressed by Frye's articulation of the importance of desire:

> Civilization is not merely an imitation of nature, but the process of making a total human form out of nature, and it is impelled by the force that we have just called desire. The desire for food and shelter is not content with roots and caves: it produces the human forms of nature that we call farming and architecture. Desire is thus not a simple response to need, for an animal may need food without planting a garden to get it. . . . It is neither limited to nor satisfied by objects, but

is the energy that leads human society to develop its own form. Desire
in this sense is the social aspect of what we met on the literal level as
emotion. . . .   (*Anatomy of Criticism*, 105–106)

Eros-Cupid confronts us with our own energy as *desire*. He serves all generations—as is made clear to Philetas in Longus' story. He seems to be in some sense
"the force that through the green fuse drives the flower." Yet he is not in nature,
whatever his relation to *natura-physis*. Longus' Eros looks *like* a nesting nightingale hidden among leaves, but is not a bird. Eros looks like "Nature" and like
something that is not "Nature" at all. He reminds us—as he does at that significant moment in Longus' narrative—that what was inchoate emotion must become artifice when given a name.

   In reading a novel we socialize our want, and we are willing to entertain
the social quality of all our emotions and needs, even when novel-reading is a
private pleasure. The element of the public and universal is one reason that critics
like D. A. Miller have objected to the Novel as policing us.[4] We are not quite
comfortable under the mocking gaze of Eros. We do not really want to make love
before those great staring carbuncle eyes.

   Eros may help us to get out of or even to rise above our labyrinth, but he
drives us on towards consciousness. Thus, though he images the social construct
of desire, he illustrates also the necessity of individual life, of that *individuation* of
which Nietzsche complains so bitterly. Here is the crossroads of the infinite desire
of the moth for the star—"I want infinitely"—and the strong particular desire
that acknowledges what is outside the self.

   "I want you to be" is an unequaled definition of love. But that want is also
and first self-directed. Each of us is minded to wish for self-being: "I want *me* to
be." That is the first great love. Without it, it would be meaningless to "love thy
neighbor as thyself." The Novel has great respect for that permanent desire, underwritten by the Novel's Eros. *Robinson Crusoe* above all novels expresses the Dionysiac intensity of that wish and need. But Robinson sells Eros when he gets the
chance—he sells the Muslim boy Xury, whose name reflects Greek words both
for "shavings, scraps" (the dispensable) and for a critical situation, the razor's
edge. Robinson, nearly insane at times in his life with himself on his island, at last
entertains relations with others when he encounters the young man whom he
names after a day important not only in the Christian calendar but also in the
pagan scheme of things. "Friday" is Freya's day, Venus' day, *vendredi*; young "Friday" is also Friday's child and Venus' boy. Eros cannot rest with the self-directed
love, Leonora Eyre's kind of narcissism, or Robinson's paranoiac desire to cut off
others.

   Francisco Coccio, who first translated Achilles Tatius, argues in favor of
the novel of love. Love offers the most copius subject for writing. And with reason, for it is Love (*Amore*) that educates us: *Amore* "is the true and most learned
master who teaches everything perfectly." "From him as from a most abundant
fountain is born the principle of all our workings" (*da lui come da uno abondantissimo fonte nasce il principio di ogni nostro operare*, in *Achille Tatio* [1560], A6ᵛ). Love
is the fountain of all our energies, and any story about our human activities is a
"love-story" of sorts. When we read a novel, we connect our individual prosaic

and diurnal life, which the novel mimics in its very prose, with our human energies. But reading a novel is a form of social or sociable event—our own energies are directed towards others in the very reading. Each reader finds a reflection of necessary self-love, while not turning in towards the sole and lonely me. Our energies move us outwards, and we apprehend a connection between our prosy life and the larger human and civilized desires for community, art, and meaning. Yet that is too grandiose—Eros always mocks pretentiousness. So Alcibiades reminds both Socrates and himself of the individual personal life, the human moments they have really shared, and will not let Socrates proceed uninterrupted with his grand universals.

A "love-story" is not necessary for Eros' presence in a novel, though it may furnish the excuse for his appearance. Eros presides over pleasure. Without Eros there could be no novel. Eros-Cupid within the story compels his victims to love *story* itself—as Charité is forced to listen to the old wife's tale of Cupid and Psyche. When we wonder "what next? And then?" we willingly engage in the story-lover's happy and playful cupidity. That cupidity is itself artificial—we know about plots, foreshadowings, denouements. Our desire for Novel is what René Girard, in *Mensonge romantique et vérité romanesque* (1961), has taught us to call "mediated desire." What we want does not originate in our own untaught emotions; we have been culturally trained to enjoy fictional narratives. For Girard, still working in the shadow of a late Romanticism, "mediated desire" is a grievance, a source of sin. Novels spread artificial desires—as novel-reading mistaught Don Quixote and Emma Bovary. We learn artificial wants. So we do. Girard seems to complain that the bread we eat is made of wheat and the wine we drink is made of grapes. Civilization *is* mediated desire. If we take Frye's definition seriously, then we see that while we may have unmediated untaught wants—like Daphnis and Chloé—our *desire* must be cultural. Not just Emma Bovary but anyone who says "I love you" has caught the same contagion.

Yet, while mediating our culture to us, Eros remains delinquent in being un-civic . . . and here I part company a little from Frye. Eros is perpetually the enemy of arrangements based on socioeconomic schemes. One of the things he tells us that we do not quite want to know is that we have no satisfactory arrangements, individually or collectively, for dealing with our loves and desires. He must always be charged as a "marriage-breaker," since he subversively acknowledges female desire as much as male. Eros reflects civilization but must always be the enemy of what is *called* "civilization" or "respectability" at any particular point. Hence Huck Finn, an Eros-bearing personage, must fly from the attempt to "sivilize" him. With Eros, we know more about human potential than society can accommodate in the here and now—but it is in the here and now that Eros is encountered. The overt presence of Eros in the novel signals a throwing-off, or a need to throw off, whatever is too stable or too strict. Eros refuses to reflect back the character's visions of success, order, or progress. Eros never seems to think we have acquired much civilization anyway; we satisfy some desire of one person by stifling the "I want," the *erōs* of another.

Eros' antipathetic or at best tangential relation to the supposed elements of civic stability is clearly delineated in Longus' novel. The parents want money—even more than they want their children. Adoptive families quarrel over money and status. The hero is somebody else's property. None of these things impresses the teasing and inescapable child who romps in the heart's garden as his own. Novels have been interested, particularly in modern times, in investigating further the ironic relation of Eros to our societies and civilization.

Damaged Eros

A strong comic expression of the suffering undergone by Eros within our "civilization," and of our cultural difficulties in dealing with him, is found in Alain-René Le Sage's satiric nonrealistic novel (partly based on a Spanish original), *Le Diable boiteux* (1707; 1726). Le Sage plays with, and plays out, the metaphor "Love is the devil!" At the outset, a young Spanish scholar, Don Cleophon Leandro Perez Zambullo, escapes through the streets of Madrid from a whore's bullies. He blunders into a conjuror's laboratory, where a spirit imprisoned in a glass jar begs for its freedom, explaining that it is a demon named Asmodée (Asmodeus, as in the Book of Tobit). This is the demon of lust, or, to speak more honorably, *le dieu Cupidon; car les poètes m'ont donné ce joli nom* (5) ("the god Cupid, for the poets have given me that pretty name"). Don Cleophon breaks the bottle. A smoky cloud appears, as in Dante's vision. Within the cloud takes shape the figure of a little man about two and one-half feet high, leaning on two crutches. This monstrous little crippled devil (*le diable boiteux*) has goat-feet and a pointed chin, little eyes like burning coals, and a red moustache. The goat-foot *daimon* thus seems a conflation of Cupid and Pan, two male figures kept separate in Longus. The absurd effect is captured in a late eighteenth-century illustration to an English version (see Plate 35). This imp's disability is, as he later explains, the result of a fight with the demon of money-interest (recalling the masque in *Don Quijote*). He is not innocently naked but elaborately overdressed. Asmodée sarcastically addresses his surprised liberator: "Well . . . you see the charming god of Love [*le charmant dieu des amours*], the sovereign master of hearts. What do you think of my air and my beauty? Aren't the poets excellent painters?" (10). The surprised young man responds frankly that the poets have flattered him a little— surely the god never appeared in *this* form to Psyche? The little devil explains that he borrowed the features of a French marquis for that adventure.

Here is a god not of *Amor* but of *amours*, of modern multiple love affairs. The devilish gossipy Asmodée entertains his naïve benefactor by taking off the house-roofs of sleeping Madrid, and telling him the secret histories of the people below. This devil of a Cupidon certainly presides over stories galore. At the end, he does unite the young Spaniard with a true beloved, Seraphine, thus replacing Don Cleophon's none-too-fortunate whoring with marriage—and to an "angel," a seraph, at that. The comic irony of Asmodeus-Cupid instructs us not to mistake the story's outcome for a solution to the problems that Asmodée's own appearance represents.

In eighteenth-century society, young men are supposed to separate sex (as an urge to be satisfied in brothels) from marriage, which is a matter of money. Le Sage raises the possibility that young men are abused in having to consent to this division of themselves. This disabling state of things—which nearly leads at the outset to the hero's permanent disablement—is only one aspect of a complex of problems reflected in the various *fabliaux* within the narrative. Eros is constantly bottled up, denied, treated as an evil. The more we deny Eros, the more crippled and false he must become in order to represent himself to us at all. Eros in Le Sage's novel presides over storytelling, in a novel set in Spain as the implied fountainhead of modern European novels. But Le Sage's image indicates that the Novel itself must be—in these circumstances of a culturally disabled Eros—a crippled product.

The challenge of Le Sage's very popular novel—frequently reprinted in eighteenth-century England as *The Devil upon Two Sticks*—is taken up in a later novel, which almost defiantly announces itself as a distorted product. Matthew Gregory Lewis's *The Monk* (1796) lays claim to the now-discredited name of "romance." It is one of the chief representatives of the "Gothic" form of narrative, a form categorized as deformed. *The Monk*, like Le Sage's novel, which it plays with and reverses, is also set in Madrid, a sort of hometown for the modern novel. When the viciously seductive and supernaturally endowed Matilda takes the victim of her lust, the monk Ambrosio, to watch with her while she raises the infernal powers, the marveling monk sees, in response to her conjuration, a most beautiful apparition:

> the cloud dispersed, and He beheld a Figure more beautiful, than Fancy's pencil ever drew. It was a Youth seemingly scarce eighteen, the perfection of whose form and face was unrivalled. He was perfectly naked: A bright Star sparkled upon his fore-head; Two crimson wings extended themselves from his shoulders; and his silken locks were confined by a band of many-coloured fires. . . . Circlets of Diamonds were fastened round his arms and ankles, and in his right hand He bore a silver branch, imitating Myrtle. His form shone with dazzling glory: He was surrounded by clouds of rose-coloured light, and at the moment that He appeared, a refreshing Air breathed perfumes through the Cavern. (276–277)

The vision is confronted within a cave—ambiguously either the womb and matrix of new existence or the hell-pit. In ironic reversal, instead of Cupid coming as the devil, the devil arrives as Cupid. This "Dæmon" or fallen Angel" must surely be Eros as Psyche saw him. Yet the power of Eros is diabolical; in loving *this* Eros, Ambrosio himself becomes demonic. Both *Le Diable boiteux* and *The Monk* articulate a resistance to Cupid and express some dismay at his works. Lewis, however, is concerned at the deepest levels of his story with expressing the fear and loathing that heterosexuality can arouse. When Cupid is conjured up by the "female" necromancer he is destructive; at the same time, this Cupid himself arouses homosexual lust, which is frightening.[5] Within the novel, erotic love—at least the love that is culturally recognized in "Madrid" (read "England")—is based on dishonesty, suppression, and fear. The Cupid that the story and the culture can officially recognize is a glamorous monstrous devil.

Doubt about Cupid—comic and monstrous doubt—had been registered in an earlier eighteenth-century English novel. Robert Lovelace, the villain-hero of Richardson's *Clarissa*, fails to seduce the brilliant and strong-minded heroine. He then is (reluctantly, as he explains) compelled (so he feels) to use force upon her. Lovelace reminds his friend Jack Belford that the affronted god of Love was on Lovelace's side early in his courtship, when Clarissa left him to freeze in her father's garden. Now, before the vengeful act of rape that will make Clarissa his, Love makes him hesitate—and Lovelace chooses to play with the personification of this emotion (V : 236–238).

Lovelace, knowingly artificial, turns his conscious (and well-managed) *psychomachia* into a masque, playing with the traditional representations of Amor. Love is the sovereign lord—as in Dante and in the sonneteers that Lovelace in youth had imitated—while still remaining the "little urchin" as in Longus. Eros now becomes Lovelace's own creation, a character scripted by him. Lovelace's confidence in dealing with this comically conceived deity is related to his egotistical belief that fundamentally he himself *is* Love. *Love*lace is his own Cupid. Robert Lovelace says of Clarissa when he thinks of marrying her that he will give her the sweetest name of all—the name of Love—that is, his own name, in which the name of "Love" appears. Earlier, Anna Howe has imagined what Lovelace was like as a child, and pictures him as "a curl-pated villain, full of fire, fancy, and mischief; an orchard-robber, a wall-climber, a horse-rider without saddle or bridle . . ." (II : 10). This description was not meant for Lovelace's eyes, but it would have delighted him.

Anna's language suggests a Cupid such as Longus had drawn—Eros the charming wall-climber and orchard-robber. Lovelace sees himself as that beguiling thief. Really, Lovelace believes, he is a thing that cannot be caught. His fate is bound up with this irresistible image of himself. As Love himself, Cupid the ever-beloved, he can do no wrong. Lovelace presents us with the temptation within self-consciousness, of falling in love with the desiring self as the emblem and energy of all desire—a danger adumbrated by Augustine's own picture of his orchard-robbing self.

EROS PROJECTED: THE DEATH IN VENICE PROBLEM

To identify Love with oneself is to commit in miniature the crime or error of society at large, which will generally acknowledge as Eros only what money-interest, Podsnappery, and other limited notions say Eros must be. Such self-identification is likely to lead to tyranny and over-control—in an individual as in society. A related but different error is involved in projecting Eros into the being of another person. In novels, this error is most likely to be committed by characters who visibly lack a central sense of self. The novel character who identifies self as Eros is almost certainly doomed to some sort of self-destruction (heroes of autobiography who make that mistake are more kindly treated by their authors). The novel character who projects Eros onto another is almost as likely to be reserved to misfortune. In *Great Expectations*, Pip (*Philip* Pirrip) falls in love with a star or "Stella" in "Estella," a love reminiscent of that in Sir *Philip* Sidney's famous cycle of love-sonnets to Stella. Philip's name contains the root of another word for love—*philia*—a love of friendship, which Pip overlooks in favor of the brighter stimulants of erotic love. Shy Pip in childhood is captivated by the child Estella, taking her for the divine illuminator: "her light came along the dark passage like a star" (89). With her aid, he hopes to transcend his labyrinth.

In an endless obsession that reflects the obsession of the still-unravished bride Miss Havisham, Pip as he grows up yearns after Estella, seeing in her not a beloved human, but the irresistible Lord of Love himself. Pip obstinately refuses to let go of this perverse vision of Eros' self, while Estella as she grows up cannot accept the burden of his projection. Only the sacrificial death of Pip's scapegoat Magwitch and the symbolic death of his old self can release Pip from that obsession. Dickens took some trouble to assure readers at the end of the novel that Pip *has* shaken his obsession. But the changed ending urged by friends leaves the ominous possibility that Pip is still subject to the mists of rising illusion, unable to get free of his own desire of Desire . . . *magis cupidine flagrans Cupidinis.*

Love of Eros' self embodied in another becomes exhausting. The same error brings on the sterner fate of Thomas Mann's Aschenbach in *Der Tod in Venedig*. Like Pip, Aschenbach falls obsessively in love with a juvenile, with the young Polish boy Tadeusz ("Tadzio"). But Aschenbach is not himself young at the time, like Pip, but old, like Philetas. He is embarrassed by and ashamed of his infatuation, and part of his story is his struggle against any conscious recognition of his desire, which involves not only a detestable homosexuality but even pederasty. It is easy to represent Aschenbach's conflict as one between the Apollonian and the Dionysiac aspects of his nature, to give it a reading from Nietzsche, an author undoubtedly on Mann's mind.

The overthrow of Aschenbach can be considered an overthrow of the specifically civic, in its German and Protestant formations. Aschenbach has been a very successful writer, whose main themes have involved control. His hero is Frederick the Great of Prussia, an image of iron control and steadfast conquest (though incidentally a man freely given to the homosexuality Aschenbach has refused to notice). Aschenbach has inherited the Protestant sense of the civic, through ancestors who were military officers, lawyers, judges, and civil servants. He has been constructed of his vision of the proper and the socially valuable. His writings proclaim total renunciation of any sympathy with the abyss, *von jeder Sympathie mit dem Abgrund* (197). Untowardly dry—his name means "Ashy Brook"—Aschenbach must seek the wetlands. In his dreams of travel in which desire begins to stir (*Reiselust*), he begins to experience his own *nostalgie de la boue*:

> he . . . saw with longing eyes a monstrous landscape, a tropical swamp under a thick misty sky, humid, luxurious, unhealthy, a sort of original wilderness shunned by mankind, with islands, morasses and mud [*Schlamm*] with thin streams winding through. The flat islands, their soil covered with leaves as thick as hands, were overwrought with huge ferns, with rich upspringing and fantastically blooming plants, and scattered hairy palm-tree trunks rising upwards . . . (189)

What Aschenbach sees in his muddy fantasia is, in short, an erotic landscape of the water margin remarkably like the Nilotic area in which *Aithiopika* opens. This is a vision of ineluctable *hylē*.

Aschenbach must make his own descent into "the abyss"—the *Abgrund*—which for him takes the topological form of that great European swamp, Venice. There he comes into contact with the alternative god glimpsed in the Dionysiac dream of "the stranger god." Falling in wild love, he can no longer moralize.

Inwardly he formulates wild reworkings of Plato, rewriting the *Phaedrus* to allow what Socrates denied, a place for the sensual and the incarnate, and acknowledging that "we poets cannot go on the path of Beauty, unless Eros himself furnishes it and constitutes himself our leader" (263). In this erratic internal monologue, near the end of his torment, Aschenbach makes his great acknowledgment of the erotic nature of the love of knowledge, and of all knowledge itself:

> For how should one be fit for a teacher, in whom an incorrigible and natural tendency towards the abyss is inborn? We might deny it and achieve dignity, but whatever way we may turn, it draws us on. So we may say something against the disintegration of Knowledge, but Knowledge, Phaidros, has neither dignity nor strength. It is knowing, understanding, apprehending, without stop or form. It has sympathy with the Abyss, it *is* the Abyss. (263)

This insight is worth something, certainly. Aschenbach has realized that what he had thought to be substantial constructs of weight and solidity are endless flow. Mocking Eros has taught him this, the Eros who loves to stir things up and likes paradoxes.

Aschenbach tries desperately to rewrite the *Phaedrus*, casting himself as the Socratic figure—a comic Socrates with his dyed hair and feverish cheek. His impassioned anti-Platonic soliloquy takes place as he sits beside a Venetian well, amidst garbage (*Abfälle lagen umher*). He has given way completely, one might say, to his role as a novelistic character, being dirt-spattered and dwelling in a marshland that he refuses to abandon. He has just been in the labyrinth in the opening of this sequence, wandering through Venice, "With a failing sense of place, there where the alleyways, waterways, bridges and squares of the Labyrinth [*des Labyrinthes*] too much resembled one another" (261).

Aschenbach is thus disoriented, because he has gazed on Eros' own body, in the person of the Polish boy Tadzio. Aschenbach's projection is evident from the time he first sees the youth in the hotel breakfast room. Like Proust's Marcel, at another seaside resort and watery margin, likewise gazing first at his love-object, Ashenbach tries to aestheticize both his response and the beloved by allusion to Greek statuary. He notes that the boy's beautiful countenance "recollected the representations of Greek art of the noblest period" (*erinnerte an griechische Bildwerke aus edelster Zeit*, 211). Shortly afterward, Aschenbach definitively connects the boy with Eros:

> From this collar, which did not match the suit's style with any particular elegance, rose the blossom of the head in incomparable love-allure [*Liebreiz*]—the head of Eros, in the warm mellowing of Parian marble [*das Haupt des Eros, vom gelblichen Schmelze parischen Marmors*], with clear and earnest brow, temples and ear covered by the perfectly placed ringlets of dark soft hair. (215–216)

Determined to make Tadzio into Eros, Aschenbach nevertheless knows all the time that this is a *representation*. With the unconscious cruelty of his gaze he wills Tadzio into the condition of a work of art—*Bildwerk*. He pursues Tadzio through the labyrinth of Venice as an image (*Bild*). He knows the terms of representation very well, though he must come to terms with the inexpressible that Eros always conceals—as Calvino notes, the mythical and unattainable. The inexpressible to which we are constantly drawn by and through the Eros-image is defined by Aschenbach as the *Abgrund*, the abyss. It is part of the irony of Aschenbach's position that he seeks abstractions and is not capable (unlike Thomas Mann) of full sensuous recognition of the world of matter jostling him in the streets. He is killed, however, by the invisible germs that rise from fecund and rotting matter.

The tone of the novel makes clear that either Tadzio or Aschenbach must be destroyed by this encounter. To identify an individual with Eros is a strangely hubristic act, as outrage may easily be done on such a person, as with the boy from Uppsala in *Ada*. The outcome of such a projecting relationship is almost certain to be disastrous. Aschenbach gains the enlightenment that there is no enlightenment, that there is no difference between knowledge and the abyss, but this insight, which is also pathetically self-justifying in its context, is of little use to him as he plunges down the unromantic and common abyss of death . . . death as an elderly man, fallen ill with a common malady. Tadzio escapes the trap of the identification and remains free—in his freedom and his flitting away again resembling Cupid himself. The lively last scene on the margin of the sea (264–266) shows Tadzio as free to enjoy the senses and at home in the world of living matter—thus alien to that smooth yellowed marble into which Aschenbach would translate him.

REDEMPTIVE PROJECTION: EROS AS BELOVED

The lot of the character who becomes another's *eidolon* of Cupid is usually unenviable, often hazardous, while, as we have seen, the lot of the character who projects Eros onto another is perilous indeed. Yet some forms of such projection may be valuable or necessary, if complex. There is no Eros-obsession more complex than in Toni Morrison's *Beloved* (1987). This novel, which deals with a group of black Americans in the period just after the end of slavery, describes a moment when culture has been most terribly rent. If the future is to be possible, there must be a revisiting and revision of Eros. The desire to live, the desire to enjoy, the desire to do and to make, must all be recaptured and redefined. The heroine, Sethe, is emotionally and morally exhausted. The ghost of her baby, killed by Sethe in order to escape a life of slavery, haunts Sethe's house, then apparently returns incarnate as a strange young woman who owns no last name, only the name "Beloved." Slaves were denied last names. But Eros too neither has nor uses a last name. The disturbing girl manifests a passion for sweet things and for stories: "It became a way to feed her. Just as Denver discovered and relied on the delightful effect sweet things had on Beloved, Sethe learned the profound satisfaction Beloved got from storytelling" (58).

In the novel, Beloved presides over Sethe's telling of her own life story; she thus forces Sethe to reconnect parts of her terribly painful life and, in the art of telling, to make that life conscious and bearable. There is of course the ironic possibility, on the realistic level, that this girl is not the dead baby returned to life, but a wandering homeless young woman. For Sethe, and for the reader, however, she is the reincarnation of the dead baby and a representation of Eros. Eros always presides over storytelling: the love of story *is* the love of being. Morrison's "Beloved" is an extreme representation of the sacred love of being. Though her mother killed her from a kind of noble instinct, the baby apparently cannot accept that death but insists on having her being. "Beloved" lives. In some aspects she is a menace, Eros as avenger. She threatens to overwhelm the lives of her family. Yet at the same time she is a promise and a liberating force. The name she chooses is found in what seems to be Morrison's favorite book of the Bible, the Song of Solomon: "My beloved is mine, and I am his" is here altered to "I am Beloved and she is mine" (214).

Eros is truly the beloved, who tells us that we can love and be loved. Sethe, at last out of the freeing shadow of "Beloved," finds that she can love her friend Paul D., despite their horrible experience of human cruelty. *Beloved* is a very great and a very painful novel. Only the presence of Eros makes the serious and true horrors of slavery bearable for the reader, as for the characters. But once Beloved has been accepted and her liberation acknowledged, Sethe must learn to free herself of love of the *eidolon*. She has begun to fall in love with Beloved herself, and the last stage of her liberation is a liberation from that misplaced fixing of the libido's energies. One must not fall in love *with* Eros. Eros must be free to point the way *to* love.

NEGATIVE AND STERILE EROS

The difficult Beloved of Morrison's novel is associated with color, fertility and sweetness. If a ghost, she is a sensuous one. She is both a character and not a character—she is not on the same level as Sethe, for instance. Eros within a novel is both vital and marginal. Looking at this embodiment of the figure, we might think that Eros as a juvenile personage must be positive. But Eros can be very negatively presented. In Goethe's *Die Leiden des jungen Werthers* (1774), the hero encounters a madman who combines the roles of old Philetas and young Eros. Under rocky crags and grey skies, the madman is searching for the flowers of his imaginary garden. But there are no roses and honeysuckles in these *Berge*. "'I seek,' he answered . . . 'flowers—and find none'" (*Die Leiden*, 90). An impotent robber of absent gardens, searching in barren rocks for unfindable blooms, treasure for an imaginary princess, the young madman as deranged mock-Eros parodies the role of Cupid and mirrors the distortions within Werther himself. The scene with the madman, like the rest of the novel, ponders not only the crippled nature of modern love, but also the crippled and deranged nature of modern desires, social and individual. Goethe indicts his own (German and Protestant) society as being incapable of dealing with either emotion or reality. The pseudo-placid reign of the civic turns Eros mad and sends him to pasture among the rocks, a sorrowful version of the naked and cruel *Amor* of the mountains imagined by Virgil's shepherd in the Eighth Eclogue.

A different figuration of a distorted Cupid can be seen in Kingsley Amis's *Jake's Thing* (1978). In this misogynistic examination of heterosexual relations, the diminutive psychiatrist Rosenberg, who attempts to cure the hero's impotence (a condition Jake does not want cured) is perpetually compared by the irritable Jake to a child or an elf. Jake thinks of Rosenberg on his bicycle, "little legs atwinkle" (248). Rosenberg's name signifies "mountain of roses," but he has no flowers on his mountain, no roses on his *berg*. Rosenberg has only a dreary official garden in which to converse with his irascible patient:

> A gravel path with bald patches took them to a rough lawn. . . . It gave extensive hospitality to buttercups, daisies, dandelions, chickweed, groundsel, charlock, viper's bugloss, plantain, moss and couch. Near its middle stood a large elm tree which might well have been on the point of toppling over from disease but for the moment kept the sun off satisfactorily. (265)

In this sunless, diseased, and weedy garden the melancholy Jake (or Jacques) resists disruption of his barren garden of self, giving the rosy-flowered facilitator his comeuppance. Eros' garden has lost its roses and is now merely a catalogue of weeds—Eros can tend nothing. There is no harmony between nature, human desire, and art. Eros is mocked.

Amis's joke has more point if we understand it in the light of Calvino and Frye, who point to Eros as a cultural as well as an individual necessity. But we should also remember Le Sage's crippled Cupidon. When society takes over and decides to fashion a civic Eros of its own, the result is a malformation. Jake dismally encounters the pseudo-benevolent pseudo-Eros of a civic-oriented idea of "therapy." Such a stunted Eros cannot preside over Philetas' garden, in which *physis*, individual desire, and communal life are in some (tentative and temporary) harmony. Jake's virile member has gone on strike; Pan is dead (temporarily). Jake is released from the erotic (simply considered) and can refuse to be either patriarchal or civil. Amis's cantankerous but clever novel protests against the reduction of heterosexuality to its civic definition. It also questions the social determination to base a number of values on the construction of the socially desirable stable marriage. The therapist serves the social régime by bringing couples (back) together, in a parody of Eros' activity.

BRINGING EROS BACK INTO THE PICTURE

We sometimes want to dismiss Eros—the Eros of our fiction—or to treat him roughly. We may pretend we can do without him. Yet as soon as we have learned to decry Eros himself (as a merely frivolous concept) or to define modern society as one in which Eros cannot function, we seem strangely impelled to recall our Eros-Cupid. Once banished, he is made visible once again. We can see this process in action in Charles Dickens's *The Pickwick Papers* (1836–1837). The major plot lines of this novel are overtly (officially, one might say) anti-erotic; we are shown how characters avoid sexual liaisons and marriage, especially how men avoid being trapped into marriage. Like Amis—and like Rabelais—Dickens here distrusts the civic heterosexual arrangements. Mr. Pickwick's major action is avoidance of marriage with Mrs. Bardell. His trial for breach of promise of marriage is set for the fourteenth of February. Sam Weller, Mr. Pickwick's faithful servant, has a great deal on his mind. But his attention is deflected by the window of a stationer's shop:

> The particular picture on which Sam Weller's eyes were fixed . . . was a highly coloured representation of a couple of human hearts skewered together with an arrow, cooking before a cheerful fire, while a male and female cannibal in modern attire, the gentleman being clad in a blue coat and white trousers, and the lady in a deep red pelisse with a parasol of the same, were approaching the meal with hungry eyes, up a serpentine gravel path leading thereunto. A decidedly indelicate young gentleman, in a pair of wings and nothing else, was depicted as superintending the cooking; a representation of the spire of the church in Langham Place, appeared in the distance; and the whole formed a "valentine," of which, as a written inscription in the window testified, there was a large assortment within . . . (403–404)

Here Cupid appears in his last resort—in the place where we would expect to find him, a pictorial "Valentine." Dante's fearsome lord who gave the beloved the poet's flaming heart to eat is transmogrified into this cheerful indelicate cook. The impish boy we knew in Longus has skewered these lovers' hearts with his arrow without disarranging their bright modern clothes or their decorum.

This detailed description constitutes a comic *ekphrasis* of some note. The love decorously celebrated is apparently safely civic, endorsed by the spire of that most fashionable and respectable temple, the church in London's Langham Place, whose name is "All Souls." To turn to "all souls" would be to turn in a Platonic direction, away from the body. As in Amis's nonerotic garden, the path is a gravel path—orderly and sterile. But this path is here still the serpentine path of a dangerous Eden, even if respectably graveled over. The image is not *too* tame. It *does* endorse desire. The cannibal couple have hungry eyes, the Cupid is energetic in his skewering and cookery. Sam's encounter with Eros, even if only through the window of a shop, galvanizes him. Instead of thinking about saving Mr. Pickwick from Eros and Mrs. Bardell, he begins to think of serving Eros himself. Cupid's reminiscent presence has redressed a balance.

Recalled to the duty of eroticism, Sam (who cannot afford to buy the valentine) writes his valentine letter to Mary the housemaid—a "valentine" sent ironically in Pickwick's name. In doing so, Sam breaks the homosocial perfection of Pickwick and his gang. Shortly, even Pickwick the leader will be drawn into assisting, instead of thwarting, an erotic liaison, acting as lightbearer in unconscious imitation of Cupid himself (499). The valentine that Sam Weller sends will bring on marriage and progeny, so that "indelicate" Eros will not be frustrated.

Eros in Sam's ekphrastic valentine may be seen as still slightly baleful, a cannibal and creator of cannibals. Nevertheless, even in this comic presentation, he is still lord of all that is—including serpentine paths and marriage in All Souls, for people still have bodies, hungers, and desires. As in the quest of Panurge in Books Three to Five of Rabelais' *Pantagruel* (a work to which *Pickwick* owes a great debt) desire must ultimately outweigh fear. "Drink!" says the Divine Bottle, that last and possibly truest oracle, and we must drink of life.

The encounter with Cupid urges us to continue, to follow the path of desiring and living. Cupid is thus a most appropriate figure for the Novel, that long form in which we must go on and on and on . . . . Our love of story, especially novelistic story, is related to our felt need to continue living. That experiential love of being reflects not mere biological fact but a conscious or half-conscious psychological desire—like the desire of a Psyche for a conscious personality. Going on is difficult, even strenuous, and uncertain—it is indeed being led or pulled towards the unknown, over Europa's deep sea.

The Cupid who lights us on our way, as he carried a torch before Europa, can look cruel, even as a light bringer. It may be our own hearts he skewers and roasts over his "cheerful fire." Cupid the light bringer will not permit our existence to go totally unexamined. Cupid's illumination may bring pain, including the humbling acknowledgment both of our own incompleteness and of our inevitable artificiality. If "Eros" or "Cupid" as we see him is always an artifice, so is our naming of our feelings an artifice. Daphnis and Chloé had but inchoate yearnings and shoots of feeling before they learned the name, and with the name a holistic—and social—construct of desire. As we name ourselves and our wants, we share in Cupid's artifice. We can bear the pain of such acknowledgment because of the lightness of touch, the assurance that all is play. "The little Loves played" (*epaizon Erōtes*) as Achilles Tatius says of the Cupidons gambling about Europa in the great painting. We not only see Eros in most novels, but want to see him, to catch a glimpse of him, to gain playful assurance that our desires are sufficiently known to be capable of representation.

Reading a novel is, then, an erotic activity that mimics and reinforces the fundamental erotic desire of living itself. We encounter in our reading, our own desire *to be*—the ontological Eros that precedes even the witting desire to love and be loved. We read on, hoping to meet Eros, to encounter the assurance that it is worthwhile to desire. Well may parents and guardians have worried over the discontent that the Novel stirs in young people!—for in it they meet the endorsement of their desiring. A novel encourages its readers to believe in the desirability of desire. To that extent, every persistent novel-reader is an Emma Bovary. And it matters not how "moral" or "good" or even "great" the particular novels read may be. A novelist may attempt to be a moralist—not necessarily a bad thing—but the Novel itself argues for desire. A morality not sympathetic to desiring will not succeed in nesting in a novel.

What might be called the fundamental theological problem of the Novel is a problem that the figure of Eros can (at least in part) help to solve. The "theological problem" can be stated thus: "Of what use is it to write or read long fictions about persons, passions, common objects and happenings, and the dirty business of this base world? How can it be good to be engaged in the passionate dust of mortality?" Such an objection can occur within an atheistic context as well as a religious one. The problem is usually only partially visible in objections to the "triviality" and "foolishness" of novels. The theological problem weighs most heavily on authors and readers from societies or groups in which religion is understood as transcendent rather than immanent. The Neoplatonic and Manichean strain in Western thought is in strong opposition to the Novel—and indeed to all fiction save parables—on that ground, as we have seen in the case of

Porphyry. The strict Neoplatonic readings of *The Golden Ass* supplied by Renaissance commentators like Johannes Andreas (Andrea de Bussi, who edited the *editio princeps* in 1469) or Beroaldus show how a novel can be interpretively tidied up to answer more perfectly this theological problem of fiction, which *The Golden Ass* itself certainly does pose.

In the novels of China, the religious objection to the Novel is most clearly posed, for Chinese authors are very aware of dealing not only with quintessentially civic Confucians but also with Buddhist readers and moralists who find any tendency towards immersion in materiality and desire distasteful. The matter is customarily picked up and examined in the frames or introduction to novels of very diverse types, from the pornographic novel *The Carnal Prayer-Mat* to such great classics as the sixteenth-century *The Journey to the West* and the eighteenth-century *The Dream of the Red Chamber*. Many classic Chinese novels have supramundane elements or frames. In Cao Xueqin's *The Dream of the Red Chamber* (also known as *The Story of the Stone*), the Goddess's discarded stone, with the spark of supernatural life in it, begins to yearn for "life in the Red Dust" (I:2). In spite of warnings that the joys of the mundane world, the Red Dust, are transitory and illusory, it begs the Buddhist priest and Taoist monk for a chance of incarnation. Despite the apparent folly of becoming incarnate at all, the Stone—like readers, the author, and all the characters of the novel—chooses incarnation. Reading the novel is to repeat that choice. The desire of living must be respected.

There is, I think, no such simple figure as Europe's Eros in the Chinese novel, although the fairy children "clad in green" who lead Song Jiang to the Queen of Ninth Heaven and then, the interview done, push him off the bridge and send him back to this world, have some characteristics of the impish child Eros (*Shui Hu Zhuan, Outlaws of the Marsh*, trans. Shapiro, I:669–674). The figure in some ways closest to Eros is Monkey—though he is a much larger character, combining qualities of Prometheus and Loki. Yet Monkey is always mischievous, as Eros is—and his avatars: Blanche Ingram angrily calls *Jane Eyre*'s Adèle "you tiresome monkey" (191).

Monkey (Hanuman) is significantly referred to very early in *The Temple of Dawn* (*Akatsuki no Tera*, 1970), the third novel in Yukio Mishima's *Sea of Fertility* tetralogy. The hero Honda sees the Monkey god in the murals of the temple in Bangkok shortly before meeting the child Princess whom he wants to identify as the reincarnation of two long-dead friends. The little Thai Princess, not quite seven years old, identifies herself with Monkey in her Ramayana game: "The Princess resembled Hanuman when she wielded a tree branch like a sword, assuming a hunchbacked stance and holding her breath in a comical way" (trans. Saunders and Seigle, 49). Her identification with Monkey under Honda's longing gaze makes the Princess the true equivalent of the character identified with Eros in the Western novel. Honda in his obsessive love suffers as do all characters in novels who fall in love with Eros' self projected in another.

The Princess is intimately bound up with the love of life itself, desire for perpetuity of individual being, a desire that in Mishma's novel also induces an excited nausea. In this highly erotic and cerebral work the *erōs* of loving another person is insistently related to religious and philosophical questions as to the reality of either "person" or world, as well as of "meaning" itself. Mishima's cycle raises the "theological question" of the Novel profoundly and intensely. He goes far beyond the realistic in proposing (through the story line) the possibility of reincarnation and transmigration. Arguably, every positive answer regarding the persistence and significance of identity or life is undercut. Immortality of recurrent existence, if true, is an exhausting project. Mishima himself pronounced that his series was called *The Sea of Fertility* in paradoxical reference to the dry infertile sea of the Moon, the "image of cosmic nihilism." Mishima's cycle itself, however, is always awake to fertile life and transformation. *The Temple of Dawn* as a novel requires and evokes a love of the living universe that is never transcended by disgust. We as readers greedily share the life of the character—even a life as cold, refined, alienated, and anxious as that of Mishima's Honda. We enjoy his detention in time and matter, his obsessive love for the Princess, that lotus arisen from the mud. We covet his series of bright recognitions, the tender visions of the Princess's Rosette Palace in Thailand, the curious fiery vision of the burning ghats at Benares. At the same time, we enjoy the paradoxes, the ironies, the strife that beset Honda's existence, and the Monkey tricks that his *daimon* author plays on him.

Monkey is an eternal plot-deviser, a perpetual troublemaker. Monkey is the distrusted medium between heaven and earth. He must be party to the holiest desire. In the sixteenth-century Chinese novel *Journey to the West* (*Hsi-yu Chi*) Monkey eventually assists in the quest to bring the Buddhist scriptures from India to China. Monkey, who may originate in a figure of lust, the "white ape," is the desirer.[6] He is *philoneikos*, a lover of strife and of paradoxes. From him emanates the possibility of story, disturbing even the great calm of the Jade Emperor in the supramundane palace. Monkey (often referred to as "dear Monkey") is our appetite, including the appetite for change. To want anything to be different from what is, to stir up life and action, is to endorse the (admittedly often violent) world of human life, where Monkey is most at home, though he never has to be human.

Perhaps each of us shares in the nature of Monkey insofar as we choose not just to act, but to be. We do not think of this as choice; it is thus a shock to read at the beginning of a recent African novel, Ben Okri's *The Famished Road*, of the hero's choosing to be born into "the world of the Living," despite its manifold disadvantages: "We disliked the rigours of existence, the unfulfilled longings, the enshrined injustices of the world, the labyrinths of love . . . the fact of dying" (3). Like the stone in *The Dream of the Red Chamber*, this hero decides to make a commitment to the Red Dust. The Novel is the genre that underwrites such commitment to the Red Dust, that is not too proud for "the world of the Living." Is it *desirable* to deal with the world of desire, change, and death—the vulgar world of the transient flesh and mistaken heart? One of the reasons for Puritanism's rejection of novels is a belief that it is foolish and wicked to celebrate the vulgar carnal life; as Ingelo indicated in the seventeenth century, in reading or writing novels, the soul prostitutes itself, seduced by Fancy in stooping to such material.

When Eros appears within a novel (even if just as a mosaic ornament, an accessory to a Victorian lady's costume) we find a sign that the theological problem is acknowledged. Yes, it is hard to deal with time, chance, and desire. At the same time, Eros himself is a guarantor of carnal existence, an assurance that the scale is already weighted in favor of the life of this mortal world. Within Plato's *Phaedrus* and *Symposium* it is already recognized that Eros represents a challenge to all flesh-shunning systems—including Platonism itself. Eros has little patience with the world-despising sort of transcendence. Eros reigns in the Red Dust. If you think, like Chariton's Dionysios or Mann's Aschenbach, that you (mere mortal!) have transcended anything so vulgar as desire, then Eros will tell you otherwise.

The indelicate young gentleman who is older than Kronos has carried on an intimate relationship with the novel from its first discernible beginnings in the West. Eros is always present in our fiction, but we may hardly notice that he is there, so subtly can he hide in the garden of prosaic narrative that is, after all, his own garden.

CHAPTER XVII

>—+◆»—O—«+—<

Ekphrasis: Looking at the Picture

>—+◆»—O—«+—<

In Lesbos while hunting I saw in the grove of the Nymphs the most
beautiful spectacle I have ever seen, a painted picture, a history of love.
—Longus, *Daphnis and Chloé*

On the fresco of the ceiling the divinities reawakened.
—Lampedusa, *Il Gattopardo*

The gallery walls of the Mahamandapa are covered with a series of
murals illustrating episodes in the *Ramayana*. . . . the monkey god,
Hanuman, the flamboyant son of the wind god, appears throughout
the painted story. The golden beauty, Sita, with teeth of jasmine flowers, is being kidnapped by the fearful *rakshasa* king. Rama fights his
many battles with fixed, bright eyes.
—Yukio Mishima, *The Temple of Dawn*

And Elstir's studio seemed to me like the laboratory of a sort of new
creation of the world . . . here a wave of the sea angrily crashing upon
the sand its lilac foam, there a young man in white duck leaning on
his elbow upon the deck railing of a ship.
—Proust, *A l'ombre des jeunes filles en fleurs*

>—+◆»—O—«+—<

*E*ros may appear to us in a novel in an *ekphrasis*—in a pictorial representation, whether the image is in a large-scale picture, or a pair of earrings. Eros so
appearing teases us, for we know we are to attend to and interpret images. The
doubt or question about the value of representing the physical and mundane
world, the quotidian life in the Red Dust, is a doubt or question resolved or answered not only in the image of Eros, but also in the invocation of a particular
visual image itself—that is, in an inset work of art.

Although other kinds of creative and created things may be invoked over
and over again within any given novel, the visual image has a special place and a
peculiar status. The function of *ekphrasis* is different from the function of, say,
music or poems recollected or created of performed by the characters—though
examples of these abound. The *ekphrasis* of the visual artistic image has a special
place in marking the order of creativity. It reminds us of the visible world, and
thus of the sensible universe, but it also speaks of stasis, and artifice—of things
out of nature. It transforms us into powerful gazers—and the power of the gaze
has recently been dealt with by Lacan, Laura Mulvey, and others.[1] But it also
humbles us, making us recall that the "real" world is visible and knowable to us
only through interpretations and re-visions. Physical sense, inward rumination,
and cultural heritage here overtly unite. *Ekphrasis*, the account of a visual artifice,
blesses the visible and sensible world while at the same time offering a non-

Platonic mode of transcendence. The artwork recalled or imagined reminds us that through art our vision of the Red Dust as meaningful can be organized. In each instance of its *ekphrasis*, a particular novel bespeaks itself a complex representation—and speaking its own representation is something a novel (even the lightest one) is bound to do.

The Novel is not the only genre capable of doing this. The epic has had a long tradition of summoning up *ekphraseis*, from the shield of Achilles on. Medieval and Renaissance narrative poets (Dante, Chrétien, Ariosto, Spenser) wrought so well in their *ekphraseis* that novelists borrowed their effects—although it may be retorted that some of these effects sprang originally from the Byzantine novel.[2] Lyric and drama both use *ekphrasis*, although drama has special problems with mere descriptive recitation—we have at least to see Hermione's "statue" on stage in *The Winter's Tale*, in a sort of *tableau vivant* in which Life triumphs over Art. *Ekphrasis* is certainly not the sole property of prose fiction. Prose fiction, however, has special obligations to—and special affinities with—*ekphrasis*. The use of it seems scarcely a matter of choice for any example of the genre, ancient or modern, realistic or magical. In dealing with the visual icon and its meaning-ful-ness, a novel must succinctly express its own drive to meaning, and its own artifice. The presentation of the visual artistic images recomplicates the case of the characters; it tests them while making us ask important questions about individuality.

THE INSET PAINTING

An *ekphrasis* may sneak up on us in the middle of a novel, or it may declare itself boldly at the outset. As has been noted earlier in this book, ancient novels are ornamented with many *ekphraseis*, many of them very knowingly and almost aggressively set out to confront the reader and demand attention. Longus' *Daphnis and Chloé* begins with a description of a painting. The entire novel is offered as a large-scale interpretation of that enigmatic painting, the whole narrative composing a large detailed *ekphrasis*. In Achilles Tatius' *Kleitophon and Leukippé*, the hero goes to great pains to describe to us exactly the paintings that he sees in the temple at Pelousion, closely inspecting the *eikona diplēn*, the double image, twin pictures of Andromeda and Prometheus (146–153). Kleitophon interprets the relationship of the pictures to each other in this duplex icon: both characters are represented in chains, both are chained to rocks, and both characters are tortured by beasts. As Shadi Bartsch points out, the paintings have complex relationships to the events of the present narrative: "the reader is aware that the paintings must foreshadow *something*" (Bartsch, *Decoding the Ancient Novel*, 58). We always know that icons in novelistic narrative mean "*something*," but we are rarely able to see the full meaning at the time—even if, as often happens, we think that a character's interpretation of an image is erroneous or inadequate.

Ekphrasis immediately introduces our own duty to interpret—a strong source of novelistic anxiety. We begin to share or imitate the characters' anxieties, for we cannot be sure of our own ground. Thus, the pleasure that we may take in a beautifully worded and evocative *ekphrasis* is simultaneously undercut by our apprehension of our own potential inadequacy in rising to significant interpretation. We may appreciate the verbal subtleties of the author in finding words equivalent to painterly effects, as Achilles Tatius does through Kleitophon in, for instance, describing the appearance of Andromeda: "Yet the paleness of her cheeks was not colorless, for there was a slight blush upon them, nor was the beauty in flower of her eyes a beauty without care, but resembled violets just starting to fade away" (148). Achilles Tatius and Kleitophon luxuriate in the contemplation of beauty in distress, the long look at Andromeda justified not only by the ingenious beauty of the painting (which we cannot see), but even more by the ingenious beauty of the language that can find metaphors not accessible to the painter.

Kleitophon is simultaneously painter (word-painter) and interpreter. Behind our hero stands the author, who is able to do what the rhetorician Philostratus was able to do so effectively—create and interpret paintings entirely through words, in a masterly display of both descriptive and hermeneutic language. Philostratus points out that he can bring us both the intellectual and the sensuous impact of the pictured garden where Cupids gather apples. The painting itself is, implicitly, hampered by restriction to visual sense. "But attend," says Philostratus, "for with my discourse the apples will approach you" (*Imagines*, 20). Words likewise evoke sensuous response in Kleitophon's description, with the synaesthesia it achieves through metaphor. Female eyes offer an idea of visual beauty, a bloom and fine flourishing caught in the word *anthos*, "flower" in its general sense. But the metaphorical maneuver turns the generalized *anthos* into particular flowers in *iois*, transforming proud flourish into pathos; the metaphor reincarnates itself in a special image, tactile and scented, very close to Keats's "Fast fading violets."

Kleitophon is in some sense showing off in his description. If *ekphrasis* unlocks the culture and the mind together, the viewer who is able to speak effectively about a painting proves that he is attuned to the culture, and possesses some power of mind. Kleitophon exhibits the intellectual and upper-class rhetorical mastery so brilliantly exhibited in Philostratus. But as interpreter he is at a decided disadvantage. Kleitophon has the basic handicap of not knowing he is *in* a work of art. He does not even see the necessity of relating these visual images to the life and experiences of himself and his beloved. The reader alone at this point is fully aware that personal ingenuity and hermeneutic qualifications are here being tested. Every time there is an *ekphrasis*, we are put on our mettle.

A certain power, including power over the plot, resides within these images themselves; the icons are numinous objects. In the most extreme case, as in Heliodorus, an icon that can be rendered to us in *ekphrasis* is substantially generative in its power to affect the babe in the womb. We talk of being "affected" by paintings, but the *Aithiopika*'s Persinna shows the extreme degree to which a viewer may be "affected," forced to incarnate the image. Icons are dangerous, for they beget. The presence of a painting of Andromeda in her bedroom was enough to make Persinna conceive a white girl. In Bernardin de Saint Pierre's *Paul et Virginie* (1788), the hero's mother has also been affected by a portrait:

> This portrait was a little miniature representing Paul the Hermit. Marguerite had a great devotion to it; she had long worn it around her neck when she was a girl; later, on becoming a mother, she had put it about the neck of her baby. It had even come to pass that, when she

was pregnant with him, and deserted by everyone, by virtue of contemplating the image of this blessed solitary, the fruit of her womb had
contracted some resemblance to it. It was this that had decided her to
make him bear the name, and to give him for his patron a saint who
had passed his life far from men, who had first abused and then abandoned her.   (*Paul et Virginie*, 116)

There seems to be a reminiscence of this passage in D. H. Lawrence's *Sons and
Lovers*, when Mrs. Morel looks upon her baby and names him: " 'I will call him
Paul,' she said suddenly; she knew not why" (37). In novels in general the icon
sustains its power to affect the fruit in the womb, for in the course of a novel (that
is, of our *reading* the novel) the image perpetually begets meaning. The novel that
at last reveals itself as fully born—reveals itself finally that is, when we arrive at
the very end—is a narrative that has incorporated and been formed by the images
it has represented.

An *ekphrasis* may certainly be introduced ironically into the novel. Tomasi
di Lampedusa's *Il Gattopardo* (1958) begins with an impressive and ironic *ekphrasis*, as we watch the aristocratic Sicilian family finish prayers (the Rosary and
the Sorrowful Mysteries) in their great salon:

> The women got up slowly and the oscillating retreat of their skirts
> ceased, little by little, to cover the mythological nudities pictured on
> the milky wall of tiles. There remained covered only the Andromeda,
> whom the cassock of Father Pirrone, delayed in his supplementary
> orisons, slightly obstructed from the view of the silvery Perseus, flying
> over the billows, who was rushing to her aid and to her kiss.
>
> On the fresco of the ceiling the divinities reawakened. Bands of Tri-
> tons and Dryads, from the mountains and the seas, precipitated them-
> selves amid raspberry and cyclamen clouds towards a transfigured
> Shell of Gold in order to exalt the glory of the house of Salina, appar-
> ently so overcome by the sudden glory of such exaltation as to trans-
> gress the simplest rules of perspective; and the major Gods, the Chiefs
> among the Gods, Jove thundering, Mars frowning, Venus languishing,
> who had preceded the crowd of minor godlets, in an orderly fashion
> supported the azure coat of arms of the Leopard.
>
> (*Il Gattopardo* [paras 2–3], 5)

Lampedusa's *ekphrasis* mocks the grandeur of the family and points a contrast
between the Christian Catholic ritual (intermittent) and the pagan permanen-
cies, ever reawakening. The provincial Renaissance frescoes are old-fashioned for
1860; the Salina family certainly lives in the past. Lampedusa is able to take advantage, in a classical novelistic manner, of the opportunity to recreate Perseus
and Andromeda—in that respect signing himself a close successor of Achilles Tatius. The declining fortunes of the house of the Leopard are in need of rescue.
The gods of the ceiling justify only the family—not the individual—and the individual, like Andromeda, may require assistance. The past may be at once both
beautiful and stifling (as it certainly is in *Il Gattopardo*) —yet any appreciation of
artistic reference depends on our participation in the past. The images have begotten us; we are not in charge of them.

Form overcomes substance in *ekphrasis*. Like the characters, we are, momentarily at least, insubstantial in comparison to the images. Members of the Salina family may temporarily obscure the images that have made them what they are, but these images persistently return, "divinities reawakened." Authors may deflect the reminder of our powerlessness in relation to cultural images by producing ignorant characters so out of contact with such imposing things that we may simply laugh at these fools. Yet as readers we know we too are defective in knowledge. A residual apprehension of our own relative ignorance, of our struggle and even failure to make perfect sense of things, remains with us. The sense of inadequacy is the more marked since the novelist, ancient or modern (unlike, say, Dante or Spenser), does not feel obliged to explain things to us.

IGNORANCE AND ALIENATION

In Zola's *L'Assommoir*, the reader may take a condescending attitude to the party of poor working people who go to visit the Louvre on a gala day. Our sense of superiority must be tempered, however, by a certain uneasiness, a sense of the weight and confusion of the past and of available meanings, not unlike the sense we get from the gigantic jumble of the antique shop in Balzac's earlier *La Peau de chagrin*. No wonder the proletarian wedding-party find the Louvre a treasure store difficult to understand. They are first amazed by the antiquities:

> And slowly the couples advanced, chin raised, eyelids batting, between the colossi in stone, the gods of black marble mute in their hieratic stiffness, monstrous beasts, half cats and half women, with the faces of dead people with thin noses and swollen lips. They found all that very ugly. People work a jolly lot better in stone nowadays. An inscription in Phoenician characters stupefied them. It wasn't possible, nobody had ever read that scribble. (100)

The comedy of the narrative is amplified by the distance between a word like *hiératique*, which the group could not know, and phrases interpolating, in *style indirect libre*, their own colloquial reactions (*joliment mieux*). The working-class party are revealed as totally inadequate interpreters of the history of Western culture; they do not understand our inheritance from Egypt and Phoenicia, they have not even acquired the word "sphinx." If we pause for a moment, we realize that the reader, like Zola himself presumably, would be just as much at a loss if set to read the Phonenican inscription—all that differentiates "us" from the proletarian group is the fact that we do believe that these signs once served as writing. We believe that we know that this script is readable—we just do not know what it means.

Signs and images (including colossi and sphinxes) belong in a cultural context, and our knowledge of contexts may fail us at a thousand points. The narrator of *Daphnis and Chloé* enjoys a painting that he cannot understand—he does not know what it all means but has to seek out an interpreter, an *exēgētēs*. We infer (but do not know) that the ensuing tale is based on what the exegete told the narrator, but our major impression is that the narrator, while gazing at the picture, was delighted but not knowledgeable. Much must be done to make a *graphē* intelligible.

Zola's little group of visitors, out of their element, are happier with modern art but still ill-equipped to understand it, even under the guidance of M. Madinier, whose slightly smaller degree of ignorance qualifies him as guide:

> With a gesture he commanded the party to halt in the middle of the square *salon*. There was nothing there but masterpieces, he murmured in hushed voice, as if in church. They made the tour of the room. Gervaise asked the subject of the *Wedding at Cana*; it was stupid not to write the subjects on the frames. Coupeau stopped in front of the *Mona Lisa* [*la Joconde*], in which he discovered a resemblance to one of his aunts. Boche and Bibi-la-Grillade laughed derisively, while showing each other, spying from the corners of their eyes, the naked women. The thighs of Antiope especially gave them a paroxysm. And, at the tail end, the Gaudron family, the man with his mouth open, the woman with her hands on her belly, remained gaping, softened and stupid, facing *The Virgin* of Murillo. (101)

Gervaise ought to understand the subject of the wedding at Cana without written explanation; her grasp of the elements of culture that should have reached her (the stories of New Testament) is very weak. The various reactions display different sorts of *ekphrastic* inadequacy; arguably, the Gaudron couple, moved to a sort of worship of the Virgin represented by Murillo, are not as out-of-the way as some of the others. The most perverse reaction, however, is that of Coupeau, who deflects a whole history of criticism—being entirely ignorant of Walter Pater, and so on. The Mona Lisa is for him not mysterious or uncanny, but homely, and representational; the picture acquires a purely new value in representing a likeness of his aunt. He privatizes the Mona Lisa for his own enjoyment. Cultural appropriation customarily occurs once we have learned the vocabulary of art criticism and history; by apparently joining in a communal (but actually exclusive) language we feel assured of our own individual rights to the work of art. Coupeau undertakes an illicit privatization. There is an added joke in Coupeau's reaction. If his aunt resembles *la Joconde*, and he knows his aunt well, then perhaps he unwittingly has the key to the "mystery" about which so much ado has been made. Zola may wish us to question our own acculturated reactions, while undoubtedly supplying a deal of class comedy in the working-class expedition. The comedy has its darker side, for one may read into it the opinion that art galleries are wasted on the poor, and should not be open to them.

Class and Art

Ekphrastic references to well-known works of art often function to display characters' class, reflected in their lack of the knowledge the cultured are supposed to possess. Sometimes, that is what we are to see in an ekphrastic invocation—we look beyond the work itself and its own vocabulary of symbolism to the social world outside it. A clear case is offered in Frances Burney's *Evelina* (1778), in which Mr. Smith functions rather like Zola's M. Madinier, the man attempting to rise from the world of the artisan with a little borrowed and inadequate culture. At Vauxhall, in the Picture Room east of the Rotunda where the party have to wait, Evelina inquires the subjects of the paintings, and her lower-class grandmother insists that Mr. Smith "can tell us all about them." Mr. Smith professes not only willingness, but also knowledge:

> "For I have attended," said he, "to all these paintings, and know every thing in them perfectly well; for I am rather fond of pictures, Ma'am; and, really, I must say, I think a pretty picture is a—a very—is really a very—is something very pretty.—"
>
> "So do I too," said Madame Duval, "but pray now, Sir, tell us who that is meant for," pointing to a figure of Neptune.
>
> "That!—why that, Ma'am, is,—Lord bless me, I can't think how I come to be so stupid, but really I have forgot his name,—and yet, I know it as well as my own, too,—however, he's a *general*, Ma'am, they are all generals." (202–203)

Mr. Smith knows just enough about art to know that one must pretend to like it, but he has not yet acquired a vocabulary of either appreciation or symbol. He is incapable of reading the symbolic language of those (then well-known) paintings, which represented in boastful eighteenth-century grand style the British naval victories of the mid-century. Mr. Smith cannot discern allegory, cannot read the inherited language. Neptune is recast as a *general* (he should at least be an *admiral*). Only the militarism of the subject has come through, but confusedly. This incident in Burney's novel not only offers us the laugh of superiority, but momentarily sets us to wondering what it would be like not to have the concept of "Neptune," at the same time realizing that multitudes do not posses this Western artistic and literary idea. It is doubly comic for Smith to say he has forgotten this figure's *name*, for "Neptune" is not a "name" in the sense that "Smith" is now a name and nothing more.

The failure of characters to perform with ekphrastic competence is a cause of mirth, a standard operation of novelistic comedy. Trimalchio proclaims his knowledge that culture is necessary: *Oportet etiam inter cenandum philologiam nosse,* he boasts (70)—"It is fitting to know one's philology even at the dinner-table," *philologia* bearing the sense "literature." Aware of the necessity of literary culture and of the vocabulary for it (*philologia*), Trimalchio is as yet unable to perform culturally accurate feats of description: "I own a hundred great cups, more or less, showing how Cassandra killed her sons, and the dead boys lying there so you'd think they were alive" (104). "We" (the cultivated we) know *of course* that it was Medea who killed her sons, not the childless Cassandra; the entire statement is the more ridiculous as Trimalchio's praise of the realism achieved by the engraver, who creates "lifelike" figures, conflicts with the fact that the figures in the story are corpses.

Conscious Alienation

The trope of *ekphrasis* may, however, be employed in order to support a character's unorthodox interpretation, in knowing defiance of cultural dictates. Nowhere is such a use clearer than in Charlotte Brontë's *Villette* (1853), in the sequence in which the heroine visits an art gallery and sardonically contemplates a "picture of pretentous size":

It represented a woman, considerably larger, I thought, than the life. I calculated that this lady, put into a scale of magnitude suitable for the reception of a commodity of bulk, would infallibly turn from fourteen to sixteen stone. She was, indeed, extremely well fed: very much butcher's meat—to say nothing of bread, vegetables, and liquids— must she have consumed to attain that breadth and height, that wealth of muscle, that affluence of flesh. She lay half-reclined on a couch: why, it would be difficult to say; broad daylight blazed round her; she appeared in hearty health, strong enough to do the work of two plain cooks; she could not plead a weak spine; she ought to have been stand- ing, or at least sitting bolt upright. She had no business to lounge away the noon on a sofa. She ought likewise to have worn decent gar- ments; a gown covering her properly, which was not the case: out of abundance of material—seven-and-twenty yards, I should say, of drapery—she managed to make inefficient raiment. Then, for the wretched untidiness surrounding her, there could be no excuse. Pots and pans—perhaps I ought to say vases and goblets—were rolled here and there on the foreground; a perfect rubbish of flowers was mixed amongst them, and an absurd and disorderly mass of curtain uphol- stery smothered the couch and cumbered the floor. On referring to the catalogue, I found that this notable production bore the name "Cleo- patra." (250)

Lucy Snowe wittily refuses to try to "make sense" of the work in the way that the culture demands, and deliberate introduces "inappropriate" material in a witty and perverse *ekphrasis*. The voluptuous physicality suggested by the Ru- benesque painting is translated into literal English weights and measure. Imagi- nary "formal" flesh treated as if it were the too-too-solid result of eating other physical solids. In order to achieve her critique, Lucy as narrator deliberately adopts a semiparodic lower-class view, refusing to accept the subject on the "edu- cated" terms that excuse the soft pornography. Her satiric persona ignores the pornography in naïve considerations of the body of the female working woman. The woman is implicitly reclassed as a housewife or servant ("two plain cooks") not as a queen, her leisurely attitude mischievously interpreted as laziness. For this obstinate observer, the woman will be only another woman, not the object of lust. Lucy Snowe misinterprets, but not like Trimalchio or Mr. Smith. Lucy *pretends* not to know why a woman is portrayed naked or nearly naked, wearing "inefficient raiment" even while luxuriating in surplus material.

The word "commodity" tips us off; the narrator is perfectly aware that the giant picture is a commodity. The gigantic odalisque is a commodity amid a riot of pictured commodities. This picture is (as the subsequent comments by M. Paul make clear) reserved for the gaze of men. Lucy is not supposed to be looking at it at all. By looking with perfect self-possession and refusing the (masculine) terms that have brought such a picture into being, lucid Lucy questions the cultural assumptions that produce both the painting and the acceptable ways of looking at it. She knows the language but rejects it, preferring, for instance to reduce the objects to "Pots and pans" rather than lending herself to the cultural formation by solemnly agreeing to call them "vases and goblets." Lucy evidently does not believe that this object necessarily has anything to do with the Egyptian queen—Lucy will not say this *is* Cleopatra, simply that the "production bore the name." This ekphrastic moment lets us see not only what our culture makes of women, but what it makes of the East, and of Africa.

Pictures make demands upon the gazers. It takes a strong mind to resist taking a picture on its own (or rather its productive culture's) terms, as Lucy resists here. Even the culturally well-bred rarely seem (in novels) to understand altogether the significance of the paintings they discuss. There is an element of Mr. Smith in almost every character in a novel who looks at a painting (real or imagined). The painting signals to the reader too, over the characters' heads, asking us to engage in another interpretation, which the character cannot—or sometimes will not—undertake, tracing the painting's meaning in relation to the entire large artwork that is this novel itself. As the presence of the work of art forcefully reminds us, nobody—not the character, not the reader—can rest for a moment from the ceaseless activity of interpretation.

The work of integrating the flow of representations can be wearying and frustrating—even when the images gazed upon represent the highest human aspirations and intuitions. In Yukio Mishima's *The Temple of Dawn* (*Akatsuki no Tera*, 1970), the hero undertakes an urgent quest to seek the meaning of human life and being. He gazes on numerous objects and representations produced by the chief Eastern religions. The description of the Bangkok temple "covered with a series of murals illustrating episodes in the *Ramayana*" not only gives the reader the benefit of a traveler's description of a wonder (like Kleitophon's description of the temple paintings), but also emphasizes the cool view and deep doubt of the hero Honda (and of his creator). The more we look at religious paintings the more fascinating they may become—but also the more alienating. Everything announces its unreality—like Rama fighting "with fixed, bright eyes." The fixed, bright world of artifice is insubstantial, yet too abundant:

> Colorful palaces, monkey gods, and battles of monsters appear against mountains painted in the manner of the southern Chinese school or in that of the somber early Venetian landscapes. Above the tenebrous *paysage* soars a god in the seven colors of the rainbow, mounted on a phoenix.   (*The Temple of Dawn*, trans. Saunders and Seigle, 9)

Everything becomes a jumble, to be sorted out by the sophisticated mind of the educated viewer. Honda knows about Chinese schools of art, about Venetian landscapes. But the knowledge itself produces detachment, and thus a kind of loss. Mishima's novels, with their almost continuous reference to artificial images as well as to sensuous objects, remind us that the flow of artistic representations is not necessarily a formal answer to the too-muchness of matter but can itself make a large contribution to that very plethora it seeks to organize. The response to all *ekphrasis* is potentially what it is in Mishima—alienation.

PORTRAYAL

The portrait may be considered a special, even restful, case of representation. Characters in novels carry about with them or encounter portraits of special persons loved by them—especially parents, children, spouses, or lovers. Characters have no anxiety about identifying what this picture is; they believe they know. In Chariton's *Chaireas and Kallirrhoé*, for instance, the heroine has the portrait of her husband, which she puts on her pregnant belly while talking to it; the portrait is a strong metonym, often treated as a part or fragment of the absent beloved. In *La Princesse de Clèves*, the Duc de Nemours steals the heroine's miniature portrait; for a portrait of him, she, however, must contemplate not a miniature but a large history painting of a battle in which he figures—his representations are public and historical. Characters in novels take pleasure in looking at portraits, including photographs of a loved one in different phases of activity.

Such references to portraiture heighten our sense of the "reality" of the character portrayed by the novelist—after all, this person is so real that just an *image* of him or her can be valued by other characters. We forget that all we *ever* have is an image, even while the trope should remind us that that is so. Of all icons, the portrait may be the simplest to be produced in a novel, although portraits themselves may be read in complex ways. In Doyle's *The Hound of the Baskervilles*, Sherlock Holmes, regarding the portraits in Baskerville Hall, detects the family similarities beneath the various costumes of the centuries, a pattern of resemblances that helps him to spot the concealed and plotting heir. Such an interpretation has its somber side: "atavism" is a key word in the subtext of Doyle's novel, which carries dark doubts about progress; we do not progress, but repeat. It takes Sherlock, the highly evolved man of reason, to dare to acknowledge his (and our) connection with the primitive man of the stone huts, and so to trace the undying similarity of a family of *types* ("Baskerville") across centuries.

In any work of novelistic *ekphrasis* we encounter our own public images, our history in the various manners in which we have represented it. We confront our own mythologies. This confrontation takes place as soon as *ekphrasis* enters even a "light" or "trifling" novel. The encounter with the public display of paintings makes us confront our human capacity for abstraction. The *ekphrasis* mimes all mimesis and formalizes our love of "form." At the same time, the internal paintings or sculptures within a novel siphon off, as it were, the work's potential abstractedness, its possible transcendence in pure form, thus curiously revalidating the novel itself as precisely *not* dry artifice. Characters looking at sculptures, mosaics, and paintings may seem more stupid than they were before, but they become more "real." We reject dry and shadowy shallow form for these characters' (purely imaginary!) substance. So in Mishima's tetralogy, the reader, character, and author may all doubt together whether there is more in the universe than a boiling sea of meaningless flux—yet, watching Honda confront the temple pictures of Monkey and Rama, we "believe" that those figures are dessicated, artificial, "fixed," and "bright"—but that the Honda who looks at them has, not fixed bright eyes, but mobile, deep, and living ones. He thus becomes more lovable and significant as incarnate. He is material, *not* formal. The contact with pure form curiously reincarnates a novel. The public display of cultural images stirs anxiety in us. Yet it may stir in us also a (perhaps unreasonable) deferred optimism about the possibility of eventual understanding—even though the encounter may thoroughly display our own (as well as the characters') consistent inadequacy in interpretation.

CHARACTERS AS ARTISTS

Characters in older novels may patronize artists or encounter them, but from the eighteenth century onward characters are more likely to be artists. They are thus producers as well as interpreters of the icons of the text. Thackeray's Clive Newcome and Charlotte Brontë's Jane Eyre are both artists. So is Dick, the hero of Kipling's *The Light That Failed* (1890), and so too is the eponymous hero of Henry James's *Roderick Hudson* (1875), a sculptor who goes into rapid artistic decline under the temptations encountered in Italy. The late twentieth century has seen a renewed emphasis upon artistic characters, who often take the central role in a novel. Elaine Risley, heroine of Margaret Atwood's *Cat's Eye* (1989), is a celebrated painter. In Tom Robbins's *Skinny Legs and All* (1990), both hero and heroine are artists.

Characters who are artists are in a difficult position, their hermeneutic task redoubled by virtue of their undertaking to articulate the icon. Very often, a character's artistic work is critically rendered in terms of failure. Jane Austen's Emma is indifferently successful in her art; of a sketch of her baby nephew she claims only, "The corner of the sofa is very good" (40), and in painting a portrait of her friend Harriet she deliberately draws an untruth and makes her taller than she should be. Artist-characters rarely succeed in providing the pleasure or the instruction they intend. They must contend with a complicated artistic history of conventions and techniques. In Flaubert's *L'Education sentimentale*, we watch Pellerin in the process of painting the portrait of Rosanette. He goes at first into a rapture of Venetian quotations, intending to mingle Titian with Veronese. He poses the woman comically nicknamed *la Maréchale* ("The Marshaless") amid a clutter of feminine objects (flowers, a chaplet of amber, a dagger) against a background of columns. It is evidently expected that the reader will be amused at this poor pilgrim Pellerin and his attempts upon "Venice." In the process of making the portrait, he loses heart:

> His first intention had been to make a Titian. But little by little, the varied coloration of his model had seduced him; and he had worked freely, accumulating paint over paint, and light upon light. Rosanette was enchanted at first; her assignations with Delmar had interrupted the sittings and allowed Pellerin time to dazzle himself. Then, his admiration subsiding, he asked himself whether his painting did not lack something in grandeur. He had looked again at the Titians, had understood the distance between them, recognized his fault; and he set himself to redraw the contours simply. Then he had tried, in blurring the lines, to lose them, to mingle the tones of the head with those of the background; and the figure took on consistency, the shades more vigor; everything seemed firmer. Finally the *Maréchale* returned. She had permitted herself some objections; the artist, naturally, had persevered. After great fury with her stupidity, he had said to himself that she could be right. Then had commenced the era of doubt, contrary pullings of thought which provoked cramps in the stomach, insomnia, fever, disgust with himself: he had had the courage to do

some retouching, but without heart, and feeling that his work was
bad. (278)

Poor Pellerin! How could he make "a Titian'? All he could do is make "a
Pellerin." If the work of the artist within a novel may be considered as a parallel
to the work of the novelist himself, a crafty *mise-en-abîme*, the artist's work as
often as not expresses the *negative* side of the novelist's sense of his or her own
art. The difficulty of creating an icon, of incorporating anything both representational and meaningful, is stressed (often comically). At the same time, the
novel in which the poor artist's icons appear overwhelms those icons, swallows
them up.

The *ekphrasis* within the novel may always be considered as a manifestation of the eternal war between poetry and painting. Literary artists in prose, as
well as poets, are anxious to vindicate the verbal art, and to give it, finally, the
higher position. As novelists like to show, the graphic can be imagined through
words. No real or actual painting needs to exist in order for an image to be shared
by author and reader. By the time Tom Robbins in *Skinny Legs and All* has got
through describing Boomer Petway's satiric piece, a "welded steel coathanger"
with "a flat, deflated skyscraper, sewn out of canvas" folded over it, we have as
good as seen Boomer's *Donald Trump's Pants Come Back From the Cleaners* (290).
After such a complete account, who needs a real artwork? In an announcement
prefixed to this novel, Robbins admits, "Some of the works of art described in
these pages are fictionalized exaggerations of pieces originally created by Patti
Warashina, Fred Bauer, and Norma Rosen." How, one may wonder, can these
artists feel about the metamorphosis of their work? What price the pieces "originally created" if they can be thus unmoored and impressed into the magical
world of *ekphrasis* that only the verbal author can know?

The possibility that the work of the graphic artist is being compared to—
and always subsumed by—the work of the novelist seems inherent in the trope:
this is already apparent in the openings of both *Daphnis and Chloé* and *Kleitophon
and Leukippé*. It would be false Romanticism to assert that a graphic artist within
a novel speaks for the creator-storyteller, and in favor of creativity in general,
even though some post-Romantic novels make gestures in that direction. It seems
more important to notice the extent to which the idea of the painting, the hard
overt graphic *form*, makes us concentrate on the *formal*. The reader's own creativity receives a check at the point at which the internal work of art is introduced.
What seemed to have been a private transaction of imagination between the
novelist and myself is now borne upward to the public realm. We think of the
external world. We remember (in novels old or new) public places for display of
images: the church or temple, the artist's studio. There is an external check on
our own imagination, as we realize that all readers are being required here to
image the same thing. The overt icon stresses our group-sense, calls upon us to
remember our shared history, legends, and meanings; we cannot stray as we are
wont to do in the delicious fields of private, imaginings, nor can we here permit
ourselves to think that reading the novel is the *same* as private imagining.

There is no more successful artist-character in fiction than Proust's Elstir
and perhaps no better example to illustrate the use of *ekphrasis* in the Novel. Elstir,

who is, Proust persuades us, a most successful major artist, offers a counterpart to the narrator Marcel as the interpreter of nature and mankind. Marcel finds great happiness in visiting this artist's studio, even though it is in a "sumptuously ugly" seaside villa, from which he turns his gaze.

> It was also in averting my eyes that I crossed the garden which had a lawn . . . a little statue of a gay gardener, some glass balls in which you could see yourself, borders of begonias and a little arbour beneath which rocking chairs were arranged around an iron table. But after all these surrounding distinguished by bourgeois ugliness, I paid no more attention to the chocolate mouldings of the plinths when I was in the studio; I felt perfectly happy, because in all the studies that surrounded me, I sensed the possibility of raising myself to a poetic knowledge, fertile in joys, of the many forms which I had not hitherto isolated in the total spectacle of reality. And Elstir's studio seemed to me like the laboratory of a sort of new creation of the world, where, from the chaos which is all the things that we see, he had drawn, in painting them on divers rectangles of canvas that were set up in all directions, here a wave of the sea angrily crashing upon the sand its lilac foam, there a young man in white duck leaning on his elbow upon the deck railing of a ship. The young man's jacket and the splashing wave had taken on a new dignity from the fact that they continued to be, even while deprived [*dépourvus*] of that in which they pretended to consist, the wave no longer being able to dampen nor the jacket to clothe anyone (*A L'ombre des jeunes filles en fleurs*), II : 222

It is only in some Keatsean sense (or Keats mediated through Ruskin) that the wave or jacket can be said to continue "to be" (*à être*), for this being has no longer a biological dimension. The new existence is figured as a deprivation, the objects are *dépourvus*; the deprivation is compensated for by the *nouvelle création du monde*, the new creation that permits us to see something instead of the mundane chaos. The Homeric wavecrash is now silent. These graphic entities have all achieved dry transcendence, from which the element of water is removed.

Yet Marcel in his introduction to the *atelier* of Elstir has altered our perceptions by deliberately including what ought to be invisible, the vulgar chaos, the forms with insufficient significance, that compose the garden. By being described, they too become part of an *ekphrasis*, and are heightened, rescued from chaos, just as the objects in the paintings have been heightened by Elstir—according to Marcel. The "extraneous" objects form new combinations with the "artistic" ones; in our mind's eye, the glass balls and begonias carry on a relationship with the pictured wave, the supremely beautiful immortal *écume lilas*.

Such an effect is foretold in the beginning of *Daphnis and Chloé*, at the point at which the narrative artist takes over, after the *ekphrasis* describing the great painting; he immediately begins to give us details not in the painting. The narrator speaks of his own sense of rivalry: his desire was "to antigraph the graphic" (*antigrapsai tēi graphēi*). So, too, Marcel's desire is to antigraph his own Elstir, and in both cases the author behind the novel (Longus, Proust) imagines the graphic artist and his work, as well as the antigraphic, the narrative riposte that is also completion. It suits both authors to make the narrators of their stories into superb interpreters. Elstir as aesthetic priest initiates Marcel and educates his taste; he has some of the functions of the *exēgētēs*. But, as in Longus, both graphic artist and exegete are surpassed by the powerful narrator.

Elstir's art is a glorification of minglings and of frontier areas: "one of his most frequent metaphors in the seascapes which he had by him at this time was precisely that which, comparing land and sea, suppressed all demarcation between them" (224). This metaphor is illustrated by the described painting representing "the harbour of Carquethuit," in which the boats seemed to be part of the town, while the churches seem to be emerging from the waters. Elstir's "metaphor" is of course Proust's own, and this "metaphor" is, as we have seen, a proper trope of the Novel. Elstir reminds us of the vital (and disturbing) quality of the damp and mingled margin, where water and land melt into each other. In some ways, all Elstir does is provide renewed focus on the well-used figure, so that it seems freshly exciting. The *idea* of the wave recoils from dry fixed transcendence, begins to combine with the image of the Madonna, and so to splash against the temple facade. The interaction of soft wave with stone icons has been evoked since the first part of *Du Côté de chez Swann*, in the description of the church at Combray: "Its sepulchral stones . . . were themselves no longer of inert and hard matter, for time had rendered them soft and made them flow like honey out of the limits of their own proper squares, which here they had overflowed in a blond flood, dragging in its drift a flowery Gothic capital letter, drowning the white violets of marble" (158). The church floor, no longer *inerte et dure*, becomes land freshly flooded, the marginal damp abode of drowning white violets. Over and over again Proust restores the Marginal Trope, for the repeated refreshments of rebirth, and as a means of ensuring that no icon should become hard and fixed. Marcel seeks moving and unstable figurations, like his magic lampshade's moving pictures, just as constantly as he resists the idea of the inflexible monolithic soul: "For if one has the sensation of being always surrounded by one's own soul, it's not as by an immobile prison: rather, it's as if one is carried away with it [*elle*] in a perpetual impulse to go beyond it [*perpétuel élan pour la dépasser*]" (107). Cambray church offers the occasion of an image of getting out, going beyond the lines. The mobile work of time and the activity of stone are incorporated for the viewer in the strangelyrenewed icon, which loses fixity and gains *élan*. Metaphor trumps static form, as the verbal lilac wave mingles unlikes and trumps Elstir's painted surf.

"Form," which is also "history," is deformed by time and the viewer, is reformed, and then launched in flux again. It is thus that Proust, with his plethora of icons, asserts against the icon the flow of life. The set images, in the hard marble, *la matière inerte et dure*, or in the inert and set painting, offer us stasis in place of flow. They create quiet moments, objective spots of time to which we should return. Yet they threaten the novel's prized individuality. While we look at an iconic image, a novelistic *graphē* in ekphrasis, we are recalled not to individuality but to typicality. The image, in its finality, its absoluteness, represents Being but at the same time presents us with Death.

CHARACTERS AS ART

Characters in novels have always had a fondness for dressing up, for pretending to be someone they are not. We have seen this since the earliest available novels, in which characters sometimes get themselves up in very ugly guise (disguised as slaves or beggars). Ancient characters do not seem to dress up as other people as often or as fully as later fictional characters will do, though the experiments with wigs and eyebrows on the part of Ascyltus and Encolpius show they can go quite a distance in remodeling themselves. In older fiction, characters dressed up as someone they are not usually are provided with an excuse in terms of the plot. From the seventeenth century there is not only a new emphasis on fashion, and thus on clothing as a kind of costume, but also a growing awareness of the possibilities of remodeling one's image for pleasure. In eighteenth-century novels, characters dress up to participate in masquerades, and in doing so they take on an abundance of deliberately dissociative as well as associative meaning. Richardson's Harriet Byron, for instance, goes to a masquerade ball as an "Arcadian Princess" (*Sir Charles Grandison*, I : 115). Is this "Princess" the Pamela of Sidney's *Arcadia*? The masquerade in life and fiction represents an escape from the demands of realism, as it does from *les convenances*. The craze for masking in Europe of the seventeenth and eighteenth centuries imports into social life not only dramatic but novelistic elements. Novelists in turn quickly responded to the *ekphrastic* possibilities of such representation.[3]

By the nineteenth century, the interest in costuming oneself led to the private theatrical display known as the *tableau vivant*. Goethe records the interest in and possibilities of the *tableau vivant* in *Die Wahlverwandtschaften* (*Elective Affinities*) (1808). The lively if foolish Luciane becomes a member of the house party; she is much given to dressing up, to appearing in *Maskenkleid* (or masquerade-dress) as peasant-girl or fisher-girl, as a fairy and a flower-maiden, or even as an old woman (all highly symbolic roles). She produces *pantomimische Stellungen und Tänze* ("pantomimic representations and dances," 144) taking on various characters. On one occasion, she insists on representing Artemisia at the tomb of Mausolus. One of her admirers persuades the Architect to draw the "tomb" on the blackboard, as background for her act, but the Architect becomes carried away by his project and goes on and on drawing his ornamented tomb. Luciane has to stand there getting flustered, holding her urn, making too many gestures, so that at last "she seemed more a Widow of Ephesus [*mehr einer Witwe von Ephesus*] than a Queen of Caria" (146). The Architect's chalked *graphē* on the blackboard offers an iconic Death in competition with the living art that Luciane want to represent. (In her impatient opposition to Death she *is* a little like the Widow of Ephesus.) It is no wonder that she is pleased when the Count makes a happy suggestion: Why should this handsome company not engage in "representing real well-known paintings" (*wirkliche, bekannte Gemälde*)? This "new art of Representation" (*neue Art von Darstellung*) is very suitable for representing Van Dyck's painting of the alms given to Belisarius (157–158). In such a representation, the "real" historic painting, as a dead piece of art, is both erased and fulfilled, its static objects replaced by the novelist's own characters—in one of the highest liberties a novelist can take with an artist. Our associations with the famous (*bekannte*) work are disturbed, new elements inserted.

A number of nineteenth-century and early twentieth-century novelists engage in such operations of replacement, invoking either well-known painterly subjects or individual paintings as their characters disport themselves in numerous drawing-rooms. A late and highly effective example of novelistic use of the *tableaux vivants* can be found in Edith Wharton's *The House of Mirth* (1905). The heroine, Lily Bart, in her last phase of social success, participates in a party given by the newly rich Wellington Brys, who trust to "*tableaux vivants* and expensive music" to attract guests. Lily's appearance comes as the climax to a sequence of *ekphraseis*, as painting after painting is represented by fashionable women and girls. The first tableau is "a group of nymphs dancing across flower-strewn sward in the rhythmic postures of Botticelli's *Spring*" (140). The living pictures, carefully and professionally mounted and choreographed, succeed each other "with the rhythmic march of some splendid frieze in which the fugitive curves of living flesh and the wandering light of young eyes have been subdued to plastic harmony without losing the charm of life" (141).

When Lily appears as Joshua Reynolds's "Mrs. Lloyd," she elicits gasps of admiration, a tribute not to Reynolds but to her own beauty. "It was as though she had stepped, not out of, but into, Reynolds' canvas, banishing the phantom of his dead beauty by the beams of her living grace" (141–142).

In Henry James's *Wings of the Dove*, the lady in the Bronzino possessed by Lord Mark strikes Milly with her dead joylessness; here Lily restores life to the "portrait of a lady."

Wharton's description captures many of the ironies and pleasures of watching characters impersonate art. When characters deliberately choose to become overtly ekphrastic, they challenge the idea of *ekphrasis* itself in a degree of free play with it. The Brys' show takes place under "the flushed splendours of the Venetian ceiling" (139): the reference to Venice invokes sensuality, freedom, and complex boundary-crossing. So too the *tableaux vivants*, we are told, afford "magic glimpses of the boundary world between fact and imagination" (140). The characters in any novel exist in the "boundary world" between the "real life" with which we supply them and the shadow-world of figment and image. They themselves are nothing other than works of art, thin abstractions with less reality than the abstract playing cards and chessmen who supply the personages of Lewis Carroll's dreamworld: "'Who cares for you?' said Alice . . . 'You're nothing but a pack of cards!'" (*Alice in Wonderland*, 114). But novel-characters can paradoxically persuade us when they choose to *embody* artistic images that they have bodies—that they are incarnation, "living grace." They replace dead form by lively history.

Such characters may be slightly comic (like Goethe's Luciane), but they gain a certain beauty. On the whole, they have more success in such lucid moments than do most of the artist-characters in creating their pictures or sculptures. At the same time, the novelist gains all the advantages of *ekphrasis*, including not only dry mythological reference but also a fresh access of mythological significance. Masquerades, charades, and *tableaux* allow the novelist renewed access to the realm of myth officially excluded from Realism. We can see this when, for instance, Thackeray has Becky Sharp impersonate Clytemnestra in the charade (*Vanity Fair*, 596), or when Flaubert has Frédéric attend Rosanette's *bal masqué*, where he can encounter pastoral impersonators and others: "A little Watteau shepherd, blue and silver as moonlight, struck his crook against the thyrsus of a Bacchante, crowned with grapes, wearing a leopard skin on her left side" (*L'Education sentimentale*, 171). Wharton's nymphs rhythmically dancing closely resemble those in Longus. The novelist, like Longus, can gesture emphatically towards the ways in which this art outperforms the graphic. The *antigraphē* is superior—the impudent embodiment of a real artwork is conducted at the expense of the painter.

The presence of the art object, however, tells us that the novelist knows his/her work is being looked at—i.e., read. The ekphrastic moment, with its filmic effects, is a moment of textual self-consciousness that is even aggressively directed toward us. Paul Willemen has analyzed cinematic moments in which the viewer undergoes an imagined gaze of the camera. As in certain forms of theater, the novels in these moments, to borrow Barbara Freedman's phrase, *"show that they know that they are showing."* [4] The moment of formal *looking* nullifies to a certain extent the simple credence we are giving to the novel. We see ourselves mirrored in the characters looking at a painting or statue; they stand in for us, the readers going at a rhetorical artwork. In a sense, thus, the moment of *ekphrasis* undoes or at least countermands the work of the Rhexis whereby we are cut off from our world and jerked into the (often violent) world of the novel. The moment of looking at an artwork is a novelistic time of calm, for character and reader, a piece of leisure reminding us to go back to ourselves, even while those "selves" seem much less stable than they were. Our delight in *ekphrasis* is paid for by a measure of forced detachment from the novel. We can not *quite* lose ourselves in the story at this point; we know that, like the characters gazing at the artwork, what we "see" is external and even alien to us.

Yet as the characters gaze earnestly at painting or statue, we see that the art object, like the novel, carries meaning as a construct, and so too does our semblance, our brother, the "character." As Lacan indicates, the "self" is always representational. As the characters gaze learnedly or ignorantly at the artwork that reflects back on them, we see how the human being is constructed into an artifice, a "self" or "personality" that can be visibly knowable. We render ourselves officially into "personality" by a reference to a cultural world. If the characters reflect artworks, so do we. The *mise-en-abîme* confronts not the characters but ourselves with the abyss, with Aschenbach's feared *Abgrund*. We fear being overwhelmed and alienated by constructs, at the same time as we begin to intuit our own constructedness. Thus, we will feel an especial pleasure at the character's resistance to an artwork (as Lucy Snowe resists the "Cleopatra") and will have an especial affection for an inferior artwork that we are easily able to resist, like Pellerin's "Venetian" portrait of Rosanette. Longus' entire novel declares itself as a kind of resistance to an artwork, or a combat with it. We need moments in which we can resist art and artifacts, so declaring ourselves as human identities; hence, perhaps, the effectiveness of Proust's introduction of the commonplace objects of the villa, as something of a relief from Elstir's perfections.

Art objects, even in the reanimated *tableaux vivants*, still carry a load of history, and forever menace us with the weight of culture to be assimilated, the many meanings to be learned. They still belong to the objective world of form, to which the character must forever be obedient. We see the characters as types that repeat themselves (genuine Baskervilles). If I think I understand Wharton's Lily better because she resembles Reynolds's Mrs. Lloyd, then Lily is a repetitive *type*. It is amusing that Goethe's Luciane, in what seems a touch of *style indirect libre*, gives herself credit for *Persönlichkeit*—Personality—when what her style of *Darstellung* takes away *is* personality. The personal is to be swallowed up in the represented, sacrificed to significance. Such mimesis is ultimately death to personality. We are reassured only when we see the static imitation broken up and the characters restored to "themselves." In Wharton's novel it is an aspect of Lawrence Selden's subtle perversity that he can admire the mimesis so wholeheartedly, seeing "the real Lily Bart, divested of the trivialities of her little world" (142). He has made and will make no effort to come to Lily through those "trivialities" which are (in the novel) her real life; his desire for her beautiful stasis contributes to her decline and death. He is fated to see her in the end "with motionless hands and calm, unrecognizing face" (338)—dead at last, she is divested of the trivialities of her little world with a vengeance.

The moment of Lily's theatrical success as a picture points to the dangers of the aesthetic desire for the perfection of still form. All *ekphraseis* in novels of course play with that desire. They challenge us with our own complicity in the creation of a "virtual reality," the virtual painting that word-painting evokes, even while they place a check upon the spirit by bringing it back to tradition, to external form, to the public manner of our legends and myths as expressed in public places. *Ekphraseis* may even haunt us with their beauty, yet they remind us that we are subjected to cultural necessity. Our personal lives are perhaps not worth very much in the light of that higher beauty, that formal perfection. We may wish for signs of imperfection, of subjugation to time, of stone flowing like honey and drowning white marble violets. The characters may be permitted to be dashed, their spirits overcrowded by the magnificent completeness and certainty of the artistic image to which they (we are assured) can never fully aspire, as long as they are—what we wish to believe them to be—living flesh. The more we gaze on perfect art, the more we realize that life in the Red Dust is not to be perfection.

CHAPTER XVIII

Ekphrasis: Dreams and Food

The great trouble in human life is that looking and eating are two different operations. Only beyond the sky, in the country inhabited by God, are they one and the same operation.

—Simone Weil, *Waiting for God*

"I shall now be convinced that there is something in dreams."

—Lovelace in Samuel Richardson's *Clarissa*

Gandelin . . . asked him to eat an *empanada* that he carried.

—Montalvo, *Amadís de Gaula*

There would never have been any end to these evils, if the last course had not been brought in, thrushes made of fine wheat flour and stuffed with raisins and nuts. There followed quinces of Crete stuck about with thorns so as to look like sea-urchins.

—Petronius, *Satyricon*

A WONDERFUL DREAM

One major work of Western fiction stages itself at the outset as an *ekphrasis*, not of a painting, as is the case with Longus' novel, but as the fulfilled description of a dream: "As I walk'd through the wilderness of this world, I lighted on a certain place, where was a Denn; And I laid me down in that place to sleep: And as I slept I dreamed a Dream. I dreamed, and behold *I saw a Man clothed with Raggs standing in a certain place, with his face from his own House, a Book in his hand, and a great burden upon his Back* . . ." (*The Pilgrim's Progress*, 8).

Picking up a common convention of medieval poetic narrative (like Chaucer's *Boke of the Duchesse* or Guillaume de Lorris' *Le Roman de la Rose*), Bunyan derives some of his strength also from the prophetic mode associated with dreaming. At the same time, he destabilizes our certainty about what we are to expect. We are not much helped in this case by Bunyan's prefatory poem, explaining and defending his use of "*Dark Figures, Allegories*," for at the end he dissolves boundaries between narrator, character and reader:

> Would'st thou be in a Dream, and yet not sleep?
> Or would'st thou in a moment Laugh and Weep?
> Wouldest thou loose thy self, and catch no harm?
> And find thy self again without a charm?
> Would'st read thy self, and read thou know'st not what. . . (7)

There are no steady categories of subject and object, symbol and thing symbolized. And there is no firm partition between reader and what is read. When thou readest a novel, thou would'st read thy self, dear Reader. We lose (and *loose*) our-selves, we are both released and abandoned. We do not know how to "make sense" of experience, which is all a dream. Lewis Carroll is to play with that sense of uneasy uncertainty in *Alice's Adventures in Wonderland*, another dream-narrative: "Oh, I've had such a curious dream!" exclaims Alice at the end (110).

In contrast to novels that are all dream, some novels have scenes which we feel ought to be termed dreams but are not so defined: "Then I felt one of the hanged men seize me by the heel of my left foot. . . . Then the monster tore the skin off it, separated all the nerves, bared them, and set to playing on them as though on a musical instrument; but since I did not render a sound that pleased him, he began to twist them, as one tunes a harp. Finally he began to play on my leg, of which he had fashioned a psaltery. . . ." (Potocki, *Tales from the Saragossa Manuscript*, trans. Donougher, 50–51). These experiences may be the mere hal-lucinations of "the demoniac" who relates them, or they may be mystic dreams shared with the main narrator, or they may be Gothic realities—Jan Potocki (or whoever the author was) is content to leave the matter indeterminate. We can urge ourselves, as we do with *Alice*, to accept all as equally "real" in surrealist narratives.

Here are the two extremes: all is a dream OR everything is non-dream. If *all* is dream, much depends on the dreamer, as we understand in *Through the Looking-Glass*, where we share some of Alice's anxiety when she sees the snoring Red King and is told "you're only one of the things in his dream. You know very well you're not real" (168). A dream-tale, far from distinguishing between life and dream, urges us to consider the possibility that (in the words of Calderón's title) *La Vida es Sueño*: Life is a Dream.

Paradoxically, we arrive at the same point in accepting stories in which hallucinatory episodes are not to be distinguished from reality. Perception of the relation Life / Dream has various aspects: On the one hand, real life becomes mere illusion, *maya*. On the other, all reality is the work of vital consciousness, and we must dream when we are awake, our world kept going through our mind-factured perceptions, constructions, arrangements. Yet we are also to feel such endeavors are not desperate individual *bricolages*, but partake of the sacred, "for everything sacred has the substance of dreams and memories," as the Siamese prince says in Yuko Mishima's *Spring Snow* (*Haru no Yuki*, 1970). The prince adds "Dreams, memories, the sacred—they are all alike in that they are beyond our grasp. Once we are even marginally separated from what we can touch, the ob-ject is sanctified; it acquires . . . the quality of the miraculous. . . . How strange man is! His touch defiles and yet he contains the source of miracles" (*Spring Snow*, trans. Gallagher, 46). There is an element of awe in the encounter with a dream, as Mishima suggests. The dream interwoven in novelistic narrative increases our awe of the human as the source of the miraculous. We sense that the miraculous and sacred emerge to us from internal and chaotic activity such as dreaming—or (as in Proust) remembering.

A novel customarily contains both tropic Moments (or Stations): the Art-work in *ekphrasis*, and the Dream. Both are tropes of contemplation. The Artwork helps us with recognition of our familiar cultural world, our public images, his-torically valuable modes of imaginative apprehension. There is a limit to the degree to which the ekphrastic art object can disturb us. The Dream is not only a greater challenge to our powers of interpretation, but also a disturber of all sorts of systems of separation, of taxonomies. In the Dream, rather more than in the Artwork, we make contact with imagination, and with the imaginative element in all consciousness. The labyrinth may have been gloomy, but we could persuade ourselves it was external to us, a prison in which the real self wanders. Now the labyrinthine is indeed thrown inward, while we are enfolded more deeply into the narrative, in what might be called an Escher-effect, thinking of works by that artist (such as *The Print-Gallery*) in which there is a collapse of boundaries between observer and observed, subject and object.

Seeing ourselves through the characters' experience, we cannot deny our own degrees of complicity and of accomplishment in making the world through imagination, through consciousness. We know, too, that consciousness is deeply irrational. Even in the most "moral" and rationally "wholesome" novels, characters live in dreamlike identifications—as in *Little Women*, where the characters identify themselves with Bunyan's personages, and their Massachusetts landscape with his mythical one. If there is a collapse of boundaries and an acknowledgment of the power of the deep mind there is not, however, in the Novel, as in the production of some theorists such as Lacan and his followers, any desire to erase the concept of "self," a motive of much recent theory. Rather, the Novel summons us to a harder task, the acknowledgment of deep self, and its connection with the selfness of others. The trope of the Dream activitates such knowledge and acknowledgment.

CHARACTERS' DREAMS

Few novels feel the need to emphasize their own dreamlikeness or the dreamlikeness of life to the extent found in the work of Bunyan and Carroll. Yet all novels participate in dreaminess and dream-likeness. Dreams loom before us in novels, posing us. Characters take up the labor of dream-work for us. Any dream once described—and a dream must be described in order to come into the narrative—works like a picture, or, rather, like a picture described. Some characters are very conscientious about describing their dreams, like Mishima's Kiyoaki Matsugae, who keeps a dream-journal. We are exhorted, in effect, to trust his dream-records because Kiyoaki is very exact, with a "compulsion for exact description" (83) and a corresponding refusal of interpretation. A lengthy dream set down in his journal in *Spring Snow* follows reader and characters through the novel and the entire series:

> I was sitting on a splendid chair in the middle of a room. . . . Throughout the dream, I felt as if I had a headache. And this was because I was wearing a tall, pointed gold crown set with all sorts of precious stones. Above my head, a huge flock of peacocks were perched on a maze of beams . . . And from time to time white droppings fell on my crown.
>
> Outside the sun was scorching. It was beating down in a desolate garden run wild. . . . I could see the trunks of palm trees and, behind them, piled-up white clouds, dazzling and unmoving.

Then I looked down at my hand and saw that I was wearing an
emerald ring. . . .   (Trans. Gallagher, 82–83)

Such a dream, full of important imagery, bright color, and sensual surprise, provides substance for mental rumination over a long period. We may feel it is almost
too good; we can envy the character for such interesting dream-work or blame
the author for letting the dream rise above the narrative. But we canot ignore the
teasing invitation to interpret, if the dreamer cannot or will not.

A dream always enters a narrative text as an *ekphrasis*. This is true in poetic
narrative, where the description of a dream as an arrangement of figures and
objects must always provide some interpretation as it continues. Medieval literature is notably rich in poetic narratives based on dream-visions. A work based on
a narrated dream is likely to include superadded art objects, *ekphrasis* within, as
in Bunyan we get the images in Interpreter's House. In Chaucer's *The Book of the
Duchess* (c. 1370), the Dreamer dreams that he awakens in his room on a lovely
May morning, and finds that his windows have been freshly glazed, the stained-
glass panes telling "hoolly al the story of Troye" (line 326). In William Langland's
Piers Plowman (1362–1400), we have a late but direct descendant of the *Kebētos
Pinax*; the Dreamer in the Malvern Hills sees not only the "Field full of Folk" but
also various objects in a landscape. Holy Church offers herself as the intepreter,
and explains, for instance, that a high tower is the home of Truth, while a deep
dungeon is the Castle of Care. The most outstanding dream artist is Dante, whose
entire *Commedia* is a form of narrated dream-vision, a complex unfolding *ekphrasis*
with many subordinate *ekphraseis* of art objects and inscriptions stored within it.

That a story is a dream assures the reader that human psychic energy is at
work here, and some degree of mystery. But the dream being told necessarily
carries with it some slight estrangement. The *reader* did not dream this dream,
any more than paint the ekphrastic picture. The reader's job is to contemplate
and analyze. In prose fictions, the dream is usually inset, very knowingly, as an
example of an *ekphrasis* to which we are to bring our own powers of judgment.
In *Du côté de chez Swann*, for instance, Swann, now at the end of his love for
Odette, tells the dream in which he is walking among strange hills with several
friends, Odette among them, but accompanied also by an unknown young man
in a fez and Napoleon III (445–447). Here the reader, like the narraator and other
characters, can join in the game of deciphering the dream—in the novel's own
terms, that is, believing in the "real" existence of Swann. We may even conclude
with Marcel that the unknown young man in the fez is another figure of Swann
himself.

The narrator, however, then amplifies his identification: "like certain novelists, he [Swann] had distributed his personality between two personages, the
one who dreamed the dream, and someone whom he saw before him" (447). We
go beyond Marcel the straightforward narrator in recognizing in this interpretation of the dream the key to Marcel Proust's own splitting of himself into the
author who actually writes the novel, and the *moi*, the character who narrates it
as if its events were lived experiences. This wink, as it were, at the audience seems
an ingeniously subtle example of what David Lodge terms "frame-breaking."

Proust opens up the possibility that the entire narrative might be an extended dream retold, or more truly that any individual human life is an extended dream and the narrative of it but a dream. "Life, what is it but a dream?" as Lewis Carroll asks in the poem that serves as *envoi* to *Through the Looking-Glass* (245). But Proust does not have to commit himself or us to any such absolute philosophy or to the reductiveness of the dream-vision category. His narrative remains alert, complex, catching numerous other dreams in its net.

Novelistic artworks, whether real, like the *Mona Lisa*, or made up by the novelist, like Boomer Petway's works, belong to the public realm. We see them in the context of the sunshine world of public order. There we publicly make sense (or pretend to make sense) of tradition, myth, and symbol. The novelistic dream is a much murkier affair. Though it too reveals itself in the terms of traditional symbols (known to dream-interpreters from Artemidorus to Jung), it allows us to consider the participation of consciousness in symbol-creation prior to the art-works that turn up on public walls. Although historically subsequent to all art objects produced by the culture, and thus derivative, the character's dream expresses itself in the ablative case, as it were, absolute, absolved from that chain of causation in which it is mere effect.

The dream-*ekphrasis* is a complement to—and opposite of—the *ekphrasis* of the artwork. The character's dream comes from within and does not impose itself from without. It pushes itself towards articulation, towards a public world that has some difficulty accommodating it. Art-*ekphrasis*, on the other hand, questions the value of the merely private and seduces us into participation in the public, shared world. The dominance of the artwork saps the notion of personality, as either ontologically true or aesthetically interesting. The rest of the novel must exist in some tension with the interpolated *ekphrasis* of an artwork. Art's challenge to the personal is (in Nietzschean terms) Apollonian. It is (and here I use Nietzsche to contradict him) the Dionysian dream which supports individuality and subscribes to the notion of the personal. The dream, insofar as it becomes intelligible at all, supports individual personality at the cost of an irruption of the inchoate and disorderly into a world of supposed order.

Were dreams universally derided as mere incoherence, they would not be interesting. But we have, historically, employed many of the same energies to examine our dreams as to examine our works of art. Dreams and artistic representations are alike in that they attract close hermeneutic examination. Long before Freud—whose reading of novels may have influenced his theories—dreams were thought to contain valuable material. Dreams had long been considered private communications by gods to particular mortals in particular circumstances (an idea that has never quite vanished). But dreams were also thought to have general content that could yield to public interpretation. Artemidorus of Daldis, in his *Oneirokritika*, or *Dream Analysis* (second century A.D.), claimed he had collected dreams from different types of people throughout most of the Roman Empire. His approach is what we today would call "psychological," but he inherited the religious wisdom of ages that held dreams to be meaningful. As John J. Winkler observes, Artemidorus inherited a "very extensive literature" on dreams, though his own theory is "pointedly empirical" and "naturalistic." "The agent who constructs the dream and sends it as a useful message is the dreamer's own soul [*psychē*]. Artemidorus' language varies between 'the dream says' and 'the soul says'" (*Constraints of Desire*, 25).

Artemidorus was the contemporary of some of our Greek novelists. If the novels that have come down to us from antiquity seem much more "modern" than Artemidorus, it may be largely because authors and readers of fiction (unlike doctors) are under no pressure to make a diagnosis. A dream's meaning can be left open, in older novels or new, as it cannot be in handbooks and case histories. Novelists and their characters *and* their readers (then and now) can share both naturalistic and "supernatural" or metanatural interpretations of a novelistic dream—and readers, like characters, can be naturalistic and "superstitious" simultaneously. A novelistic dream encourages a hermeneutics of prophecy, because we believe that this dream may very well be "fulfilled" in some way within the story. The dream can foretell the future, or act as a prompting or encouragement from the Divine. Yet a character's dream is also—and always—a message from the psyche, the soul talking to itself.

The impressive array of dreams in novels of all periods points to the interest in the internal, the subjective experience, an interest predating the arrival of the novels we possess. It was the duty of medical patients in antiquity to dream; there were special rooms set apart in the temples of Asklepios for that purpose, rooms of "incubation"; the Novel too was incubated amid important dreams.

When a dream occurs during the narration of a novel, it is likely to be much more disturbing to both characters and reader than the *ekphrasis* of a work of art. Neither reader nor character can be certain how it is to be taken. Yet, even more urgently than the work of art, the dream cries out for interpretation. The character describes the dream, invokes a nonverbal experience in words, in an *ekphrasis* that cannot be checked by the audience against some preexistent reality or model. The *Aithiopika* supplies us with a good example. "Hardly had they sipped a tiny bit of sleep so that their eyelids closed, when Charikleia was oppressed by the following dream. A man with unkempt hair, and eyes hidden in ambush, and a bloody hand with one blow of his sword took out her right eye. She immediately screamed and called to Theagenes, telling him she had lost her right eye" (I:64). Charikleia awakened touches her right eye and realizes she has not lost it. She then dismisses the illusion: *Onar ēn*, "it was a dream"; *echō ton opthalmon*, "I have my eye"; *Tharsei, Theagenes*, "Be of good cheer, Theagenes" (64–65). She then explains her dream, giving us a new *ekphrasis* of the scene already familiar to us from the narrator's account. Her own account emphasizes the huge strength of the man, stronger than Theagenes himself, and supplies erotic details we did not know before: the man attacked "even while I was resting on your knees." Charikleia then begins to interpret the dream; she would rather, she says, think it means simply that she is about to lose her eye than that it should function as a more remote allegory—for she fears it must mean she will lose Theagenes, who is her eye and her soul and all.

Knemon tries to take away this deadly apprehension by substituting another interpretation in mechanical application of the dream-books' symbol equivalents: the dream of the loss of her right eye means that her father is dead. Charikleia points out that this is also an unhappy interpretation, but she says, with the heartlessness of youth and love, she would rather it were true than the other meaning, the loss of her lover. Knemon then suggests that they leave off dream interpretation (*oneirōttein*) and inquiring into fantasies (*kai phantasias ezetazontes*) and consider their real situation (66).

Knemon thus makes a division, abrupt and absolute, between the reality, the true and the fantastic, the merely dreamlike. But of course the text cannot agree with Knemon, for we know that any dream important enough to be produced within the novel *must* have a meaning within that novel. Heliodorus' novel is well supplied with dreams produced by different characters: Kalasiris dreams of Odysseus; Charikles dreams his worrying dream that Charikleia is snatched from him and taken to the land of shadows. This latter dream produces a number of interpretations offered by Charikles himself, by Kalasiris in his pretended role, and by the reader—and all of these forecasts prove false, while the dream yet proves to be satisfactorily "true" in relation to the outcome of the novel. Charikleia's dream also stimulates us into interpretation. The rough hairy man resembles a bandit—does he represent a renewed attack of the bandit Thyamis upon her? What is her "right eye" to represent? Actual organ of sight?—Theagenes?—her father? Given the situation of her dream, the reader is urged by this text to think of the nightmare as a production of Charikleia's own *psychē*, a fantasy related to her desire for the physically close Theagenes, and her fear of losing her virginity. More than one interpretation could be right.

Theagenes also dreams. When imprisoned by the Persians, he dreams that Kalasiris—or a god assuming Kalasiris' appearance—comes to him and speaks a riddling verse, saying that he is to go to the land of Ethiopia in the company of a maiden, and will escape the prison of Arsaké tomorrow. Theagenes insists upon putting the gloomiest interpretation on this dream, connecting this maiden with *the* Maiden, Persephone; he believes he will die tomorrow (*Aithiopika*, III:24–25). Such a misinterpretation obviously adds to the reader's pleasure in the happy upshot (what Tolkien calls "eucatastrophe"). There is something comic about Theagenes' dogged pessimism as he interprets him dream—unlike most readers of their own dreams, who stretch themselves and the dream images in reaching for a favorable significance.

A salient example of such favorable misinterpretation is found in Richardson's *Clarissa*. Separated from the woman he abused and raped, Robert Lovelace has a detailed and disturbing dream, involving first confused conflict and then incapacity. Pinned down and almost stifled by his uncle's "great black mantle," Lovelace is forced to watch helplessly as Clarissa departs from him, rising into "a firmament . . . crouded with golden Cherubs and glittering Seraphs." Lovelace in the dream desperately snatches Clarissa's "azure robe" but finds himself tumbling downwards into "a hole more frightful than that of Elden. . . . I awaked in a panic" (VII, 147–148). Later, believing that he will be united with Clarissa in marriage, Lovelace reinterprets his dream. A vision like a baroque painting of the Assumption of the Virgin now turns into a cheerful rococo decoration, and the confused dream-story becomes narrative carried beyond the boundaries of the dream. The "golden Cherubims and Seraphims" now become indicators of "the charming little Boys and Girls" the married pair will have. Had he not awakened, he supposes, he would have been "soused into some river" and then, "mundified or purified," he would have been cared for by the bright angelic form who conducted Clarissa away in the original dream: "carried . . . by the same bright Form (waiting for me upon the mossy banks) to my beloved Girl; and we should have gone on cherubiming of it and carolling to the end of the chapter" (VII, 176–177).

Lovelace becomes a novelist in amplifying his dream. He re-creates it as the artist, erasing the panicky role of dreamer. His new narrative turns to the image of the river, where the Angel of the Fresh Start will await this wet swain (soused like D'Urfé's Celadon) on the "mossy banks." Angels turn into Cupidons. While he is master of the *ekphrasis*, Lovelace thinks, he is master of the dream—and of his own story, and Clarissa's story. He thus tries to take over from the novelist. But in novels, nobody is truly master of the dream.

In dealing with works of art, a character may perform a perverse interpretation and merely add to our sense of the humor of the situation—as a Mr. Smith or Trimalchio does. But perverse dream interpretation is a more serious matter, even though dreams so persistently share many of the qualities of works of art. A work of art (whether as allusion or new invention) speaks of control; it belongs to a world of objective images, and the culture bears partial responsibility for it. But a dream—even a happy dream—arises within, arises from confusion, and its vagaries when contemplated are urgent and uncomfortable.

Not to understand a painting is only that. Not to understand one's own dream is not to understand oneself. Yet *no* dream is ever felt to be perfectly understood. The characters working away at their dreams remind us of ourselves and our intimations of trouble, confusion, inconsistency that rise through our dreams and mock our pretensions to unified personality, to control of self and world. In the figure of Eros, we saw our desires, and the nature of our yearning, crystallize. In character's dreams we see the inner havoc, the necessary upheaval and discontinuity, wrought by inward desire. The dream is the work of what might be called the fluid Eros, the Eros of humors and hormones and psychological experience, pricking us towards our discomfort—Eros the lover of conflict and surprise. Watching the characters dream, we participate again—and consciously—in our sense of ourselves as dreamers.

In modern novels (e.g., Philip Roth's *Portnoy's Complaint*) a character may relate a dream to a psychiatrist, the official repository for dreams, who has high-class books on dream analysis by Freud and Jung to help him. In novels of the past, as now, dreams are related by a character to a friend most often, or to an official dream-interpreter. Hence Charikles tells his dream to the priest Kalasiris. In Montalvo's *Amadís de Gaula*, King Perion relates his dream to three trusted clerics. Each gives an interpretation, but the wisest, Ungan the Picard, derives from the dream information that has escaped the others—"Now I wish to tell you what you are keeping most hidden [*muy encubierto*] and think that nobody knows. You love where already you have accomplished your will, and she whom you love is wonderfully beautiful" (I:251). Perion has not realized that in telling the dream of the locked room (the enclosure of his secret, covered-up *encubierto* self) he was giving so much away. The heart that the lady of the locked room takes out of his breast and throws into the river is his lost child. The reader admires Ungan's deft and probing analysis, perceiving the shallowness of the first clerical interpreter, who read the dream politically, as the story of an attempt to be made on the King's kingdom. Dream-interpreters have an important job to do—a job often misperformed. But the primary interpreter is always the Dreamer, and in the Dreamer our anxiety continues to reside. Even when the dream is analyzed there is always a residue, a dream-state that cannot be explained, or controlled. Dreams tell us that the first Locked Room Mystery is the mystery of the hidden consciousness or secret unknown self.

Dreams are certainly a feature of many literary kinds other than the Novel. Dreams are found in ancient tragedy, for instance, and in epic. Obviously the earliest Western novelists were aware of these precedents. Characters in plays can tell their dreams; narrators of epics have the advantage of being able to describe them. Sometimes this is very vividly done. In the *Aeneid*, for instance, just as Troy starts to burn, Aeneas has a dream-vision of the dead Hector. Hector appears to him as in death, bloody and dust-covered, the way he looked after being dragged at Achilles' chariot wheels. There is immense pathos in Aeneas' address to this figure, the man whom he sees as terribly changed from his former self (*quantum mutatus ab illo*, II, line 274). Aeneas' first impulse, however, is to address this hopeless and bloody phantom as if Hector still were the powerful chief, the great leader. *O lux Dardaniae!* "O light of the Dardan people" (line 281). In reading this moving—because partly foolish—line, we realize the extent to which Aeneas (the unconscious Aeneas, the dreamer) has not accepted the loss of the Hector he remembers. Even though Aeneas has apparently assimilated the fact of Hector's death, that death is not entirely digested at all levels of the mind. Virgil, of all poets, knows how terribly hard it is to let anything go. But for Aeneas in his disastrous present there is no great Hector to turn to. The most that phantom can do is to warn him of the imminent destruction of Troy, and advise him to get away. This scene is one of Virgil's many strokes that tell us what loss means. David Quint points to the pattern of "the Trojans' nostalgic attempts to repeat or relive their past" in the first part of the *Aeneid* (*Epic and Empire*, 56). Aeneas voices that fruitless yearning in his first and most unguarded response to his dream.

A tragic or an epic artist can narrate a dream as well as any novelist. All of these literary dream-users are related to the religious writer who tells us prophetic dreams. Dreams in Western religious literature are works of prophetic content that look forward less to what a character is to do than to what is to happen to him. Biblical emphasis rests largely on the power of the interpreter—the dreamer is often helpless, or relatively inert. Thus, Joseph in prison interprets the dreams of two fellow-prisoners, Pharaoh's butler and his baker; one dream signifies the restoration of kingly favor, the other the imminent loss of life (Genesis 40). Yet there is nothing the butler or the baker could do at this juncture to accelerate or avert the outcomes. The emphasis is on the event, and even more on the knowledge of the outcome. The knowing Joseph himself is capable of doing something about outcome when he interprets Pharaoh's dream of the fat and lean kine and corn, but Pharaoh's dream itself just signifies what *is to happen*. No interest in this case attaches to the dreamer, Pharaoh.

Epics likewise prefer event-oriented dreams. But the point of an epic dream is customarily to make a character *do* something. The epic dreamer is customarily more active in relation to his fate than the Biblical dreamer. In novels, too, the dreamer may be called upon through a dream to act, but the action quotient is usually much lower. Emphasis is thrown on the dream it-self, and on the dreamer. Even when interpreters (like *Amadís de Gaula*'s Ungan) are present, as they often are, they are not central like Joseph, or like the Daniel who not only interprets the dream of Nebuchadnezzar but also recalls it for him (Daniel 2). In the Bible, dreamer and exegete are distinguished, and it is the prophetic exegete who matters. In novels, in contrast, the dreamer has center stage, and the interpreters—even clever ones—are peripheral. What we (inner exegete and external reader alike) are all interpreting is the complex condition of the dreamer, and not primarily action or event, even though an eventual and event-ful outcome (as in Heliodorus) may be involved. Heliodorus' whole novel is constructed on prophetic lines, as to some extent all novels must be. *Aithiopika* is perhaps not really more prophetic than, for instance, Mishima's *Spring Snow*. *Aithiopika* clearly displays the displacement of the religiously pro-phetic by the characterological. King Perion in *Amadís* cannot get rid of his dream by taking some particular action. His job is to contain the dream, to hang on to it and yet to express it. The strange residue of the dream itself re-mains, haunts us, the readers, even though *we* know all about Elisena and her pregnancy and about Child of the Sea (Amadís)—which is a lot more than Perion knows.

In a novel, the dreamer's creativity in being able to produce the dream, a moving picture in brief and cryptic narrative, is counteracted—or, rather, supple-mented by—by our sense of the weakness of the dreamer. The dreams of a novel character inevitably serve to increase our sense of that character's vulnerability. The allocation of novelistic dream to a character has the dual effect of strength-ening the impression of psychological depth while at the same time weakening the character, who becomes less controlling or heroic in direct proportion to the ability to produce vivid dreaming. The dream arises from inner disturbance. The novelistic dreamer, even if a partial exegete or expounder of the visionary expe-rience, remains to some extent a pitiful dupe, like Nebuchadnezzar, who says "I saw a dream which made me afraid, and the thoughts upon my bed and the visions of my head troubled me" (Daniel 4:5). Biblical narrative treats the hero—the expounder—we have no time to waste in sympathy for irreligious dolts. But in novelistic narrative, we do have time to give sympathy to the perturbed dream-ers and dolts—who may be the heroine or hero of our tale.

The occurrence of a dream in a novel indicates some important inner change undergone by the character, customarily some change in level of matu-rity or in aspects of self-vision or integration. In *Dream of the Red Chamber* we are given a long dream of Bao-yu, a dream of ladies and brightness ending in the vision of a dark ravine, "where only thorn-trees grew," an abyss with "demons and water monsters" that try to drag him down (I:128–148). The exciting dream culminates in ejaculation; the entire dream signifies both the illusory nature of human love and the young boy's sexual coming-of-age. Meaning is certainly sup-plied by the ending, to the comic embarrassment of the reader as well as the hero. We sympathize with the boy who is not in control of hitherto unrecognized forces within himself. If he is certainly not a hero in the grand style, in compensation he gains in our sense of his interior complexity.

If dreams effectively indicate multilayered personality, they also indicate struggles, strainings at the sutures of personality. We know that the character does not exist as a solid block but is really (like the Rock of Gibraltar itself) riven with tunnels, fissures, sibylline hollows, and caves. The dream connects with the labyrinth, bespeaks the labyrinth within. There are unknown spaces, a dark ravine rimmed by dry thorn-trees, "a hole more frightful than that of Elden"—and what is Hell but a labyrinth with no exit? There is always a fear that the character could collapse in upon itself, fall into its own inner spaces. The eighteenth century became very self-conscious and embarrassed about the matter of dreaming; as I have argued elsewhere, dreams became very largely the fictional property of female characters, or of villains, for good men, who were supposed to be "manly," in control of the real world, could not afford to be presented in dream states. A wicked Lovelace may dream, a virtuous Sir Charles Grandison should not. Epic dreams seemed no longer possible. Dreams betray the ruinous (or ruin-prone) nature of a "character." Leaving men without dreams, the eighteenth-century was in danger of constructing the male sex as the sex with no psyche. Gothic novels had to bring back male dreaming, within landscapes and stories curiously resembling the content of female dreams in fiction earlier in the period.[1]

In novels both of antiquity and of modern times, intense dreaming is associated with illness. It belongs, or may partly belong, to a state that requires a cure—although that does not discount the importance of potential revelation within a dream. In Charles Dickens's *Bleak House*, Esther Summerson, dangerously ill with smallpox, has a delirious dream that "strung together somewhere in great black space, there was a flaming necklace, or ring, or starry circle of some kind, of which *I* was one of the beads!" She speaks passionately of the "inexplicable agony and misery to be a part of the dreadful thing" (544). The reader who tries to interpret this is likely to find a disturbing meaning that will not go away just because Esther recovers. The "flaming necklace" in the "great black space" is obviously the universe itself; the dream seems to protest against existence, against survival as a lonely entity forced into an inexorable system of being—"the dreadful thing." Such a strong sense of the horror of living cannot well be erased by any particular benefits accorded the character. The reader—and I think, the author too—has to work at reconciling this vision with the more optimistic material elsewhere in the story.

True, dreams can act as omens of success. So a dream does in *Alexander Romance*, when Alexander, depressed after being first repulsed by Tyre, has an encouraging vision: "He saw in a dream a satyr, one of the attendants of Dionysus, giving him a curd cheese; he took it from him and trampled it underfoot. When he awoke, Alexander related his dream to an interpreter, who told him: 'You will rule over all Tyre, and it shall become subject to you, because the satyr gave you the cheese, and you trampled it underfoot'" (*The Greek Alexander Romance*, trans. Stoneman, 70). Dreams work in puns—long before Freud: the cheese (*tyros*) functions as *Tyre*. Here the dream shores up Alexander's power— but at his expense, too; he cannot know what his own dream means but has to consult an interpreter. Another vision, which seems even more grandiose, is darker; a visionary being who proves to be the god Serapis appears to Alexander. Serapis' very reassurances point out to Alexander his human weakness; the god asks ironically if he can move a mountain and Alexander has to reply "No."

Alexander asks to be shown how long he has left to live but the god tells him it is better for mortals not to know (66, 67, 142–143). Divine reassurances about the long life and prosperity of *Alexandria* are double-edged—for Alexander the man, this metonymy is not truly consoling. Such apparitions tie in with the cascade of rebuking omens clustering at the end of Alexander's story, admonishing the king for his *hubris* and warning him of imminent death. Contact with the divine has become ambiguous and menacing, and the punning shifts of sense seem less oracular than psychological. It would not hurt the story at all if we believed the vision of Serapis was conjured up solely by Alexander's psyche. He is helpless, not like the conquering hero to whom divine assurance is vouchsafed.

Dreams typically occur in moments of weakness, even though the dream itself may not be weakening. In the *Ephesiaka*, Habrokomes is punished by whipping, torture, and imprisonment for his refusal to make love to Manto. Abandoned in his prison while his beloved is carried off, he has a dream: "he thought he saw his own father Lykomedes in black clothing travelling across all the lands and seas, and arriving finally at his prison where he delivered him from his chains and took him from his prison-cell. Habrokomes himself became a horse and rushed along through many lands pursuing a mare, and in the end finding the female he became again a man" (28).

This dream revives hope in Habrokomes, we are told. We can readily understand this, even though there is a narrative gap between the encouraging dream and anything good actually happening to Habrokomes. There is no interpreter present, so we must work at this dream for ourselves. On the plot level: Habrokomes will be freed and will catch up with Anthia. On the psychological level: Habrokomes will grow into the maturity of his father and will achieve full manliness in regaining his wife—he needs to become a *man*. But, like all dreams in prose fiction, this has an extra content, gratuitous detail—as Virgil's vision of Hector appearing to Aeneas, for example, does not. Alexander's cream cheese is Tyre—but why the extra pun of the *satyr*? Why is Habrokomes' father dressed in black? And why does Habrokomes become a horse? His metamorphosis reminds us a little of Lucius' in *The Golden Ass*. But the word for female horse (*thēleian*) introduces the idea of the female breast—so an infantile content (colt seeks mare for the teat) is introduced into the sexual pursuit. We can contemplate the dream with interest even when we know the outcome of the story. Fictional dreams are like movies. They contain renewing images, they offer news that cannot be consumed or erased by the other news, the bigger dream, which is the novel itself.

The arrival of a fictional dream creates in the reader a heightened awareness, a pleasure in having one's hermeneutic capacities exercised, but this pleasure is rarely, if ever, unmixed with melancholy. The beginning of Proust's *A la recherche de temps perdu* deals extensively with states of sleeping and dreaming, as states that dissolve the ego:

> as I did not know where I was, I did not even know in the first instant who I was; I had only in its first simplicity the sentiment of existence as it might quiver in the depths of an animal; I was more denuded than the caveman; but then the memory—not yet of the place where I was, but of several of the places where I had lived and where I could have been—came to me like succor from on high in order to pull me from

the nothingness which I would not have been able to leave by myself; I passed in a second through centuries of civilization, and the image confusedly glimpsed of kerosene lamps, and then of shirts with turned-down collars, recomposed little by little the original traits of my *I*.

(Du côté de chez Swann, 12)

"Mon moi"—my I, the "I myself," my *me*, comes from civilization and is always in danger of flying away. This confused awaking brings a sense of loss, the melancholy of not being. The metamorphosis into an animal is included in this paragraph ("the sentiment of existence as it might quiver in the depths of an animal"). Proust also summons the cave, the pit, the hole, in his references; *l'homme des cavernes* for the "caveman" is not only one "scientificallly" defined phase of mankind on the way to civilization, but the individual thrown into the pit, naked as Joseph. In a later description of sleep and dreaming, Marcel is mourning the death of his grandmother, and the dream arranges itself about her. To dream is thus to visit the land of the dead:

World of sleep where internal consciousness, rendered dependent on the disturbances of our organs, accelerates the rhythm of the heart or of respiration, because the same dose of fright, or sadness, of remorse, acts with a hundredfold power if it is thus injected into our veins; as soon as, in order to travel the arteries of the subterranean city, we are embarked on the black waves of our own blood as on an interior Lethe of sixfold windings, great solemn figures appear before us, approach us and depart from us, leaving us in tears. I searched in vain for the form of my grandmother as soon as I had reached these sombre porches; I knew, however, that she still existed, but with a diminished life, as pale as that of memory; the obscurity increased, and the wind; my father who was to take me to her did not arrive.

(Sodome et Gomorrhe, 184–185)

Proust and Marcel recollect the sixth book of the *Aeneid*, the descent to the Underworld, conflating Styx and Lethe. The deep dark muddy place is within; the river of memory and forgetting is the river of the circulating blood, the journey downward a journey into the interior, which itself provides river, bank, pit, and labyrinth. This dream, which opens with solemnly confused recollections of the *Aeneid* and of Dante's *Inferno*, degenerates ekphrastically, refuses to maintain either a stable picture or a stable pictorial tone. The dream-narrative itself degenerates, ending in nonsense words.

The scrambling of logic that occurs with the recitation of dreams in prose narrative may be one of the most valuable properties of the recounting of such dreams in our novels. We are to be reminded of our intuitions, our emotional and physical lives, that cannot respond to argument or strict rationality. Heart and lungs move in sub-rational responses. Dream-narrative inset in regular novelistic narration changes the pulse of that narration. The dream of Habrokomes accelerates the tempo, whereas Marcel's dream about his dead grandmother acquires rhythms at once nervous and slow, and acts as a *rallentando*.

So too does the important dream of Amadís de Gaula, at a crucial point in his life. He has been enjoying great success when his lady Oriana, misled into jealousy, sends him her cruel letter of dismissal. Amadís takes off on his own, running away from his life, and on his unhappy way to nowhere has a dream:

> . . . and he started thinking about a dream which he had had the night before. It seemed to him that he was at the top of a hill covered with trees, on his horse and armed, and closely surrounded by a great crowd of people who manifested great happiness, and that there arrived among them a man who said to him "Sir, eat what I carry in this box!," and that he made him eat of it; and it seemed to taste like the most bitter thing that could be. And feeling after that much dismayed and disconsolate, he loosened the reins of his horse and went wheresoever it would go; and it seemed that the people who before had been happy became so sad that he felt grief on their account. But the horse went on with him for a distance and brought him to a forest, where he saw a place of some stones surrounded by water. And leaving the horse and his arms, he disposed himself as if hoping to take some rest there; and there came to him an old man dressed in the clothes of a religious order, and this man took him by the hand, coming close to him, showing pity, and spoke to him some words in a language he did not understand, and at that he awakened. And now it seemed to him that although he had taken it for a vain thing, it would come to pass for him as truth.
>
> (*Amadís de Gaula*, I:681)

The narrative itself tells us that this is a plotted dream, that if we watch it carefully we can guess what is going to happen; as the note in the 1987 Madrid edition points out, this is a "premonitory dream, one of the parts of which is told *a posteriori* and has been completed." Inspecting this *sueño premonitorio*, the reader knows what part refers to previous action, and we can also be sure on the plot-level that Amadís, after a time of more suffering, will be rescued from his bad state, some religious personage assisting.

   Yet it is not this *premonitory* content that interests us, but the content that is superfluous to the narrative's needs. We already know that Amadís is miserable because of Oriana's letter. The dream, however, tells us more about the experience of coming-to-grief; we dwell with Amadís' sorrow as some new thing, our attention heightened by the riddles of the dream. There is no interpreter to appear straight away and tell Amadís and ourselves what the details mean. It is up to the reader (and Amadís, of course) to divine what are the bitter contents of the mysterious box or chest—on one level it is Oriana's bitter letter, but on another it must be Amadís' own heart. The dream is both succinct and diffusive. One of the most remarkable things about it is the manner in which it shows Amadís, like Proust's Swann, dispersed among a number of dream personages. The mysterious man bearing the box may in some sense be Amadís himself, who bears his own heart in his own chest (even if on another level we might hazard a guess that this intruder is an Eros, like Dante's stern *Amor*). More remarkable still, the crowd, the *mucha gente*, is also Amadís, while his feelings are dispersed among them so that he treats those feelings as if they were partly objective, belonging to somebody else (*la gente que antes alegre estava se tornava tan triste que él havía duelo dello*). He feels grief partly because he sees that *they* are sad. Amadís himself is singularly himself, spectacularly lonely, and yet also pluralized in the dream. At some level the old man who comes to Amadís in such a friendly fashion may also an aspect of Amadís himself, but a future self that he does not yet understand, who speaks in a language he cannot comprehend. The dream itself thus reminds both Dreamer and Reader that efforts must be made to comprehend, that reality conducts itself in several languages—and the dream itself is one of the novel's "languages."

Dreams in prose fiction almost always bear some consolation with them, however slight. Some dreams, once interpreted, prove immensely consoling or hope-inspiring for the dreamer. Yet dreaming also usually means an infusion of melancholy. Literally, dreams were considered the result of *melan-cholē*, black bile, the melancholy humor, according to a medical theory that became widely known through the works of the second-century physician Galen of Pergamum. (The theory was not entirely abandoned until the nineteenth century.) The dreamer's black bile produces black and melancholy objects in the dream; it is perhaps in honor of that belief that dreams, not only in ancient but also in many modern novels, include black or dark objects or people. That is one of the jokes relating to dreams of dusky and shadowy forms in the *Aithiopika*—perhaps the dreamer's melancholy is responsible for the attribute. Habrokomes' father comes to him in his dream dressed in black. Lord M. muffles the unwilling Lovelace in his great black mantle. Proust honors the tradition, even while confounding or conflating two Galenic humors when he refers to *les flots noirs de notre propre sang*, "the black waves of our own blood." And Esther Summerson deliriously dreams of "great black space."

Dreams, however, do not really *create* sadness. They *carry* it. Dreams are the medium through which we all (Reader and Character included) can understand how hard we are to understand. In a dream we see how painful life is—or rather how pain-fully it is experienced. When Alice finds out that she is only a figment of the Red King's dream, the idea of dreaming brings special alarm. The deepest horror is (comically) evoked by our being forced to consider our existence not as Interpreters of the Character's Dream (a role we have often played) but as characters within a dream. Insubstantiality can go no further. (If Tweedledum and Tweedledee are right, incidentally, then the Red King, however choleric his name, in dreaming of the "monstrous crow, / As black as a tar-barrel" runs true to form in melancholic production.) The threat in Carroll's fable is not the ultra-modern one of "meaninglessness" but the threat of existing only within attributed meaning. We would be only dream-figures. Dream-figures are to be interpreted—they are good for nothing else. Not being real, they cannot be loved, or hated. "Meaning" is in fact all they can possess.

The pleasure of setting our ingenuity into activity consoles us for the existential melancholy of novelistic dreams. The other compensation, not unrelated to that pleasure in setting our wits to work, is the assurance that individual consciousness is deep and important. It is so deep and complex that it can produce sudden surprises, artlike works—even within a poor beaten prisoner in his cell, such as Habrokomes. The soul is always energetic—and this assurance, coming from both our own creative intelligence and the creative intelligence of the under-consciousness, binds up the wounds of melancholy and loss.

The Novel urges us to feel a relationship between the creative intelligence that both produces and interprets dreams, and the intelligence that writes and reads novels. In reading a dream—in any novel—we go through a slight ordeal, but we take heart from it. *Tharsei*. Be of good cheer. The dream is closely related to the less agreeable experiences of novel characters—frustration, loss, bereavement, illness, death. Amadís, who wants to die, goes mad and alters his name to *Beltenebros* (Beautiful Shadow). To undertake dream-life is to get near the shadows, the world of death and the grave. Yet the dream promises us that we may escape—mayhap will always escape—from the stasis that often seems the direst point of our necessity.

The dream speaks of the life continuous, the life down deep, the life unquenchable. A novel always wants to creep into our consciousness rather like a dream. Less brittle than the public work of art that is placed in a museum and proclaims our history and our respectably interpreted myths, a novel urges upon us also the private disturbances, the individual's self-mythologizing. One of the reiterated effects of such dream-scenes in fiction is to make the individual significant and exciting.

In ancient as in modern novels, the presence of dreams and dream-work creates a certain fluidity in the work itself. It also orders us to attend to the extraneous detail, as well as to plot—just as we are to attend to the extraneous, the extra, detail in the novel, and not just to a simple story line, however important that may be. If we say that in novels of modern times (considering *A La recherche*, and *Ulysses*) "the epic moves inward," why, the epic has moved inward since the appearance of the earliest Western novels. In the *Aithiopika*, Ulysses is reduced, as it were, to being a figment of a dream of Kalasiris. Dream-work is readerly work.

THE EATING GAME

The counterpart—perhaps one should say, the antidote—of Dream in the Novel is Food. When I began to deal with Food in the Novel I thought I had the field pretty much to myself; late in the day, however, I came upon Gian-Paolo Biasin's *The Flavors of Modernity: Food and the Novel* (*I sapori della modernità: Cibo e romanzo*, 1991). Biasin points out the use of food as a "realistic function" in the text, "linking the literary expression with the pretextual, historical or sociological level" (trans. Biasin, 11). Meals define characters socially and also psychologically. Furthermore, "food is used to stage the search for meaning that is carried out every time one reflects on the relationship among the self, the world, and others" (17). Within a novel, "The discourse on food inevitably becomes a discourse on pleasure and on power" (27). Moreover, the literary use of food is always figurative, the process of cooking itself being rhetorical and figurative. Biasin's account offers much food for thought, but his book deals primarily with modern Italian works, and lingers long (perhaps with too much of the lovingness of a cookbook) on particular Italian dishes in the works of D'Annunzio, Gadda, *et al.*, so that the narratological impetus of Biasin's introduction becomes dissipated. The last chapter, on Primo Levi, however, offers a valuable reminder of the reality and terror of hunger. We recollect that food figures in novels—even luxuriant playful novels—because it is essential to life. We know our incompleteness, our lack of self-sufficiency, when food comes to the table. Nobody really is *in se ipso totus, teres, atque rotundus* (see Horace, *Satires*, Book II, vii)—and that self-sufficiency, that self-satisfied, self-engaged, smooth and ball-like nature is achieved only with the aid of a good digestion.

In my terms, the presence of food in a novel serves as a special sort of *ekphrasis*, involving a particular reminder of our participation in the world through ingestion of matter. Paintings and dreams appeal to the *eye*. Food does *not* exist for the eye. A description of food is thus always to some extent or in some way an ironic *ekphrasis*, or *anti-ekphrasis*. It calls upon the writer's ability to evoke precisely what is *not* visual (shape, texture, flavor, scent). It reminds us not just of our imagination, but of need. No reader can be quite aloof from food—though that reader may (with authorial blessing) disapprove particular kinds of food in a novel, or the uses to which it is put.

Whereas dreams issue (supposedly) from the deep "interior" of the character, enabling us to posit a vivid and complex *psychic* life, and hence a human reality "within" the character, food disappears "into" the supposed physical interior of the character, persuading us that a character has a solid *physical* life. While we know that is not really true, we also know that in "real life" we ourselves possess the physical life, to which we stolidly adhere. As for the psychic "interior" of another or even of the self, that is a matter for guesswork, but the physical *interior*—that is undeniably to be deduced, the receptacle of food. Dreams move from "within" towards the world without, in being articulated and explained. Food moves from the physical objective world without (where it can be described) towards the place most truly "within." As food disappears "into" the character we are able to imagine not only that character's reality, but also his or her pleasure. Thus we participate in acknowledgment not just of a past "oral phase" but of our incessant craving need. The desire for food is *the* appetite on which other appetites, even the sexual, are figuratively based. Desire for food is the humblest and most essential aspect of *erōs*. We are brought down to our human level in the contact with novelistic food. This humanizing contact has also a certain sacramental quality.

THE USES OF EATING

Food is admittedly one of the great resorts of narrative literature of all kinds. The sensuous pleasures of food are evoked in lyric, especially in love-poetry, including the frustrating red freshness of the apple in the apple-picking sapphic and the spiced smoothness of the repast Keats's Porphyro sets up for Madeline in "The Eve of Saint Agnes": "With jellies soother than the creamy curd, / And lucent syrups, tinct with cinnamon" (lines 266–267). Porphyro in his devotion to the carnal is a notable opposite to the philosophic Porphyry. Once can imagine with what horror the philosopher would look upon this ostentatious display of *genesis*. Flaubert uses similar sticky sweets throughout *Madame Bovary*, not only in description, e.g., the list of sweet items sold by the country apothecary, but also in the narrative rhetoric, as when the shopkeeper Lheureux is described with his fat smooth face "that seemed tinted by a clear syrup of licorice" (105). The rhetoric ironically summmons the "honey of generation" into a story where the last taste sensations will pertain to rat poison. Flaubert acts almost like a satirist in this paradox, though the paradox recalls the motif of "poisoned honey" found in antique novels like Antonius Diogenes' *Wonders beyond Thule*. Satirists tradition-ally have some harsh uses for food images. Food illustrates the irrational pursuit of pleasure and power, and the absurdity of human greed. So we see in Juvenal's Satire IV, in the description of the gigantic turbot given to Domitian and of the responses to it. Juvenal concentrates on the emperor's greedy and degenerate advisors, such as Montanus, who could tell where oysters came from "at first bite," and has given his life and mind to the pleasure of the table: "no one in my time was a greater expert in the practice of eating" (*nulli maior fuit usus edendi / tempestate mea*, line 139).

All such poetic uses of food imagery are picked up by the greedy novelists. They know alike both the satirists' view of the public and social value of meals and food, and the lyric artists' suggestion of intimate connections between par-ticular foods and important moments of emotional experience. The apple-picking of Sappho's poem becomes the fruit-picking of Longus' characters (III:180–182). In mingling nuances of sensation, physical appetite, and emotion, the poem and Longus' description both lie deep behind Marcel's recognition of time's return when he takes in the *madeleine* dipped in tea. The particularity of flavor and tex-ture is insisted upon, as is the nature of the *madeleine* itself, a species of Venus-food, a vulvular shell (*coquillage*) "so plumply sensual under its severe and devout folds." The taste itself is a spiritual thing because it is constitutive of memory: "when of an ancient past nothing subsists, after the death of beings, after the destruction of things, alone . . . more persistent, more faithful, scent and taste still remain for a long time, like souls . . ." (*Du côté de chez Swann*, 60–61).

The tea-soaked *madeleine* is valued as a medium in recreating the past as a sort of special dream. Proust, then, apparently reverses the roles of dreams and food, making food participate chiefly in the special dream that is consciousness. The tea and the little cake have gone down the wrong way, to that other "inte-rior," so skilled is Marcel in the uses of eating, *nulli maior fuit usus edendi.*

Proust's treatment of the *madeleine* spiritualizes food; flavor and taste are "like souls" (*comme des âmes*). Like other things in his novel, from flowers to paint-ings, food is destined to arrive in the magic-lantern show of the mind, where alone it has true value. This value might be termed "Hegelian"; Hegel said the duty of consciousness is making matter into spirit. But the Novel cannot be happy with such a formulation, or any such formulation that would abandon matter. Even Marcel's own reaction is expressed in terms of his physical ingestion: "But at the very instant when the mouthful of tea mingled with minute fragments of cake touched my palate, I shivered, attentive to something extraordinary hap-pening within me" (58). The physical act of swallowing *la gorgée mêlée*, the mingled mouthful or throatful, must be insisted upon. What is "within me," *en moi*, is related both the spiritual interior and the physical interior of throat (*gorge*), stomach, and intestines. As James Joyce keeps trying to point out, we are a mass of tripes and cannot lay simple claim to the grandeur of an interior abyss, the *grande profoundeur* from which memory returns. Our most ascertainable profun-dity is full of meaty organs.

Marcel in partaking of the *petit coquillage de pâtisserie* shares a taste com-mon among novel characters, who tend to be rather fond of pastry (Lucius the ass goes crazy amid a pastrycook's stores). But Marcel dips the little cake into tea, turning what is dry into something wet, disintegrating what was integrated into wet crumbs, soaked little fragments (*miettes*). The *madeleine*, which may seem "devout," a Magdalen, food for repentance, is itself a paradox, a shell of the sea, a *coquillage . . . grassement sensuel*. It is further sensualized in being moved further in the direction of muddy matter, mingled earth and water. Marcel takes the dry work of the pastrycook and turns it, before digestion, visibly and sensibly into *hylē*, formless first matter. The Novel—as in this novel—ever bends back from the devout and unmixed mind towards the external world that produces ever-valuable and sustaining matter.

Food is one of the insistent and great realisms of the Novel. In this as in so much else, the Novel has some affinity with the Epic. Epic characters eat, chowing down on whole roast animals, or partaking of a more genteel repast, as when Odysseus dines with Circe. Virgil's characters, as grimly prophesied, are reduced to eating even their tables—which hard fate proves to involve nothing more alarming than eating flat pieces of bread, the product of Ceres (*Æneid* III:255–257; VI:116–134). A hero like Aeneas should not care too much for his belly, nor should his eating err in style or substance. Eating the tables is about as close as epic comes to what we may term "aberrant eating" on the part of central characters. And we do not, while reading an epic, expect to come too close to the chomping jaws of hero or heroine. The processes of chomping jaws are fearfully associated with monsters like Polyphemus, who eats men alive, raw human meat washed down (in a most unkosher manner) with milk. If the Epic has its feasts, it gives little stress to actual eating. In the Novel, on the other hand, basic eating is approved, and even "aberrant eating" may be defensible.

In novels, we are often very close to the varied and particular food a character is eating, and that character's exact mode of taking it in—as Marcel oddly eats or drinks the spoonful of tea with crumbled *madeleine* in it. Food generally tends to excite approval and we are more tolerant of overeating than satire would allow. Meals may warm the reader's memory with recollections of past pleasure, even if these seem of an unpoetic kind:

> "I hope that is what you would like," said he. "I have tried to give you food more like the food of your own land than perhaps you have had lately."
>
> "It's lovely," said Lucy, and so it was; an omelette, piping hot, cold lamb and green peas, a strawberry ice, lemon-squash to drink with the meal and a cup of chocolate to follow. But the magician himself drank only wine and ate only bread.
>
> (C. S. Lewis, *Voyage of the Dawn Treader*, 139)

In this passage from Lewis's "children's book" the reader sees the comedy in the announced Englishness of the meal as well as its appropriateness—a schoolgirl's idea of a good blowout. The English reader in particular may share recollection of such food, lending the passage an informative physicality. Lucy, who might be accused of excess, eats heartily, like Knemon in the presence of Kalasiris. Kalasiris may be a vegetarian and a teetotaler, but he is the first to suggest dinner: "Now is the hour to take care of the belly" (*Aithiopika*, I:74), although he then quotes Homer to the effect that the belly is an imperious inconvenience. Yet even abstemious characters do not pretend to rise above food.

Nor are novelistic characters always above the aftereffects of food and drink. They can get drunk or lethargic, they can vomit, they may piss and shit copiously. Joyce has been praised and blamed for showing Bloom on the privy, but it is not true that physical functions go unmentioned in older novels. Knemon gets rid of a dangerous hanger-on by saying that excessive eating has given him cramps and too much milk has brought on diarrhea. This gives him a pretext to disappear for an interval during which he makes his escape (*Aithiopika*, I:70). In Iamblichus' *Babyloniaka*, characters who have eaten poisoned honey are smitten with diarrhea and fall as if dead by the roadside, thus unwittingly deceiving their enemies. (*Bibliothēkē*, II:36). In *Kleitophon and Leukippé*, the man who is about to abduct the heroine makes an excuse to leave the room, ostensibly to attend to the needs of his digestive tract. Food in the narrative guarantees the *gaster*, not only the stomach, that inner pit, but also the whole process of food-use. If dreams often respect the body, food makes the idea of the body unignorable.

Most novelistic characters, like Carroll's Alice, take "a great interest in questions of eating and drinking" (*Alice's Adventures*, "A Mad Tea-Party," 65). Like Alice, we want to know what people "live on"—in the most basic economic sense, how their biological life is sustained from day to day. Eating plays a major part in *The Golden Ass* from the beginning, when we have Aristomenes' tale, the story of Socrates, who was killed by witches and rendered dead while still thinking he is alive. Aristomenes flatters himself that the nightmare experience was merely a bad dream—he is rudely disabused, for the dream is tested by eating, and found not dream but horrid truth. Socrates the zombie cannot eat properly, bread sticks in his throat, and one sip of running water kills him. The confusion occasioned by dreams, their lingering melancholy, can usually be cured by eating, but on this occasion that formula cannot work. Lucius himself, while still a man in the early part of the story, has difficulty in getting food. His miserly hosts do not feed him, and when he buys fish in the marketplace it is destroyed by his self-righteous old schoolmate, now a magistrate, who faults the fish as inferior goods and has it ground under foot. The sight of official boots trampling the fish into the street is offensive. The incident, not being a dream, has none of the excuses we can extend to Alexander when he trampled the cheese. Food is made dirty, changes its substance, is deprived of its essential nature according to the human scheme of things. That which should be nourishing is rendered inedible.

Cannibalism is a singular contrast to food-wasting. To render food dirty, to trample on it, is to despise other bodies by depriving them. But other bodies themselves may be turned into food, perverting the ethos of social eating and rendering the individual monstrous. That which should not be used as nutriment is rendered nourishing in an aberrant act of economy.

According to Maggie Kilgour in *From Communion to Cannibalism* (1990), cannibalism, "the most demonic image for the impulse to incorporate external reality and get everything inside a single body" (16), is pervasive in our culture. Incorporations of that which is not the self into the self can be found in diverse forms, including colonialism, Hegelian synthesis, and various kinds of sublimation and incorporation—including ambitiously encyclopedic books like hers—or my own. The Novel, I would argue, is the one form of thought that consistently recognizes the element of truth in Kilgour's view. The Novel deals consistently in its stories and tropes with the difficulty of being an "individual" without being detached from others, or ingested by them, or consuming them. But in its own cannibalizing of other texts, the Novel *plays* with incorporation; the poem by Sappho does not disappear because it is "incorporated" into *Daphnis and Chloé*.

The Novel faces up to our eating habits. Beyond the pleasure of eating lies the danger of being eaten, swallowed up. We are already in danger, however, of being consumed by the earth. Eating scenes in novels show our representatives taking world-stuff into themselves; they *become* the pit, instead of falling into the pit. But the earth's hunger to swallow is fully acknowledged in the tropes of the Novel, as within scenes in individual novels. *Great Expectations*, for instance, begins with the graves of Pip's family, and the convict who bursts forth as if from the graves is an insistent maw into which pork-pie must be crammed, as a substitute for Pip's own "fat cheeks": "Darn me if I couldn't eat 'em" (11). Earth opens its mouth for us: we have seen, for instance, the *stomion* or little mouth that is the opening of the cave into which Charikleia is thrust in the first book of *Aithiopika*, and the *estrecha boca* of the deep cave at the very beginning of *Persiles y Sigismunda*. Hans Castorp's enlightened journey takes him smoothly over "gorges" (*Schlünde*), potential swallowing pits, gullets of terra once thought to be bottomless. It is not only in former times that the earth was "bottomless." It is so now, for the earth retains its infinite capacity for swallowing human beings, and the insatiable greed of the grave remains in every sense of the word proverbial (see Proverbs 30:16). Proust's *gorgée*, Marcel's swallowing of tea and *madeleine*, has an analogue in the gorge into which we may fall. To make *Time* the eater of everything (as Ovid does, and Proust) evades the materiality of what eats the flesh and bones: the earth itself, one giant sarcophagus or flesh-eater. This gorging earth is omnipresent, so there is no use in being frightened of it as we can be frightened of its personification in Polyphemus.

Actual cannibalistic meals are relatively rare in the Novel, but they certainly do occur—in, for instance, *Phoinikika*, *The Water-Margin*, *Robinson Crusoe*. They are even found in a "girl's book" like *Anne of Windy Poplars*, in which an old sea-captain's diary shames his snobbish descendants; his cannibalism serves a positive function in putting his relatives in their place, and they repay discovery with a propitiating gift of food. Ancient novels allude to cannibalism, especially in reference to the legendary monstrous feast of Thyestes who was served his own children in a stew. Novels seem always aware of the imminent possibility that some human bodies might feed on other human bodies. While such an act overvalues the individual and breaks the social bond, it is not, as in drama or epic, unforgivable. Like Defoe's Friday, characters can promise to do so no more. In the sixteenth chapter of *Candide*, Voltaire delineated the permanent Western cartoon image of savages, captives, and the briskly boiling cooking-pot, but he also offers, through Cacambo's ironic speech, a representation of cannibalism within a tissue of anthropological practices, a defense of it in terms of economic and spiritual needs and even rights. Cannibalism in the Novel is treated as a social concern, rather than as the absolute sign of the monstrous. If everything is hungry, it is no wonder this mistake is sometimes made, that the pit people fall into forever is the esophagus of somebody else.

Characters sometimes eat other food the reader would not eat. For instance, the "furmity" that the characters eat at the fair in *The Mayor of Casterbridge*

(1886) was as unfamiliar to most of Hardy's original readers as it is to readers now, and the author as narrator must explain and normalize it. But it is important that characters regard their own food as normal, whether or not they are conscious, or somewhat conscious, of their own expectations, as Lucy recognizes her lunch with the wizard, magical in its excessive normality, as representing food of her "own land."

Food is magically "normal." Detailed references to it are semimagical bonds to the physical, the necessary, the contingent, and the valuable. Food preserves against illness. It is the sovereign remedy against dreams. It is a homage paid to the earth and to the body. For any author, of course, it is as easy to produce roast peacock as an omelette, and caviar is as affordable as chocolate pudding. But as readers we must forget that the food (whether modest lunch or grand banquet) belongs to the shadowy signs, that it has no more substance than the marks on the page. A description of an apple pie has no more reality than the *ekphrasis* of a statue of Diana. A novel's lobster salad is as unreal as its portrait of the nymphs. Its *madeleine* is as insubstantial as its nightmare. But we must not think so—we must accord food a different status, a lower and more "real" register. The credibility of prosaic food helps to endorse the more elusive credibility of dreams and art. There are magic meals in novels, but even there the elements of the gritty and the credible remain attached.

We do not think the worse of novel characters for eating bad food, even if the food is so bad that resort to it could be called "aberrant eating." We sympathize with Roderick Random, for example, when he has to endure the horrible food on shipboard: "putrid salt beef . . . bread . . . every biscuit whereof like a piece of clock-work moved by its own internal impulse, occasioned by the myriads of insects that dwelt within it" (*Roderick Random*, 211). Likewise, we "forgive" novel characters the occasional excess in eating or drinking. Bad food, we know, leads to ill-health, while a surfeit, like the feast at Rosannette's ball in *L'Education sentimentale*, can lead to lassitude or illness. At this ball Juvenal's gross fish turns up again, *un gigantesque turbot* (179). Flaubert injects food description sardonically into the *bal-masqué*; we see an "Angel," seated on a piano stool, as she "masticated placidly, without stopping" (179). The spiritual is perpetually earthed. In novels, even the Angel eats.

It is a serious matter when characters in novels do *not* eat, and we are usually told specifically what it is they are not eating. It has been mistakenly believed that characters in medieval prose fiction do not eat; Cervantes is largely responsible for that canard. *Don Quijote* certainly gives extra emphasis to eating, through the voice and figure of Sancho Panza, whose very name ("paunch," "tripes") refers to the organ or area of the body that receives food. In *Amadís de Gaula*, however, and even more in *Las Sergas de Esplandián*, there are frequent references to meals. That the defeat of a castle should upset its dining arrangements is worthy of note: "due to all the commotion, the cooking was not as good as it should have been" (*Esplandián*, trans. Little, 118). We are to note whether a knight dined well or ill. It is when Amadís is despairing because of Oriana's dismissal, after the dream discussed above, that he refuses to eat. His foster-brother, Gandalin, concerned, urges him to eat, offering a specific food: "and he asked him to eat a meat pasty [*empanada*] that he carried" (*Amadís de Gaula*, I:702).

Gandalin is here like Sancho Panza, and Amadís like Quixote—for Amadís rejects the humble empanada. The specificity of the food adds to the emphasis on the hero's *not* eating. Not taking the meat pasty, Amadís enters the dangerous shadowy state of madness and deathliness. Even in the pit, Anthia did not disdain to eat, for she fed upon the bread and water that Amphinomos gave to her (*Ephesiaka*, 55). When Amadís is recovering, redeemed by love renewed and not by religion (which nearly kills him), under the friendly care of the Damsel of Denmark, he enjoys open-air picnics.

Food is *healthy*. It is the symbol of the unshadowy. It should not be colored with the ambiguity of dreams. It is solid, like works of art, yet, unlike those, fated to disappear. It is truly *consumable*, as art, even highly purchasable art, is really not. The statue of Diana is hard marble, even her grapes are stone. The cheese polenta on which Lucius chokes is soft and viscous, adhesive, disorganized—so over-foodlike, in short, that it is hard to get down. Against the harshness of *ekphrasis*, an external image in hard material forever standing against us, to be absorbed into our minds and yet forever not absorbable, there is food. Food is subordinate, soft, compliant; it may have shape but is destined to become amorphous, it wishes to enter into us and be as nothing. Food is, we like to think, absorbed by the character who gains in credibility by eating. Sometimes characters themselves are also food-preparers. At the furthest extreme of food display, novels may even offer recipes—as in Laura Esquivel's *Like Water for Chocolate* (*Como agua para chocolate*, 1989). Dickens in *Martin Chuzzlewit* (1843–1844) attempts to offer a recipe, in describing Ruth Pinch making a steak pudding (he actually got it wrong, as readers pointed out). But, if sympathetic characters may prepare the food they eat, their real status lies in being food consumers.

The Novel's traditional emphasis on food has stimulated an equally novelistic interest in destruction through food. The truly novelistic sin with food is not overeating, nor even cannibalism—it is poisoning. The novel has produced many instances of deliberately noxious food, nutriment that seems to fulfill the demands of the normal (either homely or festive) but actually harbors death. Poisoning through food occurs in antique novels, as in the poisoning of the would-be poisoner Arsaké in Heliodorus' novel. Boccaccio's *Filocolo* offers the case of the poisoned peacock; Biancifiore is accused of attempting to murder the king. The roast peacock itself may indicate a satiric excess, counterbalanced by its present poisonous total unfitness to serve any nutritive purpose. But even totally normal (not to say "banal") meals may come under suspicion: "Sech a plain, simple dinner as it was, too . . . a good stren'thenin' drop o' soup, and a bit of nice fish and a casseroled chicken with turnips and carrots done in the gravy, and a omelette, wot could be lighter and better?" (Dorothy Sayers, *Strong Poison*, 88). The dinner eaten by Mr. Urquhart and Philip Boyes is almost exaggeratedly normal for persons of their age, class, and gender—and of course their nationality and era. This pleasant repast looks as if it could not possibly have been the source of the poison that killed Philip Boyes—but it was, through the power exercised by one deliberately aberrant eater.

The important presence of food in the Novel at large has presumably stimulated the suspicion lavished upon food in numerous detective works. Food, the guarantor of realism begins to share the perturbing qualities of art and dream.

It suddenly develops perverse (if comically perverse) hermeneutic demands. The poisoned food of the murder-mystery is a mysterious affair that leaches ekphrastic interest from more normal locations. Food here refuses to be subordinate, and starts requiring hermeneutic primacy. That it should take on any extra and unwonted significations is enough in itself to perturb the reader. Food that cannot be "taken for granted" by characters or readers becomes "poisoned" (if excitingly so) in the sense that it cannot nourish our narrative wants without losing its more comfortable and normal status.

Food—novelistic food—becomes suspicious and even repulsive, whenever it tries to transmit or reflect new and unwonted meanings. That is, hermeneutic food offends:

> We had two Courses, of three Dishes each. In the first Course, there
> was a Shoulder of Mutton, cut into an Æquilateral Triangle; a Piece of
> Beef into a Rhomboides; and a Pudding into a Cycloid. The second
> Course was two Ducks, trussed up into the Form of Fiddles; Sausages
> and Puddings resembling Flutes and Haut-boys, and a Breast of Veal in
> the Shape of a Harp. The Servants cut our Bread into Cones, Cylinders,
> Parallelograms, and several other Mathematical Figures.
>
> (Swift, *Gulliver's Travels*, Book III, 134)

In describing the Laputians' dinner, Swift is adapting Rabelais' description of a very similar dinner at the Court of the Queen of Entelechy, in which the food is cut into even more bizarre abstractions. Such manifestations of food are always comic and always disconcerting—much more so than merely lavish expenditure on the table. For the purposes of novels, the cost of food in any given situation is as much its "natural" property as its taste, and religious and festive meanings are also "naturally" applicable. But such a playing about with the food as the Laputians exhibit comes under some particular taboo that the Novel respects.

In a well-known essay of the 1950s, "Cuisine ornamentale," Roland Barthes complained of the glossy presentation of food displayed in the women's magazine *Elle*. The role of *Elle* is to present "the very dream of *chic*," and it does so by burying real foods under sleek sediment and developing repulsive refinements of ornamentation. The head and front of the offense is the transformation of the palpable and natural into the spectacular and artificial. Barthes' objections focus on the privileging of the *visual* at the expense of the physical; the real foodstuff, that which nourishes, becomes meaningless residue. *Elle* jumbles *l'aliment* with *rêve*.[2] Barthes is probably not aware that he has picked up these objections from the novel tradition, which itself has a quarrel with the *chic* that transforms food.

The Novel is always suspicious (if comically suspicious) of food that is too visually wrought up. Proust's *madeleine* itself, once we pause to look at it, shows some signs of ekphrastic excess, and it may be prudent to dissolve it into amorphousness as Marcel does. The Ass steals the baked goods, which are in various artificial shapes (*lucunculos, hamos, laterculos; The Golden Ass*, II:240). He is asking for trouble. In *The Dream of the Red Chamber*, old Grannie Liu loves "the delicately fashioned pastries" (II:310). She first takes one shaped like a peony, and then gobbles up a lot more, so that she has an upset stomach and must spend a long time on the privy (317). Grannie Liu is a poor and vulgar woman, who knows no discretion and can be understandably enchanted by the fried "little pastry-shapes," but the Novel always warns us to be wary of food got up to look like something else. Consuming (or producing) ekphrastic food holds many dangers.

Nowhere is this comic crime more fully dealt with than in *Satyricon*. Trimalchio may be a fantastic example of excess, but we are not to think of him as singular among his contemporaries. If we look at surviving ancient mosaics we can see foodstuffs reduced—or sublimated—to the visual, as fully as in *Elle*. Take, for example, what is called "The Buffet Mosaic," now in the Hatay Museum at Antioch, probably once the decoration of a dining-room. Trimalchio shares the dream of chic, and (like *Elle* and its photographers): he can arrange the visual banquet. There is something almost heroic about Trimalchio's efforts to take over the stuff of the world. As Leonard Michaels says in his novel *The Men's Club* (1981), describing a character's 1970s-style house with its acrylic paintings, orange rug, and "Porcelain sillies" including pink pigs, "The opposite of puritanical is the savage energy of bad taste" (63). Bad tase acts as if it were innocent of puritanism, and could never be world-despising. Yet bad taste tries to cut the world down to fit ridiculous molds, as if, like Cinderella's ugly sisters, needing drastic operations in order to achieve a banal success. The presence of the pigs (in Michaels and Petronius) obviously indicates the hoggish egotism at work, but this egotism is already in service of a readymade idea. Trimalchio combines both "savage energy" and dream of chic. Trimalchio and Fortunata (and their cooks) do what Barthes' *Elle* does, travestying nature and finding a substitute for it:

> There would never have been any end to these evils, if the last course had not been brought in, thrushes made of fine wheat flour and stuffed with raisins and nuts. There followed quinces of Crete stuck about with thorns so as to look like sea-urchins. These at least would have been tolerable if a far more monstrous dish had not made us wish rather to perish of hunger. For when there was placed before us what seemed to be, as far as we could tell, a fat goose surrounded by fish and all kinds of birds, "Friends," said Trimalchio, "Whatever you see set out here is made out of one body. . . my cook made all this from a pig."   (Petronius, *Satyricon*, 156)

The "thrushes are" neither birds nor any other animal, but cakes, whereas the "sea-urchins" are *simulacra* composed of quinces and thorns (the ancient version of our toothpicks). The cook has surpassed himself in contriving the appearance of different natural species (fish and fowl) out of one animal. He is a mystic wonder-worker—no marvel that Trimalchio calls him "Daedalus," after the great artificer who first wrought the labyrinth. At Trimalchio's banquet the very food (served within a labyrinth, we remember) participates in the nature of the labyrinth while at the same time assuming extraordinary ekphrastic qualities. "Natural" qualities are held in scorn—the categories are exchanged: grains become pseudo-meat, fruit becomes pseudo-meat (or fish), and one animal (pig) becomes diverse fish and fowl. Food thus is transformed into something for the vision, in hideous overrefinement of decoration.

Trimalchio has committed an offense—no less real for being a comic—in translating food into the region of both Art and Dream. Any novel whose characters start doing this is likely to be a comic novel with satiric properties. The

Novel *qua* Novel wishes to guard the sacredness of the body; the corporeal cannot be served if we translate food into an art object or dream-image. The idea of food is crucial; food must be imagined as being ingested by the characters, thus furthering the idea of their substantial nature. And not only their substantial nature—but their individuation also. Food is social, but always individual. The bread that you eat will not nourish me. That characters eat reinforces the idea of their individuality. To jumble food with dream, *l'aliment* with *rêve*, is to alter categories evidently necessary to the Novel. A novel must punish (through satire) any character who is so foolishly bold as to confuse the categories. The natural is not to be made into the spiritual in that way.

It must be admitted that a novelist such as Petronius is including his own descriptions of food in his own work of art. Why is the novelist not as guilty as Trimalchio? The novelist (any novelist) might retort that the proper use of food in the Novel is to serve and nourish the characters, and that whether it is a pretty meal or an ugly one is the characters' business. Meals within a novel can have a sacramental quality, but that quality is related to the interaction of the characters—for instance, the wine-cup shared by the newly met lovers in *Kleitophon and Leukippé*. The extreme opposite of such a meal must be the antisacramental mess that Gregor Samsa's sister gives the bug that is/was her brother. Yet in both cases the novelist sees to it that the food serves both the characters' bodies and their relationships.

Simone Weil, in the statement now standing as first epigraph to this chapter, rebukes our desire to take and eat, and makes a clear contrast between eating and beholding. Looking is for Weil a spiritual or potentially spiritual activity, whereas eating is almost its opposite, a manifestation of the base will. Sinful individualism cannot see beyond the self, and so wants to possess and absorb what should only be contemplated. "It may be that vice, depravity, and crime are nearly always, or even perhaps always, in their essence, attempts to eat beauty, to eat what we should only look at" (*Waiting for God*, 166). Only in heaven can we become one with what we adore, and in heaven anorexia will be the order of the day—there will be no need to eat. Like Barthes, her contemporary, Weil wishes to keep spectacle and eating separate. Weil, a refined and often profound religious thinker, Neoplatonically or even Gnostically gives the palm to the visual—unlike Barthes. The Novel arrives at some similar conclusions about separating eating and looking, but from a very different standpoint. The work of eating, the sacred if dangerous work, should not be cluttered by fantastic ventures into the visual. The endeavor to spiritualize food into form actually debases the eater. Matter shoud not be falsely spiritualized, should not be conceitedly perverted into object for contemplation. Perhaps, however, the Novel does agree a little with Weil; when we try to make the edible too beautiful or intricate, it is a sign of a false and dangerous desire to ingest the beautiful, to stuff the world into the self. We thus falsely and in bad faith overcome what *ekphrasis* and dream have tried to teach us in confronting us with that which is not-ourselves, or is the deep and perturbing "self." Characters must not get rid of *ekphrasis* by consuming it, as the murderess and detectives in a Dorothy Sayers short story get rid of the murder weapon (a frozen leg of lamb) by cooking and eating it.

The novelist has created imaginary food—the novelist has, as it were, sinned enough in so doing, in representing food in words that cannot nourish the reader's body. It thus behooves the novelist to make sure that food is not sinned against twice. Food that becomes a *spectacle* is food that cannot nourish or heal. Characters who even begin to move towards the preposterous transformations of food proudly engaged in by Trimalchio are (comic) reprobates. An example is Jane Austen's Mrs. Elton, rattling on about her strawberry-gathering and trying to turn it into a pictorial event (*Emma*, 321). Well may she wish to ride upon a donkey, for Augusta Elton (like Apuleius' hero) is really an ass.

A novel's food must remain at an opposite pole from that novel's paintings and even its dreams, contrivances of human wit expressed in the spectacular forms that invite interpretation. A cheese in a dream is not cheese, it is Tyre. A character may be gratified to find that this is so. But a character who is to maintain respectability in our eyes must not try to sculpt his cheese into the city of Tyre—or any other shape or thing.

Reference to food restores us to the realm of sensation, to the inner spaces of taste and digestion, to the body itself. Food, though itself entering a work of rhetoric necessarily always as image, has the job of standing up for being (*das Sein*) against spectacle or sight (*der Anblick*). It supports taste and touch against the dominant and aggressive vision. References to food, however slight or comic, pay homage to biological life as real life, in the ineluctable modality of the digestion. There *are* limits to the diaphane. To turn food into spectacle is the Novel's comic crime. The Novel must resist the reduction of all human life to spectacle and spectatorship—even while the Novel investigates these things, and is acutely aware of the role of gazing, and being gazed upon, in creating the self-conscious if somewhat shapeless entity we call the "self." If everything is spectacle, then we may as well be in the Red King's Dream, the Red Dust itself the subject of a dream, where we have meaning but at the cost of becoming only shadowy abstractions. Food reassures us that we are not phantoms—except for Aristomenes' phantasmic dead friend, an unwise Socrates who could not stand the food test. Food, bearing all these life-affirming values, begins to grow shadowy when it is rendered too spectacular.

"Do not play with your food" is the stern warning issued to all novelistic characters. The Novel itself finds this activity a travesty that denies the value of incarnation. It is in effect an insult to Eros, mocking and deluding the desires. Characters should eat first, and then go into the art-gallery. Or rather, they should probably go to the art-gallery first, like Zola's wedding-party, and then eat. In the Novel, Food is not the humble inferior of Art. It has been noted that Elstir the great painter does not return in the last volume of *A la recherche du temps perdu*; artistic representation and the *ekphrasis* of it alike prove ironically unsatisfactory, while a stumble over a paving-stone, a taste of a *madeleine*, may reassert themselves at any time. The incarnate life is not the flat life of the icon.

CHAPTER XIX

>⊶⊶○⊷⊰

The Goddess

>⊶⊶○⊷⊰

Until joking Iambe jested with her
With many broad jokes diverting the pure Lady
To smile, to laugh, and then to have a cheerful heart.
. . .
Then She ordered that barley and water
Be mixed with sweet herbs as a drink
. . .
She took it for the sake of the rite, the Allmighty Goddess.
—*Hymn to Demeter*

And the populace of Rhodes celebrated in their honor, crying aloud
the praises of the Great Goddess Isis. . . .   —Xenophon, *Ephesiaka*

She broke forth as never moon yet burst from cloud: a hand first penetrated the sable folds and waved them away; then, not a moon, but a
white human form shone in the azure, inclining a glorious brow
earthward. It gazed and gazed on me. It spoke, to my spirit . . .
—Charlotte Brontë, *Jane Eyre*

>⊶⊶○⊷⊰

DEMETER-CERES

In discussing something as lowly as food, we may seem to have wandered far
from the more imposing tropes, those lively metaphors that appear in dynamic
presence within the novelistic story. Gazing on the heaps of novelistic food—Pip's
stolen pork pie, for instance, Leopold Bloom's cheese and Burgundy, Lazarillo's
sausage and turnip—we may feel confused. We are thus in the same condition as
Psyche in the tale told within Apuleius' *The Golden Ass*, by a woman who is herself
a cook (and fond of stuffing her own belly, too). Her story, which might be called
"The Old Cook's Tale," describes the trials of Psyche, including the task set by
mocking Venus, of sorting the great heap of grains. In Psyche's ordeal she is
taunted and humiliated: "Such an ugly slave-girl [*tam deformis ancilla*] as you
seem to me, you have no other means of deserving lovers than by diligent service. Now, therefore, I myself will put your fruitfulness to the test. Separate the
seeds of this huge heap of grains: sort them out one by one and arrange them
in order. Before this evening the work must be completed to my satisfaction"
(I: 328). Poor Psyche, now described herself as de-formed, out of form, barely
touches the giant amorphous heap when the immense impossibility of this task
strikes her into paralyzed consternation. It is the little ants (female) who do the
task for her, neatly separating the seeds according to kind. Seeing that Psyche
must have had help, Venus throws her only a bit of coarse bread for supper. But

this bread is itself a product of the bounty of Ceres, as are the multitude of grains that in their abundance and diversity support human beings. Psyche has already been to the temple of Ceres. There she saw the emblems of that goddess, although they appear in some confusion:

> She saw ears of corn in heaps [*spicas frumentarias in acervo*] and others twisted into crowns, and ears of barley likewise. There were both sickles and the working tackle used by reapers throughout the whole world, but piled up together in careless confusion, as when in the heat of summer days they are thrown from the hands of the laborers. This heap Psyche carefully separated and put everything in its place, according to religious usage, reasoning, so it seems, that one ought not to neglect the temple and ceremonies of any god but should ask for the kind pity of all. (I: 312)

In piously sorting the *spicas frumentarias* and the implements, she acts as a devotee of Demeter, near the beginning of what might be called her "mystery tour." Merkelbach has emphasized the element of religious mystery and the ordeals of initiates in Apuleius's novel (see *Roman und Mysterium*, 18–55). In her work in Ceres' temple, Psyche reflects one of the very oldest of the mystery cults, the Eleusinian Mysteries.

The Eleusinian Mysteries were the rites of the mystery religion of Demeter and Persephone, the Mother and Daughter. Athenian women swore not by male gods but always by "the Two"—Demeter and the Maiden, her daughter who had descended into Hades but who returns every year for half a year. What we know of these secret Mysteries is tenuous and fragmentary.[1] Karl Kerényi studied all the then available evidence in his *Eleusis* (1960). The teasing presence of the mysteries haunts ancient culture and the antique novel. That what is secret is yet open to all, that what is hidden is powerful—these are ideas that shape the Mysteries of Eleusis.

Mythologists have assumed that the cult of Demeter and Persephone as observed in the Eleusinian Mysteries developed from a local agricultural cult into the large-scale religious observance that Eleusis offered before and during the heyday of the Roman Empire. The religion here enshrined, or some elements of the ritual, might possibly predate the prevalence of agriculture. (Not every "fertility ritual" is related to settled agriculture as we know it.) Ken Dowden remarks that the Eleusinian Mysteries, in full-blown form, were "a remarkable development from initiatory practice," and suggests that the cult arose from a practice of female initiation at Eleusis (*Death and the Maiden*, 194).

Whatever its origin, the worship at Eleusis became remarkably popular. Initiates and sightseers crowded to Eleusis, some "four hours by foot" from Athens, by a good "rut road" suitable for wheeled traffic (see Casson, *Travel in the Ancient World*, 69). There were five public days of celebration and three days of observances restricted to the initiates. A high fee (some fifteen drachmas) was charged for initiation. But initiation was open to all, male or female, Greek or foreign—as long as the candidate could speak Greek, had not committed murder, and was not a child. The participant had to *choose* initiation, and as an adult (any time after fifteen or so) should understand what was happening, as well as being physically capable of the endeavor. One could be initiated at any stage of life; old and young were *mystai* together.

The Mysteries did not mark any biological turning-point. Neither were they associated with entry into any social status, or any particular group. They are not like marriage, or coming of age, or initiation into a civic brotherhood or *phratry*. The Mysteries are thus truly singular among ancient ritual observances marking a change in the individual's life. Elsewhere in the Greco-Roman world we find plenty of "rites of passage." The Mysteries are *not* "rites of passage." They set themselves apart, alike from biological fate and from civic order. Astonishingly—and in marked contrast to Athenian cultic observances—initiation at Eleusis was open to slaves as well as to the free. Demosthenes says that when the orator Lysias was in love with a slave girl, and wished to make her a handsome present that her mistress could not confiscate, he paid for her initiation. The candidate for initiation—the *mystes*—was supposed to be guided by a *mystagogos*, someone who had formerly been initiated. The *mystagagos* was customarily a local resident; the clan of the Eumolpidai of Athens were among the suppliers of the "chief cicerones" (Parke, *Festivals of the Athenians*, 62). This well-known function may cast some light on the nature and potential of the poet Eumolpus, who becomes such a dominant figure in the latter part of the unfinished *Satyricon*.)

The initiates seem to have been prepared by a period of fasting. On the sixteenth day of the month of *Boēdromiōn* (our early September), the cry went up "*Mystai*, to the sea!" Candidates went to the beach, to undergo ritual purification in the sea at Peiraios or Phaleron. This cleansing immersion in honor of the goddess certainly resonates with the experiences of Lucius the ass at the seashore towards the end of *The Golden Ass*. This point in the beginning of the ritual also called for the sacrifice of a pig, an animal conventionally offered to Demeter and associated also with several other female goddesses. (It is not absolutely clear that each candidate necessarily had to sacrifice a personal pig.) The next days involved activities not hidden from the general populace. The long procession wound its way from Athens' Dipylon Gate, going the fourteen miles to Eleusis, the candidates and their *mystagogoi* dressed as pilgrims in simple dark clothing (*white* clothing was introduced in the second century A.D., late in the cult's history). As the procession crossed the bridge over the Kephisos river near Eleusis, a ritual important but to us indistinct took place "mockery and strange games, the *gephyrismoi*, or 'bridge jests'" (Kerényi, *Eleusis*, trans. Manheim 65).

It was probably at this moment of water-crossing that an actor (whether male or female is uncertain) engaged in an important ritualized obscenity that we know took place during the early part of the Mysteries. A woman engaged in abuse and obscene jokes. She represented Iambe, the serving woman who cheered sorrowing Demeter in mourning for her lost daughter. Demeter was *agelastos*, "laughterless," as the *Hymn to Demeter* says, but Iambe made her laugh, and the revived Mother-Goddess was able to eat a special dish based on barley, the *kykeōn*. The jokesmith's name is Iambe, which relates her to the cutting iambics of satire—she is the female as satirist. But the name of the jesting woman might also be "Baubo"—a name signifying the rocking of a child, hence a nurse. In some versions, Baubo, an old woman, is the wife of the swineherd whose herd of pigs disappeared into the earth with Persephone. Accounts of the Eleusinian clown are confused, the clearest written statements being the work of hostile witnesses relatively late in the day, like Clement of Alexandria and Eusebius, bishop of Caesarea.

The role of this bawdy entertainer seems analogous to that of the female clown, the *hàn mane'àk su*, who presides over weddings in some Polynesian cultures. Vilsoni Hereniko explains that this jester is "an older woman, past childbearing age, and non-threatening outside the boundary of privileged license" (*Woven Gods*, 131). Within one particular situation the Polynesian female clown is powerful, able to make fun of important people, even of chiefs, parodying masculinity while invoking the female forces of fertility. Like the *hàn mane'àk su*, and like the functioning Pythia who spoke the Delphic oracles, the woman who embodied the combined forces of continuity and the unexpected in Iambe-Baubo's role was clearly post-menopausal. A survivor of the goddess-work of fertility, a comically triumphant representative of a new form of sexual identity, the clown embodying Iambe-Baubo brought into the public realm the temporarily unsuppressed and unashamed voice of women's undecorous knowledge of life.

Baubo cheers sorrowful Demeter by gestural jokes, culminating in a display of her vulva, through the lifting of her garments (*anasyrma*) in revelation. As Maurice Olender points out, the Orphic verses cited by both Clement and Eusebius make it clear that Baubo displays the *sōmatos typos*, the entire body: "Baubo's action thus amounts to a display of the body as a whole"; she offers not just nudity but "a place . . . inaccessible to sight . . . that even nudity does not expose" (Olender, "Aspects of Baubo," *Before Sexuality*, 90). Winifred M. Lubell in *The Metamorphosis of Baubo* (1994) points to resemblances to certain Sumerian deities, and their connections with paleolithic vulvular symbols: "the central concept of Bau, Baalat, or Baubo—wherever and whenever she appeared—is connected with hole, entrance, cave, womb, or vulva, and her role is usually that of fecund nurturer or nurse" (24). Baubo playing before Demeter is, then, to Lubell an encouraging reminder of the everlasting fecundity of woman; the goddess is cheered by recognition of her own female power, including the powers of moon-blood and uterine reproduction. The cream of the jest of either Iambe or Baubo is that Woman is the Power, when all is said and done, and life flows from her.

Here we see, near the outset of the Eleusinian Mysteries, another entry into the pit—and another (and comic) view of it. The pit is "hole, entrance, cave, womb, or vulva," and the Pit itself, the ravening maw, is the nether mouth of earthly generation. We cannot be born without passing through that hole. The vulva-pit as mouth is emphasized in some ancient statuettes, especially those found at Priene and used in illustration by both Olender and Lubell, in which the female face with its mouth surmounts a pair of female legs. In this pun, we see that the "little mouth," the *stomion*, and the *Schlünde* or gorges, the swallowing pits, have another meaning. Novels, like the newly born or the Eleusinian *mystai*, salute that hole.

The strange moment of ritual jest at the entry into Eleusis marks a suitable overture to ceremonies in which, as Kerényi says, "both men and women seem to envisage the *feminine source of life*, but not in an intellectual way" (*Eleusis*, xxxiii). The Mysteries held their appeal to high and low from the middle of the second millennium B.C. Whatever its lost beginnings, this female cult showed itself a religion capable of theological development. What we mean by "intellectual" entails a body of writings. Eleusis offered a sacrament, a vision and an enactment.

The *mystai*, after crossing the bridge and entering Demeter's sacred precincts, proceeded with their secret rituals. As these were not open to the general public, and as each *mystes* was sworn to secrecy, our knowledge of what happened is indistinct. They underwent a journey within the temple area, part of it probably underground, and were led about and about in their own labyrinth—perhaps like pilgrims to Knossos of yore. The very name Eleusis "refers to the underworld in a favorable sense and may be translated as 'the place of happy arrival'" (Kerényi, *Eleusis*, trans. Manheim, 23). The *mystes* in Eleusis descended into the pit, and found that Hades and Elysium are one, that death is not to be feared and that life has meaning. This is an individual revelation as well as a revelation to the group. The *mystai* were led to various stations on their way. At some point they too drank of the *kykeōn*. They touched hallowed objects in the sacred *kiste* or lidded basket; these objects were perhaps pastry or ceramic images of the genital organs, though one frieze shows a snake, which the *mystes* is to touch. (See Burkert, *Ancient Mystery Cults*, 94.) In being shown the vision of the ear of corn, cut in silence, they were given a message about the meaning of the universe and, apparently, news about their own immortality.

The *mystai* wandered and wept with sorrowing Demeter, and with Demeter were reunited with the *Korē*, the Maiden, who had descended into the depths and then rose again. Demeter's is a mighty motherhood—indeed, through Persephone, she has a dual motherhood. Inside the great edifice into which the *mystai* pressed in the dark of night there was a little building, a place that opened to the display of a great light, while the voice of the Hierophant cried aloud: "The Mistress has given birth to a holy boy. Brimo has given birth to Brimos! that is, the Strong One to the Strong One" (Kerényi, *Eleusis*, 92). The *Korē* as Hekate-Brimo, Queen of the Dead, who gives birth in the midst of fire, is the true and perpetual phoenix. Through coming into the Underworld, experiencing the Pit, the *mystai* have approached the mystery of life and the power of the Great Mother.

Kerényi, pursuing the work done with Jung, sees the myth as representing *zoē*, all life, giving birth to the individual life, or *bios*, "individual human existence": "An archetypal element of *bios*, the individual human existence [*sic*], is first of all human existence itself; another is life, *zoë*, which . . . is proper not to man alone but to all species" (xxxii–xxxiii). The Mysteries celebrate not only the spring, rebirth, the growth of the grains, but also the mystery of individual life coming from all life; Kerényi's explanation offers some insight into the way late antique interest in individual personal life and salvation made a connection with Eleusis. At the same time, Kerényi reminds us, "The myth is related to the nourishment men derive from plants. . . *zoë* means not only the life of men and of all living creatures but also what is *eaten*" (xxv). The *mystes*, having fasted, then also in imitation of Demeter ate—or rather drank—the same dish she had taken after being recalled to life through the jests of Iambe-Bauto. This holy dish, the *kykeōn*, consisted of (probably roasted) barley or wheat in water with herbs. Its most immediate descendant is the modern Greek *koliva* still served at the *Mnimosino*, the memorial service for a dead person; in the U.S. wheat grains have replaced barley, the herb is now parsley, and a ritual six red pomegranate seeds are included.[2] Ovid in *Metamorphoses* (V, line 450) says this dish was sweet and made of *tosta polenta*, toasted grain. The *Hymn to Demeter* shows this meal being founded in the manner of a sacrament: "The Allmighty Goddess [*polypotnia Dēō*] took it for the sake of the rite [*hosiēs heneken*]" (line 211). This last phrase could mean "for form's sake," but here, as N. J. Richardson notes in his edition of the *Hymn*, "Demeter, in founding the rite, is also acting as the prototype of the initiates" (225–226). This *kykeōn* basically means a mixture, related to the verb *kykaō*, meaning to mix together, throw into confusion. It is evidently of the nature of this holy dish to be impure, or adulterated: it is not one thing, but elements in mixture. Near the very beginning of the *Golden Ass*, Lucius describes how he nearly choked on a glutinous food, a cheesy polenta (*polenta caseata*), perhaps indicating his very first run-in with the goddess (I : 8). The goddess of this pagan eucharist is in some sense present in what we eat, signified in the great golden sheaf of grain; the sight of the golden sheaf, a high point of the Mysteries, attached holy meaning to the food of everyday. When the initiates retraced the experience of the Suffering Mother, and, descending into the depths, celebrated the rising of the Maiden, apparently undergoing some sort of ordeal in the process, they were going through a ritual rebirth.[3] Having gone through loss and death to new life, the *Dēmētreioi*, the Demeter-people, shared an experience of the transcendent.

But "transcendence" is an uncomfortable word in this connection. The initiates were not divorced from Nature but newly reunited with it. Soul and soil, as it were, are freshly felt in relationship. Neoplatonist transcendence, and also often the Christian, is what might be called "dry transcendence." It signifies a flight from the pain and mess of the physical world—so often imaged as female. We have tended to see the world of "the mind" as holy, filled with dry white light, uncontaminated. To ascend to the spiritual is to get above what is earthy, female, dirty. The Eleusinian *mystai* took another path. In taking part in the mysteries both men and women identified themselves as "feminine," each an imitator of the Goddess. Kerényi points out, "There is historical evidence indicating that the initiate regarded himself as a goddess and not as a god" (*Eleusis*, 211). Eleusis offers an amazing counterbalance to the patriarchal Attic world, which was able to declare that a child was not of kin to his mother—the view that so profoundly astonishes Tristram Shandy's Uncle Toby. Instead of being no kin of the mother who bore him—who, according to Aristotelian biology, contributed merely house-room in her womb to the process of begetting—the initiate of Eleusis went beyond his social persona, his paternal identity, and gladly acknowledged himself the daughter of his Mother.

Both men and women in worship were in some sense to join up with or join in with both the searching Demeter and the suffering Koré, the Maiden. In Apuleius' story, Psyche, who is not a divinity, represents all readers as she undertakes her ordeal, a confrontation with the Goddess. But before the very worst of her ordeal she is somewhat consoled by the vision of the stalks of grain. The Ceres that Psyche can know at this point is powerless to interfere with the great goddess Aphrodite. The last book of Apuleius' novel, however, shows us that these goddesses are really one, or can be seen as aspects of each other.

Looking with Psyche at the grains of wheat and barley reminds us that food can have a religious as well as a "natural" meaning. Lucius, who chokes over his *polenta*, shows he is not yet worthy to ingest or understand the *kykeōn*. The holiness of food may be presented novelistically as disturbing—as indeed it is in Psyche's story. The ears of corn and of barley are in a mess. The grains present themselves as a gigantic unsortable mixed pile. We get close to this sense of mixed, confusing, and holy food in the beginning of Hardy's *The Mayor of Caster-bridge*, when the characters partake of the "furmity" made by the "haggish" woman: "The dull scrape of her large spoon was audible throughout the tent as she thus kept from burning the mixture of corn in the grain, flour, milk, raisins, currants, and what not, that composed the antiquated slop in which she dealt" (8–9). This is the mysterious meal that we partake of, the "antiquated slop," like the *kykeōn* of the Mysteries of Demeter, being both eatable and drinkable. The "furmity" is merely a slight corruption of the Roman word *frumentaria*; Hardy constantly hints at ironic connections between the Roman times and modern.

As we enter Hardy's novel, we undergo the mysterious process of imaginatively ingesting an unusual if sustaining food: "as proper a food as could be obtained within the four seas; though, to those not accustomed to it, the grains of wheat, swollen as large as lemon-pips, which floated on its surface, might have a deterrent effect at first" (9). The "furmity" which is neither solid nor liquid, is a wonderful and daunting mixture, an image in itself of primal matter, of *hylē*. Looking at the furmity-woman's product, we may better understand Proust's hero, who prepares the self-administered sacramental meal of Demeter near the beginning of Proust's giant novel. Partaking it, Marcel experiences the depth at which *bios* and *zoē* unite and separate. The *madeleine*-and-tea mixture is grain-food and water mingled (with other ingredients) in a primal "slop," a *kykeōn*.

Hardy's cook, known to us at first only as "the hag" and "the furmity woman," is a recurrent and slightly mysterious force in *The Mayor of Casterbridge*. In her appearances, she seems a stand-in for both the rowdy Baubo and sarcastic Iambe, as well as a representation of Ceres-Demeter. The magic meal she offers, neither quite liquid nor solid, is a *kykeōn* sweetened to intoxicate—as some scholars think the Eleusinian *kykeōn* was intoxicating. Her initial offering of the mixed *frumentaria* sustains us for the ordeals of the novel's characters while offering us an ironic glimpse of life's unstable mixtures. In her later appearance, the furmity-woman is arrested for an act of *anasyrma*; the foolish constable charges her "with the offence of disorderly female and nuisance" for urinating in the gutter, "on the night of the fifth instinct, Hannah Dominy" (200). The Joycean language emphasizes the truth; Hannah (or Anna), the Mother, is Dominie, mistress indeed. The hag brought before Henchard in his role as magistrate gleefully turns the tables upon him by telling the story of how he sold his wife. His masculine and structured power is powerless against her impish onslaught, and he rapidly loses his position of authority. The old woman, the "hag," acts as a witch in her micturition—like the witches who urinate over Aristomenes near the beginning of Apuleius' novel.

It should be acknowledged at the outset that the Witch is one aspect of the Goddess figure. We might wish, in Jungian terms (perhaps too sentimentally) to see the Witch as only the shadow side of the Female divinity, but that Witch and Goddess are connected is clear, as in Apuleius' novel, where the witches in the story at the beginning connect with both Milo's wife and Byrrhena, and thus with Isis at the end. In folktales such as Grimms' the witch is often singled out for detestation and destruction, but there are many stories about the "loathly lady" in which the "hag" as aspect of the Feminine must be accepted (for example, Chaucer's "Wife of Bath's Tale"). We may need to be wary of the absolutism of the Romantic period in which the brothers Grimm appear. Odd little fairy god-mothers and mysterious women encountered on a journey are also witches; in modern Hawaii the volcano goddess Pele is supposed to appear sometimes at roadsides as a little old woman who may ask you for a lift. Pele is disconcerting—but not evil.

Hags and witches abound in modern novels: Miss Havisham is one, and also a perverse Venus mothering a perverse Eros (Estella). In *Wuthering Heights* the dying Cathy sees young Nelly Dean as a hag—presumably rightly (123). Nelly's haggish qualities are an aspect of her magic power as narrator, as well as of her interventions in others' lives. Elderly female detectives like Patricia Went-worth's Miss Silver and Agatha Christie's Miss Marple are sometimes accused of being witchlike, and so they are. Jane Marple is a Nemesis. The "hag" in *The Mayor of Casterbridge* is a Fate, and she acts as both Nemesis and Tyché when she brings on Henchard's downfall. Hardy's favorite deity is, notoriously, Fate—that is, the goddess Fortuna-*Tyché* who is so well mimicked by plotting novelists themselves.

Ancient novels are visibly endeavoring to achieve or represent some sort of balance between the male and female powers. Longus achieves this balance with a graceful appearance of artlessness. We begin with the ideal—Pan *and* the Nymphs, the balance between male sexuality and female sexuality, masculine and feminine divine powers in nature. In a more lofty and labored theological exposition, Heliodorus in the ending of *Aithiopika* tries to bring into harmony both male and female powers, the Sun and Moon, and to mingle philosophies Greek, African, and Indian. The *Recognitiones* attributed to Saint Clemens, that early Christian novel, has to reject the feminine deity as represented in the sinis-ter personage Luna, Simon Magus' girlfriend; yet the goddess is not entirely to be rejected, and breathes forth again in the story of Clemens' long-lost mother, who pretends that she is from Ephesus (367). If they are not already Ephesian (like Petronius' famous widow), women in ancient fiction seem to wish to *pretend* to be Ephesian, and thus under the protection of Artemis. Charikleia pretends to Thyamis that she is a priestess of Artemis from Ephesus. *Apollonius of Tyre* ends in family reunion in the sanctuary of the temple of "Diana" at Ephesus—and Ap-ollonius finds his wife, Tharsia's mother, in the chief priestess of Diana.

As we have already seen, the Goddess is to be found everywhere in the ancient novel. Certainly, any novel may allude to gods perceived or represented as masculine. The Novel as a genre, however, has an innate desire to allude to the female deity, or rather, to allude to Divinity as Feminine. The multitude of refer-ences to goddesses in the ancient novels represents no peculiar aberration. Nor does the emphatic appearance of a goddess in any individual work of fiction in-dicate a peculiar swerve from Novel into "Romance." Rather, such references constitute a novelistic norm. We can pick up the goddess-references more readily in the oldest novels because in "pagan" antiquity there was less reason to be shy of referring to female deities by name. But the goddesses—often going under their old names—are to be found abundantly in later novels from the Middle Ages to the end of the twentieth century.

The particular goddess within any individual novel serves a multitude of necessary functions. The reader's contact with the Goddess—usually but not always brief—is different from the contact with Eros. Eros tells us about our own desire. The Goddess speaks more objectively, not only as validator of desiring, but also as assurance that our desires have objects. One of these objects is the novel itself. The Goddess in any given novel figures forth the novel as an entirety. On seeing the Goddess, even if she or the image of her is mistreated by the characters, we sense the possibility of healing the self-alienation found in most *ekphrasis*. The Goddess of prose narration stands for the subscription—on the part of author, readers, and characters alike—to the physicality of the narratable world. The goddess stands for that which is not engaged in or shut down by any "closure" that the plot can offer—to borrow from D. A. Miller, with his preference for the *narratable*, the middle of the novel, to its ending.[4]

The Goddess within the novel (any novel) stands for that which is, as it were, "bigger." Not that which is fashionably Other, for the Goddess recognizes and incorporates the perfectly this, the perfectly here-and-now. But she reflects for us, in her generous embodiment, all that is bigger than the novel, including the whole of *physis*, the realm of *zoē*. The Goddess tells us there is more to the world. In E. M. Forster's *A Passage to India* (1924), Mrs. Moore's name is picked up by the Indians, changed, and transformed, to the annoyance of her son:

> He disliked it more than he showed. It was revolting to hear his mother travestied into Esmiss Esmoor, a Hindu goddess.
>
> "Esmiss Esmoor
> Esmiss Esmoor
> Esmiss Esmoor
> Esmiss Esmoor. . . ." (219)

Mrs. Moore is transformed into the Isis of More, the goddess not only of suppressed Justice, but also of all that is to come—of the more-than-this.

The Goddess within a novel does not preside over "ending" *per se*, any more than over "beginning," but over everything, over all that is tellable, *narratable*. With and in her we recognize the universe with which we are playing here in the fiction. Though her image may turn up within the fabricated objects scattered about the novel, as in paintings or statues, she is never to be held to be strictly *within* those. Characters who treat even her images cavalierly do so with some peril to themselves—though she is wonderfully tolerant, too. The Universe, which brings the flesh into existence, also nurtures our self-reflective play with imaginary flesh-and-blood, in our toy world where neither polenta nor diamonds, neither babies nor paintings, are "real." The Goddess who is the Bigger, who can only be imaged, reminds us that we never (even in what we call "real" life) have perfect hold on reality, that all of our "realities" are partly fictional, or glimpses extreme and scattering bright of something imperfectly discoverable. We require, like Psyché, the *benivolam misericordiam* of the Goddess, her benevolent mercy on us and on our endeavors.

Late twentieth-century criticism has been fascinated by the mystique of absence. For Derrida, writing is itself absence and alienation. Todorov, in his analysis of Henry James's ghost stories, says the "ghost" is "the individual . . . that ghost which produces speech, that absence which we try in vain to apprehend . . . which produces, in its void, discourse itself" (*Poetics of Prose*, trans. Howard, 189). Roland Barthes says "the classic text" is, like the marquise in the last line of Balzac's *Sarrasine*, "pensive." "It still seems always to hold in reserve a last sense [or "final meaning," *un dernier sens*], which it does not express but whose place it keeps free and signifying: this degree zero of meaning [*sens*] . . . this supplementary meaning . . . is pensiveness [*la pensivité*]: pensiveness . . . is the signifying of the inexpressible, not of the unexpressed" (*S/Z*, 222). A text (however feeble) can attempt to supplement itself with such an "*et caetera* of plenitude." Barthes sees indicators such as the marquise's continuing thoughtfulness as a kind of trick, indicating not only a plenitude in the author's great mind, but more absurdly some plenitude in reality justifying a refusal to admit closure. Barthes may treat such signifiers of a sense beyond our discourse as cheats, but his own system depends on absences.

The post-Freudian mystique of *absence* fostered by late twentieth-century French critics can in itself be interpreted as a clever encoding of paternal power in one of its last great strongholds. "Presence" is deemed irreparably *vulgar*. It is hard to prophesy just how much energy it will take to turn Western attention back to the value of "presence," which is by definition fleshly, physical, inferior and thus "feminine." The novel—the "feminine" literary form *par excellence*—is of all literary forms the one that has the most respect for "presence." It thus puts itself in a relation of hostility to some forms of criticism recently dominant; it is noticeable, too, that the major French male critics (unlike Russian formalists) have disdained to deal very much with the novel. (Barthes in *S/Z* deals with a short story by Balzac, but not a novel.)

As a figure, the Goddess thus reveals an absence (only the *sign* of the Goddess can be here, not the Goddess). Yet as trope, as active power who reflects and endorses our reading and underlies pleasure itself, the Goddess is everywhere present within the novel, irrepressibly so. She is the signature of plenitude both in the book and in the universe. She reminds us that it is our physical selves and not just "a mind" that we bring to "a text," which is also a book—printed book or Egyptian papyri scratched with a sharp reed from the Nile. Physical being is everywhere and is never truly "absent"—this the goddess keeps saying. She is the energy by which we are present to ourselves and to the world we breathe and eat as well as to the book. It is not a dead person that turns the page, or fingers the computer keyboard. The aesthetics of the Novel—or of Novel-reading—is an aesthetics of presence, and is not going to yield to "dry transcendence" in any of its forms, including the theory that spiritualizes everything into signs. Yet the Goddess herself keeps a sharp eye on signs, which she approves in a non-Freudian manner, as she approves cheese, urine, pots and pans, and roses.

The Goddess of the novel may appear in or as a sign, as *ekphrasis* and/or dream, showing that she is known both to public consciousness and to private under-consciousness. At the end of the philosophic *Chion of Heraclea*, the hero is about to go off to kill the tyrant—a heroic deed that will surely lead to his own death. He is reassured by the vision of a goddess in a dream, an episode that closes the book: "For methought I saw a woman, divinely tall and most divinely fair [*theion ti chrēma kallous kai megethous*], who crowned me with wild olives and fillets" (78).

This divine being shows Chion his tomb, but as a sign of victory and completion. The tomb is an ending, but not the ultimate end, which is the free life of Athenians. The particular goddess here is not named; logically she should be Athena, the guardian of Athens. Chion's acceptance of his death is quite different from despair in this life.[5] A number of novel characters (Chaireas, for instance) are tempted to commit suicide (as Porphyry was in "real life"), but that response novels tend to postpone or override. Life is to be respected, to be lived without despair, and it must be endowed with both absurdity (breaking out of narrow proprieties) and significance. Chion gains meaning for his life; his goddess assures him that his individual life is deeply important. Wherever in a novel we see the Goddess, even at her most austere and uncompromising, we are assured of the significance of living. We are deeply assured of this at the same time as we recognize, on seeing her, that there is more to life than the individual existence. The Goddess as "signature of plenitude" unites the world outside the novel with the imagined world within it; she is not a hidden or reserved alibi pretending that there is something inexpressible remaining within the story (Barthes' "pensiveness"). Rather, she is the open memory—our own memory—that the world is large and full of sensations, thoughts, and meanings.

APHRODITE-VENUS

Venus—or Aphrodite—has been and continues to be the most popular single choice for Goddess-reference. Aphrodite dominates *Chaireas and Kallirrhoé* by Chariton of Aphrodite's city. She is a controlling presence: the lovers meet on her festival day, and Kallirrhoé, who looks like the goddess, prays before her image. Venus is also abundantly visible in, for example, Boccaccio's *Filocolo*. It is Venus who spurs Florio on to rescue Biancifiore from a fiery death. The grand apparition of Venus comes to console the immured heroine who earnestly prays to "santa Venus":

> "O holy Venus, to whose service my soul is entirely disposed, by your high godhead do not abandon me, and by that love you bore for your sweet Adonis, help me. . . ." Hardly had Biancifiore finished saying these words, when in her prison there suddenly appeared a great and marvelous light, within which was manifested Venus naked, save only that she was wrapped round with a purple veil, crowned with gold, with an olive branch in her hand. Once arrived, she said immediately, "Ah, beautiful girl, do not distress yourself. We will never abandon you: be comforted." (II: 202)

Venus uses the royal "we," as becomes a great personage, but her advice is kind. In Venus's *confortati* we can recognize the injunction of the ancient novel: *tharsei*. Take courage, be strong and of good cheer. Boccaccio's full and ornate manner of representing the goddess seems to call out for illustration. It is no wonder that she figures several times in the first illustrated printed version of 1478. We can see her there, her nearly naked figure (slightly big-bellied) presiding over Cupid and the lovers, as she presides over their story. (See Plate 36.) The representations of Venus in medieval fiction contributed to the desire of Renaissance artists to portray this goddess—as Botticelli does in *The Birth of Venus*, which picks up artistic, philosophical, and literary material.[6] Botticelli is certainly in line with the antique artists, inheriting conventions expressed in ancient pictures he could not have seen, like the "Birth of Venus" from Pompeii, where Venus lolls upon her famed shell, surrounded by abundant and lovely blue water. (See Plate 37.) She seems another sailor, like Europa. It is no wonder that Aphrodite-Venus, such a very representable if not uttlerly respectable personage, should figure so often in modern novels as well as ancient ones.

Venus can enter fiction in an *ekphrasis*, which is as proper a coach as her shell: "Reader, perhaps thou hast seen the Statue of the *Venus de Medicis*," Fielding suggests in *Tom Jones* (117). Susan Sontag's *The Volcano Lover* (1992) begins with the description of a picture, "a *Venus Disarming Cupid* thought to be by Correggio" (4). This picture, unsold at an auction, serves to illustrate the social class of the various characters involved and to draw attention to the egotistic possessiveness of the owner, the man who can say "My Venus" (5). But the *ekphrasis* achieved chiefly through the use of the title draws attention to the puzzles of the picture. Can Venus disarm Cupid?—and what happens to us if Venus has disarmed Cupid? Without strong desire, are we capable of love?

The Venus who turns up in an artwork may be impudently treated by the characters—who do not know the risks they run. In Balzac's *La Peau de chagrin* we are shown in Rastignac's lodgings "a clock surmounted by an admirable Venus crouched on her tortoise; but she held between her arms a half-smoked cigar" (216). No coarse abuse of the goddess's image, even thrusting a cigar into its helpless arms, can entirely conquer or put to flight the Venus who acts through slow time (her tortoise) as well as instantaneously. Venus acts upon matter generatively through time. In Charles Dickens's *Our Mutual Friend* we see a negative parody of Venus's back kitchen in Mr. Venus's shop. Mr. Venus's business card describes him as "Preserver of Animals and Birds" (83), but his "preservation" is taxidermy. He makes false dead forms out of the detritus of living—bones, mold, mummy, "dried cuticle." This "Venus" may well lament that "the world that appeared so flowery has ceased to blow" (81), since he is a mock-Venus who can give form only to death, not life. As *Mr. Venus* his other name may be Adonis, and the ancient ritual "Garden of Adonis" is a representation of death and dying.[7] "Mr. Venus" as an anti-Venus cannot supply the generative principle that the whole novel seeks.

Venus may be invoked in some ritual action or object, without her name appearing. In Forster's *Howards End* (1910), the "pigs' teeth stuck into the trunk" of the finest wych-elm in Hertfordshire" (68) are a homage to Venus and to life; the pig was sacred to the Celtic equivalent of Venus. Pigs' teeth stuck into a tree have at least the merit of sustaining the physical and living powers of the female divinity, whereas elaborate and lovely ekphrastic signs can be treated as aesthetic objects only—a fact ironically signaled in Balzac and Sontag. Joyce presents this conflict of ideas within images of Venus in the sequence of *Ulysses*, where Bloom investigates the public library's statue of Aphrodite to see if she is represented with an asshole. Bloom muses after lunch: "Lovely forms of women sculpted Junonian. Immortal lovely. And we stuffing food in one hole and out behind: food, chyle, blood, dung, earth, food: have to feed it like stoking an engine. They have no. Never looked. I'll look today" (144–145). Bloom's subsequent research is unsympathetically viewed by Buck Mulligan. Bloom's initial abstraction of ideal women as forms "sculpted Junonian" betrays the divisive Neoplatonic artthought of the West, which it is partly Joyce's business to contradict. Throughout Joyce's novel, our attention is directed to what male mankind has made of the goddesses, who turn up in works of all kinds, including *Venus in Furs*, and *Isis Unveiled*. If Aphrodite is not sculpted with an anus, she ought to be, for it is not her business to despise the work of life, which she creates and promotes. "Food, chyle, blood, dung, earth, food"—these are her business, as they are Bloom's— and Joyce's. Bloom faces Psyche's problem in relating the goddess and food, sorting and categorizing without despair and without rejection. His name shows that he is one of Venus's creatures; he is a-bloom, and his world (on June 16) blossoms.

Venus has often been appropriated as a mere art object, on the (hidden) grounds that she represents something low as well as lovely—hence a suitable repository for old cigars. The novelist also may suffer from a dual desire, to adore Venus-Aphrodite and to treat her as trash. This dual desire is never more apparent than in Zola's *Nana*, in which the heroine acts Venus in an Offenbach-style musical drama in the most vulgar of theaters. The story, the complaint of mortals against the gods because of the confusion and unhappiness love creates, is now a music-hall vulgarity appealing to a low audience, which Zola's narrative voice must reprehend: "This carnival of the gods, Olympus dragged through the mud, an entire religion, an entire poesy jeered at, seemed an exquisite treat [*un régal exquis*]" (47). An official hierarchy, a solemn tradition, is being perverted in joining with carnival, mud, and food (*régal*). The highest impertinence is that of Nana, who takes the role of Venus:

> Then, hardly had Diana found herself alone than Venus arrived. A shiver stirred the room. Nana was naked. She was naked with a tranquil audacity, certain of the omnipotence of her flesh. A single gauze enveloped her; her round shoulders, her amazonian bosom whose rosy points held themselves raised and rigid as lances, her large haunches which rolled in voluptuous balancing, her thighs of blond fat—her entire body revealed itself, let itself be seen beneath the light tissue, as of the whiteness of foam. This was Venus born of the waves, with only her hair for veil. And, when Nana raised her arms, they could see, in the footlights, the golden fleeces of her armpits. . . . A wind seemed to have passed, very soft, laden with stifled menace. Suddenly, within the good child, the woman arose, disquieting, bringing the gust of madness of her sex [*le coup de folie de son sexe*], opening the unknown of desire [*ouvrant l'inconnu du désir*]. (52–53)

Nana becomes known as the "Blonde Vénus" (she may remind us of both Marilyn Monroe and Madonna). The essence of her "act" is to appear. She is

Aphrodite-resembling Kallirrhoé rendered sinister. Like the "lilac foam" of Elstir's painting, her white flesh, described in painterly terms (*blancheur d'écume*), becomes the white foam of the Homeric wavecrash. Nana is so fascinating that she must be reprehensible; a very bodily vessel, she menaces male purity in the contamination of womankind, with its womanly smell (an image frequently invoked by Zola with repulsion) and the fleshly fullness of boundless and undisciplined life. It is Zola above all who trashes Nana, who will not let her escape with either life or beauty. At some level, her punishment comes upon her for her blasphemy against a goddess, but at another level it is the Goddess, Blonde Venus herself, that Zola would like to repudiate. Zola climaxes his novel by killing off the Goddess herself, when Nana is turned into a foul amorphous porridge (*kykeōn?*) of putrescence. This particular novel is saturated with the Goddess and can never get away from the fascinated representation of her in living enactment. The sight of Venus is terrible because it opens us to "the unknown of desire," while informing us of the body's ineluctable energies and presence.

Venus' fleshly work within the realm of matter and generation makes her forever trashy in Neoplatonist eyes. We in turn may distrust the Diotima of the *Symposium*, the Mantinean prophetess who supposedly taught Socrates the high theory of Love. (See also David Halperin, "Why Is Diotima a Woman? Platonic *Erōs* and the Figuration of Gender," in *Before Sexuality*, 257–308.) Diotima says it is *slavelike* to fasten on the beauty of an individual person or thing. Diotima's ladder, which we call "Platonic," means climbing away from the love of the individual, upward to a love of all beautiful bodies, thence to love of Beauty itself, its real being, *to kalon* (*Symposium*, 206). This prophetess seems a projection invented to take the place that might properly belong to the goddess in such a novelistic narrative as the *Symposium*. Diotima would never laugh and gain a cheerful heart with Iambe or Baubo. She forbids one to care for flesh, world, or person. In Diotima we can see a deeply intellectual counteraction of the Mysteries. The Goddess—any old goddess—knows it is not just "beauty" that people fall in love with. We are not abstractions, nor is the individual to be forsaken for some fine abstraction. In Sterne's *Tristram Shandy* these issues are debated with open reference to the *Symposium* and its interpreters; it is no surprise that Walter enthusiastically embraces Diotima's—or rather Plato's—theory:

> I wish, *Yorick*, said my father, you had read *Plato*; for there you would have learnt that there are two LOVES—I know there were two RELIGIONS, replied *Yorick*, amongst the ancients—one—for the vulgar, and another for the learned; but I think ONE LOVE might have served both of them very well—
>
> It could not; replied my father—and for the same reasons: for of these LOVES, according to *Ficinus*'s comment upon *Valesius*, the one is *rational*——
>
> ——the other is *natural*——
>
> the first ancient—without mother—where *Venus* had nothing to do: the second, begotten of *Jupiter* and *Dione*—
>
> ——Pray brother, quoth my uncle *Toby*, what has a man who believes in God to do with this? My father could not stop to answer, for fear of breaking the thread of his discourse——

This latter, continued he, partakes wholly of the nature of *Venus*.

The first, which is the golden chain let down from heaven, excites to love heroic, which comprehends in it, and excites to the desire of philosophy and truth—the second, excites to *desire*, simply——

——I think the procreation of children as beneficial to the world, said *Yorick*, as the finding out the longitude——

——To be sure, said my mother, *love* keeps peace in the world—

—In the *house*—my dear, I own——

It replenishes the earth; said my mother——

But it keeps heaven empty——my dear; replied my father.

(*Tristram Shandy*, 452–453)

Walter Shandy, who dislikes what is physical and emotional, tries to sustain a traditional Western division between intellectual-spiritual love, which leads to the life of the mind, and mere desire, which is the province of low animal lust and the business of procreation. Yorick's response regarding the "One Love" is not only democratic but philosophically subversive of the entire Neoplatonic or Stoic position. Yorick indicates that there should be no division made between the divine and the human, nor between the intellectual life and sexual love.

Tristram's mother speaks for Venus, in favor of Love's power to keep peace in the world and replenish the earth. Mrs. Shandy takes on Venus' voice here for a moment, in contradiction of Walter Shandy, who would like to eliminate the feminine if only it were possible—the first love is ancient, "without mother." As Sterne makes us see, Walter Shandy is typically Western in his impossible wish to do without mother, to get rid of the feminine in the world. Walter Shandy would like to set himself up as the patriarchal authority, with access to a spiritual system of knowledge that relegates women to such a low point of mere matter that they become invisible to Love. The irony of Sterne's novel rests partly on the fact that Walter's reiterated patriarchal assurance has a shaky base. We may believe that Mrs. Shandy was already pregnant (by Yorick) during that initial parental congress—notoriously interrupted by bored Mrs. Shandy's question about the clock. Tristram himself may insist, with anxious emphasis, on the certainty of that moment of conception, which not only explains his temperament but bestows upon him legitimacy. That "origin," however, is deducibly false, and Tristram protests too much. Mrs. Shandy, like Kallirrhoé, has taken it upon herself to reweave fatherhood. The worst that Roman or English laws regarding marriage, property, and inheritance could imagine has happened in *Tristram Shandy*. The cuckoo is in the nest—and everyone is pretty comfortable. Venus orders her world. *Tristram Shandy*, like its hero, lingers comically in the odd discomforts of incarnation, without yielding to the systems (including Neoplatonism and property law) that would devalue that incarnation.

ARTEMIS-DIANA

Venus-Aphrodite usually looks approachable; she is generously attractive, in statue or in fleshly embodiment. Artemis-Diana is another matter. In her myths, she is formidable—his own fell hounds at her command tear peeping Actaeon to pieces. She is not to be controlled by male gaze or desire. In the power of Artemis, woman regains her perpetual virginity, an independent right over her own being, which can never be taken away from her through property-exchange or sexual "possession." She may seem fiercely dominating—Mann's Felix Krull, a hermaphroditic Hermes, servant of Aphrodite, is taken sexually by the wealthy Diana, who treats him to a sexual scene closely resembling that of the ass and the lady in Apuleius.

The dangerousness of Artemis-Diana is a constant novelistic subject. Lucius in *The Golden Ass* sees the statue of Diana, dominating a room also decorated with four images of the goddess bearing the palm—i.e., Nike, or Victory. The gigantic statue of Diana, *lapis Parius in Dianam factus*, makes the spectator seem small. Absorbed into the scene the humbled viewer, peering into the pool at the goddess's feet, becomes another Actaeon. The goddess, windblown and free, surrounded by hunting dogs, commands a certain awe; *maiestate numinis venerabile* (64), she is to be venerated in the majesty of her divinity. Lucius ought to be appalled at such an encounter with this goddess, for Lucius, the new Actaeon with his soft but demanding ego, is no match for the energetic deity striding to meet him. Lucius foolishly admires the statue as a connoisseur, thinking Diana merely a work of art, a decoration for Byrrhena's hall.

In Montemayor's *Diana*, the statue of Diana is elaborated, as a decoration in the richly symbolic room of *la sabia Felicia*, "the wise Felicia" (or "the enchantress Felicia"):

> they entered another, inner chamber, which in its richness made everything they that had seen before seem like nothing in comparison, for all the walls were covered with fine gold and the floor with precious stones. Round about the rich chamber were many figures of ladies of Spain and of other nations, and the highest was the goddess Diana, life-size, made of Corinthian metal [i.e., bronze], with clothing of chased gold, ornamented with many gems and pearls of great value, with her bow in her hand and her quiver hung about her neck, surrounded by nymphs more beautiful than the sun. In such great admiration were both the shepherds and shepherdesses plunged at the things which they were seeing that they didn't know what to say, for the wealth of the house was so great. The images here were so natural, and the artfulness of the chamber and the arrangement of the ladies pictured here were such that no one could imagine anything in the world more perfect. On one side of the room there were four laurel trees of gold, enameled in green, so natural that the trees of the fields could not be more so. And beside these was a little fountain, all made of fine silver, in the middle of which was a nymph of gold who made the water clearer for the lovely fish. And seated beside the fountain was the celebrated Orpheus, singing of the age that was, at the time when his Eurydice was pursued by the importunate Aristæus. . .
> (178–179)

Montemayor's description, borrowing the mixture of living and artificial from the Byzantine (and Moorish) traditions, here undergoes delicate modulations. From the hard artifice of Diana, made of *Corinthian* metal, the bronze that hints at the name of her opposite and complement, Corinthian Venus, we move to the fountain of the solitary golden nymph, and then to Orpheus, who stands for the human fabricator in words, like the novelist himself. Through Orpheus' presence we remember his Eurydice, who was made not of metal but of vulnerable flesh, and who died from a snakebite trying to elude Aristæus. Diana presides over chastity and choice, and their consequences, over hardness and softness, over image and words. Here we find the nymphs that irritated Freud so much in Dora's case, in the proud attendants of Diana, and particularly in the solitary golden girl of the little fountain who broods over her silver pool—the muddy margin here mundified in the meeting of purer water and pure metal.

Flaubert's major goddess figure in *L'Education sentimentale* is likewise an ekphrastic Diana. In a short idyllic interlude, Frédéric and Rosanette visit Fontainebleau and tour the palace, where they see various images of Henri II's celebrated mistress, Diane de Poitiers, painted "in the form of Diana the Huntress and even as the Infernal Diana, doubtless to mark her power even beyond the tomb." The images confirm the glory of the human Diane and suggest some remaining essence of her, "an indistinct voice, a prolonged radiance. Frédéric was overtaken by a retrospective and inexpressible lust" (394). He transfers his feeling to Rosanette, who is too ignorant to have mental associations with either the goddess or the royal mistress. It is perverse to lust after Diana—and the cool images of the goddess, huntress, and controller of the Underworld, in some sense mock her avatars (Diane and Rosanette) while condemning Frédéric (like Lucius) to Actaeon's fate.

A different figure, arising out of the same convention, is the Artemis-Diana described by Kingsley Amis's Jake in *Jake's Thing*, appearing suddenly to view in the window of an Edwardian house now converted to the purposes of the therapy workshop:

> He looked at the stained-glass panel. It was divided vertically into three scenes: a kneeling girl above whom a heavily robed male figure was raising a sword, the same figure with lowered sword contemplating a quadruped about the size of a large dog, and the girl from the first scene accompanied by someone of uncertain sex carrying a curved wand and directing her towards a classical portico. He knew the subject but couldn't place it. . . .
>
> Jake had now identified the subject of the window. The curved wand was a bow, its bearer was Artemis, the portico was that of her temple at Tauris, the girl was Iphigenia, daughter of Agamemnon and Clytemnestra, and the beast was the deer supernaturally substituted for her by Artemis to forestall her sacrifice at Aulis. Shockingly rendered, but then. For a moment he felt pleased with himself. (257–259)

The work of art in Amis teases us as much as it does in Montemayor, seeming equally to call for explication and detailed commentary. On one level, in this story the saved Iphigenia is surely impotent Jake's "thing," his penis, which he can "save" from being reactivated, thus throwing in his angry lot with the goddess of chastity. Artemis herself, however, who carries her curved bow, as a magic wand, remains enigmatic, even her sex uncertain, and she gestures towards a doorway, a future where sex roles may not be as they were.[8]

As in the case of other goddesses, a character may bear the goddess's name. (In Diana's case, the name may sometimes be that of less formidable representations of moon-power, like "Phoebe.") In L. M. Montgomery's *Anne of Green Gables*, the name of the heroine's best friend is "Diana."[9] On first learning it, Anne exclaims, "What a perfectly lovely name!" but Matthew has some doubts: "Well now, I dunno. There's something dreadful heathenish about it, seems to me. I'd rather Jane or Mary or some sensible name like that. But when Diana was born there was a schoolmaster boarding there and they gave him the naming of her and he called her Diana" (30). Diana is an appropriate presiding deity for a novel about girlhood; through this invocation L. M. Montgomery can also give warning about the "dreadful heathenish" elements in her novel, which quietly refuses to share some of the Christian and practically all of the Calvinist tenets of the community it describes. Diana the character has a placid amiable sensuality that contradicts her name; it is amusing that a *Diana* should get drunk. Montgomery gives her more fiercely virginal heroine the matriarchal name of Anne.

In contrast, Witi Ihimaera, the Maori novelist, has given the name of Artemis to his matriarch (in a deliberate attempt to connect Western and Maori mythologies). This Artemis, the narrator's grandmother, is the dominant spirit of a Maori family. She breaks through conventions to assert the rights of her people; she comes to a *marae*, a public gathering, and takes part as a speaker, against custom. Artemis, as she begins to speak, clothed in black and with pearls in her black hair, becomes an awesome apparition against the evening sky: "The light lessening, lessening. The black disc of the moon closing like a gate on the sun. Suddenly the pearls in the matriarch's hair began to change colour. The lustrous pale of the pearls seemed to be becoming drenched with blood" (*The Matriarch*, 91). Diana-Artemis is associated with the moon, with pearls, and with darkness. (Even L. M. Montgomery's Diana is *black*-haired, and Montemayor's Diana statue is pearl-bedecked.) As the authority of passion, purity, and courage, Diana-Artemis is the alternative: chastity as distinct from generation, female warrior as distinct from sweet mother.

JUNO-CYBELE-MAGNA MATER

Mother may be awesome rather than sweet. Hera and Juno are connected with the menstrual phases of the moon, with female fertility, and with childbirth. These important concerns inform Juno's queenliness and make her impatient, even fierce. We encounter a manifestation of Juno near the very beginning of *Wuthering Heights*, in the "huge, liver-coloured bitch pointer" (3) with her swarm of puppies. When the silly Lockwood teases her, she flies at him; he later calls her "the villain Juno" (8). Heathcliff warns him that in the house "Juno mounts sentinel" (26). The younger Cathy may be a "Mistress of Animals," but she is aided by the bitch goddess personified within the animal.

Goddesses may be alluded to in many hints and signs. In Gabriel García Márquez's *El Amor en los tiempos del cólera* (1987), Florentino Ariza meets a madwoman and makes love to her during Carnival. This girl in the plain linen dress (like a slave or a heroine in disguise) is soon recaptured. Ariza, uselessly, tries to see her when she is immured in the asylum: "And starting from Ash Wednesday he would walk along the street of the Divine Shepherdess with a box of English chocolates for her" (234). The *Divina Pastora*, the Divine Shepherdess, might be envisaged as simply a pretty rococo figurine, but the name is more suited to Cybele, the great Mistress of Animals—or to other goddesses who adopted that office, such as Hera. In Longus' novel, Chloé as shepherdess is the *Koré*, the Maiden or daughter-figure Persephone, reflecting that divine maternal nature. In Marquez's sequence the term "Divine Shepherdess" has many ironies. The hapless Koré of Ariza's Shrove Tuesday revel has beheaded an asylum guard with a machete in making her break from the asylum. This unusual Persephone, after her one resurrection night of Carnival, disappears into the pit and never returns.

Earlier in Marquez's novel, during the beginning of Florentino's lifelong passion for Fermina Daza, he saw the girl Fermina as an image of Grecian divinity: "she wore a many-pleated linen tunic that fell from her shoulders like a peplum, and on her head she wore a garland of real gardenias that gave her the appearance of a goddess crowned [*una diosa coronada*]" (83). At the very end of the novel, during the wild, deathly, and pleasurable journey along the river, on a boat flying the yellow cholera flag, Florentino plays for Fermina their waltz, entitled "La Diosa Coronada," "The Crowned Goddess" (438). Looking on the two now aged lovers, the captain of the probably doomed boat has a tardy suspicion "that it is life more than death, which owns no limits" (443). Under the Crowned Goddess Cybele, life ceaselessly demand to be loved and enjoyed. Desire moves through perpetual renewal, traveling as in Greek novels through the swampy waterplaces of matter and renewal. Incidentally, the cover of the Spanish edition of *El Amor en los tiempos del cólera* (published by Mondadori) portrays Cupid on a riverbank shooting his arrow into a swamp—a neat combination of some major tropes of the Novel, as well as of Marquez's novel.

The original description of Fermina in her gardenias suggests her sweetness and vulnerability while counteracting any belief that these are her only aspects. We become uneasily conscious of a larger force, the awful shadow of some unseen Female Power that hovers over the characters and can be felt within the novel. The sweet garland of *naturales gardenias* is also a garland of Nature; transformed into a crown it makes Fermina a representative of the Great Mother Cybele, goddess of the Triple Crown, who is the true *Diosa Coronada*.

The Goddess may thus manifest herself not only in hints and clues, like a street sign saying "Divine Shepherdess," but also in what might be called cryptic impersonation by a character, or hidden embodiment. Customarily, if a character identifies another character (like Nana) as the Goddess, or as goddess-likeness, such identification carries no such retribution as that shadowing the unfortunate personage who identifies Eros in another's body—or in his own. The Goddess when she appears embodied for her world in a character, however, is never without mystery.

One of the most powerful instances of such embodiment is to be found in the Mother Goddess in Toni Morrison's *Beloved* (1987). The mysterious "Beloved," the girl who comes to Sethe's house, seems to be the reincarnation or wraith of the child that Sethe killed to save her from a life of slavery. But Belov-ed's nature is prismatic, undefined. There is a new revelation when her sister Denver follows the strangely resurrected Beloved and catches her gesture of *anasyrma*:

> Just ahead, at the edge of the stream, Denver could see her silhouette, standing barefoot in the water, lifting her black skirts up above her calves, the beautiful head lowered in rapt attention. . . . It took a mo-ment for her to drag her eyes from the spectacle of Beloved's head to see what she was staring at.

What Beloved watches is the gentle, determined, difficult and beautiful coupling of a pair of turtles.

> The gravity of their shields, clashing, countered and mocked the float-ing heads touching.
>   Beloved dropped the folds of her skirt. It spread around her. The hem darkened in the water. (105)

Beloved has hitherto seemed a child, with her love of sweets and stories— a mischievous Eros figure, at once destructive and creative. But is this Eros or the Goddess? Beloved now seems to be transformed, to change from Eros of the beautiful head (like Aschenbach's Tadzio) into the Goddess Genetrix, her skirts spreading over the water of generation. It is as Goddess she manifests herself in her last appearance.

> The singing women recognized Sethe at once and surprised them-selves by their absence of fear when they saw what stood next to her. The devil-child was clever, they thought. And beautiful. It had taken the shape of a pregnant woman, naked and smiling in the heat of the afternoon sun. Thunderblack and glistening, she stood on long straight legs, her belly big and tight. Vines of hair twisted all over her head. Jesus. Her smile was dazzling. (261)

The "vines" of Beloved's hair are Dionysian, perhaps, but here associated with the divinity of female in generation, as the goddess of all nature. The singing women's exclamation connects the vines with Jesus' holiness ("I am the vine, ye are the branches"). In a goddess-moment Beloved incarnates and manifests her-self before her disappearance. This is not the same as saying that Beloved throughout was a goddess, has been a goddess in disguise—only that in the leap-ing moment she is the enactment and representative of a goddess here without a name, the Goddess of Life.

ISIS

In ancient North African literature and culture, Isis is the Great Goddess who presides over life. Isis is a recurrent power in the novels of antiquity. In *Ephes-iaka*, for instance, the hero, and heroine, denizens of Artemis' city Ephesus, are reunited at last in Rhodes, and the Rhodians watch their reunion by the temple of Isis. The people (as one unit, *ho dēmos*) roars its approval and thanksgiving, praising Isis the Great Goddess: *megalēn theon anakalountes tēn Isin* (75). Apuleius, the African from Madaura, has given the greatest and most detailed expression of Isis' power.

Lucius the Ass is blessed by the vision of the Goddess after his prayer to the Queen of Heaven (*Regina caeli*). The great head comes out of the sea, then the whole body emerges. The gigantic vision wears a crown of various flowers, and just above her forehead "an image of the moon shone with white light." To left and right her crown is defined by the wrinkling of rearing snakes (*insurgentium viperarum*), and above, her head is ornamented by ears of wheat (*spicis Cerialibus*). Her robe of many shining colors is partly hidden by a gleaming black cloak: "and what more and more confounded my eyesight, a cloak of darkest black shining with a dark glow. . . . On the edges of it and on the cloak itself scattered stars were glittering, and in the midst of them a full moon breathed forth its flaming fires. Wherever streamed the verge of that singular robe, a garland of all kinds of fruits and flowers was attached with an inseparable knot" (II : 296). This Isis combines, as the Renaissance commentators on Apuleius realized, the attributes of Ceres (*déesse des bleds*), Hekate, Cybele, the lunar Diana, and others. Isis herself proclaims that she is worshipped under many names and in various rites; she is called Minerva, Venus, Diana, Proserpine, Juno, Bellona—but all these are one. The Egyptians call her by her true name, Queen Isis (*appellant vero nomine reginam Isidem*, II : 300). We can easily see that she is Medusa (with her snakes); the Divine Shepherdess, flower-crowned (reflected in Fermina Diaz); the lunar Aphrodite (reflected in Ihimaera's black-clad and glowing Matriarch); and the goddess of generation, like Morrison's Beloved, who likewise stands in dark drapery above water. Isis is Queen of Heaven as well as of earth—and of things under the earth and under the sea.

We might not expect to see or to call upon Isis very often nowadays—but a recent novel gives us the most detailed account of the Isis myth of any novel in Western literature. "Therefore, I asked my great-grandfather if he would tell the story of Osiris and of all the Gods Who lived at the beginning of our land," says the ghostly narrator of Norman Mailer's *Ancient Evenings* (45). The whole of Book II of this novel, "The Book of the Gods," is taken up with the narration of the stories of Osiris, Isis, Horus, Set, and Nephthys, with a very full account of the wanderings of Isis. Mailer has an interest in relating Israel's ancient antagonist, Egypt, to the religion and fate of the Hebrews. The Egyptian religion Mailer imagines is strongly male, but even so the presence of Isis—and of other goddess such as Astarte and Nephthys—is felt.

Mailer is a successor of Thomas Mann, whose *Joseph and His Brothers*, while designed to exalt (ultimately) male deity and Hebrew vision, yet must take the Egyptian gods seriously, and give a place to Hathor. Joseph's own vision of the Divine refuses to be purely masculine: "Was He not at once Father and Mother of the world, with two faces, one a man's, turned toward the daylight, and the other a woman's, looking into the darkness?" (trans. Lowe-Porter, 745).

Mann and Mailer deal extensively with the "matter of Egypt." The matter of Egypt, its religion and its vision, was, as we have seen, a feature of the ancient novel, although when those novels were written Egypt was a conquered province of Rome, and Greek and Roman philosophy and science seemed to have far outstripped the older civilization. Yet the novels repeatedly suggest the need to create some kind of link with Egypt, and to acknowledge a relation to Africa, including the African religious vision. That the heroine of *Aithiopika* comes from Africa, that she turns out to be part black (or black striped) was after all not ignored by most translators and readers of the Early Modern period, who literally *saw* (in illustrations) a black African in rescuing Sisimithres, and did not imagine with Merkelbach that the novel really had nothing to do with Ethiopians. (See Plate 38.) Egyptian reference persists in novels of all kinds and in various periods; for instance, we can see in Tristram Shandy's imagining himself spontaneously generated by the Nile in Nile mud (277) a hidden example of what might be called the "Nilotic desire" that returns with such great force in *Ancient Evenings*.

The Novel itself seems to yearn towards that ancient matter, and to look for its old friend Egypt and its mother Isis from time to time.

MARY

The goddesses in novel-references are not always what we call "pagan." In *Tirant lo Blanc*, the antique goddesses are certainly well represented, especially at the celebration in Constantinople with its pageant show on a platform: "There sat wise Sybil, gazing now here and now there, while other masked goddesses sat at her feet, since in the past the pagans had thought them heavenly bodies. Those ladies who had loved most truly waited upon them . . ." (trans. Rosenthal, 327). Martorell here clearly identifies these goddesses as the subject of *pagan* thought. His own book is dedicated "To the honour, praise and glory of our Lord Jesus Christ and His glorious and holy mother, Our Lady the Virgin Mary" (xxvii). Mary as a dedicatee is a "patron"—or matron—of the work. Few novelists have taken such a bold step in their dedications, but the Blessed Virgin Mother, Holy Mary, makes frequent appearances in novels.

The ambiguity that inheres in the idea of Mary as expressed and promoted within the Church and within Roman Catholicism in the latest centuries has been documented in Marina Warner in *Alone of All Her Sex* (1976). The meek, holy, and pure Virgin has often been used repressively against women. Women are sinflesh, only the Blessed One is free from the taint of stinking womanhood. But Mary the Mother of Mercy is not always so meek and pale as this (relatively modern) image makes out, and within novels she is, like Isis and Ceres, a Power. Byzantine images (i.e., images emanating from Syria–Asia Minor) long presented Mary in conjunction with the whorl of the world, the spinning of the flesh. Mary receives the red wool from the high priest in the mosaic in the Church of St. Chora, Constantinople. Mary is represented as bearing a spindle, as she is in a mosaic in the old Byzantine church on the island of Torcello, near Venice. She carries the spindle in her left hand, her right hand being raised in prayer towards the heavens, as we see her in a Byzantine statue in the Venetian Church of San Giacomo dell 'Orio. This representation of the life-spinning power acts as Frontispiece and gateway to Part III of this book (Plate 31). Mary thus represents, not the Hegelian turning of matter into spirit, but the mystic move of turning spirit into matter, rather as the whirling dervishes of Konya (Thekla's home town) in their spinning draw down the spiritual power of the universe into time and space.

What we term "the Rise of the Novel," meaning the advent of Prescriptive Realism, was Protestant enough to dismiss Mary out of hand. Despite the lofty desire to do without the feminine in the idea of Divinity, the tendency, theologically and socially, is to find some way back to it. Julia Kristeva in *Histoires d'amour* (1983) remarks, "The Mother and her attributes, evoking sorrowful humanity, thus become representatives of a 'return of the repressed' in monotheism," and she adds "it is likely that all beliefs in resurrections are rooted in mythologies marked by the strong dominance of a mother goddess" ("Stabat mater," in *Tales of Love*, trans. Roudiez, 249–251).[10] Fantasy seeks its morbid pleasure "in the area around the *hole* (Gustav Aschenbach calls it the 'abyss')—the adored and the abhorred maternal sex" (*Tales of Love*, 79). Fantasy creates a goddess, whereas what is needed is "an heretical ethics separate from morality" and a music that "swallows up the goddesses and removes their necessity" ("Stabat mater," in *Tales of Love*, 262–263). Kristeva's book itself ends with a desire for rebirth somehow through *some* kind of love. And what stronger figure have we for rebirth through love—and love here-and-now, uncelestial—than the Goddess? Kristeva marvels at the ability of the goddess-figure as Virgin to sop up the "abject" (everything that civilization throws away including birth, corpses, excreta, the flesh). It is indeed the Goddess's business to make sure we can throw nothing away. Kristeva herself is something of a romantic absolutist, and very high minded. The Goddess, who can laugh at Iambe's sharp jests and Baubo's dirty gestures, brings us to ourselves, however, unmundified.

Through the female "abyss" life returns, but never returns with pure sameness. Here both mankind and womankind are made. After all, Persephone, like Jesus, came from the womb, came through the dark labyrinth of the birth canal fluidly and confusedly into being in the world. Mary is attractive as the point at which the riddle of the transcendent and the physical can be set at rest, the two sides stitched together, or held in a solution not abstract but personal. Mary ever relates to the personal. She recurs and returns, even in novels by Protestant (or ex-Protestant rationalist) writers. Like Diana and Venus, Mary may appear in *ekphrasis*, as picture or statue, and she can likewise be invoked by the name of a character. (Mary Wollstonecraft's conscious and perpetual use of her own first name in her fictions indicates an awareness of the name's power.)

Margaret Atwood is apparently taking on (both assuming and combating with) the tradition of realism as a Protestant tradition in *Cat's Eye* (1988), a work that brings the Virgin Mary into central focus. The heroine, Elaine, as a child is on the point of freezing to death in the creek when she is saved by a vision:

> The person who was standing on the bridge is moving through the railing, or melting into it. It's a woman, I can see the long skirt now, or is it a long cloak? (202). Elaine knows who this is, because she once picked up a Roman Catholic picture in the street, presenting the Virgin Mary in a clear and conventional icon: in a long blue robe with a heart "large, red and tidy, like a satin heart pincushion":
>
> The Virgin Mary is in some of our [i.e., Protestant] Sunday school papers, but never with a crown, never with a pincushion heart, never all by herself. She is always more or less in the background. Not much fuss is made over her. . . . (195)

Fearing taunts from her schoolmates, Elaine throws the paper away, but, in a secret gesture of rebellion, she starts praying to the Virgin Mary. Elaine grows up to be an artist, and incorporates her vision in her painting entitled *Unified Field Theory*:

> Positioned above the top railing of the bridge, but so her feet are not quite touching it, is a woman dressed in black, with a black hood or veil covering her hair. Here and there on the black of her dress or cloak there are pinpoints of light. The sky behind her is the sky after sunset; at the top of it is the lower half of the moon. Her face is partly in shadow. . . .
>
> Underneath the bridge is the night sky, as seen through a telescope. Star upon star, red, blue, yellow, and white, swirling nebulae, galaxy upon galaxy: the universe, in its incandescence and darkness. Or so you think. But there are also stones down there, beetles and small roots, because this is the underside of the ground.
>
> At the lower edge of the painting the darkness pales and merges into a lighter tone, the clear blue of water, because the creek flows there, underneath the earth, underneath the bridge, down from the cemetery. The land of the dead people. (430–431)

The entire novel *Cat's Eye* helps us to understand the painting and to identify the various objects in terms of Elaine's life. But the imagined painting derives its images from traditional (especially Baroque) paintings of Mary, and from representations of the Goddess like that in Apuleius (surely Atwood has read *The Golden Ass*?). Atwood's Goddess is both Mother of the cosmos, and Persephone, Queen of the Underworld. What Atwood's novel certainly does *not* say is that the idea of the Goddess is to be understood only as convention, kept within the ekphrastic confines of the art gallery. Atwood is certainly no Roman Catholic apologist, but the Goddess is here taken seriously, in a way that can disturb readers. Atwood's novel rather shockingly chimes in with Apuleius' in reminding us what it might feel like to regard the Divine Female as a true possibility, as belonging to what we call "reality."

THE WORLD'S MOTHER

It is not only in Western novels that the Goddess appears, and the Goddess may appear in a Western novel in Eastern form. So she does, for example, in Elizabeth Goudge's *Green Dolphin Country* (1944), as Lung-mu, "the figure of the dragon goddess who keeps mortals safe when they pass to and fro upon the water" (158). Lung-mu is associated with the Virgin Mary in the form in which the young sailor from the Channel Islands best knew her, a folk divinity embodied in the "gaunt pinnacle of blue-grey rock," which is "shaped like a woman standing with a child in her arms," and is called by the islanders "Marie Tape-Tout, Marie Watch-All" (81). The Goddess may appear as Kwan-yin, or Mitsuko, names of the Goddess of Mercy. In Yukio Mishima's *The Temple of Dawn*, the notoriously unmerciful presiding goddess is Kali (who is in one avatar Durga):

> Gigantic effigies of the goddess had been erected everywhere in the city. They showed her in the act of punishing the deity of water buffaloes, and beautiful, angry eyebrows were depicted on the valiant face. . . .

The core of Kali is *shakti*, the original sense of which is "energy." This great mother goddess of the earth imparts to all female deities throughout the world her sublimity as mother, her feminine voluptousness, and her abominable cruelty, thereby enriching their divine nature.   (*The Temple of Dawn*, trans. Saunders and Seigle, 52–53)

Honda, the visitor from Japan, is deeply impressed by the Kali festival in Calcutta, and by the burning ghats of Benares, where corpses burn together in a rapture of undifferentiating flame, to be restored, mingled together, to the earth and to the holy water of the Ganges, "returned to their four elemental constituents and the vast Universe" (66). The furor of the burning has a festival quality about it, an acceptance of *hylē* and of the flow of life. It is characteristic of Mishima and of this novel that we hear of Kali, the vision of the necessary destruction in the universe. Yet every novel has its Kali aspect, in the difficulties, destruction and change the characters must experience—yes, and the deaths also. The death of Mr. B's mother at the beginning of *Pamela* is a Kali-moment, as is the battle of the burning reeds in *Aithiopika*, or the spontaneous combustion of Krook in Dickens's *Bleak House*. Mrs. Bedonebyasyoudid in Charles Kingsley's *The Water Babies* (1863) is the decisive and punishing (and thus "cruel") aspect of the Goddess, and it is she who presides over Tom's change of shape from land-boy to water baby, a transformation diagnosed by other humans as a death.

Yet, in Eastern as in Western novels, the Goddess broods over Creation— sky stars and beetles. (Or, in Kingsley, efts, newts, and corals.) The Goddess manifests herself and her works within human individuality and novelistic creation. *Hong Lou Meng* begins with the creative work of a goddess:

Long ago, when the goddess Nü-wa was repairing the sky, she melted down a great quantity of rock and, on the Incredible Crags of the Great Fable Mountains, moulded the amalgam into thirty-six thousand, five hundred and one large building blocks. . . . She used thirty-six thousand five hundred of these blocks . . . leaving a single odd block unused, which lay, all on its own, at the foot of Greensickness Peak in the aforementioned mountains.

Now this block of stone, having undergone the melting and moulding of a goddess, possessed magic powers.
                    (*The Dream of the Red Chamber*, trans. Hawkes, I: 47)

This goddess-wrought stone, which changes its shape to that of a small piece of jade, is in some sense the hero of the novel (its alternative title is *The Story of the the Stone*). Born with Bao-yu, the stone both "is" and "represents" his spirit and insight, as well as teasingly embodying in itself the nature of illusion, fiction, and fiction-writing. The goddess Nu-wa is a means whereby the author can respond to the theological question as to the value of this lowly world and of stories about it. The goddess is the creatrix or *demiurge* of the visible substantial universe, as of stories. From "her" emanate the desire to live, the desire to have consciousness, and the desire to have and write stories. The image of the goddess softens both Confucian and Buddhist theologies, adding a new element, which need not despise substance or entity.

More straightforwardly perhaps, but more unexpectedly, a goddess appears to one of the heroes of the masculine and violent *The Outlaws of the Marsh*. In the forty-second chapter the hero, Song Jiang, is taken by magical green boys and girls to the elegant palace of a beautiful lady: "In the center on a bejeweled carved couch sat the Queen. Dressed in filmy golden silks, she held a scepter of white jade. Her eyes were lovely, her countenance divine" (Shi Nai'an, *Outlaws of the Marsh*, trans. Shapiro, I : 672).

The elegant and majestic lady gives Song Jiang "Three Heavenly Books" with instructions: "defend the country and bring peace to the people. Expel wickedness and pursue justice" (673). Song Jiang is to memorize the books and burn them. If he commits no new sins, the queen can help save him and he will return at death to Heaven's Purple Palace. After his dream-vision is over, Song Jiang still possesses the three heavenly books, and can still taste the heavenly wine. He realizes that the lady he has seen is "the Mystic Queen of Ninth Heaven" (374), who has also saved his life. In this episode, the Queen of Ninth Heaven is interested in the individual, in the fate of a soul after death, and in the life of the common people. She exhorts Song Jiang to efforts in the cause of *justice*, in effect; not for her the abstract or "spiritual" reminder that all is illusion. It seems odd, if delightful, in a narrative of so much bloodshed and rebellion, to come upon such a lovely interlude—but the Mystic Queen does not detach herself from or disregard rebellion, or injustice committed against the people. Feminine divinity offers means of attachment, not detachment.

We should, at least experimentally, widen the scope of Apuleius, adding to his list of Near Eastern, Greek, Roman, and African deities the names of goddesses from India, China, Japan, the Pacific islands, and elsewhere. We remember the divine message given to Lucius, that these many are really one: "Behold I am here . . . the parent of all nature, mistress of all elements . . . whose one divinity is worshipped throughout all the world in many different forms, by various rites, and with manifold names" (II : 298).

We cannot get to where we as readers wish to go save by this route, and this knowledge: *Nous ny pouons retourner si ce nest par le moyen de la lune*, in the words of Michel, translator and editor of Apuleius in 1522. The "way of the moon" (or the means or medium of the moon) is sometimes powerfully felt, as in *Jane Eyre*:

> She broke forth as never moon yet burst from cloud: a hand first penetrated the sable folds and waved them away; then, not a moon, but a white human form shone in the azure, inclining a glorious brow earthward. It gazed and gazed on me. It spoke, to my spirit: immeasurably distant was the tone, yet so near, it whispered in my heart—
> 'My daughter, flee temptation!'
> 'Mother, I will.' (324)

It has been suggested by Elizabeth Imlay that Charlotte Brontë was directly indebted to Apuleius for this dream vision. But the whole tradition of the Novel stands behind such an appearance of the Divine Female. It would be wisest not to forget, while we say such things, that for millions on our planet this day visions of the Divine Female accord with an idea of "reality."[11] She may have been written out of Protestantism, but the Novel as a form has maintained its faith.

The Novel has a religious basis. As we have seen in discussing the ancient novels, these harbor and re-create elements of the mystery religions—above all, the religion of the Goddess. Reinhold Merkelbach in his Foreword to *Roman und Mysterium* boldly proclaims the religious origin of the Novel: "Epic, Lyric and Drama have their origin [*Ursprung*] in Religion. The learned—with the exception of Karl Kerényi—believed that the rise of the ancient novel could be otherwise explained. . . . We will demonstrate in this book that the Novel [*der Roman*] really grew out of religious roots" (vii).

Merkelbach himself hardly seems to notice that he has here switched from "the ancient Novel" to simply "the Novel." His book deals only with the ancient novels, but what he says is true of the Novel. We have indeed wanted to think that while Tragedy—for instance—is a noble form with deep religious origins, the Novel is the secular outgrowth of a secularizing age. (So Nietzsche, glorifying Dionysian drama, rejects the humanist novel with scorn.) But this is not the case.

The Novel perhaps has no exact "origin." Genealogy is after all a patriarchal exercise, and the choice of historical moments for begetting is seldom exact—as *Tristram Shandy* illustrates. The more we want to find a precise moment of origin, the less likely we are to find it. And in one biological view, the moment of conception is itself only a continuation, the activation of material already present and viable. But if the Novel has no formative instant of genesis, it has a *matrix*. The matrix is the religion of Eleusis . . . and of Isis . . . and of others. The religion in which the novel-reader participates is the religion of the Goddess. The activities we undertake (or have undertaken for us by the characters, in their name but for our sake) are religious activities. We undergo the ordeals of our pilgrimage, being cut, dirtied, muddied by some viscous mixture of wet and dry. We are thrown in a hole. We wander through the labyrinth, we cross water, we partake of holy food. Dreams are examined and interpreted, before we reach the greater vision. We are cheered on our way by the sight of Eros, and we have moments of calm meditation before iconic images. This entire ritual—which in long novels can last over a deal of time for the reader—restores and heartens us. *Tharsei.*

The "religion" of the novel—i.e., the religion *of the Novel*, as distinct from the religion of the *novelist*—is different from most other religions. It is a religion of the Goddess, a religion which prizes the very things that Porphyry despises— birth, generation, the material world, physical existence. The Goddess presides over and sustains the body and soul in this life of being and becoming. The Goddess is not without her own form of transcendence, but that transcendence is experienced only through the immanent.

She may not seem "realistic" or "naturalistic" but the Goddess underlies all realisms. The Trope of the Goddess tells us that what we are taking "for real," reading "as if real," has a value, because the real world beyond the book, the world in which we are breathing, has existence, form, and significance . . . has (or is) these things even beyond the degree to which we can recognize them in daily life. The goddess is the assurance that there is *more*.

The very existence of the cosmos, of all forms, and of significance itself can customarily only be figured, adverted to in playful irony. The Goddess's unifying and disturbing presence in vision or representation cannot remain with us too long, but we do catch the saving glimpse of her. She is our vision itself, she is in some important sense that to which the whole narrative tends. We are like pilgrims in Eleusis, and at last we do obtain our goal—which is not a "goal" as a climax, or finish, but the experience that endorses the idea and validity of experience. The Goddess Trope is far bigger than the other tropes, important as they are. The Goddess is the assurance that the reader's life has a meaning and can be made whole. Though (I as reader) be (like the character) a *deformis ancilla*, a fragmented and unshapely handmaiden, yet I can be transformed and given meaning. In the Goddess, as she tropes the novel and whirls it about her golden spindle, we see not that *this* story has point, or is well-made, or has form, but that point, and good making and form and substance are available to us—and likewise absurdity, amorphousness, and play.

The Goddess is not just a figure. If we say she "stands for" what makes the whole process of reading worthwhile—that would be to make her no more than a *mise-en-abîme*. Far from being folded into a pocket of the book, she reigns over it, as we know as soon as we see her. She is the assurance that individual life matters—that very fundamental belief that lets readers take an interest in characters, in actions, in stories. The Goddess is thus not some graceful decoration, but the looming up, the crystalizing, of the religious sensibility and passion that allow the Novel itself to be. From the particularity of her presence in any given novel many meanings shoot, like the green shoots of Ceres, but the whole meaning of the goddess invoked is larger than the particular reference in any individual work where she occurs. The Goddess tells us that bodily life is holy life. Bodily life is never insignificant, never lacks meaning.

Recognizing this pattern in the Novel at large is all the more striking, as we have long been taught to identify the Goddess of Nature with the *im*personality of material and biological existence, and we have been assured that male gods alone underwrite the identity of the person, the value of a mind and soul. Woman and Nature alike are—well, just ugly, messy, and unmeaning. One of the sharpest statements of this view ever to be made has recently been uttered by Camille Paglia, whose book *Sexual Personae* (1990) with horrific glee endorses the utter ugliness and futility of all things female. Paglia states unequivocally, "The historical repugnance to woman has a rational basis: disgust is reason's proper response to the grossness of procreative nature" (12). "Genesis hedges and does not take its misogyny far enough. . . . Nature is serpentine, a bed of tangled vines, creepers and crawlers, probing dumb fingers of fetid organic life which Wordsworth taught us to call pretty" (11). All representations of the Goddess are disgusting reminders of the ugly and sordid, of "nature's daemonic ugliness" (5). It would make sense to warn us against calling Nature "pretty" or "beautiful," but only on grounds that would make it *equally* absurd to call her "ugly." But to Paglia, "ugly" is exactly what Nature is. Paglia is a latecomer to the tradition of Porphyry, for whom Homer's cave was so dreadful. She assumes like the Neoplatonists that all "mind" is masculine and must be exercised to the defeat and abuse of "Nature."

The Novel points in the opposite direction and has always done so, however many or versatile its changes of content and ideology—for the Novel is a mistress of disguise. The Novel itself is an example of the human mind (the author's, but also the mind of character and reader) combining with the great world of Nature. The Novel endeavors to show, by pointing toward the Goddess, that there is no need to think of humans and nature in opposition. Nor is there a need to despise and subjugate the Female in order to have "civilization," for the Novel itself is "civilized" and the Goddess teaches people how to behave in a "civilized" way. (Chaireas, for instance, must learn not to kick his wife.) But the civilization of the Novel is achieved through renewed respect for *hylē*. "We have an evolutionary revulsion from slime, our site of biologic origins," says Paglia (11), again like Porphyry. But the Novel baptizes us in slime and initiates us in mud. "In aesthetic terms," says Paglia, "female genitals are lurid in color, vagrant in contour, and architecturally incoherent. Male genitals, on the other hand . . . have a rational mathematical design, a syntax" (17). There is no more reason to believe this than to think that apples are ugly and bananas orderly. If all Nature is ugly, sordid, and feminine, then actual fleshly male organs, being part of Nature, are also ugly, sordid *and* feminine. It is one of the functions of the Novel (and not just of Joyce's Bloom) to show us the beauty of the fundamental body, whether we trace it in the labyrinth or admire it in the *ekphraseis*.

A Chinese novel of 1618 expresses its appreciation of sexual organs and of pleasure in a punning title, *Chin P'Ing Mei. Chin P'ing Mei* can be properly translated as *The Plum* (or *The Plumblossoms*) *in the Golden Vase*, but as David Tod Roy, the translator, points out, "it puns with three near homophones that might be rendered as *The Glamor of Entering the Vagina*" (Introduction, *The Plum in the Golden Vase*, I: xvii). Female organs (like male ones) are displayed in novels; like the bloody grail, they are not to be dismissed and can never quite be tidied away.

A recent Italian novel bears the title of both the goddess and a physical emblem: Clara Rubbi's *La Dea del melograno* (1986)—*The Goddess of the Pomegranate*. Persephone is the Goddess of the Pomegranate. On one interpretation, that is simply because Persephone ate pomegranate seeds—or perhaps was force-fed only one seed, as in *Hymn to Demeter*—while in the underworld, and was hence condemned to stay, at least part-time. N. J. Richardson points out that the pomegranate was "symbolical of blood and death, but also of fertility and marriage" (*The Homeric Hymn to Demeter*, 276). The pomegranate is a constant attribute of Persephone, but it was also associated with Demeter at Eleusis and with Hera at Argos. The pomegranate crops up in pictorial representations of the Virgin Mary. The various associations of this fruit with deception and wounds as well as with fertility need hardly blind us to the fact that the goddess-seeking pomegranate "represents" what it resembles, woman's genitals, considered as comprising uterus and ovaries as well as vulva and vagina.[12]

In *Kleitophon and Leukippé*, Achilles Tatius achieves a balance between male and female in the odd description of a statue of Zeus carrying a pomegranate. Kleitophon adds, "There is a mystic meaning [*ho logos mystikos*] to this pomegranate" (146). The great temple at Jerusalem achieved a balance between sacred Male and sacred Female emblems with the profusion of pomegranate images within the temple (see I Kings 7:18–20), and also with the alternating gold bells and colored pomegranates on the hem of the priest's blue robe (Exodus 28:33–34). We see a pleasing alternation of male and female, masculine bell and feminine pomegranate, going round and round without any hierarchy. Strict iconoclasms within Judaism and Christianity have made us shy of using such emblems, in religious edifices, or rather of taking notice of what they mean when they are there. Protestantism tried to eliminate the feminine symbols altogether. Away with pomegranates! away with those horrid vulvular roses and rose-windows! But, even so, the images have crept back into the churches, and they have always been present in the novels. The Novel abhors no imagery of either male *or* female.

Images traditionally associated with the female body and functions and with the feminine are emblems of the classical goddesses. These have been adapted in Christian art to the images of Mary: she is often, in Italian Renaissance painting in particular, surrounded by emblems like the pomegranate, rose, egg, and dove. The peacock of Hera becomes her property. The Novel manages similar reintegrations. The heroine of *Joseph and Aseneth* is enveloped in a multitude of symbols relating to the Goddess, principally those of the Goddess Neith, known by her bees. Hardy's Fancy Day surrounded by her bees in Hardy's *Under the Greenwood Tree* (1872) comically offers another example of a bee-surrounded heroine. Aseneth devours pomegranates as well as much other fruit, pronouncing it all good (*Joseph and Aseneth*, 140). Compare Zola's Nana, the "blonde Venus" picking strawberries in the rain, crouched in the mud, her hands drenched by the downpour (*Nana*, 180). Aseneth is associated too with thickets, dense vegetation, which is the "matter of Neith." Vulvular thickets are goddess-spaces, primordial material. When Grahame's Rat and Mole go into the Wild Wood, they are entering the realm of Neith, of *hylē*, of material density.

The Goddess's emblems are everywhere, and Her genital life is not "ugly." It becomes, however, more understandable why the Novel has seemed a low, ugly mean thing to those who would keep the culture pure in officially regarding only Mind and "dry transcendence." Other arts (the paintings of goddess, pomegranate, rose) show that the female genitals are not always thought "ugly" or "incoherent." But of all arts, the Novel offers us the fullest power of the Feminine. In the Novel, at the deepest level, the Feminine fascinates. This has nothing to do with the experience of a sexual entrapment of a man within any novel (though that is a *story* that can be used in a novel). Rather, we as readers experience— whether we are male or female—a yielding of ourselves to the body and rhythms of the Mother. To read a Novel—even a very "male" novel by a great male writer—is to tune in to the wavelength of the Feminine. It is this, I believe, rather than any particular sex scenes in any particular novels, that has given the Novel a bad name. In reading (or writing) a novel, we become Demeter's people, *Dēmētreioi*—"dead" to ordinary life and initiates in a new one.

The Novel has allowed writers (male and female alike) to commit thought experiments about family, sex, and society. To some extent at least the author and reader of a novel may implicitly discount the power of a conventionally hypostasized Male Deity. This need never be done as openly as it is in, for instance, Charlotte Brontë's *Shirley* (1849), when Shirley Keeldar scorns Milton's housekeeping Eve, and the misogyny in a story which Shirley insists on re-creating (*Shirley*, 320–321). Shirley Keeldar is reacting not only against Milton but also against views of which Paglia is the most recent representative. Biological determinism can be more adamant in misogyny than belief in "Jehova," and the modern temptation to make use of the cosmos while repudiating and degrading it is more negative than the Gnosticism from which it springs.

Margaret Atwood's celebration of the Female divine in *Cat's Eye* and Paglia's degradation of the Female in *Sexual Personae* are aspects of the present and future struggle over the nature of both religion and the world. As long as that struggle persists, the Novel will be in evidence. The Novel participates, as it has always done, as a sort of undercover agent for the celebration of the Goddess, and of the mundane world. It is the openness within some novels of the 1980s and 1990s about the importance of the Goddess that allows us to see clearly and unmistakably a basic element that has always been present, even if disguised and abased, like Balzac's cigar-carrying image of Venus. Tom Robbins's *Skinny Legs and All* (1990) makes overt and continuous its argument in favor of the Goddess, of a new nonphallic religion, and of the divine powers of nature.

> Who was Astarte? She was a goddess; rather, she was *the* Goddess, the Great Mother, the Light of the World, the most ancient and widely revered divinity in human history. . . . In comparison, "God," as we moderns call Yahweh (often misspelled "Jehovah") was a Yahny-come-lately who would never approach her enormous popularity. She was the mother of God, as indeed, she was mother of all. As beloved as she was for her life-giving and nurturing qualities, the only activities of hers acceptable to the patriarchs, she was mistress over destruction as well as creation. . . .
>
> In Jezebel's native Phoenicia, the Goddess's name was Astarte. In Babylon she was Ishtar; in India, Kali; in Greece, Demeter (immature aspect: Aphrodite). If Saxon was your indigenous tongue, you would address her as Ostara; if Nordic, you'd say Freya; if Egyptian, Isis—or Nut or Hathor or Neith. Oh, the Goddess had many names, and many roles. She was virgin, bride, mother, prostitute, witch, and hanging judge, all swirled into one.   (*Skinny Legs and All*, 49–50)

This passage seems a clear recollection of Isis' self-description in *The Golden Ass*. (Though what business does Robbins have referring to Aphrodite as "immature"?)

Thomas Mann had already raised Astarte in the middle of his *Joseph*, only to set her down again in needed subjection to the Judaeo-Christian Lord and Law. In doing so he repeated the pattern of the antique *Joseph and Aseneth*. We encounter the goddess in all of Mann's novels, and likewise the "matter of Egypt," if disconcertingly conveyed. So it is in *Der Zauberberg* (1924), where Behrens's cylindrical coffee mill is decorated in a pattern that makes Hans Castorp blush, the obscene pattern repeating itself on the whole coffee-set, on each piece. Behrens explains that it was given him once by "an Egyptian princess," and it is she who supplies the doctor with cigarettes, each with a gold sphinx on it (*Der Zauberberg*, 277–278). The "Egyptian princess" teases the doctor with her mystery, and her gift of the indelicate coffee-set is a gesture of comic display linking her with Iambe-Baubo. The female jester, like the *hàn mane'àk su*, dares to confound the standards of the respectable and appropriate; it is part of her point that this motif is, as Hans Castorp says, not in its right place on coffee cups.

This episode in Mann's novel follows a chapter in which body and nature have been decried by the philosopher Settembrini, who approvingly quotes Porphyry's first sentence in the biography of Plotinus, that Plotinus was "ashamed to have a body." Settembrini makes what might now be called the Paglia case: "within the antithesis of body *and* spirit (*von Körper* und *Geist*), the body stands for evil, the diabolical principle [*das teuflische Prinzip*], for the body is Nature, and Nature—in respect of her contrast to spirit, to reason, I repeat!—is evil—mystical and evil" (*Der Zauberberg*, 264–265; cf. *The Magic Mountain*, trans. Lowe-Porter, 149).

The nameless "Egyptian princess" who gave Dr. Behrens the obscene coffee-set is a representative of Queen Isis. She reminds us that what is set before us is the body, which we cannot despise, and from which we get the power of nourishment, pleasure, and thinking. The obscene coffee-set is a *memento vitae*, a comic counterpart to the *memento mori*. As Hans Castorp remembers, "the Ancients used to have things like these put on their sarcophagi" (277). The "Ancients" remind us of the fact that we must not only die but live.

We should not end the chapter thus, on this solemn mythographic note, as if Mann or even Robbins knew all about what they were doing or had the last word. Perhaps we should end with two representations by women writers dealing with the difficulty of finding and representing the Goddess. In Dorothy L. Sayers's detective novel *The Unpleasantness at the Bellona Club* (1921), the suspected murderess (and the awkward heroine), Ann Dorland, is trying to be an artist, with indifferent success. Inspector Parker has to go through her paintings:

> He was not well acquainted with the modern school of thought in painting, and had difficulty in expressing his opinion of these curious figures, with their faces like eggs and their limbs like rubber.
> "That is the 'Judgment of Paris,'" said Miss Dorland.
> "Oh, yes," said Parker. (155)

It proved impossible for Ann to paint the three goddesses, but naturally it is difficult to capture a vision of the Goddess in a world where her only known and acknowledged aspect is Bellona, the Roman goddess of war.

The Goddess may rule all that is, but to attempt to represent her is difficult—perhaps ultimately a work of *bricolage*. Amy Tan's *The Kitchen God's Wife* (1991) is named after the goddess yet to be found. The narrator's mother, the true heroine of the story, angrily burned the picture of the Kitchen God, seeing him "smiling, so happy to see me unhappy" (529). When she burns this image of the male deity who presides over Chinese women's kitchens, she seems to hear "Kitchen God's wife, shouting, Yes! Yes! Yes!" (529). So she goes shopping for a statue of the hitherto non-existent goddess. Rejecting the images of the Eight Immortals and even the Goddess of Mercy, the seeker seems unable to find what she wants—until the shopkeeper recollects that "the factory made a mistake" in forgetting to write the name at the bottom of one statue of a goddess.

> So I bought that mistake. I fixed it. I used my gold paints and wrote her name on the bottom. And Helen bought good incense, not the cheap brand, but the best. I could see this lady statue in her new house, the red temple altar with two candlesticks lighting up her face from both sides. She would live there, but no one would call her Mrs.

Kitchen God. Why would she want to be called that, now that she and her husband are divorced? (531)

The heroine has thus created a shrine to the Unknown Goddess, an invention and a discovery transforming both the mechanical reproduction and the idle mistake of the factory. In giving this powerful good-luck image to her daughter, the Demeter-like Mother passes on the possibility not only of renewal but also of recognition. She also gives this lady a new name: "Lady Sorrowfree." This name, which emerges on the last page of Tan's novel, is obviously the Goddess of Happy Endings, who must ever be rediscovered—and even reinvented in being sought.

CHAPTER XX

⊱┈⊰─○─⊱┈⊰

Conclusion

⊱┈⊰─○─⊱┈⊰

The Novel in reality arose from religious roots.
>—Merkelbach, *Roman und Mysterium*

"Life itself is an unsolved mystery."
>—Character in Agatha Christie's *The Thirteen Problems*

Our family . . . are great Novel-readers and not ashamed of being so.
>—Jane Austen, letter of 1798

⊱┈⊰─○─⊱┈⊰

As soon as we locate the Novel in relation to its Goddess, we run into the problem of what "the Goddess" might mean. In recent years the growing interest in goddess-figures and goddess-worship has been manifest outside the academy and has become a noticeable aspect of religious life. It may thus seem too facile, too contemporary a yielding to the *Zeitgeist*, to locate the Goddess within the Novel. Within the Academy, the current interest in the Goddess, and in goddesses, has sparked debate. Some conservative historians, female as well as male, wishing to damp down dangerous fires, have insisted that the goddesses we know from classical times are neither powerful nor very meaningful. Mary Lefkowitz takes this line in *Women in Greek Myth* (1986). A similar argument is advanced in an essay by Pauline Schmitt Pantel, who argues that the Greeks, from whom we get the truly picturesque gods, are more interested in divinity than in femininity, and that in any case the only true evidence of Great Mother worship comes from dull prehistory. Besides, Pantel argues, following Neumann, the Great Mother is an invention of moderns: "The Great Mother . . . is actually an archetype, and Jung is her prophet" (Pantel, "Representations of Women," in *A History of Women*, trans. Goldhammer, p. 32). Pantel dislikes what she sees as romanticization of the Goddess: "Nothing supposedly is more edifying than the Mother (or Mothers), however terrifying she (or they) may be. Thus she is cast as a figure of reconciliation, which some people find reassuring. But one may also feel, as I do, that such a view of both the category of the feminine and the structure of the psyche give[s] short shrift to the conflict and unpleasantness that are also an essential part of life" (33).

Certainly, to see the Mother as God is hard on people who do not get along with their mothers, just as to see the Father as God is hard on people who do not get along with their fathers. But it could be argued that any religious apprehension of reconciliation, through *any* figure, would be subject to the charge that it did not allow for "conflict and unpleasantness"—which would be to argue that we could have no figures at all of reconciliation. At a time when we need such figures to realign ourselves in relation to the earth, we are not really going to cast away such a tempting figure of reconciliation as the Goddess-Mother represents. Besides, any reading of *novels* would disabuse us of the idea that getting to know the Goddess is a way of evading struggle. On the contrary, *The Golden Ass*, or *Chaireas and Kallirrhoé*, shows us that "conflict and unpleasantness" must be involved in the very approach to the Goddess, and reconciliation must be won through rebirth in mud and slime and disarray.

It is ultimately arguable that any idea of the Divine as "Feminine" is simply wrong. But that can truly be argued only on the basis that the Divine is not restricted by gender. As long as we have a masculinized God or gods, there will be need for some counterrepresentation of the feminine as divine—even if "masculine" and "feminine" are our own inventions. Modern thought (i.e., of the nineteenth and twentieth centuries), following Darwin and Marx, veered towards the supposition that "God" is not a real category, but that "masculine" and "feminine" are real. We might suppose alternately that "God" or "the Divine" is a "real" category, and that "masculine" and "feminine" are merely constructs.

The early twenty-first century will have some reasons to wish to elaborate on rather than to suppress the vision of the Goddess or the Divine as Female. The influences pressing towards this vision are behind novelists like Atwood and Robbins, who paint their Goddess in such defiantly bold strokes. No longer need Venus hover in a nineteenth-century manner as a bronze figurine; she is once more getting up and walking (or gliding) towards us: *vera incessu patuit dea.*

As long as there is a cultural insistence on enforcing an image of the Divine as Masculine, and creating institutions that faithfully reflect this vision of divine enforcement of the hypostatized masculine, so long will there be a need for a "pocket of resistance," a site where an alternative can be represented, an hypostatized feminine to prevent severe imbalance. The "femininity" or "femaleness" of the Goddess is itself perhaps only a statement about the figure's representing the alternative, that which is necessary even if denied.

An alternative—to what? My own narrative has held the Novel against what I have called "the Civic"—meaning not only an order but even an ideal. The Civic is not to be denied and cannot be erased. The political dream of a fully responsive and responsible society in which each person participates is a dream of vital importance. It is more important than ever now, when some would separate the "pursuit of happiness" from what used to be called the "public sphere," and shut down almost all public forums that exist aside from the need to make money. Cocooned in a separate dwelling, exercising on machines, phoning out for food and clothing, living by computer, and looking forward to an era in which the well-off will be independent not only of the Poor and the Other but even of Terra herself—this is the New Individual, according to some portraits. To criticize the Civic at all when it is under some heavy pressure might seem to support the idea of this cyber-lonely unit. The loneliness based on fear of crime, disease, and Otherness in general is by no means the "individuation" encouraged by the Novel. The logical outcome of such cyber-loneliness and neo-Malthusian paranoia is arguably something much more like Bosnia than anything in *Star Trek.* The Novel is qualified to represent both the horror and absurdity of our Bosnias, as we can see in works like *Candide*, or Grimmelshausen's *Simplicissimus.*

The Novel demonstrates that people can and should get out of their cocoons. Novels validate meeting people who do not belong to some originating or "natural" unit like the family, the tribe, the language group. Holy hermits, it is true, may perform a good role—but when they are the reverse of hermetic, like the fatherly befrienders of Amadís and of Simplicissimus, or like the Tibetan lama in *Kim*. Withdrawal is arguably a worse offense in the Novel than cannibalism itself. The lonely Robinson Crusoe (cast away after forsaking civic life and betraying his fellow man in slavery) feels he is in prison. Dickens's Krook in *Bleak House* dies by spontaneous combustion, a suitable end for a paranoiac who accumulated everything within himself but could divulge nothing. Miss Havisham's mad solitude is a form of destructive self-imprisonment.

To endeavor to live only with the self and the self's repetitive mental images is a disastrous proceeding. Without individual emergence from such willed cocooning, not only is general social life weakened, but madness also ensues. Women novelists have shown the forms of cocooning forced on women as forms of torture—notably in Charlotte Perkins Gilman's *The Yellow Wall Paper* (1892) and Kate Chopin's *The Awakening* (1899). The Civic idea has, ironically, often meant the enforced enclosure of women in physical luxury as expensive possessions, not to be contaminated or polluted by venturing out and mingling with others. Novelists have tended to stress the cruelty and the absurdity of this, its unhealth for the human creature. Jane Eyre thinks, "I never can bear being dressed like a doll by Mr. Rochester, or sitting like a second Danae with the golden shower falling daily round me," conventional figures of wealth and eroticism turning into ironically disagreeable images of ludicrous passivity (*Jane Eyre*, 271). The escape from others is an escape into prison, while the escape from effort is a torture. The tower that keeps one from touching terrene dirt is a barrier to life.

Arguably, the Civic ideal itself needs to be restated at this historical juncture. The realities of the Civic, however, not only inevitably fall short, but also exhibit a reluctance on the part of the powerful to relinquish power, and a great fear of the liberation of all. It is the work of fiction not to give way to the demands of the Civic when, in the name of order, it would suppress and deny not only certain groups of human beings but also elements within those individuals who are supposedly running the civic show. In saying as much, I am quite close to Mario Vargas Llosa, in his essay "La verdad de las mentiras" (1989). Vargas Llosa explains, "The lies of novels are not at all gratuitous; they fill in the insufficiencies of life. . . . When religious culture enters upon a crisis . . . that is the privileged moment for fiction. Its artificial orders supply refuge, security, and in them are freely unfolded those appetites and fears which real life incites and does not manage to get rid of or conjure away. Fiction is a temporary succedaneum for life" (12–13).

Far from looking down on this "succedaneum," or life-substitute, Vargas Llosa sees it as valuable, all the more because it cannot really tranquilize us: "at the same time as fleetingly soothing human dissatisfaction, fictions equally arouse it, spurring on desires and imagination" (13). For Vargas Llosa, fiction (particularly the Novel) is always of striking value as a protest against the way life is under any régime or ideology, "a crying testimony of its insufficiencies, of its ineptitude at fulfilling us. And thus it is a permanent corrosive of all the powers which seek to hold men satisfied and in conformity" (20). The "Truth of the Lies" is found in truths that cannot otherwise be uttered, which hold up a reproach against the system of things with which the Civic would have us pretend (at least) to be fully satisfied. Cervantes' worry (expressed in *Persiles*) about the *mentira* of fiction is here answered, as Cervantes implicitly has answered it also.

Vargas Llosa in this essay falls prey to the persistent temptation of creating a historical time for fiction; it develops *when* the unitary vision of faith is felt to fail. But this need not be a temporal or historical "when"; it may be happening at any point in history. The "faith" that fails may also be a Darwinian or other form of nontheistic faith. There was no "Age of Faith" that completely eliminated the felt need for fiction, and fiction sometimes openly expresses its protest. For instance, in *Aucassin et Nicolette*, written in the supposed "Age of Faith," the hero is rebuked by the vicomte who warns him that if he finds his woman and puts her into his bed he will have to suffer in Hell and never enter Paradise. Aucassin stoutly retorts:

> "What have I to do in Paradise? I do not wish to go there, unless I have Nicolette my sweet friend whom I love so much, for to Paradise no one goes except old priests and old cripples and one-handers who crouch night and day before the altars. . . . But I would go to Hell, for to Hell go the pretty clerks and the handsome chevaliers who died in tourneys and important wars . . . and there go the courteous ladies who have two or three friends besides their lords . . . and there go the harpers and *jongleurs* and the kings of this world; with these would I go, if I had my sweetest love Nicolette with me." (58)

The vicomte's warning has less to do with chastity than with his anxiety that Aucassin now behave and marry a suitable girl, daughter of king or count and not a foreign hussy. The vicomte's rebuke is entirely formulated as a Civic repulse of individual desire, and so Aucassin in effect reads it, in his revolt against the pinching of all desire. If Hell is the abode of the desirous, it must become (ironically) too desirable to be useful as a scare tactic. Aucassin's disorder looks forward to a new order. That is, there must be some institution that validates his individual love; this institution is really *Aucassin et Nicolette*. The Novel is the perpetual abode of a new order that is never going to be brought to actual fruition. But the presence of these imagined possibilities keeps the present order, the nonfiction discourse, the civic ideals, the religious precepts, from staleness and complacency. As Vargas Llosa says, fiction is a "permanent corrosive" of power. "The lies of literature, if they germinate in liberty, show us that it [*libertad*] was never sure." And, he concludes, the "lies of fiction" are "a permanent conspiracy" by which we will also realize in the future that freedom has not been perfectly achieved (20).

The Novelist, it might be argued, sets herself or himself too much above (or at least apart from) the Civic order to be safe. Novelists are often accused of being egotistical and reckless of the social good, as well as trifling or venal, poorly organized or poorly informed. Novelists are often, that is, treated as females, no matter how hairy and muscular the individual writer may be, for these are "feminine" sins. The Novelist may be too prosaic, caught up in dull trifles, or, if not, then inturned, narcissistic, "a mannerist," as a reviewer negatively remarked of Frances Burney. One response to this criticism is a vision of the Novelist as aloof, rather than involved, "paring his fingernails" like James Joyce's Deity. This response is already admubrated in an eighteenth-century critique, C. F. von Blanckenburg's *Versuch über den Roman* (*Exploration of the Novel*, 1774). Blanckenburg emphasizes the inevitable necessity felt in a good novel, the *Notwendigkeit* in which true verisimilitude consists. The Novelist then has, in some respects, very little control and is not involved personally in what gets written. His (one might add "her") job is to order the material rightly according to its nature; certain inevitabilities flow from certain material:

> The writer [poet, *Dichter*] himself scarcely belongs within the whole of his work; it would be extraordinary for him to stick himself into the works, as it were. . . . It is not a little wonder to me, to hear a writer say "I had need of this necessary situation, I required these developments," and so forth. . . . If he has not so ordered his work that this situation, this turning-point, follows from his personages and their characteristic qualities, and so follows that it seems to us a natural working-out, then he has truly created only a mediocre work—especially if he settles this situation merely according to his own will, his own wit, or his own fancy, without respecting his entire work and its characters. (*Versuch über den Roman*, 339–340)

Blanckenburg is a pioneer in recognizing that the genre to some extent writes the author, though his precepts point in a rather severe straight line from neoclassical principles to the kinds of "necessity" envisaged by Taine and Zola.

For Blanckenburg, the author is less a creator than someone keenly alive to the inevitable laws of psychological "Necessity." Such a formulation is partly a desire to re-poeticize the Novelist and re-create "him" as a philosopher, with an aesthetic "All breathing human passion far above." Blanckenburg is an early champion of "showing" against "telling." The characters act for themselves, if according to scientific law. But it is extremely difficult for novelists to keep themselves (or a *persona* as alibi for "self") out of their works. Some of the greatest practitioners in third-person narration (Heliodorus, e.g., or Henry Fielding, or Blanckenburg's admired Wieland) do not really try. The Novel always does seem to have a speaking voice—not the singing voice of a *vates* with his singing robes on, but a speaking voice, prosy if witty, with passions, jokes, asides, stresses. The strongest effort to break out of that cycle of personality can be found in the works of Alain Robbe-Grillet in the period after World War II. Robbe-Grillet's works thus appear like a parody of fictionality, with a keen eye for the stupidity of plots and the hopeless impasses of life when presented as a mad structure of inevitability. But such a scientifically "pure" kind of fiction was to be challenged by South America's own style of "impure" departure from High Modernist discursive realism.

Latin American writers have given us the term *el realismo mágico*. Adapted from art criticism of the 1920s, the term "magic realism" since the mid-1950s has replaced Alejo's Carpentier's term *lo real maravilloso*. As *magic* and not only *marvel*, this new mode of representation goes beyond the merely symbolic or fantastic. The customary elements of *realismo mágico*, as Isabel Allende says, are "Myths, legends, superstitions, stories, passions, obsessions, magic . . . invisible elements that affect our lives" (quoted by Gloria Bautista Gutiérrez, *Realismo mágico, cosmos Latinoamericano*, 129). Gabriel García Márquez, whose *Cien años de soledad* (1967) made the rest of the world take note of magic realism, said, "my most important problem was to destroy the line of demarcation which separates what seems real from what seems fantastic. Because in the world I was endeavoring to evoke, that barrier does not exist" (quoted by Gutiérrez, ibid., 43).

Modern Latin American writers feel a certain connection with the medieval and Renaissance classics of the Iberian peninsula, a place similarly stressed by ethnic variance and interior colonization and also, like twentieth-century South America, rich in various forms of folk belief. *Tirant lo Blanc* and *Amadís de Gaula* are to these authors not *passés*, any more than Cervantes—and the Cervantes not just of *Don Quijote* but also of his other works. The opening paragraphs of *Persiles* find a peculiar echo in the opening paragraph of *Cien Años de Soledad*.

Realismo mágico is a mode of protest against dictatorships and various other forms of tyranny and imperialism. It is a very conscious revolt, recognizing the cultural forces behind the creation of what I have termed "Prescriptive Realism." "Magic realism," which admits what was once termed "too sensational," has obviously been practiced long before the term was invented. *Asinus aureus*, for instance, is a work of "magic realism." A cultural mixture of various ethnicities and world pictures in a colonial situation may make magic realism an almost inevitable literary response; there are elements of it in the novels of Walter Scott. South American "magic realism" has now spread about the world, and has enabled the work of writers experiencing similar situations of former colonialism and impacted cultures, writers such as Witi Ihamaera and Ben Okri. It can also be found, however, in the work of modern English novelists like Jeanette Winterson, and we can recognize that when Dickens imagines Krook's spontaneous combustion he is really working in the "magical" mode (despite attempts to explain the event as scientific). The endeavor to achieve a scientific or purely "objective" novel ranks with other attempts, like that of making it more solidly epic, to masculinize the genre and render it respectable. The novel has basically resisted all such attempts to make a man of it. When Calvino plays with the Enlightenment baron who lives in the trees (*Il Barone rampante*, 1957), he enters the realm of magic realism. Isabel Allende claims that realm in *La Casa de los espíritus* (1982); we know this story is not "real" as soon as Rosa is born *con el cabello verde y los ojos amarillos*, with green hair and yellow eyes (12). As I said in the first chapter of this book, when novels by admired novelists deal with barons living in trees and girls with green hair, it is time to give up the pretense that the primary demand of a long work of prose fiction is that it should be "realistic."

Realismo mágico has arisen within the literature of regions where different cultural groups have to meet. The intermixing of various cultures (races, tribe, religions) and their stories is congenial both to the Novel as a form and to the deployment of its nonrealistic elements. Amongst these nonrealistic elements must be included what I have called the Tropes of the Novel. While I have dealt, I believe, with the most essential of these "tropes," others remain untouched. I should, for instance, have discussed the Treasure, the hidden Treasure findable in every Novel. And with the Treasure I should have liked to discuss the importance of gemstones in novels, typically pearl, amethyst, sapphire, diamond. Most especially, there is the inevitable emerald, green of life, the stone of chastity, spiritual aspiration, and immortality. This emerald is found in works by authors of very different times and places, from Heliodorus to George Eliot to Yukio Mishima. In *The Dream of the Red Chamber* (*The Story of the Stone*) the Treasure-Stone and the central character are really one, and in Hawthorne's *The Scarlet Letter* (1850), the heroine's daughter Pearl is likewise the Treasure.

Connections between novels of the East and the West can be felt very strongly in the tropes. Certain powerful novelistic images recur: the Man in Skins, the Treasure-stone, the Phoenix. We can be moved to speculate on some hidden time, long before Hellenism, when our cultures of East and West were merged in mysterious ways. The novels of the future will be more and more open to the metaphors and sacred images of various cultures—overtly so.

The Novel always does look to the future. Rooted in a deep past it may be, so it can withstand the winds of taste and fashion—including icy blasts of disapproval—but it always looks towards possibility, towards fulfillment when (and where) what is now grudging and meager may be full and generous. The Novel is the "enemy" of the Civic because it is always imagining what the Civic might come to be. Thus it urges society on, impatient of order, precepts, and maxims of the past. The Novel is the repository of our hopes. (What happens when the hopes within the Novel conflict with the "scientific" fears of the novelist in his or her era can be seen in the works of some "naturalists," not least Zola.)

The Novel as constant alternative is what its enemies have accused it of being—"escapist." It provides an escape from what the Civic order would wish to describe as Necessity. The reader retreats into another company, another order, through a "Rite of Passage" signaled by crossing a margin, a threshold, usually a watery *limen*. It is an odd "Rite of Passage," admittedly, as it provides the reader with a do-it-yourself kit to be used at will, and even privately. Within a novel, the characters themselves undergo various initiations into new life and cross (or transgress) various frontiers. An element of escape and of outlawry clings to them—as to the reader. Even when an individual novel is respectable, it is not *very* respectable. The Novel easily relapses into its old ways. It does so, not because of any particular wish of a particular author, but because of its "true story," which is the story it always must tell. If the Novel (any novel) is basically a ritual, ritual has some capacities of resistance.

As we have seen, the Novel is a ritual. Yet it is a ritual with many variables, too, and once we see the tropes we may be able to consider a novel's structure in relation to these. We can, for instance, note with pleasure the criss-crossing and multiplication of the major tropes within the first chapters of *Wuthering Heights*. We can see that the "naturalists" of a century ago work the tropes in small strokes, oft-repeated. The postponed ice cream that connects the beginning and end of Vikram Seth's *A Suitable Boy* (1993) is a particular use of the trope of food eating, while the gross banquet in Petronius is a very different use of the trope. Flaubert in *Madame Bovary* ironically unites Eros and food, in the description of the absurdly elaborate wedding cake, topped by a Cupidon (*un petit Amour*) in a chocolate swing (30). This marvelous cake even contains a representation of the erotic and novelistic wetlands, a lake of jelly with boats of nutshells. In any good novel, the permanent subtleties of a particular trope do not detract from the force of a new combination.

In the combination of tropes lies the ritual activity of the Novel. Certain specific figures or phases of the ritual appear in all novels. In entering the Novel, we break the umbilical cord, we are cast into a birth, which is repeated as rebirth or new birth at one or more intervals along the way. We begin by gazing at facades and interfaces, noting the combining of wet and dry. As we progress, we come upon mud and slime, marshy passages of possibility. Renewed contact with the earth and all its dirt is here sacred to us and to our purposes, even if it is as foul as *Our Mutual Friend*'s dirty Thames. We are buried in the hole, the womb and tomb that is the painful beginning of change. We wander through the labyrinth, which is both alien and familiar, our mother's body and our own, our life history, re-figured in the life history of the character and the interweavings of the plot. Eros directs and teases and encourages us in our wandering and our work—Eros, the stand-in for his Mother, the Goddess, and the epitome of our desire. Making contact with Eros heartens us for the great hermeneutic labor that is constantly and teasingly set before us. We make our interpretations under the guidance of Eros—who may represent as simple a desire as the desire to know how the story goes on, and always includes that. Hermeneutic labor is intensified by our contemplation of both pictures and dreams, as outer world and inner world are brought into relation.

Meanwhile, the characters have much to do. They must touch the dirt, get into the hole, wander the labyrinth, view the symbols. And the characters are active participants in their own fates. They tell great parts of the story. They have the dreams, they write the letters. They eat and go hungry and live to eat again. We explore our own lives, and our sense of the individual self as having a significant and even immortal destiny, through these teasing accounts of the mundane, which are also powerful repetitions of ritual and its hopes. If the service of that ritual is a service of the "Goddess," then we have answered Jane Austen's implied question as she reminds us how little official appreciation the Novel has had:

> Let us leave it to the Reviewers to abuse such *effusions* of fancy at their leisure, and over every new novel to talk in threadbare strains of the *trash* with which the press now *groans*. Let us not desert one another; we are an injured *body*. Although our *productions* have afforded more extensive and unaffected *pleasure* than those of any other literary *corporation* in the world, no species of composition has been so much decried. From pride, ignorance, or fashion, our foes are almost as many as our readers. (*Northanger Abbey*, 21; italics mine)

Novels are conventionally derided as "effusions," undifferentiated flow and gushing out of secretions—typically associated with the female body. The press that "groans" becomes female also, groaning in labor to produce this female "trash." The novelists are an "injured body"—and that injured *body* (in corporeal terms also a "corporation") is a female body, the compound of Austen, Burney, Edgeworth in their physical and literary bodies. Austen reverses the negative image of siren or seductress by claiming that *giving* pleasure and being pleasurable are of paramount value. Even though there seems "almost a general wish of decrying the capacity and undervaluing the *labour* of the novelist" (22), that maternal labor is always fruitful.

Austen's implicit question is "*Why* does the novel come in for such hard treatment?" The answer is that the Novel will always be felt to be feminine. Thus, it is felt to be subversive and inferior, hence "trifling," "silly," "idle." There are feeble and unsuccessful novels, it is true, but, as Austen points out, feeble nonfictional productions by the "nine-hundredth abridger of the History of England" or "the man who collects and publishes . . . some dozen lines of Milton, Pope, and Prior," are "eulogized by a thousand pens" (21–22). Despite the recent efforts of critics, the Novel has sustained considerable disrepute. It would not be a matter for pride, it would not even sound like sense to announce, "I never read nonfiction." Yet many people do proudly announce, "I never read novels," or, "I have no time for fiction." Such statements may be heard even within the groves of academe, unless the professorial business is in a modern literature department. The Novel must have its foes because it is the Great Alternative (which is another way of saying "under the Goddess"). It is the repository of our hope in something that can be stated as "feminine" if the State and Establishment are thought of as "masculine," under the sign of the phallus. Only a profound religious and social change could remove from the novel the onus of this role. Perhaps then—and only then—it would cease to exist.

Whenever we resort to a novel, we are turning to it for the pleasure of the ritual of the Alternative (or the ritual that supports alternatives), even though we who are novel-readers may peruse the books for a variety of reasons. Novels have always functioned as a form of Wisdom Literature; they offer human or spiritual truths to muse upon. (Hence Byzantine readers write *GNŌ!* in the margin.) They are stories of travel and adventure (even the tamest of them) so they give us an idea of the world beyond our doorstep. Novels are expansionist, speaking in favor of the wider life, of greater horizons.

On the other hand, the Novel constantly deals with the Family. That this is so has caused me to place at the front of this book the picture of a family adorning a fifteenth-century edition of *Apollonius of Tyre* (see frontispiece). I could have labeled it "The Nuclear Family—in Trouble as Usual," for the family that we commonly see in novels is constantly in trouble, in danger of shipwreck, on the verge of splitting up, as Apollonius' family is. The Family has been around as a unit of psychosocial thought for a long long time. The Novel, however, does not offer easy support to what are presently called "Family Values." The Novel, the genre that best describes and interprets the dynamics of family life, also displays the pain of the family. "Happy families are all alike," says Tolstoy at the beginning of *Anna Karenina*—maybe so, but we do not really see many of those. Nor does the Novel answer to Freud's "Family Romance" with its incestuous objectives. The family may be vital, it may be important for a character to return and be temporarily reunited with the original constellation—but that is never a simple homecoming. What once existed is not restored. What comes to pass is the creation of a new and more flexible compound, elaborated and amplified by new connections.

The Novel in dealing with marriage is exogamic—even if the move "outside" seems quite small. Kleitophon, for instance, runs away with a cousin instead of dutifully marrying his sister; in context this is an exogamic move. *Apollonius of Tyre* offers the starkest vision of the problem of family life when all individual energies are co-opted and contained within it. The horror of family life is incest, the riddle that is not meant to be unriddled even though it is everywhere evident. The idea of paternal ownership of children is deathly. The grip of the family must be loosened.

Novel characters are in a process of separation from the family—partial separation, which is *not* the dramatic and tragic Oedipal sort. Mother and Daughter are expected to be reunited—Demeter and Persephone, Charikleia and Persinna. Novelistic separation is daughterly separation from the Mother. Under the sign of the Mother, reunions and reinterpretations of all relations can constantly be made. The Novel takes an interest in the process of friendship whereby people not from the same family, or even tribe, nation, language-group, or religion, come together in interesting new combinations. Novel characters are constantly aerated by new acquaintance. Family reunion does not mean the loss of the new friends, lovers, and acquaintances, but a larger human constellation. In *Recognitiones*, that early Christian novel, for example, the family reunites, but they are now part of the larger group around St. Peter. The mother also has the friend she lived with, the woman who helped her scrape a living. Chariton's Kallirrhoé returns to Syracuse, her home, with her original lover-husband—but she leaves a son with her second husband. Moreover, she has acquired relationships neither of bed nor of blood. "Write to me often," she entreats the wife of the Great King, with whom she has spent time in Persia. Friendships are sustained across distances by the writing of letters. The *family* alone is never enough. Men and women, married or unmarried, need to know human beings outside the family. The ability to cultivate extrafamilial friendships is a sign of maturation. Even the most family-centered of novels (*Little Women*, for example) cannot continue without the characters' close involvement with persons alien to the family.

We sometimes speak as if we could or must choose between very stark alternatives: the Family OR the Community, the Individual OR the Group. We all need both family and community, and the individual cannot fully exist without a sustaining and educative group of some kind. Novels show this, perpetually, in exhibiting the ways in which individuals are nursed within families but seek the outside world. Novels show the ways in which friendships (and antagonisms) are formed. Novel characters are (to use a modern phrase) always networking. They exist indeed in the reticulations, the traverses of various nets; each in him- or herself is a medium of transmission of relational exchange. Novelistic relationships are rarely envisaged as truly hierarchical. Assumed hierarchies of social relation may be shown, in exhibiting, for instance, the father who takes a social and political position above his child. But the Novel hardly ever endorses such hierarchies; it is more interested in how the characters negotiate with each other. Charikles, for instance in the *Aithiopika*, thinks he knows what is right for his adopted daughter, and he is clearly wrong. His hierarchical position is subverted, and Charikleia chooses a substitute "father" in Kalasiris.

Familial relations are frequently mimicked in novels, as the characters, in happy parody of the family, set up new alliances and relationship. Yet her choice of Kalasiris in a substitute relationship that is totally without foundation in blood kinship (or even in what we would call nationality), does not preclude Charikleia's creating a new relationship with her blood father, Hydaspes, nor her resumption of a connection with her former "father," Charikles. At the end of the novel she is much richer in the sum of her connections and associations than she was at birth, or when she was given to Charikles at the age of seven. This is as it should be. Novel characters are adventurers in community, moving within and through the family in an outward direction—yet rarely utterly forsaking the family. The family itself of course may be quite dreadful, or it may reject the character as a member of it—as Gregor Samsa is largely rejected by his horrified bourgeois family. Yet even Gregor, the bug, is a part of his family. Huckleberry Finn, the abused boy, is still the son of "Pap." Characters acknowledge their birth families even when those families have been destroyed by death. Characters are not, however, going to be fixated on that acknowledgment; their energies are spent in weaving substitute families and wider groups.

Thekla is accused by her mother of being *hōs arachnē* ("like a spider"). She lives like a spider along lines of relationship, deliberately choosing to go off with Paul and forsake her family and her hometown. Her adventuring is a way of acquiring new relations, as she does in St. Paul, and in Tryphaina, the woman who looks after her when she is under sentence, and to whom she becomes a substitute daughter. It is appropriate that stories about Christians emphasize the relational life outside the family, for the Founder left his followers a model of the nonfamilial group. This aspect of Christianity is much neglected by those who would insist that Christianity not only endorses but is the source of "Family Values." In its refusal to bind its members into the life and roles allotted to them by conventional family structures, Christianity was evidently in harmony with some movements found in the new world of the Mediterranean under the Roman Empire, not only in so-called "cults," but also in the literary endorsement of the wandering and multi-relational life.

One of the many reasons why people read and reread novels is that the Novel (in its different individual forms) offers a model of coming-to-know-the-World. The World is represented not as a vicious abstract, but as a multiplicity of places, activities and—above all—persons. To know oneself as an "individual" is to know others as "individuals" also. Far from inevitably making for egotism, the "individuation" so derided by Nietzsche (himself an egotist, world-class) necessitates a curiosity about other individuals. We know ourselves as free and in some sense separate only at the moment that we know someone else is also free. The words "freedom" or "free" are not to be used lightly. Orlando Patterson has told us, with terrible logic, that the concept of "freedom" and even the words for it came into existence only in slave-owning societies. When all were "free," there was no need of the word. "Free" is the opposite of "Slave." The Novel (like the Christian religion) finds itself involved in paradox. Slaves are "really" free. The Novel is inexorably if cunningly democratic in its apprehension of the spiritual freedom of all human beings. No "individuation" really exists without such freedom being possible, at least as a concept.

Novels are the hangout of slaves and low-lifes—of servant girls and delinquent picaresque boys, of strollers and the homeless, of people down on their luck or stuck in a strange environment. The Novel may be "bourgeois" but its characters (in different levels of socioeconomic life) are often strapped for funds. This is not true merely of low-lifes like Encolpius, Huckleberry Finn, or Gil Blas, but of characters in much more settled or outwardly respectable circumstances. Amadís and Oriana send Gandalin off to town to buy food with Oriana's ring, if mainly so that they may take advantage of his absence to consummate their love. Selling personal possessions in necessity is not an uncommon activity, a novelistic activity engaged in by Clarissa (who sells her clothes to buy a coffin) and Jo March (who sells her hair to help her father). The stress of living in the economic world is known to the Novel long before the capitalist revolution of the seventeenth century. Economic concerns stand in the way of the marriage of Daphnis and Chloé—indeed, economic concerns explain why the two young people are in that pastoral world, for the children were exposed by their town-dwelling parents, who had financial reasons not to wish to support them. The economic world very frequently tries to force the sale of the novel character's self—in enslavement, in forced marriage, or in prostitution.

Novel characters, even those who are truly well-to-do, exist in perpetual dissatisfaction with their financial and social condition. Comically, Don Quixote feels that dissatisfaction acutely and tries to make himself novelistic as a cure, not realizing that material discontent is his condition of life as a novelistic character. Well-to-do Elizabeth Bennet may appear, but she is the victim of a socioeconomic system of primogeniture that will render her homeless as soon as her father dies. Tolstoy's Levin tries to make his discontent into both a divine discontent and a pastoral (or georgic) acceptance of material being.

Tragedy has not given much attention to the "prosaic" (oh, yes, prosaic) facts of life in the economic and material world, although Tragedy was readily able to conceive of heroic opposition to the Law. The Law, however, in Tragedy from Aeschylus to Racine is rarely concerned with day-to-day economic and material facts, any more than it is much concerned with spiritual states of a less-than-grand nature. Lear's peevishness and loss of household represent the closest approach of Tragedy to dealing with the kind of discontent and personal dissatisfaction that rises not to grandeur—and Lear soon rises to storm and *drang* and grandeur altogether. The Novel has always found it in its heart to be interested in less-than-heroic moments, in petulance and peevishness, in struggle with material conditions of existence and a daily life not always grandly borne. Even Charikleia breaks down into almost pettish self-pity. Even Cowgirls Get the Blues. Novel characters get depressed or anxious. They feel the perennial struggle with life. There is, however, no guarantee (happily) that their depression or moment of abasement will have a dreadful outcome—in tragedy, it must.

So attentive is the Novel to the material conditions of life, and of struggle with these, that it was (late in the day) hailed as a proper vehicle for Marxist thought and solutions. Georg Lukács, who said many good things about the Novel, based his postulates on the false premise that the Novel had arisen only in the capitalist era. Certainly, the Novel changes its form from century to century, and even from decade to decade (within and before the modern era). But the Novel is not a Communist plot. Neither is it merely a representative of bourgeois

thinking, narrowly conceived. In only the largest sense is the Novel "bourgeois"—it is of the *burgh*. Long before the eras of modern financing, the Novel
hung out in cities. It is the product of a world of city-dwellers. Cities are the place
of exchange of good and ideas, the places where people of different families, even
different races and countries, can connect with each other. The Novel is written
and read by Nietzsche's *alexandrinische Mensch*—true. Its characters, too, may be
persons from Alexandria—or just visiting. The daily world, the money concerns,
the streets and alleys of the city—yet, these are novelistic things.

In *The Rape of the Lock*, Pope, echoing Ariosto, jokingly describes the stolen
lock of hair journeying to "the Lunar Sphere":

> Since all things lost on Earth, are treasur'd there.
> There Heroes' Wits are kept in pondrous Vases,
> And Beaus' in *Snuff-boxes* and *Tweezer-Cases*.
> . . . .
> The Courtier's Promises, and Sick Man's Pray'rs,
> The Smiles of Harlots, and the Tears of Heirs,
> Cages for Gnats, and Chains to Yoak a Flea;
> Dry'd Butterflies, and Tomes of Casuistry.
> (Canto V, lines 113–122)

Pope's heterogeneous catalogue, a cross between the contents of an *Inferno* and those of a lumber-room, is a skillful rendering of the culturally abject.
The Novel performs something like the comic function of "the Lunar Sphere,"
taking in things lost elsewhere to literature, things not valued, or not believed in.
The Novel, like the loony Moon, is the great repository for what "the World"—as
Establishment, Civic order, Dignity, State, or Church, or Grand Design,—can not
find room for. What is rejected elsewhere as unimportant, or unprofitable, or
insignificant, or trifling or unpleasant—these things, like the dried butterflies and
tomes of casuistry, turn up in the Novel. Novels have been accused of misleading
us into "escape" as if they presented too perfect a world. But in fact we go to the
Novel and find such things as the following:

slaves	sticky food
housework	torn clothes
theft	chamber pots
garden tools	weak eyes
prison	bankruptcy
menstrual periods	broken beds
lost jewelry	lost love
drunkenness	overeating
hunger	scolding

This list (which applies equally to novels of any period, ancient or modern) encapsulates what we mean when we say "prosaic." To quote Charlotte
Brontë yet again, "Something real, cool, and solid, lies before you; something
unromantic as Monday morning" (*Shirley*, 5). Any novel, no matter how lyri-
cal, has something of that quality in it somewhere. That is what people often
mean by referring to the novel's "realism," though a novel has no need to tie

itself to the rules of "Prescriptive Realism," a late Whig development of the rules of the French academy. Nor need a novel be as startling in its development of physical and material experience as, for example, the early fragments of the *Phoinikika*:

> I found Persis waiting. . . . And then I had my first experience of sex . . . she took off and gave to me the golden jewelry that she was wearing . . . (for) loss of virginity. I said that I would not take it. (She) called Gla(ucetes), however, and when he came, she gave (it) to him and ordered (the steward) to bring to her two thousand (drachmas) and to count it out . . . she turned towards me and did not leave off until (satiety) took us both, and day dawned.
>
> (*Phoinikika*, trans. Gerald N. Sandy as *A Phoenician Story*, in *CAGN*, 811)

The dawning of that morning (which apparently brings the mother of the girl Persis on the scene) is not Brontë's workaday Monday morning, but the scene is "solid," "prosaic," and certainly novelistic in displaying the outbreak of altercation even on the love-bed—the couple argue about whether he should get a present from her or not, and Persis has to turn her jewelry into money.

The recognition of imperfection, of the mixed nature of experience, lies very close to the heart of the Novel, and is part of its appeal. A novel may indeed borrow the techniques of satire, and even admire satire's firm take on the material and man-made world, but does not need to act as if right customs and true hierarchies are already known. The mess in the Novel is not to be cleaned up by the broom of the Law.

In Part I (Chapter VII), I discussed the "realism" of the ancient novels as if "realism" were a known standard to which we require the ancient novel to measure up. But now we can see that much of what we call "realism" is a development emanating *from* the Novel itself. "Prescriptive Realism" extrapolated certain elements of the Novel, reinterpreted them and treated them as rules or invariable conditions. But the Novel must be "realistic" only in the sense that it deals with the tough experience of living and throws nothing away. Under the sign of the Goddess nothing is to be rejected. As the earth itself is the receptive home of all substance—bones, blood, feathers, shit, lost gold coins, and chips of earthenware—so too the Novel, which mimics its Goddess-mother, is receptive to all.

What is set a-going by writers' or readers' contact with the grand Novel, Her Great Untidiness, is not customary duty nor the formal and moral patterning for which Aristotle is sometimes produced as authority. The Novel does not necessarily demand that the bad be punished. The Novel does not need every mystery to be solved. The Novel does not require beginning, middle, and end in the manner of classical drama. A particular novel (e.g., *The Golden Ass*, *Tristram Shandy*, *Kim*) may not even have what is thought of as "an ending" at all—though here it is perhaps closer to epic than epic's fans want to admit. David Lodge mischievously suggests through one of his characters in *Small World* (1984) that "Romance" (and Lodge's own novel is subtitled "An Academic Romance") is feminine in relation to form (formal definition—especially Aristotle's—being historically the pronouncement of a hidden sexology): "Romance . . . has not one climax but many, the pleasure of this text comes and comes and comes again" (322). The "injured body" of novelistic fiction turns out to be, as Jane Austen

intimates, the body that expresses as well as gives "extensive and unaffected pleasure." In Austen's image of the productive if injured body, Novel and Novelist
combine as in an image of the Great Mother, the woman perpetually in productive pleasure if perpetually in labor. Lodge sinks the travail to emphasize the multiple orgasms of "unaffected pleasure." But if in a novel pleasure "comes and
comes again," it is intermixed with recurring anxieties, rousing the desires of the
reader (male or female) into perpetual motion and emotion, into increased consciousness. A novel *makes us feel the sense of being alive.* That, I contend, is its only
truly invariable "objective," while any given novel may have a number of designs
or even "ideas" as well as that one grand and profoundly hidden object, its real
and priceless Treasure. Our sense of "being alive" is not attained through a series
of imagined contacts with things, but through a myth that makes sense of things,
sensation and desire, together. This myth is connective. It invites pleasure, the
perceiver, and the world (*terra,* manifest in any given train, teapot, or turd). Lyric
poetry can do this too, and even brilliantly, yet but intermittently and most ego-
tistically. The Novel through the generosity of "character" enables us to enter.
The perfections of lyricism (if sometimes borrowed or parodied momentarily) are
deliberately eschewed in favor of the pained, pleasurable, imperfect, incessant,
labyrinthine reflection of consciousness working through time—through time
that is matter's reflection and sister, and not transcendant or transcended.

Throughout this book I have turned to myth to define the Novel and to
change our vision of what it is. We are all mythographers these days; the thought
of the last two centuries has been very strongly related to the interpretation of
myth, from long before Frazer's *The Golden Bough* up to and through the work of
Freud, Jung, and Lévi-Strauss. *Middlemarch*'s Mr. Casaubon reflects George Eliot
herself as mythographer. Some will regret the attachment of the Novel to myth
and religion, as we have been regarding it as our happily "secular" form. For
myself, the "secular" seems only a division of the sacred too, as life is sacred. The
"secular" is an area of the sacred where you are not to be bossed about by
the Church. I truly understand that some people do not feel that way, and dread
the incursion of anything like the "religious." Yet I think they must acknowledge the Novel's religious background and bedrock, even while attaining the reassurance that there is no reason why novels cannot be written by atheists, or
Marxist materialists, or skeptics, or Cynics. (Except that thoroughgoing Cynics
think writing a waste of time.)

Lévi-Strauss, who spent a great deal of his time categorizing myths and
explaining the nature of the mythical, said in 1977, relatively late in his career: "I
am not far from believing that, in our own societies, history has replaced mythology and fulfils the same function, that for societies without writing and without archives the aim of mythology is to ensure that as closely as possible . . . the
future will remain faithful to the present and to the past" (*Myth and Meaning,*
"The 1977 Massey Lectures," 42–43). Lévi-Strauss's statement here assumes that
there is a simple pure "history" to be written, quite independent of all "mythology." Mythology belongs, implicitly, to the "primitive" folk, and history to
the intellectually and technologically advanced. Such an assumption might well
attract eighteenth-century thinkers in earlier phases of the ongoing Enlightenment, but it should give us pause . The contention that mythology has a definable
teleology is contestable in itself, but even more dubious is the assertion that the

aim (visible and verifiable to the enlightened) of mythology is always to *stabilize*. Mythology exists in order to keep the future just like the past, or as near like it as can be managed. Such an assertion loses track of the counter-ability of mythology to enable people to explore and deal with new experience.

As a Christian, a participant in certain regular and mystical enactments and a hearer of stories regarded by the enlightened as myth, I see both mystery and myth as enabling conditions of insight and change. History, on the other hand, is various and always mixed up with the myths of the history-writer's culture. History is notoriously opinionated and unreliable, but beneath mere opinion it exemplifies the deep beliefs the historian has found most valuable, the myths that enable any sort of certainty and any sort of statement to exist.

A historian's myths may run counter to those of some readers. Plutarch in attacking Herodotus calls him a *Philobarbaros*, a "barbarian-lover," protesting that we must be on guard against Herodotus' deceptive charm "lest we take in absurd and lying opinions about the best and greatest of the cities and men of Greece" (*The Malice of Herodotus*, 28; 98). The recall to other myths, to alternative views, and to a variety of cultural perspectives is frequently felt as an affront, and heard as a blasphemy. The introduction of alternatives is genuinely felt to be dangerous.

I anticipate the charges of uttering "absurd and lying opinions" to be laid against this book. I do not wish to make a grandiose comparison between myself and Herodotus, in whose footsteps I admittedly follow, but it is already clear that disturbance of the category of the Novel (as realistic novel, begotten in the eighteenth century by British men) is upsetting to many critics. A partial outline of my thesis, when given as a lecture at Berkeley, provoked a written reaction in a hearer in whom my notions induced "paranoia"; she consoles herself with the view that the Greek novels (unread) are "cardboard love stories," as "common sense argues." The introduction of alternative myths or uncommon perspectives is always definable as an insult to "common sense." And equating the novels of Asia Minor, Africa, and the "Orient" with canonical Western novels is certainly perceived by some professors of Western literature as an outrageous act of leveling rather than as an exciting venture into wider space.[1]

History of any kind (including my own) has many defects. How much better to follow history within the Novel, where the author nothing affirmeth and therefore never lieth—and in a form whose mother-myth is so generous and all-encompassing. If you contemplate the Novel for a long time, and still more certainly if you undertake the writing of novels, you will eventually realize that it is impossible not to write History (no matter how fantastic your story may be). It is equally impossible not to write Myth (no matter how grimly realistic your prosaic narrative). The Novel represents the union between history and myth.

This union of history and myth is the more effective for being largely conscious. The Novel's own particular kind of myth allows history to be seen with some detachment, and playfully. History then becomes discussible, debatable. The myth the Novel presents, its "true story," is not teleologically rendered, but open-ended, making room for the next generation, opening out to new relations—including that between character and reader. As Michel Butor said, a novel character has to be open, rather than determined, so that "I" can put myself in the character's place. The pressure of pronouns, the grammatical element that Michel Butor seizes on as essentially novelistic (*Essais sur le roman*, 73–88), tells us of a world where many persons exist, and the final or definitive is not plausible. Hierarchies disappear, frontiers of separation become blurred in relationships.

The line between what is real and what is imaginary always gets blurred within the Novel, even destroyed as Marquez says it does in *realismo mágico*. The Novel world of artifice lusts illicitly after the real. The violets of *ekphrasis* lean insistently away from their imposed artistic transcendence. They announce their allegiance to incarnation and impermanence. In a novel's *ekphrasis* the material / immaterial division is mocked through parody. The delightful immateriality, the artifice of fiction, is itself a conscious weight, a mock ideal. Everything tends back towards the reader's own senses and sensuality, that assurance of flesh-and-bone being that underwrites the whole enterprise. If you are a saint or a prude, novels aren't written for you, as Amyot says—still less can they be yours if you are unembodied, or wish to be so. If the readers are not more than "soul" or "spirit," a novel is written in vain; its characters cannot attain their incarnation within us.

The Novel has a slippery openness appealing to us to ingest, to incarnate, to enter and be entered. Mikhail Bakhtin has expatiated on the Novel's "heteroglossia," its many-tongued nature, its aversion to what is "monoglot" and authoritarian. The Novel's openness and open-endedness make it inharmonious with totalizing answers, even the answers of mythology itself. The novelist as citizen may find himself or herself disconcerted by the recalcitrant genie that dwells in the divine fictional bottle, and may try to construct a conventional moral meaning out of it to pacify critics—including the author as contemporary reader. That is not to say the Novel is not moral. As we have seen, personal freedom is a moral value constantly represented in the novel. The strongest representation of the Eros that supports the desire for individual freedom, and for mutuality of justice, has traditionally been heterosexual love—what we call "romance." But in novels, ancient or modern, other forms of love are constantly found—not only gay love but loves neither sexual nor familial, like Charikleia's for Kalasiris, or Thekla's for Tryphaina. Unfortunately for the Novel, the "morals" that civic generations like (officially) best to hear have to do with negative moralizing—condemnation. Condemnation is rarely interesting to the Novel. The Novel may be entertained by Dante's Hell, but would not go there. It has, as it were, secret inclinations to the Eastern suggestion that even the Devil may be saved one day. The Novel's own myth, its inner story, is a story of regeneration.

In the 1930s and 1940s, that terrible time in a hectic and bloody century, Karl Kerényi and Thomas Mann exchanged a series of letters. Kerényi was an admirer of Mann's novels and sought (successfully) to interest Mann in his own current work. Kerényi discussed modern novels with Mann, remarking upon the presence and prescience of myth in works by English novelists such as Lawrence, Huxley, and Powys. But above all he recognized the myths in Mann's own work, not only in *Joseph* but also in the earlier *Zauberberg*. He sensed a kindred spirit in a writer who, though not a scholar, had in some sense anticipated him. Mann's own interest in mythology was nourished by Kerényi's epistolary friendship. He read Kerényi's book on *Die Griechisch-Orientalische Romanliteratur* with pleasure when the thirty-seven-year-old author sent it to him with the deprecating remark that it was the work of youth. Mann came up with his own ideas about the history of the novel:

> What, for example, was the relation of *Cervantes* to the Greek novel? Did he know and make use of it? As chance would have it, I am just rereading *Don Quijote*, or, oddly, for the first time really reading it thoroughly and right to the end. I found episodes in it which were conspicuously in accord with motifs in Heliodorus and in the Ass-Novel. For example, the story about the theater-dagger (p. 31 of your book) has a sufficient parallel in one of the stories in *Don Quijote*. . . . Even more striking is the story about the Ass-braying in *D.Q.*: of the two Burghers who excel and compete in imitating bellowing, and the *beating* of one of them on very account of the roars. Have you any clarification to offer about these resemblances? Perhaps it is thus: the Greek novel had strong contact with the Orient. It also made contact with the Italian novels, influenced Boccaccio and supplied him with motifs [i.e., story lines]. Boccaccio could have become the bridge between Cervantes and the Greek novel. Forgive the dilettante-ish conjecture!
> (Mann to Kerényi, 24 March 1934, *Romandichtung und Mythologie: Ein Briefwechsel* [*Novel-writing and Mythology: A Correspondence*], 29–30)

It will be seen that Mann's *dilettantische Konjektur* anticipates my own. Of course I think he is right above all in wishing to fill in the gap between ancient and modern novel. Boccaccio is a very important "bridge." There are, however, more bridges than one; Salmasius was not wrong in pointing to the transmission from the Greeks through the Moors to Spanish fiction. The ancient novel is connected with our own through a multitude of lines. As the middle part of my book demonstrates, there were ascertainable connections between ancient fiction and our own, through the work of the Middle Ages and then again in the printing Renaissance, when the surviving ancient and medieval novels became thoroughly absorbed into the bloodstream of our modern culture. Then, the English (in particular) in the mid-eighteenth century (and subsequently) created histories of fiction that cut off our view of that process and of most of the novels.

Thus, it has taken a new scholarly mythography to begin replacing what was formerly excised from our view of this literary form and its history. In a sense, what I have done is to reinvent Huet's version of the history of the Novel. Like Huet, I point to the ancient Middle East, to Syria and Egypt as well as to ancient Europe for the matrix of the Western Novel. It is, as Huet says, vain to look for the Novel's origins in modern times. From this point on, however, scholars of East and West may well join in searching for components and analogues of the Novel (if not for mythic "origins") *beyond* the Middle East as well as within it. There are striking similarities to the stories of novels, ancient and modern, in Javanese shadow-plays, in Beijing operas. The Beijing opera *Yu Tangchun*, for example, could usefully be compared with the stories of several novels.[2] The plot-motifs concerning the heroine Yu Tangchun, sold against her will into a brothel, an innocent girl who is accused of being a poisoner—these motifs resonate with elements in *Aithiopika*, *Ephesiaka*, and *Apollonius of Tyre*, as well as in *Filocolo* and *Clarissa*. Like all of these novels, the Chinese opera obviously has its roots in earlier stories. The stockpot of stories nourishing to our sense of individual value and our hope for the future was simmering long ago in the "Far East" (as Westerners call it) and not only in Egypt or Syria. The Novel, even at the point when it first becomes visible to us, would seem to be the repository of important stories and concepts that may have come first (or "first" in some form) from China, Java, Burma. . . . Let no Polynesian novelist feel like an interloper. We need not stop even at Huet's generous borders. At the same time, who can doubt that stories from the "West" have likewise traveled to the "East"? We laugh now at the Grimms' attempts to set down only purely "Germanic" folk tales. Let no one hope to have a tribally and culturally "pure" Novel. The Novel is always a mongrel mixture.

Thomas Mann, always a conscious mythographer as he points out to Kerényi regarding *Der Tod in Venedig*, felt troubled by mythography when myth of a pestilential kind, myths in vicious pursuit of purity and lordship, swirled about Europe. Mann became disturbed about Myth itself. In September 1941 he congratulates Kerényi on his work with Jung, believing that the combination of Mythology with Psychology provides a needed humanizing of Myth. "We must take Myth away from intellectual Fascism and make it function to serve Humanity. For a long time I have been doing nothing else, and nothing more" (*Briefwechsel*, 85).

Mann had reason to fear Myth on its own, and he saw psychology as a means of rescuing it, "for indeed Psychology is the means of getting Myth out of the hands of evil Fascist men and making it 'generally function' in the service of Humanity" (82). Perhaps Mann was not altogether right about psychology. Humane as it is in all apparent intentions, psychology has shown itself capable of developing its own tyrannies and falling into versions of intellectual Fascism. Jung himself was guilty of Aryan complacencies. Jeffrey Masson tellingly claims that Freud (under cultural pressure) ignored what he knew about the molestation of children in favor of a system that constructs abusive incest as the fantasy of the victim. Feminists have found in Freud a friend to the phallic order. Part of the trouble with psychology is that it is in itself a *bricolage*, made up as it goes along out of myths, beliefs, and habits culturally available at a given time. It is subject to fashion but must always sound universal. The Novel, on the other hand, announces itself as subject to fashion, as a product of its own era, even perhaps frivolously temporal. Its universality tends to be hidden. The Novel secretly offers—but does not impose—a therapy with long roots and deep ritual. So deep are its mythical sources that the Novel is much less susceptible than it looks to fashion and transitory phenomena, being itself a marvelous means of incorporating and interpreting current culture. Even aspects of the current culture that look like the Novel's rivals are partly her children. We talk of the impact of newspapers on the eighteenth-century novel, forgetting that newspapers were the invention of novel readers primed by many centuries of "Secret Histories." You have to get up pretty early to get ahead of the Novel.

Mann looked to psychology as the Perseus who was to rescue the Andromeda of Myth. But perhaps the Novel, which Mann had practiced so well—and so consciously—for so long is the more hopeful *Mittel*—the medium and means of getting Myth to circulate and function in a manner healthy for human beings. Mann was worried about the Fascists' use of mythology, and with good reason. But he also began to fear a certain *Fascismus* in Myth itself. With the horrible lessons of the twentieth century in our eyes, we must take seriously all the dangers of imposing myth. *Every* interpretation of a myth as Myth can become an imposition. This too is a danger inherent in my interpretation of the Novel and its fundamental myths of *Mythos*. In closing, I would wish to counteract anything of the Fascism of Myth by reminding us that we must not take the Goddess too seriously. I believe in her too much to want her to become a dogma.

We should treat the Goddess of the Novel lightly if she is to succeed in her task of making life bearable. Let us proceed, with Apuleius in mind, to create a vision or mock-vision of our Goddess of the Novel:

> I see her now, the Goddess of the Novel, and a novel Goddess she is. She stands in a green field, but behind and around her stretch the towers and skyscrapers of a city. Her head is rayed like the moon. Through the locks of black hair, and the golden ears of wheat rising feathery from her headgear, perky black snakes tangle and whisper in a brainy knot. On her left is a little garden which Eros is playing in, and wrecking. Her feet are on the muddy bank of a brook, and a labyrinth runs through her groin. A blue robe edged with vellum and papyrus, with paper and leather binding, adorned with Chinese inkstones and brushes and Nilotic reeds, with pencil boxes and book reviews, trails from her proud shoulders, while her iridescent dress, faintly printed in alphabetical pattern, swirls about her. She is a shape-changer, sometimes small (practically pocket-sized) and sometimes enormous. She carries a word-processor like a wallet at her hip. Near her on the greensward are a conch shell, a daisy chain, and a half-eaten cheese sandwich. In her hand she holds something like a mirror, that now and then seems to be a computer screen. Her wonderful and divine visage, indescribable on account of the poverty of human or even divine language, gazes half-kindly, half-sardonically towards the interbraidings of the nearby freeway. She is obviously a Madonna of the Future, even though she has a shepherdess' crook in her left hand, and about her gigantic right foot a little donkey plays perpetually.

Something like this kind of play is needed to guard against Myth's impositions, and to remind us that though a psychiatrist may demand belief, a novel does not. Despite Nobel Prizes, Booker Prizes, etc., novelizing has no priesthood. The myth and rituals enshrined in the Novel express our hopes for human rebirth and growth—those highest hopes never unmingled with humor at our having hopes at all. The myth, these rituals, are too valuable to be imposed. The Novel allows all sorts of things to happen—including letting itself be written by an ardent Roman Catholic, or a strict and pessimistic atheist, or a Buddhist, or a Jungian, or a dialectical materialist. The reading I have given the Novel at large interferes with no other reading of any individual novel or even (by and large) with other interpretations of the genre itself

What my sort of interpretation of the genre itself, of the novel as Novel, does *not* allow is our making narrow definitions of the genre and shutting out half of the prose fiction of the world. My reading will also not allow national and temporal boundaries to be the perdurable affairs they are often imagined to be. Like Herodotus, I wish to show that Asia and Africa were (and are) in contact with Europe, and to assure us that our literary history depends on a mixture, an interchange of all of these—with, it must now be added, the Americas, Pacific Islands, New Zealand, Australia, and so forth. The history of the Novel is never pure. The stories told by the Novel are not "pure." They are stories of mixture and variety, of boundary-crossing and changing. The Novel itself is not "pure" and refuses ever to pretend to be so. It rejoices in a rich muddy messiness that is the ultimate despair of *Fascismus*. No kind of literature has ever said more fully or firmly that there is life before death. The Goddess in her own realm is unconquerable. We make a not unimportant spiritual and political as well as personal move when we open a novel and become initiates, entering upon the marshy margins of becoming.

NOTES

>⊶⊷⊶-0-⊷⊶⊷

Abbreviations used in Notes

CAGN	*Collected Ancient Greek Novels*, edited by B. P. Reardon
ICAN	International Conference on the Ancient Novel
JHS	*Journal of the Hellenic Society*
TSAN	*The Search for the Ancient Novel*, edited by James Tatum

Introduction

1. The Anglo-American determination to separate Novel from Romance entails a certain naiveté; Michael McKeon remarks with surprise that Claude Lévi-Strauss "does not appear to use the words *roman* and *romanesque* with the intention of designating clearly either romance or novel"; see McKeon, *The Origins of the English Novel, 1600–1740*, 424. J. Paul Hunter offers a circular argument in describing a difference between French and English usage: "French, for example, encompasses both romance and novel in its term *roman*, and although the best literary historians in France have long acknowledged that quite a break occurs in French prose fiction at about the same time as in English, the distinction seems to most observers less sharp there, in part perhaps because of the history of terms" (*Before Novels* [1990], 361).

That is to say, the French or their "best historians" (who?) *would* fully acknowledge a difference if only their "terms" were not so perverse—as if the nature of the word *roman* could be set aside from a discussion of *romans*.

2. Jan Fergus's research into the contents of actual libraries, the habits of borrowers, and the size of print runs offers an invaluable corrective to a habitual overestimation of the size of the novel-reading public in the eighteenth and nineteenth centuries, and thus an exaggeration of any novel's immediate influence: Jane Austen's *Emma*, for instance, was published in a "large" run of 2,000 copies, but sold only 1,437 copies in four years, and was remaindered. See Fergus's *Jane Austen: A Literary Life* (1991), 159.

3. "Novels not only filled the leisure of those [middle-class women] without serious work but provided romantic fantasies to give meaning to their lives. . . . the epistolary formula, in particular . . . perpetuated the myth of romance in everyday life . . . inviting readers in their very form, to partake of the pleasures of fantasy" (Ruth Perry, *Women, Letters, and the Novel* [1980], 166–167). In this version of history, the Novel was not only substantially invented in England in the eighteenth century, but was invented to delude women, and is the bad by-product of bad social developments. In Gloria Steinem's bestseller *Revolution from Within* (1992), "love vs. romance" is one of the headings in the Index. Steinem seems to take it as a "natural" assumption that there is a difference between romantic erotic love and good sensible love—thus echoing some of the sexology of the seventeenth and eighteenth centuries, an era that itself is, oddly, often represented as the cradle of romantic heterosexual love.

4. Leopold Damrosch, Jr., following the Aristotelian line suggested, by, e.g., Sheldon Sacks in *Fiction and the Shape of Belief* (1964) and the Christian providential scheme employed, e.g., by Martin C. Battestin in his *The Providence of Wit: Aspects of Form in Augustan Literature and the Arts* (1974), has emphasized the sense of the Providential as distinguishing the newly emerging fiction of England in the seventeenth and eighteenth centuries. Dam-

rosch conventionally views the novel as a genre that arose out of Puritanism and "super-seded religious narrative" (5) largely by dint of first portraying the providential universe in fiction and then discarding it: see *God's Plot and Man's Stories: Studies in the Fictional Imagination from Milton to Fielding* (1985). But "religious narrative" always turns out never quite to have been superseded. The accommodation of literature and providence is a lot older than Damrosch imagines, inside and outside the Novel. "Providence," as we shall see, has played a part in the Novel and its story from the days of the Roman Empire.

5. Martin Bernal describes new developments taking place over the period 1790–1830, when a Romantic version of pure Greekness took over from older versions of Greek life and culture. The Greeks were "perceived as having transcended mundane chaos"; they were the model of what the West could be, the inner form, not to be contaminated by outsiders like the Egyptians or the Phoenicians now "increasingly perceived as 'racially' inferior." The idea that "sacred Hellas" could have been civilized by these other peoples became unthinkable. "Like the stories of sirens or centaurs, they had to be dismissed be-cause they offended against the biological and historical laws of 19th-century science." (See "Hellenomania" in Volume I of Bernal, *Black Athena*, 281–336.)

It was in the Romantic era Bernal here describes that the ancient novels, or at least the Greek ones, were absorbed by the German academy and largely lost their vital currency. I date this event from the publication of the Bipontine edition of the *Scriptores Erotici Graeci* edited by C. G. Mitscherlich in Strasbourg, in the mid 1790s, around the time of F. A. Wolf's deconstruction of Homer.

6. The case for Egypt as a center for novel-reading and novel-writing is succinctly rehearsed by Tomas Hägg in *The Novel in Antiquity*, (1983), 96–97.

J.W.B. Barns's essay in *Akten des VIII. intern. Kongr. f. Papyrologie* (Vienna, 1956) suggesting Egypt as the site of the novel's origin is discussed by Reardon, and the idea of an Egyptian origin for the novel entertained at length in *Courants littéraires grecs des IIe et IIIe siècles après J-C* (Paris, 1971), but later works by Reardon, including his "Introduction" to *Collected Ancient Greek Novels* (1989) and his book *The Form of Greek Romance* (1991), pay very little attention to the Egyptian connection.

Chapter I

1. Norman Mailer added the subtitle "A True Life Novel" to *The Executioner's Song* (1979). Truman Capote believed that in *In Cold Blood* (1965) he had solved the problem of uniting fiction and history; he claimed in an interview "that he had invented a form that used 'all the techniques of fictional art but was nevertheless immaculately factual'" (Phyllis Frus, "News and the Novel," Ph.D. dissertation [1985], 117). Frus points out that Mailer's title, by contrast, "is overt about its fictional status" and "makes no claim of absolute truth or fidelity to facts" (106). Our contemporary minglings of what is felt to be journalism (dealing with fact) and "literary" novelistic art (whose province is fiction) has led to puzzled and often disparaging coinages like "factoid" or (in Britain) "faction." But the novel has always tended to encroach on the borders of "history" and even sometimes gets itself read as history. To add to the complications, the "True Life Novel" need not ultimately be "realistic," and there are interesting forms of fantastic history, like Jeanette Winterson's *The Passion* (1987) set in the Napoleonic era.

2. "Cela vient, selon mon sens, de ce que les facultez de nostre ame estant d'une trop grande étendue, & d'une capacité trop vaste pour estre remplies par les objets presents, l'ame cherche dans le passé & dans l'avenir, dans la verité & dans le mensonge, dans les espaces imaginaires, & dans l'impossible mesme, de quoy les occuper & les exercer" (*Traité de l'Origine des Romans*, 8th ed. [Paris, 1711], 192–193).

3. "Ces règles sont connuës de si peu de gens, que les bons juges sont peut-estre plus rares que les bons Romanciers, ou les bons Poètes (100), . . . l'art de narrer, que tout le monde pratique, & que tres-peu de gens entendent, est beaucoup plus aisé d'entendre qu'à bien pratiquer" (ibid., 147).

4. "Ce n'est ni en Provence, ni en Espagne, comme plusieurs le croyent, qu'il faut esperer de trouver les premiers commencemens de cét agréable amusement des honnêtes paresseux: il faut les aller chercher dans les païs plus éloynez, & dans l'antiquité la plus reculée" (2).

5. Il fault chercher leur premiere origine dans la nature de l'espirit de l'homme, inventif, amateur des nouveautez & des fictions, desireux d'apprendre & de communiquer ce qu'il a inventé, & ce qu'il a appris; & que cette inclination est commune à tous les hommes de tous les tems, & de tous les lieux: mais que les Orientaux en ont toûjours paru plus fortement possedez que les autres, & que leur example a fait une telle impression sur les nations de l'Occident les plus ingenieux & les plus polies. Quand je dis Orientaux, j'entiens les Egyptiens, les Arabes, les Perses, les Indiens, & les Syriens. Vous l'avouerez sans doute, quand je vous auray monstré que la plupart des grands Romanciers de l'antiquité sont sortis de ces peuples. (12–13)

6. Edward Said analyzes the process of "orientalizing the Oriental" as a method of control through schematization: "How early this schematization began is clear from . . . Western representation of the Orient in classical Greece." In Western literature from the time of Aeschylus, "Europe is powerful and articulate; Asia is defeated and distant" (*Orientalism*, 68; 57). Said deals, however, with only the major canonical classical authors and does not discuss the "Greek" novelists, who offer an example of Asian thought inserting itself into the literature of the powerful Western empires and asserting its own voice or voices.

7. Erwin Rohde's *Der griechische Roman und seine Vorläufer* (1876) (translatable as *The Greek Novel and Its Forerunners*) is still a standard text and began the modern academic discussion of the ancient novel. In finding origins Rohde also sought development, and of course a chronology. The nineteenth century's ideas about the order of development are now not tenable. Rohde placed Chariton's novel, presently regarded by some as possibly the earliest surviving complete text, as late as the fifth or sixth century A.D., at the end instead of the beginning of the novel-writing era. Rohde's assumptions ought to make us wary of classifying anything according to what we regard as objective criteria of style. I have not read J. Ludvíkovský's book in Czech, *Řecký Román Dobrodružný* (*Le Roman grec d'aventures*) published in Prague in 1925, but there is a readable French summary of the contents (147–158). One of the interesting things about Ludvíkovský's study is his interest in tracing resemblances between early novels and early films. (See also Reardon, *The Form of Greek Romance*, 125).

Sophie Trenkner is interested in short forms of fiction and oral fiction, positing the circulation of oral *novelle* very like the medieval *fabliaux* that English readers know best in Chaucer. Trenkner is interested in the extent to which oral literature forms the primary "source" of written literature, and in the ways in which the oral precipitated into the written, crystallizing in what we recognize as literary forms; see her *The Greek Novella in the Classical Period* (1958). Graham Anderson's claim in *Ancient Fiction: The Novel in the Graeco-Roman World* (1984) that the Greek material repeats Sumerian religious mythology is extremely interesting and suggestive, though it is noticeable that he has to rely on translations of all his primary Eastern materials, and is particularly indebted (as we all must be) to the work of Samuel N. Kramer on Sumeria. Anderson is attentive to stylistic particulars and techniques, as can be seen also in his *Eros Sophistes: Ancient Novelists at Play* (1982).

8. "The Greek novel was the earliest writing designed to appeal to women. . . . It has also been argued that hiding behind possible pseudonyms . . . are the first female writers of the Western world. The genre's greatest vogue in the second century A.D. coincided with a significant increase in the literacy of women" (Erich Segal, "Heavy Breathing in Arcadia," *The New York Times Book Review* [29 September 1985]. Segal as classicist labors to make his disdain for all the Greek novels very clear: "the motif is identical in today's romances," he says, illustrating with the work of Rosemary Rogers. Segal does not allude to his own writing of *Love Story*. He quotes (from Hägg) B. P. Reardon's comment on Chariton (generalizing

it to cover all the novels) that this literature is "sentimental, bourgeois, and rather similar to the tone of stories in ladies' magazines today" (Hägg, *Novel in Antiquity*, 16; Segal, 48).

For the use by Theodorus Priscianus of erotic novels to cure impotence, see Rohde, *Der griechische Roman*, 242; see also Froma Zeitlin, "The Poetics of *Erōs*," *Before Sexuality* (ed. David Halperin et al.), 432. Consider, too, the hint regarding masturbation in George Thornley's Preface to his 1657 translation of *Daphnis and Chloe* (see below, Part II, Chap. XI).

9. Julian wrote to a pagan priest wishing to encourage purity of life in the revived pagan clergy; he advises the priest not to read idle histories, fictions (*plasmata*), erotic stories (or more literally "erotic supposes," *erōtikas hypotheseis*), and "all that sort of thing" (*kai panta haplōs ta toiauta*). Julian's letter (letter 89) is quoted in Reardon, *Courants Littéraires Grecs*, 324; cf. Hägg, *Novel in Antiquity*, 3. What is clear from Julian's letter is that the Greeks had no word for the novel, though they had the thing, and a variety of rather vague terms. Phrases like "that sort of thing" keep cropping up from Julian's time through the Renaissance.

10. Thomas Hägg in his splendidly illustrated *Novel in Antiquity* has been the leading exponent of the mosaics as illustrations to the novels. Such illustration exhibits a kind of popularity for the novels that seems vulgar to some scholars. Ewen Bowie argues that the mosaics may only be illustrations of mimes; see "The Readership of Greek Novels in the Ancient World," *TSAN*, 453–459. The Syrian mosiacs are thus related by Bowie to a "low" and vulgar subliterary form. When we see the mosaics we can see that the characters are being represented, as in a freeze frame of a movie or a colored photograph, *as if* they were real. If they came from theatrical works, there are no trappings of theater in the pictures— we are visually urged to treat the stories as artistic "real life," unlike some pictures of mimes at work, e.g. images from the Pompeii area now in Napoli museum. The mosaic representation well suits the mood, manner, and themes of the novels, with the emphasis on characters gazing at letters and pictures; relationship and inwardness are their themes. Any discussion of mosiac illustration is wrapped up in the contest over "popularity." If the novels were *too* popular, that militates against their true classicism. Bowie, who is University Lecturer in Greek and Latin Language and Literature at Oxford University, would evidently wish to reclaim the novels as proper "classical" material. That desire is apparent in his dating of the novels, bringing Chariton up in time and pushing Heliodorus back in order that they may fit into an appropriate frame of time around the Second Sophistic.

11. I am indebted to Dr. William Braesher of the Ägyptisches Museum and to Herr Doktor Poethke of the Bode Museum, both in Berlin, not only for showing me the fragments, but also for giving me the benefit of their learned opinion both as to the date, and as to the nature of the handwriting style and what it may signify.

12. Ewen Bowie expresses this view in his article in *TSAN*; as he acknowledges, "the evidence is desperately short" (440). In the same volume, Susan A. Stephens argues that the number of novel-readers was small, judging from the number of recovered papyri fragments of novels. Surviving bits of ancient manuscript do not emanate from the Christian community or other socially low milieu; they are well-copied and expensive. See her "Who Read Ancient Novels?" *TSAN*, 405–418. Bowie's and Stephens's articles are not entirely in harmony. Bowie wants to believe that the novels were more widely read than Stephens thinks (albeit widely read by the right people). He counters the canard that the novels were not well thought-of because there are so few references to them in the work of other writers, even positing the possibility that the Emperor Julian himself was at some point in his life a reader of novels. Bowie's sense that the novels were generally reputable automatically precludes in his paradigm any notion that they came from a feminine milieu.

Patrizia Liviabella Furiani (drawing in part on earlier work by Bowie) agrees with such a view; the novels were not written by women and what we have here is a point of view "exclusively masculine." Any "feminism" in the novels is "always filtered by masculine sensibility and experience" ("Di Donna in Donna: Elementi 'Femministi' nel Romanzo Greco d'Amore," *Piccolo mondo antico*, 43–106. A similar view is expressed in the same collection of essays in an article by Consuelo Ruiz Montero, "Cariton de Afrodisias y el Mundo Real" (107–147).

13. Arthur Heiserman, in *The Novel Before the Novel: Essays and Discussions about the Beginnings of Prose Fiction in the West* (1977), builds his argument on the idea of "erotic suffering" as story material, usable in a number of ways, including tragic, comic and didactic. He has some good arguments against the usual charges that all such "romances" are mere wish-fulfillments, pointing out that *Genesis* and *The Birds* could come under the same ban and are also "fantastic" (6). Heiserman is so taken with the importance of *pathos*, the emotional dimension of erotic suffering as a key term in the novel as a genre, that he begins his survey with an extensive discussion of the *Argonautika* by Apollonius Rhodius (d. 215 B.C.), even though the title of his own study emphasizes *prose* fiction. Heiserman claims that "the special quality of suffering" in resourceless Jason and unlucky Medea explains why this Alexandrian epic "seems most like the prose romances written centuries later" (13). But certain elements in this poem by an academic writer (royal tutor and sometime head of the Library at Alexandria) may have been current in prose form at the time; Apollonius Rhodius may have known that his love-epic already had to compete with the novel, or with forms of oral narrative very close to the novels we know.

14. See John J. Winkler, *The Constraints of Desire*, 143. Photius in his *Bibliothēkē* summarizes a major work by Ptolemy Chennos that Winkler defines as "a seven book parody of classical scholarship"; called *A Novel History*, it precedes Samuel Butler in creating a female writer of the original *Iliad* and *Odyssey*. Ptolemy Chennos "is a liar on a grand, academic scale," says Winkler (144). It is a pity Ptolemy's novel *The Sphinx* has not come down to us.

Chapter II

1. Chariton may have been the author of other novels. In the introduction to his translation Reardon suggests that Chariton was the author of *Metiochos and Parthenopé*, and *Chionē* (*CAGN*, 19). Philostratus writes an "Imaginary Epistle" to a Chariton (Epistle no. 66) saying that "Hellenes [Reardon translates: 'civilized people'] will never remember you or your writings" (*logoi*) (Reardon, "Theme, Structure and Narrative in Chariton," *Yale Classical Studies* 27 [1982], 27). Perry and others assumed Philostratus' jeer proved the general disdain for novels. But this shaft suggests rather that Chariton was popular enough to be an irritation; Ewen Bowie points out that Philostratus' statement "indicates that by his time novels and their creators had a claim to belong to the world of *logoi*, and that Philostratus might expect his cultivated readers to recognize both the individual and his genre" ("The Readership of Greek Novels in the Ancient World," *TSAN*, 445).

2. "Hermocrates, the father of the heroine Callirhoe, was a Syracusan statesman and leader in the successful resistance to the Athenian expedition against Sicily in 415–413. . . . Callirhoe herself shares this historical aura to some extent, for Hermocrates did have a daughter who died accidentally. Chaereas is not based on any known Syracusan figure, but his adventures recall, as well as those of Alexander, the exploits of an Athenian professional soldier of the early fourth century, Chabrias; and his father, Ariston, has the same name as the prominent member of the victorious Syracusan navy" (B. P. Reardon, "Introduction" to translation of *Chaireas and Kallirrhoé*, as "Chaereas and Callirhoe," *CAGN*, 18).

3. See John Boswell's historical examination of the abandonment of children in *The Kindness of Strangers* (1988); Boswell quotes Quintilian, who in his *Declamations* has a foster father in a law case challenge the natural parent: "'If it had been up to you . . . beasts would have torn him apart, or birds carried him off, or—much worse—the pimp or the gladiator-trainer would have gotten him'" (Boswell, 88). Boswell thinks that many or most of the young prostitutes in Rome were abandoned children. Child prostitution was openly practiced; as Boswell notes, "There was a holiday for boy prostitutes in Augustan Rome" (112).

4. It is *not* strictly true to say that Aphrodite-like Kallirrhoé holding the child represents a new way of seeing the goddess, although Chariton emphasizes this idea. As Marina Warner notes in *Alone of All Her Sex* (1976), "The theme of the nursing Virgin . . . probably originated in Egypt, where the goddess Isis had been protrayed suckling the infant Horus

for over a thousand years before Christ" (1983 ed., 193). A limestone carving of Aphrodite holding Eros, found in Cyprus and dating from circa 350–300 B.C. is to be seen in the Metropolitan Museum of Art in New York. Female divinities holding children include the harpies, as in the "Harpy Tomb" from Xanthus in Lykia, now in the British Museum; each harpy tenderly holds a baby, representing the soul of a person who has died. But, on the whole, goddesses and feminine *numina* are not represented holding children. The child Eros rather than a babe in arms is the usual companion of Aphrodite, and other divinities tend to hold cult objects or animals rather than children—Cybele, for instance, sometimes has a little lion in her lap.

5. Aristotle ties himself up in knots on this question; he does know that some people argue that it is detestable that merely superior power should ever constrain another human being to become a slave. (See *Politics*, 1254b–1255a.) The heroes and heroines of novels can be taken as merely illustrating Aristotle's point about the evil of enslaving the *superior* person; the amount of emphasis, however, given to the slave experience constitutes an implicit argument against slavery. At the very least, the old social system seems to be suffering from pangs of conscience. Seneca (c. 55 B.C. to A.D. 41), that anxious Spaniard always so alert to cruelty, argues that slaves should not be considered subhuman, but should be recognized as "humble friends" (*humiles amici*) and fellow human beings. Indeed, in some sense we are all slaves, being slaves to fortune: see his *Epistles*, no. 47. But it is false comfort to take Seneca's unusually highly developed moral sense as representing any kind of norm even in belief about the treatment of slaves, let alone the practice.

6. B. P. Reardon makes the peculiar objection, first posed by Rohde, that Chariton's novel lacks a villain: "nobody who is important enough is nasty enough" ("Theme, Structure and Narrative in Chariton," 13). Scholars seem actually rather to like the melodrama they professedly despise. Dionysios is certainly *not* a villain. Part of Chariton's artistry is his ability to draw mixed characters; all the major characters here are mixed, including the hero and the heroine, and of course they are all *comic* characters.

7. See John J. Winkler, "The Education of Chloe," in *The Constraints of Desire*, 105; see also Zeitlin, "The Poetics of *Erōs*," 438.

8. B. P. Reardon in a long and packed note in *The Form of Greek Romance* discusses the nature and influence of mime: "Greek mime was a realistic dramatic performance in speech, song, gesture and dance, in popular language and often farcical, generally setting out a situation from everyday life but with little sustained plot. . . . Like early romance, mime was considered sub-literary, and little remains of it." Among those remains are some papyri, including one apparent parody of Euripides' *Iphigenia in Tauris*: "a Greek girl is rescued from imprisonment in a barbarian land by her brother and a comic slave, who make her captors drunk and escape with her" (163). The material here seems to resemble elements in *Kleitophon and Leukippé* more closely than in *Ephesiaka*, which Reardon points to for comparison. There are some interesting mosaic pictures of mimes in the Pompeiian galleries in Napoli.

9. J. M. Barrie wrote the play *Peter Pan, or The Boy Who Wouldn't Grow Up* (1904) before turning the story into a narrative, *Peter and Wendy* (1911). *Peter Pan in Kensington Gardens* (1906), largely excerpted from *The Little White Bird* (1902), gives more information about Peter, aligning this Pan with the garden imagery and the pastoral goat as well as with the pan-pipes: "Gentlemen who walk home at night write to the papers to say they heard a nightingale in the Gardens, but it is really Peter's pipe they hear" (29). The musical playing of Pan, in Barrie's book and in the chapter entitled "The Piper at the Gates of Dawn" in Kenneth Grahame's *The Wind in the Willows* (1908), is strongly related to the account of Pan's playing when he terrifies the raiders and rescues Chloé and her flock in Book II of *Daphnis and Chloé*. Barrie's and Grahame's works appear to be directly and closely influenced by *Daphnis and Chloé*; Barrie's Peter in *Kensington Gardens* combines Pan with some aspects of Longus' Eros, as in his birdlike qualities. Wendy has some Chloé characteristics, but there is no Daphnis for her, Peter being a reverse foundling who left home in infancy and aligned himself with wild freedom—becoming Pan almost, one might say, by an effort of will.

Victorian and Edwardian writers (especially male) had access to antique literature about Pan, including, centrally, *Daphnis and Chloé* (see Robin Lane Fox, *Pagans and Christians*, 130–132). The popularity of the Pan figure at the beginning of the twentieth century is striking. Pan becomes the figure for natural freedom, for male sexuality and for the love that dare not speak its name. More generally, this "Pan" (whose makeup always bears some relation to the Pan of Longus) is a mode of representing the goodness of the libido, and contact with aspects of the self denied by civilization. Such a Pan turns up as the healing figure of "Dickon" in Frances Hodgson Burnett's *The Secret Garden* (1911), a children's book with a title suggesting the redemption of female genitals and libido. "Pan" is in the children's books because these are a refuge against what civilization defines as maturity; Barrie's Pan is "The Boy Who Wouldn't Grow Up." The Pan-figure does not embody a testosterone-charged violent force as masculinity, but a playfulness, the incarnate potentiality of being happy in possession of genitals and a "natural" being.

10. George Moore, for all his idealizing love of "Paganism," has a hard time translating *The Pastoral Loves of Daphnis and Chloé* (1924), his own twin gods of realism and prudery getting in his way. In the name of realism he questions Chloé's rescue of Daphnis from the wolf pit: "the reader will not be satisfied that Daphnis shall be released with the cord with which Chloe ties up her hair" ("Introduction," 27). He could have known that a *tainia* was a long strip of linen wrapped around a girl's body to support the bust—much stronger than a hair-ribbon. Moore furnishes the heroine with a rope of his own weaving: '*Chloe caught sight of one that the diggers of the pit had lost among the bushes, ran to it* and gave it to the neatherd, who threw an end of it to Daphnis" (39, italics mine). This extra rope deprives Daphnis of an important mediated contact with the heroine's person, which even the erroneous "headband" would have provided. So much for the advance of principles of translation in the twentieth century.

Chapter III

1. For a study of Ephesus in particular, and its efforts to preserve its own cultural identity with modifications suited to the imperial situation, see Guy McLean Rogers, *The Sacred Identity of Ephesos* (1991); this book is also an imaginative reconstruction of main areas of the city. Anton Bammer's *Das Heiligtum der Artemis von Ephesos* (1984) gives a general account of the archaeology with good illustrations.

2. For descriptions and discussions of the ancient civilizations of Asia Minor as archaeology has been able to reconstruct them, see A. Akurgal, *Ancient Civilizations and Ruins of Turkey* (trans., 6th ed., 1985) and *Treasures of Turkey* (1966); Everett C. Blake and Anne G. Edmonds, *Biblical Sites in Turkey* (1972); and John Boardman, *The Greeks Overseas* (1980). For anyone traveling in Turkey, the "Blue Guide," *Turkey: The Aegean and Mediterranean Coasts* (1989) by Bernard McDonagh, is an excellent guide. For Aphrodisias see Kenan T. Erim, *Aphrodisias, City of Venus Aphrodite* (1986).

3. This archaic golden image is reproduced in a color photograph in Bammer, *Das Heiligtum*, Fig. 86, facing page 192.

4. Lucy Goodison follows in the footsteps of Margaret Mead and Mary Douglas (*inter alia*) in questioning the validity and desirability of the binary system of opposites, which has informed thinking in the West in recent millenia. It was one of the functions of some modern sociologists (viz. Durkheim) to question such structures and historicize them. Contemporary thought in general (quite apart from gender studies) seems more interested in fluctuating patterns of relational flow (e.g., chaos theory) than in stable oppositions.

Thomas Laqueur in *Making Sex: Body and Gender from the Greeks to Freud* (1990) pursues what happens through the employment of traditional binary definitions (almost always hierarchical) to such "scientific" matters as anatomy, biology, and psychology—past and present. Freud's opinions on the Medusa's head can be found in a brief note written in 1922, and in an essay of 1923, "The Infantile Genital Organization."

5. Once one gets to Lykia in southwest Asia Minor, the true home of harpies, one can

see that they are images of winged creatures that care for the soul. We experience surprise at their favorable representation, for we have been bred to Virgil's version: harpies menace the hero and contaminate the food with their disgusting female ordure and foul stench (see *Aeneid* III, lines 225–262). Who could guess that such horrifying birds, obscenely expressive of all female organs and emissions, had an angelic aspect? Who could imagine anyone ever liked them? In order to understand another culture, like that of Lykia, we must temporarily "forget" what we have been told by such leading Roman mythologists as Virgil.

It must, however, be admitted that the caring harpy can still strike terror in the breasts of men. Franco Moretti in an essay entitled "The Soul and the Harpy" contemplates the bas-relief on what he calls "an ancient *Greek* tomb in the British Museum" (my emphasis). The soul can do nothing to escape from the harpy's clutches, so "prefers to delude itself about the affectionate, almost maternal nature of the creature dragging it away with her in flight" (*Signs Taken for Wonders*, 41). For Moretti, the harpy is an image of all literature (not just novelistic fiction) as it gets a grip on us and tries to persuade us that the world is a good and meaningful place. Our "consent" to be inspired by it is merely the relaxation in the grip of the harpy.

6. For worship of Mithras, see Burkert, *Ancient Mystery Cults*, 40–43; Burkert draws the "often invoked" parallel with the Masons: "In some respects the mysteries of Mithras are closer to the general type of secret societies with initiation rituals, as known in social anthropology, than the other, 'normal' Greek mysteries" (42).

7. The most impressive sacrament of the Mithraic Mysteries was the *taurobolium*, or bath in bull's blood—a rite so costly that sometimes the expense was borne by the whole brotherhood. The *taurobolium* formed part of the ritual of the Cybele-Attis cult from at least the second century, from which it may have been borrowed by the Mithraists. . . .The fullest account has been left by the Christian poet Prudentius, to whom, as to the other Christian apologists, it was an object of special detestation. . . .   (S. Angus, *The Mystery-Religions*, 94)

8. "Roman society through the time of Virgil appears to have accepted without question the right of a father to execute even a grown son" (Boswell, *The Kindness of Strangers*, 59). Boswell believes people from other parts of the empire found this Roman power distasteful. One may doubt whether the right to kill one's *grown* children was commonly invoked by Romans; the example of Lucius Junius Brutus (cited by Boswell) is poor supporting evidence. The point of the Brutus story is that he displayed true republican virtue by sacrificing his guilty sons to execution for treason, according to law and reason of state. His example could be so tremendous *because* it was taken for granted that he would want to exercise privilege to save his sons. Yet the power of the *paterfamilias* was undoubtedly very great; Boswell argues, "Their [the children's] position was structurally not unlike that of highly valued slaves" (119). The rights of parents in relation to children constitute vexed legal problems in our own time; it could be argued that the idea of a man's right to kill his children is not yet dead in the West (including the US) if we consider the number of children killed annually by their fathers or stepfathers. The laws of Rome endorsed paternal power more vigorously than the laws and customs of other nations or cultures within the region, but the power of the father was generally agreed to be extensive. Kleitophon of Tyre, though he is miserable at the prospect of his father-arranged marriage to his half-sister, has no right of protest.

9. Some legislation of the late despot of Romania, Nicolae Ceausescu, seems a deranged recollection of Augustus; Ceausescu instituted a tax on all childless women over the age of twenty-four.

10. *The Shepherd of Hermas* (*Poimēn* or *Liber Pastoris nuntii paenitentia*) is an early Christian work, written in Greek evidently by a Christian living in Italy. It was sometimes treated as Christian scripture and read in churches. *The Shepherd*, a discussion of penitence, is one of the earliest instances of the application of allegory in Christian writing and looks forward to Dante and Bunyan. The interesting beginning, with the narrator's moment of lust in his

heart for the beautiful Rhodé, bears some similarity to the novels of the period. There is scriptural precedent for the forgiveness of the erring wife as an analogy for the forgiveness of God in the Book of Hosea, where the erring wife can be read symbolically as an image of the Jewish people. Tertullian had liked the *Shepherd* at first but turned against it in his more austere phase. See *Le Pasteur*, 154.

11. Mary Wollstonecraft's heroine Maria in *The Wrongs of Woman* (1798) tries to enter in her lover's defense during an adultery case that is a legal suit by her husband as plaintiff against her "seducer." Maria argues that her lover cannot be a seducer since she herself is a free agent, who has "acted with deliberation," and she wishes to claim a divorce. Her unorthodox proceeding wins her nothing more than the judge's reprimand (195–199).

12. As the best-known cases of Roman females instituting divorce involve politically important second marriages, we must be wary of attributing real initiative to the women. No doubt Livia had formally to initiate her divorce from her first husband (even though she was pregnant by him at the time). We may, if we wish, assume that she wanted to marry Octavian (later Augustus Caesar). But in the light of Octavian's power, both she and her husband would surely have felt it unwise to cross him. Earlier, Sulla's step-daughter Aemelia divorced her husband and married Pompey, creating an alliance between Sulla and Pompey—she seems little more than a pawn in their game. What is surprising about the Romans is the acceptance of multiple sequential marriages (at least in the wealthiest classes) and male acceptance of a wife with known prior sexual experience. But it is not certain that wives could really finish with a marriage entirely of their own volition. There was likewise a procedure whereby a wife could institute a divorce in Athenian law, but MacDowell observes that the legal proceeding "gave the husband some opportunity to intervene"; he believes that in Athens "a wife could not obtain a divorce without her husband's acquiescence" (*Law in Classical Athens*, 88).

13. The Athenian woman who was seduced was punished by divorce (if she was married), and by a permanent exile from all public religious ceremonies. She was also forbidden to wear any kind of ornament: "Anyone who saw her infringing this rule could pull off her clothes and ornaments and slap her" (MacDowell, *Law in Classical Athens*, 125). She was not punishable by death, unless caught in the act by an enraged husband.

Novelists take many liberties in adjusting laws and conventions; as Brigitte Egger shows, they are anachronistic and mix various laws and social codes ("Women and Marriage in the Greek Novels: The Boundaries of Romance," *TSAN*, 260–280). Unlike Egger (who relies too much on the assumed freedom of women in Egypt as a standard), I think the novelists have a purpose in their outline of law, which is not mere authorial "androcentrism." The novelists dramatize the nature of constraint; they make us pause at the frontiers of life where the woman is going to find herself most at risk, most under the rule of necessity as law defines her role. The salad of rules and customs gains a certain coherence from this view.

14. See for example Hägg, *The Novel in Antiquity*, 154–162. Thekla has inspired at least one novelist in modern times; Hägg points out "a work by the first Swedish novelist, Jacob Mörk, which was published in Stockholm in 1749–1758 under the title of *Thecla, Eller Den Bepröfwade Trones Dygd*: 'Thecla, Or the Virtue of Well-Tried Faith.' Here it is the Emperor Nero who falls a victim to the attraction of the maiden, but is of course rebuffed" (Hägg, 159). Despite this eighteenth-century example of the attractions of Thekla to a male author, Hägg wants to argue for female authorship of the "Paul and Thekla" section of the *Acts of Paul*, suggesting that it "started as an independent piece of writing," got roped in by the compiler of the *Acts of Paul*, and then led a separate life (162).

15. It is the more surprising that Thekla's cult survives in Silifke (ancient Seleucia ad Calycadnum), since it is in a non-Christian area. But the Christian Church in the West has abandoned her; her cult was suppressed by the Roman Catholic Church in 1969. It may seem ironic that this archetypal "uppity woman" of the Christians stands a much better chance in Islamic countries. The caretaker at the Ayatekla in Silifke told me that he has seen pilgrims coming to pray here, tears pouring down their faces. A similar shrine to

St. Thekla exists near Damascus in Syria. Her feast day is 23 September—the date chosen in antiquity to celebrate the birthday of the Emperor Augustus.

St. Thekla had some success in the West; her image can be seen in the thirteenth-century mosaics of four female saints in the spandrels of the dome in the right transept of the basilica of San Marco, Venice.

16. Achilles Tatius' novel could be read as a serio-comic response to the Christians, and more specifically to the nineteenth chapter of the Acts of the Apostles, a response providing a full defense of Artemis-Diana of the Ephesians, the presiding goddess of the novel.

17. Paola Manuli, analyzing the ideological content of antique gynecology, points to the underlying idea that "the womb, an animal and most mobile god . . . is the true soul of woman, an irrational soul." This strange animal can be best appeased or tamed within marriage and in procreation. Those who do not marry or refrain from sexual contact dry up, lose their menstrual courses, become grotesquely masculine and die. The grim descriptions of virginity Manuli labels "terrorismo igienico"—medical terrorism. Descriptions of female virginity in the medical literature are terrifying; the state is likely to lead to epilepsy, a grand attack of "hysteria" or womb sickness arising from "a congenital debility repaired solely in matrimony and maternity" (P. Manuli, "La ginecologia tra Ippocrate e Sorano," in Campese et al., *Madre materia,* 157; 161–162). Helen King endorses this view in "Bound to Bleed: Artemis and Greek Women," in *Images of Women in Antiquity.* Giulia Sissa in *Le Corps virginal* (1987) argues that the ancients gave no special emphasis to virginity as either a physical or moral concept: *parthenos* only means "marriageable young woman." See also Sissa, "Maidenhood without Maidenhead" in *Before Sexuality,* 339–363. Sissa blames Christianity for the invention of a hymen-centered maidenhead.

But there is evidence that long before Christianity the word *parthenos* meant much what the English word "virgin" did in England in the time of Samuel Richardson. In Euripides' *Ēlektra,* for example, the peasant husband to whom Aegisthus has married Agamemnon's surviving daughter against her will says that he has not forced her to fulfill the marriage but that she is still a virgin: *parthenos d'et esti dē* (line 44). Compare Lovelace's story about how he is married to Clarissa but she is still a virgin (*Clarissa,* V, 95–114).

It seems evident in the surviving antique novels that the concept of untouched virginity as well as nubility existed for the ancients as for people in Early Modern Euope. Marriage to an untouched virgin has been valued in many cultures in Africa, Asia, and Europe. Some pagan priesthoods required virginity; see Robin Lane Fox, *Pagans and Christians,* 347–348. Origen points to these, as well as vigorously arguing against an opponent making the (very modern) argument that "virgin" means only "young woman" in the verses in Isaiah that Christians found prophetic (*Contra Celsum,* Book I, Secs. 33–34, 34–35). Origen certainly believes that the condition of virginity is culturally clear. Christians were unusual in allowing women to be of value without regular taming and irrigation by the male. Women were not "unclean"; a pregnant or menstruating woman was allowed by Pope Gregory to take communion, for instance.

18. Images common in the Greek novels abound in *Dora,* including the goddess (as Raphael's Madonna) and images of Nymphs. Freud interprets Dora's gazing on Raphael's picture for two hours as a sinister sign. He knows that the "Nymphs" in another modern picture in a gallery represent the female genitals, and also that they should not be looked at by Dora. (So much for Longus' vision of the Nymphs.) Dora, who resists Herr K. as Thekla resisted Alexandros, also gets into trouble with the authorities. She has been thrown into the arena that Freud created for her, in retribution for her *hubris,* her resistance both to her father and to the fatherly middle-aged man who thrust his attentions on her. Dora's story as written by Freud, based on his sessions with Ida Bauer, first appeared as *Bruchstück einer Hysterie-Analyse* in 1905.

19. Marc Philonenko in his critical edition *Joseph et Aséneth* (1968) has developed the connection of the images of Aseneth with the goddess Neith, *la déese de la couronne rouge* (63). Neith's cult is connected with bees, and with the image of a cow spangled with stars. A goddess of wisdom, she was often assimilated to Isis and was viewed by Greeks as a

parallel to Athena. The story also has astrological allegorical significance; Aseneth is a moon surrounded by seven stars for the seven nights of the week (also the Pleiades). *Joseph and Aseneth* is a Gnostic and spiritual—or spiritualized—story that has played with and rewritten an older Jewish story, in which Dinah, the daughter of Leah and Jacob, after being defiled by Shechem (Genesis 34) bore a daughter, which her vengeful brothers took from her. The daughter, placed on the altar of an Egyptian idol, was found by the priest Putiphar and brought up by him and his wife in splendor in Egypt. Unhappy Dinah's daughter "Aseneth" as the Egyptian priest's daughter is married to Joseph, and thus is restored to her rightful Jewish heritage (see Philonenko, *Joseph et Aséneth*, 32–43).

Chapter IV

1. As the first clear reference to *Apollonius* elsewhere does not occur until the sixth century A.D., and as the riddles told by Tharsia are to be found in Symphosius' riddle-book of the fourth or fifth century, this novel has been assumed to be a very late work. That the same riddles are found in another work, however, offers no proof as to which is the earlier. Certainly, narrative use of riddles is very old; cf. the story of Samson and his riddle (Judges 14:12–18). It seems likely that this novel was shaped, more or less in the form we know, during the hey-day of novel writing in the second or third centuries. It may be that we have an abridged version; some scenes seem more rushed than others. Although the Latin is simple and colloquial, references to Virgil and other poets indicate a sufficiently "literary" work. An earlier Greek form of the novel has been often, and reasonably, postulated, but not found.

2. Antiochus' riddle or "question" is as follows (the "u" is changed to "v" for easier reading):

> scelere vehor, maternam carnem vescor,
> quaero fratrem meum, meae matris virum,
> uxoris meae filium: non invenio.   (9)

"Scelere vehor" can be translated "By crime I am carried away." Antiochus' "non invenio" can mean "I do not find," or "I do not find out," or "I do not invent." The phrase combines his insatiable seeking of the impossible with a wry hint of his truthfulness. In his lust he is looking for all relations in one, and turning one relation into all.

Shakespeare is indebted to *Apollonius* for *Pericles* (c. 1606–1608; printed in 1609). (His collaborator George Wilkins in 1608 brought out a novel, *The Painfull Adventures of Pericles Prince of Tyre*, advertising itself as "The true History of the Play of *Pericles*"—as if the novel were only a novelization.) Shakespeare's *Pericles* puts the blame for the incest almost equally on father *and* daughter:

> With whom the father liking took,
> And her to incest did provoke,
> Bad child, worse father, to entice his own
> To evil should be done by none
>   (I. Chorus, lines 25–28)

The *violence* of the King's assault on his daughter has been written out of the story. She was only *enticed*. Some productions of *Pericles* have excised Antiochus and the incest theme altogether—see Arden edition of *Pericles*, ed. F. D. Hoeniger (1963), xv.

3. Myrrha's advance on her unsuspecting father (who knows only that the old nurse is going to bring him a young virgin) is narrated as if the daughter were a rapist, like Tarquin:

> She came towards her own evil deed. The golden moon
> Fled from the sky, and the stars drew
> Black curtaining of cloud to hide behind;
> Night lacked her fires.

. . .
Three times she is recalled by stumbling foot;
Three times in omen the funereal screech-owl
Sent forth its lethal song. Still on she goes,
Shadows amid dark of night diminish shame;
With her left hand she grasps her nurse, with the other
She gropes her blind way.

(Metamorphoses X, lines 448–456)

The father might seem not to be guiltless; he knows the anonymous mistress is the age of his daughter, and in their lovemaking he calls her *filia* while she calls him *pater*. But at the discovery, he is properly outraged and is going to kill her with his sword; she flees, and is changed into the ever-weeping myrrh tree. The incestuous crime is associated throughout with femaleness—the old nurse, terrified by Myrrha's threats of suicide, helps the girl plot her crime and makes the assignation for her during the festival of Ceres when the king's wife is absent:

It was the time when pious matrons were celebrating
That annual festival of Ceres, at which,
Their bodies veiled in snowy vestments, they offer
Their first fruits and the ears of standing corn,
When for nine nights sex and the touch of men
Among forbidden things are numbered.

(Lines 431–435)

The festival of the goddess seems partly responsible, and thus the goddess herself; if the pious matron had not served Ceres she would have prevented the crime by occupying her husband's bed herself. The goddess, who is associated with female chastity, is represented as antifamily, a sexually disruptive force.

4. Titles vary; this novel, like others, has alternative titles. But the author himself gives us the titles in the penultimate sentence: "Thus is the termination of the body of narrative [*syntagma*] of Ethiopia about Theagenes and Charikleia." The novel could thus be called *The Ethiopian Story* or *Theagenes and Charikleia*; we have authorial endorsement for both titles. Manuscripts supply a similar title at the ending of *Ephesiaka*, for instance, but without authorial endorsement. It was a Byzantine habit (possibly stemming from Late Antique custom) to refer to a novel by the name of its heroine. Salmasius in his edition of Achilles Tatius in 1640 noted that "Antique scholars sometimes cite this Composition [*Scriptum*] under the name of *Leukippé*, as the *Æthiopica* of Heliodorus is referred to under the title of *Charikleia*" ("Ad Lectorem," *Erōtikōn Achilleōs Tatiou* [Leiden, 1640], *8ᵛ). Achilles Tatius' novel could also be referred to as *Leukippé and Kleitophon*, a style adapted by John J. Winkler in his recent translation.

5. See Frank M. Snowden's *Blacks in Antiquity* (1970) for a well-researched investigation of Greek and Roman relations with black Africans, including without doubt those of a type later to be called "Negro." Commonplace white prejudices of the later West did not necessarily obtain in antiquity. Snowden points out that Andromeda (who figures so pointedly in the *Aithiopika*) may well have been a dark-skinned African woman in the original legend (154). Thus her portrait, even the concept of her, represents in itself an interesting nexus of black/white ideas and relations. She still is dark in Ovid's account in *Ars amatoria*, where it said "*Andromedan Perseus nigris portarit ab Indis*" (Perseus will bring his Andromeda from the black Indians). (Ovid's lightly disparaging point, however, is that there is no accounting or prescribing for sexual tastes.)

6. "You may observe there is always something which she [Clarissa] prefers to truth." Samuel Johnson made this remark about Richardson's heroine to Hester Lynch Thrale (later Piozzi), according to her *Anecdotes of the Late Samuel Johnson* (London, 1786), 221.

7. Winkler sees Kalasiris as the sophisticated narrator, and Knemon as a "naive raconteur" who is present "in order to make clear what kind of story the *Aithiopika* is *not*."

("The mendacity of Kalasiris," 107). John R. Morgan argues for the significance of Knemon and his story in "The Story of Knemon in Heliodoros' *Aithiopika,*" *JHS* 19 (1989): 99–113. Morgan's essay makes clear that Athens in this novel emerges as a rather bad place: "Athenian love . . . deals in seduction, deception, and, in the last resort, coercion" (109), but Morgan draws no political conclusions from this. Knemon might be seen as representing the inadequacy of Athenian civilization, and even he does not want to move back to Athens. The major movements of the novel are all away from Greek centers, as we keep progressing towards and into Africa.

8. "Nothing to do with Dionysius" is a catchphrase, meaning "it is irrelevant," indicating a straying from a drama or its plot line. The extra comedy here lies in the fact that *prosaic* narrative is not supposed to have much to do with Dionysius anyway —as Nietzsche so acerbically points out.

9. The priest's chastity was attacked by the beautiful and rich Rhodopis, who cast an eye on Kalasiris when she worshipped at the temple of Isis. Kalasiris is ashamed to say that he weakened inwardly, and felt overwhelmed by the *pathos erōtikon,* the emotion of love. He terms this a failing or falling into sin, and, even though it did not become action, justice decreed a sentence of exile (I:79). Good men tempted by seductive women and overcoming or abandoning that temptation are a feature of epic as of religious writing. We have Odysseus leaving Calypso, Aeneas leaving Dido, as well as virtuous Joseph. Kalasiris' Rhodopis bears some resemblance to the Rhodé who arouses the mildly sinful thought in Hermas in *The Shepherd of Hermas.* Rhodé may have been careless in asking Hermas to help her out of the river, but she makes no other advances—neither does Rhodopis try to make a move on Kalasiris, save for looking at him; we are not even *sure* that she has anything like the same feeling he does when he keeps looking at her. Kalasiris' fear of himself, with his willingness to project that fear on Rhodopis, is unpleasant—and puzzling. If this were either an epic or a religious tract, the meaning would indeed be straightforward; the texture of the novel, however, allows room for doubt. Kalasiris considers Rhodopis the beautiful as an apparition of the demon and a danger foretold in the stars. But the real demon or "danger" that leads him to death is his beloved Charikleia, to whom he admits Rhodopis compares in beauty. Kalasiris seems to have misread the stars' foretelling. Kalasiris at times exhibits ignorance and overconfidence, although he is always loveable—like Dante's Virgil.

In the novels there are many examples of men tempted by beautiful women—some fall, like Kleitophon; most resist, like Habrokomes. But the heroic theme of the man who conquers base sensuality in form of woman has changed in the novels. Just as frequently, good women in novels are tempted or attempted by the base sensuality of man—a theme for which we may search almost in vain in both Biblical and early classical literature.

10. References to Egyptian priests and kings are scattered through the ancient novels and may originate in lost Egyptian fictions. A fictional work of the second century B.C., *The Dream of Nectanebos,* is described by J.W.B. Barns; King Nektanebos (Nectanebos) sees a boat carrying Isis surrounded by other gods. The god of war complains that the pharaoh has not completed his temple; the awakened ruler then hires the best engraver in the country to finish the inscription on the temple. But this engraver, Petesis, is a drinker who likes an easy life, and near the temple he sees the prettiest girl . . . here the fragment breaks off. *The Dream of Nectanebos,* a fragment in Greek presumably translated from demotic Egyptian, indicates the strong relation of Egyptian stories to the Greek narratives. The name Nektanebos (name of the last pharaoh of Egypt, expelled by the Persians in 343 B.C.) is evidently adopted by the author or authors of the *Alexander Romance* for the priest-sorcerer-ruler who is the father of Alexander. B. P. Reardon discusses *The Dream of Nectanebos* and the Egyptian influences on the "Greek" novel in his *Courants littéraires grecs* (1971, 327–333), where he cites Barns's *Egypt and the Greek Romance* (1956).

11. Once one sees this hidden meaning of the dream it seems obvious, but it takes a long narrative time for events to fulfill this prophecy. John J. Winkler is the first modern

critic to see that Charikleia's dream is prophetic and foretells Kalasiris' death. Other critics, as he points out, have treated Charikleia's dream either as having no meaning at all and functioning as a "red herring" or as referring merely to the events of the next day; see Winkler, "The mendacity of Kalasiris,' 115. Winkler implies (rightly in my view) that modern scholarly readers can be remarkably dense in picking up something unless the author has spelled it out—this despite condescending comments about the "simplicity" of old romances.

12. "Gerald died that afternoon. He was broken up in the football match" (Forster, *The Longest Journey* 1907, 64). What makes the statement shocking is that we have been given in Forster's narrative no prophetic historical or metaphorical warning about the imminent death of Gerald, which should make us realize how much we depend on such signals.

13. Robert Lamberton prints a translation of the complete surviving text (a fragment) as "An Interpretation of the Modest Chariclea from the Lips of Philip the Philosopher," Appendix I of *Homer the Theologian* (306–311). The speaker is a teacher, an older man who takes up the concern of a young man, Nikolaos, who complains that "Charikleia's book" is being abused. The teacher then lectures the young people on the real meaning of the book. The characters represent virtues and vices, showing us what to do and what to avoid. But there is an inner meaning beyond that, once we have "lifted off the maiden's resplendent robe . . . revealing the holy chiton beneath" (309). In Charikleia we see a soul born in darkness (Ethiopia) and taken to the light (Greece); her falling in love with Theagenes is an allegory of the soul's love of the highest wisdom, while Kalasiris is the wise teacher who leads the soul to the good, until she "passes through the Egypt of ignorance" (311). Arsaké is carnal pleasure, which the soul can resist, though tried by fire.

This ingenious allegorical criticism is post-Christian and Christian-influenced, but it seems rather a Gnostic Neoplatonist production than a Christian one. We have no date for "Philip," but his essay marks the beginning of the long tradition of defending novels (like other fictions) by turning them into allegory that readers will not sneer at.

Chapter V

1. Peter Walsh in *The Roman Novel* offers a convincing reconstruction of the plot of the entire novel, based on the argument that what we have are incomplete parts of Books XIV–XVI of twenty-four books. According to Walsh, the novel probably began in Marseilles, home of Encolpius, who was betrothed to a girl called "Doris" but had to leave home in a hurry. On his wanderings he encountered the irascible Lichas and the insatiable Tryphaena, who turn up in our shipboard episode. He seduced Lichas' wife Hedyle, which explains Lichas' grudge against him; he was probably imprisoned for stealing Giton, perhaps from Tryphaena. Imprisoned, he escaped, leaving the jailer dead or wounded. Presumably the end of the novel would have recounted the *nostos* or return home of this unheroic Odysseus, who is also a mock Aeneas, urged to leave his home in an oracular warning: *linque tuas sedes* ("leave your family seat"). See Walsh, *The Roman Novel*, 73–77.

2. As Gerald N. Sandy says, *Phoinikika* provides "clear-cut evidence that the Greeks wrote . . . picaresque romances, accounts of low life . . . designed to shock moral sensibilities and conventional notions of decorum" (*CAGN*, 809). Albert Henrichs, though rightly proud of his reconstruction of the papyri, is surprisingly very critical of the *Phoinikika* as a novel:

> Lollianos only cared about sketching sharply delineated and easily comprehensible scenes, without going into any motivation and without endeavoring at characterization of the personages concerned. His novel will speak much less to the understanding and heart of the reader than to his eyes and senses. Drastic realism and coarse comedy of representation, like the commonplace sensuality not mitigated, as in Petronius, Apuleius, Longus and Achilles Tatius, by strokes of brilliance, mark the *Phoinikika* as an entertainment-product of the cheapest kind [*ein Unterhaltungs-produkt billigster Art*]   (Heinrichs, preface to *Die Phoinikika des Lollianos*, 7).

For its first editor, the *Phoinikika* represents a new low in ancient fiction, which he thinks we used to respect (!) but can now see at its lowest level of mass-produced cheap entertainment. I am much less inclined to take this negative view of *Phoinikika*. It would of course be surprising if we had much "characterization" and deeply analyzed "motivation" in three to four pages of fragments, but Henrichs, in looking in vain for "characterization" and "motivation," betrays his orientation to the nineteenth century's definitions of fiction. The conduct of (what we have of) *Phoinikika* seems "post-modernist." Appeals to the "understanding and heart" can of course be made through appeals to eyes and senses, by any writer in any century.

3. Miletus, with which the "Tales" were associated, is in the southwest corner of Asia Minor. Famous as a center of trade and commerce, Miletus is also strongly associated with philosophy and science; it was the home of Thales (636–546 B.C.), who is supposed to have originated Western geometry after a visit to Egypt. Aspasia, the *hetaira* who was a friend of Pericles, came from Miletus; she is supposed to have kept a brothel *and* taught oratory, which makes her a "Milesian" character in herself. Miletus is palpably associated not with backwoodsmen but with smartness—in all senses. The "Tales" were supposedly invented by Aristides of Miletus in the second century B.C. The fable that Eumolpus tells in *Satyricon* is a variant of a story to be found in the *Fables* of Phaedrus. Phaedrus (died c. A.D. 50), a slave from Thrace who came to Rome and served Augustus, was the author of a collection of fables; many of these, including the story of the widow, had formed part of the Aesopic canon.

4. Peter Walsh interprets the narrative pattern of *Satyricon* as indicating that in the lost earlier part of the novel Encolpius has engaged in "a series of heterosexual amours" which are then "abjured through the hero's passion for Giton"; homosexual obsession is "punished by the angry Priapus." The hero is to be healed "by the intervention of a kindly deity" and return to heterosexuality (and, presumably, Doris). (See *The Ancient Novel*, 77–78.) This *might* be the narrative pattern—or might not—but even if it were, the tone of the novel would seem to preclude serious moralizing about the choices of sexual partners. From our own moral point of view, heterosexuality produces the worst actions of the novel, in the midnight "marriage" of the seven-year-old girl Pannychis during the high jinks at the brothel. Petronius' attention seems to focus rather on questions of insatiability and satiety. Trimalchio's feast is thus relevant, even though that sequence has less sex and very little reference to homosexuality—another factor that has made it popular with schoolmasters. I think it is a mistake to imagine that Petronius considers what we call "sexual orientation" an absolute matter.

5. Photius, Patriarch of Alexandria in the ninth century, is our source of information about the earlier long *Metamorphoses*; he read and compared two Greek versions of the ass-story, he tells us: one the *Metamorphoses* by "Lucius of Patras," the other Lucian's *The Ass*. (This latter work, still extant, is no longer attributed to Lucian, but is now given the rather depressing author "pseudo-Lucian.") Photius conjectured that "Lucian" based his shorter work on the longer one, but cut it severely while retaining "phrases and constructions." See Photius, *Bibliothēkē*, II: 103–104.

6. The title "Golden Ass" has been taken to mean merely "reasonable ass"; "golden" has also been taken as reference to the excellence of the story or of its moral. It has been argued that the phrase "golden ass" refers to the Egyptian god (or demon) Seth, the enemy of Isis (see Tatum, *Apuleius*, 43–47; Winkler, *Auctor*, 305–315).

7. Nicole Loraux in *Façons tragiques de tuer une femme* (1985) has pointed out that most female death in ancient Greek tragedy involves the woman's having her throat cut or hanging herself, the throat being a kind of sexually significant part suitable for a feminine death. Men do not die by sacrificial throat-slash or strangulation. Even when a woman tries to commit a heroic suicide the story and the language will not quite let this happen. Deianara in *Trachiniae* tries to strike herself in the liver, but uncovers and strikes the *left*, or female, side. A woman who does such a deed has to be referred to as "masculine" because there is no language for female heroism. In *The Golden Ass*, Charité is certainly called masculine;

she acts suicidally in her "masculine" soul (*masculis animis,* II:80). Unlike Deianara, she *does* kill herself on the right or "masculine" side, plunging the sword "under her right pap" (*sub papillam dexteram,* II:84). The "pap," reminding us of the femininity of her breast, modifies the tragically masculine *right* side. It does not seem impossible that Apuleius is aware of the patterns pointed out by Loraux, making his virtuous widow deliberately paradoxical. Charité's murderous lover is also paradoxical, in some sense made "feminine" by being blinded; she blinds him with that feminine weapon, a pin from her hair (*acu crinali capite,* 82), and, like Antigone, he starves to death, immured alive (but "condemned by his own sentence"). Apuleius is very interested in mixtures and crossings over between masculine and feminine. It seems by no means certain that Charité is right in this acting the part of avenger and suicide, but neither is she clearly wrong; her story appears designed to stimulate debate.

8. See M. M. Bakhtin, *Rabelais and His World,* trans. Iswolsky (1968), 209. Bakhtin also deals with Apuleius in his essay "Forms of Time and Chronotope in the Novel" (see *The Dialogic Imagination,* trans. Caryl Emerson and Michael Holquist). Bakhtin wants to point out how the randomness of the adventure story, the picaresque side of *The Golden Ass,* is overtaken and subdued by the formulation of "Lucius' *individual guilt*" as spelled out by the priest of Isis, so we see the story as one of guilt-punishment-redemption. The novel's world is a private one, Bakhtin insists (evidently following Nietzsche in thinking this an impoverishment): "the everyday life that Lucius observes and studies in an *exclusively personal and private life*" (*The Dialogic Imagination,* 118, 122, emphasis in the text). But the episode of the Battle of the Wine Skins culminating in the Festival of Laughter constitutes a critique of the public world at the same time as it represents an invocation of that public world—as assembly, *polis,* law court, trial. Trial scenes (in which novels of all periods abound) may be seen as tributes to the public and social world, but they also function as critiques of the inadequacy of the conventional public social formulations. The arena near the end of *The Golden Ass* is another evocation of the public world of the Roman Empire. No novel of any era can afford to be without some tributary evocation of the "public world" but it cannot afford to submit to it.

9. See the aretology printed complete in Appendix 3 of Walsh, *The Roman Novel,* 252–253. Fragments of liturgies of Isis have come down to us; the "Hymn to Isis" by one Isidorus seems especially pertinent to Apuleius: see Appendix 3 of James Tatum's *Apuleius and the Golden Ass* (183–184).

10. See Reinhold Merkelbach, *Isisfeste in griechisch-römischer Zeit* (1963); the *Navigium Isidis* is discussed (39–41) after an account of other festivals in relation to the Egyptian calendar. He points out the use of the Nile-flood festival by Heliodorus and Achilles Tatius (16–18).

Chapter VI

1. We may divide characters into flat and round. Flat characters . . . in their purest form . . . are constructed round a single idea or quality . . . . We all want books to endure, to be refuges, and their inhabitants to be always the same, and flat characters tend to justify themselves on this account. . . .
   The test of a round character is whether it is capable of surprising in a convincing way. If it never surprises, it is flat. . . . It has the incalculability of life about it—life within the pages of a book.   (*Aspects of the Novel,* 103–118)

Forster emphasizes that *any* novel's "characters" are results of artistic construction. Characters are by definition "people whose secret lives are visible or might be visible: we are people whose secret lives are invisible" (99). "Round" characters are more aesthetically satisfying than "flat" ones, because the reader gets that subtle thrill of knowing a complex inner life: "in the novel we can know people perfectly, and . . . we can find here a compensation for their dimness in life" (98). That is, characters are most unlike life in being knowable, and those most unlike life are those we call most lifelike or "round."

2. Robert Erickson has dealt with the "Mother Midnight" as a type character in eighteenth-century novelists: see his *Mother Midnight: Birth, Sex, and Fate in Eighteenth-Century Fiction (Defoe, Richardson, and Sterne)* (1985). The phrase "Mother Midnight" comes from Defoe's *Moll Flanders* (1722), and combines ideas of the wise woman (or witch), brothel madam, and midwife.

3. Philippe Ariès, in *L'Enfant et la vie familiale sous l'ancien régime* (1960), discussing what historians tend now to call the Early Modern period in France, makes a strong point of the modern obsession with ages and dates, which he sees developing at the end of the Middle Ages and the beginning of the Renaissance. Ariès begins his study with a chapter on age and ages:

> A man of the 16th or 17th century would be astonished at the exigences of the civil state to which we submit ourselves quite naturally. We teach our children, as soon as they begin to talk, their name, that of their parents, and also their age. How proud we are when little Paul, interrogated about his age, answers correctly that he is two and a half. We think it is important that little Paul should not be mistaken: what would become of him if he no longer knew his age? In the African bush, this is still a very obscure notion, not something so important that one cannot forget it. But, in our technical civilizations, how could anyone forget the exact date of birth? . . . (1)

Ariès' point is most interesting, but somewhat weakened by a certain idyllic condescension. We are to see the looming of the modern age in the beginning of age-consciousness in the seventeenth century. Before that, however, all is darkness, pleasant obscurity, primitiveness—the "African bush." Without asking how much of *la brousse africaine* Ariès has actually seen, we might wonder whether he could not have taken some account of antiquity, early and late. Surviving evidence (including tombstones) indicates that there *was* an age consciousness in the ancient world, and, as we see in the novels, the habit of commemorating birthdays is relatively common in the Roman imperial period. Daphnis and Chloé, it could be argued, do have what Ariès considers that modern entity, a childhood, for it is considered important that the reader know that they are *adolescent* when they go to work in the pastures together, and their exact ages are certainly given.

It might be interesting to ask what the various novelistic ages signify. Does Charikleia's age (seventeen) represent a rather mature and sophisticated age for a heroine in her time, like Harriet Byron's twenty-one or Elizabeth Bennet's nineteen? Or is it more like Clarissa's eighteen years? And would not Kleitophon at nineteen commonly be considered rather old for *parthenia*?

4. Sheila Smith McKoy, paper given at Vanderbilt, 10 January 1994, based on book-length work not yet published. Paul Ricoeur has tried to pursue the questions of time and narrative, with a meditation on time based very extensively on Heidegger. Ricoeur points out that, however "objective" our thinking about time during the Enlightenment, we have come around (he thinks with Proust) to "remythicizing time." Myth, which we tried to push aside in talking about time and narration, reappears within the field of investigation itself. Ricoeur is working within the Western philosophical tradition. Yet "Western" thought has been varied, and peoples within modern nation-states have proposed and expressed (through literature, song, etc.) alternative time awareness. The Celts are an example, and not a small one. Even for Ricoeur, working faithfully within the Western philosophical tradition that McKoy would like to escape, there can, however, ultimately be no objective time, or objective investigation: "The Murmuring of mythical language has continued to resonate under the *logos* of philosophy" (*Time and Narrative*, trans. Blamey and Pellauer, III, 138).

5. Jean Hagstrum in *The Sister Arts* (1958) discusses Cebes' *Table*, "the Pilgrim's Progress of antiquity" (34), and the *Imagines* of Philostratus the Elder in the light of the influence of such Late Antique "literary pictorialism" on English poetry of the seventeenth and eighteenth century. He believes that what he calls "the Greek romance" was the vehicle that "carried classical pictorialism into the Christian era" (31). The importance of *ekphrasis*

to literature in general has often been overlooked, especially since the principles of "Romanticism" made poets feel uneasy about acknowledging descriptive models—though there is more than a hint of the ekphrastic in Shelley, for instance. Prose fiction in every era carries a large interest in *ekphrasis*, an interest that it has never seen any theoretical need to abandon.

Chapter VII

1. For Forster, the "story" springs from oral literature, which he images in Darwinian terms as belonging to a lower evolutionary stage when cavemen told each other stories until "the audience falls asleep among their offal and bones. . . . The story is primitive, it reaches back to the origins of literature, before reading was discovered, and it appeals to what is primitive in us. . . .The story is neither moral nor is it favorable to the understanding of the novel in its other aspects. If we want to do that we must come out of the cave" (*Aspects of the Novel*, 66). A post-Darwinian caveman's cave is conflated with the Platonic cave of unknowing. It is amusing to contrast Forster's disgusted view of oral literature with the horror of Derrida at writing itself, in *Of Grammatology* (1967). For Derrida, language is a kind of First Fall and writing a Second Fall. Forster contrasts the primitive life of told story to what he calls "the life by value," which is truly *literary* and which "presses against the novel from all sides," rescuing it from the low state of mere story. Forster's critique has a Gnostic tinge: "story" is body, matter, while material and "value" stand in for soul. He asserts, however (using Gertrude Stein as his example) that an endeavor to make a novel pure "value" and no "story" doesn't work: "as soon as fiction is completely delivered from time it cannot express anything at all" (67).

2. The "alert reader" may become strained, waiting for a reference or resolution of a code that does not materialize. John Winkler points out that in *Aithiopika* the reader constantly expects the second of the code words (*phoinix*) to be put to use by the characters, but that shoe never drops. Winkler suggests, however, that it turns up as a pun in the very last sentence of the novel, in which the novelist describes himself as a Phoenician man (*Phoinix*) ("The mendacity of Kalasiris," *Yale Classical Studies* [1982], 157). "Phoinix" is a word rich in pun-potential, as it can mean purple-red or date-palm, or date-fruit, or a musical instrument, or the fabulous bird the phoenix, also referred to in *Aithiopika* in the pun on *phoinikopteros* ("red-wing," i.e., flamingo) and *phoinix* (II:88–89).

3. The author as he writes should be like the ideal reader described by Hume in "The Standard of Taste," who . . . considers himself as "man in general" and forgets, if possible, his "individual being" and his peculiar circumstances.
    To put it in this way, however, is to understate the importance of the author's individuality. As he writes, he creates not simply an ideal, impersonal "man in general" but an implied version of "himself" that is different from the implied authors we meet in other men's works. . . . the picture the reader gets of this presence is one of the author's most important effects.
    (Booth, *The Rhetoric of Fiction* [1961], 70–71)

Booth's definition of the "implied author" has been helpful in novel criticism, though one may quarrel with the Enlightenment (and masculinist) bias lurking behind the Hume quotation and coloring Booth's definition. It is sometimes useful to notice that "by distinguishing between the author and *his* implied image . . . we can avoid pointless and unverifiable talk about such qualities as 'sincerity' or 'seriousness' in the author" (75, emphasis mine)—but some readers will always want to reach towards the individual biological and social entity behind the masks. Booth further points out how the "implied author" educates the reader ("he makes his reader, as he makes his second self," 138), shaping the ideal reader for this particular work. Wolfgang Iser has carried on the discussion in his *The Implied Reader* (*Der Implizite Leser*, 1972).

4. I chanced to be reading for pleasure Fay Weldon's *The Hearts and Lives of Men* (1987) when I was seriously annotating Chariton, and found that Weldon's book chimed ex-

tremely well with the classic novel. Weldon's treatment of traditional—and classic—novelistic material (the trials of love, the lost child, the miraculous rescues and restorations) has a significant playfulness quite in Chariton's vein. See my essay "Classic Weldon," in *Fay Weldon's Wicked Fictions*, ed. Regina Barrecca (Hanover, N.H.: University Press of New England, 1994), 37–58.

5. Stefan Merkle's article, "Telling the True Story of the Trojan War: The Eyewitness Account of Dictys of Crete" (*TSAN*, 183–194), is a detailed and appreciative account of a neglected novel. Merkle is original in envisaging a political as well as a moral theme in the novel—most commentators on ancient novels have fought shy of any consideration of political elements. In his paper, the basis of this essay, and the discussion that followed in the 1989 International Conference on the Ancient Novel at Dartmouth College, Stefan Merkle seemed even more strongly to emphasize the resistance to war he saw expressed in the novel. Either the speaker or a sympathetic auditor drew a parallel with the film *Full Metal Jacket*.

6. Ben Edwin Perry thinks that "comic romances" are "told in the person of the principal character speaking about his own experiences" because "the authors . . . are deterred by the conventions of historiography from telling an obviously fictitious tale on their own authority." Perry argues that a prose story was thought of as a true history for which the author took responsibility; thus, the wilder or more fabulous stories had to be told in first-person, by a visibly fictitious someone who took the responsibility. Perry accords with Sophie Trenkner in thinking that "wonder stories" coming from oral tradition had oral narrative forms which writers such as Apuleius capture and subsume. (See Perry, *The Ancient Romances*, 327–329.)

7. See, e.g., Walsh, in *The Roman Novel*: "built into the sensational adventures of the Greek anti-hero is a series of vignettes of the types whom he encounters. This pattern is already a commonplace in the fiction of Petronius, Lucian and Apuleius some fifteen hundred years before it is 'invented' (according to some modern critics) in the first Spanish picaresque novel *Lazarillo de Tormes*" (4).

8. Wolfgang Iser explains the role and activities of the reader created by the text: "In the act of reading, we are to undergo a kind of transformation . . . the role of the reader . . . is fulfilled through the continual instigation of attitudes and reflections on those attitudes. As the reader is maneuvered into this position, his reactions . . . bring out the meaning of the novel; it might be truer to say that the meaning of the novel only materializes in these reactions, since it does not exist per se" (*The Implied Reader*, 30–32). Iser closely analyses the process of reading:

> . . . the reader actually causes the text to reveal its potential multiplicity of connections. These connections are the product of the reader's mind working on the raw material of the text, though they are not the text itself—for this consists just of sentences, statements, information, etc.
> This is why the reader often feels involved in events which, at the time of reading, seem real to him, even though in fact they are very far from his own reality . . . literary texts transform reading into a creative process that is far above mere perception of what is written. . . . The product of this creative activity is what we might call the virtual dimension of the text, which endows it with its reality. This virtual dimension is not the text itself, nor is it the imagination of the reader: it is the coming together of text and imagination. (278–279)

Linda Hutcheon points out that there is a problem with Iser's view that the reader creates "the autonomous world of fiction" only by dint of "the reader's temporarily leaving his personality and experience behind." Modern fiction, "self-conscious fiction" is, she claims, less likely to ask the reader to do so, but "tries actively to *prevent* even a temporary abandoning of human experiential responses, while also trying, it is true, simultaneously to lure the reader into an overtly fictive universe" (*Narcissistic Narrative*, 149). The problem now is that after all this emphasis on the flattered role of the reader, narcissism is the way for the reader to go; Hutcheon wants to defend narcissism as helpful in certain ways, while believing that certain intricate—and politically informed—texts can allow "a total breaking out of the limits of introverted self-informing narcissism" (161).

Yet, perhaps the readerly narcissism so particularly popular in the self-regarding 1970s and 1980s is always tempered—however unwillingly—by an intuition that the author is really (if temporarily) our superior, and does have a control that we cannot directly reciprocate. I can do anything with an author's literary allusion, for instance, except round on that author with a literary allusion of my own that he/she must ponder and digest. There *are* limitations to the reader's capacity to make the meaning of a novel, though there is no limit to our freedom to walk away from it. The author who insults the reader of the novel (Hutcheon admiringly cites John Barth) had better be pretty damn good. The novel text is not "raw material" as Iser (and Co.) would have it, but very well-cooked by the author, as Fielding knew when he invited us to the feast.

Chapter VIII

1. The Phoenix is a "New Age" creature; it comes every 1,461 years and begins a new era. The disquisition upon the Phoenix in *Kleitophon and Leukippé* (Book III, 184–188) has, as Merkelbach points out, an important place in pointing to the theme of resurrection: "The Phoenix is an image of *apokatastasis* [complete reestablishment of things]. Its epiphany happens simultaneously with the swelling of the Nile" (*Roman und Mysterium*, 131). In *Aithiopika*, the characters come upon a man running along with a *phoenikopter* (flamingo) under his arm; his mistress asked him to get one, and they joke that it's good she didn't ask him to fetch a *phoinix* (*Aithiopika*, II:88). Even this jest is significant: "The episode must have a mystic sense. The red-feathered bird obviously represents the Phoenix; the loved Isias, Isis. . . . One can interpret the episode as meaning that to a zealous servant of the goddess (Isis-Selene) even the apparently hardest task, the capture of the Phoenix (immortality), would be possible" (267). More flippantly, the underarm flamingo recalls to us the croquet game in *Alice's Adventures in Wonderland* (Chap. 8); I would not be prepared to swear that Lewis Carroll had never come upon Heliodorus' book.

2. This apocryphal work, the *Protevangelion* with its *Gennesis [sic] Marias Tēs Hagias Theotokou* (*Nativity of Mary, Holy God-Bearer*) was popular and influential, especially but not only in the Eastern Church. A number of ideas about Mary stem from it. Emile Amann, editing the work in 1910 and drawing on other scholarship, suggests that, although there are many Jewish references, the author is not from a Jewish milieu: "under Hebrew clothing is hidden a spirit profoundly impregnated with paganism" (an interesting imagery). Amann suggest that the basic ideas came from Egypt:

> It is in Egypt from the beginning of the fourth century that we find the development of the ideas of *purity* and *impassability*, which have served to compose the portrait of Mary; it is in the Alexandria region, classic home of religious syncretism, that we must look for a terrain favorable to the flowering of these pagan legends relative to the Jewish or Christian mysteries. . . . The *Protevangelion of James* is nothing other than the legend of Isis, but in its latest state, when that divinity was considered as a *numen virginale*. . . . Naturally Mary is no different from Isis, Jesus is in short nothing other than Osiris; apparently in the last state of the Isaic legend the relations between Isis and Osiris were those of mother and son. . . .
>
> As for the object of the author of the *Protevangelion*, . . . it was to offer to the cult of Isis a restoration of youthfulness and contemporaneity [*actualité*] by the infusion of new ideas. . . . The author of the *Protevangelion*, more or less conscious of the progress of Christianity in that epoch . . . believed he could do good in presenting the legend of Isis under features recognizable by the Christians, in attracting them towards the grotto in Bethlehem.
>
> (Introduction to *Le Protévangile de Jacques*, 93–94)

Amann has a more conspiratorial view of priests of Isis busy in Jerusalem and Bethlehem than we might wish to adopt, but the suggestion of an Isaic design is most interesting.

Chapter IX

1. Corinne Jouanno, in a paper given at the second International Conference on the Ancient Novel, Dartmouth College, July 1989, remarked on the use of mirrors in this Byzantine fiction, noting "the theme of the mirror offers in effect rich possibilities to an author wishing to play on the confusion between appearance and reality." These Byzantine authors "also amuse themselves in confounding the boundaries between nature and art" (*à brouiller les frontières entre nature et art*). They enjoy describing art works that seem natural, and nature that seems artistically wrought. "The universe created by the ekphrases of the novelistic Byzantines is then a strongly artificial universe, where the word almost always takes precedence over the object." (Jouanno, "L'Univers des Descriptions Romanesque Byzantines ou le Règne du Faux-Semblant," ICAN paper.) The effects of these Byzantine narrative elaborations can be traced in Western European fiction.

2. Panagiotis A. Agapitos passed out copies of Greek passages of *Kallimachos and Chrysorrhoé* and treated us to a detailed discussion in his paper "The Erotic Bath in the Byzantine Vernacular Romance" at ICAN-II at Dartmouth College, 1989.

3. Jean Bodel of Arras, who retired into a house for lepers in 1202, was the author of the *Chanson de Saisnes* (*Song of the Saxons*), a *chanson de geste* in which this couplet appears near the very beginning in a discussion of the poem's subject.

4. Jessie L. Weston's *From Ritual to Romance* (1920), now best known for inspiring a cryptic footnote to T. S. Eliot's *The Waste Land* (1922), is a work of symbolic anthropology, stimulated by, but not to be identified with, *The Golden Bough*. According to Weston, pagan fertility rituals inspired the Grail legends found in the literary form that subsumed such religious rituals, i.e., "romance."

5. Dante in his letter to Can Grande, traditionally taken as the Preface to the *Divina Commedia*, explains that his work does not have one simple meaning (*non est simplex sensus*), but could be called polysemous (*polysemous*)—that is, having several meanings. Taking his cue from modes of reading Scriptures, Dante suggests that his book should be read not just for *literal* meaning but also for *allegorical* and *moral* and *anagogical* meanings. Thus, the exodus of the children of Israel from Egypt signifies allegorically our redemption by Christ; morally, the conversion of the soul from the misery of sin to a state of grace; and anagogically, the exodus of saved souls from this earthly state of corruption and slavery into the liberty of everlasting glory (see *Opere Minori*, 798–799). Dante's four levels have offered modes of reading various kinds of literature of the Middle Ages. The system he here suggests offers an ideal of literature as *polysemous*, but at the same time as strictly controlled by an absolute meaning that the author fully knows before he begins. At the moment, we are less likely to find appealing a vision of literature as so firmly controlled by the author and even by God in advance, while yet we must admit that narrative stories, and also drama and film, are often allegorical in Dante's way. We do see the point, so energetically made by Dante, that a good work is not likely to have a *simplex sensus*.

6. D. W. Robertson in *A Preface to Chaucer: Studies in Medieval Perspectives* (1962) forcefully proposes that there is a strict Christian way of reading Western medieval literature, and that no other way will do. This has had its appeal, not least to non-Christian readers and teachers who are relieved at finding an exact set of formulas. Robertson's ideal Christian reader is passionless and transcendentalist, never swayed by senses or sin. The way real Christian believers of various periods actually deal with their art is a much more complex matter than Robertson can allow. Nashville's country music is a better analogy than a "Robertsonian" could contemplate.

7. Tony Tanner's interesting study *Adultery in the Novel* (1979) suggests a connection, although Tanner, taking the customary British definition of "novel," does not concern himself much with literature before the eighteenth century. What he has to say about the adulterous and the novelistic could be applied to the loves of Melitté and Kleitophon. He has some interesting comments on *Satyricon* (52–57) but does not examine the case of the widow of Ephesus.

8. Alexandre Micha's introduction to the 1968 edition of *Cligès* says "Chrétien wanted to give an Arthurian tincture to adventures foreign to the matter of Bretagne"; this editor thinks that "the Byzantine atmosphere and *décor* dominate in this work where sumptuous luxury, the harem and its eunuchs and a certain perfume of exoticism evoke the city that enflamed the imagination of Villehardouin's contemporaries" (*Cligès*, ed. Alexandre Micha, viii–ix). Villehardouin was a historian who participated in the Fourth Crusade.

9. The Grimms' "Rapunzel" offers an interesting story from the Germanic and Celtic traditions that seems close in motifs to Mediterranean material. Rapunzel, as her name somewhat comically signifies, is connected with vegetation, like green-shoot Chloé. She is bred by an old witch, who claims she will care for the Maiden "like a Mother." The witch resembles "mother" Venus, in "Cupid and Psyche." At the age of twelve (puberty) the girl is separated not only as formerly from her real mother but also from her witch-mother, seeing her only periodically, like a Persephone. She is not in an underworld, but is in—or above—a deep wood, in a tower with only one window. Rapunzel memorably lets down her long hair, which is "fine as spun Gold"; she is like the moon with her rays (though as she is *das schönste Kind unter der Sonne*, the golden-haired girl has some Sun characteristics as well). She is also like a Phoenix (a Fenice): the sneering witch tells the girl's lover, "the beautiful Bird sits on her Nest no longer, and sings no more" (*der schöne Vogel sitzt nicht mehr im Nest und singt nicht mehr*—note the masculinity of *Vogel*, unmodified by diminutives; the Phoenix contains both male and female within it). The lovely bird of course rises again in the waste land (*Wüstenei*) as both Maiden and Mother, and her very tears have power to restore her lover's sight (see *Die Märchen der Brüder Grimm*, 57–60).

It should not be forgotten that stories like the Grimm's *Tales* were in oral circulation during the Middle Ages and Renaissance. Fairy tales and folk-tales were first categorized and published in quantity during the Enlightenment (Charles Perrault, *Contes de ma Mère l'Oye*, 1697; Jakob and Wilhelm Grimm, *Märchen*, Vol. I, 1812; Vol. II, 1814). Such publications gave novelists ready access to a well of images, plots, and sayings, but earlier writers likewise had drawn on this tradition, if in ways not readily traceable by us. We should also never assume that reciters of tales in the oral tradition, either in the antiquity discussed by Sophie Trenkner or in more modern times, were altogether cut off from all contact with what we call "literature"—i.e., written works—once works were set down in writing.

Girls in towers crop up in new and old works of fiction, and not only "romantic" or Gothic fiction, like Poe's "Annabel Lee" (1849). Tower-dwellers include L. M. Montgomery's Anne Shirley, who lives for three years during her prenuptial state in a tower room in a house (named after trees) guarded by three old ladies. Fay Weldon's Mary Fisher, trying to be remote and ethereal, dwells in an ill-fated tower in *The Life and Loves of a She-Devil* (1984). The Moon-Lady character is always in a state of transition and suspension. The lady's tower is a place for undergoing alteration or preparation, whereas for the male a tower is a site of observation, control, and scientific imagination (as in Milton's *Il Penseroso*).

10. "Cum duo sint genera facetiarum: alterum fusum: alterum peracutum et breuem: in illo genere leporis perpetuo excellens est Lucius noster: . . . ut non minus his facetiis placeat: lepidisque narraciunculis: quam serii scriptores doctrina seria et graui: hic est illo sermo milesius: cuius in principio huisce operis affatim commemini: quem Lucianus *logon milesian* appellat: quo fabularis narratio concinniter explicat." *Apulieus cum commento Beroaldi* (Venice, 1516), 116ʳ. I greatly admire C. S. Lewis's achievement in translating "neo-Latin authors . . . into sixteenth-century English," and I agree that the translation of passages of Latin writers into the modern vernacular can lead to the false impression "that the Latinists are somehow more enlightened, less remote, less limited by their age than those who wrote English" (*English Literature in the Sixteenth Century, Excluding Drama*, v). But here, as in the translations from other writers in European languages while I have resisted the strict fidelity that would lead to apparently archaic "thee" and "thou," I have endeavored not to smooth out temporal coloration and quirks of style. Renaissance writing in Latin is not the work of ancient Romans. Acommodating a word like "narraciunculis" tempts one to translate it as "mini-narratives," but I try not to modernize unduly.

11. "Iohannes Boccatius eloquio uernaculo disertissimus: condidit centum fabulas argumento & stilo lepidissimo festiuissimoque: inter quas Apuleianam hanc inseruit: transposuitque commodissime: non ut interpres: sed ut conditor: quam foeminae nostrates non surdis auribus audiunt: neque inuitae legunt. . . ." *Apuleius cum commento Beroaldi*, 1516, 116[r].

12. "nos quoque mythopolon: hoc est opificem fabellae Lucium nostrum latialiter personantem & graphice lepidissimeque explicantem inaudiamus; legamus: pensitemus auribus: oculis: animis lubentibus: cum talibus eggressionum amoenitatibus non solum lectores: uerum etiam commentatores reficiantur. . . ." (1516, 116[r]).

13. Samuel Richardson to Lady Bradshaigh, 25 February 1754, commenting on his own novel *Sir Charles Grandison*, now finishing publication: "The whole Story abounds with Situations and Circumstances debatable. It is not an unartful Management to interest the Readers so much in the Story, as to make them differ in Opinion as to the Capital Articles, and by Leading one, to espouse one, another, another, Opinion, make them all, if not Authors, Carvers" (Forster Collection XI, f.87). If Richardson, like Beroaldus, acknowledges the role played by the reader, he also resembles Chrétien de Troyes in his teasing interest in solutions to the problems of love. Richardson also says, "I have lost a great Part of my Aim, if I do not occasion many Debates upon different parts of my Management" (to Lady Bradshaigh, 8 December 1753, XI, f.53). Chrétien could have said the same. We are obviously meant to discuss whether, for instance, Fenice's solution is better than Yseult's, worse, or practically the same.

Chapter X

1. Eisenstein writes:

> Paradoxically enough, the same presses which fanned the flames of religious controversy also created a new vested interest in ecumenical concord and toleration; the same wholesale industry which fixed religious, dynastic, and linguistic frontiers more permanently also operated most profitably by tapping cosmopolitan markets. Paradoxically also, the same firms made significant contributions to Christian learning by receiving infidel Jews and Arabs, schismatic Greeks and a vast variety of dissident foreigners into their shops and homes. Circles associated with the firms of Daniel Bomberg or Aldus Manutius in Venice . . . with Plantin in Antwerp or the Wechels in Frankfurt point to formation of 'polyglot' households in scattered urban centers throughout the continent. In the age of religious wars, such print shops represented miniature 'international houses.'
>
> (*The Printing Press as an Agent of Change*, 139)

Eisenstein describes the earlier decline of the monastic scriptoria, noting (as other historians have done) that the Abbot of Sponheim wrote a treatise *De Laude Scriptorum* exhorting his monks to copy books and praising the longevity of manuscripts—but "He had had his *Praise of Scribes* promptly printed, as he did his weightier works" (15).

2. "Quo utique factum est, ut qui in eo conflictu ex graecis et latinis autoribus [*sic*] immane id incœndium subterfugerint, hi (ut in prœliis solet accidere) uel undequaque mutili, uel cum innumeris penè uulneribus superfuerint. Quorum in numero noster hic Apuleius . . ." ([Florence], 1512, aii[r]).

3. & ipse apud latinos consimili argumento stiloque nitidissimo condidit undecim uolumina de Asino aureo: siue metamorphoseon: In quibus elegans est: eruditus: emunctus. Et cum haud dubie ex racimis Luciani sibi fecerit uindemiam: eoque uno archetypo prope peculiariter sit usus: magna tamen inter graecum latinumque asinum differentia. Ille breuis. Hic copiosus. Ille uniformis & summatim ex homine in asinum: ex asino in hominem transformationem reformationemque praescribens. Noster uero multiplex & fabellis tempestiuiter intersertis omnem aurium fastidium penitus abstergit.   (Venice, 1516, aiii[r])

4. Et sane nouator plerumque verborum est elegantissimus tantoque cum decore & venere: ut nihil decentius: nihil uenustius fieri possit. Denique hic noster asinus: sicut uerbo dicitur: ita re ipsa aureus conspicitur: tanto dicendi lepore: tanto cultu: tanto uerborum minime triuialium elegantia concinnatus compositusque: ut de eo id dici meritissimo possit: Musas apuleiano sermone loquuturas fuisse si latine loqui uellent. . . (Ibid.)

5. In Beroaldus' edition of 1512, for instance but not in that of 1516, we find

> At ego tibi sermone isto milesio
> Varias fabellas conseram, atque auras tuas
> Beneuolas lepido susurro permulceam. . .

and so on down to "Exordior." In other such editions, e.g., a late (1621) version of the *Opera* published in Frankfurt, what is felt to be prologue to the main narrative is written in this "verse" form all the way down to *Lector intende, laetaberis*. This is technically an example of *cola*, the writing of clauses according to a measure; nobody thought Apuleius was writing strict Latin verse, but the treatment of these lines, often set off by a different typeface, strongly suggests that they were seen as a kind of "found poetry" or semipoetry. The constant turning of this section into verse by translators may persuade us that the opening was indeed read as if it were some sort of poem.

Firenzuola prints the intial opening as poetic or, more truly, doggerel verses:

> Io ordirò col mio parlar festeuole
> Varie nouelle, empiendoti l'orecchie.
> . . . riuolger gli occhi
> A queste carte pien di ciancie, & scritte
> Con lagrime de calami d'Egitto.
>   ([1549], f4ʳ)

6. "Firenzuola posta a pie delle Alpi, che sono tra Fiorenza, & Bologna, è picciolo Castello, ma come il nome, & le sue insegne dimostrano, nobilitato . . . . Et Sebastiano mio padre in assai stato, & abondanza de beni della Fortuna" (f4ʳ⁻ᵛ).

7. That is, Apuleius' passage, "reputans me media Thessaliae loca tenere, quo artis magicae nativa cantamina totius orbis consono ore celebrentur," is rendered thus: "et pensando intra me d'esser nell mezzo di Bologna; doue per detto d'ogn'uno come in propria prato fioriscono gli incantamenti dell'arte Magica . . ." (f16ʳ).

8. Nous ny pouons retourner si ce nest par le moyen de la lune. Cest a entendre la glorieuse Vierge Marie: qui finablement nous ayde car iamais ne delaisse ceulx qui linuocquent. Parquoy il la fault appeller sur la mer damaritude, douleur et desplaisance de ses peches en se lauant sa conscience dedans celle mer de contriction: comme fit Apuleius qui se plongea dedans comme il inuoquoit sa deesse. Puis par son moyen nous enuoye vers le grant prebstre Vicaire de dieu tout puissant: qui nous baillera le chappeau de fleurs et couronne de roses qui pend au Sistre de lymaige de la deesse Ceres, cest assauoir de la croix de Jesucrist qui tant est sauoureuse. Voila la couronne des roses quil nous fault avoir si nous voullons reprendre nostre belle forme dinnocence. Puis quant nous laurons reprise: demeurons en continuelle louange de la glorieuse deesse Ceres, & la Lune qui au ciel diuin et eglise militante resplandist. Sacrons nous en ses immortelles louanges. Bonnorons & celebrons l'honneur de dieu son espoux & delle: comme fit Lucius Apuleius lhonneur de Osiris: & de son espouse la grande deesse Ceres aultrement nommee. Ceste deesse soubz une seule deite auoit et contenoit plusieurs noms, aussi fait la glorieuse Vierge sacree mere de dieu. Cest Ceres la deesse des bleds, cest Juno qui a chascun aide. Cest aussi Triuie par les trois voyes quelle a par sa nuissance, car elle est royne du ciel, des enfers & du monde. Cest cette lune qui si fort reluyt de nuyt qui est exposee entre les tenebres de peche, en esclarissant ses seruiteurs. Cest en terre Dyane la deesse de la chasse: qui des iadis Acteon mua en cerf & le chassa,

cest assauoir le dyable denfer en confusion, & le chassa de la forestz qui est la conscience des pecheurs et ceste en enfer Proserpine per sa puissance, car tous les dyables luy obeyssent & se disparent de ladicte temptation de ses seruiteurs. Laquelle vueille si bien prier pour nous que nous ayons remission de noz pechez. Au nom du pere & du fils, & du benoist sainct esprit. AMEN. (Paris, 1522, OOv^v–OOvi^r)

9. "Si quis aurum paratus & gemmas ex stercore legere, is demum aptus huic libello continget lector. . . . Multa in ipsa fabula absurdè excogitata, multa in sermone barbarè posita, quae tamen quibusdam melioris interdum notae stellulis distincta, & antiqui moris ritusque vestigiis nunnullis interspersa . . ." ("Editoris Censura" [Augsburg, 1595], A2^r). Professor William Race informs me that this proverbial expression (to find gold in a dunghill) is first found in the work of the late Roman Christian writer Cassiodorus, in his *Institutiones*.

10. "Neque uero mediocrem gratiam & ille debebit uestrae Reipub. si per uos quodammodo renatus, & tanquam ab inferis reductus, hoc est à blattis & tineis, à carcere & tenebris, à situ, squalore, & interitu, cui proximus erat, liberatus in lucem emerserit . . ." (1534, a2^r–a2^v).

11. "praeter quàm quod in hac historia omnium humanorum affectuum absolutissimam quandam imaginem (quos omnes exacte cognoscere non extrema sapientiae pars habenda est) & coniugalis amoris ac fidei, & constantiae pulcherrimum exemplar in Theagene & Chariclia adumbrauit: mitto uerborum ornatum & compositionem, et dicendi artificium, caeterasque orationis uirtutes, quibus nulli Graecorum authorum secundus est . . ." (ibid., a2^r).

12. De argumento quod & uarium est & multiplex, nihil non polliceor, quod praeter festiuam & amoenam & puram & castam historiam, quam perpetua narratione exequitur: multorum quoque locorum situs cosmographica ratione scitissime depingit: non paucarum rerum caussas [*sic*] easque occultissimas eruit & aperit: nonnullorum populorum ritus & mores erudite describit: plerorumque fluminuum, montium, lapidum, herbarum & regionum naturas, Aegypti nimirum & Aethyopiae huic conterminae, uulgo haud cognitas explicat: omnia pulcherrimis digressionibus, & amoenissimis parergis & exornationibus ita miscens & temperans . . . (Ibid., a3^r)

13. What we know as the *Old Arcadia* was written when Sidney was in his early twenties; one of the complicating factors of the production of his novel is that between the writing of the first *Arcadia* and the printing of the new one Sir Philip had not only died but become a national monument. Katherine Duncan-Jones crisply defines the relations between old and new versions and the manuscript "publication" of the *Old Arcadia*: Fulke Greville in 1586 thought the *Old Arcadia* had become "so common," for, Duncan-Jones suggests "the nine surviving manuscripts of the *Old Arcadia* probably represent dozens which were in circulation in the 1580s" (Introduction, *Old Arcadia*, viii). Jean Robertson points to a manuscript comment supporting the idea that copies of the *Old Arcadia* circulated, "'emparted to some few of his frends in his lyfe time and to more sence his vnfortunat deceasse'" (General Introduction, *The Countess of Pembroke's Arcadia*, xl). The circulation of the first *Arcadia* in the 1580s should help us remember that the manuscript culture did not utterly cease with the advent of the printing press. It has never quite ended.

14. Est enim cùm ad uoluptatem lectoris, tum uerò etiam ad utilitatem mirificè accommodata narratio, elegantia & uenustate sermonis eximia, & mira uarietate consiliorum, euentuum & affectuum. Nec solum fortunae uices, sed etiam uirtutum imagines multae hic propositae sunt. In quibus & Hydaspes describitur, rex Æthiopum, cui non solum laus fortitudinis, sed etiam iustitiae, clementiae, & pietatis erga subditos tribuitur" (1552, a3^v).

15. "Oratio est nitida, & non tumida. Et mira est uarietas, consiliorum, occasionum, euentuum & adfectuum: & uitae imagines multas continet. Itaque à multis eam legi utile est, & uarietas lectores inuitare potest" (a4^r).

Warschewiczki in his preface echoes Melancthon, leading one to wonder whether he is just borrowing, or whether Melancthon's suppositious epistle was largely of the editor-translator's own composition (ibid., a4ʳ).

16. "CON LA TAVOLA NEL FINE delle cose piu [sic] notabili," this edition of *Fiammetta* is apparently edited by its publisher Filippo Giunti. The dedication to *Fiametta* is dated the end of July 1594, while the dedication to Giunti's edition of Boccaccio's *Corbaccio* is dated 1 August 1594; evidently the publisher was putting out a set. *Corbaccio* also offers "Tavola Delle Cose Degne di Memoria" ("Table of Things Worthy of Memory") (Florence, 1594, I: 2ʳ–4ᵛ).

17. Samuel Johnson wrote to Richardson on 9 March 1751, "I wish You would add an *Index Rerum* that when the reader recollects any incident he may easily find it . . . for Clarissa is not a performance to be read with eagerness and laid aside for ever, but will be occasionally consulted by the busy, the aged, and the studious, and therefore I beg that this Edition by which I suppose Posterity is to abide, may want nothing that can facilitate its use" (*Letters of Samuel Johnson*, ed. Redford, I:48). Commelinus' 1611 edition of Heliodorus has endnotes followed by "Index Rerum in Hoc Opusculo Insigniorem" ("Index of Remarkable Things in This Work," running-title, "Index Rerum"). Johnson may have come upon this edition. Commelinus' title-page announces, "Accessit huic editione Sententiarum ex hoc opusculo Collectarum series" ("Added to this edition is an ordered list of Observations collected out of this Work"). Richardson met the demand for an index of *sententiae* (aphorisms, observations, or sentiments), and created his own *Trésor*, when in March 1755 he published *A Collection of the Moral and Instructive Sentiments, Maxims, Cautions, and Reflections, Contained in the Histories of Pamela, Clarissa, and Sir Charles Grandison.*

18. "Philostratus le surnomme Arabe, & que Heliodorus luy mesme à la fin de son liure dit qu'il estoit Phoenicien, natif de la ville d'Emessa [sic], laquelle est située es confins de la Phoenicie, & de l'Arabie" (Paris, 1547, Aiiiᵛ).

19. "Tiercement en la fiction, dont la fin est l'esbahissement, & la delectation, qui procede de la nouuelleté des choses estranges & pleines de merueilles." (1547, Aiiiᵛ).

20. "& par tout les passions humaines paintes au vif, auecq' si grande honnesteté, que l'on n'en sçauroit tirer occasion, ou exemple de mal faire. Pource que de toutes affections illicites, & mauuaises, il a fait l'yssue malheureuse: & au contraire des bonnes, & honnestes, la fin desirable & heureuse" (Aiiiʳ).

21. Mais sur tout la disposition en est singuliere: car il commence au mylieu de son histoire, comme font les Poëtes Heroïques. Ce qui cause de prime face vn grande esbahissement aux lecteurs, & leur engendre vn passionné desir d'entendre le commencement: & toutesfois il les tire si bien par l'ingenieuse liaison de son conte, que l'on n'est point resolu de ce que l'on trouue tout au commencement du premier liure iusques à ce que l'on ayt leu la fin du cinquiesme. Et quand on est là venu, encore a l'on plus grande enuie de voir la fin, que l'on n'auoit au parauant d'en voir le commencement: De sorte que tousiours l'entendement demeure suspendu, iusques à ce que l'on vienne à la conclusion, laquelle laisse le lecteur satisfait, de la sorte que le sont ceux, qui à la fin viennent à iouyr d'vn bien ardemment desiré, & longuement atendu [sic].   (1547, Aiiiʳ)

22. Mais au regard de ceux qui sont si parfaitement composez à la vertu qu'ilz ne cognoissent, ny ne reçoiuent aucun autre plaisir, que le deuoir, ou de ceux qui par vne fieüre d'austerité intraitablé ont le goust si corrumpu, qu'ilz ne treuuent rien bon, & se desplaisent à eux mesmes, si d'auanture ilz viennent à reprendre ceste mienne entremise, ie me contenteray de leur respondre. Que ce liure n'a iamais esté escrit, ne traduit pour eux: les vns, pource qu'ilz n'en ont que faire, les autres pource qu'ilz ne le valent pas.   (1547, Aiiiᵛ)

23. "ita variis implexum ambagibus, vt vix lectione tertia quicquam nisi per nebulam consequereris" (Paris, 1619, aviᵛ).

24. "Minimè autem necessarium arbitror ea refellere quae in autorem nostrum dicuntur friuola, eum scilicet peccasse saepius in narrationibus suis, dum imbellem Theagenem exhibet" ("Lectori Fauenti" ["To the Well-Disposed Reader"], *Heliodori Æthiopicorum* [1619], aviii ʳ).

25. Bourdelotius' prefatory essay continues: "Nec enim vident poëtica haec imitatione succedere: aliis, qui sub nominibus humanis Chymicam describi testantur, nihil omnino respondeo. Quo enim argumento huic mendacio fides esset habenda? An uiri clarissimi qui materiam Amatoriam tractandam susceperunt, vt nunc politissimum Barclaium audio, nugas Chymicas corporum pestem, animorum detrimentum sibi proposuere?" (*Heliodori Æthiopicorum* [1619], aviii ʳ). ["For they do not see that this kind of poetic work succeeds by imitation: To others, who would assert that under the names of human beings Chymistrie (i.e., alchemical elements and processes, also processes of Paracelsian medicines) is being described, I shall not respond at all. How can we give any faith to such a lying argument? Did the most celebrated men who undertook the treatment of the matter of Love— as I now hear of the most accomplished Barclay—set themselves to deal with Chymick trumpery, bodily sickness and mental damage?"] Clifton Cherpack, in *Logos in Mythos: Idea and Early French NArrative* (1983), comments on the scientific thought in Barclay's *Euphormio.*

26. The most detailed study was undertaken by Samuel Lee Wolff, *The Greek Romance in Elizabethan Prose Fiction* (1912). All recent editions of Sidney's novel refer to its relation to Heliodorus; editors sometimes have a harder time admitting the relationship to Achilles Tatius.

27. In the "Prologo Lector" prefixed to his *Novelas Ejemplares* (1613), Cervantes advertised the new work soon to appear as *libro que se atreve a competir con Heliodoro* (I:53). Note that this is not only to be taken as an aesthetic reality for the author, but also as a come-on to the reader. For the relation of Cervantes' last novel to the antique novel tradition, see Diana de Armas Wilson, *Allegories of Love: Cervantes's "Persiles and Sigismunda'* (1991), as well as her essay "Homage to Apuleius: Cervantes' Avenging Psyche," in *TSAN*, 88–100; and also James Romm's "Novels beyond Thule: Antonius Diogenes, Rabelais, Cervantes" in the same volume, 101–116.

28. "Recvrri proximis canicularis vacationis diebus ad Æthiopica Heliodori: partim, vt animum iucundissima lectione a laboribus reficerem: partim, vt rursus meam modicam Graecae linguae facultatem, ex eloquentissimo Scriptore alerem" (Frankfurt, 1584, 3).

29. "*Omne tulit punctum* (inquit Venusinus) *qui miscuit utile dulci.* Hoc quanquam de Poëtis dictum est: tamen non malè ad hunc quoque Scriptorem transferri potest: cùm liber eius non dissimilis poëmati sit, licet soluta oratione constans. Non enim ex metro potius, quàm fictione, Poëma spectari conuenit" (ibid., 5).

30. "Deinde, suam cuique culpam, malorum & calamitatum causam esse: vt, quòd Theagenes Thessalus hanc virginem Delphis rapiens, cum ea multis durissimis casibus conflictatur. Factum puellae non laudabile illud quidem: deferentis eum, qui loco parentis erat: & promissione matrimonij, iuuenum ad incerta casuum sequentis (.sicut ipsa tandem agnoscit.) insignis tamen inter haec castitas, fides, constantia, in amore vtriusque: donec ad extremum optata tranquillitate, & dulci coniugio, potiuntur" (ibid., 6).

31. "Totam verò Historiam, veluti Tragicocomoediam dicentes, haud errauerimus: sicut ex Theagenis verbis lib. 5 patet" (ibid., 8).

32. "Achille Tatio pare che nella locutione & componimento sia ornato. percioche ella è chiara & significante, & quando usa li traslati, gli usa molto acconciamente. i giri delle sue sentenze per lo piu sono concisi, aperti, & soaui, & col lor suono porgono dilettatione a gli orecchi, & serba gran similitudine nello apparecchio & forma delle narrationi con quelle di Heliodoro" (Venice, 1560, A5 ʳ). I have not been able to find a copy of the 1550 translation.

33. "Amore è il uero e dotto maestro, che insegna ciascuna cosa perfettamente. da lui come da uno abondantissimo fonte nasce il principio di ogni nostro operare, & egli troua il

mezzo, & conduce tutte le nostri attioni a glorioso fine" (*Achille Tatio Alessandrino Dell' Amore di Leucippe et di Clitophonte* [Venice, 1560], A6ᵛ). ("Love is the true and learned master, who teaches every thing perfectly. From him as from a most abundant fountain springs the principle [or beginning] of all our works, and he both finds the means and conducts all our actions to the glorious end . . .") *Amore* is thus inner libidinousness, the well-spring of all possibility of desiring, as well as the highest desire that leads the human to heaven. Coccio proposes that, far from putting love-stories away from us, we ought to want to think about Love, for without contemplation of Love's meaning we will make a poorer job of living. Others would argue against him that he is disingenuously conflating the false fleshly sensual love and the highest Platonic love. Coccio is neither alone nor new in his admiration of Cupid-*Amor*, for many of the Renaissance artists of Italy have preceded him.

34. See Michael Danahy, *The Feminization of the Novel* (1991), and English Showalter, *The Evolution of the French Novel, 1641–1782* (1972). In assuming a change to a feminine audience to have taken place in the seventeenth century, both are following the arguments of Antoine Adam in *Romanciers de XVIIᵉ Siècle* (1958). Donahy takes issue with Adam's condescension, but believes that the novel (*le roman*) *did* become gendered as feminine: "Novels were construed as a womanish cover-up, while history was a grave matter, stately and manly, strong and serious" (*Feminization of the Novel*, 19). Partly as a result of such gendering, Danahy believes, the novel became a cultural *anima* in the Jungian sense.

In the seventeenth century various forms of fiction came under the suspicion of being both feminine and dangerous to females. Perrault in his "Préface" of 1695 defends his own stories, which resemble those of antiquity, as more moral, a better influence on women. The moral of the story of the Matron of Ephesus is that even the most apparently virtuous women are not so. "Who does not see that this Moral is very bad, and that it can only serve to corrupt women by the bad example [*corrompre les femmes par le mauvais exemple*] and make them believe that in failing in their duty they do but follow the common path." As for any moral in the Fable of Psyche, the story makes no sense, it is *une enigme impénétrable* (Perrault, *Contes*, 4–5). Perhaps male readers in the late seventeenth and eighteenth centuries made a habit of reading stories *"as if"* they were women—that is, imagining how a weak woman might be influenced by this or that. It is ironic that one of the points against love-stories in modern times is that they are "merely fairy tales," when Perrault thought his tales could be healthier than novels or romances.

Chapter XI

1. See Barclay, *Euphormio's Satyricon*, edited and translated by Paul Turner. There is a brief discussion of Barclay's work in Clifton Cherpack's *Logos in Mythos: Ideas and Early French Narrative* (1983); Cherpack points out the autobiographical content within the Petronian outline, as well as the relation to Spanish picaresque models (89). But Firenzuola's autobiographical takeover of Apuleius seems the important model for Barclay's assimilation of Petronius.

2. "Criticorum praeludia Petronius Arbiter, nec vllus est, cuius ingenium non senserit, aut ungues. Declarat ipsa moles Emendationum, Coniecturarum, Notarum, Animaversionum, Collectaneorum, Praecidaneorum, Racemationum, Spicilegiorum, Symbolarum, & tot noua nomina vestis, quae lectorem quaerunt iam cibos validiores fastidientem" ("Blande lectorem meum admoneo" [Paris, 1618], aiᵛ.

I have taken the liberty in translating of assuming a misprint in the Latin, reading "non senserit, aut ungues" as "non censerit, ad ungues" (or "ad unguem"); thus, it means, "who will not appraise his wit to a nicety," i.e., with the test of the fingernail running over a sculpture, as in Horace, "non castigavit ad unguem," *Ars poetica*, 1:294.

3. I find it interesting that the hero of Frances Burney's first novel, *Evelina* (1778), is named "Orville"—possibly after Chariton's first editor? But any influence Chariton may have had was relativity slight.

4. See my article, "Heliodorus Rewritten: Samuel Richardson's *Clarissa* and Frances Burney's *Wanderer*," in *TSAN*, 117–131.

5. "Non fœdiore habitu fuit ejus Leucippe, cum verberata, detonsa, & servili schema induta suo Clitophonti non agnoscenda se in eius conspectum stitit" (Leiden, 1640, "Praefatio," *3 ᵛ).

6. ". . . certum tamen est, tum non fuisse Christianum, cum hunc librum composuit. Quæ de amoribus puerorum disserit, & quod de suo adulterio fatetur Clitophon, satis arguunt, hominem a Christi disciplina esse alienum. Quin postea potuerit sacramentum Christo dicere, nolo inficiari, quia non possum, qui aliter dixerit, refutare" ("Ad Lectorem," *8 ᵛ).

7. Heliodorus isto disertior, & in operosiore dicendi genere eloquentiam, quam promittit ac præstat, etiam venditans. Certe abundantior est, & tractu limpido & amœno diffusæ orationis, lectorem suum allicit ac tenet. Iste simplicioris & magis inaffectatæ elegantiæ sectator, ut plane in eo agnoscas peculiares Alexandrinis vernulis argutias & delicias nativi sermonis, miro sale ac suavitate conditi. Succinctior ubique est, & vibrantes sententias ex abrupto intorquens. Argumenti varietas & accidentium mutatio in Heliodoro mirabilior, quamvis nec Achilles hac in parte sibi defuerit. Hic noster *epeisodia* intermiscuit paullo lasciviora, cum semper sit castus Heliodorus. Vetus omnino hoc genus scribendi fuit, ac a multis populis politioribus olim hodieque frequentatum. (Ibid., *8 ᵛ–9 ʳ)

8. "Persae in primis ista amatoria affectant, qua prosa, qua versu, sive rythmis, in quibus excellunt. Et videntur ab omni ævo fabulis ad hunc modum scriptitandis studuisse. In Asiam olim, quam regebant, fabularum Milesiarum originem intulisse, non frustra credas. Arabibus certè hunc eundem scribendi morem ac genium dedere. Hi transmisere Hispanis. A quibus nos porro Galli accepimus. Verum de his alibi" (ibid., *9 ʳ).

9. Huet's *Traité de l'origine des romans* made its first appearance as the preface to a novel, *Zayde, histoire espagnole* (1670). It is one of the ironies of Huet's treatise, so sympathetic to the "feminine" literary form under attack, that it was addressed to the nominal *male* author of *Zayde*, Jean Regnault de Segrais. (Segrais was a kind of accommodation address for fiction-writing women, being the putative author of two novels by the duchesse de Montpensier, as well as the titular author of *La Princesse de Clèves*.) The *Traité* was first published separately still bearing the alternative title *Lettre de Monsieur Huet à Monsieur de Segrais.* Joan DeJean deals with this appearance of a history of the novel as "a classic literary history: a man-to-man discourse, a story between men about male literary endeavors" (*Tender Geographies*, 170). She points out that both Huet and Segrais were aware that the real author of *Zayde* was a woman, Mme. de Lafyette. Yet Huet also unveils the gender of "Scudéry," discussing that author, whom he admires, as a woman: "With this tribute, Huet enacts the initial public inscription of Scudéry's name in the ranks of the modern authors to be included in French literature's first canon . . ." (170). DeJean points out that Boileau's *L'Art poetique* of 1674 has to take Huet's argument into account in the attack on the novel and most particularly on Scudéry; see DeJean, *Tender Geographies*, 169–178.

10. "De ce grand nombre de Romanciers que l'on vit en France sur le commencement de la troisième race de nos Rois, nous sont venus tant & tant de vieux Romans, dont une partie est imprimée, une autre pourrit dans les Bibliotheques, & le reste a esté consumé par la longueur des années. Et c'est de nous que l'Italie, & l'Espagne, qui a esté si fertile en Romans, tient l'art de les composer" (Paris, 1711, 166).

11. "Feu Monsieur de Saumaise, dont la memoire m'est en singuliere vénération, & pour sa grande érudition, & pour l'amitié qui a esté entre nous, a crû que l'Espagne, après avoir appris des Arabes l'art de romaniser, l'avoit enseigné par son exemple à tout le reste de l'Europe" (ibid., 168–169).

12. Miguel de Cervantes, l'un des plus beaux esprits que l'Espagne ait produits, en a fait une fine & judicieuse Critique dans son Dom Quixote [*sic*], qu'il feint d'avoir

traduit de l'Arabe de Cid Achmed ben Engeli, faisant voir par là son erreur touchant l'origine de la Romancerie Espagnole. A peine le Curé du village de son
Heros, & maistre Nicolas le Barbier, en trouvent-ils dans ce grand nombre six qui
meritent d'estre conservez. . . . Mais tout cela est recent en comparaison de nos
vieux Romans, qui vray-semblablement en furent les modeles. . . .

(Ibid., 174–176)

13. "Ce n'est ni en Provence, ni en Espagne, comme plusieurs le croyent, qu'il faut
esperer de trouver les premiers commencemens de cét agréable amusement des honnestes
paresseux: il faut les aller chercher dans les païs plus éloignez, & dans l'antiquité la plus
reculée" (2).

14. The King's Arcadian prayer begins a section on prayers in his captivity, and heads
the "Appendix" or post-mortem section of *Eikon Basilike: The Portraiture of His Sacred Majesty
in His Solitudes and Sufferings*; see edition by Philip Knachel (1966). John Milton sets himself
up as the detective of this piece of plagiarism on the part of the dead king, who could
"immediately before his death . . . pop into the hand of that grave Bishop who attended
him . . . a Prayer stol'n word for word from the mouth of a heathen fiction. . . . & that in
no serious Book, but the vain amatorious poem of Sr *Philip Sidneys Arcadia*: a Book in that
kind full of worth and witt, but among religious thoughts, and duties, not worthy to be
nam'd; nor to be read at any time without good caution; much less in time of trouble and
affliction to be a Christian's Prayer Book" (*Eikonoklastes*, in *Complete Prose Works of John
Milton*, III:362–363). Milton, so well versed in *Arcadia* that he immediately caught the
echoes, cannot utterly reprobate the "vain" book, but suggests that it is dangerous and
needs to be read with caution and, implicitly, under guidance. King Charles was a mad
misreader who read the wrong thing in the wrong way and at the wrong time.

15. Si tu sçaurois quelles sont les peines & difficultez qui se rencontrent le long du
chemin que tu entreprens . . . peut estre t'arresterois-tu sagement, où tu as esté
si longuement & doucement cherie. Mais ta ieunesse imprudente & qui n'a point
d'experience de ce que ie te dis, te figure peut-estre des gloires & des vanitez qui
produisent en toy. . . . Toutefois, puisque ta resolution est telle, & que si ie m'oppose, tu me menaces d'une prompte desobeyssance, ressouviens toy pour le moins
que ce n'est point par volonté: mais par souffrance que ie te le permèts. Et pour te
laisser à ton despart quelques arres de l'affection paternelle que je porte, mets bien
en ta memoire de que je te vay dire. . . .   (*L'Astrée* [Rouen, 1616], aiii^r–aiii^r)

The tone of intimacy achieved by the use of "tu" throughout is striking enough, if untran-
slatable into modern English.

16. "C'est tousiours la mesme Astree qui se presente deuant vous auec le mesme desir
de vous plaire, qu'elle a tousiours eu. Il est vray qu'elle a perdu ses ornements. . . . Il est
vray qu'elle ne veut plus qu'on luy parle de pierreries ny de perles. En fin il est vray qu'elle
est toute cachée dans les crespes & les voiles de son dueïl" (*L'Astrée*, Sixiesme Partie [Paris,
1626], a vii^v–a viii^r).

17. "Je supplierois l'illustre Auteur de Cénie & des Lettres Péruviennes, d'adopter
CLARISSE HARLOVE. L'aimable Famille! Un lieu cheri du Ciel, qui rassemblent ZILIA,
CENIE & CLARISSE, sous les ailes de cette excellente Mère, seroit le Temple de la VERTU
& du SENTIMENT" (Prévost, "Introduction," *Lettres angloises, ou Histoire de Miss Clarisse Harlove* [Dresden, 1751], I, p. x^v [*sic*]). Henry Fielding, defending his *Amelia*, held a mock-trial
of the case in his periodical *The Covent-Garden Journal* (January 1752). He presents himself
as "the Father of this poor Girl the Prisoner at the Bar . . . of all my Offspring she is my
favorite Child."

18. Nina Auerbach argues in *Woman and the Demon: The Life of a Victorian Myth* (1982)
that the idea of literary character, of characters having, as we say, an existence of their
own, is an invention of the Victorian period in unconscious response to the disapearance
of religion: "literary characters of both sexes provided the same image as women did of a
magic life within yet beyond the human. The religious and the literary imaginations con-

verge in woman to envision a transcendence that does not involve the death of time" (192–193). Auerbach sees literary "character" as sort of repository for "soul," and views Modernist literature and criticism of the earlier twentieth century as getting rid of the idea of "character," if only to serve other myths. But the idea of literary character is older than the nineteenth century. Ideas about literary "character" change, even within the works of the same author, but "character" has been around for a long time, and is still with us.

Chapter XII

1. The unknown "A. Allan," author of a set of verses "On *Clitophon* and *Leucippe's* Loves" prefixed to the 1638 version, tries to defend this novel as a "love toy" while presenting its chief value as its moral warning to males about dangerous women:

> Are *Clitophons* so scarce? doth not each street
> Afford us *Melites*? Every cloak you meet
> May wrap *Thersanders* rising forehead: though
> Exc'lent *Leucippes* peere we scarce can show.
> Thus may some sager Criticke, who would have
> Vs straight from Cradle thinke upon the Grave,
> Condemne our youths delight: we must expect
> The worst of censures for the least defect.
> Love is a Passion, and who e're will touch
> Ought that is his, must looke to finde him such.
> Nor shall the wounded onely bleed, but *Hee*
> That dares describe *Cupids* Artillerie.
> And yet he shall not suffer, let me call
> Lovers, the better part o'th' world, who all
> Will vindicate our Author. . . .
> (*The Loves of Clitophon and Leucippe*
> [Oxford, 1638], A7ᵛ–A8ʳ)

2. In Western Europe of the eighteenth century there was a general perception of an increase in popular fiction coming off the presses—a persistent impression may be just as important as any statistical facts. Little has yet been done to ascertain the number of novels printed and their print runs. Some recent studies have concentrated on literacy and readership. See, e.g., Margaret Spufford's *Small Books and Pleasant Histories: Popular Fiction and Its Readership in Seventeenth-Century England* (1981). Jan Fergus's *Jane Austen* casts some light on the printing and reading of novels in Jane Austen's time. J. Paul Hunter makes some interesting speculations on the readership available for novels as well as for other printed works in eighteenth-century England in his *Before Novels*. Elizabeth Eisenstein, in some general remarks on novel-printing in Europe, reminds us that "novelists are apt to be novel readers" (*The Printing Press as an Agent of Change*, 153). Novelists on the whole are intertextual creatures. If print runs of novels were small (from 500 or less to 2000 in each issue, even in the eighteenth century), targeted readers included other writers. A great curiosity about fiction ensured that almost every novel of any note got translated (sooner or later) into at least one other European language. Major writers (Sidney, Cervantes, Scudéry, Marivaux, Richardson, Fielding) were repeatedly translated. *Translation* is a key to the understanding of Renaissance and Enlightenment culture. Not all translation is hack work; that Prévost would translate Richardson is significant. Renaissance and Enlightenment translators took liberties we would find indefensible, in compression or addition. For instance, James Mabbe (sometimes signed "Puede-Ser," "Maybe"), translator of Cervantes and of Alemán, and a leading transmitter of Spanish culture to England, adds enormously to his original, feeling quite free to interlard his own opinions at length with those of the narrator or author.

3. Much of the work on this rests on the groundbreaking and still useful study by Alice Clark, *The Working Life of Women in the Seventeenth Century* (London, 1919).

4. Nancy Armstrong in *Desire and Domestic Fiction: A Political History of the Novel* (1987) takes the division between "private" and "public" and the idea of purely "domestic" fiction very seriously. The rise of the propaganda about women's place in the domestic sphere and their devotion to the private in the late eighteenth century is traced by Claudia Johnson, who sees an increase in the intensity of this prescription as part of the backlash during and after the French Revolution; see *Jane Austen: Women, Politics, and the Novel* (1988). The aftermath of the French Revolution had a somewhat chilling effect on female writing on the Continent as well as on England; intellectuals like Mme. de Staël were not to be encouraged by the new order. We should note, however, the importance of George Sand (Lucile-Aurore Dupin, 1804–1876), who refused to acknowledge the difference of spheres and openly dealt with both "public" and "private" material in her fiction. It is, however, also true that the nineteenth century sees the phenomenon of female writers appearing under deliberately composed male pseudonyms such as "George Sand," "George Eliot," "Currer Bell." This is a somewhat different practice from that of seventeenth-century writers appearing anonymously or under the real names of brothers or friends (Segrais, Georges de Scudéry), though Georges de Scudéry perhaps lent his name ultimately to the generic pseudonym. The adoption of such fake masculinity acknowledges the theory that women belong to the "private" and do *not* meddle with the "public" world, as well as exhibiting a playful awareness that there is no such distinction. We should also remember an older distinction between "public" and "private," which is that between high nobles or aristocracy who run the country (these are the "public") and all others—male shopkeepers and small landowners included, who are merely "private" persons, however extensive (socially and geographically) their dealings with the wider world.

5. Mary Delany (née Granville) was married off at age seventeen to Alexander Pendarves, who was nearly sixty, to suit the prospective political convenience of her uncle, Lord Lansdowne. Many years later she told the story of her early life and this unhappy marriage in a written account for her friend Margaret Duchess of Portland, using pseudonyms and tropes adapted from novels, more particularly from Scudéry's kind of novel. See *The Autobiography and Correspondence of Mary Granville, Mrs. Delany* (1861), I: 1–112.

6. See, e.g., Janice A. Radway, *Reading the Romance: Women, Patriarchy and Popular Literature* (1984). Radway is not entirely negative about the reading performed on the cheap Harlequin and other brand-name "romances" (Mills and Boon, Silhouette). Investigators seem always to find with some sense of shock that the readership for such products, like the audience for soap-operas, is not as underprivileged or uneducated as the intelligentsia would readily assume. Holly Montagu tries to apply the forms of contemporary reading of these prefabricated "romances" to the "ancient romances," but her essay, though it starts by equating these romances as two equal kinds, in the end shows that there are great differences between them ("From *Interlude in Arcady* to *Daphnis and Chloe*: Two Thousand Years of Erotic Fantasy," *TSAN*, 391–401). If there is anything "wrong" with Harlequins etc. it is not that they are "love-stories," for life can certainly be examined in stories of love, courtship, sexual adventure or misfortune. The deficiency lies in the fact that the stories are closely prescribed by publishers and set out as piecework, and the authors are not allowed to wander out of the formula—they cannot, for instance, be intertextual. The little books are thus not novels (or "romances") but sketches or scenarios. The reader, however, gets a "quick hit" of certain material important to the Novel itself as well as to real novels. In getting such a "hit" the reader is inevitably cooperating with the organization that cynically designs the books, and she is thus submitting to civic propriety in that form. Certain forms of "male romance" (westerns, war-stories, etc.) are produced in the same manner.

7. La première est desmenée aux Princes & aux Héros célèbres: la seconde a été abandonée à tous les Sujets du second Ordre, voyageurs, avanturiers, hommes & femmes de médiocre vertu. Il faut même l'avouer à l'honte du genre humain. La haute Romancie est depuis long-tems presque deserte, . . . au lieu que la basse Romancie se peuple tous les jours de plus en plus. Aussi, les Fées & les Génies se

voyant abandonnés, & presque sans pratique, ont pris la plûpart le parti de s'en aller, les uns dans les espaces imaginaires, les autres dans le pays des Songes. C'est ce qui fait que vous ne voyez plus la Romancie ornée come elle étoit autrefois.

(*Voyage Merveilleux du Prince Fan-Férédin* . . ., 107)

8. "cette funeste lecture nous accoûtume à confondre les idées du bien avec celles du mal, celles du vice avec celles de la vertu. . . . Ouvrez ces ouvrages, & vous y verrez, presque dans tous, les droits de la justice divine & humaine violés; l'autorité des parens sur leurs enfans méprisée; les liens sacrés du mariage & de l'amitié rompus" (*Entretiens sur les Romans*, 225).

9. "chaque Lecteur se crut fondé à s'arroger le même droit . . . laissant au caprice & aux passions le soin de dicter les maximes de sa croyance: tant il est vrai qu'il n'est qu'une route qui conduit au sanctuaire de la vérité, & que celles qui mènent à l'erreur sont sans nombre!" (212–213).

10. "De tous les poisons, celui qu'on présente dans une coupe dorée & sous des dehors pleins de charmes, est souvent le plus dangereux" (289).

11. "Avois-je donc tort de vous prophétiser que le Roman de *Paméla* seroit bien-tôt oublié? Vous en étiez idolâtre pour lors; & cependant, sans votre petite chienne, que vous appellâtes de ce nom, vous en resteroit-il encore quelqu'idée? Il en fut de même il y a trois ans de *Tom-Jones* & de *Clarice*" (101).

12. F. A. Wolf's *Prolegomena ad Homerum* "proves" not only that the *Iliad* and the *Odyssey* were not written by the same author, but also that each work was an amalgam of a number of oral poems and only lightly unified at a much later period than that of the original lays. In making the epics seem more uncertain, more folk-based, and more "Oriental," Wolf in a way does for the Epic what Huet had done for the Novel. As the Romantic Age highly valued individual voice and mind, the deconstructed "Homeric" poems lost heavily in this new rendering, which signals the advent of the "Higher Criticism," soon to tackle the Bible systematically. Modern literature became increasingly valued as offering the only guaranteed contact with the individual creative mind. The appearance of Johnson's edition of Shakespeare in the anniversary year (1765) and the "Shakespeare Jubilee" produced by Garrick at Stratford in 1769 both mark the new value being accorded to Shakespeare, and even the beginning of the "Shakespeare Industry" still so profitable to Stratford.

13. See my article, "Shakespeare's Novels: Charlotte Lennox Illustrated," *Studies in the Novel*, 19 (Fall 1987), 296–307. It is noticeable that English women writers such as Aphra Behn, Eliza Haywood, and Charlotte Lennox exhibit a thorough knowledge of Boccaccio, Bandello, and the other writers who were the target of Roger Ascham's complaint against the lewd Italian books.

14. Walpole's friend Henry Seymour Conway teased Walpole about his proclivity for novel-reading when they were both schoolboys at Eton: "I remember you buried in romances and novels; I really believe you could have said all the *Grand Cyrus*'s, the *Cleopatra*'s and the *Amadis*'s in the world by heart" (18 April 1745 OS, *Horace Walpole's Correspondence*, XXXVII:189). Walpole himself, from the eminence of eighteen years, looks back fondly on the way in which the landscape of Eton College was colored for him by his quixotic reception of his reading matter: "At first I was content with a visionary flock. . . . As I got further into Virgil and *Clelia*, I found myself transported from Arcadia to the Garden of Italy, and saw Windsor Castle in no other view than the *capitoli immobile saxum*" (6 May 1736, *Correspondence*, IX:3). Walpole was at Eton from 1727 to 1734; at that time the whole tradition of modern Western fiction was still available, from *Amadís* to the works of D'Urfé and Scudéry, and on up to *Oroonoko, Robinson Crusoe*, and *Lettres Persanes*.

15. *Frères humains* is the beginning of François Villon's well-known *Ballade des Pendus* (c. 1462), in which he imagines himself and his fellow rogues executed on the gallows,

their flesh also rotten (*pourrie*): "You human brothers, who live after us / Do not have hearts hardened against us." But the civic ideal necessitates the hardening of the heart, which Zola imposes on the death of his heroine.

16. Vineta Colby, *The Singular Anomaly: Women Novelists of the Nineteenth Century* (1970); Elaine Showalter, *A Literature of Their Own: British Women Novelists from Brontë to Lessing* (1977); Sandra M. Gilbert and Susan Gubar, *The Madwoman in the Attic: The Woman Writer and the Nineteenth-Century Literary Imagination* (1979). Armstrong's book has already been cited. Mary Poovey deals with the restrictions the women encounter in writing while inhibited by a felt duty to be modest and submissive: see *The Proper Lady and the Woman Writer: Ideology as Style in the Works of Mary Wollstonecraft, Mary Shelley and Jane Austen* (1984). The recuperation of the history of women's writing was undertaken in the 1970s primarily by critics and historians centered in nineteenth-century studies, a fact productive of some limitation. The recuperation of women's writing on the Continent has proceeded later than in the Anglo-American world.

17. "To promote this Design, the Reader will find in the following Treatise, the Best Instructions for composing ROMANCES . . ." (*The History of Romances*. Made English by Mr. Stephen Lewis [London, 1715], ix).

18. "It was half-way through the second term of my fourth year at school that I suddenly discovered a friend. Our teacher began reading stories about Winnie the Pooh every Wednesday. From then on, I was never sick on Wednesdays. In a way, discovering Pooh was my salvation. He made me feel more normal. I suppose I saw something of myself in him" (Sally Morgan, *My Place*, 45). *Winnie-the-Pooh* (1926) could be seen—*has* been seen—as a book entirely limited to its class and time, a whimsy arising out of upper middle-class Home Counties English life between the wars. But the power of the book itself apparently goes beyond its limitations. Part of the strength of *Winnie-the-Pooh* the novel is that as a "children's book" it is not limited by Prescriptive Realism and thus may be the more culturally portable. It is unsafe to assume that the appeal of *any* novel will be strictly limited to the country, class, and cultural subgroups from which it emerged.

Chapter XIII

1. Shall I recount to you his [Sidney's] pastoral epic, the *Arcadia*? It is a mere relaxation, a sort of poetic novel written in the country for the amusement of his sister, a fashionable work which, like our *Cyrus* and *Clélie* at home, is not a monument but a document. Such works display only the externals, the elegance and current politeness, the jargon of the *beau monde*, in short what one has to talk about in the presence of women; nevertheless, one sees there the tendencies of the cultural spirit [*l'esprit public*]: in *Clélie*, the oratorical development, the fine and coherent analysis, the abundant conversation of people serenely seated in elegant armchairs; in *Arcadia*, tormented imagination, excessive feelings, pell-mell events which suit men hardly emerged from a semi-barbaric way of life [*la vie demi-barbare*]. In fact, in London people still shot off pistols in the streets, and under Henry VIII, under his son and his daughters the queens, and a protector, the first amongst the nobility knelt before the executioner's axe.

   (*Histoire de la littérature anglaise*, I: 283–284)

   It will be noted that Taine gains an unfair national advantage by fast-forwarding some forty years between the writing of *Arcadia* and the publication of *Clélie*. His account of *Clélie* omits all that is violent, and he refrains from noting the war and revolution that mark *Le Grand Cyrus*. England is to be perturbed and violent; France, tranquil. Taine takes a leaf from Ruskin's book, but reverses the national (and sectarian) praise and disparagement.

   Throughout his work Taine emphasizes the difference between a "monument," which is an admirable work of lasting value, and a "document,' a work interesting to us only because of social history. Female works tend to be mere "documents," if mentioned at all. *Clélie* may be superior to *Arcadia* as a French work, but it is still merely a "document."

2. Henry James was discussing absence of "composition" in referring to certain long nineteenth-century novels as "such large loose baggy monsters, with their queer elements of the accidental and the arbitrary." Specifically, he cites Thackeray's *The Newcomes*, Dumas' *Les Trois Mousquetaires*, and Tolstoy's *War and Peace* as examples of novels that have life but want art. (Preface, 1907, to New York Edition of *The Tragic Muse*; see *The Art of the Novel*, 84). James was not describing the genre, but (he felt) defective examples. On the contrary, it was James's declared objective to show how formally beautiful a novel could be. But perhaps there is something "loose and baggy" about the Novel, as well as something slightly monstrous. James's own genius, ironically, led him to proliferation; the New York Edition of his novels involved gigantic rewritings. James's elaborations of his aesthetic constitute a major expression of the formalism of the late nineteenth century. (One can forgive James anything except his disciples, such as Percy Lubbock, who begin to turn James's inspiring suggestions into something more like rules: see Lubbock's *The Craft of Fiction*, 1921). It should be noted in favor of the nineteenth-century seekers after *form* that their search for the aesthetic provided a coded context for a gay sensibility denied elsewhere in the culture. The aesthetes who tried "to burn always with this hard, gemlike flame," as Walter Pater famously suggested in his essay on Leonardo da Vinci, were trying to demonstrate that gay art could be "hard"—a reclamation of a prized cultural "masculinity."

3. Sir James Frazer thus produced what George Eliot's Mr. Casaubon was vainly hunting for, "A Key to All Mythologies." Casaubon's concerns are in keeping with the era in which *Middlemarch* was written—the era of Nietzsche and Frazer—rather than of the 1820s and 1830s in which Casaubon's supposedly exists. The thought of the twentieth century has been dominated by the leading ideas of the nineteenth century. Many of those ideas were deeply affected by academic classical study, but this was a classicism such as Bernal describes, developing in an era when Greece became the totem of the Ayrans. Anthropologists and mythographers developed strategies often based on the strategies of the classical writers. Frazer, for instance, published an edition of Ovid's *Fasti* (an account of festivals and religious observances) with a commentary in 1929.

The nineteenth century was fascinated by *morphology*; the very word elevates the idea of *form* to its dominant Greek position. The one remains, the many change and pass. Gillian Beer succinctly explains this fascination in her *Darwin's Plots* (1983): Victorians wondered, "is there a morphology of the unconscious yet to be discovered, as insistent and inescapable as that of physical organic life?" (197). Vladimir Propp's work is significantly entitled *The Morphology of the Folktale* (1928); he claimed he could "make an examination of the forms of the tale which will be as exact as the morphology of organic formations" (quoted by Beer, 197). Morphological thought (even that derived from Darwin) tended to encode or suppose an "ultimate fixity" (Beer, 217). Stories studied in the formalist method could easily seem "dead" (like Taine's empty shell) as well as neatly unified.

Modern anthropology inherits this approach, as well as the entire Western tradition of examining "savage" or "barbaric" peoples. Claude Lévi-Strauss applied his inherited methods to the ways of life and the tales of "Third World" peoples, at the end of the colonial era. The anthropologist's assumed objectivity is betrayed in the emotions running through Lévi-Strauss's work, including at last the typically 1950s nausea that characterizes *Tristes Tropiques* (1955). Lévi-Strauss here laments the unity and fixity of the modern world, in which civilization is no longer a rare flower but a dull and aggressive necessity: "Mankind has opted for monoculture; it is in the process of creating a mass civilization" (*Tristes Tropiques*, trans. Weightman, 38). Yet Lévi-Strauss does not lament his own and his profession's part in this development. Rereading Lévi-Strauss, we may now doubt whether matters (savage or civilized) ever were as unified as he supposes, as well as whether his accounts of rites and stories and their meanings are satisfactory. The gynecological tale of the shaman, for instance, in *Structural Anthropology*, leaves the woman out of the narrative (186–205).

Late twentieth-century structuralism comes to us chiefly from anthropology and chiefly from France, though structuralism can be employed in various ways. Barthes, for example, with a style agreeably reminiscent of that of seventeenth-century wits like La Rochefoucault, examines public myths and cultural strategies. while remaining somewhat wary of mythographers like Sigmund Freud, the chief of the deep mythographers, who shares many of the concerns and approaches of the High Nineteenth Century into which he was born (in 1856).

4. Jessie L. Weston's *From Ritual to Romance* (1920) investigates the Grail legends, proposing a religious ritual underlying stories that became attached to certain knights of the *Table Ronde*. Using the anthropology and mythography of the age of Frazer, Weston proposes that fertility rituals are at the basis of the story and are expressed in the symbols of the Lance and the Cup: "the Lance, or Spear, representing the Male, the Cup, or Vase, the Female, reproductive energy" (75). She is hampered by the coyness of her era—the closest she gets to blunt expression of what the Cup may actually represent is the use of the word *yoni* within somebody else's expression in a footnote (75). Her suggestion that the "romances" of the Grail are the last repository of an old religion that refused absolutely to die out is most interesting. Denials—as by the introducer of the most recent edition (1993; xix–xxxv)—seem to be motivated less by any new knowledge than by an unease at supposing that these great European stories might rest on a search for the female genital organs. Yet—is that not pretty well understood already by Rabelais, in his version of the Quest in Books III–V of *Pantagruel*? Weston might have made her argument stronger had she been less hindered by politeness; the Sangraal is the Sang-grail, the blood cup, the everbleeding and inexhaustible container of life.

I would not deny some parallel between Weston's study and my own, but her definition of "romance" is quite narrow, and she is not interested in literature outside the Grail stories.

5. When referring to non-Western works, however, I have tried to go over the passages quoted or alluded to with readers conversant with the original-language versions. I am extremely indebted to Yu-Fang Han for her assistance with the Chinese novels, not only in translation but in explanation of cultural background.

Chapter XIV

1. John Bender in *Imagining the Penitentiary: Fiction and the Architecture of Mind in Eighteenth-Century England* (1987) has made a point of "liminal" rites of passage as characteristic features of English eighteenth-century culture and novel. John Bender is indebted, as I must also be, to the attention paid by anthropologists of the twentieth century to the role of the "liminal" in what have come to be called, in Arnold van Gennep's phrase, "rites of passage." The "liminal" marks the ritual necessity for the initiate to enter momentarily a state of being distinct and separate from other categories, and distinguished by its transience, as a frontier zone between one state and another. That such zones can be unpleasant is illustrated in Bender's discussion of Newgate prison; entry into prison is an initiation, being on Death Row a liminal state.

Victor Turner's terms, the basis for all such recent studies, are found in "Betwixt and Between: The Liminal Period in *Rites de Passage*" (1964), reprinted in *The Forest of Symbols: Aspects of Ndembu Ritual* (1967), Chapter IV, 93–111. Turner himself was commenting on van Gennep's *Les Rites de Passage* (1909). Anthropological and sociological studies have had their effect upon classical studies, as one sees in Ken Dowden's *Death and the Maiden: Girls' Initiation Rites in Greek Mythology* (1989).

2. When Lichas' corpse is carried by a gentle eddy and cast up on the strand, Encolpius reacts appropriately: he cries, beats his breast, and utters a valedictory speech. But his speech, though it follows the formulae of mourning addresses, is a comic apostrophe, as Encolpius cannot help remembering all Lichas' unpleasant qualities, particularly the disagreeably macho qualities (*vires*), which have led to this pass. The other characters—including even lascivious Tryphaena—are all saved; for them this beach is quite agreeable.

3. The body is often treated as a despicably dirty production, especially (as far as the West is concerned) in Stoic and Gnostic thought. Origen, strong defender of the Incarna-

tion, quotes his opponent Celsus as sneering at the very idea of God uniting with a human body: "Then was the mother of Jesus beautiful? And because she was beautiful did God have sexual intercourse with her, although by nature he cannot love a corruptible body?" (*Contra Celsum*, Book I, Sec. 39, 37). Celsus denies that God needed the womb of a woman: "He could have formed a body for this man [Jesus] without having to thrust his own spirit [*pneuma*] into such foul pollution [*miasma*]" (Book VI, Sec. 73, 386).

The body itself is evidently always on the "feminine" or dirty side of things, and the female generative parts are the dirtiest of the dirty. Origen's reply here is somewhat weak; it is absurd, he argues, to think the rays of the sun are defiled by shining on dung heaps. Passages and images like these (if not Origen's own statements) seem to have been on Joyce's mind.

Chapter XV

1. Merkelbach first comments on the "Fischer" motif in relation to the Sicilian fisherman who befriends Habrokomes. "Schließlich scheint auch die Gestalt des 'Fischers' einen mystischen Sinn zu haben: Wie der Fischer den Fisch aus dem Meer zieht, so der geistliche Vater bei der Weihe seinen 'Sohn' aus dem Taufwasser . . ." ("Finally, the image of the 'Fisherman' seems also to have a mystic sense: As the Fisherman pulls the Fish from the sea, so the spiritual Father by consecration draws his 'Son' from the baptismal water . . .") (*Roman und Mysterium*, 108). By "baptismal water" (*Taufwasser*) Merkelbach does not mean Christian baptismal water, though that can be included, and the Christian tradition, especially through Peter and his successors, enshrines the notion of the rescuing fisherman, spiritual fisher of men. The idea, however, does not in Merkelbach's view originate with Christians.

2. Much of Louisa May Alcott's writing consisted in the sort of Gothic fiction, "thrillers" and "shockers," that she has Jo repudiate; see Madeleine Stern, *The Hidden Louisa May Alcott*, Introductions to Volumes I (ix–xxxv) and II (281–299). The inclusion of Jo's play and its setting in *Little Women* may be considered as a case of ironic *mise-en-abîme*.

3. Castleden interprets the Minotaur legend as an aspect of religious history. The story of Pasiphaë and the Minotaur is about "collective personalities, each one a personification of a powerful, large-scale cultural force at work in the Aegean world in the second millennium B.C. Daidalos, for example . . . represents the Cretan genius for all kinds of crafts . . . King Minos is the secular and commercial power of Crete." Pasiphaë, then, represents "the love of nature and strength and the intense sexuality of the Minoans," whereas the Minotaur is "the embodiment of the terrifying, sacrifice-demanding, tribute-consuming deities of the Minoan pantheon." Theseus enters the picture as "the vigorous young mainland culture whose destiny it is to pluck away the heart of the Minoan culture and leave the rest to perish . . ." (*The Knossos Labyrinth*, 175). Such an allegory removes the antifeminist theme so noticeable in most retellings of the legend. But perhaps there was another version of the Minotaur and Pasiphae altogether, before the Theseus plot developments were added; it is possible to imagine a version of Woman's union with Earth that does not treat the sacred Woman as merely driven by demented lust. Why may not the Minotaur have been an earthen Poseidon, a god of earth and earthquakes that only the woman-goddess could master and appease?

4. These passages are taken from an edition of Balzac's novel based on the first edition of 1831. Pierre Barbéris, editor of the present text, argues that the mature Balzac, revising and trying to integrate this early novel with his Comédie Humaine, systematized the novel too much, and "radically transformed" it (ii). Richardson, Balzac, and Henry James are the most glaring instances of major novelists revising their own earlier works. Currently we tend to suspect such authorial work as meddling. No writer can entirely agree that a living writer has *no* right to edit and reissue his or her own work—yet I, too, share the general prejudice in favor of the author's first production of a work, unless circumstance argues against accepting this simple solution—as in the case of Richardson's *Clarissa* or Lawrence's *Lady Chatterley's Lover*.

Chapter XVI

1. Interestingly, the idea of getting above a maze or labyrinth, as Eros does in this illustration, is reflected in D'Alembert's *Discours préliminaire* to the *Enclyclopédie* (1751). According to D'Alembert, it is the enlightened man who must desire to get above the labyrinth—desire here taking an intellectual turn.

2. Goethe said it was a book "in comparison with which the good Virgil truly falls back a little" (*wogegen der gute Virgil freilich ein wenig zurücktritt*, Eckermann, *Gespräche mit Goethe*, 409). He praised *Daphnis and Chloé* in conversations of the spring of 1831, when he apparently encountered a new translation, but his knowledge of the book is so detailed, his comparisons of Courier's version with Amyot's so confident, that we may take it that Goethe had long been familiar with Longus' novel. Goethe valued in *Daphnis and Chloé* the landscape depicted in the manner of Poussin (*im Poussinischen Stil*, Eckermann, 409), and the creation of an independent and believable world (*eine vollständige Welt*, Eckermann, 417) including various professions and ages, as well as the delicate combination of plot-events with motives and feelings. He told Eckermann, "One would have to write a whole book in order to appreciate all the great merits of this poem [*dieses Gedichts*]. One should indeed read it over again every year, in order to learn from it over again, and to experience afresh the impression of its great beauty" (Eckermann, 418).

3. Augustine, who went to school in Apuleius' own city, Madaura, makes a rather puzzling reference to *The Golden Ass* in *De Civitate Dei* (*The City of God*), in a section where he is arguing against pagan gods and pagan beliefs in metamorphoses. He writes as if Apuleius really claimed in *Asinus Aureus* to have experienced what his hero experiences—and then adds that this may be taken as fact or fiction. As odd as the fact that Augustine cannot *quite* dismiss the possibility of metamorphosis is his determination to lump Lucius and Apuleius together as one entity—the "I" narration has certainly impressed one who was no mean artist in "I narration" himself. See *De Civitate Dei*, Book XVIII, Chap. 18; see also Winkler, *Auctor & Actor*, 293–294, where Augustine's remark is used as evidence that tradition supports the title *The Golden Ass*.

4. See D. A. Miller, *The Novel and the Police* (1988). Miller evidently regards the Novel—especially the nineteenth-century novel—as officiously busy in normalizing heterosexual desire, as well as directing heterosexual inclinations into approved institutions. The Novel thus engages in various policing activities, conducting us to morally and socially approvable objectives. Hence, in Miller's view, we have the rise of the policeman in novels such as *Bleak House* and *The Moonstone*.

In my terms, Miller is recording some of the efforts made by the Novel under Prescriptive Realism to remain on good terms with the civic ideal while covertly exploring the civic ideal itself. Policemen in detective fiction of the era of High Realism are notoriously somewhat dim-witted. Dickens's Bucket is by no means brilliant, and he is, as his name implies, a *receptacle* of cultural beliefs and commands. Classic detective fiction gives us Doyle's Gregson and Lestrade of Scotland Yard, "quick and energetic, but conventional—shockingly so" as Sherlock says (*A Study in Scarlet*, 21); Christie's Inspector Japp is the same bustling but slow-minded type. A *private* detective can operate within both public and private spheres and is not ultimately fully answerable to the *civitas* or to the civic idea.

5. Within his novel, Lewis introduces another reference to Cupid—in the poem written by the beautiful boy Theodore. In Theodore's Anacreontic verses, Cupid arrives and persuades the aged Anacreon that he is not too old for poetry or for love: "Again beloved, esteemed, carest, / Cupid shall in thine arms be prest" (197). A pattern established within *The Monk* indicates that good Eros is associated with Greek literature and with homosexuality, and bad Eros with Northern literature, particularly the German ballads of heterosexual love that end in death, like the ballad of Lenore.

6. Anthony C. Yu discusses the background of Monkey in the Introduction to his edition and translation of *Hsi-yu Chi* as *The Journey to the West* (Chicago, 1977). Yu draws on the work of Glen Dudbridge concerning the "white ape" figure in earlier Chinese litera-

ture. As Yu paraphrases Dudbridge, "the essential role of the white ape emerging from the tales . . . is one of abductor and seducer of women," and Dudbridge is quoted as concluding "the white ape is from first to last a monstrous creature which has to be eliminated" (*Journey to the West*, I:9). But could it not be that the "white ape" represents the virile member?—and thus it must certainly *not* be "eliminated" but should be brought into harmony with other elements and qualities, as, in Longus, Pan (the virile member) must be brought into harmony with the Nymphs and Eros. Although the Monkey of the *Hsi-yu Chi* is not lustful, he preserves the erotic qualities of mischievousness, curiosity, and quickness of action. Such erotic qualities are put into the service of religious aspiration, but they are not eradicated.

Chapter XVII

1. Lacanian thought about self-representation has affected many important works such as Stephen Greenblatt's *Renaissance Self-Fashioning* (1980). The emphasis on the element of the "spectacular" forces our attention upon the element of the representational and theatrical in common life; as Barbara Freedman points out, summarizing Lacan, "The French rereading of Freud reminds us that the ego is a delusory centric point, always already in representation" (*Staging the Gaze: Postmodernism, Psychoanalysis, and Shakespearean Comedy*, 30). Recent work by Teresa de Lauretis and Laura Mulvey has dealt with spectatorship and gazing in film; see particularly Mulvey's original essay, "Visual Pleasure and Narrative Cinema," *Screen* 16 (1975), reprinted in *Narrative, Apparatus, Ideology*, ed. Rosen, 198–209.

2. Corinne Jouanno, in her paper "L'Univers des déscriptions romanesques Byzantines, ou le Règne du Faux-semblant," at the International Conference on the Ancient Novel at Dartmouth in 1989, has developed the characteristic qualities of *ekphrasies* in the Byzantine novel. This kind of novel deals with the frontiers of nature and art: *les frontières se brouillent souvent entre les deux domaines* (Abstract, in *The Ancient Novel: Classical Paradigms and Modern Perspectives*, ed. Tatum and Vernazza, 119). Jouanno points out the frequent use of natural and metallic materials in a blend or mixture, as well as the motif of the looking glass. Effects such as those she describes can be found plentifully in Spenser, for instance, and one sees that descriptions like those of Acrasia's bower (with its metallic grapes) or the house of Busyrane are really "Byzantine"—but for Spenser, as *not* for the Byzantine novelists, such play with imitation and the spectacular is always to be denounced. The reader may enjoy such effects, but must be prepared also to enjoy virtuously casting them from him—as Guyon tramples upon and destroys Acrasia's bower in one of the more disturbing sections of *The Faerie Queene* (Book II, Canto XII, stanzas 81–87).

3. See Terry Castle, *Masquerade and Civilization: The Carnivalesque in Eighteenth-Century English Culture and Fiction* (1986). Castle's excellent study is based chiefly on the Bakhtinian idea of the "carnivalesque," but the masquerade lends itself equally well to a Lacanian interpretation; characters construct themselves by being seen, as by seeing. None of these theoretical approaches seems, however, quite to capture the sense of boundless possibility, the potential for multiple personalities within one individual, that such exercises as the masquerade suggest. It is as if people in the seventeenth and eighteenth centuries (when the appeal of the masquerade registered in a number of social classes) had participated in an experiment permitting play with identity, and exploring the possibility of a richer psychology. Recent social and psychological theories ignore, on the whole, the more positive suggestions of this experiment.

4. See Paul Willemen, "Voyeurism, the Look and Dwoskin" in *Narrative, Appearance, Ideology*, as well as Laura Mulvey's essay. Barbara Freedman elaborates on Mulvey and Willemen in *Staging the Gaze*. Self-consciousness is currently considered not only inevitable but desirable in all forms of art, not only in film or theater, which Freedman believes always "displays a fractured gaze, or *shows that it knows that it is showing*" (69). Post-Modern criticism values a similarly "fractured" narrative. Critics have become cool to the notion so important to the Jamesian Modernists, that narrative has a duty to "show" instead of

"tell." Both *telling* and *showing* are artificial, but "telling" has the advantage of registering its own artificial self-consciousness. Formerly popular devices of storytelling, such as addresses to the reader, once thought the clichés of mere narrative inadequacy, have all returned.

Chapter XVIII

1. See my article, "Deserts, Ruins and Troubled Waters: Female Dreams in Fiction and the Development of the Gothic Novel," *Genre* 10 (1977):529–572.

2. Roland Barthes' essay "Cuisine ornamentale" is included in his *Mythologies*, from which it is quoted here. Barthes calls *Elle* a *précieux* journal (carrying on the history of the war against the *précieuses* as Boileau interpreted it); he wants to see in this cuisine of sleek sediments and refinements a false style of ornamentation proceeding from bourgeois taste: "It's the same movement that one finds elsewhere in the elaboration of petty-bourgeois trinkets (ashtrays in the form of saddles, lighters in the form of cigarettes, earthenware cooking pots in the form of hares)". Barthes errs, however, if he believes that making objects look like something else is a product only of the petty-bourgeoisie in a late capitalist culture. Cooking pots in the shape of hens, rabbits, etc., have come down to us from the time of the Greeks, and earlier. The art of recalling another object through a common object is both widespread and ancient, and was certainly not initiated by a women's magazine.

Chapter XIX

1. The initiates were prohibited from describing the central acts of the mysteries, which explains why they remain so puzzling. The official written culture tends to bypass the Mysteries. Aeschylus was tried for having revealed the secret in one of his plays (possibly his *Oedipus*) but, as he could prove he had not been initiated, he was not found guilty (Kerényi, *Eleusis*, 99). Breezes from Eleusis blow to us from Sophocles' *Oedipus at Colonus*, and from the Platonic dialogues, especially the *Phaedrus*, where Socrates borrows the terms of Eleusinian initiation to describe the beatific vision of the soul in the upper world (cap. 250, *Phaedrus*, 68). The *Hymn to Demeter*, formerly attributed to Homer (not recovered until the eighteenth century), is the work of a poet probably of the late seventh century B.C., to whom the established Mysteries are very well known. Evidently an initiate, he concludes his poem with a prayer to the deity who is its addressee, in which he asks the goddesses *bioton thymēre opazein*: "to grant a living that warms the heart" or "to grant spiritually a life" (line 494; see N. J. Richardson, *The Homeric Hymn to Demeter*, 135). As her poet, he may ask Demeter for worldly assistance, but as her initiate also he can remind her of the promise of fullness of life after death.

2. For the *kykeōn* see Karl Kerényi's Appendix I, "The Preparation and Effect of the *Kykeon*," in his book *Eleusis: Archetypal Image of Mother and Daughter* (1991), trans. Ralph A. Manheim (177–180). (This book first appeared in Dutch as *Elusis: de heiligste mysteriën van Griekenland* [1960], and in German as *Die Mysterien von Eleusis* [1962].) The *Hymn to Demeter* says Demeter asked for barley mixed with water, with some pennyroyal (lines 208–209, in Richardson, ed., *The Homeric Hymn to Demeter*, 112). Kerényi suggests "Roasted barley in water produces malt and a drink which may . . . become alcoholic after short fermentation" (*Eleusis*, 178). He offers, further, the idea that herbs could have enhanced the mood-altering nature of the beverage drunk by the *mystai*. Demeter would thus be the symbolic founder and inventor of ale or beer, in contrast to the wine of Hades. Helene P. Foley, in the notes to her edition and translation, takes issue with Kerényi's view, suggesting instead that the "mild and medicinal" drink is connected with the feminine treatment of feminine processes, and is appropriate to the new profession of Demeter as Nurse to Metaneiré's child (Foley, *The Homeric Hymn to Demeter: Translation, Commentary, and Interpretive Essays*,

47). Richardson in his edition has extensive commentary on the Eleusinian rituals (12–30), as does Foley (84–97).

The use of the *koliva* in modern Greek Orthodox memorial services supports Foley against Kerényi. I am indebted for my knowledge of this dish to Angela Saylor; the recipe for an American version may be found in Sophia Clikas, *A Southern Lady Cooks with a Greek Accent*, 189–190. It is now cooked into a fairly solid pudding and served as a mound decorated with the six "ruby red pomegranate seeds"—an interesting contact with Persephone. The use of wheat is justified with a reference to John 12:24.

3. One of the chief sources of information of the vision of Eleusis is an antagonistic Christian account by one Hippolytos, who makes fun of the vision of the ear of grain as "the great, admired, and most perfect epoptic Mysterion at Eleusis." But the connection of the grain of wheat and the hope of life after death can be found in the Gospel of John 12:24. (See *Eleusis*, 106.)

4. See D. A. Miller's *Narrative and Its Discontents: Problems of Closure in the Traditional Novel* (1981). Miller's "narratable" covers "the instances of disequilibrium, suspense, and general insufficiency from which a given narrative appears to arise" (ix). This term is in contrast to "closure," which supposes (in Miller's view) some kind of recovered stasis at the end of a novel. He sees in narratives a "radical incompatibility between desire (desire for narrative) and the law (law of closure)"; this incompatibility "determines the narrative structure" of different novels (272). Miller's "narrative" coincides in many respects with Victor Turner's "liminal state"; we prefer to participate in the activity "betwixt and between" supposedly stable states.

5. Chion thinks he will be honored by the Athenians "if by that death I purchase their freedom for them" (*ei tōi idiōi thanatōi tēn eleutherian autois ōnēsometha*, 78). Chion's language is very like that of Christian theology: he is to ransom, to redeem (*ōneomai*) lost freedom through his own death. It is thought that the novel was written by a Neoplatonist under some Stoic influences, probably in the first century A.D. (see Düring's preface, 20). The editor suggests that *Chion* might have been one of the "pamphlets" circulated "in the political struggle under Domitian," but rejects this hypothesis for lack of further evidence (25). When the author, however, has Chion refer to "tyrants" and "tyranny" he probably expects his readership to fill in these words with a modern instance. The epistolary story can, however, be regarded as only a historical novella about the assassination of Clearchus in 352 B.C.

6. The recovery of the "Homeric" *Hymn to Aphrodite* and other discoveries in the Renaissance increased the visibility and acceptability of goddess-reference in art and in fiction. Such reference is by no means lacking in medieval literature, in Chaucer's "Knight's Tale," for example. The effloresence of images of Venus, etc. in the Renaissance was a result of a very conscious effort to recover and amplify valuable symbols. Such a "revival" may seem artificial, but what we call "revival" is a constant human mode of recapturing what we feel we need at any given moment. Botticelli's painting of Venus arriving on her shell is part of "the history of Venus" or of Venus-consciousness. Painters and sculptors rarely explain openly that Venus' shell is the representation of the female genitals, but I have seen at least one Late Antique statue (in Asia Minor) that makes the matter perfectly clear.

7. The best succinct explanation of the matter may be found in Winkler's *Constraints of Desire*, in an essay entitled "The Laughter of the Oppressed" in the subsection "The Gardens of Adonis" (189–193). English readers have generally been somewhat misled by Spenser, who in *The Fairie Queene* presents the "Garden of Adonis" (in Canto VI of Book III) as the eternal locus of the great work of generation of all forms in matter. But the original "Gardens of Adonis" had a different function. During the celebration of the Adonia in July, the women made little gardens in terracotta pots, of quick-springing green herbs like fennel and lettuce. These herbs, left in the sun and air, would quickly wither and were cast away in a common grave. "Gardens of Adonis—applies to things untimely and not rooted" (Diogenianos, quoted by Winkler, 192). Rather than being the permanent garden of con-

stant generation, these little "Gardens of Adonis" are gardens of death, memorials of decay—which is what Mr. Venus's shop is.

8. In Aeschylus' version of the story of Orestes, his sister Iphigenia was actually killed, sacrificed to Artemis by her father Agamemnon to bring about a favorable change in the wind. Euripides, in *Iphigenia in Tauris*, picks up another version of the story, according to which Artemis rescued the girl at the point of sacrifice and carried her off to be her priestess in the Crimea, where she was required to sacrifice other victims. Iphegenia then saves her brother and his friend, who are ordered to be sacrificed. Iphigenia is thus victim, killer, and rescuer. It would make sense if Amis emphasized both Artemis and the girl as dangerous to men, but he does not; the emphasis seems to be rather on the release found in serving Artemis from bondage to sex.

In Sara Paretsky's detective series the heroine, V. I. Warshawski, is really named "Victoria Iphigenia." She is thus an expression of Nike and of Iphigenia, always in danger of being sacrificed, but herself a deliverer.

9. L. M. Montgomery had not planned this name for the best friend when she started writing; the manuscript shows she wrote first "Laura" and then "Gertrude" before she hit on "Diana."

10. For Kristeva, the image of the Divine Female, the Divine Mother, is (not so simply) another means of endorsing narcissism while answering "the requirements of a new society based on exchange and . . . increased production, which require the contribution of the superego and rely on the symbolic paternal agency" (*Tales of Love*, trans. Roudiez, 259). The symbolic paternal agency is itself failing to produce. We would re-create a faith in Mum, having lost confidence in dear old Dad. For Kristeva, as for an old-time Puritan (though for somewhat different reasons), all activities and expressions of human love are deeply contaminated, expressions of paranoia, narcissism, and psychosis. Her response at the end of *Histoires d'amour* is the Post-Modernist one: we must get rid of all stable structures, seeing them as imaginary, countering their pseudo-unity with a number of wittingly imaginary constructions. Like any good Romantic, Kristeva has a powerful faith in *imagination*; she may not quite realize how powerful a faith she has in what could be called the creative power of the individual soul. But whence? But why?

11. A number of persons living on this planet at the present time pay heed to the Divine Lady, and within the Christian world there has been a resurgence of interest in the Virgin Mary. Many Americans were startled in 1992 by news of apparitions of Mary in the United States—a country which likes to regard itself as rationalist-Protestant. People of many nationalities have taken an interest in Mary's appearances to school children, reported in Medjugorje (in what was Yugoslavia), beginning in June 1981. A book by two Roman Catholic apologists gives an account of what the children have said, which includes statements about what she looked like. There seems to be a consensus that she wore a gray robe, white veil, and a crown of stars; some of her characteristics or symbols are not very distant from those reported of the appearance of Isis in Apuleius' story. She is not, however, gigantic, and has curly black hair and blue eyes. The association with the stars reminds us that Mary is Queen of Heaven. It is a mistake to associate the manifestations of the divine Female with *earth* only—she is Queen of Air and Heaven too (see René Laurentin and Ljudevit Rupčič, *Is the Virgin Mary Appearing at Medjugorje?* trans. Francis Martin, 44–46).

12. Gaselee, annotating Achilles Tatius, notes, "Some have supposed that the large number of seeds in a pomegranate typify the fertility and productivity of nature" (146–147). Shadi Bartsch notices that St. John Chrysostom stressed the deceptiveness of the pomegranate rind. She points out that the pomegranate viewed by Kleitophon connects with the false belly, the device by which Leukippé will escape death (*Decoding the Ancient Novel*, 60–61). But the false belly of Leukippé parodies her real second belly, her uterus. Artemidorus in his dream-interpretation identifies pomegranates as emblems of wounds and as prognostics of suffering because of their spines, and, he adds, "because of the story of Eleusis, they are signs of slavery and submission" (*La Clef des songes*, 78). Christian reli-

gious iconography connects the pomegranate with Mary, with femininity, and with the Church because of the perpetual increase of the faithful.

Chapter XX

1. As noted earlier, J. Paul Hunter in *Before Novels* expresses a sense that getting rid of the categories "Novel" and "Romance" would be "dangerous." He expresses a fear of a "new literary history built *thoughtlessly* on the *rubble* of the old" (4; my italics). A change in the categories would be a kind of bomb, reducing structures to leveled rubble and encouraging the mushrooming of jerry-built hutments. The attack on my lecture at Berkeley in February 1992 is contained in an article by Victoria Nelson, "The Hermeticon of Umbertus E," *Raritan* 12 (Summer 1993), 87–101.

When I gave a talk on the early novels and their influence on eighteenth-century literature at a meeting of the American Society for Eighteenth Century Studies in Providence, R.I., in April 1993, I was asked during the question period "why I wanted to bash everything down to one level?" I had not hitherto thought of my thesis in that way, but I could see that, to anyone used to the Rise of the Novel as a story of hierarchy and of spatial erection, my narrative could seem like a loss of attributed eminence. I tried to reply that my own spatial metaphor was different—I saw it in terms of leaping over a paddock fence and escaping into a larger space.

2. I am grateful to Elizabeth Wichmann for allowing me to read her translation of *Yu Tangchun*; this version (in English, with Chinese songs) was staged in Honolulu in 1990. *Yu Tangchun* (*The Jade Hall of Spring*) was composed as an opera in the nineteenth century, but the story is old. "One of the first printed versions was the tale 'Su San Meets with Misfortune and Finds Her Husband' ('Su San Iuo non feng fu'), published in 1624 in Feng Mengdong's *Words of Warning to Society* (*Jing shi tongyan*), a collection of cautionary and didactic stories from the tenth through the seventeeth centuries" (Wichmann, program note, 1990).

I also want to thank Roger Long for information about Javanese dramatic tradition.

BIBLIOGRAPHY

>─+●>─O─<●+─<

The first section (I A) of this Bibliography gives the base text for ancient novels that are frequently quoted in this work, in my own translation (unless otherwise noted) from original-language versions. Many of these base texts exist in a modern dual-language version, with some modern titles, but I employ throughout a standardized English version of the title of each ancient novel, although various editions provide their own. Other versions and translations of these ancient novels that may be quoted but do not function as base text are cited in the following section (I B), in chronological order from the fifteenth to the twentieth century.

In treating modern works from the Renaissance on, I have kept a distinction between nonfiction discourse and fiction. Works by the same author are cited in alphabetical order. In the text, the date given after the first citation of a title is the first date of publication; the Bibliography gives dates of texts used for quotations within this study.

I. THE ANCIENT NOVEL AND THE ANCIENT WORLD

I A. Ancient Novels: Original-language Versions (Including Dual-language) Sources of Original-language Quotations

Achilles Tatius. *Kleitophon and Leukippé* as *Achilles Tatius*. Edited with translation by S. Gaselee. London: William Heinemann, 1917.

Antonius Diogenes. *Apista hyper Thulēn* (*Wonders beyond Thule*). In Photius, *Bibliothēkē*, as *Bibliothèque*. Edited by René Henry. 11 vols. Paris: Belles Lettres, 1960. Vol. II, 140–149.

Apuleius. *Metamorphoses* (also known as *The Golden Ass*). Edited with translation by J. Arthur Hanson. 2 vols. Cambridge, Mass.: Harvard University Press, 1989.

Chariton. *Chairéas and Kallirrhoé*, as *Le Roman de Chairéas et Callirhoe*. Edited by Georges Molinié and Alain Billault. Paris: Belles Lettres, 1989 [first printed 1979].

Chion of Heraklea, as *Chion of Heraclea*. Edited with translation by Ingemar Düring. Gothenburg: Wettergren and Kerbers, 1951.

"Clemens" ["Pseudo-Clemens"]. *S. Clementis Romani Recognitiones*. Edited by E. G. Gersdorf. Leipzig: Tauchnitz, 1838.

"Dictys Cretensis." *Dictys Cretensis Ephemeridos Belli Troiani libri sex*. Edited by Ferdinand Meister. Leipzig: Teubner, 1958.

Heliodorus. *Aithiopika*, as *Les Ethiopiques* (*Theagène et Chariclée*). Edited by R. M. Rattenbury, T. W. Lumb, and J. Maillon. 3 vols. Second edition. Paris: Belles Lettres, 1960.

Historia Apolonii Regis Tyri. Edited by David Konstan and Michael Roberts. Bryn Mawr: Bryn Mawr College, 1985.

Iamblichus. *Babyloniaka*, summary in Photius, *Bibliothēkē*, as *Bibliothèque*. Edited by René Henry. 11 vols. Paris: Belles Lettres, 1960. Vol. II, 34–48.

Joseph and Aseneth (*Exomolgēsis kai Proseuchē Aseneth Thugatros Pentephrē Iereōs*), as *Joseph et Aséneth*. Edited and translated by Marc Philonenko. Leiden: E. J. Brill: 1968.

Lollianus. *Phoinikika*, as *Die Phoinikika des Lollianos*. Edited by Albert Henrichs. Bonn: Rudolf Habelt, 1972.

Longus. *Daphnis and Chloe*, as *Daphnis and Chloé*. Translated by George Thornley, edited and revised by J. M. Edmonds. Cambridge, Mass.: Harvard University Press, 1978 [first printed 1916].

Lucian. *Vera Historia*. In *Lucian*. Translated by A. M. Harmon. 8 vols. London: William Heinemann Ltd., 1961. Vol. 1, 297–358.

Ninus and Semiramis, as "The Ninus Romance." Edited and Translated by S. Gaselee. In *Daphnis and Chloé and Parthenius*, edited by J. M. Edmons and S. Gaselee. London: William Heinemann Ltd., 1978 [rpt. of Loeb, 1916].

Metiochos and Parthenope. In H. Maehler, "Der Metiochos-Parthenope-Roman." *Zeitschrift für Papyrologie und Epgraphik* 23 (1976):1–20.

Paul and Thekla. In *Les Actes de Paul*. Edited and translated by Léon Vouaux. Paris: Librairie Letouzey et Ané, 1913.

Petronius (Petronius Arbiter). *Satyricon*, as *Petronius*. Edited and revised by R. H. Warmington. Translated by Michael Heseltine. London: William Heinemann, 1975.

Xenophon. *Cyropaedia*. Edited and translated by Walter Miller. 2 vols. London: William Heinemann, 1983.

"Xenophon of Ephesus." *Ephesiaka*, as *Les Ephésiaques, ou Le Roman d'Habrocomès et d'Anthia*. Edited by Georges Dalmeyda. Second edition. Paris: Belles Lettres, 1962.

I B. Other Printings and Translations of Ancient Novels Cited in Text, Fifteenth–Twentieth Centuries, Chronologically under Author

Achilles Tatius

Achilles Statii Alexandrini de Clitophontis et Leucippes amoribus Libri VIII. Translated by L. Annibale Cruceius. Basel: Ioannes Heruagius, 1554.

Achille Tatio Alessandrino Dell'Amore Di Leucippe e Di Cliophonte, Novamente Tradotto dalle Linguae Greca. Translated by Francisco Angelo Coccio. Venice: Francesco Lorenzini da Turino, 1560.

Les Amovrs de Clytophon, et de Levcippe. Paris: Tovssainct Quinet, 1635.

The Loves of Clitophon and Leucippe. A Most Elegant History. . . Translated by Anthony Hodges. Oxford: William Turner for John Allam, 1638.

Erōtikōn Achilleōs Tatiou Sive de Clitophontis et Levcippes Amoribus. Edited by Claude Salmasius. Leiden: Franciscus Hegerus, 1640.

The Amours of Clitophon and Leucippe. Illustrated, in Six Novels. London: T. Bickerton, 1720.

"Leucippe and Clitophon." Translated by John J. Winkler. *CAGN*, 170–284.

Alexander

The Greek Alexander Romance. Translated by Richard Stoneman. London: Penguin Books, 1991.

Apuleius

Opera. Edited by Ioannes Andrae. Rome: Conradus Sweynheym and Arnoldus Pannartz, 1469.

L. Apuleii Madaurensis Enchiridio. Edited and in part translated by Marsilio Ficino, with a Dedication by Marianus Tuccius. Florence: Philippe de Giunta, 1512.

Apuleius cum commento Beroaldi. Figuris noviter additis [With illustrations newly added]. Venice: I. Tacuinus de Tridino, 1516.

Lucius Apulei de Lasne dore autrement dit de la Couronne Ceres, contenante maintes belles histoires, delectantes fables et subtilles inventions. . . . Translated by Guillaume Michel. Paris: Phillippe le noir, 1522.

Lucio Apuleyo del asno de oro corregido y anadido. En el qual se traitan muchos hystorias y fabulas alegres. Medina del Campo: Pedro de Castro for Juan de Espinosa, 1543.

Apuleio dell'Asino D'Oro. Translated by Agnolo Firenzuola. Venice: Gabriel Golito de Ferrari, 1550.

Les Metamorphoses, autrement L'Asne d'Or. Translated by George de la Bouthière Autunois. Lyon: I. de Tournes & Gazeau, 1553.

The eleven Bookes of the Golden Asse, Containing the metamorphosie of Lucius Apuleius, enterlaced with sundry pleasant and delectable tales. Translated by William Adlington. London: Valentine Symmes, 1586.

L. Apvleii Madavrensis Opera Omnia. Edited by Petrus Colvus. Leiden: Plantin, 1588.

Chariton

Charitōnos Aphrodisieōs tōn peri Chairean kai Kallirroēn Erōtikōn Diēgēmatōn Logio Ē. Edited with notes by Jacobus Philippus D'Orville. Amsterdam: Petrus Mortier, 1750.

Di Caritone Afrodisieo De'Racconti Amorosi Di Cherea e Di Callirroe Libri otto. Venice: Luigi Pavini, 1755.

Les Amours de Chereas et de Callirrhoé. Traduites du Grec de Chariton. Translation and commentary by Pierre-Henri Larcher. Paris: Guillaume, 1763.

The Loves of Chaereas and Callirrhoe. 2 vols. London: T. Becket and P. A. De Hondt, 1764.

"Chaereas and Callirrhoe." Translated B. P. Reardon. *CAGN,* 17–127.

"Dictys Cretensis"

De Bello Troiano. Leiden: Ioannes Marion, 1530.

Heliodorus

Heliodōrou Aithiopikēs Historias Biblia Deka. Heliodori Historiae Æthiopicae libri decem, nunquam antea in lucem editi. Edited by Vincentus Obsopoeus. Basel: ex officina Hervagiana, 1534.

L'Histoire Æthiopique de Heliodorus, Contenant dix Livres, Traitant des Loyales et Pudiques Amours de Theagenes Thessalien, et Chariclea Æthiopienne. Translated by Jacques Amyot. Paris: E. Groulleau, 1547.

Heliodori Æthiopicae libri decem, nunc primum e Graeco Sermone in Latinum translati. Translated by Stanislaus Warschewiczski. Basel: Johannes Oporinus, 1552.

Historia de Heliodoro delle Cose Ethiopiche. Translated by M. Leonardo Ghini. Venice: G. G. de Ferrari, 1560.

An Æthiopian Historie, written in Greek by Heliodorus: very wittie and pleasaunt. Translated by Thomas Underdowne. London: Henry Wykes for Fraunces Coldocke, 1569.

An Æthiopian Historie, written in Greeke by Heliodorus, no lesse wittie than pleasant . . . newly corrected and augmented with divers and sundrie new additions. Translated by Thomas Underdowne. London: Henry Middleton for Fraunces Coldocke, 1577.

Martinus Crvsii Æthiopicae Heliodori Historia Epitome. Epitome and commentary by Martinus Crusius. Frankfurt: Ioannes Wechelus, 1584.

Heliodori Æthiopicorum Libri X. Edited by Hieronymus Commelinus. Leiden: A. de Harsy, 1611.

Heliodōrou Aithiopikōn Biblia Deka. Heliodori Æthiopicorum Libri X. Edited with notes by Johannes Bourdelotius. Paris: P. L. Febvrier, 1619.

The Aethiopian History of Heliodorus. Translated by "a Person of Quality" and Nahum Tate. London: J. L. for E. Poole, 1686.

The Adventures of Theagenes and Chariclia. A Romance. 2 vols. London: W. Taylor, E. Curll, et al., 1717.

Aethiopian Adventures: Or, The History of Theagenes and Chariclea. London, 1753 [reissue of 1686 translation].

The Adventures of Theagenes and Chariclea. A Romance. 2 vols. London: George Stafford, sold by Thomas Payne and Son, 1789.

An Ethiopian Romance. Translated by Moses Hadas. Ann Arbor: University of Michigan Press, 1957.

"An Ethiopian Story." Translated by J. R. Morgan. *CAGN,* 349–588.

Historia Apollonii

———. *Kynge Appolyn of Thyre.* Translated by Robert Copelande. London: Wynkyn de Worde, 1510.

———. *The Patterne of painefull Aduentures: Containing the most excellent, pleasant and variable Historie of the strange accidents that befell vnto the Prince Apollonius, the Lady Lucina his wife, and Tharsia his daughter. Wherein the uncertaintie of this world, and the fickle state of mans life are liuely described.* Translated by Laurence Twine. London: Valentine Simmes for the Widow Newman, [1594].

———. *Narratio Eorum quae Contingervnt Apollonio Tyrio.* Augsburg: ad insigne pinus, 1595.

———. "The Story of Appollonius King of Tyre." Translated by Gerald N. Sandy. *CAGN*,
    736–772.

Iamblichus

"A Babylonian Story." Translated by Gerald N. Sandy. *CAGN*, 783–797.

Longus

Gli' Amori Innocenti di Dafni, e della Cloe. Favola Greca. . . . Edited and translated by Giovanni
    Battista Manzini. Bologna: Giacomo Mant, 1643.
Daphnis and Chloe. A Most Sweet, and Pleasant Pastorall Romance for Young Ladies. Translated
    by George Thornley. London: John Garfield, 1657.
Les Amours de Daphnis et de Chloe. Avec Figures par un Elève de Picart. Amsterdam: n.p., 1749
    [Probably printed in France, not "Amsterdam."]
Moore, George. *The Pastoral Loves of Daphnis and Chloe.* London: William Heinemann Ltd.,
    1927.

Lucian

———. *Vera Historia* in *Opera.* Translated into Latin by Lilius Castellanus. Venice: Simon
    Bevilaqua, 1494. (Copy illustrated by Benedetto Bordon for Mocenico family, Ös-
    terreichische Nationalbibliothek Inc. 4 G 27.)

Petronius

*Petronii Arbitri Massiliensis Satyrici Fragmenta Restituta et Aucta, ex Bibliotheca Johannis Sam-
    bucci.* Antwerp: Christopher Plantin, 1565.
Petronii Arbitri Satyricon. Paris: Mamertus Patissonius, King's Printer, 1587.
T. Petronii Arbitri Satyricon. Edited with commentary by Johannes Bourdelotius. Paris: Isaac
    Mesnier, 1618.
T. Petronii Arbitri Satyricon; cum fragmentis Albae Graecae recuperatis anno 1688. Cologne: Jo-
    seph Gooth, 1691. [The "fragments discovered at Belgrade" were the forgery of
    François Nodot.]
The Works of Titius Petronius Arbiter, In Prose and Verse. Made English by Mr. Wilson, Mr. Th.
    Brown . . . and several others. And adorned with Cuts. London: Sam. Briscoe,
    1708.

Xenophon of Ephesus

Degli Amori Di Abrocome e d'Anthia. "London": n.p., 1723. [Probably printed in Florence.]
Xenophon's Ephesian History: or the Love-Adventures of Abrocomas and Anthia. Third edition.
    London: J. Millan, 1727.

I C. Modern Studies of the Ancient Novel.

Anderson, Graham. *Eros Sophistes: Ancient Novelists at Play.* Chico: Scholars Press, 1982.
———. *Ancient Fiction: The Novel in the Graeco-Roman World.* London: Croom Helm, 1984.
Bartsch, Shadi. *Decoding the Ancient Novel: The Reader and the Role of Description in Heliodorus
    and Achilles Tatius.* Princeton: Princeton University Press, 1989.
Beaton, Roderick. "The Greek Novel in the Middle Ages." In *The Greek Novel AD 1–1985,*
    ed. Roderick Beaton. Beckenham, Kent: Croom Helm, 1988.
Egger, Brigitte. "Women and Marriage in the Greek Novels: The Boundaries of Romance."
    TSAN, 260–280.
Fusillo, Massimo. *Il Romanzo greco: Polifonia ed eros.* Venice: Marsilio, 1989.
Hägg, Tomas. *The Novel in Antiquity.* Oxford: Blackwell, 1983.
Halperin, David, et al., ed. *Before Sexuality.* Princeton: Princeton University Press, 1990.
Heiserman, Arthur. *The Novel before the Novel: Essays and Discussions about the Beginnings of
    Prose Fiction in the West.* Chicago: University of Chicago Press, 1977.
Jouanne, Corinne. "L'Univers des déscriptions romanesques Byzantines, ou le Règne de

Faux-Semblant." Typescript of paper given at International Conference on the Ancient Novel, Dartmouth College, Hanover, N.H., July 1989.

Kehayióglou, George. "Translations of Eastern 'Novels' and their Influence on Later Byzantine and Modern Greek Fiction." In *The Greek Novel AD 1–1985*, ed. Roderick Beaton. Beckenham, Kent: Croom Helm, 1988.

Kerényi, Karl. *Die Griechisch-Orientalische Romanliteratur in religionsgeschichtlicher Beleuchtung*. Darmstadt: Wissenschaftliche Buchgesellschaft, 1962 [reprint of Tübingen, 1927].

Konstan, David. "*Appollonius, King of Tyre* and the Greek Novel.' *TSAN*, 173–182.

———. *Sexual Symmetry: Love in the Ancient Novel and Related Genres*. Princeton: Princeton University Press, 1994.

Liviabella Furiani, Patrizia. "Di Donna in Donna: Elementi 'Feministi' nel Romanzo Greco d'Amore." In *Piccolo mondo antico*, ed. P. Liviabella Furiani and A. M. Scarcella. Perugia: Edizioni Scientifiche Italiane, 1989, 43–106.

Ludvíkovský, Jaroslav. *Řecký Román Dobrodružný (Le Roman grec d'aventures)* Prague: University of Prague, 1925).

Merkelbach, Reinhold. *Roman und Mysterium in der Antike*. Munich: Beck, 1962.

Montague, Holly W. "From Interlude in Arcady to Daphnis and Chloe: Two Thousand Years of Erotic Fantasy." *TSAN*, 391–401.

Montero, Consuelo Ruiz. "Caritón de Afrodisias y el Mundo Real." In *Piccolo mondo antico*, ed. P. Liviabella Furiani and A. M. Scarcella. Perugia: Edizioni Scientifiche Italiane, 1989, 107–149.

Morgan, J. R. "The Story of Knemon in Heliodoros' *Aithiopika*." *JHS* 19 (1989):99–113.

Neumann, Erich. *Amor and Psyche: The Psychic Development of the Feminine*. Translated by Ralph Manheim. New York: Pantheon, 1956.

Perry, Ben Edwin. *The Ancient Romances: A Literary-Historical Account of Their Origins*. Berkeley: University of California Press, 1967.

Reardon, B. P. *Courants littéraires grecs des IIe et IIIe siècles après J.-C.* Paris: Belles Lettres, 1971.

———. *The Form of Greek Romance*. Princeton: Princeton University Press, 1991.

———. "Theme, Structure, and Narrative in Chariton." *Yale Classical Studies* 27 (1982): 1–27.

———, ed. *Collected Ancient Greek Novels*. Berkeley: University of California Press, 1989.

Rohde, Erwin. *Der griechische Roman und seine Vorläufer*. Hildesheim and New York: Georg Olms Verlag, 1974 [reprint of 1914 edition].

Rollo, David. "From Apuleius's Psyche to Chrétien's Erec and Enide." *TSAN*, 347–369.

Romm, James. "Novels beyond Thule: Antonius Diogenes, Rabelais, Cervantes.' *TSAN*, 101–116.

Roueché, Charlotte. "Byzantine Writers and Readers: Storytelling in the Eleventh Century." In *The Greek Novel AD 1–1985*, ed. Roderick Beaton. Beckenham, Kent: Croom Helm, 1988.

Saïd, Suzanne. "The City in the Greek Novel." *TSAN*, 216–236

Segal, Erich. "Heavy Breathing in Arcadia." *The New York Times Book Review*, 29 September 1985, p. 1; pp. 48–49.

Snowden, Frank M. *Blacks in Antiquity: Ethiopians in the Greco-Roman Experience*. Cambridge, Mass.: Belknap Press, 1970.

Stephens, Susan A. "Who Read Ancient Novels?" *TSAN*, 405–418.

Tatum, James. *Apuleius and the Golden Ass*. Ithaca: Cornell University Press, 1979.

———. *Xenophon's Imperial Fiction: On the Education of Cyrus*. Princeton: Princeton University Press, 1989.

———, ed. *The Search for the Ancient Novel*. Baltimore: The Johns Hopkins University Press, 1993.

Tatum, James, and Gail M. Vernazza, eds. *The Ancient Novel: Classical Paradigms and Modern Perspectives. Proceedings of the Second International Conference on the Ancient Novel*. Hanover: Dartmouth College, 1990.

Trenkner, Sophie. *The Greek Novella in the Classical Period*. Cambridge: Cambridge University Press, 1958.

Walsh, P. G. *The Roman Novel: The Satyricon of Petronius and the Metamorphoses of Apuleius.* Cambridge: Cambridge University Press, 1970.

Winkler, John J. *Auctor and Actor: A Narratological Reading of Apuleius's "The Golden Ass."* Berkeley: University of California Press, 1985.

———. "The mendacity of Kalasiris and the narrative strategy of Heliodoros' *Aithiopika.*" *Yale Classical Studies* 27 (1982):93–158.

Zeitlin, Froma. "The Poetics of *Erōs*: Nature, Art, and Imitation in Longus' *Daphnis and Chloe.*" In *Before Sexuality,* ed. David Halperin, et al. Princeton: Princeton University Press, 1990, 417–464.

I D. Literary Works of Antiquity Excluding Novels.

Artemidorus of Daldis. *Oneirokritika,* in *La Clef des songes.* Edited and translated by A. J. Festugière. Paris: Librairie Philosophique, 1975.

"Cebes." *Cebes' Tablet.* Edited by Richard Parsons. Boston: Ginn and Co., 1889.

———. *Cebes in England: English Translations of Cebes from Three Centuries.* Edited by Stephen Orgel. New York: Garland, 1980.

Euripides. *Elektra.* In *Euripides.* Edited and translated by Arthur S. Way, 4 Vols. Cambridge, Mass.: Harvard University Press, 1978 [reprint of 1912], Vol. 2, 1–119.

Herodotus, *Histories.* Translated by A. D. Godley. 4 vols. London: William Heinemann, 1921.

Homer. *The Iliad.* Edited with a translation by A. T. Murray. 2 vols. London: William Heinemann, 1924.

———. *The Iliad.* Translated by Richmond Lattimore. Chicago: University of Chicago Press, 1962.

———. *The Odyssey.* Edited and translated by A. T. Murray. 2 vols. London: William Heinemann, 1984 [reprint of 1919].

———. *The Odyssey of Homer.* Translated by Richmond Lattimore. New York: Harper & Row, 1967.

Horace. *Satires, Epistles and Ars Poetica.* Edited and translated by H. R. Fairclough. Cambridge, Mass.: Harvard University Press, 1970 [first printed 1926].

Hymn to Demeter. Translated by N. J. Richardson. Oxford: Oxford University Press, 1974.

The Homeric Hymn to Demeter: Translation, Commentary, and Interpretative Esays. Translated and with commentary by Helen P. Foley. Princeton: Princeton University Press, 1993.

Juvenal. *Satires.* In *Juvenal and Persius.* Edited and translated by G. G. Ramsay. Cambridge, Mass.: Harvard University Press, 1979 [first printed 1918].

Ovid. *Metamorphoses.* Edited and Translated by Frank Justus Miller. 2 vols. Cambridge, Mass.: Harvard University Press, 1968 [first printed 1916].

Philostratus. *Philostratus, Imagines: Callistratus, Descriptiones.* Edited and translated by Arthur Fairbanks. London: William Heinemann, 1931.

———. *Philostrate: La Galerie de Tableaux.* Translated by Auguste Bougot and François Lissarrague, with Preface by Pierre Hadot. Paris: Les Belles Lettres, 1991.

Plato. *Phaedrus.* Edited and translated by C. J. Rowe. Warminster, England: Aris and Phillips, 1986.

———. *Symposium.* In *Plato.* Edited and translated by W.R.M. Lamb. Vol. 3. Cambridge, Mass.: Harvard University Press, 1975.

Plutarch. *Life of Alexander.* In *Plutarch's Lives.* Translated by Bernadotte Perrin. Vol. 8. London: William Heinemann; New York: G. P. Putnam's Sons, 1918.

———. Plutarch. *The Malice of Herodotus.* Edited and translated by Anthony Bowen. Warminster, England: Aris and Phillips, 1992.

Porphyry. *On the Cave of the Nymphs.* Translated with an Introduction by Robert Lamberton. Barrytown, New York: Station Hill Press, 1983.

Seneca. *Epistulae,* as *Lettres à Lucilius.* Edited by François Préchac and translated by Henri Noblot. 2 vols. Second edition. Paris: Belles Lettres, 1956.

Virgil. *P. Vergili Maronis Opera.* Edited by R.A.B. Mynors. Oxford: Clarendon Press, 1976.

I E. Early Christian Works.

Augustine of Hippo. *St. Augustine's Confessions*. Edited and translated by William Watts. 2 vols. London: William Heinemann, 1931 [first printed 1912].

———. *The City of God Against the Pagans (De Civitate Dei contra Paganos)*. Edited and translated by George E. McCracken. 7 vols. London: William Heinemann, 1966.

"Hermas." *Le Pasteur*. Edited and translated by Robert Joly. 2d edition. Paris: Les Editions du Cerf, 1968.

———. *The Shepherd of Hermas*. Translated by Charles H. Hoole. London: Rivingtons, 1870.

"James" (falsely attributed to Saint James). *Protevangelion*, as *Le Protévangile de Jacques et ses Remaniements Latins*. Edited and translated by Emile Amann. Paris: Letouzey et Ané, 1910.

James, M. R. *The Apocryphal New Testament*. Oxford: Clarendon Press, 1924.

Origen. *Origen: Contra Celsum*. Translated with an Introduction and Notes by Henry Chadwick. Cambridge: Cambridge University Press, 1953.

"Paul" (falsely attributed to Saint Paul). *Les Actes de Paul et Ses Lettres Apocryphes*. Edited and translated by Léon Vouaux. Paris: Librairie Letouzey et Ané, 1913.

I F. Modern Studies of the Ancient World.

Angus, S. *The Mystery-Religions: A Study in the Religious Background of Early Christianity*. New York: Dover, 1975 [reprint of 1925].

Bammer, Anton. *Das Heiligtum des Artemis von Ephesos*. Graz: Akademische-Druck-und-Verlagsanstalt, 1984.

Bernal, Martin. *Black Athena: The Afroasiatic Roots of Classical Civilization*. 2 vols. New Brunswick: Rutgers University Press, 1987; 1991.

Boswell, John. *The Kindness of Strangers: The Abandonment of Children in Western Europe from Late Antiquity to the Renaissance*. New York: Vintage Books, 1990.

Bowersock, G. W. *Greek Sophists in the Roman Empire*. Oxford: Clarendon Press, 1969.

———. *Hellenism in Late Antiquity*. Ann Arbor: University of Michigan Press, 1990.

———. *Julian the Apostate*. Cambridge, Mass.: Harvard University Press, 1978.

Bowie, Ewen. "The Readership of Greek Novels in the Ancient World." *TSAN*, 435–459.

Bradley, Keith R. *Discovering the Roman Family: Studies in Roman Social History*. Oxford: Oxford University Press, 1991.

Brown, Peter. *The Body and Society: Men, Women, and Sexual Renunciation in Early Christianity*. New York: Columbia University Press, 1991.

———. *The Making of Late Antiquity*. Cambridge, Mass.: Harvard University Press, 1978.

Burkert, Walter. *Ancient Mystery Cults*. Cambridge, Mass.: Harvard University Press, 1987.

———. *The Orientalizing Revolution: Near Eastern Influence on Greek Culture in the Early Archaic Age*. Translated by Margaret E. Pinder and Walter Burkert. Cambridge, Mass.: Harvard University Press, 1992.

Campese, Silvia, with Paola Manuli and Giulia Sissa. *Madre materia: Sociologia e biologia della donna Greca*. Turin: Boringhieri, 1983.

Canfora, Luciano. *The Vanished Library: A Wonder of the Ancient World*. Translated by Martin Ryle. London and Sydney: Hutchinson Radius, 1989 [first published as *Biblioteca scomparsa*, Palermo, 1987].

Casson, Lionel. *Travel in the Ancient World*. London: George Allen and Unwin, 1974.

Castleden, Rodney. *The Knossos Labyrinth: A New View of the Palace of Minos at Knossos*. London: Routledge, 1990.

Couliano, Ioan P. *The Tree of Gnosis: Gnostic Mythology from Early Christianity to Modern Nihilism*. Translated by Couliano and H. S. Weisner. New York: HarperCollins, 1991 [first published as *Les Gnoses dualistes d'Occident*].

Countryman, L. William. *Dirt, Greed, and Sex: Sexual Ethics in the New Testament and Their Implications for Today*. Philadelphia: Fortress Press, 1990.

Crook, A. J. "Women in Roman Succession." In *The Family in Ancient Rome*, ed. Beryl Rawson. Ithaca: Cornell University Press, 1986, 58–82.

Crouzel, Henri. *Origen.* Translated by A. S. Worrall. San Francisco: Harper & Row, 1989 [first published as *Origène,* Paris, 1985].

Dowden, Ken. *Death and the Maiden: Girls' Initiation Rites in Greek Mythology.* London and New York: Routledge, 1989.

Fox, Robin Lane. *Pagans and Christians.* London: Viking, 1986.

Goodison, Lucy. *Death, Women and the Sun: Symbolism of Regeneration in Early Aegean Religion.* London: University of London Institute of Classical Studies, 1989.

Gould, John. *Herodotus.* London: Weidenfeld and Nicolson, 1989.

Halperin, David M. "Why Is Diotima a Woman?" Platonic *Erōs* and the Figuration of Gender." In *Before Sexuality,* ed. David Halperin, et al. Princeton: Princeton University Press, 1990, 257–308.

Kerényi, Karl. *Eleusis: Archetypal Image of Mother and Daughter.* Translated by Ralph Manheim. Princeton: Princeton University Press, 1991.

King, Helen. "Bound to Bleed: Artemis and Greek Women." In *Images of Women in Antiquity,* ed. Averil Cameron and Amelie Kurt. Beckenham, England: Croom Helm, Ltd., 1987, 109–127.

Lacey, W. K. "Patria Potestas." In *The Family in Ancient Rome,* ed. Beryl Rawson. Ithaca: Cornell University Press, 1986, 121–144.

Lamberton, Robert. *Homer the Theologian: Neoplatonist Allegorical Reading and the Growth of the Epic Tradition.* Berkeley: University of California Press, 1986.

Lefkowitz, Mary R. *Women in Greek Myth.* London: Duckworth, 1986.

Liviabella Furiani, Patrizia, and A. M. Scarcella. *Piccolo mondo antico: Le donne, gli amori, i costumi, il mondo reale nel romanzo antico.* Università degli Studi di Perugia. Napoli: Edizioni Scientifiche Italiane, 1989.

Lubell, Winifred Milius. *The Metamorphosis of Baubo: Myths of Woman's Sexual Energy.* Nashville: Vanderbilt University Press, 1994.

MacDowell, Douglas M. *The Law in Classical Athens.* Ithaca: Cornell University Press, 1978.

Manuli, Paola. "Donne masculine, femmine sterili, vergini perpetua: La ginecologia greca tra Iippocrate e Sorano." In *Madre Materia: Sociologia e biologia della donna greca.* Turin: Boringhieri, 1983, 149–191.

Merkelbach, Reinhold. *Isisfeste in griechisch-römischer Zeit.* Meisenheim am Glan: Anton Hain, 1963.

Merkle, Stefan. "Telling the True Story of the Trojan War: The Eyewitness Account of Dictys of Crete." In *TSAN,* 183–196.

Montero, Consuelo Ruiz. "Cariton de Afrodisias y el mundo real." In *Piccolo mondo antico,* ed. P. Liviabella Furiani and A. M. Scarcella. Perugia: Edizioni Scientifiche Italiane, 1989, 107–149.

Olender, Maurice. "Aspects of Baubo: Ancient Texts and Contexts." In *Before Sexuality,* ed. David Halperin, et al. Princeton: Princeton University Press, 1990, 83–113.

Owens, E. J. *The City in the Greek and Roman World.* London and New York: Routledge, 1991.

Padel, Ruth. *In and Out of the Mind: Greek Images of the Tragic Self.* Princeton: Princeton University Press, 1992.

Pagels, Elaine. *Adam, Eve, and the Serpent.* New York: Random House, 1988.

Pantel, Pauline Schmidt, ed. *A History of Women in the West.* Vol. I: *From Ancient Goddesses to Christian Saints.* Translated by Arthur Goldhammer. Cambridge, Mass.: Harvard University Press, 1992.

Parke, H. W. *Festivals of the Athenians.* Ithaca: Cornell University Press, 1977.

Rawson, Beryl. "The Roman Family." In *The Family in Ancient Rome: New Perspectives,* ed. Beryl Rawson. Ithaca: Cornell University Press, 1986, 1–57.

———, ed. *The Family in Ancient Rome: New Perspectives.* Ithaca: Cornell University Press, 1986.

Rogers, Guy MacLean. *The Sacred Identity of Ephesos: Foundation Myths of a Roman City.* London and New York: Routledge, 1991.

Winkler, John J. *The Constraints of Desire: The Anthropology of Sex and Gender in Ancient Greece.* New York: Routledge, 1990.

II. THE MIDDLE AGES THROUGH THE PRESENT
(the first edition mentioned is standard work for quotations; it is succeeded by other editions in chronological order).

II A. *Novels, Poetry, and Dramatic Fiction and Nonfiction of the Middle Ages*

El Abencerraje. Edited by Francisco López Estrada. Fifth edition. Madrid: Cátedra, 1987.

Alighieri, Dante. *Convivio* and *Epistole.* In *Opere Minori.* Edited by Alberto del Monte. Second edition. Milan: Rizzoli, 1966.

———. *La Divina Commedia,* as *The Divine Comedy.* Edited and translated by John Sinclair (Italian-English). 3 vols. Oxford and New York: Oxford University Press, 1981.

———. *La Vita Nuova.* In *Opere Minori.* Edited by Alberto Del Monte. Second edition. Milan: Rizzoli, 1966.

Aucassin et Nicolette. Edited by Jean Dufournet. Paris: Garnier-Flammarion, 1973.

Boccaccio, Giovanni. *Il Corbaccio.* Florence: Filippo Giunti, 1594.

———. *Decameron.* In Vol. IV of *Tutte le opere di Giovanni Boccaccio.* Edited by Vittore Branca. Verona: Arnold Mondadori, 1976.

———. *Elegia di Madonna Fiammetta.* In Vol. III of *Giovanni Boccaccio opere minori in volgare.* Edited by Mario Marti. Milan: Rizzoli, 1971.

———. *La Fiametta.* Padua: Bartholomaeus de Valdezoccho and Martinus de Septem Arboribus, 1472.

———. *Fiammetta.* Edited by "Hieronymo Squarzasigo Alexandrino." Venice: Maximo di Papia, 1491.

———. *La Fiameta de Juan Vocacio.* Salamanca: n.p., 1497.

———. *Amorous Fiammetta.* Translated by "B. Giovano" [Bartholemew Yong]. London: I. C. for Thomas Gubbin and Thomas Newman, 1587.

———. *Fiammetta.* Edited by Filippo Giunti. Florence: Filippo Giunti, 1594.

———. *Filocolo.* In Vol. I of *Tutte Le Opere di Giovanni di Boccaccio.* Edited by Vittore Branca. Verona: Arnold Mondadori, 1967.

———. *Il Philocolo.* Venice: Gabriel di Pietro e Filippo, 1472.

———. *Il Philocolo.* Napoli: Russinger, 1478.

———. *Le Philocope de Messire Jehan Boccace Florentin, Contenant l'histoire de Fleury et Blanche-fleur.* Paris: Jehan Baptiste for Deni Ianot, 1542.

———. *Il Filocolpo. Con la Tavola di tutte le materie che nell'opera si contengono.* Edited by Francesco Sansovino. Venice: Giovanni Antonio Bertano, 1575.

Chaucer, Geoffrey. *Chaucer's Major Poetry.* Edited by Albert C. Baugh. New York: Meredith Publishing, 1963.

Chrétien de Troyes. *Cligès.* Edited by Alexandre Micha. Paris: Librairie Honoré Champion, 1968.

Eustathius Macrobilites. *Eustathiou Kath' Hysminian kai Hysminēn Drama/Eustathii de Ismeniae et Ismenes Amoribus.* Paris: Hieronymus Drouart, 1617.

———. *Ismene and Ismenias, A Novel.* Translated from the French by L. H. Le Moine Esq.: First Valet de chambre of his most Christian Majesty. London [? Paris], 1788.

Fulgentius. *Mythologiae* and other works. In *Fulgentius the Mythographer.* Translated by Leslie George Whitbread. N.p.: Ohio State University Press, 1971.

Lancelot do Lac: The Non-Cyclic Old French Prose Romance. Edited by Elspeth Kennedy. 2 vols. Oxford: Clarendon Press, 1980.

Lorris, Guillaume de, and Jean de Meung. *Le Roman de la Rose,* "version Attribuée a Clement Marot." Edited by Sylvio F. Baridon, with Introduction by Antonio Viscardi. 2 vols. Milan: Istituto Editoriale Cisalpine, 1957.

Lull, Ramon. *Blanquerna.* Translated with an Introduction by E. A. Peers, edited by Robert Irwin. London and New York: Daedalus/Hippocrene Books, n.d.

Malory, Sir Thomas. *Works.* Edited by Eugene Vinaver. Second edition. London: Oxford University Press, 1971.

Marie de France. *Lais.* Edited by Alfred Ewert. Oxford: Basil Blackwell, 1969.

Martorell, Joanot, and Martí Joan de Galba. *Tirant lo Blanc*. Translated by David H. Rosenthal. New York: Schocken Books, 1984.

Montalvo, Garci Rodríguez de. *Amadís de Gaula*. Edited by Juan Manuel Cacho Blecua. 2 vols. Madrid: Cátedra, 1987.

————. *The Labors of the Very Brave Knight Esplandián*. Translated by William Thomas Little. Medieval and Renaissance Texts and Studies, Vol. 92. Binghampton: SUNY Binghampton Press, 1992.

————. *The most excellent and pleasaunt Booke, entituled: The treasurie of Amadis of Fraunce*. [Translated by T. Paynell.] London: Henry Bynneman, for Thomas Hacket [? 1567].

————. *Amadis of Gaul: A Novel of Chivalry of the Fourteenth Century*. Translated by Edwin B. Place and Herbert C. Behm. Lexington: University of Kentucky Press, 1974.

Murasaki, Shikibu. *The Tale of Genji [Genji Monogatori]*. Translated by Edward G. Seidensticker. New York: Alfred A. Knopf, 1977.

Polo, Marco. *The Travels*. Translated and edited by Ronald Latham. London: Penguin Books, 1990.

Pródromos, Theodoros. *Les Amours de Rhodante et de Dosiclés*. Translated by Pierre François Godart de Beauchamps [version in prose]. Paris: n.p., 1746.

La Queste del Saint Graal. Edited by Albert Pauphilet. Paris: Librairie Honoré Champion, 1965.

Le Roman de Tristan en Prose. Edited by Philippe Menard. Geneva: Librairie Droz, 1987.

Shi Nai'an and Luo Guanzhong. *Marsh Chronicles [Shui Hu Zhuan]*, as *Outlaws of the Marsh*. Translated by Sidney Shapiro. 2 vols. Beijing and Bloomington: Indiana University Press and Foreign Languages Press, 1981.

Teresa, Saint. *El Libro de la Vida*. Madrid: Editorial de Espiritualidad, 1962.

II B. Works of the Renaissance, 1500–1600

II B 1. Novels, Poetry, and Dramatic Fiction

Alemán, Mateo. *Guzmán de Alfarache. Prima parte de la vida del picaro Guzmán de Alfarache Çaraqoça*. Madrid: Varez de Castro, 1599.

————. *The Rogue, or the Life of Guzmán de Alfarache*. Translated by James Mabbe. London: Edward Blount, 1622.

Florius, Franciscus. *De amore Camilli et Emilie aretinorum. . . ex Boccaccio transfiguratus*. Paris: Petrus de Caesaris, 1473.

The Journey to the West [Hsi-yu Chi]. Translated and edited by Anthony C. Yu. 4 vols. Chicago: University of Chicago Press, 1980.

Lanforde, James. *Amorous Tales and Sentences of the Philosophers*. London: Henrie Bynneman for Leonard Maylarde, 1567.

Lyly, John. *Euphues: The Anatomy of Wit*. In *The Complete Works of John Lyly*. Edited by R. Warwick Bond. 3 vols. Oxford: Oxford University Press, 1967.

Montemayor, Jorge de. *Los Siete Libros de la Diana*. Edited by Francisco Lopez Estrada. Madrid: Espasa-Calpe, S.A., 1962.

————. *Diana of George of Montemayor*. Translated by Bartholemew Yong. London: Ed. Bollifant, 1598.

Rabelais, François. *Oeuvres Complètes*. Edited by Pierre Jourda. 2 vols. Paris: Editions Garnier, 1962.

Shakespeare, William. *The Complete Works*. Edited by Stanley Wells and Gary Taylor. Oxford: Clarendon Press, 1988.

Sidney, Sir Philip. *The Countess of Pembroke's Arcadia (The Old Arcadia)*. Edited by Jean Robertson. Oxford: Oxford University Press, 1973.

————. *The Old Arcadia*. Edited by Katherine Duncan-Jones. Oxford: Oxford University Press, 1985.

Spenser, Edmund. *The Poetical Works of Edmund Spenser*. Edited by J. C. Smith and E. De Selincourt. London: Oxford University Press, 1961 [first printed 1912].

Lazarillo de Tormes as *La Vida de Lazarillo de Tormes, y de sus fortunas y adversidades*. Edited by Alberto Blecua. Madrid: Clasicos Castalia, 1987.

II B 2. Nonfictional Works

Ascham, Roger. *The Schoolmaster*. Edited by Lawrence V. Ryan. Charlottesville: University Press of Virginia, 1974.

Burton, Robert. *The Anatomy of Melancholy: What it is, with all the kinds, causes, symptomes, prognostickes & severall cures of it*. Edited by Holbrook Jackson. New York: Vintage Books, 1977 [edition first printed 1932].

Castiglione, Baldassare. *Il Cortegiano*. Edited by Vittorio Cian. Florence: G. C. Sansoni, 1929.

Cinthio, Giambattista Giraldi. *Discorsi intorno al comporre de i Romanzi, delle Comedie, e delle Tragedie, e di altre Maniere di poesie*. Venice: Gabriel Giolito de Ferrari e Fratelli, 1554.

Firenzuola, Agnolo. *On the Beauty of Women*. Translated and edited by Konrad Eisenbichler and Jacqueline Murray. Philadelphia: University of Pennsylvania Press, 1992.

Sidney, Sir Philip. *An Apologie for Poetrie*. London: Henry Olney, 1595.

II C. Novels, Poetry and Dramatic Fiction, and Folk Tales of the Seventeenth Century

Barclay, John. *Euphormio-Satyricon*. Edited by Paul Turner. London: Golden Cockerel Press, 1954 [first published 1603–1607].

———. *Argenis*. Edited by Theandro Bugnotius. 2 vols. Leiden and Rotterdam: Hackiana, 1664 [first published 1621].

Behn, Aphra. *Oroonoko, or The Royal Slave*. Introduction by Lore Metzger. New York: W. W. Norton, 1973.

Boileau-Despréaux, Nicolas. *Oeuvres*. Edited by Georges Mongrédien. Paris: Garnier Frères, 1961.

Bunyan, John. *The Pilgrim's Progress*. Edited with an Introduction by N. H. Keeble. Oxford: Oxford University Press, 1984.

Cavendish, Margaret (Duchess of Newcastle). *The Description of the New World, Called the Blazing World*. London: A. Maxwell, 1666.

Cervantes, Miguel de (Saavedra). *Don Quijote de la Mancha*. Edited by Martin de Riquer. Barcelona: Editorial Juventud, S.A., 1968.

———. *The History of the Valorous and Wittie Knight-Errant, Don-Quixote of the Mancha*. Translated by Thomas Shelton. London: William Stansby, for Edward Blount, 1612.

———. *L'Ingenieux Don Quixote De la Manche*. Translated by Cesar Ouden. Paris: Iean Foüet, 1614.

———. *The History of the most Ingenious Knight Don Quixote*. Translated by John Stevens. London: R. Chiswell, R. Battersby, et al., 1700.

———. *Novelas ejemplares*. Edited by Harry Sieber. 2 vols. Madrid: Cátedra, 1980.

———. *Exemplarie Novells. In sixe Books. . . Full of Various Accidents both Delightfull and Profitable*. Translated by "Don Diege Puede-Ser" [James Mabbe]. London: John Dawson for R. M. and sold by Laurence Blacklocke, 1640.

———. *Los Trabajos de Persiles y Sigismunda*. Edited by Juan Bautista Avalle-Arce. Madrid: Clásicos Castalia, 1970.

———. *The Travels of Persiles and Sigismunda. A Northern History*. London: H. L. for M. L., 1619.

———. *Persiles and Sigismunda. A Celebrated Novel. Intermixed with a great Variety of Delightful Histories and Entertaining Adventures*. London: C. Ward, R. Chandler and C. Woodward, 1741.

Godwin, Francis. *The Man in the Moone: or a Discourse of a Voyage thither by Domingo Gonsales, the speedy messenger*. London: J. Norton for K. Kirton and T. Warren, 1638.

Guilleragues, Gabriel-Joseph de Lavergne, Vicomte de [attrib.]. *Lettres Portugaises*. Edited by Bernard Bray and Isabelle Landy-Houillon. Paris: Flammarion, 1983.

Ingelo, Nathaniel. *Bentivolio and Urania, in Four Bookes*. London: Richard Marriot, 1660.

Lafayette, Marie-Madeleine, Comtesse de. *La Princesse de Clèves*. Edited by Antoine Adam. Paris: Garnier-Flammarion, 1966.

——. *Zayde*, as *Zaide Histoire espagnole*. Edited by Janine A. Kreiter. Paris: Librairie A.-G. Nizet, 1982.

Milton, John. *Paradise Lost*. In *John Milton: Complete Poems and Major Prose*. Edited by Merritt Y. Hughes. New York, Macmillan Publishing Company, 1957.

Molière, Jean-Baptiste Poquelin. *Les Femmes savantes*. Edited by Jean Lecomte. Paris: Librairie Larousse, 1971.

——. *Les Précieuses ridicules*. Edited by Denis A. Canal. Paris: Librairie Larousse, 1990.

Perrault, Charles. *Contes*. Edited by Gilbert Rouger. Paris: Garnier Frères, 1967.

Scarron, Paul. *Le Roman comique*. Edited by Emile Magne. Paris: Garnier Frères, 1967.

Scudéry, Madeliene de. *Artamène, ou Le Grand Cyrus*. 10 vols. Paris: A. Covrbé, 1650–1655.

——. *Artamenes, or The Grand Cyrus, that Excellent Romance*. Englished by F. G. Esq. London: J. Darby, et al., 1691.

——. *Clélie, Histoire romaine*. 10 vols. Paris: Covrbé, 1658–1662.

——. *Ibrahim, or The Illustrious Bassa. An Excellent New Romance*. Translated by Henry Cogan. London: J. R. for P. Parker and T. Guy, 1674.

Urfé, Honoré d'. *L'Astrée*. Rouen, Jean Boulley, 1616.

——. *L'Astrée*. Sixiesme Partie. Paris: Robert Fouet, 1626.

——. *The History of Astrea*. The First Part. In Twelve Bookes. Translated by John Pyper. London: N. Okes for John Pyper, 1620.

——. *Astrea. A Romance*. Written in French by Messire Honoré d'Urfé, and translated by a Person of Quality [John Davies of Kidwelly]. London: W. W. for H. Moseley, T. Dring and H. Herringman, 1657.

II D. Novels, Poetry, and Dramatic Fiction of the Eighteenth Century

Bernardin de Sainte-Pierre, Jacques-Henri. *Paul et Virginie*. Edited by Robert Mauzi. Paris: Garnier-Flammarion, 1966.

Burney, Frances. *Evelina, Or the History of a Young Lady's Entrance into the World*. Edited by Edward A. Bloom. Oxford: Oxford University Press, 1970.

Cleland, John. *Memoirs of a Woman of Pleasure*. Edited by Peter Sabor. Oxford: Oxford University Press, 1985.

Defoe, Daniel. *The Life and Strange Surprizing Adventures of Robinson Crusoe, of York, Mariner*. Edited by J. Donald Crowley. Oxford: Oxford University Press, 1972.

Fielding, Henry. *The History of the Adventures of Joseph Andrews, And of His Friend Mr. Abraham Adams*. Written in Imitation of the Manner of Cervantes. Edited by Homer Goldberg. New York: W. W. Norton, 1987.

——. *The History of Tom Jones, A Foundling*. Edited by Sheridan Baker. New York: W. W. Norton, 1973.

Goethe, Johann Wolfgang von. *Die Leiden des Jungen Werthers*. Edited by E. L. Stahl. Second edition. Oxford: Basil Blackwell, 1972.

Goldsmith, Oliver. *The Vicar of Wakefield*. Edited with an Introduction by Arthur Friedman. Oxford: Oxford University Press, 1981.

Graffigny (or Grafigny), Françoise d'Issembourg d' Happoncourt, Dame de. *Lettres d' une Péruvienne*. Edited by Bernard Bray and Isabelle Landy-Houillon. Paris: Flammarion, 1983.

Griffith, Elizabeth. *A Collection of Novels. Selected and Revised by Mrs. Griffith*. 2 vols. London: G. Kearsley, 1777.

Haywood, Eliza F. *The Adventures of Eovaai, Princess of Ijaveo*. Introduction by Josephine Grieder. New York: Garland, 1972.

——. *Fantomina, or Love in a Maze*. In Vol. III of *Secret Histories, Novels, and Poems*. Second edition. 4 vols. London: Brown and Chapman, 1725.

——. *Love in Excess; or the Fatal Enquiry*. Edited by David Oakleaf. Orchard Park, N.Y.: Broadview Press, 1994.

Laclos, Choderlos de. *Liaisons dangereuses*. In Laclos, *Oeuvres complètes*. Edited by Laurent Versini. Paris: Gallimard, 1979.

Lennox, Charlotte. *The Female Quixote or The Adventures of Arabella*. Edited by Margaret Dalziel with an introduction by Margaret Anne Doody, notes by Duncan Isles. Oxford: Oxford University Press, 1989.

———. *The Life of Harriet Stuart*. London: A. Millar, 1751 [actually published in December 1750].

Le Sage, Alain-René. *Le Diable boiteux*. Paris: Garnier Frères, 1909.

Lewis, Matthew G. *The Monk*. Edited by Howard Anderson. Oxford: Oxford University Press, 1973.

Marivaux, Pierre Carlet de Chamblain de. *La Vie de Marianne, ou Les Aventures de Madame La Comtesse de ****. Edited by Frédéric Deloffre. Paris: Garnier Frères, 1963.

Montesquieu, Charles Louis de Secondat de. *Lettres Persanes*. Edited by Paul Vernière. Third edition. Paris: Garnier Frères, 1960.

Pope, Alexander. *The Poems of Alexander Pope*. Edited by John Butt [1-vol. Twickenham edition]. London: Methuen, 1970.

Prévost, Antoine-François (Prévost d'Exiles). *Histoire d'une Grecque moderne*. Edited by Jean Sgard. Grenoble: Presses Universitaires de Grenoble, 1989.

Radcliffe, Ann. *The Mysteries of Udolpho. A Romance Interspersed with Some Pieces of Poetry*. Edited with an Introduction by Bonamy Dobrée, notes by Frederick Garber. Oxford: Oxford University Press, 1970.

Richardson, Samuel. *Clarissa. Or, the History of a Young Lady: Comprehending the most important Concerns of Private Life*. Reproduction of third edition [1751]. Introduction by Florian Stuber. 8 vols. New York: AMS Press, 1990.

———. *Lettres Angloises, ou Histoire de Miss Clarissa Harlove*. Translated by A. F. Prevost d'Exiles. 6 vols. Dresden: Conrad Walther, 1751–1752.

———. *The History of Sir Charles Grandison*. Edited with an Introduction by Jocelyn Harris. 3 vols. London: Oxford University Press, 1972.

———. *Pamela, or Virtue Rewarded*. Edited by T. C. Duncan Eaves and Ben D. Kimpel. Boston: Houghton Mifflin, 1971.

Rousseau, Jean-Jacques. *Julie, ou La Nouvelle Héloïse. Oeuvres complètes*. Edited by Henri Coulet and Bernard Guyon. Paris: Gallimard, 1960, Vol. III.

Schiller, Friedrich. *Der Geisterseher Aus den Memoires des Grafen von O**. Sämtliche Werke*. Munich: Carl Hanser Verlag, 1967, Vol. 5.

Sterne, Laurence. *The Life and Opinions of Tristram Shandy, Gentleman*. Edited by Ian Watt. Boston: Houghton Mifflin, 1965.

Swift, Jonathan. *Gulliver's Travels*. Edited by Robert A. Greenberg. New York: W. W. Norton, 1970.

Voltaire, François-Marie Arouet de. *Candide, ou L'Optimisme*, and *Zadig ou La Destinée* in *Romans et Contes de Voltaire*. Edited by René Pomeau. Paris: Flammarion, 1966.

Voyage Merveilleux du Prince Fan-Férédin dans le Romancie; Contenant Plusieurs Observations Historique, Géographiques, Physiques, Critiques, and Morales. Paris: P. G. Le Mercier, 1735.

Walpole, Horace. *The Castle of Otranto. A Gothic Story*. Edited with an Introduction by W. S. Lewis, notes by Joseph W. Reed. Oxford: Oxford University Press, 1969.

Wieland, Christoph Martin. *Geschichte des Agathon*. In *Werke*, 12 vols. Edited by Klaus Manger. Frankfurt am Main: Deutscher Klassiker Verlag, 1986; Vol.3, edited by Gonthier Louis Fink et al.

Wollstonecraft, Mary. *Mary, and the Wrongs of Woman*. Edited by Gary Kelly. Oxford: Oxford University Press, 1976.

Xueqin, Cao. *The Dream of the Red Chamber*, as *The Story of the Stone*. Edited and translated by David Hawkes. 5 vols. London: Penguin Books, 1993 [translation of 1973].

II E. Novels, Poetry, Dramatic Fiction, and Folk Tales of the Nineteenth Century

Alcott, Louisa May. *The Hidden Louisa May Alcott*. Edited by Madeleine Sterne. 2 vols. in one. New York: Avenel Books, 1984.

————. *Little Women*. Edited by Elaine Showalter. London: Penguin Books, 1986.

Austen, Jane. *Emma*. Edited by James Kinsley with an Introduction by David Lodge. Oxford: Oxford University Press, 1990.

————. *Northanger Abbey, Lady Susan, The Watsons, and Sanditon*. Edited by John Davie with an Introduction by Terry Castle. Oxford: Oxford University Press, 1980.

————. *Pride and Prejudice*. Edited by James Kinsley with an Introduction by Isobel Armstrong and notes by F. W. Bradbrook. Oxford: Oxford University Press, 1990.

Balzac, Honoré de. *Eugénie Grandet*. Edited by Samuel S. de Sacy. Paris: Gallimard, 1972.

————. *La Peau de chagrin*. Edited by Pierre Barberis. Paris: Librairie Générale Francaise, 1984.

Brontë, Anne. *The Tenant of Wildfell Hall*. Edited by Herbert Rosengarten with an Introduction by Margaret Smith. Oxford: Oxford University Press, 1993.

Brontë, Charlotte. *Jane Eyre*. Edited by Margaret Smith. Oxford: Oxford University Press, 1980.

————. *Shirley*. Edited by Margaret Smith and Herbert Rosengarten, Oxford: Oxford University Press, 1981.

————. *Villette*. Edited by Margaret Smith and Herbert Rosengarten with an Introduction by Margaret Smith. Oxford: Oxford University Press, 1990.

Brontë, Emily. *Wuthering Heights*. Edited by Ian Jack. Oxford: Oxford University Press, 1981.

Browning, Elizabeth Barrett. *Aurora Leigh*. New York and Boston: C. S. Francis, 1857.

Bulwer-Lytton, Sir Edward. *The Last Days of Pompeii*. With an Introduction by T. H. Feder. New York: T. H. Feder, 1993 [photocopy of 1834 edition].

Carroll, Lewis [Charles Lutwidge Dodgson]. *Alice's Adventures in Wonderland and Through the Looking-Glass*. Edited with an Introduction by Roger Lancelyn Green. Oxford: Oxford University Press, 1982.

Dickens, Charles. *Bleak House*. Edited by Norman Page with an Introduction by J. Hillis Miller. London: Penguin Books, 1985.

————. *David Copperfield*. Edited by Trevor Blount. London: Penguin Books, 1988.

————. *Great Expectations*. With an Afterword by Angus Wilson. New York: New American Library, 1980.

————. *Our Mutual Friend*. Edited with an Introduction by Michael Cotsell. Oxford: Oxford University Press, 1989.

————. *The Pickwick Papers*. Edited with an Introduction by Robert L. Patten. London: Penguin Books, 1986.

————. *A Tale of Two Cities*. Edited with an Introduction by George Woodcock. London: Penguin Books, 1986.

Dostoevsky, Fedor. *Crime and Punishment*. Translated by Jessie Coulson with an Introduction by John Jones. Oxford: Oxford University Press, 1980.

————. *The Idiot*. Translated by Henry and Olga Carlisle with an Introduction by Harold Rosenberg. New York: New American Library, 1980.

Doyle, Arthur Conan. *A Study in Scarlet*. In *The Complete Sherlock Holmes Long Stories*. London: John Murray, 1966.

Eliot, George. *Daniel Deronda*. Edited by Barbara Hardy. Harmondsworth, England: Penguin Books, 1967.

————. *Middlemarch*. Edited by Bert G. Hornback. New York: W. W. Norton, 1977.

————. *The Mill on the Floss*. Edited with an Introduction by A. S. Byatt. Harmondsworth, England: Penguin Books, 1979.

————. *Silas Marner the Weaver of Raveloe*. Edited by Q. D. Leavis. Harmondsworth, England: Penguin Books, 1967.

Flaubert, Gustave. *L'Education sentimentale, Histoire d'un Jeune Homme*. Edited by Claudine Gothot-Mersch. Paris: Flammarion, 1985.

————. *Madame Bovary*. Edited by Claudine Gothot-Mersch. Paris: Garnier, 1971.

————. *Salammbô*. Edited by Pierre Moreau with a Preface by Henri Thomas. Paris: Gallimard, 1970.

Goethe, Johann Wolfgang von. *Die Wahlverwandtschaften. Ein Roman*. Edited by Erich Trunz. Munich: Deutscher Taschenbuch Verlag, 1984.

Grimm, Jacob, and Wilhelm Grimm. *Die Märchen der Brüder Grimm*. With an Introduction by Kurt Waselowsky. Munich: Goldman Verlag. 1989.

Hardy, Thomas. *The Mayor of Casterbridge*. Edited by Dale Kramer. Oxford: Oxford University Press, 1987 [first published in 1886].

———. *The Return of the Native*. Edited by Simon Gatrell with notes by Nancy Barrineau. Oxford: Oxford University Press, 1990.

———. *Tess of the D'Urbervilles*. Edited by Juliet Grindle and Simon Gatrell with an Introduction by Simon Gatrell and notes by Nancy Barrineau. Oxford: Oxford University Press, 1983.

James, Henry. *Portrait of a Lady*. Harmondsworth, England: Penguin Books, 1970.

———. *The Wings of the Dove*. Harmondsworth, England: Penguin Books, 1965.

Keats, John. *John Keats: The Complete Poems*. Edited by John Barnard. Second edition. Harmondsworth, England: Penguin Books, 1977.

Kipling, Rudyard. *The Light That Failed*. Edited with an Introduction by John M. Lyon. London: Penguin Books, 1988.

Potocki, Jan. *Tales from the Saragossa Manuscript*. Translated by Christine Donougher with an Introduction by Brian Stableford. Sawtry, England, and New York: Dedalus/Hippocrene, 1990.

Tennyson, Alfred (Lord). *Poems and Plays*. Oxford: Oxford University Press, 1968.

Thackeray, William Makepeace. *Vanity Fair*. Edited with an Introduction by J.I.M. Stewart. London: Penguin Books, 1985.

Tolstoy, Leo. *Anna Karenina*. Translated by David Magarshack. New York: New American Library, 1980.

———. *War and Peace*. Translated with an Introduction by Rosemary Edmonds. London: Penguin Books, 1988.

Trollope, Anthony. *Barchester Towers*. With an Afterword by Robert W. Daniel. New York: New American Library, 1963.

Twain, Mark [Samuel Clemens]. *Adventures of Huckleberry Finn*. Edited with an Introduction by John Seelye. London: Penguin Books, 1988.

———. *The Adventures of Tom Sawyer*. With an Introduction by John Seelye. London: Penguin Books, 1986.

———. *The Tragedy of Pudd'nhead Wilson*. With a Foreword by Wright Morris. New York: New American Library, 1964.

Zola, Emile. *L'Assommoir*. Edited by Henri Mitterand, preface by Jean-Louis Rory. Paris: Gallimard, 1978.

———. *Nana*. With an Introduction by Roger Ripoll. Paris: Flammarion, 1968.

———. *Thérèse Raquin*. Paris: Livre de Poche, 1961.

Yu Tangchun (*The Jade Palace of Heaven*; nineteenth-century Beijing opera based on a story collected in seventeenth century.) Translated by Elizabeth Wichmann, typescript of acted version.

II F. The Twentieth Century

II F 1. Novels, Poetry, and Dramatic Fiction

Achebe, Chinua. *Arrow of God*. New York: Anchor Books, 1974.

Allende, Isabel. *La Casa de los espíritus*. Barcelona: Plaza and Janes Editores, SA, 1982.

Amis, Kingsley. *Jake's Thing*. Harmondsworth, England: Penguin Books, 1978.

Atwood, Margaret. *Cat's Eye*. New York and Toronto: Bantam Books, 1989.

Barrie, J. M. *Peter Pan in Kensington Gardens / Peter and Wendy*. Edited with an Introduction by Peter Hollindale. Oxford: Oxford University Press, 1991.

Borges, Jorge Luis. *Ficciones*. New York: Grove Press, 1962.

———. *Labyrinths: Selected Stories and Other Writings*. Edited by Donald A. Yates and James E. Irby, with a Preface by Andre Maurois. New York: New Directions, 1964.

Brookner, Anita. *A Friend from England*. London: Grafton Books, 1987.

Burnett, Frances Hodgson. *The Secret Garden*. New York: Harper & Row, 1987.

Christie, Agatha. *Death Comes As the End*. New York: Harper Paperbacks, 1992.

———. *Death on the Nile*. New York: Harper Paperbacks, 1992.

———. *The Thirteen Problems*. London: Fontana, 1965.

Conrad, Joseph. *Lord Jim*. Edited by Thomas Moser. New York: W. W. Norton, 1968.

Doody, Margaret. *Aristotle Detective*. New York: Harper & Row, 1978.

Doyle, Arthur Conan. *The Hound of the Baskervilles*. London: Penguin Books, 1988.

Eco, Umberto. *Il Nome della rosa*. Milan: Bompiani, 1980.

Forster, E. M. *Howards End*. New York: Penguin Books, 1968.

———. *The Longest Journey*. Edinburgh and London: W. Blackwood and Sons, 1907.

———. *A Passage to India*. Harmondsworth, England: Penguin Books, 1961.

Grahame, Kenneth. *The Wind in the Willows*. With an Introduction by Roger Sale. New York: Bantam Books, 1982.

Goudge, Elizabeth. *Green Dolphin Country*. London: Hodder and Stoughton, 1989.

Heller, Joseph. *Catch-22*. New York: Simon and Schuster, 1955.

Ihimaera, Witi. *The Matriarch*. Auckland: Pan Books, 1990.

Joyce, James. *Ulysses*. The Corrected Text. Edited by Hans Walter Gabler with Wolfhard Steppe and Claus Melchior. New York: Vintage Books, 1986.

Kafka, Franz. *Die Verwandlung*. In *Sämtliche Erzählungen*. Edited by Paul Raabe. Frankfurt am Main: Fischer Taschenbuch Verlag, 1970.

———. *Die Verwandlung* as *The Metamorphosis*. Translated by Stanley Corngold. New York and Toronto: Bantam Books, 1972.

Kennedy, William. *Ironweed*. New York: Viking Penguin, 1988.

Kundera, Milan. *The Book of Laughter and Forgetting*. Translated by Michael Henry Heim. New York: Alfred A. Knopf, 1980.

Lampedusa, Tomasi di. *Il Gattopardo*. Milan: Feltrinelli, 1984.

Lawrence, D. H. *The Rainbow*. Harmondsworth, England: Penguin Books, 1968.

Lewis, C. S. *The Voyage of the Dawn Treader*. Harmondsworth, England: Penguin Books, 1971.

Lodge, David. *Small World: An Academic Romance*. London: Secker & Warburn, 1984.

Mailer, Norman. *Ancient Evenings*. Boston: Little, Brown, 1983.

Mann, Thomas. *Bekenntnisse des Hochstaplers Felix Krull*. Frankfurt am Main: Fischer Taschenbuch Verlag, 1989.

———. *Joseph und seine Brüder*. Edited by Albert von Schirnding. 4 vols. Frankfurt am Main: S. Fischer Verlag, 1983.

———. *Joseph und seine Brüder* as *Joseph and His Brothers*. Translated by H. T. Lowe-Porter. Harmondsworth, England: Penguin Books, 1984.

———. *Der Tod in Venedig*. In *Schwere Stunde und Andere Erzählungen*. Frankfurt am Main: Fischer Taschenbuch Verlag, 1990.

———. *Der Zauberberg*. Frankfurt am Main: Fischer Taschenbuch Verlag, 1982 [first published 1924].

———. *Der Zauberberg* as *The Magic Mountain*. Translated by H. T. Lowe-Porter. New York: Vintage Books, 1969.

Márquez, Gabriel García. *El Amor en los tiempos del cólera*. Madrid: Mondadori, 1990.

———. *El General en su laberinto*. Madrid: Mondadori, 1989.

———. *El General en su laberinto* as *The General in His Labyrinth*. Translated by Edith Grossman. New York: Alfred A. Knopf, 1990.

Michaels, Leonard. *The Men's Club*. New York: Farrar, Straus, and Giroux, 1981.

Mishima, Yukio. *Spring Snow* [*Haru no Yuki*]. Translated by Michael Gallagher. New York: Vintage Books, 1990.

———. *The Temple of Dawn* [*Akatsuki no Tera*]. Translated by E. Dale Saunders and Cecilia Segawa Seigle. New York: Vintage Books, 1990.

Montgomery, L. M. *Anne of Green Gables*. Halifax, Nova Scotia: Nimbus, 1992.

Morrison, Toni. *Beloved*. New York: Alfred A. Knopf, 1987.

———. *Jazz*. New York: Alfred A. Knopf, 1992.

Nabokov, Vladimir. *Ada or Ardor: A Family Chronicle*. New York: McGraw-Hill, 1981.

Okri, Ben. *The Famished Road*. New York: N. A. Talese, 1992.

Proust, Marcel. *A la recherche du temps perdu*. 8 vols. Paris: Gallimard, 1954.

Pym, Barbara. *The Sweet Dove Died*. New York: Dutton, 1979.

Robbe-Grillet, Alain. *Les Gommes*. Paris: Editions de Minuit, 1985.

Robbins, Tom. *Skinny Legs and All*. New York and Toronto: Bantam Books, 1991.

Rubbi, Clara. *La Dea del melograno*. Genoa: ECIG, 1986.

Rushdie, Salman. *The Satanic Verses*. New York: Viking Penguin, 1989.

Sayers, Dorothy L. *Strong Poison*. New York: Harper & Row, 1987.

———. *The Unpleasantness at the Bellona Club*. London: New English Library, 1973.

Seth, Vikram. *The Golden Gate: A Novel in Verse*. New York: Random House, 1986.

———. *A Suitable Boy: A Novel*. New York: Harper Collins, 1993.

Sontag, Susan. *The Volcano Lover: A Romance*. New York: Farrar, Straus, and Giroux, 1992.

Tan, Amy. *The Kitchen God's Wife*. New York: Ivy Books, 1991.

Weldon, Fay. *The Hearts and Lives of Men*. New York: Dell, 1987.

Wharton, Edith. *The House of Mirth*. With an Afterword by Louis Auchincloss. New York: New American Library, 1964.

Winterson, Jeannette. *The Passion*. London: Penguin Books, 1988.

II F 2. Nonfiction, Excluding Literary History and Criticism

Ariès, Phillipe. *L'Enfant et la vie familiale sous l'Ancien Régime*. Paris: Plon, 1960.

Bernheimer, Charles, and Claire Kehane, eds. *In Dora's Case: Freud—Hysteria—Feminism*. New York: Columbia University Press, 1985.

Clikas, Sophia. *A Southern Lady Cooks with a Greek Accent*. Memphis, Tenn.: Wimmer Bros., 1980.

Erim, Kenan. *Aphrodisias, City of Venus Aphrodite*. Introduction by John Julius Norwich. London: Muller, Blond and White, 1986.

Freud, Sigmund. *Bruchstück einer Hysterie-Analyse*. In *Gesammelte Werke*. Edited by Anna Freud, et al. Frankfurt am Main: S. Fischer Verlag, 1942, Vol. V.

———. *Civilization and Its Discontents*. Translated by James Strachey. New York: W. W. Norton, 1961.

Hereniko, Vilsoni. *Woven Gods: Female Clowns and Power in Rotuma*. Honolulu, Hawaii: University of Hawaii Press, 1995.

Kerényi, Karl, ed. *Romandichtung und Mythologie; ein briefwechsel mit Thomas Mann, herausgegeben zum siebzigsten geburtstag des dichters*. Zurich: Rhein-Verlag, 1945.

Kilgour, Maggie. *From Communion to Cannibalism*. Princeton: Princeton University Press, 1990.

Lacan, Jacques. *Ecrits: A Selection*. Translated by Alan Sheridan. New York: W. W. Norton, 1977.

Ladurie, Emmanuel Le Roy. *Montaillou: The Promised Land of Error*. Translated by Barbara Bray. New York: Vintage Books, 1979 [*Montaillou, village occitan de 1294 à 1324*, Paris, 1975].

Laqueur, Thomas. *Making Sex: Body and Gender from the Greeks to Freud*. Cambridge, Mass.: Harvard University Press, 1990.

Laurentin, René, and Ljudevic Rupčič. *Is the Virgin Mary Appearing at Medjugorje?* Translated by Francis Martin. Gaithersburg, Md.: The Word Among Us Press, 1984.

Lévi-Strauss, Claude. *Myth and Meaning: Five Talks for Radio*. The 1977 Massey Lectures. Toronto; Buffalo, N.Y.: University of Toronto Press, 1978.

———. *Tristes Tropiques*. Translated by John and Doreen Weightman. New York: Atheneum, 1974 [originally published Paris, 1955].

———. *Structural Anthropology*. Translated by Claire Jacobson and Brooke Grundfest Schoepf. New York: Basic Books, 1963.

Masson, Jeffrey Moussaieff. *The Assault on Truth: Freud's Suppression of the Seduction Theory*. New York: Farrar, Straus, and Giroux, 1984.

Patterson, Orlando. *Freedom: Volume I: Freedom in the Making of Western Culture*. New York: Basic Books, 1991.

Steinem, Gloria. *Revolution from Within: A Book of Self-Esteem*. Boston and London: Little, Brown, 1993.

Warner, Marina. *Alone of All Her Sex: The Myth and the Cult of the Virgin*. New York: Vintage, 1983.

Weil, Simone. *Waiting for God* (translation of *L'Attente de Dieu*). Translated by Emma

Crauford with an introduction by Leslie A. Fiedler. New York: Harper & Row, 1973.

Williams, Rowan. *Teresa of Avila*. Harrisburg, Pa.: Morehouse Publishing, 1991.

III. LITERARY CRITICISM, LITERARY AND CULTURAL HISTORY, AND COMMENTARY

III A. 1500–1995

Adam, Antoine. *Histoire de la littérature francaise au XVIIe siècle*. 5 vols. Paris: Del Duca, 1949–1956.

———. *Romanciers du xviii siècle: Sorel, Scarron, Furetière, Madame de Lafayette*. Paris: Gallimard, 1958.

Adams, Percy G. *Travel Literature and the Evolution of the Novel*. Lexington: University Press of Kentucky, 1983.

Addison, Joseph, and Richard Steele. *The Spectator*. Edited by Gregory Smith with an Introduction by Peter Smithers. 4 vols. London and New York: Dent and Dutton, 1967.

Alkon, Paul K. *Origins of Futuristic Fiction*. Athens, Ga.: University of Georgia Press, 1987.

Armstrong, Nancy. *Desire and Domestic Fiction: A Political History of the Novel*. Oxford: Oxford University Press, 1987.

Arnold, Matthew. *Complete Prose Works*. Edited by R. H. Super. Ann Arbor: University of Michigan Press, 1960–1976.

Auerbach, Erich. *Mimesis: The Representation of Reality in Western Literature*. Translated by Willard R. Trask. Princeton: Princeton University Press, 1974 [reprint of 1953].

Auerbach, Nina. *Woman and the Demon: The Life of a Victorian Myth*. Cambridge, Mass.: Harvard University Press, 1982.

Austen, Jane. *The Letters of Jane Austen*. Edited by R. W. Chapman. Second edition. Oxford: Oxford University Press, 1979.

Baker, Ernest. *The History of the English Novel*. London: F. F. and G. Witherby, 1934.

Bakhtin, M. M. *The Dialogic Imagination: Four Essays*. Edited by Michael Holquist, translated by Caryl Emerson and Michael Holquist. Austin: University of Texas Press, 1982.

Barthes, Roland. *Mythologies*. Paris: Editions du Seuil, 1957.

———. *Le plaisir du texte*. Paris: Editions du Seuil, 1973.

———. *S/Z*. Paris: Editions du Seuil, 1970.

Battestin, Martin. *The Providence of Wit: Aspects of Form in Augustan Literature and the Arts*. Oxford: Clarendon Press, 1974.

Bayle, Pierre. *Dictionnaire historique et critique*. 2 vols. Rotterdam: Reinier Leers, 1697.

Beer, Gillian. *Darwin's Plots: Evolutionary Narrative in Darwin, George Eliot, and Nineteenth-Century Fiction*. London and Boston: Routledge and Kegan Paul, 1983.

Bender, John. *Imagining the Penitentiary: Fiction and the Architecture of Mind in Eighteenth-Century England*. Chicago: University of Chicago Press, 1987.

Bersani, Leo. *The Culture of Redemption*. Cambridge, Mass.: Harvard University Press, 1990.

Biasin, Gian-Paolo. *The Flavors of Modernity: Food and the Novel* [translated from *I Sapori della modernità: Cibo e romanzo* (Bologna, 1991)]. Princeton: Princeton University Press, 1993.

Blanckenburg, Christoph Friedrich von. *Versuch über den Roman*. Edited by Eberhard Lammert. Stuttgart: J. B. Metzlersche Verlagsbuchhandlung, 1965.

Blumenfeld-Kosinski, Renate. "The Earliest Developments of the French Novel: The *Roman de Thèbes* in Verse and Prose." In *The French Novel: Theory and Practice*. French Literature Series Vol XI. Columbia, S.C.: University of South Carolina Press, 1984, 1–10.

Booth, Wayne C. *The Rhetoric of Fiction*. Chicago: University of Chicago Press, 1961.

Brooks, Peter. *Body Work: Objects of Desire in Modern Narrative*. Cambridge, Mass.: Harvard University Press, 1993.

———. *Reading for the Plot: Design and Intention in Narrative*. New York: A. A. Knopf, 1984.

Butor, Michel. *Essais sur le roman*. Paris: Gallimard, 1969.

Calasso, Roberto. *Le Nozze di Cadmo e Armonia*. Milan: Adelphi Edizioni, 1988.

Calvin, Jean. *Institutes*. Edited by Julien Reinach. Paris: Belles Lettres, 1950.

———. *Treatises against the Anabaptists and against the Libertines*. Edited and translated by Benjamin W. Farley. Grand Rapids, Mich.: Baker Book House, 1982.

Calvino, Italo. *The Uses of Literature*. Essays translated by Patrick Creagh. New York: Harcourt Brace Jovanovich, 1987.

Castle, Terry. *Masquerade and Civilization: The Carnivalesque in Eighteenth-Century English Culture and Fiction*. Stanford: Stanford University Press, 1986.

Cherpack, Clifton. *Logos in Mythos: Ideas and Early French Narrative*. Lexington, Ky.: French Forum, 1983.

Cixous, Hélène. "The Laugh of the Medusa." *Signs* 1:4 (1976):875–894.

Cixous, Hélène, and Catherine Clement. *The Newly Born Woman*. Translated by Betsy Wing with an Introduction by Sandra M. Gilbert. Minneapolis: University of Minnesota Press, 1986 [*La Jeune née* (Paris), 1975].

D'Alembert, Jean le Rond. "Discours preliminaire à l'Encyclopédie." *Encyclopédie ou dictionnaire raisonné des sciences, des arts et des metiers (articles choisis)*. Selected and edited by Alain Pons. 2 vols. Paris: Flammarion, 1986, Vol. 1.

Damrosch, Leopold. *God's Plot and Man's Stories: Studies in the Fictional Imagination from Milton to Fielding*. Chicago: University of Chicago Press, 1985.

Danahy, Michael. *The Feminization of the Novel*. Gainesville, Fla.: University of Florida Press, 1991.

DeJean, Joan. *Tender Geographies: Women and the Origins of the Novel in France*. New York: Columbia University Press, 1991.

Delany, Mary. *The Autobiography and Correspondence of Mary Granville, Mrs. Delany*. Edited by Lady Llanover. 3 vols. London: Richard Bentley, 1861.

Derrida, Jacques. *Of Grammatology*. Translated by Gayatri Spivack. Baltimore: Johns Hopkins University Press, 1976.

Doody, Margaret Anne. "Beyond *Evelina*: The Individual Novel and the Community of Literature." *Eighteenth-Century Fiction* 3 (1991):359–371.

———. "Classic Weldon." In *Fay Weldon's Wicked Fictions*. Edited by Regina Barrecca. Hanover, N.H.: University Press of New England, 1994, 37–58.

———. "Deserts, Ruins and Troubled Waters: Female Dreams in Fiction and the Development of the Gothic Novel." *Genre* 10 (1977):529–572.

———. *A Natural Passion: A Study of the Novels of Samuel Richardson*. Oxford: Clarendon Press, 1974.

———. "Shakespeare's Novels: Charlotte Lennox Illustrated." *Studies in the Novel* 19 (Fall 1987):296–307.

Eckermann, Johann Peter. *Gespräche mit Goethe in den letzten Jahren seines Lebens*. Berlin and Weimar: Aufbau-Verlag, 1982.

Eisenstein, Elizabeth L. *The Printing Press as an Agent of Change: Communications and Cultural Transformations in Early-Modern Europe*. 2 vols. in one. Cambridge: Cambridge University Press, 1982 [reprint of 1979].

Erickson, Robert. *Mother Midnight: Birth, Sex and Fate in Eighteenth-Century Fiction (Defoe, Richardson and Sterne)*. New York: AMS Press, 1986.

Fergus, Jan. *Jane Austen: A Literary Life*. New York: St. Martin's Press. 1991.

Fielding, Henry. *The Covent Garden Journal*. By Sir Alexander Drawcansir, Knt. Edited by Bertrand A. Goldgar. Middletown, Conn.: Wesleyan University Press, 1988.

Forster, E. M. *Aspects of the Novel*. New York: Harcourt, Brace, 1927.

Foucault, Michel. *The Care of the Self*. As Vol. 3 of *The History of Sexuality*. Translated by Robert Hurley. New York: Random House, 1988.

———. "Introduction" to *The History of Sexuality*. Translated by Robert Hurley. New York: Vintage Books, 1990.

Freedman, Barbara. *Staging the Gaze: Postmodernism, Psychoanalysis, and Shakespearean Comedy*. Ithaca: Cornell University Press, 1991.

Frus, Phyllis. "News and the Novel." Ph.D. dissertation. New York University. 1985.

Frye, Northrop. *Anatomy of Criticism*. Princeton: Princeton University Press, 1971 [reprint of 1957].

———. *The Great Code: The Bible and Literature*. New York: Harcourt Brace Jovanovich, 1982.

———. *The Secular Scripture: A Study of the Structure of Romance*. Cambridge, Mass.: Harvard University Press, 1976.

Gilbert, Sandra M., and Susan Gubar. *The Madwoman in the Attic: The Woman Writer and the Nineteenth Century Literary Imagination*. New Haven and London: Yale University Press, 1979.

Girard, René. *Mensonge romantique et vérité romanesque*. Paris: Grasset, 1961.

Greetham, D. C. *Textual Scholarship: An Introduction*. New York: Garland Publishing, Inc., 1992.

Gutiérrez, Gloria Bautista. *Realismo magico, cosmos Latinoamerico*. Santafé de Bogotá, D.C.: America Latina, 1991.

Hagstrum, Jean. *The Sister Arts: The Tradition of Literary Pictorialism and English Poetry from Dryden to Gray*. Chicago: University of Chicago Press, 1958.

Hobbes, Thomas. *Leviathan*. Edited by Richard Tuck. Cambridge: Cambridge University Press, 1991.

Huet, Pierre-Daniel. *The History of Romances*. Translated by Stephen Lewis. London: J. Hooke, 1715

———. *Traité de l'origine des romans. Revue et augmentée d'une Lettre touchant Honoré d'Urfé, Auteur de l'Astrée*. Eighth edition. Paris: Jean Mariette, 1711.

Hunter, J. Paul. *Before Novels: The Cultural Contexts of Eighteenth Century English Fiction*. New York: W. W. Norton, 1990.

Hutcheon, Linda. *Narcissistic Narrative: The Metafictional Paradox*. New York: Methuen, 1984.

———. *A Theory of Parody: The Teachings of Twentieth-Century Art Forms*. New York: Methuen, 1985.

Imlay, Elizabeth. *Charlotte Brontë and the Mysteries of Love*. New York: St. Martin's Press, 1989.

Iser, Wolfgang. *The Act of Reading: A Theory of Aesthetic Response*. Translated by W. Iser. Baltimore: The Johns Hopkins University Press, 1978.

———. *The Implied Reader: Patterns of Communication in Prose Fiction from Bunyan to Beckett*. Translated by W. Iser. Baltimore: The Johns Hopkins University Press, 1974.

Jacquin, Abbé Armand-Pierre. *Entretiens sur les Romans. Ouvrage moral et critique, Dans lequel on traite de l'origine des Romans, et de leurs différentes espèces*. Paris: Duchesne, 1755.

James, Henry. *The Art of the Novel*. Introduction by Richard P. Blackmur. New York and London: Charles Scribner's Sons, 1934.

———. *The House of Fiction: Essays on the Novel*. Edited with an Introduction by Leon Edel. Westport, Conn.: Green Wood Press, 1973.

Johnson, Claudia. *Jane Austen: Women, Politics, and the Novel*. Chicago: University of Chicago Press, 1988.

Johnson, Samuel. *The Letters of Samuel Johnson*. Edited by Bruce Redford. 5 vols. Princeton: Princeton University Press, 1992–1994.

———. *The Rambler*. Vols. 4–6 of *The Works of Samuel Johnson, LL.D.* Edited by Arthur Murphy. 12 vols. London: Thomas Tegg, et al., 1824.

Kermode, Frank. *The Art of Telling: Essays on Fiction*. Cambridge, Mass.: Harvard University Press, 1983.

———. *Poetry, Narrative, History*. Oxford: Basil Blackwell, 1990.

———. *The Sense of an Ending: Studies in the Theory of Fiction*. Oxford: Oxford University Press, 1967.

Kristeva, Julia. *Strangers to Ourselves*. Translated by Leon S. Roudiez. New York: Columbia University Press, 1991.

———. *Tales of Love*. Translated by Leon S. Roudiez. New York: Columbia University Press, 1987.

Lenglet-Dufresnoy, Nicolas [under pseudonym "M. Le C. Gordon de Percel"]. *De l'usage des romans, où l'on fait voir leur utilité, et leurs differens caracteres*. 2 vols. Amsterdam: La veuve de Poilras, 1734 [possibly not "Amsterdam"].

Létoublon, Françoise. "La Modernité de la Grecque de Prévost et la Tradition Grecque du Genre Romanesque." *Cahiers Prevost d'Exiles*, No. 6, 1989.

Lewis, C. S. *The Allegory of Love: A Study in Medieval Tradition*. London: Oxford: Oxford University Press, 1938

———. *English Literature in the Sixteenth Century, Excluding Drama*. Oxford: Clarendon Press, 1954.

———. *An Experiment in Criticism*. Cambridge: Cambridge University Press, 1992 [reprint of 1961].

Lodge, David. *Language of Fiction: Essays in Criticism and Verbal Analysis of the English Novel*. New York: Columbia University Press, 1966.

Lukács, Georg. *The Theory of the Novel: A Historico-Philosophical Essay on the Forms of Great Epic Literature*. Translated by Anna Bostock. Cambridge, Mass.: MIT Press, 1971 [originally published Berlin, 1920].

McKeon, Michael. *The Origins of the English Novel 1600–1740*. Baltimore: The Johns Hopkins University Press, 1987.

Miller, D. A. *Narrative and Its Discontents*. Princeton: Princeton University Press, 1981.

———. *The Novel and the Police*. Berkeley and Los Angeles: University of California Press, 1988.

Miller, Nancy. *The Heroine's Text: Readings in the French and English Novel, 1722–1782*. New York: Columbia University Press, 1980.

Milton, John. *Eikonoklastes. Complete Prose Works of John Milton*. Edited by Douglas Bush, et al. 8 vols. New Haven and London: Yale University Press, 1952, Vol. III, 1982.

Moretti, Franco. *Signs Taken for Wonders: Essays in the Sociology of Literary Forms*. Translated by Susan Fischer, David Forgacs, and David Miller. London: Verso, 1988.

Mulvey, Laura. "Visual Pleasure and Narrative Cinema." *Screen* 16 (1975):6–18; reprinted in *Narrative, Apparatus, Ideology: A Film Theory Reader*. Edited by Phillip Rosen. New York: Columbia University Press, 1986.

Nelson, Victoria. "The Hermeticon of Umbertus E." *Raritan* 13:1 (Summer 1993):87–101.

Neusner, Jacob. *What Is Midrash?* Philadelphia: Fortress Press, 1987.

Nietzsche, Friedrich. *Die Geburt der Tragödie aus dem Geiste der Musik*. Edited by Peter Putz. Munich: Goldmann, 1990.

Osborne, Dorothy. *The Letters from Dorothy Osborne to Sir William Temple*. Introduction by Edward A. Parry. London: J. M. Dent & Sons, Ltd., 1914.

Paglia, Camille. *Sexual Personae: Art and Decadence from Nefertiti to Emily Dickinson*. New York: Vintage Books, 1991.

Parker, Patricia A. *Inescapable Romance: Studies in the Poetics of a Mode*. Princeton: Princeton University Press, 1979.

———. *Literary Fat Ladies: Rhetoric, Gender, Property*. New York and London: Methuen, 1987.

Patterson, Annabel. *Censorship and Interpretation: The Conditions of Writing and Reading in Early Modern England*. Madison: University of Wisconsin Press, 1984.

Perry, Ruth. *Women, Letters, and the Novel*. New York: AMS Press, 1980.

Porcelli, Bruno. *La Novella del Cinquecento*. Rome and Bari: Editori Latera, 1973.

Propp, Vladimir Iakovlevich. *Morphology of the Folktale*. Translated by Laurence Scott. Austin: University of Texas Press, 1968.

Quint, David. *Epic and Empire: Politics and Generic Form from Virgil to Milton*. Princeton: Princeton University Press, 1993.

———. *Origin and Originality in Renaissance Literature: Versions of the Source*. New Haven and London: Yale University Press, 1983.

Radway, Janice. *Reading the Romance: Women, Patriarchy and Popular Literature*. Chapel Hill: University of North Carolina Press, 1984.

Reeve, Clara. *The Progress of Romance through Times, Countries, and Manners, with Remarks on the Good and Bad Effect of it on them Respectively*. 2 vols. Colchester: Printed for the Author by W. Keymer, 1785.

Reyes, Graciela. *Polifonía textual: La Citación en el relato literario*. Madrid: Editorial Gredos, 1984.

Richardson, Samuel. *A Collection of the Moral and Instructive Sentiments, Maxims, Cautions, and Reflections, Contained in the Histories of Pamela, Clarissa, and Sir Charles Grandison*. With an Introduction by Benjamin Kennicott. London: printed for Samuel Richardson, 1755.

Ricoeur, Paul. *Time and Narrative*. Translated by Kathleen Blarney and David Pellauer. 3 vols. Chicago: University of Chicago Press, 1988.

Sacks, Sheldon. *Fiction and the Shape of Belief: A Study of Henry Fielding, with Glances at Swift, Johnson & Richardson*. Berkeley: University of California Press, 1964.

Said, Edward. *Orientalism*. New York: Vintage Books, 1979.

Salzman, Paul. *English Prose Fiction 1558–1700: A Critical History*. Oxford: Oxford University Press, 1985.

Sanguineti White, Laura. *Boccaccio e Apuleio: caratteri differenziali nelle strutture narrativa del Decameron*. Bologna: EDIM, 1977.

Showalter, English. *The Evolution of the French Novel 1641–1782*. Princeton: Princeton University Press, 1972.

Spufford, Margaret. *Small Books and Pleasant Histories: Popular Fiction and Its Readership in Seventeenth-Century England*. Athens, Ga.: University of Georgia Press, 1982.

Sternberg, Meir. *The Poetics of Biblical Narrative: Ideological Literature and the Drama of Reading*. Bloomington: Indiana University Press, 1985.

Stone, Lawrence. *The Family, Sex and Marriage in England 1500–1800*. New York: Harper & Row, 1977.

Stuart, Charles (King Charles I). *Eikon Basilike: The Portraiture of His Sacred Majesty in His Solitudes and Sufferings*. Edited by Philip A. Knachel. Ithaca: Cornell University Press for the Folger Shakespeare Library, 1966.

Taine, Hippolyte. *Histoire de la littérature anglaise*. 3 vols. Paris: Librairie Hachette, 1877.

Tanner, Tony. *Adultery in the Novel: Contract and Transgression*. Baltimore: The Johns Hopkins University Press, 1979.

———. *Venice Desired*. Cambridge, Mass.: Harvard University Press, 1982.

Todorov, Tzevetan. *The Poetics of Prose*. Translated by Richard Howard with a Foreword by Jonathan Culler. Ithaca: Cornell University Press, 1977.

Turner, Victor Witter. *The Forest of Symbols: Aspects of Ndumba Ritual*. Ithaca: Cornell University Press, 1967.

Vargas Llosa, Mario. *La Verdad de las mentiras*. Barcelona: Seiz Barral, 1990.

Walpole, Horace. *Correspondence*. Edited by R. B. Lewis, et al. 48 vols. Oxford: Oxford University Press, 1937–1983.

Warner, Marina. *Alone of All Her Sex: The Myth and the Cult of the Virgin Mary*. New York: Vintage Books, 1983.

Watt, Ian. *The Rise of the Novel: Studies in Defoe, Richardson and Fielding*. Harmondsworth, England: Penguin Books, 1963.

Weston, Jessie L. *From Ritual to Romance*. With a Foreword by Robert Segal. Princeton: Princeton University Press, 1993.

White, Hayden. *The Content of the Form: Narrative Discourse and Historial Representation*. Baltimore: The Johns Hopkins University Press, 1987.

Wilson, Diana de Armas. *Allegories of Love: Cervantes's "Persiles and Sigismunda."* Princeton: Princeton University Press, 1991.

Wolff, Samuel Lee. *The Greek Romance in Elizabethan Prose Fiction*. New York: Columbia University Press, 1912.

Wolf, F. A. *Prolegomena ad Homerum*. Translated with an Introduction by Anthony Grafton, Glen W. Most, and James E. G. Zetzel. Princeton: Princeton University Press, 1985.

IV. MANUSCRIPTS CONSULTED

Achilles Tatius (see also under Heliodorus)

"Achilleōs Tatiou." Vatican GR 1349. Byzantine, thirteenth cent. (?). "Ex libris Juliuii Ursini." With copious side notes in Greek.

"Achilleōs Alexan. tou Tatiou. Ton kata Leukippēn, kai Kleitophōnta." Vatican GR 1348. Begins at f. 96.
With Longus. "Daphnis and Chloe." Byzantine, fourteenth cent. (?). ff. 1–65.

Alexander (History of)

Codex, Istituto Ellenico, Venice. Rec. gamma, MS D. Byzantine, fourteenth cent. probably for ruler of Trebizond, with Turkish inscriptions from later Turkish owner(s).
Armenian ms., collection of Mechitarist Congregation, MS 424. S. Lazzaro degli Armeni, Venice. Parchment; illustrated.

Apuleius

"Apuleius de asino aureo scriptus in mccclxxxviii." Marcian Library, Venice. MS Latin Z 468 1967. Parchment, with illustration; bound with Macrobius. 1388.

Boccaccio

"Filocolo." Vatican MS Ross. 547. Parchment, fourteenth cent. No chapter title headings, unlike printed versions, e.g., Venice 1472. Blue capital letter at beginning of new chapter, first part has ornamented first page.

Chariton

"Chariton Aphrodisi": "excriptus manu A. Maria Salvini." Marcian Library GR VIII 16. coll. 1194. Greek transcription by Salvinius, early modern with endnotes on language, and marginal notes, in Latin.

Homer

"Iliad": "Homer Ilias cum scholis marginalibus." Marcian Library, Venice. Codex 454. coll. 822. Parchment; illustrated. Tenth cent. A fragment of Heliodorus' *Aithiopika*, written later, is inserted in this Codex.

Heliodorus

"Heliodorou aithiopika, hē Charikleia." Marcian Library GR 409 coll. 838 sepia on parchment. Eleventh cent. (?):Bessarion. Same collocation offers Achilles Tatius, beginning f. 164: "Logos protos Achilleōs Alexandreus Tatiou tōn peri Leukippēn kai Kleitophōnta."
"Hēliodōrou aithiōpikōn." Vatican GR 157. Thirteenth cent. With end notes in Greek about author as Bishop of Tricca. Latin note inserted dated 29 October 1546 gives recent history of manuscript.
"Aithiopika." Marcian Library, Venice. Codex 410. Coll. 522. Sepia on parchment, fifteenth cent. Bessarion.
"Aithiopika." Marcian Library. Codex 411. Fifteenth cent.
"Aethiopica; Agathaiae Scholastica Daphniaca; Achilles Tatius; Leucippe et Clitophontis amoribus." Marcian Library. GR 607 coll. 809. Fourteenth cent.

Lucian

"Lucius vel asino." Under "Lucianus" in Marcian Library, Venice. GR 436 coll. 314. Bessarion. ff. 76–84.

Petronius

"Satyricon." Vienna Bibliothek. MS 4755. Parchment, Italian, late fifteenth cent. Illuminated first page, border in pink, blue, green and gold.

Richardson, Samuel

Letter to Lady Bradshaigh, 25 Feb. 1754. Forster Collection, Victoria and Albert Museum, London. FC XI, f. 87.

Index

>-+◆>-0-<◆+-◄

Potocki, Jan, *Tales from the Saragossa Manuscript*, 406
Poussin, Nicolas, 524
Powys, John Cowper, 481
pre-Adamitic language, 279
préciosité, 20, 265–267, 275, 289, 526
Presbyterianism, 233
Prescriptive Realism, 287–288, 292, 296, 298,
331, 453, 470, 477–478, 520, 524; escape
from Prescriptive Realism, 293–296. *See
also* realism
Prester John, 210
Prévost, Antoine-François, Abbé, 272, 277,
298, 517; *Histoire d'une Grecque moderne*,
256; *Lettres angloises, ou Histoire de Miss Clar-
isse Harlove*, 272, 516; *Manon Lescaut*, 286,
291; *Philosophie Anglais ou les Mémoires de
Cleveland*, 284
Priapus, 107, 109–110, 501
Priene, 435
Princeton University, 23
"Print, Age of," 224, 226
printing press, 214, 232, 278, 509, 511, 517;
print culture, 214
Prior, Matthew, 473
Priscianus, Theodoros, 21, 490
private sphere, public sphere, 278, 291, 518
probability in novels, 281–287, 292
Pródromos, Theodoros, 259; *Rodanthé and
Dosikles*, 177, 257
Prometheus, 139, 384, 388
propaganda, 210, 272, 518
prophecy, 97–98, 101, 105, 134, 410, 499–
500
Propp, Vladimir, 142, 306–307, 521
prostitutes and prostitution, 71, 84–86, 108–
109, 362, 374, 462, 476, 482, 491, 501, 503
Protestantism, 154, 164, 214, 224, 227–233,
238, 241, 243, 246, 267–268, 276, 285,
304, 377, 380, 453–454, 457, 461, 528. *See
also* Calvinism; Lutheranism; Presbyterianism; Puritanism
Proteus, 94
Proust, Marcel, 144, 258, 503; *A la recherche
du temps perdu*, 324, 406, 416, 420, 431;
Du côté de chez Swann, 258, 330, 400, 408–
409, 416–418, 422–423, 425, 428, 438; *A
l'ombre des jeunes filles en fleurs*, 325, 378,
387, 398–400, 403, 445; *La Prisonnière*,
325; *Sodome et Gomorrhe*, 417, 419
Provence, 17, 261, 489, 516
Providence, divine, 6, 124, 245, 487
Providence, Rhode Island, 529
Prudentius, 494
"Pseudo-Clemens," *Recognitiones*, 32, 79, 81,
86–88, 133, 151, 160–161, 170, 223, 439,
474
"Pseudo-Lucian." *See Onos*
pseudonyms, 489, 518
psychiatry, 381, 412, 484; psychoanalysis,
307; psychotherapy, 307
psychology, 4, 183, 304, 306, 409, 483, 493,

525; psychological criticism, 10
Ptolemy Chennos: *Novel History, A*, 491;
Sphinx, The, 31, 491
Puritanism, 1, 6, 231, 242, 262, 264, 266–
270, 286, 385, 429, 488, 528
Pushkin, Alexander Sergeevich, *Evgeny One-
gin*, 10
Pym, Barbara, *Crampton Hodnet*, 212; *The
Sweet Dove Died*, 370–372
Pyper, John, 326, 357, 365
Pyramus and Thisbe, 211
Pyrenees, 181
Pythia, 435

"Queen of Heaven" (*Regina caeli*), 121, 452,
528
Queste del Saint Graal, 186
Quint, David, 413
Quintilian, *Declamations*, 491
quipus, 157
Quixotic reading, 268, 271–273

Rabelais, François, 220, 225–226, 254, 257–
258, 299, 381, 428, 513; *Pantagruel*, 113,
237, 314, 382; *Tiers Libre*, 113, 248, 522;
Quart Libre, 113, 235, 247–248, 522;
Quint Livre, 237, 522; *Le Dive bouteille*,
220
Race, William, 511
race, 89, 104–105, 164, 292, 303–304, 498
Racine, Jean, 267, 279, 282, 476, *Phèdre*, 99
Radcliffe, Ann, 351–352; *Mysteries of Udolpho,
The*, 330, 345; *Sicilian Romance, A*, 294
Radway, Janice A., 518
Rambouillet, Catherine, marquise de, 266
rape, 64, 70, 83–85, 289, 362
Raphael (Raffaello Sanzio), 365, 496
Rapunzel, 195, 198, 508
rationalism, 454, 528
Rawson, Beryl, 68, 71
reading aloud, 201, 212, 224
realism, 3, 15, 27, 106, 127, 134, 136–137,
158, 161, 273–274, 284–291, 293–297,
300, 308, 330–331, 352, 354, 393, 402,
423, 427, 454, 458, 477–478, 488, 493,
500, 524; "realism of content," 134, 294;
"realism of presentation," 134, 294. *See also*
Prescriptive Realism
realismo mágico, el, 469–470, 481
Reardon, B. P., 21, 29, 488–490, 492, 499;
ed., *Collected Ancient Greek Novels* (*CAGN*),
xviii, 27, 29, 86, 478, 488, 491, 500
reason, 353, 459, 463; Age of Reason, 172
Reeve, Clara, *The Progress of Romance*, 262,
298
Reformation, 267
Reiskius (J. J. Reiske), 254–255
religion, 62–68, 89, 102, 127, 129, 160–172,
181, 282, 303, 305, 329, 348, 413, 427,
462, 468, 473–474, 479, 488, 499, 509,
516, 523, 525. *See also* Buddhism; Christianity; Confucianism; Goddess; Hinduism;

About the Author

*M*argaret Anne Doody, who decided at the age of six to be "a writer," is the author of two published novels. *The Alchemists*, written in the 1960s, when she was a graduate student at Oxford, was published in 1980. *Aristotle Detective*, first published in the United Kingdom in 1978, appeared in an American edition in 1980 and in a paperback, as well as being translated into three other languages.

In the course of writing the (unpublished) sequel to *Aristotle Detective*, tentatively entitled "Aristotle and Poetic Justice," and dealing with literary kinds, the author ran into the fascinating problem of the history and status of the novel itself in antiquity, and began the researches that would lead to *The True Story of the Novel*, She thinks of this as "the book I was born to write."

Margaret Doody is a graduate of Dalhousie University (which also gave her an honorary LL.D. in 1985) and of Oxford University (B.A.:D.Phil.). She has held permanent appointments at Victoria University, British Columbia; University College of Swansea, Wales; University of California at Berkeley; as well as visiting appointments at Stanford and Columbia. She was a Professor in the English Department at Princeton University (1980–1989), and since 1989 has been Andrew W. Mellon Professor of Humanities and Professor of English at Vanderbilt University, where she is currently Director of the Program in Comparative Literature.